Volkswagen GTI, Golf, and Jetta

Service Manual
1985, 1986, 1987, 1988, 1989

Gasoline, Diesel, and Turbo Diesel
Including 16V

Volkswagen Service Manuals
from Robert Bentley

GTI, Golf, and Jetta Service Manual: 1985-1989 Gasoline, Diesel, and Turbo Diesel including 16V. Robert Bentley. ISBN 0-8376-0338-2
Volkswagen Part No. LPV 800 109

Scirocco, Cabriolet Service Manual: 1985–1989, including 16V. Robert Bentley. ISBN 0-8376-0344-7
Volkswagen Part No. LPV 800 110

Volkswagen Fox Official Factory Repair Manual: 1987–1989, including Wagon and Sport. Volkswagen United States. ISBN 0-8376-0361-7
Volkswagen Part No. LPV 800 502

Quantum Official Factory Repair Manual: 1982-1988, Gasoline and Turbo Diesel, including Wagon and Syncro. Volkswagen United States. ISBN 0-8376-0341-2
Volkswagen Part No. LPV 800 202

Vanagon Official Factory Repair Manual: 1980-1989, including Air-cooled, and Water-cooled Gasoline Engines, Diesel Engine, Syncro, and Camper. Volkswagen United States. ISBN 0-8376-0345-5
Volkswagen Part No. LPV 800 147

Rabbit, Jetta Service Manual: 1977-1984, Diesel Models, including Pickup Truck and Turbo Diesel. Robert Bentley. ISBN 0-8376-0184-3
Volkswagen Part No. LPV 800 122

Rabbit, Scirocco, Jetta Service Manual: 1980-1984 Gasoline Models, including Pickup Truck, Convertible and GTI. Robert Bentley. ISBN 0-8376-0183-5
Volkswagen Part No. LPV 800 104

Rabbit, Scirocco Service Manual: 1975-1979 Gasoline Models. Robert Bentley. ISBN 0-8376-0107-X
Volkswagen Part No. LPV 997 174

Dasher Service Manual: 1974-1981, including Diesel. Robert Bentley. ISBN 0-8376-0083-9
Volkswagen Part No. LPV 997 335

Super Beetle, Beetle and Karmann Ghia Official Service Manual Type 1: 1970-1979. Volkswagen United States. ISBN 0-8376-0096-0
Volkswagen Part No. LPV 997 109

Beetle and Karmann Ghia Official Service Manual Type 1: 1966-1969. Volkswagen United States. ISBN 0-8376-0416-8
Volkswagen Part No. LPV 997 169

Station Wagon/Bus Official Service Manual Type 2: 1968-1979. Volkswagen United States. ISBN 0-8376-0094-4
Volkswagen Part No. LPV 997 288

Fastback and Squareback Official Service Manual Type 3: 1968-1973. Volkswagen United States. ISBN 0-8376-0057-X
Volkswagen Part No. LPV 997 383

Audi Service Manuals
from Robert Bentley

Audi 80, 90 Official Factory Repair Manual: 1988. Audi of America. ISBN 0-8376-0367-6
Audi Part No. LPV 800 601

Audi 5000S, 5000CS Official Factory Repair Manual: 1984-1988 Gasoline, Turbo, and Turbo Diesel, including Wagon and Quattro. Audi of America. ISBN 0-8376-0370-6
Audi Part No. LPV 800 445

Audi 5000, 5000S Official Factory Repair Manual: 1977-1983 Gasoline and Turbo Gasoline, Diesel and Turbo Diesel. Audi of America. ISBN 0-8376-0352-8
Audi Part No. LPV 800 443

Audi 4000S, 4000CS, and Coupe GT Official Factory Repair Manual: 1984-1987, including Quattro and Quattro Turbo. Audi of America. ISBN 0-8376-0348-X
Audi Part No. LPV 800 423

Audi 4000, Coupe Official Factory Repair Manual: 1980-1983, Gasoline, Diesel, and Turbo Diesel. Audi of America. ISBN 0-8376-0349-8
Audi Part No. LPV 800 422

Audi Fox Service Manual: 1973-1979. Robert Bentley. ISBN 0-8376-0097-9
Audi Part No. LPA 997 082

Volkswagen GTI, Golf, and Jetta

Service Manual
1985, 1986, 1987, 1988, 1989

Gasoline, Diesel, and Turbo Diesel
Including 16V

Robert Bentley
Cambridge, Massachusetts

Published and distributed by:

Robert Bentley, Inc.
1000 Massachusetts Avenue
Cambridge Massachusetts 02138

Copies of this manual may be purchased from authorized Volkswagen dealers, from selected booksellers and automotive accessories and parts dealers, or directly from the publisher by mail.

This publication contains the essential removal, installation and adjustment procedures for the 1985 through 1989 Volkswagen GTI, Golf and Jetta sold in the USA and Canada.

NOTE TO USERS OF THIS MANUAL

The publisher encourages comments from the readers of this manual. These communications have been and will be carefully considered in the preparation of this and other manuals. Please write to Robert Bentley, Inc., at the address on this page.

This manual was published by Robert Bentley, Inc., which has sole responsibility for its content. Volkswagen has not reviewed and does not vouch for the accuracy of the technical specifications and procedures described in this manual.

CAUTION

It is assumed that the reader is familiar with basic automotive repair procedures.

Before attempting any work on your Volkswagen, read the cautions and warnings on page ix and any caution or warning which may accompany a procedure in the service manual.

Special tools required in performing certain service operations are identified in the manual and recommended for use.

Use of tools or procedures other than those recommended in this service manual may be detrimental to the car's safe operation as well as the safety of the person servicing the car.

Part numbers listed in this manual are for reference only. Always check with your authorized dealer to verify part numbers.

Robert Bentley, Inc., the publisher, has made every effort to ensure the accuracy of this manual. The publisher cannot be responsible for the result of any error in this manual.

Library of Congress Catalog Card No. 88-71601
ISBN 0-8376-0338-2
VWoA Part No. LPV 800 109
Bentley Stock No. VG89
91 90 89 88   10 9 8 7 6 5 4 3 2 1

Manufactured in the United States of America

Fundamentals 1

Lubrication and Maintenance 2

Engine 3

Cooling System 4

Fuel System — Gasoline 5

Fuel system — Diesel 6

Exhaust System and Emission Control 7

Ignition 8

Manual Transmission and Clutch 9

Automatic Transmission 10

Suspension and Steering 11

Brakes 12

Body and Interior 13

Electrical System 14

Index 15

Foreword

Service to Volkswagen owners is of top priority to the Volkswagen organization and has always included the continuing development and introduction of new and expanded services. In line with this purpose, Robert Bentley, Inc. in cooperation with Volkswagen United States, Inc. has introduced this Volkswagen Service Manual.

This GTI, Golf, and Jetta manual covers the model years 1985, 1986, 1987, 1988, and 1989, including Golf and Jetta GL, Golf GT, Jetta GLI and Carat, and 16-valve models. This manual is specifically written to cover U.S. and Canada models only.

For the Volkswagen owner with basic mechanical skills, this manual gives detailed maintenance and repair information along with the same complete and accurate specifications that were available in an authorized Volkswagen dealer service department as this manual went to press. In addition, the Volkswagen owner who has no intention of working on his or her car will find that reading and owning this manual will make it possible to be better informed and to discuss repairs more intelligently with a professional automotive technician. This manual has been prepared from the repair information that the Volkswagen organization provides to its own factory-trained technicians and has been developed primarily with the do-it-yourself Volkswagen owner in mind. The aim throughout has been clarity and understanding with practical functional descriptions, step-by-step procedures, and accurate specifications.

The Volkswagen owner intending to do maintenance and repair should have a set of tools including metric wrenches and sockets, screwdrivers, a torque wrench, and feeler gauges, since these basic hand tools will be used for the majority of the maintenance and repair described in this manual. This manual includes more detailed information on basic tools and other tips for the beginner in the first section of the manual, entitled Fundamentals. Volkswagen technicians use special tools for some of the repairs described in this manual. The text will note when a repair requires special tools and, where possible, will recommend practical alternatives.

This manual is organized so that, whenever possible, when a change has been made within a model year, the vehicle identification number (VIN) of the first car with this change is given. The digits you need to know for this parts and service information are taken from the seventeen-digit VIN number. If, for example, the VIN is 1VWDB9170FV000001, you will need only nine of the last eleven digits of this number—or, more specifically, the digits 17 F 000001. Your Volkswagen's VIN is found on the left doorjamb and on a plate mounted on the driver's side of the instrument panel padding where the number can be seen through the windshield. The VINs assigned to GTIs, Golfs, and Jettas for model years 1985, 1986, 1987, 1988 and 1989 which are covered by this manual are:

Golf, GTI

1985: . . . 17 F 000001 to . . . 17 F 999999
1986: . . . 17 G 000001 to . . . 17 G 999999
1987: . . . 17 H 000001 to . . . 17 H 999999
1988: . . . 17 J 000001 to . . . 17 J 999999
1989: . . . 17 K 000001 to . . . 17 K 999999

Jetta

1985: . . . 16 F 000001 to . . . 16 F 999999
1986: . . . 16 G 000001 to . . . 16 G 999999
1987: . . . 16 H 000001 to . . . 16 H 999999
1988: . . . 16 J 000001 to . . . 16 J 999999
1989: . . . 16 K 000001 to . . . 16 K 999999

Every human effort has been made to ensure the highest degree of accuracy possible. When the vast array of data presented in this manual is taken into account, however, no claim to infallibility can be made. We therefore cannot be responsible for the result of any errors that may have crept into the text. The Publisher encourages comments from the readers of this manual in regard to any errors and, also, suggestions for improvement in the presentation of the technical material. These communications have been and will be carefully considered in the preparation of this and other manuals. Please write to Robert Bentley, Inc., Cambridge, Massachusetts 02138.

Volkswagen offers extensive warranties, especially on components of the fuel delivery and emission control systems. Therefore, before deciding to repair a Volkswagen that may still be covered wholly or in part by any warranties issued by Volkswagen United States, Inc., consult your authorized Volkswagen dealer. You may find that he can make the repair either free or at minimum cost. Regardless of its age, or whether it is under warranty, your Volkswagen is both an easy car to service and an easy car to get serviced. So if at any time a repair is needed that you feel is too difficult to do yourself, a trained Volkswagen technician is ready to do the job for you.

Robert Bentley, Inc.

Please read these warnings and cautions before proceeding with maintenance and repair work.

WARNING—

• Never work under a lifted car unless it is solidly supported on stands intended for the purpose. Do not support a car on cinder blocks, hollow tiles, or other props that may crumble under continuous load. Do not work under a car that is supported solely by a jack.

• If you are going to work under a car on the ground, make sure that the ground is level. Block the wheels to keep the car from rolling. Disconnect the battery ground strap to prevent others from starting the car while you are under it.

• Never run the engine unless the work area is well ventilated. Carbon monoxide kills.

• Friction materials such as brake and clutch linings or brake pads may contain asbestos fibers. Do not create dust by grinding, sanding or by cleaning with compressed air. Avoid breathing asbestos fibers and asbestos dust. Breathing asbestos may result in serious diseases, such as asbestosis or cancer, and cause severe injury and death.

• Tie long hair behind your head. Do not wear a necktie, scarf, loose clothing, or necklace when you work near machine tools or running engines. If your hair, clothing, or jewelry were to get caught in the machinery, severe injury could result.

• Disconnect the battery ground strap whenever you work on the fuel system or the electrical system. When you work around fuel, do not smoke or work near heaters or other fire hazards. Keep an approved fire extinguisher handy.

• Illuminate your work area adequately but safely. Use a portable safety light for working inside or under the car. Make sure its bulb is enclosed by a wire cage. The hot filament of an accidentally broken bulb can ignite spilled fuel or oil.

• Catch draining fuel, oil, or brake fluid in suitable containers. Do not use food or beverage containers that might mislead someone into drinking from them. Store flammable fluids away from fire hazards. Wipe up spills at once, but do not store the oily rags, which can ignite and burn spontaneously.

• Finger rings should be removed so that they cannot cause electrical shorts, get caught in running machinery, or be crushed by heavy parts.

• Keep sparks, lighted matches, and open flame away from the top of the battery. If hydrogen gas escaping from the cap vents is ignited, it will ignite gas trapped in the cells and cause the battery to explode.

• Always observe good workshop practices. Wear goggles when you operate machine tools or work with battery acid. Gloves or other protective clothing should be worn whenever the job requires it.

CAUTION—

• If you lack the skills, tools, and equipment, or a suitable workshop for any procedure described in this Manual, we suggest you leave such repairs to an Authorized Volkswagen Dealer or other qualified shop. We especially urge you to consult your Authorized Volkswagen Dealer before attempting any repairs on a car still covered by the new-car warranty.

• Volkswagen is constantly improving its cars and sometimes these changes, both in parts and specifications, are made applicable to earlier models. Therefore parts numbers listed in this manual are for reference only. Always check with your Authorized Volkswagen Parts Department for the latest information.

• Before starting a job, make certain that you have all necessary tools and parts on hand. Read all instructions thoroughly; do not attempt shortcuts. Use tools appropriate to the work and use only replacement parts meeting Volkswagen specifications. Makeshift tools, parts, and procedures will not make good repairs.

• Use pneumatic and electrical tools only to loosen threaded parts and fasteners. Never use such tools to tighten fasteners, especially on light alloy parts.

• Be mindful of the environment and ecology. Before you drain the crankcase, find out the proper way to dispose of the oil. Do not pour oil onto the ground, down a drain, or into a stream, pond, or lake. Consult local ordinances that govern the disposal of wastes.

FUNDAMENTALS

Contents

Introduction 3

1. General Description 4
1.1　Body 4
1.2　Engine 4
　　Engine Systems 5
　　Ignition System 6
　　Fuel System 6
　　Cooling System 6
　　Lubrication System 7
　　Exhaust System 7
1.3　Drivetrain 7
　　Clutch or Torque Converter 8
　　Transmission 8
　　Final Drive 8
　　Drive Axles 9
1.4　Suspension and Steering 9
1.5　Brakes 10
1.6　Electrical System 11
　　Battery 11
　　Alternator 11
　　Wiring Harness and Circuits 11

2. How To Use This Manual 11
2.1　Fundamentals 11
2.2　Lubrication and Maintenance 12
2.3　Repair Sections 12
　　General Description 12
　　Maintenance 12
　　Troubleshooting 12
2.4　Index 12
2.5　Notes, Cautions, and Warnings 12

3. Getting Started 12
3.1　Safety 12
　　Lifting The Car 13
3.2　General Advice For The Beginner 14
　　Planning Ahead 14
　　Cleanliness 14
　　Tightening Bolts 14
　　Bolt Torque 15
　　Gaskets 15
　　Seals 15
　　Wire Repairs 15
　　Cleaning 16
　　Electrical Testing 16
　　Making An LED Test Light 17
　　Disconnecting Wiring Harness Connectors . . . 17
3.3　Buying Parts 17
　　Genuine Volkswagen Parts 17
　　Volkswagen Remanufactured Parts 18
　　Non-returnable Parts 18
　　What Information You Need To Know 18

4. Tools 19
　　Basic Tool Requirements 19
　　Jack Stands 21
　　Oil Change Equipment 22
　　Torque Wrench 22
　　Timing Light 22
　　Tachometer 22
　　Duty Cycle Meter or Dwell Meter 23
　　Feeler Gauges 23
　　Micrometers 23
　　Test Light 23

2 FUNDAMENTALS

Volt-Ohm Meter or Multimeter 23
Jumper Wires 24
Volkswagen Special Tools 24

5. Troubleshooting Fundamentals 24
  5.1 Starting 24
  5.2 Running 25
  5.3 Driving 25

6. Emergencies 25
  6.1 Changing a Tire 25
  6.2 Car Will Not Start 26
  6.3 Jump-Starting 26
  6.4 Coolant Temperature Warning Light—
       Overheating 27
  6.5 Oil Pressure Warning Light 27
  6.6 Dim Lights 27
  6.7 Towing 27
  6.8 Spare Parts Kit 28

Fundamentals

Introduction

Although Volkswagens are sophisticated and complex machines, nearly all of their basic maintenance and most repairs can be accomplished by any interested owner with basic mechanical skills and the right information. While some of the repairs covered in this manual are complicated and require special knowledge and equipment, most of the care that is required in the lifetime of the average Volkswagen is well within the capabilities of the do-it-yourselfer.

This section of the manual is dedicated to helping the beginner get started smartly and safely with Volkswagen maintenance and repair. Of interest to all owners, the section begins with a **General Description** of the car, broken down into its individual systems so that it can be more easily understood, and a discussion on **How To Use This Manual** — a simple directory of the kind of information you can expect to find and where to find it.

The section continues with extensive information on **Safety** and **General Advice For The Beginner**, including a number of tips on mechanic's skills and workshop techniques which can help the beginner do a faster, complete, and more thorough job. Also for the beginner, this section includes a discussion of **Tools** with information on the tools needed to do 90% of the jobs in this manual, and advice on how to buy them wisely and use them effectively.

Finally, and once again of interest to any owner, this section ends with a quick reference guide to emergencies — what to do when the car won't start or when a warning light comes on, including basic troubleshooting and information on how to gauge the seriousness of the problem.

1. GENERAL DESCRIPTION

Volkswagen's GTI, Golf, and Jetta models are sophisticated examples of the state of today's automotive engineering art, blending advanced design and manufacturing to provide an outstanding combination of performance, economy, roadholding, and reliability at very reasonable cost. In spite of this sophistication, much of the necessary maintenance and repair can be accomplished by the average owner using this manual. While the complexity of the car may seem to make this a difficult challenge for the novice mechanic, it can be simplified and more easily understood by viewing the car as a well-designed assembly of simpler systems, each performing its own independent functions.

Fig. 1-1. Modern Volkswagen unitized body.

1.1 Body

The body is the basic building block. All of the models covered in this manual feature unitized body construction, meaning that they do not have a separate frame. A complex body shell, shown in Fig. 1-1, is the main structural platform to which all the other systems are attached. Fig. 1-2 shows some of the subassembly used to attach engine, drivetrain, suspension, and steering systems to the basic body structure. For comfort, convenience, and safety, the body itself has several additional subsystems and substructures. The doors, the instrument panel, the seats, and other interior trim pieces are all added to the basic body shell. Other parts of the body shell function as mounting points for the other major and minor subsystems. For more information, see **BODY AND INTERIOR**.

1.2 Engine

The engine is the system which produces the power to move the car. It does so by burning a precise mixture of fuel and air, converting the fuel's stored energy into mechanical work, and delivering that mechanical work in a useful form.

All of the Volkswagen engines covered in this manual are of reciprocating-piston design, and operate on the four-stroke cycle. The combustion of the air/fuel mixture creates tremendous pressure in a closed space above a piston, forcing the piston downward in its cylinder, and translating the energy of combustion into a mechanical force. The crankshaft converts each piston's motion into rotating motion, in much the same way that the up-and-down motion of a person's legs rotates the

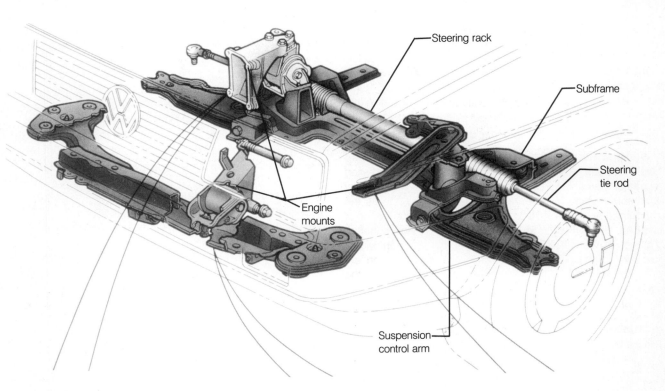

Fig. 1-2. Front subframe, engine mounts and steering gear, examples of subsystems which mount to basic unitized body structure.

pedals of a bicycle. The power, transmitted in this rotary form, can then be used to move the car. The four-stroke cycle, the heart of how and why this all happens, is illustrated in Fig. 1-3.

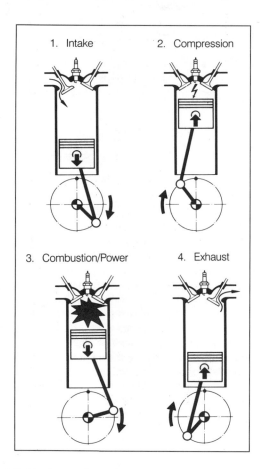

Fig. 1-3. The four-stroke cycle.

Intake Stroke. The piston, traveling downward, creates low pressure inside the cylinder. With the intake valve open, this low pressure causes the fresh air/fuel mixture to rush in. When the piston is near the bottom of its travel the intake valve closes, leaving the cylinder sealed, full of air and vaporized fuel.

Compression Stroke. As the piston begins its upward travel in the sealed cylinder, the air/fuel mixture is compressed to a small percentage of its original volume, creating a very flammable mixture in a very small space, referred to as the combustion chamber. Just before the piston reaches the top of its travel, the air/fuel mixture is ignited. In gasoline-fueled, spark-ignition engines, a spark plug causes ignition with a precisely timed spark. In diesel or compression-ignition engines, the air/fuel mixture is compressed so severely that the heat generated is, by itself, enough to cause ignition. In either case, the ignited air/fuel mixture begins to burn very rapidly.

Combustion or **Power Stroke**. As the confined air/fuel mixture burns, temperature and pressure rise very rapidly,

forcing the piston downward, turning combustion energy into work. Generally, the faster an engine runs and the more often this combustion cycle happens, the more power is produced.

Exhaust Stroke. At the end of the power stroke, the piston is near the bottom of its travel and the cylinder is filled with the waste products of combustion which have little energy value and must be expelled to make way for a fresh load of air/fuel mixture. The exhaust valve opens and the piston, now traveling back upward, pushes the burned gasses out into the exhaust system. Near the top of the piston's travel, the exhaust valve closes, the intake valve opens, and the process begins anew with another intake stroke.

Engine Systems

The engine, which seems so complex, is a collection of simpler systems whose sole purpose is to efficiently perform the engine's power-making and power-transmitting functions. Virtually all automobile engines are multi-cylinder designs, in which a number of individual pistons and cylinders are joined together in a common housing or cylinder block, transmitting their power to a common crankshaft.

A camshaft, driven by the crankshaft, precisely times and controls the opening and closing of the intake and exhaust valves. Since each valve must cycle open and closed once for every two turns of the crankshaft, camshafts always turn at one-half crankshaft speed. The rest of the engine assembly is made up of systems which supply the essential fuel, air, and ignition, and provide for continuous operation of the pistons, crankshaft, and valves. A cutaway view of the engine is shown in Fig. 1-4. For more information, see **ENGINE**.

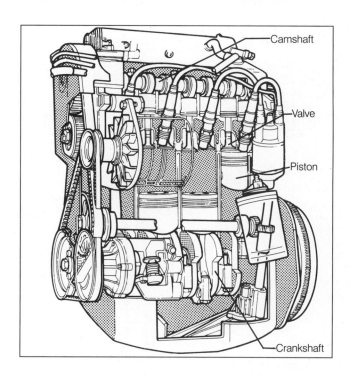

Fig. 1-4. Cutaway view of 4-cylinder overhead-cam engine.

Ignition System

In the case of gasoline-fueled, spark-ignition engines, the ignition system creates the high-voltage spark necessary to ignite the combustible mixture in the cylinders. An ignition distributor, synchronized to the rotating parts of the engine, delivers the spark to the right cylinder at precisely the right time. Since each cylinder has to have a spark once for every two revolutions of the crankshaft, the distributor always turns at one-half crankshaft speed. The basic system is shown schematically in Fig. 1-5. For more information, see **IGNITION**.

Fuel System

To run smoothly and produce power most efficiently, the engine requires the proper mixture of air and fuel — the proper air/fuel ratio. Depending on conditions, the optimum ratio for gasoline-fueled engines is about 15:1, fifteen parts of air for every one part of fuel. The throttle controls the amount of air entering the engine. The fuel system's job is to deliver and disperse fuel in the proper ratio to the incoming air.

Traditionally, the job of fuel delivery has been handled by a carburetor, a device carefully calibrated to dispense and atomize fuel in proportion to the amount of air passing through it. To meet the increasing demand for performance with economy and reduced exhaust emissions, many modern engines, including the Volkswagen engines covered in this manual, use a more sophisticated fuel injection system. It measures the incoming air more precisely, and in turn meters fuel more precisely for better control of the air/fuel ratio. This precise control means greater efficiency over a wider variety of operating conditions. In spite of all this sophistication, the fundamental task of the fuel injection system is still simply to control the ratio of fuel and air entering the engine's combustion chambers.

The fuel system of the automobile also includes a fuel storage, the fuel tank, and a network of pump and lines to transfer the fuel from the tank to the injection system.

A diesel engine's fuel system operates differently. It is free to intake as much air as it needs. The accelerator pedal controls the amount of fuel injected into the cylinders.

For more information on the fuel system, see **FUEL SYSTEM (Gasoline)** or **FUEL SYSTEM (Diesel)**.

Cooling System

Even the most advanced engines lose some of their combustion energy as heat, which must be dissipated to prevent damage to the engine parts. Some heat is carried away in the exhaust, but much of it is absorbed by the valves, the pistons, and the rest of the combustion chamber. Most modern automobile engines are liquid-cooled, using a network of passages around the cylinders and combustion chambers, filled with circulating water-based coolant, to carry away heat. Circulation is provided by an engine-driven coolant pump, often called the water pump. The heat which the coolant absorbs from the hot engine is eventually dissipated to the surrounding atmosphere by the radiator at the front of the car. A smaller radiator-like heater core, located near the interior of the car, radiates heat to warm the passenger compartment. A basic cooling system layout, similar to that used on cars covered by this manual, is shown in Fig. 1-6.

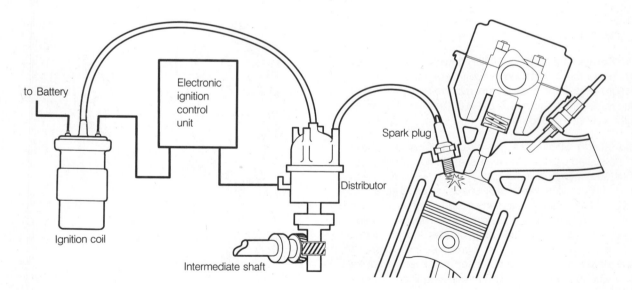

Fig. 1-5. Schematic representation of basic spark-ignition system. Ignition coil boosts voltage, electronic control unit and distributor control timing, and distributor delivers spark to spark plugs.

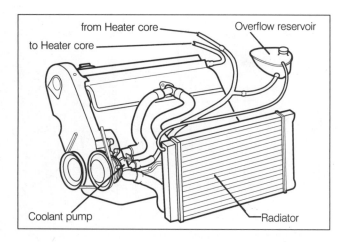

Fig. 1-6. Cooling system. Heat from engine is absorbed by coolant which is circulated by coolant pump and cooled by radiator.

Since some heat is necessary for the engine to run most efficiently, a thermostat in the cooling system restricts the flow of coolant through the radiator until the engine has reached normal operating temperature. For more information on the entire engine cooling system, see **COOLING SYSTEM**.

Lubrication System

The crankshaft and camshaft rotate at speeds up to several thousand revolutions per minute (rpm). Valves and pistons accelerate at tremendous rates, abruptly changing direction between velocities of hundreds of feet per second. In order to endure these harsh conditions, the parts are manufactured to exact dimensions, assembled with precision clearances, and

lubricated by a pressurized oiling system. An engine-driven oil pump supplies oil under pressure to the engine where it is routed through a network of small passages which deliver it to each critical bearing surface.

A filter to clean the oil and a system to warn the driver of low oil pressure are part of the oil system. A secondary function of the oil in the lubrication system is to help carry away excess heat, and some lubrication systems contain an oil cooler for reducing oil temperature before it is recirculated back to the engine. More information on the lubrication system is found in **ENGINE**. For information on oil and oil filter replacement intervals, see **LUBRICATION AND MAINTENANCE**.

Exhaust System

The exhaust system serves several functions, but the primary one is to carry spent gasses from the engine and to route them away from the passenger compartment. Modern automobiles' exhaust systems include muffling devices to reduce noise, chemically reactive components to reduce harmful emissions, and sensors which can evaluate the exhaust gasses and provide information on engine efficiency to the fuel injection system. Fig. 1-7 shows a typical Volkswagen exhaust system. For more information, see **EXHAUST SYSTEM AND EMISSION CONTROLS**.

1.3   Drivetrain

The drivetrain is a series of mechanisms which takes the power developed by the engine and delivers it to the wheels in order to actually move the car. It consists of the clutch or torque

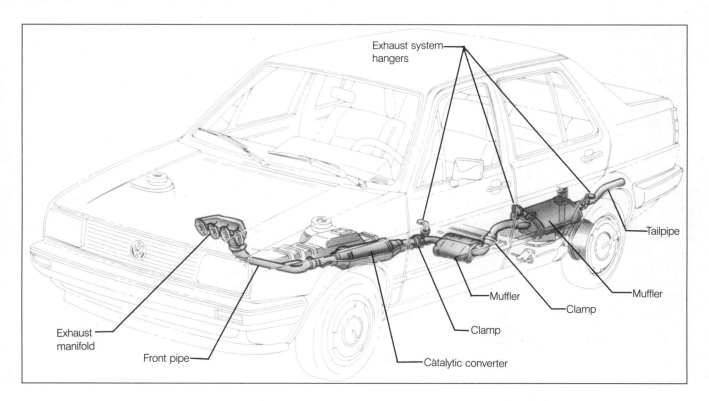

Fig. 1-7. Typical exhaust system.

converter, the transmission, the final drive, the drive axles, and the wheels and tires. The Volkswagens covered by this manual, like most front-wheel-drive cars, combine the transmission and the final drive in one unit called a transaxle. A manual transaxle is shown in Fig. 1-8.

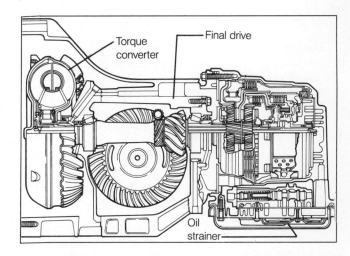

Fig. 1-9. Cutaway view of automatic transaxle showing torque converter, automatic transmission, and final drive.

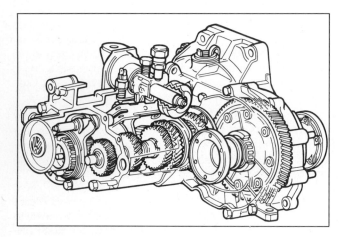

Fig. 1-8. Cutaway view of manual transaxle. Transmission and final drive are combined in one major assembly.

Clutch or Torque Converter

The clutch provides a way to connect or disconnect the engine and the rest of the drivetrain. A friction disc, attached to the input shaft of the transmission, gets squeezed between the heavily spring-loaded clutch and the flywheel, both positively attached to the engine. Normally, the friction between the clutch, friction disc, and flywheel, aided by the heavy spring, makes the transmission input shaft turn at the same speed as the engine. For stopping, starting, and shifting gears, depressing the clutch pedal works against the clutch spring, reducing the friction bond and disconnecting the engine from the drivetrain. In normal use the clutch and flywheel wear, much like brakes, and need periodic maintenance or replacement. More information on the clutch is found in **MANUAL TRANSMISSION AND CLUTCH**.

Cars with automatic transmission achieve the same result with a sophisticated fluid clutch called a torque converter. With one part attached to the engine and another to the transmission, power is transmitted between the two by the action of a viscous fluid. The design of the torque converter is such that it allows the engine to turn at idle speeds without transmitting much driving force to the transmission. A slight forward tug may be noticed when the car is in a forward gear, but at idle speed it is barely enough to drive the car. Above idle speeds, the torque converter becomes increasingly resistant to slip, and transmits power through the fluid coupling to the transmission, delivering power to the wheels. Fig. 1-9 is a cutaway view of the automatic transaxle showing the torque converter. For more information, see **AUTOMATIC TRANSMISSION**.

Transmission

Although the engine develops a substantial amount of power, it does so best at relatively high revolutions per minute (rpm). To handle all driving conditions, it is necessary to use gearing to change the ratio of engine rpm to vehicle speed. A manual transmission is simply a mechanism which contains several sets of gears in a compact assembly, each suited to a particular range of driving speeds, and a mechanism to allow the driver to change from one gear ratio to the next on the move as vehicle speed requirements change. For information on manual transmission maintenance and adjustments, see **MANUAL TRANSMISSION AND CLUTCH**.

An automatic transmission has the same purpose, but uses hydraulic fluid under pressure in a complex network of passages, valves, and hydraulically operated control mechanisms to engage and disengage constantly meshed planetary gear sets. Hydraulic controls select the appropriate gear based on vehicle speed, engine load, throttle position, and gear shift position. For information on automatic transmission maintenance and adjustments, see **AUTOMATIC TRANSMISSION**.

Final Drive

The final drive is another gearset which delivers transmission output to the drive axles, and includes the differential. When a car turns, the wheels on the outside of the turn have to turn slightly faster than those on the inside, since they have to travel a larger arc in an equal amount of time. The drivetrain must be able to transmit power to the wheels and still allow for these variations in wheel speed when cornering. The device which allows this, called the differential, uses a system of gears to allow a speed differential between wheels on opposite sides of the car.

Drive Axles

The final step in the transfer of power from the engine to the wheels is the drive axles, which provide a connection between the differential and the wheel hubs. Information on the drive axles is found in **SUSPENSION AND STEERING**.

1.4 Suspension and Steering

The suspension and steering systems are what allow the wheels to move independent of the body structure for improved ride, stability, and directional control. In addition, these systems limit and control that movement.

The suspension system is the combination of springs, shock absorbers, and other stabilizing devices which separate the wheels from the body structure and support its weight. The springs cushion the effects of bumps. For added control, the suspension system also includes dampers, or shock absorbers, to resist excessive movement of the springs. Volkswagen's strut-type suspension, like that of many modern cars, combines the spring and shock absorber into a single unit, performing the same jobs in less space with fewer individual components. Stabilizer bars aid stability by causing the forces acting on the suspension to be more uniformly distributed.

The remainder of the suspension system are the parts that link it all together, designed with bushings, bearings, and joints which purposefully allow or restrict movement.

The steering system is an assembly of gearbox mechanism and linkage which translates the rotating motion of the steering wheel into the side-to-side motion of the front wheels. Cars covered by this manual use a rack-and-pinion type of steering mechanism. A pinion gear, connected to the steering column, moves a toothed rack from side to side. The rack can be thought of as a long, straight gear. The entire assembly is also referred to as the steering rack. Power-assisted steering uses hydraulic fluid under pressure to do some of the work normally done by the driver turning the steering wheel.

Fig. 1-10, Fig. 1-11, and Fig. 1-12 show the typical compact system of front suspension and steering, and their proximity to other systems in the car. For more information, see **SUSPENSION AND STEERING**.

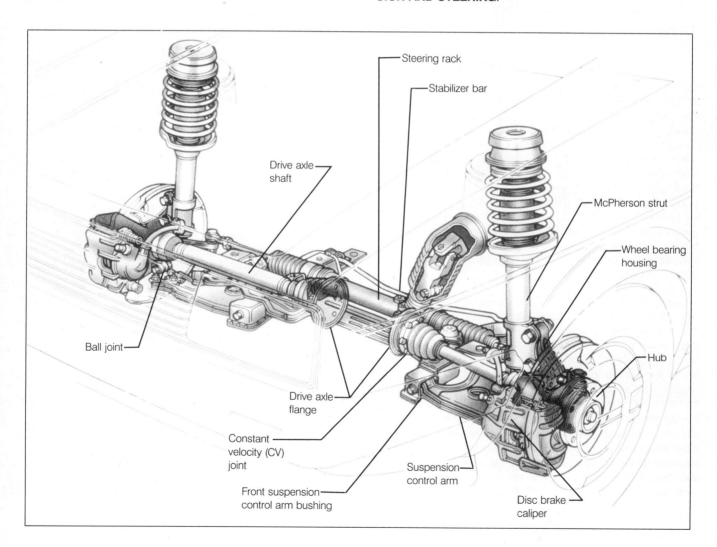

Fig. 1-10. Front suspension and steering of a front-wheel-drive car, showing drive axles and brakes.

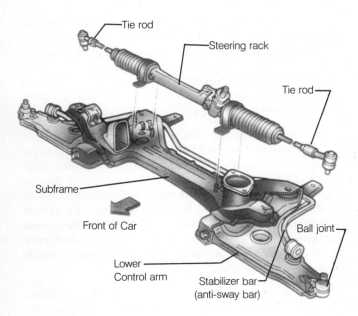

Fig. 1-11. Front subframe showing attachment of suspension control arms and stabilizer bar, and placement of the steering rack.

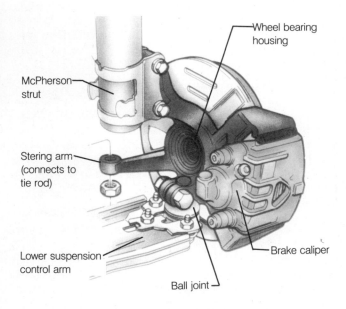

Fig. 1-12. Front suspension and brakes.

1.5 Brakes

The system for slowing and stopping the car is, not surprisingly, completely independent of the systems which make it go. Although the brakes are located at the wheels where they can act most directly, and they mount to parts of the suspension system, the brakes and suspension are completely separate systems.

The brakes act to slow or stop the car by causing friction. Since cars are relatively heavy, the amount of friction required to stop it safely and effectively is quite high, and requires

considerable force. Virtually all modern cars use a system of hydraulics to multiply the force applied to the brake pedal and to distribute it uniformly to the four wheels.

The brake pedal is connected by a mechanical linkage to the first major hydraulic component, the master cylinder, usually mounted on the firewall at the back of the engine compartment. A piston in the master cylinder creates hydraulic pressure in the brake lines going to the wheels. Because the brakes are located at the wheels and move relative to the body, the final length of brake line at each wheel is flexible, so that it follows the movement. At each wheel, the hydraulic pressure acts on the brake mechanism to cause friction and slow the wheel. The hydraulic components are sized in such a way that the driver's force applied to the brake pedal is highly multiplied by the time it acts on the wheels.

Two types of brake mechanisms are in common use in modern cars. Both create braking friction by forcing a stationary friction material against a larger, rotating member attached to the wheel. A drum brake forces semi-circular shoes, lined with friction material, against the inside of a round brake drum. A disc brake squeezes pads lined with friction material against both sides of a flat, round brake disc. Both types are shown below in Fig. 1-13 and Fig. 1-14. A disc brake is generally capable of generating higher braking forces for a given size, is self-adjusting and self-cleaning, and dissipates heat more easily. Heat is a major enemy of brake efficiency which affects the friction materials ability to grip. Under extreme conditions, excess heat from repeated heavy braking can cause the brake fluid to boil, resulting in severely diminished braking capability, called brake fade. Disc brakes, because of their greater ability to dissipate heat, are more resistant to brake fade.

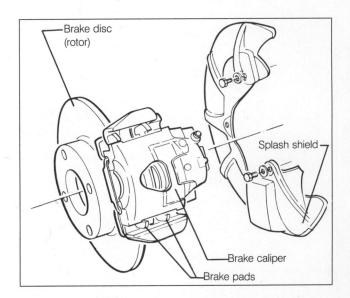

Fig. 1-13. Disc brake assembly showing disc, caliper, and splash shield. Caliper holds pads with friction material.

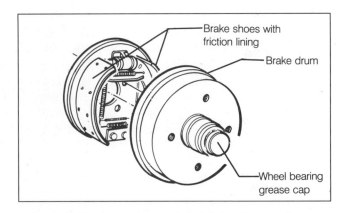

Fig. 1-14. Drum brake assembly with brake drum removed to show brake shoes. Friction material on brake shoes contacts inner surface of brake drum.

1.6 Electrical System

Many components, including accessory items, are powered electrically. The power comes from the car's electrical system. The electrical system uses a battery to store energy, an engine-driven alternator to generate electricity and recharge the battery, and various wiring harnesses and other circuits to distribute electric power to the rest of the car. The electrical system is represented in Fig. 1-15.

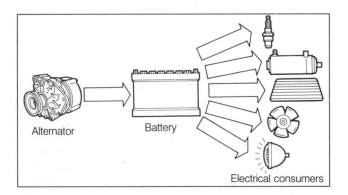

Fig. 1-15. In electrical system, alternator generates electricity to recharge battery and power other electrical consumers.

Battery

Almost every electrical component in the car operates from 12 volt direct current (DC). The battery converts electrical energy into chemical energy for storage, and converts its stored chemical energy back into electrical energy on demand.

Alternator

Left alone to meet all the electrical demands of an automobile, the battery would soon be completely discharged, therefore, the electrical system includes an alternator. Once the running engine is turning the alternator, it takes over supplying electrical energy to the various electrical components. When the power generating capability of the alternator exceeds demand, as it usually does at driving speeds, the extra energy recharges the battery to its full potential.

Wiring Harness and Circuits

The flow of electricity depends upon a closed-loop path—a complete circuit. Electrical current flows through wires to the consumer, a light bulb for example, and back to the battery in a complete circuit. The electrical route back to the source, which completes the circuit, is called a path to ground. Every consumer of electrical power in the car must have a source of power and a path to ground in order to operate. In this manual, the electrical circuits are represented by current flow diagrams which illustrate electrical current flow from voltage source to ground for each circuit.

Commonly, the electrically conductive metal structure of the automobile is used as a ground path. The negative (−) terminal of the battery connects to the car body, and all of the electrical consumers in the car make a ground connection to the car body, thus eliminating the need for many feet of additional wire. Electrical components near the engine are often grounded directly to the engine, which is then grounded to the body. Some components are grounded through their housings which are bolted to a ground. Electrically, the effect is the same.

2. HOW TO USE THIS MANUAL

The manual is divided into 14 sections, **FUNDAMENTALS**, **LUBRICATION AND MAINTENANCE**, and 12 repair sections, each covering a particular system or portion of the car. Thumbtabs on the page margins help locate each section. A page listing section titles and showing their thumb-tab locations is near the front of the manual. An Index is located at the back of the manual.

Each section has a Table of Contents listing the major subject headings within the section, and the pages on which they begin. Page numbers always refer to pages within the same section. References to numbered headings always refer to headings in the same section. Reference to a procedure in another section is by section title only.

2.1 Fundamentals

This first section is **FUNDAMENTALS**. It contains basic information on equipment and safety which is important to any do-it-yourselfer, regardless of experience, as well as information on getting started and helpful suggestions for the novice. Anyone can use this manual. This section helps show how.

2.2 Lubrication and Maintenance

LUBRICATION AND MAINTENANCE is the section dedicated to taking care of the car and preventing future problems. Volkswagen specifies certain periodic maintenance to prevent trouble and keep the car at its best. This section details those maintenance tasks, shows how they are done, and tells what is needed to do them.

2.3 Repair Sections

The 12 repair sections give more involved and more detailed information about system function, troubleshooting, and repair. For clarity and ease of use, each repair section begins with **1. General Description, 2. Maintenance**, and **3. Troubleshooting**.

General Description

The General Description is an overview of the system's technical features. It describes the general layout and function of the system, discusses unique aspects of different versions, and gives information on identifying each version and the repair information which applies to it.

Maintenance

Maintenance is a brief checklist of all the routine maintenance tasks which pertain to the system being discussed. Each listed maintenance item also includes a reference to the part of the manual which covers the work procedure.

Troubleshooting

A systematic approach to problem solving, based on observing trouble symptoms and isolating their causes, is called troubleshooting. The Troubleshooting heading of each repair section begins with a discussion of the system's basic operating principles. Following that general discussion is a more specific list of symptoms—particular problems which affect the car—and their probable causes. Suggested corrective actions include references to the numbered heading or section where the repair information can be found.

2.4 Index

A comprehensive index is found at the back of the manual. Each index entry is followed by a page reference giving the section and the section page number. For example, **3:16** refers to section three, **ENGINE**, and page 16 of that section.

2.5 Notes, Cautions, and Warnings

Throughout this manual are many passages with the headings **NOTE**, **CAUTION**, or **WARNING**. These very important headings have different meanings.

> **NOTE ——**
>
> A note contains helpful information about the job, tips which will help in doing a better job and completing it more easily.

> **CAUTION ——**
>
> *A caution calls attention to important precautions to be observed during the repair work which will prevent accidently damaging the car.*

> **WARNING ——**
>
> *A warning is the most serious of the three. It warns of unsafe practices which will very possibly cause injury, either by direct threat to the person(s) doing the work or by increased risk of accident or mechanical failure while driving.*

Please read every **NOTE**, **CAUTION**, and **WARNING** at the front of the manual and as they appear in repair procedures. They are very important. Read them before you begin any maintenance or repair job. Some **CAUTION**s and **WARNING**s are repeated wherever they apply. Read them all and do not skip any. These messages are important, even to the owner who never intends to work on the car.

3. GETTING STARTED

Most of the necessary maintenance and minor repair that a Volkswagen will need through the years can be accomplished with ordinary tools, even by owners with little or no experience in car repair. Below is some important information on how to work safely, a discussion of what tools will be needed and how to use them, and a series of mechanic's tips on methods and workmanship.

3.1 Safety

Although an automobile presents many hazards, common sense and good equipment can ensure safety. Accidents happen because of carelessness. Pay attention, and stick to these few important safety rules.

> **WARNING ——**
>
> *•Never run the engine in the work area unless it is well-ventilated. The exhaust should be ducted to the outside. Carbon Monoxide (CO) in the exhaust kills.*

• *Remove all neckties, scarfs, loose clothing, or jewelry when working near running engines or power tools. Tuck in shirts. Tie long hair and secure it under a cap. Severe injury can result from these things being caught in rotating parts.*

• *Remove rings, watches, and bracelets. Aside from the dangers of moving parts, metallic jewelry conducts electricity and may cause shorts, sparks, burns, or damage to the electrical system when accidently contacting the battery or other electrical terminals.*

• *Disconnect the battery negative (−) terminal whenever working on the fuel system or anything that is electrically powered. Accidental electrical contact may damage the electrical system or cause fire.*

• *Never work under a lifted car unless it is solidly supported on jack stands which are intended for that purpose. Do not support a car on cinder blocks, bricks, or other objects which may shift or crumble under continuous load. Never work under a car that is supported only by the lifting jack.*

• *The fuel system is designed to retain pressure even when the ignition is off. When working with the fuel system, loosen the fuel lines very slowly to allow the residual pressure to dissipate gradually. Avoid spraying fuel.*

• *Fuel is highly flammable. When working around fuel, do not smoke or work near heaters or other fire hazards. Keep an approved fire extinguisher handy.*

• *Illuminate the work area adequately and safely. Use a portable safety light for working inside or under the car. A fluorescent type is best because it gives off less heat. If using a light with a normal incandescent bulb, use rough service bulbs to avoid breakage. The hot filament of an accidently broken bulb can ignite spilled fuel or oil.*

• *Keep sparks, lighted matches, and open flame away from the top of the battery. Hydrogen gas emitted by the battery is highly flammable. Any nearby source of ignition may cause the battery to explode.*

• *Never lay tools or parts in the engine compartment or on top of the battery. They may fall into confined spaces and be difficult to retrieve, become caught in belts or other rotating parts when the engine is started, or cause electrical shorts and damage to the electrical system.*

Lifting The Car

For those repairs that require raising the car, the proper jacking points should be used to raise the car safely and avoid damage. To use the jack supplied with the car by Volkswagen for changing wheels, there are four jack points—two on each side of the car—marked by dimples in the lower panel sheet metal just behind the front wheel or just in front of the rear wheel. See Fig. 3-1.

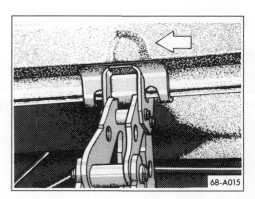

Fig. 3-1. Jacking point for use with Volkswagen-supplied jack. Dimple in lower panel marks exact point just behind front wheel or just ahead of rear wheel.

To lift the car with a floor jack or hydraulic lift, use the lifting points shown in Fig. 3-2 and Fig. 3-3. At the front, use only the small round member protruding at the bottom of the car under the front door hinge pillar. At the rear, use the flat surface just ahead of the mounting for the rear axle assembly.

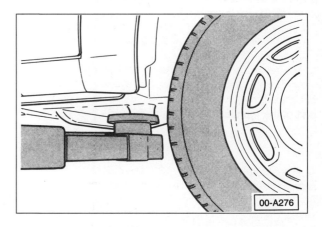

Fig. 3-2. Front lifting point for use with floor jack or hydraulic lift. Lift on round member under front door hinge pillar.

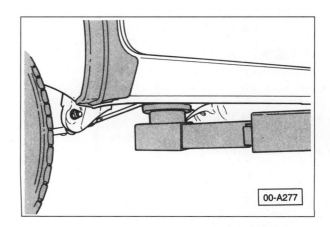

Fig. 3-3. Rear lifting point for use with floor jack or hydraulic lift. Lift on flat surface directly in front of rear axle mount.

To raise the car safely:

1. Park the car on a flat, level surface.

2. Place the jack in position. Make sure the jack is resting on flat, solid ground. Use a board or other support to provide a firm surface for the jack, if necessary.

3. Raise the car slowly.

> *WARNING*———
>
> *Watch the jack closely. Make sure that it stays stable and does not shift or tip. As the car is raised, the car, or the jack if it is on wheels, will want to roll slightly.*

4. Once the car is raised, block the wheel that is opposite and farthest from the jack to prevent the car from unexpectedly rolling.

> *WARNING*———
>
> *Do not rely on the transmission or the emergency brake to keep the car from rolling. While they will help, they are not a substitute for blocking the opposite wheel.*

> *WARNING*———
>
> *Never work under car that is supported only by a jack. Use jack stands which are properly designed to support the car. See* **4. Tools**.

To safely work under a car:

1. Disconnect the battery negative (-) terminal so that no one else can start the car. Let others know what you will be doing.

2. Use at least two jack stands to support the car. A jack is a temporary lifting device and should not be used alone to support the car while you are under it. Use positively locking jack stands which are designed for the purpose of supporting a car. For more information on jack stands, see **4. Tools**.

> *WARNING*———
>
> *Do not use wood, concrete blocks, or bricks to support a car. Wood may split. Blocks or bricks, while strong, are not designed for that kind of load, and may break or collapse.*

3. Place jack stands on a firm, solid surface, just like the jack. If necessary, use a flat board or similar solid object to provide a firm footing.

4. After placing the jack stands, lower the car slowly until its weight is fully supported by the jack stands. Watch to make sure that the jack stands do not tip or lean as the car settles on them, and that they are placed solidly and will not move.

5. Observe all jacking precautions again when raising the car to remove the jack stands.

3.2 General Advice For The Beginner

The tips in the paragraphs which follow are general advice to help any do-it-yourself Volkswagen owner perform repairs and maintenance tasks more easily and more professionally.

Planning Ahead

Most of the repairs and maintenance tasks described in this manual can be successfully completed by anyone with basic tools and abilities. Some can not. To prevent getting in too deep, know what the whole job requires before starting. Read the procedure thoroughly, from beginning to end, in order to know just what to expect and what parts will have to be replaced.

Cleanliness

Keeping things organized, neat, and clean is essential to doing a good job, and a more satisfying way to work. When working under the hood, use fender covers to protect the finish from scratches and other damage. Make sure the car is relatively clean so that dirt under the cover does not scratch.

Avoid getting tools or clothing near the battery. Battery electrolyte is a corrosive acid. Be careful with brake fluid. If it comes in contact with paint, it will cause permanent damage. Finally, keep rubber parts such as hoses and belts free from oil or gasoline, as they will cause the material to soften and fail prematurely.

Tightening Bolts

When tightening the bolts or nuts which attach a component, it is always good practice to tighten the bolts gradually and evenly to avoid overstressing any one portion of the component. For components sealed with gaskets, this method helps to ensure that the gasket will seal properly and completely. With several fasteners, tighten them in a sequence alternating between opposite sides of the component. Fig. 3-4 shows such a sequence for tightening six bolts attaching an imaginary component.

For some repairs, a specific tightening sequence is necessary, or a particular order of assembly is required. Such special conditions are noted in the text, and the necessary sequence is described or illustrated.

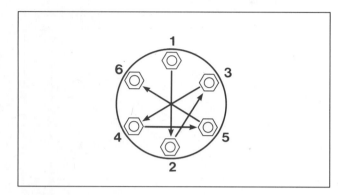

Fig. 3-4. Sequence for tightening alternating opposite fasteners attaching component. Repeat sequence until all are evenly tightened to desired specification.

Bolt Torque

Tightening bolts and nuts to a specified torque value, as measured with a torque wrench, is a way to ensure that they are tight enough without being in danger of going too far and breaking the fastener or stripping the threads.

Vibration of assembled parts causes stress. A fastener which is simply holding things together will be subjected to stress alternating in opposite directions which will eventually cause it to become loose. To counter this loosening, fasteners are tightened more, and actually stretched, in order to pre-stress them. When tightened this way, they are always stressed in one direction, in spite of vibration, and will not work loose.

The proper torque for a fastener is related to the amount of stretch necessary to prevent the fastener from working loose in normal use. To do the best work, use a torque wrench and follow Volkswagen's torque specifications whenever possible. See **4. Tools** for more information on torque wrenches.

Gaskets

The smoothest metal mating surfaces still have imperfections which can allow leakage. To try to prevent leakage at critical joints, gaskets of soft, form-fitting material are used to fill in the imperfections.

To be most effective at their task, gaskets are designed to "crush", to become thinner as they are pressed together between mating parts. Once a gasket has been used and crushed, it is no longer capable of making as good a seal as when new, and is much more likely to leak. For this reason, gaskets should not be reused. Always plan to use new gaskets for any reassembly.

This same logic applies to any part used for sealing, including rubber O-rings and copper sealing washers.

Seals

In places where a shaft must pass through a housing, flexible lip seals are used to keep the lubricating oil or grease from leaking out past the rotating shaft. With a little consideration for the seals and the job they have to do, future leaks can be avoided.

Seals are designed to be installed in the housing only once, and should never be reused once they have been removed. As long as they are not removed from the housing and not leaking, they need not be replaced, however, there is no easier time to replace seals than when the car is already apart for some other repair.

When doing repairs that require removing a seal, be very careful not to scratch or otherwise damage the metal sealing surfaces. Even minor damage can cause seal damage and leakage.

The whole key to seal installation is to get the seal in straight and without damage. Use an object that is the same diameter as the seal to gently and evenly drive it into place. A socket of the right size works well. Coat the entire seal with a little grease or oil to help it go in more easily. Seals are directional. Make sure that it is being installed with the lip facing the correct way. Normally the lip faces the inside. Notice the installation direction of the old seal before removing it.

Wire Repairs

Repairs to a wiring harness to reconnect broken wires or correct shorts to ground deserve special care to make the repair permanent.

The wire ends must be clean. If frayed or otherwise damaged, cut off the end. If necessary, to maintain proper length splice in a new piece of wire of the same size and make two connections.

Use connectors which are designed for the purpose. Crimped-on or soldered-on connectors are best. Crimp connectors and special crimping pliers can be found at most electronics supply or hardware stores. If soldering, use a needle-nose plier to hold the wire near the solder joint and create a "heat dam", keeping the solder from "wicking" up the wire. Use a solder specifically for electronics, without acid flux which will promote corrosion. Twisting wires together is a temporary repair at best, since corrosion will eventually spoil the connection.

Insulate the finished connection. Electronics stores can supply heat-shrinkable insulating tubing which can be placed onto the wire before connecting, slid over the finished joint, and shrunk to a tight fit with a heat gun or hair dryer. The next best alternative is electrical tape. Make sure the wire is clean and free of solder flux or other contamination. Wrap the joint tightly and completely to seal out moisture.

Cleaning

Any repair job is more enjoyable and less likely to be troublesome if the parts are clean. For cleaning old parts, there are any number of solvents and parts cleaners available commercially.

For cleaning parts prior to assembly, commercially available aerosol cans of carburetor cleaner or brake cleaner are handy to use, and the cleaner will evaporate completely leaving no residue.

WARNING ——

Virtually all solvents used for cleaning parts are highly flammable, especially in aerosol form. Use with extreme care. Do not smoke. Do not use these products near any source of sparks or flame.

Let any solvent or cleaning product dry completely. Low-pressure, dry compressed air is helpful if available. Also, use only lint-free rags for cleaning and drying.

WARNING ——

When drying roller or ball bearings with compressed air, do not allow them to spin. Unlubricated, they may fail and come apart, causing injury.

Electrical Testing

A great many electrical problems can be understood and solved with only a little fundamental knowledge of how electrical circuits function.

Electric current only flows in a complete circuit. To operate, every electrical device in the car requires a complete circuit including a voltage source and a path to ground. The positive (+) side of the battery is the original voltage source, and ground is any return path to the negative (−) side of the battery, whether through the wiring harness or the car body. Except for portions of the charging system, all electrical current in the car is direct current (DC) and flows from positive (+) to negative (−). Switches are used to turn components on or off by completing or interrupting the circuit. A switch is "open" when the circuit is interrupted, and "closed" when the circuit is completed. Fig. 3-5 shows a complete circuit schematically.

The first step in tracing an electrical system problem is to check with a test light, a voltmeter, or a multimeter (DC volts scale) to see that voltage is reaching the component. If so, then the circuit is sound as far as that point. If voltage is not reaching the component, that indicates that the circuit is open (interrupted) somewhere between the battery positive (+) terminal and the component. Look for a blown fuse, an open switch, a broken wire, or a failed component earlier in the same circuit. Isolate the location of the problem by doing more voltage measurements at different points in the circuit. Voltage found at any point in the circuit means that the circuit is good at least up to that point. Look for problems after the point in the circuit where voltage is found.

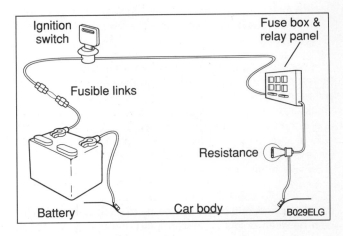

Fig. 3-5. Schematic representation of simple circuit for lightbulb. Switch is shown closed, making circuit complete.

To test for voltage:

1. Start with an electrical connection closest to the component in question. If necessary, remove the terminal cover or disconnect the harness connector.

2. Connect the clip lead of a test light or the black (−) probe of a voltmeter or multimeter to ground (any clean, unpainted metal part of the engine or car).

3. Touch the probe of the test light or the red (+) probe of the meter to the terminal being tested. A meter reading or the test light lighting indicates that voltage is present in the circuit up to that point.

4. Double check a no-voltage indication by wiggling the probes and connections to make sure adequate contact is being made.

Once it is confirmed that voltage is reaching the component, check the remainder of the circuit by testing for continuity to ground. If the component is grounded through its physical mounting, make sure that the contact area is clean, dry, and free of corrosion.

To check component ground:

1. If the component is grounded through the wiring harness (usually a brown or brown striped wire), disconnect the harness connector or the ground wire. Connect the clip lead of a test light or the black (−) probe of a meter to the removed ground terminal.

2. If the component is grounded by its mounting to the car, connect one end of a test light or the black (−) probe of a meter to the clean metal surface of the component.

3. Briefly touch the remaining probe to a known source of battery voltage. If the previous test for voltage reaching the component was successful, that terminal is a suitable connection.

4. A meter reading or the test light lighting indicates current flow in a complete circuit and, therefore, a good connection to ground.

A continuity test, performed with an ohmmeter, is a universal test of any wire, connection, or component which will tell if current can flow through it. It can be used to check wires for breaks, to find out whether switches are open or closed, to find poor connections, and many other things. Continuity is a measure of resistance. A complete circuit has continuity—resistance is nearly zero. An open circuit due to a broken wire or an open switch has infinite resistance—there is no continuity.

To test the continuity of any conductor between any two points, connect one ohmmeter probe to each test point. If the path between points is uninterrupted, the ohmmeter should read nearly zero. If it reads significantly above zero, there may be a component in the circuit which is supposed to have some resistance. If not, there may be a poor connection or a damaged wire somewhere between the test points.

Making An LED Test Light

Many of the electrical tests in this manual require the use of a special LED test light, since the use of a more conventional test light with incandescent bulb can damage sensitive electronic circuits in the ignition, fuel injection, and emission control systems. One suitable test light is Volkswagen special tool no. US 1115 (order no. TU1 115 000 28 ZEL).

A lower-cost alternative is to make an LED test light, using parts available from an electronics supply outlet. Assemble the components as shown in Fig. 3-6. Use a needlenose plier to hold the parts and to act as a heat dam while soldering, as described above in **Wire Repairs**. Insulate all connections with heat-shrinkable tubing or electrical tape.

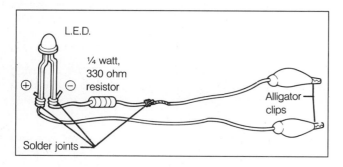

Fig. 3-6. Do-it-yourself LED test light for safe testing of ignition, fuel injection, and emission control circuits.

Parts

1. (1) LED.

2. (1) ¼ watt, 330 ohm resistor.

3. Wire and two alligator clips. (Purchase a jumper wire with an alligator clip on each end, and cut it in half).

4. Solder and soldering iron.

5. Heat-shrinkable tubing or electrical tape.

Disconnecting Wiring Harness Connectors

Volkswagen harness connectors used throughout the car are designed to positively lock into place to prevent coming loose. One type, shown in Fig. 3-7, is equipped with an easy disconnect feature. To disconnect this type of connector, press on the wire clip to release the lock and carefully pull the connector loose.

CAUTION ——

Always pull only on the connector body to disconnect it. Never pull on the wires themselves.

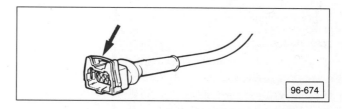

Fig. 3-7. Harness connector with quick disconnect feature. Push on wire lock (arrow) and gently pull on connector to release.

3.3 Buying Parts

Many of the maintenance and repair tasks in this manual call for the installation of new parts, or the use of new gaskets and other materials when reinstalling parts. Most often, the parts which will be needed can be on hand before beginning the job. Read the introductory text and the complete procedure to determine which parts will be needed.

NOTE ——

For some bigger jobs, partial disassembly and inspection is required in order to determine a complete parts list. Read the procedure carefully and, if necessary, make other arrangements to get the necessary parts while your car is disassembled.

Genuine Volkswagen Parts

Without any doubt, the best parts for maintenance and repair of Volkswagens are genuine Volkswagen parts, from an authorized Volkswagen dealer.

Genuine Volkswagen replacement parts from an authorized Volkswagen dealer are designed and manufactured to the same high standards as the original parts. They will be the correct material, manufactured to the same specifications, and guaranteed to fit and work as intended by the engineers who designed the car. Volkswagen is constantly updating and improving their cars, often making improvements during a given model year. So, when Volkswagen recommends a newer, improved part as a replacement, your authorized dealer's parts department will know about it and provide it.

The Volkswagen parts organization is best equipped to deal with any Volkswagen parts needs. Most parts, if not immediately available at an authorized dealer, are available through Volkswagen's highly computerized parts distribution system in less than 48 hours.

Most reputable independent repair shops also make a point of using genuine Volkswagen parts. They know the value of doing the job right with the right parts. So, even if someone else is buying parts for your Volkswagen, make sure they are genuine Volkswagen parts from an authorized Volkswagen dealer.

Volkswagen Remanufactured Parts

If major repairs become necessary, one attractive alternative to expensive new parts is to install genuine Volkswagen remanufactured parts. They are remanufactured—not just rebuilt—to the same exact standards as new parts and usually covered by a warranty, but are available at lower cost than new through authorized Volkswagen dealers. In most cases, the old assembly, called a "core", can be turned in for partial credit against the cost of the remanufactured unit, sometimes even if it is severely damaged.

Volkswagen remanufactured parts which are available from an authorized Volkswagen dealer include:

Alternators	Fuel Distributors
Brake Calipers	Fuel Injectors
Coolant Pumps	Power Steering Pumps
Crankshafts	Starters
Cylinder Heads	Steering Gears
Diesel Injection Pumps	Torque Converters
Distributors	Transaxles
Drive Axles	Turbochargers
Engines	Windshield Wiper Motors
Flywheels	

Non-returnable Parts

Some parts cannot be returned for credit, even if it is the wrong part for the car or it was not required. The best example is electrical parts, which are almost universally considered non-returnable because they are so easily damaged internally.

Buy electrical parts carefully, and be as sure as possible that a replacement is needed, especially for expensive parts such as control units. It may be wise to let an authorized dealer confirm your diagnosis before replacing a part which cannot be returned.

What Information You Need To Know

Model Year. This is not necessarily the same as date of manufacture or date of sale. A 1986 model could have been manufactured in late 1985, or perhaps sold as late as early 1987. It would still be a 1986 model. If in doubt, consult the vehicle identification number (VIN), explained below.

Model. GTI, Golf, and Jetta are all model names. In some cases, buying trim parts for example, it may be helpful to know more model details, such as GL, Wolfsburg Edition, etc.

Vehicle Identification Number (VIN). This is a combination of 17 letters and numbers which identify the particular vehicle. The VIN appears on the state vehicle registration document, and on the car itself. One location is shown in Fig. 3-8.

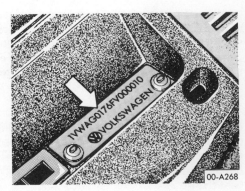

Fig. 3-8. Location (arrow) of vehicle identification number (VIN) on 1985-1989 Volkswagen GTI, Golf, and Jetta cars. Number, on driver's side of instrument panel, is most easily viewed from outside, through windshield.

Copy down the VIN and have it along whenever buying parts. If there was a mid-year change in specifications which affects replacement parts, the change will often be defined in terms of VIN.

In addition, each of the 17 letters and numbers indicates certain facts about the car and its manufacture. Some are useful to know for buying parts. For example, in the 10th space is a letter indicating model year. "F" is for 1985, "G" is for 1986, "H" is for 1987, "J" is for 1988, and "K" is for 1989. The next letter, the 11th, indicates where the car was made. Cars with the letter "V" are U.S.-built.

Engine Code. All GTI, Golf, and Jetta engines are very similar, but subtle differences mean that some parts of the engines and related systems are different. The different engines are identified by a two-letter code, part of the engine number stamped on the cylinder block, as shown in Fig. 3-9. For a complete explanation of the engine codes and how to find them, see the section titled **ENGINE**.

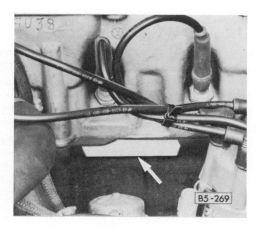

Fig. 3-9. Location (arrow) of stamped engine number on all except 16-valve engines. First two letters are engine indentifying code. All 16-valve engines are code "PL".

Transmission Number. Although most internal repairs to the transaxle are beyond the scope of this manual, the transmission number with its identifying code may be important when buying clutch parts, seals, gaskets, and other transmission-related parts for repairs which are covered. The location of the transmission number is shown in Fig. 3-10. The number consists of two or three transmission code letters followed by a number signifying date of manufacture. For example, "AGB18117" identifies an AGB transaxle built on the 18th of November, 1987. More information on transmission codes and their meanings can be found in **MANUAL TRANSMISSION AND CLUTCH** and **AUTOMATIC TRANSMISSION**.

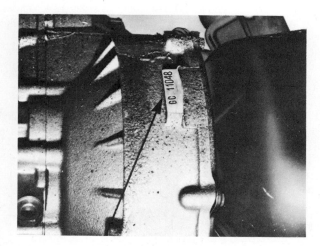

Fig. 3-10. Location (arrow) of transmission number. First characters are transmission code letters.

Volkswagen dealers are uniquely qualified to provide the best possible service for Volkswagen cars. Their ongoing relationship with the large Volkswagen service organization means that they are constantly receiving new tools and equipment, together with the latest and most accurate repair information.

The Volkswagen dealer's service technicians are highly trained and very capable. In addition to periodic Volkswagen Service Training courses which keep them up to date on all the latest technical features and service methods, Volkswagen dealers recognize and actively promote professional technician certification by the National Institute for Automotive Service Excellence (ASE).

Unlike independent repair shops, authorized Volkswagen dealers are intensely committed to supporting the Volkswagen product. They share every owner's interest in Volkswagen value, performance, and reliability.

4. TOOLS

Most maintenance can be accomplished with a small selection of the right tools. Tools range in quality from inexpensive junk, which may break at first use, to very expensive and well-made tools which, to the professional, are worth every bit of their high cost. The best tools for most do-it-yourself Volkswagen owners lie somewhere in between.

Cheap tools are no bargain. They often do not hold up to even casual use, and they present a greater risk of personal injury. If they fit poorly, they can actually damage the fasteners they are intended to remove, making it that much harder to use a good tool the next time around.

Many reputable tool manufacturers offer good quality, moderately priced tools with a lifetime guarantee. A broken tool can be exchanged for a new one, for the life of the tool. These are your best buy. They cost a little more, but they are good quality tools which will do what is expected of them. Sears' Craftsman™ line is one such source of good quality, reasonably priced, and guaranteed tools.

Basic Tool Requirements

The basic hand tools described below can be used to accomplish most of the simple maintenance and repair tasks.

Screwdrivers. Two types, the common flat-blade type and the Phillips type, will handle 99% of all screws used on Volkswagens. Two or three different sizes of each type will be best, since a screwdriver of the wrong size will damage the screw head. Screwdrivers are for screws. Do not use them for anything else, such as prying or chiseling. A complete set of screwdrivers can often be purchased for about the same money as the four or six individual ones that are really necessary. See Fig. 4-1.

For the more complete tool box, include "stubby" screwdrivers or offset screwdrivers for use in tight spots where a normal length screwdriver will not easily fit.

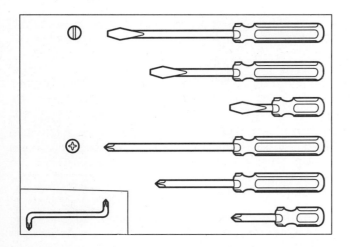

Fig. 4-1. Common flat-blade (top) and Phillips (bottom) screwdrivers. Offset screwdriver (inset) is used for screws with limited access.

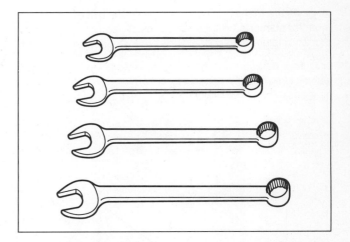

Fig. 4-3. Combination wrenches with one open-end and one 12-point box end. 12-point box end is more universal than 6-point.

Wrenches. Wrenches come in different styles for different uses. Fig. 4-2 shows several. The basic open-end wrench is most widely useful, but grips on only two sides. It can spread apart and slip off more easily. The box wrench has better grip, on all six sides of a nut or bolt, and is much less prone to slip. A 12-point box end can loosen a nut or bolt with less movement, while a 6-point box end provides greater grip for tight fasteners. For hex fasteners on fluid lines, like brake lines and fuel lines, a flare-nut wrench offers better grip and less chance of fastener damage, but will still fit over the line.

Sockets. Sockets perform the same job as box wrenches, but offer greater flexibility. Normally used with a ratchet handle for speed and convenience, they can be combined with extensions to reach fasteners more easily. Standard sockets come in 6-point and 12-point styles. For use with a ratchet, the universal nature of the 12-point is unnecessary, and the 6-point type offers better grip on tight nuts and bolts. Sockets are also characterized by their drive size, the size of the connection to a handle or extension. To start, choose 6-point sockets with a ⅜ in. square drive, two or three extensions of different lengths, and a ⅜ in. drive ratchet handle. As with wrenches, 6mm to 15mm, 17mm, and 19mm are the most needed sizes. See Fig. 4-4.

For the more complete tool box, add deep sockets and a greater variety of handles and extensions. A universal joint extension can allow access from an angle where a straight extension will not quite fit.

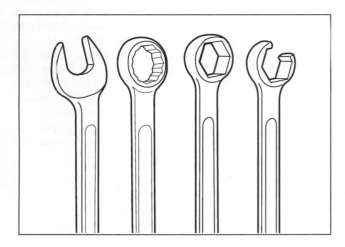

Fig. 4-2. Types of wrench heads. From left, open-end, 12-point box, 6-point box, flare nut.

Most universal is the combination wrench, shown in Fig. 4-3, with one open-end and one 12-point box end. For Volkswagens, 10mm and 13mm wrenches are the most common sizes needed. A 19mm wrench is needed to loosen and tighten the engine oil drain plug. A complete set should also include 6mm, 7mm, 8mm, 9mm, 11mm, 12mm, 14mm, 15mm, and 17mm.

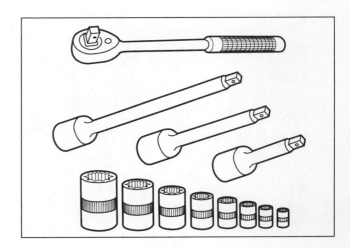

Fig. 4-4. Sockets, handles, and extensions.

Spark Plug Socket. A special socket for spark plugs is the correct size, is deep enough to accomodate a spark plug's length, and contains a rubber insert to both protect the spark plug from damage and grip it for easy removal. This gripping feature is especially necessary on 16-valve engines. A spark plug socket is shown in Fig. 4-5.

The spark plugs used in all Volkswagen engines except 16-valve require a $^{13}/_{16}$ in. socket. The spark plugs used in 16-valve engines require a $^5/_8$ in. socket. Get one with a drive size to match the socket handle and extensions.

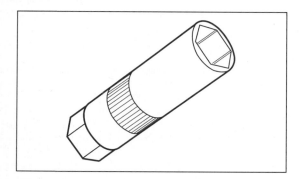

Fig. 4-5. Spark plug socket.

Pliers. A few of the many types of pliers are shown in Fig. 4-6. Most all are used for holding irregular objects, bending, or crimping. Some have special applications. A needlenose plier is used for gripping small and poorly accessible objects, and is useful for wiring and other electrical work. A locking plier, such as the famous Vise-Grip™ is useful because it can grip tightly all by itself. Snap-ring pliers with special tipped jaws are used to remove and install snap-rings or circlips. A channel lock or water pump plier has adjustable jaws which can be quickly changed to match the size of the object being held to give greater leverage. There are many different types and sizes of pliers. Start with a small selection of different types of medium size.

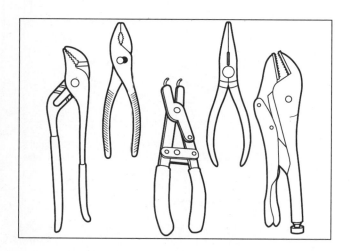

Fig. 4-6. Pliers. From left, channel lock, common, snap-ring, needlenose, locking.

Adjustable wrench. An adjustable wrench, shown in Fig. 4-7, can be a useful addition to a small tool kit. It can substitute in a pinch if, for example, two wrenches of the same size are needed to remove a nut and bolt. Use extra care with adjustable wrenches, as they especially tend to loosen, slip, and damage fasteners if not used carefully. Compared to a wrench of the correct size, an adjustable wrench is always second best. Choose one of average size range, about 6 to 8 inches in length.

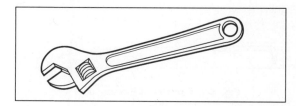

Fig. 4-7. Adjustable wrench is useful if used with care. Adjust for best possible fit. Use only when correct size wrench is not available.

Jack Stands

Strong jack stands are extremely important for any work that is done under the car. A jack should never, ever be used alone to support the car while working underneath.

Use only jack stands which are designed for the purpose. Blocks of wood, concrete, bricks, etc. are not safe or suitable substitutes.

Jack stands are available in several styles. A typical jack stand is shown in Fig. 4-8. The best ones are made of heavy material for strength, have a wide base for stability, and are equipped to positively lock in their raised positions. They also cost more. Think about their purpose. Get the best ones available.

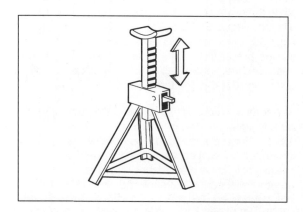

Fig. 4-8. Jack stand for safely supporting car to work underneath.

Oil Change Equipment

Changing oil requires a box wrench or socket to loosen and tighten the drain plug (19mm or ¾ in.), a drain pan (at least 5 qt.), and an oil filter wrench. These items are shown in Fig. 4-9. A wide, low drain pan will fit more easily under the car. Use a funnel to pour the new oil into the engine.

An oil filter wrench is used to remove the oil filter. Volkswagen oil filters are of smaller diameter than many others. Be sure to get a filter wrench which will grip the smaller Volkswagen filter tightly.

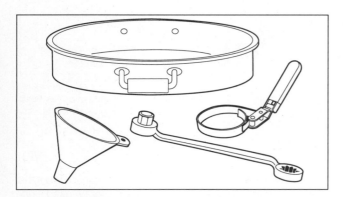

Fig. 4-9. Oil change equipment includes drain plug wrench (19mm or ¾ in.), 5 qt. drain pan, oil filter wrench, and funnel.

Torque Wrench

A torque wrench is used to precisely tighten threaded fasteners to a predetermined value. Nearly all of the repair procedures in this manual include Volkswagen's recommended torque values, in Newton-meters (Nm) and foot-pounds (ft. lb.), to be used during reassembly.

Several types of torque wrenches are widely available. They all do the same job, but offer different convenience features at different prices. Some typical torque wrenches are shown in Fig. 4-10. The most convenient ones have a built-in ratchet, and can be preset to indicate when a specific torque value has, been reached. Follow the wrench manufacturer's directions for use to achieve the greatest accuracy.

A torque wrench with a range up to about 250 Nm (185 ft. lb.) has adequate capacity for all of the repairs covered in this manual. For recommended torque values of 10 Nm or below, the English system equivalent is given in inch-pounds (in. lb.). These small values may be most easily reached using a torque wrench calibrated in inch-pounds. To convert foot-pounds to inch-pounds, multiply by 12. To convert inch-pounds to foot-pounds, divide by 12.

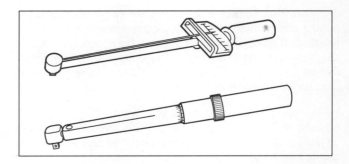

Fig. 4-10. Torque wrenches. Inexpensive beam-type (top) is adequate but must be read visually. Ratchet-type (bottom) can be preset to indicate when torque value has been reached.

Timing Light

A timing light connects to the battery and to the #1 spark plug wire to check ignition timing. A bright strobe light flashes in sequence with the firing of the #1 spark plug. One example is shown in Fig. 4-11. Guard against less expensive models with lights which are too dim to be seen in daylight.

An attractive feature of the more expensive models is an inductive pickup which just clamps on over the spark plug wire to get its signal, rather than needing a more positive connection.

An adjustable timing light is a more sophisticated instrument used to actually measure the timing and the advance and retard characteristics in engine crankshaft degrees. This type is only necessary for detailed analysis of the ignition system's function.

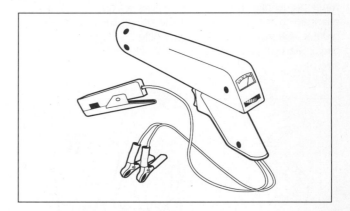

Fig. 4-11. Timing light and electrical connections, including inductive pickup. Dial shown is found on sophisticated adjustable timing lights.

Tachometer

An external tachometer is used to precisely measure engine speed (rpm) for various tests and adjustments. Most tachometers are powered by connection to the battery, and measure engine rpm through a connection to terminal 1 of the ignition coil. To locate terminal 1, see **IGNITION**.

Duty Cycle Meter or Dwell Meter

The duty cycle meter is used on today's Volkswagens to measure the functions of certain components of the fuel injection system and emission controls. A dwell meter, the same type used on older cars to measure ignition breaker point dwell, can also be used for this purpose. Some tachometers can also be used as a dwell meter.

Duty cycle is measured on a 0 to 100 % scale. Using a dwell meter (0° to 90° scale), multiply duty cycle by ⅘ to get the dwell equivalent, and multiply dwell readings by ⅘ to convert to duty cycle percentage.

Feeler Gauges

Feeler gauges are thin metal strips of precise thickness, used to measure small clearances. They are normally available as a set, covering a range of sizes. For Volkswagens, metric feeler gauges (in millimeters) are the best choice. Fig. 4-12 shows a set of feeler gauges.

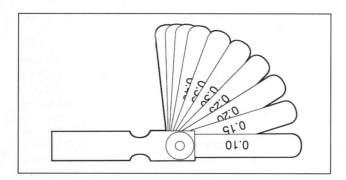

Fig. 4-12. Feeler gauge set, used for precise measurement of clearances between parts.

Micrometers

Precision measurements of internal engine parts and other critical dimensions are made with micrometers, some of which can accurately measure to within thousandths of a millimeter. These are expensive instruments, and are only recommended for those who plan to be repeatedly involved in engine overhauls or other similar work requiring detailed measurement. If such measurements are necessary on a one-time basis, a qualified machine shop can be called upon to make these measurements, particularly if they are also going to be doing the necessary machine work.

Test Light

A test light, shown in Fig. 4-13, is a simple tool used to check electrical circuits for voltage or continuity to ground when actual voltage values are unimportant. A bulb in the handle will light whenever current is flowing through the circuit. The use of a test light is described in **3.2 General Advice For The Beginner.**

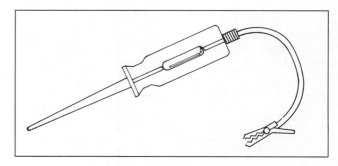

Fig. 4-13. Test light with alligator clip test lead.

CAUTION ━━━

Electrical tests of the ignition, fuel injection, and emission control electronics may be damaged by a test light with a normal incandescent bulb. For these applications, use a high input impedence tester such as Volkswagen special tool no. US 1115 (order no. TU1 115 000 28 ZEL), or build one as described in **3.2 General Advice For The Beginner** *under* **Making An LED Test Light.**

Volt-Ohm Meter or Multimeter

Many of the electrical tests in this manual call for the measurement of resistance (ohms) or voltage values. For tests of ignition, fuel injection, and emission control systems, the multimeter should be a digital, high input impedance type. One good example of this type of meter is Volkswagen special tool no. US 1119 (order no. TU1 119 000 00 KTM), shown in Fig. 4-14.

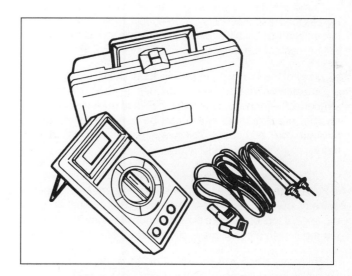

Fig. 4-14. Multimeter with test probes and case. Volkswagen special tool no. US 1119 (order no. TU1 119 000 00 KTM).

Jumper Wires

Some of the electrical tests in this manual require the use of extra jumper wires to bypass a component or a portion of the wiring harness. For most basic electrical tests, jumper wires with alligator clips at each end (made or purchased) are sufficient. For tests involving harness connectors, hookup of jumper wires may damage the connector and cause inferior connections later on. To avoid this damage, jumper connections to harness connectors should be made using a small, flat-blade terminal which will mate properly with the connector. Use Volkswagen part no. N 17 457 2. See Fig. 4-15.

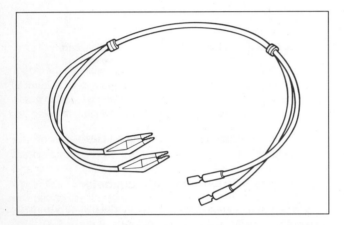

Fig. 4-15. Jumper wires with alligator clips. Flat connectors shown (Volkswagen Part No. N 17 457 2) are for electrical testing at harness connectors.

Volkswagen Special Tools

Some of the more challenging repairs covered in this manual call for the use of Volkswagen special tools. This, however, does not automatically mean that the job is too complicated or out of reach of the novice.

Many of the Volkswagen special tools shown in this manual are inexpensive and are simply the best thing to use to do the job correctly. In these cases, the tool is identified with a Volkswagen order number which can be used to order the tool through your authorized Volkswagen dealer's parts department.

Often, the procedure involves the use of a tool which is used in Volkswagen dealer service departments to make a job easier or faster, but which is not really essential. This manual will show the special tool but, where possible, describe how to complete the repair with a substitute tool or method at lower cost.

There are some jobs for which expensive special tools are essential, and not a cost-effective purchase for one-time repair by the do-it-yourself owner. This manual includes such repairs for the benefit of those with the necessary experience and access to tools. For the do-it-yourselfer, the need for special tools is noted in the text, and Volkswagen dealer service is recommended.

The special tools can be ordered from your authorized Volkswagen dealer parts department using the order numbers provided. The dealer does not stock tools for resale and will most likely have to order them.

As an alternative, the tools mentioned in this manual can probably be ordered from their manufacturers using the Volkswagen special tool number. Check with:

Zelenda Machine and Tools Corp.
66-02 Austin Street
Forest Hills, NY 11374
(212) 896-2288

or

Assenmacher Specialty Tools
5725 Olde Stage Road
Boulder, CO 80302
(303) 444-3958

5. TROUBLESHOOTING FUNDAMENTALS

Troubleshooting, the systematic approach to identifying and solving a problem, depends primarily on the individual circumstances and on direct observation of the symptoms. Careful attention to exactly what is happening, and under what conditions, is the most powerful tool available to get to the problem.

The basic rule for troubleshooting is: never overlook the obvious. Always start with the basics and work toward the more complex. Lots of time and money has been wasted on exotic testing only to find, eventually, that the problem was a loose wire or an empty fuel tank.

The discussions below are intended to help in the initial analysis of a problem and to provide some direction to the right section or sections for more detailed troubleshooting information.

5.1 Starting

There are three main requirements for starting the engine:

1. The starting system (battery and starter) must provide adequate engine cranking speed.

2. The ignition system must function properly.

3. The fuel system must correctly deliver fuel.

Observing the symptoms of a starting problem will give clues to its cause. Too low cranking speed indicates problems with the electrical system—probably the battery or starter. Further troubleshooting should focus on the electrical system—tests of the ignition or fuel systems at this point would be meaningless. See **ELECTRICAL SYSTEM**.

An engine that cranks normally is confirmation that the battery and starter are fine, so starting problems suggest an ignition or fuel system problem. If there is no sign whatsoever of starting, make sure there is adequate fuel in the tank. On gasoline engines, check for loose wires around the coil and distributor. Check to see that the distributor cap and spark plug wires are dry.

Unless this basic inspection turns up a cause, the cause could be in either the ignition system or the fuel system. For gasoline engines, the ignition system is the more likely culprit and is also easier to evaluate. The condition and function of the ignition system should always be confirmed before suspecting the fuel system. For diesel engines, the most likely cause of starting trouble is the glow plugs. For either gasoline or diesel engines, see **IGNITION**. If troubleshooting of the ignition or glow plug system indicates that all is well, proceed to **FUEL SYSTEM**.

5.2 Running

Problems with the way the engine runs may be caused by either ignition system or fuel system faults. The fuel injection system is far more likely to be influenced by temperature. Symptoms which are present only when the engine is cold, or only when it is warm, tend to suggest fuel system problems. For gasoline engines, the ignition system should be investigated and confirmed to be in good condition prior to beginning any work on the fuel system. For troubleshooting diesel engine running problems, see the fuel system troubleshooting information in **FUEL SYSTEM (Diesel)**.

For an engine which has recorded a high number of miles, the general mechanical condition of the engine may also be a factor. Particularly in cases where running problems have developed slowly over time, troubleshooting should include evaluation of the engine's mechanical condition with a compression test. See **ENGINE**.

When attempting to evaluate noise or vibration problems which exist when the engine is running, try to eliminate other possible causes. With a manual transaxle, if the symptoms change depending on whether or not the clutch is engaged, the problem may be in the clutch disc, the clutch release mechanism, or the transaxle. See **MANUAL TRANSMISSION AND CLUTCH**. With an automatic transaxle, check for the symptoms in different shift positions. If the symptoms differ, the problem may be in the torque converter or the transaxle. See **AUTOMATIC TRANSMISSION**.

5.3 Driving

To track down noise and vibration problems which occur while driving, first try to learn more about the symptom. Does it occur all the time, or only at certain speeds? If the symptom is speed-dependent, the first step is to find out whether it is related to engine speed or vehicle speed. Compare driving in different gears at the same approximate engine speed. A symptom which persists at a certain engine speed or speed range regardless of gear selection suggests an engine or exhaust system problem. See **ENGINE** or **EXHAUST SYSTEM AND EMISSION CONTROLS**.

For more analysis, try driving the car at the speed which creates the symptom, and then briefly shifting into neutral and coasting. If the symptom continues unchanged, then it is the car's speed which is a factor, and not engine speed. Symptoms which are related to vehicle speed suggest problems with running gear. See **SUSPENSION AND STEERING** for more detailed troubleshooting information.

6. EMERGENCIES

6.1 Changing a Tire

If the tire goes flat while driving, pull well off the road. Changing a tire on a busy street or highway can be dangerous. If necessary, drive a short distance on the flat tire to get to a safe place. It is much better to ruin a tire or rim than to risk being hit.

Stop the car on as flat a surface as possible, turn on the emergency flashers, and set out flares or emergency markers well behind the car. Passengers should get out of the car and stand well away from the road. Take the jack, tools, and spare wheel from the trunk. If you have wheel chocks, chock the wheel diagonally opposite to the one being changed. If not, use whatever is available, including large rocks or pieces of wood.

Remove the hubcap from the wheel using either a puller clip and wheel wrench supplied with the tool kit or, on 16V models, a special wrench (Fig. 6-1) which should be in the glove compartment. If using the puller clip, insert the clip into the holes at the hubcap rim. Put the wheel wrench on the wheel rim and pull lightly on the other end.

Fig. 6-1. Special wrench being used to remove hubcap. Insert wrench into locking bolt and remove bolt counterclockwise.

Loosen the wheel bolts about one turn, but do not remove them. Place the jack under the lifting point nearest the wheel being changed (lifting points are described in **3.1 Safety**). Use a board to provide a firm footing for the jack if the ground is soft. Raise the jack until it is just touching the notch at the lifting point, and adjust the jack so that its base is slightly under the car. Raise the car only far enough so that the wheel is off the ground, and then remove the wheel bolts and the wheel.

Install the spare wheel and the wheel bolts; tighten them by hand, then lower the car. With all wheels on the ground, fully tighten the bolts in a cross-wise pattern. If a torque wrench is available, torque the bolts to 110 Nm (80 ft. lb.).

Check the inflation pressure of the spare tire. The compact spare should be inflated to 60 psi. Inflation pressures for other tires are given in **LUBRICATION AND MAINTENANCE**.

> **WARNING** —
>
> *The compact spare supplied with the car is for temporary use only. Do not drive at speeds in excess of 50 mph (80 km/h), and avoid rapid acceleration, hard cornering, and hard braking. Do not use two or more compact spares at one time. Failure to heed these warnings may result in tire failure and loss of car control.*

6.2 Car Will Not Start

If the engine turns over slowly or not at all, especially on cold mornings, it may be because the battery is not sufficiently charged. Jump-starting the battery from another car may help. Jump-starting is described below in **6.3 Jump-Starting**.

If the starter seems to be operating but the engine does not turn over (indicated by a high-pitched whine or grinding when the ignition key is turned to START), then there is a problem with the starter; jump starting will not help.

> **CAUTION** —
>
> *Volkswagen does not recommend "bump starting" the engine by pushing the car or driving it down a hill. Damage to the catalytic converter and other parts of the car may result.*

If the engine is turning over at normal speed, it indicates that the battery and starter are fine. Check to make sure that there is fuel in the tank. Don't rely on the fuel gauge, it may be faulty. Instead, remove the gas filler cap and rock the car. If there is gas in the tank, you should hear a sloshing sound from the filler neck. If so, turn the ignition on and listen for the sound of the fuel pump. It should run for a few seconds, then stop. If not, then fuel may not be reaching the engine.

The engine may have difficulty starting because it has too much fuel, because the fuel system is vapor-locked on a hot day, or because the ignition system is wet on a very damp day. There will probably be a strong smell of gas if the engine is flooded. Repeatedly cranking the engine with the gas pedal floored may damage the catalytic converter. Instead, wait for a few minutes, and then try starting the engine again. If you suspect vapor lock, raise the hood, let the engine cool, and then try to start the engine. On damp days, check the distributor cap and spark plug wires for condensation. If they are wet, remove and replace the wires one at a time and dry them off with a clean dry cloth, then remove the distributor cap and wipe it dry inside and out.

6.3 Jump-Starting

Cars with partially discharged or completely dead batteries can be jump-started using the good battery from another car. When jump-starting the engine, always heed the following warnings.

> **WARNING** —
>
> • *Battery acid (electrolyte) can cause severe burns, and will damage the car and clothing. If electrolyte is spilled, wash the surface with large quantities of water. If it gets into eyes, flush them with water for several minutes and call a doctor.*
>
> • *Batteries produce explosive gasses. Keep sparks and flames away. Do not smoke near batteries.*
>
> • *Do not jump-start the engine if you suspect that the battery is frozen; trapped gas may explode. Allow the battery to thaw first.*

To jump-start the engine, place the cars close together, but do not allow the cars to touch. With the engine of the car with the good battery off, remove the battery cover from the dead battery and connect the jumper cables as shown in Fig. 6-2. First connect the end of one cable to the positive post of the good battery, and the other end of the same cable to the positive post of the dead battery. The positive post is the fatter of the two posts and is usually marked with a plus (+) sign. Connect one end of the other cable to the negative (−) post of the good battery, and connect the other end of the same cable to the engine block of the car with the dead battery. Make the connection as far away from the battery as possible, as there may be sparks.

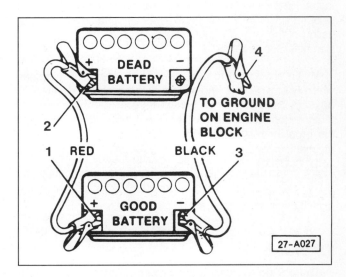

Fig. 6-2. Battery jumper cables connections. Numbers indicate correct sequence for cable attachment.

Have a helper start the car with the good battery and rev the engine slightly, then start the car with the dead battery. Leave the cars running and disconnect the cables in the reverse order in which they were installed. The car with the dead battery should be run for at least a half an hour to recharge the battery.

6.4 Coolant Temperature Warning Light - Overheating

If the coolant warning light on the instrument panel flashes, the engine may be overheated. Even if the temperature gauge is not indicating a high temperature, find a safe place to stop, stop the engine, and inspect cooling system. Open the hood to help cool the engine. Continuing to drive an overheated car can cause expensive damage.

> **WARNING** ──
>
> *Do not remove the coolant reservoir or radiator caps with the engine hot. Undoing either could spray hot coolant, and cause burns, or damage the engine.*

> **WARNING** ──
>
> *Do not touch the radiator fan blades. They will rotate spontaneously when the thermoswitch turns the fan on, even with the ignition off, until the engine has cooled sufficiently. This may take ten minutes or more.*

> **CAUTION** ──
>
> *Do not add cold water or coolant to a hot engine. Severe engine damage could result from the sudden temperature change.*

The radiator fan should be running. If not, then this may be the cause of overheating, especially if the warning light came on while the car was in slow traffic. Let the engine cool, and check the coolant level as described in **LUBRICATION AND MAINTENANCE**. The car can still be driven, but it should only be as far as is necessary until repairs are made. Watch the temperature gauge closely, and stop to cool the engine if the warning light comes on again.

If the fan is running and everything seems normal in the engine compartment, then the overheating may be caused by the driving conditions, such as operating the air conditioner in slow traffic, or by a low coolant level or damaged V-belt. Turn off the air conditioner. Let the engine cool and check the coolant and V-belt as described in **LUBRICATION AND MAINTENANCE**.

If no coolant is visible in the coolant reservoir, then remove the radiator cap to check the level and add coolant. The car can be driven, but have the cooling system thoroughly checked as soon as possible. If replacement coolant is not available, then plain water can be used, but the coolant should eventually be drained and refilled with coolant of the proper anti-freeze/water ratio.

If steam comes from the engine compartment then there most likely is a burst coolant hose or a large leak in the cooling system. To find the hole, look for signs of coolant leakage on hoses, at hose connections, or on the radiator. Let the engine cool thoroughly, then add coolant or water to fill the system and start the engine. If a great deal of water or coolant flows out of the hole, then the car should not be driven until repairs are made. If there is a slight seepage, then it may be possible to drive a short distance, adding coolant as needed.

If none of the above conditions apply, and the coolant gauge does not indicate a hot engine, then the warning light system may be faulty. The car can be driven, but closely watch the temperature gauge.

6.5 Oil Pressure Warning Light

If the oil pressure warning light comes on while driving the car, stop the engine immediately to prevent severe engine damage. Check the oil level as described in **LUBRICATION AND MAINTENANCE**. If the level is low, add oil to the correct level and start the engine. If the light still flashes, do not operate the car at all. Have it towed to the nearest authorized Volkswagen dealer or qualified repair shop.

6.6 Dim Lights

Headlights that are dim or gradually getting dimmer generally indicate a problem with the battery or charging system. The red alternator warning light may come on as the lights are dimming. In either case, the engine and accessories are running off of the battery alone, and will soon discharge it altogether.

If possible, do not turn the engine off, unless you have the capability to jump start it. There may not be enough power in the starting system to restart the engine. Instead, turn off as many electrical consumers as possible. This will reduce the current drain and will allow the car to be driven further before you lose all battery power.

With the engine and ignition off, check to see if the battery cables are firmly attached, or if there are any loose wires leading to the battery or to the alternator. If any of the wires look heavily corroded (covered by fluffy white deposits), then disconnecting, cleaning, and reinstalling them may solve the problem. Also check V-belt tension as described in **LUBRICATION AND MAINTENANCE**.

6.7 Towing

The cars covered by this manual can be towed either flat, on all four wheels, or by a tow truck using typical sling-type towing equipment.

If flat-towing the car, use the towing eyes at the front of the car under the bumper (Fig. 6-3). Set the transmission in neutral.

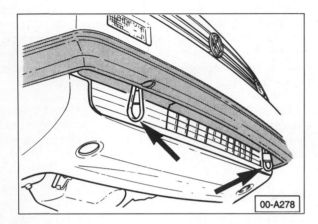

Fig. 6-3. Front towing eyes (arrows) used when flat-towing cars.

If using sling-type towing equipment, attach grab hooks to the towing eyes under the bumper, position a four-foot-long piece of 4 x 4 against the eyes and under the bumper, and raise the car four inches off the ground as shown in Fig. 6-4. Attach safety chains at the front to the lower control arms, and at the rear to the rear axle. Set the transmission in neutral.

CAUTION ━━

GTI models should not be towed from the rear using sling-type towing equipment. Damage to the exhaust pipe or lower body panel may result.

WARNING ━━

Do not allow passengers to ride in a car being towed by sling.

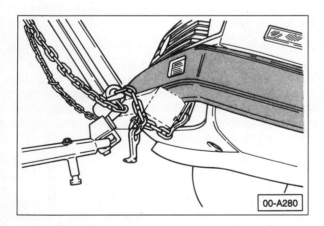

Fig. 6-4. Correct installation of sling-type towing equipment at front of car. Rear hook up is similar.

Cars with automatic transmission should not be towed faster than 30 mph or further than a distance of 30 miles (48 km/h, 48 km) if the front wheels are on the ground. Damage to the transmission could result. If exceeding the limits, use wheel dollies, or remove the drive axles and support the front wheel bearings as described in **SUSPENSION AND STEERING**. There are no speed or distance restrictions when towing cars with manual transmission, provided the transaxle is filled to the correct level with lubricant.

6.8 Spare Parts Kit

Carrying a basic set of spare parts with you in your car can prevent a minor breakdown from turning into a major annoyance. Many of the following items won't allow you to do major repair work on the car, but they will help in the event of the failure of something which can disable the car or compromise its safety.

Spare Parts Kit - Basic Contents:

1. V-belt(s) for the alternator and/or water pump (on some models there is one belt, on others two separate belts)

2. one or two quarts of engine oil

3. a gallon container of engine coolant (pre-mixed anti-freeze and water)

4. spare fuel pump relay

5. a new, unopened bottle of brake fluid

6. 10 amp, 15 amp, and 20 amp fuses

7. upper and lower radiator hoses

Spare Parts Kit - Additional Contents:

1. replacement headlight (sealed beam or bulb)

2. brake light, turn signal light, and tail light bulbs

3. other relays such as headlight, turn signal, or load reduction

4. wiper blades

5. distributor cap and rotor

LUBRICATION AND MAINTENANCE

Contents

Introduction		3
1. General Description		4
1.1	Scheduled Maintenance	4
1.2	Fluid and Lubricant Specifications	4
1.3	Engine Oil Change	4
1.4	Tune-up	4
1.5	Engine Compartment Maintenance	4
1.6	Under-car Maintenance	4
1.7	Body and Interior Maintenance	4
1.8	Cleaning and Preserving	4
2. Scheduled Maintenance		4
3. Fluid and Lubricant Specifications		10
	Engine Oil	11
	Gear Oil - Manual Transmission and Final Drive	11
	Brake Fluid	11
	Engine Coolant (Anti-freeze)	11
	Gasoline Additive	12
	Greases	12
4. Engine Oil Change		12
4.1	Changing Engine Oil and Filter	12
5. Tune-up		14
5.1	Air Filter	14
5.2	Spark Plugs	15
5.3	Distributor Cap, Rotor, and Spark Plug Wires	16
5.4	Fuel Filters	16
	Main Fuel Filter (gasoline)	16

	Mini Fuel Filter	16
	Diesel Fuel Filter	17
5.5	EGR System (Canada 90 H.P. engine w/automatic transmission only)	17
5.6	Idle Speed	17
5.7	Compression Test	17
5.8	Diesel Fuel Water Separator	17
	Draining Water From Diesel Fuel Filter	18
5.9	Valve Adjustment (diesel and turbo diesel only)	18
6. Engine Compartment Maintenance		18
6.1	Battery	18
	Checking and Cleaning Battery	18
	Replacing Battery	19
	Charging Battery	19
6.2	V-Belts	19
	Inspecting and Adjusting	19
	Replacing V-Belts	20
6.3	Cooling System	20
	Checking Coolant Level	20
	Inspecting Hoses	20
6.4	Power Steering	21
6.5	Oxygen Sensor (gasoline engines only)	21
	Replacing Oxygen Sensor	21
	Resetting OXS Warning Light Counter	21
6.6	Clutch Adjustment	22
7. Under-Car Maintenance		22
7.1	Tires and Wheels	22
	Tire Inflation Pressure	22
	Tire Rotation	22

Wheel Alignment 23

7.2 Brakes 23
Checking Brake Fluid Level 23
Inspecting Brake Hoses and Lines 23
Checking Disc Brake Pad Wear 23
Checking Rear Drum Brake Lining Wear 23
Replacing Brake Fluid 24

7.3 Exhaust System 24
7.4 Constant Velocity Joints 24
7.5 Manual Transaxle Service 24
Checking and Filling Transaxle Lubricant 24

7.6 Automatic Transaxle Service 25
Checking and Filling ATF 25
Draining and Replacing ATF, and Cleaning ATF Strainer 26
Checking and Filling Final Drive Lubricant 26
Checking Kickdown Operation 26

7.7 Front Suspension and Steering 27

8. Body and Interior Maintenance 27
8.1 Windshield Wiper Blades 27
8.2 Body Lubrication 28
8.3 Seat Belts 28

9. Cleaning and Preserving 28
9.1 Care of Exterior Finish 28
Washing 28
Waxing 28
Polishing 28
Washing Chassis 28
Special Cleaning 28
9.2 Care of Interior 28
Leatherette Upholstery and Trim 28

Tables

a. Scheduled Maintenance (Cars with gasoline engines) 5
b. Scheduled Maintenance (cars with diesel engines) . . . 7
c. Oil Viscosity Requirement vs. Temperature (Gasoline engines except 16-valve) 10
d. Oil Viscosity Requirement vs. Temperature (16-valve gasoline engines) 10
e. Oil Viscosity Requirement vs. Temperature (Diesel engines) 10
f. Fluids and Lubricants 11
g. Engine Oil Change Specifications 13
h. Spark Plug Specifications 15
i. DIN and SAE Battery Rating Equivalents 19
j. V-Belt Deflection Specifications 20
k. Recommended Wheel and Tire Specifications 22
l. Brake Pad and Lining Minimum Thickness (Including brake pad backing plate or brake shoe) 23
m. Kickdown Shift Points 27

Lubrication and Maintenance

Introduction

The service life of your car depends on the kind of maintenance it receives. The procedures described in this section of the manual include all periodic checks and maintenance steps necessary for long and reliable operation of your car, as well as instructions for basic car care.

The Owner's Manual, the Maintenance Record, and the Warranty Booklet originally supplied with the car contain the maintenance schedules that apply to your Volkswagen. Following these schedules will ensure safe and dependable operation. In addition, many of the maintenance items are necessary to maintain warranty protection. Volkswagen is constantly updating their recommended maintenance procedures and requirements. The information contained here is as accurate as possible at the time of publication. If there is any doubt about what procedures apply to a specific model or model year, or what intervals should be followed, always take the Owner's Manual, the Maintenance Record, and the Warranty Booklet as your guide, and remember that an authorized Volkswagen dealer always has the latest maintenance information.

Some maintenance procedures, such as oil change service, require no special tools and can be carried out by almost all Volkswagen owners, regardless of mechanical experience. Certain other diagnostic and maintenance tasks require special tools and equipment. Cylinder compression tests, idle speed and idle mixture (% CO) checks, wheel alignment, and ignition timing are some examples. If you lack the skills, the tools, or a suitable workplace for performing any of the maintenance described in this section, we suggest you leave this work to an authorized Volkswagen dealer or other qualified shop. We especially urge you to consult an authorized Volkswagen dealer before beginning any repairs on a car that is still subject to Volkswagen's extensive warranty coverage.

Although the Volkswagens covered by this manual generally require less maintenance than those of five or ten years ago, all of the maintenance work described here is important and should be performed promptly and correctly. Your Volkswagen should not be thought of as a maintenance-free machine. Correct care will protect your investment and help you to get many years of reliability and enjoyable driving from your Volkswagen.

1. GENERAL DESCRIPTION

Lubrication and maintenance is the performance of those routine procedures which are necessary to keep a car operating at its peak and to maintain the requirements for full warranty coverage.

This section of the manual contains information about all of the routine maintenance that is specified for the Volkswagens covered by this manual.

1.1 Scheduled Maintenance

These are the tables which list all of the routine maintenance required for a particular model or model year, and the mileage and time intervals at which particular maintenance tasks should be performed.

1.2 Fluid and Lubricant Specifications

The fluids and lubricants used in Volkswagens have been carefully chosen for their ability to perform and adequately protect. To maintain these high standards of performance, and to ensure that Volkswagen's warranty coverage remains in effect, use only the fluids and lubricants which meet the standards set forth by Volkswagen and listed under this heading.

1.3 Engine Oil Change

Regular changing of the engine lubricating oil and the engine oil filter is perhaps the single most important kind of maintenance that a car can receive. It is also simple and easy.

1.4 Tune-up

Much of what has traditionally been considered part of a tune-up has been rendered obsolete by sophisticated Volkswagen technology. Therefore, tune-ups have become a less frequent and simpler part of Volkswagen maintenance.

The heading **5. Tune-up**, covers those few parts of the traditional tune-up which are still included by Volkswagen as scheduled maintenance.

1.5 Engine Compartment Maintenance

Many of the most important routine maintenance tasks are performed under the hood within easy reach. They are grouped together so that complete maintenance can be planned and carried out most efficiently.

1.6 Under-car Maintenance

Thorough maintenance requires periodic inspection and servicing of parts which are only accessible by raising the car. Since a suitable level workspace and equipment to raise the car are required, this maintenance requires a little more planning. As a convenient alternative, you may wish to leave these items to an authorized Volkswagen dealer or other qualified and suitably equipped repair shop.

1.7 Body and Interior Maintenance

Periodic service and inspection of certain safety-related body and interior equipment is specified by Volkswagen and covered under this heading.

1.8 Cleaning and Preserving

Keeping a car clean not only improves its appearance, it can also reduce harmful effects of dirt and other contaminants and actually preserve the car's appearance. Information on recommended cleaning materials and methods can be found under this heading.

2. SCHEDULED MAINTENANCE

The maintenance schedules below list all of the routine maintenance tasks specified by Volkswagen, as well as the mileage and time intervals at which they should be performed. Maintenance should be performed according to the specified time **or** mileage interval, whichever comes first. In any instance where the publisher has recommended maintenance or a maintenance interval which differs from that specified by Volkswagen, such recommendations are more conservative, and still meet Volkswagen's maintenance requirements.

> *CAUTION* ━━
> *Aside from keeping Volkswagens in the best possible condition, the scheduled maintenance plays a role in maintaining full coverage under Volkswagen's extensive warranties. If in doubt about the terms and conditions of your car's warranty, an authorized Volkswagen dealer can explain them.*

Except where noted, the maintenance items listed apply to all models covered by this manual. The boldface numbers which appear after each listing are the headings in this section where the maintenance procedure is discussed in more detail. The columns on the right side of each table give quick-reference information about the job—whether tools are needed, whether the procedure requires new parts, whether the engine should be warm, and in some cases a recommendation, because of the need for special equipment or expertise, that the job be turned over to an authorized Volkswagen dealer.

Table a. Scheduled Maintenance (cars with gasoline engine)

every 7,500 miles (12,000 km) or 6 months	every 15,000 miles (24,000 km) or 12 months	every 30,000 miles (48,000 km) or 2 years	every 60,000 miles (96,000 km) or 4 years	maintenance item		Tools required	New parts required	Engine warm	Dealer service recommended
Oil Change Service									
*	*	*	*	Change oil	4.1	*	*	*	
*	*	*	*	Change oil filter **	4.1	*	*	*	
Tune-up									
	*	*	*	Clean air filter (recommended for California models)	5.1				
		*	*	Replace air filter	5.1		*		
		*	*	Check engine compression (recommended for California models)	5.7	*			*
	*	*	*	Check EGR system (Canada 90 H.P. engine only)	5.5				
	*	*	*	Check idle speed, adjust if necessary (except California models)	5.6	*		*	*
*				Remove mini fuel filter (at first 15,000 mi. service, if so equipped)	5.4	*	*		
		*	*	Replace spark plugs	5.2	*	*		
	*	*	*	Replace spark plugs (Canada 90 H.P. engine only)	5.2	*	*		
		*	*	Replace gasoline fuel filter **	5.4	*	*		
		*	*	Inspect ignition distributor cap, rotor and spark plug wires, and replace as necessary **	5.3				
Engine Compartment Maintenance									
	*	*	*	Check automatic transmission fluid (ATF) level and add as necessary	7.6			*	
	*	*	*	Check brake fluid level and add as necessary	7.2				
*	*	*	*	Adjust clutch (except models with self-adjusting clutch cable; adjust at first 7,500 mi. service and every 15,000 mi.)	6.6				
	*	*	*	Check engine coolant level and add as necessary	6.3	*			
	*	*	*	Engine: Inspect for leaks around seals and gaskets					
		*	*	Replace oxygen sensor and reset OXS indicator light (1985 models, 1986 models, and 1987 models except 16-valve	6.5	*	*		*

**Maintenance recommended by the publisher which meets or exceeds Volkswagen requirements

(continued on next page)

Table a. Scheduled Maintenance (cars with gasoline engine) (cont'd)

every 7,500 miles (12,000 km) or 6 months	every 15,000 miles (24,000 km) or 12 months	every 30,000 miles (48,000 km) or 2 years	every 60,000 miles (96,000 km) or 4 years	maintenance item		Tools required	New parts required	Engine warm	Dealer service recommended
Engine Compartment Maintenance (cont'd)									
			*	Replace oxygen sensor (1987 16-valve models, and all 1988 1989 models)	6.5	*	*		*
	*	*	*	Check power steering fluid level and add as necessary	6.4			*	
		*	*	Inspect V-belt tension and condition, and adjust or replace as necessary	6.2	*	*		
			*	Replace camshaft timing belt **	see **ENGINE**	*	*		*
		*	*	Drain and flush cooling system and replace coolant **	see **COOLING SYSTEM**	*	*		
			*	Replace cooling system hoses**	6.3	*	*		
			*	Replace V-belts **	6.2	*	*		
Under-car Maintenance									
	*	*	*	Automatic transaxle final drive: check for leaks. Check oil level if leaks are present	7.6	*			
		*	*	Drain automatic transmission fluid (ATF), replace filter and ATF (recommended for transmission subjected to severe service)	7.6	*	*	*	*
	*	*	*	Inspect brake system for damaged hoses or leaks, check brake pad and brake shoe wear	7.2				
		*	*	Replace brake fluid	7.2	*	*		*
*		*	*	Inspect exhaust system	7.3				
*		*	*	Inspect front suspension ball joint dust seals, tie rod ends, tie rods (1985 models)	7.7	*			
		*	*	Inspect front suspension ball joint dust seals, tie rod ends, tie rods (1986–1989 models)	7.7	*			
*		*	*	Manual transaxle: check for leaks, check oil level if leaks are present	7.5	*			
		*	*	Replace oxygen sensor and reset OXS indicator light (1985 models, 1986 models, and 1987 models except 16-valve	6.5	*	*		*
			*	Replace oxygen sensor (1987 16-valve models, and all 1988 1989 models)	6.5	*	*		*

**Maintenance recommended by the publisher which meets or exceeds Volkswagen requirements

(continued on next page)

Table a. Scheduled Maintenance (cars with gasoline engine) (cont'd)

every 7,500 miles (12,000 km) or 6 months	every 15,000 miles (24,000 km) or 12 months	every 30,000 miles (48,000 km) or 2 years	every 60,000 miles (96,000 km) or 4 years	maintenance item		Tools required	New parts required	Engine warm	Dealer service recommended
Under-car Maintenance (cont'd)									
*	*		*	Inspect steering and drive axles, steering rack, constant velocity (CV) joint boots	7.7				
*	*		*	Inspect wheels and tires (1985 models)	7.1				
Body and Interior Maintenance									
*	*		*	Lubricate door check rods (1985 models)	8.2				
*	*		*	Check headlight aiming and adjust as necessary (1985 models)	see **BODY AND INTERIOR**	*			*
*	*		*	Sliding sunroof: clean guide rails, lubricate with silicone spray (1988–1989 models)	see **BODY AND INTERIOR**				
Road Test									
*	*		*	Check braking performance, steering, heating and ventilation efficiency, and automatic transmission kickdown					*

NOTE —

The maintenance schedules, published by Volkswagen, list what Volkswagen considers to be the minimum maintenance requirements based on typical expected use at reasonable speeds and in moderate climates. If the car is subjected to frequent short trips or extended use under conditions such as temperature extremes or excessive dust, more frequent maintenance intervals are necessary. See an authorized Volkswagen dealer for service advice.

Table b. Scheduled Maintenance (cars with diesel engine)

every 5,000 miles (8,000 km) or 6 mo.	every 7,500 miles (12,000 km) or 6 months	every 15,000 miles (24,000 km) or 12 months	every 30,000 miles (48,000 km) or 2 years	every 60,000 miles (96,000 km) or 4 years	maintenance item		Tools required	New parts required	Engine warm	Dealer service recommended
Oil Change Service										
	*	*	*	*	Change engine oil (except turbo diesel models)	4.1	*	*	*	
	*	*	*	*	Change oil filter (except turbo diesel models)**	4.1	*	*	*	
*	*	*	*	*	Change engine oil (turbo diesel models)	4.1	*	*	*	
*	*	*	*	*	Change oil filter (turbo diesel models)**	4.1	*	*	*	

**Maintenance recommended by the publisher which meets or exceeds Volkswagen requirements

(continued on next page)

Table b. Scheduled Maintenance (cars with diesel engine) (cont'd)

every 5,000 miles (8,000 km) or 6 mo.	every 7,500 miles (12,000 km) or 6 months	every 15,000 miles (24,000 km) or 12 months	every 30,000 miles (48,000 km) or 2 years	every 60,000 miles (96,000 km) or 4 years	maintenance item	ref.	Tools required	New parts required	Engine warm	Dealer service recommended
Tune-up										
			*	*	Check idle speed and adjust if necessary (except California models)	5.6	*		*	*
		*	*	*	Clean air filter (recommended for California models)	5.1				
			*	*	Replace air filter	5.1		*		
*		*	*	*	Drain water from fuel filter (1985 Golf models without water separator only)	5.8	*			
			*	*	Replace fuel filter	5.4	*	*		
		*	*	*	Drain water separator	5.8	*			
		*	*	*	Check valve clearance and adjust if necessary, replace cylinder head cover gaskets (1985 and 1986 models with adjustable mechanical cam followers only)	5.9	*	*	*	
Engine Compartment Maintenance										
	*	*	*	*	Adjust clutch (except models with self-adjusting cable)	6.6	*			
*	*	*	*	*	Adjust clutch (turbo diesel only, except models with self-adjusting cable)	6.6	*			
			*	*	Check engine coolant level and add as necessary	6.3		*		
			*	*	Check battery electrolyte level (1985 models)	6.1				
			*	*	Inspect V-belt tension and condition, and adjust or replace as necessary	6.2	*			
			*	*	Check brake warning light switch function (1985 models)	see **BRAKES**				
		*	*	*	Engine: check for leaks around seals and gaskets					
		*	*	*	Check brake fluid level and add as necessary	7.2				
		*	*	*	Check automatic transmission fluid (ATF) level and add as necessary	7.6			*	
		*	*	*	Check power steering fluid level and add as necessary	7.7			*	
				*	Replace camshaft timing belt **	see **ENGINE**	*	*		*
			*	*	Drain and flush cooling system and replace coolant **	6.3	*	*		
				*	Replace cooling system hoses **	6.3	*	*		
				*	Replace V-belts **	6.2	*	*		

**Maintenance recommended by the publisher which meets or exceeds Volkswagen requirements

(continued on next page)

Table b. Scheduled Maintenance (cars with diesel engine) (cont'd)

every 5,000 miles (8,000 km) or 6 mo.	every 7,500 miles (12,000 km) or 6 months	every 15,000 miles (24,000 km) or 12 months	every 30,000 miles (48,000 km) or 2 years	every 60,000 miles (96,000 km) or 4 years	maintenance item	ref	Tools required	New parts required	Engine warm	Dealer service recommended
Under-car Maintenance										
			*	*	Replace brake fluid	7.2	*	*		*
		*	*	*	Inspect steering and drive axles, steering rack, and constant velocity (CV) joint boots	7.7				
		*	*	*	Inspect front suspension ball joint dust seals, tie rod ends, and tie rods (1985 models)	7.7				
		*	*	*	Inspect front suspension ball joint dust seals, tie rod ends, and tie rods (1986–1989 models)	7.7				
		*	*	*	Engine: check for leaks around seals and gaskets					
		*	*	*	Manual transmission: check for leaks, check oil level if leaks are present	7.5			*	
		*	*	*	Automatic transaxle final drive: check for leaks, check oil level if leaks are present	7.6			*	
			*	*	Drain automatic transmission fluid (ATF), replace filter and ATF (1985 models, also recommended for transmission subjected to severe service)	7.6	*	*	*	*
		*	*	*	Inspect exhaust system for damage and leaks	7.3				
		*	*	*	Inspect brake system for damaged hoses or leaks, check brake pad and brake shoe wear	7.2				
		*	*	*	Inspect wheels and tires (1985 models)	7.1				
Body and Interior Maintenance										
		*	*	*	Lubricate door check rods (1985 models)	8.2				
		*	*	*	Check headlight aiming and adjust as necessary (1985 models)	see **BODY AND INTERIOR**	*			*
		*	*	*	Sliding sunroof: clean guide rails, lubricate with silicone spray (1988–1989 models)	see **BODY AND INTERIOR**				
Road Test										
		*	*	*	Check braking performance, steering, heating and ventilation efficiency, and automatic transmission kickdown					*

**Maintenance recommended by the publisher which meets or exceeds Volkswagen requirements

NOTE

The maintenance schedules published by Volkswagen, list what Volkswagen considers to be the minimum maintenance requirements based on typical expected use at reasonable speeds and in moderate climates. If the car is subjected to frequent short trips or extended use under conditions such as temperature extremes or excessive dust, more frequent maintenance intervals are necessary. See an authorized Volkswagen dealer for service advice.

3. FLUID AND LUBRICANT SPECIFICATIONS

The fluids and lubricants listed in the tables which follow are those specified by Volkswagen for use in the cars covered by this manual.

CAUTION

The use of fluids which do not meet Volkswagen's specifications may impair performance and reliability, and may void warranty coverage.

Table c, **Table d**, and **Table e** give engine oil viscosity (SAE grade) vs. operating temperature range for the different Volkswagen engine types covered in this manual. **Table f** lists fluid and lubricant specifications.

CAUTION

Avoid high-speed long distance driving when using SAE 5W-20 or SAE 10W oil, especially if the outside temperature rises above the indicated limits. If maximum loads on the engine or continuous speeds above 60 mph (100 km/h) are expected, use an oil with the next higher viscosity rating.

Table c. Oil Viscosity Requirement vs. Temperature
(Gasoline engines except 16-valve)

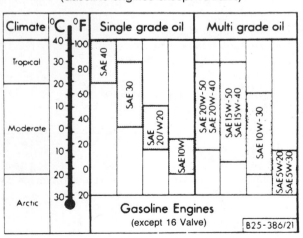

Table d. Oil Viscosity Requirement vs. Temperature
(16-valve gasoline engines)

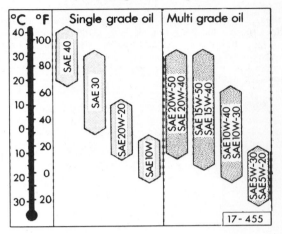

Table e. Oil Viscosity Requirement vs. Temperature
(Diesel engines)

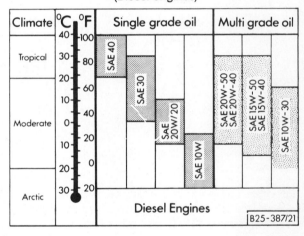

Table f. Fluids and Lubricants

	Specification	Approximate Capacity
gasoline engines except 16-valve	API service SE	4.0 L (4.2 US qt.) with filter change
16-valve engines	API Service SF	4.0 L (4.2 US qt.) with filter change
diesel engines	API Service CC	4.5 L (4.7 US qt.) with filter change
turbo diesel engines	API Service CD	4.5 L (4.7 US qt.) with filter change

continued on next page

Table f. Fluids and Lubricants (cont'd)

	Specification	Approximate Capacity
manual transmission and final drive	SAE 80W or 80W/90 hypoid oil API service GL-4, Mil-L-2105	2.0 L (2.1 US qt.)
final drive (with automatic transmission)*	SAE 80W/90 or 90 hypoid oil, API service GL-5, Mil-L-2105B	0.8 L (0.8 US qt.)
automatic transmission fluid (ATF)	Dexron®; or Dexron II®	3.0 L (3.2 US qt.) refill 6.1 l (6.4 US qt.) dry fill
power steering fluid	Dexron®; or Dexron II® ATF or equivalent	0.85 L (0.85 US qt.)
brake fluid	DOT 4, SAE J 1703, FMVSS 116	—
engine coolant	50% phosphate-free ethylene glycol "G 11" anti-freeze (VW part no. ZVW 237 102) 50% distilled water	7.0 L (7.3 US qt.)

Engine Oil

Oil is essential to the engine. It provides a lubricating film between all moving parts, and also has a cooling function. Maintaining an adequate supply of clean oil is one of the best ways of making an engine last. Some engine oil is consumed during normal operation, making it necessary to regularly check and "top up" the oil supply. Since oil also becomes contaminated and breaks down over time, regular oil changes are necessary.

Engine oil requirements are defined by the oil's American Petroleum Institute (API) service rating, and by its Society of Automotive Engineers (SAE) viscosity rating. This information can be found on the oil can or bottle, often on a standard label as shown in Fig. 3-1.

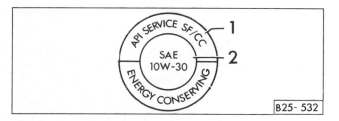

Fig. 3-1. Engine oil label showing API service rating (**1**) and SAE viscosity number (**2**).

The API service rating designates the type of use for which the oil is suited. It is based on the additives that are used to resist oil break-down and carbon formation, inhibit corrosion, resist foaming, neutralize acids, and help remove deposits and keep contaminants suspended in the oil.

For gasoline engines, the service ratings range from SA to SF, with SF rated for the most demanding applications. For diesel engines, the ratings range from CA to CD, with CD rated for the most severe use. Oils may have service ratings for both gasoline and diesel engines, SF/CC for example.

The SAE viscosity rating indicates resistance to flow. An oil designated SAE 40 has a higher viscosity, greater resistance to flow, than an oil designated SAE 30. While higher viscosity oils will generally offer greater engine protection, they may be too thick and resistant to flow, and may inhibit starting during cold weather.

The correct engine oil viscosity depends on the operating temperature range. See the viscosity vs. temperature tables elsewhere in this section. Select a viscosity rating for the lowest anticipated temperature at which the engine must start.

Multi-viscosity oils have additives that make them suitable for use over a wider range of temperatures. For example, an oil rated SAE 10W-30 offers the flow characteristics of SAE 10 at low temperatures, but the protection capability of SAE 30 at engine operating temperature. The "W" in the SAE rating indicates that the oil is suitable for winter use.

Oils of different viscosity ratings can be mixed, but mixing oils of different API service ratings or brands is not recommended.

Gear Oil—Manual Transmission and Final Drive

Gear oil requirements are also defined by API service rating and SAE viscosity rating, as described in **Engine Oil** above.

Manual transmissions and final drives share a common oil supply. Automatic transmissions and final drives are separate. With an automatic transmission, only the final drive uses gear oil.

Brake Fluid

Brake fluid deserves special consideration because it absorbs moisture easily, and moisture in the fluid affects brake performance and reliability. When replacing or adding brake fluid, use only new fluid from previously unopened containers. Do not use brake fluid that has been bled from the system, even if it is brand new. Volkswagen does not recommend the use of DOT 5 synthetic brake fluids.

Engine Coolant
(Anti-freeze)

Volkswagen recommends coolant that is a mixture of water and phosphate-free anti-freeze containing ethylene glycol. Anti-freeze raises the boiling point and lowers the freezing point of the coolant. It also contains additives which help prevent cooling system corrosion.

Gasoline Additive

Because many gasolines do not contain the necessary additives to help prevent carbon deposits in the fuel injection system, Volkswagen recommends the periodic use of Autobahn Gasoline Additive, Volkswagen part no. ZVW 246 001, which is available from any authorized Volkswagen dealer.

CAUTION ━━

Follow all label directions. Do not use more than once every 2500 mi. (4000 km).

Greases

Two different types of grease are used for lubrication of drive train and brake components. Multipurpose grease (lithium grease) has a wider temperature tolerance range than ordinary grease and should be used for most general lubrication purposes, including roller bearings.

Molybdenum grease is lithium grease with a friction-reducing molybdenum disulfide additive. This special grease, Volkswagen part no. G 000 602, is recommended for certain applications including lubrication of the drive axle constant velocity (CV) joints.

4. ENGINE OIL CHANGE

The engine oil level is checked with a dipstick, located in the engine block behind the alternator. To check the level, pull out the dipstick, wipe it clean, reinsert it all the way, and withdraw it again. The oil level is correct if it is between the two marks near the end of the stick. The location of the dipstick and the level marks are shown in Fig. 4-1. The upper (max) mark indicates full, the highest acceptable oil level. The lower mark (min) indicates the minimum acceptable level. The difference between the marks is approximately 1 liter (1 US qt.).

Always check the oil with the car on a level surface, after the engine has been stopped for at least a few minutes. For the most accurate check, especially on 16-valve engines, wait a few hours or overnight.

Add oil through the filler cap on the top of the cylinder head cover shown in Fig. 4-2. Add only the amount needed to bring the oil level to the "max" mark on the dipstick, using an oil of the correct viscosity and grade as described above in **Engine Oil**. Too much oil is just as harmful as too little.

The amount of oil which needs to be added between oil changes varies from one engine to another. Generally, a new engine or an engine operated routinely at high speeds will consume more oil. It is helpful to become familiar with the rate at which a particular engine requires oil. A sudden increase may be an early warning of engine mechanical problems.

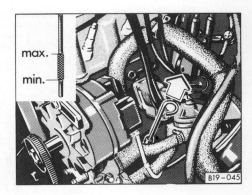

Fig. 4-1. Engine oil dipstick location in engine compartment. Withdraw in direction of arrow. Inset shows maximum (**max**) and minimum (**min**) marks on dipstick used in determining correct oil level.

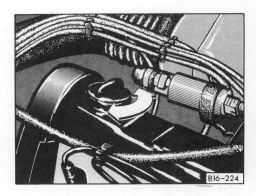

Fig. 4-2. Location of oil filler cap. Remove and install by turning (arrows). 16-valve engine (not shown) is similar.

4.1 Changing Engine Oil and Filter

The 7,500-mile or 6 month oil change interval specified in the maintenance schedule should be the basic guide to scheduling oil changes. Do not rely on the color of the oil on the dipstick to indicate when a change is needed. Because of the detergent additives in the oil, fresh oil will look dark after only a few hundred miles.

If the car is used primarily for short trips, or routinely operated in dusty conditions or slow-moving traffic, the oil should be changed more frequently. In general, changing the oil at more frequent intervals will help better protect the engine, and promote longer engine life. For diesel engines using SAE 10W-40 oil in winter, the oil should be changed every 3,000 miles (4800 km).

Although it is an acceptable practice to change the oil filter at every other oil change, reusing the old filter leaves about ½ quart of old oil in the lubrication system. The publisher recommends also changing the oil filter with every oil change, no matter what the interval.

A complete oil change requires approximately 5 US qt. of new oil (see **3. Fluid and Lubricant Specifications**), a new oil filter, and a new drain plug sealing washer. Part numbers and oil capacities are given in **Table g**. The equipment needed, a drain plug socket or box wrench (19 mm), a drain pan of at least 6 US qt. (5.6 L) capacity, and an oil filter wrench, is described in **FUNDAMENTALS**.

Table g. Engine Oil Change Specifications

Engine Oil Capacity (approximate)	
gasoline engines	
(with filter change)	4.0 liters (4.2 US qt.)
(without filter change)	3.5 liters (3.7 US qt.)
diesel engines	
(with filter change)	4.5 liters (4.8 US qt.)
(without filter change)	4.0 liters (4.2 US qt.)
Oil Filter	
gasoline engines	Volkswagen part no. 056 115 561 G
diesel engines	Volkswagen part no. 068 115 561 B
Oil Pan Drain Plug Sealing Washer	
gasoline and diesel engines	Volkswagen part no. N 013 849 2

To change oil and filter:

1. Run the car for a few minutes to slightly warm the engine and the oil, then shut the engine off.

2. With the car on level ground, place a drain pan under the oil drain plug shown in Fig. 4-3.

> **NOTE** ——
>
> If a shallow enough drain pan is used, the car will not need to be raised off the ground.

3. Using a 19 mm socket or box wrench, loosen the drain plug. By hand, remove the plug and let the oil drain into the pan.

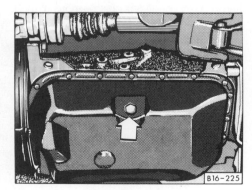

Fig. 4-3. Engine oil drain plug (arrow) in oil pan underneath engine (shown from rear).

> **CAUTION** ——
>
> *Pull the loose plug away from the hole quickly to avoid being burned by the hot oil. It will run out quickly when the plug is removed.*

4. When the oil flow has diminished to an occasional drip, reinstall the drain plug with a new metal sealing washer and torque the plug to 30 Nm (22 ft. lb.).

5. Move the drain pan slightly forward so that it is directly under the oil filter, shown in Fig. 4-4. Using an oil filter wrench, loosen the filter by turning it counterclockwise (as viewed from below), then remove it by hand.

Fig. 4-4. Engine oil filter located in front of engine, behind radiator. (Shown viewed from below).

6. After the oil stops dripping, wipe clean the oil filter gasket surface on the filter mounting flange. Lubricate the rubber gasket of the new oil filter with a light coating of clean engine oil.

7. Install the filter by hand until the gasket contacts the mounting flange, then turn the filter another ¾ turn to tighten it.

> **CAUTION** ——
>
> *Overtightening the oil filter will make the next change much more difficult, and may deform the gasket, causing leaks.*

8. Refill the crankcase with oil. Approximate oil capacity is given in **Table g.** above. Use the dipstick to check for the correct oil level. Oil specifications are found in **3. Fluid and Lubricant Specifications**.

9. Start the engine and allow it to run for three to five minutes to circulate the new oil, then check for leaks at the drain plug and around the oil filter. Stop the engine and recheck the oil level.

NOTE ——

Dispose of the used oil properly. Use tight-sealing containers and mark them clearly. Check with a local service station or oil retailer about proper disposal.

5. TUNE-UP

A tune-up is regular maintenance of the ignition and fuel systems to compensate for normal wear. Modern Volkswagen electronic ignition and fuel injection systems have eliminated much work involved in a tune-up. For the Volkswagens covered by this manual, only limited tune-up maintenance is necessary to maintain peak performance and economy.

5.1 Air Filter

The specified maintenance intervals for the air filter are based on "normal" use. If the car is operated primarily in dusty conditions, the air filter should be serviced more frequently. A dirty air filter element starves the engine for air, reducing power output and increasing fuel consumption. Fig. 5-1, Fig. 5-2, and Fig. 5-3 show the locations of the air filter housing for the engines covered by this manual.

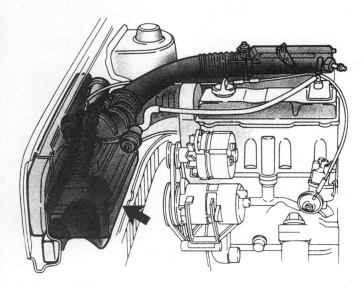

Fig. 5-1. Air filter housing (arrow) for CIS and CIS-E fuel injection systems used on all 1985–1987 cars with gasoline engines, and 1988–1989 cars with 16-valve engines. The correct replacement filter element is Volkswagen part no. 113 129 620.

The upper and lower parts of the air filter are fastened together with spring-clips around the outside edge. To replace the air filter element, unfasten the clips that separate the air filter housing. Take note of the filter's installed position, then remove the old filter element and wipe the inside of the air cleaner housing using a lint-free cloth. On gasoline engines, the filter element is installed with the gasket side facing up. On diesel engines, filter element is installed with the gasket side facing down. Make sure that the two halves of the air filter housing are mated correctly, and refasten the spring-clips.

On California models, clean the element at the specified interval by tapping it lightly, dirty-side down, on a hard surface to remove the dirt. Do not blow it clean with compressed air, as this can cause small tears which will lead to engine contamination. Do not clean it in gasoline or cleaning solvents, and do not coat it with oil.

CAUTION ——

It is especially important when reinstalling a used air filter element that it be in the same position as when it was removed. Reversed installation will allow accumulated dirt to be drawn into the engine.

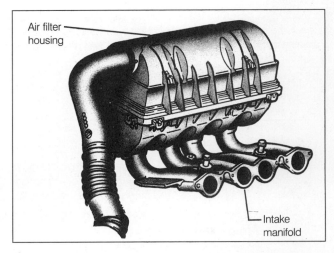

Fig. 5-2. Air filter housing used on diesel engines. The correct replacement filter element is Volkswagen part no. 069 129 620.

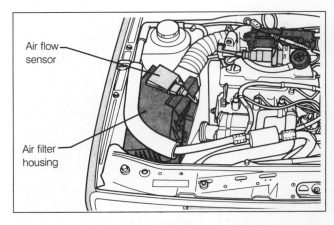

Fig. 5-3. Air filter housing for Digifant II fuel injection systems used on 1988–1989 gasoline engines (except 16-valve).

5.2 Spark Plugs

High temperature and high voltage sparks eventually wear out the spark plug electrodes, and the spark plugs must be replaced. To replace a spark plug, gently remove the spark plug wire by pulling on the protective boot, and blow or brush away any dirt from around the base of the plug to prevent it from entering the engine when the plug is removed.

CAUTION ——

Label the spark plug wires so that each one can be reinstalled on the correct spark plug.

Use a ¹³⁄₁₆ in. spark plug socket to remove spark plugs on all except 16-valve engines. On 16-valve engines, use a ⅝ in. spark plug wrench with a rubber insert that will hold the plugs for installation and removal in the deep spark plug recesses.

The correct spark plugs for the different engines covered by this manual are listed in **Table h**. Use a spark plug gap gauge to check the gap. If necessary, bend the outer electrode slightly to adjust the gap to meet the specification. Do not bend or file the center electrode.

NOTE ——

The electrode gap on the triple-electrode spark plugs used on 16-valve engines cannot be adjusted.

Lightly lubricate the new spark plug threads with a little oil or grease, and thread the plugs in the engine by hand, to prevent cross-threading. Torque the spark plugs to no more than 20 Nm (15 ft. lb.).

Table h. Spark Plug Specifications

Engine Code*	Bosch	Spark Plug Beru	Champion	Electrode Gap
GX	W7 DTC WR 7DS	RS 35	N8GY	0.6–0.8 mm (.024–.031 in.)
MZ	W8 DO	14 8DU	—	0.6–0.8 mm (.024–.031 in.)
HT, RD	W7 DTC	14 7DTU	N8GY	0.7–0.9 mm (.028–.035 in.)
PL	F6 DTC	—	—	0.7–0.9 mm (.028–.035 in.)
RV, PF	W7 DCO	—	—	0.7–0.9 mm (.028–.035 in.)
*See **ENGINE** for more information on engine codes				

For California models, it is recommended for emission control that the spark plugs be removed and cleaned every 15,000 miles (24,000 km). Checking the plugs at this interval on all models can be informative, as the condition of the spark plug is a good indicator of combustion quality which can help diagnose engine faults. Fig. 5-4 shows some examples of spark plug condition and what they mean.

Normal

Normal spark plug has gray or light tan color which indicates proper combustion.

Oil-fouled

Oil-fouled spark plug has wet, oily black deposits caused by excess engine oil getting into combustion chamber, probably due to worn piston rings or valve guide oil seals.

Carbon-fouled

Carbon-fouled spark plug has dry sooty black deposits caused by too much fuel which may indicate fuel injection or ignition problems.

Worn out

Worn out spark plug may have correct gray or light tan color, but shows physical deterioration (enlarged gap, eroded electrodes).

Fig. 5-4. Spark plug appearance which may indicate engine condition. For more information on interpreting spark plug condition, see **ENGINE**. Photos courtesy of Champion Spark Plug Co.

NOTE ——

Any of the abnormal spark plug conditions described above could also result from spark plugs of the wrong specification being installed. Check replacement plugs carefully and follow the spark plug manufacturer's recommendations.

Clean lightly-fouled spark plugs with a light wire brush, and remove all debris from around the electrode. Do not chip the ceramic insulator. Badly fouled spark plugs should be replaced, and the cause of the fouling should be investigated and corrected.

5.3 Distributor Cap, Rotor, and Spark Plug Wires

The distributor cap, the rotor, and the spark plug wires deliver high-voltage spark to the spark plugs. They are subject to insulation breakdown, corrosion fouling, and electrode wear and damage. Inspection every 30,000 miles (48,000 km) or 2 years, and replacement as necessary, are recommended to ensure maximum ignition system efficiency. Guidelines for visual inspection and testing, and instructions for replacement are found in **IGNITION**.

5.4 Fuel Filters

Main Fuel Filter
(gasoline)

Because of varying quality of available gasoline, the fuel filter may become clogged enough during normal operation to restrict fuel flow. To prevent any such problems, and to guarantee continued good performance, the filter should be replaced at the specified interval. The main fuel filter is located beneath the car, just in front of the fuel tank as shown in Fig 5-5.

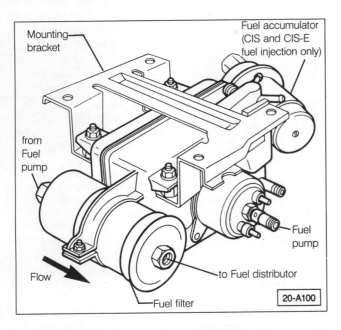

Fig. 5-5. Main gasoline fuel filter. Direction of flow (arrow) is indicated by arrow on filter housing.

When replacing the fuel filter, disconnect the battery negative (−) terminal and clamp the filter inlet and outlet hoses to lessen fuel spillage. Use new hose clamps. On cars where the inlet and outlet hoses are attached with banjo fittings, torque the inlet fitting to 25 Nm (18 ft. lb.) and the outlet fitting to 20 Nm (15 ft. lb.).

Mini Fuel Filter

Many Volkswagens equipped with CIS or CIS-E fuel injection have a mini fuel filter installed in the system to collect any contaminants which may have been trapped in the system during manufacturing. The filter, shown in Fig. 5-6, is a small mesh screen built into the fuel inlet union bolt on the fuel distributor. The bolt with the mini filter is identified by a disc shape on its head. Removal of the mini filter is a one-time procedure. The old bolt/filter is replaced with a new union bolt (Volkswagen part no. N 021 071 2) and two new sealing washers (Volkswagen part no. N 013 812 2). Torque the new union bolt to 20 Nm (15 ft. lb.).

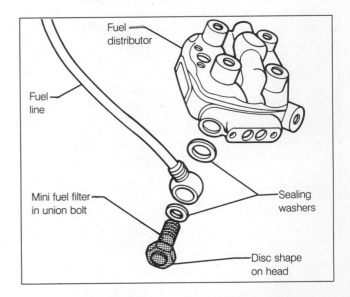

Fig. 5-6. Fuel line union bolt with mini fuel filter. (CIS-E fuel injection shown, CIS fuel injection is similar).

Diesel Fuel Filter

The diesel fuel filter is located in the engine compartment, in the fuel line, before the injection pump. See Fig. 5-7. The correct replacement filter is Volkswagen part no. 191 127 401. For information on draining water from the diesel fuel filter, see **5.8 Diesel Fuel Water Separator**.

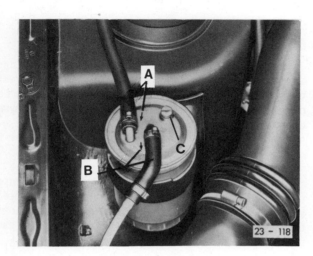

Fig. 5-7. Diesel fuel filter installed in engine compartment. Small arrows, indicating direction of fuel flow, should point to front of engine compartment. **A** is supply line from fuel tank. **B** is outlet line to diesel injection pump. **C** is vent screw, used when draining water from filter. Drain screw is at bottom of filter (not shown).

When replacing the filter, disconnect the battery negative (−) terminal, then remove the two hoses at the top of the filter. Remove the bracket with the filter, then remove the filter. Install the fuel hoses on the new filter, making sure that they are routed as shown in Fig. 5-7. Torque the bracket mounting nuts to 25 Nm (18 ft. lb.).

CAUTION ━

Diesel fuel is damaging to rubber. Immediately wipe up any fuel that spills on belts or hoses. Extreme cleanliness should be observed when working on the diesel fuel system. Even the smallest particle of dirt may damage the system.

5.5 EGR System

(Canada 90 H.P. engine with automatic transmission only)

The exhaust gas recirculation (EGR) system is a type of emission control. EGR system testing is described in **EXHAUST SYSTEM AND EMISSION CONTROLS**.

5.6 Idle Speed

Engine idle speed can change due to a number of factors, including normal wear of engine and fuel injection components. On most of the models covered in this manual, a check of idle speed simply confirms that the electronic idle speed stabilizer system is functioning correctly. See **FUEL SYSTEM** for detailed information on checking engine idle speed.

5.7 Compression Test

A check of engine cylinder compression is recommended for California models. For any engine, however, a compression test is a good indicator of overall valve and piston ring condition. In some cases it can pinpoint specific problems. See **ENGINE** for detailed information on engine compression testing.

5.8 Diesel Fuel Water Separator

The diesel models covered by this manual (except some 1985 Golf Diesels) are equipped with an in-line water separator between the fuel tank and the diesel injection pump. The separator collects the water that it separates from the fuel, and it must be periodically drained. Under normal use with good quality fuel, the specified maintenance interval is sufficient, however, a blinking glow plug light also indicates that the water separator should be drained. If the light blinks again within a few miles after draining, the fuel is most likely contaminated, and the fuel tank should be flushed.

CAUTION ━

Diesel fuel is damaging to rubber. Immediately wipe up any fuel that spills on belts or hoses. Extreme cleanliness should be observed when working on the diesel fuel system. Even the smallest particle of dirt may damage the system.

To drain water from the water separator, use the drain hose and plastic bag supplied with the car. Attach the hose to the drain valve outlet, route it to the plastic bag, as shown in Fig. 5-8. If the original hose is not available, use a piece of clear hose approximately 300 mm (12 in.) long and a suitable container. Open the separator drain valve (three turns maximum) and let the fluid drain until clear fuel enters the hose. Close the drain valve and remove the hose. Disconnect it from the water separator first. If the water separator is being drained because the glow plug light was blinking, then the fuel filter should also be drained as described in **Draining Water From Diesel Fuel Filter**.

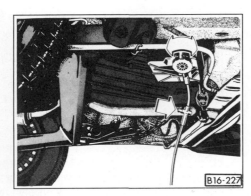

Fig. 5-8. Diesel fuel water separator, located in front of right rear wheel. When draining, open valve a maximum of three turns (top arrows), and drain until fuel is clear. Lower arrow indicates valve on drain hose.

Draining Water From Diesel Fuel Filter

After draining the water separator, or on 1985 Golf Diesels without a water separator, it is necessary to drain the water that collects in the fuel filter. First, loosen the vent screw on the top of the filter. Do not remove the fuel hoses. Place a container under the filter and open the drain at the bottom of the filter. It may be necessary to remove the bracket mounting nuts and raise the filter in order loosen the drain screw. Let the fluid drain until approximately 100 ml (about 3.5 oz.) has been collected, or until clean fuel appears. Close the drain and the vent when finished, and retighten the mounting bracket nuts. Also see **5.4 Fuel Filters**.

5.9 Valve Adjustment

(diesel and turbo diesel only)

Depending on their date of manufacture, the diesel engines covered by this manual may require periodic valve clearance adjustment. The engines which require valve adjustments, all 1985 and some 1986 diesels and turbo diesels, are identified by a sticker on the cylinder head cover, shown in Fig. 5-9.

> ADJUST VALVES EVERY 15,000 MILES (24,000 km).
> VERIFIER LE JEU DES SOUPAPES TOUS LES
> 15,000 MILES (24,000 km).   176 010 005

Fig. 5-9. Sticker found on cylinder head cover of 1985 and some 1986 diesel and turbo diesel engines which require valve adjustment.

The complete valve adjustment procedure is covered in **ENGINE**.

6. ENGINE COMPARTMENT MAINTENANCE

The information under this heading describes the routine maintenance—other than oil change and tune-up—which is performed in the engine compartment. It is not necessary that the car be raised and supported off the ground. For information on oil change and tune-up, see **4. Engine Oil Change** and **5. Tune-up**.

6.1 Battery

Simple maintenance of the battery and its terminal connections will ensure maximum starting performance, especially in winter when colder temperatures reduce battery power. For a more detailed discussion of the battery and charging system, see **ELECTRICAL SYSTEM**.

Checking and Cleaning Battery

Terminal clamps should be tight. The terminals, the terminal clamps, and the battery case should be clean and free of the white deposits which indicate corrosion and acid salts. Even a thin layer of dust containing conductive acid salts can cause the battery to discharge.

To remove corrosion, disconnect the battery terminals, negative (−) terminal first. Clean the terminal posts and the terminal clamps with a wire brush. Corrosion can be washed away with a baking soda and water solution which will neutralize the acid. Avoid getting the solution into the battery cells through vent holes. It will also neutralize the acid inside the battery. Reconnect the terminal clamps, positive (+) terminal first, then lightly coat the outsides of the terminals and clamps with petroleum jelly, grease, or a commercial battery terminal corrosion inhibitor.

> **WARNING**——
> *Battery acid is extremely corrosive. Take care to keep it from contacting eyes, skin, or clothing. Wear eye protection.*

> **CAUTION**——
> *Disconnecting the battery cables with the engine running, or reconnecting the cables to the incorrect posts will damage the electrical system.*

Battery electrolyte should be maintained at the correct level just above the battery plates and their separators. On conventional and low-maintenance batteries, the level can be checked using the indicator marks on the side of the battery, or through a filler hole, as shown in Fig. 6-1. The correct level is approximately 5 mm (¼ in.) above the battery plates. If the electrolyte level is low, replenish it by adding distilled water only.

On the low-maintenance batteries which are factory-installed in the cars covered by this manual, the filler caps are removed using the tip of a flat-bladed screwdriver, as shown in Fig. 6-2. Maintenance-free batteries, because of the sealed case, cannot have their electrolyte levels adjusted. For additional information on batteries, see **ELECTRICAL SYSTEM**.

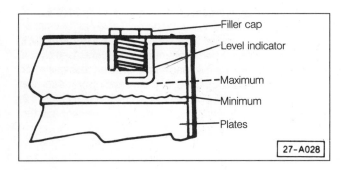

Fig. 6-1. Proper level for battery electrolyte.

Fig. 6-2. Screwdriver being used to open filler cap on low-maintenance batttery. Turn upper part of filler cap counterclockwise to its stop. Install cap by hand.

Replacing Battery

Batteries are rated by ampere hours (Ah), the number of hours they can sustain a specific current drain before complete discharge, or by cold cranking amps (CCA), the number of amps they produce to crank the engine in cold weather conditions. They may be rated according to European (DIN) standards, by Society of Automotive Engineers (SAE) standards, or both. **Table i** lists approximate rating equivalents. Replacement batteries should always be rated equal or higher than the original battery.

Table i. DIN and SAE Battery Rating Equivalents

Cold Cranking Amps DIN	SAE	Ampere Hours
220A	365A	45 Ah
265A	440A	54 Ah
300A	500A	63 Ah
320A	535A	50 Ah
380A	635A	63 Ah
395A	660A	88 Ah

The battery is held in place by a single hold-down bolt and plate. A secure battery hold-down is important in order to prevent vibrations and road shock from damaging the plates. Always disconnect the negative (−) terminal first, and connect it last. While changing batteries, clean away any corrosion in or around the battery tray using a baking soda and water solution.

Charging Battery

A discharged battery is not necessarily faulty. It may be restored by recharging, using a battery charger. There are some limitations on the rate at which low-maintenance and maintenance-free batteries may be charged. Frozen batteries should be recharged only after they have thawed. For complete information on battery charging, as well as applicable cautions and warnings, see **ELECTRICAL SYSTEM**.

6.2 V-Belts

V-belts and pulleys transfer power from the engine crankshaft to various accessories. Cars covered by this manual have at least one V-belt, and may have as many as four, depending on the number of accessories.

Inspecting and Adjusting

Proper V-belt maintenance, by correcting loose or overtight belts, can extend the life of the belt and the component it drives. Inspect belts with the engine off, and twist the belt to see its sidewalls and bottom. Belt structural damage, glazed or shiny sidewalls caused by a loose belt, or separation caused by oil contamination are all reasons to replace a belt. Some of these faults are illustrated in Fig. 6-3.

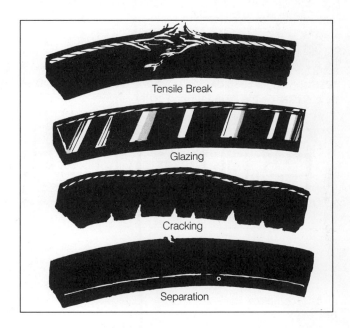

Tensile Break

Glazing

Cracking

Separation

Fig. 6-3. Examples of belt failure.

V-belt squealing is normally caused by incorrect belt tension (too loose) or by dirt between the belt and pulley. Extremely loud squealing may only be corrected by replacing the belt. Belt dressings should not be used to correct the problem. Many dressings contain oil-based compounds which can soften the rubber and reduce belt life.

Check V-belt tension by checking the amount of deflection when the belt is pressed midway between two pulleys. Specifications are given in **Table j**. Alternator V-belt adjustment is described in **ELECTRICAL SYSTEM**.

Table j. V-Belt Deflection Specifications

Belt	Approximate deflection
Alternator	2 to 5 mm (5/64 to 3/16 in.)
Power steering	10 mm (3/8 in.)
Air conditioning	10 mm (3/8 in.)

The power steering pump and air conditioning compressor V-belts are each adjusted using a tensioning bolt that is part of each of the component mounting brackets. To adjust the tension, loosen the mountings and turn the tensioning bolt, clockwise to tighten the belt or counterclockwise to loosen it.

Replacing V-Belts

To reduce the chance of V-belt failure while driving, replacement of the belts every four years is recommended. Loosen the mounting bolts and adjust until the belt tension is very loose, then remove the belt by slipping it over the pulleys. In some cases it may be necessary to remove one V-belt to replace another. Cross section and length determine belt size. Use the old belt for comparison, or make sure that the new belt fits into the pulley groove as shown in Fig. 6-4.

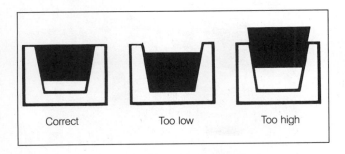

Correct   Too low   Too high

Fig. 6-4. Cross-section of correct V-belt position in pulley.

With the belt off, remove dirt and grease from the belt pulleys using a suitable solvent. Inspect the pulleys for wear or damage which may cause premature failure of the new belt. This is also a good opportunity to inspect the belt-driven accessory, checking for bearing wear and excess play, for example. When installing the new belt, gently pry it over the pulleys. Too much force may damage the belt. Tension the belt(s), run the engine for about 15 minutes, then recheck the tension.

6.3 Cooling System

Cooling system maintenance consists of maintaining the coolant level and inspecting the hoses. Because the coolant's anti-corrosion and anti-freeze additives gradually lose their effectiveness, replacement of the coolant every 2 years is recommended. As a preventive measure, replacement of the cooling system hoses every 4 years is recommended.

CAUTION ▬
Use only phosphate-free anti-freeze when filling the cooling system. Use of anti-freeze containing phosphates is considered to be harmful to the cooling system and may void warranty coverage.

Checking Coolant Level

Because the expansion tank is transluscent, the coolant level can be checked visually without opening the system. With the engine cold, the coolant level should be between the **MIN** and **MAX** marks on the expansion tank, as shown in Fig. 6-5. If it is necessary to add coolant, remove the cap and add it to the expansion tank only.

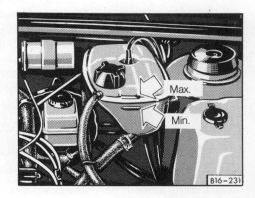

Fig. 6-5. Correct coolant level indicated by **MAX** and **MIN** marks on expansion tank.

Inspecting Hoses

Connections should be tight and dry. Coolant seepage indicates either that the hose clamp is loose, that the hose is damaged, or that the connection is dirty or corroded. Hoses should be firm and springy. Replace any hose that is cracked, that has become soft and limp, or has been contaminated by oil. See Fig. 6-6.

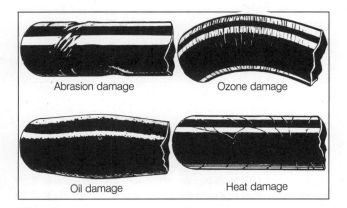

Fig. 6-6. Examples of damage to coolant hoses. Any of conditions shown is cause for replacement.

6.4 Power Steering

Check the power steering fluid level in the fluid reservoir, just to the right of the battery as shown in Fig. 6-7. Park the car on level ground and start the engine. The fluid level is correct if it is between the **MAX** and **MIN** marks on the fluid reservoir. If the level is below the **MIN** mark, add fluid to the reservoir to bring the level up. Hand-tighten the reservoir cap.

NOTE ──

The power steering fluid does not routinely need to be changed.

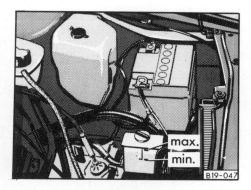

Fig. 6-7. Power steering fluid reservoir showing **MIN** and **MAX** marks which indicate correct fluid level.

6.5 Oxygen Sensor

(gasoline engines only)

The oxygen sensor monitors engine combustion efficiency by measuring the oxygen content of the exhaust gasses. That information in turn helps to control the fuel injection system. Any problems with the oxygen sensor will directly affect how well the engine runs and how well emissions are controlled.

Replacement of the oxygen sensor at the specified interval ensures that the engine and emission control system will continue to perform correctly with no interruption. Failure to replace the oxygen sensor on schedule may void the emission control warranty coverage.

On 85 H.P. engines (engine code GX), the sensor is mounted in the exhaust manifold and is accessible from inside the engine compartment. On all other engines, the sensor is mounted in the exhaust system at the inlet to the catalytic converter. See **EXHAUST SYSTEM AND EMISSION CONTROLS** for more information on the oxygen sensor system.

Replacing Oxygen Sensor

An in-line connector disconnects the sensor wiring. The sensor itself is threaded into place. When installing, apply a light coat of anti-seize compound to the threads, but be careful not to get any into the slits of the probe. Torque the sensor to 50 Nm (37 ft. lb.) and reconnect the wiring.

Resetting OXS Warning Light Counter

The counter is located in the engine compartment, in-line with the speedometer cable, behind the coolant overflow reservoir. To reset the counter, first remove the reservoir by pulling it straight up from its mounting bracket, and then push in the counter reset button as shown in Fig. 6-8. It is not necessary to disconnect any of the cooling system hoses to reach the counter.

NOTE ──

On models with a 60,000 mile (96,000 km) oxygen sensor replacement interval, the mileage counter and warning light have been eliminated.

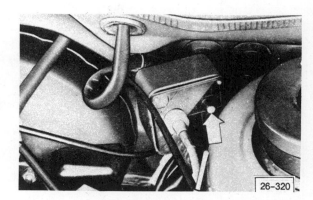

Fig. 6-8. Reset button (arrow) on mileage counter for OXS warning light. (Car shown is slightly different from those covered by this manual.)

6.6 Clutch Adjustment

Those cars which are not equipped with a self-adjusting clutch cable require periodic adjustment to compensate for the wear of the clutch friction material. See **MANUAL TRANSMISSION AND CLUTCH** for information on identifying the two cable types and for the clutch cable adjustment procedure.

7. UNDER-CAR MAINTENANCE

7.1 Tires and Wheels

For stability and car control, the wheels and tires must be of the correct size and in good condition. Tires must be inflated to the correct recommended air pressures, and the wheels must be in proper alignment. For maximum safety and best all-around handling, always install replacement radial tires that are of the same specifications. When possible, all four tires should be replaced at once, or at least in pairs on the front or rear. New tires do not provide maximum traction, and should be broken in gently for the first 100 miles (160 kilometers) or so. Volkswagen warns against mixing tires of different design on the same car, i.e., bias ply with radial ply.

Tire Inflation Pressure

Correct tire inflation pressures are important to handling and stability, fuel economy, and tire wear. Tire pressures change with temperature. Pressures should be checked often during seasonal temperature changes. The correct inflation pressures for cars covered by this manual are given in **Table k**, and can also be found on a sticker in the glove box or on the rear edge of the right door. Notice that the pressures should be higher when the car is more heavily loaded.

WARNING ——

Do not inflate any tire to a higher pressure than the tire's maximum inflation pressure listed on the sidewall.

All inflation pressures given are for cold inflation, that is, when the car has not been driven for at least three hours, or for more than one mile after sitting for at least three hours. Inflate radial snow tires (M + S) to 3 psi above normal pressure, and inflate all-season radials to normal pressures.

Tire Rotation

Volkswagen recommends tire rotation every 7,500 miles (12,000 km) to promote even wear and maximum tire life. Though it is a minor added expense, it is prudent to also have the tires balanced at the same time, to correct any imbalance due to wear. Rotate the tires as shown in Fig. 7-1.

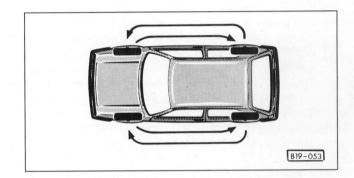

Fig. 7-1. Recommended tire rotation pattern, showing tires rotated from front to rear and rear to front on same side of car.

Table k. Recommended Wheel and Tire Specifications

Model	Wheels	Offset	Tires	Tire pressures psi (bar), cold			
				Half load		Max. load	
				front	rear	front	rear
Golf diesel	5J X 13	45mm	155/80SR13	29 (2.0)	26 (1.8)	29 (2.0)	35 (2.4)
Golf fuel inject. Golf diesel (optional) Jetta	5 ½J X 13 (steel)	38mm	175/70SR13	29 (2.0)	26 (1.8)	32 (2.2)	35 (2.4)
Jetta (optional)	5 ½J X 13 (alloy)	38mm	175/70SR13	29 (2.0)	26 (1.8)	32 (2.2)	35 (2.4)
GTI Jetta GLI Jetta 16V	6J X 14 (alloy)	38mm	185/60HR14	29 (2.0)	26 (1.8)	32 (2.2)	35 (2.4)

Wheel Alignment

Volkswagen makes no specific recommendation of how often the car should have a wheel alignment. It is a good idea to have the wheels aligned whenever they are rotated, or at least once a year. See **SUSPENSION AND STEERING** for a more detailed discussion of alignment requirements and specifications.

7.2 Brakes

Routine maintenance of the brake system includes maintaining an adequate level of brake fluid in the reservoir, checking brake pads and brake shoes for wear, and inspecting the system for fluid leaks or other damage.

> **WARNING**
>
> •*Friction materials such as brake linings may contain asbestos fibers. Do not create dust by grinding, sanding, or cleaning the pads with compressed air. Avoid breathing asbestos fibers and asbestos dust, as it may result in serious diseases such as asbestosis and cancer, or in death.*
>
> •*Brake fluid is poisonous. Wear gloves when working with brake fluid to prevent contamination of cuts.*

Checking Brake Fluid Level

The level of the brake fluid will drop slightly as the brakes wear. The level is checked at the brake fluid reservoir, located to the left of the coolant reservoir as shown in Fig. 7-2. Use only new brake fluid from previously unopened containers. See **3. Fluid and Lubricant Specifications** for brake fluid specifications.

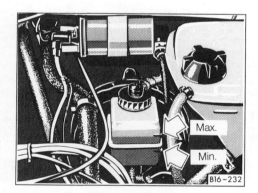

Fig. 7-2. Level indicators on brake fluid reservoir. Correct level is between **MIN** and **MAX** marks.

Inspecting Brake Hoses and Lines

Gently bend the hoses to check for cracks, and make sure that they are routed correctly to avoid chafing or kinking.

Inspect the unions and the brake calipers for signs of fluid leaks. Inspect the lines for corrosion, dents, or other damage. Replace faulty hoses or lines as described in **BRAKES**.

> **WARNING**
>
> *Incorrect installation or overtightening hoses, lines, and unions may cause chafing or leakage, leading to partial or complete brake system failure.*

Checking Disc Brake Pad Wear

In most cases, brake pads can be inspected by looking through a hole in the wheel as shown in Fig. 7-3 to inspect the outer pad, and using a small mirror to inspect the inner pad. For a more thorough inspection, or to view the pads when the wheels have no suitable holes, raise the car and remove the wheel. Minimum brake pad thickness specifications are given in **Table I**.

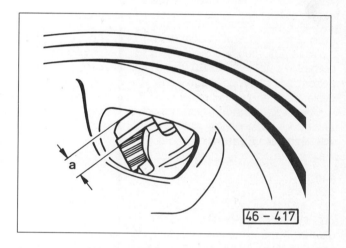

Fig. 7-3. Outer disc brake pad wear being checked through opening in wheel.

Table I. Brake Pad and Lining Minimum Thickness (Including brake pad backing plate or brake shoe)

Front Disc Brake Pads	7 mm (.276 in.)
Rear Disc Brake Pads	7 mm (.276 in.)
Rear Drum Brake Linings	2.5 mm (.098 in.)

Checking Rear Drum Brake Lining Wear

Drum brake lining wear can be checked from behind the brake backing plate after removing a rubber plug, as shown in Fig. 7-4. Minimum thickness specifications are givin in **Table I** above.

Fig. 7-4. Rear brake lining thickness being checked through hole in backing plate after removing rubber plug.

Replacing Brake Fluid

Volkswagen recommends replacement of the brake fluid every 2 years, to protect against corrosion and the effects of moisture absorbed into the brake fluid. The procedure is described in detail in **BRAKES**. If you lack suitable equipment to perform this job properly, service by an authorized Volkswagen dealer or other qualified repair shop is recommended.

7.3 Exhaust System

Exhaust system life varies widely according to driving habits and environmental conditions. If short-distance driving predominates, the moisture and condensation in the system will not fully dry out, leading to corrosion damage and more frequent replacement of systems or system components. Scheduled maintenance of the exhaust system is limited to inspection. Check for restrictions due to dents or kinks. Check for weakness or perforation due to rust. Check to see that all the hangers are in place and properly supporting the system and that the system does not strike the body. Alignment of the system and the location of the hangers are described in **EXHAUST SYSTEM AND EMISSION CONTROLS**.

7.4 Constant Velocity Joints

The protective boots must be closely inspected for cracks and any other damage which will allow contaminants to get into the joint. If the rubber boots fail, the water and dirt which enter the joint will quickly damage it. Replacement of the CV joint boots and inspection of the CV joints are described in **SUSPENSION AND STEERING**.

7.5 Manual Transaxle Service

The areas where leaks are most likely to occur are around the drive axle mounting flanges on the final drive, and at the bottom of the bellhousing, between the transmission and the engine. For more information on identifying oil leaks and their causes, see **MANUAL TRANSMISSION**.

Checking and Filling Transaxle Lubricant

Because the manual transaxle oil is not contaminated by combustion by-products, the lubricant does not need to be routinely changed. There is no dipstick to check the oil level, and there should be no need to check the level or fill the transaxle unless leaks are detected. The oil filler and checking hole is angled downward. This means that oil will run out of the checking hole, even when the transmission is filled to the proper level. Checking transaxle lubricant level always requires replacing some of the lubricant.

Check and fill the transaxle with the car on level ground. Place a drain pan under the oil filler plug, which is located on the left side of the transmission and use a 17 mm hex wrench to remove the plug as shown in Fig. 7-5.

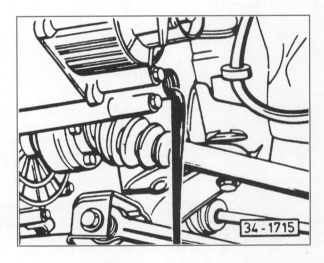

Fig. 7-5. Oil filler plug removed to check transaxle lubricant level. Use 17 mm hex wrench to remove plug.

Allow the oil to drain off until it is level with the edge of the filler hole. If no oil flows out when the plug is removed, add oil until it is level with the edge of the hole. When the level is correct, reinstall and torque the oil filler plug to 25 Nm (18 ft. lb.). Remove the speedometer drive cable from top of the transaxle and pour 0.5 l (.53 US qt.) of gear lubricant into the transaxle as shown in Fig. 7-6. Then, reinstall the speedometer drive cable.

2

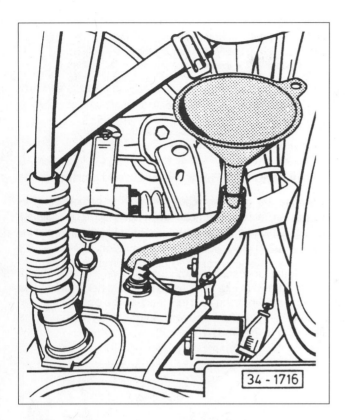

Fig. 7-6. Transaxle lubricant being filled though speedometer drive cable hole. After level is even with drain plug hole, install plug and add another 0.5 L (.53 US qt.).

7.6 Automatic Transaxle Service

Smooth and efficient operation of the automatic transmission relies on the automatic transmission fluid (ATF). Many automatic transmission problems can be traced to an incorrect fluid level, a clogged ATF strainer, or contaminated fluid. With regular preventative maintenance, expensive and unnecessary automatic transmission repair may be avoided.

Before checking the ATF level, inspect for leaks. ATF leaks are most likely to occur around the ATF pan gasket and at the bottom of the bellhousing, where the transaxle joins the engine. Final drive lubricant leaks will most likely occur around the drive flanges. All leaks should be corrected. If necessary, replace a leaky ATF pan gasket as described below. For more information, see **AUTOMATIC TRANSMISSION**.

> **CAUTION** ——
>
> *Extreme cleanliness is important when working on the automatic transmission. Use lint-free rags to check the level, and use a clean funnel when adding fluid.*

Checking and Filling ATF

The location of the dipstick for checking the ATF is shown in Fig. 7-7. Two types of dipsticks used on cars covered by this

manual are shown in Fig. 7-8. The level should be checked with the car on a level surface, the ATF warm, the engine idling, the parking brake firmly set, and the transmission selector lever in park. The ATF level is correct if it is between the **MIN** and **MAX** marks on the dipstick. The ATF is sufficiently warm if the car is driven approximately 6 mi. (10 km) prior to checking the level.

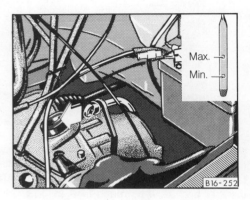

Fig. 7-7. ATF dipstick (arrow). Inset shows marks on ATF dipstick. Level should be between **MIN** and **MAX** marks.

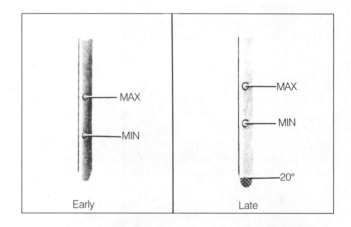

Fig. 7-8. Two versions of automatic transmission dipsticks used on earlier and later transmissions. Difference between marks is 0.33 L (.35 US qt.) on early version and 0.23 L (.24 US qt.) on later version.

If the level is too low, use a clean funnel to add ATF as specified in **3. Fluid and Lubricant Specifications** until it indicates between the two marks on the dipstick.

> **NOTE** ——
>
> If the ATF level is incorrect, and a visual inspection does not indicate any external leaks, then an internal oil seal between the transmission and final drive may be faulty. Correcting the ATF level will not eliminate the problem. See **AUTOMATIC TRANSMISSION** for more information on faulty oil seals.

Check the condition of the ATF by rubbing some between fingers and sniffing it. The ATF should not be foamy, gritty, or have a burnt odor. Contaminated ATF should be drained and replaced to prevent further damage, but doing so will not repair any internal transmission damage that has already occurred.

NOTE ━━

Because Dexron II® ATF is a red/brown color that discolors to black/brown during normal use, ATF color may not be a good indicator of its condition.

Draining and Replacing ATF, and Cleaning ATF Strainer

With the car raised and supported securely on jack stands, place a drain pan of at least 5.6 L (6 US qt.) capacity under the transmission and remove the two rear pan bolts. See Fig. 7-9. Loosen the two front pan bolts, then pull the ATF pan down at the rear and allow as much fluid as possible to drain, then remove the front bolts and remove the pan and gasket. Pour out the fluid remaining in the pan.

CAUTION ━━

Towing the car or running the engine with no fluid in the transmission will ruin the transmission bearings.

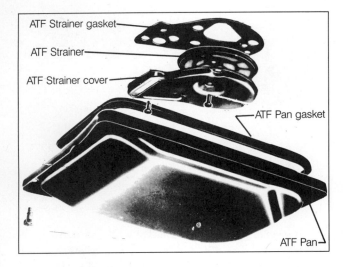

ATF Strainer gasket
ATF Strainer
ATF Strainer cover
ATF Pan gasket
ATF Pan

Fig. 7-9. Exploded view of ATF pan and strainer components. Always use new gasket without sealer.

Clean the pan and dry it completely. Remove the two screws retaining the strainer and remove the cover and the strainer. The strainer can be cleaned if it is dirty or clogged. Replace a damaged strainer or one that cannot be thoroughly cleaned. Remount the strainer using a new gasket. Torque the screws to 4 Nm (35 in. lb.). Using a new gasket without any sealer, install the ATF pan. Working diagonally, tighten the pan bolts to 20 Nm (15 ft.lb.). Refill the transmission with fluid according to the type and amount specified in **3. Fluid and Lubricant Specifications**. Then check the fluid level as described above.

NOTE ━━

On 1985 and 1986 models, transmission slippage during cornering or at stops may only be caused by a low ATF level, however, if the level is correct and the problem still occurs, there may be another problem. A redesigned strainer cover (Volkswagen part no. 010 325 429A) and gasket (Volkswagen part no. 010 325 443) to correct the problem are available from authorized Volkswagen dealers.

Checking and Filling Final Drive Lubricant

Because the oil is not contaminated by combustion by-products, the final drive lubricant does not need to be routinely changed. Checking the lubricant level should only be necessary if hypoid oil leaks are discovered.

Check the lubricant level with the car level. Remove the oil filler plug, shown in Fig. 7-10, using a 17 mm hex wrench. The level is correct when the fluid just reaches the edge of the filler hole. See **3. Fluid and Lubricant Specifications**. Torque the oil filler plug to 25 Nm (18 ft. lb.).

Oil filler plug

Fig. 7-10. Oil filler plug location on automatic transaxle final drive, behind right-side drive flange. Remove with 17 mm hex wrench.

Checking Kickdown Operation

Kickdown operation is a feature designed into the transmission which gives maximum acceleration when the accelerator pedal is depressed to the full-throttle position. Depending on road speed and engine speed, kickdown either delays the upshift or downshifts into the next lower gear. The kickdown specifications vary with the exact type of transmission installed. See **AUTOMATIC TRANSMISSION** for information on how to identify a particular transmission.

Table m gives the kickdown shift points in mph (km/h). Shifts should be smooth and positive. Incorrect shift points may simply mean that the accelerator cable is misadjusted. Slow shifting may mean that the bands or clutches are slipping. See **AUTOMATIC TRANSMISSION** for more testing and troubleshooting information.

Table m. Kickdown Shift Points

Shift points in mph (km/h)		
	Transmission Code	
Shift	**TJ**	**TNA**
1–2	44–47 (71–75)	40–43 (65–69)
2–3	76–77 (122–124)	69–71 (112–114)
3–2	71–73 (114–118)	66–67 (106–108)
2–1	34–36 (55–58)	31–33 (50–53)

7.7 Front Suspension and Steering

Inspection of the front suspension and steering includes a check of all moving parts for wear and excessive play, as well as checks of the condition of rubber seals and boots which are designed to keep the joints free of dirt, water, and other wearing contaminants. Complete front suspension inspection and troubleshooting information can be found in **SUSPENSION AND STEERING**.

8. BODY AND INTERIOR MAINTENANCE

8.1 Windshield Wiper Blades

Common problems with the windshield wipers include streaking or sheeting, water drops after wiping, and blade chatter. Streaking, illustrated in Fig. 8-1, is usually caused when wiper blades are coated with road film or car wash wax. The blades can be cleaned with alcohol or an alcohol-based cleaning solution, using a lint-free cloth or hard-bristle brush. If cleaning the blades does not cure the problem then they should be replaced.

Drops which remain behind after wiping, as shown in Fig. 8-2, are caused by oil, road film, or diesel exhaust coating the windshield. Again, use an alcohol or ammonia solution, or a non-abrasive cleanser to clean the windshield.

Wiper blade chatter, illustrated in Fig. 8-3, may be caused by dirty or worn blades, by a dirty windshield, or by bent or twisted wiper arms. Clean the blades and windshield as described above. Adjust the wiper arm so that there is even pressure along the blade, and so that the blade is perpendicular to the windshield at rest. If the problem persists, the blades are excessively aged or worn and should be replaced.

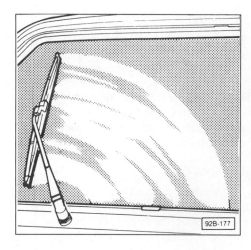

Fig. 8-1. Streaking caused by dirty, worn, or damaged wiper blades.

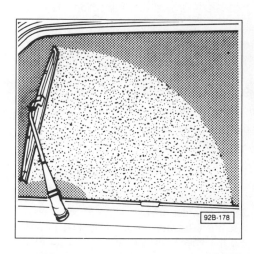

Fig. 8-2. Water beading after wiping caused by oil and dirt contaminating windshield.

Fig. 8-3. Blade chatter caused by dirty or worn blade, or by twisted or bent wiper arm.

8.2 Body Lubrication

The door locks and lock cylinders can be lubricated with an oil that contains graphite. The body and door hinges, the hood latch, and the door check rods should be lubricated with SAE 30 or SAE 40 engine oil. Lubricate the seat runners with multipurpose grease. Do not apply any oil to rubber parts. Lubricate the sunroof guide rails with silicone spray. If door weatherstrips are sticking, lubricate them with silicone spray or talcum powder.

8.3 Seat Belts

Dirt and other abrasive particles will damage seat belt webbing. If it is necessary to clean seat belts, use a mild soap solution. Bleach and other strong cleaning agents may weaken the belt webbing.

The condition of the belt webbing and the function of the retractor mechanisms should be inspected. See **BODY AND INTERIOR** for seat belt inspection information.

9. CLEANING AND PRESERVING

9.1 Care of Exterior Finish

The longer dirt is left on the paint, the greater the risk of damaging the glossy finish, either by scratching or by the chemical effect dirt particles may have on the painted surface.

Washing

Washing the car in direct sunlight is not recommended. Beads of water not only leave spots when dried rapidly by the sun, but also act as tiny magnifying glasses that can burn spots into the finish. Use plenty of water, a mild soap, and a soft sponge.

Begin by spraying water over the dry finish to remove all loose dirt. Wash with lukewarm soapy water. Special car wash soap can be used, but a gentle soap such as Ivory® can do the job just as well at less expense. The idea is to get rid of the dirt without removing the wax underneath. Rinse using plenty of clear water under as little pressure as possible. Wipe the body dry with a soft terry-cloth towel or chamois to prevent water-spotting.

Waxing

For a long-lasting, protective, and glossy finish, apply a hard wax after the car has been washed and dried. Waxing is not needed after every washing. You can tell when waxing is required by looking at the finish when it is wet. If the water coats the paint in smooth sheets instead of forming beads that roll off, the old wax is gone and a new coat of wax is needed.

Polishing

Use paint polish only if the finish assumes a dull look after long service. Polish can be used to remove tar spots and tarnish, but afterwards a coat of wax should be applied to protect the clean finish. Do not use abrasive polish or cleaners on aluminum trim or accessories.

Washing Chassis

Periodic washing of the underside of the car, especially in winter, will help prevent accumulation of road salt and rust. The best time to wash the underside is just after the car has been driven in wet conditions. Spray the chassis with a powerful jet of water to remove dirt and de-icing salt that may have accumulated there. Commercial or self-service car washes may not be best for this, as they may recycle the salt-contaminated water.

Special Cleaning

Tar spots can be removed with tar remover. Never use gasoline, kerosene, nail polish remover, or other unsuitable solvents. Insect spots also respond to tar remover. A bit of baking soda dissolved in the wash water will facilitate their removal. This method can also be used to remove spotting from tree sap.

9.2 Care of Interior

Clean the carpet with a vacuum cleaner or whisk broom. Dirt spots can usually be removed with lukewarm soapy water. Use spot remover for grease and oil spots. Do not pour the liquid directly on the carpet, but dampen a clean cloth and rub carefully, starting at the edge of the spot and working inward. Do not use gasoline, naptha, or other flammable substances to clean the carpeting.

Leatherette Upholstery and Trim

Use a dry foam cleaner. Grease or paint spots can be removed by wiping with a cloth soaked with this cleaner. Use the same cleaner, applied with a soft cloth or brush, on the headliner and side trim panels. For cloth-covered seat areas, use the techniques described previously for cleaning the carpeting.

ENGINE

Contents

Introduction 3

1. General Description 4
   1.1 Engine Components 4
       Crankshaft and Bearings 4
       Connecting Rods and Pistons 4
       Cylinder Head 4
       Valve Train 4
       Intermediate Shaft 4
       Lubrication System 4
   1.2 16-valve Engine 4
       Cylinder Block 4
       Pistons 5
       Cylinder Head 5
       Valve Train 5
       Intermediate Shaft 5
   1.3 Diesel and Turbo Diesel Engines 5
       Cylinder Head and Valve Train 5
       Connecting Rods and Pistons 5
       Valve Train 6
   1.4 Engine Identification Codes and
       Specifications 6
       Finding Engine Letter Codes 6

2. Maintenance 7

3. Troubleshooting 7
   3.1 Basic Troubleshooting Principles 7
       Noise 7
       Fluid Leaks 8
       Smoking 8
       Excessive Oil Consumption 8

Poor Fuel Consumption and Low Power 9
Engine Not Running 9
   3.2 Diagnostic Testing 10
       Compression Test 10
       Wet Compression Test
       (gasoline engines only) 11
       Leak-down Test 11

4. Cylinder Head 11
   4.1 Cylinder Head Cover and Gasket 12
   4.2 Camshaft Drive Belt (except diesel engines) . . 12
   4.3 Camshaft Oil Seal 15
   4.4 Valve Adjustment (1985 and early 1986 diesel
       and turbo diesel only) 15
   4.5 Removing and Installing Camshaft 17
   4.6 Hydraulic Cam Followers 18
       Checking Hydraulic Cam Followers 19
   4.7 Valve Stem Oil Seals 19
   4.8 Removing and Installing Cylinder Head 20
   4.9 Disassembly, Assembly, and Reconditioning . . 22
       Cylinder Head Assembly (16-valve engine) . . . 22
       Cylinder Head Assembly (gasoline engines
       except 16-valve) 23
       Cylinder Head Assembly (diesel and turbo
       diesel engines) 24
       Camshaft and Cam Followers 24
       Valves and Valve Springs 25
       Valve Guides 26
       Valve Seats 26

5. Removing and Installing Engine and Transaxle . . . 28
       Removing 28
       Separating Engine and Transaxle 31

Installing 32
Aligning Engine and Transaxle Assembly 33

6. Cylinder Block and Pistons 33
6.1   Cylinder Block Oil Seals 33
Replacing Front Crankshaft Oil Seal 33
Replacing Intermediate Shaft Oil Seal 34
6.2   Disassembly, Assembly, and Reconditioning . . 34
Pistons and Connecting Rods 34
Piston Rings 36
Diesel and Turbo Diesel Piston Height 36
Crankshaft and Intermediate Shaft 37
Flywheel or Drive Plate 38

7. Lubrication System 39
7.1   Dynamic Oil Pressure Warning System 40
Checking Low Oil Pressure Warning System . 40
Checking Dynamic Oil Pressure Warning
System (high rpm) 40
Testing Oil Pressure Switches 40
7.2   Oil Pump 40
Oil Spray Nozzles 41
7.3   Oil Cooler 41

8. Engine Technical Data 42
I.   Tightening Torques 42
II.   Crankshaft, Intermediate Shaft, and Bearing
Specifications 43
III.   Piston, Piston Ring, and Cylinder
Specifications 43

IV.   Camshaft, Valve, and Cylinder Head
Specifications 43
V.   Lubrication System Specifications 44

TABLES

a.   GTI, Golf, and Jetta Engines 6
b.   Engine Troubleshooting 9
c.   Compression Pressure Specifications - psi (bar) 11
d.   Valve Adjusting Discs 16
e.   Valve Clearance Specifications (1985 and early 1986,
diesel and turbo diesel) 17
f.   Valve and Valve Spring Specifications 25
g.   Minimum Dimensions for Calculating Valve Seat
Refacing Dimensions 27
h.   Valve Seat Dimensions (gasoline engines except
16-valve) 27
i.   Valve Seat Dimensions (16-valve engines) 27
j.   Valve Seat Dimensions (diesel and turbo diesel
engines) 28
k.   Cylinder and Piston Diameter Specifications 35
l.   Connecting Rod Specifications 36
m.   Piston Ring End Gap 36
n.   Piston Ring Side Clearance 36
o.   Cylinder Head Gasket vs. Piston Height
Specifications 37
p.   Crankshaft Journal Diameter 38
q.   Crankshaft and Intermediate Shaft Clearance 38
r.   Crankshaft and Cylinder Block Tightening Torques . . . 38

Engine

Introduction

The four-cylinder engine is front-mounted and water-cooled. Valves are operated by a belt-driven overhead camshaft. Several versions of this engine are covered in this section of the manual. The basic 1985-1989 gasoline-fueled engines are all of 1781 cc (109 cu. in.) displacement, commonly referred to as 1.8 liter, with horsepower ratings (SAE net) ranging from 85 to 102. The 16-valve engine also displaces 1.8 liters, but features a cross-flow cylinder head design wit dual overhead camshafts and four valves per cylinder (two intake and two exhaust) which raises rated horsepower to 123. In addition, there are diesel engines of 1588 cc (96.9 cu. in.) displacement or 1.6 liters. The naturally-aspirated diesel is rated at 52 horsepower. The turbocharged diesel, or turbo diesel, is rated at 68 horsepower. Additional information on all these engines appears in **1. General Description**.

The transverse-mounted engine is bolted to a bellhousing on the transaxle and is inclined toward the rear of the car—thereby permitting a lower hood line and improving weight distribution. The engine and the transaxle are supported as a single unit by bonded rubber and hydraulic mounts which reduce the transmission of noise and vibration to the rest of the car. The engine and transaxle are removed as a unit, although the transaxle alone can be removed without removing the engine.

The engine's crosswise placement makes possible a roomier passenger compartment and concentrates weight over the (front) driving wheels where it will improve traction in mud or snow. Despite a slight forward weight bias when the vehicle is empty, total vehicle weight is distributed about equally on the front and rear wheels when the car is loaded. Equal weight distribution increases vehicle stability and assures precise handling.

The information in this section of the manual is intended to serve as a guide both to car owners and to professional mechanics. Some of the operations may require special equipment and experience. If you lack the skills, tools, or a suitable workplace for servicing or repairing the engine, we suggest you leave these repairs to an authorized Volkswagen dealer or other qualified shop. We especially urge you to consult your authorized Volkswagen dealer before beginning any repairs to a vehicle still covered by the manufacturer's new-car warranty.

1. GENERAL DESCRIPTION

The in-line four-cylinder overhead cam engine is water-cooled and transmits power through a piston-driven crankshaft. The cylinder block is made of cast iron with integral cylinders completely exposed on all sides to the coolant that circulates through the water jacket. A separate cast aluminum alloy cylinder head contains the belt-driven camshaft and the entire valve train. On diesel engines, the camshaft drive belt also drives the fuel injection pump. A cutaway view of the engine appears in Fig. 1-1.

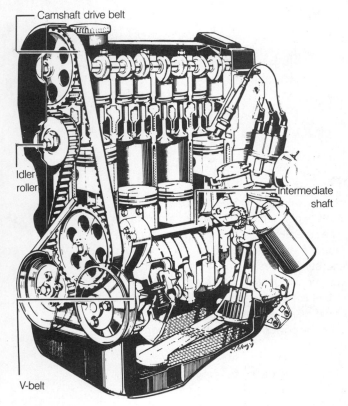

Fig. 1-1. Cutaway view of engine.

1.1 Engine Components

Crankshaft and Bearings

The fully counterweighted crankshaft rotates in five replaceable split-shell main bearings. A 6-piece center main bearing (upper shell, lower shell, and four thrust bearings) controls crankshaft end thrust. Flexible lip seals, pressed into light alloy seal carriers, are used at both ends of the crankshaft to prevent oil leakage.

Connecting Rods and Pistons

The connecting rods are steel forgings. Replaceable split-shell bearings are used at the crankshaft end and lead-bronze coated steel bushings at the piston pin end. The pistons are of the three-ring type with two upper compression rings and a lower one-piece oil scraper ring. Full-floating piston pins are retained at each end by circlips.

Cylinder Head

The cylinder head is an aluminum alloy casting. Replaceable valve guides are press-fit, while the bearing surfaces for the overhead camshaft and the bores for the cam followers (or valve lifters) are machined directly into the cylinder head casting.

Valve Train

The single overhead camshaft is driven by the crankshaft via a toothed, steel-reinforced belt. The cam lobes operate the intake and the exhaust valves directly through hydraulic cam followers which use engine oil, supplied under pressure by the lubrication system, to maintain correct valve clearances. Dual valve springs and both upper and lower spring seats are used on the intake and exhaust valves.

Intermediate Shaft

The intermediate shaft, turning in the cylinder block, is located above and parallel to the crankshaft. It is driven at half crankshaft speed by the camshaft drive belt, and in turn drives the oil pump and the ignition distributor shaft.

Lubrication System

A gear-type oil pump driven by the intermediate shaft draws oil through a strainer in the bottom of the oil pan and forces it through a spin-on replaceable filter and into the engine's oil passages. A pressure relief valve limits the pressure in the system, and a filter bypass valve assures lubrication even if the filter is plugged. Diesel engines and high performance gasoline engines feature an oil cooler attached to the filter housing through which engine coolant circulates to help moderate oil temperature. In addition to a warning system for low oil pressure, a more sensitive dynamic oil pressure warning system operates at elevated engine rpm.

1.2 16-valve Engine

The 16-valve engine is a highly developed version of the basic 1.8 liter engine, sharing most of its major design features. There are several differences, in the cylinder head as well as other related systems, which distinguish the 16-valve version.

Cylinder Block

The cylinder block used for the 16-valve engine has several modifications to help make it more suitable to the higher power output, primarily in the lubrication system. The passageways connecting the crankcase and the upper cylinder head are larger, to allow better ventilation and oil return, and an additional oil passage in the block supplies oil to a series of spray nozzles, one below each cylinder. At oil pressure above 3.5 bar (50 psi), the nozzles open and small streams of oil are sprayed at the underside of each piston to provide additional cooling. The cylinder block casting is also modified to accept a larger crankcase breather.

Pistons

The 16-valve engine, because of its different cylinder head design and valve arrangement, uses a different piston than the other 1.8 liter engines to achieve the necessary combination of compression ratio and valve clearance.

Cylinder Head

The cylinder head is, of course, the 16-valve engine's major departure from Volkswagen's other 1.8 liter engines. Its cross-flow design features four valves per cylinder, versus the usual two, operated by two overhead camshafts. The result is more efficient air flow into and out of the combustion chambers, and an engine with greater efficiency and power over a wide RPM range.

The cylinder head is an aluminum alloy casting with sintered steel valve seats. Press-fit valve guides are replaceable, while the bearing surfaces for the dual camshafts and the bores for the cam followers are machined directly into the cylinder head casting. Fig. 1-2 shows the 16-valve cylinder head and its four-valve combustion chambers.

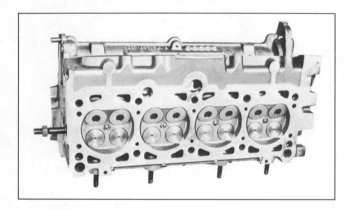

Fig. 1-2. 16-valve cylinder head showing orientation of intake valves (top) and exhaust valves (bottom).

Valve Train

The camshafts are driven by the crankshaft via a single toothed, steel-reinforced belt. The belt drives a single sprocket attached to the exhaust camshaft. The exhaust camshaft in turn drives the intake camshaft through a roller chain and sprockets at the other end of the cylinder head. The drive belt and sprockets, although similar to those of the other 1.8 liter engines, are modified to handle the extra loads of the 16-valve valve train. Fig. 1-3 shows the orientation of the camshafts and drive mechanisms in the assembled cylinder head. The cam lobes operate the intake and exhaust valves directly through hydraulic cam followers which use engine oil, supplied under pressure by the lubrication system, to maintain correct valve clearances. A spray-jet assembly, similar to that used to cool the pistons, is used in the cylinder head to prevent oil from draining out of the supply gallery for the cam followers. Sodium-filled exhaust valves aid heat transfer and reduce valve seat temperature. Dual valve springs and both upper and lower spring seats are used on the intake and exhaust valves.

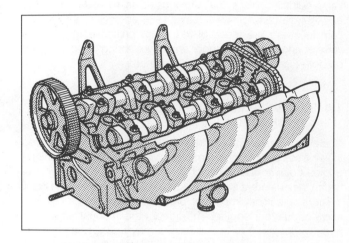

Fig. 1-3. 16-valve cylinder head and valve train.

Intermediate Shaft

The ignition distributor on the 16-valve engine is driven directly by the exhaust camshaft. The intermediate shaft, which drives only the oil pump, is driven at 60% of crankshaft speed by the camshaft drive belt.

1.3 Diesel and Turbo Diesel Engines

In many respects, the Volkswagen diesel and turbo diesel engines are very similar to the Volkswagen spark-ignition engine. The most notable differences are smaller cylinder bore diameters, and the oil supply gallery of the turbo diesel block which is modified to accept piston-cooling oil spray nozzles.

Cylinder Head and Valve Train

The cylinder head for the turbo diesel uses a different gasket and is cast from a special stronger alloy. Different materials are also used for the turbo diesel cylinder head's valves, valve seats, and combustion pre-chambers.

Connecting Rods and Pistons

Although the forged-steel connecting rods are similar to those used in the spark-ignition engines, the pistons are of far more robust dimensions and are totally different in design, since they must be capable of attaining very high compression pressures and withstanding the loads of compression ignition. As on other Volkswagen engines, full-floating piston pins are secured by circlips. The connecting rods for the turbo diesel engine have greater piston pin clearances, however, and the piston skirts are notched for clearance with the piston-cooling oil jets.

Valve Train

The camshaft and valve train layout is identical to that of the spark-ignition engines. On 1985 and early 1986 diesel and turbo diesel engines, the cam lobes operate on hardened steel valve adjusting discs that are located in recesses atop the bucket-type cam followers. Later 1986 engines use hydraulic cam followers like those of the spark-ignition engines. Dual valve springs and both upper and lower spring seats are used on both diesel and turbo diesel engines.

1.4 Engine Identification Codes and Specifications

Several versions of the basic four-cylinder engine are used in vehicles covered by this manual. Volkswagen uses a unique engine code to identify each version and to distinguish between their different parts and specifications. The engine code is the single most important piece of information for you to know about your engine. Throughout this manual, where different procedures or specifications may apply, references to the engine code letters are used to identify the correct information for each engine version.

Finding Engine Letter Codes

The code letters which identify an engine can be easily viewed in the engine compartment. The code letters, GX for example, are given at the beginning of the engine number which is stamped on a flat area of the top of the engine block, just below the lower edge of the cylinder head and located approximately between the No. 3 and No. 4 cylinders. The location of the engine number stamp is shown in Fig. 1-4. **Table a** lists engine codes, application information, and major specifications.

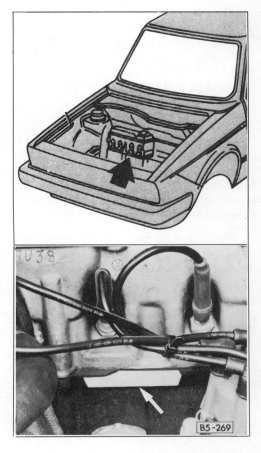

Fig. 1-4. Location of stamped engine number and identifying code letters

GTI, Golf, and Jetta Engines

Engine code letters	GX	MZ	HT	RD	RV	PF	PL	ME	MF
Number of cylinders	4	4	4	4	4	4	4	4	4
Bore mm (in.)	81.0 (3.19)	81.0 (3.19)	81.0 (3.19)	81.0 (3.19)	81.0 (3.19)	81.0 (3.19)	81.0 (3.19)	76.5 (3.012)	76.5 (3.012)
Stroke mm (in.)	86.4 (3.40)	86.4 (3.40)	86.4 (3.40)	86.4 (3.40)	86.4 (3.40)	86.4 (3.40)	86.4 (3.40)	86.4 (3.40)	86.4 (3.40)
Displacement cc (cu. in.)	1781 (109)	1781 (109)	1781 (109)	1781 (109)	1781 (109)	1781 (109)	1781 (109)	1588 (97)	1588 (97)
Compression Ratio	9.0:1	9.0:1	10.0:1	9.0:1	10.0:1	10.0:1	10.0:1	23.0:1	23.0:1
Horsepower SAE net @ RPM	85@ 5250	90 @ 5500	100 @ 5500	102 @ 5250	100 @ 5400	102 @ 5400	123 @ 5800	52 @ 4800	68 @ 4500

continued on next page

GTI, Golf, and Jetta Engines (continued)

Engine code letters	GX	MZ	HT	RD	RV	PF	PL	ME	MF
Torque lbs-ft @ RPM SAE net	96 @ 3000	98 @ 3250	105 @ 3000	110 @ 3250	107 @ 3400	110 @ 3400	120 @ 4250	71 @ 2500	98 @ 2500
Fuel Injection System	CIS/ CIS-E	CIS	CIS-E	CIS-E	Digifant II	Digifant II	CIS-E	Diesel	Diesel
Fuel Required	Unleaded	Leaded Regular	Unleaded	Unleaded	Unleaded	Unleaded	Unleaded	No. 2 Diesel	No. 2 Diesel
Application Notes		Canada only	GTI, Jetta GLI (1985)	GTI Jetta GLI			16-valve	Diesel	Turbo Diesel

3

2. MAINTENANCE

The following routine maintenance steps are covered in detail in **LUBRICATION AND MAINTENANCE** or in this section under the bold numbered headings.

1. Checking engine oil level

2. Changing engine oil and filter

3. Replacing spark plugs

4. Checking compression pressure **3.2**

5. Adjust valve clearance (diesel, turbo diesel) **4.4**

6. Replace cylinder head cover gasket (with valve adjustment above) **4.1**

7. Check cylinder head bolt torque (diesel, turbo diesel) **4.8**

3. TROUBLESHOOTING

This troubleshooting section applies to problems affecting the basic engine assembly—the cylinder block, cylinder head, and their internal moving parts.

Only a few basic functions are required of the engine. The block, cylinder head, and their moving parts must fit together properly, operate smoothly, seal well enough to create and maintain compression, and keep pistons, valve train, and ignition properly timed. The problems discussed in this troubleshooting section are those which affect one or more of these functions.

Troubleshooting specifically for the lubrication system can be found in this section in **7. Lubrication System**. To troubleshoot overheating and other cooling system problems, see **COOLING SYSTEM**. Troubleshooting for other general starting and running problems can be found in **FUEL SYSTEM, IGNITION**, and **ELECTRICAL SYSTEM**.

3.1 Basic Troubleshooting Principles

As with any troubleshooting, analysis of the observed symptoms is the key to isolating and identifying engine problems. Begin with careful observation, keeping in mind the following questions:

How has the symptom developed? A symptom which develops quickly is probably caused by a problem which can be corrected by simple maintenance or repair. A symptom which has developed gradually over time, especially after fifty or sixty thousand miles, is more likely an indication of general wear and the need for more comprehensive overhaul work.

Is the symptom rpm-dependent? A noise which is caused by an engine mechanical problem will be dependent mainly on engine speed, with similar symptoms regardless of changes in vehicle speed. Noises which repeatedly occur only in a certain rpm range suggest a vibration problem. Noises which change with vehicle speed are more likely due to drivetrain or running gear problems.

Is the symptom load dependent? Forces at work inside a running engine vary as the demand for power varies. Symptoms which are more severe during hard acceleration indicate certain kinds of problems. Symptoms which are more apparent at no load or high vacuum (example: coasting at high rpm) point to other problems. Note that higher engine loads also affect the fuel and ignition systems, which may be responsible for high-load performance problems.

Is the symptom temperature dependent? Does it only occur when the engine is cold? Does it change as the engine warms up? How? Metal parts expand and contract with changes in temperature. Clearances change. Oil viscosity and cooling system pressure change. In troubleshooting symptoms which change as the engine gets warm, look for an engine characteristic that changes with temperature.

Noise

In order to run reliably and smoothly under harsh conditions, the internal engine parts are manufactured to precise dimensions, assembled with precision clearances between moving parts, and lubricated by a pressurized oiling system.

Most unidentified engine noises result from clearances which have become too large due to worn or failed parts, lack of adequate lubrication, or both. The importance of lubrication cannot be over-emphasized. For best results, troubleshooting engine noises should only be done when the oil and filter have been recently changed and the oil level is correct.

High-pitched metallic tapping noises are caused by relatively small, lightweight parts and are most likely an indication of excessive clearances in the valve train. Valve train noise accompanied by burning oil (blue-gray smoke in the exhaust), particularly at startup or when decelerating from high RPM, is an indication of worn valve guides which can only be remedied by overhaul or replacement of the cylinder head. In a high-mileage engine, a light metallic rattle or chatter under acceleration, accompanied by increased oil consumption and smoking, may indicate severely worn or broken piston rings. Since this diagnosis means overhaul or replacement of the engine, the problem should be further investigated with a compression or cylinder leakage test. See **3.2 Diagnostic Testing**.

Deep, metallic knocking sounds are caused by excessive clearances between heavier components. Closer analysis of the noise will often help identify the problem. Piston slap, caused by excessive piston skirt to cylinder wall clearance, is worse when the engine is cold and may be accompanied by increased oil consumption and reduced compression due to accelerated piston ring wear. A double knock, most pronounced at idle or low load, is due to excessive clearance at the piston pin and upper connecting rod bushing.

Crankshaft bearing problems produce a deep, hollow knock that is worst when the engine is warm. A noise that is very pronounced under load, perhaps louder during the transition from acceleration to coasting, is most likely caused by a damaged connecting rod bearing. Crankshaft main bearings produce a lower, dull knock. An intermittent knock, indicating excessive crankshaft end play, may be most apparent when depressing or releasing the clutch. These problems seldom occur as isolated failures. They are almost always an indication of the overall engine condition which can only be properly corrected by complete engine overhaul or replacement.

Rumbling or groaning from the engine compartment may not indicate engine problems at all, but rather a worn bearing or bushing in an engine-driven accessory. They include the coolant pump, alternator, and may include a power steering pump and air conditioning compressor. The air conditioning compressor is equipped with an electrically-switched clutch-type pulley, so a bad compressor will only be noisy when the air conditioning is on. To check other accessories, run the engine briefly with the drive belt disconnected and see if the noise has stopped. Once the drive belt is removed, turning the pulley and shaft by hand may also reveal a bad bearing or bushing. A properly functioning accessory should turn smoothly.

Fluid Leaks

Fluid leaking from and around the engine is most likely either oil, coolant, or brake fluid. Look for wet spots on the engine to help pinpoint the source. It may be helpful to start by cleaning the suspected area.

The most likely sources of engine oil leaks are the oil filter gasket, the crankcase oil seals, the cylinder head cover gaskets, or the oil pan gaskets. See **6. Cylinder Block and Pistons** for more information on the gaskets and seals.

The power steering system is another possible source of oil leaks near the engine. For repairs to the power steering system, see **SUSPENSION AND STEERING**.

Coolant is a mixture of water and anti-freeze, yellow-green in color or perhaps brown if the cooling system is corroded. A pressure test of the cooling system is the best way to discover and pinpoint leaks. See **COOLING SYSTEM**.

Brake fluid is clear, perhaps slightly purple, and a little slippery. Look for wet spots around the master cylinder or brake lines. Especially check the flexible hoses near the wheels. See **BRAKES** for repair information.

Smoking

Smoke which is visible under the hood will be either blue-gray smoke from burning oil, or white steam from the cooling system. Both symptoms indicate a leak. See **Fluid Leaks** above.

Smoke in the exhaust indicates something getting into the combustion chamber and being burned which does not belong there. The color of the smoke identifies the contaminant.

Blue-gray smoke is from oil. Oil smoke, probably accompanied by increased oil consumption and oil residue on spark plugs, indicates that engine oil is getting past piston rings, valve guides, the cylinder head gasket, or some combination of the three. Use a compression test for diagnosis. See **3.2 Diagnostic Testing**. Compression pressures in an older engine which are even, but below specifications, point to piston ring and cylinder wall wear and the need for engine overhaul or replacement. If the smoking is most obvious under high engine vacuum, such as while coasting at high RPM, and compression pressures are within specifications, leaking valve guide oil seals or valve guides are a probable cause. See **4. Cylinder Head** for repair information.

Oil smoke or steam appearing suddenly in the exhaust, along with low compression pressure in one cylinder or two adjoining cylinders, is very probably due to a failed cylinder head gasket. Look also for coolant loss, oil in the radiator, or water in the oil (which turns the oil an opaque, creamy brown). See **4.8 Removing and Installing Cylinder Head** for repair procedures.

Black smoke is caused by the engine getting too much fuel. See **FUEL SYSTEM** for more troubleshooting information.

Excessive Oil Consumption

Some oil consumption is normal and indicates healthy flow and distribution of the vital lubricant in the engine. This is why oil level must be checked, and occasionally corrected, between oil changes. Aside from leaks, increased oil consumption will usually be accompanied by some smoking, however slight, and the causes of excessive oil consumption are the same as those for oil smoke in the exhaust. As with smoking symptoms, gradual increases are caused by worn piston rings and/or valve guides. Sudden high oil consumption suggests broken rings or a failed cylinder head gasket. See **Smoking** above for more troubleshooting information.

Poor Fuel Consumption and Low Power

Poor fuel consumption and low power can, of course, suggest problems with the fuel or ignition systems, particularly on a low-mileage engine. On an engine with high mileage, suffering the effects of wear, low compression may be the cause.

Normal wear of the valves, piston rings, and cylinder walls decreases their ability to seal. The intake and compression of the air/fuel mixture becomes less efficient, and the engine has to work harder, using more fuel, to produce the same amount of power. Engine condition can be evaluated with a compression test. See **3.2 Diagnostic Testing**.

Engine Not Running

An engine problem which affects timing may prevent the engine from starting or running. The camshaft drive belt and sprockets are responsible for timing the actions of the valves and the ignition system relative to the pistons and crankshaft. On diesel engines, the camshaft drive belt also drives the fuel injection pump. A worn belt and sprockets may jump teeth, throwing off all the engine's timing functions, and still appear to be perfectly normal. To check camshaft and ignition timing of gasoline engines, see **4.2 Camshaft Drive Belt** and **IGNITION**. To check camshaft and injection pump timing of diesel engines, see **FUEL SYSTEM (diesel)**. Other troubleshooting information for an engine which fails to start can be found in **ELECTRICAL SYSTEM**, **FUEL SYSTEM**, and **IGNITION**.

Table b lists symptoms of engine problems, their probable causes, and suggested corrective actions. The boldface numbers in the corrective action column indicate the heading in this section of the manual where the applicable test and repair procedures can be found.

Table b. Engine Troubleshooting

Symptom	Probable cause	Corrective action
1. Pinging or rattling noise under load, uphill or accelerating, especially from low speeds. Indicates detonation or pre-ignition	**a.** Ignition timing too far advanced **b.** Fuel does not meet manufacturer's octane requirements **c.** Overheating **d.** Spark plugs damaged or wrong heat range **e.** Air/fuel mixture too lean	**a.** Correct ignition timing. See **IGNITION** **b.** Switch to higher octane fuel. See **FUEL SYSTEM** for fuel octane requirements **c.** See **COOLING SYSTEM** **d.** Replace spark plugs. See **IGNITION** **e.** See **FUEL SYSTEM**
2. Screeching or squealing noise under load. Goes away when coasting. Indicates slipping V-belt	**a.** Loose, worn, or damaged V-belt(s) **b.** Excessive belt loads due to failed engine-driven component	**a.** Inspect, replace, or tighten belt(s). See **LUBRICATION AND MAINTENANCE** **b.** Locate and replace failed component. **3.2**
3. Growling or rumbling, varies with engine rpm. Bad bearing or bushing in an engine-driven accessory	**a.** Coolant pump **b.** Alternator **c.** Power steering pump **d.** Camshaft drive belt tensioner bearing **e.** Air conditioning compressor	**a.** See **COOLING SYSTEM** **b.** See **ELECTRICAL SYSTEM** **c.** See **SUSPENSION AND STEERING** **d.** Replace belt tensioner. **4.2** **e.** Replace compressor
4. Light metallic tapping noise, varies directly with engine speed. Oil pressure warning light **not** illuminated	**a.** Low oil pressure and defective warning light circuit **b.** Valve lash out of adjustment (1985 and early 1986 diesel and turbo diesel only) **c.** Defective cam follower(s)	**a.** See **7. Lubrication System** **b.** Adjust valve lash. **4.4** **c.** Check cam followers and replace as required. **4.6**
5. Light metallic knock, varies directly with engine speed. Oil pressure warning light blinking or fully illuminated (may be most noticeable after hard stops or during hard cornering) indicates lack of sufficient oil supply	**a.** Low oil level **b.** Restricted (dirty) oil filter **c.** Insufficient oil pressure	**a.** Check and correct oil level. See **LUBRICATION AND MAINTENANCE** **b.** Change engine oil and filter. See **LUBRICATION AND MAINTENANCE** **c.** Check oil pressure. **7.**

continued on next page

Table b. Engine Troubleshooting (continued)

Symptom	Probable cause	Corrective action
6. Blue-gray exhaust smoke, oily spark plugs. Indicates oil burning in combusion chamber	**a.** Leaking valve stem oil seals **b.** Worn valve guides **c.** Worn or broken pistons or piston rings	**a.** Replace valve stem oil seals. **4.7** **b.** Overhaul or replace cylinder head. **4.** **c.** Overhaul or replace engine
7. Blue-gray smoke and/or white steam in exhaust	**a.** Failed cylinder head gasket (probably accompanied by low compression readings) See **3.2 Diagnostic Testing** **b.** Warped or cracked cylinder head (probably accompanied by low compression readings) See **3.2 Diagnostic Testing** **c.** Cracked cylinder block	**a.** Replace cylinder head gasket. **4.8** **b.** Resurface or replace cylinder head gasket. **4.8** **c.** Replace engine or short block. See **5. Removing and Installing Engine and Transaxle**
8. Black exhaust smoke	**a.** Rich air/fuel mixture	**a.** See **FUEL SYSTEM**
9. Engine runs badly, pops and backfires	**a.** Spark plug wires installed incorrectly **b.** Incorrect valve timing	**a.** Install wires correctly. See **IGNITION** **b.** Check camshaft drive belt and camshaft timing. **4.2**
10. Engine will not start or run. Starter operates, engine turns over at normal speed	**a.** Failed ignition system **b.** Broken camshaft drive belt **c.** Incorrect camshaft timing due to jumped belt or misassembly	**a.** See **IGNITION** **b.** Check cam sprocket rotation as engine turns over. Install camshaft drive belt as necessary. **4.2** **c.** Check camshaft timing. Replace belt and sprockets as necessary. Adjust belt tension. **4.2**

3.2 Diagnostic Testing

The tests that follow can be used to help isolate engine problems, to better understand a problem before starting expensive repairs, or just to periodically check engine condition.

Compression Test

A test of compression pressures in the individual cylinders will tell a lot about the condition of the engine without the need for taking it apart. For gasoline engines, the text is relatively simple. It requires a compression tester, a spark plug wrench, a screwdriver, and a jumper wire to disable the ignition system. Diesel and turbo diesel engines with their higher compression pressures require a more expensive tester. For diesels and turbo diesels, it may be more economical to have a compression test performed by a Volkswagen dealer or other qualified shop.

For a compression test of either type of engine, the battery and starter must be copable of turning the engine at normal cranking speed to achieve meaningful results. The area around the spark plugs or injectors should be clean, to avoid getting debris inside the engine when they are removed. Because engine temperature may affect compression, the most accurate results are obtained when the engine is at normal operating temperature.

To test compression (gasoline engine):

1. With the ignition off, disconnect the coil wire from the center tower of the distributor cap and connect it to ground on the engine block using a jumper wire. This is to disable the secondary circuit of the ignition system.

2. Disconnect one end of the duct between the air flow sensor and the throttle body to disable the fuel injection system.

3. Remove the spark plug wires from the spark plugs. Use care to pull on both the wire and the boot at the same time to avoid damage to the connectors. Label the wires so that they can be reattached to the correct spark plugs.

4. Remove the spark plugs and set them aside, in order corresponding to the cylinders from which they were removed.

5. Thread the compression tester into the first cylinder's spark plug hole, just tight enough to seal around the spark plug hole. Use cafe not to damage the seal on the gauge line.

6. With the transmission in neutral and the throttle held wide open, crank the engine with the starter. The gauge reading should increase with each engine revolution. Continue cranking until the gauge reading stops increasing (agout 4 to 5 revolutions). Record the highest value indicated by the gauge.

7. Release the pressure, either with the gauge valve or by slowly removing the gauge, allowing the pressure to bleed off while threading it out of the spark plug hole.

8. Repeat the test for each of the other cylinders. Record the data and compare with **Table c**.

9. Reinstall the spark plugs and the spark plug wires in their original locations. Reinstall the air duct. Reconnect the coil wire.

To test compression (diesel engine):

1. Disconnect the wire from the fuel shutoff solenoid on the injector pump.

2. Unscrew the fuel pipe union nuts from the injection pump and the fuel injectors. Remove the fuel pipes as a unit, taking care not to bend them.

> **WARNING** ━━
>
> *Fuel will be expelled as you loosen the unions. Do not smoke or work near heaters or other fire hazards. Have a fire extinguisher handy.*

3. Using a 27 mm deep socket, remove the injectors, and then remove the heat shields from each injector hole.

> **WARNING** ━━
>
> *If the heat shields are not removed along with the injectors, compression pressure will expel them with dangerous force when the engine is turned over.*

4. Thread the compression tester, with an injector heat shield, into the first cylinder's injector hole. Thread the gauge in tight enough to seal.

5. With the transmission in neutral, crank the engine with the starter. The gauge reading should increase with each engine revolution. Continue until the gauge reading stops increasing (about 4 to 5 revolutions). Record the highest value indicated by the gauge.

6. Release the pressure, either with the gauge valve or by slowly removing the gauge, allowing the pressure to bleed off while threading it out of the injector hole.

7. Repeat the test for each of the other cylinders. Record the data and compare with **Table c**.

8. Reinstall the injectors with new heat shields. Torque the injectors to 70 Nm (51 ft. lb.). For correct heat shield installation position, see **FUEL SYSTEM (diesel)**.

9. Reconnect the fuel lines and torque the fittings to 25 Nm (18 ft. lb.). Reconnect the wire to the fuel shutoff solenoid.

Table c. Compression pressure specifications psi (bar)

Engine code	GX,MZ	HT,RD,PL, RV,PF	ME,MF
New engines	131–174 (9.0–12.0)	145–189 (10.0–13.0)	500 (34.0)
Wear limit	102 (7.0)	109 (7.5)	412 (28.0)
Maximum difference between cylinders	45 (3.0)	45 (3.0)	73 (5.0)

Low compression is evidence of poorly sealed combustion chambers. The characteristics of the test results help isolate the cause or causes. Generally, compression pressures which are relatively even but below acceptable specifications indicate worn piston rings and/or cylinder walls. Low but erratic values tend to indicate valve leakage. Dramatic differences, such as acceptable values in some cylinders and very low values in one or two cylinders are the sign of a localized failure, probably of a head gasket. There are two more tests which can further isolate the problem.

Wet Compression Test

(gasoline engines only)

To analyze poor compression and further identify the source of the leakage, repeat the compression test, this time with about a tablespoon of oil squirted into each cylinder. The oil will temporarily help seal between the piston rings and the cylinder wall, practically eliminating leakage past the rings for a short time. If this test yields higher compression readings than the "dry" compression test, the difference can be attributed to leakage between the piston rings and cylinder walls, due either to wear or to broken piston rings. Little or no change in compression readings indicates other leakage, probably from the valves or a failed cylinder head gasket.

> **CAUTION** ━━
>
> *Do not attempt a wet compression test on a diesel engine. The oil in the cylinder may be ignited by compression pressure.*

Leak-down Test

The most conclusive diagnosis of low compression symptoms requires a leak-down test. Using a special tester and a supply of compressed air, each cylinder is pressurized. The rate at which the air leaks out of the cylinder, as well as the sound of the air escaping, can more accurately pinpoint the magnitude and source of the leakage. Any engine compression diagnosis which will require major disassembly should first be confirmed by the more accurate leak-down test. Because the test requires special equipment and experience, it may be desirable to have it performed by a Volkswagen dealer or other qualified repair shop.

4. CYLINDER HEAD

The cylinder head can be removed from the engine for repairs without first removing the engine from the car, and many cylinder head repairs can be accomplished without removing the cylinder head from the engine. The cylinder head cover gasket, the camshaft(s), the camshaft drive belt, the camshaft oil seal, the valve guide oil seals, and the cam followers are all accessible with the cylinder head installed.

Reconditioning the cylinder head is not overly complicated, but requires time and an extensive tool selection. If good machine shop services are not available in your area, or time is a factor, installation of a remanufactured cylinder head is an alternative. Remanufactured cylinder heads are available from an authorized Volkswagen dealer.

4.1 Cylinder Head Cover and Gasket

Because the cylinder head cover gasket is deformed as it is compressed, it is not reusable. It should be replaced any time the cylinder head cover is removed and any time there is evidence of leaks. A thorough visual inspection will usually detect a faulty cylinder head cover gasket. The gasket used on most engines is a three-piece set. A two-piece gasket set is used on 16-valve engines.

To remove and install cylinder head cover and gaskets (except 16-valve engines):

1. Remove the eight 10 mm nuts and the reinforcing strips.

2. Remove the socket-head flanged nut from the camshaft drive belt upper cover.

3. Lift off the cylinder head cover and its gasket. Raise the camshaft drive belt upper cover slightly for clearance. If the gasket is stuck to the cylinder head, use a gasket removing tool to separate the gasket from the head. Remove the sealing plug from the rear of the cylinder head and remove the semi-circular gasket piece from inside the front of the cover.

> **CAUTION** —
> Use care when removing a stuck gasket. Damage to either surface will cause leaks. Use only a gasket removing tool designed for the purpose.

4. Installation is the reverse of removal. Make sure the tabs on the semi-circular piece correctly mate the slots on the gasket to ensure a good seal. Torque the eight nuts and the socket head flanged nut to 10 Nm (7.5 ft.lb. or 87 in. lb.).

To remove and install cylinder head cover and gasket (16-valve engine only):

1. Remove spark plug wire connectors. Remove the intake air boot from the throttle housing and remove the small rubber hose between the intake air boot and the idle air valve.

2. Disconnect the electrical connector for the charcoal canister control valve, and the large vacuum hose from the back of the upper intake manifold.

3. Remove the support bolt from the back of the upper intake manifold, then remove the five nuts and washers that join the upper intake manifold to the lower intake manifold.

4. Rotate the upper manifold up and away from the engine. Remove and label electrical connections or vacuum hoses as required. Then secure the manifold out of the way.

5. Remove the two inner bolts and the six outer bolts from the cover, and lift the cover from the cylinder head. If necessary, use a soft hammer to loosen the cover. Remove the center gasket from the cylinder head or the cover.

> **CAUTION** —
> Use care when removing a stuck gasket. Damage to either surface will cause leaks. Use only a gasket removing tool designed for the purpose.

6. Installation is the reverse of removal. Torque the eight cover bolts to 10 Nm (87 in. lb.). Torque the five manifold nuts and the manifold support bolt to 20 Nm (15 ft. lb.). Torque the support bolt last.

4.2 Camshaft Drive Belt
(except diesel engines)

The camshaft drive belt and its related parts are shown in Fig. 4-1. Although no maintenance interval is specified, the publisher recommends periodic inspection of the belt, and replacement at 60,000 to 75,000 miles (96,000 to 120,000 km), or every 4 to 5 years. Diesel camshaft drive belt replacement can be found in **FUEL SYSTEM (Diesel)**.

Removal of the belt is the best way to perform a thorough inspection. Drive belt replacement does not require any special tools for most engines covered in this manual. On 16-valve engines, a special wrench is required to adjust the camshaft drive belt tensioner. On all engines, the drive belt can be replaced without removing the drive belt sprockets.

Whenever the drive belt is installed, the camshaft and intermediate shaft timing must be adjusted.

To remove and inspect camshaft drive belt (except diesel):

1. Remove the socket-head shouldered nut securing the upper camshaft drive belt cover, and remove the cover.

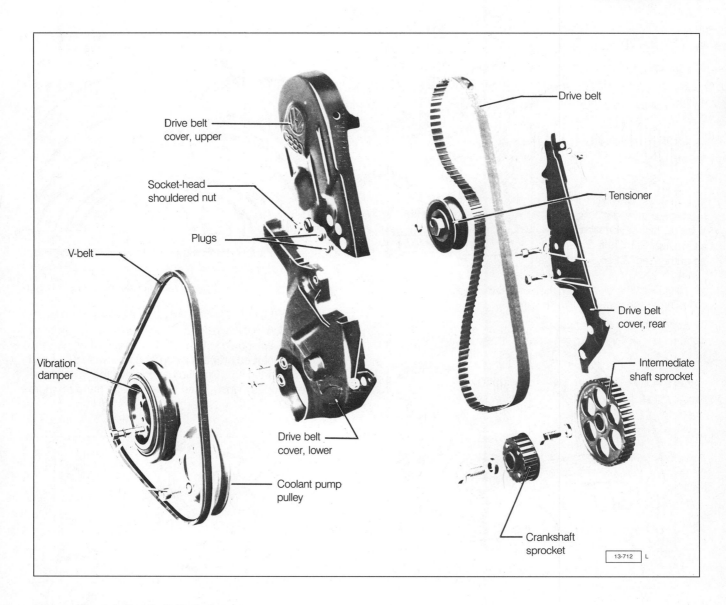

Fig. 4-1. Camshaft drive belt and cover.

2. Loosen the coolant pump pulley bolts, and remove the V-belts as described in **LUBRICATION AND MAINTE-NANCE**. Remove the coolant pump pulley.

3. Using a socket wrench on the crankshaft vibration damper bolt, rotate the engine by hand to set the No.1 piston at Top Dead Center (TDC), and remove the vibration damper from the crankshaft.

> **CAUTION** ━━
>
> *Rotating the crankshaft or the camshaft with the drive belt removed may cause interference which can damage pistons and valves.*

4. Remove the two nuts and bolt that hold the lower camshaft drive belt cover to the coolant pump and to the front of the engine. Remove the lower cover.

5. Loosen the camshaft drive belt tensioner locknut. Turn the tensioner counterclockwise so that the tension is removed from the drive belt. Then remove the drive belt by working it off the sprockets.

6. Inspect the tensioner bearing and the belt. Spin the bearing to check that it runs smoothly. Inspect the drive belt for any visible damage such as stretch, exposed threads, missing teeth, or any other visible damage. A damaged belt or worn tensioner should be replaced.

To install and adjust camshaft drive belt (except diesel):

1. Use a socket wrench to rotate the camshaft sprocket by hand until the timing mark is aligned. The timing marks for 16-valve engines are shown in Fig. 4-2. The timing mark for all other engines is shown in Fig. 4-3.

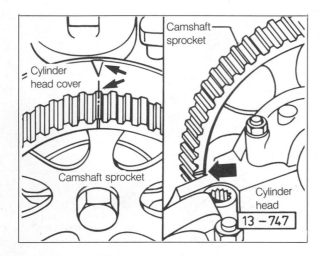

Fig. 4-2. Camshaft timing marks on 16-valve engine.

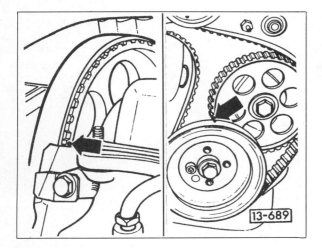

Fig. 4-3. Camshaft timing marks (arrows) for all except 16-valve engines.

2. Loosely install the camshaft drive belt over the crankshaft and intermediate shaft sprockets. Then temporarily install the crankshaft vibration damper onto the crankshaft.

3. Use a socket to rotate the crankshaft and the intermediate shaft by hand until the timing marks line up. The timing marks for the crankshaft on 16-valve engines are shown in Fig. 4-4. The timing marks for the crankshaft and the intermediate shaft on all other engines are shown in Fig. 4-3, above.

NOTE ——

It is not necessary to time the intermediate shaft on 16-valve engines.

4. Install the camshaft drive belt. Start on the crankshaft and intermediate shaft sprockets. Install the belt so that it is as tight as possible between the crankshaft and the intermediate shaft sprockets, and between the intermediate shaft and the camshaft sprockets.

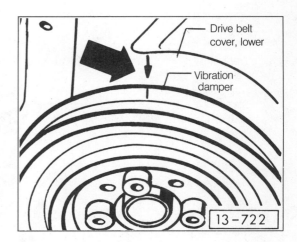

Fig. 4-4. Crankshaft timing marks on vibration damper and lower drive belt cover on 16-valve engines.

5. Tighten the belt. Turn the tensioner clockwise and lock it in position with the locknut. Check the tension by twisting the belt, as shown in Fig. 4-5. On 16-valve engines, the belt is tightened properly when it can be twisted by hand no more than 45°. On all other engines the belt is tightened properly when it can be twisted by hand no more than 90°.

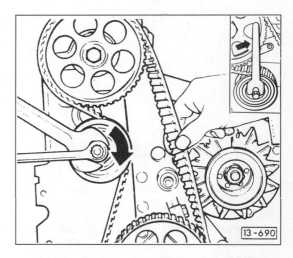

Fig. 4-5. Camshaft drive belt tension being adjusted. Check tension halfway between the camshaft and the intermediate shaft sprockets. On 16-valve engines, use spanner wrench to engage holes in tensioner (inset).

6. Torque the tensioner locknut to 45 Nm (33 ft. lb.). Turn the crankshaft two full revolutions and recheck the tension and the timing marks.

NOTE ——

Some movement of the sprockets and their marks is to be expected as belt tension is adjusted. Keep in mind that the smallest possible increment of adjustment is one whole tooth of the belt or sprocket.

7. The remaining installation is the reverse of removal. Remove the vibration damper to install the lower drive belt cover. On 16-valve engines, torque the upper belt cover bolt to 6 Nm (53 in. lb.). Torque all other belt cover nuts and bolts to 10 Nm (87 in. lb.). Torque the coolant pump pulley bolts and the crankshaft vibration damper bolts to 20 Nm (15 ft. lb.). Install the V-belts as described in **LUBRICATION AND MAINTENANCE**.

4.3 Camshaft Oil Seal

To save disassembly, the camshaft oil seal can be removed using a seal extractor such as Volkswagen special tool no. 2085, shown in Fig. 4-6. The procedure that follows involves more disassembly and does not require special tools.

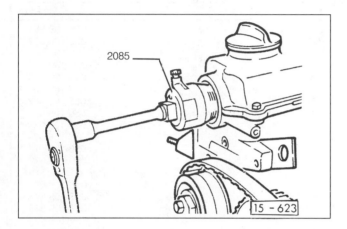

Fig. 4-6. Oil seal extractor being used to remove camshaft oil seal.

To replace camshaft oil seal

1. Remove the camshaft drive belt. For gasoline engines, see **4.2 Camshaft Drive Belt (except diesel engines)**. For diesel engines, see **FUEL SYSTEM (Diesel)**.

2. Remove the cylinder head cover as described in **4.1 Cylinder Head Cover and Gasket**.

3. Remove the camshaft sprocket. Loosen the center sprocket bolt 1/2 turn and, using a soft-faced hammer, tap the sprocket loose. On all except 16-valve engines, take care also to remove the woodruff key from the shaft.

4. On 16-valve engines only, remove the ignition distributor from the cylinder head, as described in **IGNITION**.

5. Loosen the camshaft bearing caps in exact order as described in **4.5 Removing and Installing Camshaft**, so that the camshaft is loose and free to move slightly.

> *CAUTION* ——
>
> *Failure to loosen and tighten the bearing caps in the order prescribed may damage the bearing caps or warp the camshaft.*

6. Lift slightly on the sprocket end of the camshaft and remove the oil seal. A small screwdriver may help to pry it loose. On 16-valve engines, use care not to disturb the camshaft drive chain at the other end of the cylinder head.

7. Tighten the camshaft bearing caps in xact order as described in **4.5 Removing and Installing Camshaft**.

8. Install the cylinder head cover, with a new gasket, as described in **4.1 Cylinder Head Cover and Gasket**. On 16-valve engines, first check to see that the markings on the camshaft chain sprockets are correctly aligned. See **4.5 Removing and Installing Camshaft**.

9. Lightly oil the seal lip and camshaft's sealing surface. Fit the seal into position, and carefully drive it into place until it is flush with the front of the cylinder head. Use care not to distort the seal as it is installed. For best results, use a seal driver such as Volkswagen special tool no. 10-203, shown in Fig. 4-7.

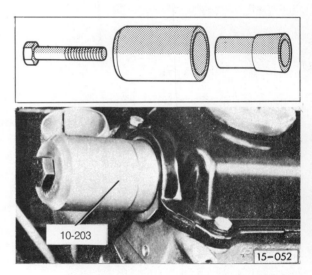

Fig. 4-7. Camshaft oil seal being installed. Inset shows parts of Volkswagen special tool no. 10-203

10. Reinstall the camshaft drive belt sprocket. On 16-valve engines, one side of the integral key is curved. The curved part of the key faces the engine. Torque the sprocket bolt to 65 Nm (48 ft. lb.) on 16-valve engines. On all gasoline engines except 16-valve, torque the sprocket bolt to 80 Nm (59 ft.lb.). On diesel engines, torque the sprocket bolt to 45 Nm (33 ft. lb.).

11. Reinstall the camshaft drive belt. For gasoline engines, see **4.2 Camshaft Drive Belt**. For diesel engines, see **FUEL SYSTEM (Diesel)**.

4.4 Valve Adjustment

(1985 and early 1986 diesel and turbo diesel only)

1985 and early 1986 diesel and turbo diesel engines require periodic valve lash adjustment. A label on the cylinder head cover, as shown in Fig. 4-8, identifies the type of cam followers installed on diesel and turbo diesel engines. **LUBRICATION**

AND MAINTENANCE. gives the recommended adjustment interval. Valve clearance should also be checked 1000 mi. (1500 km) after any repairs to the cylinder head.

All other 1985 through 1989 engines covered in this manual have hydraulic cam followers that do not require adjustment. To check hydraulic cam followers, see **4.6 Hydraulic Cam Followers**.

> ADJUST VALVES EVERY 15,000 MILES (24,000 km).
> VERIFIER LE JEU DES SOUPAPES TOUS LES
> 15,000 MILES (24,000 km). 176 010 005

Fig. 4-8. Identifying label found on cylinder head cover of diesel and turbo diesel engines requiring periodic valve adjustment.

Valve clearance is adjustable by means of a replaceable disc on the top of each cam follower. Different clearance is achieved with discs of different thicknesses. Fig. 4-9 shows the orientation of the cam lobe, the cam follower, and the disc.

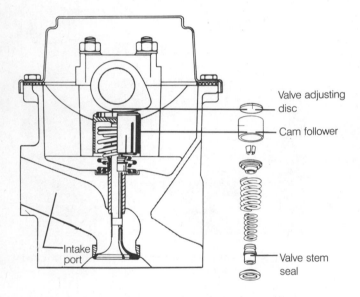

Valve adjusting disc

Cam follower

Intake port

Valve stem seal

Fig. 4-9. Cross-section of cylinder head showing the cam lobe and cam follower. Adjusting disc fits in recess in follower.

The adjusting discs are available in twenty thicknesses from 3.30 to 4.25 mm (.130 to .167 in.), in increments of .05 mm (.002 in.). **Table d** lists thicknesses and part numbers of the available adjusting discs. The thickness of each disc is etched on its underside. The procedure which follows requires two Volkswagen special tools. These are no. 2078, used to compress the valve spring, and no. 10-208, used to replace the adjusting disc.

Valve clearance should be measured with the engine warm. Coolant temperature should be at least 35°C (95°F) or the engine should be at least warm to the touch. The clearance changes with engine temperature, so more precise adjustment is possible when the engine is warm. Because it may be necessary to adjust the valves when the engine is cold, such as after cylinder head repairs, specifications for both hot and cold engines are given.

To adjust valve clearance:

1. Remove the cylinder head cover, as described in **4.1 Cylinder Head Cover and Gasket**.

2. Using a socket wrench on the crankshaft vibration damper bolt, hand-turn the crankshaft clockwise until both the No. 1 cylinder's cam lobes are pointing approximately upward (valves fully closed).

   NOTE ━
   No. 1 cylinder is the one closest to the camshaft drive belt.

Table d. Valve Adjusting Discs

Thickness mm (in.)	Part No.
3.30 (.1299)	.056 109 561
3.35 (.1319)	.056 109 562
3.40 (.1339)	.056 109 563
3.45 (.1358)	.056 109 564
3.50 (.1378)	.056 109 565
3.55 (.1398)	.056 109 566 *
3.60 (.1417)	.056 109 567 *
3.65 (.1437)	.056 109 568 *
3.70 (.1457)	.056 109 569 *
3.75 (.1476)	.056 109 570 *
3.80 (.1496)	.056 109 571 *
3.85 (.1516)	.056 109 572
3.90 (.1535)	.056 109 573
3.95 (.1555)	.056 109 574
4.00 (.1575)	.056 109 575
4.05 (.1594)	.056 109 576
4.10 (.1614)	.056 109 577
4.15 (.1634)	.056 109 578
4.20 (.1654)	.056 109 579
4.25 (.1673)	.056 109 580
* most commonly used adjusting discs	

3. Measure the valve clearances. Insert feeler gauges between the cam lobe and the adjusting disc on the top of the cam follower, as shown in Fig. 4-10. Compare the measured clearance values with the specifications given in **Table e**.

Fig. 4-10. Valve clearance being measured. Both valves are closed. Both cam lobes are pointing up, away from cam followers. Feeler gauge is inserted between cam lobe and adjusting disc on top of cam follower.

4. If valve clearance is not within the specifications, replace the adjusting disc. Depress the cam follower and lift out the disc as shown in Fig. 4-11.

**Table e. Valve Clearance Specifications
(1985 and early 1986 diesel and turbo diesel)**

engine warm	
intake . . . . .0.20–0.30 mm (.008–.012 in.)	
exhaust . . . . .0.40–0.50 mm (.016–.020 in.)	
engine cold	
intake . . . . .0.15–0.25 mm (.006–.010 in.)	
exhaust . . . . .0.35–0.45 mm (.014–.018 in.)	

Fig. 4-11. Adjusting disc being removed from cylinder head. Volkswagen tool no. 2078 is used to depress cam followers. Tool no. 10-208 is used to remove adjusting disc.

NOTE ——

To calculate the correct adjusting disc thickness, first determine the thickness of the old disc. Read the thickness, in millimeters, that is etched on its underside, or measure it with a micrometer. The change in thickness required is the same as the difference between the measured clearance and the specification given in **Table e.** above. A thicker disc will reduce valve clearance. A thinner disc will increase valve clearance.

5. Install the correct adjusting disc. Lightly oil the contact surfaces. Depress the cam follower and install the disc the same way it was removed, as shown in Fig. 4-11, above. The etched disc thickness numbers should face down.

6. Rotate the engine by hand for two complete turns, to ensure that the adjusting disc is properly seated, and recheck the clearance.

7. Using a socket wrench, hand-turn the crankshaft clockwise 180° (1/2 turn) and repeat the procedure on the valves for No. 3 cylinder. Turn another 180° to adjust the No. 4 cylinder, and another 180° to adjust the No. 2 cylinder.

8. Install the cylinder head cover with new gaskets, as described in **4.1 Cylinder Head Cover and Gasket**.

4.5 Removing and Installing Camshaft

The camshaft can be removed without removing the cylinder head. Removing the camshaft allows access to the cam followers, the valve springs, and the valve stem oil seals. When removed, the camshaft should be checked for wear and other visible damage as described in **4.9 Disassembly, Assembly, and Reconditioning**.

**To remove and install camshaft
(except 16-valve engines):**

1. Turn the engine over by hand until the No. 1 cylinder is at Top Dead Center (TDC), and remove the camshaft drive belt from the camshaft sprocket. For gasoline engines, see **4.2 Camshaft Drive Belt**. For diesel engines, see **FUEL SYSTEM (diesel)**.

2. Remove the cylinder head cover and gasket as described in **4.1 Cylinder Head Cover and Gasket**.

3. On gasoline engines, remove bearing caps 1 and 3, in that order. Loosen the nuts on each of the two remaining caps, a little at a time so that valve spring tension is relieved evenly.

4. On diesel engines, remove bearing caps 1, 3 and 5, in that order. Loosen the nuts on each of the two remaining caps, a little at a time so that valve spring tension is relieved evenly.

CAUTION ——

To avoid uneven and accelerated wear, the bearing caps must be reinstalled in their exact original positions. Although each bearing cap is numbered, the numbers are not always marked in the same place on the cap.

5. To install, begin with bearing caps 2 and 5 on gasoline engines, or 2 and 4 on diesel engines. See Fig. 4-12. Install the washers and nuts, gradually tightening all four nuts until the camshaft is drawn down fully and evenly into the bearing saddles. Install the remaining bearing caps with washers and nuts. Torque all the nuts to 20 Nm (15 ft. lb.).

6. Reinstall the camshaft drive belt. For gasoline engines, see **4.2 Camshaft Drive Belt**. For diesel engines, see **FUEL SYSTEM (diesel)**. Reinstall the cylinder head cover with a new gasket, as described in **4.1 Cylinder Head Cover and Gasket**.

**To remove and install camshafts
(16-valve engine):**

1. Turn the engine over by hand until the No. 1 cylinder is at Top Dead Center (TDC), and remove the camshaft drive belt from the camshaft sprocket as described in **4.2 Camshaft Drive Belt**.

2. Remove the cylinder head cover and gasket as described in **4.1 Cylinder Head Cover and Gasket**.

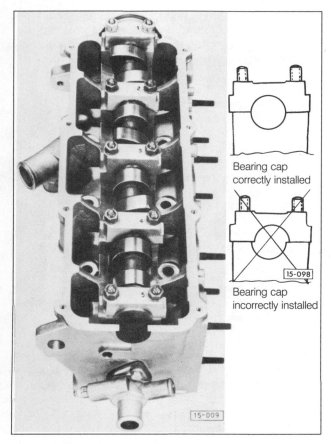

Fig. 4-12. Camshaft bearing caps. Diesel engine shown. Gasoline engines are similar, except that bearing cap no. 4 is not used.

3. Remove the ignition distributor from the rear of the cylinder head as described in **IGNITION**.

4. Remove bearing caps 1, 3, 5 and 7, as illustrated in Fig. 4-13.

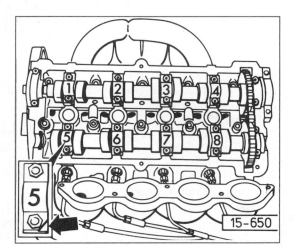

Fig. 4-13. Top view of 16-valve cylinder head showing camshaft bearing cap identification. Inset shows proper installation of bearing caps (beveled corners facing intake side).

5. Gradually and evenly loosen each of the eight nuts from bearing caps 2, 4, 6 and 8, a little at a time so that valve spring tension and cam chain tension are relieved evenly.

CAUTION ——

Removal of camshaft bearing caps by any other method may damage the camshafts, the camshaft chain, or the bearing caps.

6. Installation is the reverse of removal. Install the camshafts and the drive chain so that the markings on the chain sprockets face each other and align with the top of the cylinder head, as shown in Fig. 4-14.

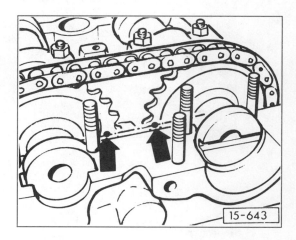

Fig. 4-14. Camshaft drive chain sprockets correctly aligned in 16-valve cylinder head.

7. Torque the bearing cap nuts to 15 Nm (11 ft. lb.). Reinstall the cylinder head cover with a new gasket, as described in **4.1 Cylinder Head Cover and Gasket**.

8. Install the camshaft drive belt and adjust the camshaft timing as described in **4.2 Camshaft Drive Belt**.

9. Install the ignition distributor and adjust ignition timing as described in **IGNITION**.

4.6 Hydraulic Cam Followers

All 1985 through 1989 gasoline engines, and all diesel engines since late 1986, are equipped with hydraulic cam followers which automatically maintain proper valve adjustment. The cylinder head cover label which identifies these engines is shown in Fig. 4-15.

Hydraulic cam followers are pumped up by engine oil pressure, expanding as necessary to fill the gap between valve and camshaft lobe. If the space between the valve and the camshaft lobe becomes smaller, due to wear for example, some oil escapes through a small orifice and the follower bleeds down slightly.

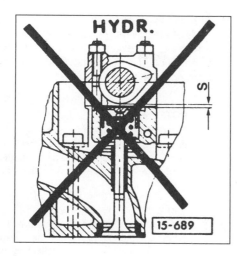

Fig. 4-15. Identifying label found on cylinder head cover of engines with hydraulic cam followers. These engines do not require valve adjustment.

Some valve noise at startup is normal, due to hydraulic cam followers which have bled down while the engine was not running. Before checking noisy cam followers, check to see that the engine oil level is correct and allow a minute or so with the engine running for the lubrication system to properly pump up the cam followers.

CAUTION ━━━

After installing new cam followers, the engine should not be started for at least 30 minutes. New cam followers are at full height and must be allowed to bleed down to their proper height. Failure to do this may cause valve or piston damage.

Checking Hydraulic Cam Followers

Cam followers should only be checked when the engine is fully warm. Run the engine, preferably drive the car, for 20 to 30 minutes. Shut the engine off and proceed immediately while the engine is still warm.

To check the hydraulic cam followers, remove the cylinder head cover as described in **4.1 Cylinder Head Cover and Gasket**. Turn the engine by hand until both the camshaft lobes of one cylinder are pointing approximately up. Using a non-metal object such as wood or plastic, lightly apply pressure to the top of the cam follower, as shown in Fig. 4-16.

If the follower can be pushed down more than 0.1 mm (.004 in.) with hand pressure, it is faulty and should be replaced. Repeat the test for the other cylinders. Replace a faulty cam follower by removing the camshaft, as described in **4.5 Removing and Installing Camshaft** and pulling the follower from the cylinder head. Hydraulic cam followers are non-adjustable and non-repairable, and are replaced only as complete assemblies.

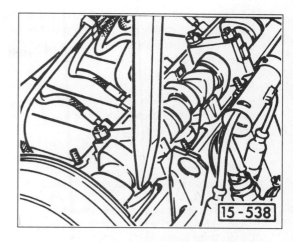

Fig. 4-16. Hydraulic cam follower being checked with a non-metal object.

NOTE ━━━

When hydraulic cam followers are removed, place them on a clean surface with the camshaft contact surface facing down, to prevent bleed down, and cover them.

4.7 Valve Stem Oil Seals

The sign of faulty valve stem oil seals are excessive oil consumption and blue-gray oil smoke from the exhaust after starting and during sudden deceleration. For more information on excessive oil consumption and smoking, see **3. Troubleshooting**.

Replacement of the valve stem oil seals requires that the camshaft(s), the cam followers, and the valve springs be removed. Valve springs can be removed while the cylinder head is installed with the use of compressed air to hold the valves closed, or with the cylinder head removed. Either method requires the use of a valve spring compressor. An additional special tool is highly recommended for installation of the new seals. If the special tools are not available, an alternative is to remove and partially dismantle the cylinder head, following the procedures in this section, and have the valve spring and valve stem oil seal work performed by an authorized Volkswagen dealer or other qualified repair shop.

NOTE ━━━

Diesel engines do not require compressed air to hold the valve on its seat. The valve can rest on the piston at Top Dead Center (TDC).

To replace valve stem oil seals:

1. If working with the cylinder head installed, remove the cylinder head cover, as described in **4.1 Cylinder Head Cover and Gasket**. Otherwise, remove the cylinder head as described below in **4.8 Removing and Installing Cylinder Head**.

2. Remove the camshaft, as described in **4.5 Removing and Installing Camshaft**, and remove the cam followers. Keep all parts so that they can be reinstalled in their original locations.

3. Remove the valve springs as shown in Fig. 4-17. The valve spring compressors shown are Volkswagen special tools, designed specifically for use on Volkswagen engines.

   NOTE ━━

   To support the valves with compressed air and remove the valve springs with the cylinder head installed, install an air hose adapter in the spark plug hole. Position the piston for the cylinder at top dead center (TDC). Apply a constant air pressure of at least 6.0 bar (85 psi).

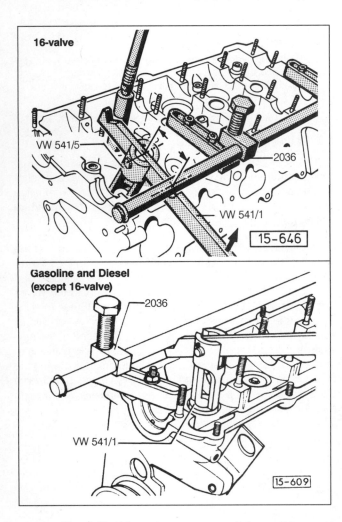

Fig. 4-17. Valve spring compressors being used to remove valve springs on 16-valve engine (top), and all other gasoline and diesel engines (bottom). On 16-valve engines, it may be necessary to notch the tool's handle as shown to prevent it from slipping. Dimension **a** is 50.0 mm (1.97 in.). Numbers identify Volkswagen special tools.

4. Remove the valve stem oil seals. Volkswagen recommends the use of a slide hammer, special tool no. 3047A, to remove the seals without damage to the valve stems.

5. Install each new valve stem oil seal by temporarily fitting the protective plastic cap over the valve stem end, and then hand-pressing the seal onto the valve stem as shown in Fig. 4-18. Remove the protective cap for use on the next valve.

   NOTE ━━

   The protective cap protects the seal from being damaged by the keeper grooves in the valve stem. In the absence of a protective cap, temporarily wrap the valve stem with plastic tape.

   NOTE ━━

   The use of an inexpensive hand-held tool will guard against damaging the new seals on installation. Such a tool is Volkswagen special tool no. US 5042 (order no. TU5 042 000 15 ZEL).

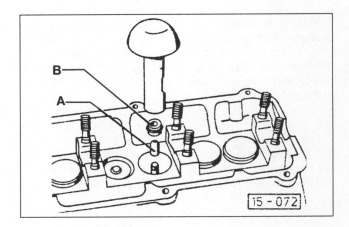

Fig. 4-18. Protective cap **A**, new valve stem oil seal **B**, and installing tool.

6. Reinstall the valve springs. The closely spaced coils of the outer valve springs face down, toward the lower spring seats.

7. Repeat the procedure for each pair of valves. Assembly is the reverse of disassembly. See **4.5 Removing and Installing Camshaft**, **4.8 Removing and Installing Cylinder Head**, and **4.1 Cylinder Head Cover and Gasket**. Torque spark plugs to 20 Nm (15 ft. lb.).

4.8 Removing and Installing Cylinder Head

The cylinder head can be removed without removing the engine from the vehicle, and without removing the camshaft(s). On diesel engines, new cylinder head bolts should be used every time the cylinder head is installed.

If a failed head gasket or warped head is suspected, a compression test, as described in **3.2 Diagnostic Testing**, may aid diagnosis and should be performed before the cylinder head is removed. A failed head gasket may be caused by a warped cylinder head. When replacing a failed head gasket, always check the cylinder head for straightness. Specifications for maximum permissible warpage can be found in **4.9 Disassembly, Assembly, and Reconditioning**.

To remove cylinder head:

1. Disconnect the battery negative (−) terminal from the battery. Disconnect the ground strap from the cylinder head or intake manifold.

2. On gasoline engines, disconnect the intake air duct from the throttle body on the intake manifold.

3. On diesel engines, remove the air cleaner and the intake air duct. On turbo diesel engines, remove the turbocharger as described in **EXHAUST SYSTEM AND EMISSION CONTROLS**.

4. Drain the coolant as described in **COOLING SYSTEM**.

5. Remove the camshaft drive belt. For gasoline engines, see **4.2 Camshaft Drive Belt**. For diesel engines, see **FUEL SYSTEM (diesel)**.

6. On diesel engines only, disconnect the accelerator cable and the fuel injection pipes as described in **FUEL SYSTEM (diesel)**. Disconnect the wire from the glow plug bus.

7. On gasoline engines, pull out the fuel injectors and remove the cold start valve from the intake manifold, leaving the fuel lines attached. Cover the injectors and the cold start valve to keep them clean and plug the openings. Disconnect the throttle cable and throttle switches from the throttle body. Disconnect and label the hoses and wires connected to the throttle body and the intake manifold. For more information on fuel injection components, see **FUEL SYSTEM (gasoline)**.

8. Disconnect the exhaust pipe from the exhaust manifold, as described in **EXHAUST SYSTEM AND EMISSION CONTROLS**.

9. Loosen the alternator mounting bolts and remove the upper alternator mounting bracket.

10. Disconnect the coolant hoses from the outlet on the front of the cylinder head and from the heater outlet on the left (driver's side) end of the cylinder head. Disconnect the wires from the temperature and oil pressure sending units, and label them.

11. On gasoline engines, disconnect the spark plug connectors from the spark plugs. On 16-valve engines, also disconnect the high voltage lead from the coil, and then remove the distributor as described in **IGNITION**.

12. Remove the cylinder head cover, and the upper intake manifold on 16-valve engines, as described in **4.1 Cylinder Head Cover and Gasket**.

13. Gradually and evenly loosen the cylinder head bolts, beginning with the outer bolts and working toward the center, and remove the cylinder head. If the head is stuck, use a soft-faced mallet or pry gently with a wooden stick to loosen it.

To install cylinder head:

1. Clean the cylinder head and the gasket surface of the cylinder block. Clean the threads of the head bolts and bolt holes with thread chasers, and remove all foreign matter from the holes. Avoid letting debris into the cylinders or oil passages in the cylinder block.

3

CAUTION ▬

Do not use a metal scraper or wire brush to clean the aluminum cylinder head. These may damage the cylinder head. Instead, use a solvent to soften carbon deposits and old sealing materials. If necessary, use a wooden or plastic scraper.

2. Check the gasket surfaces of the cylinder head and the cylinder block for warpage. See **4.9 Disassembly, Assembly, and Reconditioning**.

3. On diesel engines, reinstall the combustion pre-chamber inserts, if they were removed while cleaning the cylinder head.

4. Place a new cylinder head gasket on the surface of the cylinder block. The word "OBEN", found imprinted on the gasket near the part number, should face up.

CAUTION ▬

Cylinder head gaskets will give a reliable seal only once. Always use a new gasket that has not previously been compressed by tightening the cylinder head bolts.

CAUTION ▬

*Three different cylinder head gaskets are available for use on diesel engines, identified by a number of notches or holes in the gasket near the part number. When reassembling the same cylinder head and cylinder block, make sure that the new gasket matches the one it replaces. When assembling a new cylinder head, a new cylinder block, or an overhauled cylinder block, the correct gasket must be selected by measuring piston protrusion. See **6. Cylinder Block and Pistons**.*

5. Place the cylinder head in position on the cylinder block. Loosely install all the head bolts, with the special washers, then thread them in until they are finger-tight.

NOTE ▬

To be sure of proper alignment of the installed cylinder head, place two 200 mm long, 9 mm diameter (8 in. x 3/8 in.) wooden dowels into two of the outermost head bolt holes to hold the gasket and serve as guides as the cylinder head is installed. Thread in several bolts, then remove the dowels and install the remaining bolts.

6. Torque the bolts to 40 Nm (30 ft. lb.), in the sequence shown in Fig. 4-19. Repeat the sequence, torquing the bolts to 60 Nm (43 ft. lb.). Repeat the sequence a third time, tightening each bolt an additional 1/2 turn. Alternatively, this last step may be done as two 1/4 turns.

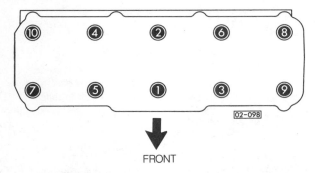

FRONT

Fig. 4-19. Cylinder head bolt tightening sequence for all 1985–1988 gasoline and diesel engines.

NOTE ——

On diesel engines, the cylinder head bolts should be retorqued (1/4 turn without loosening) after the engine has been run and is at operating temperature. After approximately 1,000 mi. (1,500 km) the cylinder head bolts should be torqued an additional 1/4 turn, without loosening and without interruption.

7. Installation of the remaining parts is the reverse of removal. See **4.2 Camshaft Drive Belt**, **4.1 Cylinder Head Cover and Gasket**, **FUEL SYSTEM (diesel)**, **FUEL SYSTEM (gasoline)**, and **EXHAUST SYSTEM AND EMISSION CONTROLS**. For installation of the ignition distributor on 16-valve engines, see **IGNITION**.

8. Refill the cooling system as described in **COOLING SYSTEM**.

4.9 Disassembly, Assembly, and Reconditioning

Disassembly, assembly, and reconditioning procedures for the cylinder heads used on 1.6 and 1.8 liter Volkswagen engines covered in this manual are similar to those for most other modern 4-cylinder, water-cooled engines. For anyone with the proper tools and equipment and basic experience in cylinder head reconditioning, this section provides the specifications and special reconditioning information necessary to repair these Volkswagen engines.

Those who are without the necessary tools, or unfamiliar with reconditioning procedures, will still find this information to be important to the qualified machinist who does the work. If machine shop services are not readily available, one alternative is to install a Volkswagen remanufactured cylinder head, available from an authorized Volkswagen dealer parts department.

Cylinder Head Assembly

(16-valve engine)

Fig. 4-20 shows the cylinder head and valve train assembly found on PL (16-valve) engines.

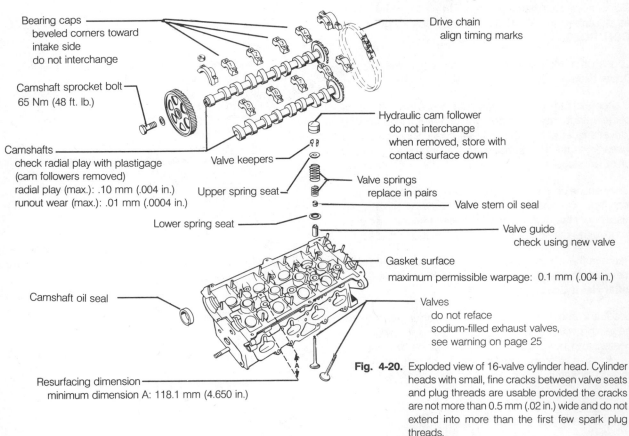

Bearing caps
beveled corners toward
intake side
do not interchange

Drive chain
align timing marks

Camshaft sprocket bolt
65 Nm (48 ft. lb.)

Hydraulic cam follower
do not interchange
when removed, store with
contact surface down

Camshafts
check radial play with plastigage
(cam followers removed)
radial play (max.): .10 mm (.004 in.)
runout wear (max.): .01 mm (.0004 in.)

Valve keepers

Valve springs
replace in pairs

Upper spring seat

Valve stem oil seal

Lower spring seat

Valve guide
check using new valve

Gasket surface
maximum permissible warpage: 0.1 mm (.004 in.)

Camshaft oil seal

Valves
do not reface
sodium-filled exhaust valves,
see warning on page 25

Resurfacing dimension
minimum dimension A: 118.1 mm (4.650 in.)

Fig. 4-20. Exploded view of 16-valve cylinder head. Cylinder heads with small, fine cracks between valve seats and plug threads are usable provided the cracks are not more than 0.5 mm (.02 in.) wide and do not extend into more than the first few spark plug threads.

Cylinder Head Assembly
(gasoline engines except 16-valve)

Fig. 4-21 shows the cylinder head and valve train assembly found on all GTI, Golf, and Jetta gasoline engines except 16-valve.

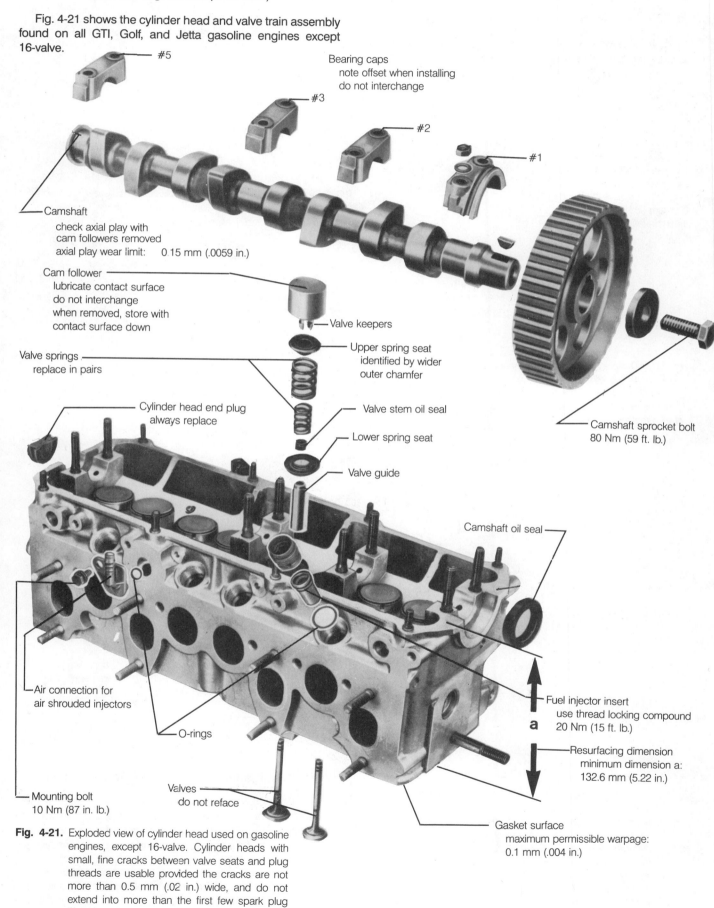

#5

Bearing caps
note offset when installing
do not interchange

#3

#2

#1

Camshaft
check axial play with
cam followers removed
axial play wear limit: 0.15 mm (.0059 in.)

Cam follower
lubricate contact surface
do not interchange
when removed, store with
contact surface down

Valve keepers

Upper spring seat
identified by wider
outer chamfer

Valve springs
replace in pairs

Valve stem oil seal

Cylinder head end plug
always replace

Lower spring seat

Valve guide

Camshaft sprocket bolt
80 Nm (59 ft. lb.)

Camshaft oil seal

Air connection for
air shrouded injectors

Fuel injector insert
use thread locking compound
20 Nm (15 ft. lb.)

a

O-rings

Resurfacing dimension
minimum dimension a:
132.6 mm (5.22 in.)

Mounting bolt
10 Nm (87 in. lb.)

Valves
do not reface

Gasket surface
maximum permissible warpage:
0.1 mm (.004 in.)

Fig. 4-21. Exploded view of cylinder head used on gasoline engines, except 16-valve. Cylinder heads with small, fine cracks between valve seats and plug threads are usable provided the cracks are not more than 0.5 mm (.02 in.) wide, and do not extend into more than the first few spark plug threads.

Cylinder Head Assembly

(diesel and turbo diesel engines)

Fig. 4-22 shows the cylinder head and valve train assembly found on the 1.6 L diesel and turbo diesel engines.

Fig. 4-22. Exploded view of cylinder head used on diesel and turbo diesel engines. Cylinder heads with small, fine cracks between valve seats are usable provided the cracks are not more than 0.5 mm (.02 in.) wide.

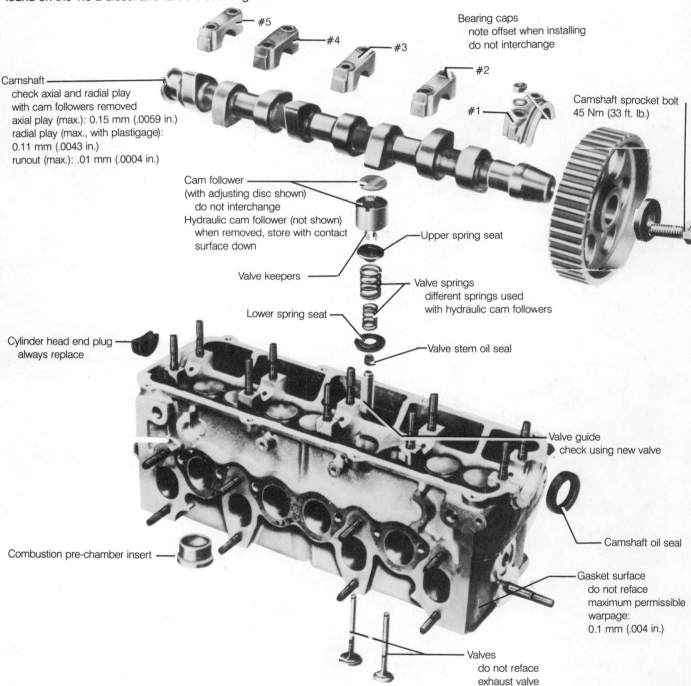

Bearing caps
note offset when installing
do not interchange

#5
#4
#3
#2
#1

Camshaft
check axial and radial play
with cam followers removed
axial play (max.): 0.15 mm (.0059 in.)
radial play (max., with plastigage):
0.11 mm (.0043 in.)
runout (max.): .01 mm (.0004 in.)

Camshaft sprocket bolt
45 Nm (33 ft. lb.)

Cam follower
(with adjusting disc shown)
do not interchange
Hydraulic cam follower (not shown)
when removed, store with contact
surface down

Upper spring seat

Valve keepers

Valve springs
different springs used
with hydraulic cam followers

Lower spring seat

Cylinder head end plug
always replace

Valve stem oil seal

Valve guide
check using new valve

Camshaft oil seal

Combustion pre-chamber insert

Gasket surface
do not reface
maximum permissible
warpage:
0.1 mm (.004 in.)

Valves
do not reface
exhaust valve

CAUTION

Three different cylinder head gaskets are available for use on diesel engines, identified by a number of notches or holes in the gasket near the part number. When reassembling the same cylinder head and cylinder block, make sure that the new gasket matches the one it replaces. When assembling a new cylinder head, a new cylinder block, or an overhauled cylinder block, the correct gasket must be selected by measuring piston protrusion. See 6. Cylinder Block and Pistons.

Camshaft and Cam Followers

To measure camshaft axial play, relieve the tension on the cam lobes by first removing the cam followers. Store hydraulic cam followers with the camshaft contact surface face down. Lubricate the cam follower's contact surfaces before installing.

Do not interchange camshaft bearing caps or cam followers. Note the bearing cap offset when installing. On 16-valve engines, the beveled corners on the bearing caps face the intake side of the cylinder head. On 16-valve engines, align the camshaft chain sprockets as shown in Fig. 4-23. Camshaft identifying marks for gasoline engines, except 16-valve, are shown in Fig. 4-24.

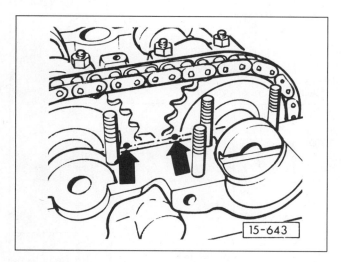

Fig. 4-23. Camshaft chain sprocket timing marks on 16-valve engines. Marks should align with each other and cylinder head top surface.

CAUTION ━━

After installing new cam followers, the engine should not be started for at least 30 minutes. New cam followers are at full height and must be allowed to bleed down to their proper height. Failure to do this may cause valve or piston damage.

Valves and Valve Springs

Only intake valves in diesel engines may be refaced by machine. Diesel exhaust valves, and all gasoline engine valves, should be hand-lapped only. Valve and valve spring specifications are given in **Table f.**

Exhaust valves used in 16-valve engines are sodium-filled. Disposal of used valves is dangerous and requires special care to avoid personal injury.

15 - 684

Engine code	Arrow **A**	Arrow **B**
RD	G	026
GX, HT, MZ	026	—
	OR	
	A	026

Fig. 4-24. Camshaft identifying marks used on gasoline engines, except 16-valve.

WARNING ━━

Dispose of 16-valve engine sodium-illed exhaust valves properly. By hand, cut off the valve stem near the head of each valve. Use only a hack saw. Do not use a power saw. Do not let water contact the valve while cutting. Throw the valve parts (no more than 10 valves at a time) into a bucket of water and stand clear. Discard the valves when the reaction has ceased.

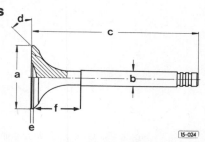

Table f. Valve and Valve Spring Specifications

Engine code	GX, MZ	HT, RD, RV, PF	PL	ME, MF (with hydraulic cam followers)	ME, MF (with mechanical cam followers)
Valve head diameter (a)					
intake	38.00 mm (1.496 in.)	40.00 mm (1.575 in.)	32.00 mm (1.259 in.)	34.00 mm (1.339 in.)	34.00mm (1.339 in.)
exhaust	33.00 mm (1.299 in.)	33.00 mm (1.299 in.)	28.00mm (1.102 in.)	31.00 mm (1.220 in.)	31.00 mm (1.220 in.)

continued on next page

Table f. Valve and Valve Spring Specifications (continued)

Engine Code	GX, MZ	HT, RD, RV, PF	PL	ME, MF with hydraulic cam followers	ME, MF with mechanical cam followers
Valve stem diameter (**b**)					
intake	7.97 mm (.3138 in.)	7.97 mm (.3138 in.)	6.97 mm (.2744 in.)	7.97 mm (.3138 in.)	7.97 mm (.3138 in.)
exhaust	7.95 mm (.3130 in.)	7.95 mm (.3130 in.)	6.94 mm (.2732 in.)	7.95 mm (.3130 in.)	7.95 mm (.3130 in.)
Valve length (**c**)					
intake	91.00 mm (3.583 in.)	91.00 mm (3.583 in.)	95.50 mm (3.760 in.)	95.00 mm (3.740 in.)	104.80 mm (4.126 in.)
exahust	90.80 mm (3.575 in.)	90.80 mm (3.575 in.)	98.20 mm (3.866 in.)	95.00 mm (3.740 in.)	104.60 mm (4.118 in.)
Valve face angle (**d**)					
intake	45°	45°	45°	45°	45°
exhaust	45°	45°	45°	45°	45°
Valve margin (**e**)	-	-	-	0.5 mm (0.020 in.)	0.5 mm (0.020 in.)
Valve spring length					
inner	-	-	-	32.5 mm (1.28 in.)	33.9 mm (1.33 in.)
outer	-	-	-	37.0 mm (1.46 in.)	40.2 mm (1.58 in.)

Valve Guides

Special tools and a press are required to replace valve guides. Check valve guide wear with a new valve, as shown in Fig. 4-25. Inspect the valve seats to ensure that the cylinder head can be reconditioned before installing new valve guides.

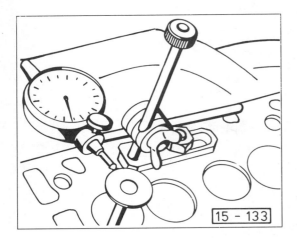

Fig. 4-25. Valve guide wear being checked with a new valve. Insert valve until stem end is flush with end of guide. Maximum play for intake valves on all gasoline engines is 1.0 mm (.039 in.). Maximum play for exhaust valves on all gasoline engines, and both intake and exhaust valves on diesel engines, is 1.3 mm (.051 in.)

Original valve guides, without shoulders, are pressed out from the camshaft side of the cylinder head. Replacement valve guides, with shoulders, are pressed out from the combustion chamber side of the cylinder head. Lubricate new valve guides with oil and press them in from the camshaft side. On all except 16-valve engines, remove and install guides with Volkswagen special tool no. 10-206 (order no. T10 206 000 15 ZEL).

On 16-valve engines, remove and install guides with Volkswagen special tool no. 3121 (order no. T03 121 000 15 ZEL), and ream guides with Volkswagen special tool no. 3120 (order no. T03 120 000 15 ZEL). To remove and install intake valve guides, support the cylinder head at an angle as shown in Fig. 4-26, using Volkswagen special tool no. 3123 (order no. T03 123 000 15 ZEL).

Valve Seats

When resurfacing valve seats on engines with hydraulic cam followers, there is a limit to the amount of material which can be removed. If too much material is removed, the final assembly will leave too little space for the hydraulic cam follower to function correctly. The maximum refacing dimension, the maximum amount of material that can be removed from the valve seat, is calculated from the measurement shown in Fig. 4-27.

Measure dimension **a**, and subtract the minimum dimension, as given in **Table g**. The difference is the maximum amount of material that can be removed from the valve seat.

3

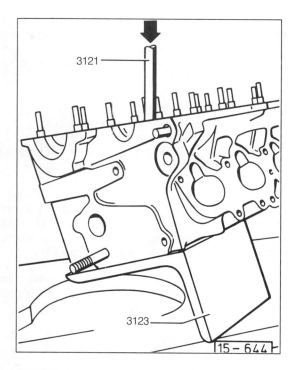

Fig. 4-26. Angle plate (Volkswagen special tool no. 3123) used to support 16-valve cylinder head when removing and installing intake valve guides.

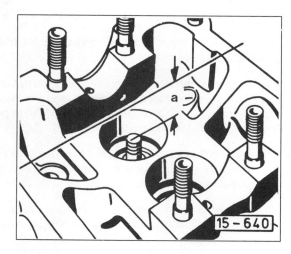

Fig. 4-27. Top view of cylinder head. Dimension **a**, distance between top of valve stem and upper (gasket) surface of cylinder head, is used to calculate maximum refacing dimensions.

Table g. Minimum Dimensions for Calculating Valve Seat Refacing Dimensions.

Engine Code	Intake	Exhaust;
GX MZ HT RD RV PF	33.8 mm (1.331 in.)	34.1 mm (1.343 in.)
PL (16-valve)	34.4 mm (1.354 in.)	34.7 mm (1.366 in.)
ME (diesel) MF (turbo diesel)	35.8 mm (1.409 in.)	36.1 mm (1.421 in.)

Valve seat dimensions are given in the tables that follow. **Table h** lists dimensions for all gasoline engines, except 16-valve. **Table i** lists dimensions for 16-valve engines. **Table j** lists dimensions for diesel and turbo diesel engines.

Table h. Valve Seat Dimensions (gasoline engines except 16-valve)

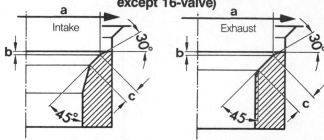

Engine code . . . . .GX, MZ, HT, RD, RV, PF

diameter **a**
     intake (GX, MZ only) . . . . .37.2 mm (1.465 in.)
     intake (HT, RD only). . . . . .39.2 mm (1.543 in.)
     exhaust. . . . . .32.4 mm (1.276 in.)

Maximum permissible
   refacing depth **b** . . . . .calculate
     See Fig. 4-27, **Table g.**

Seat width **c**
     intake. . . . . .approx. 2.0 mm (.080 in.)
     exhaust. . . . . .approx. 2.4 mm (.094 in.)

Valve seat angle. . . . . .45°
Upper correction angle . . . . .30°

Table i. Valve seat dimensions (16-valve engines)

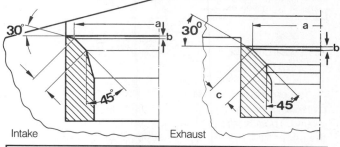

Engine code. . . . . .PL

diameter **a**
     intake . . . . .31.2 mm (1.228 in.)
     exhaust .27.6 mm (1.087 in.)

Maximum permissible
   refacing depth **b** . . . . .calculate
     See Fig. 4-27, **Table g**

Seat width **c**
     intake . . . . .1.5 to 1.8 mm
     (.06 to .07 in.)
     exhaust .approx. 1.8 mm
     (.07 in.)

Valve seat angle. . . . . .45°
Upper correction angle . . . . .30°
Lower correction angle   intake . . . . .75°

Table j. Valve seat dimensions (diesel and turbo diesel engines)

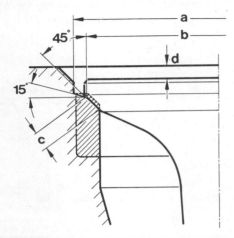

Engine Code . . . . .ME, MF	
Maximum seat angle correction diameter **a**	
intake . . . . .35.2 mm (1.386 in.)	
exhaust . . . . .33.2 mm (1.307 in.)	
Diameter **b**	
intake . . . . .32.8 mm (1.291 in.)	
exhaust . . . . .30.4 mm (1.197 in.)	
Seat width **c**	
intake . . . . .2.0 mm (.080 in.)	
exhaust . . . . .2.4 mm (.094 in.)	
Valve depth below gasket surface (maximum) . . . . .1.5 mm (0.059 in.)	
Valve seat angle. . . . . .45°	
Upper correction angle . . . . .15°	

5. REMOVING AND INSTALLING ENGINE AND TRANSAXLE

The engine and transaxle are removed as a unit, and separated from each other for additional work once they are removed. The assembly is lifted out from the front, requiring that the upper front apron (radiator support) be removed. It is not necessary to remove the hood, unless it will interfere with the type of lifting equipment being used.

Removing

On air-conditioned cars, the air conditioning compressor and condenser should be removed and set aside without disconnecting refrigerant lines, as described below, before removing the engine and transaxle. On cars with power steering, dismount the power steering pump and fluid reservoir, and set them aside without disconnecting the power steering fluid lines.

On cars with automatic transmissions, if the engine and transaxle are going to be separated, the torque converter drive plate needs to be marked for reinstallation. It may be easier to do this prior to removing the engine and transaxle. Mark the drive plate with the engine at Top Dead Center (TDC).

To remove:

1. Disconnect the negative (−) battery terminal, and then the positive (+) terminal. Remove the battery.

2. Working under the car, disconnect the drive axle inner constant velocity joints from the transaxle drive flanges, as described in **SUSPENSION AND STEERING**. Suspend the axles from the body with stiff wire to avoid damage to the outer constant velocity joints.

3. Disconnect the exhaust pipe from the exhaust manifold, as described in **EXHAUST SYSTEM AND EMISSION CONTROLS**.

4. Drain the cooling system as described in **COOLING SYSTEM**, and remove the coolant hoses connected to the engine.

5. On gasoline engines, remove fuel injection components as described in **4.8 Removing and Installing Cylinder Head**. With the main fuel lines attached, remove the air flow sensor and air filter housing and set it aside.

6. Remove the lower apron bolt and unclip the lower trim piece. See Fig. 5-1.

7. Disconnect the electrical connectors for the radiator cooling fan, the radiator thermoswitch, and the headlights. Disconnect the hood release cable and the upper radiator mounts. See Fig. 5-2.

8. Remove the grill and the front apron. Remove the radiator with air ducts and fan shroud, as described in **COOLING SYSTEM**.

9. On cars with air conditioning, remove the condenser mounting bolts as shown in Fig. 5-3. Without disconnecting any refrigerant lines, remove the condenser and remove the air conditioning compressor from the engine. Set them aside as shown in Fig. 5-4, using care to avoid kinking the refrigerant lines.

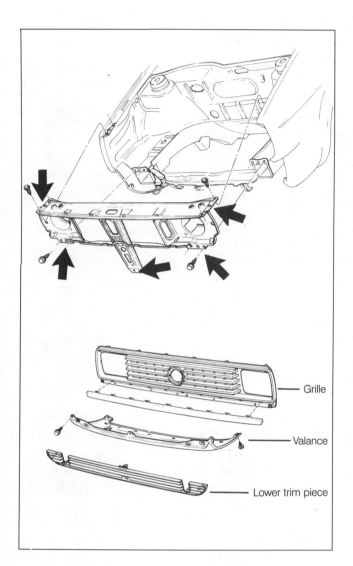

Fig. 5-1. Front apron (radiator support) mounting points (arrows). Lower trim piece and grille snap in place.

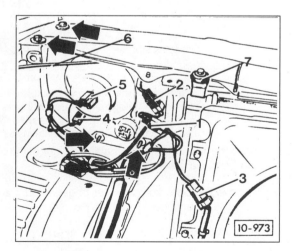

Fig. 5-2. Items to be disconnected for removal of front apron. Connectors **1** and **2**, radiator cooling fan plug **3**, headlight connections **4** and **5**, hood release cable from hood latch **6**, radiator mounts **7**, and front apron mounting bolts **(arrows)**.

Fig. 5-3. Air conditioning condenser mounting bolts (arrows).

Fig. 5-4. Air conditioning compressor and condenser set aside for engine removal with refrigerant lines still connected. Tie in place. Use padding to protect paint.

10. Disconnect all remaining electrical connections to the engine and transaxle. Typical engine and transaxle connections are shown in Fig. 5-5. For diesel fuel injection connections, see **FUEL SYSTEM (diesel)**.

11. On turbo diesel engines, detach the air cleaner duct from the turbocharger's air intake. Remove the air cleaner assembly and detach the electrical connector from the blow-off valve.

12. On 16-valve engines, remove the upper intake manifold, as described in **4.1 Cylinder Head Cover and Gasket**.

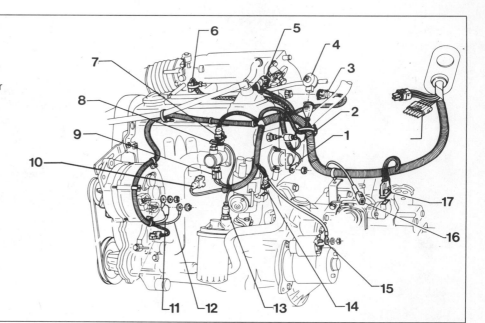

1. Ground
2. Oil pressure switch
3. Auxilary air regulator
   (CIS)
4. Vacuum switch for upshift indicator
   (manual transmission only)
5. Cold start valve
6. After-run thermo switch
   (where applicable)
7. Thermo-time switch
8. Coolant temperature sensor
9. Thermoswitch
10. Control pressure regulator (CIS)
11. B+ alternator connection
12. D+ alternator connection
13. Oil pressure sending unit
14. Hall ignition sender
15. Starter cable
16. Positive (+) battery cable
    (automatic transmission)
17. Upshift and back-up light
    switch (manual transmission)

Fig. 5-5. Engine and transaxle items to be disconnected. 8-valve gasoline engine shown. Other engines are similar.

13. On gasoline engines, disconnect the oxygen sensor connector behind the cylinder head. Remove and label the ignition coil connectors. Remove all engine ground connections.

14. Remove the speedometer drive cable from the transaxle housing. On models with manual transmission, detach the clutch cable and shift linkage as described in **MANUAL TRANSMISSION AND CLUTCH.**

15. On models with automatic transmissions, place the selector lever in the "Park" position. Remove the accelerator cable and the selector lever cable as shown in **AUTOMATIC TRANSMISSION.**

16. Install an engine lifting device, using the lifting points illustrated in Fig. 5-6 and, for 16-valve engines, Fig. 5-7.

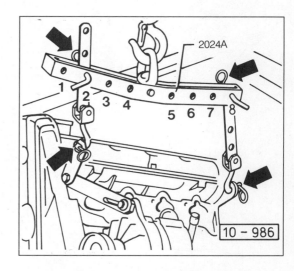

Fig. 5-7. Engine hoist (Volkswagen special tool no. 2024A) installed on 16-valve engine. Use of hoist as shown is necessary for proper weight distribution. Always use securing cotter pins and holding pins, as shown.

17. Raise the hoist slightly, so that the weight of the engine and transaxle assembly is supported by it.

18. Remove the bolts from the rear engine mount and the transaxle mounting as shown in Fig. 5-8.

Fig. 5-6. Engine hoist chain properly attached for lifting gasoline and diesel engines, except 16-valve.

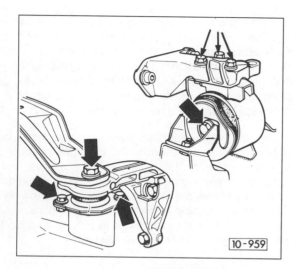

Fig. 5-8. Rear engine mounting bolts (right) and transaxle mounting bolts (left). The rear engine mount is attached to passenger-side of subframe behind engine. Transaxle mount is attached to transaxle and left side subframe.

19. Remove the front engine mounting nut or bolt as shown in Fig. 5-9.

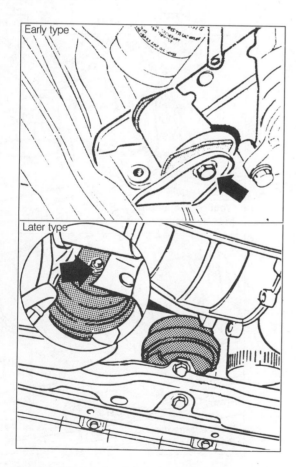

Fig. 5-9. Front engine mounting (arrows). Early type (top) uses rubber bushing. Later type (bottom) is hydraulic mount.

20. Raise and remove the engine and transaxle assembly from the car. Proceed slowly. Check frequently to make sure no hoses or wires are interfering with engine removal. If the car has been raised on jack stands, check often see that it remains stable and adequately supported.

Separating Engine and Transaxle

Both the engine and the transaxle should be supported. On cars with automatic transmission, remove the three bolts holding the torque converter to the drive plate. These bolts are near the outside diameter of the torque converter, and are accessible from the bottom as shown in Fig. 5-10.

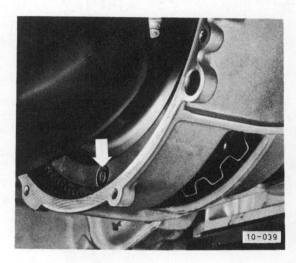

Fig. 5-10. One of three bolts (arrow) that hold torque converter to drive plate. Use crankshaft pulley bolt to turn engine for access to bolts.

On all models, remove the cover plate shown in Fig. 5-11, and remove the bolts which hold the transaxle to the engine. Separate the engine and transaxle using care not to place any strain on the transmission mainshaft.

CAUTION ―

On models with automatic transmission, be sure that the drive plate separates cleanly from the torque converter without pulling the torque converter off its support. As soon as the engine and transaxle are separated, install a bar across the open bellhousing to keep the torque converter from falling.

CAUTION ―

On models with manual transmission, at no time should the weight of either the engine or the transaxle be supported by the transmission mainshaft. If it is, the clutch, the clutch pushrod, or the mainshaft may be damaged.

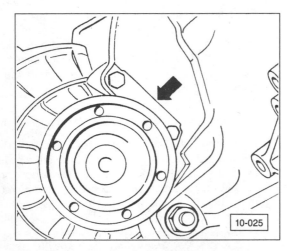

Fig. 5-11. Cover plate (arrow) to be removed when separating engine and transaxle.

Installing

Engine and transaxle installation is the reverse of removal. On models with automatic transmission, make certain during reassembly that the torque converter has not slipped from its support. See Fig. 5-12.

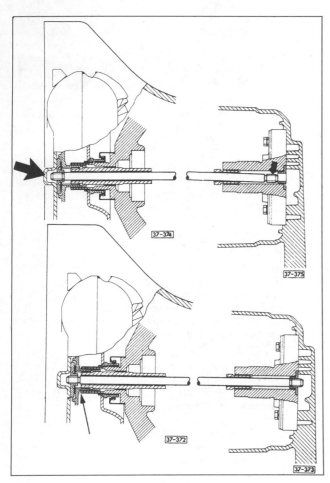

Fig. 5-12. Torque converter positions. Top: converter slipped off support; pilot projects at left arrow, pump driveshaft may be disengaged, as at right arrow. Bottom: converter correctly positioned on support (arrow).

The engine-to-transaxle bolts are two sizes, 10 mm and 12 mm. Torque the larger (12 mm) bolts to 80 Nm (59 ft. lb.) and the smaller (10 mm) bolts to 45 Nm (33 ft. lb.). On models with automatic transmission, torque the bolts holding the engine drive plate to the torque converter to 30 Nm (22 ft. lb.). Torque starter mounting bolts to 25 Nm (18 ft. lb.). On all models, torque the cover plate mounting bolts to 15 Nm (11 ft. lb.).

With the engine and transaxle in position, install the rear engine mount first, then install the transaxle mount. Roughly align the engine and transaxle on these mounts, and then install the remaining mounts. The mounting bolts and nuts and their torque values are identified in Fig. 5-13. Following installation of the remaining engine and transaxle parts and fluids, the assembly should be aligned in its mounts as described in **Aligning Engine and Transaxle Assembly**.

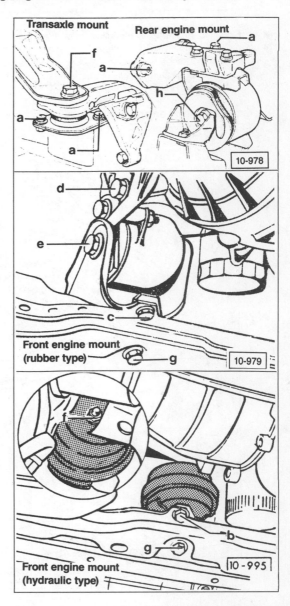

Fig. 5-13. Engine/transaxle mounting bolts. Torque **a** to 25 Nm (18 ft. lb.), **b** to 30 Nm (22 ft. lb.), **c** to 35 Nm (25 ft. lb.), **d** to 45 Nm (33 ft. lb.), **e** to 50 Nm (36 ft. lb.), **f** to 60 Nm (43 ft. lb.), **g** to 70 Nm (51 ft. lb.), and **h** to 80 Nm (59 ft. lb.),

Aligning Engine and Transaxle Assembly

It is normally necessary to align the engine and transaxle mounts only after the assembly has been installed, or after the mounts have been loosened as part of another repair.

To align:

1. Loosen the mounting bolts and nuts as indicated in Fig. 5-14. Loosen the center bolts for the engine mount **A** and the transaxle mount **B** first.

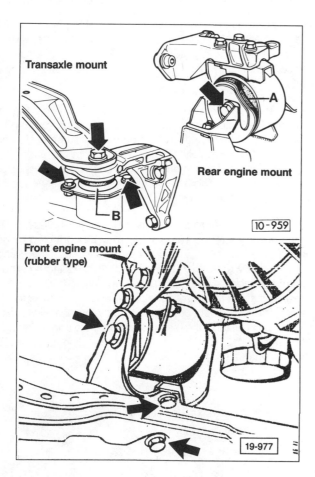

Fig. 5-14. Nuts and bolts (arrows) loosened for engine and transaxle alignment. Center bolts for engine mount **A** and transaxle mount **B** are loosened first.

2. With the car sitting on the ground, lightly shake the engine and transaxle assembly to allow it to shift and find its own position.

3. Tighten the mounting bolts and nuts. Tighten the center bolts, shown in Fig. 5-14 above, first. Torque all the bolts and nuts to the specifications given earlier in Fig. 5-13.

NOTE ——

After the alignment, check gearshift function. If necessary, adjust the shift mechanism as described in either **MANUAL TRANSMISSION AND CLUTCH** or **AUTOMATIC TRANSMISSION.**

6. CYLINDER BLOCK AND PISTONS

Although the pistons and connecting rods can be reached with the engine in the car by removing the cylinder head and oil pan, any internal engine work should be done with the engine removed from the car.

Cylinder block problems normally result from wear due to high mileage. Low compression pressures and noise due to excessive clearances are signs of a seriously worn engine. For more information, see **3. Troubleshooting.**

6.1 Cylinder Block Oil Seals

The front crankshaft and intermediate shaft oil seals can be replaced with the engine installed. Replacement of the rear crankshaft oil seal requires that the transaxle be removed. The mounting location of the rear oil seal and oil seal carrier is shown in Fig. 6-7, below.

Replacing Front Crankshaft Oil Seal

To reach the seal, remove the camshaft drive belt as described in **4.2 Camshaft Drive Belt** for gasoline engines or **FUEL SYSTEM (diesel)** for diesel engines, and remove the crankshaft sprocket bolt and the sprocket.

There are three ways to remove the seal. Volkswagen special tool no. 2085, shown being used in Fig. 6-1, is designed to remove the seal without removing the seal carrier or damaging the sealing surface on the crankshaft. Alternatively the seal carrier, fastened by bolts to the cylinder block and the oil pan, can be removed to make seal removal easier. This requires care during reassembly to prevent oil leaks. Use a new seal carrier gasket. Finally, some experienced mechanics can pry out the seal with a screwdriver or similar tool. Use great care not to damage the alloy seal carrier or the sealing surface of the crankshaft.

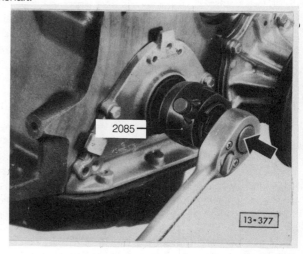

Fig. 6-1. Crankshaft front oil seal being removed using Volkswagen special tool no. 2085. Rotate tool clockwise to remove seal.

3

Install the new seal, lubricated with clean engine oil, with the lip on the inside and the closed side facing out. Fit the seal into position, and carefully drive it into place until it is fully seated in the seal carrier. Use care not to distort the seal as it is installed. For best results, use a seal driver such as Volkswagen special tool no. 3083, shown in Fig. 6-2. If reinstalling the seal carrier, torque the top three bolts to 10 Nm (87 in. lb.) and all other bolts to 20 Nm (15 ft. lb.).

Fig. 6-2. Front crankshaft oil seal being installed, using Volkswagen special tool no. 3083.

Replacing Intermediate Shaft Oil Seal

Remove the camshaft drive belt, as described in **4.2 Camshaft Drive Belt** for gasoline engines or **FUEL SYSTEM (diesel)** for diesel engines. Loosen the intermediate shaft sprocket bolt and, using a soft faced hammer, tap the sprocket loose. Remove the bolt and the sprocket. Remove the two bolts holding the oil seal carrier to the cylinder block and pull out the seal carrier. Pry or hand-press the seal out of the carrier.

Reinstall the seal carrier with a new O-ring. Torque the bolts to 25 Nm (18 ft. lb.). To install the seal, lightly oil the seal and shaft's sealing surface. Fit the seal into position, and carefully drive it into place. Use care not to distort the seal as it is installed. For best results, use a seal driver such as Volkswagen special tool no. 10-203.

6.2 Disassembly, Assembly, and Reconditioning

Disassembly, assembly, and reconditioning procedures for the 1.6 and 1.8 liter Volkswagen engines covered in this manual are simiar to those for most other modern 4-cylinder, water-cooled engines. For anyone with the proper tools and equipment and basic experience in engine reconditioning, this section provides the specifications and special reconditioning information necessary to repair these Volkswagen engines.

Those who are without the necessary tools, or unfamiliar with reconditioning procedures, will still find this information to be important to the qualified mechanic who does the work. If machine shop services are not readily available, one alternative is to install a Volkswagen remanufactured engine or short block, available from an authorized Volkswagen dealer parts department.

To minimize wear during engine start-up, clean engine oil should be used to lubricate all friction surfaces during engine assembly.

Pistons and Connecting Rods

Pistons, piston pins, piston rings, connecting rods, and bearings, if they are to be reused, should never be interchanged. Mark the cylinder numbers on connecting rods and connecting rod caps before removal. Mark the piston tops as shown in Fig. 6-3 (avoid scratching the piston). Components of one piston and connecting rod assembly are shown in Fig. 6-4.

The piston pin should fit such that, with the piston heated to approximately 60°C (140°F) in an oil bath, a light push will move the pin. Replace the piston and the pin if the fit is excessively loose. Connecting rods should always be replaced in complete sets.

Measure cylinder bores at approximately the top, the middle, and the bottom of piston travel, and at right angles (90°), as shown in Fig. 6-5. The top and bottom measurements should be made approximately 10 mm (⅜ in.) from the ends of the cylinder. Nominal piston and cylinder bore diameter specifications are given in **Table k**. Nominal piston diameters are also marked on the piston crowns.

Maximum out-of-round variation in any one cylinder is 0.04 mm (.0016 in.). Minor irregularities may be corrected by honing. If the diameter of any one cylinder exceeds the nominal dimension by more than 0.08 mm (.003 in.), all four cylinders should be rebored and honed to accept new oversized pistons. Visually inspect the bores for scoring and other imperfections which will also prevent good piston ring to cylinder wall sealing. When fitting pistons, the piston-to-cylinder clearance should be 0.03 mm (.0012 in.). Maximum piston-to-cylinder clearance is 0.07 mm (.0028 in.).

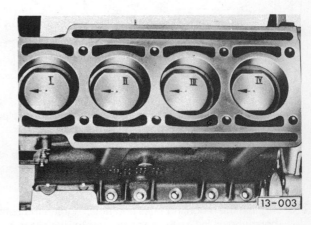

Fig. 6-3. Cylinder numbers and arrows marked on piston crowns. Used pistons should always be installed in their original orientation.

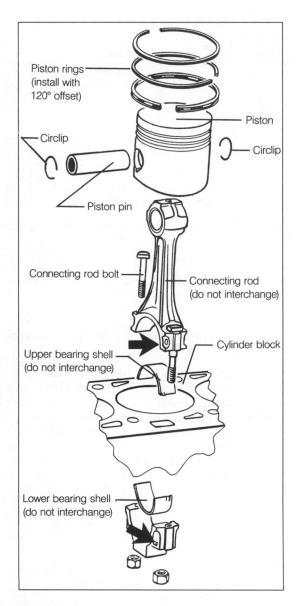

Fig. 6-4. Components of piston and connecting rod assembly. Connecting rod markings (arrows) face camshaft drive belt.

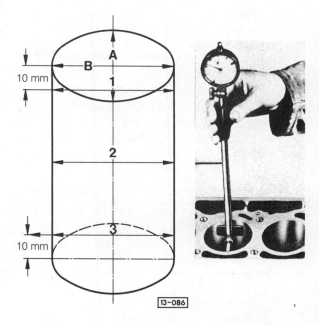

Fig. 6-5. Cylinder bore measuring points. Top (**1**) and bottom (**3**) measurements should be made at least 10 mm (3/8 in.) from ends of cylinder, first in direction **A** and then in direction **B**.

CAUTION ━

Mounting the bare cylinder block to an engine stand will distort its shape and cause inaccurate cylinder bore measurements.

CAUTION ━

Oversized pistons for diesel engines with hydraulic cam followers have a 15° chamfer on the piston crown for cylinder head gasket clearance. Use only chamfered pistons for repairs using oversized pistons.

Table k. Cylinder and Piston Diameter Specifications

Engine Code	Repair Stage	Piston Diameter	Cylinder Bore
GX, MZ, HT, RD, RV, PF	Basic Dimension (standard)	80.98 mm (3.1882 in)	81.01 mm (3.1894 in.)
	1st oversize	81.23 mm (3.1980 in.)	81.26 mm (3.1992 in.)
	2nd oversize	81.48 mm (3.2079 in.)	81.51 mm (3.2091 in.)
PL	Basic Dimension	80.98 mm (3.1882 in.)	81.01 mm (3.1894 in.)
ME, MF	Basic Dimension	76.48 mm (3.0110 in.)	76.51 mm (3.0122 in.)
	1st oversize	76.73 mm (3.0209 in.)	76.76 mm (3.0220 in.)
	2nd oversize	76.98 mm (3.0307 in.)	77.01 mm (3.0319 in.)
	3rd oversize	77.48 mm (3.0504 in.)	77.51 mm (3.0516 in.)

NOTE

At the time of printing, only standard size pistons are available for 16-valve engines. Check with an authorized Volkswagen dealer parts department for the latest information on parts availability.

Measure connecting rod bearing clearances using Plastigage®. Inspect the connecting rods for any bending, distortion, or other visual damage. Connecting rod specifications are listed in **Table l**.

Table l. Connecting Rod Specifications

Radial Clearance Wear Limit . . . . .0.12 mm (.0047 in.)	
Side Clearance Wear Limit . . . . .0.37 mm (.0145 in.)	
Checking Torque . . . . .30 Nm (22 ft. lb.)	
Assembly Torque . . . . .30 Nm (22 ft. lb.)	
	+ 1/4 turn (90°)

NOTE

When checking radial clearance, lubricate the contact surface of the nut before tightening.

If connecting rod radial clearance is excessive, the crankshaft connecting rod journals should be checked as described in **Crankshaft and Intermediate Shaft**. If the crankshaft journal diameters are within specifications, recheck radial clearance using new bearing shells.

When installing each connecting rod to the crankshaft, the two bearing shells' retaining tabs should be on the same side of the journal, and the marks on the connecting rods, shown earlier in Fig. 6-4, should face the drivebelt side of the engine.

Piston Rings

Piston ring end gaps are checked with the piston rings inserted approximately 15mm (5/8 in.) from the top of the cylinder. The piston ring gap specifications are listed in **Table m**.

Table m. Piston Ring End Gap

	Gap	Wear limit
Compression Rings	0.30 to 0.45 mm (.012 to .018 in.)	1.0 mm (.039 in.)
Oil Scraper Rings (bottom ring)	0.25 to 0.45 mm (.010 to .018 in.)	1.0 mm (.039 in.)

Piston ring side clearance is checked using feeler gauges. Measure each ring in its original groove. Piston ring side clearance specifications are listed in **Table n**.

Table n. Piston Ring Side Clearance

Engine code	Ring	Clearances (new parts)	Wear limit
GX, MZ, HT RD, RV, PF, PL	all	0.02–0.05 mm (.0008–.0019 in.)	0.15 mm (.0059 in.)
ME, MF	Upper compression ring	0.06–0.09 mm (.0024–.0035 in.)	0.20 mm (.0079 in.)
	Lower compression ring (middle ring)	0.05–0.08 mm (.0020–.0031 in.)	0.20 mm (.0079 in.)
	Oil scraper ring (bottom ring)	0.03–0.06 mm (.0012–.0024 in.)	0.15 mm (.0059 in.)

Install the piston rings with the gaps offset from each other by 120°, as illustrated earlier in Fig. 6-4.

Diesel and Turbo Diesel Piston Height

Assembling or replacing a diesel engine short block requires that the height of the pistons be measured in order to select the proper cylinder head gasket. Using a dial indicator, measure the amount that each piston protrudes above the top of the cylinder block at Top Dead Center, as shown in Fig. 6-6. Cylinder head gaskets are available in three thicknesses. Select the correct gasket from **Table o** based on the largest piston height measurement. The different gaskets are identified by the number of marks, either notches or holes, located near the part number stamped on the gasket face.

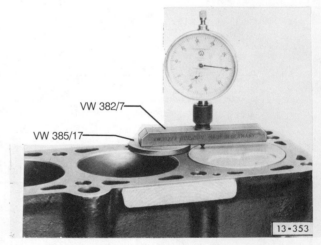

Fig. 6-6. Piston height being measured on diesel engines.

Table o. Cylinder Head Gasket vs. Piston Height Specifications

	Piston height above cylinder block	Gasket identification notches or holes
Engines with mechanical cam followers	0.67–0.80 mm (.0264–.0315 in.)	1
	0.81–0.90 mm (.0319–.0354 in.)	2
	0.91–1.02 mm (.0358–.0402 in.)	3
Engines with hydraulic cam followers	0.66–0.86 mm (.0260–.0339 in.)	1
	0.87–0.90 mm (.0343–.0354 in.)	2
	0.91–1.02 mm (.0358–.0402 in.)	3

Crankshaft and Intermediate Shaft

Fig. 6-7 shows the assembly of the crankshaft and the intermediate shaft in the cylinder block. To remove the crankshaft, both crankshaft oil seal carriers must be removed from the ends of the cylinder block. Crankshaft main bearing caps must not be interchanged. Crankshaft main bearing shells, if they are to be reused, should only be installed in their original positions. On gasoline engines except 16-valve, the ignition distributor must be removed in order to remove the intermediate shaft.

NOTE ——

On models with automatic transmission, mark the position of the driveplate on the crankshaft before removing the driveplate.

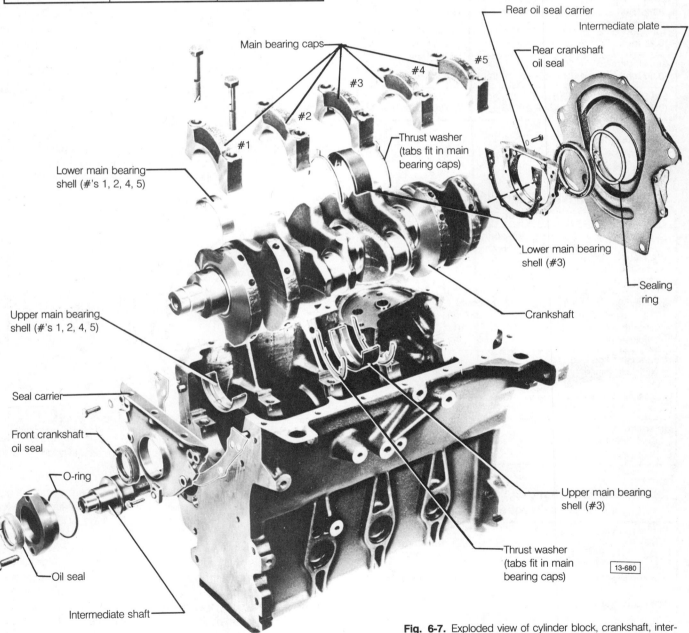

Fig. 6-7. Exploded view of cylinder block, crankshaft, intermediate shaft, and related parts.

NOTE ━━

Replacement No. 3 main bearing shells are one-piece with integral thrust washers.

Crankshaft journal specifications are listed in **Table p**. Crankshaft and intermediate shaft clearance specifications are listed in **Table q**. Crankshaft bearings are available in three undersizes to fit reconditioned crankshafts. Tightening torques are listed in **Table r**. If a crankshaft must be replaced, a Volkswagen remanufactured crankshaft is available from an authorized Volkswagen dealer.

Table p. Crankshaft Journal Diameter

	Main bearing journal diameter	Connecting rod journal diameter
Basic dimension	53.958–53.978 mm (2.1243–2.1251 in.)	47.758–47.778 mm (1.8802–1.8810 in.)
1st Undersize (0.25 mm)	53.708–53.728 mm (2.1145–2.1153 in.)	47.508–47.528 mm (1.8704–1.8712 in.)
2nd Undersize (0.50 mm)	53.458–53.478 mm (2.1046–2.1054 in.)	47.258–47.278 mm (1.8606–1.8613 in.)
3rd Undersize (0.75 mm)	53.208–53.228 mm (2.0948–2.0956 in.)	47.008–47.028 mm (1.8507–1.8515 in.)

Table q. Crankshaft and Intermediate Shaft Clearance

	New parts	Wear limit
Crankshaft main bearings		
radial clearance	0.03–0.08 mm (.0012–.0031 in.)	0.17 mm (.0067 in.)
axial (thrust) clearance (gasoline engines)	0.07–0.17 mm (.0028–.0067 in.)	0.25 mm (.0098 in.)
axial (thrust) clearance (diesel engines)	0.07–0.17 mm (.0028–.0067 in.)	0.37 mm (.0146 in.)
Connecting rod bearings		
radial clearance	–	0.12 mm (.0047 in.)
axial (side) clearance	–	0.37 mm (.0146 in.)
Intermediate shaft		
axial clearance	–	0.25 mm (.0098 in.)

Table r. Crankshaft and Cylinder Block Tightening Torques

Crankshaft Oil Seal Carrier Bolts
M6 .10 Nm (87 in. lb.)
M8 .20 Nm (15 ft. lb.)

Intermediate Shaft Oil Seal Carrier Bolts . . . . .25 Nm (18 ft. lb.)

Main Bearing Cap Nuts. . . . . .65 Nm (48 ft. lb.)

Oil Pan Bolts. . . . . .20 Nm (15 ft. lb.)

Flywheel or Drive Plate

The correct flywheel or torque converter drive plate tightening sequence is shown in Fig. 6-8. Fig. 6-9 illustrates the use of a holding fixture, Volkswagen special tool no. VW 558 (order no. TV0 558 000 13 ZEL) to remove and install the flywheel or drive plate. Apply thread locking compound and torque the bolts to 100 Nm (74 ft. lb.). If the rear crankshaft oil seal is leaking, replace the oil seal before installing the flywheel or drive plate.

CAUTION ━━

Always replace flywheel or drive plate mounting bolts.

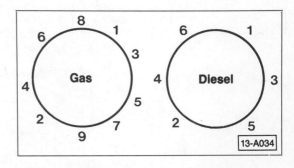

Fig. 6-8. Flywheel or drive plate bolt torque sequence. Removal is reverse of installation. Apply thread locking compound when installing.

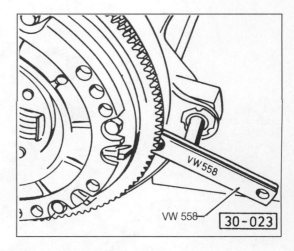

Fig. 6-9. Flywheel or drive plate secured with holding fixture VW 558.

Replacement flywheels for gasoline engines may not have an ignition timing mark. On new flywheels, make a timing mark 12 mm (0.47 in.) arc length to the left of the TDC mark, as shown in Fig. 6-10.

On models with automatic transmission, mark the drive plate during disassembly and reinstall it with the same orientation. Install as shown in Fig. 6-11, with the notch in the washer facing the drive plate. Install two of the six bolts and then check drive plate to cylinder block clearance as shown in Fig. 6-12. If necessary, use a shim (part no. 056 105 303) to achieve a dimension of 30.5 to 32.1 mm (1.20 to 1.26 in.).

Fig. 6-10. Location on replacement flywheel to make new ignition timing mark. **a** is arc length from Top Dead Center (TDC) mark.

Fig. 6-11. Exploded view of drive plate assembly. Notch in washer **1** faces drive plate. Shim **2**, used to achieve correct installation dimension, is optional.

Fig. 6-12. Drive plate to cylinder block dimension being measured. Dimension **a** should be 30.5-32.1 mm (1.20-1.26 in.). Adjust distance by adding or removing shim.

NOTE —

Part numbers are subject to change. Always rely on an authorized Volkswagen dealer parts department for the latest information.

3

7. LUBRICATION SYSTEM

The primary function of the lubrication system is to lubricate the internal moving parts of the engine. The circulation of oil also aids engine cooling. Proper lubrication relies on a constant supply of oil, fed to the moving parts under pressure. Pressure is supplied by a gear-type oil pump located inside the oil pan. Engine oil returns to the oil pan where it is stored for pickup by the pump. It is cleaned by circulating through a replaceable filter. Fig. 7-1 is a schematic view of the lubrication system showing the paths of pressurized oil supply to the engine bearings.

This section covers inspection, repair, and assembly of the parts of the lubrication system. Oil change, oil filter changes, and engine oil specifications are covered in greater detail in **LUBRICATION AND MAINTENANCE**.

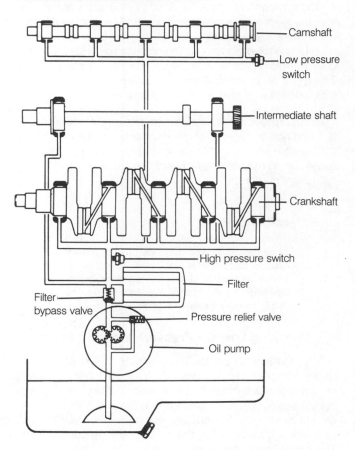

Fig. 7-1. Schematic view of lubrication system. On 16-valve engines, both oil pressure switches are located on oil filter flange. On turbo diesel engines, additional oil supply line and return line lubricate turbocharger bearings. On all models, pressure relief valve is integral with pump.

To prevent serious engine damage, a dynamic oil pressure warning system warns the driver of insufficient oil pressure. Other safety features include a filter by-pass, to guard against bursting the filter due to over pressure, and an oil pump pressure relief valve to prevent excessive system pressure.

On models equipped with multi-function indicators, an oil temperature sensor, located on the oil filter flange, monitors the oil temperature. On 16-valve engines, the sensor is located on the end of the cylinder head.

Lubrication system problems result from the system's inability to create oil pressure, the engine's inability to maintain it, or faults with oil pressure warning systems. Because proper lubrication is directly related to engine life, its importance cannot be overemphasized. Change the engine oil and oil filter regularly, at least as often as specified by Volkswagen's recommended maintenance intervals, and periodically check engine oil level between oil changes. See **LUBRICATION AND MAINTENANCE**.

7.1 Dynamic Oil Pressure Warning System

The components of the dynamic oil pressure warning system are the pressure switches, the electronic control unit, the low oil pressure indicator, and the warning buzzer. A 0.3 bar pressure switch provides warning when the oil pressure falls to near zero at any time, including at idle. A 1.8 bar pressure switch (1.4 bar on diesels) provides earlier warning, at elevated rpm, whenever oil pressure falls below a minimum safe level.

The low pressure switches are located on the oil filter flange (0.3 bar) and on the end of the cylinder head (1.4 or 1.8 bar). On 16-valve engines, both switches are located on the filter flange. On all models, the electronic control unit is behind the instrument cluster.

CAUTION ━━

If the warning indicator stays on after the engine is started, or flashes on while driving, always assume that there is insufficient oil pressure. Check oil level and test oil pressure before proceeding with tests of the warning system. See **8. Engine Technical Data**.

Checking Low Oil Pressure Warning System

With the ignition off, the low pressure switch (0.3 bar) is closed (complete circuit to ground). When the ignition is turned on, the indicator flashes (no oil pressure). When the engine is started and oil pressure rises, it opens the switch (opening the ground circuit), and the indicator goes out. With insufficient oil pressure or a stuck switch, the indicator will continue to flash. The switch opens and closes at specific pressures. See **Testing Oil Pressure Switches**.

To quick-check the pressure switch, simulate a closed switch by removing the blue/black wire and grounding it. With the ignition on, the indicator should flash. If not, the problem is in the circuit or the indicator. If the indicator flashes only when tested in this way, replace the switch.

If the indicator flashes with the engine running, and the oil pressure tests OK, remove the blue/black wire from the switch with the engine running. The indicator should go out. If not, the circuit is shorted to ground between the wire and indicator. If the indicator does go out, the switch is stuck closed and should be replaced.

Checking Dynamic Oil Pressure Warning System

(high rpm)

The 1.8 bar pressure switch (1.4 bar in diesels) is normally open (no circuit to ground). When the engine is running above 2000 rpm (ignition distributor input to control unit), oil pressure closes the switch (completing the circuit to ground). If oil pressure is insufficient to close the pressure switch, or the switch is stuck open, the indicator will flash and the buzzer will sound. The pressure switch opens and closes at specific pressures. See **Testing Oil Pressure Switches**.

To quick-check the pressure switch, raise the engine speed above 2000 rpm and disconnect the yellow wire from the switch. The indicator should flash and the buzzer should sound. If the wire is connected to ground, the warning should stop. Disconnect the wire from ground and connect it to the switch. If the indicator does not go out, replace the switch.

Testing Oil Pressure Switches

The oil pressure at which the pressure switches react can be tested by temporarily installing an oil pressure gauge in parallel with the switch with a T-fitting and monitoring switch performance with a multimeter or test light, as shown in Fig. 7-2. See **8. Engine Technical Data**.

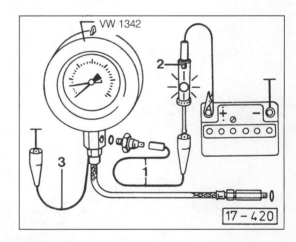

Fig. 7-2. Pressure gauge and test light being used to test oil pressure switches.

7.2 Oil Pump

The oil pump is located inside the engine oil pan, and draws engine oil through a pickup tube from near the bottom of the pan. The pump can be removed for inspection of its internal clearances (a potential source of low oil pressure problems) by removing the oil pan.

There is normally no need to remove and inspect the oil pump unless oil pressure is inadequate. Check the oil pressure by installing a pressure gauge in place of one of the oil pressure switches and run the engine. Engine oil pressure at normal operating temperature should be at least 2.0 bar (29 psi) at 2000 rpm.

To inspect the oil pump, drain the oil and remove the oil pan. Remove the pump and disassemble it. See Fig. 7-3.

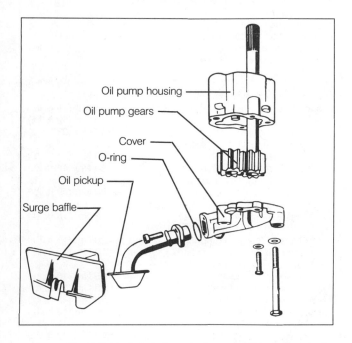

Fig. 7-3. Exploded view of oil pump. Note long mounting bolts and short cover bolts.

With the oil pump removed and disassembled, use feeler gauges to check the clearances. Backlash, shown being measured in Fig. 7-4, should be between 0.05 and 0.20 mm (.002 and .008 in.). If not, replace the gears or the pump. Oil pump gear axial play, shown being measured with a straight-edge in Fig. 7-5, should not exceed 0.15 mm (.006 in.). If it does, replace the pump.

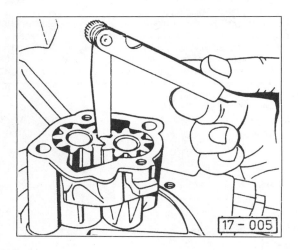

Fig. 7-4. Oil pump gear backlash being measured using feeler gauge.

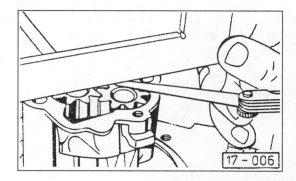

Fig. 7-5. Oil pump gear axial play being measured using straight-edge and feeler gauge.

If the oil pickup has been removed from the pump cover, replace the O-ring when installing the pickup. Torque the pickup bolts and cover bolts to 10 Nm (87 in. lb.). Torque the oil pump mounting bolts to 20 Nm (15 ft. lb.).

Replace the oil pan gaskets and install the oil pan. Torque the oil pan bolts to 20 Nm (15 ft. lb.) and the drain plug to 30 Nm (22 ft. lb.). Add engine oil, as described in **LUBRICATION AND MAINTENANCE**.

Oil Spray Nozzles

Turbo diesel and 16-valve gasoline engines are equipped with oil spray nozzles which, above a certain oil pressure threshold, spray oil from the main oil galley against the bottoms of the pistons for added cooling.

Install these nozzles with sealing paste, Volkswagen part no. AMV 188 100 02, and torque the bolts to 10 Nm (87 in. lb.).

NOTE ——

Part numbers are subject to change. Always rely on an authorized Volkswagen dealer parts department for the latest information.

7.3 Oil Cooler

The oil cooler used on some models is an oil-to-coolant heat exchanger. Engine oil flows through one part of the cooler and gives up heat to the engine coolant flowing through the other part of the cooler. The cooler is a potential source of leakage between the lubrication system and the cooling system, and should be considered whenever such leakage is suspected.

Fig. 7-6 is an exploded view of the oil cooler, the oil filter, and the mounting parts. Remove the oil cooler only if it needs to be cleaned, inspected, or replaced. On installation, use sealing paste, Volkswagen part no. AMV 188 100 02, on the sealing surfaces and check to see that there is adequate space for the coolant hose connections. Torque the oil cooler mounting nut to 25 Nm (18 ft. lb.).

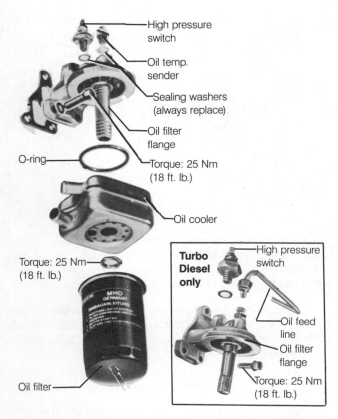

Fig. 7-6. Exploded view of oil cooler and related parts used on gasoline and diesel engines, except 16-valve. 16-valve engines are similar. Inset shows filter flange with oil line used on turbo diesel engines.

8. ENGINE TECHNICAL DATA

I. Tightening Torques

Air conditioning components to Engine . .See **5. Removing and Installing Engine and Transaxle**
Air connection to cylinder head for
   gasoline engines except 16V engines (bolt) .10 Nm (87 in. lb.)
Alternator to adjusting bracket of
   vehicle (bolt) . . . . .35 Nm (26 ft. lb.)
Alternator to lower mounting of vehicle (bolt) . .26 Nm (19 ft. lb.)
Camshaft bearing caps to cylinder head (nut)
   ex. 16V engine . . . . .20 Nm (15 ft. lb.)
   16V engine . . . . .15 Nm (11 ft. lb.)
Camshaft drive belt sprocket to camshaft or
   intermediate shaft (bolt)
   gasoline engines except 16V engine . . . .80 Nm (59 ft. lb.)
   16V engine . . . . .65 Nm (48 ft. lb.)
   diesel engines . . . . .45 Nm (33 ft. lb.)
Camshaft drive belt tensioner locknut. . . . . .45 Nm (33 ft. lb.)
Clutch pressure plate assembly or torque converter
   drive plate to crankshaft
   (with thread locking compound). . . . . . .100 Nm (74 ft. lb.)
Connecting rod cap to connecting rod . . . . .30 Nm (22 ft. lb.)
   + 1/4 turn
Cover plate to transaxle . . . . .15 Nm (11 ft. lb.)
Crankshaft oil seal carrier to cylinder block
   M 6 bolt .10 Nm (87 in. lb.)
   M 8 bolt .20 Nm (15 ft. lb.)

I. Tightening Torques (continued)

Crankshaft sprocket to crankshaft
   (lubricated)
   gasoline engines. . . . . .200 Nm (148 ft. lb.)
   diesel engines . . . . .180 Nm (130 ft. lb.)
Cylinder head cover to cylinder head (nut) . . .10 Nm (87 in. lb.)
Cylinder head to engine block (engine cold). . .60 Nm (43 ft. lb.)
   + 1/2 turn
Drive belt rear cover to stud in cylinder head
   (socket-head bolt) . . . . .10 Nm (87 in. lb.)
Drive belt upper and lower front cover to rear
   cover (bolt)
   ex. front bolt on 16V engine . . . . .10 Nm (87 in. lb.)
   front bolt on 16V engine . . . . .6 Nm (53 in. lb.)
Drive shaft to transaxle drive flange . . . . . . .45 Nm (33 ft. lb.)
Engine to transaxle bellhousing
   M10 . . . . .45 Nm (33 ft. lb.)
   M12 . . . . .80 Nm (59 ft. lb.)
Engine front mount to body (bolt)
   short bolt . . . . .35 Nm (26 ft. lb.)
   long bolt. . . . . .70 Nm (52 ft. lb.)
Engine front mount to engine (bolt) . . . . . . .45 Nm (33 ft. lb.)
Engine front mounting to rubber
   center bushing (through bolt) . . . . .50 Nm (37 ft. lb.)
Engine front mount (to hydraulic mount) . . . .60 Nm (44 ft. lb.)
Engine mount (right rear) to rubber
   center bushing (M10 bolt) . . . . .80 Nm (59 ft. lb.)
Engine mount (right rear) to bushing bracket
   or engine (M8 bolt) . . . . .25 Nm (18 ft. lb.)
Fuel injector insert to cylinder head
   (with thread locking compound) . . . . . . .20 Nm (15 ft. lb.)
Flywheel to clutch pressure plate . . . . .20 Nm (15 ft. lb.)
Intermediate shaft oil seal
   carrier to cylinder block . . . . .25 Nm (18 ft. lb.)
Manifolds to cylinder head . . . . .25 Nm (18 ft. lb.)
Main bearing caps to cylinder block . . . . . . .65 Nm (48 ft. lb.)
Oil cooler to oil filter flange (nut). . . . . .25 Nm (18 ft. lb.)
Oil filter mounting flange to engine
   block (socket-head bolt) . . . . .25 Nm (18 ft. lb.)
Oil pickup to oil pump housing cover (bolt) . . .10 Nm (87 in. lb.)
Oil pressure switches. . . . . .25 Nm (18 ft. lb.)
Oil pan to cylinder block . . . . .20 Nm (15 ft. lb.)
Oil drain plug in oil pan. . . . . .30 Nm (22 ft. lb.)
Oil pump to cylinder block (M8 bolt) . . . . . .20 Nm (15 ft. lb.)
Oil pump cover bolt . . . . .10 Nm (87 in. lb.)
Power steering pump to mount (bolt) . . . . . .20 Nm (15 ft. lb.)
Spark plug. .20 Nm (15 ft. lb.)
Starter to bellhousing (manual transmission) . .60 Nm (44 ft. lb.)
Transaxle mount (left rear)
   M8 bolt .25 Nm (18 ft. lb.)
   M10 bolt. . . . . .60 Nm (43 ft. lb.)
Torque converter to drive plate . . . . .30 Nm (22 ft. lb.)
Upper intake manifold to lower intake
   manifold (16-valve engine). . . . . .20 Nm (15 ft. lb.)
Upper intake manifold to support bracket
   (16-valve engine) . . . . .20 Nm (15 ft. lb.)
V-belt pulleys to coolant pump or
   crankshaft sprocket . . . . .20 Nm (15 ft. lb.)

3

II. Crankshaft, Intermediate Shaft, and Bearing Specifications

Crankshaft main journals and main bearings
Main bearing journal diameter
    basic dimension . . . . .53.958–53.978 mm
    (2.1243–2.1251 in.)
    1st undersize (0.25 mm) . . . . .53.708–53.728 mm
    (2.1145–2.1153 in.)
    2nd undersize (0.50 mm) . . . . .53.458–53.478 mm
    (2.1046–2.1054 in.)
    3rd undersize (0.75 mm) . . . . .53.208–53.228 mm
    (2.0948–2.0956 in.)
Main bearing radial clearance
(Plastigage®)
    new parts. . . . . .0.03–0.08 mm
    (.0012–.0031 in.)
    wear limit . . . . .0.17 mm (.0067 in)
Crankshaft axial play (side clearance)
    new parts. . . . . .0.07–0.17 mm
    (.0028–.0067 in.)
    wear limit (gasoline) . . . . .0.25 mm (.0098 in.)
    wear limit (diesel) . . . . .0.37 mm (.0146 in.)
Crankshaft connecting rod journals and bearings
Journal diameter
    basic dimension . . . . .47.758–47.778 mm
    (1.8802–1.8810 in.)
    1st undersize (0.25 mm) . . . . .47.508–47.528 mm
    (1.8704–1.8712 in.)
    2nd undersize (0.50 mm) . . . . .47.258–47.278 mm
    (1.8606–1.8613 in.)
    3rd undersize (0.75 mm) . . . . .47.008–47.028 mm
    (1.8507–1.8515 in.)
Connecting rod bearing radial clearance
(Plastigage®)
    wear limit . . . . .0.12 mm (.0047 in.)
Connecting rod bearing
    axial clearance (side clearance)
    wear limit . . . . .0.37 mm (.0145 in.)
Intermediate shaft
    axial clearance (side clearance) . . . . . .0.25 mm (.0098 in.)

III. Piston, Piston Ring, and Cylinder Specifications

Cylinder diameter
GX, MZ, HT, RD, RV, PF engines
    basic dimension . . . . .81.01 mm (3.1894 in.)
    1st oversize (0.25 mm). . . . . .81.26 mm (3.1992 in.)
    2nd oversize (0.50 mm) . . . . .81.51 mm (3.2091 in.)

PL engine
    basic dimension . . . . .81.01 mm (3.1894 in.)

ME, MF engines
    basic dimension . . . . .76.51 mm (3.0122 in.)
    1st oversize (0.25 mm). . . . . .76.76 mm (3.0220 in.)
    2nd oversize (0.50 mm) . . . . .77.01 mm (3.0319 in.)
    3rd oversize (1.00 mm) . . . . .77.51 mm (3.0516 in.)

Piston diameter
GX, MZ, HT, RD, RV, PF engines
    basic dimension . . . . .80.98 mm (3.1882 in.)
    1st oversize (0.25 mm). . . . . .81.23 mm (3.1980 in.)
    2nd oversize (0.50 mm) . . . . .81.48 mm (3.2079 in.)

PL engine
    basic dimension . . . . .80.98 mm (3.1882 in.)

III. Piston, Piston Ring, and Cylinder Specifications (continued)

ME, MF engines
    basic dimension . . . . .76.48 mm (3.0110 in.)
    1st oversize (0.25 mm). . . . . .76.73 mm (3.0209 in.)
    2nd oversize (0.50 mm) . . . . .76.98 mm (3.0307 in.)
    3rd oversize (1.00 mm) . . . . .77.48 mm (3.0504 in.)

Piston to Cylinder clearance
    with new parts . . . . .0.03 mm (.0012 in.)
    wear limit . . . . .0.08 mm (.003 in.)

Piston rings side clearance
GX, MZ, HT, RD,
RV, PF, PL engines . . . . .0.02–0.05 mm
    (.0008–.0019 in.)
ME, MF engines
    upper compression ring . . . . .0.06–0.09 mm
    (.0024–.0035 in.)
    lower compression ring . . . . .0.05–0.08 mm
    (.0020–.0031 in.)
    oil scraper ring. . . . . .0.03–0.06 mm
    (.0012–.0024 in.)

Piston ring end gap (in cylinder)
    compression ring . . . . .0.30–0.45 mm
    (.0118–.0177 in.)
    compression ring wear limit . . . . .1.0 mm (.039 in.)
    oil scraper ring. . . . . .0.25–0.45 mm
    (.0098–.0177 in.)
    oil scraper ring wear limit. . . . . .1.00 mm (.039 in.)

Piston height vs. Cylinder head gasket
(gasket selection for diesel engines)
with mechanical cam followers
    0.67–0.80 mm (.0264–.0315 in.) . . .gasket 1 (1 notch or hole)
    0.81–0.90 mm (.0319–.0354 in.) .gasket 2 (2 notches or holes)
    0.91–1.02 mm (.0358–.0402 in.) .gasket 3 (3 notches or holes)
with hydraulic cam followers
    0.66–0.86 mm (.0260–.0339 in.) . . .gasket 1 (1 notch or hole)
    0.87–0.90 mm (.0343–.0354 in.) .gasket 2 (2 notches or holes)
    0.91–1.02 mm (.0358–.0402 in.) .gasket 3 (3 notches or holes)

IV. Camshaft, Valve, and Cylinder Head Specifications

Camshaft
    axial play, maximum
    (except PL engine). . . . . .0.15 mm (.0059 in.)
    runout, maximum permissible
    ME, MF engines. . . . . .0.01 mm (.0004 in.)
    radial clearance (Plastigage®)
    wear limit. . . . . .0.11 mm (.0043 in.)

Cylinder head
    warpage, maximum . . . . .0.1 mm (.004 in.)
    thickness, minimum
    GX, MZ, HT, RD, RV,
    and PF engines . . . . .132.6 mm (5.221 in.)
    PL engine . . . . .118.1 mm (4.650 in.)
    ME, MF engines . . . . .cannot be refaced

Cylinder block
    deck warpage, maximum . . . . .0.1 mm (.004 in.)

Valve spring dimensions (ME, MF engines)
    outer spring free length
    with hydraulic cam followers . . . . . . .37.0 mm (1.46 in.)
    with mechanical cam followers . . . . . .40.2 mm (1.58 in.)

continued on next page

IV. Camshaft, Valve, and Cylinder Head Specifications (continued)

Valve spring dimensions (ME, MF engines)
inner spring free length
with hydraulic cam followers . . . . . . .32.5 mm (1.28 in.)
with mechanical cam followers . . . . . .33.9 mm (1.33 in.)

Valve seat dimensions
seat angle . . . . .45°
upper correction angle
gasoline engines . . . . .30°
diesel engines . . . . .15°
lower correction angle (PL engine)
intake . . . . .75°
upper correction cut, maximum diameter (diesel)
exhaust . . . . .33.2 mm (1.307 in.)
intake . . . . .35.2 mm (1.386 in.)
seat width, intake
GX, MZ, HT, RD, ME, MF engines . . . . .2.00 mm (.080 in.)
PL engine . . . . .1.5-1.8 mm (.06 -.07 in.)
seat width, exhaust
GX, MZ, HT, RD, RV,
PF, ME, MF engines . . . . .2.4 mm (.094 in.)
PL engine . . . . .approx. 1.8 mm (.07 in.)
outside seat diameter of 45° face, intake
GX, MZ engines . . . . .37.2 mm (1.465 in.)
HT, RD, RV, PF engines . . . . .39.2 mm (1.543 in.)
ME, MF engines . . . . .32.8 mm (1.291 in.)
PL engine . . . . .31.2 mm (1.228 in.)
outside diameter of 45° face, exhaust
GX, MZ, HT, RD, RV, PF engines . . . .32.4 mm (1.276 in.)
ME, MF engines . . . . .30.4 mm (1.197 in.)
PL engine . . . . .27.6 mm (1.087 in.)
minimum dimension used to calculate maximum
refacing dimension
GX, MZ, HT, RD, RV, PF engines
exhaust . . . . .34.1 mm (1.343 in.)
intake . . . . .33.8 mm (1.331 in.)
PL engine
exhaust . . . . .34.7 mm (1.366 in.)
intake . . . . .34.4 mm (1.354 in.)
ME, MF engines
exhaust . . . . .36.1 mm (1.421 in.)
intake . . . . .35.8 mm (1.409 in.)

Valve guide wear, maximum
(measure with new valve)
gasoline engines
intake .1.0 mm (.039 in.)
exhaust . . . . .1.3 mm (.059 in.)
diesel engines
intake and exhaust . . . . .1.3 mm (.059 in.)

Intake valve dimensions
stem diameter
except PL engine . . . . .7.97 mm (.3138 in.)
PL engine . . . . .6.97 mm (.2744 in.)
length
GX, MZ, HT, RD, RV, PF engines . . .91.00 mm (3.583 in.)
PL engine . . . . .95.50 mm (3.760 in.)
ME, MF engines
w/hydraulic cam followers . . . . . . .95.00 mm (3.740 in.)
ME, MF engines
w/mechanical cam followers . . . . .104.80 mm (4.126 in.)
head diameter
GX, MZ engines . . . . .38.00 mm (1.496 in.)
HT, RD, PF engines . . . . .40.00 mm (1.575 in.)
ME, MF engines . . . . .34.00 mm (1.339 in.)
PL engines . . . . .32.00 mm (1.259 in.)
head margin, minimum after grinding
(diesel intake valves only) . . . . .0.5 mm (.02 in.)

IV. Camshaft, Valve, and Cylinder Head Specifications (continued)

Exhaust valve dimensions
stem diameter
except PL engine . . . . .7.95 mm (.3130 in.)
PL engine . . . . .6.94 mm (.2732 in.)
length
GX, MZ, HT, RD, PF engines . . . . . .90.80 mm (3.575 in.)
PL engine . . . . .98.20 mm (3.846 in.)
ME, MF engines
w/hydraulic cam followers . . . . .95.00 mm (3.740 in.)
ME, MF engines
w/mechanical cam followers . . . . . .104.60 mm (4.118 in.)
head diameter
GX, MZ, HT, RD, PF engines . . . . . .33.00 mm (1.299 in.)
ME, MF engines . . . . .31.00 mm (1.220 in.)
PL engine . . . . .28.00 mm (1.102 in.)

Valve clearance, ME and MF w/adjustable
cam followers
engine cold
intake . . . . .0.15–0.25 mm (.006–.010 in.)
exhaust . . . . .0.35–0.45 mm (.014–.018 in.)
engine hot (coolant temp. 95°F (35°C) min.
intake . . . . .0.20–0.30 mm (.008–.012 in.)
exhaust . . . . .0.40–0.50 mm (.016–.020 in.)

V. Lubrication System Specifications

Oil pump gears backlash . . . . .0.05–0.20 mm (.002–.008 in.)
Oil pump gears axial play, wear limit . . . . . .0.15 mm (.006 in.)
Oil pressure, minimum at 2000 rpm
with SAE 10W oil at 140°F (68°C) . . . . .2.0 bar (28 psi)
Oil pressure warning system switch pressures
low pressure switch opens . . . . .0.15–0.45 bar (2.1–6.4 psi)
(0.3 bar nominal)
dynamic (high rpm) pressure switch closes
gasoline engines . . . . .1.6–2.0 bar (23.2–29 psi)
(1.8 bar nominal)
diesel engines . . . . .1.2–1.6 bar (20.3–23.2 psi)
(1.4 bar nominal)

COOLING SYSTEM

Contents

Introduction 3

1. General Description. 4
    Coolant Pump and Thermostat 4
    Radiator. 4
    Radiator Cooling Fan. 4

2. Maintenance. 4

3. Troubleshooting. 4
   3.1 Basic Troubleshooting Principles. 4
   3.2 Diagnostic Tests 5
       Pressure Testing Cooling System and
       Expansion Tank Cap 5
       Temperature Gauge and Sending Unit
       Quick-Check 6

4. Cooling System Service 6
   4.1 Coolant and Cooling System Hoses 6
       Draining and Filling Coolant 7
   4.2 Thermostat 8
       Removing and Installing Thermostat 8

Testing Thermostat 8
   4.3 Coolant Pump. 9
       Inspecting and Replacing Coolant Pump 9
   4.4 Radiator Cooling Fan. 10
       Testing Cooling Fan and Radiator
       Thermoswitch 10
       Radiator Cooling Fan After-Run System
       (gasoline engine only, late 1986 Jetta, all
       1987–1989 models except 16V) 11
       Removing and Installing Radiator
       Cooling Fan. 11
   4.5 Radiator. 11
       Removing and Installing Radiator 11

5. Cooling System Technical Data 12
    I. Cooling System Specifications 12
    II. Tightening Torques 12

TABLES

a. Cooling System Troubleshooting. 5
b. Anti-Freeze-to-Water Proportions 7
c. Radiator Cooling Fan Switching Temperatures 10

Cooling System

Introduction

Volkswagen GTI, Golf, and Jetta engines are liquid-cooled, and rely on a closed system of circulating coolant to maintain an even engine temperature and help transfer heat away from the engine. To provide adequate cooling systemperformance over a range of temperature conditions, to supply lubrication to the system's moving parts, and to prevent the buildup of mineral deposits and other contaminants, the coolant recommended for use year-round is a mixture of phosphate-free anti-freeze and clean water. The closed system becomes pressurized as its temperature increases. The pressure in turn raises the boiling point of the coolant and allows engine temperature to exceed the coolant's normal boiling point.

The coolant pump is mechanically driven by the engine, and operates whenever the engine is running. Coolant circulates through the engine to the radiator, the heat exchanger or heater core in the passenger compartment heating system, and back to the pump. On some models, coolant is also circulated through a heat exchanger in the engine's lubrication system to help moderate engine oil temperature. Before the engine is up to normal operating temperature, the flow of coolant is controlled by a thermostat. The thermostat forces coolant flow to bypass the radiator, returning directly to the coolant pump, until the engine is warm.

A radiator cooling fan provides auxiliary air flow through the radiator. For compatibility with the transverse engine design, and to minimize power consumption, the fan is electrically operated and thermostatically controlled so that it runs only when the extra air flow is required to maintain proper coolant temperature.

Proper care of the cooling system is easy. Simple preventive maintenance can keep the system operating at its best and help prevent temperature-related problems from shortening engine life. If you lack the tools or a suitable workplace for servicing the cooling system, we suggest you leave this work to an authorized Volkswagen dealer or other qualified shop. We especially urge you to consult your authorized Volkswagen dealer before beginning any repairs on a vehicle still covered by warranty.

1. GENERAL DESCRIPTION

Fig. 1-1 is a schematic view of the cooling system and hose routing. Arrows indicate the direction of coolant flow.

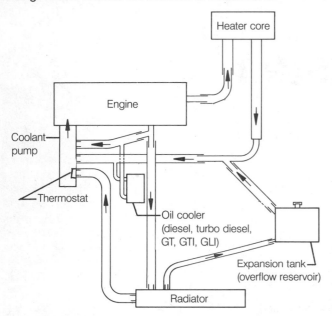

Fig. 1-1. Schematic view of cooling system components and hose routing showing coolant flow (arrows).

Coolant Pump and Thermostat

A centrifugal-type coolant pump and its housing are mounted to the cylinder block. The pump is crankshaft-driven by a V-belt, and circulates coolant through the system whenever the engine is running.

A thermostat is located in the coolant pump housing and controls coolant flow into the pump. When the engine is cold, the thermostat is closed and coolant bypasses the radiator, recirculating from the engine directly back to the pump inlet. When the engine reaches normal operating temperature, the thermostat opens and coolant circulates through the whole system, including the radiator.

Radiator

The radiator is a cross-flow type constructed of an aluminum core and plastic side tanks. A translucent expansion tank, or overflow reservoir, provides for the expansion of the coolant at higher temperatures and easy monitoring of coolant level.

Radiator Cooling Fan

An electric radiator coolin fan, operating independently of the engine, is controlled by a thermoswitch located in the bottom of the radiator. At high coolant temperatures, the switch closes to start the cooling fan. The cooling fan is wired directly to the battery. Any time the coolant temperature is excessive, the fan will start and continue to run until coolant temperature is in the correct range. On models with air conditioning, high refrigerant pressure can also activate the cooling fan.

is in the correct range. On models with air conditioning, high refrigerant pressure can also activate the cooling fan.

On some models with gasoline engines, a cooling fan after-run system, operated by a control unit on the fuse/relay panel, runs the cooling fan for as long as 15 minutes after the engine is shut off, as a guard against starting problems which may be caused by high engine compartment temperatures.

2. MAINTENANCE

The following routine maintenance steps are covered in detail in **LUBRICATION AND MAINTENANCE**.

1. Checking coolant level

2. Inspecting coolant pump V-belt tension and condition

3. Inspecting coolant hoses

4. Replacing engine coolant

3. TROUBLESHOOTING

This troubleshooting section applies to problems affecting the cooling system, which includes those components which store, pump, and regulate the circulation of engine coolant.

While coolant also circulates through the heater core in the passenger compartment, problems associated with the operation and repair of the heater system are covered in **BODY AND INTERIOR**. Similarly, while this section may help to isolate a problem to a faulty coolant temperature gauge, replacement of the gauge is covered in **ELECTRICAL SYSTEM**.

Overheating problems may also be caused by an engine fault that leaks hot combustion gasses into the cooling system, or by ignition timing that is out of specification. See **ENGINE** or **IGNITION** for additional information on these subjects.

3.1 Basic Troubleshooting Principles

When investigating the cause of overheating or coolant loss, begin with a visual inspection of the system. Check coolant level and for evidence of coolant leaks. Leaks can occur at any place in the cooling system where there is a bolted housing or other connection. An occasional drop of coolant found under the coolant pump is normal, and is not cause for concern.

The system becomes pressurized at normal operating temperatures, and this pressure is important to system function. Leaks may prevent the system from becoming pressurized and allow the coolant to boil at a lower temperature. If visual evidence is inconclusive, a cooling system pressure test will determine whether the system leaks, and may help to indicate the source. See **3.2 Diagnostic Tests**.

If the cooling system is full of coolant and holds pressure, the next most probable cause of overheating is bad coolant circulation caused by a broken V-belt, a failed thermostat, a pinched or restricted hose, or a clogged system. In warm weather, virtually all clogs are caused by neglect of the coolant, or by the addition of substances to the coolant that are not recommended by Volkswagen. In cold weather, a clogged cooling system may also be the result of frozen coolant due to an inadequate amount of anti-freeze.

The engine-driven coolant pump is subject to the same wear as any other rotating engine parts. Complete failure of the pump to circulate coolant is unusual, but excessive wear often results in noise or coolant leaks at the pump shaft.

An otherwise sound cooling system may still have overheating problems, particularly with prolonged idling, if the radiator cooling fan is inoperative. The cooling fan should cycle on and off whenever the coolant temperature is above normal. If the fan does not cycle, test the fan as described in **4.4 Radiator Cooling Fan**.

Table a lists overheating and underheating symptoms, their probable causes, and suggested corrective actions. The bold numbers in the corrective action column refer to headings in this section where the suggested repairs are described.

3.2 Diagnostic Tests

These system tests are used to help isolate and diagnose cooling system problems, and pinpoint their causes.

Pressure Testing Cooling System and Expansion Tank Cap

A pressure test will help find any leaks and show whether the cooling system can maintain pressure. If the system cannot maintain pressure, the boiling point of the coolant is reduced and the engine will overheat more easily. Various kinds of cooling system pressure testers are available. Follow the instructions supplied by the tester's manufacturer. The unique design of the Volkswagen system requires a special adapter. If these tools are not available, a Volkswagen dealer or other qualified repair shop can perform this test inexpensively.

4

Table a. Cooling System Troubleshooting

Symptom	Probable cause	Corrective action
1. Engine overheats	a. Low coolant level	a. Fill the radiator to the **Max.** mark. Check cooling system for leaks with pressure tester. **3.2**
	b. Burst hose	b. Replace hose. Refill radiator to **Max.** mark. **4.1**
	c. Radiator hose restricted (lower hose may collapse only at highway speeds)	c. Replace hose. **4.1**
	d. V-belt loose or broken	d. Adjust or replace V-belt. **4.3**
	e. Faulty thermostat	e. Remove and test thermostat. Replace if necessary. **4.2, 4.3**
	f. Electric fan not switching on	f. Test thermoswitch and fan. Replace faulty part. **4.2, 4.5**
	g. Faulty radiator cap	g. Test pressure relief valve in cap. Replace faulty caps. **4.2**
	h. Clogged radiator	h. Replace radiator or have heater core cleaned. **4.2, 4.3**
	i. Incorrect ignition timing or valve timing	i. Check camshaft drivebelt installation. Adjust ignition timing and check spark advance. See **ENGINE**.
	j. Coolant pump faulty	j. Test coolant pump. Repair or replace if necessary. **4.2 and 4.3** or **4.4**
2. Temperature gauge reads low, inadequate heater output	a. Faulty thermostat	a. Remove and test thermostat. **4.2, 4.3**
	b. Electric fan not switching off	b. Replace thermoswitch for fan. **4.4**
3. Temperature gauge reads low, heater output normal	a. Faulty temperature gauge or sending unit	a. Test temperature gauge and sending unit. Replace faulty part. **4.2**
4. Temperature gauge reads normal, inadequate heater output	a. Installed position of heater hoses reversed	a. Install heater hoses. **4., 4.1**
	b. Heater hose restricted	b. Replace hose. **4.1**
	c. Heat exchanger (heater core) clogged	c. Replace heater exchanger or have core cleaned. See **BODY AND INTERIOR**.
	d. Heater control out of adjustment	d. Adjust control cables. See **BODY AND INTERIOR**.

Pressurize the system to approximately 1.25 bar (18 psi). Loss of pressure indicates leaks which should be apparent by the seepage of coolant. If the pressure drops rapidly and there is no sign of coolant leaks, the cylinder head gasket may be faulty. To check for a faulty gasket, see **ENGINE**.

CAUTION ━

Do not exceed the specified test pressure. Higher pressure could damage the radiator or other cooling system components.

To test the cap, install it on the pressure tester as shown in Fig. 3-1. Increase pressure to 1.20 to 1.35 bar (17 to 19 psi). The cap's pressure relief valve should open within this range, but not below. Faulty caps should be replaced.

Fig. 3-1. Expansion tank cap installed on pressure tester pump (**A**) using adapter US 4467. Adapter is also used to pressure test the cooling system.

Temperature Gauge and Sending Unit Quick-check

A quick, easy test will determine whether the coolant temperature gauge is correctly representing engine temperature.

If the temperature gauge needle remains at its rest position even though the engine is fully warmed, test the gauge as follows. With the ignition on and the engine not running, disconnect the gauge wire (yellow with red stripe) from the sending unit in the coolant outlet on the cylinder head. On 16-valve engines, the sending unit is on the driver's-side end of the cylinder head. Ground the wire. This simulates a high engine temperature signal to the gauge. If the gauge needle moves upward, the sending unit is faulty and should be replaced. If the needle still does not move, either the wire to the gauge is broken (open circuit) or the gauge is faulty.

If the gauge reads high when the engine is cold and the ignition is switched on, disconnect the temperature sending unit wire from the sending unit. If the needle drops to a lower reading, the sending unit is faulty. If the needle does not drop, the wire or the gauge is shorted to ground. See **ELECTRICAL SYSTEM** for electrical system troubleshooting.

4. COOLING SYSTEM SERVICE

Most repairs to the cooling system are easy and require relatively little time. Always plan to replace gaskets and seals and have them on hand before beginning.

WARNING ━

The cooling system at high temperature operates under pressure. If it is necessary to open the hot cooling system, do so very slowly to allow safe release of pressure. Use heavy gloves or other hand protection.

CAUTION ━

Avoid adding cold water to the coolant while the engine is hot or overheated. If it is absolutely necessary to add coolant to a hot system, do so only with the engine running and coolant pump turning.

4.1 Coolant and Cooling System Hoses

To guard against cooling system trouble, the coolant level and the hoses should be periodically inspected, as described in **LUBRICATION AND MAINTENANCE**. Hoses deteriorate with time, and periodic inspection will help prevent unexpected failure. When adding or replacing coolant, Volkswagen recommends the use of phosphate-free anti-freeze, formulated to prohibit the formation of harmful, clogging deposits in the cooling system.

CAUTION ━

Use of anti-freeze containing phosphates is considered by Volkswagen to be harmful to the cooling system and may void warranty coverage.

Always mix anti-freeze with clean water. Distilled water is best because of its reduced mineral content. Oil in the coolant will encourage the formation of sludge which can clog the system and damage rubber parts. Oil should not be added as a lubricant. If using leak sealer as a precaution against leaks, the system should never contain more than one can. The additives that plug leaks can also plug radiators and heater cores.

Draining the coolant is a first step in almost all cooling system repairs. The coolant can be reused provided it is drained into a clean pan. New coolant is recommended every 2 years. Replacing hoses, or draining and filling the coolant, requires only a medium-sized flat bladed screwdriver, a pliers, and a 3-gallon drain pan.

Draining and Filling Coolant

To drain the coolant, disconnect the coolant hoses indicated in Fig. 4-1. To refill the system, first reinstall the lower radiator hoses and their clamps. Then fill the system with the coolant and water mixture until the level reaches the **Max** mark on the coolant reservoir as shown in Fig. 4-2. Mixture proportions are given in **Table b**. Start the engine and let it idle, rechecking the coolant level after it has had a chance to circulate. After the engine has cooled, check the coolant level and add coolant as necessary.

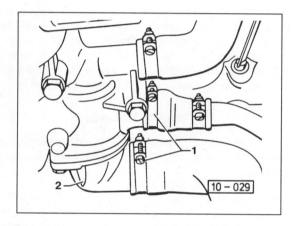

Fig. 4-1. Hoses (**1**) to be removed for draining coolant from coolant pump and thermostat housing (**2**).

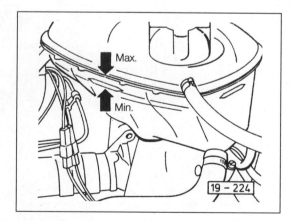

Fig. 4-2. Fill level marks on coolant expansion tank. Level should be between **Max** and **Min** marks (arrow) with engine cold.

Table b. Anti-Freeze-to-Water Proportions

Protection level (outside temperature)	Anti-freeze quarts (liters)	Water quarts (liters)
−13°F (−25°C)	2.7 (2.6)	4.1 (3.9)
−22°F (−30°C)	3.1 (3.0)	3.75 (3.5)
−31°F (−35°C)	3.4 (3.25)	3.4 (3.25)

To replace a hose:

1. Drain the coolant as described above.

2. Remove the hose. Using a screwdriver, or pliers in the case of spring clamps, loosen each hose clamp and slide the clamps away from the hose ends.

   NOTE ——

   If a radiator hose is stuck to the radiator connection by sealer, cut the old hose off the connection, as shown in Fig. 4-3. Prying the hose loose may damage the connection or the radiator.

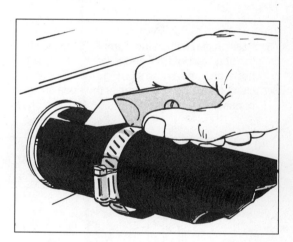

Fig. 4-3. Stuck hose being removed by cutting.

3. Clean the hose connections. Make sure any bits of old hose and sealer are removed. Clean them with a wire brush if necessary.

4. Install the new hose. Lightly coat the connections with water-resistant sealer. Place the loose hose clamps onto the new hose before fitting the hose ends to the connections.

NOTE ━━

Spring clamps should be used only with hoses and connections designed for their use. See Fig. 4-4.

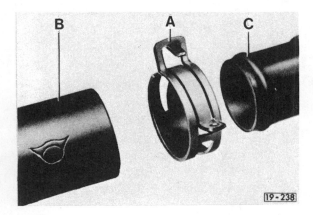

Fig. 4-4. Identification of hose and connection suitable for use with spring clamp (**A**). Hose (**B**) bears spring clamp symbol and is smooth on inside (instead of corrugated). Connection (**C**) has larger bead and is about 5 mm (¼ in.) longer.

5. Position and tighten the clamps. Place the clamp as near the bead as possible and at least 4 mm (5/32 in.) from the hose end, as shown in Fig. 4-5. Tighten screw-type clamps enough to compress the hose firmly around the connections.

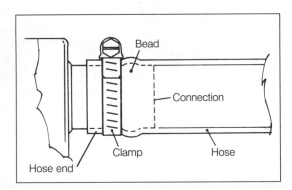

Fig. 4-5. Hose clamp correctly installed on hose end.

CAUTION ━━

Do not overtighten clamps. Tighten just enough to seal. Overtightening may cause hose damage and failure.

6. Refill the radiator as described in **Draining and Filling Coolant**. Run the engine until warm and check for leaks. Check again after the engine has cooled.

4.2 Thermostat

The thermostat controls the coolant temperature by regulating coolant flow to the radiator. A thermostat stuck open will cause the engine to warm up slowly and run below normal temperature at highway speed. A thermostat stuck closed will restrict coolant flow to the radiator and cause overheating.

Replacement is only necessary if the thermostat is faulty. In addition to the tools required for draining the coolant, a wrench or a socket is required to remove the thermostat housing. Use a new O-ring, Volkswagen Part No. 059 121 119, when the thermostat housing is reinstalled.

Removing and Installing Thermostat

Drain the coolant as described in **Draining and Filling Coolant**. Remove the two thermostat housing bolts and separate the housing from the coolant pump. See Fig. 4-1, above.

To install the thermostat, position the thermostat in the coolant pump housing with a new O-ring and install the thermostat housing. Torque the bolts to 10 Nm (87 in. lb.). Reinstall any disconnected hoses. Fill the cooling system as described in **Draining and Filling Coolant**. Warm the engine and check for leaks. Check again after the engine has cooled.

Testing Thermostat

Test the thermostat when it is removed from the engine. It is also wise to perform this simple test to a new thermostat before installation.

Measure the thermostat to determine the change in length between cold and hot conditions, as shown in Fig. 4-6. Heat the thermostat in a pan of water as shown in Fig. 4-7 while monitoring temperature with a thermometer.

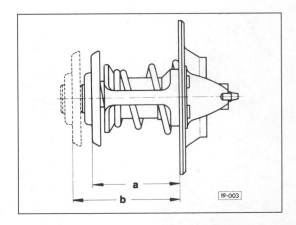

Fig. 4-6. Thermostat length. Dimension **a** is closed (cold) length; dimension **b** is open (hot) length.

Fig. 4-7. Testing thermostat in hot water.

The thermostat should begin to open at approximately 185°F (85°C). At boiling temperature, approximately 212°F (100°C), the length as shown in Fig. 4-6 should be at least 7 mm (⁹⁄₃₂ in.) greater than the cold length measured earlier. A thermostat which does not open the full amount should not be installed.

4.3 Coolant Pump

Fig. 4-8 is an exploded view of the coolant pump and its related parts. The pump can be removed from the housing and replaced separately, however, it is easier to remove the pump and housing from the engine as a unit and separate them later.

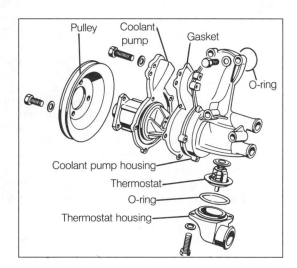

Fig. 4-8. Exploded view of coolant pump and related parts.

Only basic hand tools are required to replace the coolant pump. It is replaced as a unit, as parts for rebuilding are not generally available. A Volkswagen remanufactured pump is available. Always use a new gasket between the pump and housing, and a new O-ring between the housing and engine.

When replacing the coolant pump on cars with power steering, the power steering pump and mounting brackets must be removed first. For more information, see **SUSPENSION AND STEERING**. On cars with air conditioning, replacement of the coolant pump will be considerably easier if the alternator and air conditioning compressor are removed. Remove the alternator as described in **ELECTRICAL SYSTEM**. The air conditioning compressor should be removed from its mountings and set out of the way without loosening or removing the compressor hoses. This procedure is described as part of the engine removal procedure in **ENGINE**.

Inspecting and Replacing Coolant Pump

To inspect the coolant pump, first remove the V-belt. See **LUBRICATION AND MAINTENANCE**. Firmly grasp the coolant pump pulley and check for play in all directions. Rotate the pulley and check that the shaft turns smoothly. It should rotate smoothly. Inspect the pump for leaks. An occasional drop of coolant from the pump shaft is acceptable. A larger leak or a shaft that is excessively loose or noisy, indicating a worn bushing, means that the pump is faulty and should be replaced. Also, replace the V-belt if it is worn or damaged.

To remove coolant pump:

1. Drain the cooling system. See **4.1 Coolant and Cooling System Hoses**. Remove the V-belt. See **LUBRICATION AND MAINTENANCE**.

2. Remove the nut and T-bolt that fastens the camshaft drive belt cover to the coolant pump. Disconnect the remaining hoses from the pump housing.

3. Remove pump and housing assembly. Four bolts hold the coolant assembly to the engine.

4. Disassemble the pump and housing assembly. Remove the pulley(s) from the coolant pump shaft. Remove the seven bolts and washers and separate the pump from the housing.

Assembly is the reverse of disassembly. Use a new gasket between the coolant pump and housing. Tighten the seven bolts evenly until all are torqued to 10 Nm (87 in. lb.). Install the pulley(s). Torque the bolts to 20 Nm (15 ft. lb.).

> **NOTE ▬**
>
> The power-steering V-belt pulley attached to the coolant pump is marked with the word **KLIMA**. The mark faces outward (away from the pump) on vehicles with air conditioning, and inward on vehicles without air conditioning.

To install coolant pump:

1. Clean the surface of the engine block where it will be contacted by the pump housing and the O-ring. Install a new O-ring in the recess that surrounds the water outlet.

   NOTE ———

   The O-ring between the coolant pump housing and the engine block does not require sealer.

2. Loosely install the coolant pump on the engine. The two short bolts are used at the top of the pump housing. Torque the four bolts evenly to 20 Nm (15 ft. lb.). Refasten the camshaft drive belt cover to the coolant pump.

3. Install the hoses and refill the cooling system as described in **4.1 Coolant and Cooling System Hoses**. Install and adjust the V-belt as described in **LUBRICATION AND MAINTENANCE**.

4.4 Radiator Cooling Fan

The cooling fan provides additional air flow through the radiator. A faulty cooling fan motor or thermoswitch may be the cause of insufficient air flow and, therefore, overheating. Models covered by this manual have either a single-speed or a two-speed cooling fan.

Some gasoline-engined models (late 1986 Jettas, and all 1987– 1989 models except 16-valve) have a radiator cooling fan after-run system, designed to run the cooling fan for up to 15 minutes after the engine is shut off, to aid in restarting a hot engine. A thermoswitch mounted on the cylinder head monitors engine compartment temperature.

In either case, the cooling fan can come on at any time, even if the key is out of the ignition. To avoid personal injury, cooling fan and thermoswitch tests should be performed with extreme caution, and preferably with the engine cold. The tests below simulate a warm engine by electrically bypassing the thermoswitch with a jumper wire. Switching temperatures are given in **Table c**.

Testing Cooling Fan and Radiator Thermoswitch

Note that the electric cooling fan will operate only when the temperature is high enough to close the radiator thermoswitch or, on cars so equipped, the after-run thermoswitch. If a faulty thermostat is not allowing the coolant to bypass the radiator and warm up to the switching tmperature, the thermoswitch will not close and the cooling fan will not run.

Table c. Radiator Cooling Fan Switching Temperatures

Specification	Without Air Conditioning	With Air Conditioning
Radiator thermoswitch two-terminal)		
On	198°–207°F (92°–97°C)	
Off	183°–196°F (84°–91°C)	
Radiator thermoswitch (three-terminal)		
Low Speed On (continuity on switch terminals 2 and 3)	198°–208°F (92°–98°C)	183°–207°F (84°–97°C)
Low Speed Off	183°–196°F (84°–91°C)	
High Speed On (continuity on switch terminals 1 and 3)	210°–221°F (99°–105°C)	201°–226°F (94°–108°C)
High Speed Off	196°=220°F (91°–104°C)	
After-run thermoswitch		
On	230°F (110°C)	230°F (110°C)
Off	217°F (103°C)	217°F (103°C)

To test the cooling fan, disconnect the radiator thermoswitch connector and use a jumper wire (with switch) to make connnection between terminals to simulate a closed switch. On three-terminal connectors used with two-speed fans, the fan should run at low speed when the red wire is jumpered to the red/white wire. It should run at high speed when the red wire is jumpered to the red/black wire. Thermoswitch location is shown in Fig. 4-9.

WARNING ———

Always keep clear of the fan blades. The cooling fan may run at any time, even with the ignition off.

If the fan does not run, check for voltage at the thermoswitch connector. There should be battery voltage (approx. 12 V) at terminal no. 3 (red wire) whenever the battery is connected. If not, check fuse no.1 in the fuse/relay panel. For more information on the cooling fan circuit, see **ELECTRICAL SYSTEM**.

If the fan runs only when powered directly by the jumpered connector, the radiator thermoswitch should be replaced.

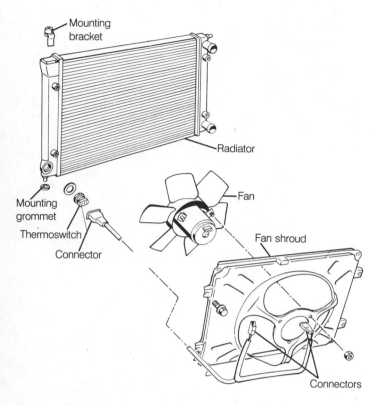

Fig. 4-9. Radiator and cooling fan used on 16-valve models. Other models are similar.

Radiator Cooling Fan After-Run System

(gasoline engine only, late 1986 Jetta, all 1987–1989 models except 16V)

The after-run system uses a cylinder head mounted thermoswitch to sense excessive engine compartment temperature. High temperature closes the switch, making a ground connection for the after-run control unit, turning on the cooling fan for up to 15 minutes. The control unit is located on the fuse/relay panel.

Test the system, with the ignition off, by disconnecting the black wire from the thermoswitch and grounding it. The thermoswitch is mounted near the top of the engine, behind the cylinder head cover, between no.2 and no.3 cylinders. The fan should run on low speed. If not, check for battery voltage (approx. 12 V) from the control unit (terminal 8/87) to the fan (terminal no.2, red/white wire). If there is no voltage from the control unit, it is faulty and should be replaced.

If, with the thermoswitch connected normally, the fan runs continuously (more than 15 minutes), disconnect the black wire from the thermoswitch. If the fan stops, the thermoswitch is faulty, permanently shorted to ground, and should be replaced. If the fan continues running with the wire detached, the control unit is faulty and should be replaced.

Removing and Installing Radiator Cooling Fan

To remove the cooling fan without removing the radiator, disconnect the negative (−) battery cable and the fan's electrical connector. See Fig. 4-9 above. On cars with air conditioning, remove the connector leading to the series resistor and the cooling fan relay. See Fig. 4-10. Unbolt the fan shroud from the radiator and remove the shroud and fan together. Installation is the reverse of removal. Torque the mounting bolts to 10 Nm (87 in. lb.).

4

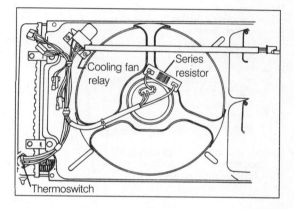

Fig. 4-10. Radiator and related electrical components found on models with air conditioning.

4.5 Radiator

To perform efficiently, the radiator must not be blocked with dirt or debris, and it must be firmly mounted. Excess vibration due to loose, broken, or missing fasteners may damage the radiator.

If the engine overheats and no other cooling system tests indicate trouble, the radiator may have plugged passages restricting coolant flow. Consult a qualified radiator repair shop about repairs.

Removing and Installing Radiator

Drain the cooling system and disconnect the upper and lower radiator hoses, as described in **4.1 Coolant and Cooling System Hoses**. Disconnect the negative (−) battery cable from the battery and the harness connectors from the thermoswitch and cooling fan motor. On models with air conditioning, disconnect the connectors to the series resistor and cooling fan relay. See Fig. 4-10 above. Remove the bolts from the upper radiator mounts. Lift the radiator out from the top, complete with the fan and radiator shroud, tilting it toward the engine.

Installation is the reverse of removal. Torque the mounting bolts to 10 Nm (87 in. lb.).

5. COOLING SYSTEM TECHNICAL DATA

I. Cooling System Specifications

Cooling system leakage test
  maximum test pressure . . . . .1.25 bar (18 psi)
Expansion tank cap relief
  opening pressure . . . . .1.20 to 1.35 bar
                                                       17 to 19 psi)
Thermostat opening temperature
  gasoline engines
    begins to open . . . . .185°F (85°C)
    fully open. . . . . .N/A
    thermostat stroke. . . . . .7 mm (0.275 in.)
  diesel engines
    begins to open . . . . .189°F (87°C)
    fully open. .216°F (102°C)
    thermostat stroke . . . . .7 mm (9/32 in.)
Thermoswitch switching temperature (two-terminal)
  models without air conditioning
    ON (switch closed). . . . . .198° to 207°F
                                                       (92° to 97°C)
    OFF (switch open) . . . . .183° to 196°F
                                                       (84° to 91°C)
Thermoswitch switching temperature (three-terminal)
  models without air conditioning
    ON (switch closed)
    1st stage(low speed) . . . . .198° to 208°F
                                                       (92° to 98°C)
    2nd stage(high speed) . . . . .210° to 221°F
                                                       (99° to 105°C)
    OFF (switch open)
    1st stage (low speed) . . . . .183° to 196°F
                                                       (84° to 91°C)
    2nd stage (high speed) . . . . .196° to 220°F
                                                       (91° to 104°C)
  models with air conditioning
    ON
    1st stage(low speed) . . . . .183° to 207°F
                                                       (84° to 97°C)
    2nd stage(high speed) . . . . .201° to 226°F
                                                       (94° to 108°C)
After-run thermoswitch
  models without air conditioning
    ON . . . . .230°F (110°C)
    OFF. . . . . .217°F (103°C)
  models with air conditioning
    ON . . . . .230°F (110°C)
    OFF. . . . . .217°F (103°C)
Coolant system capacity . . . . .6.5 liters (1.7 gal.)
V-belt tension, deflection under thumb
  pressure at a midpoint between alternator
  and crankshaft pulleys
  models without air conditioning
    with new belt. . . . . .2 mm (5/64 in.)
    with used belt . . . . .5 mm (3/16 in.)
  models with air conditioning
    with new or used belt. . . . . .10 mm (3/8 in.)
Coolant Type. . . . . . .Phosphate-free, containing ethylene glycol

II. Tightening Torques

Coolant outlet to
  cylinder head (bolt) . . . . .10 Nm (87 in. lb.)
Coolant pump housing to
  engine (bolt). . . . . .20 Nm (15 ft. lb.)
Coolant pump pulley to
  coolant pump (bolt) . . . . .20 Nm (15 ft. lb.)
Coolant pump to
  coolant pump housing (bolt) . . . . .10 Nm (87 in. lb.)
Coolant temperature sending unit to
  cylinder head water outlet. . . . . .10 Nm (87 in. lb.)
Radiator shroud mounting to
  radiator (bolt). . . . . .10 Nm (87 in. lb.)
Thermostat housing to
  coolant pump housing (bolt) . . . . .10 Nm (87 in. lb.)
Upper radiator mounts
  to body (bolt). . . . . .10 Nm (87 in. lb.)

FUEL SYSTEM – GASOLINE

5

Contents

Introduction		3
1. General Description		4
	Fuel Storage	4
	Fuel Pump and Fuel Circuit	4
	Air Filter	4
1.1	Continuous Injection System (CIS)	4
1.2	Continuous Injection System-Electronic (CIS-E)	4
1.3	Digifant II Engine Management System	4
1.4	Applications-Identifying Features	5
2. Maintenance		6
3. Troubleshooting		6
3.1	Basic Troubleshooting Principles	6
3.2	CIS Troubleshooting	7
3.3	CIS-E Troubleshooting	8
3.4	Digifant II Troubleshooting	10
4. Fuel Supply		11
4.1	Fuses and Relays	11
	Operating Fuel Pump For Test	12
4.2	Transfer Pump	12
4.3	Fuel pump	14
	Fuel Pump Electrical Tests	15
	Replacing Fuel Pump	16
	Replacing Fuel Pump Check Valve (CIS and CIS-E only)	17
4.4	Fuel Pressure Regulator	18
	CIS Pressure Relief Valve	18
	CIS-E Diaphragm Pressure Regulator	18

	Digifant II Fuel Pressure Regulator	18
4.5	Evaporative Emission Controls	19
	Testing Charcoal Canister Bypass Valve	20
4.6	Accelerator Cable	20
4.7	CIS and CIS-E Fuel Injectors	21
	Removing and Installing Fuel Injectors	21
	Quick-checking Injectors	22
	Testing Injector Fuel Delivery	22
	Cleaning Injectors	23
4.8	Digifant II Fuel Injectors	23
	Testing Injectors	24
	Removing and Installing Injectors	25
5. Continuous Injection System (CIS)		26
5.1	Air Flow Measurement and Fuel Metering	27
	Throttle Valve Basic Adjustment	27
	Air Flow Sensor	28
	Fuel Distributor	28
5.2	Cold Start Enrichment	30
5.3	Cold Running Enrichment	32
	Testing and Replacing Control Pressure Regulator	32
5.4	Idle Speed	32
	Idle Air Bypass Adjustment	33
	Auxiliary Air Regulator	34
	Idle Speed Boost Valve	35
5.5	Fuel Pressure Tests and Specifications	35
	System Pressure	36
	Control Pressure	37
	Residual Pressure	38
5.6	Idle Specifications (rpm and % CO)	38

6. Continuous Injection System - Electronic (CIS-E) . 39
6.1　Air Flow Measurement and Fuel Metering 40
　　　Throttle Valve Basic Adjustment 40
　　　Throttle Switches (HT, RD, and PL engines
　　　only) 41
　　　Air Flow Sensor 41
　　　Fuel Distributor 43
　　　Differential Pressure Regulator 45
6.2　Cold Start Enrichment 46
6.3　Idle Speed 48
　　　Adjusting Idle Air Bypass (engine code
　　　GX only) 49
　　　Idle Air Stabilizer Valve (engine codes HT,
　　　RD, and PL) 49
6.4　Electrical Tests 51
　　　After-start and Cold Running Enrichment 51
　　　Cold Acceleration Enrichment 52
　　　Full-throttle Enrichment (engine codes HT, RD,
　　　and PL only) 53
　　　Deceleration Fuel Shutoff (engine codes HT,
　　　RD, and PL only) 53
　　　Control Unit Inputs 53
6.5　Fuel Pressure Tests and Specifications 56
　　　System Pressure 56
　　　Differential Pressure 56
　　　Residual Pressure 57
6.6　Idle Specifications (rpm and % CO) 57

7. Digifant II Fuel Injection 59
7.1　Air Flow Measurement 60
　　　Air Flow Sensor 60
　　　Throttle Valve Basic Adjustment 61
　　　Throttle Valve Vacuum Hoses 61

7.2　Cold Start and Cold Running Enrichment 61
　　　Coolant Temperature Sensor 61
　　　Intake Air Preheat System 62
7.3　Idle Speed 62
　　　Idle Air Bypass idle speed adjustment 63
　　　Idle Air Stabilizer Valve 63
　　　Idle and Full-Throttle Switches 64
7.4　Electrical Tests 64
7.5　Fuel Pressure Tests and Specifications 67
　　　System Pressure and Residual Pressure 67
　　　Replacing Pressure Regulator 68
7.6　Idle Specifications (rpm and % CO) 68

8. Fuel System Technical Data 69
　　I. CIS Fuel Injection Specifications 69
　　II. CIS-E Fuel Injection Specifications 70
　　III. Digifant Fuel Injection Specifications 70

TABLES

a.　CIS Troubleshooting 7
b.　CIS-E Troubleshooting 8
c.　Digifant II Troubleshooting 10
d.　Digifant II Fuel Injector Resistance 24
e.　Idle Specifications 39
f.　CIS-E Electrical Tests 54
g.　Idle Specifications 59
h.　Digifant II Electrical Tests 65
i.　Idle Specifications 69

Fuel System—Gasoline

5

Introduction

The fuel system handles four main functions necessary for proper engine operation: (1) it provides storage space for the fuel; (2) it delivers fuel to the engine; (3) it admits filtered air to the engine to be mixed with fuel; (4) it mixes fuel and air in precise proportions and delivers the mixture to the cylinders as a combustible vapor. On all gasoline-fueled cars covered by this manual, the fourth function is performed by one of three types of sophisticated fuel injection systems.

Unlike a carburetor, which depends on the velocity of the incoming air to vaporize the fuel and draw it into the engine, a fuel injection system injects atomized fuel into the intake air stream under pressure. This method of active fuel metering means that the fuel mixture entering the engine can be controlled more precisely and used more efficiently, yielding improved driveability, fuel economy, and performance.

Three types of gasoline fuel injection systems are used on the cars covered by this manual. Each has its own unique features and methods, but all achieve the same result. Although at first look these systems appear complicated, they operate on simple principles and can be easily understood. This section provides separate and thorough descriptions of each system, making it simple to identify and understand the system used on a particular car. Troubleshooting and repair are covered in detail. Test procedures for individual components also explain their function, so that the purpose of each test can be understood.

Special equipment is necessary for some servicing of the fuel injection system. Please read the information carefully before beginning any test or repair. If the equipment required to accurately perform the job is not readily available, we suggest leaving those tests or repairs to an authorized Volkswagen dealer or other qualified repair shop. We especially urge you to consult an authorized Volkswagen dealer before beginning any work on a car which may be subject to Volkswagen's warranty coverage.

1. GENERAL DESCRIPTION

Each of the cars covered by this manual is equipped with one of three different types of fuel injection systems. The main components of the fuel system and the three fuel injection systems are described below. For help in identifying the fuel injection system on a particular car, see **1.4 Applications-Identifying Features**.

Fuel Storage

The fuel tank is located beneath the car, behind the rear seat, and is constructed of plastic to avoid corrosion problems. The capacity of the fuel tank is 55 liters (14.5 gallons). Included with the fuel tank are the fuel gauge sending unit, the transfer pump which supplies fuel to the main fuel pump, connecting lines for the evaporative emission control system, and a fuel return line.

Fuel Pump and Fuel Circuit

The electric transfer pump, mounted in the fuel tank, pumps fuel to the fuel reservoir which houses the main fuel pump. The fuel reservoir is located beneath the car in front of the fuel tank. The fuel filter is mounted next to the fuel reservoir. The main fuel pump delivers fuel to the fuel injection system.

On models with CIS and CIS-E fuel injection systems, the fuel reservoir also houses the fuel accumulator. In these high-pressure systems, the fuel accumulator absorbs pressure surges and maintains fuel pressure in the system after the engine is turned off.

A pressure regulator controls fuel pressure to the fuel injection system and allows surplus fuel to flow back to the fuel reservoir.

Air Filter

All of the cars covered by this manual have rectangular, dry-type pleated paper air filter elements housed beneath the fuel injection system's air flow sensor.

1.1 Continuous Injection System (CIS)

CIS is a fully mechanical fuel injection system, in which the amount of fuel metered to the engine is controlled mechanically by the air flow sensor and fuel pressure.

The main components of the system are the air flow sensor, the fuel distributor, and the fuel injectors. The air flow sensor is moved by the flow of intake air, in effect measuring the volume of air entering the engine. Based directly on the movement of the air flow sensor, the fuel distributor then allocates a proportional amount of fuel to the fuel injectors. All fuel metering is done by the fuel distributor. The fuel injectors are actually precise nozzles through which fuel flows continuously while the engine is running.

Several auxiliary components are used to further adapt the fuel mixture to various operating conditions by making changes in fuel pressure. For more detailed information on CIS and its function, see **5. Continuous Injection System (CIS)**.

1.2 Continuous Injection System-Electronic (CIS-E)

CIS-E is a mechanical continuous-flow fuel injection system, in which the fuel metering—controlled by the air flow sensor and fuel pressure—is further refined by precise electronic control of fuel pressure. The main components of CIS-E are the air flow sensor, the fuel distributor, the fuel injectors, the differential pressure regulator, and the electronic control unit.

The air flow sensor measures the volume of air entering the engine. Based directly on the movement of the air flow sensor, the fuel distributor then allocates a proportional amount of fuel to the fuel injectors. The fuel metering done by the fuel distributor is fine-tuned by the differential pressure regulator, an electro-hydraulic valve which makes small and continuous changes to fuel pressure based on signals from the electronic control unit.

The electronic control unit controls the action of the differential pressure regulator by analyzing engine coolant temperature, engine speed, throttle position, and oxygen content in the exhaust. For more detailed information on CIS-E and its function, see **6. Continuous Injection System-Electronic (CIS-E)**.

1.3 Digifant II Engine Management System

The Digifant II engine management system—so called because both fuel injection and ignition are controlled by one integral system—includes fuel injection that is completely electronically controlled. As illustrated in Fig. 1-1, several sensors supply information to the central electronic control unit which then electrically operates the solenoid-type fuel injectors. Fuel is metered to the engine by controlling the amount of time that the injectors are open. All functions, including the amount of fuel injected, are controlled electronically by the control unit.

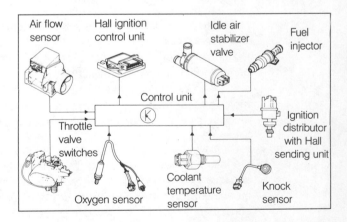

Fig. 1-1. Main components of electronic Digifant II engine management system.

For more detailed information on the fuel injection functions of the Digifant II system, see **7. Digifant II Fuel Injection**. Additional information on the oxygen sensor is covered in **EXHAUST SYSTEM AND EMISSION CONTROLS**. The ignition functions of the system, including the knock sensor, are covered in **IGNITION**.

1.4 Applications-Identifying Features

Three different fuel injection systems—CIS, CIS-E, and Digifant II—are used on the cars covered by this manual. Each has its own distinct components, specifications, and testing procedures. It is essential to be aware of exactly which system is on the car before performing repairs or adjustments.

Nearly all 1985, 1986, and 1987 models are equipped with either CIS or CIS-E fuel injection. All 1987–1989 16-valve engines have CIS-E. CIS and CIS-E are very similar in appearance. See Fig. 1-2. The most obvious visual differences are at the fuel distributor. The steel CIS fuel distributor is painted black and has no electrical components. The CIS-E fuel distributor is aluminum-colored and has harness connectors attached to its differential pressure regulator and sensor plate potentiometer, as shown in Fig. 1-3.

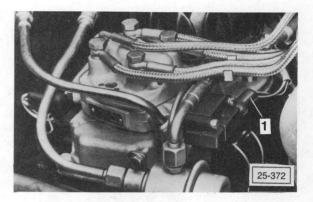

Fig. 1-3. CIS-E fuel distributor. Notice aluminum color and differential pressure regulator with harness connector (**1**).

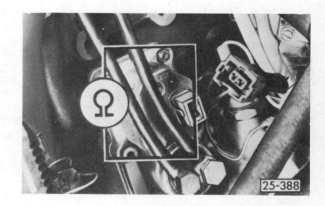

Fig. 1-4. CIS control pressure regulator, mounted to engine cylinder block near oil filter flange with two fuel lines connected to fuel distributor. (Shown with harness connector disconnected for test.)

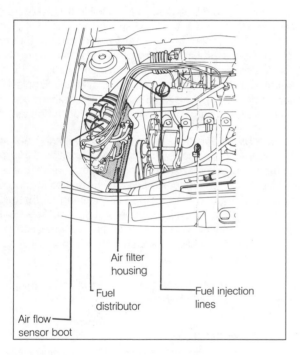

Fig. 1-2. Engine compartment layout on models with CIS-E fuel injection. CIS features are very similar.

An additional distinguishing feature of CIS is the control pressure regulator. The control pressure regulator is mounted to the front side of the engine cylinder block. Two fuel lines connect it to the fuel distributor. See Fig. 1-4. CIS-E has no such component.

A few 1987 and all 1988–1989 models, except those with 16-valve engines, are equipped with the Digifant II system. This system, shown in Fig. 1-5, appears quite different from CIS or CIS-E. There is no fuel distributor atop the air filter housing. The fuel injectors are all connected to a common fuel rail, so there are no individual fuel lines. The Digifant II air filter housing and air flow sensor are shown in Fig. 1-6.

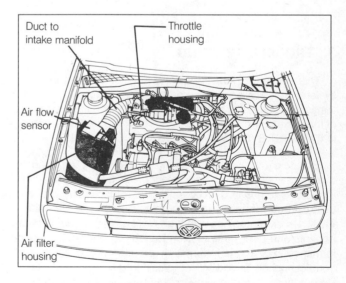

Fig. 1-5. Engine compartment layout on models with Digifant II fuel injection.

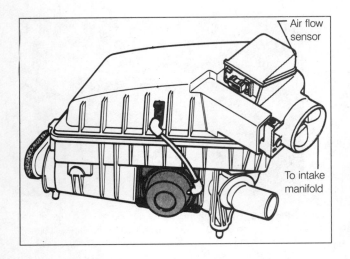

Fig. 1-6. Digifant II air filter housing and air flow sensor.

2. MAINTENANCE

There are only a few maintenance operations that should be carried out at a specified mileage or time interval. These items, listed below, are covered in **LUBRICATION AND MAINTENANCE** or under the listed headings in this section of the manual.

1. Servicing the air filter

2. Replacing the fuel filter

3. Inspecting fuel system for leaks

4. Checking idle speed and idle mixture (CO). **5.6**, **6.6**, or **7.6**

3. TROUBLESHOOTING

This section covers troubleshooting for the fuel injection system, specifically for those parts of the system whose function is to measure air flow and meter fuel. One important part of the system, the oxygen sensor, is covered more thoroughly in **EXHAUST SYSTEM AND EMISSION CONTROLS**.

Engine compression and ignition are also very important to overall driveability and performance. Always verify that the ignition system is in good condition and functioning properly before troubleshooting the fuel injection system. See **IGNITION**. On older engines with high mileage, worn engine components and poor compression may be a factor in poor performance. For more information on engine problems and troubleshooting, including compression testing, see **ENGINE**. Do not try to correct engine trouble by making simple adjustments to the idle speed or the idle mixture (CO). Changing these settings without the proper measuring equipment will only be a hindrance when trying to locate the real fault.

3.1 Basic Troubleshooting Principles

The basic function of each of the three fuel injection systems is to meter the correct amount of fuel to the engine in proportion to the amount of air being drawn into the engine to achieve an optimum air/fuel mixture. Since proper fuel system operation depends on accurately sensing or measuring the intake air, any unmetered air entering the system will cause poor running.

Inspect the entire system for disconnected or damaged hoses, loose connections, or other air leaks. CIS and CIS-E, in particular, are very sensitive to fuel pressure. Check the fuel lines and connections for signs of leaks. Especially inspect the electrical connections to the various components. Aside from loose connections, many problems can be caused by contamination at the connectors which affect the electrical signals. Make sure all connections are clean, tight, and dry.

Generally, fuel system problems fall into one of four symptom categories: cold start, cold running, warm running, and hot start. Warm running is the most basic condition. Before troubleshooting a problem in any other catagory, make sure that the system is working well and properly adjusted for normal warm running. If the car will not start, even the simplest potential problem cannot be ruled out. Make certain that the battery is adequately charged and that there is fuel in the tank.

Various modifications to the basic fuel metering are required to adapt to other than warm running conditions, and certain components are responsible for adapting the fuel metering in certain ways. By concentrating on the sensors and components that adapt or correct the fuel metering for the particular condition, troubleshooting can be greatly simplified. For example, if the engine will not start when cold, the components responsible for cold start enrichment are most likely to be at fault, and should be tested first.

Please abide by the following cautions and warnings whenever servicing the fuel system.

WARNING —

During many fuel system test procedures, fuel will be discharged. Do not smoke or work near heaters or other fire hazards. Have a fire extinguisher handy.

CAUTION —

•Before making any electrical tests with the ignition turned on, disconnect the high-voltage cable from the center tower of the distributor and ground it to some clean metal surface to prevent sparks.

• To prevent damage to the ignition system or the electronic fuel system components, connect and disconnect wires and test equipment only with the ignition off.

3.2 CIS Troubleshooting

This information applies specifically to CIS fuel injection. For troubleshooting other systems, see **3.3 CIS-E Troubleshooting** or **3.4 Digifant II Troubleshooting**.

The basic adjustments of engine idle speed, ignition timing, and idle mixture (% CO) are critical to all other phases of CIS fuel injection performance. Before making any other adjustments to the system, make certain that these parameters are within specifications. See **5.4 Idle Speed**, **5.6 Idle Specifications**, and **IGNITION**.

Table a lists symptoms of CIS fuel system problems, their probable causes, and suggested corrective actions. The boldface numbers in the corrective action column indicate the heading in this section of the manual where the applicable test and repair procedures are found.

5

Table a. CIS Troubleshooting

Symptom	Probable cause	Corrective action
1. Cold start - Engine starts hard or fails to start when cold	a. Cold start valve or thermo-time switch faulty	a. Test cold start valve and thermo-time switch. Replace faulty parts. **5.2**
	b. Fuel pump not running	b. Check fuel pump fuse and fuel pump relay. **4.1, 4.3**
	c. Air flow sensor plate rest position incorrect	c. Inspect air flow sensor plate rest position and adjust if necessary. **5.1**
	d. Fuel pressure incorrect	d. Test system pressure and cold control pressure. **5.5**
2. Hot start - Engine starts hard or fails to start when warm	a. Cold start valve leaking or operating continuously	a. Test cold start valve and thermo-time switch. **5.2**
	b. Fuel pressure incorrect	b. Test warm control pressure. Replace control pressure regulator if necessary. **5.5**
	c. Air flow sensor plate rest position incorrect	c. Inspect air flow sensor plate rest position and adjust if necessary. **5.1**
	d. Insufficient residual fuel pressure	d. Test residual fuel pressure. Replace fuel pump check valve or fuel accumulator as necessary. **5.5**
	e. Fuel leak(s)	e. Inspect fuel lines and connections. Correct leaks as required
3. Engine misses and hesitates under load	a. Fuel injector clogged	a. Test fuel injectors. Check for clogged injector lines. Replace faulty injectors. **4.7**
	b. Fuel pressure incorrect	b. Test system pressure and warm control pressure. Adjust system pressure regulator or replace control pressure regulator as necessary. **5.5**
	c. Fuel leak(s)	c. Inspect fuel lines and connections. Correct leaks as required
4. Engine starts but stalls at idle	a. Incorrect fuel pressure	a. Test system pressure and control pressure. **5.5**
	b. Cold start valve leaking	b. Test and, if necessary, replace cold start valve. **5.2**
	c. Auxiliary air regulator faulty	c. Test and, if necessary, replace auxiliary air regulator. **5.4**
	d. Vacuum (intake air) leak	d. Inspect intake air components for leaking hoses, hose connections, and cracks or other leaks. Repair as required
5. Engine idles too fast	a. Accelerator pedal, cable, or throttle valve binding	a. Inspect for worn or broken parts, kinked cable, or other damage. Replace faulty parts. **4.6** Also see **BODY AND INTERIOR**
	b. Auxiliary air regulator faulty	b. Test and, if necessary, replace auxiliary air regulator. **5.4**
	c. Air leaking past throttle valve	c. Inspect throttle valve and adjust or replace as required. **5.1**
6. Hesitation on acceleration	a. Vacuum (intake air) leak	a. Inspect intake air components for leaking hoses, hose connections, and cracks or other leaks. Repair as required
	b. Fuel injectors clogged	b. Test injector spray pattern and quantity. Replace faulty injectors. **4.7**
	c. Cold start valve leaking	c. Test and, if necessary, replace cold start valve. **5.2**
	d. Control plunger in fuel distributor binding or fuel distributor faulty	d. Check air flow sensor plate movement and, if necessary, replace fuel distributor. **5.1**
	e. Air flow sensor plate out of adjustment	e. Inspect air flow sensor plate position and adjust if necessary. **5.1**
	f. Fuel pressure incorrect	f. Test system pressure and warm control pressure. If necessary, replace control pressure regulator. **5.5**
	g. Idle mixture (% CO) incorrectly adjusted	g. Check and adjust CO. **5.6**

continued on next page

Table a. CIS Troubleshooting (continued)

Symptom	Probable cause	Corrective action
7. Poor fuel mileage	a. Idle speed, ignition timing, and idle mixture (% CO) out of adjustment b. Cold start valve leaking c. Fuel pressure incorrect	a. Check and adjust. **5.6** Also see **IGNITION** b. Test and, if necessary, replace cold start valve. **5.2** c. Test system pressure and warm control pressure. If necessary, replace control pressure regulator. **5.5**
8. Engine continues to run (diesels) after ignition is turned off	a. Incorrect ignition timing or faulty ignition system b. Engine overheated	a. See **IGNITION** b. See **COOLING SYSTEM**

3.3 CIS-E Troubleshooting

This information applies specifically to CIS-E fuel injection. For troubleshooting other systems, see **3.2 CIS Troubleshooting** or **3.4 Digifant II Troubleshooting**.

The basic adjustments of engine idle speed, ignition timing, and idle mixture (% CO) are critical to all other phases of CIS-E fuel injection performance. Before making any other adjustments to the system, make certain that these parameters are within specifications. See **6.3 Idle Speed**, **6.6 Idle Specifications**, and **IGNITION**.

Table b lists symptoms of CIS-E fuel system problems, their probable causes, and suggested corrective actions. The boldface numbers in the corrective action column indicate the heading in this section of the manual where the applicable test and repair procedures are found.

Table b. CIS-E Troubleshooting

Symptom	Probable cause	Corrective action
1. Cold start - Engine starts hard or fails to start when cold	a. Cold start valve or thermo-time switch faulty b. Fuel pump not running c. Air flow sensor plate rest position incorrect d. Fuel pressure incorrect e. Coolant temperature sensor faulty or wire to sensor broken	a. Test cold start valve and thermo-time switch. Replace faulty parts. **6.2** b. Check fuel pump fuse and fuel pump relay. **4.1, 4.3** c. Inspect air flow sensor plate rest position adjust as necessary. **6.1** d. Check differential pressure regulator, system pressure, and differential pressure. **6.1, 6.4, 6.5** e. Test coolant temperature sensor and wiring. Repair wiring or replace sensor as required. **6.4**
2. Hot start - Engine starts hard or fails to start when warm	a. Cold start valve leaking or operating continuously b. Fuel pressure incorrect c. Insufficient residual fuel pressure d. Oxygen sensor system faulty e. Air flow sensor plate rest position incorrect f. Fuel injector faulty or clogged g. Fuel pump delivery inadequate h. Fuel leak(s)	a. Test cold start valve and thermo-time switch. **6.2** b. Check differential pressure regulator, system pressure, and differential pressure. **6.1, 6.4, 6.5** c. Test residual fuel pressure. Replace fuel pump check valve or fuel accumulator as necessary **6.5** d. See **EXAHUST SYSTEM AND EMISSION CONTROLS** e. Inspect air flow sensor plate rest position and adjust if necessary. **6.1** f. Test injector spray patterns and quantity. Replace faulty injectors. **4.7** g. Check fuel pump delivery. **4.3** h. Inspect fuel lines and connections. Correct leaks as required
3. Engine stalls or idles rough (cold or warm)	a. Fuel pressure incorrect b. Cold start valve faulty c. Fuel injector faulty or clogged d. Coolant temperature sensor faulty or wiring to sensor broken e. Vacuum (intake air) leak	a. Check differential pressure regulator, system pressure, and differential pressure. **6.1, 6.4, 6.5** b. Test cold start valve. Replace if leaking or otherwise faulty. **6.2** c. Test injector spray patterns and quantity. Replace faulty injectors. **4.7** d. Test coolant temperature sensor and wiring. Repair wiring or replace sensor as required. **6.4** e. Inspect intake air components for leaking hoses, hose connections, and cracks or other leaks. Repair as required

continued on next page

Table b. CIS-E Troubleshooting (continued)

Symptom	Probable Cause	Corrective Action
3. Engine stalls or idles rough (cold or warm)	f. Control plunger in fuel distributor binding or fuel distributor faulty	f. Check air flow sensor plate movement and, if necessary, replace fuel distributor. 6.2
	g. Auxiliary air regulator faulty (GX, MZ engines only)	g. Test auxiliary air regulator and replace if faulty. 6.3, 5.4
	h. Idle air stabilzer valve not operating (HT, RD, and PL engine only)	h. Test idle switch. 6.1 Test idle air stabilizer valve. 6.3
	i. Air flow sensor plate rest position incorrect	i. Visually inspect air flow sensor plate rest position and adjust if necessary. 6.1
4. Engine misses and hesitates under load	a. Fuel injector clogged	a. Test injector spray patterns and quantity. Replace faulty injectors. 4.7
	b. Fuel pressure incorrect	b. Check differential pressure regulator, system pressure, and differential pressure. 6.1, 6.4, 6.5
	c. Oxygen sensor system faulty	c. See **EXHAUST SYSTEM AND EMISSION CONTROLS**
	d. Fuel leak(s)	d. Inspect fuel lines and connections. Correct leaks as required
	e. Coolant temperature sensor faulty or wire to sensor broken	e. Test coolant temperature sensor and wiring. Repair wiring or replace sensor if faulty. 6.4
5. Engine idles too fast	a. Accelerator pedal, cable, or throttle valve binding	a. Inspect for worn or broken parts, kinked cable, or other damage. Replace faulty parts. 4.6, Also see **BODY AND INTERIOR**
	b. Auxiliary air regulator faulty (GX, MZ engines only)	b. Test auxiliary air regulator and replace if faulty 6.3, 5.4
	c. Idle boost valve faulty (GX, MZ engines only)	c. Test idle boost valve system and replace faulty components. 5.4
	d. Idle air stabilizer valve not operating (HT, RD, and PL engine only)	d. Test idle switch. 6.1, Test idle air stabilizer valve. 6.3
	e. Air leaking past throttle valve	e. Inspect throttle valve and adjust or replace as required. 5.1
6. Hesitation on acceleration	a. Vacuum (intake air) leak	a. Inspect intake air components for leaking hoses, hose connections, and cracks or other leaks. Repair as required
	b. Fuel injectors clogged	b. Test injector spray pattern and quantity. Replace faulty injectors. 4.7
	c. Cold start valve leaking	c. Test and, if necessary, replace cold start valve. 6.2
	d. Control plunger in fuel distributor binding or fuel distributor faulty	d. Check air flow sensor plate movement and, if necessary, replace fuel distributor. 6.1
	e. Air flow sensor plate out of adjustment	e. Inspect air flow sensor plate position and adjust if necessary. 6.1
	f. Fuel pressure incorrect	f. Check differential regulator, system pressure, and differential pressure. 6.1, 6.4, 6.5
	g. Air flow sensor plate potentiometer faulty or incorrectly adjusted	g. Test air flow sensor plate potentiometer and adjust if necessary. Replace a faulty potentiometer. 6.4
7. Low power	a. Coolant temperature sensor faulty or wire to sensor broken	a. Test coolant temperature sensor and wiring. Repair wiring or replace sensor if faulty. 6.4
	b. Fuel pressure incorrect	b. Check differential pressure regulator, system pressure, and differential pressure. bd;6.1, 6.4, 6.5
	c. Throttle plate not opening fully	c. Check throttle cable adjustment to make sure throttle is opening fully. Adjust cable if necessary. 4.6
	d. Full throttle switch faulty or incorrectly adjusted (HT, RD, and PL engines only)	d. Check throttle switch and adjust if necessary. Replace a faulty switch. 6.1
8. Poor fuel mileage	a. Idle speed, ignition timing, and idle mixture (% CO) out of adjustment	a. Check and adjust. 5.6, Also see **IGNITION**
	b. Cold start valve leaking	b. Test and, if necessary, replace cold start valve. 6.2
	c. Fuel pressure incorrect	c. Check differential pressure regulator, system pressure, and differential pressure. 6.1, 6.4, 6.5
9. Engine continues to run (diesels) after ignition is turned off	a. Incorrect ignition timing or faulty ignition system	a. See **IGNITION**
	b. Engine overheated	b. See **COOLING SYSTEM**

5

continued on next page

3.4 Digifant II Troubleshooting

This information applies specifically to the fuel injection part of the Digifant II engine management system. For troubleshooting other fuel injection systems, see **3.2 CIS Troubleshooting** or **3.3 CIS-E Troubleshooting**. For troubleshooting the Digifant II ignition components, see **IGNITION**. The oxygen sensor system is covered in **EXHAUST SYSTEM AND EMISSION CONTROLS**.

The basic adjustments of engine idle speed, ignition timing, and idle mixture (% CO) are critical to all other phases of Digifant II performance. Before making any other adjustments to the system, make certain that these parameters are within the specifications. See **7.3 Idle Speed**, **7.6 Idle Specifications**, and **IGNITION**.

Table c lists symptoms of Digifant II fuel system problems, their probable causes, and suggested corrective actions. The boldface numbers in the corrective action column indicate the heading in this section of the manual where the applicable test and repair procedures are found.

Table c. Digifant II Troubleshooting

Symptom	Probable cause	Corrective action
1. Cold start - Engine starts hard or fails to start when cold	a. Coolant temperature sensor faulty.	a. Test coolant temperature sensor and replace if necessary. **7.1**
	b. Fuel pump not running.	b. Check fuel pump fuse and fuel pump relay. **4.1, 4.3**
	c. Fuel filter clogged.	c. Check fuel filter. See **LUBRICATION AND MAINTENANCE**
	d. Vacuum (intake air) leak.	d. Inspect intake air components for leaking hoses, hose connections, and cracks or other leaks. Repair as required. Check for loose oil fill cap or dip stick. **7.1**
	e. Low fuel pressure.	e. Test fuel pressure. **7.5**
	f. Electronic control unit faulty.	f. Make electrical tests at control unit connector. Replace faulty control unit. **7.4**
2. Cold running - Engine starts when cold but stalls at idle	a. Coolant temperature sensor faulty.	a. Test coolant temperature sensor and replace if necessary. **7.2**
	b. Electronic control unit faulty.	b. Make electrical tests at control unit connector. Replace faulty control unit. **7.4**
3. Engine idles rough or stalls (cold or warm)	a. Vacuum (intake air) leak.	a. Inspect intake air components for leaking hoses, hose connections, and cracks or other leaks. Repair as required. Check for loose oil fill cap or dip stick. **7.1**
	b. Air flow sensor flap binding or faulty.	b. Check air flow sensor flap. Check air flow sensor resistance. **7.1**
	c. Inadequate fuel being delivered to engine.	c. Test fuel pump. **4.3**
	d. Blocked fuel filter.	d. Replace fuel filter. See **LUBRICATION AND MAINTENANCE**
	e. Idle air stabilizer valve faulty.	e. Test idle switch. **7.3** Test idle air stabilizer valve. **7.3**
	f. Low fuel pressure.	f. Test fuel pressure. **7.5**
	g. Electronic control unit faulty.	g. Make electrical tests at control unit connector. Replace faulty control unit. **7.4**
4. Engine misses, hesitates or stalls under load	a. Air flow sensor flap binding or faulty.	a. Check air flow sensor flap. Check air flow sensor resistance. **7.1**
	b. Intake air preheating system faulty.	b. Test intake air preheating system and replace faulty components as required. **7.2**
	c. Vacuum (intake air) leak.	c. Inspect intake air components for leaking hoses, hose connections, and cracks or other leaks. Repair as required. Check for loose oil fill cap or dip stick. **7.1**
	d. Low fuel pressure.	d. Test fuel pressure. **7.5**

continued on next page

Table c. Digifant II Troubleshooting (continued)

Symptom	Probable cause	Corrective action
5. Engine idles too fast	a. Accelerator pedal, cable, or throttle valve binding. b. Coolant temperature sensor wire disconnected or broken. c. Idle air stabilzer valve faulty.	a. Inspect for worn or broken parts, kinked cable, or other damage. Replace faulty parts. **4.6** Also see **BODY AND INTERIOR**. b. Check wiring between control unit and sensor. **7.2**. c. Test idle switch. **7.3** Test idle air stabilizer valve. **7.3**
6. Low power	a. Air intake restricted. b. Air flow sensor flap not fully opening. c. Throttle plate not opening fully. d. Full throttle switch faulty or incorrectly adjusted. e. Electronic control unit faulty.	a. Check intake air element, housing, and preheating system. **7.2** b. Check movement of air flow sensor plate. Replace air flow sensor. **7.1**. c. Check throttle cable adjustment. to make sure throttle is opening fully. Adjust cable if necessary. **4.6**. d. Check throttle switch and adjust if necessary. Replace a faulty switch. **6.1**. e. Make test at control unit connector. Replace the control unit if it is faulty. **7.4**.
7. Engine continues to run (diesels) after ignition is turned off	a. Incorrect ignition timing or faulty ignition system. b. Engine overheated.	a. See **IGNITION**. b. See **COOLING SYSTEM**.

4. FUEL SUPPLY

Aside from the fuel injection system which controls the amount of fuel metered to the engine, the remainder of the fuel system is dedicated to storing and supplying fuel.

An electric transfer pump, located in the fuel tank, supplies fuel to the fuel reservoir and the main electric fuel pump. The main pump supplies fuel under pressure to the fuel injection system. If, for any reason, adequate electric power is not available to run these pumps, the engine will not run. The fuel injectors, which deliver fuel from the fuel injection system to the engine, are also covered in this section.

Fig. 4-1 shows the fuel reservoir, together with the main fuel pump, the fuel filter, and the fuel accumulator. On Digifant II models, the accumulator is not used.

Absolute cleanliness is essential when working with the fuel system. Even a minute particle of dirt can cause trouble if it reaches an injector. Thoroughly clean the unions before disconnecting any of the fuel line connections. Use only clean tools. Keep removed components clean, and seal or cover them with a clean, lint-free cloth, especially if the repair cannot be finished immediately. When replacing parts, install only new, clean components. Do not use compressed air nearby, and do not move the car while the fuel system is open. Always replace seals, O-rings, and clamps.

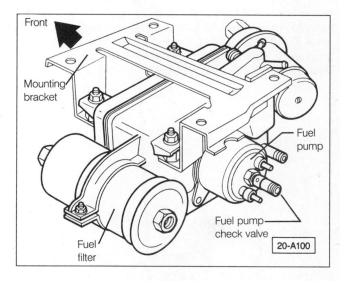

Fig. 4-1. Fuel reservoir, main fuel pump, fuel filter, and accumulator used on models with CIS and CIS-E fuel injection. Reservoir assembly on models with Digifant II is similar.

4.1 Fuses and Relays

Both the transfer pump and the main fuel pump are electric, and operated by a fuel pump relay. If either pump is not running, the cause may be a faulty fuse or a faulty fuel pump relay. In cold weather, water in the fuel may freeze in the pump, causing the circuit to overload and the fuse to fail. Troubleshooting of any fuel pump fault should begin with checking the fuel pump fuse and the fuel pump relay.

For relay and fuse locations and identification, see **ELECTRICAL SYSTEM**. To test the fuel pump relay, see **4.3 Fuel Pump**. For information on testing the Digifant II power supply relay, see **7.4 Electrical Tests**.

CAUTION ——

Fuse and relay locations are subject to change and may vary due to production line changes. Use care when troubleshooting the electrical system at the fuse/relay panel. To resolve problems in identifying a relay, see an authorized Volkswagen dealer.

Operating Fuel Pump For Test

Unless the fuel pump relay receives an rpm signal from the ignition system indicating that the engine is running, the fuel pumps will operate for only a few seconds when the ignition is on. To operate the pumps longer, for fuel system tests without the engine running, the relay must be bypassed to power the pumps directly.

One method is to remove the relay and connect two sockets on the fuse/relay panel. The sockets used are those corresponding to terminals 30 (power input) and 87 (output) of the relay. Fig. 4-2 shows the terminals on some Golf and GTI fuse/relay panels. For fuse/relay panel information on a specific model, see **ELECTRICAL SYSTEM**.

NOTE ——

The jumper wire should be 1.5 mm (16 ga.) and include an in-line fuse holder with a 20 amp fuse (15 amp for Jetta). To avoid fuse/relay panel damage from repeated connecting and disconnecting, also include a toggle switch. A commercially available jumper, Volkswagen special tool no. US 4480/3 (order no. TU4 480 003 25 ZEL), is also available.

With the ignition off and the fuel pump relay removed, use the jumper (toggle switch off) to bridge the sockets in the fuse/relay panel. Turn on the toggle switch to operate the fuel pumps. If the fuel pump does not run except when the jumper is connected, the relay or relay wiring is faulty. If the pump does not run with the jumper in place of the relay, the fault could be in the fuel pump or the electrical wiring to the fuel pump. For more fuel pump electrical testing, see **Fuel Pump Electrical Tests**.

4.2 Transfer Pump

The transfer pump is mounted in the fuel tank and is an integral assembly with the fuel gauge sender. The pump is cooled and lubricated by fuel and may therefore be damaged if allowed to run dry or if the fuel pickup strainer becomes blocked. Access to the transfer pump is from the top of the fuel tank, reached by removing the rear seat bottom.

WARNING ——

When removing the transfer pump and fuel gauge sending unit, the fuel level must be below 3/4 full. If higher, fuel will be spilled when the transfer pump is removed.

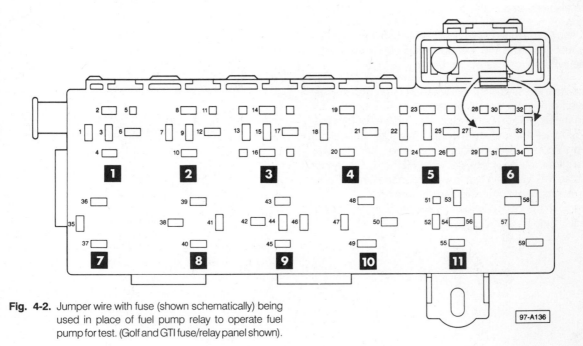

Fig. 4-2. Jumper wire with fuse (shown schematically) being used in place of fuel pump relay to operate fuel pump for test. (Golf and GTI fuse/relay panel shown).

NOTE ─────

Some 1986 Golfs and 1985 through 1987 Jettas have been recalled for transfer pump replacement. On affected cars, the transfer pump may seize in hot weather, causing the engine to stall. To prevent this, a modified fuel pump and filter are installed. If in doubt about whether a particular car is affected or has been repaired, check with an authorized Volkswagen dealer.

To test transfer pump:

1. Remove the rear seat bottom as described in **BODY AND INTERIOR**. Remove the transfer pump and fuel sender gauge access cover by removing the three mounting screws.

2. With the ignition off, disconnect the coil wire fron the center tower of the distributor cap and connect it to ground on the engine block using a jumper wire.

3. With the transmission in neutral, and the parking brake set, operate the starter for 3 to 4 seconds. While the starter is running, and for a few seconds afterward, the running transfer pump should be audible.

4. If the pump is not operating, bypass the fuel pump relay as described in **4.1 Fuses and Relays**.

5. If the transfer pump still does not run, check for voltage at the transfer pump harness connector, as shown in Fig. 4-3. If voltage is reaching the connector, the transfer pump is probably faulty and should be replaced.

NOTE ─────

On the harness connector, one wire is for input voltage, one is to ground, and one is for fuel gauge sending unit output. See the current flow diagrams in **ELECTRICAL SYSTEM** for specific terminal and wire identification.

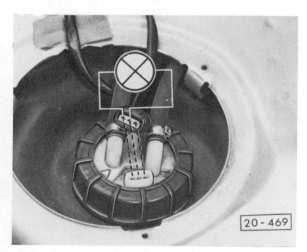

Fig. 4-3. Voltage supply to transfer pump being checked at harness connector using test light (shown schematically).

6. If the transfer pump runs, check its fuel delivery rate. Remove the fuel filler cap. Remove and plug the black transfer pump output hose.

7. Temporarily connect a hose leading to a measuring container, as shown in Fig. 4-4.

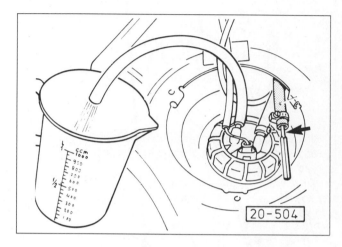

Fig. 4-4. Transfer pump fuel delivery rate being measured. Disconnect and plug output hose (arrow) and temporarily connect test hose.

8. With the fuse/relay panel jumper described in **4.1 Fuses and Relays**, run the pump for exactly 10 seconds. Models with Digifant II should deliver at least 300 cc (10 oz.) of fuel. All others should deliver at least 400 cc (13 ½ oz.).

9. If too little fuel is delivered in the preceding step, remove the transfer pump as decribed below and inspect the pickup strainer/filter for blockage. If when retested the fuel delivery is still too low, the transfer pump is faulty and should be replaced.

To remove and install transfer pump:

1. Disconnect the negative (−) battery terminal.

2. Remove the rear seat bottom as described in **BODY AND INTERIOR**. Remove the access cover and the harness connector as described above.

3. Remove the fuel hoses and discard the hose clamps. Label the hoses so they can be reconnected correctly.

WARNING ─────

Fuel will be exposed. Do not smoke or work near heaters or other fire hazards. Keep a fire extinguisher handy.

4. Loosen and remove the large lock ring on the transfer pump and fuel gauge sending unit assembly by turning it counterclockwise. See Fig. 4-5. Remove the assembly from the fuel tank.

5. Inspect and, if necessary, clean the strainer/filter. Inspect the sealing gasket on the top of the fuel tank. Replace a damaged gasket.

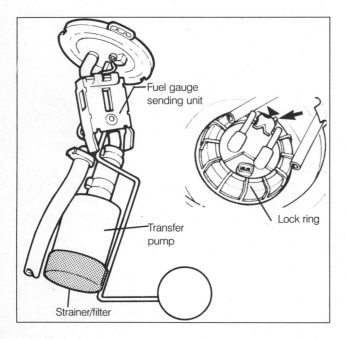

Fig. 4-5. Transfer pump and fuel gauge sending unit assembly shown removed from fuel tank. Inset shows alignment of matching marks (arrow).

6. Place the transfer pump assembly with gasket in position on the tank with the matching marks aligned as shown in Fig. 4-5 above.

7. Install the lock ring and tighten clockwise until snug. Using new hose clamps, connect the fuel hoses. Reconnect the harness connector. Install the access cover and its mounting screws. Install the rear seat bottom and reconnect the negative (−) battery terminal.

4.3 Fuel pump

The electric fuel pump is mounted in the fuel reservoir. The pump is cooled and lubricated by fuel and therefore may be damaged if allowed to run dry. During starting, the pump runs as long as the ignition switch is in the start position and continues to run once the engine starts. Pressure and volume of fuel flow are the important fuel pump performance measurements.

Another important aspect of fuel system performance is residual pressure—the pressure which stays in the system after the engine is off to help prevent vapor lock and hard starting. On cars with CIS and CIS-E, residual fuel pressure is maintained by a fuel pump check valve and an accumulator, shown in Fig. 4-6 and located on the side of the fuel reservoir. On Digifant II models, residual pressure is maintained by a one-way check valve at the fuel pump outlet, and a one-way check valve in the fuel pressure regulator.

On models with CIS and CIS-E, the fuel pump check valve is replaceable. On models with Digifant II, the fuel pump check valve is not replaceable. The procedure for testing fuel delivery rate appears below. To test fuel system pressure and residual pressure, see the headings covering pressure tests under **5. Continuous Injection System (CIS), 6. Continuous Injection System - Electronic (CIS-E),** or **7. Digifant II Fuel Injection.** Before testing the main fuel pump, check that the transfer pump is working correctly as described above in **4.2 Transfer Pump.**

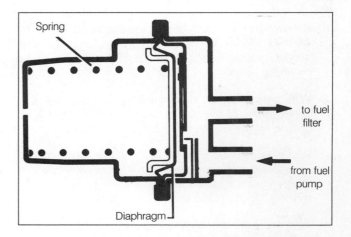

Fig. 4-6. Schematic cross-section of fuel accumulator to damp pressure pulses and maintain residual pressure in CIS and CIS-E fuel systems.

To test fuel pump delivery rate:

1. Disconnect the fuel return line as shown in Fig. 4-7 or Fig. 4-8 and route the end of the fuel return line to a measurement container of at least 1000 ml (1 qt.).

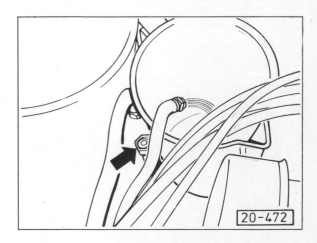

Fig. 4-7. Container being used to measure fuel delivery rate at CIS or CIS-E return line. Return line connection (**arrow**) is located near right (passenger side) front suspension strut tower.

WARNING ——

Fuel will be expelled under pressure as the line is disconnected. Do not disconnect wires that could cause sparks. Do not smoke or work near heaters or other fire hazards. Keep a fire extinguisher handy.

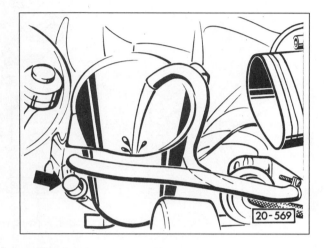

Fig. 4-8. Container being used to measure fuel delivery rate at Digifant II return line. Return line from fuel pressure regulator (lower right) is disconnected (**arrow**) near right (passenger side) front suspension strut tower.

2. Run the fuel pump, as described in **4.1 Fuses and Relays**, for exactly 30 seconds.

3. On models with Digifant II, the pump should deliver at least 500 cc (17 oz.) of fuel.

4. On CIS and CIS-E models, the pump should deliver an amount of fuel according to the chart in Fig. 4-9.

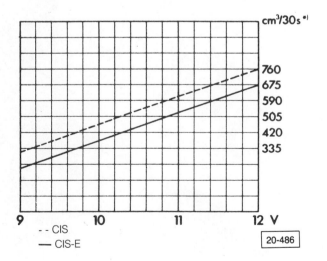

Fig. 4-9. Minimum amount of fuel to be delivered by fuel pump in 30 seconds of operation. Chart shows fuel delivery vs. voltage at fuel pump with pump running (approximately 2 volts less than battery voltage).

If the fuel pump does not run, test as described below under **Fuel Pump Electrical Tests**. If fuel delivery is below specifications, check for leaks, blocked or kinked lines, a blocked filter, or a blocked transfer pump strainer/filter. If no such faults are found, the fuel pump is probably faulty and should be replaced. For more information on the fuel filter, see **LUBRICATION AND MAINTENANCE**.

Fuel Pump Electrical Tests

These tests are for use in finding out why the main fuel pump does not run. If the pump will run with the relay jumper connected as described in **4.1 Fuses and Relays** but not with the fuel pump relay installed, then the fuel pump relay or wiring for the relay is faulty.

The first step is to check the fuel pump fuse (no. 10 on Golf and GTI, no. 5 on Jetta). Replace a failed fuse and test the fuel pump again. If the fuel pump fuse is good, make voltage tests at the fuse/relay panel as described below. The GTI, Golf, and Jetta relay panels are shown in Fig. 4-10.

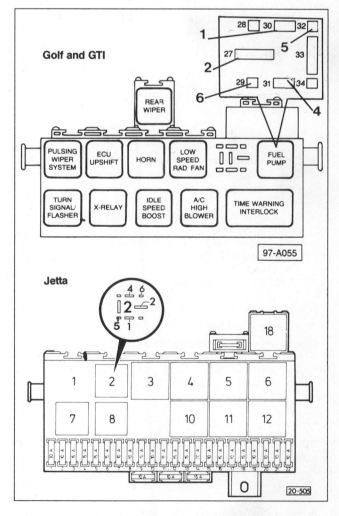

Fig. 4-10. Fuel pump relay location on Golf and GTI (top) and Jetta (bottom). Insets show terminal designations used for testing.

To test fuel pump circuit:

1. Remove the fuel pump relay (no. 6 on Golf and GTI, no. 2 on Jetta) and note whether it has four terminals or five terminals.

2. Turn the ignition on.

3. Using a test light or a voltmeter, check that the voltage between socket 2 and ground and between socket 4 and ground is equal to battery voltage (approximately 12 VDC). See Fig. 4-10 above.

> **NOTE**
>
> If voltage is not present, power is not reaching the fuel pump relay. See the current flow diagrams in **ELECTRICAL SYSTEM** for help in finding and repairing the fault.

4. On cars with five-terminal relays, check that the voltage between sockets 2 and 1, and between sockets 4 and 1 is equal to battery voltage (approximately 12 VDC).

> **NOTE**
>
> If voltage is not present, the socket 1 connection to ground is faulty. See the current flow diagrams in **ELECTRICAL SYSTEM** for help in finding and repairing the fault.

5. On cars with five-terminal relays, check between sockets 5 and 1 for a voltage signal from the ignition system (approximately 12 VDC).

> **NOTE**
>
> If voltage is not present, the ignition signal is not reaching the relay to make the fuel pump keep running. See the current flow diagrams in **ELECTRICAL SYSTEM** for help in finding and repairing the fault.

6. On cars with four-terminal relays, turn the ignition off and connect an LED test light or a voltmeter between sockets 4 and 6. Turn the ignition on and check that there is voltage for approximately 1 second. If not, check the wiring to the knock sensor control unit or, on cars with the Digifant II system, the Digifant control unit.

If the fuel pump will run only with the jumper connected, as described in **4.1 Fuses and Relays**, and no faults are found in the wiring to the relay, then the relay itself is faulty and should be replaced.

If the pump still will not run with the jumper connected, check to see whether voltage is reaching the fuel pump. Disconnect the harness connector from the fuel pump. With the relay removed, the jumper wire connected, and the ignition on, check for voltage at the fuel pump connector as shown in

Fig. 4-11. If there is voltage, then the connection or the fuel pump is faulty. Replace a faulty fuel pump. If there is no voltage, look for a faulty wire or connection between the fuel pump relay and the fuel pump connector.

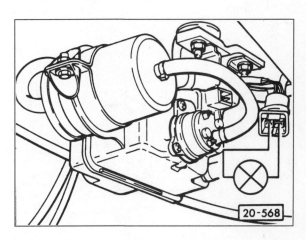

Fig. 4-11. Voltage supply to fuel pump being checked with test light (shown schematically) at fuel pump harness connector. Digifant II pump shown. Others are similar.

Replacing Fuel Pump

Fig. 4-12 is an exploded view of the fuel pump assembly used with CIS and CIS-E. On these pumps, the check valve is available for replacement as a separate part. The pump used with Digifant II is similar, but the check valve is not replaceable.

Always use a new O-ring when installing a new fuel pump or reinstalling the old one. On CIS and CIS-E fuel pumps, always use new sealing washers on the fuel line connections.

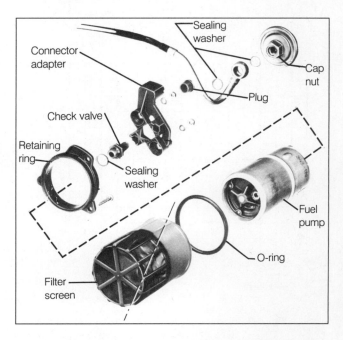

Fig. 4-12. Exploded view of fuel pump assembly used with CIS and CIS-E. Digifant II pump is similar.

To replace:

1. Disconnect the negative (−) battery cable from the battery.

2. Working beneath the car, disconnect the harness connector from the fuel pump. Thoroughly clean the fuel line unions.

3. Temporarily pinch shut the supply line that comes from the transfer pump to the fuel reservoir. See Fig. 4-13 or Fig. 4-14. Place a large container beneath the fuel reservoir for catching fuel.

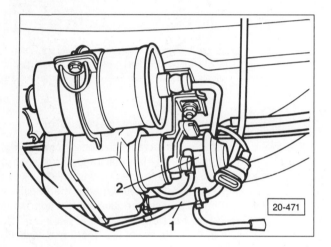

Fig. 4-13. Fuel pump and filter used with CIS and CIS-E. Pinch shut fuel supply line from transfer pump **1** and remove cap nut **2** to drain fuel.

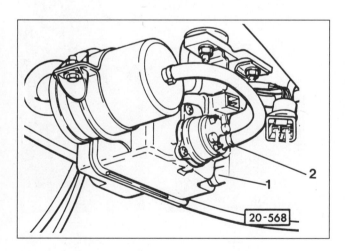

Fig. 4-14. Fuel pump and filter installed on cars with Digifant II. Pinch shut fuel supply line from transfer pump **1** and remove output fuel line **2** to drain fuel.

4. Remove the output fuel line to drain the reservoir. On models with CIS and CIS-E, remove the cap nut, the fuel line, and its two sealing washers. On Digifant II models, remove the hose clamp and the fuel line.

WARNING —

Fuel will be discharged. Do not smoke or work near heaters or other fire hazards. Keep a fire extinguisher handy.

5. Remove the three mounting screws from the fuel pump retaining ring and pull the fuel pump assembly from the fuel reservoir.

NOTE —

Compare the replacement pump to the old pump. If the new pump is equipped with the new positive-lock connector, the mating connector in the wiring harness will have to be changed. Check with an authorized Volkswagen dealer parts department.

6. Moisten the new O-ring with fuel and install it over the fuel pump. After making sure the fuel pump filter screen is clean, install the pump in the fuel reservoir. Secure the retaining ring with three screws. Tighten the screws evenly, checking that the fuel pump is correctly seated.

7. Reconnect the fuel line and the harness connector. Use new sealing washers and hose clamps as required. On CIS and CIS-E models, torque the cap nut to 20 Nm (15 ft. lb.).

8. Reconnect the negative (−) battery cable. Run the engine and check for leaks.

Replacing Fuel Pump Check Valve (CIS and CIS-E only)

All CIS and CIS-E fuel pumps have a check valve at the outlet to help maintain pressure in the fuel system, particularly as an aid to hot starting. This replaceable check valve is one of the most likely causes of low residual fuel pressure and difficult hot starting.

Cars with CIS-E fuel injection have an additional check valve at the fuel reservoir, in the supply line from the transfer pump. This valve is also replaceable. It should be replaced if hot start problems persist, even though the residual fuel pressure meets specifications.

The location of the pump check valve is shown in Fig. 4-15. To replace it, clean and disconnect the fuel line as described above in **Replacing Fuel Pump**. With the line disconnected, the check valve can be removed from the pump. Use new sealing washers for both the check valve and the fuel line union. Torque both parts to 20 Nm (15 ft. lb.).

The CIS-E fuel reservoir check valve is shown in Fig. 4-16. Remove the line from the transfer pump, as shown, to gain access to the valve.

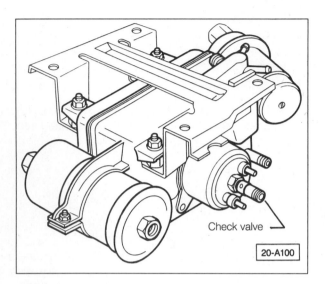

Fig. 4-15. CIS and CIS-E fuel reservoir assembly showing location of fuel pump check valve.

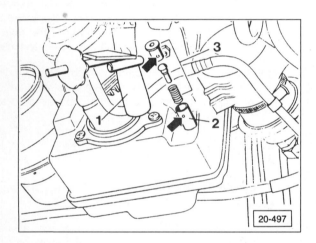

Fig. 4-16. Fuel reservoir check valve **3** found in hose **1** from transfer pump on CIS-E models. Bump (top arrow) must fit into hole (bottom arrow) in tube **2**.

4.4 Fuel Pressure Regulator

Each of the three different fuel injection systems covered in this section uses a different type of fuel pressure regulator to maintain a constant system pressure. All three recirculate excess fuel back to the fuel reservoir near the main fuel pump.

CIS Pressure Relief Valve

CIS system pressure is determined by the pressure relief valve mounted in the fuel distributor. See Fig. 4-17. System pressure can be adjusted by adding or subtracting shims. To measure and adjust system pressure, see **5.5 Fuel Pressure Tests and Specifications**.

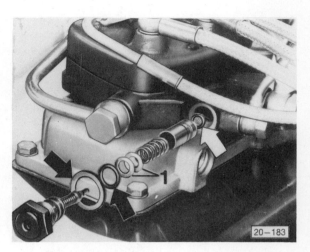

Fig. 4-17. Exploded view of CIS pressure relief valve showing location of adjusting shims (**1**). O-rings and sealing washer (arrows) should always be replaced.

CIS-E Diaphragm Pressure Regulator

The CIS-E diaphragm pressure regulator, shown in Fig. 4-18, is mounted externally on the fuel distributor. In addition to controlling system pressure, it acts as a one-way check valve to maintain residual pressure in the system after the engine is turned off. The diaphragm pressure regulator is not adjustable and should be replaced if system pressure is not within the specifications given in **6.5 Fuel Pressure Tests and Specifications**.

Fig. 4-18. CIS-E diaphragm pressure regulator (**A**)

Digifant II Fuel Pressure Regulator

The Digifant II fuel pressure regulator shown in Fig. 4-19 is a diaphragm-type, similar to that used on CIS-E. The most significant differences are that Digifant II operates at a much lower system pressure, and that system pressure varies with engine load (vacuum) because of a connection to the intake manifold.

The pressure regulator is mounted to the end of the fuel rail which supplies the fuel injectors. It is not adjustable and should be replaced if system pressure is not within specifications given in **7.5 Fuel Pressure Tests and Specifications.**

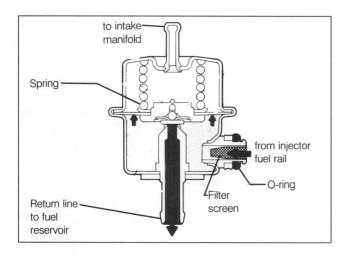

Fig. 4-19. Schematic view of Digifant II pressure regulator. Vacuum hose connection to engine intake manifold adjusts fuel pressure at high engine loads.

4.5 Evaporative Emission Controls

Fig. 4-20 is an exploded view of the fuel tank and its evaporative emission control components. The evaporative emission system is a closed system that provides venting for the fuel tank but traps the fuel vapors that would otherwise be vented into the atmosphere.

The system collects fuel vapors from the fuel tank in a charcoal canister which is then vented to the engine air intake. The main components of the system are the charcoal canister (located in engine compartment), the bypass valve (near the charcoal canister), and the gravity valve and breather valve (both located in the top of the fuel tank filler neck).

The charcoal canister collects fuel vapors from the tank when the engine is idling or stopped. During normal driving, the fuel vapors are drawn into the engine. The gravity/vent valve is connected to the charcoal canister and is normally open. In the event the car is inverted during an accident, the valve closes to prevent fuel and fuel vapors from escaping.

The breather valve vents the vapors from the filler neck area to the expansion tank. The valve is open when the fuel filler cap is installed and closed when the cap is removed. This prevents the tank from being overfilled if the car is parked on an incline.

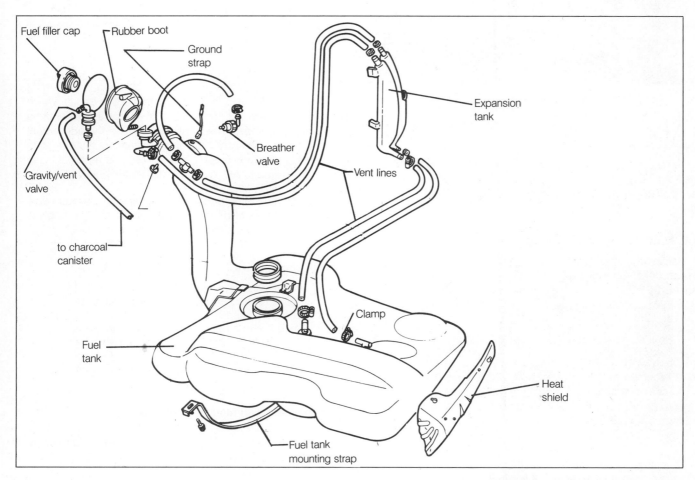

Fig. 4-20. Exploded view of fuel tank and evaporative emission control components.

To inspect the breather valve, remove the vent hose from the valve and connect an auxiliary hose to the valve's port. Blow into the hose. With the fuel filler cap installed air should pass through the valve. With the fuel filler cap removed, air should not flow through the valve.

To inspect the gravity valve, first remove the valve. Working from inside the rear cargo area, pull the valve up and out of the filler neck. With the valve in a vertical position, air should pass through the valve. With the valve tilted at a 45° angle, no air should pass through the valve.

Testing Charcoal Canister Bypass Valve

The charcoal canister connections and the bypass valve are shown in Fig. 4-21. The valve is tested by trying to pass air through it to determine when it is open or closed.

Fig. 4-21. Charcoal canister **1** and bypass valve **6**, canister mounting bolts **2**, line to gravity/vent valve **3**, line to intake manifold **4**, and vacuum line **5** to spacer on throttle body.

To test the bypass valve disconnect the gravity/vent valve line from the bypass valve, as shown in Fig. 4-22, and blow into the open port of the valve. It should be closed and not pass any air.

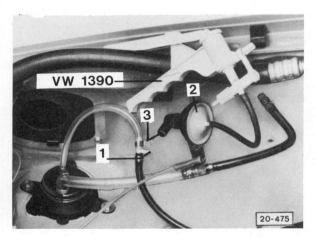

Fig. 4-22. Connector **1** disconnected from charcoal canister bypass valve **2** at port **3** for testing. (Shown with vacuum pump connected to valve to test valve function).

Apply vacuum to the small vacuum hose connection on the bypass valve. See Fig. 4-22 above. When vacuum is applied, the valve should be open and air should be able to pass through. Replace a bypass valve which fails either of these tests.

The charcoal canister and bypass valve hose routing is slightly different for cars with Digifant II. The system is shown in Fig. 4-23. The valve can be tested as described above.

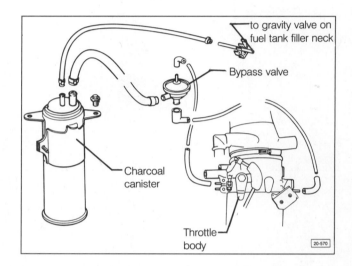

Fig. 4-23. Charcoal canister and bypass valve used with Digifant II system.

4.6 Accelerator Cable

Cars with automatic transmission have two cables which connect the accelerator pedal to both the throttle valve and the transmission kickdown mechanism. Because the adjustment of the accelerator and throttle cables may affect the operation of the automatic transmission, adjustment and repair of these cables is covered in **AUTOMATIC TRANSMISSION**.

Cars with manual transmission have one accelerator cable linking the accelerator pedal to the throttle body. This cable is easily adjusted or replaced using ordinary hand tools.

> **CAUTION** ——
>
> *The throttle valve idle bypass screw is factory-set and should not be adjusted in an attempt to correct idle speed. For more information on idle speed adjustments, see the appropriate heading under **5. Continuous Injection System (CIS)**, **6. Continuous Injection System-Electronic (CIS-E)**, or **7. Digifant II Fuel Injection***

To adjust (cars with manual transmission):

1. Have a helper push the accelerator pedal down to its full-throttle position.

2. If the cable requires adjustment, remove the retaining clip and the grommet from the bracket atop the cylinder head cover. See Fig. 4-24.

NOTE ——

With the pedal fully depressed, the throttle valve should barely reach the full-throttle stop on the housing, leaving a maximum clearance of 1 mm (.04 in.). If the throttle valve reaches the stop before full-throttle, the cable will be overstressed and may fail.

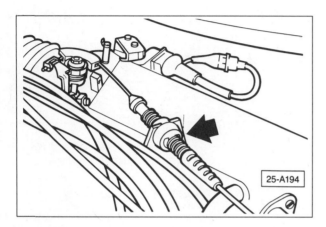

Fig. 4-24. Retaining clip and grommet (arrow) used to adjust accelerator cable tension.

3. Adjust cable tension by repositioning the grommet and retaining clip in a different groove. Use a groove closer to the throttle valve to tighten the cable. Use a groove farther from the throttle valve to loosen it.

To remove and install the cable, remove the retaining clip and the grommet to slacken the cable, and disconnect the cable end from the throttle valve lever. Working from inside the car, pull the cable end from its ball socket in the accelerator pedal assembly. Pull the cable through the firewall from the engine compartment. Installation is the reverse of removal. Adjust the new cable as described above. Finally, depress the accelerator pedal several times to check for binding before driving.

4.7 CIS and CIS-E Fuel Injectors

The mechanical fuel injectors used with CIS and CIS-E fuel injection are actually precision nozzles. Above a certain minimum pressure, the injector nozzles open and continuously spray fuel into the engine's intake ports.

The injectors fit into two-piece inserts which thread into the cylinder head (intake manifold on 16-valve engines). The injectors are held in place in the inserts by thick rubber O-rings. One injector, its two-piece insert, and the O-rings are shown in Fig. 4-25.

The most common fuel injector problems are low fuel flow or an uneven spray pattern, both caused by contaminated fuel or carbon deposits. Some signs of faulty injectors are rough idle, poor starting, and detonation (pinging) at full throttle. Keep injectors functioning properly by eeping them clean. See **LU-**

BRICATION AND MAINTENANCE for information on fuel filter maintenance, and on a fuel additive which Volkswagen recommends for reducing and preventing carbon deposits.

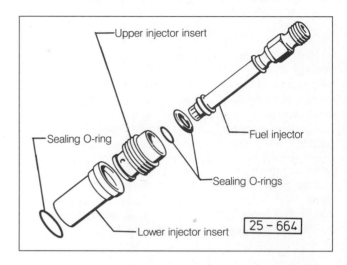

Fig. 4-25. Components of CIS and CIS-E fuel injector.

Removing and Installing Fuel Injectors

The fuel injectors must be removed for inspection or testing. As described above, the injectors are held in the inserts by thick rubber O-rings. To remove the injectors simply pull them straight out, forcing them out of the O-rings, as indicated in Fig. 4-26. Leave the fuel lines attached. Pull straight and pull only on the injectors themselves, not on the fuel lines.

Fig. 4-26. CIS and CIS-E fuel injectors. Remove by pulling straight out (arrow). Do not pull on fuel line.

It is not normally necessary to remove the injector inserts, except to replace the O-rings and cure air leaks which can cause rough idling. The inserts have an integral hex socket and are removed using a hex wrench—12 mm on CIS and all 16-valve engines and 13 mm on all other CIS-E engines. Replace all the O-rings. See Fig. 4-25 above. Moisten the O-rings with fuel for installation. Clean the threads of the upper insert and reinstall using Loctite® T primer and Loctite® 620 thread locking compound, or equivalent. Torque the upper injector insert to 20 Nm (15 ft. lb.).

Injector installation is the reverse of removal. Replace the thick rubber O-rings, soaking the new ones in fuel for several minutes before installing them. Then press the injector into the insert until the O-ring is fully seated in its groove.

Quick-checking Injectors

Each individual injector can be easily quick-checked to evaluate its spray pattern and to check for leakage. A more involved test, using special equipment, compares the injection quantity from all four injectors to check that both the fuel distributor and the injectors are supplying the same amount of fuel to each cylinder. Finally, a special injector tester can be used to clean injectors, measure opening pressure, or check and flush new injectors prior to installation.

If the quick-check suggests that more testing is necessary and the special equipment is not available, we suggest having the injectors tested by an authorized Volkswagen dealer or other qualified and properly equipped repair shop.

To quick-check injectors:

1. Remove one injector, leaving the fuel hose connected, as shown in Fig. 4-26 above. Aim the removed injector into a fuel-resistant container.

2. Remove the large rubber duct from the top of the air flow sensor.

3. Remove the fuel pump relay from the fuse/relay panel and install a fused jumper wire to run the fuel pump, as described in **4.1 Fuses and Relays**.

4. Using a magnetic tool such as the one shown in Fig. 4-27, lift the air flow sensor plate and observe the injector's spray pattern. The injector should discharge a fine mist of fuel in an even, cone-shaped pattern.

> **WARNING ▬**
>
> *Fuel will be discharged from all four injectors during this check. Keep the test time short and discharge as little fuel as possible. Do not smoke or work near heaters or other fire hazards. Keep a fire extinguisher handy.*

5. Release the sensor plate and hold the injector in a horizontal position. It should not drip fuel.

6. Disconnect the fuel pump jumper wire to stop the pump.

> **NOTE ▬**
>
> An injector that has an irregular spray pattern, or drips when the sensor plate is at rest with the fuel pump running, should be replaced.

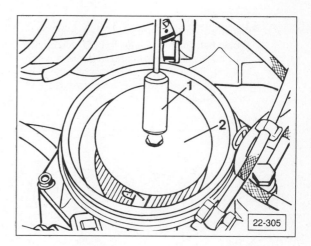

Fig. 4-27. Magnetic tool (**1**) being used to lift air flow sensor plate (**2**) for fuel injector quick-check.

Testing Injector Fuel Delivery

A similar but more complicated test is used to compare the rate of fuel delivery from all four injectors as a means of isolating a bad injector or fuel distributor. Remove all four injectors from the engine, with fuel lines attached, and connect them to four identical measuring containers as shown in Fig. 4-28.

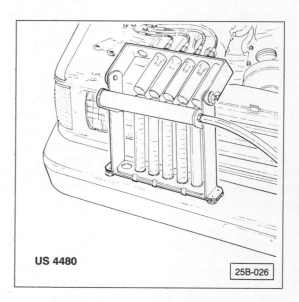

Fig. 4-28. Volkswagen special tool US 4480 being used to collect and measure fuel injectors' output. Injectors are inserted at top.

Use a jumper wire in place of the fuel pump relay to run the fuel pump during the test as described in **4.1 Fuses and Relays**. Use Volkswagen special tool no. VW 1348/1 (order no. TV1 348 001 25 ZEL), to raise and hold the sensor plate in the various test positions.

Install the Volkswagen special tool as shown in Fig. 4-29. Carefully push the center sleeve all the way down, then turn the adjusting knob clockwise until the tool's magnetic tip just contacts the sensor plate center bolt. Turn the adjusting screw counterclockwise to raise the sensor plate to a point just before any of the injectors start spraying.

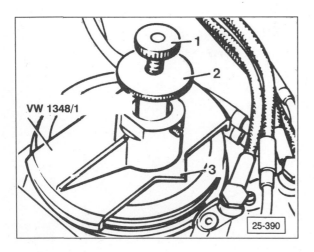

Fig. 4-29. Volkswagen special tool VW 1348/1 with adjusting knob (**1**) and sleeve (**2**) being used to simulate sensor plate position at idle, full throttle, or any point between. Pointer (**3**) faces fuel distributor.

WARNING ━━

Do not smoke or work near heaters or other fire hazards. Keep a fire extinguisher handy.

Run the fuel pump and raise the sensor plate to conduct the test. The tool's center sleeve has two detents—one raises the plate to a position simulating idle and the second raises it higher to simulate full throttle. At the idle setting, with 20 ml collected from each injector (approximately 2 minutes) there should be no more than 3 ml difference between any two. At the full throttle setting, with 80 ml collected from each injector (approximately 40 seconds) there should be no more than 8 ml difference.

If the difference in fuel quantity is greater than allowed, select the two injectors with the lowest and highest values. Loosen the unions, remove them from their fuel lines, exchange them, and repeat the test. If the same injector delivers a low amount of fuel, it is faulty and should be replaced. If the same container collects a low amount from a different injector, then that fuel line is blocked or kinked, or the fuel distributor is faulty. When reinstalling fuel line unions to injectors, torque them to 25 Nm (18 ft. lb.).

Cleaning Injectors

A special tool for cleaning injectors and testing their opening pressure is shown in Fig. 4-30. Remove the injector from its fuel line by loosening the union, and install the injector on the tester line as shown. Pump several times to purge the air from the line. When spraying normally the injector will make a high-pitched squeal. Pump slowly and read the injector opening pressure on the gauge as the injector starts to spray. It should open at 3.0 to 4.1 bar (44 to 59 psi). Any injector which opens or leaks at a lower pressure or has an uneven spray pattern should be replaced.

WARNING ━━

Use only Shell mineral spirit 135 or equivalent when testing or cleaning injectors using pressure tester. Shell mineral spirit 135 is flammable. Do not smoke or work near heaters or other fire hazards. Keep a fire extinguisher handy.

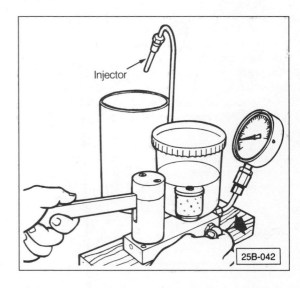

Fig. 4-30. CIS and CIS-E fuel injector pressure tester (Volkswagen special tool no. US 8034) being used to clean and test fuel injector.

4.8 Digifant II Fuel Injectors

The injectors used on models with Digifant are electrically operated solenoid valves which are turned on and off by the Digifant II control unit. Fig. 4-31 shows a cut-away view of one injector. The four injectors are connected to a common fuel supply, called the fuel rail, shown in Fig. 4-32.

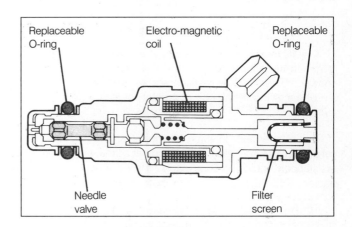

Fig. 4-31. Schematic view of fuel injector used on models with Digifant.

5

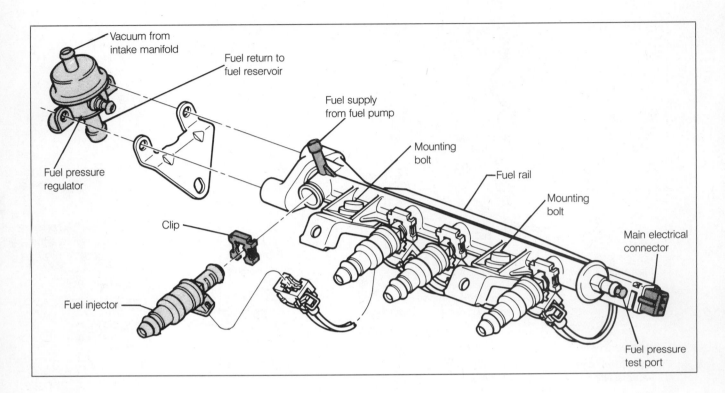

Fig. 4-32. Digifant II fuel rail is common fuel supply and wiring to all four injectors.

The injectors are switched on and off (open and closed) by the Digifant control unit. In each injector, the solenoid opens the needle valve to spray fuel into the intake port. All four injectors open at the same time and are synchronized to engine rpm. The control unit regulates fuel delivery to the engine by controlling how long the injectors are open each time. The injectors are not repairable, and must be replaced if found to be faulty.

Testing Injectors

A faulty injector can be detected by checking resistance at the main electrical connector on the end of the fuel rail, as shown in Fig. 4-33. The resistance should be between 3.7 and 5.0 ohms. If the resistance is greater, at least one injector is faulty.

To isolate a faulty injector, disconnect the individual electrical connectors from the injectors, one at a time, and retest. The resistance should increase each time an injector is disconnected. **Table d** lists the approximate resistance values.

If the resistance does not increase when a particular injector is disconnected, check the resistance directly at that injector. The resistance should be between 15 and 20 ohms. If it is, check the wiring between the main connector and the injector connector. If it is not, the injector is faulty and should be replaced.

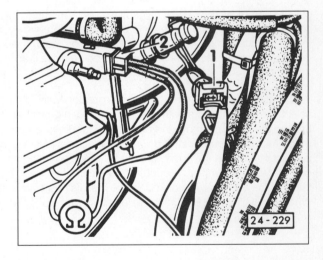

Fig. 4-33. Digifant II fuel injector resistance being checked. Harness connector (**1**) is disconnected and ohmmeter (shown schematically) is connected across terminals of main electrical connector (**2**).

Table d. Digifant II Fuel Injector Resistance

Number of injectors connected	Resistance at main electrical connector
4	3.7 to 5.0 ohms
3	5.0 to 6.7 ohms
2	7.5 to 10.0 ohms
1	15.0 to 20.0 ohms

To check if the injectors are receiving battery voltage, connect a LED test light to the wiring harness connector as shown in Fig. 4-34. With the transmission in neutral and the parking brake set, activate the starter and check that the LED flickers. If not, test the Digifant control unit as described in **7.4 Electrical Tests** or check for a fault in the wiring harness to the injector connector.

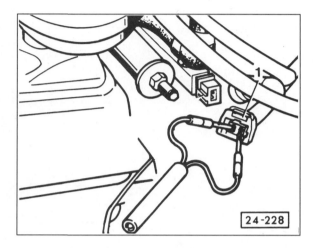

Fig. 4-34. LED test light connected to injector wiring harness (**1**) to check for battery voltage.

Removing and Installing Injectors

The fuel injectors are removed and installed by removing the fuel rail. Although the entire assembly of fuel rail and injectors can be removed as a unit, it may be easier to first remove the fuel rail from the injectors and then remove the individual injectors from the engine.

To remove injector fuel rail and injectors:

1. Disconnect the negative (−) battery terminal, and disconnect the main electrical connector at the fuel rail.

2. Remove the idle stabilizer valve. Disconnect the electrical connector, then remove the hoses and mounting bracket. See Fig. 4-35.

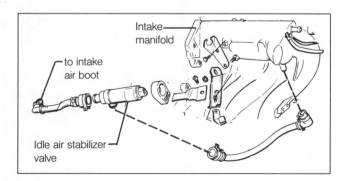

Fig. 4-35. Exploded view of idle air stabilizer system showing mounting brackets and hose connections.

3. Loosen the hose clamp and disconnect the crankcase ventilation hose from the throttle body. Swing the hose out of the way.

4. Remove the vacuum hose and the blue fuel return hose from the fuel pressure regulator. See Fig. 4-36.

> **WARNING** ——
>
> *Fuel will be expelled. Do not smoke or work near heaters or other fire hazards. Keep a fire extinguisher handy.*

5. Remove two Phillips-head screws and remove the pressure regulator. Using a 6-mm hex wrench, remove the socket-head mounting bolt and the pressure regulator mounting bracket.

> **NOTE** ——
>
> It may be easier to remove the rubber intake air boot to gain better access to the pressure regulator. To remove the boot, remove the clamps and pull the boot from the engine. Cover the openings with a clean, lint-free cloth.

6. Using a 5-mm hex wrench, remove the two socket-head fuel rail mounting bolts. Pry off the injector mounting clips using a small, flat-bladed screwdriver.

7. Remove the black fuel supply line from the connection atop the fuel rail.

> **WARNING** ——
>
> *Fuel will be expelled. Do not smoke or work near heaters or other fire hazards. Keep a fire extinguisher handy.*

8. Disconnect the injector connectors and pull the fuel rail from the injectors.

> **NOTE** ——
>
> If necessary, cut the wire ties which secure the wiring harness to the fuel rail, and disconnect the connectors after removing the fuel rail.

9. Remove each injector from its insert, and check the insert tightness. Remove any that are loose using a 10 mm hex wrench.

Installation is reverse of removal. Replace injector or pressure regulator O-rings that are hard, cracked, or otherwise damaged. Clean the threads of the injector inserts, apply thread locking compound to the threads, and install and torque them to 20 Nm (15 ft. lb.). Be sure the injector's electrical connections are aligned correctly and that the injectors are fully seated prior to installing the fuel rail. Use new hose clamps.

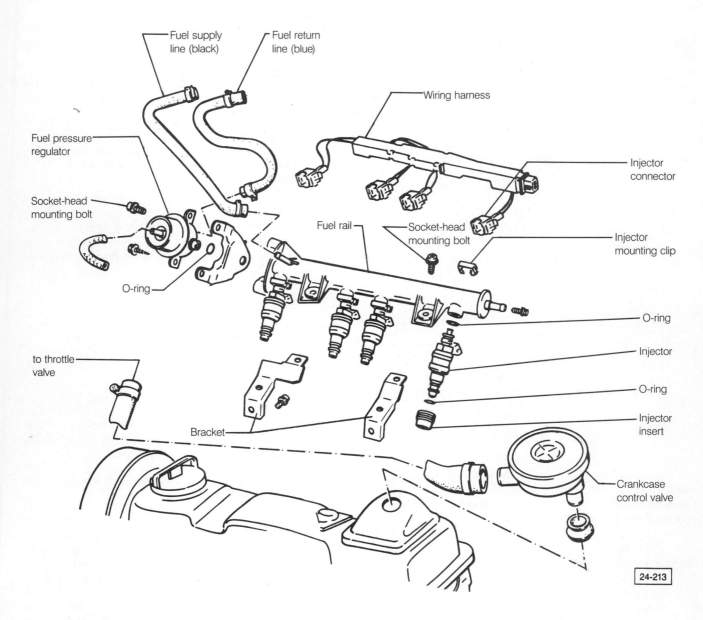

Fig. 4-36. Exploded view of Digifant II fuel rail and fuel injector mounting components.

Torque the fuel rail mounting bolts to 10 Nm (7 ft. lb.) and the pressure regulator mounting bolt to 15 Nm (11 ft. lb.). Mount the idle stabilizer valve and torque the mounting bolt to 10 Nm (7 ft. lb.). Reconnect the main electrical connector and the negative (−) battery terminal. Recheck the resistance of the injectors as described above in **Testing Injectors**.

5. CONTINUOUS INJECTION SYSTEM (CIS)

Fig. 5-1 is a schematic view of CIS fuel injection. The system is almost entirely mechanical, utilizing the influence and control of fuel pressure to accurately meter fuel. Other than the main fuel pump, electrically operated components are only used in an auxiliary role, to help adapt the fuel mixture to such extreme conditions as cold weather starting and warm-up.

The continuous injection system (CIS) is so-called because, unlike many other fuel injection systems, the injectors do not open and close—they deliver fuel continuously. The main function of the fuel injectors is to atomize the continuous flow of fuel being supplied under pressure from the fuel distributor.

The heart of CIS is the mixture control unit, consisting of the air flow sensor and the fuel distributor. Air entering the engine raises the air flow sensor plate. A lever connected to the sensor plate raises the control plunger in the fuel distributor, increasing the quantity of fuel flowing to the injectors in proportion to the air flow. Fuel pressure working against the control plunger, called control pressure, helps regulate the plunger's movement and pushes it back down for less fuel flow when there is less air flow.

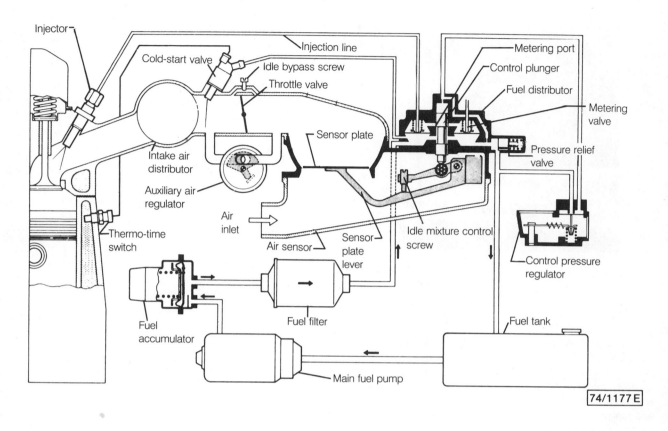

Fig. 5-1. Schematic view of CIS fuel injection. Arrows indicate direction of fuel flow.

The cold start valve, the auxiliary air regulator, and the control pressure regulator are used to adapt the system to different operating conditions. The cold-start valve is like a fifth injector, and performs a choke-like function. It injects additional fuel into the intake manifold during starting to provide a richer fuel mixture when the engine is cold. The cold-start valve is operated electrically.

The auxiliary air regulator opens when the engine is cold to allow a small amount of additional air to bypass the throttle plate and boost the idle speed. The control pressure regulator improves driveability when the engine is cold by reducing control pressure. This not only creates a greater pressure differential across the metering valves, causing more fuel flow for a given air flow (a richer mixture), but also improves throttle response by allowing the control plunger in the fuel distributor to rise more easily.

CIS is designed so that all the auxiliary electrical components can be tested using only a test light and an ohmmeter, but the basic fuel metering system is highly dependent on fuel pressure. Evaluation of the system's basic function requires the use of a fuel pressure gauge. See **5.5 Fuel Pressure Tests and Specifications** for more information.

5.1 Air Flow Measurement and Fuel Metering

The throttle valve, which is operated by the accelerator cable, regulates the amount of air drawn in by the engine. The

most basic function of the fuel injection system is to measure that incoming air and precisely meter a proportional amount of fuel. The components responsible for air flow measurement and fuel metering are the air flow sensor and the fuel distributor.

The throttle valve is adjusted at the factory. It does not require routine adjustment and should not be used to adjust idle speed. The procedure below for the throttle valve's basic adjustment is provided in the event that the factory adjustment has been altered. The air flow sensor plate can be adjusted if it is found to be out of alignment. After the adjustment, idle speed and idle mixture (% CO) will need to be adjusted also. The fuel distributor is precisely calibrated when it is manufactured and, except for adjusting system pressure, it cannot be adjusted or repaired.

Throttle Valve Basic Adjustment

The purpose of the throttle valve adjusting screw is to provide a positive stop and prevent the valve from closing so far that it becomes worn or damaged.

To correct a faulty throttle valve adjustment, use a screwdriver to back off the throttle valve adjusting screw until there is clearance between its tip and the throttle valve lever. The adjusting screw is shown in Fig. 5-2. Place a thin piece of paper between the throttle valve adjusting screw and the throttle valve lever. With the throttle valve closed, turn the screw in until it lightly contacts the paper. From this position, remove the paper and turn the screw in an additional ½ turn.

Fig. 5-2. Location of adjusting screw (arrow) for throttle valve basic adjustment (not used to adjust idle speed).

Air Flow Sensor

The air flow sensor measures all the air being drawn in by the engine. Air flows past the air flow sensor plate and the plate is lifted, in turn lifting the control plunger in the fuel distributor to meter the fuel. The sensor plate and its cone-shaped venturi are carefully designed to achieve the proper balance of air flow and fuel metering for all flow rates from idle to full throttle. If the sensor plate is off-center or binding, or the lever has too much resistance, the fuel distributor cannot respond properly to the air flow sensor.

To check and adjust:

1. Remove the rubber intake air boot from the top of the air flow sensor.

2. Disconnect the coil wire from the center tower of the distributor cap and connect it to ground, using a jumper wire if necessary. Actuate the starter for approximately 10 seconds to pressurize the fuel system.

3. Using a magnetic tool, lift the sensor plate slowly to check that the resistance, due to fuel pressure resisting movement of the control plunger, is uniform throughout the entire range of travel. Move the sensor plate quickly back to its rest position. There should be no resistance.

4. If the sensor plate binds as it is moved through the air cone, loosen the center bolt and center the sensor plate. Push down on the plate lightly to check that it is correctly centered in the air cone.

5. If the sensor plate is hard to move or moves with uneven resistance, remove the air flow sensor from the air filter housing. Clean and lubricate the sensor plate lever pivot so that it moves smoothly.

6. If the resistance encountered in moving the sensor plate is caused by a binding control plunger, remove and clean the plunger as described below in **Fuel Distributor**. If it still binds, replace the fuel distributor.

7. Reconnect the coil wire and run the engine until it reaches normal operating temperature. Then ground the coil wire and pressurize the fuel system as described in step 2.

8. Check the height of the air flow sensor plate. At rest, the front edge of the plate should be aligned with the narrowest point in the venturi as shown in Fig. 5-3. Adjust the height by bending the spring clip below the plate.

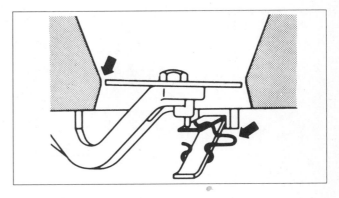

Fig. 5-3. Correct air flow sensor plate rest position. Front edge of plate (left arrow) should be neither above nor more than 0.5 mm (.020 in.) below narrowest point of venturi cone. Adjust height by bending wire spring stop (right arrow).

9. Check and, if necessary, adjust idle speed and idle mixture (% CO). See **5.6 Idle Specifications (RPM and % CO)**.

Fuel Distributor

The fuel distributor's control plunger, moving up or down in its cylinder, uncovers or covers the metering ports leading to the four metering valves—one for each injector. The metering valves maintain a constant pressure differential for precise control at all fuel flow rates. A cross-section of one metering valve is shown in Fig. 5-4.

The fuel distributor is not normally a source of problems. It is, however, a precision device that is easily damaged by plugging or corrosion from contaminated fuel. For fuel filter maintenance information, see **LUBRICATION AND MAINTE-NANCE**. On some cars, a mini-filter is installed during manufacture in the fuel inlet bolt at the fuel distributor. This filter should be removed and a normal bolt installed in its place at a specified interval. For more information on identifying and replacing the mini-filter, see **LUBRICATION AND MAINTE-NANCE**. Check fuel distributor function by measuring injection quantity, as described in **4.7 CIS and CIS-E Fuel Injectors**.

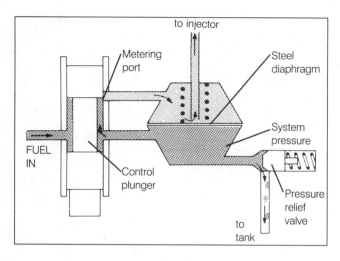

Fig. 5-4. Cross-section of one fuel distributor metering valve. Pressure in upper chamber, combined with spring pressure, deflects diaphragm and increases opening to injector.

Fig. 5-5 illustrates the fuel distributor's fuel line connections and mounting detail. If either the fuel distributor or the air flow sensor is repaired or replaced, the idle speed and idle mixture (% CO) should be adjusted. See **5.6 Idle Specifications (RPM and % CO)..** Before making the adjustments, make sure the air flow sensor plate position is correctly adjusted as described above in **Air Flow Sensor**.

To remove and clean the control plunger, remove the two mounting screws from the top of the fuel distributor and pull the fuel distributor from the air flow sensor assembly. Remove the control plunger and clean it with carburetor cleaner or equivalent. Lubricate the control plunger with a light coat of fuel and reinstall it with the small end facing down toward the air flow sensor plate lever.

5

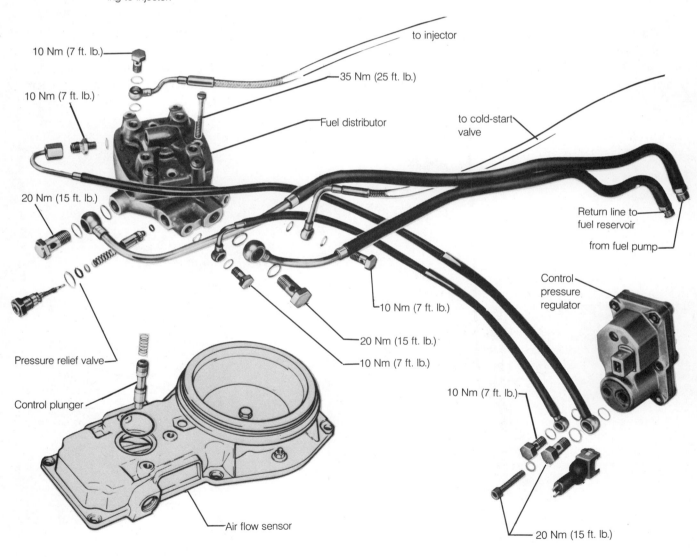

Fig. 5-5. CIS fuel distributor mounting and fuel line connections. Torque values shown are for installation.

5.2 Cold Start Enrichment

The electrically operated cold-start valve sprays extra fuel into the intake manifold for several seconds when the starter is actuated and the engine is cold. The valve is controlled by the thermo-time switch, located in the cylinder head coolant outlet. When the engine is cold, the switch is closed allowing power to reach the valve and open it. When the engine is warm, the switch is open and the valve does not operate. To limit valve operation and prevent flooding, the electric current also warms the switch and opens the circuit after a few seconds. The cold-start valve and the thermo-time switch are shown in Fig. 5-6.

If the cold-start valve fails to inject fuel during cold starting, it will be difficult or impossible to start the engine. If the cold-start valve leaks, the engine may receive extra fuel at the wrong time and become flooded, especially if the engine is hot.

To test cold start valve:

1. Make sure engine coolant temperature is below 86°F (30°C). Preferably the engine should sit for several hours.

2. Remove the two screws holding the cold start valve to the intake manifold. Without disconnecting the fuel line or the harness connector, remove the cold start valve from the intake manifold.

3. Disconnect the coil wire from the center tower of the distributor cap and connect it to ground, using a jumper wire if necessary.

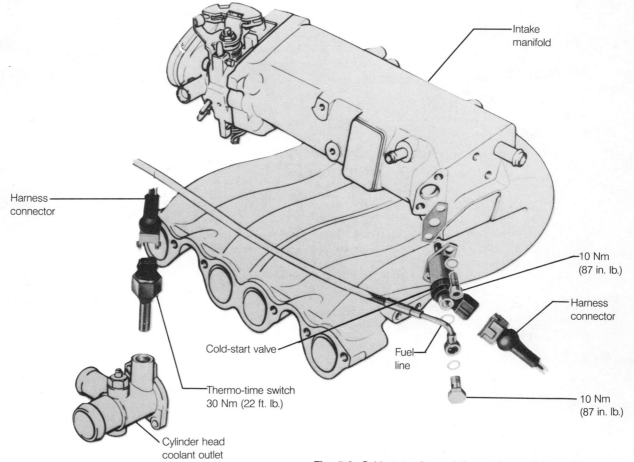

Harness connector

Intake manifold

10 Nm (87 in. lb.)

Harness connector

Cold-start valve

Fuel line

Thermo-time switch 30 Nm (22 ft. lb.)

10 Nm (87 in. lb.)

Cylinder head coolant outlet

Fig. 5-6. Cold-start valve and thermo-time switch used to provide extra fuel for cold starting.

4. Wipe dry the nozzle of the cold start valve. Point the valve into a transparent container, and have a helper actuate the starter. See Fig. 5-7.

WARNING ――

Fuel will be expelled. Do not smoke or work near heaters or other fire hazards. Keep a fire extinguisher handy.

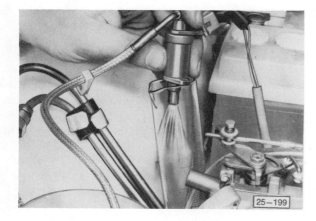

Fig. 5-7. Cold-start valve operation being checked.

NOTE ――

The valve should spray in an even, cone-shaped pattern until the thermo-time switch interrupts the circuit. An irregular spray pattern indicates a dirty or faulty cold start valve. If the valve does not spray, test the thermo-time switch as described below.

5. Wipe the nozzle dry. The valve should not drip for at least a minute. If it does, it is faulty and should be replaced.

To test thermo-time switch:

1. Make sure engine coolant temperature is below 86°F (30°C). Preferably the engine should sit for several hours.

2. Disconnect the coil wire from the center tower of the distributor cap and connect it to ground, using a jumper wire if necessary.

3. Disconnect the cold-start valve harness connector and connect a test light across the connector terminals, as shown in Fig. 5-8.

4. Actuate the starter while observing the test light. The test light should light for several seconds, then go out. The amount of time that the light should stay on depends on coolant temperature. See the graph in Fig. 5-9.

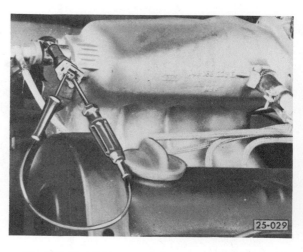

Fig. 5-8. Test light connected across cold-start valve harness connector. Location shown is different than on cars covered by this manual.

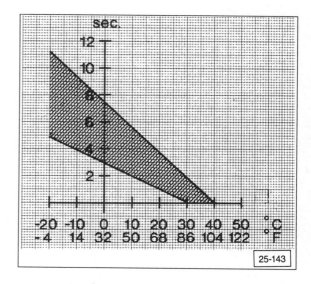

Fig. 5-9. Graph of thermo-time switch response to coolant temperature. Switch completes circuit to open cold-start valve for number of seconds shown. Example: at coolant temperature of 68°F (20°C), switch is closed for 1 to 3.7 seconds.

NOTE ――

If the test light does not light, it is either because voltage is not reaching the connector due to faulty wiring, or because the path to ground (through the thermo-time switch) is interrupted by a faulty switch or wire. Consult the current flow diagrams in **ELECTRICAL SYSTEM** for help in identifying wires and terminals.

To replace the thermo-time switch, first drain the coolant from the engine as described in **COOLING SYSTEM**. Use a thread sealant and torque the new switch to 30 Nm (22 ft. lb.). Then, refill the cooling system with coolant.

5.3 Cold Running Enrichment

To compensate for cold running conditions, the control pressure regulator provides a richer mixture (higher proportion of fuel) when the engine is cold. The function of the control pressure regulator is similar to that of the choke on a carburetor. The control pressure regulator is mounted to the cylinder block near the oil filter flange. See Fig. 5-5 above.

Fig. 5-10 is a schematic diagram that shows the relationship of the control pressure regulator to the fuel distributor. When the engine is cold, the control pressure regulator allows more fuel to be delivered to the injectors by reducing the control pressure above the control plunger. Above the desired pressure, the control pressure regulator bypasses excess fuel to the fuel return line.

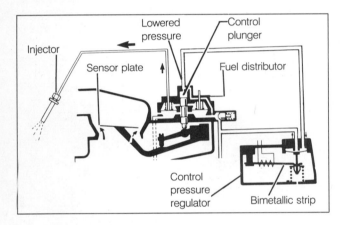

Fig. 5-10. Schematic diagram of control pressure regulator and fuel distributor. When powered with ignition on and engine running, heating element reduces valve opening to increase control pressure to normal warm-engine level.

When the engine is cold, a bimetallic strip holds the regulator wide open to minimize control pressure and provide the richest mixture. When the engine is started and running, electric current warms a heating element that surrounds the bimetallic strip. This in turn slowly closes the regulator's valve, increases control pressure, and leans the fuel mixture. When the regulator is fully warmed, the control pressure reaches a fixed value.

Testing and Replacing Control Pressure Regulator

To test the heating element of the control pressure regulator, disconnect the harness connector and measure the resistance across the regulator terminals, as shown in Fig. 5-11. If the resistance is not approximately 22 ohms, the control pressure regulator is faulty and should be replaced.

Also check to see that the control pressure regulator heating element is receiving voltage. Disconnect the harness connector and ground the coil wire as described above to prevent the engine from starting. When the starter is actuated, there should be a minimum of 8 VDC across the harness connector, as shown in Fig. 5-12.

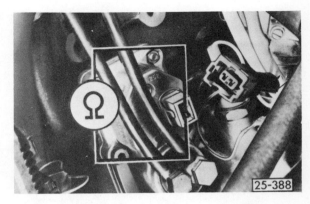

Fig. 5-11. Resistance of control pressure regulator heating element being checked with ohmmeter (shown schematically).

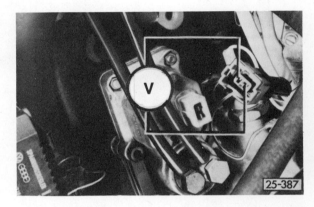

Fig. 5-12. Voltmeter (shown schematically) being used to check for voltage at control pressure regulator harness connector.

To replace the control pressure regulator, disconnect the fuel union bolts from the regulator, disconnect the electrical plug, and remove the mounting bolts that hold the control pressure regulator to the engine block. Use new sealing washers. Torque the larger fuel line union bolt and the two mounting bolts to 20 Nm (15 ft. lb.). Torque the smaller fuel line union bolt to 10 Nm (87 in. lb.).

WARNING ——
Fuel will be expelled as fuel unions are disconnected. Do not smoke or work near heaters or other fire hazards. Keep a fire extinguisher handy.

5.4 Idle Speed

Engine idle speed is controlled not by a fine adjustment of the throttle valve, but by the idle air bypass controlling a small amount of air that is allowed to bypass the throttle valve. By this method, idle speed is more reliable, as it is independent of accelerator cable stretch or wear in the throttle valve mechanism. The idle air bypass is shown schematically in Fig. 5-13. The need for additional inlet air during cold running is handled much the same way, by the auxiliary air regulator which allows additional air to bypass the throttle valve. Fig. 5-14 shows the locations of both the idle air bypass adjusting screw and the auxiliary air regulator.

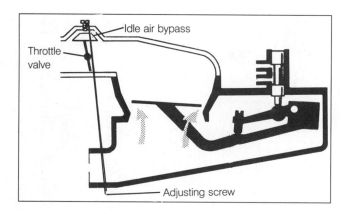

Fig. 5-13. Schematic view of air flow sensor and throttle valve showing idle air bypass and adjusting screw.

A separate component, the idle speed boost valve, maintains engine idle speed by controlling air flow to compensate for varying engine loads at idle due to, for example, high demands on the charging system. Cars with air conditioning have two idle speed boost valves.

Idle Air Bypass Adjustment

Idle speed adjustment is somewhat complicated, due to the sensitivity of emission controls and the effects of idle on emissions. Idle speed, ignition timing, oxygen sensor duty cycle, and idle mixture (% CO) must be checked and adjusted together. Check and, if necessary, adjust ignition timing first. See **IGNITION**. Then check and adjust idle speed, oxygen sensor duty cycle, and CO, repeating the adjustments until all four are simultaneously within specifications. For idle mixture (% CO) specifications, see **5.6 Idle Specifications (rpm and % CO)**. For more information on the oxygen sensor duty cycle, see **EXHAUST SYSTEM AND EMISSION CONTROLS**.

Making these four checks and adjustments together is very important to both driveability and emission control. If the equipment necessary to accurately perform this work is not available, we suggest turning the job over to an authorized Volkswagen dealer or other qualified repair shop. In a properly equipped shop, these checks and adjustments can be made quickly, accurately, and at reasonable cost.

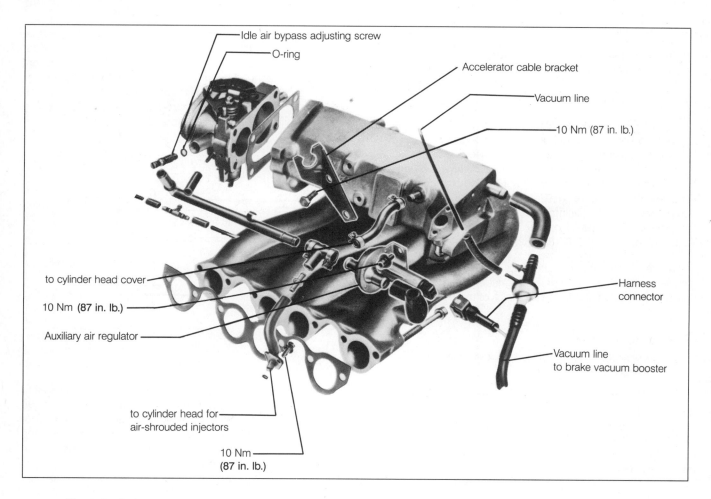

Fig. 5-14. Exploded view of intake manifold and throttle valve showing location of idle air bypass adjusting screw and auxiliary air regulator.

When adjusting the idle speed, as a part of the procedure outlined above, the following requirements apply:

1. The engine must be at normal operating temperature (oil temperature at least 176°F (80°C)). The radiator fan should have cycled on and off at least once.

2. All electrical accessories should be off (including the radiator cooling fan—make adjustments only when the fan is not on).

3. Fuel pressure measuring equipment should not be connected.

4. The exhaust system must be free of leaks.

5. The oxygen sensor system must be functioning correctly.

NOTE ━━

If repairs have been made to the fuel system, raise the engine speed over 3000 rpm a few times, then let it idle for approximately 2 minutes. This will bleed any trapped air from the fuel system.

Make sure that the auxiliary air regulator is fully closed. The engine rpm should not change when the hose to the auxiliary air regulator is pinched shut. If the rpm drops when the hose is pinched, check the auxiliary air regulator as described below.

Fig. 5-15 shows additional preparations for idle adjustment. Pinch off the hose leading from the idle speed boost valve(s). Disconnect the crankcase ventilation hoses from the intake manifold and the air flow sensor. Remove the charcoal canister line "T" fitting from the air flow sensor boot and turn it to insert the side with the 1.5 mm (.059 in.) restrictor hole. If the car is not equipped with the "T" fitting, remove the hose and fit a restrictor plug with the proper size hole. Such a plug is available from Volkswagen, part no. 026 133 382D.

Connect a tachometer according to the instrument manufacturer's instructions. The ignition signal lead from the tachometer should be connected to terminal 1 of the coil.

CAUTION ━━

Connect and disconnect the test leads only with the ignition off.

Idle speed should be between 800 and 1000 rpm. If not, adjust it to 900 ± 30 rpm by turning the idle air bypass screw—clockwise to decrease idle speed, and counterclockwise to increase it. When all adjustments are complete, restore the hose and fitting connections described in Fig. 5-15 to their original configurations.

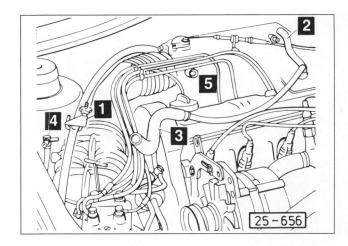

Fig. 5-15. Preparations for idle speed adjustment. Pinch shut idle boost valve hose (**1**), disconnect crankcase ventilation hose (**2** and **3**), remove "T" fitting (**4**) and reinsert restrictor. Idle air bypass adjusting screw is at **5**.

Auxiliary Air Regulator

Fig. 5-16 is a schematic diagram of the auxiliary air regulator. When open, the auxiliary air regulator lets additional air bypass the throttle valve to raise idle speed. Electrical current warms the heating element and causes the bimetallic strip to deflect gradually, closing the rotary valve and cutting off the additional air. The auxiliary air regulator is mounted on the intake manifold. See Fig. 5-14 above.

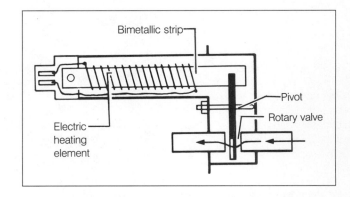

Fig. 5-16. Schematic view of auxiliary air regulator. Arrows indicate direction of air flow through valve.

Check the function of the auxiliary air regulator by checking its effect on engine idle speed under various conditions. When the engine is cold (engine coolant temperature below 30°C or 86°F), disconnect the auxiliary air regulator harness connector. Start the engine and pinch shut the hose from the auxiliary air regulator to the intake manifold as shown in Fig. 5-17. The valve should be open and the engine should lose rpm and perhaps stall.

When the engine is fully warm, with the harness connector attached, pinch shut the hose as shown in Fig. 5-17. The valve should be closed and engine rpm should not change.

Fig. 5-17. Auxiliary air regulator hose being pinched shut with wire-loop pliers.

If in doubt about the results, the valve can be inspected in place using a light and a small mirror. When the valve is open (cold engine), it should be possible to see light through the valve port. When the valve is closed (engine warm), it should not be possible to see through the valve port. If the valve remains open when the engine warms, check to see that the auxiliary air regulator is receiving voltage at the harness connector. There should be battery voltage (approximately 12VDC) at the connector any time the ignition is on.

To remove the auxiliary air regulator, disconnect the harness connector. Loosen the hose clamps and remove the hoses, then remove the socket-head mounting bolts. Installation is reverse of removal. Torque the bolts to 10 Nm (87 in. lb.).

Idle Speed Boost Valve

The idle speed boost valve maintains the idle speed within a 300 rpm range, compensating for varying engine loads at idle. A second valve is used on air-conditioned cars to boost idle speed when the air conditioning is on. The electrically operated valves, shown in Fig. 5-18, allow additional air to bypass the throttle plate and increase idle speed whenever the idle speed drops below 750 rpm. Above 1050 rpm, the valves close and idle speed is reduced.

The idle speed boost valve is a solenoid valve controlled by an electronic control unit on the fuse/relay panel that turns the valve on and off according to an engine speed signal from the coil. Below 750 rpm, the control unit sends a voltage signal which opens the valve. The valve should open with an audible click. When engine speed exceeds 1050 rpm, the control unit cuts the voltage signal to the valve and it closes. The second boost valve on cars with air conditioning is switched on and off at the same time as the air conditioning compressor.

If the valve does not respond as specified, check the voltage signal to the valve at the harness connector, using a test light or a voltmeter. If the valve is receiving a voltage signal below 750 rpm and not opening, the valve is faulty and should be replaced. If the valve is not receiving voltage below 750 rpm,

check the signals to and from the control unit as described below. On Jettas, the system also has its own fuse (check fuse no. 18).

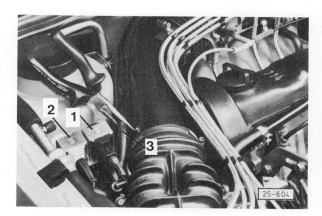

Fig. 5-18. Idle speed boost valve (**1**) and connecting hoses. Cars with air conditioning are equipped with additional boost valve (**2**). (Shown with connecting hose (**3**) pinched off for test).

Using the terminal numbers on the back of the control unit as a guide, test at the fuse/relay panel sockets. Test for continuity to ground at the socket for terminal 31. With the ignition on, check for battery voltage (approximately 12 VDC) at the socket for terminal 15. With the engine running, test for voltage between the socket for terminal 1 and ground. Also check the continuity of the wiring between the panel and the valve's harness connector. If no wiring faults are discovered, and the system does not function properly, then the control unit is faulty and should be replaced. See the current flow diagrams in **ELECTRICAL SYSTEM** for help in troubleshooting the wiring.

5.5 Fuel Pressure Tests and Specifications

As described earlier in this section, much of the function of CIS is dependent on precise fuel pressure. Fuel pressure influences all engine operating characteristics, such as idle, partial-throttle and full-throttle response, starting and warm-up, engine power, and emission levels. Any significant troubleshooting or repair of the system requires the use of a pressure gauge to measure fuel pressure in different parts of the system under different operating conditions.

There are three significant CIS fuel pressure values: 1) System pressure—the basic fuel pressure created by the main fuel pump and maintained by the pressure relief valve in the fuel distributor, 2) Control pressure—determined by the control pressure regulator and used to counter system pressure and regulate the movement of the control plunger, and 3) Residual pressure—the amount of pressure which remains in the closed system after the engine (and fuel pump) are shut off. Testing of each of these pressures is described below.

The pressure gauge shown in Fig. 5-19 (Volkswagen special tool no. VW 1318) has a range of 0 to 10 bar (150 psi) and a valve in one line. It is connected between the fuel distributor and the control pressure regulator. At the fuel distributor, disconnect the line that runs from the center of the fuel distributor to the control pressure regulator. Connect the gauge line without the valve to the fuel distributor. Connect the gauge line with the valve to the end of the control pressure regulator line. Bleed any air from the gauge by hanging it upside down while opening and closing the valve several times. Leave the gauge connected this way for all three pressure tests.

WARNING —

Fuel will be expelled when fuel lines are disconnected. Do not disconnect wires that could cause sparks. Do not smoke or work near heaters or other fire hazards. Keep a fire extinguisher handy.

CAUTION —

Absolute cleanliness is essential when working with fuel circuit components of the CIS. Even a minute particle of dirt can cause trouble if it reaches an injector. Before disconnecting any of the fuel line connections, thoroughly clean the unions. Use clean tools.

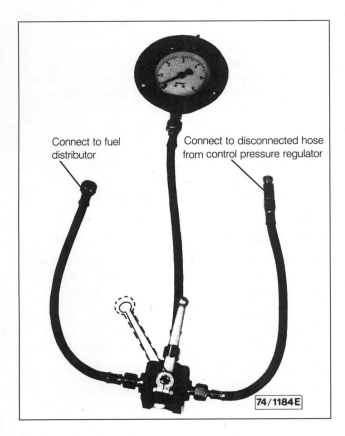

Connect to fuel distributor

Connect to disconnected hose from control pressure regulator

74/1184E

Fig. 5-19. Pressure gauge used to test system pressure, control pressure, and residual pressure.

System Pressure

To measure system pressure, install a pressure gauge as described above and close the valve in the line to the control pressure regulator, as shown in Fig. 5-20. Start the engine and let it idle. System pressure should be 4.7 to 5.4 bar (68 to 77 psi). System pressure is preset during fuel distributor manufacture and should not require routine adjustment.

Fig. 5-20. Pressure gauge valve lever in position (**B**) with flow to control pressure regulator blocked.

If system pressure is too low, look for fuel leaks, a clogged fuel filter, or a damaged fuel line blocking fuel flow. Check fuel pump delivery rate as described in **4.3 Fuel Pump**. If no other cause for low system pressure can be found, the pressure can be adjusted by adding shims to the pressure relief valve. See Fig. 5-21. An additional 0.50 mm (.020 in.) shim will increase system pressure by about 0.30 bar (4 psi). An additional 1.00 mm (.040 in.) shim will increase it by about 0.60 bar (8 psi).

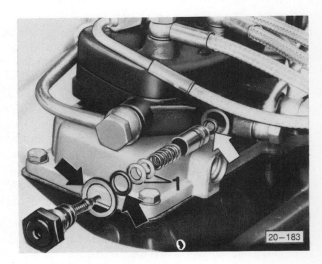

Fig. 5-21. Exploded view of pressure relief valve showing location of adjusting shims at (**1**). Always replace the sealing washer and the O-rings (arrows).

If system pressure is too high, check for a blocked or damaged fuel return line. If the fuel return line is in good condition, the pressure can be adjusted by reducing the thickness of the shims on the pressure relief valve. See Fig. 5-21 above. A change of 0.50 mm (.020 in.) total shim thickness will decrease system pressure by about 0.30 bar (4 psi). A change of 1.00 mm (.040 in.) total shim thickness will decrease it by about 0.60 bar (8 psi).

5

If the fuel pressure cannot be accurately adjusted, the fuel distributor is faulty and should be replaced. See **5.1 Air Flow Measurement and Fuel Metering**.

Control Pressure

Control pressure is that which is determined by the control pressure regulator. It helps regulate the response of the control plunger and, therefore, influences the fuel mixture. Measurement of control pressure is the primary way of evaluating the control pressure regulator. Control pressure is not adjustable, and if the pressure is not within specifications the control pressure regulator should be replaced.

System pressure influences control pressure, and should be checked, as described above, prior to checking control pressure. Check control pressure with the pressure gauge connected as described above at the beginning of **5.5 Fuel Pressure Tests and Specifications**, and the gauge valve pen. A major function of the control pressure regulator is to adapt the fuel mixture for cold starting and cold running, so control pressure should first be checked with the engine completely cold.

To check cold control pressure, disconnect the harness connectors from control pressure regulator and the auxiliary air regulator, then start the engine. Cold control pressure varies with temperature. On U.S. cars, the measured control pressure should correspond to the chart in Fig. 5-22. On Canada cars with engine code MZ, the cold control pressure should be approximately 0.3 bar (4.4 psi) below the value shown in Fig. 5-22. For example, at 68°F (20°C) a Canada car with MZ engine should have a cold control pressure of 1.2±0.15 bar (17.4±2 psi).

If cold control pressure is too high, check for a blocked or kinked fuel line. Also, remove the fuel union at the control pressure regulator and check for a plugged filter screen. If no such faults are found, the control pressure regulator is faulty and should be replaced.

> **WARNING** ━━
>
> *Fuel will be expelled as the unions are disconnected. Do not smoke or work near heaters or other fire hazards. Keep a fire extinguisher handy.*

To check warm control pressure, reconnect the harness connectors to the control pressure regulator and the auxiliary air regulator. Run the engine until the control pressure is no longer increasing (about 2 minutes). The warm control pressure should be between 3.4 and 3.8 bar (49 and 55 psi). U.S. cars with engine code GX, except those sold new in California, have control pressure regulators which compensate for changes in altitude. Fig. 5-23 is a graph of warm control pressure vs. altitude above sea level.

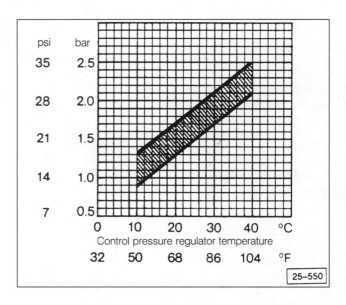

Fig. 5-22. Graph of cold control pressure vs. temperature. Example: at 86°F (30°C), control pressure should be between 1.7 and 2.1 bar (24 and 30 psi).

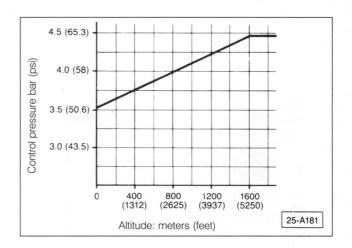

Fig. 5-23. Graph of warm control pressure vs. altitude above sea level, for U.S. cars except California. Example: at 800 meters (2625 ft.) above sea level, warm control pressure should be approximately 4.0 bar (58 psi).

If the warm control pressure is too high, check for a blocked or kinked fuel line. Also, remove the fuel union at the control pressure regulator and check for a plugged filter screen. If no such faults are found, the control pressure regulator is faulty and should be replaced.

If warm control pressure is too low, or takes more than about 2 minutes to reach its peak, test the resistance of the heating element and test for voltage reaching the harness connector, as described in **5.3 Cold Running Enrichment**.

Residual Pressure

The closed fuel system is designed to maintain pressure after the engine is shut off to help prevent the fuel in the injector lines from overheating, causing vapor lock and hard starting. The fuel pump's one-way check valve and the fuel accumulator help maintain this residual pressure. See **4. Fuel Supply**.

Check residual pressure with the pressure gauge connected as described above for measuring control pressure. When the engine is fully warm (control pressure between 3.4 and 3.8 bar (49 and 55 psi), shut off the engine. Leave the gauge connected.

After ten minutes, the pressure should not have dropped below 2.6 bar (38 psi). If the pressure drops excessively, check for leaks in the fuel lines, the fuel distributor including the pressure relief valve O-rings, the injectors, the cold-start valve, and the oxygen sensor frequency valve. To further isolate the cause, check residual pressure at the fuel supply line from the pump. See Fig. 5-5, shown earlier. Disconnect the gauge from the fuel distributor and the control pressure regulator line, and reconnect that line to the fuel distributor. Connect the pressure gauge as shown in Fig. 5-24.

WARNING —

The gauge line with the valve is left disconnected. Be sure to close the valve.

Fig. 5-24. Pressure gauge connected to fuel supply line from fuel pump for residual pressure test of fuel pump, check valve, fuel accumulator, and fuel line. Gauge valve must be closed. Gauge shown (Volkswagen special tool no. VW 1318) is connected using adapter (Volkswagen special tool no. VW 1318/23).

Run the fuel pump using a fused jumper wire at the fuse/relay panel, as described in **4.1 Fuses and Relays**, until fuel pressure indicated by the gauge reaches 5 bar (78 psi). Then, turn the fuel pump off. Once again, after ten minutes, the pressure should not have dropped below 2.6 bar (38 psi).

If the pressure drops excessively and no leaks are found between the fuel pump and the gauge, repeat the test. This time shut off the pump and immediately pinch closed the fuel hose between the tank and the pump. If residual pressure now stays within specifications, the fuel pump check valve is faulty and should be replaced. See **4.3 Fuel Pump**.

If the residual pressure still drops off too quickly, the fuel accumulator may be faulty. For a quick check, remove the plug from the end of the accumulator. If fuel drips out, then the diaphragm is leaking and the accumulator should be replaced.

5.6 Idle Specifications (rpm and % CO)

Idle speed, ignition timing, oxygen sensor duty cycle, and idle mixture (% CO) must be checked and adjusted together. See **5.4 Idle Speed**. Making these four checks and adjustments together is very important to both driveability and emission control. If the equipment necessary to accurately perform this work is not available, we suggest turning the job over to an authorized Volkswagen dealer or other qualified repair shop. In a properly equipped shop, these checks and adjustments can be made quickly, accurately, and at reasonable cost.

Fuel mixture at idle (% CO) is adjusted by raising or lowering the position of the control plunger relative to the air flow sensor plate lever, in order to adjust the amount of fuel delivered to the injectors for a given air flow. This is done by means of an adjusting screw inside the air flow sensor as shown in Fig. 5-25. A small CO test pipe connection to the exhaust manifold provides a place to connect a CO meter. The pipe is about 8 in. long with a blue rubber plug on the end.

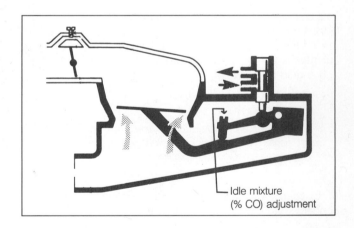

Fig. 5-25. Cut-away view of air flow sensor showing idle mixture (% CO) adjusting screw.

The idle mixture screw can only be reached and adjusted after removing the anti-tampering plug in the top of the air flow sensor housing. This is a small plug with a soft aluminum top and a hard steel bottom, removed by drilling a 2.5 mm (³⁄₃₂ in.) hole in the aluminum and using a sheet metal screw to extract the plug.

CAUTION ▬

Do not drill through the steel bottom. Do not allow metal shavings to fall into the air flow sensor.

With the plug removed, the adjustment is made using a long 3 mm hex wrench as shown in Fig. 5-26. Turning the screw clockwise makes the mixture richer (higher % CO). Turning it counterclockwise makes the mixture leaner (lower % CO). **Table e** lists idle speed and % CO specifications. A new plug should be installed when the adjustment is complete.

CAUTION ▬

Do not accelerate the engine or push on the adjusting wrench while it is in place. Doing so may damage the air flow sensor. Remove the wrench and briefly accelerate the engine after each adjustment.

NOTE ▬

The U.S. government and some states consider it ''illegal tampering'' for the car to leave a commercial repair facility without the anti-tampering plug correctly installed.

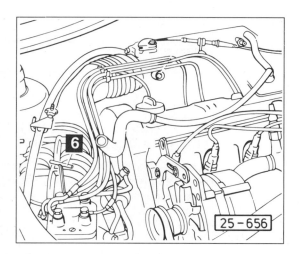

Fig. 5-26. Engine idle mixture (% CO) being adjusted with 3 mm hex wrench (**6**).

Table e. Idle Specifications (CIS)

	Checking Value	Adjusting Value
Engine code GX		
Idle speed	800 to 1000 rpm	900 ± 30 rpm
% CO	0.3 to 1.2%	——
Oxygen sensor duty cycle	20 to 70% (fluctuating)	50 ± 8%
Oxygen sensor duty cycle (measured with dwell meter)	18° to 63° (fluctuating)	45° ± 7°

Table e. Idle Specifications (continued)

	Checking Value	Adjusting Value
Engine code MZ (Canada only)		
Idle speed	800 to 1000 rpm	900 ± 30 rpm
% CO manual transmission	1.5% max.	1.0 ± 0.2%
automatic transmission	1.0% max.	0.7 ± 0.2%

6. CONTINUOUS INJECTION SYSTEM — ELECTRONIC (CIS-E)

Fig. 6-1 is a schematic view of CIS-E fuel injection. Much like the simpler CIS fuel injection described earlier, the basic part of CIS-E is mechanical, utilizing the influence and control of fuel pressure to accurately meter fuel. As the system's name implies, however, electronic control also plays a role in precisely adapting the fuel mixture to the running conditions.

The continuous injection system - electronic (CIS-E) is called continuous because, unlike many other fuel injection systems, the injectors do not open and close — they deliver fuel continuously. The main function of the fuel injectors is to atomize the flow of fuel being supplied under pressure from the fuel distributor. CIS-E differs from the earlier CIS system in that it also uses electronic controls to regulate fuel pressures and therefore control fuel mixture more precisely.

The heart of CIS-E is the mixture control unit, consisting of the air flow sensor and the fuel distributor. Air entering the engine raises the air flow sensor plate. A lever connected to the sensor plate raises the control plunger in the fuel distributor, increasing the quantity of fuel flowing to the injectors in proportion to the air flow. The differential pressure regulator is controlled by a fluctuating signal from the oxygen sensor control unit, based on inputs from various sensors. By regulating electric current flow in the differential pressure regulator circuit, fuel pressure in the lower chamber of the fuel distributor is used to control the volume of fuel delivered to the injectors by the metering valves.

In addition to the differential pressure regulator's constant inputs, the cold start valve, the auxiliary air regulator or idle air stabilizer, and the air flow sensor plate potentiometer (not shown in Fig. 6-1) help adapt the system to different operating conditions. The cold-start valve is like a fifth injector, and performs a choke-like function. It injects additional fuel into the intake manifold during starting to provide a richer fuel mixture when the engine is cold. The cold-start valve is operated electrically.

The auxiliary air regulator opens when the engine is cold to allow a small amount of additional air to bypass the throttle plate and boost the idle speed. On some models, the auxiliary air regulator is replaced by an idle air stabilizer which maintains a constant idle speed under all conditions.

The air flow sensor plate potentiometer provides the control unit with a signal indicating sensor plate position. The signal is primarily used for cold acceleration enrichment.

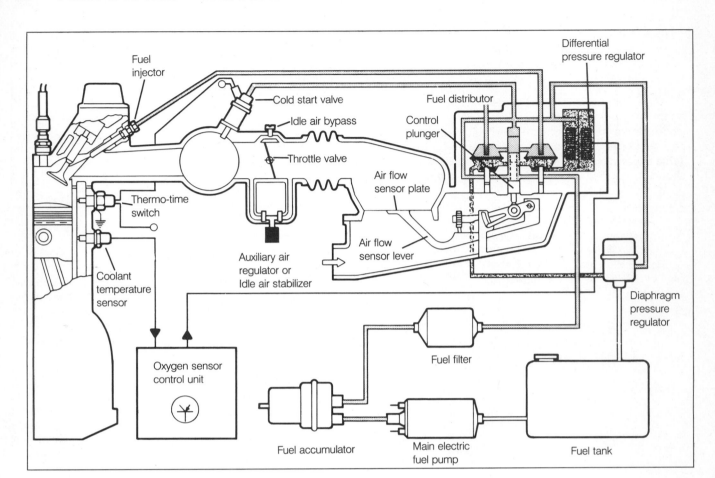

Fig. 6-1 Schematic view of CIS-E fuel injection.

CIS-E is designed so that all the electrical components can be tested using only a low-current LED test light and a multimeter, but the basic fuel metering system is highly dependent on fuel pressure. Evaluation of the system's basic function requires the use of a fuel pressure gauge. See **6.5 Fuel Pressure Tests and Specifications** for more information.

6.1 Air Flow Measurement and Fuel Metering

The throttle valve, which is operated by the accelerator cable, regulates the amount of air drawn in by the engine. The most basic function of the fuel injection system is to measure that incoming air and precisely meter a proportional amount of fuel. The components responsible for air flow measurement and fuel metering are the air flow sensor and the fuel distributor.

The throttle valve is adjusted at the factory. It does not require routine adjustment and should not be used to adjust idle speed. The procedure below for the throttle valve's basic adjustment is provided in the event that the factory adjustment has been altered. The air flow sensor plate can be adjusted if it is found to be out of alignment. After the adjustment, idle speed and idle mixture (% CO) will need to be adjusted also. The fuel distributor is precisely calibrated when it is manufactured and, except for adjusting system pressure, it cannot be adjusted or repaired.

Throttle Valve Basic Adjustment

The purpose of the throttle valve adjusting screw is to provide a positive stop and prevent the valve from closing so far that it becomes worn or damaged.

To correct a faulty throttle valve adjustment, use a screwdriver to back off the throttle valve adjusting screw until there is clearance between its tip and the throttle valve lever. The adjusting screw is shown in Fig. 6-2.

Fig. 6-2. Location of adjusting screw (arrow) for throttle valve basic adjustment (not used to adjust idle speed).

Place a thin piece of paper between the throttle valve adjusting screw and the throttle valve lever. With the throttle valve closed, turn the screw in until it lightly contacts the paper. From this position, remove the paper and turn the screw in an additional ½ turn.

Throttle Switches (HT, RD, and PL engines only)

Engines with code letters HT, RD, and PL are equipped with an idle switch and a full throttle switch mounted on the throttle valve housing. The idle switch supplies the control unit with a signal when the throttle is fully closed, used for idle air stabilizer control and deceleration fuel shut-off. The full-throttle switch supplies the control unit with a signal when the throttle valve is fully open, used for full-throttle enrichment.

Fig. 6-3 shows Volkswagen special tool no. VW 1501 (order no. TV1 501 000 24 ZEL) attached to the throttle switch harness connectors. The harness, if available, is a useful test aid, but the switches can be tested without it.

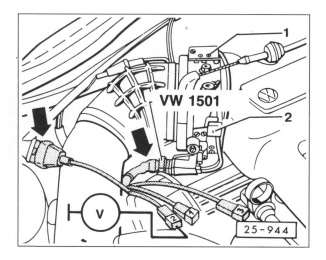

Fig. 6-3. Test harness (Volkswagen special tool no. VW 1501) connected to both sides of harness connector (arrows) for full throttle switch (**1**) and idle switch (**2**) on PL engine. (HT and RD engines are similar.)

First, check to see that voltage is reaching the switches when the ignition is on. Using the test harness, check for voltage between test lead no. 2 and ground. Without the test harness, check for voltage between the center terminal of the harness connector and ground. With the ignition on, there should be battery voltage (approximately 12 VDC). If not, check for a failed fuse (no. 17 on Jetta, no. 22 on Golf GT and GTI) or damage to the wiring harness.

Next, check the switches. Using the test harness, check for voltage between each of the other two test leads and ground to indicate when each switch is open or closed. Test lead no. 1 is for the idle switch. Test lead no. 3 is for the full throttle switch.

Without the test harness, check at the switch connector for continuity between the center terminal and each of the outer terminals to indicate when each switch is open or closed.

Terminal 1 is for the idle switch. Terminal 3 is for the full-throttle switch. Use the wire colors indicated on the current flow diagrams in **ELECTRICAL SYSTEM** to help identify the proper terminals.

To check the idle switch, open the throttle valve about half-way and slowly let it close. The idle switch should close, completing the circuit (and indicating voltage or continuity), when the throttle valve lever gets to within 0.15 to 0.5 mm (.006 to .020 in.) of its stop. Check the gap at which the switch closes with a feeler gauge as shown in Fig. 6-4. If necessary, the switch can be repositioned to adjust the switch-on point by loosening the switch mounting screws.

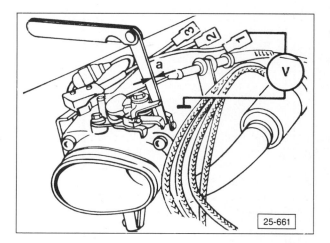

Fig. 6-4. Idle switch **1** being checked and adjusted using feeler gauge to measure gap (**a**) between throttle lever and stop. (VW 1501 test harness on HT or RD engine shown, PL engine is similar.)

To check the full-throttle switch, slowly open the throttle valve to the maximum, full-throttle position. The full-throttle switch should close, completing the circuit (and indicating voltage or continuity), when the throttle is 10°±2° from full open. Check the angle using a protractor as shown in Fig. 6-5. If necessary, the switch can be repositioned to adjust the angle by loosening the switch mounting screws.

Air Flow Sensor

The air flow sensor measures all the air being drawn in by the engine. Air flows past the air flow sensor plate and the plate is lifted, in turn lifting the control plunger in the fuel distributor to meter the fuel. The sensor plate and its cone-shaped venturi are carefully designed to achieve the proper balance of air flow and fuel metering for all flow rates from idle to full throttle. Although it is seldom necessary, the sensor plate is easily adjusted. If the sensor plate is off-center or binding, or the lever has too much resistance, the fuel distributor cannot respond properly to the air flow sensor. If the sensor plate is adjusted, the idle speed and idle mixture (% CO) should be checked and adjusted, as described in **6.3 Idle Speed** and **6.6 Idle Specifications (rpm and % CO)**.

5

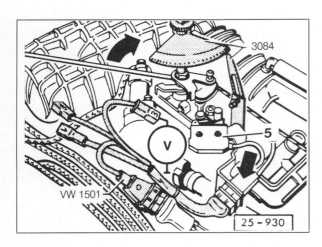

Fig. 6-5. Full throttle switch (**5**) being checked and adjusted using protractor (left arrow, Volkswagen special tool no. 3084, order no. T03 084 000 25 ZEL). (VW 1501 test harness connected to throttle switch connector (right arrows) on HT or RD engine shown. PL engine is similar.

The sensor plate potentiometer provides the control unit with information on the position of the sensor plate. This signal is primarily used for cold acceleration enrichment. For information on repair and adjustment of the air flow sensor plate potentiometer, see **Cold Acceleration Enrichment** under **6.4 Electrical Tests**.

To check the air flow sensor plate with the engine at normal operating temperature, remove the rubber intake air boot from the top of the air flow sensor. Using a magnetic tool, lift the sensor plate slowly and check to see that there is uniform resistance throughout the plate's entire range of travel. Move the sensor plate quickly from its raised position to its rest position. There should be no resistance.

If the sensor plate binds in the air cone, remove the bolt in the center of the sensor plate. Apply thread locking compound to the bolt and reinstall it, centering the plate before tightening the bolt. If the plate cannot be centered, release the clamps to separate the air flow sensor housing from the air filter housing. Remove the clamp bolt from the end of the air flow sensor lever as indicated in Fig. 6-6. Coat the bolt threads with thread locking compound and reinstall the bolt hand-tight. Center the air flow sensor lever on the shaft and tighten the clamping bolt.

If the sensor plate is hard to move or moves with uneven resistance, clean and lubricate the sensor plate lever pivot so that it moves smoothly. If the resistance encountered in moving the sensor plate is caused by a binding control plunger, remove and clean the control plunger as described below in **Fuel Distributor**.

Check the sensor plate rest position with the engine at normal operating temperature. Check the position of the plate in the air cone as shown in Fig. 6-7. When correctly adjusted, the sensor plate should be 1.9 mm (.075 in.) below the narrowest point of the air cone. Up to 2.1 mm (.083 in.) is permissible. Adjust the height by bending the wire spring stop indicated in Fig. 6-8.

NOTE —

An ordinary U.S. nickel (approximately 2 mm thick) can be used to gauge the CIS-E sensor plate height adjustment.

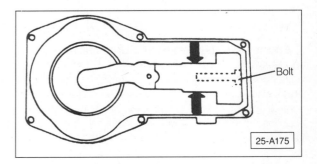

Fig. 6-6. Bottom view of air flow sensor showing location of clamping bolt. Center sensor plate lever (arrows) and tighten clamping bolt.

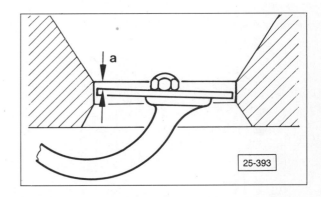

Fig. 6-7. Correct sensor plate position (**a**) is 1.9 mm (.075 in.) below narrowest point of cone. As much as 2.1 mm (.083 in.) is permissible.

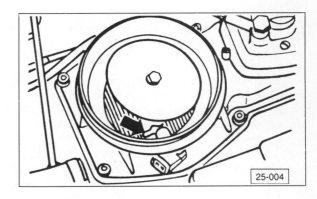

Fig. 6-8. Height of sensor plate can be adjusted by bending wire spring stop (arrow).

When the engine is turned off, there should be a small gap between the sensor lever and the fuel distributor's control plunger, as shown in Fig. 6-9. This gap ensures that the control plunger seats against the O-ring at the bottom of its bore. The plunger seats on the O-ring to help maintain fuel pressure at the injectors, thus helping to eliminate fuel vaporization and hard starting.

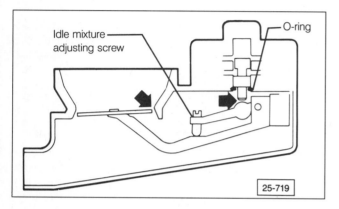

Fig. 6-9. Cut-away view of sensor plate housing showing gap between lever and control plunger (right arrow). Adjust gap by altering position of idle mixture screw. Use sensor plate position (left arrow) to check gap.

Check the gap with the engine at normal operating temperature. Slowly lift the air flow sensor plate until there is some resistance. There should be a small amount of free play, but no more than 2.0 mm (.079 in.) at the edge of the plate. In other words, the free play should be just enough for the sensor plate to rise and be even with the narrowest point in the air cone. If the free play is incorrect, the fuel distributor must be removed from the air flow sensor assembly to make further adjustments, which are described below in **Fuel Distributor**.

Fuel Distributor

The fuel distributor's control plunger, moving up or down in its cylinder, uncovers or covers the metering ports leading to the four metering valves—one for each injector. The differential pressure regulator controls pressure in the lower chambers to control the metering valves which meter fuel to the injectors. A cross-section of the fuel distributor showing the differential pressure regulator and one metering valve is shown in Fig. 6-10.

The fuel distributor is not normally a source of problems. It is, however, a precision device that is easily damaged by plugging or corrosion from contaminated fuel. For fuel filter maintenance information, see **LUBRICATION AND MAINTENANCE**. On some cars, a mini-filter is installed during manufacture in the fuel inlet bolt at the fuel distributor. This filter

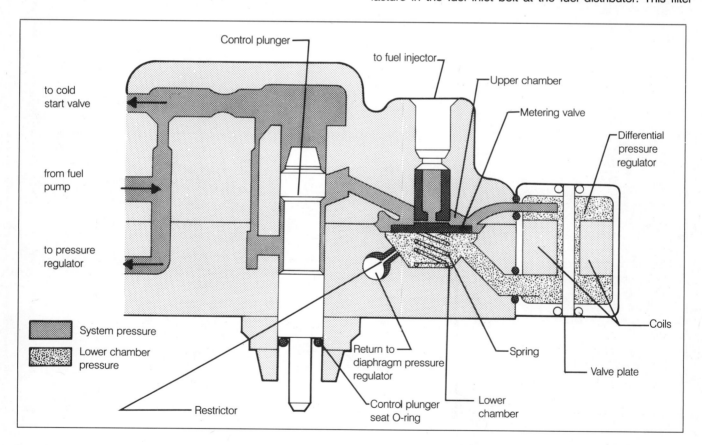

Fig. 6-10. Cross-section of fuel distributor showing differential pressure regulator and one metering valve. Varying pressure in lower chamber regulates metering valve opening and therefore fuel flow to injectors.

should be removed and a normal bolt installed in its place at a specified interval. For more information on identifying and replacing the mini-filter, see **LUBRICATION AND MAINTENANCE**. Check fuel distributor function by measuring injection quantity, as described in **4.7 CIS and CIS-E Fuel Injectors**.

Fig. 6-11 illustrates the fuel distributor's fuel line connections and mounting detail. If either the fuel distributor or the air flow sensor is repaired or replaced, the idle speed and idle mixture (% CO) must be adjusted. See **6.3 Idle Speed** and **6.6 Idle Specifications (rpm and % CO)**. Before making the adjustments, make sure the air flow sensor plate position is correctly adjusted as described above in **Air Flow Sensor**.

If the fuel distributor is removed or replaced, or the air flow sensor plate free play is incorrect as described earlier in **Air Flow Sensor**, basic adjustments to the air flow sensor lever and control plunger will be required. See the checking and adjusting procedure below.

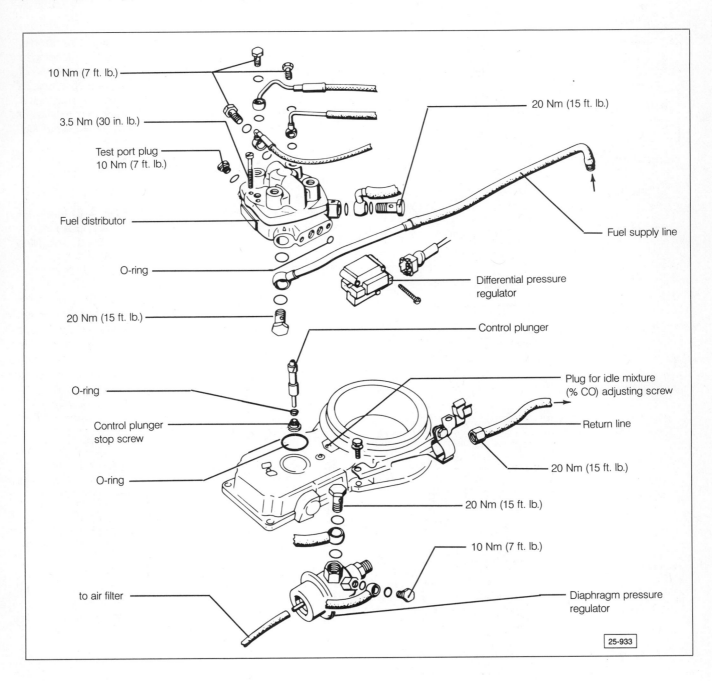

Fig. 6-11. Exploded view of CIS-E fuel distributor and related components. Tightening torques are given for removal and installation of fuel distributor and related components.

To remove and clean the control plunger, remove the two mounting screws from the top of the fuel distributor and pull the fuel distributor from the air flow sensor assembly. Remove the stop screw and the O-ring. Remove the control plunger. Inspect the O-ring and replace it if it is deformed or otherwise damaged. Clean the plunger with carburetor cleaner or equivalent, and then lubricate the plunger with a light coat of fuel and install it. Install the O-ring with the smaller diameter side facing the control plunger. Install the stop screw and make the control plunger basic adjustment as described below.

WARNING ——

Fuel will be expelled when disconnecting fuel unions. Disconnect the battery negative (−) terminal. Do not smoke or work near heaters or other fire hazards. Keep a fire extinguisher handy.

CAUTION ——

When removing the fuel distributor from the air flow sensor housing, be careful not to let the control plunger fall. If the control plunger is allowed to fall, it may be damaged — rendering the entire fuel distributor unserviceable. The fuel distributor is precision calibrated at the factory and should not be disassembled.

To check the air flow sensor lever basic adjustment, measure the distance from the fuel distributor mounting surface to the sensor plate lever roller when the sensor plate is at rest, as shown in Fig. 6-12. The height should be 19.0 ± 0.1 mm (0.75 ± 0.004 in.). If the height is incorrect, remove the tamper-proof plug in the top of the air flow sensor housing and turn the idle mixture adjusting screw, using a 3 mm hex wrench, until the measurment is correct.

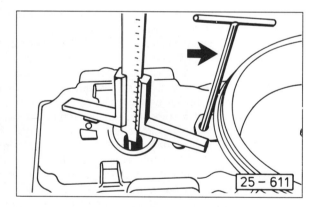

Fig. 6-12. Air flow sensor lever basic adjustment being measured. Adjust by turning idle mixture screw using 3 mm hex wrench (arrow).

To check the control plunger basic adjustment, measure the distance from the gland nut to the stop screw as shown in Fig. 6-13. It should be approximately 0.6 mm (0.024 in.). If not,

adjust it to this height by turning the stop screw. Turning the screw in (clockwise) will increase free play; turning the screw out will reduce free play.

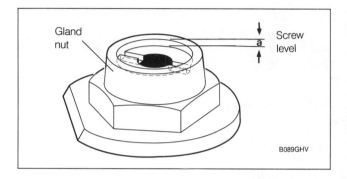

Fig. 6-13. Control plunger basic adjustment measured at dimension **a**. (Gland nut and stop screw shown with control plunger deleted for clarity).

NOTE ——

If any adjustments or repairs are made to the fuel distributor or the air flow sensor lever, the idle must be checked as described in **6.3 Idle Speed** and **6.6 Idle Specifications (rpm and %CO).**

Differential Pressure Regulator

The differential pressure regulator controls pressure in the lower chamber of the fuel distributor, thereby controlling the pressure differential across the metering valves and the volume of fuel that is delivered to the injectors. It is operated by the control unit which continuously makes adjustments based on information received from the oxygen sensor and other inputs. Fig. 6-14 is a cut-away view of the fuel distributor showing the differential pressure regulator. Information on testing the actual differential pressure with a pressure gauge is found in **6.5 Fuel Pressure Tests and Specifications**.

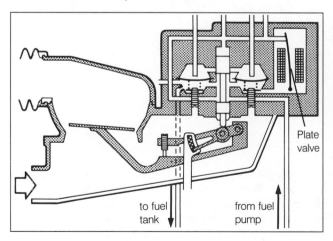

Fig. 6-14. Cut-away view of fuel distributor showing differential pressure regulator. Position of plate valve is controlled by varying electrical current flow.

The differential pressure regulator is an electro-mechanical valve which responds to changes in electrical current flow. The control unit controls it by varying the amount of current flowing in the circuit. In the event that the differential pressure regulator does not receive a signal from the control unit, due to an electrical failure for example, the differential pressure regulator mechanically reverts back to a constant pressure value which will still allow the car to be driven, but perhaps with the engine running roughly.

The action of the differential pressure regulator is the single most important factor controlling and adapting fuel mixture. The measurement of differential pressure regulator current is, therefore, the most important and significant means of checking the operation of CIS-E fuel injection.

Fig. 6-15 shows the connection of a test harness, Volkswagen special tool no. VW 1315A/1 (order no. TV1 315 0A1 25 ZEL), used to measure differential pressure regulator current. The harness and a schematic representation of the test circuit are shown in Fig. 6-16. Alternately, a harness can be fabricated to allow hookup of an ammeter as shown.

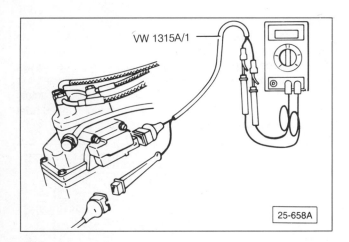

Fig. 6-15. Test harness (Volkswagen special tool no. VW 1315A/1) and multimeter shown connected for measuring differential pressure regulator current.

Complete electrical tests and current specifications are found in **6.4 Electrical Tests**. The differential pressure regulator cannot be repaired and if found to be faulty should be replaced. To replace the regulator, remove the harness connector and the two mounting screws. Remove the regulator and the O-rings from the fuel distributor. Installation is the reverse of removal. Replace the two O-rings.

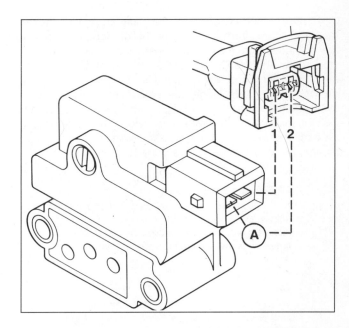

Fig. 6-16. Differential pressure regulator with harness connector removed for connection of ammeter (shown schematically) for current measurement. Numbers shown (**1** and **2**) identify terminals and are found on regulator housing.

NOTE ──

The differential pressure regulator mounting screws are special anti-magnetic screws. If a screw must be replaced, obtain a correct replacement part from an authorized Volkswagen dealer.

6.2 Cold Start Enrichment

The electrically operated cold-start valve sprays extra fuel into the intake manifold for several seconds when the starter is actuated and the engine is cold. The valve is controlled by the thermo-time switch which senses engine coolant temperature. When the engine is cold the switch is closed, allowing power to reach the valve and open it. When the engine is warm, the switch is open and the valve does not operate. To limit valve operation and prevent flooding, the electric current also warms the switch and opens the circuit after a few seconds. The location and mounting of the cold-start valve and the thermo-time switch for all CIS-E engines except 16-valve are the same as for CIS, shown earlier in Fig. 5-6. On 16-valve engines, the cold-start valve is located in the intake manifold and the thermo-time switch is mounted in the end of the cylinder head, as shown in Fig. 6-17.

If the cold-start valve fails to inject fuel during cold starting, it will be difficult or impossible to start the engine. If the cold start valve leaks, the engine may receive extra fuel at the wrong time and become flooded, especially if the engine is hot.

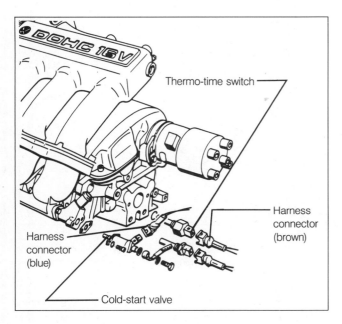

Fig. 6-17. Locations of cold-start valve and thermo-time switch on 16-valve engines with CIS-E fuel injection.

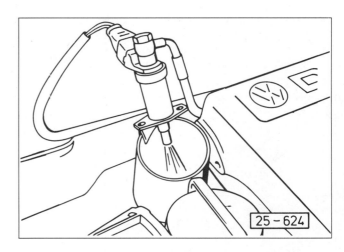

Fig. 6-18. Cold-start valve being checked by observing as fuel sprays into transparent container. (16-valve shown, other CIS-E engines are similar).

To test cold start valve:

1. Make sure engine coolant temperature is below 86°F (30°C). Preferably the engine should sit for several hours.

2. Remove the two screws holding the cold start valve to the intake manifold. Without disconnecting the fuel line or the harness connector, remove the cold start valve.

3. Disconnect the coil wire from the center tower of the distributor cap and connect it to ground, using a jumper wire.

4. On 16-valve models, use a jumper wire to connect the metal cold-start valve housing to ground.

5. Wipe dry the nozzle of the cold start valve. Point the valve into a transparent container, and have a helper actuate the starter. See Fig. 6-18.

> **WARNING** ——
>
> *Fuel will be expelled. Do not smoke or work near heaters or other fire hazards. Keep a fire extinguisher handy.*

> **NOTE** ——
>
> The valve should spray in an even, cone-shaped pattern until the thermo-time switch interrupts the circuit. An irregular spray pattern indicates a dirty or faulty cold start valve. If the valve does not spray, test the thermo-time switch as described below.

6. Wipe the nozzle dry. The valve should not drip for at least a minute. If it does, it is faulty and should be replaced.

When replacing the cold-start valve, the sealing washers on either side of the fuel line fitting should be replaced. Torque the fuel line bolt and the valve's mounting bolts to 10 Nm (87 in. lb.).

To test thermo-time switch:

1. Make sure engine coolant temperature is below 86°F (30°C). Preferably the engine should sit for several hours.

2. Disconnect the coil wire from the center tower of the distributor cap and connect it to ground, using a jumper wire if necessary.

3. Disconnect the cold-start valve harness connector and connect a test light across the connector terminals, as shown in Fig. 6-19.

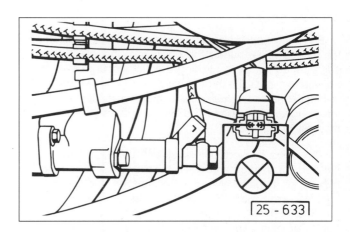

Fig. 6-19. Test light (shown schematically) connected to cold start valve connector.

4. Actuate the starter while observing the test light. The test light should light for several seconds, then go out. The amount of time that the light should stay on depends on coolant temperature. See the graph in Fig. 6-20.

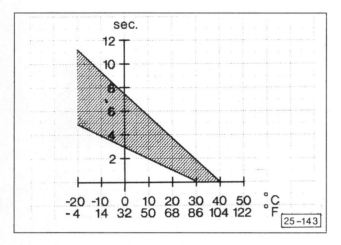

Fig. 6-20. Graph of thermo-time switch response to coolant temperature. Switch completes circuit to open cold-start valve for number of seconds shown. Example: at coolant temperature of 68°F (20°C), switch is closed for 1 to 3.7 seconds.

NOTE ──

If the test light does not light, it is either because voltage is not reaching the connector due to faulty wiring, or because the path to ground (through the thermo-time switch) is interrupted by a faulty switch or wire. Consult the current flow diagrams in **ELECTRICAL SYSTEM** for help in identifying wires and terminals.

To replace the thermo-time switch, first drain the coolant from the engine as described in **COOLING SYSTEM**. Use a thread sealant and torque the new switch to 30 Nm (22 ft. lb.). Then, refill the cooling system with coolant.

6.3 Idle Speed

Engine idle speed is controlled not by a fine adjustment of the throttle valve, but by the position of the idle air bypass adjusting screw. By controlling a small amount of air that is allowed to bypass the throttle, idle speed is more reliable, as it is independent of accelerator cable stretch or wear in the throttle valve mechanism. The idle air bypass is shown schematically in Fig. 6-21.

The need for additional inlet air during cold running is handled much the same way, by allowing additional air to bypass the throttle valve. For this function, the basic CIS-E engine (engine code GX) uses the same system of auxiliary air regulator and idle speed boost valves found on CIS engines. For repair information on these components, see **Idle Speed Boost Valves** and **Auxiliary Air Regulator** under **5.4 Idle Speed**. See **Adjusting Idle Air Bypass** below for information on adjusting idle speed on these engines.

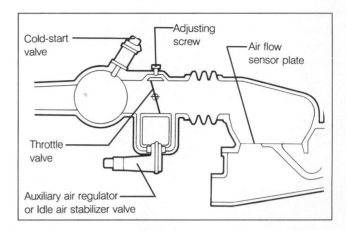

Fig. 6-21. Schematic view of air flow sensor and throttle valve showing idle air bypass and adjusting screw.

The other CIS-E engines (engine codes HT, RD, and PL), use an electronically controlled idle air stabilizer valve to maintain idle speed within a prescribed range. Idle speed itself is subject to electronic control and is not adjustable. See **Idle Air Stabilizer Valve** below for information on checks and adjustments to engines equipped with the idle air stabilizer. Fig. 6-22 shows one example of the idle air stabilizer.

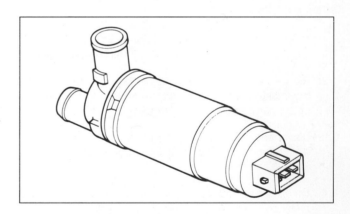

Fig. 6-22. Electronically controlled idle air stabilizer valve used with CIS-E fuel injection (engine codes HT, RD, and PL).

Idle adjustment is somewhat complicated, due to the sensitivity of emission controls and the effects of idle on emissions. Idle must be checked and adjusted together with ignition timing, differential pressure regulator current, and idle mixture (% CO). Check and, if necessary, adjust ignition timing first. See **IGNITION**. Then check and adjust idle speed, differential pressure regulator current, and CO, repeating the adjustments until all are simultaneously within specifications. For information on measuring differential pressure regulator current, see **Differential Pressure Regulator** under **6.1 Air Flow Measurement and Fuel Metering**. For idle mixture (% CO) specifications, see **6.6 Idle Specifications (rpm and % CO)**.

Making these checks and adjustments together is very important to both driveability and emissions control. If the equipment necessary to accurately perform this work is not available, we suggest turning the job over to an authorized Volkswagen dealer or other qualified repair shop. In a properly equipped shop, these checks and adjustments can be made quickly, accurately, and at reasonable cost.

When adjusting idle, the following requirements apply:

1. The engine must be at normal operating temperature (oil temperature at least 176°F (80°C)).The radiator fan should have cycled on and off at least once.

2. All electrical accessories should be off (including the radiator cooling fan—make adjustments only when the fan is not on).

3. Fuel pressure measuring equipment should not be connected.

4. The exhaust system must be free of leaks.

5. The oxygen sensor must be functioning correctly.

NOTE ▬

If repairs have been made to the fuel system, raise the engine speed over 3000 rpm a few times, then let it idle for approximately 2 minutes. This will bleed any trapped air from the fuel system.

Connect a tachometer according to the instrument manufacturer's instructions in order to accurately measure rpm. The ignition signal lead from the tachometer should be connected to terminal 1 of the coil.

CAUTION ▬

Connect and disconnect the test leads only with the ignition off.

Adjusting Idle Air Bypass
(engine code GX only)

Make sure that the auxiliary air regulator is fully closed. Engine rpm should not change when the hose to the auxiliary air regulator is pinched shut. If the rpm drops when the hose is pinched, the regulator's function should be checked as described in **Auxiliary Air Regulator** under **5.4 Idle Speed**.

Fig. 6-23 shows the temporary set-up necessary for idle speed adjustment. Pinch off the hose leading from the idle speed boost valve(s). Disconnect the crankcase ventilation hoses from the intake manifold and the air flow sensor. Remove the charcoal canister line "T" fitting from the air flow sensor boot and turn it to insert the side with the 1.5 mm (.059 in.) restrictor hole. If the car is not equipped with the "T" fitting, remove the hose and fit a restrictor plug with a 1.5 mm (.059 in.) hole. Such a plug is available from Volkswagen. Ask for part no. 026 133 382D.

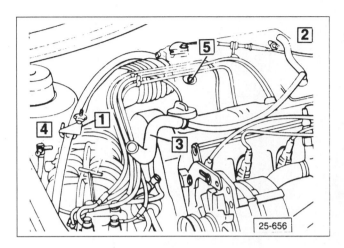

Fig. 6-23. Temporary set-up for idle speed adjustment (engine code GX). Pinch shut idle boost valve hose (**1**), disconnect crankcase ventilation hoses (**2** and **3**), remove "T" fitting (**4**) and reinsert restrictor. Idle air bypass adjusting screw is at **5**.

Idle speed should be between 800 and 1000 rpm. If not, adjust it to 900 ± 30 rpm by turning the idle air bypass screw—clockwise to decrease idle speed, and counterclockwise to increase it. When all adjustments are complete, restore the hose and fitting connections described in Fig. 6-23 above to their original configurations.

Idle Air Stabilizer Valve
(engine codes HT, RD, and PL)

The electronic idle air stabilizer valve controls the amount of air allowed to bypass the throttle valve and increase engine idle speed. Whenever the throttle valve idle switch is closed, the valve receives a cycled voltage signal from the oxygen sensor control unit based on engine rpm and other inputs, as shown in Fig. 6-24. This voltage signal cycles on and off to incrementally open or close the valve to adjust idle speed. This on/off signal is referred to as the valve's duty cycle, and is measured with a duty cycle meter or a dwell meter.

When the idle air stabilizer valve is functioning correctly, it should vibrate and hum slightly whenever the engine is running at idle. If not, turn the engine off, check for a voltage signal reaching the valve, and check the valve's resistance.

Check for a voltage signal at the valve's harness connector as shown in Fig. 6-25. With the ignition on, there should be battery voltage (approximately 12 VDC) between the center terminal and ground, and approximately 10 VDC between the center terminal and each of the two outer terminals. If not, see **6.4 Electrical Tests**.

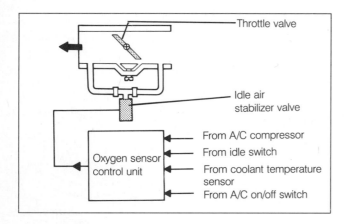

Fig. 6-24. Schematic representation of idle air stabilizer valve and electronic control inputs.

Check resistance at the connector terminals on the valve as shown in Fig. 6-25. There should be continuity between the center terminal and each of the outer terminals. If not, the valve is faulty and should be replaced.

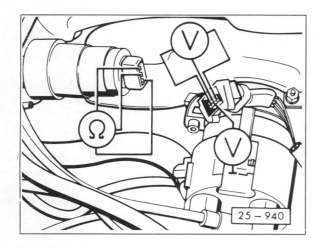

Fig. 6-25. Ohmmeter and voltmeter (shown schematically) being used to test idle stabilizer valve resistance and voltage signal.

Adjustment of the idle air stabilizer system is limited to measuring the duty cycle and adjusting it to specification by adjusting the idle air bypass. Duty cycle measures the on time of the cycling on/off voltage signal, and is expressed as a percentage. It is measured by connecting a duty cycle meter, such as the Siemans 451, to a test connector in the wiring harness near the ignition coil. Connect the duty cycle meter according to the instrument manufacturer's instructions.

A common dwell meter can also be used to measure duty cycle. The 90° scale of a dwell meter corresponds to the 100% scale of a duty cycle meter. For example, a 50% duty cycle would be read as 45° on a dwell meter. The tests below express test values for both instruments. Connect a dwell meter by connecting the meter's positive (+) lead to the test connector and the negative (−) lead to ground.

Fig. 6-26 and Fig. 6-27 show the temporary set-ups necessary to make accurate idle checks. Disconnect the crankcase ventilation hoses as shown. Remove the charcoal canister line "T" fitting from the air flow sensor boot and turn it to insert the side with the 1.5 mm (.059 in.) restrictor hole, as shown in Fig. 6-28. If the car is not equipped with the "T" fitting, remove the hose and fit a restrictor plug with a 1.5 mm (.059 in.) hole. Such a plug is available from Volkswagen. Ask for part no. 026 133 382D.

With the engine running, the duty cycle should be 26 to 30% (23° to 27° on a dwell meter). If the duty cycle is incorrect, adjust it by turning the idle air bypass adjusting screw as shown in Fig. 6-29.

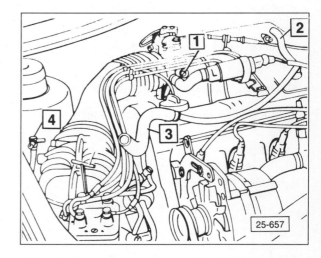

Fig. 6-26. Temporary set-up for idle speed adjustment (engine codes HT and RD). Disconnect crankcase ventilation hoses (**2** and **3**), remove "T" fitting (**4**) and reinsert restrictor. Idle air bypass adjusting screw is at **1**.

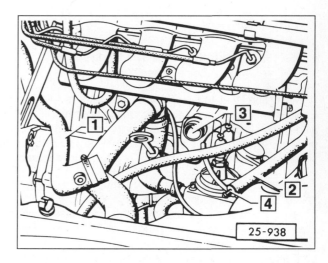

Fig. 6-27. Temporary set-up for idle speed adjustment (16-valve engine code PL). Disconnect crankcase ventilation hose (**2**) and connector (**4**) from hose **1**. Disconnect hose (**1**) from ventilation housing (**3**).

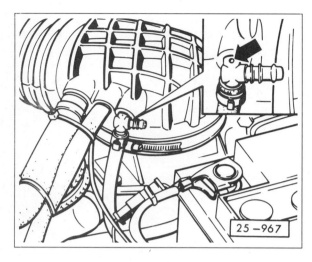

Fig. 6-28. Charcoal canister "T" fitting shown turned with 1.5 mm (.059 in.) restrictor in place in boot.

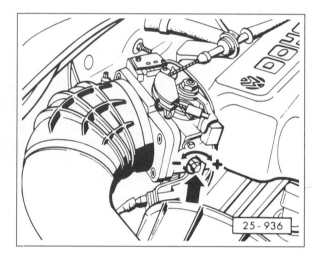

Fig. 6-29. Idle air bypass adjusting screw on throttle valve. (16-valve engine shown, other engines with CIS-E are similar).

NOTE ⏤

If the idle stabilizer valve is diagnosed as faulty, it should be replaced with the improved version, which was introduced by Volkswagen as a running change during 1986 production. The improved valve carries the same part number, but is identified by a green or yellow dot.

6.4 Electrical Tests

Two types of electrical tests are described here. First, several fuel injection electronic control functions can be checked and evaluated by measuring differential pressure regulator current under different running conditions. Next, the voltage and continuity tests listed under **Control Unit Inputs** can be used to help determine whether there are faults in the wiring or components which provide information to the control unit. If all control unit inputs are found to be correct and the system does not perform as specified, the control unit itself may be faulty.

For purposes of general troubleshooting, the electrical tests below are arranged in a specific order designed to logically

isolate the cause of a problem. For best results, the tests should be carried out in the order in which they appear. All tests of differential pressure regulator current require connecting an ammeter in series with the differential pressure regulator as described in **Differential Pressure Regulator** under **6.1 Air Flow Measurement and Fuel Metering**.

After-start and Cold Running Enrichment

To ensure smooth running, the system supplies additional fuel to a cold engine by increasing differential pressure regulator current for a short period after starting and during warm-up. A coolant temperature sensor provides the control unit with temperature information. The starter provides an additional signal for after-start enrichment. After-start enrichment lasts approximately 40 seconds. Cold running enrichment decreases gradually as the engine warms up, finally reaching the normal warm running value.

To test either function, remove the harness connector from the coolant temperature sensor to simulate a cold engine, as shown in Fig. 6-30. To check cold running enrichment, turn the ignition on. Differential pressure regulator current should be 80 to 100 mA on 16-valve engines, and 80 to 110 mA on all other engines.

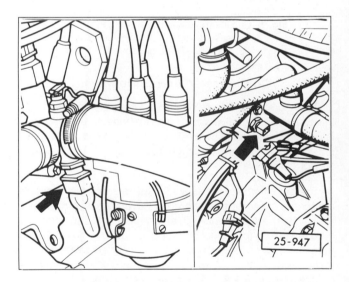

Fig. 6-30. Location of coolant temperature sensor. Left: bottom of cylinder head coolant outlet on all except 16-valve engines. Right: left side of cylinder head on 16-valve engines.

After-start enrichment is checked after operating the starter. To prevent the engine from starting during the test, disconnect the ignition coil wire from the center of the distributor cap and use a jumper wire to connect it to ground. Actuate the starter for 2 to 3 seconds, then leave the ignition on. The differential pressure regulator current should increase to more than 120 mA for 20 to 50 seconds and then return to the cold running value given above. On 16-valve engines, the after-start enrichment lasts slightly longer (30 to 60 sec.). When the test is complete, turn the ignition off. Reconnect the coil wire and the coolant temperature sensor harness connector.

Test the coolant temperature sensor by detaching its harness connector and checking resistance across the sensor's terminals. The correct resistance varies with engine coolant temperature. A sensor with resistance not corresponding to the values given in the chart in Fig. 6-31 is faulty and should be replaced. When replacing the sensor, drain and refill the engine coolant as described in **COOLING SYSTEM**.

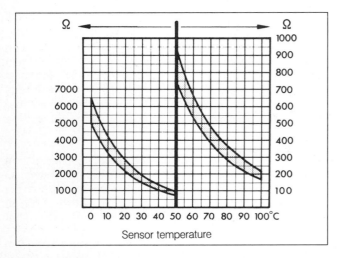

Fig. 6-31. Graph showing coolant temperature sensor resistance (ohms) vs. temperature (°C). Example: at 50°C (122°F), resistance is 725 to 925 ohms.

Cold Acceleration Enrichment

To ensure good throttle response when the engine is cold, the system briefly delivers additional fuel when the throttle valve is opened suddenly. The air flow sensor plate potentiometer, shown in Fig. 6-32, sends a signal to the control unit based on sensor plate travel.

The potentiometer is adjusted at the factory and the mounting screws are sealed. Its operation can be checked by making resistance measurements with an ohmmeter. No adjustment is required unless the potentiometer is replaced. Adjusting a new potentiometer requires the use of an accurate voltmeter. First make certain that the air flow sensor plate is correctly adjusted, as described in **6.1 Air Flow Measurement and Fuel Metering**.

CAUTION ——

Do not attempt to adjust the potentiometer unless it is necessary because of replacement. The mechanism is very sensitive to position and precise adjustment may take several tries.

To test cold acceleration enrichment, disconnect the coolant temperature sensor harness connector and remove the black rubber intake air boot from above the air flow sensor plate. On engines with throttle valve switches (code letters HT, RD, and PL), open the throttle so that the idle switch is not contacted by the throttle lever. Turn the ignition on and quickly raise the air flow sensor plate to its stop. The differential pressure regulator current should briefly exceed and then return to the cold

running enrichment value given above. Turn the ignition off and reconnect the temperature sensor harness connector.

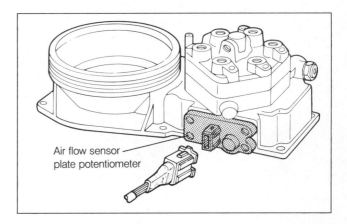

Fig. 6-32. Air flow sensor plate potentiometer mounted to air flow sensor housing. No adjustment is necessary unless it is replaced.

To check the potentiometer's operation, detach the harness connector and use an ohmmeter to measure resistance between terminals, as shown in Fig. 6-33. The resistance between terminals 1 and 2 should be greater than 4000 ohms. The resistance between terminals 2 and 3 should be less than 1000 ohms. Check the resistance between terminals 2 and 3 while slowly and evenly lifting the sensor plate. The resistance should steadily increase, without any flat spots, to approximately 4000 ohms. A potentiometer which does not perform as specified is faulty and should be replaced.

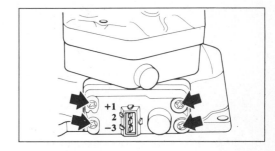

Fig. 6-33. Air flow sensor plate potentiometer terminal identification. When replacing potentiometer, leave mounting screws (arrows) slightly loose to allow adjustment.

To replace the potentiometer, remove its mounting screws and pull it from the fuel distributor. Install the new potentiometer with the mounting screws, leaving them just loose enough to allow some position adjustment. Lift the air flow sensor plate until it is flush with the narrowest point in the air cone, as shown in Fig. 6-34, and hold the plate steady in this position.

On all except 16-valve engines, adjust the position of the potentiometer until the voltage between the center terminal and ground is 0.2 to 0.3 volts. On 16-valve engines only, adjust the position of the potentiometer until the voltage between the center and bottom terminals is 0.02 to 0.2 volts. Carefully tighten the mounting screws and recheck the voltage reading.

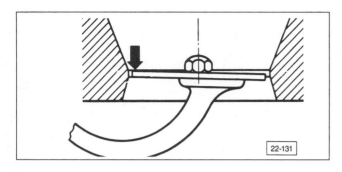

Fig. 6-34. Air flow sensor plate correctly positioned prior to adjusting potentiometer.

Raise the sensor plate fully to its stop. The voltage should increase to approximately 7.0 volts. If not, check the rest position of the sensor plate and recheck the initial position setting of the potentiometer.

Full-throttle Enrichment
(engine codes HT, RD, and PL only)

The full-throttle enrichment function operates only when the engine is warm, when engine speed is above 4000 rpm (above 2500 rpm on 16-valve engines), and when the throttle is fully open. The full-throttle switch supplies a signal to the control unit when the throttle is fully open.

To check full-throttle enrichment, disconnect the harness connector from the coolant temperature sensor and, using a jumper wire, bridge the connector terminals. The sensor is shown earlier in Fig. 6-30. Start the engine. With the engine speed raised to above 4000 rpm (above 2500 rpm on 16-valve engines), actuate the full-throttle switch on top of the throttle valve by hand, as shown in Fig. 6-35. The differential pressure regulator current should increase to approximately 14 mA (approximately 16 mA on 16-valve engines).

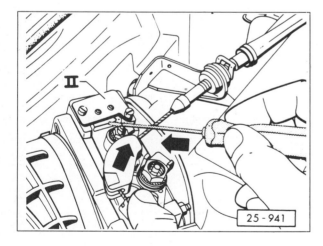

Fig. 6-35. Small screwdriver being used to operate full-throttle switch on throttle valve and test full-throttle enrichment.

If the differential pressure regulator current reads excessively high, recheck the installation of the jumper wire at the temperature sensor connector. If the current does not increase when the full-throttle switch is closed, check for a faulty full throttle switch or a faulty rpm signal from the ignition control unit as described below under **Control Unit Inputs**.

Deceleration Fuel Shutoff
(engine codes HT, RD, and PL only)

When decelerating, fuel flow to the injectors is shut off to improve fuel economy. At normal operating temperature, fuel flow is shut off when the throttle is closed at engine speeds above 1600 rpm, and fuel flow resumes when rpm drops to below 1300 rpm. Below normal oprating temperature, these limits are higher. The closed throttle signal is provided to the control unit by the idle switch mounted underneath the throttle body.

To check the deceleration fuel shutoff function, disconnect the harness connector from the coolant temperature sensor and bridge the connector terminals with a jumper wire as described above under **Full-throttle Enrichment**. Start the engine and increase engine speed to about 3000 rpm, then release the throttle. The positive differential pressure regulator current should briefly change to a negative value (approximately -45 mA) and then return to its normal positive value.

If the current does not temporarily change to a negative value, check for a faulty or incorrectly adjusted idle switch or a faulty rpm signal from the ignition control unit as described below in **Control Unit Inputs**.

Control Unit Inputs

The circuit information in the table below can help diagnose a faulty CIS-E oxygen sensor control unit by checking the components and the wiring harness which supply information to the control unit. The terminals of the control unit connector are identified in Fig. 6-36.

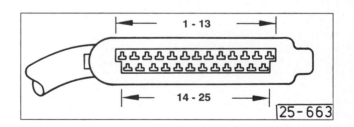

Fig. 6-36. Identification of terminals on CIS-E oxygen sensor control unit.

As a general rule, a complete absence of the voltage or continuity specified in the table suggests an open circuit in the wiring harness. For more specific information, consult the current flow diagrams in **ELECTRICAL SYSTEM**.

Test results which differ from the value specified in the table do not necessarily mean that a component is faulty. Check for loose connections or connections which are inadequate due to contamination or corrosion.

CAUTION ▬▬▬

Use only a high input impedance voltmeter, ohmmeter, or multimeter. The electrical characteristics of other types of test equipment may cause inaccurate results or damage to the electronic components. For more information, see **FUNDAMENTALS**.

Use care to avoid damaging the delicate connector terminals with meter probes during testing. For best and safest results, fabricate a set of test leads as shown in Fig. 6-37. Use the flat connectors (Volkswagen part no. N 17 457 2 or equivalent) to make contact with female connector terminals, then connect the meter leads to the insulated alligator clips.

Before performing the tests indicated by the table, disconnect the coil wire from the center tower of the distributor cap and connect it to ground on the engine block with a jumper wire. With the ignition turned off, disconnect the 25-point connector from the oxygen sensor control unit and test as indicated in **Table f**. The control unit is located in the upper left side of the engine compartment, beneath the drip tray. The drip tray is clipped into place. Pull it up carefully to remove it for access to the control units.

CAUTION ▬▬▬

Always connect or disconnect the control unit connector and the meter probes with the ignition off, to avoid damage to the electronic components.

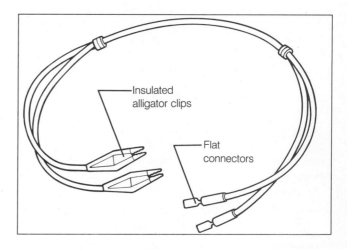

Fig. 6-37. Test leads made with flat connectors (Volkswagen part no. N 17 457 2 or equivalent) and alligator clips, used to make contact without connector damage.

Table f. CIS-E Electrical Tests

Component or Circuit	Test Terminals	Test Conditions	Correct test value
All 1985 to 1988 with CIS-E			
Voltage supply and control unit ground	1 and 2	Ignition on	Battery voltage (approximately 12 VDC)
	1 and 2	Starter operated	8 volts minimum
Signal from starter to control unit	2 and 24	Starter operated	8 volts minimum
Differential pressure regulator	10 and 12	Ignition off	17-22 ohms
Air flow sensor plate potentiometer	17 and 18	Air flow sensor plate at rest	more than 4000 ohms
	14 and 17	Air flow sensor plate at rest	less that 1000 ohms
	14 and 17	Air flow sensor plate lifted to stop	more than 4000 ohms
Coolant temperature sensor	2 and 21	Ignition off	Resistance per Fig. 6-31

continued on next page

Table f. CIS-E Electrical Tests (continued)

Component or Circuit	Test Terminals	Test Conditions	Correct test value
All 1985 to 1988 with CIS-E (cont'd)			
Wire from oxygen sensor to control unit	2 and 8	Green oxygen sensor wire disconnected and touched to ground	Continuity
	2 and 8	Green oxygen sensor wire connected to black wire	No continuity
Ground connection to intake manifold for ground cable bridge	2 and 15	Ignition off	Continuity
Ground connection to intake manifold for oxygen sensor cable shield	2 and 7	Ignition off	Continuity
Ground connection to intake manifold (manual transmission only)	2 and 9	Ignition off	Continuity
1985 to 1988 with engine codes HT, RD, and PL			
Idle air stabilizer valve	2 and 3 2 and 4	Ignition on	Battery voltage (approximately 12 VDC)
Full throttle switch	2 and 5	Ignition on; Throttle fully open (full-throttle switch closed)	Battery voltage (approximately 12 VDC)
Idle switch	2 and 13	Ignition on; Throttle closed	Battery voltage (approximately 12 VDC)
RPM signal from knock sensor control unit	2 and 25	LED test light connected between terminals 2 and 25; Starter operated	LED must flicker
Ground connection to intake manifold (automatic trans. only)	2 and 22	Ignition off	Continuity
Voltage signal from air conditioning system	2 and 6	Ignition on	Continuity
	2 and 16 2 and 19	Ignition on; A/C switch on	Continuity
Battery ground	2 and 20	Ignition off	Continuity

5

6.5 Fuel Pressure Tests and Specifications

As described earlier in this section, much of the function of the CIS-E fuel injection system is dependent on precise fuel pressure. Fuel pressure influences all engine operating characteristics, such as idle, partial throttle and full-throttle response, starting and warm-up, engine power, and emission levels. Any significant troubleshooting or repair of the system requires the use of a pressure gauge to measure fuel pressure in different parts of the system under different operating conditions.

There are three significant CIS-E fuel pressure values: 1) System pressure—the basic fuel pressure created by the main fuel pump and maintained by the diaphragm pressure regulator, 2) Differential pressure—the pressure ratio in the fuel distributor, controlled by the differential pressure regulator, which regulates the flow of fuel to the injectors, and 3) Residual pressure—the amount of pressure which remains in the closed system after the engine (and fuel pump) are shut off. Testing of each of these pressures is described below.

The pressure gauge shown in Fig. 6-38 (Volkswagen special tool no. VW 1318) has a range of 0 to 10 bar (150 psi) and a valve in one line. It is connected between the fuel distributor test port and the end of the fuel line which supplies the cold-start valve. Bleed any air from the gauge by hanging it upside down while opening and closing the valve several times. Leave the gauge connected this way for all three pressure tests.

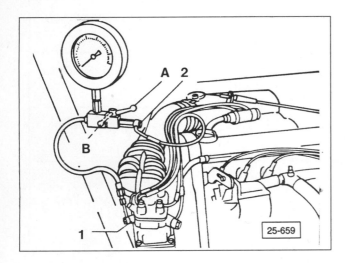

Fig. 6-38. Fuel pressure gauge and valve installed between fuel distributor test port (**1**) and cold-start valve supply line (**2**, removed from cold-start valve). Gauge valve is open in position **A** and closed in position **B**.

CAUTION ━━
Fuel will be expelled when fuel lines are disconnected. Do not disconnect wires that could cause sparks. Do not smoke or work near heaters or other fire hazards. Keep a fire extinguisher handy.

CAUTION ━━
Absolute cleanliness is essential when working with fuel circuit components of CIS-E. Even a minute particle of dirt can cause trouble if it reaches an injector. Before disconnecting any of the fuel line connections, thoroughly clean the unions. Use clean tools.

System Pressure

System pressure is the pressure created by the fuel pump and regulated by the diaphragm pressure regulator shown in Fig. 6-39. Above the predetermined pressure limit of the regulator, the regulator opens and routes fuel back to the fuel reservoir. System pressure is not adjustable and a faulty pressure regulator must be replaced as described in **4.4 Fuel Pressure Regulator**.

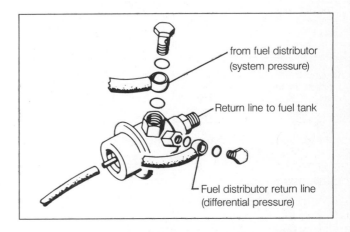

Fig. 6-39. CIS-E diaphragm pressure regulator and fuel line connections. Always use new sealing washers.

To check system pressure, connect the fuel pressure gauge as described above and disconnect the harness connector from the differential pressure regulator. See **6.1 Air Flow Measurement and Fuel Metering**. Run the fuel pump, to pressurize the fuel system, using a jumper wire at the fuse/relay panel as described in **4.1 Fuses and Relays**. System pressure should be 5.2 to 5.6 bar (75 to 82 psi). After reading system pressure on the gauge, disconnect the fuel pump jumper.

If the system pressure is too high, check for a blocked or damaged fuel return line. If the system pressure is too low, look for fuel leaks, a clogged fuel filter, or a damaged fuel line blocking fuel flow. Check fuel pump delivery rate as described in **4.3 Fuel Pump**. If no faults are found with the return line or the fuel pump, the pressure regulator is faulty and should be replaced.

Differential Pressure

Differential pressure is the pressure difference between the upper and lower chambers of the fuel distributor, regulated by the differential pressure regulator, which controls the air/fuel mixture by regulating fuel flow to the injectors.

Check differential pressure with the gauge connected as described above and the gauge valve closed. Also, connect an ammeter to measure differential pressure regulator current as described in **Differential Pressure Regulator** under **6.1 Air Flow Measurement and Fuel Metering**. To test, run the fuel pump using a fuse/relay panel jumper wire as described in **4.1 Fuses and Relays**. The differential pressure should be 0.2 to 0.5 bar (2.9 to 7.0 psi) less than the system pressure measured above. Disconnect the fuel pump jumper wire to stop the fuel pump.

If the differential pressure is too low, measure the volume of fuel coming from the fuel distributor return line. Disconnect the fuel distributor return line from the diaphragm pressure regulator (see Fig. 6-39 above) and place the disconnected line in a measuring container suitable for catching fuel. Plug the open port on the diaphragm pressure regulator and run the fuel pump. After exactly one minute, there should be 130 to 150 cc (4.4 to 5.1 oz.) of fuel in the container. When reconnecting the line, use new sealing washers and torque the union to 10 Nm (87 in. lb.).

If the fuel quantity is correct, the differential pressure regulator is faulty and should be replaced. If system pressure is within specifications but the fuel quantity is incorrect, the fuel distributor is faulty and should be replaced. See **6.1 Air Flow Measurement and Fuel Metering**.

The differential pressure is lower at lower temperatures. Using Volkswagen special tool no. VW 1490 (order no. TV1 490 000 25 ZEL) as shown in Fig. 6-40, with the 15,000 ohm side plugged into the coolant temperature sensor harness connector and testing as described above, the differential pressure should be 0.7 to 1.2 bar (10 to 17.5 psi.) below system pressure and the differential pressure regulator current should be 50 to 80 mA.

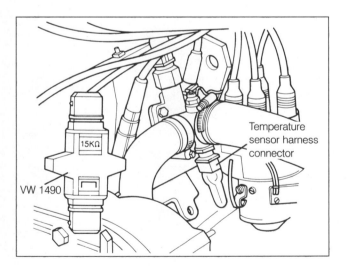

Fig. 6-40. Volkswagen special tool no. VW 1490 used to simulate cold temperature condition with 15,000 ohm resistor side inserted into coolant temperature sensor harness connector. On 16-valve engines (not shown), coolant temperature sensor is located on end of cylinder head.

If the differential pressure regulator current is within specifications but the differential pressure is not, the differential

pressure regulator is faulty and should be replaced. If both the pressure and the regulator current are out of specifications, look for an electrical problem. Check that the resistance across the terminals of the differential pressure regulator is between 17.5 and 21.5 ohms. Check all wires and connections. Check for a good ground connection at the cold-start valve. If no other faults can be found, the oxygen sensor control unit is probably faulty.

Residual Pressure

The closed fuel system is designed to maintain pressure after the engine is shut off to help prevent the fuel in the injector lines from overheating, causing vapor lock and hard starting. The fuel pump's one-way check valve and the fuel accumulator help maintain this residual pressure. See **4. Fuel Supply**.

Check residual pressure with the pressure gauge connected as described above for measuring system pressure. Pressurize the fuel system by operating the fuel pump using a jumper wire at the fuse/relay panel, as described in **4.1 Fuses and Relays**, then disconnect the jumper wire. After ten minutes, the pressure should not have dropped below 2.6 bar (38 psi). If the pressure drops excessively, check the fuel pump check valve and the fuel accumulator as described below. Also check for leaks in the fuel lines, the fuel distributor O-rings, and the injectors. If no leaks are found, check the air flow sensor plate clearance as described in **6.1 Air Flow Measurement and Fuel Metering.**

To check the fuel pump check valve and the fuel accumulator, check residual pressure at the fuel supply line from the pump. See Fig. 6-11, shown earlier. Connect the pressure gauge to the fuel supply line coming from the pump.

> **WARNING** ——
> *One gauge line (the one with the valve) is left disconnected. Be sure to close the valve.*

Run the fuel pump using a jumper wire at the fuse/relay panel, as described in **4.1 Fuses and Relays**, until fuel pressure indicated by the gauge reaches 5 bar (78 psi). Then turn the fuel pump off. Once again, after ten minutes, the pressure should not have dropped below 2.6 bar (38 psi).

If the pressure drops excessively and no leaks are found between the fuel pump and the gauge, repeat the test. This time shut off the pump and immediately pinch closed the fuel hose between the tank and the pump. If residual pressure now stays within specifications, the fuel pump check valve is faulty and should be replaced. See **4.3 Fuel Pump**.

If the residual pressure still drops off too quickly, the fuel accumulator may be faulty. For a quick check, remove the plug from the end of the accumulator. If fuel drips out, then the diaphragm is leaking and the accumulator should be replaced.

6.6 Idle Specifications (rpm and % CO)

Idle speed, ignition timing, differential pressure regulator current, and idle fuel mixture (% CO) must be checked and adjusted together. See **6.3 Idle Speed**. Making these checks and adjustments together is very important to both driveability and emissions control. If the equipment necessary to accurately perform this work is not available, we suggest turning the job over to an authorized Volkswagen dealer or other qualified repair shop. In a properly equipped shop, these checks and adjustments can be made quickly, accurately, and at reasonable cost.

Fuel mixture at idle (% CO) is adjusted by raising or lowering the position of the control plunger, relative to the air flow sensor plate lever, in order to adjust the amount of fuel delivered to the injectors for a given air flow. This is done by means of an adjusting screw inside the air flow sensor as shown in Fig. 6-41. A small CO test pipe connection to the exhaust manifold provides a place to connect a CO meter. The pipe is about 8 in. long with a blue rubber plug on the end.

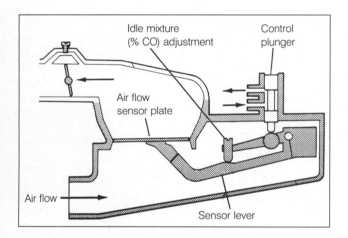

Fig. 6-41. Cut-away view of air flow sensor showing idle mixture (% CO) adjusting screw.

The idle mixture screw can only be reached and adjusted after removing the anti-tampering plug in the top of the air flow sensor housing. This is a small plug with a soft aluminum top and a hard steel bottom, removed by drilling a 2.5 mm (3/32 in.) hole in the aluminum and using a sheet metal screw to extract the plug.

CAUTION ▬

Do not drill through the steel bottom. Drill only about 3.5 to 4.0 mm (9/64 to 5/32 in.) deep. Do not allow metal shavings to fall into the air flow sensor.

With the plug removed, the adjustment is made using a long 3 mm hex wrench as shown in Fig. 6-42. Turning the screw clockwise makes the mixture richer (higher % CO). Turning it counterclockwise makes the mixture leaner (lower % CO). **Table g** lists idle speed and % CO specifications.

CAUTION ▬

Do not accelerate the engine or push on the adjusting wrench while it is in place. Doing so may damage the air flow sensor. Remove the wrench and briefly accelerate the engine after each adjustment.

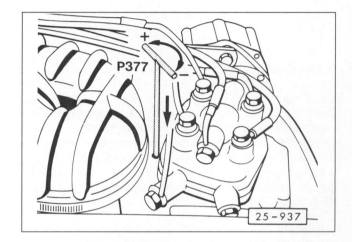

Fig. 6-42. Engine idle mixture (% CO) being adjusted with 3 mm hex wrench. (Volkswagen special tool no. P377, order no. TP0 377 000 25 ZEL, shown.)

Table g. Idle Specifications

	Checking Value	Adjusting Value
Engine code GX		
Idle speed	800 to 1000 rpm	900 ± 30 rpm
% CO	0.3 to 1.2%	—
Differential pressure regulator current	4 to 16 mA (fluctuating)	10 ± 1 mA (average)
Engine codes HT, RD		
Idle speed	800 to 900 rpm	—
% CO	0.3 to 1.2%	—
Differential pressure regulator current	4 to 16 mA (fluctuating)	10 ± 1 mA (average)
Idle air stabilizer valve duty cycle	26 to 30%	28 ± 1%
Idle air stabilizer valve duty cycle (measured with dwell meter)	23° to 27°	25° ± 1°

continued on next page

Table g. Idle Specifications (continued)

	Checking Value	Adjusting Value
Engine code PL		
Idle speed	800 to 900 rpm	—
% CO	0.3 to 1.2%	—
Differential pressure regulator current	4 to 16 mA (fluctuating)	10 ± 1 mA (average)
Idle air stabilizer valve duty cycle	26 to 30%	29 ± 1%
Idle air stabilizer valve duty cycle (measured with dwell meter)	23° to 27°	26° ± 1°

7. DIGIFANT II FUEL INJECTION

Fig. 7-1 shows the main components of the Digifant II engine management system. The Digifant II system combines the engine's ignition and fuel injection functions into one system, managed by a single electronic control unit.

In the Digifant II system, basic fuel metering is determined by engine rpm and by the volume and temperature of the air entering the engine. The Digifant II control unit receives air flow volume and temperature data from the air flow sensor and engine rpm data from the ignition distributor, and distributes fuel to the engine through electrically-operated solenoid valve fuel injectors.

Four injectors, one for each cylinder, are triggered simultaneously at a rate that is proportional to engine RPM. Fuel mixture is controlled by the length of the electrical impulse from the control unit—the length of time that the injectors are open. The injectors are mounted to a common fuel supply—called the fuel rail. Fuel pressure is regulated by a fuel pressure regulator mounted to the end of the fuel rail. Information on fuel injectors is found in this section under **4.8 Digifant II Fuel Injectors**. The fuel pressure regulator is covered separately under **4.4 Fuel Pressure Regulator**.

The Digifant II control unit makes additional adjustments to the amount of fuel delivered by the injectors based on input from various sensors. The oxygen sensor system provides the control unit with information on engine combustion efficiency by measuring the amount of oxygen in the exhaust stream. Switches on the throttle valve inform the control unit when the throttle is fully open or fully closed (at idle). A coolant temperature sensor, located on the engine cylinder head, provides the control unit with engine temperature information for adjustments during starting and warmup. For information on the oxygen sensor system, see **EXHAUST SYSTEM AND EMISSION CONTROLS**.

In order for the system to operate properly, the basic adjustments to idle speed, ignition timing, idle mixture (% CO), and throttle switches must be correct. If these basic settings are faulty, the Digifant II system will compensate for any differences, and any other test results will be misleading. These basic settings are all related and all adjustments should be made together, as described in **7.3 Idle Speed** and **7.6 Idle Specifications (rpm and % CO)**.

5

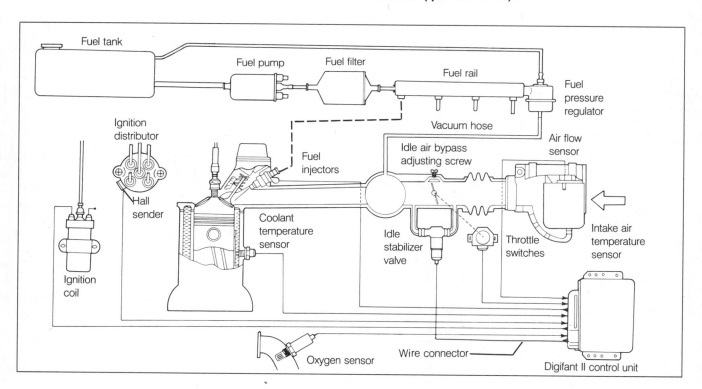

Fig. 7-1. Schematic view of Digifant II engine management system. Knock sensor (mounted to engine and connected to control unit) not shown.

The Digifant II system has been designed so that almost all electrical components can be tested using a low-current LED test light and a multimeter. Most of these tests can be performed right at the Digifant II control unit harness connector. The only other major piece of test equipment required is a fuel pressure gauge. Incorrect system fuel pressure can directly affect engine performance.

7.1 Air Flow Measurement

Fig. 7-2 is an exploded view of the air flow sensor, the throttle valve, and their connecting air duct. As intake air is drawn past the air flow sensor flap, the flap opens and in turn actuates the potentiometer. The varying resistance of the potentiometer provides a signal to the control unit that is proportional to air flow. The air flow sensor also contains an intake air temperature sensor which measures the temperature of the incoming air.

The throttle valve is operated by the accelerator pedal via the accelerator cable, and controls the amount of air drawn in by the engine. The throttle valve is adjusted during manufacture and does not require any routine adjustment. The throttle valve can be adjusted if the factory settings have been tampered with.

Air Flow Sensor

The sensor's mechanical operation depends upon the free movement of the spring-loaded stator flap inside the main air passage. To check the flap movement, loosen the clamps, remove the rubber intake air duct, and move the stator flap through its range of travel. If the flap binds at any point, remove the intake air flow sensor, as described later under this heading, and check for any foreign material that may be interfering with the flap's movement. If the flap cannot be made to move freely, the air flow sensor is faulty and should be replaced.

Check the air flow sensor potentiometer by measuring resistance across its electrical terminals. Disconnect the harness connector from the sensor and connect an ohmmeter. See Fig. 7-2 for terminal identification. The resistance between terminals 3 and 4 should be 500 to 1000 ohms. The resistance between terminals 2 and 3 should vary as the stator flap is moved by hand.

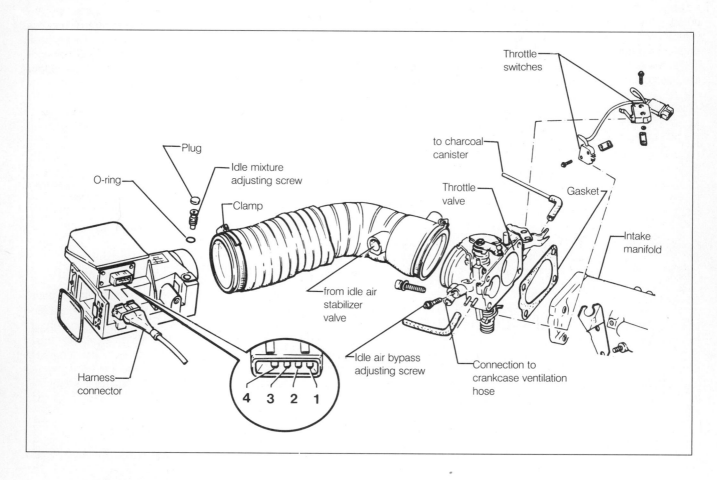

Fig. 7-2. Exploded view of throttle valve and air flow sensor. Inset shows air flow sensor terminals used for electrical testing.

Check the intake air temperature sensor by measuring resistance between terminals 1 and 4. The proper resistance value depends on the air temperature. See the graph in Fig. 7-3. If the resistance values are not as specified for any of the tests above, the air flow sensor is faulty and should be replaced.

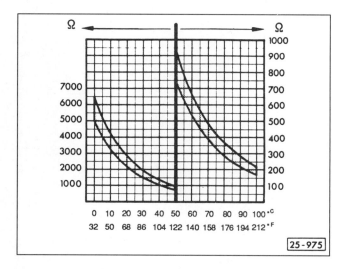

Fig. 7-3. Graph showing intake air temperature sensor resistance vs. outside air temperature. Example: At 68°F (20°C), resistance should be 2200 to 2800 ohms.

To remove the air flow sensor, disconnect the electrical harness connector. Remove the large hose clamp and disconnect the intake air duct. Separate the upper air filter housing from the lower air filter housing. Working from inside the upper air filter housing, remove the air flow sensor mounting bolts and remove the sensor and its gasket. Installation is the reverse of removal. Replace a gasket that is deformed or otherwise damaged. Use care not to overtighten the mounting bolts. The correct torque is only 5 Nm (44 in. lb.).

Throttle Valve Basic Adjustment

The factory-set throttle valve adjusting screw is not used to adjust idle speed. Its only function is to provide a mechanical stop for the linkage to prevent damage to the throttle plate and housing. It should be adjusted only if the factory setting has been changed.

To correct a faulty throttle valve adjustment, loosen the locknut and back off the throttle valve adjusting screw until there is clearance between its tip and the throttle valve lever. See Fig. 7-4. Place a thin piece of paper between the screw and the lever and turn the adjusting screw in. When the screw is just barely gripping the paper, remove the paper and turn the screw in an additional ½ turn. Tighten the locknut.

Throttle Valve Vacuum Hoses

Fig. 7-5 illustrates the correct vacuum hose connections to the throttle valve. Use care to not interchange the lines.

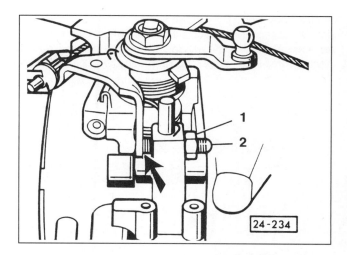

Fig. 7-4. Throttle valve adjusting screw (**2**) and locknut (**1**). Set by contact (arrow) with throttle valve lever.

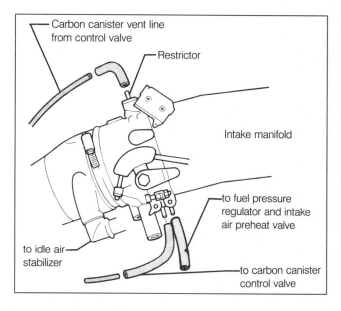

Fig. 7-5. Vacuum line connections to throttle valve.

7.2 Cold Start and Cold Running Enrichment

To ensure good starting and smooth running, the Digifant II system provides extra fuel to a cold engine. The coolant temperature sensor gives the control unit information on engine temperature. The control unit, in turn, makes an adjustment to injector opening time to provide the necessary richer mixture. For additional cold running driveability and fuel economy, the intake air preheat system warms the air entering the engine in cold weather.

Coolant Temperature Sensor

The coolant temperature sensor is located on the front side of the cylinder head. To test the sensor, disconnect the harness connector as shown in Fig. 7-6 and measure resistance across the sensor terminals. The proper resistance value depends on engine coolant temperature. A graph of resistance vs. temperature is shown in Fig. 7-7. If the resistance of the coolant temperature sensor is incorrect, the sensor is faulty and should be replaced. Replacing the sensor will require draining and replacing some of the engine coolant. See **COOLING SYSTEM**.

Fig. 7-6. Harness connector shown disconnected from coolant temperture sensor (arrow).

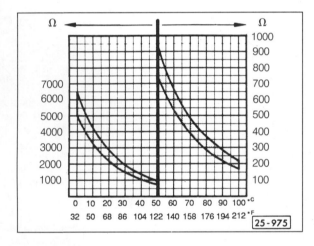

Fig. 7-7. Graph showing coolant temperature sensor resistance vs. temperature. Example: At 68°F (20°C) resistance should be 2200 to 2800 ohms.

Intake Air Preheat System

The intake air preheat system operates a regulator flap in the lower part of the air filter housing. In cold weather the regulator flap opens so that the engine can draw in preheated air from around the warm exhaust system. The system is shown in Fig. 7-8 below. Vacuum from the throttle valve which opens or closes the regulator flap is controlled by the temperature regulator valve in the side of the upper air filter housing.

Test the temperature regulator valve by applying vacuum to the upper port. When the engine is cold, the valve should be open and air should easily pass through. When the engine compartment is warm, the valve should be closed. A faulty temperature regulator valve can be replaced separately.

To check the regulator flap, remove the vacuum hose from the lower port on the temperature regulator valve. Separate the upper part of the air filter housing from the lower part and remove the air filter so the regulator flap is visible. Apply vacuum to the disconnected vacuum hose and check that the flap moves smoothly. If the regulator flap mechanism is faulty, the lower air filter housing should be replaced.

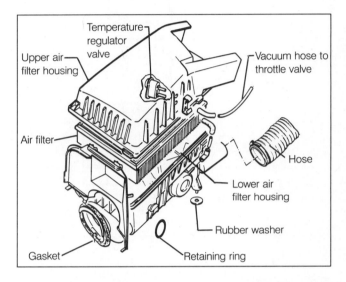

Fig. 7-8. Intake air preheat system fitted to air filter housing. Cutaway shows temperature regulator valve inside housing.

7.3 Idle Speed

Engine idle speed is controlled not by a fine adjustment of the throttle valve, but by the idle air bypass controlling a small amount of air that is allowed to bypass the throttle valve. By this method, idle speed is more reliable since it is independent of accelerator cable stretch or wear in the throttle valve mechanism. The idle air bypass is shown schematically in Fig. 7-9.

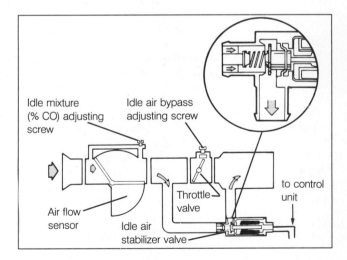

Fig. 7-9. Schematic view of air flow sensor and throttle valve showing idle air bypass and idle air stabilizer valve.

The need for additional inlet air during cold running is handled much the same way, by allowing additional air to bypass the throttle valve. An idle air stabilizer valve, controlled by the Digifant control unit, maintains idle speed within a prescribed range.

Idle adjustment is somewhat complicated, due to the sensitivity of emission controls and the effects of idle on emissions. Idle must be checked and adjusted together with ignition timing and idle mixture (% CO). Check and, if necessary, adjust ignition timing first. See **IGNITION**. Then, check and adjust idle speed and CO, repeating the adjustments until both are within specifications. For idle mixture (% CO) specifications, see **7.6 Idle Specifications (rpm and % CO)**.

Making these checks and adjustments together is very important to both driveability and emissions control. If the equipment necessary to accurately perform this work is not available, we suggest turning the job over to an authorized Volkswagen dealer or other qualified repair shop. In a properly equipped shop, these checks and adjustments can be made quickly, accurately, and at reasonable cost.

When adjusting idle, the following requirements apply:

1. The engine must be at normal operating temperature (oil temperature at least 176°F (80°C)). The radiator fan should have cycled on and off at least once.

2. All electrical accessories should be off (including the radiator cooling fan — make adjustments only when the fan is not on).

3. The idle stabilizer valve must be operating correctly. (It should vibrate and hum slightly when the ignition is on).

4. The throttle valve idle switch must be operating correctly. (Idle speed changes noticeably when switch harness connector is disconnected and reconnected).

5. The exhaust system must be free of leaks.

6. There must be no engine vacuum leaks.

7. The oxygen sensor must be operating correctly.

8. When the engine is started, briefly raise the engine speed to over 2100 rpm four times, to cancel the electronic control unit's built-in hot-start high idle.

Connect a tachometer according to the instrument manufacturer's instructions in order to accurately measure rpm. The ignition signal lead from the tachometer should be connected to terminal 1 of the coil.

CAUTION —

Connect and disconnect the test leads only with the ignition off.

Idle Air Bypass
idle speed adjustment

The idle air bypass screw is located in the throttle valve as shown in Fig. 7-10. Adjusting the screw changes the amount of air which is allowed to bypass the throttle plate, which in turn changes idle speed.

NOTE —

Ignition timing should be adjusted to specifications (as described in **IGNITION**) before making any adjustments to idle speed.

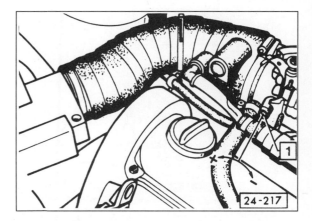

Fig. 7-10. Idle air bypass adjusting screw (**1**) on throttle valve housing. Turning screw clockwise will decrease idle speed; turning screw counterclockwise will increase idle speed.

To adjust idle speed, disconnect the harness connector from the coolant temperature sensor. The idle speed should be 975 ± 50 rpm. If not, turn the idle air bypass adjusting screw as shown in Fig. 7-10 until the idle speed is 975 ± 25 rpm. When the coolant temperature sensor harness connector is reconnected, the idle speed should drop to 820 ± 50 rpm. If not, check the idle air stabilizer valve.

Idle Air Stabilizer Valve

The idle air stabilizer valve operates continuously when the ignition is on and the coolant temperature sensor is connected. To check that the valve is functioning, start the engine. The valve should vibrate and hum slightly. If the valve is not operating, check that the idle switch on the throttle valve is closed and functioning correctly as described below. If no faults are found with the idle switch, turn the engine off, disconnect the harness connector from the valve, and check for continuity at the terminals on the valve. If there is no continuity, the valve is faulty and should be replaced.

To check the idle stabilization function of the control unit, measure the current flow to the valve. Fig. 7-11 shows a special wire harness used to hook up an ammeter (0 to 1000 mA range). Alternately, a harness can be fabricated to allow hookup of an ammeter as shown.

5

Start the engine and briefly raise the engine speed to over 3000 rpm at least three times, then let the engine return to idle. With the engine running, the current reading should fluctuate between 400 and 460 mA. Disconnect the harness connector from the coolant temperature sensor. The current reading should be steady at approximately 430 mA.

CAUTION ━━

The small female terminals in the differential pressure regulator harness connector are easily damaged. If fabricating a test harness, use the appropriate male terminals (Volkswagen part no. N 174572) to make connections with the harness connector.

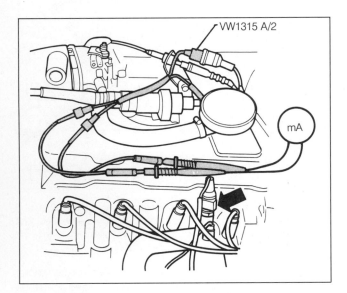

Fig. 7-11. Test harness Volkswagen special tool no. VW 1315 A/2 (order no. TV1 315 0A2 025 ZEL) being used to connect ammeter and measure idle air stabilizer current from control unit.

NOTE ━━

Idle air stabilizer current will fluctuate between 400 and 1000 mA if the engine is too cold, if the coolant temperature sensor is faulty, if idle speed is incorrectly adjusted, if there is an engine vacuum leak, or if electrical accessories are on.

Idle and Full-Throttle Switches

The idle and full-throttle switches are mounted on the throttle valve as shown in Fig. 7-12. Through them, the control unit receives a signal whenever the throttle valve is fully closed (idle) or fully open (full-throttle). With the ignition on, there should be at least 5 VDC across the terminals of the switch harness connector. Test and adjust both switches by checking for continuity at the connector terminals.

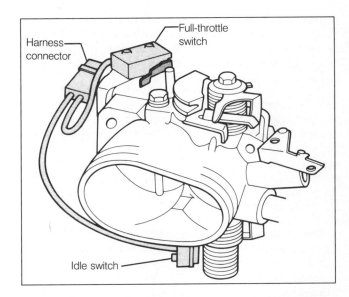

Fig. 7-12. Digifant II throttle valve showing idle switch and full throttle switch.

To test and adjust the idle switch, open the throttle part way by hand. Slowly let the throttle return to its idle stop. There should be continuity at the connector terminals when the throttle lever is 0.20 to 0.60 mm (.008 to .024 in.) from the idle stop.

To test and adjust the full-throttle switch, open the throttle slowly. There should be continuity when the throttle is within 10° ± 2° of the full-throttle position.

If the operating characteristics of the switches do not meet these specifications, adjust switch position by loosening the mounting screws and repositioning the switch. Tighten the mounting screws and recheck the adjustment.

7.4 Electrical Tests

The voltage and continuity tests described under this heading can be used to help determine whether there are faults in the wiring or components which provide information to the Digifant control unit. If all control unit inputs are found to be correct and the system still does not perform as specified, the control unit itself may be faulty.

As a general rule, a complete absence of the voltage or continuity specified in **Table h** suggests an open circuit in the wiring harness. For more specific information, consult the current flow diagrams in **ELECTRICAL SYSTEM**.

Test results which differ from the value specified in **Table h** do not necessarily mean that a component is faulty. Check for loose connections or connections which are inadequate due to contamination or corrosion.

Use care to avoid damaging the delicate connector terminals with meter probes during testing. For best and safest results, fabricate a set of test leads as shown in Fig. 7-13. Use the flat connectors (Volkswagen part no. N 17 457 2 or equivalent) to make contact with female connector terminals, then connect the meter leads to the insulated alligator clips.

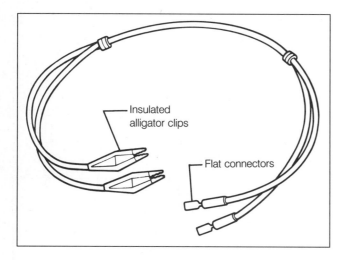

Fig. 7-13. Test leads made with flat connectors (Volkswagen part no. N 17 457 2 or equivalent) and alligator clips, used to make contact without damaging connector.

Before performing the tests indicated by **Table h**, disconnect the coil wire from the center of the distributor cap connect it to ground with a jumper wire. With the ignition turned off, disconnect the 25-point connector from the Digifant control unit and the 7-point connector from the ignition control unit and test as indicated in **Table h**. The Digifant control unit and the smaller ignition control unit are mounted together in the upper left side

of the engine compartment, beneath the drip tray. Carefully remove the drip tray for access to the control units. Remove the control unit from its mounting bracket to disconnect the control unit connector. The test terminals are identified in Fig. 7-14 and Fig. 7-15.

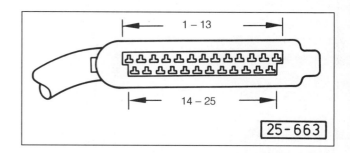

Fig. 7-14. Terminal identification for 25-point Digifant control unit connector. Use care to not damage connector terminals with test probes.

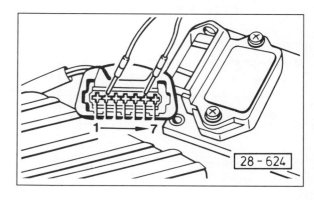

Fig. 7-15. Terminal identification for 7-point ignition control unit. Use care not to damage connector terminals with test probes.

Table h. Digifant II Electrical Tests

Component or Circuit	Test Terminals (at Digifant connector unless otherwise specified)	Test Conditions	Correct test value
Voltage supply to control unit	13 and 14	Ignition on	Battery voltage (approximately 12 VDC)
	14 and 19	Ignition on	Battery voltage (approximately 12 VDC)
Wire from starter solenoid (terminal 50)	1 and 13	Actuate starter	8 VDC (minimum)

continued on next page

Table h. Digifant II Electrical Tests (continued)

Component or Circuit	Test Terminals (at Digifant connector unless otherwise specified)	Test Conditions	Correct test value
Fuel injectors	12 and 14		3.7 to 5.0 ohms
Ignition control unit	25 (Digifant control unit) and 6 (ignition control unit)	Ignition off	Continuity
Coolant temperature sensor	6 and 10		Resistance according to Fig. 7-7 given earlier
Throttle switches	6 and 11	Throttle closed	Continuity
		Open throttle slowly to half-open position	No continuity
		Full-throttle	Continuity
Air flow sensor	6 and 17 17 and 21	Move sensor flap or actuate starter	500 to 1000 ohms Resistance must fluctuate
Intake air temperature sensor	6 and 9	Resistance according to Fig. 7-3 given earlier	
Fuel pumps and fuel pump relay	3 and 13	Bridge terminals with jumper wire; Switch ignition on	Fuel pumps run (audibly)
Ignition (Hall sender)	6 and 8 6 and 18	Remove connector at distributor and bridge all three wires with jumper wire	Continuity
Knock sensor	4 and 5 4 and 7	Disconnect knock sensor harness connector and bridge all three wires with jumper wire	Continuity
Idle air stablizer valve	22 and 23		Continuity
Oxygen sensor	2 and 13	Separate connector and connect green wire to ground	Continuity
		Green wire connected	No continuity

7.5 Fuel Pressure Tests and Specifications

Although the quantity of fuel delivered to the engine is controlled primarily by how long the injectors are open, fuel pressure also has some influence. The fuel pressure created by the fuel pump is regulated by a diaphragm-type pressure regulator mounted to the end of the fuel rail.

A vacuum hose connected to the top of the regulator helps to control the fuel pressure as a function of engine vacuum. When the throttle is opened and vacuum drops suddenly, fuel pressure increases slightly to richen the air/fuel mixture for improved throttle response. For more information on the pressure regulator, see **4.4 Fuel Pressure Regulator**.

CAUTION ——

Cleanliness is essential when working with Digifant II fuel circuit components. Before disconnecting any fuel lines, thoroughly clean the unions. Use clean tools.

System Pressure and Residual Pressure

System pressure is the pressure value which is maintained in the system by the pressure regulator. When fuel pressure from the pump exceeds the desired system pressure, the regulator opens and routes fuel back to the fuel reservoir surrounding the fuel pump. System pressure is not adjustable and the pressure regulator should be replaced if it is faulty.

To avoid fuel vaporization and hard starting when the engine is hot, the system is designed so that fuel pressure is retained for a time after the engine has stopped running. This residual pressure is maintained by check valves in the pressure regulator and in the fuel pump. Neither the pressure regulator check valve nor the fuel pump check valve are serviceable as individual parts.

To test fuel pressure:

1. Loosen and remove the service port sealing screw shown in Fig. 7-16, and connect a fuel gauge.

   ### WARNING ——

   Fuel will be expelled. Use a clean rag to soak up fuel. Do not disconnect any wires that could cause electrical sparks. Do not smoke or work near heaters or other fire hazards. Keep a fire extinguisher handy.

   ### NOTE ——

   The fuel pressure gauge must have a range of at least 0 to 3.5 bar (0 to 50 psi) and must be securely connected to prevent it coming loose under pressure.

2. Start the engine and allow it to idle. Fuel pressure should be approximately 2.5 bar (36 psi).

3. Disconnect the vacuum hose from the top of the fuel pressure regulator. Fuel pressure should increase to approximately 3.0 bar (44 psi).

4. Turn the engine off. After ten minutes, residual pressure should be at least 2 bar (29 psi).

5

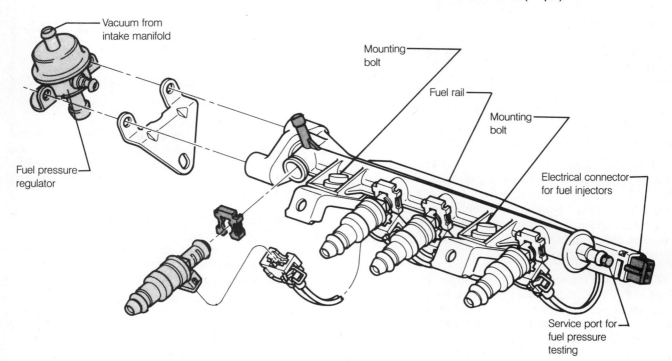

Vacuum from intake manifold

Mounting bolt

Fuel rail

Mounting bolt

Fuel pressure regulator

Electrical connector for fuel injectors

Service port for fuel pressure testing

Fig. 7-16. Digifant II fuel rail showing location of sealing screw for service port. Service port is used for fuel pressure testing.

If the system pressure is too high, the pressure regulator is faulty and should be replaced. If the system pressure is too low, run the engine briefly to build up fuel pressure, then turn the engine off and quickly pinch shut the blue fuel return line. If the pressure holds, then the pressure regulator is faulty and should be replaced.

If the pressure still drops, check for leaks in the fuel system. If no leaks are found, the fault may be due to a leaky fuel injector, a faulty fuel injector O-ring, or a faulty fuel pump check valve.

To conclude the fuel pressure testing, disconnect the gauge from the fuel rail service port and catch any spilling fuel with a clean rag. Install the sealing screw with a new seal.

Replacing Pressure Regulator

The fuel pressure regulator attaches to the fuel rail with two Phillips-head screws. Disconnect the vacuum hose and the blue fuel return hose. Discard the hose clamp. Remove the screws and pull the regulator from the fuel rail. Inspect the O-ring for damage and replace it if necessary. Installation is the reverse of removal. Connect the blue fuel return line with a new hose clamp.

> **WARNING ——**
>
> *Fuel will be expelled. Use a clean rag to soak up fuel. Do not disconnect any wires that could cause electrical sparks. Do not smoke or work near heaters or other fire hazards. Keep a fire extinguisher handy.*

7.6 Idle Specifications (rpm and % CO)

Idle speed, ignition timing, and idle fuel mixture (% CO) must be checked and adjusted together. See **7.3 Idle Speed**. Making these checks and adjustments together is very important to both driveability and emissions control. If the equipment necessary to accurately perform this work is not available, we suggest turning the job over to an authorized Volkswagen dealer or other qualified repair shop. In a properly equipped shop, these checks and adjustments can be made quickly, accurately, and at reasonable cost.

To check % CO, remove the cap from the CO tap tube that comes from the exhaust manifold and connect an exhaust gas analyzer. Disconnect the oxygen sensor harness connector. Disconnect and plug the crankcase ventilation hose as shown in Fig. 7-17. Start the engine and briefly raise the engine speed to at least 2100 rpm four times to cancel the control unit's hot-start fast idle function.

At idle, the CO reading should be within the specifications shown in Fig. 7-18. Notice that the correct value varies with altitude above sea level. The fuel mixture (% CO) is adjusted by turning the idle mixture screw, changing the amount of air allowed to bypass the air flow sensor flap. This changes the opening force acting on the flap, which changes the potentiometer signal to the control unit. Since the injector opening time is influenced by the potentiometer signal, the idle mixture is altered.

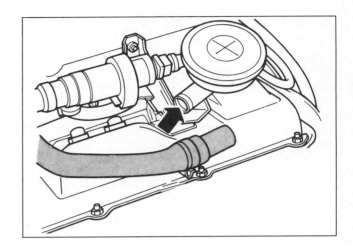

Fig. 7-17. Crankcase ventilation hose disconnected from emission control valve (arrow) and plugged for idle mixture (% CO) adjustment.

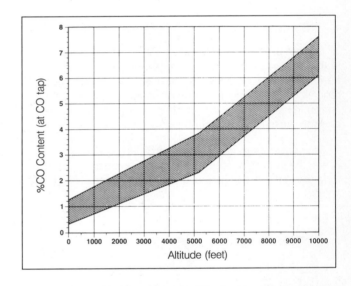

Fig. 7-18. Idle mixture (% CO) checking tolerance vs. altitude.

The idle mixture screw can only be reached and adjusted after removing the anti-tampering plug in the top of the air flow sensor housing. This small plug is removed by drilling with a 2.5 mm (3/32 in.) drill bit and threading a screw into the plug so that it can be extracted with pliers.

With the plug removed, adjust the idle mixture using a 5 mm hex wrench as shown in Fig. 7-19. Turning the screw counterclockwise makes the mixture richer (higher % CO). Turning it clockwise makes the mixture leaner (lower % CO). **Table i** lists idle speed specifications. Fig. 7-20 is a graph of % CO adjusting value vs. altitude.

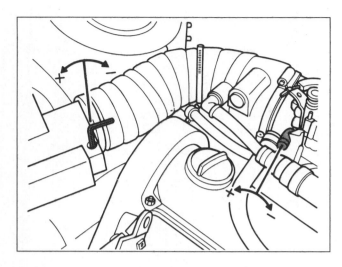

Fig. 7-19. Idle mixture (% CO) being adjusted by turning air flow sensor adjusting screw with 5 mm hex wrench.

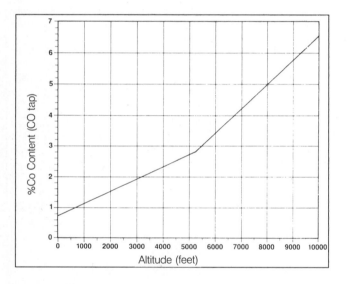

Fig. 7-20. Idle mixture (% CO) adjusting specification vs. altitude.

Table i. Idle Specifications

	Checking Value	**Adjusting Value**
Engine codes RV, PF		
Idle speed (with coolant temperature sensor disconnected)	975 ± 50 rpm	975 ± 25 rpm
Idle speed (with coolant temperature sensor connected)	820 ± 50 rpm	—
% CO	See Fig. 7-18	See Fig. 7-20

Reconnect the oxygen sensor harness connector and check the idle speed. See **7.3 Idle Speed**. Readjust idle speed and mixture until both are within specifications. Then, reconnect the crankcase ventilation hose to the emission control valve. Turn the engine off and remove the test equipment.

NOTE ——

If the % CO drastically increases when the crankcase ventilation hose is reconnected, it is not due to incorrect adjustment. It is probably caused by engine oil contaminated by fuel due to short distance driving. Changing the oil is a temporary solution.

8. FUEL SYSTEM TECHNICAL DATA

I. CIS Fuel Injection Specifications

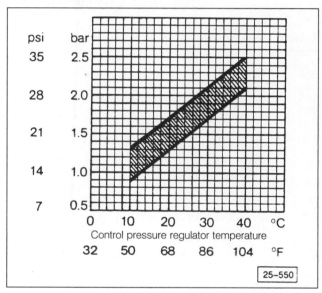

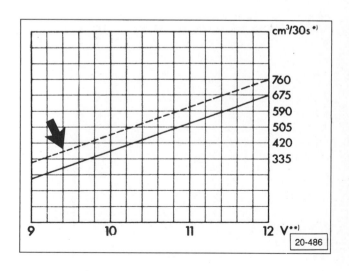

I. CIS Fuel Injection Specifications (continued)

Fuel pump delivery rate fuel pump
operated for 30 seconds,
minimum permissible. . . . . .See graph

note
Delivery rate varies with voltage. . . . . .See graph
System pressure . . . . .4.7 to 5.4 bar
(68 to 78.3 psi)

Control pressure (cold)
Harness connector removed
from control pressure regulator
and auxiliary air regulator . . . . .See graph

note
Control pressure varies with ambient temperature.
Variations of not more than 0.05 bar
(or 1 psi) are not significant . . . . .See graph
Control pressure (warm) . . . . .3.4 to 3.8 bar
(49.3 to 55 psi)

Residual pressure
  after 10 min., minumum pressure . . . . . .2.6 bar (37.7 psi)
  after 20 min., minimum pressure . . . . . .2.4 bar (34.8 psi)
Idle speed. . . . . .800 to 1000 rpm
Idle mixture (% CO)
  manual transmission, maximum permissible 1.5%
  automatic transmission, maximum permissible 1.0%

II. CIS-E Fuel Injection Specifications

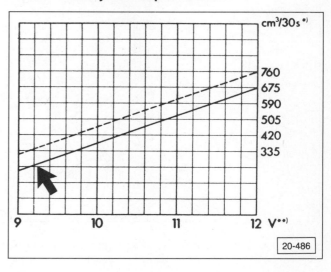

Fuel pump delivery rate
note
Fuel pump delivery rate varies with voltage.
Fuel pump operated for 30 seconds,
minimum permissible . . . . .See graph
System pressure . . . . .5.2 to 5.6 bar (75 to 82 psi)
Differential pressure
  differential pressure regulator
  harness connector
  disconnected . . . . .0.2 to 0.5 bar (2.9 to 7.0 psi)
             less than system pressure
  differential pressure regulator harness
  connector connected,
  and special fixed resistor
  tool connected to removed
  coolant temperature
  sensor harness connector. . . . .0.7 to 1.2 bar (10 to 17.5 psi)
             less than system pressure
Residual pressure
  after 10 min., minimum pressure . . . . . . .2.6 bar (37.7 psi)
Idle speed
  GX engine . . . . .800 to 1000 rpm
  HT,RD, and PL engine (duty cycle) . . . . .26 to 30%
             (850±50 rpm)
Idle mixture (% CO)
  Differential pressure regulator
  current . . . . .4 to 16 mA (fluctuating)
             (0.3 to 1.2 % CO)

III. Digifant Fuel Injection Specifications

Fuel pump delivery rate
  Fuel pump operated for 30 seconds,
  minimum permissible . . . . .500 cc (17 fl. oz.)
System pressure . . . . .2.5 bar (36 psi)
Residual pressure
after 10 min., minimum pressure . . . . .2.0 bar (29 psi)
Idle Speed . . . . .820±30
  Idle stabilzer valve control current . . . . .430±30 mA
Idle mixture (% CO). . . . . .0.3 to 1.1 %CO

FUEL SYSTEM – DIESEL

Contents

Introduction 3

1. General Description 4
    Fuel Storage and Supply 4
    Fuel Injection 4
    Injectors 4
    Air Cleaner 4
    Emission Controls 4
    Applications and Identification Codes 4

2. Maintenance 4

3. Troubleshooting 4
  3.1 Basic Troubleshooting Principles 5
  3.2 Diagnostic Testing 6
      Checking Fuel Supply to Injectors 6
      Idle Speed Drop Test 7

4. Fuel Supply 8
  4.1 Fuel Tank Vents 9
  4.2 Fuel Gauge Sender 9

5. Fuel Injection 10
  5.1 Idle Speed and Maximum RPM Adjustments . 10
      Checking and Adjusting Idle Speed (1985 models without idle speed boost) 10
      Checking and Adjusting Idle Speed (1986 and later models with idle speed boost) 11

      Checking and Adjusting Maximum RPM (all 1985 through 1989 diesel and turbo diesel models . 12
  5.2 Accelerator Cable 12
      Replacing Accelerator Cable 12
      Checking and Adjusting Accelerator Cable . . . 13
  5.3 Cold Start System 13
      Removing, Installing and Adjusting Cold Start Cable 13
  5.4 Camshaft/Injection Pump Drive Belt (diesel engines only) 14
  5.5 Injection Pump 17
      Checking and Adjusting Injection Pump Timing 19
      Inspecting and Replacing Stop Solenoid 20
      Stop Solenoid Quick-Check 20
      Injection Pump Valves 21
  5.6 Injectors 21
      Removing and Installing Injectors 22
      Pressure Testing Injectors 22
      Inspecting and Repairing Injectors 22
  5.7 Turbo Diesel Boost Enrichment 23

6. Technical Data 24
    I. Tightening Torques 24
    II. Diesel Fuel System General Technical Data . . 24

TABLES

a. Diesel Engine Fuel Injection Troubleshooting 5
b. Injection Pump Timing 20
c. Diesel Fuel Injector Opening Pressure 22

Fuel System — Diesel

6

Introduction

The fuel system handles two main tasks necessary for diesel engine operation: (1) it provides storage space for the diesel fuel, (2) it delivers the correct quantities of filtered diesel fuel to the cylinders. It is also responsible for admitting an unrestricted supply of filtered air to the engine. The second function — delivering fuel to the cylinders — is handled by a high-pressure fuel injection system that is totally unlike the fuel injection systems used on contemporary spark-ignition engines

Because the diesel engine relies on a high compression ratio (23:1) to generate heat that will ignite vaporized diesel fuel, the maximum possible quantity of air must be admitted to each cylinder on every air intake stroke. So the diesel engine has no throttle to restrict airflow as on spark-ignition engines; the intake ports are always "wide open." In the case of the optional turbo-diesel engine, a turbocharger is used to pump air into the engine under pressure. The diesel engine's power output — hence its rpm — is determined solely by the quantity of fuel injected into the superheated air inside the combustion pre-chambers. At idle, the air-to-fuel ratio may be greater than 100:1; even at top speed, the mixture never approaches the comparatively rich stoichiometric air-to-fuel ratio of approximately 14.5:1 that is common to spark-ignition engines. This lean operation is largely responsible for the diesel engine's excellent fuel economy. (A stoichiometric ratio is one in which all fuel and oxygen are consumed in combustion; a diesel always has oxygen left over.)

The diesel engine's fuel injection pump draws fuel through a water separator and filter from the tank. This fuel is then put under very high pressure. The fuel distributor portion of the pump selects (according to the engine's firing order) the cylinder to which the fuel will go. Finally, the pressurized fuel enters the combustion pre-chamber of the correct cylinder via an injector. Because diesel fuel is not a particularly volatile liquid, thorough vaporization is necessary to obtain efficient burning. Each injector is designed both to restrict the admission of fuel until a pressure of about 125 bar (1786 psi) has been attained and also to spray the fuel into the pre-chamber with a uniform pattern of highly vaporized fuel.

Special equipment is necessary for nearly all kinds of diesel injection system work. So if you lack the skills, the tools, or a clean workshop for diesel fuel injection tests, adjustments, and repairs, we suggest you leave this work to an authorized dealer or other qualified shop. We especially urge you you attempt to consult your authorized dealer before repairs on a vehicle still covered by the new-car warranty.

1. GENERAL DESCRIPTION

The diesel engine's fuel system can be divided into two main parts according to their functions. These are fuel storage and supply, and fuel injection.

Fuel Storage and Supply

The molded plastic fuel tank is located beneath the car, ahead of the rear axle. The fuel tank capacity is 53 liters (14.0 U.S. gallons). When the fuel gauge indicates reserve there is approximately 7 liters (1.8 U.S. gallons) of fuel left in the tank. The correct fuel to use under most conditions is diesel fuel No. 2. See **LUBRICATION AND MAINTENANCE** for more information on fuel requirements.

The tank is equipped with a sending unit for the electrical fuel gauge, incorporating a pickup tube for the transfer of fuel to the engine, and a connection for the return of surplus fuel from the fuel injection pump. To prevent exposing the injector pump to harmful contaminants, the fuel system also contains an efficient water separator and fuel filter. An exploded view of the fuel supply system appears in **4. Fuel Supply**.

Fuel Injection

The injection pump is engine-driven by the same toothed belt that drives the camshaft. It handles virtually all engine fuel functions including pumping fuel from the tank, and controlling the timing and the quantity of fuel injected. A timing advance mechanism changes injection timing in response to engine speed and during cold-start conditions. The pump meters fuel to the injectors at an operating pressure in excess of 120 bar (1706 psi) and incorporates check valves to prevent backflow of fuel from the injectors. All the internal moving parts are lubricated by the diesel fuel, so routine maintenance is not required.

Repairs to the injection pump require specialized knowledge and equipment, and parts for rebuilding are not generally available. Faulty pumps must be serviced by the pump manufacturer or other qualified diesel fuel injection repair shop. Internal problems usually require replacement of the pump.

Injectors

The fuel injectors are complex and very precise devices. They open at a specific pressure, in excess of 120 bar (1706 psi), and close quickly to ensure complete fuel vaporization. The injectors can be disassembled for cleaning and repair, and Volkswagen replacement parts are available.

Air Cleaner

The diesel engine has a rectangular, dry-type pleated paper air filter, held in a plastic housing bolted directly to the intake manifold. Intake air is drawn from inside the passenger-side fender well, through an adapter, in order to reduce the noise caused by intake air resonance.

Emission Controls

Diesel engines are equipped with a closed, Positive Crankcase Ventilation (PCV) system to keep harmful emissions from entering the atmosphere. Crankcase emissions are vented through a PCV valve on the cylinder head cover back into the air intake.

Because of the low volatility of diesel fuel, evaporative emission controls like those found on cars with gasoline engines are not required.

Applications and Identification Codes

When discussing repairs to the fuel system or replacement parts, it may be necessary to differentiate between the different fuel injection systems. Golf and Jetta diesel models use the same basic Volkswagen fuel system. Turbo diesel Jettas use a modified version of that system. In this section, the distinction will be pointed out only in those specific instances where a difference exists. Otherwise, all procedures apply equally to fuel systems for both engines. When ordering parts, distinctions may be made by the engine code at the beginning of the engine number. ME is the code for normally aspirated diesels. MF is the code for Jetta turbo diesels.

2. MAINTENANCE

The following routine Maintenance steps are covered in detail in **LUBRICATION AND MAINTENANCE** or in this section under the numbered headings listed.

1. Draining the water separator.

2. Replacing the fuel filter.

3. Replacing the air filter element.

4. Checking and adjusting idle and maximum rpm. **5.1**

5. Checking the fuel system for leaks. **4.**

6. Replacing the camshaft drive belt. **5.4**

3. TROUBLESHOOTING

This troubleshooting section applies to the diesel fuel system and problems such as hard starting, rough idle, and poor overall performance.

In the diesel engine, good compression is especially necessary for the engine to run well. Engine mechanical faults leading to poor compression can cause problems that seem to be injection related. Engine lubricating oil that leaks past worn piston rings or valve stem seals may produce exhaust smoke that is mistaken for the sign of a misadjusted fuel injection system. For more information on diesel engine problems, see **ENGINE**.

A faulty glow plug system may contribute to cold starting problems. Troubleshooting for the glow plug system can be found in **IGNITION**. Battery and starter troubleshooting can be found in **ELECTRICAL SYSTEM**. Low power symptoms on Jetta turbo diesels may be the result of turbocharger problems, which are covered in **EXHAUST SYSTEM AND EMISSION CONTROLS**.

3.1 Basic Troubleshooting Principles

Proper operation of the diesel engine requires that it be supplied with clean fuel, that it have an unrestricted supply of air, and that the fuel be delivered, at high pressure, at the right time. The battery and starting system are also important. For starting, they must be able to turn the engine fast enough (at least 150 RPM) to begin compression ignition.

Fuel must be of the correct grade, properly winterized when necessary for cold-start conditions, and clean. Dirt and water can interfere with combustion and cause problems much more readily than in a gasoline engine.

Because the diesel engine's speed is controlled by the amount of fuel injected, and not by the amount of air admitted past a throttle plate, the air intake must be unrestricted. A clogged air filter or incorrect valve clearance can restrict the air and cause power loss.

The injection pump produces the high pressure necessary to open the injectors and spray and vaporize the fuel. Fuel leaks or air in the fuel lines, because it is compressible, may inhibit system pressure. Since power is controlled by the amount of fuel injected, low fuel pressure may cause sluggish performance.

Injection timing controls the amount of time the fuel has to burn. For cold starting, when the compression heat necessary for combustion is dissipated quickly by the cold engine, injection timing is advanced to give the fuel more time to burn. At higher rpm, there is less time for fuel to burn, so injection timing is advanced to start the fuel burning sooner. Since the injection pump is driven by the engine and externally mounted, its precise fuel metering and timing can be degraded by such things as a loose timing belt, worn sprocket, or loose mounting bolts.

Table a lists symptoms, their probable causes, and corrective actions. The boldface numbers in the corrective action column refer to headings in this section where the repairs are described.

Table a. Diesel Engine Fuel Injection Troubleshooting

Problem	Probable cause	Corrective action
1. Engine does not start	**a.** Cranking speed too low	**a.** Repair starting system or charge or replace battery. See **ELECTRICAL SYSTEM.**
	b. No voltage at stop solenoid on injection pump	**b.** Check for voltage with test light. If necessary, replace faulty wires. See **ELECTRICAL SYSTEM**
	c. Stop solenoid on injection pump loose or faulty	**c.** Tighten solenoid. Check that solenoid clicks when key is turned off and on. Replace faulty solenoids
	d. No voltage at glow plug bus	**d.** If test light shows no voltage at bus with key at "preglow" position, test relay and wiring. See **IGNITION**
	e. Glow plugs faulty	**e.** Test and, if necessary, replace glow plugs. See **IGNITION.**
	f. Air in fuel system	**f.** Check fuel supply line from fuel tank for crack
	g. Injection pump not delivering fuel	**g.** If no fuel emerges from a loosened injector line during cranking, check camshaft drive belt and fuel supply from filter. **5.3**
	h. Injector lines misconnected	**h.** Connect lines in correct locations. **5.5**
	i. Injection timing incorrect	**i.** Adjust injection timing. **5.4**
	j. Faulty injectors	**j.** Check and, if necessary, repair or replace injectors. **5.5**
	k. Engine mechanical faults, as described earlier under this heading	**k.** Test compression. See **ENGINE**
	l. Faulty injection pump	**l.** Replace pump. **5.4**
2. Glow plug warning light not working	Bulb burned out or trouble in glow plug relay circuit	Test and repair as described in **IGNITION**
3. Idle speed incorrect or idle rough or irregular	**a.** Idle speed incorrectly adjusted	**a.** Check and, if necessary, adjust the idle speed. **5.1**
	b. Accelerator control binding	**b.** Check that governor lever on pump is not loose, then adjust accelerator cable. **5.2**
	c. Loose fuel hose between filter and injection pump	**c.** Replace hose or secure with clamps
	d. Injection pump bracket (rear mounting) cracked or broken	**d.** Check and, if necessary, replace bracket. **5.4**
	e. Air in fuel system	**e.** Check fuel supply line from fuel tank for cracks, kinks, or leaks
	f. Inadequate fuel supply owing to clogged fuel filter, or fuel return line and injection pipes leaking, dirty, kinked, or squeezed at connectors	**f.** Inspect and, if necessary, replace lines and hoses, replace fuel filter. See **LUBRICATION AND MAINTENANCE**

continued on next page

Table a. Diesel Engine Fuel Injection Troubleshooting (cont'd)

Symptom	Probable cause	Corrective action
3. Idle speed incorrect or idle rough or irregular (cont'd)	**g.** Faulty injectors **h.** Injection timing incorrect **i.** Engine mechanical faults, as described earlier under this heading **j.** Faulty injection pump	**g.** Check and, if necessary, repair or replace injectors. **5.5** **h.** Adjust injection timing. **5.4** **i.** Test comprssion. See **ENGINE** **j.** Replace pump. **5.4**
4. Smoky exhaust (black, blue, or white)	**a.** Engine lugging in too high a gear **b.** Engine not reaching correct operating temperature **c.** Maximum RPM incorrectly adjusted **d.** Faulty injectors **e.** Injection timing incorrect **f.** Restricted exhaust system **g.** Engine mechanical faults, as described earlier under this heading **h.** Faulty injection pump	**a.** Observe correct shift speeds as given in Owner's Manual **b.** Check and, if necessary, replace cooling system thermostat. See **COOLING SYSTEM** **c.** Check and, if necessary, adjust maximum RPM. **5.1** **d.** Check and, if necessary, repair or replace injectors. **5.5** **e.** Adjust injection timing. **5.4** **f.** Check exhaust system for dents and obstructions. **EXHAUST SYSTEM AND EMISSION CONTROLS** **g.** Test compression. See **ENGINE** **h.** Replace pump. **5.4**
5. Poor power output, slow acceleration or top speed (speedometer accurate, clutch not slipping)	**a.** Injection pump governor lever loose or not reaching maximum rpm adjusting screw **b.** Maximum rpm incorrectly adjusted **c.** Air filter dirty **d.** Inadequate fuel supply owing to clogged filter; or fuel return line and injection pipes leaking, dirty, kinked, or squeezed at connections **e.** Air in fuel system **f.** Ice or solidified wax in fuel lines (wintertime only) **g.** Faulty injectors **h.** Injection timing incorrect **i.** Engine mechanical faults, as described earlier under this heading **j.** Faulty injection pump	**a.** Tighten lever, check that accelerator pedal travel is not restricted, then adjust accelerator cable. **5.2** **b.** Check and, if necessary, adjust maximum RPM. **5.1** **c.** Clean or replace air filter. See **LUBRICATION AND MAINTENANCE** **d.** Inspect and, if necessary, replace lines and hoses, replace fuel filter **e.** Check fuel supply line between fuel tank and fuel injection pump **f.** Move car to warm garage until ice or wax has become liquid **g.** Check and, if necessary, repair or replace injectors. **5.5** **h.** Adjust injection timing. **5.4** **i.** Test compression. See **ENGINE** **j.** Replace pump. **5.4**
6. Excessive fuel consumption (markedly below 44 mpg (19 km/L) in mixed traffic at temperatures above 32°F (0°C))	**a.** Air filter dirty **b.** Fuel leaks **c.** Return pipe blocked **d.** Idle speed too fast or maximum rpm too high **e.** Faulty injectors **f.** Injection timing incorrect **g.** Engine mechanical faults, as described earlier under this heading **h.** Faulty injection pump	**a.** Clean or replace air filter. See **LUBRICATION AND MAINTENANCE** **b.** Check and, if necessary, replace or tighten all pipes, hoses and connections. **1., 5.** **c.** Check return line for kinks and dents; replace faulty lines. If line is clogged, blow it out with compressed air, then bleed fuel system **d.** Check and, if necessary, adjust idle speed and maximum RPM. **5.1** **e.** Check and, if necessary, repair or replace injectors. **5.5.** **f.** Adjust injection timing. **5.4** **g.** Test compression. See **ENGINE** **h.** Replace pump. **6.4**

3.2 Diagnostic Testing

These system tests are used to isolate and diagnose diesel fuel system problems, and to help pinpoint their causes. It is assumed that the glow plug system is functioning correctly, that the engine and drive belt are sound, and that injection pump timing and valve timing are correct.

Checking Fuel Supply to Injectors

When troubleshooting starting problems, check to determine whether fuel is being delivered to the injectors. First check visually for fuel leaks at the injector pipe unions or around the injector pump timing plug. To test fuel delivery, slightly loosen the fuel union nut on the fuel injector pipe for No. 1 cylinder, either at the pump or at the injector. See Fig. 3-1. Crank the engine and look for signs of fuel leakage at the loosened union.

WARNING ━━

Loosen the nut only about one-quarter to one-half turn to limit the amount of fuel leakage. The fuel injection system operates at very high pressure. Keep hands and eyes clear. Wear heavy gloves and eye protection.

WARNING ━━

Fuel will be expelled. Do not smoke or work near heaters or other fire hazards. Have a fire extinguisher handy.

CAUTION ━━

Diesel fuel is damaging to rubber. Wipe off any fuel that spills on hoses, wiring, and rubber steering and suspension parts, and wash with soap and water.

Fig. 3-1. Open end box wrench (Volkswagen special tool no. 3035 or equivalent) being used to loosen fuel union nut at the injector.

If no fuel is observed during this test, the most likely cause is a restriction or air leak in the fuel lines between the fuel tank and the injection pump, or a clogged fuel filter.

If fuel is observed but the engine still fails to start, possible causes are incorrect valve timing (see **ENGINE**) or incorrect injection pump timing (see **5.5 Injection Pump**).

When finished testing, tighten the fuel union nut and torque to 25 Nm (18 ft. lb.).

Idle Speed Drop Test

A defective or clogged injector may be the cause of hard starting, rough idling and running, knocking, or loss of power. An idle speed drop test is used to identify faulty injectors.

To test:

1. Run the car at fast idle. On 1985 models pull the cold start handle out. On later models pull the cold start handle out to the first detent.

2. Slightly loosen one of the fuel union nuts on a fuel injector pipe, either at the pump end or the injector end, as shown in Fig. 3-1, above.

WARNING ━━

Loosen the nut only about one-quarter to one-half turn to limit the amount of fuel leakage. The fuel injection system operates at very high pressure. Keep hands and eyes clear. Wear heavy gloves and eye protection.

WARNING ━━

Fuel will be expelled. Do not smoke or work near heaters or other fire hazards. Have a fire extinguisher handy.

3. Observe the condition of the idle. Idle speed should roughen and drop, due to loss of pressure at that injector. No change indicates that the injector was already malfunctioning.

4. Tighten the fuel union nut and torque it to 25 Nm (18 ft. lb.). Repeat the test for the other three injectors.

CAUTION ━━

Diesel fuel is damaging to rubber. Wash or wipe off any fuel that spills on hoses, wiring, and rubber steering and suspension parts.

Injectors which fail the test should be rebuilt or replaced. See **5.6 Injectors**.

6

4. FUEL SUPPLY

Fig. 4-1 is an exploded view showing the fuel tank, the fuel sender gauge, the expansion tank, and the tank vents. Fuel is drawn from the tank through a pickup tube in the fuel gauge sender assembly. Surplus fuel from the injection pump is returned to the tank, which also aids in warming the fuel during cold weather. Vents and the expansion tank compensate for expansion and contraction of the fuel volume.

When reinstalling the fuel tank after cleaning or repairs, it is important that the connections leading to the tank be installed correctly, without kinks and in their original locations. Errors can cause fuel starvation, a collapsed fuel tank, or faulty operation of the fuel injection system.

Fuel from the tank passes through a fuel filter and a water separator enroute to the injection pump in order to remove water and other harmful contaminants. The fuel filter, the water separator, and their connections are shown in Fig. 4-2. Information on maintenance of the water separator and the fuel filter can be found in **LUBRICATION AND MAINTENANCE**.

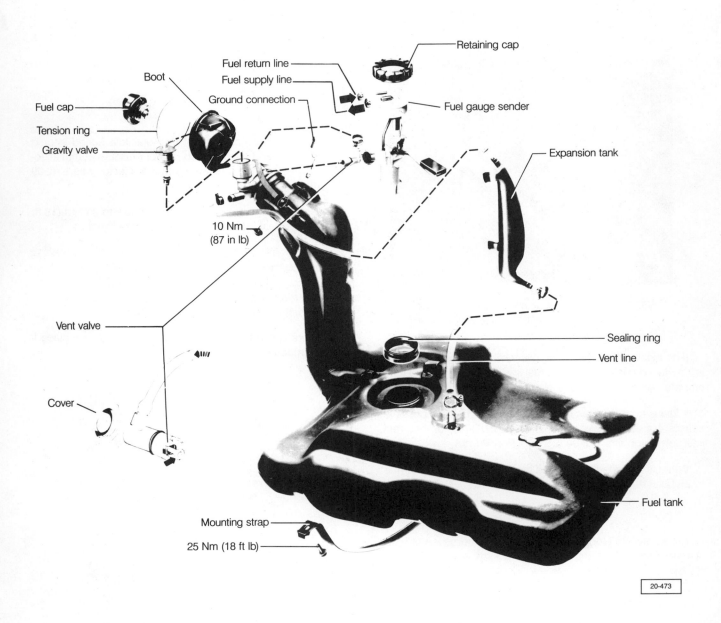

20-473

Fig. 4-1. Exploded view of diesel fuel system, including fuel tank, expansion tank, fuel gauge sender, and vent hoses.

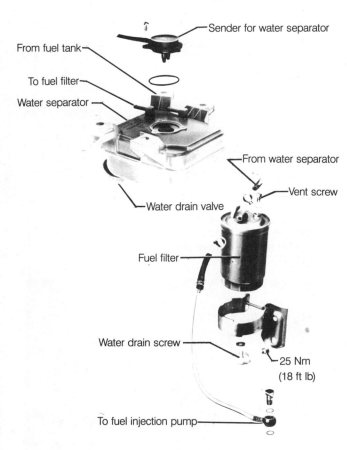

Fig. 4-2. Fuel filter and water separator, showing connections and direction of fuel flow.

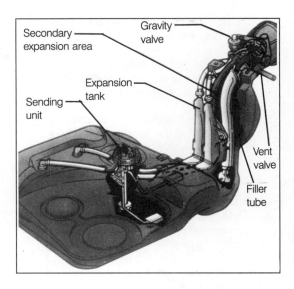

Fig. 4-3. View of fuel tank showing secondary expansion area. When vent valve is closed (filling), fuel in expansion area will rise no further than bottom of filler tube, due to back pressure.

A two-way pressure relief valve in the fuel cap prevents pressure build-up in the tank in the event of a failure of the normal tank ventilation. While vent problems are rare, failure of either vent could allow filling of the fuel tank to dangerous levels.

4.1 Fuel Tank Vents

There are two fuel tank vents, shown earlier in Fig. 4-1. Both vents are accessible by reaching up inside the rear fender on the fuel cap side.

The gravity valve is the main tank vent. It is normally open, but automatically closes when tilted more than 45°—such as in an accident—to prevent fuel spillage. The gravity valve is removed by unclipping it and pulling it straight up from its mounting. The vent valve is removed by first unscrewing its cover, and then pulling it straight out. You should be able to blow through the gravity valve when it is held vertically, but not when it is tilted past 45°.

The vent valve is operated by the insertion and removal of the fuel cap: inserting the cap opens the valve, removing it closes the valve. The vent valve controls the pressure in the expansion tank and the secondary expansion area around the filler tube. See Fig. 4-3. When the tank is being filled, the valve is closed, preventing fuel from entering the expansion tank or the secondary expansion area. When the vent valve is open, it allows the expansion of fuel into the expansion tank, and the venting of pressure through the gravity valve. You should be able to blow through the vent valve tube when the spring-loaded lever is pushed in (arrow, Fig. 4-1 above), but not when the lever is released.

4.2 Fuel Gauge Sender

It may become necessary to remove the fuel gauge sending unit to inspect the fuel pickup screen for blockage, or to replace the unit. The sender is removed and replaced as a unit, and is not repairable.

To remove fuel gauge sending unit:

> **CAUTION** ━━
> *The fuel tank should be no more than ¾ full.*

1. Disconnect the battery negative (−) terminal.

> **WARNING** ━━
> *Do not smoke or work near heaters or other fire hazards during any part of this procedure. Have a fire extinguisher handy.*

2. Remove the rear seat. Access to the fuel gauge sender is through a cover plate secured by three screws.

3. Unplug the wiring connector from the sending unit and disconnect the fuel lines.

4. By hand, or using a strap wrench if necessary, turn the knurled locking ring counter-clockwise to remove the ring. Remove the sending unit.

5. Installation is the reverse of removal. Use a new gasket when installing the sending unit. Refer to Fig. 4-4 for proper alignment of the sender unit.

NOTE ——

The fuel pickup is spring-loaded against the bottom of the fuel tank. When installing, slight downward pressure may be necessary to engage the locking ring.

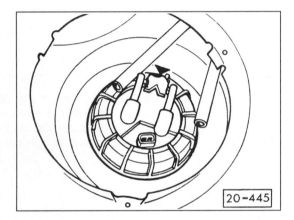

Fig. 4-4. Fuel gauge sending unit with cover plate removed and fuel lines and wiring connector unplugged. When installing, arrow markings on tank and sending unit align as shown.

5. FUEL INJECTION

This section covers adjustments and repairs to the diesel and turbo diesel fuel injection systems, including the injection pump and related parts, the camshaft drive belt, and the fuel injectors. Adjustments or repairs to the injection system are similar for all model years covered by this manual. 1986 and later injection pumps feature an additional idle speed boost system. All turbo diesel injection pumps employ a boost pressure enrichment feature.

Adjustments to the diesel engine's fuel injection system should be made carefully. Haphazard adjustments may not improve engine operation, and can cause serious engine and fuel injection trouble. Cleanliness is especially important. Always clean fuel unions before removing lines, and use lint-free cloths. If you lack the skills or the correct tools and instruments for adjusting the diesel engine's fuel injection, we suggest that you leave these sensitive adjustments to an authorized dealer or other qualified and properly equipped shop.

5.1 Idle Speed and Maximum RPM Adjustments

Although the fuel injection pump is self-lubricating and long-wearing, some wear occurs. Over time, periodic adjustment of the idle speed and maximum rpm may be necessary. Adjustments are also necessary if a new pump is installed.

Because the diesel engine has no electrical ignition system, special methods and equipment are required to be able to measure engine rpm. Volkswagen special tool no. VW 1367 measures rpm by detecting timing marks on the engine's flywheel through an access hole in the top of the bellhousing. VW 1324, shown in Fig. 5-1, is another Volkswagen special tool which converts engine vibrations to electrical signals which can be read as engine rpm with a conventional tachometer. While the latter method is much less expensive, the cost may still make dealer service a more cost-effective alternative.

Fig. 5-1. Tachometer connected to diesel rpm sensor, Volkswagen special tool no. VW 1324.

Checking and Adjusting Idle Speed
(1985 models without idle speed boost)

The engine should be at normal operating temperature. Oil temperature should be 122°F (50°C) minimum, or the cooling fan should have cycled on and off at least once. The cold start handle should not be pulled out, and all electrical accessories should be shut off. Engine speed on all 1985 diesels and turbo diesels should be 920 to 980 rpm. To adjust, loosen the locknut, shown in Fig. 5-2, and turn the adjusting screw, clockwise to increase idle speed or counterclockwise to reduce idle speed. Lock the adjusting screw in place by tightening the locknut. Finally, check the accelerator cable adjustment as described in **5.2 Accelerator Cable**.

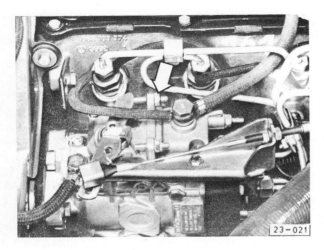

Fig. 5-2. Idle adjusting screw and locknut (arrow). On turbo diesel, assembly is integral with base of boost pressure enrichment housing.

Checking and Adjusting Idle Speed
(1986 and later models with idle speed boost)

Diesels since 1986 employ an injection pump with an idle speed boost system, as shown in Fig. 5-3, allowing manual idle boost for cold running. The old idle speed adjustment is sealed, and the cold start handle now has two detents. The first detent boosts the idle speed by about 100 rpm without cold start timing advance. The second detent increases idle by about 200 rpm and advances injection timing.

To measure idle, the engine should be at normal operating temperature. Oil temperature should be 122°F (50°C) minimum, or the cooling fan should have cycled on and off at least once. The cold start handle should not be pulled out, and all electrical accessories should be shut off. Engine speed on all 1986 and later diesels and turbo diesels should be 820 to 880 rpm. To adjust, turn the cap nut on the adjusting linkage as shown in Fig. 5-3. Turn the nut clockwise to increase idle speed and counterclockwise to decrease idle speed. Finally, check the accelerator cable adjustment as described in **5.2 Accelerator Cable**.

The basic pump adjustments performed by the manufacturer should allow idle to be adjusted within specifications. If, however, the idle speed cannot be brought below 900 rpm, the linkage must be adjusted. First, loosen the locknut on the stop screw (number 3 shown in Fig. 5-3) and turn it two turns counterclockwise. Next, turn the cap nut on the linkage counterclockwise to adjust idle. Finally, turn the stop screw clockwise until it just touches the low idle stop and tighten the locknut.

Quick-check idle speed boost with the engine running. With the cold start handle at the first detent, idle speed should increase to 880 to 940 rpm. With the handle at the second detent, idle speed should be 1000 to 1100 rpm. If not correct, first check the adjustment of the cold start cable as described in **5.3 Cold Start System**. To adjust, loosen the locknut on the stop screw (number 4 shown in Fig. 5-3) and adjust idle by turning the stop screw. Tighten the locknut.

6

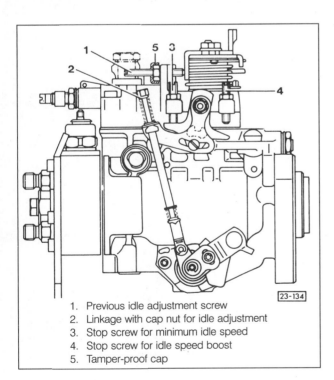

1. Previous idle adjustment screw
2. Linkage with cap nut for idle adjustment
3. Stop screw for minimum idle speed
4. Stop screw for idle speed boost
5. Tamper-proof cap

Fig. 5-3. 1986 and later diesel injection pump with idle speed boost, showing locations of idle adjustment mechanisms.

Checking and Adjusting Maximum RPM
(All 1985 through 1989 diesel and turbo diesel models)

The engine should be at normal operating temperature. Oil temperature should be 122°F (50°C) minimum, or the cooling fan should have cycled on and off at least once. The cold start handle should not be pulled out, and all electrical accessories should be shut off. With the transmission in neutral and the hand brake set, move the throttle lever on the injection pump until the engine is operating at its maximum speed without load. Maximum speed for all except turbo diesel is 5300 to 5400 rpm. Maximum speed for turbo diesel is 5050 to 5150 rpm. To adjust, loosen the locknut indicated in Fig. 5-4 and turn the adjusting screw until engine rpm is within the specified range. Finally, check the accelerator cable adjustment as described in **5.2 Accelerator Cable**.

Fig. 5-4. Maximum rpm adjusting screw and locknut (arrow). On turbo diesel, assembly is integral with base of boost pressure enrichment housing.

CAUTION ━━
At no time should engine speed exceed the specified maximum rpm. Turn adjusting screw to reduce rpm as necessary before final adjustment.

5.2 Accelerator Cable

This section covers replacement and adjustment of the accelerator cable for cars with manual transmission only. For cars with automatic transmission, the adjustment is part of the transmission adjustments described in **AUTOMATIC TRANS-AXLE**.

Cable adjustment is relatively simple and is usually required only after the idle speed and maximum rpm have been adjusted, after a new pump is installed, or when installing a new cable.

Replacing Accelerator Cable

Attachment and detachment of the cable at the pump, as well as complete replacement of the cable, are simple. Fig. 5-5 illustrates cable routing and attachments.

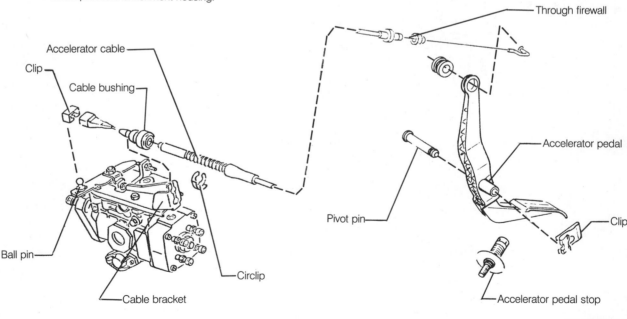

Fig. 5-5. Accelerator cable routing and attachment.

To detach the cable from the pump, slide the metal retainer clip off the end of the cable to free it from the ball pin, and remove the circlip to free the cable from the bracket. If removing the cable only to work on the pump, move the cable aside, taking care not to kink it. If the pump is being replaced, some cable attachment parts may need to be removed from the old pump and reused. Installation on the new pump is the reverse of removal. The cable adjustment should be checked as described in **Checking and Adjusting Accelerator Cable**.

When installing a new cable, disengage the cable from the accelerator pedal and withdraw it through the firewall, taking care to note the routing of the cable through the engine compartment.

Checking and Adjusting Accelerator Cable

Check the adjustment of the accelerator cable with the engine not running. First, with a helper pressing the accelerator pedal all the way down, check to see that the governor portion of the linkage mechanism just contacts the maximum rpm adjustment screw. If, at full throttle, the lever does not reach the stop, or reaches it too soon and strains the cable, then adjustment is necessary. Remove the cable-retaining circlip shown in Fig. 5-6 and relocate the accelerator cable in its bracket until the lever just contacts the stop. Reinstall the circlip on the cable so that it holds the cable in position. Depress the accelerator pedal a few times to recheck the adjustment and re-adjust if necessary.

Fig. 5-6. Circlip (arrow) used to adjust accelerator cable.

5.3 Cold Start System

Since the diesel engine relies on the heat of compression to ignite its fuel, it is harder to start in cold weather when the cold engine dissipates heat quickly. To compensate for hard cold starting conditions, the diesel injection pump includes a manually-operated timing advance feature. By means of a cable, pulling the cold start handle—one detent only on 1985 cars, the second detent on 1986 and later cars—advances injection timing by about 5°. The fuel is injected sooner and given more time to burn, offsetting most of the negative effects of a cold

engine. The cold start feature affects injection timing up to about 2200 rpm.

Cold starting difficulty can also be a symptom of other problems with the engine or injection system. See **3. Troubleshooting**.

Removing, Installing, and Adjusting Cold Start Cable

To detach the cold start cable from the pump, first loosen the clamping screw, then remove the lock washer and withdraw the cable from the bracket. See Fig. 5-7. Note the position of the washer on the cable. Attachment is the reverse of removal.

Fig. 5-7. Cold start cable attachment to diesel injection pump, top view. Washer (**1**) and lock washer (**2**) secure cable. Locking screw and pivot pin (**3**) used for adjustment. Turbo diesels are similar.

6

To replace the cold start cable, first remove the handle and lock nut and withdraw the cable from the dashboard. The cable components are shown in Fig. 5-8. Remove the cable from the pump as described above, and draw the entire cable through the firewall into the passenger compartment. Note the cable routing in the engine compartment. Installation is the reverse of removal.

To adjust the cold start cable, push the cold start handle all the way in, then loosen the clamping screw shown in Fig. 5-8. Without moving the lever, pull taught the end of the cable that comes through the pivot pin, and tighten the clamping screw.

5.4 Camshaft/Injection Pump Drive Belt
(diesel engines only)

Although Volkswagen's maintenance schedule does not specify a replacement interval, the publisher recommends, as preventative maintenance, that the drive belt be inspected periodically and replaced every 60,000 to 75,000 miles (96,000 to 120,000 km) or 4 to 5 years. Removal of the belt is the best way to thoroughly inspect it, and is required for some repairs, such as injection pump or cylinder head removal. To simply replace the belt, the sprockets need not be removed.

Any time the camshaft drive belt is installed, camshaft timing and injection pump timing must be checked and adjusted. Some special tools are required.

To remove:

1. Remove the upper drive belt cover. One bolt holds the cover on its mount. Three spring clips hold the upper cover to the rear drive belt cover. See Fig. 5-9.

2. Remove the cylinder head cover and gaskets as described in **ENGINE**.

3. Using a socket on the crankshaft pulley bolt, rotate the engine by hand to set the No.1 piston at Top Dead Center (TDC), and remove the pulley from the crankshaft. Check TDC removing the plug from the top of the flywheel bellhousing and aligning the marks on the flywheel, as shown in Fig. 5-10. Both valves for No. 1 cylinder should be closed (both cam lobes pointing approximately upward).

4. Lock the camshaft in position. Fig. 5-11 illustrates the use of a Volkswagen special tool, no. 2065A, inserted in the slot at the end of the camshaft to hold it in position.

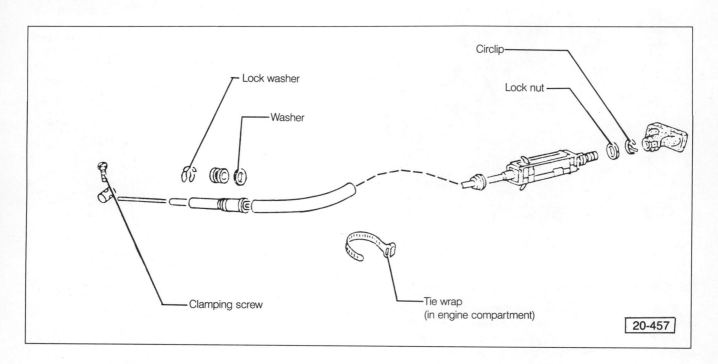

Fig. 5-8. Components of diesel cold start cable.

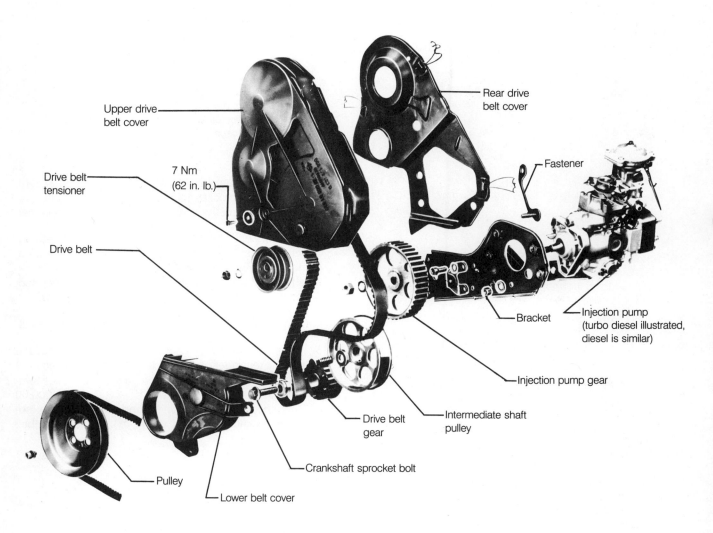

Upper drive belt cover

Rear drive belt cover

Drive belt tensioner

7 Nm (62 in. lb.)

Fastener

Drive belt

Injection pump (turbo diesel illustrated, diesel is similar)

Bracket

Injection pump gear

Drive belt gear

Intermediate shaft pulley

Crankshaft sprocket bolt

Pulley

Lower belt cover

Fig. 5-9. Camshaft and injection pump drive belt, sprockets, and covers.

23-081

Fig. 5-10. Alignment of marks (arrow) indicating TDC.

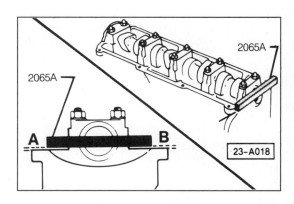

2065A

2065A

A   B

23-A018

Fig. 5-11. Volkswagen special tool no. 2065A used to hold camshaft position. Shim tool at **A** and **B** with feeler gauges of equal thickness, until there is no play.

5. Lock the injection pump in position. Insert a lock pin through the injection pump sprocket and the rear drive belt cover to keep the pump from turning, as shown in Fig. 5-12. If the drive belt is broken or has jumped time, do not attempt to lock the sprocket in position.

Fig. 5-12. Injection pump sprocket locked in position with pin. Volkswagen special tool no. 2064 (order no. T02 064 000 00 ZEL) shown. Snug fit is required, allowing no movement.

6. Loosen the coolant pump pulley bolts. Remove the V-belts as described in **LUBRICATION AND MAINTE-NANCE**. Remove the coolant pump pulley.

7. Remove the two bolts and one nut holding the lower drive belt cover, then remove the cover.

8. Loosen the camshaft drive belt tensioner's locknut. Turn the tensioner counterclockwise to remove tension from the belt, and remove the belt. Work it off the sprockets away from the engine.

9. Temporarily tighten the tensioner locknut to inspect the tensioner. Check for smooth rotation and no play. Replace a worn tensioner.

10. Inspect the drive belt for damage such as stretched cords, exposed threads, missing teeth, or other visible damage. Do not reinstall a worn or otherwise faulty belt.

11. Inspect the area around the camshaft oil seal for leaks. If the seal is leaking, it is easiest to replace it before installing the camshaft drive belt. See **ENGINE**.

To install and adjust:

CAUTION ━━

The cold start cable must be completely pushed in, in the off position, during the installation procedure.

1. If not done previously, set the crankshaft to TDC (No. 1 cylinder) and lock the camshaft and the injection pump at their TDC positions as described above under **To remove:**.

CAUTION ━━

Special care must be taken when rotating the camshaft or the crankshaft independently. Mistimed rotation could cause the pistons to hit the valves, damaging either or both.

2. Loosen the camshaft drive belt sprocket bolt ½ turn. Loosen the sprocket from the camshaft end by tapping the back side of the sprocket with a soft-faced hammer.

3. Install the drive belt. There should be no slack between the camshaft sprocket and the injection pump sprocket, or between the injection pump sprocket and the crankshaft sprocket. Temporarily tighten the drive belt tensioner, just enough to keep the belt firmly in place.

4. Remove the lock pin from the injection pump sprocket.

5. Tension the drive belt. Loosen the tensioner locknut and turn the tensioner clockwise, using a spanner wrench as shown in Fig. 5-13. The tension gauge shown, Volkswagen special tool no. VW210 (order no. TV0 210 000 00 ZEL) should read between 12 and 13. Torque the tensioner locknut to 45 Nm (33 ft. lb.). Remove the belt tension gauge.

NOTE ━━

An approximate measure of belt tension can be made without a tension gauge by twisting the belt by hand. At the center between the injection pump sprocket and the crankshaft sprocket, if the belt can be twisted 45° but no further, it is tensioned correctly.

Fig. 5-13. Spanner wrench (arrow) being used to adjust belt tension. Volkswagen special tool no. VW210 is belt tension gauge.

6. Tighten the camshaft sprocket bolt to and remove the locking tool from the camshaft.

NOTE —

Torque hex (six-sided) camshaft sprocket bolts to 45 Nm (33 ft. lb.). Torque twelve-sided camshaft sprocket bolts to 90 Nm (67 ft. lb.) **plus** ½ turn (180°). During repairs, a twelve-sided bolt should always be replaced.

7. Turn the engine by hand, two full revolutions in the direction of crankshaft rotation (clockwise). Using a soft-faced hammer, strike the camshaft drive belt once, between the camshaft sprocket and the injection pump sprocket. Recheck drive belt tension and adjust if necessary.

8. Check and adjust injection pump timing as described in **5.5 Injection Pump**.

The remainder of installation is the reverse of removal. Torque the bolt for the upper drive belt cover to 7 Nm (62 in. lb.), and the lower belt cover bolts to 10 Nm (89 in. lb.). Torque the V-belt pulley attachment bolts to 20 Nm (15 ft. lb.). Install and adjust the V-belts as described in **LUBRICATION AND MAINTENANCE**.

5.5 Injection Pump

The diesel fuel injection pump performs three functions. It pressurizes the fuel, precisely times the delivery of fuel to the injectors, and meters the amount of fuel delivered. The pump is driven by the camshaft drive belt at ½ crankshaft speed. Internal parts are lubricated by the diesel fuel, so no routine maintenance is required. If clean fuel is used, and the fuel filter and water separator properly maintained, the pump can be expected to operate reliably for a long time.

Most diesel fuel system problems are caused by a problem outside the injection pump. If injection pump problems do occur, it will most likely be due to wear and high mileage. Internal injection pump wear is most often characterized by an unsteady idle, or the inability to precisely adjust pump timing. Internal repairs to the injection pump require specialized knowledge and equipment, and parts for rebuilding are not generally available. Faulty pumps must be serviced by the pump manufacturer or other qualified diesel fuel injection repair shop.

Parts are available to service the stop solenoid, the external throttle and advance mechanisms, and the outlet check valves. Adjusting injection pump timing requires some special tools. More serious problems generally require replacement of the injection pump.

Turbo diesel injection pumps use an additional boost-pressure-operated enrichment device. See **5.7 Turbo Diesel Boost Enrichment**. Diesel fuel injection pumps for cars with automatic transmissions also incorporate a manual fuel shut-off valve that can be used to stop the engine should the pump's electrical stop solenoid fail. See **AUTOMATIC TRANSMISSION**.

To remove:

1. Remove the camshaft drive belt as described in **5.4 Camshaft/Injection Pump Drive Belt**.

2. Loosen the injection pump sprocket retaining nut, but do not completely remove it. Using a puller, as shown in Fig. 5-14, apply tension to the sprocket. Lightly tap the puller bolt until the sprocket pops loose from the tapered shaft. Remove the puller, the nut and washer, and the sprocket.

Fig. 5-14. Puller installed on fuel injection pump sprocket. Tension puller and tap bolt (arrow) to remove sprocket. Spacer between nut and puller screw prevents damage to pump shaft.

3. Disconnect the battery negative (−) terminal from the battery.

4. Detach all fuel pipes and hoses from the injection pump, including the fuel intake line from the fuel filter, and the fuel return line. Remove the fuel pipes to the injectors as a unit, taking care not to bend them. Cover the unions with a clean, lint-free cloth.

WARNING —

Fuel will be expelled when the fuel lines are loosened. Do not smoke or work near heaters or other fire hazards. Have a fire extinguisher handy.

CAUTION —

Thoroughly clean all unions before disconnecting fuel lines.

5. On turbo diesels, remove the bolt and hose at the top of the boost pressure enrichment housing leading from the housing to the intake manifold.

6. Disconnect the electrical wire from the stop solenoid. On the cars with an upshift indicator, disconnect the wires attached to the idle and full throttle switches.

7. Disconnect the accelerator cable and the cold start cable as described in **5.2 Accelerator Cable** and **5.3 Cold Start System**.

8. Remove the bolt from the injection pump rear support (Fig. 5-15). Remove the bolts from the front injection pump mounting plate and remove the pump.

Fig. 5-15. Injection pump rear support bolt (**1**). To avoid damage to the distributor plunger, do not loosen the bolts (arrows) on the fuel distributor head.

To install:

1. Install the pump on the front and rear mounting plates, and loosely tighten the bolts. Align the marks indicated in Fig. 5-16, then torque the bolts to 25 Nm (18 ft. lb.).

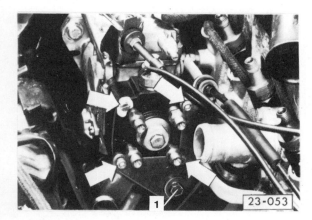

Fig. 5-16. Mark on fuel injection pump aligned with mark on mounting plate (broken line).

2. Reconnect the fuel lines and the fuel pipes to the injectors. Torque the connections to 25 Nm (18 ft. lb.).

> **NOTE** ——
>
> The fuel return line connection is labeled OUT. On normally-aspirated diesels, the return line connection is on the pump housing. On turbo diesels, the return line connection is on the boost pressure enrichment housing. Do not interchange the fuel supply union bolt with the return line union bolt.

> **NOTE** ——
>
> The injector line connections on the pump are marked A, B, C, D. Connect No. 1 cylinder to A, No. 3 to B, No. 4 to C, and No. 2 to D. In reconnecting the fuel hoses, take care not to interchange the fuel supply union bolt with the return line union bolt, which is marked OUT on its head and contains a restrictor.

3. On turbo diesels, reconnect the hose leading from the intake manifold to the boost pressure enrichment housing and torque it to 10 Nm (89 in. lb.).

4. Reconnect the electrical wires to the stop solenoid, and upshift sensors where applicable. Reconnect the accelerator cable and the cold start cable as described in **5.2 Accelerator Cable** and **5.3 Cold Start System**.

5. Position the injection pump sprocket on the shaft and loosely install the nut. Hand-turn the sprocket until it lines up with the mounting plate and the pump body as shown in Fig. 5-17. Lock the sprocket in position as shown in Fig. 5-12 above, and torque the nut to 45 Nm (33 ft. lb.).

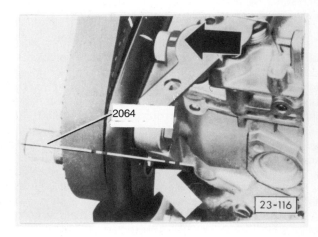

Fig. 5-17. Mark on injection pump sprocket aligned with mark on mounting plate and pump (black arrow). Installation of locking pin (white arrow) also shown.

6. Install the camshaft drive belt as described in **5.4 Camshaft/Injection Pump Drive Belt**.

7. Check and adjust injection pump timing as described below in **Checking and Adjusting Injection Pump Timing.**

8. Check and adjust idle speed and maximum rpm as described in **5.1 Idle Speed and Maximum RPM Adjustments.**

Checking and Adjusting Injection Pump Timing

Precise injection timing is critical, since it also determines when combustion begins. Checking and adjustment of injection timing is necessary any time the injection pump or the timing belt have been loosened or replaced, and may be necessary at other times to maintain precise timing.

Injection timing is checked by measuring the injection pump plunger's stroke at TDC with a dial indicator. Adjustment, if necessary, is based on this measurement. Before adjusting injection pump timing, the cold start cable must be all the way in, and the camshaft drive belt must be properly installed and tensioned. See **5.4 Camshaft/Injection Pump Drive Belt.**

To check and adjust:

1. Using a socket on the front crankshaft bolt, hand-turn the engine clockwise until No. 1 cylinder is at TDC. Both valves should be closed and the TDC mark on the flywheel should be aligned, as shown in Fig. 5-18 if the engine is installed and in Fig. 5-19 if it is not installed.

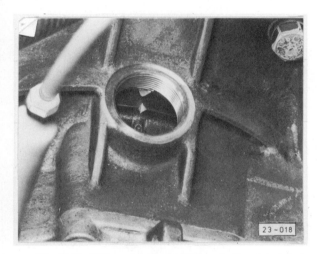

Fig. 5-18. TDC mark on flywheel aligned with pointer in hole in bellhousing (engine installed).

2. Remove the timing-check plug from the pump cover, shown in Fig. 5-20, and install a dial indicator with (3 mm range) as shown in Fig. 5-21. The gauge should be installed so that it indicates about 2.5 mm (preload).

> **WARNING** ━━
>
> *Fuel will be expelled when the timing plug is removed. Do not smoke or work near heaters or other fire hazards. Have a fire extinguisher handy.*

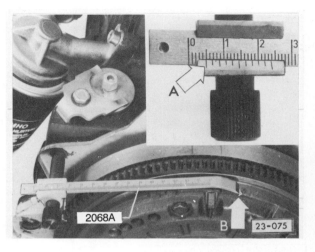

Fig. 5-19. Volkswagen special tool no. 2068A (order no. T02 068 A00 23 ZEL) being used to align TDC mark on flywheel (**B**) with engine removed. Use left notch (**A**) as measurement point. TDC is indicated when scale reads 5 mm for vehicles with manual transmission; 85 mm for vehicles with automatic transmission.

Fig. 5-20. Timing check plug (white arrow) to be removed for installation of dial indicator. Only the small central plug and its gasket should be removed. The black arrows indicate the fuel injection pump check valves.

Fig. 5-21. Dial indicator mounted on fuel injection pump. Adapter shown is Volkswagen special tool no. 2066 (order no. T02 066 000 00 ZEL).

3. Hand-turn the crankshaft counterclockwise (opposite normal engine rotation) until the dial indicator stops moving. Zero the dial indicator.

4. Hand-turn the crankshaft clockwise (normal rotation), stopping precisely at TDC. With the engine at TDC, the dial indicator should read within the checking limits given in **Table b**.

Table b. Injection Pump Timing

Model	Timing
1985 (standard diesel)	
checking	0.90–1.05 mm
adjusting	0.95 ± 0.02 mm
1986–1989 (standard diesel)	
checking	0.83–0.97 mm
adjusting	0.90 ± 0.02 mm
Turbo diesel (all)	
checking	0.95–1.05 mm
adjusting	1.00 ± 0.02 mm

5. If the dial indicator reading is within the checking values given, it is not necessary to adjust the injection timing.

6. If the dial indicator reading is out of specification, a timing adjustment is necessary. With the engine at TDC, slightly loosen the injection pump rear support bolt, shown earlier in Fig. 5-15, and the front mounting plate bolts as shown in Fig. 5-22. Rotate the pump, either clockwise or counterclockwise, until the dial indicator reading is within the adjusting specification tolerance.

Fig. 5-22. Lower mounting plate bolt (arrow) accessible through hole in the injection pump sprocket.

7. Tighten the mounting bolts and torque them to 25 Nm (18 ft. lb.). Rotate the engine by hand through two complete revolutions (clockwise), and then repeat the checking procedure. Repeat the timing adjustment if necessary.

8. Remove the dial indicator. Reinstall the timing check plug with a new gasket, and torque it to 15 Nm (11 ft. lb.).

9. Start the engine and check for leaks around the timing check plug. If any is seen, the timing check plug may be retorqued to 25 Nm (18 ft. lb.).

Inspecting and Replacing Stop Solenoid

A diesel engine is normally stopped by cutting off its fuel supply. On Volkswagen diesels, this is done by means of an electrical solenoid valve operated by the "ignition" key. The valve is normally closed. An electrical signal from the ignition switch (key ON) opens the valve. A failure of the solenoid may cause an inability to start the engine, or to stop it even if the key is turned off.

Stop Solenoid Quick-Check

A quick-check of the stop solenoid can be made by turning the key on and off, without operating the starter. The stop solenoid should click (open) when the key is turned on, and click again (closed) when the key is turned off. If a solenoid seems faulty, first clean the solenoid as described below and test it again before replacing it. When working on the injection system, all fuel unions must be kept clean, and lint-free cloths should be used, as dirt and lint can cause internal parts to bind.

To inspect and replace:

1. Disconnect the battery negative (−) terminal.

2. Disconnect the electrical wiring from the stop solenoid. Clean the area around the solenoid, and remove it. See Fig. 5-23.

WARNING ──

Fuel may be expelled. Do not smoke or work near heaters or other fire hazards. Have a fire extinguisher handy.

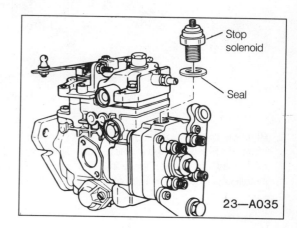

Fig. 5-23. Stop solenoid removed from injection pump.

3. Clean and inspect the solenoid plunger and seat. If the plunger does not move freely after cleaning, the solenoid should be replaced.

4. Install the stop solenoid using a new seal. Torque the solenoid to 40 Nm (29 ft. lb.), and reconnect the wiring.

5. Reconnect the battery negative (−) terminal.

6. Quick-check the solenoid again as described above. If no clicking noises are heard, check the wire for battery voltage (approximately 12V) when the key is on. If there is voltage and the stop solenoid still does not operate, replace the solenoid.

Injection Pump Valves

The injection pump check valves shut off the fuel supply to the injectors at the end of injection to prevent pressure build up and fuel "dribble" at the injector nozzles, which can cause pre-ignition and high exhaust emissions. The location of the valves is shown earlier in Fig. 5-20. The valves do not generally fail. However, their seals can become loose over time, and should be replaced or the valve body tightened if leakage is seen around them. Leaks around the injection pump valves can also cause a pressure drop in one or more injectors leading to hard starting and rough running.

> **CAUTION** ━━
>
> *Diesel fuel is damaging to rubber and plastic, and should be cleaned off of hoses and wiring after the leaks are corrected.*

To correct leaks:

1. Thoroughly clean the fuel pipes, the unions, and the pump head.

2. Loosen the nuts holding the injection pipes to the pump valve housings, then torque the housings to the pump to 45 Nm (33 ft. lb.).

> **WARNING** ━━
>
> *Fuel will be expelled when the nuts are loosened. Do not smoke or work near heaters or other fire hazards. Have a fire extinguisher handy.*

3. Re-tighten the injection pipe nuts and torque them to 25 Nm (18 ft. lb.).

4. Run the engine and check for leaks. If there is still leakage, replace the sealing washers in the pump valves.

5. Loosen the fuel pipe unions at the injectors and at the injection pump. Remove the fuel pipes as a unit, using care not to bend or kink them.

6. Loosen and remove the leaking pump valve. If more than one housing is removed, be careful not to interchange parts. Fig. 5-24 is an exploded view of one valve.

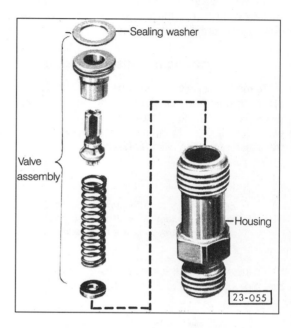

Fig. 5-24. Exploded view of injection pump valve.

7. Install a new sealing washer and reinstall the valve housing. The washer is Volkswagen Part No. 068 130 787 A. Torque to 45 Nm (33 ft. lb.).

8. Reinstall the fuel pipes. Torque to 25 Nm (18 ft. lb.).

9. If leakage continues, replace the entire valve assembly. (Volkswagen Part No. 068 130 795).

5.6 Injectors

The injectors are nozzles which open under great pressure, about 130 bar (1849 psi). They are lubricated by the fuel that flows through them and do not usually fail mechanically. They can, however, become partially or totally clogged due to contaminated fuel. The first signs of injector trouble usually appear as knocking noises from one or more of the injectors or cylinders, engine overheating, loss of power, smoky black exhaust, increased fuel consumption, engine misfire, or excessive blue smoke during cold start. Other problems can cause similar symptoms. See **3. Troubleshooting** before beginning repairs. Test injectors with an idle speed drop test, as described in **3.2 Diagnostic Testing.**

The injectors can be disassembled for inspection and repair and parts are available, however, any time an injector is repaired its opening pressure must be readjusted by adding or subtracting internal shims.

When working on any part of the injection system, but especially the injectors, everything must be kept absolutely clean. Wipe clean all pipe unions before disconnecting. Use lint-free cloth to dry the injector components. Removal and disassembly of the injectors requires a 27 mm deep-well socket.

Removing and Installing Injectors

To remove an injector, first unscrew the fuel pipe union nuts at both the injection pump and the injectors, and detach the fuel pipes as a unit. Then remove the fuel return hoses from between the injectors. Using a 27 mm deep-well socket, unscrew the injector from the cylinder head.

CAUTION ▬

Be absolutely sure to remove the heat shield from the bottom of each injector hole. When reinstalling, always use a new heatshield. See Fig. 5-25.

To install, torque the injectors to 70 Nm (51 ft. lb.), and the fuel pipe union nuts to 25 Nm (18 ft. lb.).

NOTE ▬

Bleeding air from the system is not necessary.

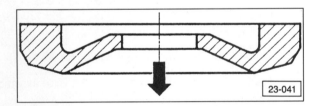

Fig. 5-25. Proper installation of the fuel injector heat shield. Arrow points down, away from injector.

Pressure Testing Injectors

Once removed, the injectors can be tested for correct spray pattern, leakage, and correct opening pressure. Fig. 5-26 illustrates an injector being tested with a hand pressure pump. If the injectors fail any of the pressure tests that follow, see **Inspecting and Repairing Injectors**, later in this section.

WARNING ▬

Keep hands or other parts of your body clear of the injector spray. Working pressure can cause the fuel oil to penetrate the skin. Work carefully. Do not smoke or work near heaters or other fire hazards. Have a fire extinguisher handy.

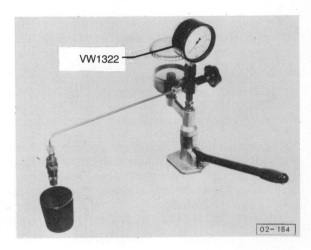

Fig. 5-26. Injector installed on hand pressure pump. Volkswagen special tool (VW1322 or US1111) shown.

Check general injector performance using rapid, short strokes of the testing pump lever (4 to 6 strokes per second). Check that the injector sprays in an even, compact cone pattern and stops cleanly, and that it does not drip after spraying.

To check injectors for leaking, slowly press down on the pump lever to a pressure of about 110 bar (1564 psi). Maintain that pressure for about 10 seconds. During that time, no fuel should drip from the injector nozzle.

To measure injector opening pressure, slowly push the pump lever down. Watch the gauge and read the value when the injector begins to spray. Opening pressure specifications are given in **Table c**. Any injector which does not meet the specifications should be rebuilt or replaced.

Table c. Diesel Fuel Injector Opening Pressure

Diesel	
new injectors.	.130 to 138 bar (1849 to 1963 psi)
wear limit.	.120 bar (1706 psi)
Turbo diesel	
new injectors.	.155 to 163 bar (2248 to 2364 psi)
wear limit.	.140 bar (2030 psi)

Inspecting and Repairing Injectors

Mount the injector in a vise, clamping the upper body as shown in Fig. 5-27. Using a 27 mm deep-well socket, loosen— but do not remove—the lower body. Turn the injector over and clamp the lower body in the vise. The upper and lower bodies can now be separated without scattering the internal parts. Assembly is the reverse of disassembly. Torque the upper and lower bodies together at 70 Nm (51 ft. lb.)

CAUTION —

When disassembling more than one injector, keep the parts separate. Interchanging parts from one injector to the other can result in faulty operation or make necessary a lengthy testing and adjustment procedure.

Fig. 5-27. Upper injector body clamped in vise so that lower body can be loosened.

A disassembled injector is shown in Fig. 5-28. Clean the disassembled injector parts in solvent, using brass scrapers and brushes if necessary to remove hardened deposits. Take care not to scratch or damage the needle or its seat. Inspect the parts carefully—for worn or rough needle seat, worn-out nozzle bottom, cavities on the needle seat, out-of-round spray drilling, grooves and pressure marks on the needle, tempering colors on the nozzle—and replace them as required.

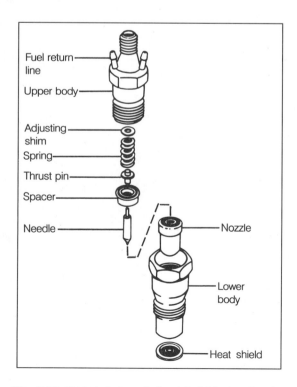

Fig. 5-28. Exploded view of diesel fuel injector. Opening pressure is adjusted by changing shim.

Test the reassembled injector's opening pressure and change adjusting shim thickness as necessary to adjust to specifications. A thicker shim increases opening pressure, and a thinner shim reduces it. An increase in shim thickness of 0.05 mm will increase pressure by approximately 5.0 bar (71 psi). Shims are available in thicknesses from 1.00 mm to 1.95 mm in 0.05 mm increments. Refer to the opening pressure specifications in **Table c** above.

5.7 Turbo Diesel Boost Enrichment

Volkswagen turbo diesel engines incorporate a boost pressure enrichment mechanism on the fuel injection pump, to increase the amount of fuel injected when the turbocharger is providing more air. The boost enrichment housing, shown in Fig. 5-29, incorporates a diaphragm and push rod connected to the injection pump distributor plunger and to intake manifold pressure. An increase in manifold pressure, due to turbocharger boost, acts on the boost enrichment diaphragm, and in turn the injection pump distributor plunger, to increase the amount of fuel delivered to each injector.

Turbo diesel boost enrichment is pre-set at the factory, and the boost enrichment housing can only be replaced as a unit with the fuel injection pump. The only maintenance necessary is to see that the housing vent is open when a new pump is installed. See Fig. 5-29.

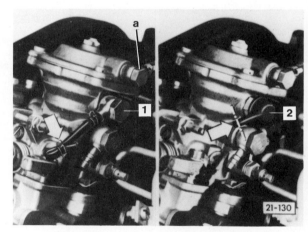

Fig. 5-29. Boost pressure enrichment housing. Connection from intake manifold shown at **a**. New injection pump with a vent hose (**1**) must have sealing clamps (left arrow) removed. Rubber cap (**2**) must have tip cut off cap (right arrow) for venting.

6. TECHNICAL DATA

I. Tightening Torques

Alternator adjuster (bolt)	.35 Nm (26 ft. lb.)
Alternator adjusting bracket (bolt)	.20 Nm (15 ft. lb.)
Alternator pivot (bolt)	.26 Nm (19 ft. lb.)
Camshaft drive belt cover (upper, bolt)	.7 Nm (5 ft. lb.)
Camshaft drive belt cover (lower, bolts)	.10 Nm (7.5 ft. lb.)
Camshaft drive belt tensioner (bolt)	.45 Nm (33 ft. lb.)
Camshaft sprocket (bolt) six-sided	.45 Nm (33 ft. lb.)
twelve-sided	.90 Nm (67 ft. lb.) **plus** ½ turn (180°)
Fuel IN and Fuel OUT lines (bolt)	.25 Nm (18 ft. lb.)
Fuel tank mounting strap (nut)	.25 Nm (18 ft. lb.)
Injection pump check valves	.45 Nm (33 ft. lb.)
Injection pump sprocket (bolt)	.45 Nm (33 ft. lb.)
Injection pump to mounting plate (bolt)	.25 Nm (18 ft. lb.)
Injector in cylinder head (always use new heatshield with recess towards injector)	.70 Nm (51 ft. lb.)
Injector pipe to injector (nut)	.25 Nm (18 ft. lb.)
Injector pipe to injection pump (nut)	.25 Nm (18 ft. lb.)
Injector upper body to lower body	.70 Nm (51 ft. lb.)
Stop solenoid to injection pump	.40 Nm (29 ft. lb.)
Timing check plug normal	.15 Nm (11 ft. lb.)
if leaking	.25 Nm (18 ft. lb.)
Turbo boost pressure enrichment housing (from intake manifold)	.10 Nm (7.5 ft. lb.)
V-belt pulley (bolt)	.20 Nm (15 ft. lb.)

II. Diesel Fuel System General Technical Data

Fuel requirement	.Diesel fuel No. 2
Fuel tank capacity	.53 liters (14.0 U.S. gallons)
Engine idle speed	
1985	.920–980 rpm
1986–1989 (with idle speed boost)	.820–880 rpm
1986–1989 idle speed boost at first detent	.880–940 rpm
1986–1989 idle speed boost at second detent	.1000–1100 rpm
Engine maximum speed	
1985–1989 except turbo diesel	.5300–5400 rpm
1985–1989 turbo diesel only	.5050–5150 rpm
Injection pump plunger movement at Top Dead Center (TDC) with injection timing and valve timing correct	
1985 (standard diesel engine) checking	.0.90–1.05 mm
adjusting	.0.95 ± 0.02 mm
1986–1989 (standard diesel with idle speed boost) checking	.0.83–0.97 mm
adjusting	.0.90 ± 0.02 mm
1985–1989 (turbo diesel engine) checking	.0.95–1.05 mm
adjusting	.1.00 ± 0.02 mm
Injection pump timing advance with cold start knob pulled out	.5° at pump
Injector pipe connections between pump and injectors:	
Pump connection A to injector for cylinder No. 1	
Pump connection B to injector for cylinder No. 3	
Pump connection C to injector for cylinder No. 4	
Pump connection D to injector for cylinder No. 2	
Injector leakage test specification	
No leakage after 10 seconds at 110 bar (1564 psi)	
Injector opening pressure	
Standard diesel engine	.130–138 bar (1849–1963 psi)
Wear limit	.120 bar (1706 psi)
Turbo diesel	.155–163 bar (2248–2364 psi)
Wear limit	.140 bar (2030 psi)

EXHAUST SYSTEM AND EMISSION CONTROLS

Contents

Introduction 3

1. General Description 4
  1.1   Exhaust System 4
        Turbocharger 4
  1.2   Emission Controls 4
        Catalytic Converter 4
        Oxygen Sensor System 5
        EGR System 5
  1.3   Exhaust System and Emission Control
        Identification 5

2. Maintenance 5

3. Troubleshooting 5
  3.1   Basic Troubleshooting Principles 5

4. Exhaust System 7
  4.1   Removing and Installing Exhaust System ... 10
        Removing Exhaust System 10
        Removing and Installing Front Pipe Spring
        Clamps 10
        Installing Exhaust System 12
  4.2   Catalytic Converter 12
        Removing and Installing Catalytic Converter .. 13
        Checking Catalytic Converter 13

5. Oxygen Sensor System 13
  5.1   Testing Oxygen Sensor System (CIS) 14
        Measuring Frequency Valve Duty Cycle 14
        Quick Checking Oxygen Sensor System 14
        Checking Thermoswitch 14

        Checking Frequency Valve 15
        Checking Oxygen Sensor System
        Control Unit 15
        Checking Oxygen Sensor 16
        Troubleshooting Oxygen Sensor Circuits ... 16
        Replacing Oxygen Sensor Control Unit 16
  5.2   Testing Oxygen Sensor System (CIS-Electronic)
        (CIS-Electronic) 17
        Testing Oxygen Sensor 17
        Checking Control Unit Response 17
        Replacing Oxygen Sensor 18
        Replacing Oxygen Sensor Control Unit 18
  5.3   Testing Oxygen Sensor System (Digifant II) ... 18
        Testing Oxygen Sensor Function 18
        Replacing Oxygen Sensor 19
        Replacing Digifant Control Unit 19

6. Exhaust Gas Recirculation System 19
        Testing and Replacing EGR Valve 19
        Testing and Replacing EGR Thermo-pneumatic
        Valve 20

7. Turbocharger (turbo diesel only) 20
  7.1   Removing and Installing Turbocharger 21
  7.2   Testing Turbocharger Wastegate and Blow-Off
        Valve 22

**8. Exhaust System and Emission Control Technical
    Data** 24
    I.   Tightening Torques
         (engine codes: RD, PF, PL) 24
    II. Tightening Torques
         (engine codes: GX, HT, RV, MZ) 24
    III. Tightening Torques (engine codes: ME, MF) .. 24

2 Exhaust System and Emission Controls

IV. Turbocharger Technical Data
(engine code: MF) 24

V. Oxygen Sensor System Technical Data (CIS) . 24

VI. Oxygen Sensor System Technical Data
(CIS-E) 24

TABLES

a. Exhaust and Emission Control Troubleshooting 6

Exhaust System and Emission Controls

7

Introduction

The exhaust system has two main functions: first, to provide a conduit for the rapidly expanding gasses of combustion, and second, to quiet the noise and cool the temperature of the exhaust. On cars equipped with a catalytic converter, the exhaust system and the emission control system remove most of the pollutants resulting from combustion.

Exhaust system function depends on each component being free from holes, with airtight seals at all joints. Emission control system function depends on proper adjustment of the fuel injection system and the ignition system, as well as on the action of the catalytic converter. Any misadjustment of the fuel injection or ignition systems can adversely affect the emission control system.

During operation, all exhaust system components are subjected to extremes in temperature and pressure, vibration, and damaging contact with all manner of road hazards. Even though the exhaust system is designed for relatively maintenance-free operation, the environment to which it is exposed means that regular inspection is warranted. The only scheduled recommended emission control maintenance is the replacement of the oxygen sensor.

This section covers the maintenance, troubleshooting, and repair of the exhaust system and the emission controls. Special tools are required to remove and install the front pipe spring clamps on certain models, but otherwise only basic hand tools are required for complete servicing. Testing of the emission control system requires special equipment and skills. If you lack the necessary skills or equipment, we suggest you leave these tests or repairs to an authorized Volkswagen dealer or other qualified and properly equipped repair shop. We especially urge you to consult your authorized Volkswagen dealer service department before attempting any repairs on a car that may be subject to Volkswagen's warranty coverage.

1. GENERAL DESCRIPTION

1.1 Exhaust System

The basic exhaust system components (Fig. 1-1) are an exhaust manifold, front pipe, and muffler with integral tailpipe. All gasoline models have an additional middle muffler, or resonator, and all U.S. models have a catalytic converter. Some Canada cars have a pre-muffler in place of the catalytic converter. On turbo diesel models, the turbocharger is mounted between the exhaust manifold and front pipe.

The exhaust manifold is mounted to the cylinder head and channels exhaust from the four exhaust ports to the front pipe. The manifold is made of cast iron to withstand the extreme heat, vibration, and pressures of combustion. The corrosion-resistant alloy steel front pipe mounts to the exhaust manifold at the top, and to the catalytic converter or pre-muffler at the bottom. On some models, the catalytic converter and the front pipe are one piece. The converter housing is stainless steel. The remainder of the exhaust system is mild steel treated to resist corrosion.

The front end of the system is supported by attachment to the exhaust manifold, while the middle and rear mufflers are suspended by six rubber retaining rings or hangers from the underbody of the car. The retaining rings provide positive but non-rigid mounting, allowing expansion and contraction of the system due to changes in temperature and helping to isolate noise and vibration from the body.

Turbocharger

The turbocharger has a cast housing with separate chambers in the intake and exhaust systems, each housing has an impeller. The impellers are linked by a common shaft mounted in roller bearings. The turbine impeller on the exhaust side is driven by the flow of exhaust gasses, and in turn drives the compressor impeller on the intake side. The compressor impeller pressurizes the intake air up to a specified limit, controlled by a pressure relief mechanism called a wastegate.

1.2 Emission Controls

Emission controls are used on gasoline-engined cars to reduce harmful exhaust emissions. The diesel-engined cars covered in this manual do not require such equipment. All U.S. models are equipped with a catalytic converter and an oxygen sensor system. Canada cars with automatic transmission have an exhaust gas recirculation (EGR) system. U.S. models equipped with the Digifant II engine management system include a crankcase control valve (Fig. 1-2) as part of the crankcase emission control system.

Catalytic Converter

The catalytic converter is similar in appearance to a small muffler. Its honeycombed ceramic core contains hundreds of tiny passages whose surfaces are coated with precious metal catalysts. The catalysts react with the exhaust gasses to reduce the quantity of harmful pollutants in the exhaust.

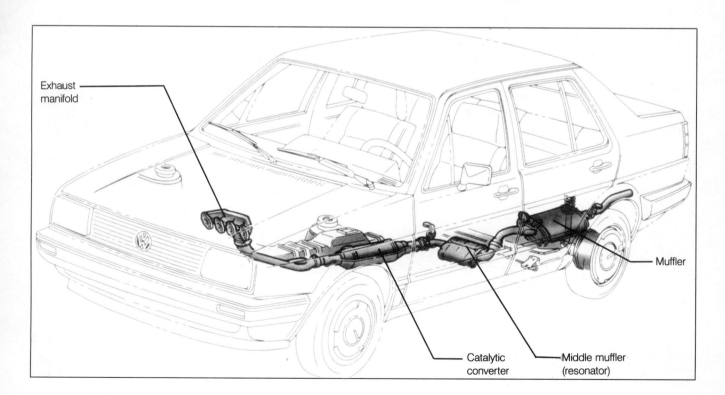

Fig. 1-1. Basic exhaust system with catalytic converter used on U.S. models.

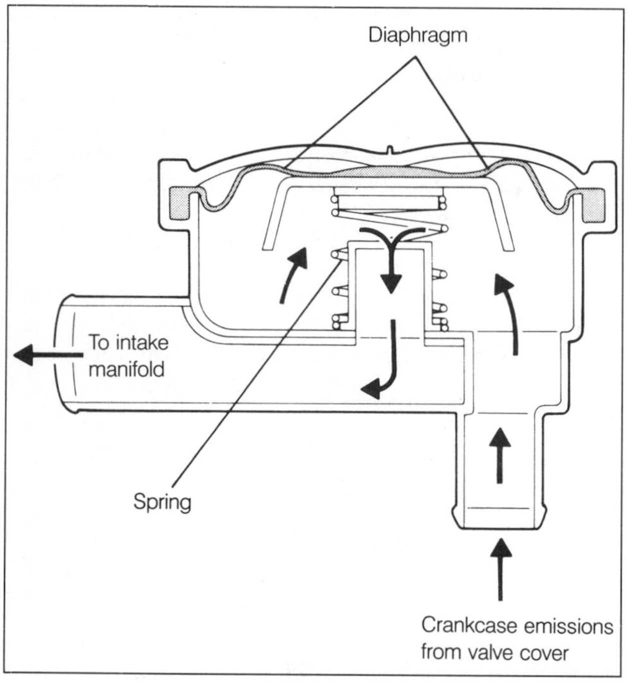

Fig. 1-2. Crankcase emission control valve used on engines with Digifant II. Valve routes crankcase emissions to intake manifold.

Oxygen Sensor System

The catalytic converter reduces emissions most efficiently when the percentage of oxygen in the exhaust falls within a certain narrow range. The oxygen sensor system is part of a closed-loop system which regulates fuel mixture to maintain peak combustion efficiency and proper oxygen content in the exhaust. The oxygen sensor continuously measures the amount of oxygen in the exhaust stream and sends a proportional signal to the fuel injection system which in turn adjusts the fuel mixture. The oxygen sensor system consists of an oxygen sensor which is mounted in the exhaust system and linked electrically to a control unit and, in turn, to the fuel injection system.

EGR System

The EGR system used on some Canada models reduces emissions by recirculating some exhaust gas back into the engine under certain conditions. The system consists of a vacuum-operated valve mounted on the intake manifold and linked to the exhaust system. At part-throttle the EGR valve opens, allowing exhaust gas to be drawn into the intake manifold.

1.3 Exhaust System and Emission Control Identification

Specific exhaust system features vary according to engine specifications. In this section procedures, specifications, and system illustrations are identified by the engine code for the engine to which they apply. Where no engine code is provided,

it can be assumed that the information applies to all engines in vehicles covered by this manual. For information on locating the engine code on a specific car, see **ENGINE**.

Emission controls vary depending mainly on the fuel injection system used, and are identified accordingly. For help in identifying fuel injection systems, see **FUEL SYSTEM (Gasoline)**.

2. MAINTENANCE

There are only a few exhaust system and emission control maintenance operations which should be carried out at specified mileage intervals, or after a certain period of service.

Volkswagen recommends inspection of the exhaust system every 15,000 miles (24,000 km), but it is a good idea to inspect it whenever the underside of the car is made accessible for other repair work. The system should be inspected immediately whenever it becomes unusually noisy, if exhaust can be smelled inside the car, or if damage is suspected.

More information on maintenance schedules and requirements for the exhaust system and emission controls can be found in **LUBRICATION AND MAINTENANCE** or under the numbered headings in this section listed below.

1. Inspecting exhaust system

2. Checking EGR system. **6.**

3. Replacing oxygen sensor. **5.2**

3. TROUBLESHOOTING

This troubleshooting section pertains to the exhaust and emission control systems, including the exhaust manifold and pipes, the muffler, the catalytic converter, and the oxygen sensor system.

Problems such as exhaust leakage or excessive noise are self-evident as relating to the exhaust system. Problems such as poor performance, rough running, or increased emissions may have more complex causes. Troubleshooting for running and performance problems can also be found in **IGNITION**, **ENGINE**, and **FUEL SYSTEM**. For help in selecting the appropriate section, see the discussion of troubleshooting in **FUNDAMENTALS**.

3.1 Basic Troubleshooting Principles

As with any troubleshooting, analysis of the observed symptoms is the key to isolating and identifying exhaust and emission systems problems. Begin with careful observation, keeping in mind the following questions:

How has the problem developed? A symptom which develops quickly usually indicates damage or failure of an isolated part. In the case of the exhaust system, such damage or failure may be due to striking a road hazard. Noise is, of course, the main indicator of exhaust system problems. A gradual increase in noise level is more likely a general indication of the condition of the whole system. More extensive repair, perhaps complete replacement, may be necessary.

Is the symptom rpm dependent? The correct amount of backpressure helps the engine produce power smoothly over a wide range of engine speeds. Excessive backpressure due to failed or damaged components may cause poor performance, rough idling, or stalling. The catalytic converter with its small passages is especially susceptible to plugging if it gets over-heated or if the car accidently burns leaded fuel. On turbo diesels, loss of power at higher rpm may indicate a failed turbocharger.

Is the symptom temperature dependent? Cold running problems are almost certainly not caused by the oxygen sensor system, since the fuel injection system operates without it when the engine is cold.

Table a lists problems commonly associated with the exhaust and emission control systems, their probable causes, and suggested corrective actions. The numbers in bold type in the corrective action column refer to the numbered headings in this section of the manual where the suggested repairs are described.

Table a. Exhaust and Emission Control Troubleshooting

Symptom	Probable cause	Corrective action
1. Hissing, rumbling, loud noise during acceleration	a. Exhaust system leaks b. Internally damaged muffler or catalytic converter	a. Examine all system joints (see **LUBRICATION AND MAINTENANCE**). Replace faulty components. **4.1** b. Replace faulty components. **4.1**
2. Exhaust system rattles	a. Exhaust system out of alignment b. Missing or broken rubber exhaust system retaining ring	a. Re-align exhaust system. **4.1** b. Replace retaining ring(s). **4.1**
3. Reduced power, poor mileage, hesitation on initial acceleration, rough idle	a. Oxygen sensor system faulty/out of adjustment b. Faulty EGR valve c. Excessive backpressure due to plugged catalytic converter d. Excessive backpressure due to damaged muffler or pipes	a. Test oxygen sensor system function, replace faulty components. **5.1, 5.2** b. Test EGR system and repair or replace faulty components. **6.** c. Replace catalytic converter. **4.2** d. Inspect components and replace as required. **4.1**
4. Cold running hesitation, stalling at idle	a. Faulty oxygen sensor thermoswitch (CIS)	a. Test and replace if necessary. **5.1**
5. Failed emissions test	a. Oxygen sensor system faulty/out of adjustment b. Catalytic converter failed	a. Test system and replace faulty components. **5.1** or **5.2** b. Replace catalytic converter. **4.2**
6. Severe power loss (turbo diesel)	a. Failure of turbocharger wastegate b. Failure of blow-off vale	a. Test wastegate and, if necessary, replace turbocharger. **7.2** b. Test and replace blow-off valve as required. **7.2**

4. EXHAUST SYSTEM

The exhaust system is bolted together at welded flanges or clamped together at slip-joints. Slots and dimples are incorporated into the mating flanges to ensure proper alignment. An individual gasket is used at each of the four exhaust manifold ports for mounting to the cylinder head. One gasket is also used at the front pipe to exhaust manifold joint, fastened with either spring clamps or a bolted flange, depending on the engine, as shown in Fig. 4-1, Fig. 4-2 and Fig. 4-3. The metal heat shield is attached to the front pipe at the mounting flange.

From the catalytic converter back, the mufflers and pipes are joined together with slip-joints secured with circular clamps, as shown in Fig. 4-4, Fig. 4-5, and Fig. 4-6. Brackets welded to the pipes and mufflers support the system by rubber retaining rings connected to brackets on the body.

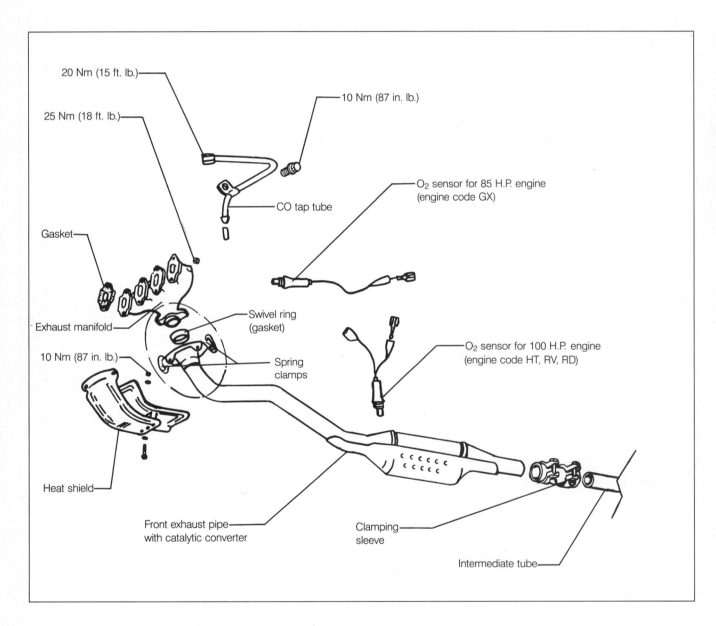

Fig. 4-1. Manifold and front pipe assembly used on GTI, Golf, and Jetta with GX, HT, and RV engines, and GTI with RD engine.

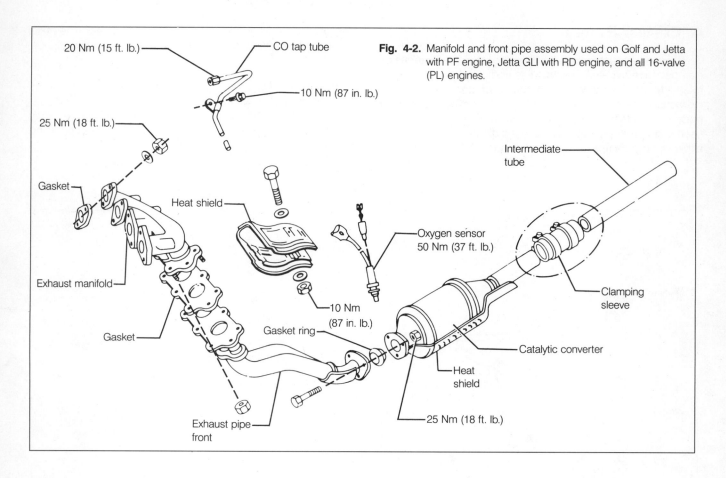

Fig. 4-2. Manifold and front pipe assembly used on Golf and Jetta with PF engine, Jetta GLI with RD engine, and all 16-valve (PL) engines.

20 Nm (15 ft. lb.)

CO tap tube

10 Nm (87 in. lb.)

25 Nm (18 ft. lb.)

Gasket

Heat shield

Intermediate tube

Exhaust manifold

Oxygen sensor
50 Nm (37 ft. lb.)

Clamping sleeve

Gasket

10 Nm (87 in. lb.)

Gasket ring

Catalytic converter

Heat shield

Exhaust pipe front

25 Nm (18 ft. lb.)

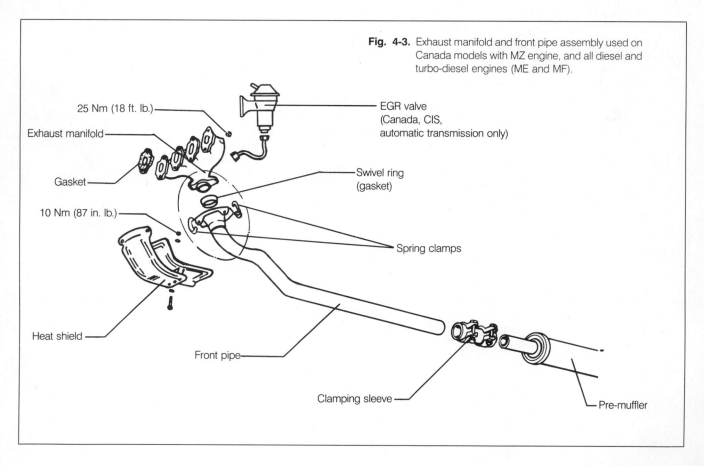

Fig. 4-3. Exhaust manifold and front pipe assembly used on Canada models with MZ engine, and all diesel and turbo-diesel engines (ME and MF).

25 Nm (18 ft. lb.)

Exhaust manifold

EGR valve
(Canada, CIS,
automatic transmission only)

Gasket

Swivel ring
(gasket)

10 Nm (87 in. lb.)

Spring clamps

Heat shield

Front pipe

Clamping sleeve

Pre-muffler

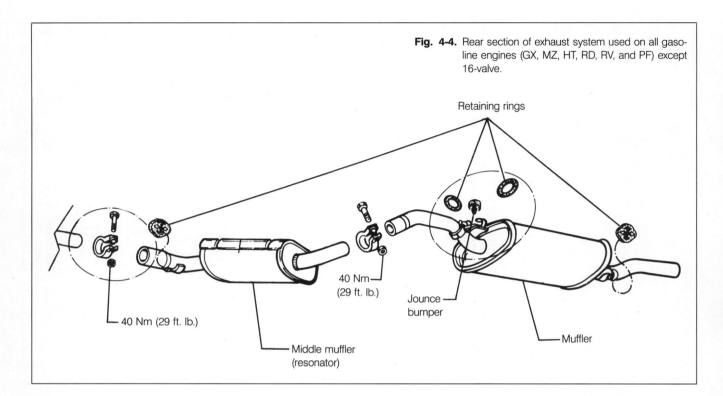

Fig. 4-4. Rear section of exhaust system used on all gasoline engines (GX, MZ, HT, RD, RV, and PF) except 16-valve.

Retaining rings

40 Nm (29 ft. lb.)

40 Nm (29 ft. lb.)

Jounce bumper

Middle muffler (resonator)

Muffler

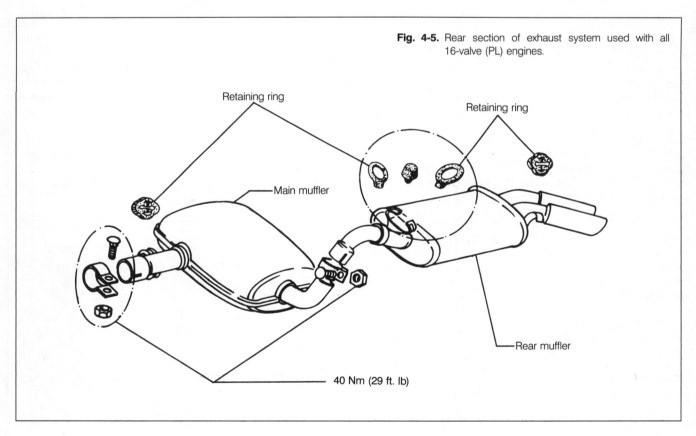

Fig. 4-5. Rear section of exhaust system used with all 16-valve (PL) engines.

Retaining ring

Retaining ring

Main muffler

Rear muffler

40 Nm (29 ft. lb)

7

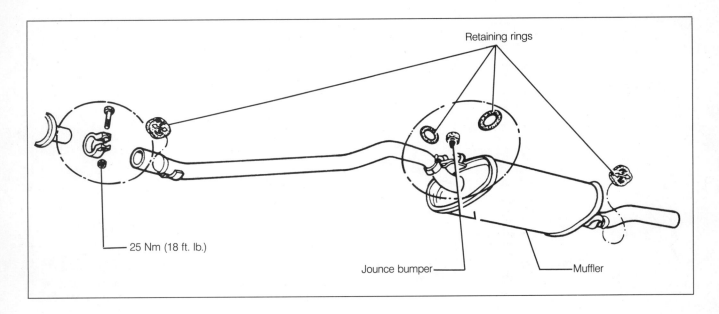

Fig. 4-6. Rear section of exhaust system used with diesel and turbo diesel (ME and MF) engines.

4.1 Removing and Installing Exhaust System

Because the front pipe and catalytic converter are made of special corrosion-resistant materials, the mufflers and other pipes tend to deteriorate more quickly. This deterioration also tends to affect the system as a whole. If any one part of the system is perforated by rust, it is very likely that other parts are similarly affected.

If replacing only part of the system, make sure that the new parts will fit properly with the old before removal. Parts from different sources may not mate properly. For partial replacement, genuine Volkswagen parts from an authorized Volkswagen dealer will mate best with the original parts.

New bolts and clamps are always recommended. The chance of getting the old ones off in reusable condition is slim anyway. If removing the front pipe, the gasket should be inspected and, if damaged or leaking, replaced. Use eye protection and heavy gloves to work on the rusty parts of the old exhaust system.

If it is necessary to remove the front pipe, there may be a need for special tools. 1986, 1987, 1988, and 1989 models with GX, MZ, RV, ME, and MF engines require a special wedge tool set to safely remove the front pipe spring clamps. Their removal is hazardous without the proper tools. See the procedure below for more details.

Removing Exhaust System

Individual components can be removed without completely dismantling the system. The rubber retaining rings allow some movement—enough to remove front components without removing the rear also. Removal of the left rear tire will improve access to the joint between the middle and rear mufflers. A penetrating oil applied to all bolts and slip joints several hours before performing the work will make removal easier.

Removing and Installing Front Pipe Spring Clamps

On all engines with spring clamps (Fig. 4-7) fastening the front pipe to the exhaust manifold, the clamps must be expanded to remove them. To avoid personal injury or damage, use of the expanding wedge set, Volkswagen special tool no. 3140, is highly recommended for removal and installation of both old and new clamps.

WARNING ——

Due to the spring tension in the clamps, serious injury may result from improper handling or from attempts to remove or install the clamps without proper tools.

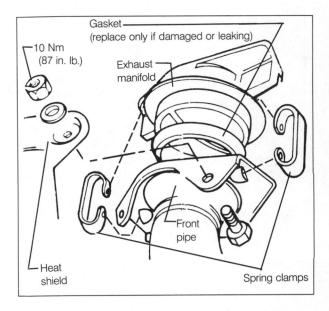

Fig. 4-7. Exploded view of front pipe connection with spring clamps.

To remove:

1. Push the front pipe to one side to expand the opposite clamp. Insert one short wedge in the expanded clamp as shown in Fig. 4-8. Push the pipe the opposite way to expand the other clamp and insert the other short wedge.

   CAUTION —

   When inserting wedge into spring clamp be sure it is completely inserted. The shoulders of the wedge should butt against the edge of the clamp.

   WARNING —

   Use extra caution when handling the expanded spring clamps. Spring tension can expel the wedges with considerable force and may cause serious injury. Wear safety goggles or safety glasses.

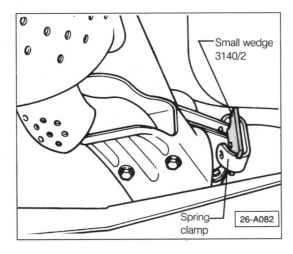

Fig. 4-8. Short wedge being installed in expanded spring clamp.

2. Push the front pipe to one side, and use a pair of locking pliers to grasp the clamp and wedge on the opposite side and remove them as a unit.

3. Repeat the operation to remove second clamp and wedge.

4. If the old clamps are to be reused, the wedges should remain in the clamps until they are reinstalled. If it is necessary to replace the clamps, place the old clamp with the installed wedge between the jaws of a vise, as shown in Fig. 4-9. Open the jaws of the vise approximately 15 mm (⁹⁄₁₆ in.).

5. Use a soft-faced mallet to drive the longer starting wedge into the clamp next to the short wedge, to further expand the clamp.

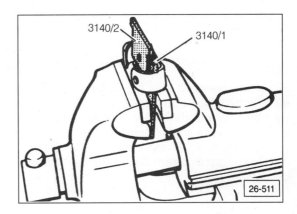

Fig. 4-9. Removing short wedge 3140/2 with longer starting wedge 3140/1.

6. Turn clamp over, knock out the short wedge, then knock out longer starting wedge. Repeat this process to remove the wedge from the other clamp.

   WARNING —

   The wedge will be expelled with considerable force. Provision should be made to catch the wedge in a safe container or trap to avoid injury.

To install:

1. If the spring clamps are being replaced, place a new clamp on its side in vise jaws and, using a soft-faced mallet, drive the longer starting wedge into clamp until it is spread enough to allow insertion of the short wedge next to the starting wedge. Drive in the short wedge until its shoulder butts against the edge of the spring clamp.

   WARNING —

   Do not attempt to insert the short wedge until first spreading the clamp with the starting wedge. Serious injury and tool and clamp damage may result.

2. Turn the clamp over and knock out the starting wedge, leaving the short wedge in place. Repeat the operation for the second clamp.

3. To install the clamps, position the front pipe against the exhaust manifold. If the gasket has been removed, it should be placed in position at this time. Push the pipe to one side and install an expanded clamp and wedge on that side.

4. Push the pipe to the other side and install the remaining clamp and wedge on that side. With the pipe in this position, remove the first wedge from its clamp. Use the mallet if necessary.

5. Push the pipe to the other side and remove the second wedge.

Installing Exhaust System

Loosely install and align the complete system before tightening any clamps or mounting bolts. Anti-seize compound used on all joints and threaded fasteners will extend service life and make any future replacement easier. Align the clamping sleeve and slip joints as shown in Fig. 4-10 and Fig. 4-11. Make sure that no part of the exhaust system contacts any part of the car body.

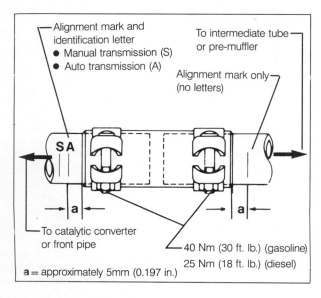

Fig. 4-10. Alignment of clamping sleeve.

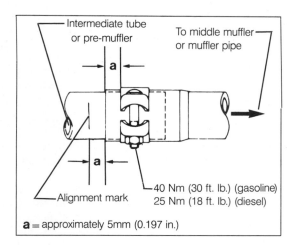

Fig. 4-11. Alignment of slip-joint.

The rubber retaining rings should be installed as indicated in Fig. 4-12. They should be evenly stressed. The jounce bumper should have the clearance shown in Fig. 4-13. Always use new rubber retaining rings when reinstalling the exhaust system.

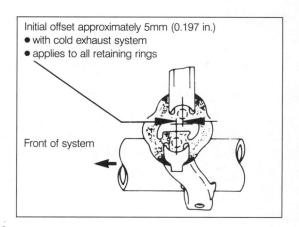

Fig. 4-12. Alignment of retaining rings.

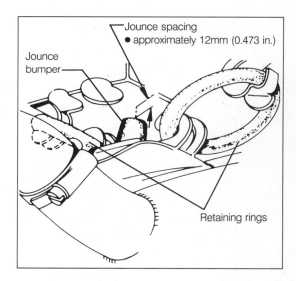

Fig. 4-13. Jounce bumper clearance.

After the system is loosely installed and aligned, tighten the bolts and clamps. Torque values are given in Fig. 4-1 through Fig. 4-6 above. After completing the installation, start the engine and check for any exhaust leakage. Some slight smoking and odor as the new parts become hot for the first time are normal. System alignment can be checked by driving the car over a rough road and listening for sounds of the exhaust system striking the body.

4.2 Catalytic Converter

All of the cars covered by this manual which have an oxygen sensor system also have a three-way catalytic converter in the exhaust system. Fig. 4-14 shows the construction of the catalytic converter and illustrates the chemical reaction that turns harmful compounds into nitrogen, carbon dioxide, and water.

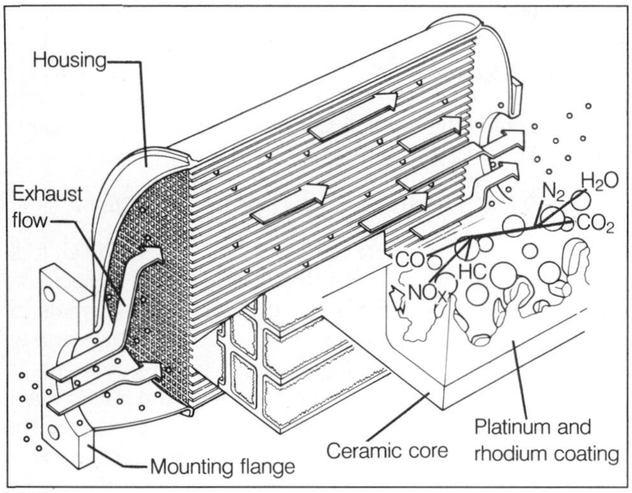

Fig. 4-14. Cutaway view of catalytic converter illustrating re-action of harmful compounds to form nitrogen, carbon dioxide, and water.

The catalytic converter is designed to be maintenance free, and under normal operating conditions it should last at least 60,000 miles (96,000 km). However, conditions which result in elevated temperature in the converter can cause damage and leave the catalytic converter partially plugged or inoperative. Some of those conditions are: incorrect ignition timing, incorrect fuel injection CO adjustment, engine misfiring, prolonged idling, prolonged high load such as towing, and the use of leaded gasoline.

Reduced power, stalling at idle, rattles in the exhaust system, and measured excessive emissions are all possible indications of a faulty catalytic converter. The converter can be removed and visually inspected if converter failure is suspected. See **Checking Catalytic Converter** below.

Removing and Installing Catalytic Converter

The catalytic converter is one of the components of the exhaust system and can be removed and installed with the rest of the system as described in **4.1 Removing and Installing Exhaust System**. On cars where the converter is an integral part of the front pipe, removal of the front pipe is required to thoroughly inspect the converter.

Checking Catalytic Converter

To check a one-piece front pipe and converter, remove the pipe and hold it vertically with the outlet down. Firmly tap the end on a block of wood, then turn the pipe over and tap the other end in the same manner. A knocking sound inside the converter housing indicates that the ceramic core has become dislodged, and the converter should be replaced.

In addition to the check above, a separate catalytic converter can be visually inspected by holding it up to a strong light and looking through both ends. If the core appears broken or melted down as shown in Fig. 4-15, the converter should be replaced.

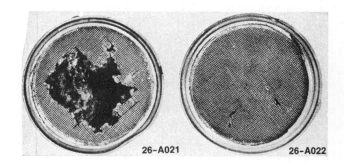

Fig. 4-15. Examples of catalytic converter cores showing severe meltdown (left) and minor meltdown (right).

5. Oxygen Sensor System

The Oxygen sensor system provides the fuel injection system with information about combustion efficiency by measuring the oxygen content in the exhaust. The exhaust-mounted oxygen sensor is constructed of ceramic material coated with platinum. One surface is exposed to the exhaust gas, while the other is exposed to atmosphere. The difference in oxygen content between the two surfaces causes a chemical reaction which generates a low-voltage signal (100–1000mv). This signal is monitored by the control unit which, in turn, signals for changes in the air/fuel ratio in the fuel injection system.

Since the oxygen sensor system relies on low-voltage signals, it is very sensitive to contamination or poor connections. Making sure that the electrical contacts are clean and dry may cure system problems easily and preclude the need for time-consuming testing.

Because the oxygen sensor system is different for each fuel injection type, the repair information in this section is organized according to fuel injection type. For help in identifying the fuel injection system, see **FUEL SYSTEM (Gasoline)**.

Replacement of the oxygen sensor is a scheduled maintenance procedure. The specified replacement interval varies depending on model year. On 1985–1987 models, the sensor's replacement interval is signalled by an indicator light on the instrument panel coming on as a service reminder. After the oxygen sensor is replaced, the mileage counter must be reset. On 1988 and 1989 models with oxygen sensors, the service reminder light has been omitted. See **LUBRICATION AND MAINTENANCE** for more information on the oxygen sensor replacement interval and the mileage counter resetting procedure.

NOTE ——

Emission controls, including the oxygen sensor system, are covered by an extended warranty. See **LUBRICATION AND MAINTENANCE** for maintenance requirements. Consult an authorized Volkswagen dealer about warranty coverage before beginning any repairs.

5.1 Testing Oxygen Sensor System
(CIS)

The system has four main components: the oxygen sensor, the oxygen sensor control unit, the frequency valve, and the thermoswitch. The oxygen sensor is located in the exhaust manifold, near the connection to the front pipe. The control unit, located in the cowling behind the engine compartment, monitors the signal from the oxygen sensor and controls the frequency valve. The frequency valve, mounted in a fuel line near the airflow sensor, opens and closes at a variable rate to finely adjust fuel pressure, and therefore air/fuel ratio. The thermoswitch, mounted on the cylinder head coolant outlet, interrupts the circuit and places the system in a stand-by mode whenever engine coolant temperature is below 82°F (28°C).

The most obvious indication of system function is the on/off action of the frequency valve, referred to as its duty cycle. To quick-check the system's function, listen for the hum of the frequency valve cycling on and off while the engine runs. Measurement of the duty cycle requires a duty cycle meter or a dwell meter. For more information, see **Measuring Frequency Valve Duty Cycle** below.

The tests should be carried out in the sequence that follows. Testing of an individual component is possible, but without knowing the status of the other components in the system, the results may not be conclusive. Also, testing is completely valid only if idle speed and ignition timing are correct.

Most component electrical testing can be accomplished with a multimeter and jumper wires. Some control unit testing requires the use of a 1.5 volt "D" size battery as an external power source. Frequency valve testing requires running the fuel pump without running the engine. Information on how to run the fuel pump for testing purposes can be found in **FUEL SYSTEM (Gasoline)**.

Measuring Frequency Valve Duty Cycle

The measurement of frequency valve function is called its duty cycle, expressed as the percentage of time that the valve is open. It is measured by connecting a duty cycle meter, such as the Siemans 451, to a test connector. As an alternative, duty cycle can be measured with an ordinary dwell meter, such as the Sun TDT-11. The 90° scale of the dwell meter corresponds to the 100% scale of the duty cycle meter. For example, a duty cycle of 50% would be read as 45° on a dwell meter. The tests that follow express test values for both instruments.

To connect a duty cycle meter, attach the meter's positive and negative leads to the positive and negative battery terminals respectively. Connect the meter's signal lead to the duty cycle test connector.

To connect a dwell meter, attach the meter's positive lead to the duty cycles test connector. Connect the negative lead to ground. Set the meter to the four-cylinder scale.

The duty cycle test connector is found in the engine compartment. On Jettas, the test connector wires are blue/white and brown/blue. On Golfs, the wires are blue/white and brown. A test adapter is available to make an easy, positive connection to the test connector. It is Volkswagen special tool no. US1112 (order no. TU1 112 000 00 HRN).

Quick Checking Oxygen Sensor System

Checking the duty cycle for fluctuation gives a quick indication that the system is functioning as intended. To check, the engine should be fully warmed up. Attach a duty cycle meter or dwell meter as described above, then start the engine and let it run for at least two minutes to warm the oxygen sensor. Remove the crankcase ventilation hose from the intake manifold as shown in Fig. 5-1 and plug the manifold connection. The duty cycle reading should drop and then fluctuate within a range of 25-65% (23-59° on a dwell meter). If the reading does not fluctuate, rev the engine several times. The reading should then fluctuate. Stop the engine and reconnect the hose. If the reading is incorrect, test the system in the sequence which follows.

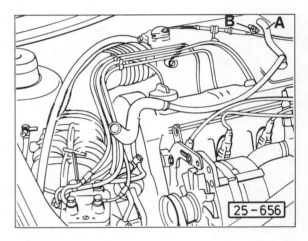

Fig. 5-1. Crankcase ventilation hose **A** removed for duty cycle measurement. Intake manifold connection **B** should be plugged for test.

Checking Thermoswitch

The thermoswitch inhibits the oxygen sensor system when the engine is cold and the sensor signal is unstable. A faulty thermoswitch may also prevent proper operation at normal operating temperature. To check the thermoswitch, remove the wiring connectors and test for continuity between the two terminals on the switch. The thermoswitch is mounted on the cylinder head coolant outlet, as shown in Fig. 5-2.

When engine coolant temperature is below 59°F (15°C), there should be continuity (switch closed). At normal operating temperature, there should be no continuity (switch open). A thermoswitch which fails either test should be replaced. To continue testing the oxygen sensor system, go to the next test.

Fig. 5-2. Location of thermoswitch on cylinder head coolant outlet. (Wire connectors **2** shown disconnected from switch terminals **1** and bridged for later test.)

To replace the thermoswitch, allow the engine to cool. Use a wrench on the large hex portion of the switch. Install with sealing compound on the threads, and use a new sealing washer.

NOTE ——

Coolant may be lost when the thermoswitch is replaced. When finished, check and correct the coolant level as described in **LUBRICATION AND MAINTENANCE**.

Checking Frequency Valve

To check the frequency valve, jumper the fuel pump relay to operate the fuel pump without running the engine, as described in **FUEL SYSTEM (Gasoline)**. On Golf models, it is also necessary to turn on the ignition to operate the pump. With the pump running, the frequency valve should make a repeating clicking or buzzing sound, indicating that the valve is operating correctly. If so, disconnect the fuel pump jumper and reinstall the relay. To continue testing the oxygen sensor system, go to the next test, **Checking Oxygen Sensor System Control Unit**.

If no clicking sound is heard, remove the frequency valve harness connector and, using an ohmmeter, measure the resistance of the valve's windings as shown in Fig. 5-3. If the resistance is not 2 to 3 ohms, replace the frequency valve as described below.

Check that the valve is getting power by testing for voltage at the harness connector (Fig. 5-3). Once again, operate the fuel pump by jumpering the relay terminals. There should be voltage at one of the two connector terminals. If not, the system wiring or the power supply relay or the control unit is faulty. See **Troubleshooting Oxygen Sensor Circuits** below.

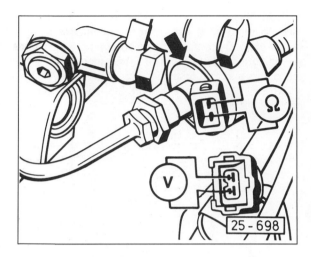

Fig. 5-3. Duty cycle valve resistance being measured with ohmmeter, and voltage at harness connector being measured with voltmeter (shown schematically). Duty cycle valve is located on right side of mixture control unit when viewed from front of car. Check connector for loose or damaged contacts.

To replace the frequency valve, clean and disconnect the fuel line unions. Loosen the mounting clamp bolt and press the valve out of the rubber bushing in the clamp. Installation is the reverse of removal. Use new sealing washers when reconnecting the fuel lines.

WARNING ——

Fuel will be expelled when the lines are disconnected. Do not smoke or work near heaters or other fire hazards. Have a fire extinguisher handy.

Checking Oxygen Sensor System Control Unit

Control unit function and regulation of the system can be checked by simulating the thermoswitch and oxygen sensor signals to the control unit. All tests require measuring the frequency valve duty cycle with the fuel pump jumpered, as described above.

To test the cold start enrichment function of the control unit, detach the wires from the thermoswitch and bridge the terminals of the disconnected plug with a jumper wire as shown previously in Fig. 5-2. With the fuel pump running and the ignition turned on, the duty cycle should be a steady 80% ± 2% (72° ± 2° on a dwell meter).

To test the control unit's stand-by or limp-home mode, remove wires from the thermoswitch, but do not bridge them. Run the fuel pump and turn on the ignition. The duty cycle should be a steady 50% ± 2% (45° ± 2° on a dwell meter).

7

To test the control unit's normal running, mixture regulating function, remove the wires from the thermoswitch, but do not bridge them. Disconnect the green wire from the oxygen sensor, and ground the green wire as indicated in Fig. 5-4. Run the fuel pump, and turn on the ignition. The duty cycle should be above 87% (78° on a dwell meter). Stop the fuel pump and turn off the ignition.

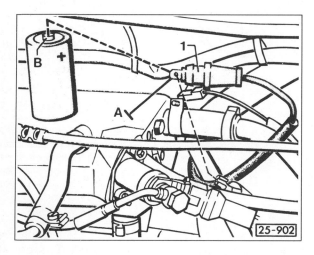

Fig. 5-4. Oxygen sensor green wire (**1**) grounded (**A**), and connected to "D" size 1.5 volt flashlight battery for test (**B**). Negative (−) end of battery should contact ground.

Next, connect the green oxygen sensor wire to a 1.5 volt "D" size flashlight battery, as indicated in Fig. 5-4. The negative (−) end of the flashlight battery should contact ground. Run the fuel pump and turn on the ignition. The duty cycle should be below 20% (18° on a dwell meter).

Incorrect duty cycle readings mean either that some part of the oxygen sensor system wiring is faulty, or that the oxygen sensor control unit has failed. The system wiring can be checked as described in **Troubleshooting Oxygen Sensor Circuits**. Make repairs as necessary, and repeat the tests. If the wiring is not faulty but improper duty cycle measurements persist, the control unit is faulty and should be replaced. Reconnect the green oxygen sensor wire and the wire connectors to the thermoswitch. Reinstall the fuel pump relay.

Checking Oxygen Sensor

Oxygen sensor function is also checked by measuring the duty cycle, as described in the tests above. To properly evaluate the oxygen sensor, the rest of the oxygen sensor system must first be tested in the sequence described above.

Start the engine and let it run until it reaches normal operating temperature. If the engine is already warm, run it for at least two minutes. With the engine running, remove the crankcase ventilation hose from its connection at the intake manifold,

as shown in Fig. 5-1 above. When the open port on the intake manifold is plugged, the duty cycle reading should drop. If it does not respond, the oxygen sensor is faulty and should be replaced.

To replace the oxygen sensor, wait for the exhaust system to cool. Disconnect the wiring from the sensor and remove it using a wrench on the hex portion of the sensor. Apply an anti-seize compound to the threads of the new part. On installation, torque sensor to 50 Nm (37 ft. lb.). Reconnect the oxygen sensor wiring.

CAUTION ▬

Do not let anti-seize compound come into contact with the slit portion of the sensor body.

Troubleshooting Oxygen Sensor Circuits

If system and component testing does not directly indicate any defects, it may be necessary to check the system wiring and the power supply relay using the information below along with the appropriate circuit diagrams found in **ELECTRICAL SYSTEM**.

If there is no voltage reaching the frequency valve connector as described in **Checking Frequency Valve**, remove the fuel injection power supply (or lambda) relay from its position on the fuse/relay panel. Check for voltage from the battery to the relay when the fuel pump operates. Check for continuity between the relay and the frequency valve. If both conditions are met, the relay should be replaced.

The control unit also receives voltage via the fuel injection power (or lambda) relay. With the harness connector to the control unit disconnected, there should be voltage reaching the connector from the relay whenever the fuel pump is running. In addition, there must be continuity in the wires from the frequency valve, the thermoswitch, the control unit ground, and the green oxygen sensor wire to the control unit connector. If not, repair any faulty wiring and then redo the test.

Replacing Oxygen Sensor Control Unit

The oxygen sensor control unit is located on the driver's side of the car above the firewall, under the windshield cowl. Lift out the plastic drip tray for access to the control unit and its connector. Disconnect the battery negative (−) terminal. Disconnect the control unit connector, remove the mounting screws at the base, and lift out the control unit. Installation is the reverse of removal. Make sure that the connector and socket are clean and dry, that the connector is solidly attached, and that no wires are bent or pinched.

5.2 Testing Oxygen Sensor System

(CIS-Electronic)

With CIS-Electronic (CIS-E) fuel injection, the oxygen sensor control unit operates the oxygen sensor system in addition to many other CIS-E functions. The signal from the oxygen sensor is just one of many inputs the control unit receives and processes in order to properly control the air/fuel mixture. For more information on the operation of the control unit and the rest of the CIS-E system, see **FUEL SYSTEM (Gasoline)**.

Testing Oxygen Sensor

Because of the integral nature of the fuel injection system and the oxygen sensor system, the basic measurement of fuel injection function—differential pressure regulator current—is also used to evaluate oxygen sensor performance. See **FUEL SYSTEM (Gasoline)** for information on measuring differential pressure regulator current.

This is a sensitive measurement. In the interest of accuracy, the engine must be fully warmed up, the exhaust system must be free of leaks, and all electrical consumers (fan, air conditioning, lights, etc.) must be off.

To test:

1. Disconnect the harness connector from the differential pressure regulator. Install the test harness and connect a multimeter or ammeter for measuring differential pressure regulator current.

2. Remove the crankcase ventilation hose from the intake manifold, as shown in Fig. 5-5, and leave it open to the atmosphere. Remove the "T" connector from the intake air boot, turn it 90°, and insert the blank side (with 1.5 mm restrictor hole) into the hole in the boot.

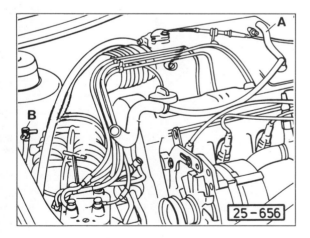

Fig. 5-5. Crankcase ventilation hose (**A**) and "T" connector (**B**) removed for testing oxygen sensor system. "T" connector (**B**) is removed, turned 90°, and reinserted. See Step 2 above.

3. Start the engine and let it idle. After about two minutes, the meter reading should be fluctuating. If not, raise the engine speed to 3000 rpm and look again. In either case, a fluctuating current reading indicates that the oxygen sensor is operating correctly.

4. Stop the engine. Reinstall the hoses in their original configurations. Remove the test harness and reconnect the harness connector.

No fluctuation in the meter reading (differential pressure regulator current) indicates a problem. Either the control unit, the oxygen sensor, or the wiring is faulty. To troubleshoot the system, continue testing using the procedures which follow.

Checking Control Unit Response

If, in the test above, the multimeter shows little or no fluctuation, check the control unit's response to a dramatic change in signal from the oxygen sensor. With the ignition off and the test harness connected, disconnect the harness connector from the coolant temperature sensor and bridge the connector terminals. See Fig. 5-6. Disconnect the green oxygen sensor wire.

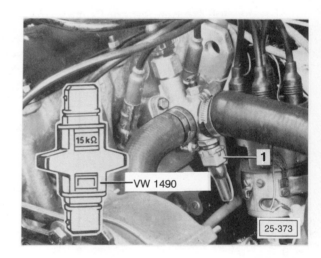

Fig. 5-6. Coolant temperature sensor harness connector (**1**). Volkswagen special tool no. VW 1490 (order no. TV1 490 000 25 ZEL) is available to bridge harness connector terminals for test.

Turn the ignition on. Differential pressure regulator current should be 9 to 11 mA. Ground the oxygen sensor connector (at the end of the green wire). After about 20 seconds, the current should increase to 19 to 20 mA. Correct measured values confirm that the control unit is responding normally, and if the differential pressure regulator current still does not fluctuate when tested as described above, the oxygen sensor or its wire is faulty and should be replaced.

If the current reading does not increase to 19 or 20 mA when the oxygen sensor wire is grounded, turn off the ignition and check for continuity between the green oxygen sensor wire and terminal 8 of the control unit connector. If there is no continuity, the wiring between the oxygen sensor and the control unit is faulty. Repair as necessary and repeat the test. If there is continuity and the control unit is still not responding when the oxygen sensor wire is grounded, then the control unit is faulty and should be replaced.

Replacing Oxygen Sensor

On cars with engine code HT, RD, or PL, the oxygen sensor is located in the front of the catalytic converter housing. On cars with engine code GX, the oxygen sensor is located in the exhaust manifold, just above the front exhaust pipe connection. To replace an oxygen sensor in either case, disconnect the wiring to the oxygen sensor and use a wrench on the hex portion of the sensor housing. Apply an anti-seize compound to the threads of the new sensor. Install the sensor, torque to 50 Nm (37 ft. lb.), and reconnect the wiring.

CAUTION ▬

Do not let anti-seize compound come into contact with the slit portion of the sensor body.

Replacing Oxygen Sensor Control Unit

The oxygen sensor control unit for models with CIS-E fuel injection is located on the driver's side of the car above the firewall, under the windshield cowl. Disconnect the battery negative (−) terminal. Lift out the plastic drip tray for access to the control unit. Disconnect the harness connector, remove the mounting screws at the base, and lift out the unit. Installation is the reverse of removal. Make sure that the connector and socket are clean and dry, that the connector is solidly attached, and that no wires are bent or pinched.

5.3 Testing Oxygen Sensor System

(Digifant II)

With the Digifant II engine management system, the oxygen sensor provides just one of many inputs to the Digifant control unit which it receives and processes in order to properly control the air/fuel mixture. Because there is no way to directly measure the injector opening time, which adjusts the air/fuel mixture, there is no direct way to observe or measure the operation of the oxygen sensor.

Oxygen sensor function can only be evaluated indirectly, using a carbon monoxide (CO) meter in the exhaust. If the necessary equipment and an experienced operator are not available, we recommend that the oxygen sensor be checked by an authorized Volkswagen dealer.

For more information on the operation of the Digifant II control unit and the rest of the Digifant II system, see **FUEL SYSTEM (Gasoline)**.

Testing Oxygen Sensor Function

This is a sensitive measurement. In the interest of accuracy, the engine must be fully warmed up, with idle speed, ignition timing, and CO content adjusted to specifications. The exhaust system between the engine and the catalytic converter must be free of leaks, the engine coolant temperature sensor should be connected normally, the voltage supply to the oxygen sensor heater must be OK, and all other electrical consumers including air conditioning should be switched off. In addition, test measurements should only be made when the radiator cooling fan is not running.

Run the engine and record a baseline CO measurement. With the engine running, raise the engine oil dipstick slightly. This allows extra air into the closed crankcase ventilation system and, therefore, into the intake manifold. If the oxygen sensor is performing correctly, the CO reading should drop for a few seconds, then return to the original value.

To check oxygen sensor wiring:

1. Disconnect the harness connector from the Digifant control unit, as shown in Fig. 5-7.

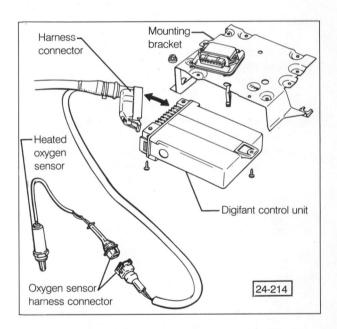

Fig. 5-7. Digifant control unit and oxygen sensor showing mounting and harness connectors.

2. Using an ohmmeter or a multimeter set to the 20kΩ scale, check continuity between terminals 2 and 13 of the Digifant control unit harness connector. See Fig. 5-8. There should be no continuity. If there is, there is a short to ground in the oxygen sensor wiring.

Fig. 5-8. Digifant control unit harness connector terminal identification.

3. Disconnect the oxygen sensor harness connector. Connect a jumper wire between ground and the green wire (terminal 1) on the harness side of the connector. There should be continuity. If not, there is a break in the oxygen sensor wiring between the harness connectors.

Replacing Oxygen Sensor

On cars with engine code PF, the oxygen sensor is located in the front of the catalytic converter housing. On cars with engine code RV, the oxygen sensor is located in the exhaust manifold, just above the front exhaust pipe connection. To replace an oxygen sensor in either case, disconnect the oxygen sensor harness connector and use a wrench on the hex portion of the sensor housing. Apply an anti-seize compound to the threads of the new sensor. Install the sensor, torque to 50 Nm (37 ft. lb.), and reconnect the harness connector.

CAUTION ━━

Do not let anti-seize compound come into contact with the slit portion of the sensor body.

Replacing Digifant Control Unit

The Digifant control unit is located on the driver's side of the car above the firewall, under the windshield cowl. See Fig. 5-7 above. Disconnect the battery negative (−) terminal. Lift out the plastic drip tray for access to the control unit. Disconnect the harness connector, remove the mounting screws, and lift out the unit. Installation is the reverse of removal. Make sure that the connector and socket are clean and dry, that the connector is solidly attached, and that no wires are bent or pinched.

6. EXHAUST GAS RECIRCULATION SYSTEM

The vacuum-operated exhaust gas recirculation (EGR) valve, used on Canada model Jettas with engine code MZ and automatic transmission, operates only at part throttle to direct a small amount of exhaust gas into the intake manifold. The exhaust gas displaces a small volume of the air/fuel mixture, resulting in lower combustion chamber temperatures and a reduction of certain harmful emissions. A thermo-pneumatic valve in the EGR system permits system operation only when engine coolant temperature is above 142°F (61°C).

Testing and Replacing EGR Valve

The EGR valve should open only under part-throttle vacuum. A rough idle may indicate that the valve is incorrectly opening at idle. To check, loosen the union and disconnect the EGR line to the exhaust manifold at the bottom of the EGR valve. Then plug the open bottom port of the EGR valve. If the idle smooths out, it is because the valve was leaking and should be replaced.

WARNING ━━

The EGR valve operates at high temperature and may cause severe burns if handled without adequate protection. Use heavy gloves when working with the EGR valve.

The normal part-throttle operation of the EGR valve is tested by artificially supplying vacuum to the valve and observing the response. Pinch shut the hose leading from the idle speed boost valve to the throttle body as shown in Fig. 6-1. Remove the vacuum line from the thermo-pneumatic valve and temporarily reconnect it to a vacuum port on the brake booster line. See Fig. 6-2.

Fig. 6-1. Idle speed boost valve vacuum line (**1**) being pinched shut.

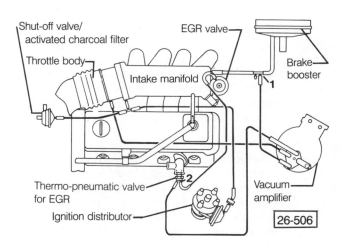

Fig. 6-2. Vacuum hose routing for Jetta (Canada only), engine code MZ, automatic transmission. To test valve, disconnect vacuum line from port on brake booster line (**1**) and connect hose end (**2**) to port.

At normal operating temperature with the vacuum lines connected as described, the engine should idle roughly or stall. If not, loosen the union and disconnect the EGR line from the bottom of the EGR valve. If the idle then becomes rough the EGR valve is operating correctly, but the line to the exhaust manifold is clogged and should be cleaned or replaced. If the idle is still smooth, then the EGR valve is defective.

To replace the EGR valve allow the engine to cool, then disconnect the vacuum line and the EGR line to the exhaust manifold. Use a hex wrench to remove the two socket-head mounting screws. Install the new valve with a new gasket, using a high-temperature anti-sieze lubricant on the screw threads. Reconnect the EGR line. Reconnect the vacuum lines as shown in Fig. 6-2.

Testing and Replacing EGR Thermo-pneumatic Valve

Locate the two vacuum lines leading from the thermo-pneumatic valve as shown in Fig. 6-2 above. Disconnect these vacuum lines from the EGR valve and from the vacuum amplifier. Blow into one and listen for airflow from the other. With the engine coolant temperature below 112°F (45°C), no air should pass through the valve. With the engine at normal operating temperature, air should pass through the valve. If the valve appears to be faulty, first check for damaged or kinked lines. If the vacuum lines are clear, the valve is defective and should be replaced.

If the thermo-pneumatic valve must be replaced, use a new sealing washer. Use a sealing compound on the threads of the new valve. Reconnect the vacuum lines. Some engine coolant may leak out when the valve is removed. If so, check and correct the coolant level as described in **LUBRICATION AND MAINTENANCE**.

7. TURBOCHARGER
(turbo diesel only)

The turbocharger is shown in Fig. 7-1. The small-diameter turbine and impeller rotate at over 100,000 rpm. The shaft turns in floating bearings, pressure-lubricated by engine oil. Maximum turbocharger pressure (boost) is regulated by the wastegate, which vents excess (overpressured) intake air directly to the exhaust system. As an additional safety feature, the intake manifold is fitted with a blow-off valve which also opens to limit intake air pressure.

The turbocharger/wastegate unit and the blow-off valve are mechanically simple systems which should be maintenance-free. The turbocharger operates at high temperature, and it is important that the oil surrounding its bearings be of the correct type and quality. Any failure of the turbocharger will most likely be caused by either a lubrication problem or a boost control problem. For repair, the entire turbocharger assembly is replaced as a unit. Remanufactured turbochargers are available from an authorized Volkswagen dealer at lower cost than a new part, and the old unit can usually be exchanged for partial credit.

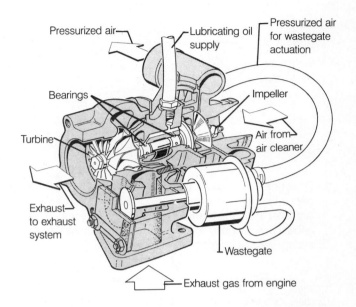

Fig. 7-1. Cutaway view of turbocharger. Notice bearings with multiple oil holes, and pressurized oil supply line. Faulty turbocharger is replaced as a unit; wastegate is press-fit and not available separately.

The high operating temperature and high rotating speed of the turbocharger make extra caution necessary during repairs.

WARNING ———

The turbocharger and related components operate at very high temperature. Always allow the system to cool or use proper protective clothing to prevent severe burns.

CAUTION ———

●Thoroughly clean all joints, pipe unions and connections, before disconnecting or reconnecting the turbocharger.

●Take measures to prevent dust and dirt contamination. Cover all components with dust-free paper or seal them in plastic bags. Do not use cloths. Avoid nearby use of compressed air. Do not move the car or work in dusty conditions while the turbocharger is open or removed.

7.1 Removing and Installing Turbocharger

Fig. 7-2 shows the turbocharger and related components.

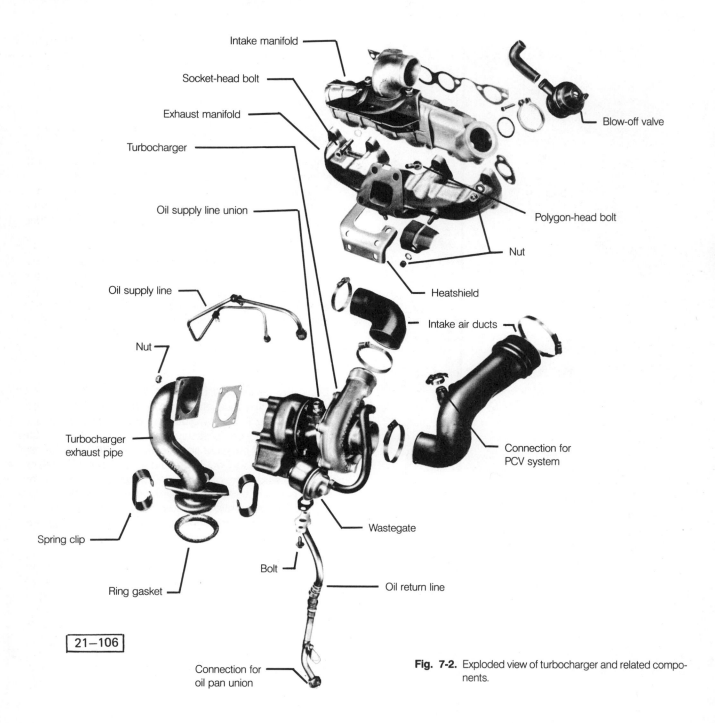

Intake manifold

Socket-head bolt

Exhaust manifold

Turbocharger

Oil supply line union

Oil supply line

Nut

Turbocharger
exhaust pipe

Spring clip

Ring gasket

Bolt

Connection for
oil pan union

Blow-off valve

Polygon-head bolt

Nut

Heatshield

Intake air ducts

Connection for
PCV system

Wastegate

Oil return line

21—106

Fig. 7-2. Exploded view of turbocharger and related components.

7

To remove:

1. Disconnect the battery negative (−) terminal. On cars with automatic transmission, remove the starter as described in **ELECTRICAL SYSTEM**.

2. Disconnect the turbocharger exhaust pipe from the turbocharger by removing the four mounting nuts. Remove the gasket.

3. Disconnect the oil supply line and its bracket from the top of the turbocharger. Plug the oil hole in the turbocharger, and seal the end of the detached oil line.

4. Loosen the clamps and remove the air ducts that connect the air cleaner to the turbocharger and the turbocharger to the intake manifold.

5. Disconnect the oil return line from the engine oil pan. Plug the end of the disconnected line and the connection on the oil pan.

6. Working from under the vehicle, use a 12mm, 12-point socket wrench to remove the four polygon-head mounting bolts shown in Fig. 7-3 that hold the turbocharger to the exhaust manifold. Remove the turbocharger.

Fig. 7-3. Polygon-head bolts (arrows) to be removed.

To install:

1. Loosely connect the turbocharger with oil return line to the turbocharger exhaust pipe. Use a new gasket. Thread the mounting nuts on only finger tight.

   NOTE ━━

   If the oil return line has been removed from the turbocharger, reinstall it now using a new gasket. Torque the bolts to 30 Nm (22 ft. lb.).

2. Thoroughly clean the mating surfaces between the turbocharger and the exhaust manifold, and make sure that they are undamaged. This is important as no gasket is used.

3. Apply a high-temperature anti-seize compound to the threads of the polygon-head bolts. Connect the turbocharger to the exhaust manifold, evenly torquing the four bolts to 45 Nm (33 ft. lb.).

4. Torque the turbocharger exhaust pipe nuts to 25 Nm (18 ft. lb.).

5. Reconnect the oil return line to the engine oil pan. Torque the union to 30 Nm (22 ft. lb.).

6. Reinstall the intake air ducts. Replace any that is deformed or cracked. On cars with automatic transmission, reinstall the starter, as described in **ELECTRICAL SYSTEM.**

7. Pre-lubricate the turbocharger by pouring clean engine oil into the oil hole, filling it as full as possible. Reconnect the oil supply line. Torque the oil supply line unions to 30 Nm (22 ft. lb.).

8. Start the engine and let it idle for at least one minute prior to any higher speed operation. Check for oil leaks or exhaust leaks and make any necessary repairs before returning the car to use.

7.2 Testing Turbocharger Wastegate and Blow-Off Valve

The wastegate and blow-off valve are both normally closed, opening only when the boost pressure becomes too high. Not opening will allow the turbocharger to create too much boost pressure, which can cause prompt and serious engine damage. Opening too soon will limit boost pressure and reduce engine power.

Before testing wastegate and blow-off valve regulating functions, inspect the system for leaks and make sure that the control line to the wastegate is not plugged, loose, or leaking. To achieve meaningful test results, other engine performance factors such as injection timing and valve clearance should be within specification or adjusted correctly. The engine should be warmed up to normal operating temperature for the pressure tests.

Boost pressure specifications in this test procedure are "overpressure" specifications, given in relation to normal atmospheric pressure. In other words, zero pressure on the gauge is actually atmospheric pressure or 1 bar (14.5 psi) absolute pressure. A boost pressure specification of 0.70 bar (10.2 psi) as given in this manual would be read as 0.70 bar (10.2 psi) on an overpressure type gauge, or 1.70 bar (24.7 psi) on an absolute pressure gauge. Make sure to identify the gauge type and, if necessary, convert the specifications and readings to the same scale using the conversion graph given in Fig. 7-4.

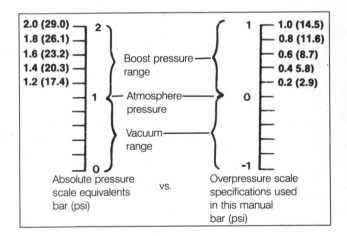

Fig. 7-4. Conversion graph for converting between absolute pressure scale and overpressure scale. Specifications given are for overpressure.

To test:

1. Use a T-fitting to install a pressure gauge in the air pressure line that links the air intake manifold with the boost enrichment device on the fuel injection pump (Fig. 7-5).

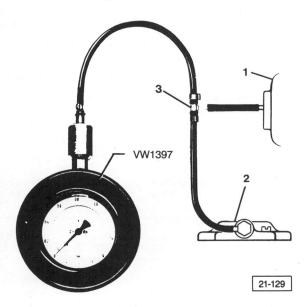

Fig. 7-5. Pressure gauge installed with T-fitting (**3**) between intake manifold port (**1**) and boost enrichment valve (**2**) on injection pump. Use long hose to place gauge in passenger compartment. Gauge shown is Volkswagen special tool no. VW 1397.

2. Install a tachometer so that it can be seen from the driver's seat. See **IGNITION**.

3. Place the pressure gauge inside the vehicle where it can be easily seen from the driver's seat. Take care not to kink or pinch the hose.

4. Start the engine and open the gauge's valve, if so equipped.

5. To road test, use the brakes or a steep hill to hold the car at 35 mph (60 kph) with the accelerator floored; in 2nd gear with a manual transmission, or in drive range 1 with an automatic transmission.

> **WARNING**
>
> *For the sake of safety during a road test, take a helper along to read the gauge, or if the gauge is equipped with a valve, close the valve at peak boost and record the value later.*

6. If testing on a dynamometer, hold the engine at 4000 rpm with the accelerator pedal floored; in 3rd gear with a manual transmission, or in drive range 2 with an automatic transmission.

> **CAUTION**
>
> *To avoid unnecessary engine strain, the road-test or dynamometer measurement time should be limited to a maximum of 10 seconds.*

7. The boost pressure should be 0.64 to 0.72 bar (9.3 to 10.4 psi). If the pressure indicated is greater, the waste-gate is faulty and the turbocharger should be replaced. If the maximum boost pressure is lower, the blow-off valve may be sticking open. Proceed with the steps which follow.

8. Disconnect the blow-off valve outlet hose from the intake air duct. Plug the hose (inside diameter approximately 25 mm or 1 in.) and secure the plug with a hose clamp, as shown in Fig. 7-6.

Fig. 7-6. Blow-off valve outlet hose disconnected and plugged (arrow).

9. Repeat the test. Correct boost pressure at this point indicates that the blow-off valve is faulty and should be replaced. Boost pressure which is still below specification indicates that the turbocharger is faulty and should be replaced.

To replace blow-off valve:

1. Allow the engine to cool.

2. Disconnect the outlet hose from the blow-off valve and loosen the clamp securing the valve to the intake manifold.

3. Remove the valve and O-ring from the intake manifold.

4. Installation is the reverse of removal. Always use a new O-ring.

8. EXHAUST SYSTEM AND EMISSION CONTROL TECHNICAL DATA

I. Tightening Torques (engine codes: RD, PF, PL)

Exhaust manifold to cylinder head (nut)	.25 Nm (18 ft. lb.)
Exhaust pipe to exhaust manifold (nut)	.40 Nm (30 ft. lb.)
Slip-joint clamps (nut or bolt)	.40 Nm (30 ft. lb.)
Front pipe to catalytic converter (nut and bolt)	.25 Nm (18 ft. lb.)
Heatshield mounting (nut or bolt)	.10 Nm (87 in. lb.)
CO tap tube clamp (bolt)	.10 Nm (87 in. lb.)
CO tap tube union to exhaust manifold	.20 Nm (15 ft. lb.)
Oxygen sensor	.50 Nm (37 ft. lb.)

II. Tightening Torques (engine codes: GX, HT, RV, MZ)

Exhaust manifold to cylinder head (nut)	.25 Nm (18 ft. lb.)
Slip-joint clamps (nut or bolt)	.40 Nm (30 ft. lb.)
Heatshield mounting (nut or bolt)	.10 Nm (87 in. lb.)
CO tap tube clamp (bolt)	.10 Nm (87 in. lb.)
CO tap tube union to exhaust manifold	.20 Nm (15 ft. lb.)
Oxygen sensor	.50 Nm (37 ft. lb.)

III. Tightening Torques (engine codes: ME, MF)

Exhaust manifold to cylinder head (nut)	.25 Nm (18 ft. lb.)
Slip-joint clamps (nut or bolt)	.25 Nm (18 ft. lb.)
Heatshield mounting (nut or bolt)	.10 Nm (87 in. lb.)
Oil supply line to turbocharger or to fitting on cylinder head (union nut)	.30 Nm (22 ft. lb.)
Oil return line flange to turbocharger (bolts)	.30 Nm (22 ft. lb.)
Turbocharger oil return line to fitting on engine oil pan	.30 Nm (22 ft. lb.)
Exhaust pipe to turbocharger (nut)	.25 Nm (18 ft. lb.)
Turbocharger to exhaust manifold (polygon-head bolt with high-temperature anti-seize compound)	.45 Nm (33 ft. lb.)

IV. Turbocharger Technical Data (engine code: MF)

Turbocharger maximum delivery pressure, regulated by wastegate (boost)	.0.64–0.72 bar (9.3–10.4 psi) above atmospheric pressure
Maximum intake manifold pressure allowed by blow-off valve	.0.77–0.87 bar (11.2–12.6 psi) above atmospheric pressure

V. Oxygen Sensor System Technical Data (CIS)

Thermoswitch Resistance	∞ ohms (over 28°C or 82°F)
Frequency valve resistance	.2–3 ohms
Frequency valve voltage requirement	.approx. 12VDC
Control unit duty cycle equivalent: (dwell)	
cold enrichment function	.80% ± 2% (72 ± 2°)
stand-by mode function	.50% ± 2% (45 ± 2°)
rich-mixture limiting function	> 87% (> 78°)
lean-mixture limiting function	< 20% (< 18°)
CO percent	.0.3%–1.2%

VI. Oxygen Sensor System Technical Data (CIS-E)

Differential pressure regulator current (fluctuating)	.10 mA ± 6 mA

IGNITION

Contents

Introduction 3

1. General Description 4
  1.1   Electronic Ignition System 4
  1.2   Knock Sensor System 4
  1.3   Digifant II Ignition System 4
  1.4   Glow Plug System 5
  1.5   System Identification and Applications 5

2. Maintenance 6

3. Troubleshooting 6
  3.1   Basic Troubleshooting Principles 6
        Test Equipment 7
        Quick-Check of Ignition System 7
  3.2   Ignition System Visual Inspection 8
  3.3   Testing Coil and Spark Plug Wires 9
  3.4   Testing Hall Sender and Ignition Control Unit . . 10
        Voltage Supply and Ground to Ignition Control
        Unit 10
        Voltage Supply and Ground to Hall Sender . . . 11
        Hall Sender Switching Function 11
        Ignition Control Unit Voltage to Coil 11
        Ignition Control Unit Response to Hall Sender
        Signal 12

4. Transistorized Coil Ignition (TCI-h) System 12
  4.1   Ignition Timing 15
  4.2   Centrifugal and Vacuum Spark Advance (basic
        TCI-h only, engine codes GX and MZ) 17
  4.3   Electronic Timing Advance (TCI-h with knock
        control, engine codes HT, RD, PL, RV, PF) . . . 17

        Checking RPM-dependent Timing Advance
        (engine codes HT, RD, PL) 17
        Checking Vacuum-dependent Ignition Timing
        Advance (engine codes HT, RD, PL) 17
        Checking Digifant II Ignition Timing Advance
        (engine codes RV and PF) 17
  4.4   Knock Sensor System Diagnosis (engine codes
        HT, RD, PL) 18
  4.5   Troubleshooting Knock Sensor System 18
        Checking Knock Sensor System Wiring 18
        Knock Sensor System Voltage Checks 19
        Checking Knock Sensor System
        Components 20
  4.6   Removing and Installing Knock Sensor 20

5. Distributor 21
  5.1   Removing and Installing Distributor Cap, Rotor,
        and Spark Plug Wires 22
        Replacing Spark Plug Wires 22
        Replacing Distributor Cap and Rotor 22
  5.2   Removing and Installing Distributor 23
  5.3   Disassembling and Assembling Distributor . . . 23
        All Engines except 16-valve 24
        16-valve Engines 24

6. Diesel Glow Plug System 24
  6.1   Testing and Replacing Glow Plugs 24
  6.2   Testing and Repairing Glow Plug System
        Circuits 25
        Checking Wiring 25
        Glow Plug System Voltage Checks 25
        Checking Glow Plug Relay 26

2   IGNITION

7. Technical Data 26
    I. Ignition System Specifications 26
    II. Knock Sensor Specifications. 27

TABLES

a. Ignition System Applications 5
b. Ignition System Troubleshooting 8
c. Ignition Coil Resistance 9

d.. Basic TCI-h Ignition System Specifications (engine codes GX and MZ). 15
e. Ignition System Specifications TCI-h with Knock Control (engine codes HT, RD, PL) 15
f. Ignition System Specifications TCI-h with Knock Control Digifant II (engine codes RV and PF). 15
g. Maximum RPM-Dependent Ignition Timing Advance (engine codes HT, RD, PL) 17
h. Knock Sensor System Voltage Checks 19
i. Knock Sensor System Resistance Checks 20
j. Knock Sensor Specifications 21

Ignition

Introduction

The ignition systems used on the gasoline-engine cars covered by this manual incorporate many technologically advanced components to maximize engine performance and reliablity in the face of increasing restrictions on engine exhaust emissions. The ignition system, in cooperation with the fuel system, precisely controls engine operation to ensure maximum power and efficiency from the engine under all operating conditions.

While diesel-engined cars do not have a spark-ignition system, the glow plug system is essentially an ignition assist system, and is therefore covered here also. Proper function of the glow plug system is essential for starting a cold diesel engine, and greatly enhances the process no matter what the temperature.

Due to the use of sophisticated electronics to operate and control these modern ignition systems, the need for routine maintenance is reduced and troubleshooting can be more difficult. Any service or repair work must be carried out carefully, with special attention to the cautions and warnings and proper working procedures. Most necessary service and repair information is provided here, although some of the operations that are described may be of practical value only to professional mechanics. If you lack the skills, or the special tools and equipment, we suggest you leave the service and repair of the ignition system to an authorized Volkswagen dealer or other qualified repair shop. We especially urge you to consult your authorized Volkswagen dealer before attempting any repairs on a vehicle still covered by any warranties.

1. GENERAL DESCRIPTION

The spark-ignition system for a gasoline engine provides each spark plug with a precisely timed high-voltage charge to ignite the air/fuel mixture in the combustion chamber. The system also makes adjustments to the ignition timing in response to changes in engine speed and load.

The diesel engine by comparison has no ignition system, but rather an ignition assist system. To start a cold engine, the glow plugs pre-heat the combustion chamber to assist combustion. Once the engine starts running and becomes warm, normal diesel compression-ignition takes over, air and fuel being ignited by the heat of compression.

1.1 Electronic Ignition System

The basic ignition system used on vehicles covered by this manual is a transistorized coil ignition with Hall sender (TCI-h), as shown in Fig. 1-1. The Hall sender in the distributor is the electronic equivalent of breaker points, but it has no moving parts and does not wear out. The ignition control unit, based on the signal from the Hall sender, switches the 12-volt ignition coil primary circuit to discharge the high-voltage spark. Vacuum and centrifugal advance mechanisms in the distributor adjust the ignition timing in response to engine load and speed.

1.2 Knock Sensor System

TCI-h ignition with knock sensor differs from the basic TCI-h system with the addition of an engine knock sensor and knock sensor control unit (Fig. 1-2). With this system, the distributor has no vacuum or centrifugal advance mechanisms, and all adjustments to ignition timing are done electronically. The knock sensor system detects pre-ignition or detonation (commonly called knock or ping), and adjusts ignition timing electronically to eliminate it. The system also makes the timing advance adjustments which are necessary at higher engine speeds. On engines with the Digifant II engine management system, knock control is an integral function of the Digifant control unit.

1.3 Digifant II Ignition System

The Digifant II ignition system is also TCI-h with knock control, however, all ignition functions including the knock sensor system are combined with the fuel injection control functions in the Digifant electronic control unit. Ignition timing is based on engine load, engine speed, ignition quality, and coolant temperature.

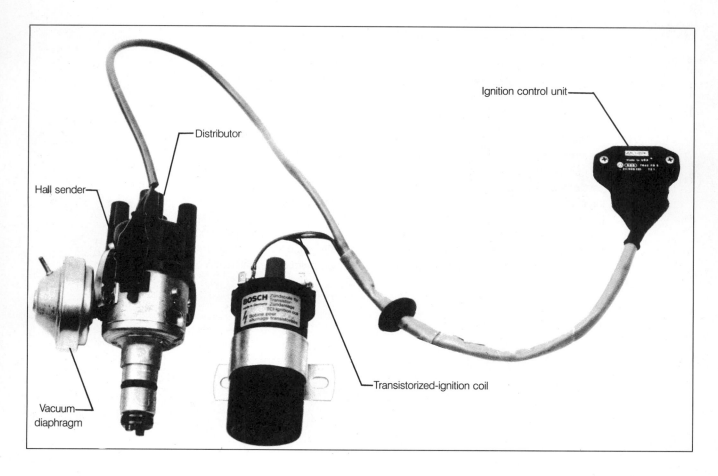

Fig. 1-1. Components of basic Transistorized Coil Ignition with Hall sender (TCI-h).

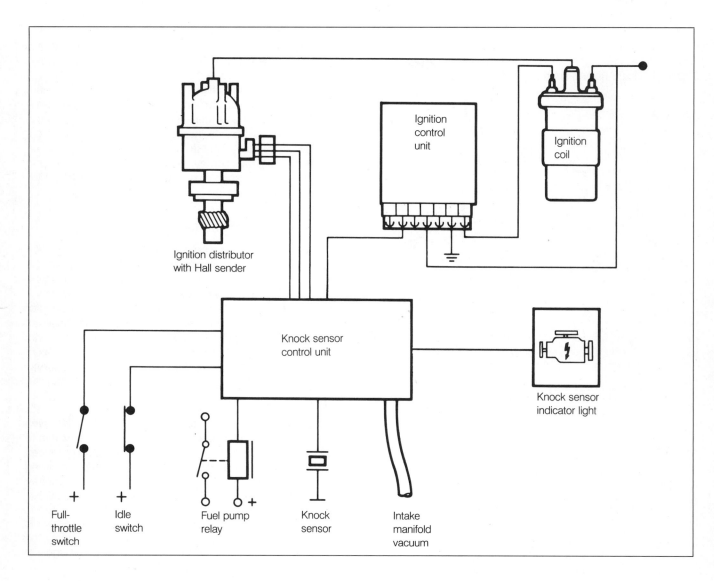

Fig. 1-2. Schematic view of Transistorized Coil Ignition (TCI-h) with knock sensor system.

1.4 Glow Plug System

The glow plug system for diesel engines includes four glow plugs, a connecting electrical bus bar, a time-delay relay, an engine temperature sender, and a warning light. The system is activated by turning the ignition switch on.

1.5 System Identification and Applications

The type of ignition system used is determined by engine type. **Table a** lists the engine codes for cars covered by this manual, and the corresponding ignition system. For more information on engine identification, see **ENGINE**.

Table a. Ignition System Applications

Engine code	Ignition system
GX, MZ	TCI-h
HT, RD, PL	TCI-h with knock sensor
RV, PF	TCI-h with knock sensor (Digifant II)
ME, MF	Glow plug system

The different ignition systems used on gasoline engines can also be quickly identified by their appearance. The basic TCI-h ignition system has a vacuum diaphragm mounted on the side of the distributor, as shown in Fig. 1-1 above. The ignition systems with knock control have a knock sensor mounted to the front of the engine block between cylinders 1 and 2 as shown in Fig. 1-3, and a separate knock sensor control unit located in the passenger-side cowl area above the firewall. The Digifant II system has no such separate control unit.

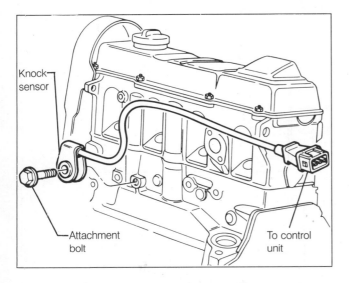

Fig. 1-3. Knock sensor mounted on front of engine cylinder block.

2. MAINTENANCE

The following recommended scheduled maintenance for the ignition system is covered in detail in **LUBRICATION AND MAINTENANCE**, or in this section under the bold numbered headings.

1. Replacing spark plugs

2. Inspecting and replacing distributor cap and rotor **3.2**

3. Inspecting and replacing spark plug wires **3.3**

3. TROUBLESHOOTING

This troubleshooting section applies to starting and running problems caused by faults in the ignition system, including the Hall sender, the ignition control unit, the coil, the distributor cap and rotor, and the spark plug wires. Troubleshooting for the diesel glow plug system is covered in **6. Diesel Glow Plug System**.

The ignition system's primary function is to provide a properly timed high-voltage spark. The distributor's basic timing adjustment gives the Hall sender and the electronic system its baseline ignition timing. The Hall sender signals the ignition control unit which in turn switches the coil primary circuit, causing the coil to discharge high voltage to the spark plugs through the distributor cap and spark plug wires. In this sensitive electronic ignition system, corroded or loose connections may interfere with any part of this function.

A complete failure of the ignition system to produce spark at the spark plugs is self-evident as an ignition system problem; however, for other problems such as rough idle, misfiring, or poor starting, the cause is not so clear. Start by testing and evaluating the ignition system, but if no ignition problems are discovered, proceed elsewhere. Inadequate engine compression or a malfunctioning fuel system will cause similar problems. See **ENGINE** for information on checking compression. See **FUEL SYSTEM (Gasoline)** for information on troubleshooting the fuel injection system. For more general help in determining what section may best apply, see **FUNDAMENTALS** at the front of the manual.

3.1 Basic Troubleshooting Principles

An engine that starts and runs indicates that the ignition system is fundamentally working – delivering voltage to the spark plugs. A hard-starting or poor-running engine, however, may indicate a problem with how well the spark is delivered. A faulty coil, poor spark plug wires, a worn or cracked distributor cap or rotor, and worn or fouled spark plugs are all causes of reduced spark intensity and inefficient combustion. For cars with catalytic converters, this is an especially serious problem since the poorly burned mixture can overload the catalytic converter. This may cause the converter to overheat, causing plugging or presenting a fire hazard.

An engine that has good cranking speed but will not even begin to start may indicate a complete failure of the system to produce spark. A basic check to see if spark is being produced will be the most important first troubleshooting step. If a strong spark is observed, then the failure to start is due to another cause, perhaps incorrect timing or engine mechanical failure.

The TCI-h ignition system contains very sensitive electronic components. To protect the system, and for general safety, the following cautions should be observed during any ignition system troubleshooting, maintenance, or repair work.

CAUTION ——

• *Do not touch or disconnect any of the high tension cables from the coil, distributor, or spark plugs while the engine is running or being cranked by the starter.*

• *Connect or disconnect ignition system wires, multiple connectors, and ignition test equipment leads only while the ignition is off.*

• *Before operating the starter without starting the engine (as when making a compression test), disconnect the wire from the center of the distributor cap and positively connect it to ground on the engine. Cranking the engine with the high-voltage secondary wiring disconnected may damage the ignition system.*

CAUTION ━━━

•*Do not connect test instruments with a 12-volt current supply to terminal 15 (+) of the ignition coil. The voltage backflow will damage the ignition control unit. In general, make test connections only as specified by Volkswagen, as described in this manual, or as described by the instrument's manufacturer.*

• *Do not connect a condenser to terminal 1, the negative (−) coil terminal. This may cause misfiring or ignition system damage.*

• *Do not disconnect the battery while the engine is running.*

• *The ignition systems in Volkswagens covered by this manual use a special distributor rotor with 1000 ± 400 ohms resistance. Take care to use the correct part. Do not substitute any other Volkswagen or Bosch part.*

• *Do not quick-charge the battery (for boost starting) for longer than one minute, and do not exceed 16.5 volts at the battery with the boosting cables attached. Wait at least one minute before boosting the battery a second time.*

• *Do not tow a vehicle suspected of having a defective ignition system without first disconnecting the ignition control unit.*

• *Do not wash the engine while it is running, or anytime the ignition is switched on.*

• *Disconnect the battery when doing any electric welding on the vehicle.*

• *Do not try to start the engine of a car which has been heated above 176°F (80°C), (for example, in a paint drying booth) until allowing it to cool to normal temperature.*

• *Do not conduct ignition system tests with a test lamp that uses a normal incandescent bulb. The high electrical consumption of these test lamps may damage the electronic components.*

Test Equipment

Many of the tests of ignition system components require the use of high-impedance test equipment to prevent damage to the electrical components. An LED test light which meets these requirements is Volkswagen special tool no. US 1115, available from an authorized Volkswagen dealer parts department (order no. TU1 115 000 28 ZEL). A multimeter (for voltage, current, and resistance measurements) which meets these requirements is Volkswagen special tool no. US 1119, a digital multimeter (order no. TU1 119 000 00 KTM).

Many tests require checking for voltage, continuity, or resistance at the terminals of the components' harness connectors. The blunt tips of a multimeter's probes can damage the terminals, and cause poor connections. To prevent damage, use flat male connectors to probe the harness connector terminals. A suitable flat connector is Volkswagen part no. N 017 457 02.

NOTE ━━━

Tool numbers and order numbers are subject to change. Always rely on an authorized Volkswagen dealer parts department for the latest and most accurate information.

Quick-check of Ignition System

If the engine does not start, the most fundamental step in troubleshooting the ignition system is to determine whether or not the system is creating any kind of spark at the spark plug. If a spark is present, then it is the ignition system's efficiency and accuracy or another system's function that is in question. If no spark is present, then more detailed testing of the ignition system is necessary.

To check for spark, turn the ignition off and remove a connector from one of the spark plugs. Connect it to a known good spark plug, preferably a new plug, and hold the spark plug with insulated pliers so that the outer electrode is grounded on the engine.

CAUTION ━━━

Any test set-up other than the one described above may cause damage or inconclusive tests.

While a helper actuates the starter, look for spark in the spark plug gap. A bright blue spark indicates a healthy ignition system. A yellow-orange spark is weaker and indicates that, while spark is present and the system is functioning, it is not operating at peak efficiency. Check the condition of the ignition system components as described in **3.2 Ignition System Visual Inspection** and replace any faulty components.

WARNING ━━━

If ignition system failure is not the problem, the engine may start during this test. Be prepared to turn off the ignition immediately. Also, running the engine with a spark plug wire disconnected will damage the catalytic converter.

NOTE ━━━

Before checking the ignition system when there is no spark or a weak spark, make sure that the battery is fully charged. See **ELECTRICAL SYSTEM**.

If there is no spark, test for primary voltage at the ignition coil. Connect a test light between terminal 1 (−) of the ignition coil and ground. While the starter is actuated, the test light should flash, indicating that the coil is receiving primary voltage. If not, there is a fault in the wiring harness or the ignition switch. If the coil is receiving voltage, or if a strong spark is observed but the engine still will not start, refer to **Table b** for more troubleshooting information. Bold numbers in the corrective action column refer to numbered headings in this section where repair information is located.

3.2 Ignition System Visual Inspection

The spark plug wires, the distributor cap, and the distributor rotor are subject to wear and electrical breakdown which will impair their ability to deliver a crisply timed and powerful spark. Many of these conditions are most easily detected by a thorough visual inspection. Dirt and moisture on any of these components are also potential causes of poor spark at the spark plugs.

Table b. Ignition System Troubleshooting

Symptom	Probable cause	Corrective action
1. Engine will not start—cranking speed too low	**a.** Starting system fault	**a.** See **ELECTRICAL SYSTEM**.
2. Engine will not start—cranking speed OK	**a.** No spark	**a.** Spark test ignition. **3.1**
	b. Wet distributor cap and/or spark plug wires	**b.** Remove cap and wires. Dry and reinstall. **5.1**
	c. Weak coil	**c.** Test and replace as needed. **3.3**
	d. Defective spark plug wires	**d.** Test and replace as needed. **3.3**
	e. Faulty Hall sender	**e.** Test and replace as needed. **3.4**
	f. Incorrect ignition timing	**f.** Check and adjust timing. **4.1**
	g. Engine mechanical failure	**g.** See **ENGINE**
	h. Fuel system fault	**h.** See **FUEL SYSTEM (Gasoline)**
3. Engine starts but runs badly, misfires, loses power, backfires	**a.** Incorrect ignition timing	**a.** Check and adjust timing. **4.1**
	b. Wet distributor cap and/or spark plug wires	**b.** Remove cap and wires. Dry and reinstall. **5.1**
	c. Fouled spark plugs	**c.** Replace spark plugs. See **LUBRICATION AND MAINTENANCE**
	d. Weak coil	**d.** Test and replace as needed. **3.3**
	e. Defective spark plug wires	**e.** Test and replace as needed. **3.3**
	f. Worn distributor cap/rotor	**f.** Inspect and replace as needed. **3.2**
	g. Faulty knock sensor control unit (TCI-h with knock sensor only)	**g.** Test knock sensor system. **4.3**
	h. Faulty centrifugal advance mechanism (TCI-h only)	**h.** Test and replace as needed. **4.2**
	i. Faulty control unit	**i.** Test and replace as needed. **4.**
	j. Faulty throttle switches	**j.** Test switches and replace as needed. See **FUEL SYSTEM (Gasoline)**
	k. Engine mechanical damage	**k.** See **ENGINE**
4. Knocking or pinging noise while accelerating	**a.** Incorrect ignition timing	**a.** Check and adjust timing. **4.1**
	b. Faulty centrifugal advance mechanism (TCI-h only)	**b.** Test and replace as needed. **4.2**
	c. Faulty ignition control unit	**c.** Test and replace as needed. **3.4**
	d. Faulty knock sensor and/or control unit	**d.** Test knock sensor system. **4.3**
	e. Faulty control unit	**e.** Test and replace as needed.
	f. Pre-ignition due to carbon buildup or burned valves in engine combustion chambers	**f.** Overhaul or replace cylinder head. See **ENGINE**

To check the distributor cap and rotor, remove the cap as described in **5. Distributor**. Inspect the contacts inside the distributor cap and at the tip of the rotor for corrosion, wear, or pitting. Parts with corroded contacts can be cleaned and re-used, but for wear, pitting, or heavy corrosion, replacement is highly recommended. The center black carbon brush inside the cap should spring back when compressed.

Cracks or carbon tracks in the distributor cap may cause shorts to ground. The cracks may be fine and difficult to see. Check carefully, especially around the contacts. Carbon tracks are the faint black lines, usually running between two contacts or to ground, left over from high-voltage arcing. Replace a distributor cap that shows any sign of cracks or carbon tracking. For a thorough inspection, be sure also to check under the black radio-suppression shield around the outside of the cap.

To visually check the spark plug wires, gently bend them in several places to expose cracks in the insulation which may cause spark "leaks". Remove the rubber boots and check them for pliancy and the ability to seal out dirt and moisture. Replace any wire that is cracked, oil-soaked, or dry and brittle.

For a quick-check of distributor cap and spark plug wire condition, listen for the sound of the arcing or watch while the engine runs at night. In darkness, the arc of high voltage to ground because of a crack in the cap or a poorly insulated wire may be visible as a blue spark. For another quick check of cap and wire condition, use a spray bottle to spray a fine mist of water around them while the engine runs. If the cap and wires are in good condition and insulated properly, the added moisture should have no effect. If their condition is marginal, the added moisture may promote arcing and cause the engine to run roughly.

The coil should be examined for cracks, burns, carbon tracks, and for any leaking fluid. The coil tower, terminal 4, should be clean and dry. If necessary, remove the coil for cleaning and closer examination.

3.3 Testing Coil and Spark Plug Wires

Use an ohmmeter to test the ignition coil primary and secondary resistance as shown in Fig. 3-1. Resistance values are given in **Table c**. Replace any coil which has higher primary or secondary resistance.

Fig. 3-1. Primary coil resistance being measured with an ohmmeter (shown schematically) between terminals 1 and 15. Measurement of secondary resistance is similar.

Table c. Ignition Coil Resistance

TEST	Engine	Terminals	Resistance
Primary resistance	All except PL	1 (−) and 15 (+)	.52 to .76 ohms
	PL	1 (−) and 15 (+)	.60 to .80 ohms
Secondary resistance	GX, MZ, HT, and RD	1 (−) and 4 (center tower)	2400 to 3500 ohms
	PL	4 (center tower) and 15 (+)	6500 to 8500 ohms
	RV, PF	4 (center tower) and 15 (+)	2400 to 3500 ohms

To check each spark plug wire, disconnect the ends from the spark plug and from the distributor cap and use an ohmmeter to check resistance as shown in Fig. 3-2. Spark plug wires should have 4600 to 7400 ohms resistance. The coil wire should have 1200 to 2800 ohms resistance.

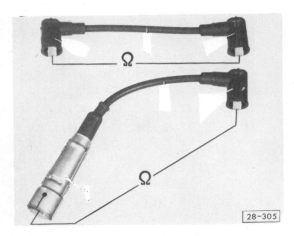

Fig. 3-2. Resistance of spark plug wire (bottom) and coil wire (top) being measured with an ohmmeter (shown schematically).

If the measured resistance is too high, check the wire and the connectors separately, as shown in Fig. 3-3. Also check for corrosion at the connections. Remove the connectors carefully. Twist, then pull. If the metal wire end stays in the connector, the connection is ruined and both connector and wire must be replaced. The resistance of the spark plug connectors should be 4000 to 6000 ohms. The resistance of the suppression connectors which connect to the distributor cap should be 600 to 1400 ohms. The resistance of the wire alone should be nearly zero ohms. Wires or connectors with too much resistance should be replaced. Individual connectors and wires are available from authorized Volkswagen dealers, but may not be stocked by all dealers.

CAUTION ━━

To avoid damaging the distributor cap, do not wiggle the connectors when removing them. If necessary, twist to loosen. Then, pull straight out from the cap.

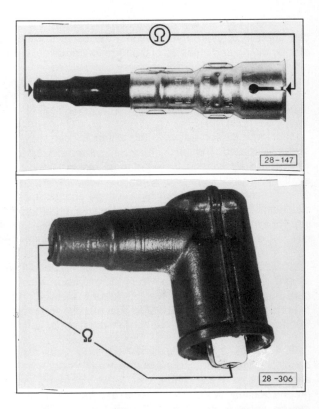

Fig. 3-3. Resistance measurement of spark plug connector (top) and distributor cap suppression connector (bottom) shown schematically.

3.4 Testing Hall Sender and Ignition Control Unit

The Hall sender and ignition control unit only need to be tested if there is no spark at the spark plugs when tested. For these tests, the spark plug wires and ignition coil should be in good condition as described in **3.3 Testing Coil and Spark Plug Wires**. The ignition control unit is located in the driver's side cowling, above and behind the firewall, beneath the drip tray. The Hall sender connector is on the side of the distributor.

These tests require the use of a high-impedence voltmeter or low-current LED test light. For more information, see **3.1 Basic Troubleshooting Principles**. The sequence of the tests below is important. Follow the test sequence as it is presented in order to logically isolate the faulty component.

CAUTION ━━

Always turn the ignition off before connecting or disconnecting ignition test equipment. Switch multimeter functions or measurement ranges only with the test probes disconnected.

Voltage Supply and Ground to Ignition Control Unit

With the ignition off, remove the harness connector from the ignition control unit. Check for voltage between connector terminals 2 (−) and 4 (+) as shown in Fig. 3-4. There should be battery voltage when the ignition is turned on. If there is no voltage, check for wiring faults. Check the continuity of the wire from terminal 2 to ground, and from terminal 4 of the connector to terminal 15 of the coil. Repair wiring as necessary. For current flow diagrams, see **ELECTRICAL SYSTEM**.

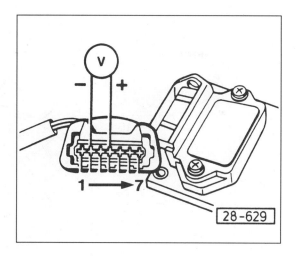

Fig. 3-4. Ignition control unit voltage supply being checked at connector terminals 2 and 4.

Voltage Supply and Ground to Hall Sender

The three ignition systems covered by this manual each get power to the Hall sender a different way. The basic TCI-h system powers the Hall sender through the ignition control unit. On the TCI-h system with knock sensor, the Hall sender receives power from the knock sensor control unit. On Digifant II system, the Digifant control unit powers the Hall sender.

With the ignition off and the ignition control unit connected, disconnect the harness connector from the Hall sender at the distributor. Check for voltage between terminals 1 (−) and 3 (+) of the connector, as shown in Fig. 3-5. There should be voltage when the ignition is switched on.

If there is no voltage, use the current flow diagrams in **ELECTRICAL SYSTEM** to check the wiring between the Hall sender connector and the control unit, between the voltage source and the control unit, and between the control unit and ground. If all of these wires have continuity and there is still no voltage reaching the Hall sender, the control unit which provides power to the sender is faulty and should be replaced.

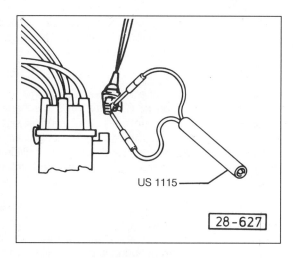

Fig. 3-5. Checking voltage supply at Hall sender connector. LED test light shown.

Hall Sender Switching Function

To check Hall sender function, check its ability to switch the primary circuit. Remove the coil wire from the center of the distributor and connect it to ground with a jumper wire. With the Hall sender connected, carefully push back the rubber connector boot to expose the back of the wire connections. Connect an LED test light between the center terminal and the positive (+) battery terminal, as shown in Fig. 3-6. When the starter is actuated, the LED should flicker. If there is no reaction, the Hall sender is defective and should be replaced as described in **5.3 Disassembling and Assembling Distributor**.

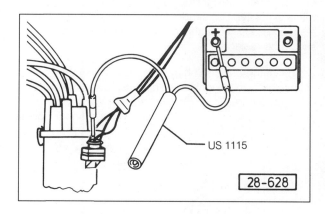

Fig. 3-6. Hall sending unit switching function being tested with LED test light.

Ignition Control Unit Voltage to Coil

With the ignition off, connect the probes of a multimeter (20 DCV scale) to terminal 1 (−) and terminal 15 (+) of the ignition coil, as shown in Fig. 3-7. Do not disconnect the existing coil wiring. On models with the basic TCI-h system, disconnect the Hall sender connector at the distributor. On models with TCI-h and knock sensor, disconnect the harness connector from the knock sensor unit. On Digifant II models, disconnect the harness connector from the Digifant control unit.

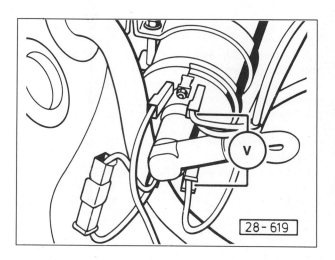

Fig. 3-7. Voltage being measured at ignition coil terminals 1 (−) and 15 (+) (shown schematically).

8

When the ignition is switched on, the meter should display a reading of at least 2 volts for approximately 1 to 2 seconds, and then drop to 0 volts. If not, either the ignition coil or the ignition control unit is defective. Check the coil as described earlier in **3.2 Ignition System Visual Inspection** and **3.3 Testing Coil and Spark Plug Wires**. If no coil faults are discovered, the ignition control unit is faulty and should be replaced.

Ignition Control Unit Response to Hall Sender Signal

With the voltmeter or multimeter connected as in the previous test, check the ignition control unit function by providing it with a simulated Hall sender signal. If the control unit does not respond as indicated, the ignition control unit is defective and should be replaced.

To test the basic TCI-h system, disconnect the Hall sender connector. Turn the ignition on and, using a jumper wire, briefly connect the center terminal of the Hall sender connector to ground, as shown in Fig. 3-8. The voltage should briefly increase to at least 2 volts.

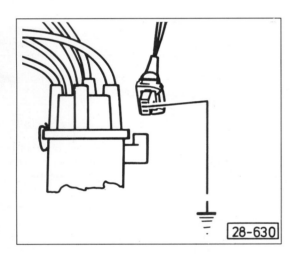

Fig. 3-8. Center terminal of Hall sender connector being briefly connected to ground to test ignition control unit on TCI-h ignition system (shown schematically).

To test the TCI-h system with knock sensor, disconnect the knock sensor control unit harness connector. Turn the ignition on and, using a jumper wire, briefly connect terminal 12 of the knock sensor control unit connector to ground as shown in Fig. 3-9. The voltage should briefly increase to at least 2 volts.

To test the Digifant II ignition system, disconnect the Digifant control unit harness connector. Turn the ignition on and, using a jumper wire, briefly connect terminal 25 of the Digifant control unit connector to ground. Terminal locations are shown in Fig. 3-10. The voltage should rise briefly to at least 2 volts.

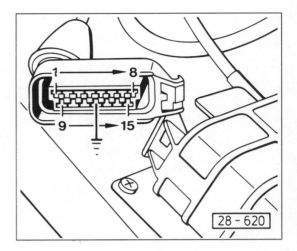

Fig. 3-9. Terminal 12 of the knock sensor control unit connector being briefly connected to ground to test ignition control unit on TCI-h ignition system with knock sensor. (Test shown schematically).

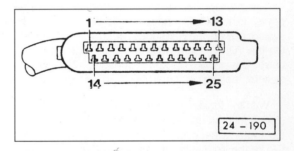

Fig. 3-10. Terminal locations on Digifant control unit harness connector.

4. TRANSISTORIZED COIL IGNITION (TCI-H) SYSTEM

The TCI-h system has four major components: the distributor with Hall sender, the ignition control unit, the coil, and the spark plugs. The TCI-h system with knock control used on engines with CIS-E fuel injection also includes the knock sensor and knock sensor control unit. With the Digifant II engine management system, the Digifant control unit controls the knock sensor.

This section covers checking and adjusting the ignition timing, checking the basic TCI-h system's mechanical and vacuum timing advance functions, and troubleshooting the knock sensor system. Testing of the basic ignition system electronics, including the Hall sender and the ignition control unit, is covered in **3.4 Testing Hall Sender and Ignition Control Unit**.

The components of the basic TCI-h ignition system are illustrated in Fig. 4-1. Ignition timing is mechanically adjusted to compensate for changes in engine speed and load. The centrifugal advance system of spring-loaded rotating weights advances ignition timing as engine rpm increases. The vacuum advance mechanism adjusts ignition timing to adapt to changes in engine load.

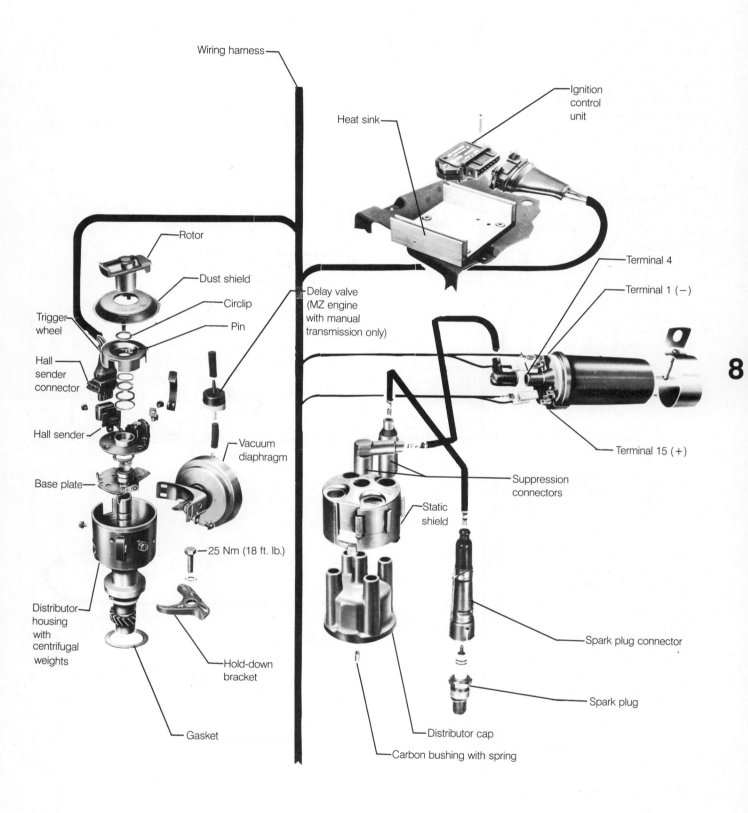

Fig. 4-1. Transistorized coil ignition with Hall sender (TCI-h)
and mechanical advance distributor used on Golf
and Jetta engines (GX and MZ engine codes).

The components of the TCI-h ignition system with knock control used on engines with CIS-E fuel injection are illustrated in Fig. 4-2. The similar Digifant system includes the Digifant control unit which replaces the knock sensor control unit. Both systems are similar to the basic TCI-h system, except that all timing advance control is done electronically. The distributor has no timing advance capability. Instead, the signal from the Hall sender to the ignition control unit is manipulated electronically to adjust timing advance in response to engine load,

engine speed, throttle position, knock sensor signals, and on Digifant II engines, coolant temperature. The timing advance function is controlled by the knock sensor control unit or, on Digifant II engines, by the Digifant control unit. These control units also have an rpm-limiting function.

Specifications for the transistorized coil ignition systems with and without knock control are given in **Table d**, **Table e**, and **Table f**.

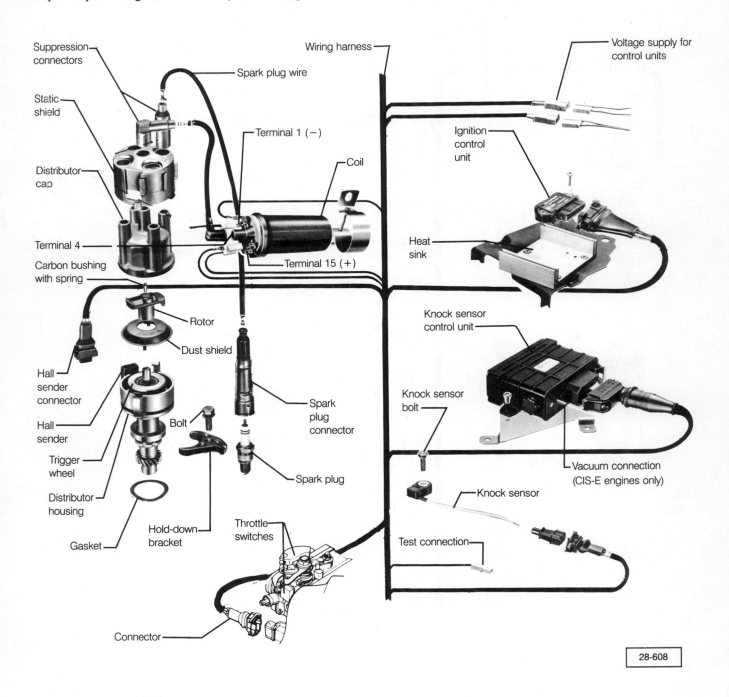

28-608

Fig. 4-2. Transistorized coil ignition with Hall sender (TCI-h) and knock control. System shown is used on engines with HT and RD engine codes. 16-valve (PL engine code) and Digifant (RV and PF engine codes) systems are similar.

Table d. Basic TCI-h Ignition System Specifications (engine codes GX and MZ)

Distributor part number	.027 905 205 F
Ignition Timing	
Test value	.4 – 8° BTDC
Adjusting value	.6 ± 1° BTDC
Engine idle speed, checking	.800 – 1000 rpm
adjusting	.900 ± 30 rpm
Vacuum hose	.connected
Centrifugal advance	
Start (rpm)	.@ 1100 – 1350
Degrees advance @ rpm	.12 – 17° @ 2600 rpm
End	.23 – 27° @ 6000 rpm
Vacuum advance	
Start	.4 – 8° @ 100 – 160 mbar
End	.10 – 14° @ 240 – 260 mbar
Firing order	.1 - 3 - 4 - 2
Spark plugs (Engine GX)	
Bosch	.W7DTC, WR7DS
Beru	.RS 35
Champion	.N8GY
Spark plugs (Engine MZ)	
Bosch	.W8DO
Beru	.14-8DU
Spark plug gap	.0.6–0.8 mm (.024–.031 in.)
Spark plug tightening torque	.20 Nm (15 ft. lb.)

Table e. Ignition System Specifications TCI-h with Knock Control (engine codes HT, RD, PL)

Distributor part no. (HT, RD, engines)	.026 905 205 S
Distributor part no. (PL engines)	.027 905 205 P
Knock sensor control unit part no.	
(HT, RD engines)	.811 907 397
(PL engines)	.811 907 397 E
Ignition timing	
Test value	.4 – 8° BTDC
Adjusting value	.6 ± 1° BTDC
Engine idle speed	.800 – 900 rpm
Control unit vacuum hose	.connected
Firing order	.1 - 3 - 4 - 2
Spark Plugs (Engine HT-RD)	
Bosch	.W7 DTC
Beru	.14-7 DTU
Champion	.N8GY
Spark plugs (Engine PL)	
Bosch	.F6 DTC
Spark plug gap	.0.7–0.9 mm (.027–.035 in.)
Spark plug tightening torque	.20 Nm (15 ft. lb.)
Engine RPM limit	
HT engine	.6200 – 6400 rpm
RD engine	.6570 – 6630 rpm
PL engine	.7200 – 7300 rpm

Table f. Ignition System Specifications TCI-h with Knock Control (Digifant II) (engine codes RV and PF)

Distributor part no.	.037 905 205
Ignition timing (coolant temperature sensor disconnected)	
Test value	.4 – 8° BTDC
Adjusting value	.6 ± 1° BTDC
Engine idle speed (radiator fan not running)	.750 – 850 rpm
Firing order	.1 - 3 - 4 - 2
Spark Plugs:	
Bosch	.W7 DCO
Spark plug gap	.0.6–0.8 mm (.024–.032 in.)
Spark plug tightening torque	.20 Nm (15 ft. lb.)
Engine rpm limit	.6500

4.1 Ignition Timing

Correct ignition timing is essential to proper engine performance. Checking and adjusting ignition timing is an important part of any engine tune-up. Ignition timing also needs to be adjusted whenever the distributor has been removed or taken apart, and whenever the camshaft drive belt has been adjusted or replaced.

Ignition timing has a significant effect on engine exhaust emissions. Ignition timing should always be adjusted only in conjunction with idle speed and idle mixture (exhaust carbon monoxide or CO level). See **FUEL SYSTEM (Gasoline)**.

Since CO measurement and adjustment requires special skills and equipment, most do-it-yourselfers are advised to leave these adjustments to an authorized Volkswagen dealer service department or other qualified repair shop, to ensure compliance with emissions regulations as well as maximum performance.

To check basic ignition timing:

1. On cars with manual transmission, use a 27 mm hex wrench to remove the plastic plug from the timing check hole at the top of the transaxle bellhousing.

   NOTE ——

   The entire plug must be removed. The small center plug is for use with a special timing indicator used by Volkswagen dealer technicians.

2. With the ignition off, connect a tachometer and timing light to the battery positive (+) terminal and to the coil terminal 1 (−), according to the instrument manufacturer's instructions.

8

3. On cars with the Digifant II system, disconnect the harness connector to the coolant temperature sensor as shown in Fig. 4-3 and, disconnect and plug the hose from the crankcase emission valve, as shown in Fig. 4-4.

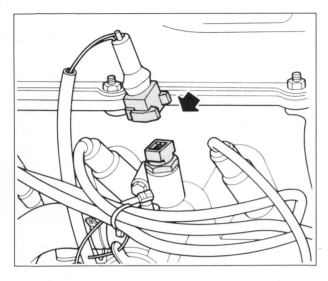

Fig. 4-3. Coolant temperature sensor connector (arrow) on Digifant II system (engine codes RV and PF) disconnected for test.

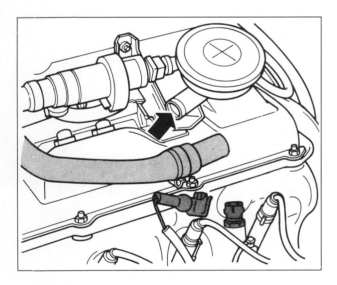

Fig. 4-4. Crankcase emission valve hose (arrow) on Digifant II system (engine codes RV and PF) disconnected and plugged for ignition timing check.

4. Start the engine and allow it to fully warm up. Oil temperature should be at least 140°F (60°C) or the radiator cooling fan should cycle on and off at least once.

NOTE ━

On GX and MZ engines with the basic TCI-h system, the vacuum hose should remain connected to the distributor's vacuum advance diaphragm unit when checking ignition timing.

5. Briefly raise the engine speed above 3000 rpm three or four times.

6. With the engine idling, aim the timing light at the timing check hole in the bellhousing. The timing mark on the flywheel should appear adjacent to the pointer in the hole as shown in Fig. 4-5.

WARNING ━

Keep hands and other objects clear of the radiator cooling fan. The fan may start at any time, even when the ignition is switched off.

NOTE ━

The basic timing indications are only valid when engine idle speed is within specifications.

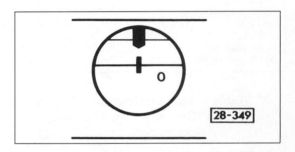

Fig. 4-5. Timing mark on flywheel aligned with pointer in timing check hole (top of bellhousing).

7. If ignition timing is within specifications, switch off the ignition and disconnect the test equipment. On Digifant II system, reconnect the coolant temperature sensor harness connector and the crankcase ventilation hose.

To adjust basic ignition timing:

1. With the ignition off, loosen the distributor hold-down bolt. On 16-valve engines, there are two.

CAUTION ━

The distributor should be just loose enough to be moved by hand, but tight enough that it can only be moved by deliberate effort. The distributor must not move by itself while the engine is running.

2. Start the engine and let it run at idle. Gradually turn the distributor housing until the timing mark, viewed with the timing light, lines up with the bellhousing pointer. See Fig. 4-5 above.

3. Stop the engine and tighten the distributor hold-down bolt without moving the distributor. On all except 16-valve engines, torque the bolt to 25 Nm (18 ft. lb.). On 16-valve engines, torque the bolts to 10 Nm (87 in. lb.).

4. Start the engine and recheck the ignition timing. Repeat the adjustment if necessary.

5. Turn the ignition off and remove the test equipment. On cars with manual transmission, replace the plastic plug in the timing check hole.

Ignition timing which varies continuously may be an indication of worn distributor shaft bearings. These bearings are not available as separate replacement parts. Repair is by replacement of the distributor housing only.

4.2 Centrifugal and Vacuum Spark Advance
(basic TCI-h only, engine codes GX and MZ)

The centrifugal advance mechanism advances ignition timing as rpm increases. To check centrifugal advance, disconnect the vacuum advance hose at the distributor and plug the hose. Then observe the change in ignition timing at speeds above idle.

Precise measurement requires an adjustable timing light which can accurately indicate how much timing changes from the basic timing value. See **Table d** above for centrifugal advance specifications. If the distributor's centrifugal advance mechanism is not performing properly, the distributor housing assembly should be replaced.

The vacuum advance mechanism changes ignition timing according to intake manifold vacuum, an indication of the load on the engine. To check vacuum advance, remove the vacuum hose from the vacuum diaphragm on the side of the distributor and connect a substitute hose to the diaphragm. Then observe the change in ignition timing while applying vacuum to the hose.

It is important that the vacuum advance diaphragm not leak. Check the diaphragm with a vacuum pump and gauge if necessary. It should hold vacuum of approximately 500 mbar, losing no more than 50 mbar in one minute. The vacuum diaphragm is available as a separate replacement part.

To further check both mechanisms, remove the distributor cap. When the plate on which the Hall sender is mounted is moved counterclockwise, it should move smoothly without sticking and spring back to its original position when released. If it doesn't, then the plate is binding or the vacuum advance diaphragm is faulty. The mechanism for the centrifugal advance can be checked by twisting the distributor rotor clockwise. The movement of the rotor should be smooth and it should spring back to its original position when released.

4.3 Electronic Timing Advance
(TCI-h with knock control, engine codes HT, RD, PL, RV, PF)

The timing advance functions are most accurately checked using specialized equipment. An adjustable timing light or an engine analyzer such as Volkswagen special tool no. VW 1367 can be used to accurately read ignition timing throughout the range of advance. Follow the operating instructions provided by the instrument's manufacturer.

Checking RPM-dependent Timing Advance
(engine codes HT, RD, PL)

Start the engine and let it idle for a few minutes to establish a base timing value in the control unit. Check this base reading with the timing light. Disconnect the vacuum hose from the knock sensor control unit. Raise the engine rpm and compare the maximum timing advance with the values given in **Table g**. Turn off the engine and reinstall the vacuum hose to the knock sensor control unit.

On HT engines, if the values are not as specified, remove the harness connector from the knock sensor control unit and check for continuity between terminal 11 and ground. If there is no continuity, repair the wiring and repeat the test. See **ELECTRICAL SYSTEM** for current flow diagrams.

Timing which does not advance as specified indicates that either the knock sensor control unit or the knock sensor is faulty. See **4.4 Knock Sensor System Diagnosis** for information on using the system's built-in diagnostic capability to help pinpoint the problem.

Table g. Maximum RPM-Dependent Ignition Timing Advance
(engine codes HT, RD, PL)

Engine code	Engine rpm	Total timing advance (approx.)
HT	4300	14°
RD	3000	16°
PL	2500	13°

Checking Vacuum-dependent Ignition Timing Advance
(engine codes HT, RD, PL)

Check the vacuum advance function only after determining that the rpm dependent timing advance is correct. Start the engine and increase engine speed to approximately 3400 rpm. Record the amount of timing advance and let the engine return to idle. Remove the vacuum hose from the knock sensor control unit and again raise the engine to 3400 rpm. The timing should advance approximately 6° more than the previous reading. If it does not, check the vacuum hose for kinks or leaks. If the hose is not kinked or broken, then the knock sensor control unit may be faulty.

Checking Digifant II Ignition Timing Advance
(engine codes RV and PF)

Start the engine and run it for at least two minutes at normal operating temperature. Remove the coolant temperature sensor connector. Raise the engine speed to 2300 rpm, and record the timing value. Reconnect the coolant temperature sensor connector and briefly raise the engine speed above 3000 rpm. Raise the engine speed again to 2300 rpm and recheck the timing. The timing should now be 30° ± 3° more advanced than it was with the coolant temperature sensor connected.

If the timing does not advance as specified, check the knock sensor mounting bolt torque as described in **4.6 Removing and Installing Knock Sensor**, and check the knock sensor resistance and wiring as described in **4.5 Troubleshooting Knock Sensor System**. If torque and resistance are within specification and there are no breaks in the wiring, then the Digifant control unit is probably faulty.

If connecting or disconnecting the coolant temperature sensor has no effect on timing advance, check the continuity of the coolant temperature sensor wire as described in **4.5 Troubleshooting Knock Sensor System**. If there are no breaks in the wire, then either the Digifant control unit or the temperature sensor is faulty. See **FUEL SYSTEM (Gasoline)** for information on testing the coolant temperature sensor.

4.4 Knock Sensor System Diagnosis

(engine codes HT, RD, PL)

The knock sensor control unit has a fault memory which records and communicates certain system faults. This information is displayed by connecting an LED test light to the test connection of the wiring harness near the ignition coil. The test connection is a single wire, either blue or blue/brown, leading to pin 4 of the knock sensor control unit.

To read the fault memory, connect an LED test light between the test connection and the battery positive (+) terminal, as shown in Fig. 4-6. When the ignition is turned on, the LED should light, indicating that the control unit is responding. If it doesn't, check the connections and check for continuity of the wire from the test connector to terminal 4 of the knock sensor control unit connector. If there is continuity, the knock sensor control unit may be faulty.

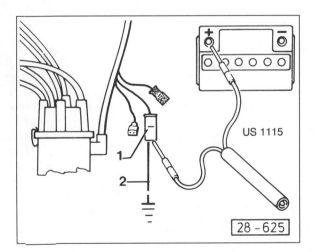

Fig. 4-6. LED test light connected to knock sensor control unit test connection (**1**), and test connection connected by jumper wire (**2**) to ground. LED test light shown is Volkswagen special tool no. US 1115.

Start the engine and briefly raise the engine speed to at least 3000 rpm. If the LED test light goes out, there is no fault information stored, and the system is operating correctly. If it

does not go out, or if it goes out and comes back on, there is a fault in the system. Leave the engine idling and the LED test light connected, and connect a jumper wire from the test connector to ground, as shown in Fig. 4-6 above. Hold the connection for at least three seconds. The test light should flash in coded intervals. If the light does not flash, the control unit is faulty and should be replaced.

NOTE ——

Do not turn off the ignition during this procedure. Doing so will permanently erase the fault memory.

Two flashes per interval indicates a fault in either the circuit wiring, the knock sensor, or the knock sensor control unit. See **4.5 Troubleshooting Knock Sensor System** below for additional troubleshooting.

Three flashes per interval indicates a problem with the vacuum connection to the knock sensor control unit. Check the vacuum hose for breaks and replace it if necessary. If there are no breaks, the control unit is faulty and should be replaced.

4.5 Troubleshooting Knock Sensor System

This heading outlines the final steps for troubleshooting faults in the knock sensor system. The sequence of the tests is important. Follow the test sequence as it is presented in order to logically isolate the faulty component.

Checking Knock Sensor System Wiring

With the ignition off, disconnect the harness connectors from the ignition control unit, the Hall sender at the distributor, the throttle switches, and the knock sensor. The ignition control unit is in the cowl, above and behind the firewall on the driver's side, mounted atop the larger control unit. The throttle switches are on the throttle valve, near the accelerator cable and throttle valve actuating mechanism.

On HT, RD, and PL engines, disconnect the harness connectors from the knock sensor control unit and the oxygen sensor control unit. These control units are located in the cowl above and behind the firewall, on the right and left sides respectively.

On RV and PF engines, disconnect the harness connectors from the Digifant control unit and the coolant temperature sensor. The Digifant control unit is located in the cowl above and behind the firewall on the driver's side. The coolant temperature sensor is shown earlier in Fig. 4-3.

Check continuity of the knock sensor system wiring harness between all the component wiring connectors, using the appropriate current flow diagrams in **ELECTRICAL SYSTEM** as a guide. Fig. 4-7 and Fig. 4-8 identify the terminals of the knock sensor control unit connector and the oxygen sensor control unit connector for HT, RD, and PL engines. Fig. 4-9 identifies the terminals of the Digifant control unit connector for RV and PF engines. Repair any defective wiring and reconnect the harness connectors.

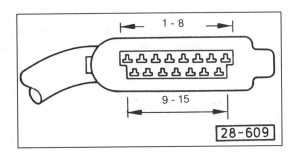

Fig. 4-7. Knock sensor control unit connector terminal orientation (HT, RD, and PL engines).

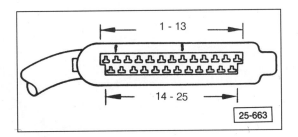

Fig. 4-8. Oxygen sensor control unit connector terminal orientation (HT, RD, and PL engines).

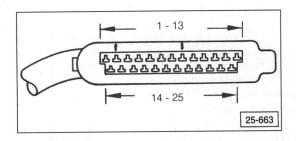

Fig. 4-9. Digifant control unit connector terminal orientation (RV and PF engines).

Knock Sensor System Voltage Checks

With the knock sensor control unit or Digifant control unit disconnected, make voltage checks at the connector terminals as specified below. Voltage at all of the specified terminals should be approximately 12 volts. **Table h** lists terminals to be tested at the control unit connector, as well as possible causes for no voltage at a particular terminal. To prevent damage to the sensitive electronic components, always connect or disconnect the meter probes with the ignition off.

8

Table h. Knock Sensor System Voltage Checks

Terminals	Test conditions	Probable causes if not approximately 12 volts
CIS-E (HT, RD, and PL) engines		
3 and 5	Ignition on	Fuse 17 defective (Jetta only) Wire from terminal 5 to ignition switch open
3 and 8	Ignition on, full-throttle switch on throttle valve closed	Fuse 22 faulty (all except Jetta) Middle wire to throttle switches open Full-throttle switch defective
3 and 6	Ignition on, idle switch closed	Fuse 22 faulty (all except Jetta) Middle wire to throttle switches open Idle switch improperly adjusted or defective (see **FUEL SYSTEM (Gasoline)**)
3 and 10	Ignition on	Wire from terminal 10 to fuel pump relay open Fuel pump relay faulty (see **ELECTRICAL SYSTEM**)
Digifant II (RV and PF) engines		
13 and 14	Ignition on	Fuse 17 faulty Ground wire to battery negative terminal faulty Wire from terminal 14 to relay panel faulty Digifant control unit relay faulty
14 and 19	Ignition on	Ground wire to intake manifold faulty
3 and 19	Ignition on	Wire from terminal 3 to relay panel faulty Fuel pump relay faulty

Checking Knock Sensor System Components

If the wiring and voltage signals are as specified, the final step in troubleshooting the knock sensor system is to check the resistance of the system components. Test terminals and resistance specifications are given in **Table i**. Fig. 4-10 gives the resistance values for the coolant temperature sensor, which vary according to temperature. If the resistance values are correct and the knock sensor system is still not operating correctly, check the knock sensor mounting torque as described in **4.6 Removing and Installing Knock Sensor**. If the torque is correct, the control unit is probably defective.

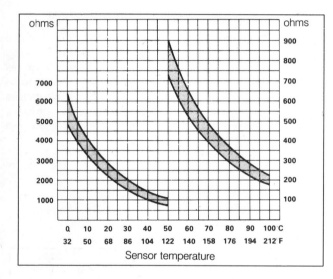

Fig. 4-10. Graph of Digifant coolant temperature sensor resistance versus sensor temperature. If the wiring, voltage checks, and sensors are not faulty, and there is still a problem with the knock sensor system or the fault diagnosis system indicates a system fault, then the control unit is probably faulty.

4.6 Removing and Installing Knock Sensor

The knock sensor detects the unusual engine vibrations caused by detonation, often referred to as knock or ping. The knock causes the sensor to generate a low-voltage signal which is monitored by the knock sensor control unit. The control unit retards ignition timing electronically in small steps until the detonation ceases.

The two types of knock sensors used on engines covered by this manual are shown in Fig. 4-11. Correct mounting bolt torque is critical. The knock sensor will not operate correctly if the mounting bolt torque is too low or too high.

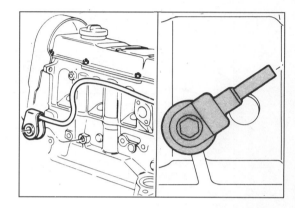

Fig. 4-11. Type I knock sensor (left) and Type II knock sensor (right). See Table j for correct mounting torque.

Table i. Knock Sensor System Resistance Checks

Terminals	Resistance	If resistance not as specified
CIS-E (HT, RD, and PL) engines		
2 and 3	90,000 to 100,000 ohms	Check oxygen sensor control unit See **FUEL SYSTEM (Gasoline)**
3 and 13	at least 1,000,000 ohms	Knock sensor or sensor wiring faulty
13 and 14	Type I knock sensor: 300,000 ohms Type II knock sensor: ∞ ohms (See **4.6 Removing and Installing Knock Sensor** for type identification)	Replace knock sensor
Digifant II (RV and PF) engines		
6 and 11	0 ohms with throttle closed or fully opened ∞ ohms at part throttle	Replace idle and full-throttle switches Replace idle and full-throttle switches
6 and 10	per graph in Fig. 4-10	Replace coolant temperature sensor See **FUEL SYSTEM (Gasoline)**
2 and 13	∞ ohms	Replace knock sensor

The two sensor types have different torque specifications, so the sensor type must be identified prior to installation. It is also advisable to check the knock sensor with an ohmmeter prior to installation. **Table j** lists the resistance values and tightening torques for the two types of sensors. If it becomes necessary to replace the knock sensor, or to remove it for other repair work, the following cautions should be observed.

CAUTION ━━

•*Disconnect battery negative (−) terminal before loosening or tightening the knock sensor.*

• *Do not use washers when mounting the knock sensor.*

• *Knock sensor mounting bolt torque must be strictly observed during installation.*

Table j. Knock Sensor Specifications

Type	Resistance value	Mounting bolt torque
I	approx. 300k ohms	10–12 Nm (7–9 ft. lb.)
II	approx. ∞ ohms	15–25 Nm (11–18 ft. lb.)

5. DISTRIBUTOR

This heading covers the removal and installation of the distributor, the distributor cap and rotor, the spark plug wires, and the Hall sender. Inspection and testing procedures for these components are covered in **3. Troubleshooting**.

The different ignition systems and engines covered in this manual use different distributors. The basic TCI-h system uses a distributor with mechanical advance mechanisms, as shown in Fig. 5-1. The distributor used for the TCI-h system with knock control is very similar—many parts are interchangeable—but since timing advance is controlled electronically, the Hall sender is rigidly mounted and there are no mechanical advance mechanisms. The same type of distributor is used on 16-valve engines (engine code PL), although there are some physical differences resulting from its unique mounting location on the cylinder head. This distributor is illustrated in Fig. 5-2. Fig. 5-3 shows the distributor cap and suppression shield used on distributors for all engines covered by this manual.

The distributor cap and rotor are generally replaced as a part of normal maintenance. See **LUBRICATION AND MAINTENANCE** for recommended replacement intervals.

The Hall sender, the trigger wheel, the vacuum diaphragm, the suppression shield, and the dust shield are all available as replacement parts, but replacement is not routinely necessary. The distributor housing parts, including the centrifugal advance mechanism and shaft bushings, are not available. The distributor housing must be replaced as a unit.

Whenever the distributor is disassembled, all of the shims, circlips, gaskets, and O-rings should be replaced. Any disassembly or removal of the distributor will require checking and adjusting the ignition timing, as described in **4.1 Ignition Timing**.

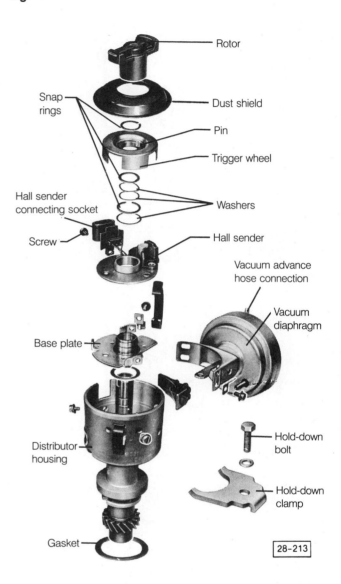

28-213

Fig. 5-1. Distributor assembly used with basic TCI-h ignition system. Distributor used for TCI-h with knock control is similar, but distributor housing has no vacuum diaphragm.

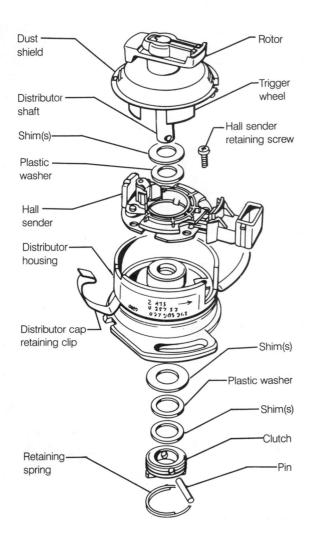

Dust shield
Rotor
Distributor shaft
Trigger wheel
Shim(s)
Hall sender retaining screw
Plastic washer
Hall sender
Distributor housing
Distributor cap retaining clip
Shim(s)
Plastic washer
Shim(s)
Clutch
Retaining spring
Pin

Fig. 5-2. Distributor used on 16-valve engines (engine code PL).

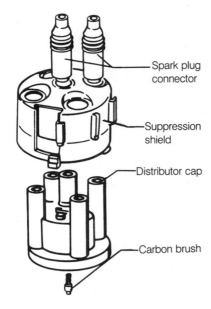

Spark plug connector
Suppression shield
Distributor cap
Carbon brush

Fig. 5-3. Distributor cap with suppression shield used on all engines. Suppression shield is grounded by distributor cap attachment clips.

5.1 Removing and Installing Distributor Cap, Rotor, and Spark Plug Wires

These components all carry high voltage to the spark plugs and proper engine performance depends on getting the best possible spark at the spark plug. Worn and corroded contacts or poor insulation which allows the spark to short to ground are the primary reasons for replacement of these components.

Replacing Spark Plug Wires

Each spark plug wire leads from a specific terminal on the distributor cap to a specific spark plug. When removing the wires, label their positions so that they can be reinstalled in the proper places.

The spark plug wires are removed from the distributor cap and spark plugs by pulling the boots straight up. Pull only on the connector, not on the wire itself. On particularly old wires, twisting the connector or peeling back the rubber boot from the distributor cap tower may ease removal.

CAUTION ━━

Wiggling the connectors from side to side when removing the spark plug wires from the distributor cap may damage the cap.

Replacing Distributor Cap and Rotor

The distributor cap is held in place with two spring clips which can be pried loose using the blade of a screwdriver. Avoid bending the clips. To replace the cap remove the spark plug wires, then remove the suppression shield by releasing the spring clips and sliding it off the cap.

On all except 16-valve engines, simply pull straight up on the rotor to remove it. When installing a new rotor, make sure that the key inside the rotor fits into the notch on the distributor shaft.

On 16-valve engines, the rotor is permanently attached to the distributor shaft. To replace the rotor, the part which fits over the distributor shaft must be carefully crushed using a pair of pliers.

CAUTION ━━

Do not hit the rotor or distributor shaft with any tool.

Clean off all of the old adhesive. When installing a new rotor, use an instant adhesive such as Loctite® 325 Speed Bonder, and make sure that the key inside the rotor fits into the notch on the distributor shaft.

Spark plug wires must be installed so that the spark plugs have the proper firing order. For all engines covered by this manual, the firing order is 1-3-4-2. That is, looking at the top of the distributor cap, the spark plug wires go to cylinders no. 1, no. 3, no. 4, and no. 2, in clockwise order.

NOTE ━━

Cylinder no. 1 is the one closest to the camshaft drive belt.

5.2 Removing and Installing Distributor

Ignition timing must be checked and adjusted any time the distributor is disassembled or removed. See **4.1 Ignition Timing**.

To remove:

1. Rotate the engine by hand until the distributor rotor tip is aligned with the No. 1 cylinder Top Dead Center (TDC) mark on the distributor housing, as shown in Fig. 5-4.

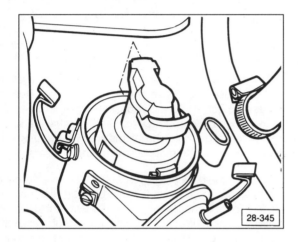

Fig. 5-4. Distributor rotor aligned with No. 1 cylinder mark on distributor housing.

2. Disconnect all electrical connections from the distributor. On GX and MZ engines, disconnect the vacuum line from the vacuum diaphragm.

3. Remove the distributor hold-down, and remove the distributor by pulling it straight out. Retrieve the sealing washer or O-ring from the bottom of the distributor. Cover the opening.

   NOTE ——

   On all except 16-valve engines, the distributor will want to rotate counterclockwise as the beveled drive gears disengage. Notice how far the distributor turns as it is removed, in order to reinstall it approximately the same way.

To install:

1. If the crankshaft has been turned since the distributor was removed, rotate the crankshaft so that the cylinder no. 1 is at TDC. If necessary, see **ENGINE**.

2. On all except 16-valve engines, align the oil pump drive shaft so that it is parallel to the crankshaft as shown in Fig. 5-5. Use a screwdriver to turn it if necessary.

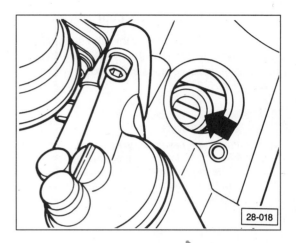

Fig. 5-5. Lug (arrow) on oil pump drive shaft aligned parallel to engine crankshaft.

3. Using a new sealing washer or O-ring, install the distributor. Align the rotor with the distributor housing, as shown in Fig. 5-4 above. Be sure that the distributor housing is seated firmly and that the distributor shaft engages properly.

   NOTE ——

   The rotor will rotate as the beveled drive gears engage, so check for proper alignment after installation.

   NOTE ——

   On 16-valve engines, be sure that the distributor drive clutch on the distributor shaft is properly engaged with the notch in the camshaft.

4. Install the distributor hold-down and the distributor cap. Reconnect the electrical connections and, on GX and MZ engines, the vacuum line.

5. Adjust the ignition timing as described in **4.1 Ignition Timing**.

5.3 Disassembling and Assembling Distributor

Some disassembly of the distributor is required to replace the Hall sender. It will require a snap-ring plier and, for 16-valve engines, a thin drift or punch. It is possible to disassemble the base plate, the distributor shaft, and the centrifugal advance mechanism on GX and MZ engines for cleaning and inspection, but these are not available as individual replacement parts. Fig. 5-1 and Fig. 5-2 above illustrate the distributor assemblies.

First remove the distributor cap and suppression shield, the rotor, and the dust shield as described in **5.1 Removing and Installing Distributor Cap, Rotor, and Spark Plug Wires.**

8

All Engines except 16-valve

Use a snap-ring plier to remove the snap-ring retaining the trigger wheel. To remove the wheel, use two screwdrivers positioned at opposite sides of the trigger wheel to pry it up as shown in Fig. 5-6.

CAUTION ━━

Push the screwdrivers in as far as possible, and pry up only under the strongest, center portion of the trigger wheel. Take care not to lose the small pin which keys the trigger wheel to the shaft.

NOTE ━━

A bent trigger wheel must be replaced.

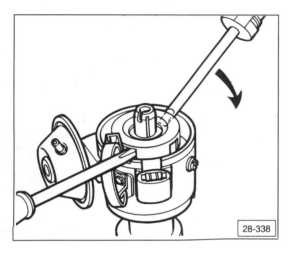

Fig. 5-6. Trigger wheel being pried off of distributor shaft. Pry evenly under center of trigger wheel, from both sides with two flat-bladed screwdrivers.

Remove the Hall sender by removing the screws holding it to the base plate.

16-valve Engines

Use a thin drift or punch to drive out the retaining pin in the distributor drive clutch, and pull the distributor shaft, the rotor, the dust shield, and the trigger wheel out from the top as a unit. The Hall sender is removed from the base of the distributor housing by removing the mounting screws.

6. DIESEL GLOW PLUG SYSTEM

The four glow plugs are small heating elements, one for each cylinder, mounted in the cylinder head with the tips projecting into the combustion pre-chambers. The glow plugs assist combustion during cold starts by providing additional heat for ignition. Voltage to the bus bar connecting the glow plugs is supplied by the glow plug relay whenever the ignition key is turned on. The glow plug relay is located on the fuse/relay panel. An indicator light on the instrument cluster signals that the system is operating, and also indicates when the engine is ready to start when it goes out. The length of time that the system operates and the indicator remains lit is controlled by an engine temperature sensor. Above a certain temperature, the system does not operate.

This heading covers testing the glow plug system, including the wiring and the glow plug relay, and glow plug replacement. In order for these tests to give meaningful results, the battery must be fully charged. For more information on troubleshooting diesel cold-starting problems, see **FUEL SYSTEM (Diesel)**.

6.1 Testing and Replacing Glow Plugs

The glow plugs themselves are the part of the system most likely to cause a problem during normal use. Due to their constant exposure in the combustion chamber, they are subject to carbon build-up and wear, and they have a limited life. Other potential glow plug problems are over-torquing on installation, or wear due to malfunctioning fuel injectors.

To check the glow plugs, disconnect the wire from the glow plug bus bar, and remove the bus bar from each of the glow plug terminals. Connect one probe of a test light to the battery's positive (+) terminal, and touch the other probe to each of the glow plugs. The test light should come on when it is touched to each glow plug. If not, that plug is faulty and should be replaced. If the test light does not light at all, voltage may not be reaching the bus bar connection due to a problem in the system circuit. See **6.2 Testing and Repairing Glow Plug System Circuits**.

Another test of glow plugs is how much electrical current they draw. Disconnect the engine temperature sensor and reconnect the bus bar. Connect an ammeter in series between the glow plug bus bar and the wire which connects to it. Turn the ignition on, for a maximum of 15 seconds, and notice the current measurement. After an initial surge, the total current draw should drop to a steady 48 amperes (12 amps per glow plug). If the current draw is not steady, or is less than 48 amperes, one or more glow plugs is faulty. To find the faulty glow plug, remove the bus bar and repeat the previous test, measuring current flow to each individual glow plug. Replace any plug that is drawing less than 12 amperes.

Finally, check the glow plugs by removing and inspecting them. Replace a glow plug if it has been over-torqued, as shown in Fig. 6-1, or if the tip is burned away, as shown in Fig. 6-2. Worn away tips can be caused by malfunctioning fuel injectors. See **FUEL SYSTEM (Diesel)** for fuel injector pressure testing.

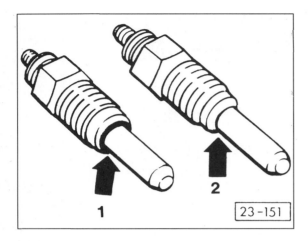

Fig. 6-1. Glow plug ring gap closed (**2**) after incorrect torquing. Correct gap (**1**) is approximately 0.5 mm (.02 in.).

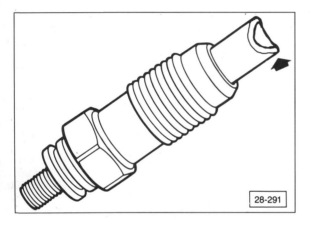

Fig. 6-2. Example of glow plug with burned away tip (arrow).

Clean off carbon deposits before reinstalling used glow plugs. When installing glow plugs, clean the glow plug holes and seats in the cylinder head. Tighten the plugs to the correct torque of 30 Nm (22 ft. lb.). Use new self-locking nuts when installing the bus bar.

CAUTION ━━━

Exceeding the recommended tightening torque will damage the glow plugs and lead to premature failure.

6.2 Testing and Repairing Glow Plug System Circuits

The glow plug system circuits should be suspected if the glow plug indicator does not light, or if the glow plug bus bar does not receive voltage. A test light, or multimeter, and a jumper wire are used for testing. See the current flow diagrams in **ELECTRICAL SYSTEM** for a complete diagram of the glow plug electrical circuits including the glow plug relay, fuses, and connector identification. The sequence of the tests which follow is important. Perform the tests, in order, to isolate the cause of a problem.

Fig. 6-3 is a rear view of the glow plug relay used on the diesel models covered by this manual. The numbers shown appear on the back of the relay and are used to identify the terminals. In the procedures which follow, these numbers are also used in reference to the corresponding terminals on the fuse/relay panel.

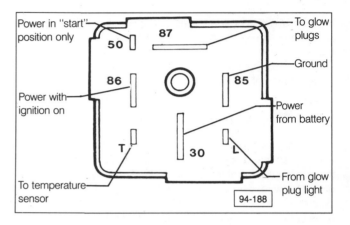

Fig. 6-3. Back side of glow plug relay used to control diesel engine glow plug system.

Checking Wiring

To check the continuity of the wiring, remove the glow plug relay from the relay panel. There should be continuity (zero ohms resistance) between the fuse/relay panel socket for terminal 87 and the bus bar connection at glow plug No. 1. If not, then there is a break or short in the wire. On Jettas, check the in-line fuse which is in the wire to the bus bar.

Check for continuity between the fuse/relay panel socket for terminal T and ground. There should be continuity at engine coolant temperature below 122°F (50°C), and no continuity when coolant temperature is above that mark. If not, either the temperature sensor or the wire from the temperature sensor is faulty.

Glow Plug System Voltage Checks

With the glow plug relay removed, check for voltage between the fuse/relay panel sockets for terminals 30 and 85. If there is no voltage, either the fuses are blown, there is a break or short in the wiring to the battery positive terminal, or the ground from terminal 85 is faulty.

Disconnect the wire from the stop solenoid on the fuel injection pump and check for voltage between fuse/relay panel sockets for terminals 50 and 85. There should be approximately 12 volts when the starter is actuated. If not, either there is a break or a short in the wiring from socket 50 to the starter, or the ignition switch is faulty. See **ELECTRICAL SYSTEM** for more information on testing the ignition switch. Reconnect the wire to the stop solenoid.

Check for voltage between the fuse/relay panel sockets for terminals L and 85. When the ignition is turned on, there should be approximately 12 volts and the glow plug indicator should light. If not, either the wiring is damaged, the fuse has failed, the ignition switch is faulty, or the glow plug indicator is faulty. See **ELECTRICAL SYSTEM** for testing and replacing the glow plug indicator and the instrument cluster.

Check for voltage between the fuse/relay panel sockets for terminals 85 and 86. With the ignition on, there should be approximately 12 volts. If not, the wiring is damaged or the fuse is faulty.

If the wiring is not damaged and the voltage checks at the fuse/relay panel are as specified, but there is still no voltage at the bus bar with the glow plug relay in place, the temperature sensor disconnected, and the ignition on, then the relay is faulty and should be replaced.

Checking Glow Plug Relay

With the glow plug relay installed, disconnect the wire from the stop solenoid on the fuel injection pump, and disconnect the engine temperature sensor. Check voltage between the glow plug wire, where it connects to the bus, and ground. Turn on the ignition and watch the glow plug warning light. When it goes out, there should still be voltage at the glow plug bus wire for approximately five seconds.

Next, turn off the ignition and ground the temperature sensor wire. When the starter is actuated, there should be voltage at the glow plugs bus wire. If the results of either test are not as specified, the relay is faulty and should be replaced.

7. TECHNICAL DATA

I. Ignition System Specifications

```
Basic TCI-h system
(engine codes GX and MZ)

Distributor part number . . . . . . . . . . . . . . .027 905 205 F
Ignition Timing
    Test value. . . . . . . . . . . . . . . . . . . . . . . .4 – 8° BTDC
    Adjusting value . . . . . . . . . . . . . . . . . . . . .6 ± 1° BTDC
Engine idle speed, checking . . . . . . . . . .800 – 1000 rpm
    adjusting . . . . . . . . . . . . . . . . . . . . . . . .900 ± 30 rpm
Vacuum hose . . . . . . . . . . . . . . . . . . . . . . .connected
Centrifugal advance
    Start (rpm). . . . . . . . . . . . . . . .@ 1100 – 1350
    Degrees advance @ rpm. . . . . . .12 – 17° @ 2600 rpm
    End. . . . . . . . . . . . . . . . . . . .23 – 27° @ 6000 rpm
Vacuum advance
    Start . . . . . . . . . . . . . . . . .4 – 8° @ 100 – 160 mbar
    End . . . . . . . . . . . . . .10 – 14° @ 240 – 260 mbar
Firing order. . . . . . . . . . . . . . . . . . . . .1 - 3 - 4 - 2
Spark plugs (Engine GX)
    Bosch . . . . . . . . . . . . . . . . . .W7DTC, WR7DS
    Beru . . . . . . . . . . . . . . . . . . . . . . . . . . . .RS 35
    Champion . . . . . . . . . . . . . . . . . . . . . . . .N8GY
Spark plugs (Engine MZ)
    Bosch . . . . . . . . . . . . . . . . . . . . . . . . . . .W8DO
    Beru . . . . . . . . . . . . . . . . . . . . . . . . . . .14-8DU
                                                    continued
```

I. Ignition System Specifications (cont'd)

```
Spark plug gap . . . . . . . . . . .0.6–0.8 mm (.024–.031 in.)
Spark plug tightening torque. . . . . . . . . . .20 Nm (15 ft. lb.)
Ignition coil resistance
    Between terminals 1 and 15. . . . . . . . . . .52–.76 ohms
    Between terminals 1 and 4 . . . . . . . . . .2400–3500 ohms

TCI-h with knock control
(engine codes HT, RD, and PL)

Distributor part no. (HT, RD, engines) . . . . . . .026 905 205 S
Distributor part no. (PL engines) . . . . . . . . .027 905 205 P
Knock sensor control unit part no.
    (HT, RD engines) . . . . . . . . . . . . . . . .811 907 397
    (PL engines) . . . . . . . . . . . . . . . . .811 907 397 E
Ignition timing
    Test value. . . . . . . . . . . . . . . . . . .4 – 8° BTDC
    Adjusting value . . . . . . . . . . . . . . . .6 ± 1° BTDC
Engine idle speed . . . . . . . . . . . . . . . .800 – 900 rpm
Control unit vacuum hose . . . . . . . . . . . . . .connected
Firing order. . . . . . . . . . . . . . . . . . . .1 - 3 - 4 - 2
Spark Plugs (Engine HT-RD)
    Bosch . . . . . . . . . . . . . . . . . . . . . . .W7 DTC
    Beru . . . . . . . . . . . . . . . . . . . . . . .14-7 DTU
    Champion . . . . . . . . . . . . . . . . . . . . . .N8GY
Spark plugs (Engine PL)
    Bosch. . . . . . . . . . . . . . . . . . . . . . . .F6 DTC
Spark plug gap . . . . . . . . . . .0.7–0.9 mm (.027–.035 in.)
Spark plug tightening torque. . . . . . . . . . .20 Nm (15 ft. lb.)
Ignition coil resistance (HT, RD engines)
    Between terminals 1 and 15 . . . . . . . . .52–.76 ohms
    Between terminals 1 and 4 . . . . . . . . .2400–3500 ohms
Ignition coil resistance (PL engines)
    Between terminals 1 and 15 . . . . . . . . .52–.76 ohms
    Between terminals 4 and 15 . . . . . . . . .6500–8500 ohms
Engine RPM limit
    HT engine. . . . . . . . . . . . . . . . . .6200 – 6400 rpm
    RD engine. . . . . . . . . . . . . . . . . .6570 – 6630 rpm
    PL engine . . . . . . . . . . . . . . . . . .7200 – 7300 rpm

TCI-h with knock control
(engine codes RV and PF)

Distributor part no. . . . . . . . . . . . . . . . .037 905 205
Ignition timing (coolant temperature sensor disconnected)
    Test value. . . . . . . . . . . . . . . . . . .4 – 8° BTDC
    Adjusting value . . . . . . . . . . . . . . . .6 ± 1° BTDC
Engine idle speed (radiator not running) . . . . .750 – 850 rpm
Firing order. . . . . . . . . . . . . . . . . . . .1 - 3 - 4 - 2
Spark Plugs:
    Bosch . . . . . . . . . . . . . . . . . . . . . .W7 DCO
Spark plug gap . . . . . . . . . . .0.6–0.8 mm (.024–.032 in.)
Spark plug tightening torque. . . . . . . . . . .20 Nm (15 ft. lb.)
Ignition coil resistance
    Between terminals 1 and 15 . . . . . . . . . .52–.76 ohms
    Between terminals 4 and 15 . . . . . . . . .2400–3500 ohms
Engine rpm limit . . . . . . . . . . . . . . . . .6450 – 6550 rpm
```

II. Knock Sensor Specifications

Type	Resistance Value	Tightening Torques
I	approx. 300k ohms	10–12 Nm (7–9 ft. lb.)
II	approx. ∞ ohms	15–25 Nm (11–18 ft. lb.)

MANUAL TRANSMISSION AND CLUTCH

Contents

Introduction 3

1. **General Description**........................ 4
   1.1   Clutch 4
   1.2   Transaxle........................... 5
          Five-Speed Manual Transmission 5
          Final Drive 5
   1.3   Identification Codes and Specifications 5

2. **Maintenance**................................ 6

3. **Troubleshooting**............................ 6
   3.1   Basic Troubleshooting Principles........... 6
   3.2   Diagnostic Tests 6

4. **Shift Mechanism** 8
   4.1   Disassembling, Assembling, and Adjusting Shift
          Mechanism 8
          Shift Mechanism Adjustment............. 8

Removing and Installing Shift Lever and Shift
Rod 10

5. **Clutch**.................................... 10
   5.1   Clutch Cable 10
   5.2   Removing and Installing Clutch........... 13

6. **Transmission and Final Drive** 15
   6.1   External Adjustments.................. 16
   6.2   Transaxle Oil Seals 16
   6.3   Removing and Installing Transaxle 20

7. **Technical Data** 22
   I.   Tightening Torques 22
   II.   Clutch Tolerances, Wear Limits and Settings.. 22
   III. Gear Ratios For Five-speed Manual
         Transaxles.......................... 23

TABLES

a. Manual Transaxle Specifications 5
b. Manual Transaxle Troubleshooting 7

9

Manual Transmission and Clutch

Introduction

The five-speed manual transmission, standard on the cars covered by this manual, is fully synchronized in all forward gears. A two-piece lightweight alloy case houses both the gear train and the final drive. As a unit, the transmission, the final drive, and the case are called the transaxle. From the transaxle, power is transmitted to the drive wheels by the drive axles and constant velocity joints. The service and repair of drive axles and constant velocity joints is covered in **SUSPENSION AND STEERING**.

The transaxle can be removed and installed without removing the engine, or the engine and transaxle can be removed as a unit, using the procedure given in **ENGINE**, and separated later.

Though internal repair of the transaxle requires specialized knowledge and equipment, significant expense may be saved by removing and installing the transaxle, using the procedures described in this section. Once removed and cleaned, the transaxle can be taken to an authorized Volkswagen dealer or other qualified shop for repairs. A partially disassembled transaxle in a box is a mechanic's nightmare, and partial disassembly is not a way to save money. Do not attempt to begin a job which cannot be properly finished.

If performing work on the transaxle, make sure that the correct tools are available before beginning the job—particularly for procedures given only with metric specifications. Volkswagen vehicles, and especially their drivetrains, are covered by an extensive new-car warranty. We urge you to consult an authorized Volkswagen dealer before beginning any repairs on a car which may still be covered by the new-car warranty.

9

1. GENERAL DESCRIPTION

Fig. 1-1 is a cross-section of the transaxle with five-speed manual transmission. The gears on the mainshaft and the drive pinion shaft are called the transmission gear train. The drive pinion, the ring gear, and the differential gears—all of which carry driving torque from the transmission gear train to the front wheel driveshafts—are called the final drive.

1.1 Clutch

The clutch is cable-operated. Two types of clutch-actuating cable are used on cars covered by this manual. On some models, the conventional clutch cable has been upgraded with a self-adjusting mechanism. The clutch release mechanism, on the driver's side of the transaxle, activates a push rod through a hollow mainshaft. This pushrod moves the release plate of the pressure plate assembly to engage or disengage the clutch.

The pressure plate assembly consists of a diaphragm-spring type pressure plate, a release plate, and a retaining ring to hold them together. The friction clutch disc is splined to accept the mainshaft of the transmission and has integral cushion springs and dampening springs. The cushion springs—which are between the friction surfaces of the disc—help to reduce the shock when the clutch is engaged. The dampening springs—which are visible in the center hub—help to absorb the rotating power pulses of the engine. Unlike most other cars, the clutch's pressure plate assembly is bolted to the crankshaft with the flywheel bolted to the periphery of the pressure plate assembly. The ring gear, used to engage the starter, is integral with the flywheel and cannot be separated.

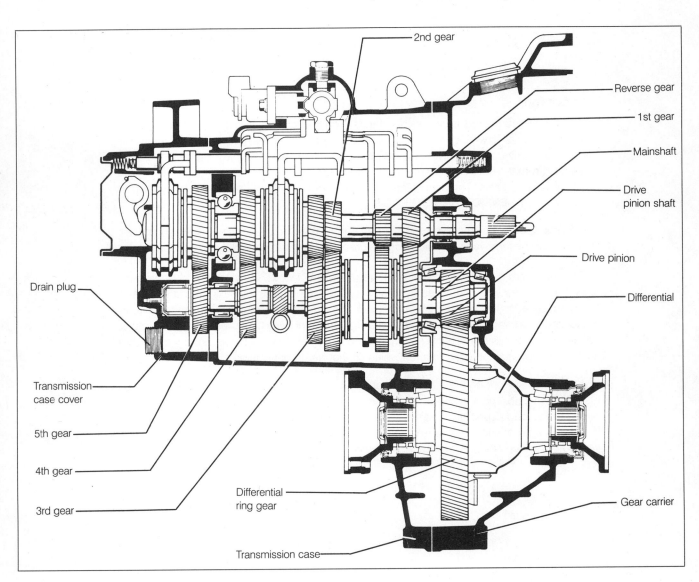

Fig. 1-1. Cross-section of transaxle with manual transmission.

1.2 Transaxle

The transaxle case, which contains the transmission gear train and the final drive gears, is a lightweight alloy die casting with an integral flywheel bellhousing. There is no partition between the transmission gear train and the final drive, as both are lubricated by the common hypoid gear oil supply in the transaxle case.

Five-Speed Manual Transmission

The transmission gears are of the constant-mesh type with balk ring synchronizers. Each gear (1st through 5th) is actually a mating pair of gears, and constant-mesh simply means the mating gears are always meshing. When shifting, synchronizers cause the moving parts to rotate at the same speed before engaging. This prevents damage to the gears, minimizes wear, and eases shifting. The 3rd, 4th, and 5th gear synchronizers are on the mainshaft; the 1st and 2nd gear synchronizers are on the pinion shaft. Gear selection is made through the gearshift lever in the passenger compartment, which is linked to the transmission by the gearshift linkage.

Final Drive

The ring and pinion gear set consists of two helical-cut gears (curved teeth), designed for quiet running. The driven gear, or ring gear, is mounted on the differential housing. The driving gear, or pinion, is an integral part of the pinion shaft. The differential gear set, which consists of two differential sidegears and two differential pinions, allows the front wheels to turn at different speeds, as is necessary when making turns (the outside wheel must travel farther than the inside wheel in the same amount of time).

1.3 Identification Codes and Specifications.

Transaxles are identified by letters and numbers stamped on the case. The letters, given first, identify the transaxle code and the numbers reveal the date of manufacture. They are located on the bottom of the bellhousing as shown in Fig. 1-2. A manual transmission type number is located on the driver's side of the transmission case near the drive flange as shown in Fig. 1-3. All of the manual transmissions used in cars covered

by this manual are type 020. **Table a** lists manual transmission specifications.

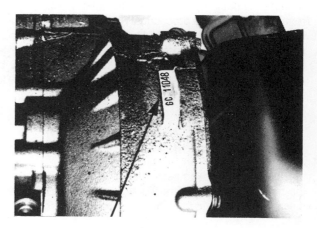

Fig. 1-2. Transaxle code letters and date of manufacture on five speed manual transmissions. Example shows code letters GC and date 11 (day), 04 (month, April), 8 (year 1978).

Fig. 1-3. Transaxle type number (020) on five-speed manual transmission.

9

Table a. Manual Transaxle Specifications.

Engine type and model year	1.6 L Diesel (1985)	1.6 L Diesel (1986 – 1989)	1.8 L Gasoline (except GT/ GTI/GLI)	1.8 L Gasoline (except GT/ GTI/GLI)	1.8 L GT/GTI/GLI except 16-valve	1.8 L (GTI/GLI 16-valve)
Transmission type no. and code letters	020 ACH	020 AGS 020 AOP 020 4S	020 ACN 020 AON 020 ASF	020 ACL	020 9A 020 ACD 020 AEN	020 AGB 020 2Y
Gear Ratios						
1st Gear	3.45	3.45	3.45	3.45	3.45	3.45
2nd Gear	1.94	1.94	1.94	1.94	2.12	2.12
3rd Gear	1.37	1.29	1.37	1.37	1.44	1.44
4th Gear	1.03	.91	1.03	1.03	1.13	1.13
5th Gear	.75	.75	.75	.75	.89	.91
Final Drive Ratio	3.94	3.94	3.67	3.67	3.67	3.67

2. MAINTENANCE

Checking clutch pedal freeplay at a prescribed mileage, except on models with self-adjusting clutch cable, is the only required maintenance procedure. The transaxle is designed to be lubricated for its operational life, so checking and correcting the transaxle oil level is not necessary unless the transaxle is leaking or has been repaired. Checking pedal freeplay and checking transaxle oil level are described in **LUBRICATION AND MAINTENANCE**.

3. TROUBLESHOOTING

This troubleshooting section applies to problems affecting the correct functioning of the transaxle—including the gearshift mechanism, the gear train, and the final drive—as well as the clutch.

The source of most transaxle problems is apparent from the symptoms. For example, difficulty in engaging a gear, shuddering when releasing the clutch, or a vague shifting mechanism are all transaxle problems. Other symptoms, such as power loss or noises from the front end, are less specific. Power loss may be due to an engine problem, or to a slipping clutch. Noises may be the result of a failure in the gear train, worn constant velocity joints, or a bad wheel bearing. What appears to be a transmission oil leak may be engine oil leaking from a faulty rear crankshaft oil seal, especially if the leak is near the bottom of the transaxle bellhousing. See **ENGINE** for information on crankshaft oil seals. See **SUSPENSION AND STEERING** for information on constant velocity joints and wheel bearings.

3.1 Basic Troubleshooting Principles

Transaxle problems fall into two catagories: those that can be fixed by external adjustments, and those which require removal and disassembly of the transaxle. Problems which at first appear to be caused by internal faults, such as gear shifting difficulty or noisy operation, may be correctable with external adjustments.

Begin any transaxle troubleshooting with a thorough visual inspection, both in the engine compartment and from beneath. Check all parts of the gearshift mechanism for wear which might cause misalignment and shifting difficulty. Look for wet spots which may indicate oil leaks. Low lubricant level may be the cause of hard shifting or noise. Accurate pinpointing of leaks may require that the suspected area be cleaned and reinspected.

To avoid removing the transaxle unnecessarily, check and adjust the gearshift mechanism and correct leaks and oil level before acting on suspected internal problems. The gearshift mechanism is covered in **4. Shift Mechanism**. Replacement of oil seals is covered in **6.2 Transaxle Oil Seals**. Checking and correcting oil level is covered in **LUBRICATION AND MAINTENANCE**.

NOTE ——
It is not necessary to routinely check the transaxle oil level unless a leak is suspected. Due to the installed position of the transaxle, the correct oil level is above the filler plug and will leak out if the plug is removed.

As with most other troubleshooting, logical analysis of the observed symptoms is the key to isolating and identifying transaxle problems. A road test is an important step when troubleshooting the transaxle. Determining whether the problem is present in all gears, only during acceleration, when the clutch is engaged, or in some other special conditions may help isolate the source of the problem.

Table b lists manual transmission, final drive, and clutch symptoms, their probable causes, and recommended corrective actions. The numbers in bold type in the corrective action column refer to the numbered headings in this section where the suggested repairs are described.

3.2 Diagnostic Tests

Most internal transaxle problems cannot be accurately diagnosed unless the unit is removed and disassembled; however, a quick test can be used to determine whether the clutch is performing satisfactorily or slipping.

To quick-check clutch performance, start the engine and set the parking brake. Depress the clutch pedal and place the gearshift lever in 3rd or 4th gear, then slightly accelerate the engine and slowly release the clutch pedal. The engine should immediately stall, indicating that the clutch is engaging properly and will not slip enough to allow the engine to continue to run.

If the engine stalls slowly, or does not stall at all, the clutch is probably faulty. Adjust the clutch pedal freeplay, as described in **5.1 Clutch Cable**, and repeat the test. If the clutch is still slipping, the transaxle will have to be removed to make further repairs to the clutch.

Table b. Manual Transaxle Troubleshooting

Symptom	Probable cause	Corrective action
1. Difficult or noisy shifting	a. Clutch not fully releasing	a. Adjust clutch pedal freeplay. **5.1**
	b. Clutch disc binding on transmission mainshaft	b. Remove transaxle and inspect splines of clutch disc and transmission mainshaft. Lubricate splines. If necessary, replace clutch disc. **5.**
	c. Worn or misadjusted gearshift linkage	c. Adjust shift mechanism and, if necessary, replace worn parts. **4.1** and **6.1**
	d. Insufficient gear oil	d. Check for transmission oil leaks. Check and correct gear oil level if needed. See **LUBRICATION AND MAINTENANCE**
	e. Worn or damaged internal transmission components	e. Remove and repair transmission. **6.3**
2. Transaxle noisy	a. Insufficent gear oil	a. Check for transmission oil leaks. Check and correct gear oil if needed. See **LUBRICATION AND MAINTENANCE**
	b. Worn or damaged internal transaxle components	b. Remove and repair transaxle. Especially check the differential gears. **6.3**
3. Grinding noise when shifting (1st or reverse gears)	a. Excessive idle speed	a. Adjust idle speed. See **FUEL SYSTEM (gasoline)** or **FUEL SYSTEM (diesel)**
	b. Worn or damaged internal transmission components	b. Remove and repair transmission. Especially checking the synchronizers of the noisy gear. **6.3**
4. Transmission fails to engage a gear or jumps out of gear	a. Worn or misadjusted gearshift linkage	a. Adjust shift mechanism and, if necessary, replace worn parts. **4.1** and **6.1**
	b. Worn or damaged internal transmission components	b. Remove and repair transmission. **6.3**
5. Poor acceleration, clutch slipping on hills or when accelerating	a. Clutch friction surfaces worn or burnt	a. Inspect clutch components and replace faulty parts. **5.2**
	b. Clutch not fully engaging	b. Adjust clutch pedal freeplay. **5.1**
	c. Clutch disc, pressure plate or flywheel are oil soaked	c. Inspect clutch components. If necessary, clean pressure plate and flywheel; replace clutch disc. **5.2**
6. Clutch grabs or chatters when the pedal is released	a. Binding clutch cable	a. Inspect the clutch cable. Replace the cable if it is severely bent or otherwise faulty. **5.1**
	b. Clutch disc binding on transmission mainshaft	b. Remove transaxle and inspect splines of clutch disc and transmission mainshaft. Lubricate splines. If necessary, replace clutch disc. **5.**
	c. Contaminated or glazed (overheated) clutch lining	c. Inspect clutch components and replace faulty parts. **5.2**
	d. Faulty engine mount	d. Inspect and, if necessary, replace broken engine mounts. See **ENGINE**

9

4. Shift Mechanism

The transverse mounting of the transaxle in vehicles covered by this manual requires a relatively complex mechanism of shafts and levers to transmit the movements of the gearshift lever to the transmission for gear changes. For any shifting problems, the gearshift mechanism should be inspected for wear and misalignment which might affect smooth or accurate shifting. Fig. 4-1 shows the arrangement of the shift mechanism and its directions of movement.

4.1 Disassembling, Assembling, and Adjusting Shift Mechanism

Fig. 4-2 is an exploded view of the shift mechanism used with five-speed manual transmissions which can be used as a guide for disassembling and assembling the linkage, to replace any worn bushings, or when removing the transaxle. When removing the selector rods, use a screwdriver to press back the clips on the plastic rod ends before pulling them off of the ball pins on the levers. When assembling, remove any white grease from the linkage and lubricate all joints and pivot points with molybdenum disulphide grease (Volkswagen part no. G 000 602). A special Volkswagen gauge is required to accurately adjust the shift mechanism after installing new parts, or to correct shifting difficulties.

NOTE ——

Early 1985 models can be fitted with the newer style relay shaft/selector lever assembly. When refitting early models, replace the selector lever and the relay shaft together, using a new sealing washer on the selector lever ball pin.

Shift Mechanism Adjustment

The position of the selector lever on the shift rod is the only adjustment that can be made to the shift mechanism. The adjustment procedure uses a Volkswagen special tool to correctly position the shift lever while the transmission is in neutral. Before adjusting the shift rod to correct shifting difficulties, first check for any worn or broken parts of the shift mechanism.

To adjust:

1. Park the car on a level surface. Set the parking brake and place the transmission in neutral.

2. Loosen the shift rod clamp bolt, shown in Fig. 4-3, so that the shift rod moves freely in the selector lever.

3. Unscrew the shift knob from the gearshift lever. Remove the gearshift boot by detaching it at the bottom and pulling it up over the lever.

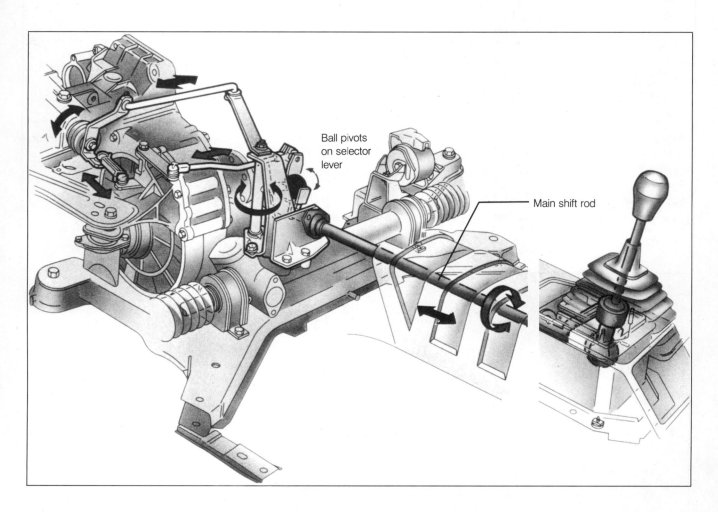

Ball pivots on selector lever

Main shift rod

Fig. 4-1. Shift mechanism and movement of linkage as gears are selected (indicated by arrows).

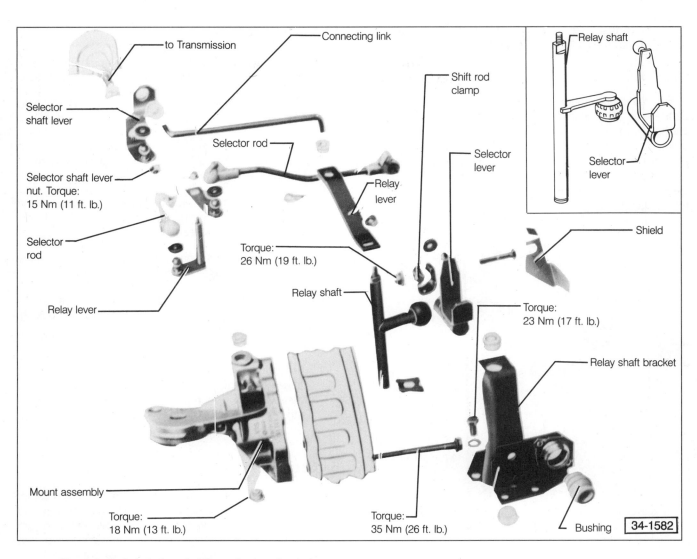

Fig. 4-2. Exploded view of shift mechanism. Inset shows new relay shaft and selector lever used on models produced since mid-1985.

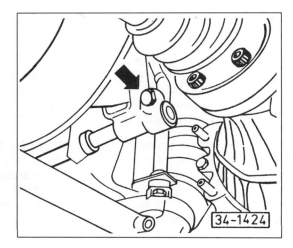

Fig. 4-3. Shift rod clamp bolt (**arrow**).

4. Position the gearshift lever. If possible, use Volkswagen special tool no. 3104 and place it in the position shown in Fig. 4-4 at the base of the gearshift lever. Without disturbing the alignment, torque the clamp bolt to 26 Nm (19 ft. lb.).

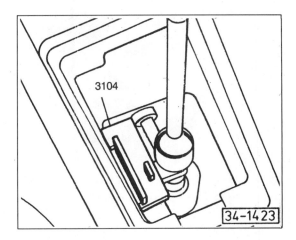

Fig. 4-4. Volkswagen alignment gauge (special tool no. 3104, order no. T03 104 000 34 ZEL) being used to align shift lever and selector lever.

5. Check that all the gears engage smoothly and easily. Reinstall the shift lever boot and the shift knob.

Removing and Installing Shift Lever and Shift Rod

Fig. 4-5 is an exploded view of the shift lever and related parts. Removal is necessary to replace the bearing assembly or the ball if either is determined to be cracked or worn. The exhaust pipe will need to be removed. See **EXHAUST SYSTEM** and note the special tool requirements. After installing the shift lever and shift rod, the mechanism should be adjusted using the special Volkswagen gauge as described in **Shift Mechanism Adjustment**.

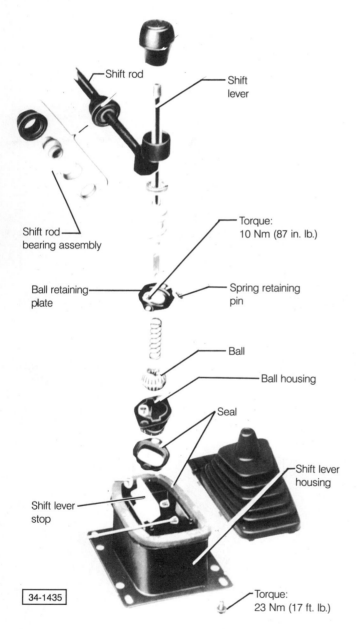

Fig. 4-5. Exploded view of gearshift lever and related parts.

Shift rod

Shift lever

Shift rod bearing assembly

Torque: 10 Nm (87 in. lb.)

Ball retaining plate

Spring retaining pin

Ball

Ball housing

Seal

Shift lever housing

Shift lever stop

Torque: 23 Nm (17 ft. lb.)

34-1435

To remove and install:

1. Unscrew the shift knob. Remove the boot by detaching it at the bottom and pulling it off over the gearshift lever.

2. Remove the center console as described in **BODY AND INTERIOR**.

3. Remove the exhaust pipe from the exhaust manifold as described in **EXHAUST SYSTEM**. Remove the exhaust heat shield.

4. Loosen the shift rod clamp bolt (see Fig. 4-3 above) and remove the bolts holding the relay shaft bracket to the body. Slide the bracket off the shift rod.

5. Working beneath the car, remove the bolts holding the shift lever housing to the body.

6. Working inside the passenger compartment, remove the two nuts holding the ball retaining plate to the housing. Push the rear shift rod bearing into the shift housing, and pull out the shift lever with the shift rod.

7. Installation is the reverse of removal. Remove any old grease from the joints and pivot points, and lubricate them with molybdenum disulphide grease (Volkswagen part no. G 000 602).

5. CLUTCH

Except for replacement or adjustment of the clutch cable, any repairs to the clutch require that the transaxle be removed from the car. The flywheel and the clutch assembly remain bolted to the crankshaft when the transaxle is separated from the engine. The clutch release bearing and its related parts are located at the opposite end of the transaxle, and operate the clutch by means of a pushrod running through the center of the mainshaft. Fig. 5-1 is an exploded view of the clutch components.

5.1 Clutch Cable

Two types of clutch cables are used on the vehicles covered by this manual. The more conventional, manually-adjusted cable needs periodic adjustment to compensate for the wear of the clutch friction material. For mileage intervals, see **LUBRICATION AND MAINTENANCE**.

Some models are equipped with a self-adjusting clutch cable. It has a built-in mechanism which automatically compensates for wear, adjusting every time the clutch pedal is actuated. The self-adjusting cable can be identified by the rubber boot atop the clutch cable sleeve on the transaxle end of the cable, as shown in Fig. 5-2. The two cables are not interchangeable.

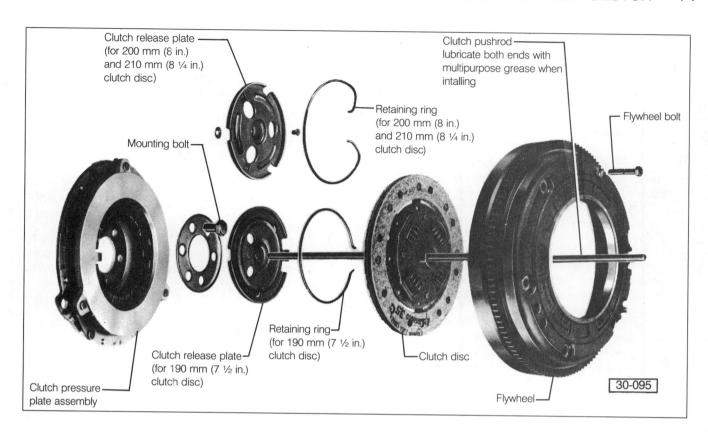

Fig. 5-1. Exploded view of flywheel and clutch.

9

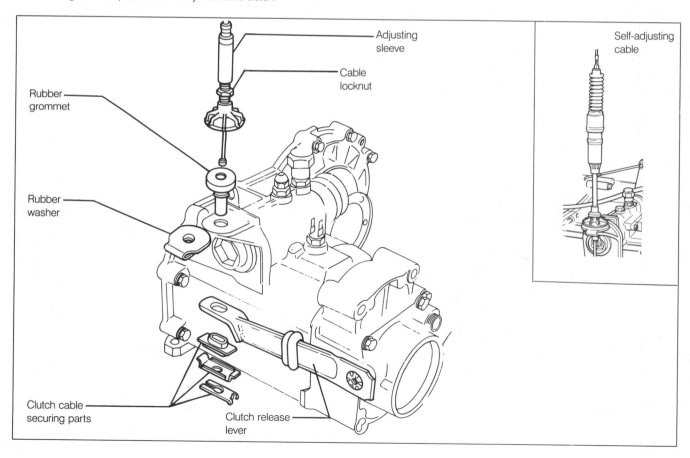

Fig. 5-2 Exploded view of clutch cable and related parts.
Inset shows self-adjusting cable.

Removal and installation of the clutch cable can be accomplished without any special tools. Replacement self-adjusting cables come with a holding strap that relieves the spring tension and allows easy installation. If the cable does not have the strap attached, a helper may be needed during installation.

To replace clutch cable:

1. On manually-adjusted cables, loosen the adjusting sleeve locknut and turn the sleeve clockwise until the cable's tension is relieved. Remove the securing parts from the cable end beneath the clutch release lever and pull the cable end from the lever.

2. On self-adjusting clutch cables, depress the clutch pedal several times. Compress the spring (under the rubber boot) and have a helper remove the securing parts from beneath the clutch release lever. Pull the cable end from the lever.

> **CAUTION** ━
>
> *Do not open the automatic adjustment mechanism. If the adjustment mechanism is opened, the cable assembly will need to be replaced.*

3. Unhook the cable end from the top of the clutch pedal and pull the cable through the firewall from the engine compartment side.

4. Install the clutch cable. Lubricate both ends with multi-purpose grease, then insert the clutch cable end through the firewall grommet and hook the cable onto the clutch pedal.

5. Position the rubber washer and the rubber grommet as shown in Fig. 5-3.

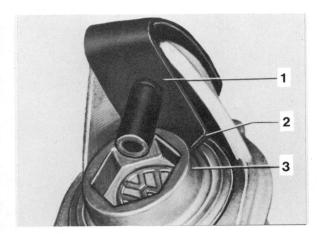

Fig. 5-3. Rubber washer and rubber grommet correctly installed. Rubber washer **1** is fitted with lip **2** parallel to selector shaft cover **3** to protect vent.

> **CAUTION** ━
>
> *The rubber parts must be installed correctly. If not, the transaxle vent which is protected by the washer may become clogged, and cause oil leakage past the seals.*

6. If reinstalling a used self-adjusting cable, compress the spring (beneath the rubber boot).

7. Insert the cable end through the rubber grommet and the release lever. Attach the securing parts to the end of the cable.

8. On self-adjusting cables, adjust clutch pedal freeplay by removing the spring retaining strap or relieving the spring tension, and then operating the clutch pedal several times.

To adjust (except self-adjusting clutch cable):

1. Operate the clutch pedal several times. Raise the clutch release lever by hand until resistance is felt.

2. Adjust freeplay by turning the adjusting sleeve counter-clockwise, as shown in Fig. 5-4, until the clearance between the cable's large plastic flange and the transaxle housing is 12 mm ($^{15}/_{32}$ in.).

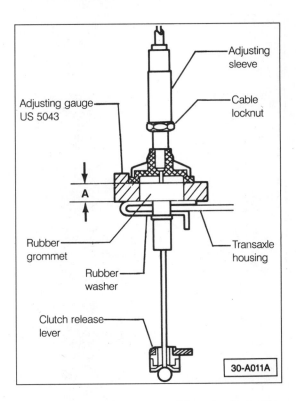

Fig. 5-4. Adjusting clutch freeplay. Dimension **A** should be 12 mm ($^{15}/_{32}$ in.) while raising clutch release lever by hand. Adjusting gauge shown is Volkswagen special tool no. US 5043 (order no. TU5 043 000 30 ZEL).

3. Hold the adjusting sleeve and tighten the locknut against the sleeve. Freeplay at the clutch release lever should now be approximately 6 mm (¼ in.). Torque the locknut to 4 to 6 Nm (36 to 48 in. lb.).

5.2 Removing and Installing Clutch

The transaxle must be removed from the engine to gain access to the clutch. See **6.3 Removing and Installing Transaxle**. It is normally recommended that the pressure plate be replaced when a new clutch disc is installed. If the clutch pressure plate is removed from the crankshaft, new mounting bolts should be used to reinstall it.

The flywheel should be carefully inspected when replacing the clutch. Replacing the clutch disc without replacing other worn components may accelerate clutch disc wear.

An inexpensive alignment tool is used to install and center the clutch disc. Use of this tool or its equivalent will greatly aid the installation of the transaxle. For 16-valve engines, use Volkswagen special tool no. 3178 (order no. T03 178 000 30 ZEL). For all except 16-valve engines, use Volkswagen special tool no. VW 547 (order no. TV0 547 000 30 ZEL).

Some lubrication is recommended when reassembling the clutch. To avoid accelerated failure of the new parts, use only the Volkswagen-recommended lubricants. If signs of oil are present at the bottom of the transaxle, carefully inspect the rear crankshaft oil seal while the clutch is removed. A faulty oil seal should be replaced.

To replace clutch:

1. Remove the transaxle from the engine as described in **6.3 Removing and Installing Transaxle**.

2. Remove the flywheel, clutch disc, and release plate. A holding fixture, Volkswagen special tool number VW 558 (order no. TV0 558 000 13 ZEL), is shown in Fig. 5-5. Loosen the flywheel mounting bolts evenly, one-quarter turn at a time, until the clutch pressure is relieved. Remove the flywheel and the clutch disc.

3. Use a screwdriver to pry out the retaining ring for the clutch release plate.

WARNING ——

The retaining ring is a spring which will be released with some force. To avoid injury, hold on to it firmly while prying it loose.

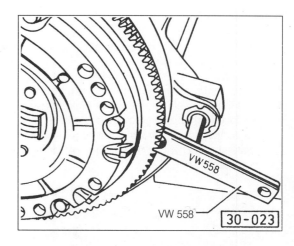

Fig. 5-5. Holding fixture being used while loosening flywheel bolts.

4. Remove the six center mounting bolts and remove the clutch pressure plate from the crankshaft. Use of the holding fixture is illustrated in Fig. 5-6.

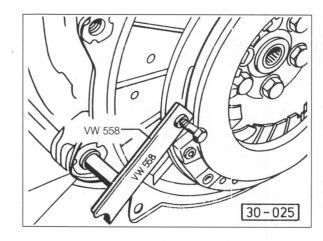

Fig. 5-6. Holding fixture used to remove clutch pressure plate assembly.

9

To inspect and install:

1. Inspect the clutch pressure plate. Check the release levers for bending or misalignment. Using a straightedge as shown in Fig. 5-7, check that the mating surface does not taper inward more than 0.30 mm (.012 in.). Check to see that no rivets are loose. Carefully inspect the friction surface for cracks, scoring, discoloration due to heat or oil contamination, or other damage. A clutch pressure plate showing any of these signs of damage should be replaced.

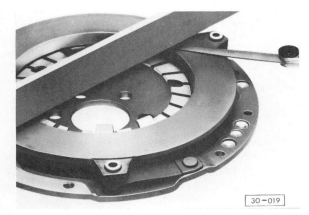

Fig. 5-7. Pressure plate being checked for taper. If feeler gauge over 0.30 mm (.012 in.) can be inserted between pressure plate and straightedge on inside edge, pressure plate should be replaced.

2. Clean the flywheel friction surface and inspect it for wear, cracks, and grooves. Check for loose or worn dowel pins. Replace a flywheel with any of these faults.

3. Check the thickness, runout, and general condition of the clutch disc. See Fig. 5-8. If runout exceeds 0.40 mm (.016 in.), or if there is any evidence of contamination by oil, the disc should be replaced.

Fig. 5-8. Dial indicator being used to measure clutch disc runout while disc is rotated.

NOTE ━━

The clutch disc is a relatively low-cost part which commonly wears out and requires replacement. Many experienced mechanics routinely install a new clutch disc anytime the transaxle is removed.

4. Inspect the splines of the clutch disc and the transmission input shaft. Check that the clutch disc is free to slide on the shaft. If the clutch disc is in any way unserviceable, it should be replaced. Clean all traces of grease from the shaft and clutch splines.

5. Position the clutch pressure plate on the crankshaft. Using thread locking compound on new bolts, position the washer and thread the bolts into place. The holding fixture shown earlier in Fig. 5-6 can be used to hold the pressure plate. Torque bolts without shoulders to 75 Nm (55 ft.lb.). Torque bolts with shoulders to 100 Nm (74 ft. lb.).

CAUTION ━━

Always use new pressure plate mounting bolts. Once torqued, they are deformed and should not be reused.

6. Place the clutch release plate in position and install the retaining ring. Lightly lubricate the contact surface of the plate and the center seat for the clutch pushrod with lithium grease. Align the ends of the retaining ring as shown in Fig. 5-9.

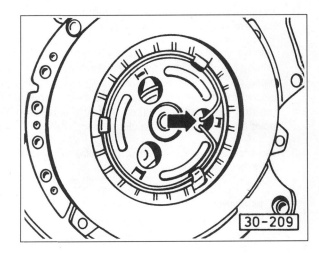

Fig. 5-9. Installation of clutch release plate retaining ring. Ends of ring rest in hole of release plate (**arrow**).

7. Lightly lubricate the transmission mainshaft splines and the clutch splines using molybdenum disulphide grease, Volkswagen part no. G 000 602, then place the clutch disc inside the flywheel.

CAUTION ━━

Use only the recommended molybdenum disulphide grease on the splines. Otherwise the clutch disc may bind on the input shaft and cause hard shifting. Other lubricants may contaminate the clutch disc.

NOTE ━━

The projecting part of the clutch hub faces the flywheel, away from the engine.

8. Install the flywheel. Position the flywheel on the dowel pins and start the mounting bolts in their holes. Leave the bolts loose enough so that the clutch disc can still move.

CAUTION ━━

The two guide pins in the flywheel must align with the corresponding holes in the clutch pressure plate, or the pressure plate will be damaged during installation. Do not mistake balancing holes for guide pin holes.

9. Center the clutch disc. The Volkswagen special tool used to accurately center the disc is shown in Fig. 5-10. Tighten the flywheel mounting bolts evenly until the clutch disc is firmly held in place.

Fig. 5-10. Clutch disc being centered in flywheel with centering tool, Volkswagen special tool no. VW 547 (order no. TV0 547 000 30 ZEL). For 16-valve engines, use Volkswagen special tool no. 3178 (order no. T03 178 000 30 ZEL).

10. Remove the centering tool, if used, and torque the bolts to 20 Nm (15 ft. lb.) in the sequence shown in Fig. 5-11.

NOTE ━━

New replacement flywheels for gasoline engines have no timing mark. They are marked only with a 0° TDC mark. Before installing, make a timing mark as shown in Fig. 5-12.

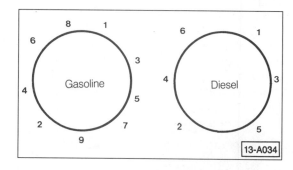

Fig. 5-11. Flywheel bolt torque sequences.

Fig. 5-12. Location of timing mark to be made on new replacement flywheels. Dimension **a** (arc length) is 12 mm (.472 in.).

11. Reinstall the transaxle as described in **6.3 Removing and Installing Transaxle**.

6. TRANSMISSION AND FINAL DRIVE

This section covers external adjustments, the replacement of oil seals, and the removal and installation of the transaxle. Internal repairs require knowledge and special equipment which are beyond the scope of this manual. Once removed, the transaxle can be repaired by an authorized Volkswagen dealer or other qualified shop, or replaced with a Volkswagen remanufactured unit.

Testing of the reverse/upshift indicator light switch, located on the top of the transaxle housing, is covered in **ELECTRICAL SYSTEM**. It is not adjustable. The only remedy for a faulty switch is replacement.

6.1 External Adjustments

External adjustment of the transmission—which includes adjusting the selector shaft detent plunger and the fifth gear lockout plunger—may correct shifting problems that are not fully remedied by adjusting the shifting mechanism. In addition, the adjustments will be necessary if the transaxle has been partially disassembled. The selector shaft adjusters are located on the transaxle housing as illustrated in Fig. 6-1. Some later models retain the selector shaft with a bolt; only the 5th gear lockout plunger is adjustable. The adjustments should be made with the transaxle removed, or with the shift linkage removed from the selector shaft.

Fig. 6-1. Location of selector shaft adjusters. Selector shaft detent plunger **1** with plastic cap, 5th gear lockout plunger **2**, and selector shaft lever **3**. Inset shows screwdriver being used to remove selector rod.

The selector shaft detent plunger is shown in Fig. 6-2. To adjust, place the transmission in neutral, remove the plastic cap, and loosen the locknut. Turn the adjusting bolt clockwise until the lockring lifts away from the adjusting bolt, then turn the adjusting bolt counterclockwise until the lockring just contacts the adjusting bolt. While holding the adjusting bolt stationary, torque the locknut to 20 Nm (15 ft. lb.). To check the adjustment, hand turn the selector shaft slightly. If the lockring does not lift as soon as the selector shaft is turned, repeat the adjustment. When satisfied with the adjustment, reinstall the plastic cap.

The fifth gear lockout plunger is shown in Fig. 6-3. To adjust, place the transmission in neutral, remove the plastic cap, and loosen the locknut. Tighten the adjusting sleeve until the detent just begins to move out. From this position, loosen the adjusting sleeve ½ turn, then hold the sleeve stationary and tighten the locknut.

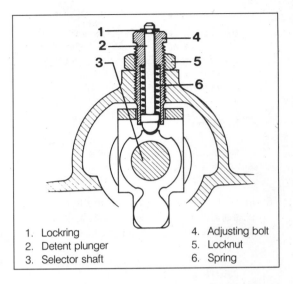

1. Lockring
2. Detent plunger
3. Selector shaft
4. Adjusting bolt
5. Locknut
6. Spring

Fig. 6-2. Cross-section of main selector shaft detent plunger.

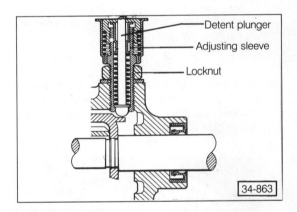

Detent plunger
Adjusting sleeve
Locknut

Fig. 6-3. Cross-section of 5th gear lockout plunger.

6.2 Transaxle Oil Seals

Oil leakage due to faulty transaxle oil seals may be the cause of problems such as hard shifting, jumping out of gear, and transaxle noise. The final drive oil seals, the selector shaft oil seal, and the clutch release shaft oil seal can all be replaced while the transaxle is installed in the car. Read the procedure to determine what other new parts are required before beginning repairs. When replacing the clutch release shaft oil seal, some disassembly of the transaxle will make the repair easier. The procedure for replacing the final drive oil seals includes the use of Volkswagen special tools which are helpful, but not essential, to the repair.

To replace final drive oil seals:

1. Detach the drive axle from the transaxle as described in **SUSPENSION AND STEERING**.

Suspend the detached drive axle from the car body with a stiff wire hook to prevent damage to the outer constant velocity joint.

2. Pry the dust cap from the center of the drive flange. Remove the circlip and the spring washer.

3. Remove the drive flange from the transaxle using a puller as shown in Fig. 6-4. Inspect the flange and plan to replace it if there is a groove worn where it contacts the oil seal.

The internal threads of the shaft are used to reinstall the drive flange. Avoid thread damage during removal.

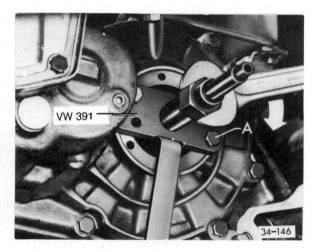

Fig. 6-4. Drive flange being removed. Puller VW 391 shown. Puller mounts to drive flange with M8 x 30 bolts (**A**).

4. Pry the faulty seal from its recess using a hooked seal removal tool, as shown in Fig. 6-5, or a large screwdriver.

Fig. 6-5. Drive flange oil seal being removed. Volkswagen special tool VW 681 shown.

5. Make sure the new seal has a spring behind its lip. Then pack the open side of the new seal with multipurpose grease. Drive the new seal into place until it is fully seated.

6. Install the drive flange as shown in Fig. 6-6.

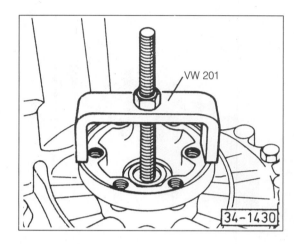

Fig. 6-6. Drive flange being installed. Installation tool shown (VW 201) threads into shaft.

7. Install the spring washer, a new circlip, and a new dust cap. Attach the drive axle as described in **SUSPENSION AND STEERING**.

To replace selector shaft oil seal:

1. Shift the transmission into neutral.

2. Remove the selector shaft lever. Unscrew the nut holding the lever to the selector shaft, then disconnect the connecting link from the top of the selector shaft lever. (See the earlier Fig. 4-2.)

3. Pull the lever off the selector shaft, noting its position on the shaft. Remove the flexible boot and clean the exposed end of the selector shaft.

4. Remove the detent plunger (or bolt) from the top of the transaxle housing, then remove the 5th gear lockout plunger. See Figs. 6-1, 6-2, and 6-3 above. Remove the reverse/upshift light switch by removing the two mounting bolts.

5. Remove the clutch cable and rubber stop/guide from the transaxle as described in **5.1 Clutch Cable**.

9

6. To gain access to the selector shaft, remove the selector shaft cover as shown in Fig. 6-7. Use care to avoid losing the spring as the cover is removed. Remove the selector shaft by hand-pressing it out through the cover opening.

Fig. 6-7. Selector shaft cover being removed. Hex socket size is 27mm. Use short bolt (27mm head) and locknuts with wrench in place of special tool shown.

7. Pry out the old seal, as shown in Fig. 6-8, and install a new seal.

Fig. 6-8. Selector shaft oil seal being removed.

8. Lubricate the new oil seal and all surfaces of the selector shaft with multipurpose grease, then carefully install the selector shaft in the transaxle case. See Fig. 6-9.

9. The rest of the installation is the reverse of removal. Torque the selector shaft cover to 50 Nm (37 ft. lb.). Adjust the selector shaft adjusters as described in **6.1 External Adjustments**. Torque the selector shaft lever mounting nut to 15 Nm (11 ft. lb.).

Fig. 6-9. Selector shaft (arrow) being installed. Bent coat hanger wire or welding rod (**A**) can be inserted as shown to keep shaft components from moving while engaging shift forks.

To replace clutch release shaft oil seal:

1. Remove the clutch cable from the clutch release shaft as described in **5.1 Clutch Cable**, then remove the stop clip from side of the release lever. Drain the transaxle as described in **LUBRICATION AND MAINTENANCE**.

2. Pierce the end cap and pry the cap out of its recess in the 5th gear/clutch release bearing housing. See Fig. 6-10.

3. Remove the circlip from each side of the clutch release shaft, then pull the clutch release shaft from the transaxle case. Remove clutch lever and the return spring.

4. Remove the oil seal as indicated in Fig. 6-11. Drive in a new oil seal as shown in Fig. 6-12.

5. Position the clutch lever and the return spring in the housing. The central hook of the return spring should lie atop the lug on the clutch lever, and the spring's end hooks should point downward so that the clutch lever is held away from the clutch release bearing.

6. Lightly coat the release bearing with multipurpose grease. Then lubricate the seal lip and pack the lubricant into the seal's open side.

7. Insert the clutch release shaft, being careful that the splines do not damage the oil seal, and engage its splines with the clutch lever. The splines will mate only one way.

8. Install the retaining circlips and check that the return spring is correctly tensioned when the operating lever is lifted to its normal operating position.

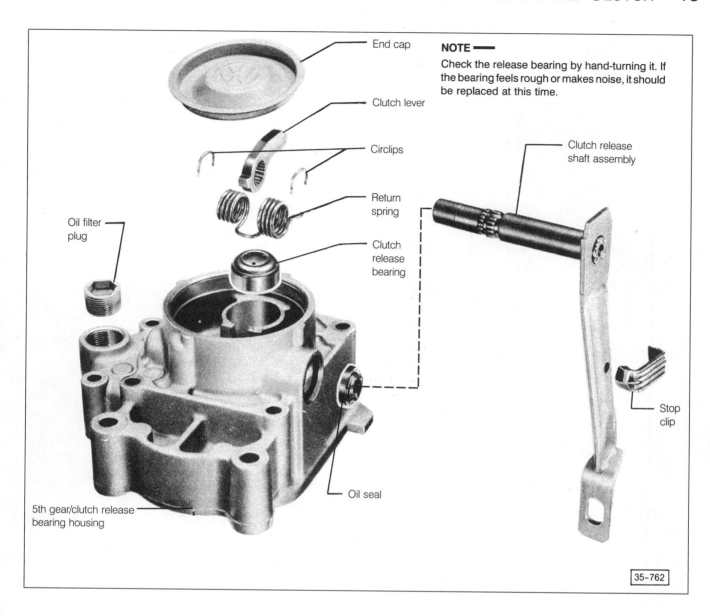

End cap

NOTE

Check the release bearing by hand-turning it. If the bearing feels rough or makes noise, it should be replaced at this time.

Clutch lever

Circlips

Return spring

Clutch release bearing

Oil filter plug

Clutch release shaft assembly

Stop clip

Oil seal

5th gear/clutch release bearing housing

35-762

9

Fig. 6-10. Exploded view of clutch release mechanism.

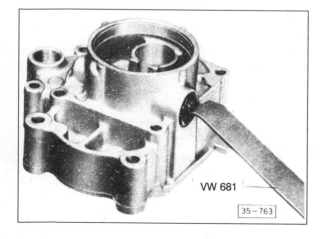

VW 681

35-763

Fig. 6-11. Clutch release shaft oil seal being removed.

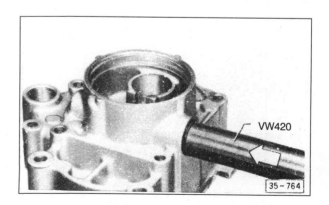

VW420

35-764

Fig. 6-12. Clutch release shaft oil seal being installed.

9. Install a new end cap as shown in Fig. 6-13. Use Volkswagen special tool no. VW 792/2 or equivalent to install the cap evenly.

Fig. 6-13. New end cap being installed.

10. Install the stop clip and the clutch cable to the clutch release lever. If necessary, adjust the clutch pedal free-play as described in **LUBRICATION AND MAINTENANCE**.

6.3 Removing and Installing Transaxle

The transaxle must be removed from the car for most internal repairs or for replacement. In the procedure given below, the transaxle is separated from the engine, supported on a jack, and removed from below. Alternatively, the engine and transaxle assembly can be removed, as described in **ENGINE**, and the transaxle then separated from the engine.

Removal of the transaxle requires a means of lifting the engine, a transmission jack or a floor jack with transmission adaptor, and jack stands to support the car. The engine lift is necessary because the engine mounts are removed. Use extreme caution when working beneath the car and lowering the transaxle.

To remove:

1. Disconnect the battery negative (−) terminal. Disconnect the ground strap from the transaxle. Disconnect the electrical connector from the reverse/upshift light switch atop the transaxle.

2. Remove the speedometer cable and insert a plug in the hole to prevent loss or contamination of the transaxle lubricant.

3. Disconnect the clutch cable from the clutch release lever as described in **5.1 Clutch Cable**.

4. Loosen the left front wheel lug bolts. Then jack up the front of the vehicle, support it securely, and remove the left front wheel.

5. Remove the starter as described in **ELECTRICAL SYSTEM**.

6. Remove the short selector rod and the long connecting link from the two relay levers of the shift linkage. If necessary, see **4. Shift Mechanism**.

7. Install an engine support, as shown in Fig. 6-14, and increase tension until it supports the weight of the engine.

Fig. 6-14. Engine being supported by support tool. Volkswagen special tool no. 10-222A shown.

8. Remove the upper bolts that hold the transaxle to the engine.

9. Remove the three bolts from the right rear engine mount as shown in Fig. 6-15.

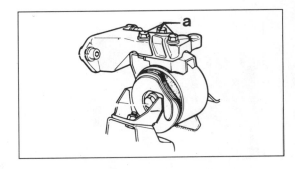

Fig. 6-15. Right rear engine mounting bolts **a**.

10. Remove the center bolt from the left rear transaxle mount as shown in Fig. 6-16, then remove the two through-bolts and nuts holding the mount's support arm to the transmission.

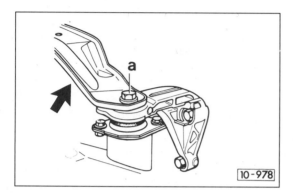

Fig. 6-16. Left transaxle mounting bolt **a** that needs to be removed. The arrow indicates the support arm.

11. Detach the drive axles from the transaxle drive flanges as described in **SUSPENSION AND STEERING**.

CAUTION

Suspend the detached drive axles from the car body with stiff wire hooks to avoid damaging the outer constant velocity joint.

12. Remove the left wheelhouse liner mounting screws and washers, and remove the wheelhouse liner.

13. Remove the bolts from the clutch cover plate as indicated in Fig. 6-17 (the cover plate will remain on the engine when the transaxle is removed). Remove the bolts from the small cover plate (located behind the left drive flange).

Fig. 6-17. Clutch cover plate bolts at **1** and small cover plate bolts at **2**.

14. Place a transmission jack or a floor jack with transmission adaptor beneath the transaxle. Raise the jack just enough to support the transaxle. Do not raise the engine.

15. Remove the front engine and transaxle mount as shown in Fig. 6-18. Completely remove it from the car.

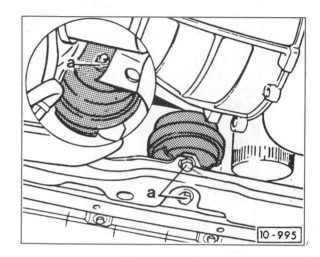

Fig. 6-18. Front hydraulic engine/transaxle mounting bolts **a**. Earlier rubber mount is similar.

16. Slightly lower the transaxle and remove the left mounting bolt that was concealed by the small cover plate.

CAUTION

At no time should the weight of the transaxle be supported by the transmission mainshaft. Such a load will damage the clutch and transaxle components.

17. Push the engine and transaxle assembly as far as possible toward the passenger side of the car (approximately 4 mm or 5/32 in.). Remove the remaining lower mounting bolts holding the transaxle to the engine.

18. Separate the transaxle from the engine, taking care not to place any strain on the transmission mainshaft, and either lower the jack or raise the car until there is enough clearance to remove the transaxle. Pull the transaxle out from under the car.

WARNING

Make sure the car is stable and well supported at all times during the removal procedure. Use jack stands which are designed for the purpose. A floor jack alone is not adequate support.

9

To install:

1. Lightly lubricate the input shaft splines with molybdenum disulphide grease, then position the transaxle on the engine, being careful not to damage any of the clutch components. Check that the large clutch plate is correctly positioned. If necessary, use a wrench on the crankshaft pulley to align the splines of the mainshaft to the splines of the clutch disc.

2. Install the lower transaxle to engine mounting bolts and then install the upper bolts. Torque the M12 bolts to 75 Nm (55 ft. lb.). Install the small cover plate for the concealed bolt.

3. Install the left rear transaxle mount, but do not fully tighten the bolts and nuts.

4. Reconnect the drive axles to the transaxle drive flanges. Torque the 8mm 12-point socket-head bolts to 45 Nm (33 ft. lb.).

5. Install and torque the clutch cover bolts to 15 Nm (11 ft. lb.).

6. Install the left wheelhouse liner with mounting screws and washers.

7. Install the bolts to the right engine mount and install the front transaxle/engine mount, but do not fully tighten the bolts and nuts.

8. Install the starter. Torque the M10 bolts to 60 Nm (44 ft. lb.). Install the reverse gear/upshift light switch and attach its connector. Torque the bolts to 10 Nm (87 in. lb.). If removed, install the plastic plug in the timing check hole.

9. Reinstall the left front wheel and tighten the lug bolts. Lower the car to the ground and torque the bolts to 110 Nm (81 ft. lb.).

10. Reconnect the shift mechanism and loosely install the clutch cable to the release lever. Connect the speedometer cable to the transaxle housing.

11. Remove the engine lift or hoist. Reconnect the battery negative (−) terminal and the ground strap.

12. Align the engine and transaxle mounts as described in **ENGINE**. With the mounts aligned, and the fasteners properly torqued, adjust clutch pedal freeplay as described in **5.1 Clutch Cable**, and adjust the shifting mechanism as described in **4. Shift Mechanism**.

13. Refill the transaxle with the appropriate lubricant before starting or towing the car. See **LUBRICATION AND MAINTENANCE** for information on the proper lubricant and how to check the level or fill the transaxle.

7. TECHNICAL DATA

I. Tightening Torques

Shift rod to selector lever (clamp bolt and nut)	.26 Nm (19 ft.lb.)
Shift lever retaining plate to shift lever housing (bolt)	.10 Nm (87 in. lb.)
Gearshift lever housing to body (bolt)	.23 Nm (17 ft. lb.)
Relay shaft bracket to body (nut)	.23 Nm (17 ft. lb.)
Relay lever to relay shaft (nut)	.18 Nm (13 ft. lb.)
Selector shaft lever to selector shaft (nut)	.15 Nm (11 ft. lb.)
Pressure plate to crankshaft with shoulder (bolt)	.100 Nm (74 ft. lb.)
without shoulder(bolt)	.75 Nm (55 ft. lb.)
Flywheel to pressure plate (bolt)	.20 Nm (15 ft. lb.)
Clutch cable locknut to cable sleeve (nut)	.4-6 Nm (36–48 in. lb.)
Selector shaft cover	.50 Nm (37 ft. lb.)
Driveshaft to drive flange (socket-head bolt)	.45 Nm (33 ft. lb.)
Transaxle to engine (M12 bolt)	.75 Nm (55 ft. lb.)
Starter to transaxle (M10 bolt)	.60 Nm (44 ft. lb.)
Selector shaft detent plunger to transaxle housing (locknut)	.20 Nm (15 ft. lb.)
5th gear lockout plunger to transaxle housing (locknut)	.20 Nm (15 ft. lb.)
Reverse gear/upshift light switch to transaxle (bolt)	.10 Nm (87 in. lb.)
5th gear/release housing to transaxle case (bolt)	.25 Nm (18 ft. lb.)

II. Clutch Tolerances, Wear Limits and Settings.

Clutch pedal freeplay	.6 mm (¼ in.)
Clutch disc runout (maximum)	.0.4 mm (.016 in.)
Pressure plate taper (max. inward)	.0.3 mm (.012 in.)

III. Gear Ratios For Five-speed Manual Transaxles

Engine type and model year	1.6 L Diesel (1985)	1.6 L Diesel (1986 – 1989)	1.8 L Gasoline (except GT/ GTI/GLI)	1.8 L Gasoline (except GT/ GTI/GLI)	1.8 L GT/GTI/GLI except 16-valve	1.8 L (GTI/GLI 16-valve)
Transmission type no. and code letters	020 ACH	020 AGS 020 AOP 020 4S	020 ACN 020 AON 020 ASF	020 ACL	020 9A 020 ACD 020 AEN	020 AGB 020 2Y
Gear Ratios						
1st Gear	3.45	3.45	3.45	3.45	3.45	3.45
2nd Gear	1.94	1.94	1.94	1.94	2.12	2.12
3rd Gear	1.37	1.29	1.37	1.37	1.44	1.44
4th Gear	1.03	.91	1.03	1.03	1.13	1.13
5th Gear	.75	.75	.75	.75	.89	.91
Final Drive Ratio	3.94	3.94	3.67	3.67	3.67	3.67

AUTOMATIC TRANSMISSION

Contents

Introduction 3

1. General Description 4
   1.1 Automatic Transmission 010 4
       Torque Converter 5
       ATF Pump 5
       Planetary Gear System 5
       Hydraulic Controls 6
       Final Drive 6
   1.2 Identification Codes and Specifications 6

2. Maintenance 6

3. Troubleshooting 7
   3.1 Basic Troubleshooting Principles 7
   3.2 Diagnostic Tests 9
       Stall Speed Test 9
       Pressure Test 10

4. Controls 10
   4.1 Removing and Installing Control Cables 11

Selector Lever Cable 11
Accelerator Cable and Throttle Cable 12
   4.2 External Transmission Adjustments 12
       Adjusting Selector Lever Cable 12
       Adjusting Accelerator and Throttle Cables 12
       Adjusting 2nd Gear Brake Band 14

5. Transaxle Assembly 14
   5.1 Removing and Installing Transaxle 14
   5.2 Oil Seals 17
       Torque Converter Oil Seal 17
       Drive Flange Oil Seals 18

6. Automatic Transmission Technical Data 19
   I. Automatic Transmission Test Data 19
   II. Tightening Torques 19
   III. Automatic Transmission Specifications 20

TABLES
a. Automatic Transaxle Specifications 7
b. Automatic Transmission Troubleshooting 8

Automatic Transmission

Introduction

The automatic transmission is housed in a cast aluminum alloy case that is attached by studs to a separate final drive housing. Taken as a unit, the transmission and final drive assembly are called the transaxle. Though the transaxle with automatic transmission operates on entirely different principles from those of the transaxle with manual transmission, the constant velocity joints and the front wheel drive axles of the two transaxles are identical. Please consult **SUSPENSION AND STEERING** for repairs related to the drive axles and constant velocity joints.

Cleanliness and a careful approach are very important when repairing the transaxle. Become familiar with the procedure before beginning a job and make sure that you have the necessary tools—particularly for procedures with specifications given in metric units only. Specifications that lack U.S. equivalents require that the related work be carried out using metric tools and instruments.

With normal use and regular maintenance, the transaxle with automatic transmission is very reliable and does not require internal repairs. Repairs to the internal sections of the transaxle require special knowledge and equipment, and as such are beyond the scope of this manual. In the event that internal repairs or overhaul are required, you may be able to save service time and expense by removing the transaxle for repair by a properly equipped and qualified repair shop. The procedures for transaxle removal and installation, as well as the necessary external adjustments are included in this manual. We recommend that the transaxle be thoroughly cleaned on the outside and taken to the shop as is—partial disassembly will not save money and may complicate repairs. We especially urge you to consult an authorized Volkswagen dealer before beginning any work on a car that may be subject to Volkswagen's warranty coverage.

10

1. GENERAL DESCRIPTION

The transaxle with automatic transmission is shown in Fig. 1-1. At the right end of the transaxle is the final drive housing, which has an integral bellhousing for the torque converter. Inside the final drive housing are the differential, the ring and pinion gearset, and the intermediate gear—which is between the drive pinion and the ring gear. The governor for the automatic transmission is located beneath the round cover atop the final drive housing.

The final drive housing, containing hypoid gear oil for lubricating the final drive gears, is completely sealed off from the transmission case, which contains automatic transmission fluid (ATF). The transmission case contains the ATF pump, the hydraulic controls, and the planetary gear system. The planetary gear system is lubricated solely by the ATF that is circulated through the transmission by the ATF pump. The ATF does not circulate unless the engine is runnning, so the transmission parts are only partially lubricated when the engine is turned off.

CAUTION ——

Towing a Volkswagen with an automatic transmission while the front wheels are on the ground can cause damage due to lack of lubrication. Volkswagen recommends that cars with automatic transmission be flat-towed (four wheels on the ground) for no more than 30 miles (48 km), at no more than 30 mph (48 km/h). Do not flat-tow the car backward.

1.1 Automatic Transmission 010

All automatic transmissions used on the Volkswagens covered by this manual are type number 010 and are hydraulically controlled with three forward speeds. The automatic transmission can best be described and understood by dividing it into five subsystems. These are the torque converter, the ATF pump, the planetary gear system, the hydraulic controls, and the final drive. See Fig. 1-2.

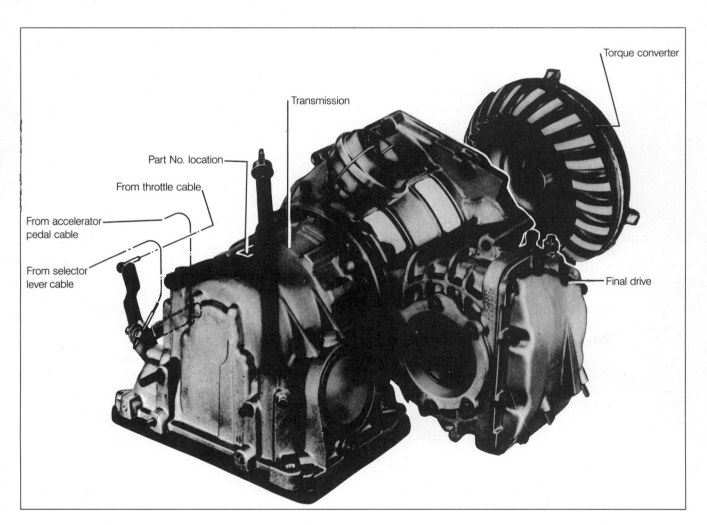

Fig. 1-1. Transaxle with automatic transmission.

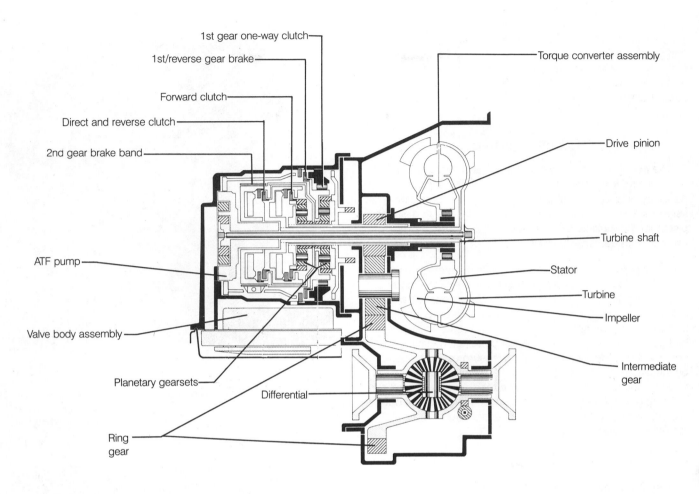

Fig. 1-2. Cross-section of transaxle with automatic transmission showing orientation of internal parts.

Torque Converter

The torque converter is a doughnut-shaped assembly located between the engine and the transaxle inside the bellhousing. The torque converter transmits engine output to the transmission, and also multiplies engine torque at low vehicle speeds. The torque converter is a fluid coupling. Curved impeller vanes inside the housing set up a flow of ATF that drives another vaned wheel opposite it, called the turbine. The turbine drives a hollow shaft that transmits power to the planetary gear system in the transmission. The central set of vanes in the torque converter is called the stator. At low speeds, a one-way clutch keeps the stator stationary so that its curved vanes will redirect the flow of ATF in such a way that torque is multiplied. At higher speeds, when there is no longer a speed differential between the impeller vanes and the turbine, the stator freewheels and torque multiplication ceases.

ATF Pump

The automatic transmission fluid (ATF) circulates through the transmission under pressure. The ATF pump that creates this pressure is located in the extreme left-hand end of the transaxle case, the end farthest from the engine. A long pump driveshaft passes through the center of the hollow turbine shaft to drive the ATF pump. The splined pump driveshaft is connected directly to the torque converter housing, so ATF circulates whenever the engine is running.

Planetary Gear System

A torque converter alone cannot supply the torque multiplication needed for all driving conditions. The torque converter therefore drives through a planetary gear system which can operate at different drive ratios. The planetary gear system consists of two clutches, two brakes, and two planetary gearsets—one gearset for forward operation of the vehicle and the other gearset for reverse.

The two hydraulically-operated multiple-disc clutches control the routing of power to the planetary gearsets. The clutch at the right-hand end of the transmission is called the forward clutch because it transfers power to the planetary gears in all forward gears. The clutch at the left-hand end of the transmission is called the direct and reverse clutch because it transfers power to the planetary gears only when the transmission is in direct drive (3rd or top gear) or reverse.

The first of the two brakes is the 2nd-gear brake band. It contracts around the direct and reverse clutch drum to provide 2nd gear. The second of the two brakes is the 1st/reverse gear brake. It is applied hydraulically to obtain reverse. This brake is also applied when the selector lever is at **1** in order to provide additional engine braking by locking the normally freewheeling 1st gear one-way clutch.

Hydraulic Controls

The hydraulic control system directs and regulates hydraulic pressure from the ATF pump to control shifting of the planetary gear system. Shifts are produced by the piston-type servo for the second gear brake band, by the ring shaped piston for the multiple-disc 1st/reverse gear brake, and by the two ring-shaped clutch pistons.

Three primary control devices regulate the movement of the control valves in the automatic transmission's valve body assembly. The first is the manual valve, which is connected to the selector lever by a flexible cable. Moving the lever changes the setting of the valve and produces the necessary application of hydraulic pressure for the drive range selected. The second primary control device, the throttle pressure valve, is operated by the accelerator cable and makes the transmission responsive to engine speed and load. The third primary control device, the governor, controls ATF pressure relative to the output shaft rotational speed, making the transmission responsive to rear wheel speed.

Final Drive

The final drive consists of the drive pinion — which is mounted around the turbine shaft and the ATF pump driveshaft — the intermediate gear, the ring gear, and the differential. The teeth on the ring gear, the intermediate gear, and the drive pinion are helically-cut for quieter running. The differential allows the front wheels to turn at different speeds, as is necessary when turning.

1.2 Identification Codes and Specifications

Due to different power characteristics and performance requirements of various engine/model combinations, there are minor variations of the basic automatic transmission transaxle, including the torque converter. The different versions are identified by code letters.

The transmission code letters and a transmission number corresponding to date of manufacture are located on the top of the bellhousing. The automatic transmission type number 010 is found atop the transmission case near the dip stick. See Fig. 1-3. Torque converter code letters are found on the converter as shown in Fig. 1-4. **Table a** lists transmission specifications for all automatic transmission models covered by this manual. If replacing the transaxle or the torque converter, the replacement part's code letters should correspond to those of the original part.

Fig. 1-3. Automatic transmission type number (**A**) and code letters with date of manufacture (**B**). In example shown, code letters are EG. Numbers indicate date of manufacture, 15 is day, 08 is month, and 8 is last digit of year.

Fig. 1-4. Torque converter code letter location (arrow). Code letter "K" shown.

Table a. Automatic Transaxle Specifications.

Engine and engine code (model year)	1.8 L Gasoline GX, MZ (1985 - 1987)	1.6 L Diesel ME (Canada) (1985 - 1987)	1.8 L Gasoline HT, RD, RV, PF (1985 - 1989)
Transmission type no. and code letter	010 TJ	010 TL	010 TNA 010 TN
Torque converter code letter	K	U	K

Gear ratios
  1st gear
  2nd gear
  3rd gear
	
	2.71
	1.50
	1.00
		
		2.71
		1.50
		1.00
			
			2.71
			1.50
			1.00

Final drive ratio	3.12	3.41	3.41

2. MAINTENANCE

The following routine maintenance should be performed at the time or mileage intervals prescribed in **LUBRICATION AND MAINTENANCE**. Maintenance procedures are provided there, as are the specifications and quantities for the required lubricants.

1. Checking ATF level and adding ATF

2. Checking kickdown operation

3. Checking final drive hypoid oil level

4. Changing ATF

3. TROUBLESHOOTING

This troubleshooting section applies to problems affecting the transaxle, including the torque converter, the automatic transmission, and the final drive. The basic functions of the automatic transmission are to circulate clean ATF under pressure, to provide the correct drive ratio in response to both the hydraulic and mechanical controls, and to transfer engine power to the front wheels.

The troubleshooting information in this section applies to the diagnosis of problems which are remedied either by external adjustment or by internal disassembly and repair. Most external adjustments to the transmission, as well as removal and installation of the transaxle, are covered in this manual; however, internal transmission repairs require specialized knowledge and equipment and should be left to an authorized Volkswagen dealer or other qualified automatic transmission repair shop.

3.1 Basic Troubleshooting Principles

In order for automatic transmission troubleshooting to provide meaningful results, the engine must be in good condition and properly tuned. See **ENGINE** for troubleshooting engine problems.

Inspect the transaxle for external damage, loose or missing fasteners, and for any obvious leaks. Check both the ATF and the final drive hypoid oil levels. The transmission and final drive use completely separate fluids. If the ATF level is too low and there is no sign of leakage, it may be because ATF is leaking into the final drive. Check for abnormally high final drive oil level. See **LUBRICATION AND MAINTENANCE**.

Many automatic transmission problems can be traced to an incorrect ATF level, to contaminated ATF, or to misadjusted transmission controls. Check for leaks, check the ATF level, and check to see if the fluid is dirty or has a burned odor. A burned odor indicates overheated fluid, which may be accompanied by burned clutches or brake bands. Friction material may be clogging the valve body passages.

Less severe automatic transmission problems may be solved merely by correcting the ATF level, by draining the ATF and refilling the transmission with new fluid as described in **LUBRICATION AND MAINTENANCE**, or by inspecting the adjustment and operation of the controls as described in **4.2 External Transmission Adjustments**.

Table b on the following two pages lists symptoms of automatic transmission and final drive problems, their probable causes, and recommended corrective action.

10

NOTE ———

Probable causes and corrective actions may discuss specific internal transmission faults for reference only. We recommend that internal transmission repair and overhaul be left to an authorized Volkswagen dealer or other qualified repair shop.

Table b. Automatic Transmission Troubleshooting

Symptom	Probable cause	Corrective action
1. No drive (car will not move)	**a.** ATF level low	**a.** Check and, if necessary, correct ATF level. See **LUBRICATION AND MAINTENANCE**
	b. Drive plate or torque converter not correctly installed	**b.** Check and correct drive plate and torque converter installation. See **ENGINE**
	c. Selector lever cable detached from manual valve	**c.** Connect and adjust cable **4.2**
	d. Sticking main pressure valve, faulty ATF pump, or broken gear or shaft — no pressure	**d.** Test ATF pressure. **3.2** Remove, disassemble, and inspect transaxle. To remove and install, see **5.1**
2. Irregular drive in all forward gears	**a.** ATF level low	**a.** Check and correct ATF level. See **LUBRICATION AND MAINTENANCE**
	b. ATF pump pickup strainer partially clogged	**b.** Remove ATF pan. Clean or replace strainer. See **LUBRICATION AND MAINTENANCE**
3. No drive in 1st gear (shift position **D** or **2**)	**a.** Forward clutch or 1st gear one-way clutch faulty	**a.** Overhaul or replace transmission. To remove and install transaxle, see **5.1**
4. No drive in 1st gear (shift position **1**)	**a.** 1st/reverse gear brake defective	**a.** Overhaul or replace transmission. To remove and install transaxle, see **5.1**
5. No drive in 2nd gear (shift position **D** or **2**)	**a.** 2nd gear brake band incorrectly adjusted	**a.** Adjust band. **4.2**
	b. 2nd gear brake band damaged	**b.** Overhaul or replace transmission. To remove and install transaxle, see **5.1**
6. No drive in 3rd gear (shift position **D**)	**a.** Direct/reverse clutch faulty	**a.** Overhaul or replace transmission. To remove and install transaxle, see **5.1**
7. No drive in reverse	**a.** 1st/reverse gear brake, direct/reverse clutch, or forward clutch faulty	**a.** Overhaul or replace transmission. To remove and install transaxle, see **5.1**
8. No upshift into 2nd or 3rd gear	**a.** Faulty governor or governor drive	**a.** Replace governor shaft
	b. Governor dirty	**b.** Remove, clean, and reinstall governor
	c. Shift valve(s) sticking	**c.** Remove and clean valve body
	d. Faulty valve body	**d.** Repair or replace valve body
9. No downshift into 2nd or 1st gear	**a.** Governor dirty	**a.** Remove, clean, and reinstall governor
	b. Shift valves sticking	**b.** Remove and clean valve body
10. Downshift to 1st gear delayed (jerky engagement)	**a.** 1st gear one-way clutch slipping	**a.** Overhaul or replace transmission. To remove and install transaxle, see **5.1**
11. Gear engagement delayed in upshift to all gears	**a.** ATF level low	**a.** Check and correct ATF level. See **LUBRICATION AND MAINTENANCE**
	b. Valve body contaminated	**b.** Remove and clean valve body
	c. 2nd gear brake band incorrectly adjusted	**c.** Adjust band. **4.2**
	d. 2nd gear brake band faulty	**d.** Overhaul or replace transmission. To remove and install transaxle, see **5.1**
12. Gear engagement jerky when moving selector lever from **N** to **D**, or from **N** to **R**	**a.** ATF level low	**a.** Check and correct ATF level. See **LUBRICATION AND MAINTENANCE**
	b. Engine idle speed too high	**b.** Adjust idle. See **FUEL SYSTEM (Gasoline)** or **FUEL SYSTEM (Diesel)**
13. Kickdown fails to operate	**a.** Accelerator cable incorrectly adjusted	**a.** Adjust cable. **4.2**

continued on next page

Table b. Automatic Transmission Troubleshooting (continued)

Symptom	Probable cause	Corrective action
14. Poor acceleration, poor high speed performance	a. Engine out of tune b. Throttle cable incorrectly adjusted c. Accelerator cable incorrectly adjusted	a. Tune up engine. See **LUBRICATION AND MAINTENANCE** b. Adjust cable. **4.2** c. Adjust cable. **4.2**
15. Transmission slips during hard cornering or after hard stops	a. ATF level low b. Clogged ATF pump strainer, incorrect strainer cover	a. Check and correct ATF level. See **LUBRICATION AND MAINTENANCE** b. Remove and clean strainer. Install new strainer cover as described in **LUBRICATION AND MAINTENANCE**
16. Chronic low ATF level with no visible leaks	a. ATF leaking into final drive housing	a. Check final drive hypoid oil level. See **LUBRICATION AND MAINTENANCE**. Remove transaxle, separate transmission and final drive, and replace oil seals, O-ring, or gaskets as required. **5.2**
17. ATF appears dirty, smells burnt	a. Contaminated ATF b. Damaged clutch and brake friction linings	a. Drain and replace ATF. Remove and clean ATF strainer. See **LUBRICATION AND MAINTENANCE** b. Overhaul or replace transmission. To remove and install transaxle, see **5.1**
18. Parking lock fails to engage	a. Parking lock mechanism damaged b. Selector lever cable misadjusted	a. Overhaul or replace transmission. To remove and install transaxle see **5.1** b. Adjust cable. **4.2**
19. Selector lever will not move	a. Selector lever cable binding b. Internal transmission failure	a. Remove and re-route cable. **4.1** b. Overhaul or replace transmission. To remove and install transaxle, see **5.1**

3.2 Diagnostic Tests

Although most internal transaxle problems cannot be fully diagnosed unless the unit is removed and disassembled, these tests may help further diagnose transaxle trouble prior to its removal. To obtain accurate test results, the ATF must be clean, in good condition (not previously overheated or burnt), and at the proper level.

Stall Speed Test

This test is used to check for faults in the torque converter and planetary gear system when there is no other apparent cause for poor performance and acceleration. The test results are meaningless if the engine is not running properly. A precise tachometer must be used for the rpm measurements, as dashboard instruments are not sufficiently accurate.

CAUTION ▬

The stall speed test should be as short as possible, and should never extend beyond 20 seconds maximum. Prolonging the test may overheat the transmission and damage the seals or internal components.

To test:

1. Drive the vehicle to warm the engine and transmission to normal operating temperature.

2. Connect a tachometer according to the instrument manufacturer's instructions, so that it can be read from the driver's seat, then start the engine.

3. Set the parking brake and depress the foot brake firmly to hold the vehicle stationary.

4. Place the selector lever in **D**.

5. While holding the car stationary with the brakes, floor the accelerator for no more than 20 seconds. Notice the tachometer readings. The rpm should increase, and then hold steady. For transmission code TJ the rpm should be between 2200 and 2500. For transmission code TL, between 2110 and 2460. For transmission code TNA, between 2320 and 2570. For transmission code TN, between 2200 and 2500 rpm. Maximum rpm achieved under these conditions is the stall speed.

NOTE ▬

It is normal for the stall speed to be 125 rpm lower than specified for each 1000 meters (3200 ft.) above sea level. High ambient air temperature will also cause a slight drop in stall speed.

10

A stall speed that is a few hundred rpm below the specified range is probably due to reduced engine performance. A stall speed that is 400 rpm or more below the specified range indicates a faulty torque converter.

If the stall speed is above the specified range, there is slippage in the forward clutch or in the 1st gear one-way clutch. To determine which is faulty, repeat the test, this time with the selector lever in **1**. If the stall speed is now within specifications, then the 1st gear one-way clutch is defective. If the stall speed rpm is still high, then the forward clutch is defective.

The test can also be made with the selector lever in **R**. If the stall speed is too high, it indicates slippage in either the direct/reverse clutch or in the 1st/reverse clutch.

All of these faults require that the transaxle be removed and disassembled for repair.

Pressure Test

A main pressure test will reveal internal leaks, sticking control valves, or other troubles in the hydraulic controls. Although the full-throttle part of this test can be performed while driving the car, whenever possible this test should be carried out on a dynamometer. The pressure gauge should have a range of at least 0 to 15 bar or 0 to 200 psi, and a hose long enough to allow it to be read from the passenger compartment. Engine idle speed must be correctly adjusted.

To test:

1. Connect the pressure gauge to the main pressure tap on the transmission, as shown in Fig. 3-1. Route the hose so that the gauge can be read from inside the car.

Fig. 3-1. Main pressure tap on transmission case, located on rear of transaxle near driver's side drive axle flange.

2. Drive the car to warm the engine and transmission to normal operating temperature. Stop the car and set the parking brake.

3. Place the selector lever at **D**. With car stationary and idling, the main pressure should be between 2.90 and 3.00 bar (41 and 43 psi).

4. Place the selector lever at **R**. With the car stationary and idling, the main pressure should be between 9.00 and 10.00 bar (130 and 145 psi).

5. Either on a dynamometer or during a road test, with the selector lever at **D**, and the speedometer indicating a speed over 25 mph (40 km/h), floor the accelerator. During full-throttle acceleration the main pressure should be between 5.85 and 5.95 bar (85 and 86 psi).

6. Shut off the engine. Disconnect the pressure gauge hose and reinstall the plug for the pressure tap. Torque the plug to 10 Nm (87 in.. lb.).

Any pressure that is higher or lower than specification usually indicates a malfunctioning valve body and valves, probably due to contamination. The valve body can be removed, cleaned, and reinstalled with the transaxle in place by removing the ATF pan and strainer. However, it contains many precision parts which must be reassembled in their exact locations. Because of the complexity of the valve body assembly, we recommend that these repairs be left to an authorized Volkswagen dealer or other qualified repair shop.

Low pressure may also indicate a worn ATF pump or internal ATF pump leaks past seals, gaskets, and metal mating surfaces. These repairs require that the transaxle be removed and disassembled.

4. CONTROLS

The automatic transmission controls include the selector lever cable, the accelerator cable, and the throttle cable. The selector lever cable allows the transmission to be manually shifted from inside the passenger compartment. The accelerator cable and the throttle cable make the transmission responsive to throttle position.

The selector lever cable activates the manual valve on the transmission. When the lever is moved out of park, the parking mechanism is released and the manual valve is correctly positioned according to the gear selected.

The accelerator cable and the throttle cable are connected to an operating lever on the side of the transmission. This operating lever controls both the movement of the throttle and the engagement of the kickdown valve. The lever is connected to a shaft which runs through the center of the manual valve. On the opposite end of the shaft is the operating lever for the kickdown valve.

The accelerator and throttle cables are shown in Fig. 4-1. When the accelerator pedal is depressed the accelerator cable changes the position of the operating levers, which in turn change the position of the throttle valve (gasoline engines) or the speed control lever (diesel engines) via the throttle cable. The kickdown device allows for maximum acceleration when the accelerator pedal is fully depressed either by downshifting to a lower gear or by delaying the shift into a higher gear.

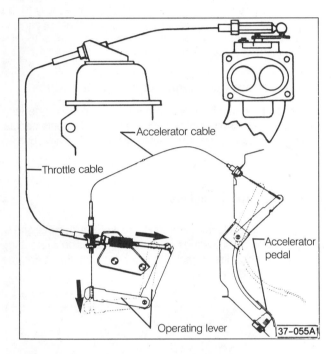

Fig. 4-1. Accelerator and throttle cable layout used with gasoline engine with automatic transmission. Arrows show movement of operating levers as accelerator pedal is depressed. Diesel engine with automatic transmission is similar.

4.1 Removing and Installing Control Cables

All three cables operate within a conduit or sheath. They are available for replacement only as a complete assembly, with conduit.

Selector Lever Cable

The selector lever cable and related parts are shown in Fig. 4-2. The neutral/park/reverse light switch prevents the car from starting when the selector lever is in gear. The switch also actuates the reverse lights when the selector lever is in reverse. For information on testing the switch, see **ELECTRICAL SYSTEM**.

To replace:

1. Place the selector lever in **P**. If the cable is broken, select park by hand-moving the operating lever on the transaxle all the way to the left.

2. Remove the knob on the top of the selector lever by removing the set screw, and then pry off the indicator plate. Remove the selector cable from the lever by prying off the E-clip.

3. Working beneath the vehicle, remove the screws holding the selector support to the body and lower the support. Pull back the rubber boot covering the selector cable and loosen and remove the cable conduit nut so the conduit is free from the support.

4. Working in the engine compartment on the transmission end of the cable, loosen the nut on the clamping sleeve, then loosen and remove the cable from the transmission bracket. Pull the cable through to the engine compartment.

Fig. 4-2. Exploded view of automatic transmission selector lever and related parts. Inset shows end of cable which attaches to transmission operating lever.

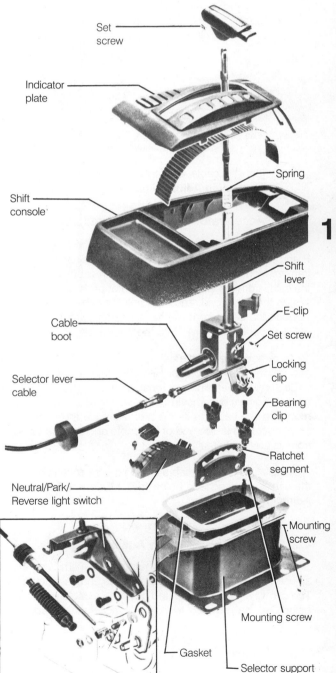

10

5. Installation of the cable is the reverse of removal. Torque the selector support mounting bolts to 23 Nm (17 ft. lb.). Make sure the selector cable is routed correctly around the speedometer cable, or it may bind and jam the lever. See Fig. 4-3.

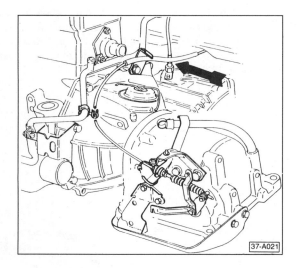

Fig. 4-3. Correct installation of selector lever cable, routed to outside of speedometer cable (arrow).

6. Adjust the cable as described below in **4.2 External Transmission Adjustments**.

Accelerator Cable and Throttle Cable

To remove the accelerator cable, place the selector lever in **P** and set the parking brake. Loosen the adjusting nut on the transmission operating lever to make the cable slack. Unhook the cable from the top of the accelerator pedal by prying off the clip on the cable end, and then pull the cable from the pedal. Unhook the cable from the transmission operating lever and pull it through the firewall into the passenger compartment.

To remove the throttle cable, place the selector lever in **P** and set the parking brake. Remove the cable end from the throttle valve (gasoline engines) or the speed control lever (diesel engines) by removing the retaining clip. Loosen the nuts mounting the cable to its bracket. Remove the retaining clip from the transmission end of the cable and pull the cable end from its ball socket.

Installation of either cable is the reverse of removal. Adjust the cables as described below in **4.2 External Transmission Adjustments**.

4.2 External Transmission Adjustments

External adjustments to the automatic transmission include adjustments of the control cables and the 2nd gear brake band. The cables should be adjusted any time a cable is installed. A helper will be required to hold the accelerator pedal at full throttle while adjustments are made. These external adjustments may correct imprecise shifting without the need for removal of the transaxle or costly overhaul work.

Adjusting Selector Lever Cable

Adjust the selector lever cable with the shift lever in **P**. Loosen the nut clamping the cable to the actuating lever on the transmission. Make sure that the transmission lever is in the Park position by hand-pushing the actuating lever fully to the left. Tighten the nut to 8 Nm (71 in. lb.). Check that the cable is correctly adjusted by starting the engine and moving the selector lever through all shift positions.

Adjusting Accelerator and Throttle Cables

Proper throttle control and transmission operation depend on accurate adjustment of the accelerator and throttle cables. Cable adjustments for gasoline and diesel engines are covered separately.

To adjust (gasoline engines only):

1. Place the selector lever in **P** and set the parking brake. Loosen the adjusting nut on the transmission's operating lever and disconnect the accelerator cable from the lever. See Fig. 4-4.

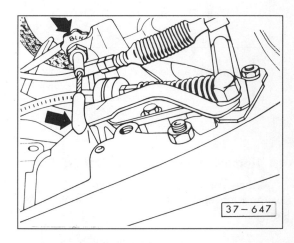

Fig. 4-4. Accelerator cable adjusting nut (top arrow) and accelerator cable end attachment to operating lever (bottom arrow).

2. Loosen the locknuts that hold the cable conduit to the bracket on the cylinder head cover. Make certain that the cable moves freely and that the throttle valve is fully closed.

3. Lightly tension the throttle cable as shown in Fig. 4-5, until there is no free-play in the cable. Turn the locknut (**1**) against the bracket, making sure the throttle valve is still fully closed. Tighten the other locknut (**2**) and torque to 10 Nm (87 in. lb.).

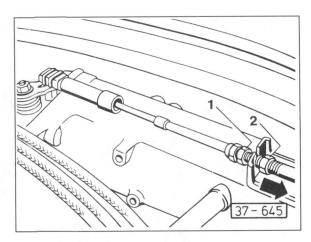

Fig. 4-5. Accelerator cable being adjusted on gasoline engine with automatic transmission. Move cable in direction of arrow before tightening locknuts **1** and **2**.

4. Connect the hooked end of the accelerator cable to the transmission operating lever. With the accelerator pedal depressed to its kickdown position (contacting the floor stop), push the transmission lever to its kickdown stop and turn the adjusting nut on the accelerator cable until there is no free play in the cable. See Fig. 4-6.

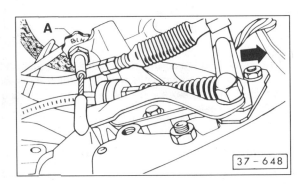

Fig. 4-6. Accelerator cable being adjusted. Move operating lever of automatic transmission to kickdown position (in direction of arrow until it contacts stop) and adjust cable to remove slack. Cable adjusting nut is at **A**.

5. Release and depress the accelerator pedal several times to check that the cable operates smoothly and that the operating lever rests against the kickdown stop when the pedal is fully depressed.

To adjust (diesel engines only):

1. Place the selector lever at **P** and set the parking brake. Check, and if necessary adjust, the engine idle speed and maximum rpm as described in **FUEL SYSTEM (Diesel).**

2. Loosen the accelerator pedal cable adjusting nut and detach the cable from the operating lever. See Fig. 4-4 above.

3. Loosen the locknuts that hold the cable conduit in its bracket on the injection pump and pull the rubber boot back from the spring housing. See Fig. 4-7.

Fig. 4-7. Accelerator cable adjustment on diesel engine with automatic transmission. Loosen locknuts (**1** and **2**), and remove rubber boot (arrow). Turbo diesel shown.

4. With the transmission operating lever held against its closed throttle stop (pedal released) as indicated in Fig. 4-8, hold the injection pump's speed control lever against the idle speed adjusting screw.

10

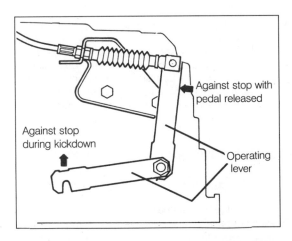

Fig. 4-8. Operating lever showing positions used for cable adjustment on diesel engine with automatic transmission.

5. Slide the accelerator cable conduit as far as possible away from the pump lever without compressing the kickdown spring, as shown in Fig. 4-9, then tighten the locknuts without moving the cable.

Fig. 4-9. Cable conduit being pulled (in direction of white arrow) for adjustment with locknuts **1** and **2**. During adjustment, do not move cable conduit so far that kickdown spring at throttle lever is compressed.

6. Hook the end of the accelerator cable onto the operating lever of the transmission. With the accelerator pedal fully depressed to the kickdown position, turn the accelerator cable adjuster so that the transmission lever just contacts the kickdown stop. See Fig. 4-5 above.

> **NOTE** ——
>
> At full throttle, (with the injection pump lever just contacting the maximum RPM adjusting screw), the kickdown spring should not be compressed. With the pedal in the kickdown position (all the way to the floor stop), the kickdown spring should be compressed and the transmission lever should just contact the kickdown stop.

7. Tighten the adjuster locknut and refit the cable boot.

Adjusting 2nd Gear Brake Band

The 2nd gear brake band can be adjusted with the transaxle installed or removed. In either case, the transaxle must be in its normal horizontal position or the brake band may jam during adjustment. The 2nd gear brake band adjusting screw is located just to the left of the operating lever, as viewed from the front of the car.

1. Loosen the locknut and temporarily torque the adjusting screw to 10 Nm (87 in. lb.), as shown in Fig. 4-10, to center the brake band.

2. Loosen the screw and retorque it to 5 Nm (44 in. lb.).

3. Back the screw off (counterclockwise) exactly 2 ½ turns. Hold the adjusting screw stationary and tighten the locknut, torquing it to 20 Nm (15 ft. lb.).

Fig. 4-10. 2nd gear brake band being adjusted.

5. TRANSAXLE ASSEMBLY

Repair of internal transmission or final drive components requires that the transaxle be removed for disassembly. Once removed, the final drive and transmission can be separated and replaced or repaired individually. Remanufactured transaxles are available through authorized Volkswagen dealers, and offer some savings over the outright purchase of a new unit.

To correct fluid leaks, the drive flange oil seals and the governor O-ring are replaceable with the transaxle installed in the vehicle. The transaxle must be removed to replace any other faulty oil seals.

5.1 Removing and Installing Transaxle

In the procedure given here, the transaxle assembly is separated from the engine, supported on a floor jack, and taken out from below. Alternately, the engine/transaxle assembly may be removed from above, and the transaxle then separated from the engine as described in **ENGINE**.

The procedure which follows requires a means of externally supporting the weight of the engine, a transmission jack or floor jack with a transmission adaptor, and jack stands designed for the purpose of solidly supporting the raised car. The engine support device is necessary because, in this procedure, all of the engine mounts are removed.

> **CAUTION** ——
>
> *The car must be raised and supported off its front wheels during the removal procedure. Use extreme caution when working beneath the car.*

To remove:

1. Disconnect the negative (−) and positive (+) battery cables from the battery, in that order. Disconnect the speedometer cable from the transaxle.

2. Set the parking brake and loosen the left and right drive axle nuts. Loosen the left and right front wheel lug bolts.

3. Raise the car and support it on jack stands, and remove both driveshaft nuts, the wheel lug bolts, and the front wheels. For more drive axle and front suspension information, see **SUSPENSION AND STEERING**.

> **CAUTION** ━━
>
> *Moving the car even a short distance with the drive axle nuts loosened or removed may cause wheel bearing damage and lead to premature wheel bearing failure.*

4. Install a device to support the engine, as shown in Fig. 5-1.

Fig. 5-1. Engine support installed. Volkswagen special tool no. 10-222A shown.

5. Remove the bolts from the rear transaxle mount and remove the mounting arms as shown in Fig. 5-2.

6. Place a transmission jack or a floor jack with a transmission adaptor beneath the transaxle. Raise the jack just enough to support the transaxle, but do not raise the engine.

7. Remove the upper bolts from the front engine/transaxle mount as shown in Fig. 5-3. If necessary, also remove the bolt holding the coolant pipe to the mount. Remove the lower bolts from the front mount and remove the mount.

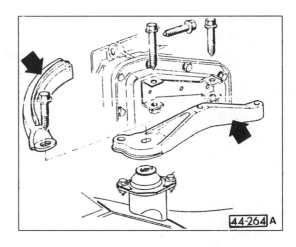

Fig. 5-2. Left rear transaxle mounts (arrows).

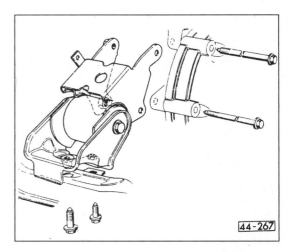

Fig. 5-3. Front engine/transaxle mounting bolts removed from early-type rubber mount. Later hydraulic mount is similar.

8. Remove the bolts that hold the transmission protection plate, the torque converter cover plate, and the driveshaft cover plate to the transaxle, then remove the plates.

> **NOTE** ━━
>
> The transmission protection plate is at the lower left (driver's side) front of the transaxle; the torque converter cover plate is at the bottom of the bellhousing; the driveshaft cover plate is above the right (passenger) side transaxle drive flange.

9. With the selector lever at **P**, remove the selector lever cable and the accelerator and throttle cables from the transmission as described in **4.1 Removing and Installing Control Cables**.

10

10. Remove the bolts from the right rear engine mount and remove the mount. See Fig. 5-4.

11. Remove the upper transaxle-to-engine mounting bolts.

12. Remove the starter heat shield and the brackets. Disconnect the starter wiring and then remove the starter mounting bolts and the starter.

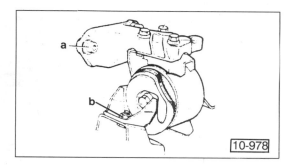

10-978

Fig. 5-4. Right rear engine mounting bolts (**a** and **b**) removed.

13. Detach the drive axles from the transmission drive flanges.

14. Separate the left and right lower ball joint from the wheel bearing housing as described in **SUSPENSION AND STEERING**. Remove the drive axles.

15. Working through the lower opening in the bellhousing, remove the three bolts that hold the torque converter to the drive plate. See Fig. 5-5.

NOTE ———

Use a socket wrench on the crankshaft sprocket bolt and turn the crankshaft clockwise to move the bolts into position for removal.

16. Working beneath the car, remove the subframe mounting bolts and allow the subframe to hang freely.

17. Remove the lower engine-to-transaxle mounting bolt. Slide the transaxle off its dowels and lower it out of the car.

To install:

1. To avoid serious damage when installing the transaxle, make certain the torque converter has not slipped off of its support. Turn the converter back and forth to check that it has engaged its splines.

2. Position the transaxle until it can pushed onto its locating dowels. Install and evenly tighten all the engine-to-transaxle mounting bolts until the transaxle is firmly in place. Torque the smaller M 10 bolts to 45 Nm (33 ft. lb.) and the larger M 12 bolts to 75 Nm (55 ft. lb.).

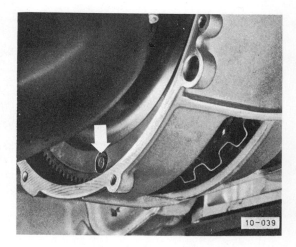

10-039

Fig. 5-5. Bolt (arrow) fastening torque converter to drive plate. Remove three bolts.

3. Install all of the transaxle and engine mounts and their bolts. Remount the coolant pipe to the front engine/transaxle mount. Snug the bolts, but do not tighten them.

4. Install the driveshafts first into the wheel bearing housing and then onto the drive flanges. Install the socket- head inner mounting bolts and torque them to 45 Nm (33 ft. lb.). Align the subframe and install, but do not fully torque, the mounting bolts. Position the lower ball joints into the wheel bearing housing. Install the clamp bolt and torque it to to 50 Nm (37 ft. lb.).

5. Install the mounting bolts which attach the torque converter to the drive plate. Using a wrench on the front crankshaft bolt, turn the crankshaft (clockwise only) to align the bolt holes. Torque the bolts to 30 Nm (22 ft. lb.).

6. Remove the transmission jack and install the transmission protection plate, the torque converter cover plate, and the driveshaft cover plate, torquing the smaller M 8 bolts to 20 Nm (15 ft. lb.) and the larger M 10 bolts to 25 Nm (18 ft. lb.).

7. Install the starter with its heat shield and brackets, torquing the bolts to 20 Nm (15 ft. lb.), then reconnect the starter wires.

8. Install the washers and the drive axle nuts on the ends of the driveshafts until they are snug. Install the road wheels and lower the car to the ground. Torque the wheel lug bolts to 110 Nm (81 ft. lb.) and the drive axle nuts to 230 Nm (170 ft. lb.). Torque the subframe mounting bolts to 130 Nm (96 ft. lb.).

9. Reconnect the battery cables. Reconnect the speedometer cable to the transaxle and torque it to 10 Nm (87 in. lb.).

10. Align the engine/transaxle mounts, as described in **ENGINE**. With the mounts aligned and the nuts and bolts torqued, install and adjust the selector lever cable and the accelerator and throttle cables as described earlier in **4.2 External Transmission Adjustments**.

5.2 Oil Seals

The torque converter oil seal and the drive flange oils seals can be replaced without extensive disassembly of the transaxle. The drive flange oil seals can be replaced without removing the transaxle from the car; torque converter oil seal replacement requires that the transaxle be removed. See **5.1 Removing and Installing Transaxle**.

Torque Converter Oil Seal

A leaking torque converter oil seal is often caused by a worn bushing in the torque converter hub. The bushing should always be checked if the seal is replaced. A worn bushing will promote rapid wear of the new seal.

To replace oil seal and check bushing:

1. Pry the seal from the final drive housing using a chisel as shown in Fig. 5-6.

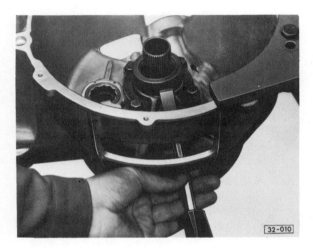

Fig. 5-6. Faulty torque converter seal being removed with chisel.

2. Coat the new seal in ATF and drive the seal into place as far as it will go. See Fig. 5-7.

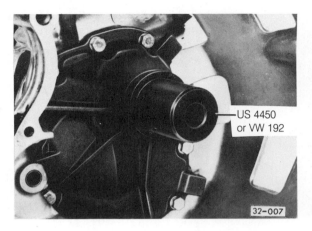

Fig. 5-7. Seal driver being used to install new torque converter seal onto one-way clutch support on final drive housing. Volkswagen special tool no. US 4450 or VW 192 shown. Use tool of approximate seal diameter to apply even installation pressure.

3. Check the torque converter oil seal hub for wear. See Fig. 5-8. Remove sharp edges and burrs with emery cloth. If the hub is deeply scored, the torque converter should be replaced.

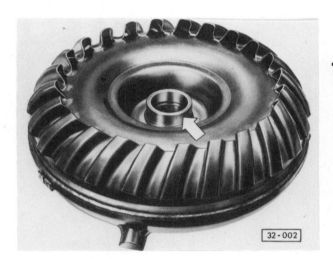

Fig. 5-8. Torque converter oil seal hub (arrow).

4. Measure the bore of the bushing inside the torque converter hub using an inside micrometer. If the diameter exceeds 34.25 mm (1.348 in.) or if the bore is out of round by more than 0.03 mm (.001 in.), the bushing should be replaced.

10

5. To replace the bushing, remove it using the Volkswagen special tools shown in Fig. 5-9. Press in the new bushing as shown in Fig. 5-10.

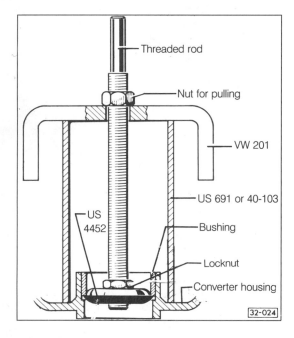

Fig. 5-9. Torque converter bushing being removed. Numbers shown identify Volkswagen special tools.

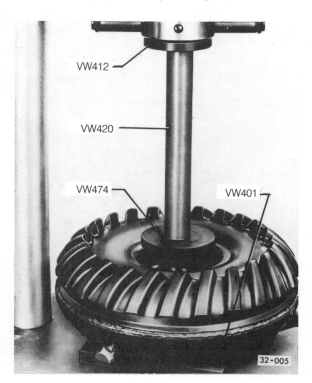

Fig. 5-10. Torque converter bushing being installed. Numbers shown identify Volkswagen special tools used with hydraulic press.

NOTE ━━━

Replacement bushings are manufactured to the correct size and do not require additional reaming or honing.

Drive Flange Oil Seals

The drive flange oil seals can be replaced without removing the transaxle from the car. Check the new seals prior to beginning the job to make sure that each is equipped with a tension spring behind the seal lip.

To replace:

1. Remove the socket-head bolts to separate the front drive axle and constant velocity joint from the transaxle drive flange. Suspend the detached end of the drive axle with a stiff wire hook to avoid outer constant velocity joint damage.

CAUTION ━━━

Do not let the driveshaft hang freely. This may damage the outer constant velocity joints, causing them to fail soon after the vehicle is returned to service.

NOTE ━━━

It may be necessary or at least helpful to separate the ball joint from the lower control arm to allow moving the drive axle farther out of the way. For additional information, see **SUSPENSION AND STEERING**.

2. Pry the dust cap from the center of the drive flange. Remove the circlip which retains the flange, and remove the spring washer. Using a puller such as that shown in Fig. 5-11, pull the drive flange from the drive flange shaft.

NOTE ━━━

Notice the way that the spring washer is installed so that it can be reinstalled the same way.

3. Pry the oil seal from its recess using a hooked tool or a screwdriver, using care not to damage the sealing surface.

4. Pack the open side of the new seal with multipurpose grease, and then drive the seal into place, as shown in Fig. 5-12, until it is fully seated.

5. Inspect the drive flange for wear at the point where it is contacted by the oil seal. Replace the drive flange if the seal contact area is grooved.

Fig. 5-11. Drive flange being pulled from drive flange shaft. Volkswagen special tool no. VW 391 shown. If another puller is used, be careful not to damage threaded hole in drive flange shaft.

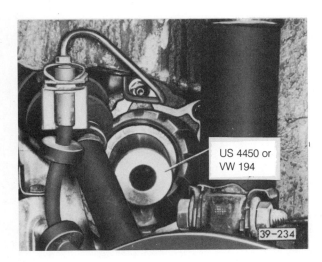

Fig. 5-12. Seal driver (Volkswagen special tool no. US 4450 or VW 194) being used to install new drive flange oil seal. Alternately, use tool of approximate seal diameter to apply even installation pressure.

6. Install the drive flange as shown in Fig. 5-13.

7. Install the spring washer. Fit a new circlip over the end of the drive flange shaft.

8. Lightly drive the circlip into place until it is firmly seated in its groove in the drive flange shaft.

9. Reattach the drive axle to the drive flange. Torque the socket-head bolts to 45 Nm (33 ft. lb.).

10. If the ball joint was disconnected, raise the lower suspension control arm and insert the ball joint stud into the bearing housing. Install the clamp bolt and nut, and torque to 50 Nm (37 ft. lb.).

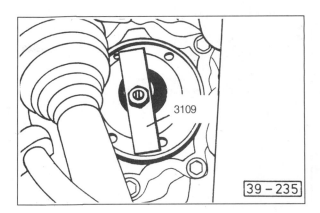

Fig. 5-13. Drive flange being installed. Volkswagen special tool no. 3109 (shown) threads into center of drive flange shaft. Nut is tightened to pull flange into place evenly and avoid seal damage.

6. TECHNICAL DATA

I. Automatic Transmission Test Data

Stall speed (brakes locked, wide-open throttle)
  Transmission TJ . . . . .2200 to 2500 rpm
  Transmission TL . . . . .2110 to 2460 rpm
  Transmission TNA . . . . ,2320 to 2570 rpm
Main pressures
  At idle (stationary, selector lever
  at **D**) . . . . .2.90 – 3.00 bar (41 – 43 psi) (lead1)
  At idle (stationary, selector lever
  at **R**) . . . . .9.00 – 10.00 bar (130 – 145 psi) (lead1)
  Full throttle (indicated speed above 25 mph
  (40 km/h), selector lever at **D**) . . . . .5.85 – 5.95 bar
                                                        (85 – 86 psi)

10

II. Tightening Torques

Main pressure tap plug in
  transmission case (threaded plug) . . . . . . .10 Nm (87 in. lb.)
Locknut for 2nd gear brake band
  adjusting screw (nut) . . . . .20 Nm (15 ft. lb.)
Engine to transaxle (bolt and/or nut)
  M 10 . . . . .45 Nm (33 ft. lb.)
  M 12 . . . . .75 Nm (55 ft. lb.)
Torque converter to drive plate (bolt) . . . . . .30 Nm (22 ft. lb.)
Torque converter cover plate to
  bellhousing (bolt) . . . . .15 Nm (11 ft. lb.)
Protection plate to transaxle (bolt)
  M 8 . . . . .20 Nm (15 ft. lb.)
  M 10 . . . . .25 Nm (18 ft. lb.)
Starter to bellhousing (bolt) . . . . .20 Nm (15 ft. lb.)
Transmission case to final drive
  housing (nut) . . . . .30 Nm (22 ft. lb.)
Throttle cable to valve cover or
  speed lever (locknuts) . . . . .10 Nm (87 in. lb.)
Selector support to floor board (bolt) . . . . . .23 Nm (17 ft. lb.)
Selector lever cable to transmission
  operating lever (nut) . . . . .8 Nm (71 in. lb.)
Driveshaft to drive flange
  (socket-head bolt) . . . . .45 Nm (33 ft. lb.)
Lower ball joint to wheel bearing
  housing (clamp bolt) . . . . .50 Nm (37 ft. lb.)
Driveshaft to wheel hub (bolt) . . . . .230 Nm (170 ft. lb.)
Subframe to body (bolt) . . . . .130 Nm (96 ft. lb.)

III. Automatic Transaxle Specifications.

Engine and engine code (model year)	1.8 L Gasoline GX, MZ (1985 - 1987)	1.6 L Diesel ME (Canada) (1985 - 1987)	1.8 L Gasoline HT, RD, RV, PF (1985 - 1989)
Transmission type no. and code letter	010 TJ	010 TL	010 TNA 010 TN
Torque converter code letter	K	U	K
Gear ratios 1st gear 2nd gear 3rd gear	 2.71 1.50 1.00	 2.71 1.50 1.00	 2.71 1.50 1.00
Final drive ratio	3.12	3.41	3.41

SUSPENSION AND STEERING

Contents

Introduction 3

1. General Description 4
  1.1   Front Suspension 4
  1.2   Rear Suspension 5
  1.3   Steering 5

2. Maintenance 6

3. Troubleshooting 6
  3.1   Basic Troubleshooting Principles 6
  3.2   Diagnostic Inspection and Testing 8
       Tire Wear 8
       Isolating Pulling Symptoms 8
       Vibration 8

4. Wheels, Tires, and Alignment 8
  4.1   Wheels and Tires 8
       Wheels 8
       Tires 9
       Winter Tires 9
  4.2   Alignment 9
       Four-wheel Alignment 10
       Camber Adjustment 10
       Toe Adjustment 10
       Centerline Adjustment
       (four-wheel alignment only) 10
  4.3   Alignment Specifications 11

5. Front Suspension 11
  5.1   Front Suspension Struts 11

Checking Shock Absorbers 12
Removing and Installing Front Suspension
Struts 12
Disassembling and Assembling Front
Suspension Strut 13
  5.2   Drive Axles and Constant Velocity Joints 13
Removing and Installing Drive Axles 14
Removing and Installing Constant Velocity
Joints 14
Disassembling and Inspecting Constant
Velocity Joints 16
Removing and Installing Drive Axle Vibration
Damper 19
  5.3   Ball Joints 19
Inspecting and Replacing Control Arm Ball
Joints 19
  5.4   Bearings and Bushings 20
Removing and Installing Wheel Bearing
Housings and Wheel Bearings 20
Control Arm Bushings 22
Repairing Subframe Mounting 23

6. Rear Suspension 23
  6.1   Rear Shock Absorbers and Springs 24
Removing and Installing Rear Shock
Absorbers and Springs 24
  6.2   Rear Wheel Bearings 24
Removing and Installing Rear Wheel
Bearings 24
Adjusting Rear Wheel Bearings 27
  6.3   Rear Axle Beam 27
Removing and Installing Rear Suspension
as a Unit 27
Replacing Axle Beam Bushings 28

11

2 SUSPENSION AND STEERING

7. Steering 29

  7.1   Steering Column 30

        Removing and Installing Steering Wheel 30

        Removing and Installing Steering Column
        Switches 31

        Replacing Ignition/Steering Lock Cylinder 32

  7.2   Steering Gear and Tie Rods 32

        Inspecting Tie Rod Ends 32

        Replacing Inner Tie Rod Boots 32

        Replacing and Adjusting Tie Rods 33

        Centering Manual Steering Rack 34

        Adjusting Steering Gearbox 34

        Removing and Installing Steering Gearbox . . . 35

  7.3   Power-Assisted Steering 35

        Draining and Filling Power Steering Fluid 37

        Pressure Testing Power Steering System 37

        Power Steering Pump 37

8. Suspension and Steering Technical Data 38

    I. Tightening Torques 38

TABLES

a. Suspension and Steering Troubleshooting 6

b. Alignment Specifications 11

Suspension and Steering

Introduction

GTIs, Golfs, and Jettas are equipped with a strut-type independent front suspension and a torsion-type rear axle beam with trailing arms. The front suspension struts are integral spring and shock absorber units, while the rear suspension has separate shock absorbers mounted inside coil springs. This type of suspension system is one of the most commonly used systems in contemporary automotive design for the specific reason that it provides excellent steering and handling in a compact size with comparatively light weight.

The front suspension struts have been designed to provide a negative steering roll radius. That is, the steering axis of each strut intersects the road surface at a point outboard of the wheel's vertical centerline. This suspension geometry tends to steer the car automatically in the direction of a skid caused by unequal front wheel traction. Conventional front suspension geometry, which places the steering axes inboard of the tire centerlines, tends to steer the car in the opposite direction, thereby increasing the severity of the skid.

The rear suspension has been designed for low unsprung weight, easy replacement of springs and shock absorbers, and good ride and handling qualities. The main axle beam is somewhat flexible. Uneven rear suspension loads cause the axle beam to twist slightly, thus acting as a stabilizer bar. This suspension design yields many desired performance benefits which are otherwise only available from more complicated and expensive kinds of independent suspension.

The steering uses a rack and pinion steering gear with tie rods connecting to the front suspension to minimize weight and space requirements. The steering column is connected to the steering gear by a universal joint shaft. The universal joint shaft is angled in order to prevent collision impacts from forcing the steering wheel toward the driver.

The front suspension struts and control arms can be disassembled for repair, but much of this work requires special tools and experience. If you lack the skills, tools, or a suitable workshop for suspension and steering work, we suggest you leave such repairs to an authorized Volkswagen dealer or other qualified repair shop. We especially urge you to consult your authorized Volkswagen dealer before beginning any repairs on a car that may be subject to Volkswagen's warranty coverage.

11

1. GENERAL DESCRIPTION

The GTI, Golf, and Jetta suspension and steering systems are designed to provide excellent handling and comfort while minimizing weight and space requirements. Although the front and rear suspension systems are independent sub-systems, and are of completely different designs, they work together to achieve Volkswagen's outstanding combination of precise handling and ride comfort. Troubleshooting, maintenance, and repair should always consider the condition of both front and rear suspension systems, as well as the steering system.

1.1 Front Suspension

Fig. 1-1 shows the components of the front suspension system. The lower control arms, sometimes called wishbones or A-arms, connect to mounting points on the subframe.

Each front suspension strut is a hydraulic shock absorber inside a tubular strut housing and a concentrically-mounted coil spring. The front wheel bearing housing with its integral steering arm is a separate component that is bolted to the lower end of the strut and mounted to the control arm with a ball joint. Suspension travel is limited by rubber bump stops which are integral to the strut assemblies.

The two Y-shaped control arms control the position of the lower ends of the suspension struts. The ball joints are riveted to the control arms during manufacture—replacements are installed with bolts. There are no adjustments for front wheel alignment on the control arms. Toe is adjusted by altering the length of the right-hand steering tie rod. Camber is not normally adjusted. Caster is non-adjustable. A stabilizer bar mounted in rubber bushings is connected to both control arms and reduces body roll during cornering.

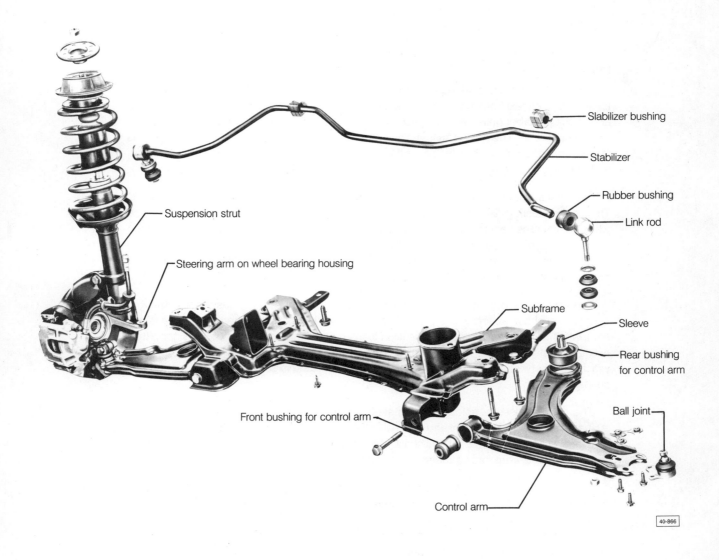

Fig. 1-1. Front suspension assembly showing subframe and control arm bushing detail.

1.2 Rear Suspension

The rear suspension system is shown in Fig. 1-2. The beam-type rear axle is a one-piece welded assembly of axle beam and trailing arms which yields constant toe and camber throughout the range of suspension travel. The axle beam itself acts as a stabilizer bar, its torsional stiffness helping to reduce body roll during cornering. Rear wheel stub axles are bolted to the trailing arms. The rear suspension "struts" are actually separate coil springs mounted concentrically with shock absorbers. They are easily removed and installed and, unlike the front struts, do not require a special spring compressor for assembly and disassembly.

1.3 Steering

The rack and pinion steering gear is located behind the engine and the transaxle. This location protects the steering gear from weather and from damage in all but the most severe collisions. Neither the steering gear nor the tie rod ends require lubrication during their normal service lives. Although there is an adjusting screw on the steering gear, adjustment is not necessary unless the steering either rattles, or is stiff and does not self-center. On some models, the steering gear is power-assisted to reduce steering effort.

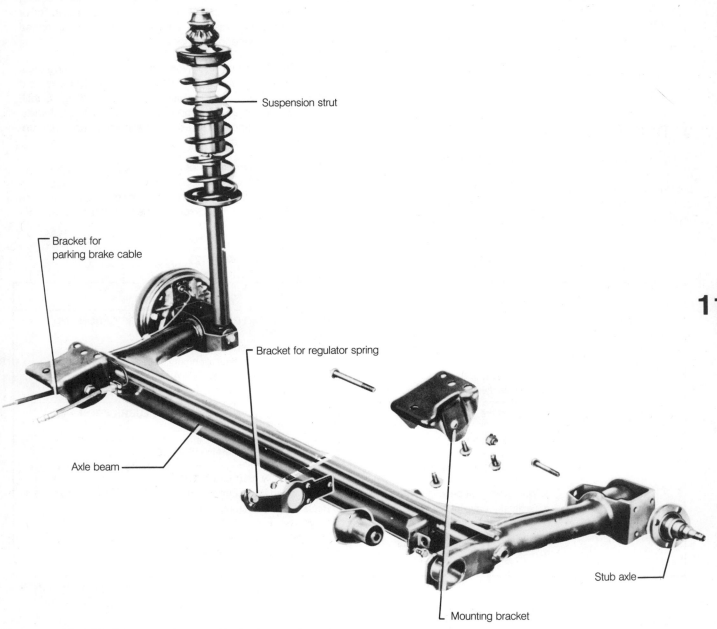

Fig. 1-2. Rear suspension assembly showing one-piece axle beam and trailing arm assembly.

11

2. Maintenance

Scheduled maintenance of the suspension and steering systems consists of periodic inspections of the components for wear and damage. Another periodic requirement is precision adjustment of wheel alignment by an authorized Volkswagen dealer or other qualified shop.

The following items should be checked at the intervals prescribed in **LUBRICATION AND MAINTENANCE**. Information on making these checks can be found either in **LUBRICATION AND MAINTENANCE** or under the listed headings in this section of the manual.

1. Checking power steering fluid level.

2. Inspecting constant velocity (CV) joints and boots. **5.2**

3. Inspecting ball joints. **5.3**

4. Inspecting tie rods and tie rod boots. **7.2**

3. TROUBLESHOOTING

This troubleshooting section applies to problems affecting ride comfort, handling and stability, and steering. That such problems are caused by suspension or steering systems is usually self-evident, although a problem such as consistently pulling to one side may be caused by faulty brakes. Excessive vibration may be caused by a misaligned engine and transaxle assembly. For brake system troubleshooting, see **BRAKES**. For information on engine and transaxle alignment, see **ENGINE**. For more basic help in determining which is the appropriate section to use for troubleshooting a particular symptom, see **FUNDAMENTALS** at the front of the manual.

3.1 Basic Troubleshooting Principles

Ride comfort and stability both depend on the suspension and steering systems controlling the positions and movements of the wheels. These systems must allow controlled movement so that the wheels can steer and react to bumps, but they also limit and precisely locate the wheels so that the car is stable, controllable, and predictable. Any symptom of instability or imprecise road feel may be caused by worn or damaged suspension and steering components.

Aside from inspection for worn parts, troubleshooting must also consider tires, wheels, and their alignment. Tire wear and inflation pressures can dramatically affect handling. Subtle irregularities in wheel alignment angles also affect stability. Tires of mixed brands or sizes affect alignment and may unbalance a car's handling.

Table a lists symptoms of suspension and steering problems and their probable causes, and suggests corrective actions. The boldface numbers in the corrective action column refer to headings in that section where the repairs are described.

Table a. Suspension and Steering Troubleshooting

Symptom	Probable cause	Corrective action
1. Pull to one side, wandering	a. Incorrect tire pressure	a. Check and correct tire pressures. See **LUBRICATION AND MAINTENANCE**
	b. Defective/unevenly worn tire	b. Inspect tires and replace as needed. **4.1**
	c. Incorrect wheel alignment	c. Check and adjust wheel alignment. **4.2**
	d. Worn rear axle beam pivot bushings	d. Replace axle beam bushings. **6.4**
	e. Faulty brakes	e. See **BRAKES**
2. Steering heavy, poor self-centering	a. Incorrect tire pressure	a. Check and correct tire pressures. See **LUBRICATION AND MAINTENANCE**
	b. Low power steering fluid	b. Check power steering fluid and add as required. See **LUBRICATION AND MAINTENANCE**
	c. Loose or broken power steering pump V-belt	c. Inspect V-belt. Tighten or replace as necessary. See **LUBRICATION AND MAINTENANCE**
	d. Worn front strut bearing(s)	d. Remove and disassemble front struts. Replace strut bearings. **5.1**
	e. Faulty universal joint shaft	e. Replace shaft assembly. **7.1**
	f. Binding steering gear	f. Adjust steering gear **7.2**
	g. Faulty power steering pump	g. Test and, if necessary, replace pump. **7.3**
	h. Air in power steering fluid	h. Repair air leak and, if necessary, add fluid. **7.3**

continued on next page

Table a. Suspension and Steering Troubleshooting (continued)

Symptom	Probable cause	Corrective action
3. Front-end vibration or shimmy	a. Incorrect tire pressure	a. Check and correct tire pressures. See **LUBRICATION AND MAINTENANCE**
	b. Loose wheel lug bolts	b. Tighten lug bolts to proper torque. **4.**
	c. Bent wheel rim	c. Inspect wheels and replace as necessary. **4.**
	d. Unbalanced wheels/tires	d. Balance tires. Check for uneven wear patterns. **4.1**
4. Shudder or vibration when accelerating	a. Faulty inner constant velocity (CV) joint(s)	a. Replace inner CV joint(s). **5.2**
5. Steering loose, imprecise	a. Incorrect tire pressure	a. Check and correct tire pressures. See **LUBRICATION AND MAINTENANCE**
	b. Worn tie rod end(s)	b. Replace tie rod(s) and align. **7.2**
	c. Worn control arm ball joint(s)	c. Replace ball joint(s) and align. **5.3**
	d. Faulty front wheel bearing(s)	d. Replace wheel bearing(s). **5.4**
	e. Worn steering gear	e. Check and adjust steering gear. **7.2**
	f. Worn universal joint shaft	f. Replace shaft assembly. **7.1**
6. Poor stability, repeated bouncing after bumps, suspension bottoms out easily	a. Weak shock absorbers	a. Replace shock absorbers. **5.1, 6.1**
	b. Worn front strut bearing(s)	b. Replace strut bearings. **5.1**
7. Uneven ride height	a. Bent or damaged suspension components	a. Inspect and repair/replace as necessary.
	b. Sagging coil springs	b. Replace front and/or rear springs in pairs. **5.1, 6.1**
8. Front wheel noise, continuous growling, may be more noticeable when turning	a. Worn front wheel bearing(s)	a. Replace front wheel bearing(s). **5.4**
	b. Faulty transaxle	b. See **MANUAL TRANSMISSION AND CLUTCH** or **AUTOMATIC TRANSMISSION**
9. Front wheel noise, ratcheting, clicking most severe when turning and accelerating	a. Failed outer constant velocity (CV) joint(s)	a. Replace outer CV joint(s). **5.2**
10. Rear wheel noise, scraping, dragging	a. Worn/improperly adjusted rear wheel bearings	a. Adjust or replace bearings. **6.2**
	b. Faulty rear brakes	b. See **BRAKES**
11. Steering surges or makes noise when turning (power-assisted steering only)	a. Low power steering fluid level	a. Check power steering fluid and add as required. See **LUBRICATION AND MAINTENANCE**
	b. Loose power steering pump V-belt	b. Inspect V-belt. Tighten or replace as necessary. See **LUBRICATION AND MAINTENANCE**
	c. Faulty power steering pump	c. Test and, if necessary, replace pump. **7.3**
	d. Air in power steering fluid	d. Repair air leak and, if necessary, add fluid. **7.3**

11

3.2 Diagnostic Inspection and Testing

Suspension and steering problems can usually be isolated and at least partially diagnosed by careful consideration of the symptoms and inspection of the components which are most likely to cause such a symptom.

Tire Wear

Tire tread wear, while not a source of immediate feedback, can be an indicator of suspension and steering problems. Proper tire tread wear is difficult to notice, so tires are made with wear indicator bars which visually indicate when the tire is nearly worn-out. These wear indicator bars show up as evenly spaced bald "stripes" running across the tread surface, as shown in Fig. 3-1.

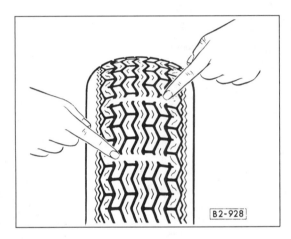

Fig. 3-1. Tread wear indicator bars showing on worn-out tire.

Uneven tire wear usually indicates improper tire inflation pressures or a misalignment condition. Fig. 3-2 illustrates how tire inflation pressures influence tire wear. Tire wear that is uneven across the tread—one side worn more than the other or unusual wear of individual tread blocks—probably indicates an alignment problem. Cupping or scalloping—wear that is uneven around the circumference of the tire—is a telltale sign of a tire balance problem or a worn-out shock absorber.

Isolating Pulling Symptoms

Consistent pulling to one side in a car driven straight ahead on a level road may be caused by either suspension misalignment or a faulty tire. In more unusual cases, a brake problem may be the cause.

To help decide whether tires or alignment are at fault, temporarily swap the front tires and then road test the car. If a tire problem is the cause of the pulling symptom, the problem should switch to the other side of the car when the tires are switched, and it should now pull to the other side. If the symptom is unchanged, then the problem is probably alignment, which is unaffected by swapping tires.

Vibration

Abnormal vibration, if not caused by a mechanical problem, will most often be the result of one or more unbalanced wheels.

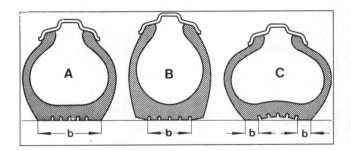

Fig. 3-2. Effect of tire inflation pressure on wear pattern. Condition **A** is normal. Condition **B** is overinflation which increases wear in center of tire tread. Condition **C** is underinflation which increases wear on outer edges of tire tread. Dimension **b** is tire contact area.

Before spending the money for wheel balancing, look for an obvious cause of wheel imbalance. Caked-on mud or ice and snow can dramatically affect wheel balance. Clean the wheels and tires and road test the car before investigating more serious causes.

4. WHEELS, TIRES, AND ALIGNMENT

For stability and control, wheels and tires must be in good condition and be properly aligned. Tire inflation pressures, tire wear, and wheel alignment will all influence how the car feels and responds on the road.

Precise wheel alignment can only be accomplished when the tires, the suspension, and the steering are in good condition. Uneven tire wear, different size tires, or worn suspension and steering parts all affect wheel alignment. Reputable wheel alignment technicians will always inspect the suspension and steering for worn parts before an alignment, and will recommend that any necessary repairs be made before proceeding. A wheel alignment on a car with excessively worn suspension and steering parts is a complete waste of time and money.

4.1 Wheels and Tires

Wheels and tires are subject to many stresses. They will perform as intended only if undamaged, properly inflated, and correctly balanced. Properly maintained, the factory-installed tires will provide long service with comfort and safety. See **LUBRICATION AND MAINTENANCE** for information on wheel size, tire size, and recommended inflation pressures.

Wheels

The wheels on all models covered by this manual are designed for use with tubeless, radial tires of a specific size. Replacement tires of non-standard size or construction should be used only if the tire manufacturer specifies them for your make and model. See **LUBRICATION AND MAINTENANCE** for information on the original equipment wheel sizes for cars covered by this manual.

When installing accessory wheels, be sure to install wheels with the proper offset. Measured across the width of the wheel rim, the offset is how far the center of the wheel is offset from the wheel mounting surface. The wheels on Volkswagens covered by this manual have negative offset. In other words, from the wheel mounting surface the wheel rim is offset to the inside. The use of other than original equipment wheels requires special care since many aftermarket wheels do not have the correct offset. Incorrect offset may cause the tires to interfere with the body, overload the wheel bearings, or affect the steering.

Tires

Radial-ply tires are factory-installed on all vehicles covered by this manual. To retain the car's excellent handling characteristics, it is recommended that the tires only be replaced with those of radial-ply construction and of the original size.

Winter Tires

Though inferior to regular tires for dry-road wear and handling, winter (mud and snow) tires offer a big improvement on snowy winter roads. Studded winter tires improve traction on icy surfaces, but may be more dangerous on dry roads. They should be used only if icy conditions predominate. Check local laws. The use of studded tires may be restricted or completely prohibited in your area.

> **WARNING** ——
>
> *When winter tires are installed on only two of the four wheels, they should be installed on the front driving wheels. To prevent dangerous handling characteristics, they must be of the same type of (radial-ply) construction as those on the rear of the car.*

4.2 Alignment

Wheel alignment is the precise adjustment of wheel angles, used to achieve the best compromise between comfort, control, and tire wear. Alignment specifications differ from model to model, depending on suspension design. The alignment can also be fine-tuned for specific driving conditions. For example, if the car consistently carries only one person, or is consistently heavily loaded, this information will be useful to the alignment technician. Like tire pressure, wheel alignment also has some influence on fuel economy, because of the effect on rolling resistance.

The important alignment angles are camber, caster, and toe. Camber is the angle that the wheels tilt from vertical when viewed from front or rear, as illustrated in Fig. 4-1. Wheels which tilt out at the top have positive (+) camber. Wheels which tilt in at the top have negative (−) camber. On the Volkswagens covered by this manual, camber adjustment is not normally required, although there are provisions for making camber adjustments if necessary. See **Camber Adjustment**

below. Camber influences cornering, directional stability, and tire wear. Different camber on the two front wheels may cause the car to pull to one side. Misadjusted camber will cause uneven tire wear.

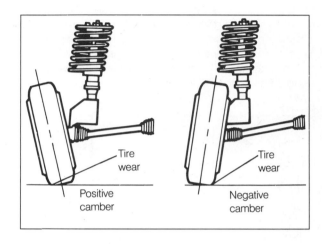

Fig. 4-1. Camber angle viewed from front or rear.

Caster, the angle by which the steering axis deviates from vertical, is illustrated in Fig. 4-2. The steering axis is an imaginary line about which the front wheels turn. Most cars are designed with a steering axis which is inclined toward the rear at the top (positive caster), giving them directional stability and self-centering steering. Caster should be checked as part of any alignment. It is not, however, an adjustable angle on cars covered by this manual. Caster which is out of specification suggests worn or damaged components. Uneven front wheel caster will cause the car to pull to one side. Too little caster reduces directional stability. Too much caster increases turning effort.

11

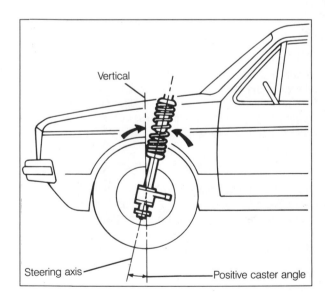

Fig. 4-2. Caster is angle of steering axis inclination from vertical. Caster on Volkswagens covered by this manual is non-adjustable.

Toe is a measurement of the amount that two wheels point toward each other (toe-in) or away from each other (toe-out), as viewed from above or below. Toe-in and toe-out are illustrated in Fig. 4-3. Toe affects directional stability and tire wear, and at the front wheels also has some effect on how the car responds to steering changes. Toe is the primary alignment adjustment for cars covered by this manual. See **Toe Adjustment** below for information on adjusting toe. Too much toe will cause the tires to "scrub" and to wear unevenly and more quickly. Too little toe—too near zero—may cause the car to be less stable and wander from side to side.

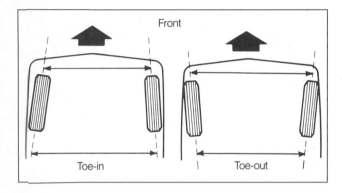

Fig. 4-3. Front wheel toe.

Because of the emphasis on precision, wheel alignment has become very sophisticated. Modern computerized equipment, using special optics or laser beams for measurement, help the qualified technician do the job more quickly and more accurately than is possible for the do-it-yourselfer. For this reason, this manual covers only the specific adjustment methods, and not the basic procedures for measuring wheel alignment angles. The reasonable cost of a professional wheel alignment is money well spent.

Four-wheel Alignment

A four-wheel alignment considers not just the individual wheels or pairs of wheels, but also the alignment of the wheels relative to the car's centerline and the relationships between front and rear wheels. Four-wheel alignment is more sophisticated and slightly more expensive, but is also the best, most precise alignment for any car.

Camber Adjustment

Routine camber adjustment is not normally necessary on cars covered by this manual. If measurements indicate that front wheel camber deviates from the specification, adjustment is possible by replacing the upper strut mounting bolt with a special Volkswagen replacement bolt. See Fig. 4-4.

CAUTION ———

The slotted control arm ball joint mounting holes should never be used to adjust camber. Ball joint location is factory set to match drive axle length. Moving the ball joint may cause premature CV joint wear.

Fig. 4-4. Upper strut mounting bolt (arrow) which can be replaced to allow for camber adjustment.

The new bolt, Volkswagen part no. N 903 334.01, has a slightly smaller diameter shank. Using the lower strut mounting bolt as a pivot and the new upper bolt with its larger clearance, camber adjustment of approximately ± ½° is possible. If greater adjustment is necessary, the smaller-shank replacement bolt may also be used in the lower mounting hole, for a total adjustment range of approximately ± 1°.

Rear wheel camber is not adjustable. Rear wheel camber which does not meet specifications suggests a damaged rear axle beam or rear stub axle. See **6. Rear Suspension** for more information.

Toe Adjustment

Toe at the front wheels is adjusted by changing the length of the right (passenger-side) steering tie rod. Because camber also affects toe, toe adjustments should be made only after camber adjustments are final. Loosen the locknut, and turn the tie rod to thread it into or out of the tie rod end, increasing or decreasing the overall tie-rod length. Large toe adjustments may also require centering the steering rack or the steering wheel. See **7. Steering** for more information.

Rear wheel toe is not adjustable. Rear wheel toe which does not meet specifications suggests a damaged rear axle beam or rear stub axle. See **6. Rear Suspension** for more information.

Centerline Adjustment
(four-wheel alignment only)

Although individual rear wheel toe is not adjustable, loosening the mounting bolts which hold the beam axle mounting brackets to the car body will allow a small amount of movement which can be used to adjust the rear wheel centerline.

4.3 Alignment Specifications

Alignment specifications for all models covered by this manual are listed in **Table b**. See **4.2 Alignment** for more information.

5. FRONT SUSPENSION

Though the cars covered by this manual have front wheel drive, the front suspension is no more complex than that of a rear-drive car. All of the front suspension parts that are subject to wear can be easily replaced. Some of these repairs require special tools and equipment. To avoid starting a job that may be difficult to complete, please read the entire procedure before beginning any repairs.

When doing any front suspension maintenance or repair, please observe the following general cautions.

CAUTION ━━

●Do not install bolts and nuts coated with undercoating wax, as correct tightening torque cannot be assured on installation. Always clean the threads of removed bolts and nuts with solvent before installation, or replace them with new parts.

●Do not attempt to weld or straighten the suspension strut, wheel bearing housing, control arm, or subframe. Damaged parts should be replaced.

5.1 Front Suspension Struts

Fig. 5-1 is an exploded view of the front strut assembly. The spring and the upper strut bearing are replaceable separately. If the shock absorber is worn-out or the strut itself is damaged, then the entire strut must be replaced. To maintain even side-to-side shock absorber performance, the struts should always be replaced in pairs.

The entire strut assembly is removed from the car as a unit for disassembly. To disassemble the strut, special tools are required. Most importantly, the coil spring must be compressed with a spring compressor before removing the strut's top nut.

WARNING ━━

If you lack the tools or experience necessary to safely disassemble and reassemble the front suspension struts, we strongly urge that this work be left to an authorized Volkswagen dealer or other qualified repair shop. Attempts to disassemble the struts without proper tools are likely to cause serious injury.

Table b. Alignment Specifications

	Golf, Jetta		Golf GT, GTI, Jetta GLI	
Front wheels	specification	tolerance	specification	tolerance

Caster (not adjustable)
  wheels straight ahead
(corresponds to camber difference from 20°
  left lock to 20° right lock)
maximum permissible difference between sides
	+ 1° 30'
	
	1°
		± 30'
		
		—
			+ 1° 33'
			
			1°
				± 30'
				
				—

Camber wheels straight ahead maximum permissible difference between sides	− 30' 30'	± 20' —	− 35' 30'	± 20' —

Toe
  total toe, wheels not pressed
toe angle difference at 20° lock
  (each side, wheels not pressed)
	0°
	
	+ 1° 20'
		± 10'
		
		± 30'
			0°
			
			+ 1° 20'
				± 10'
				
				± 30'

Rear Axle (not adjustable)				
Camber each side maximum permissible difference between sides	− 1° 40' 30'	± 20' —	− 1° 40' 30'	± 20' —
Toe total maximum permissible deviation from driving direction	+ 25' 25'	± 15' —	+ 25' 25'	± 15' —

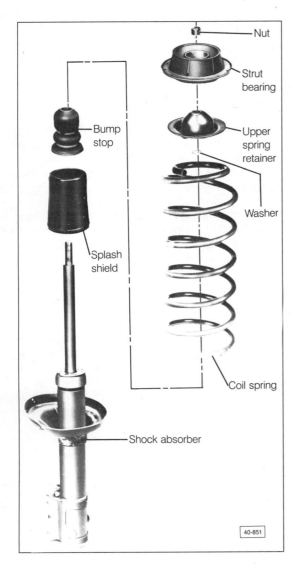

Fig. 5-1. Front strut assembly showing coil spring, strut bearing, and related parts removed.

Checking Shock Absorbers

Springs are what support the car and allow the suspension to bounce smoothly over bumps and other road irregularities. The shock absorber's function is to moderate the spring action—to quickly slow the bounce and help the spring return to its normal position. Shock absorbers do not require maintenance. An adequate supply of fluid is placed in them during manufacturing to compensate for small leaks. Minor leakage is acceptable if the shock absorber still functions correctly. Shock absorbers cannot be serviced, and need to be replaced when they lose their ability to control the suspension.

To the careful observer, a decline in shock absorber performance can be detected in normal driving. Worn shock absorbers will cause extra skittishness over bumps, and a less-controlled and wallowing feel in corners and after bumps. When seriously worn, the shock absorbers present little resistance to spring oscilations. Because they easily reach the limits of their travel, they may knock when going over bumps.

For more deliberate evaluation, the most common—though not entirely accurate—test of shock absorber function involves vigorously bouncing each end or corner of the car, and then releasing and observing how quickly the bouncing stops. More than one bounce usually indicates shock absorbers that need replacing.

Some evaluation of a shock absorber's condition can be made by removing and disassembling the strut and checking the shock absorber's resistance to movement. When held vertically, the shock absorber shaft should move smoothly and very firmly over its entire range of travel. If possible, compare the movement of a used shock absorber to a new one.

Removing and Installing Front Suspension Struts

The struts can be easily removed for replacement or for access to other components. Special tools may be necessary to remove the top flange nut. See the procedure below for more information. Use a stiff wire, or equivalent, to support the free-hanging lower control arm and avoid damage to the flexible brake lines. Use new self-locking flange nuts. Also, the strut mountings affect wheel alignment. Any time the struts have been removed and reinstalled, a wheel alignment is highly recommended.

To remove front struts:

1. Loosen the wheel lug bolts, then raise the car and support it with jack stands which are designed for the purpose. The front wheels should be off the ground so that the suspension is not bearing any weight.

2. Remove the wheel.

3. Remove the nuts from the two bolts that hold the bottom of the strut to the wheel bearing housing, leaving the bolts in place. Remove the brake line from its guide at the bottom of the strut and secure it out of the way.

4. Support the suspension and brake assembly so that it will not fall when the strut is removed.

5. Using a hex wrench to hold the shock absorber rod, remove the flange nut and flange, as shown in Fig. 5-2.

6. Remove the bolts from the bottom of the strut, and remove the strut.

WARNING——
Further disassembly of the strut requires special tools and great care to avoid serious personal injury. Do not proceed without thoroughly reading the procedure below.

Installation is the reverse of removal. Use a new self-locking nut to secure the flange to the top of the shock absorber rod and torque it to 60 Nm (44 ft. lb.). Torque the bolts and nuts that hold the strut to the wheel bearing housing to 80 Nm (59 ft. lb.).

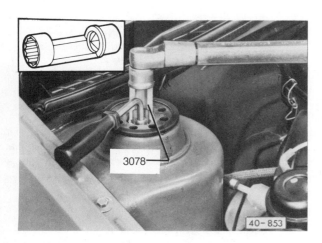

Fig. 5-2. Flange nut being loosened with hex wrench holding shock absorber shaft. Cutaway 22 mm deep socket shown (see inset) is Volkswagen special tool no. 3078 (order no. T03 078 000 40 ZEL).

Disassembling and Assembling Front Suspension Strut

In the assembled strut, the coil spring is under some compression, even when the strut is removed from the car. Attempting to disassemble the strut without first compressing the spring is extremely dangerous. Read the procedure carefully. Do not attempt to disassemble the struts without a proper spring compressor.

To disassemble front strut:

1. Install a spring compressor that is designed for the purpose. Relieve the pressure on the upper spring retainer by compressing the coil spring, as shown in Fig. 5-3.

> **WARNING** ——
>
> *Work slowly. Keep watch to make sure the spring compressor stays firmly in place on the spring.*

2. Remove the slotted nut on the shock absorber rod, using Volkswagen special tool no. VW 524 or equivalent. Use a hex wrench to hold the shock absorber shaft.

> **WARNING** ——
>
> *Do not remove the slotted nut from the shock absorber rod until the coil spring is compressed enough that there is no force pushing on the upper spring retainer.*

3. Slide the strut bearing, the upper spring retainer, the washer, the rubber bump stop, and the splash shield off the shock absorber rod.

4. Carefully release and remove the spring compressor. Remove the coil spring.

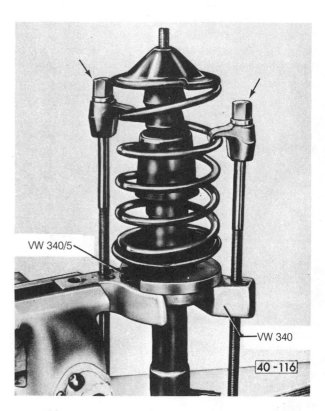

Fig. 5-3. Spring compressor being used to safely disassemble front suspension strut. On compressor shown (Volkswagen special tool no. VW 340), turn nuts (arrows) on threaded shafts to compress spring.

Assembly is the reverse of disassembly. First, check the strut bearing for signs of wear and replace it if it does not turn smoothly. Fully extend the shock absorber rod by hand. With the spring compressed and no pressure on the upper spring retainer, torque the slotted nut to 40 Nm (30 ft. lb.). Align the ends of the coil spring to mate properly with the spring retainers. If the coil springs are to be replaced, note the paint color code on the coils and always replace springs in matched pairs.

5.2 Drive Axles and Constant Velocity Joints

On cars with front wheel drive, the drive wheels must also be able to turn for steering. The drive axles are equipped at each end with constant velocity (CV) joints which allow power to be continuously delivered to the drive wheels — even when all the connections are not precisely straight. The CV joint is similar in function to older-type universal joints, but it operates much more smoothly at more radical drive axle angles.

The inner CV joints attach to the transaxle drive flanges, while the outer CV joints are equipped with splined stub axles which engage the splines of the wheel hubs and are secured by the large nut. Each joint is packed with a special molybdenum disulfide grease and completely sealed by a rubber boot. Although some inspection of the CV joints — and even replacement of the inner joints — is possible while the drive axles are installed, complete inspection and thorough lubrication of the joints require that the drive axles be removed from the car.

11

If the drive axles themselves are damaged, complete remanufactured drive axle assemblies are available from an authorized Volkswagen dealer at lower cost than a new unit.

CAUTION ——

Moving a car with drive axles removed will quickly damage the wheel bearings. If moving the car is necessary, always secure the bearing races by temporarily installing an old outer CV joint in the hub, or hold the bearing races in place with two large washers and a suitable bolt and nut.

Removing and Installing Drive Axles

The large nut securing the stub axle and outer CV joint to the hub is very tight. Removing it and torquing it properly on installation may require special tools. The inner CV joints are mounted with 8 mm, 12-point socket-head bolts which require a special wrench. Both inner and outer CV joints are held onto the drive axle shafts with circlips which should be replaced any time the joints are removed and installed. Use a new gasket when installing the inner CV joints to the transaxle drive flanges.

To remove:

1. With the vehicle on the ground, pry off the dust cap in the center of the front wheel hub and loosen, but do not remove, the axle shaft nut.

WARNING ——

Loosen axle shaft nuts only while the car is on the ground. The leverage required to do this could topple the car from a lift or jack stand.

2. Raise the front end of the vehicle and support it securely on jack stands. Make matching marks on the control arm and ball joint so that the ball joint can be reinstalled in the same location on the control arm. Remove the two ball joint mounting nuts.

3. Clean around the inner CV joint and remove the six 8 mm, 12-point socket-head bolts that hold the inner CV joint to the transaxle drive flange. Support the inner end of the drive axle to prevent damage to the outer CV joint.

4. Remove the axle shaft nut and pull the drive axle out of the wheel hub. Cover the exposed inner CV joints to prevent contamination.

NOTE ——

A light tap with a soft-faced mallet will help dislodge a stubborn axle.

Installation is the reverse of removal. Stick a new adhesive-backed gasket onto the clean inner CV joint. Torque the 8 mm, 12-point socket-head bolts to 45 Nm (33 ft. lb.). Torque the control arm ball joint clamping bolt to 50 Nm (37 ft. lb.). Torque the axle shaft nut to 230 Nm (170 ft. lb.).

WARNING ——

Torque the axle shaft nut only while the car is on the ground. The leverage required to do this could topple the car off a lift or jack stand.

Removing and Installing Constant Velocity Joints

Fig. 5-4 is an exploded view of a drive axle and its two constant velocity joints. Notice the ridges that are forged into the shaft for the purpose of holding the rubber boots in place. New circlips should be used when reinstalling the joints, and new clamps should be used to fasten the boots.

NOTE ——

Because the CV joints must be removed to replace the boots, it is good preventive maintenance to replace the boots whenever the CV joints are removed.

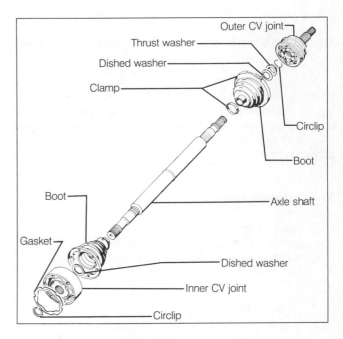

Fig. 5-4. Drive axle assembly showing inner and outer constant velocity joints and attachment parts.

To remove and install the CV joints, it is necessary to first remove the drive axles as described above. CV joints are not rebuildable, and must be replaced as complete units. Volkswagen specifies a special molybdenum disulfide grease for packing CV joints. See **LUBRICATION AND MAINTENANCE** for more information on CV joint lubricant. Some special tools and equipment are required to remove and install CV joints. Read the procedure carefully before starting work. If you lack the necessary tools and equipment, or a suitable workplace, we suggest leaving these repairs to an authorized Volkswagen dealer or other qualified repair shop.

To remove and install outer CV joint:

1. Cut and remove the large clamp holding the rubber boot to the CV joint. Fold the boot back from the joint, inside out over the shaft.

2. Clamp the shaft in a vise, and drive the joint off the shaft, as shown in Fig. 5-5, using a soft-faced mallet. Remove the thrust washer, the dished washer, and the circlip from the axle and inspect the shaft for wear.

NOTE ———

The CV joint is secured to the shaft with a circlip that is inaccessible. The force used to drive the joint off the shaft must be sufficient to override the clip, but not enough to cause damage to the joint.

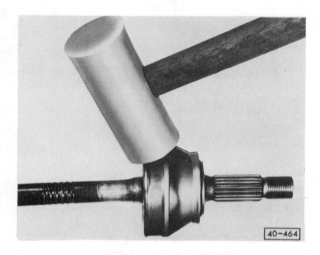

Fig. 5-5. Outer CV joint being driven off axle shaft with soft-faced mallet (shown with boot removed for clarity).

3. When installing the joint, use a new circlip in the groove at the end of the axle shaft. See Fig. 5-6. Drive the joint onto the shaft until the circlip is seated. Fold the boot back over the joint, using a new clamp to hold it.

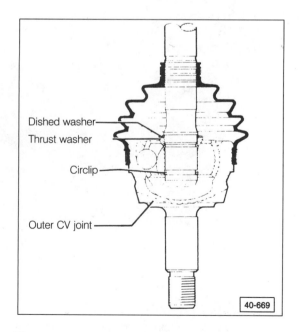

Fig. 5-6. Cutaway view of outer CV joint, showing positions of circlip and washers.

To remove and install inner CV joint:

1. Remove the circlip from the end of the axle shaft, as shown in Fig. 5-7.

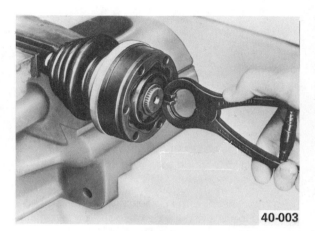

Fig. 5-7. Removing circlip which holds inner CV joint to axle shaft.

2. Drive the protective cap off of the outer ring of the joint, as shown in Fig. 5-8, and fold the boot away from the joint, inside out over the axle shaft.

CAUTION ———

Do not pivot the ball hub more than 20° in the outer ring of the joint. The balls will fall out if the hub is pivoted too far.

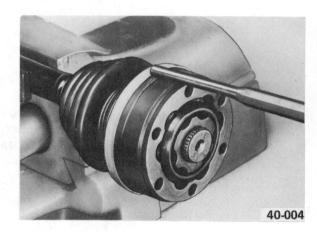

Fig. 5-8. Driving off CV joint protective cap with drift and hammer.

3. Support the hub of the CV joint and press the axle shaft out of the joint, as shown in Fig. 5-9.

4. Remove the dished washer and inspect the shaft and the splines for wear and damage.

11

Fig. 5-9. Driving axle shaft out of inner CV joint with punch (drift) and thrust plate (support).

5. When installing the CV joint, use a new dished washer and install it with the concave surface facing the end of the shaft, as shown in Fig. 5-10.

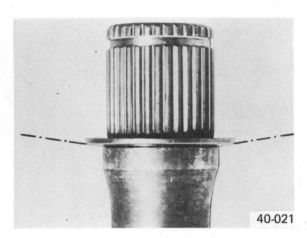

Fig. 5-10. Correct installation of dished washer used with inner CV joint on end of drive axle.

6. Press the joint onto the shaft as shown in Fig. 5-11. While using the press to hold the hub of the CV joint against the dished washer, install the circlip in the groove on the end of the shaft.

7. Release the press and make sure that the circlip is completely seated in the groove. Install the protective cap around the edge of the CV joint.

Disassembling and Inspecting Constant Velocity Joints

The components of each CV joint are precisely matched during manufacture and they cannot be serviced individually. The joints can, however, be disassembled for cleaning, inspection, and repacking with lubricant. Begin the inspection of a CV joint before it is disassembled. The balls and grooves allow the inner hub to move relative to the outer housing, but the parts should fit snugly and move with some effort. A joint with obvious freeplay should be replaced. Polished interior surfaces or visible ball tracks are not necessarily cause for replacement.

Fig. 5-11. Pressing inner CV joint onto drive axle shaft. Press tool shown, Volkswagen special tool no. VW 522 (order no. TV0 522 000 00 ZEL), allows installation of circlip while CV joint and washer are being pressed.

To disassemble outer CV joint:

1. With the CV joint removed from the drive axle as described above, mark the relative positions of the hub, the cage, and the outer housing.

2. Swivel the cage and hub as shown in Fig. 5-12 to remove the balls one at a time. Keep track of the removed balls so that they can be reinstalled in the same relationship to each other and to the marked hub and cage.

Fig. 5-12. Hub and cage of outer CV joint swivelled for removal of balls. Notice mark on outer housing. Similar marks should be made on hub and cage.

3. Remove the hub and cage as a unit, turning them so that the two large rectangular openings in the cage are positioned as shown in Fig. 5-13, and remove the hub and cage.

Fig. 5-13. Large rectangular openings in cage (arrow) in position for cage and hub removal.

4. Remove the hub from the cage. Turn the hub so that one of the splines is in line with one of the large rectangular openings in the cage. See Fig. 5-14. The hub now has sufficient clearance to be tipped out of the ball cage.

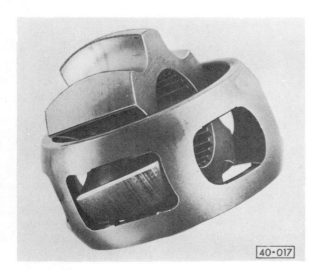

Fig. 5-14. Hub in position for removal or installation. Rectangular opening just accommodates spline of hub.

5. Clean and inspect the joint for galling, pitting, and other wear or damage. Replace any joint that is worn or damaged in these ways.

Assembly of the outer CV joint is the reverse of disassembly. Thoroughly coat all parts with molybdenum disulfide grease, and pack the joint with approximately 45 grams (1 ½ oz.) of the grease. This is half the total amount required for one CV joint. Make sure that the markings made on the housing, hub, and cage during disassembly line up. Install the joint on the drive axle as described in **Removing and Installing Constant Velocity Joints**. Finish packing the joint with another 45 grams of molybdenum disulfide grease.

To disassemble inner CV joint:

1. With the CV joint removed from the drive axle as described above, mark the relative positions of the hub, the cage, and the outer housing.

2. Pivot the hub and cage 90° to the housing, as shown in Fig. 5-15, and then push it out of the housing.

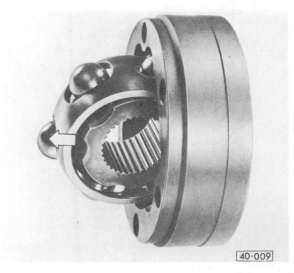

Fig. 5-15. Inner CV joint hub and cage with balls being separated from housing. Pivot hub and cage until perpendicular to housing, then push in direction indicated by arrow.

3. Remove the balls one at a time. Keep track of the removed balls so that they can be reinstalled in the same relationship to each other and to the marked hub and cage.

11

CAUTION ━━

The cage, housing, and balls are precisely matched during manufacture. When disassembling more than one joint, do not intermix components between joints.

4. Rotate the ball hub into the position shown in Fig. 5-16. The ball grooves on the hub must be in line with the outer edge of the cage. The hub now has sufficient clearance to be rotated out of the cage.

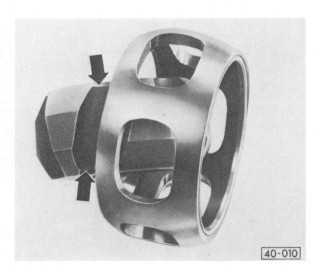

Fig. 5-16. Hub being removed or installed. Arrows indicate alignment of hub ball groove with edge of cage.

To assemble inner CV joint:

1. Clean and inspect the joint for galling, pitting, and other wear or damage. Replace any joint that is worn or damaged in these ways.

2. Thoroughly coat all components with molybdenum disulfide grease, and install the hub in the cage as illustrated in Fig. 5-16 above.

3. Install the balls in the cage, as shown in Fig. 5-17, using the adhesion of the molybdenum disulfide grease to hold the balls in place.

Fig. 5-17. Balls being installed in inner CV joint cage and hub.

4. Insert the hub and cage with the balls into the outer housing.

> **CAUTION** ━━
>
> *The chamfer on the inner splines of the hub (visible in Fig. 5-17) must face the drive axle and the larger diameter side of the outer housing.*

> **NOTE** ━━
>
> Align the components so that when the hub and cage are rotated into place, the widely-spaced grooves in the hub will line up with the widely-spaced grooves in the outer housing (**a**), and the closely-spaced grooves in the hub (**b**) will line up with the closely-spaced grooves in the outer housing, as shown in Fig. 5-18.

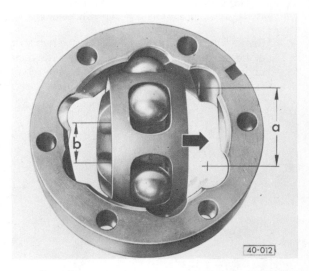

Fig. 5-18. Inner CV joint hub and cage positioned for assembly in outer housing. Wide grooves in housing (**a**) mate with wide grooves in hub. Narrow grooves in hub (**b**) mate with narrow grooves in housing. Arrow indicates direction in which hub and cage assembly is turned to install.

5. Pivot the hub and cage, as shown in Fig. 5-19, until the balls align with the grooves in the outer housing.

6. When the alignment is correct, press on the cage as indicated in Fig. 5-20 until it swings into place.

> **CAUTION** ━━
>
> *The CV joint should go together firmly but smoothly. Heavy force should not be required. If in doubt, start over and recheck the alignment. A joint which is forced together incorrectly may not come apart again.*

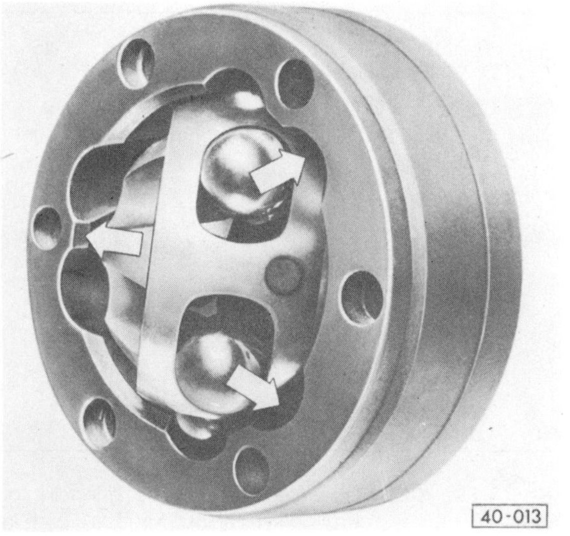

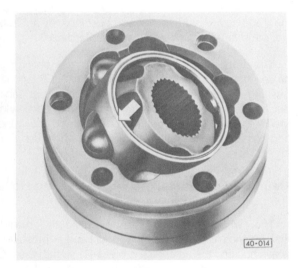

Fig. 5-19. Hub being rotated within cage to align balls with grooves of outer housing (arrows).

Fig. 5-20. Balls being engaged in grooves of outer housing. Apply only hand pressure at point indicated by arrow.

7. Check the operation of the joint. The hub should be able to move smoothly throughout its entire range of travel.

8. Pack the joint with 90 grams (3 oz.) of molybdenum disulfide grease, using 2/3 of the grease on the outer side of the joint, and the remaining 1/3 on the other side.

Removing and Installing Drive Axle Vibration Damper

On some models, a vibration damper is installed on the right (passenger-side) drive axle to help reduce vibration. No maintenance is required. Its installation is shown in Fig. 5-21.

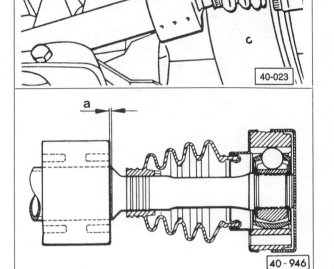

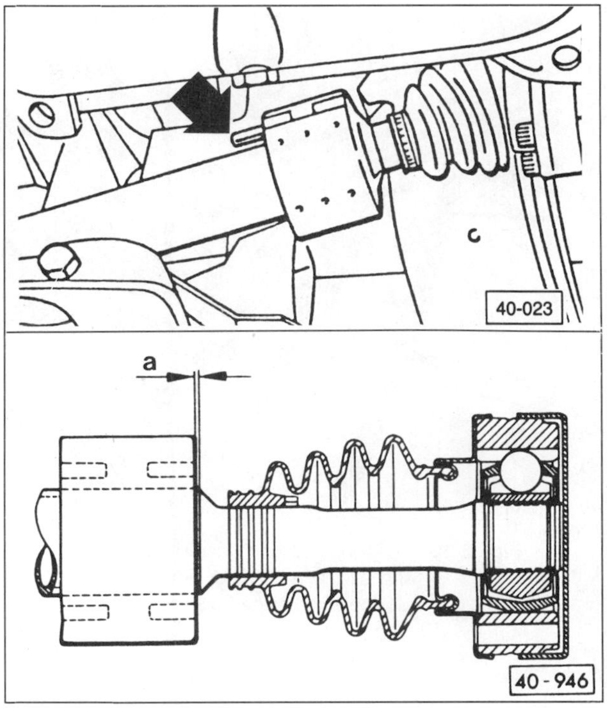

Fig. 5-21. Drive axle vibration damper held in place by pin (arrow, top). Remove pin to separate halves of absorber. On installation, dimension **a** is 4.0 mm (.157 in.).

5.3 Ball Joints

The ball joints provide a precise but moveable connection between the wheel bearing housing and the lower suspension control arm. The ball joints are permanently lubricated and surrounded by a protective rubber boot. No ball joint maintenance is required, except for periodic inspection to check for wear.

Inspecting and Replacing Control Arm Ball Joints

The ball joints should be checked regularly for freeplay. A simple inspection of the ball joints involves using a pry bar to check freeplay and a caliper or ruler to measure it. Replacing a ball joint requires a new lockplate and bolts and, following the repair, a wheel alignment.

To inspect:

1. Lift the front end of the car and support it securely on jack stands which are designed for the purpose.

2. Place the tip of the pry bar directly under the socket of the ball joint, and place the metal spacer between the shank of the pry bar and the wheel rim as shown in Fig. 5-22.

3. Check for movement of the ball joint socket relative to the wheel bearing housing. Replace any ball joints that can be compressed 2.5 mm (.10 in.) or more. For reference, the freeplay in new ball joints is about 1.0 mm (.04 in.).

11

Fig. 5-22. Checking ball joint wear with pry bar on ball joint, and spacer on wheel rim for use as support. Moving lever (arrow) will compress joint.

To replace:

1. With the front of the car raised and supported securely on jack stands, remove the wheel.

2. Disconnect the stabilizer bar link rod from the control arm.

3. Loosen and remove the clamping bolt that holds the ball joint stud in the wheel bearing housing, and then pull or pry the stud out of the housing.

> **NOTE** ———
>
> If the old ball joint is to be reinstalled, mark its position on the control arm for reinstallation. Use a marker. Do not scratch the paint.

4. Remove the three bolts holding the ball joint to the control arm, and remove the old ball joint. Remove the lockplate from the top of the control arm and discard it.

Installation is the reverse of removal. Install the new ball joint as shown in Fig. 5-23, using M8 x 24 bolts and a new lockplate. Torque the bolts to 25 Nm (18 ft. lb.). Torque the stabilizer bar link rod nut to 25 Nm (18 ft. lb.) and the ball joint clamping bolt to 50 Nm (37 ft. lb.).

> **CAUTION** ———
>
> The position of the ball joint in the slotted mounting holes is set during manufacture to match drive axle length. When installing a replacement ball joint, position the joint in the center of the slotted mounting holes.

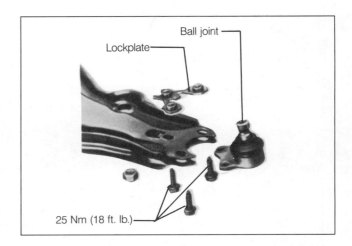

Fig. 5-23. Replacement ball joint being installed on control arm. Center replacement ball joint in slotted mounting holes.

5.4 Bearings and Bushings

The front suspension includes wheel bearings, strut bearings, and suspension control arm bushings. All are subject to wear and deterioration, and all are replaceable.

The strut bearings are replaced by disassembling the struts as described in **5.1 Front Suspension Struts.** The control arm bushings are press-fit into the control arms and can be replaced after removing the control arms. The wheel bearings are press-fit into the wheel bearing housing and the wheel hub, and can be replaced after removing the wheel bearing housing.

Removing and Installing Wheel Bearing Housings and Wheel Bearings

The wheel bearings are permanently sealed and maintenance-free. The bearing inner race is press-fit on the wheel hub and the outer race is press-fit into the wheel bearing housing. The bearing, therefore, is normally destroyed as it is removed.

Removal of the wheel bearing and installation of the new one both require a press. If a press is not available, arrangements should be made to have this press work done at an authorized Volkswagen dealer or other automotive machine shop.

Plan to use new self-locking nutson the tie rod end and ball joint clamping bolt, as well as new circlips to install the new wheel bearing.

To remove wheel bearing housing:

1. With the vehicle on the ground, pry off the dust cap in the center of the front wheel hub and loosen, but do not remove, the axle shaft nut.

> **WARNING** ———
>
> Loosen axle shaft nuts only while the car is on the ground. The leverage required to do this could topple the car off a lift or jack stand.

2. Raise the front end of the vehicle and support it securely on jack stands.

3. Remove the two bolts holding the brake caliper to the bearing housing, and suspend it from the coil spring using a stiff wire. Remove the countersunk screw that holds the brake rotor to the wheel hub and remove the brake rotor. Also see **BRAKES** for more information on disassembly and assembling the brake components.

> **CAUTION** ▬
>
> *Do not allow the caliper to hang by the brake line. Doing this could damage the line and cause brake failure.*

> **NOTE** ▬
>
> By leaving the brake line attached to the caliper, there will be no need to bleed the brake system.

4. Remove the nut holding the tie rod end to the steering arm, and use a puller to remove the tie rod end, as shown in Fig. 5-24.

> **CAUTION** ▬
>
> *The puller is used to prevent thread damage. Do not use a hammer.*

Fig. 5-24. Puller being used to disconnect tie rod end (car shown is not one of those covered by this manual).

5. Disconnect the stabilizer bar from the control arm.

6. Remove the nut and clamping bolt holding the ball joint stud in the bottom of the wheel bearing housing, and remove the ball joint from the housing so that the control arm hangs free.

7. While supporting the bearing housing and drive axle, remove the bolts mounting the strut to the bearing housing.

8. Remove the axle shaft nut and pull the bearing housing off the stub axle.

> **NOTE** ▬
>
> A light tap with a soft-faced mallet will help dislodge a stubborn splined stub axle.

Installation is the reverse of removal. Torque the bolts holding the strut to the bearing housing to 80 Nm (59 ft. lb.). Install the ball joint with a new self-locking nut and torque the clamping bolt to 50 Nm (37 ft. lb.). Torque the stabilizer bar link rod nut to 25 Nm (18 ft. lb.). Install the tie rod end in the steering arm with a new self-locking nut and torque to 35 Nm (26 ft. lb.). Remount the brake caliper to the wheel bearing housing and torque the mounting bolts to 25 Nm (18 ft. lb.). Install a new axle nut and torque it to 230 Nm (170 ft. lb.). Torque the wheel lug bolts to 110 Nm (81 ft. lb.).

> **WARNING** ▬
>
> *Always loosen or tighten axle nuts while the car is on the ground. The leverage required to do this could topple the car from a lift or jack stand.*

To remove and install front wheel bearings:

1. Remove the wheel bearing housing from the car as described above, then remove the brake disc splash shield.

2. From behind, press the hub out of the wheel bearing housing.

3. Remove the inner bearing race from the hub using a bearing puller as shown in Fig. 5-25.

11

Fig. 5-25. Wheel bearing inner race being removed from hub. Clamping-type puller, as shown, is highly recommended.

4. Remove the circlips from the bearing housing on either side of the bearing outer race, and then press out the rest of the bearing, as shown in Fig. 5-26.

Fig. 5-26. Wheel bearing outer race being pressed out of bearing housing after circlips are removed. Numbers shown identify Volkswagen special tools for press work.

5. Install a new circlip into the innermost groove in the wheel bearing housing. Lubricate the bearing seat with the molybdenum disulfide grease that is supplied with the new bearing, and press in the new bearing, as shown in Fig. 5-27, making sure to press only on the bearing outer race. Then install a new circlip in the outer groove of the housing.

Fig. 5-27. New wheel bearing being pressed into wheel bearing housing. Press on outer bearing race only.

6. Press the hub into the bearing as shown in Fig. 5-28. Be sure to support the bearing on the inner race only.

7. Reinstall the wheel bearing housing on the car as described above.

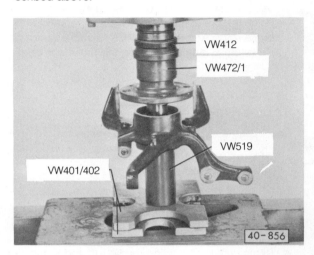

Fig. 5-28. Wheel hub being pressed into bearing. Press tool must support bearing inner race only.

Control Arm Bushings

The control arm and the control arm bushings are shown in Fig. 5-29. The control arm bushings are replaced by removing the control arms from the car. The rubber bushings are somewhat flexible, but they are a tight fit and a press is recommended for removal and installation. If a press is not available, arrangements should be made to have this press work done at an authorized Volkswagen dealer or other automotive machine shop.

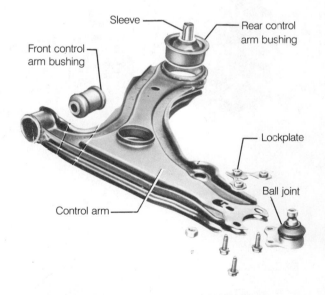

Fig. 5-29. Exploded view of control arm showing control arm bushings. Ball joint should not be loosened except when being replaced.

To replace the control arm bushings, raise the car and support it on jack stands. Remove the control arm mounting bolts and remove the sleeve from the rear control arm bushing. Disconnect the stabilizer bar. Remove the ball joint clamping bolt and separate the ball joint from the wheel bearing housing.

NOTE ——

Leave the ball joint attached to the control arm unless it too is being replaced.

Press out the old control arm bushings, using a press as shown in Fig. 5-30. Alternately, a hand puller may be used to press out the bushings as shown in Fig. 5-31. On installation, the rear bushing must be oriented as shown in Fig. 5-32. Use soft soap to lubricate new control arm bushings for installation.

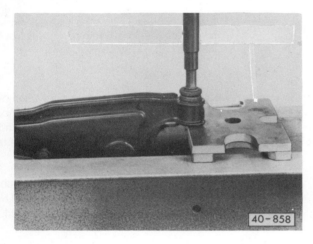

Fig. 5-30. Front bushing being pressed out of control arm with hydraulic press and punch. New bushing is installed in same manner.

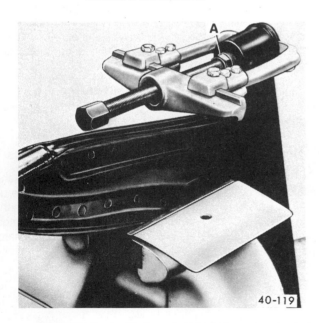

Fig. 5-31. Front control arm bushing being pressed out of control arm using hand puller. Use bolt (**A**) with depression in head to keep puller centered. Car shown is not one of those covered in this manual.

NOTE ——

To aid in removing a siezed bushing, cut through the rubber, and through the metal sleeve of the bushing, taking care not to cut into the control arm.

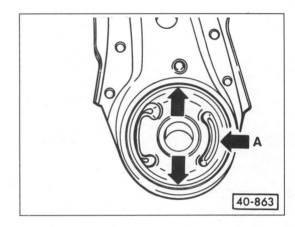

Fig. 5-32. Correct orientation of rear bushing in control arm. Align with indentation in control arm (arrows). Kidney-shaped opening in bushing (**A**) must face toward center of car.

Install the control arm using a new sleeve in the rear control arm bushing. Use a new self-locking nut on the ball joint clamping bolt and torque the bolt to 50 Nm (37 ft. lb.). Connect the stabilizer bar and torque the nut to 25 Nm (18 ft. lb.). Torque the control arm mounting bolts to 130 Nm (96 ft. lb.).

Repairing Subframe Mounting

If the rear control arm mounting bolt threads in the subframe become stripped or damaged, a longer bolt is available to replace the old bolt, precluding the need to weld a new cap nut to the body of the vehicle. Drill through the cap nut with a 10.2 mm (13/32 in.) bit, and use an M12 x 1.5 tap to cut new threads. The new longer bolt is Volkswagen part no. N 101 030.01.

11

6. REAR SUSPENSION

The cars covered by this manual have rear shock absorbers and springs assembled concentrically, in a strut arrangement. Unlike the front suspension, the rear springs and shock absorbers can be safely separated without the use of a spring compressor.

The rear wheel bearings do not routinely require maintenance. However, cleaning, repacking with grease, and adjusting the rear wheel bearings are necessary parts of rear brake service and much of the work described here will be performed in conjunction with work described in **BRAKES**.

The rear suspension components which are most likely to require maintenance or repair are readily accessible and can be removed with standard tools. The wheel bearing outer races, however, should be removed and installed in the brake drum or rotor using a press. When performing any maintenance or repair of the rear suspension or brakes, please observe the following general cautions.

CAUTION ━━

●*Do not reinstall bolts and nuts coated with undercoating wax as correct tightening torque cannot be assured on installation. Always clean the threads of removed bolts and nuts with a solvent before installation, or replace them with new parts.*

● *If the axle beam has been removed, or if for any other reason the brake lines have been disconnected, reassembly must include bleeding air from the brake system and readjusting the brakes as described in* **BRAKES.**

● *Do not weld or attempt to straighten a damaged rear axle beam or rear stub axles.*

● *Use only multipurpose (lithium) grease to lubricate the rear wheel bearings. Other greases will not maintain adequate lubrication and may lead to premature bearing failure.*

6.1 Rear Shock Absorbers and Springs

The rear shock absorbers are removed and installed like any conventional stand-alone shock absorber. In this case, the coil spring is removed or installed at the same time. When the rear suspension is fully extended, as when the car is supported on jack stands, the springs will no longer be compressed and can be removed safely.

For information on checking shock absorbers and determining when replacement is necessary, see **Checking Shock Absorbers,** found under **5.1 Front Suspension Struts.**

Removing and Installing Rear Shock Absorbers and Springs

The rear shock absorbers are mounted with conventional hardware which should not require any special tools for removal and installation, however, a Volkswagen special tool is available for use in removing and installing the top nut which is difficult to reach.

Remove and install the shock absorber and spring assemblies one side at a time only, in order to prevent the rear axle assembly from hanging unsupported and damaging the brake lines.

To remove and install:

1. Inside the car, snap off the plastic cap that covers the upper shock absorber mount. See Fig. 6-1. Loosen and remove the nut and the dished washer beneath the nut.

2. Raise the car slowly until the coil spring is unloaded and the top of the shock absorber and spring assembly begins to pull away from the body.

NOTE ━━

When jacking, do not use any part of the suspension for a lifting point. The axle beam and trailing arms must not be supporting the car.

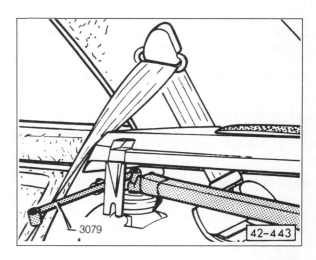

Fig. 6-1. Rear shock absorber mounting nut being removed from inside car using Volkswagen special tool no. 3079 (order no. T03 079 000 42 ZEL).

3. Position jack stands to support the car securely. Remove the nut and bolt that mount the bottom of the shock absorber to the trailing arm, and remove the assembly from the car. Fig. 6-2 illustrates the components of the shock absorber and spring assembly.

4. On installation, use a new self-locking nut at the bottom shock absorber mount. Torque the bolt and nut to 70 Nm (52 ft. lb.). Torque the top mounting nut to 15 Nm (11 ft. lb.).

6.2 Rear Wheel Bearings

The rear wheel bearings are dual tapered roller bearings. The inner bearing races fit on the stub axles. The replaceable outer races are pressed into the brake drum or rotor. Fig. 6-3 is an exploded view of the rear wheel bearings and drum brakes. Cars with rear disc brakes are similar.

Rear wheel bearing service consists of removing the bearings, cleaning and inspecting the bearings and outer races, repacking with fresh grease, and adjusting.

Removing and Installing Rear Wheel Bearings

The rear wheel bearings can be removed, installed, and adjusted using ordinary hand tools. If the bearings are to be replaced, the bearing outer races (which are provided with the new bearings) should be replaced also. The races are most easily and properly installed using a press. The axle nut hardware is locked in place with a cotter pin which should always be replaced rather than reused.

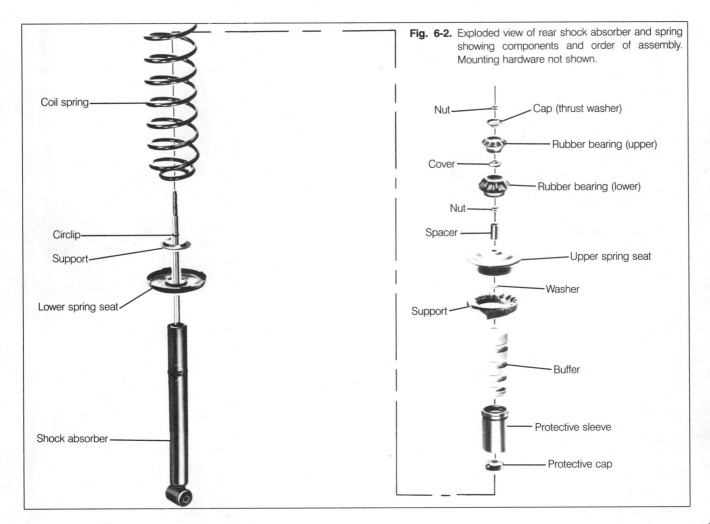

Coil spring

Circlip

Support

Lower spring seat

Shock absorber

Fig. 6-2. Exploded view of rear shock absorber and spring showing components and order of assembly. Mounting hardware not shown.

Nut — Cap (thrust washer)

Rubber bearing (upper)

Cover

Rubber bearing (lower)

Nut

Spacer

Upper spring seat

Washer

Support

Buffer

Protective sleeve

Protective cap

11

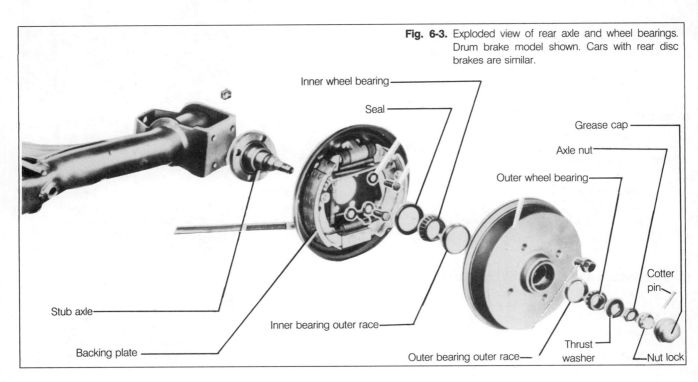

Fig. 6-3. Exploded view of rear axle and wheel bearings. Drum brake model shown. Cars with rear disc brakes are similar.

Inner wheel bearing

Seal

Grease cap

Axle nut

Outer wheel bearing

Cotter pin

Stub axle

Inner bearing outer race

Backing plate

Outer bearing outer race

Thrust washer

Nut lock

To remove:

1. Raise the rear of the car, support it securely on jack stands which are designed for the purpose, and remove the wheel.

2. On cars with drum brakes, fully back off the brake adjuster (adjust the brake shoes away from the drum) as described in **BRAKES**.

3. On cars with rear disc brakes, remove the rear brake caliper, as described in **BRAKES**, and hang it out of the way without disconnecting the brake line, using a stiff wire or equivalent.

4. Pry off the grease cap in the center of the brake drum or disc, remove the cotter pin and nut lock, and then remove the axle nut, the thrust washer, and the outer bearing.

   NOTE ━━
   If the thrust washer and outer bearing are reluctant to move, thread the axle nut back on, leaving a slight gap between it and the thrust washer. A slight jerk on the brake drum, pulling away from the car, will loosen the bearing and thrust washer. The nut will prevent scattering the parts on the ground.

5. Remove the brake drum or rotor. Pull it straight off the stub axle to prevent damage to the bearing races and the threads of the stub axle.

6. Working on the back side of the brake drum or rotor, pry the grease seal out of the recess in the hub. Lift out the inner bearing.

7. If the brake drum or rotor is being replaced, or if the bearings are being replaced, use a brass drift or punch to drive the outer bearing races out of the hub. A brass drift is used to avoid damaging the machined surfaces of the hub.

To install:

1. Clean the hub and the bearings in solvent and let dry thoroughly. Dry with compressed air if available.

   CAUTION ━━
   Do not use gasoline as a solvent as it will remove all lubrication. Also, do not let blasts of compressed air spin the unlubricated bearings.

2. Inspect the bearing rollers and races. Replace any that is pitted, burred, rough, or heat-blued.

3. Install the outer bearing races in the hub, using a hydraulic press as shown in Fig. 6-4 and 6-5.

4. Pack the inner bearing with multipurpose grease. Coat the bearing outer races in the hub with grease, and lightly coat the interior of the hub to prevent corrosion.

Fig. 6-4. New outer wheel bearing outer race being pressed into hub. Brake drum shown. Installation in disc brake rotor is similar.

Fig. 6-5. New inner wheel bearing outer race being pressed into hub. Brake drum shown. Installation in disc brake rotor is similar.

CAUTION ━━
Use only multipurpose (lithium) grease to lubricate the rear wheel bearings. Other greases will not maintain adequate lubrication and may lead to bearing failure.

NOTE ━━
When packing bearings, cup the grease in the palm of your hand and force it into the bearing all possible ways, especially around the rollers from the ends, until the bearing is completely filled with grease and it oozes out the other side. If in doubt, pack in some more.

5. Place the inner bearing in its outer race on the back side of the hub, and press in a new grease seal.

6. Lightly coat the surface of the stub axle with grease, and slide the brake drum or rotor onto the stub axle. Move carefully to avoid damaging the grease seal or the bearing races on the threads of the stub axle.

7. Pack the outer bearing with multipurpose grease, and slide it over the stub axle and into its outer race. Install the thrust washer and the axle nut. Tighten the nut until the bearings just contact their outer races and the assembly just starts to become snug.

8. Adjust wheel bearing end thrust as described in **Adjusting Rear Wheel Bearings** below.

9. Fill the grease cap with approximately 10 grams (5/16 oz.) of multipurpose grease. Install the grease cap using a soft-faced mallet.

10. On cars with disc brakes, install the rear brake caliper as described in **BRAKES**.

11. On cars with drum brakes, adjust the brakes as described in **BRAKES**.

12. Install the wheel and tire. Torque the lug bolts to 110 Nm (81 ft. lb.).

Adjusting Rear Wheel Bearings

The rear wheel tapered roller bearings must be adjusted to work smoothly and minimize wear. This adjustment must be made any time the rear brake drum or rotor has been removed. Other periodic bearing adjustments to compensate for wear may help to increase bearing life or give early warning of excessive wear and the need for replacement. The only materials needed are a little extra multipurpose grease for the grease cap, and new cotter pins.

To adjust:

1. Raise the rear of the car, support it securely on jack stands which are designed for the purpose, and remove the wheel.

2. Pry off the grease cap in the center of the brake drum or disc, remove the cotter pin and nut lock, and then loosen the axle nut.

3. If the wheel bearings, especially new ones, have just been installed, temporarily torque the axle nut to 10 Nm (87 in. lb.), while turning the brake drum or rotor by hand.

> **CAUTION** ━━
>
> *Avoid overtorquing the axle nut, as this may damage the bearings and bearing races.*

4. Tighten the axle nut again, slowly and in small increments, until the thrust washer can just barely be moved

back and forth with the tip of a screwdriver, as shown in Fig. 6-6.

> **NOTE** ━━
>
> Do not twist or pry with the screwdriver. Use hand pressure only.

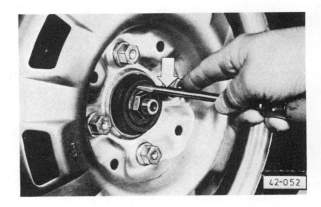

Fig. 6-6. Wheel bearing adjustment being checked. Axle nut is tightened correctly when thrust washer moves with slight pressure.

5. After the wheel bearings are correctly adjusted, install the nut lock so that its projections do not cover the cotter pin hole. If necessary, tighten the axle nut slightly so that the nut lock will align with the hole in the stub axle. Then install a new cotter pin.

6.3 Rear Axle Beam

The rear suspension can be removed and installed as a unit for replacement or for facilitating rear body repairs. The axle beam is mounted to the body by brackets at the front of the axle, cushioned and supported by replaceable rubber bushings. Replacement of the axle beam bushings also requires removal of the axle assembly and mounting brackets.

Removing and Installing Rear Suspension as a Unit

The car must be raised high enough to remove the axle assembly, so a lift or a jack and suitable jack stands are required. Removal of the axle assembly also requires disconnecting brake lines to the rear wheels, and bleeding the brakes when reinstallation is complete.

To remove:

1. Disconnect the parking brake cables at the parking brake lever between the front seats. See **BRAKES**.

> **NOTE** ━━
>
> If the car can be raised and safely supported high enough, the shock absorber and spring units can stay attached to the axle beam at the bottom and be removed with the axle beam.

11

2. Remove the rear shock absorbers and springs as described above in **Removing and Installing Rear Shock Absorbers and Springs**.

3. Disconnect the flexible rear brake hoses from the rigid brake lines near the forward edge of the axle beam. Cap both ends of the open connection to prevent contamination.

4. On GTI and all Jetta models, disconnect the brake pressure regulator spring from the bracket attached to the axle beam. See **BRAKES**.

5. While supporting the front of the axle beam so that it cannot fall, loosen and remove the bolts which hold the axle beam mounting brackets to the car body.

6. Remove the rear suspension assembly by pulling it out to the rear.

To install:

1. If the axle beam mounting brackets have been removed from the axle beam, or if the pivot bolts have been loosened, align the mounting brackets at 12°±2° as shown in Fig. 6-7, then torque the pivot bolts and their nuts to 60 Nm (44 ft. lb.).

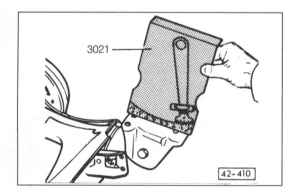

Fig. 6-7. Axle beam mounting brackets being aligned at 12°±2° angle to axle beam prior to axle beam installation. Protractor shown is Volkswagen special tool no. 3021.

2. Position the rear suspension assembly under the car and loosely install the mounting bolts. Position the right (passenger-side) mounting bracket so that the bolts are centered in the elongated holes, and torque them to 85 Nm (63 ft. lb.).

3. Using two prybars, push the left (driver's-side) mounting bracket to the left, leaving only a slight gap between the inside of the bushing and the mounting bracket, as shown in Fig. 6-8. Torque the mounting bracket bolts to 85 Nm (63 ft. lb.).

4. Clean the brake line unions and reconnect the flexible brake hoses to the rigid brake lines. Torque the unions to 15 to 20 Nm (11 to 15 ft. lb.).

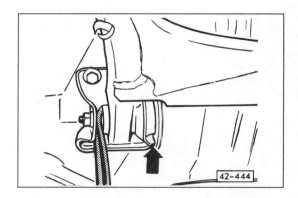

Fig. 6-8. Positioning left axle beam mounting bracket with prybars. Move bracket to left, leaving slight gap (arrow).

5. Remount the rear shock absorbers and springs. Carefully lower the car while guiding the top shock absorber mounts into their mounting holes.

6. Reconnect the top shock absorber mounts as described in **Removing and Installing Rear Shock Absorbers and Springs**. Torque the nuts to 15 Nm (11 ft. lb.).

7. Reconnect the parking brake cables.

8. Bleed the brakes and adjust the parking brake as described in **BRAKES**.

Replacing Axle Beam Bushings

To replace the axle beam bushings, remove the rear suspension as a unit, as described above. Remove the pivot bolts and the mounting brackets and press out the bushings as shown in Fig. 6-9.

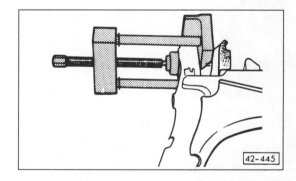

Fig. 6-9. Rear axle bushing being pressed out of rear axle beam.

The new bushings should be aligned with the larger rubber portion facing front, as shown in Fig. 6-10. Press the new bushings into place so that the bushing protrudes 8.0 mm (5/16 in.), as shown in Fig. 6-11. Reinstall the axle beam as described in **Removing and Installing Rear Suspension as a Unit**, above.

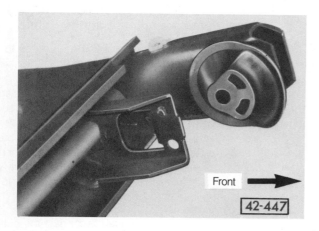

Fig. 6-10. New axle beam bushing correctly installed. Larger rubber section faces front, as shown.

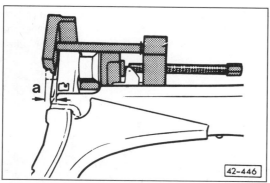

Fig. 6-11. Rear axle beam bushing being pressed in. Bushing protrusion dimension (**a**) is 8.0 mm (5/16 in.).

7. STEERING

The steering wheel and steering column are connected to the rack and pinion steering gear by a flexible universal joint shaft. When the steering wheel turns, the steering rack moves the tie rods to turn the wheels. Power-assisted steering operates the same way, except that hydraulic pressure is used to boost the response of the steering gear and reduce steering effort. Fig. 7-1 is an exploded view of the basic steering system without power assist. The steering column connects to the upper end of the universal joint shaft.

Wear and excessive play or clearance anywhere in the system will cause sloppy, loose-feeling, and imprecise steering. The steering gearbox itself can be adjusted to compensate for wear. Otherwise, the steering system is serviced only by the replacement of worn parts.

Except where specifically noted, sections **7.1 Steering Column** and **7.2 Steering Gear and Tie Rods** apply to both manual and power-assisted steering. The hydraulic components which are unique to the power-assisted steering system are covered in **7.3 Power-assisted Steering**.

11

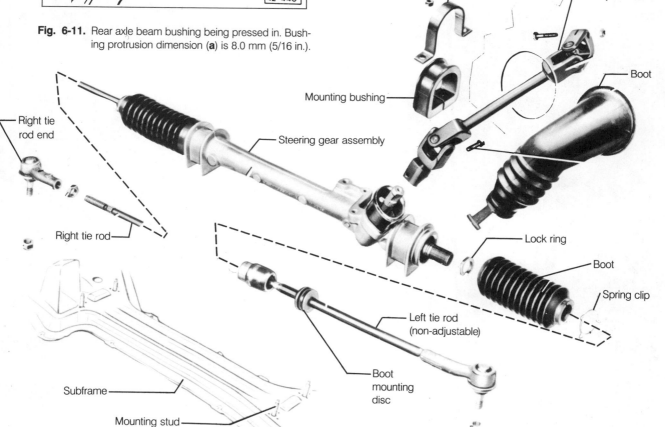

Fig. 7-1. Exploded view of steering gear and tie rods showing subframe mounting and universal joint shaft for connection to steering column.

If the steering requires excessive effort, or if the steering lacks precision, the steering system may not be to blame. Faulty front suspension strut bearings or other worn front suspension parts may cause or contribute to the problem. Before checking for any suspension or steering problems, check the tires and tire inflation pressures. For more information, see **3. Troubleshooting** or **5. Front Suspension**.

7.1 Steering Column

Fig. 7-2 is an exploded view of the steering column. The steering column connects the steering wheel to the steering gear. Several accessory switches are also mounted on the tube which houses the steering column. The steering column tube is bolted to the body with shear bolts which are designed to break in the event of a collision.

Removal and installation of the steering column switches, including the windshield wipers and washers, the turn signals, the headlight high beam switch, and in some models the cruise control and multi-function indicator, is covered here. The electrical function and troubleshooting of these switches is covered in **ELECTRICAL SYSTEM**.

Removing and Installing Steering Wheel

The steering wheel must be removed for access to the steering column switches and the ignition switch. The splined connection between the steering wheel and the steering column also allows the steering wheel position to be adjusted as the final step in the wheel alignment process. The steering wheel should only be repositioned after the steering rack and tie rods are centered and adjusted as described in **7.2 Steering Gear and Tie Rods**, and if the front wheel alignment is correct. These checks are especially important for cars with power-assisted steering because the system is sensitive to the centered, straight-ahead steering wheel position.

To remove the steering wheel, first disconnect the battery negative (−) terminal. Then pry off the center cover of the steering wheel. On models with four horn pads, use a screwdriver under the center cover to pry it up.

Disconnect the wiring from the horn pad or pads. Holding the steering wheel, remove the nut and washer that hold it to the steering column. Pull the steering wheel straight off the steering column.

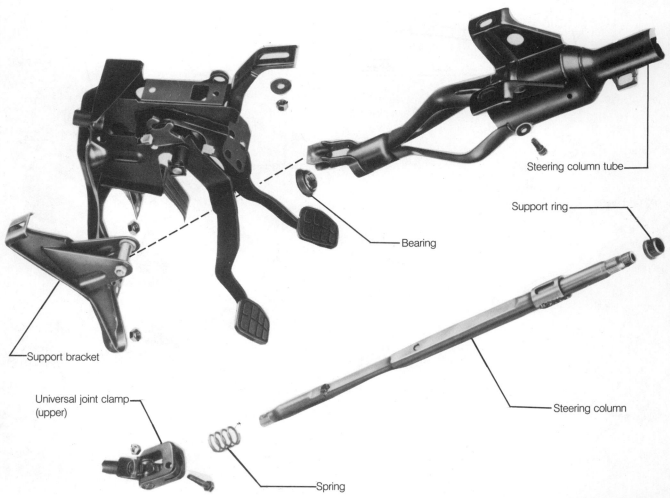

Support bracket

Universal joint clamp
(upper)

Spring

Steering column tube

Support ring

Bearing

Steering column

Fig. 7-2. Exploded view of steering column and steering column tube.

NOTE ——

Before removing the steering wheel, mark the hub and the shaft so that, unless it is being adjusted, the steering wheel can be reinstalled in exactly the same position.

Installation is the reverse of removal. When aligning the steering wheel, be sure the wheels are pointed straight ahead. Torque the nut on the steering column to 40 Nm (30 ft. lb.).

Removing and Installing Steering Column Switches

Fig. 7-3 is an exploded view of the steering wheel and steering column switches. The turn signal switch and the windshield wiper and washer switch are fastened to the top of the steering column housing by three screws. They can be replaced individually if necessary, but individual parts for repairing the switches are not available.

The ignition switch and lock cylinder also mount to the steering column housing, which in turn clamps to the steering column tube. There is no provision for adjusting the height of the steering wheel or the switches on the steering column.

To remove:

1. Remove the steering wheel as described in **Removing and Installing Steering Wheel**.

2. Remove the Phillips-head screws that hold the two halves of the steering column switch cover together, and remove the lower cover.

3. Remove the three screws that hold the turn signal and windshield wiper switch assemblies to the steering column housing. Disconnect the harness connectors from the switches and remove the switches from the steering column.

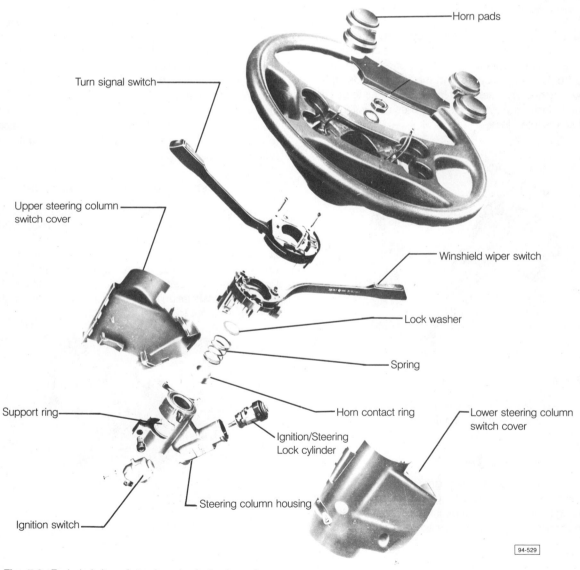

Fig. 7-3. Exploded view of steering wheel, steering column housing, and switches.

4. Remove the lock washer, the spring, and the horn contact ring. Remove the socket head bolt that clamps the steering column housing to the steering column tube.

5. Disconnect the wiring from the ignition switch. Insert the ignition key and unlock the steering. Remove the steering column housing and the ignition/steering lock, together with the upper half of the steering column switch cover.

6. Remove the ignition switch by removing the screw that holds it to the steering column housing.

Installation is the reverse of removal. Use a new lock washer on the steering column. Torque the socket-head steering column housing clamping bolt to 10 Nm (87 in. lb.). Avoid overtightening the three switch mounting screws.

Replacing Ignition/Steering Lock Cylinder

The steering column housing does not need to be removed from the steering column in order to replace or repair the lock cylinder, but removal of the entire assembly may make it easier.

To replace the ignition/steering lock cylinder, drill a 3 mm (1/8 in.) hole in the lock cylinder housing at the point indicated in Fig. 7-4. Insert a pin through the hole and press down on the spring that holds the lock cylinder in the housing. Using the ignition key may help by inserting it into the cylinder to pull the cylinder out. To install the cylinder, simply press it in without the key until it snaps into place.

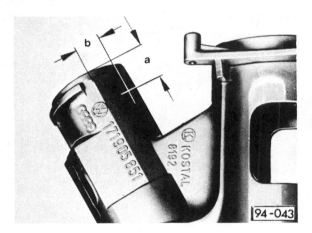

Fig. 7-4. Location of 3 mm (1/8 in.) hole to be drilled in housing for access to ignition/steering lock cylinder retaining spring. Dimension **a** is 12 mm (15/32 in.); dimension **b** is 10 mm (3/8 in.).

7.2 Steering Gear and Tie Rods

In the rack and pinion steering gear, the steering pinion translates rotary motion of the steering wheel into lateral motion of the steering rack. Tie rods connect the ends of the steering rack to the steering arms near the wheels.

The inner and outer tie rod ends are ball-jointed to combine precise steering with flexibility for suspension movement. Rub-

ber boots protect the joints and retain lubricant. Other than periodic inspections for wear or damage, no maintenance or additional lubrication is required for the life of the joints.

Adjustments to the steering rack, and adjustment or replacement of tie rods will virtually always affect wheel alignment. Plan to include a wheel alignment as the final step in any such work.

Inspecting Tie Rod Ends

There are two concerns when inspecting tie rod ends and protective boots. First, wear and excess play in the tie rod ball joints and, second, damage to the protective boot which will accelerate that wear.

Check the conditon of the inner and outer tie rod boots. Cracked or ripped inner tie rod boots can be replaced separately, perhaps prolonging the life of the tie rod end. See **Replacing Inner Tie Rod Boots**. Outer tie rod boots are not separately available. Replacement of damaged outer tie rod boots is accomplished only by replacing the tie rod.

To inspect the tie rod ends, look for unwanted play between the steering rack and the tie rods or between the tie rods and the steering arms. At the outer tie rod ends, there should be little or no vertical freeplay. At all four tie rod ends, inner and outer, there should be little or no lateral play. Any turning motion of the wheel should be directly translated to the steering rack with no freeplay in between. Try forcing mating parts in opposite directions and looking for freeplay. Replace any tie rod that fails these tests, as described in **Replacing and Adjusting Tie Rods**.

Replacing Inner Tie Rod Boots

The inner tie rod boots can be replaced without removing the tie rod from the steering rack, and alignment adjustments are not necessary as long as tie rod length is unchanged. Disconnect the outer tie rod end from the steering arm. Use a puller as shown in Fig. 7-5 to avoid damage to the threads. Remove the boot clamps and slide the boot off over the outer tie rod end. Installation is the reverse of removal. Torque the tie rod end stud nut to 35 Nm (26 ft. lb.).

Fig. 7-5. Outer tie rod end being disconnected from steering arm with puller to avoid thread damage (car shown is not one covered by this manual).

Replacing and Adjusting Tie Rods

Only complete tie rods are supplied as replacement parts. Tie rod ends for the adjustable right-side tie rod are not separately available. All replacement tie rods are adjustable. When replacing a non-adjustable left-side tie rod, the new adjustable tie rod must first be adjusted to a standard length. Use a puller to disconnect outer tie rod ends from the steering arms, as shown in Fig. 7-5 above. Use a thread locking compound such as Volkswagen's D6 when installing tie rods.

On cars with power-assisted steering, tie rod ends are torqued directly to the steering rack. Locknuts are not used. For this reason, the rack itself must be securely held when loosening or tightening the tie rod ends, to avoid damaging the steering gear. The steering gear assembly should be removed from the car and secured in a soft-jawed vise to remove and install the tie rod ends, as shown in Fig. 7-6.

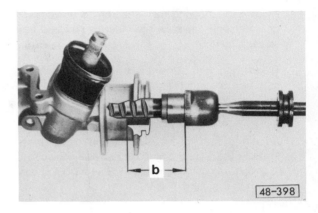

Fig. 7-7. Positioning new ball joint on manual steering rack. With rack centered, dimension **b** is 70.5 mm (2.77 in.).

6. Adjust the length of the adjustable left-side tie rod by loosening the outer tie rod end locknut and screwing the tie rod end in or out. Adjust the length to 379 mm (14.921 in.), as shown in Fig. 7-8.

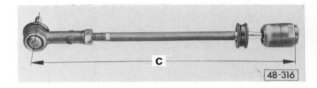

Fig. 7-8. Setting length of adjustable left-side tie rods for manual steering. Dimension **c** is 379 mm (14.921 in.).

7. On cars with manual transmission, adjust the basic right-side tie rod length to 379 mm (14.921 in.)

8. On cars with automatic transmission, adjust the basic right-side tie rod length to 381 mm (15.00 in.).

9. Reposition the inner boot on the tie rod and the steering gear housing and install the clamps. Make sure that the boot is not twisted.

10. Reconnect the tie rod end to the steering arm. Install a new self-locking nut and torque it to 35 Nm (26 ft. lb.).

11. Adjust the toe to the specifications in **4. Wheels, Tires, and Alignment**.

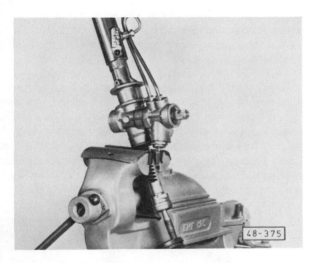

Fig. 7-6. Steering rack for power-assisted steering mounted in soft-jawed vise for removal of tie rod.

To replace and adjust (manual steering only):

1. Remove the nut from the outer tie rod end in the steering arm, and press the stud out using a puller, as shown in Fig. 7-5 above.

2. Remove the clamps that hold the tie rod boots to the steering gear housing and slide the boots back over the tie rod to expose the inner tie rod end.

3. Loosen the locknut on the inner tie rod end and unscrew the tie rod from the steering rack.

4. Center the steering gear housing, as described in **Centering Manual Steering Rack**.

5. With a new inner boot in place on the tie rod, thread the new tie rod onto the steering rack, adjusting the position of the tie rod as shown in Fig. 7-7. Tighten the locknut to hold this position.

To replace and adjust (power-assisted steering only):

1. Remove the nut from the outer tie rod end in the steering arm, and press the stud out using a puller, as shown in Fig. 7-5 above.

2. Remove the clamps that hold the tie rod boots to the steering gear housing and slide the boots back over the tie rod to expose the inner tie rod end.

11

3. Holding the steering rack securely to prevent steering gear damage, unscrew the inner tie rod end from the steering rack.

4. Clean the threads of the rack, then coat the threads of the new tie rod with locking compound. Thread the tie rod onto the rack and torque to 70 Nm (52 ft. lb.). Make sure that the boot is correctly installed and not twisted.

5. Adjust the length of the adjustable tie rods by loosening the outer tie rod end locknut and screwing the tie rod end in or out. Adjust the length to 379.5 mm (14.938 in.), as shown in Fig. 7-9.

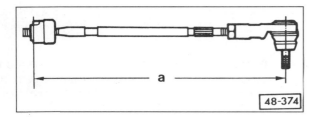

Fig. 7-9. Setting basic length of adjustable tie rods for power-assisted steering. Dimension **a** is 379.5 mm (14.938 in.).

6. Reposition the boot on the tie rod and the steering rack housing and install the clamps. Make sure that the boot is not twisted.

7. Reconnect the tie rod end to the steering arm. Install a new self-locking nut and torque it to 35 Nm (26 ft. lb.).

8. Adjust the toe to the specifications in **4. Wheels, Tires, and Alignment**.

Centering Manual Steering Rack

Centering the steering rack on a manual steering car should be the first step in any mechanical adjustments to the steering system. The rack should be centered whenever the steering gear has been installed and prior to installing tie rods.

Before centering the rack, make sure that the steering gear is firmly mounted and that the universal joint shaft is correctly installed on the pinion shaft of the gearbox.

The steering rack is properly centered when the rack protrudes an equal length from each end of the steering gear housing, as shown in Fig. 7-10. When the steering rack is centered, the steering wheel spokes should be approximately horizontal. If not, see **Removing and Installing Steering Wheel**.

Fig. 7-10. Centering manual steering rack. Dimension **a** is measured from ends of steering rack and must be equal on both ends.

Adjusting Steering Gearbox

The rack and pinion housing of the manual steering gearbox has an adjustment to correct steering play. If the steering rattles or there is play in the steering wheel with the front wheels pointed straight ahead, an adjustment of the steering gearbox may help. If the steering seems too stiff or tends not to center itself after turning, the steering adjustment may be too tight. The power-assisted steering gearbox has a similar adjustment, but it is made using a special tool with the steering gearbox removed from the car.

To adjust the manual steering gearbox, turn the front wheels to the staight ahead position. Turn the adjusting bolt shown in Fig. 7-11 clockwise to tighten the steering and counterclockwise to loosen the steering. Make a small change and road test the car. Turn the adjusting bolt no more than 20° (approximately 1/16 turn) at any one time. If the steering becomes too stiff, back off the adjusting bolt in small steps until the steering effort feels comfortable.

Fig. 7-11. Manual steering gearbox adjustment bolt (arrow) as seen from behind and beneath steering gearbox.

To adjust the power-assisted steering gearbox, remove it from the car, as described in **Removing and Installing Steering Gearbox**. Loosen the locknut and, using Volkswagen special tool VW 524 (order no. TV0 524 000 40 ZEL) as shown in Fig. 7-12, turn the hex socket head adjusting bolt until the steering rack can be moved in the housing by hand without binding. Tighten the locknut and reinstall the steering gearbox in the car.

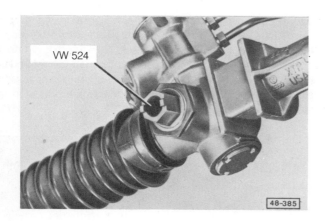

Fig. 7-12. Power-assisted steering gearbox being adjusted using Volkswagen special tool no. VW 524.

Removing and Installing Steering Gearbox

No special tools are required for removing and installing the steering gearbox, although removing and installing the power-assisted steering gearbox requires supporting the engine and transaxle from above and loosening or removing some engine and transaxle mounts.

It is not necessary to remove the steering gearbox to replace the mounting bushings. The bushings are split at the bottom and the clamps can be removed from above.

On cars with power-assisted steering, a May 1985 production change resulted in a larger universal joint clamping bolt at the connection to the steering gear. Only the later parts are available. Fitting a new universal joint shaft to an early 1985 car may require that the pinion shaft notch for the universal joint clamp bolt be made larger by approximately 1 mm (.04 in.).

To remove:

1. Disconnect the tie rod ends from the steering arms, as described in **Replacing and Adjusting Tie Rods**.

2. On cars with power-assisted steering, drain the power steering fluid as described in **7.3 Power-assisted Steering**.

3. On cars with manual transmission, remove the gearshift relay shaft bracket from the steering gear housing. See **MANUAL TRANSMISSION**.

4. On cars with power-assisted steering, clean the pressure hose and return hose unions at the steering gearbox and remove them. Do not bend the rigid tubing.

5. On cars with power-assisted steering, support the engine and transaxle as shown in Fig. 7-13, remove the rear transaxle mount, and loosen the center bolt of the rear engine mount.

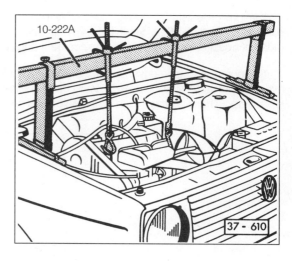

Fig. 7-13. Volkswagen special tool no. 10-222A used to safely support engine and transaxle while mounts are removed for steering gear removal on cars with power-assisted steering.

6. Remove the boot from the steering pinion housing to expose the universal joint shaft. Remove the clamp bolt and nut from the lower end of the shaft and remove the universal joint.

7. Remove the U-shaped steering gear housing mounting clamps (one right-side clamp and the left-side housing mounting on power-assisted steering cars), free the steering gear housing from the mounting studs on the subframe, and remove the steering gear housing from beneath the car.

Installation is the reverse of removal. If the rubber mounting bushings are hard and cracked or oil-soaked, they should be replaced before installation of the steering gear. Make sure that the universal joint shaft lines up with the splined shaft on the steering gearbox as it is being installed. On cars with manual steering, center the steering rack as described in **Centering Manual Steering Rack**. Torque the mounting nuts to 30 Nm (22 ft. lb.).

Torque the universal joint clamping bolt to 30 Nm (22 ft. lb.). Torque the power steering line unions to 20 Nm (15 ft. lb.). Install the relay shaft bracket and check the gearshift linkage as described in **MANUAL TRANSMISSION**. Fill the power steering system with new fluid as described in **7.3 Power-assisted Steering**. Torque the outer tie rod end nuts to 35 Nm (26 ft. lb.). When the installation is complete, a check of front wheel toe as described in **4. Wheels, Tires, and Alignment** is highly recommended, particularly if the steering gear and tie rods have been disassembled.

7.3 Power-Assisted Steering

This section covers the hydraulic portion of the power steering system, including the pump, the fluid reservoir and connecting hoses, and draining and filling the system. The mechanical part of the steering system is covered in **7.2 Steering Gear and Tie Rods**. Information on tightening or replacing the V-belt is found in **LUBRICATION AND MAINTENANCE**.

11

The power-assisted steering gear is available only as a complete assembly. Service of the steering gear, including repair of housing seal leaks, is by replacement only.

The pump is engine-driven by a V-belt, and provides the hydraulic pressure which is used to assist the movement of the steering rack. Fluid is drawn from the reservoir and pressurized by the pump. Then, depending on the position of the spool valve in the steering gearbox, fluid is directed to either side of the work piston to help move the rack. Fluid which is not doing work flows back to the fluid reservoir through the return line. Fig. 7-14 is a schematic representation of the power-assisted steering system. The system components are shown in exploded view in Fig. 7-15.

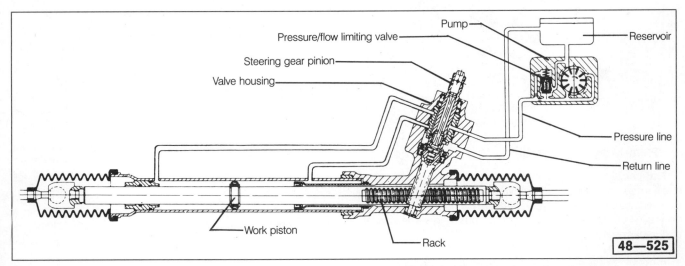

Fig. 7-14. Power steering system operation.

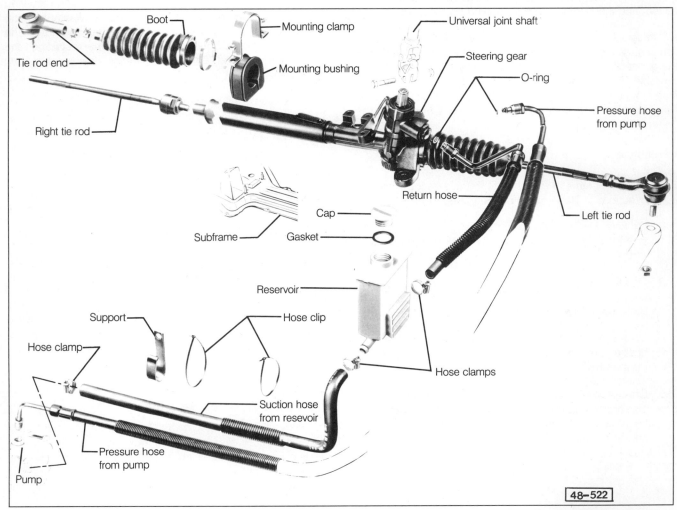

Fig. 7-15. Power-assisted steering system components

Draining and Filling Power Steering Fluid

The fluid should be drained any time the system is to be opened or fluid-bearing components removed. Refilling with new fluid is recommended. The system is essentially self-bleeding, although a simple bleeding step when refilling the system will help remove air from the fluid. Air in the system causes noisy and inconsistent operation.

To drain the fluid from the system, disconnect the suction hose from the pump, as shown in Fig. 7-16. Drain the fluid and dispose of it.

Fig. 7-16. Suction hose (arrow) to be removed from pump for draining fluid.

Refill the system with new power steering fluid, Volkswagen part no. ZVW 239 902 or equivalent, until the fluid in the reservoir is at the MAX mark. See **LUBRICATION AND MAINTENANCE** for more information on Volkswagen-approved fluids.

To bleed the system, make sure the fluid level in the reservoir is at the MAX mark and start the engine. With the help of an assistant, turn the steering wheel back and forth from full left to full right, adding fluid to the reservoir as the level drops. When the fluid level remains constant, continue turning the steering wheel until no more air bubbles appear in the reservoir. Add fluid until the fluid level is at the MAX mark. Replace the cap gasket if it is damaged.

Pressure Testing Power Steering System

The pump is tested by measuring its output pressure, as shown in Fig. 7-17. This test requires a pressure gauge with a minimum range of 0-100 bar (0-1500psi) and a valve between the gauge and the pressure line to the steering gear. Connect the gauge, with the valve open, between the pump and the pressure hose. Center the steering. Start the engine and let it idle.

To test the pump, close the valve on the gauge and quickly read the pressure. Then, open the valve. The pressure should be 76 to 82 bar (1102 to 1189 psi). If not, replace the pump.

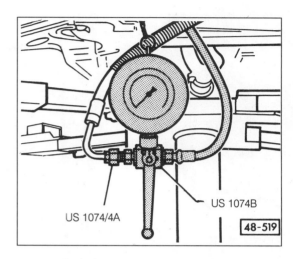

Fig. 7-17. Pressure gauge connected for measuring power steering pump pressure. Gauge shown is Volkswagen special tool no. US 1074B with US 1074/4A adapter.

CAUTION ━━

The valve should be closed for no more than 5 seconds. A longer test risks damaging the pump and/or the V-belt.

To test system pressure, leave the gauge valve open and have a helper turn the steering wheel full right and full left. At each position, the pressure with the valve open should be 76 to 82 bar (1102 to 1189 psi). If not, the steering gear should be replaced.

CAUTION ━━

Hold the steering at full left or right for no more than 5 seconds.

Power Steering Pump

The power steering pump is mounted on a bracket at the lower front side of the engine, below the coolant pump. The pump and mounting and belt-tensioning brackets are shown in exploded view in Fig. 7-18. For information on V-belt tensioning or replacement, see **LUBRICATION AND MAINTENANCE**.

11

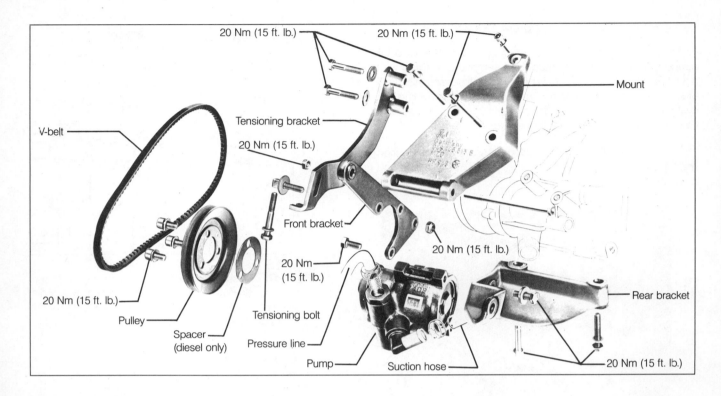

Fig. 7-18. Exploded view of power steering pump and mounting brackets.

8. SUSPENSION AND STEERING TECHNICAL DATA

I. Tightening Torques

Outer tie rod end stud to steering arm self-locking nut	.35 Nm (26 ft. lb.)
Tie rod end to tie rod locknut	.50 Nm (37 ft. lb.)
Control arm ball joint to control arm bolt and lockplate	.25 Nm (18 ft. lb.)
Control arm ball joint clamping bolt bolt and nut	.50 Nm (37 ft. lb.)
Stabilizer bar link rod to control arm nut	.25 Nm (18 ft. lb.)
Stabilizer bar bushing clamp to subframe bolt	.25 Nm (18 ft. lb.)
Front suspension strut top mounting flange self-locking nut	.60 Nm (44 ft. lb.)
Front suspension strut to wheel bearing housing bolt and nut	.80 Nm (59 ft. lb.)
Front brake caliper to wheel bearing housing socket-head bolt	.25 Nm (18 ft. lb.)
Front control arm mount to subframe bolt	.130 Nm (96 ft. lb.)
Rear control arm mount to subframe bolt	.130 Nm (96 ft. lb.)
Subframe to body bolt	.130 Nm (96 ft. lb.)
Constant velocity (CV) joint to drive flange socket-head bolt	.45 Nm (33 ft. lb.)
Drive axle to front hub self-locking nut	.230 Nm (170 ft. lb)

I. Tightening Torques (continued)

Wheel lug bolts	.110 Nm (81 ft. lb.)
Rear stub axle and brake backing plate or splash shield to trailing arm bolt and spring washer	.60 Nm (44 ft. lb.)
Rear brake caliper mount socket-head bolt	.65 Nm (48 ft. lb.)
Rear shock absorber lower mount bolt and nut	.70 Nm (52 ft. lb.)
Rear shock absorber rod upper mount nut	.15 Nm (11 ft. lb.)
Coil spring retainer to rear shock absorber nut	.15 Nm (11 ft. lb.)
Rear axle beam pivot bolt bolt and self-locking nut with captive washer	.60 Nm (44 ft. lb.)
Rear axle mounting bracket to body collar bolt	.85 Nm (63 ft. lb.)
Universal joint shaft to steering column clamp bolt and self-locking nut	.30 Nm (22 ft. lb.)
Universal joint shaft to steering gear pinion clamp bolt	.30 Nm (22 ft. lb.)
Steering gear housing to subframe nut	.30 Nm (22 ft. lb.)
Power steering hoses hose union	.20 Nm (15 ft. lb.)
Power steering pump to mounting bracket bolt	.20 Nm (15 ft. lb.)
Power steering pump pulley socket-head bolt	.20 Nm (15 ft. lb.)
Steering column housing clamping bolt socket-head bolt	.10 Nm (87 in. lb.)
Steering wheel to steering column nut and washer	.40 Nm (30 ft. lb.)
Steering column tube mount shear bolt	Tighten until heads shear

BRAKES

Contents

Introduction 3

1. General Description 4
    Master Cylinder, Vacuum Booster, and
    Brake Lines 4
    Disc Brakes 4
    Rear Drum Brakes 5
    Pressure Regulator and Proportioning Valves . 5
    Parking Brakes 5
  1.1   Brake Applications and Identification 5

2. Maintenance 5

3. Troubleshooting 5
  3.1   Basic Troubleshooting Principles 5
  3.2   Diagnostic Tests 7
  3.3   Brake Noise 7

4. Brake System Service 8
  4.1   Brake Fluid 8
  4.2   Bleeding Brakes 8
    Pressure Bleeding 9
    Vacuum Bleeding 9
    Manual Bleeding 9
    Replacing Brake Fluid 9
    Flushing the Brake System 9
  4.3   Master Cylinder and Vacuum Booster 9
    Removing and Installing Master Cylinder 10
    Removing and Installing Vacuum Booster 10
  4.4   Brake Pressure Regulator and
    Proportioning Valves 11
    Quick-checking Brake Pressure Regulator . . . 11

Pressure Testing Regulator or Proportioning
Valves 11

5. Front Disc Brakes 11
    Checking Brake Pad Wear 13
  5.1   Reconditioning Front Disc Brakes 13
    Removing and Installing Brake Pads 13
    Removing, Reconditioning, and Installing
    Brake Rotors 14
  5.2   Calipers 14

6. Rear Drum Brakes 15
    Checking Brake Lining Wear 16
  6.1   Reconditioning Rear Drum Brakes 16
    Removing and Installing Brake Shoes 16
    Reconditioning Brake Drums 18
    Inspecting and Replacing Wheel Cylinder 18
  6.2   Parking Brake (Drum Brakes) 18
    Adjusting Parking Brake 18
    Replacing Parking Brake Cables 19

7. Rear Disc Brakes 19
    Checking Brake Pad Wear 20
  7.1   Reconditioning Rear Disc Brakes 20
    Removing and Installing Rear Brake Pads 20
    Removing, Reconditioning, and Installing
    Rear Brake Rotors 21
  7.2   Parking Brake (Disc Brakes) 21
    Adjusting Parking Brake 21
    Replacing Parking Brake Cable 22
  7.3   Calipers 22

2 BRAKES

8. Technical Data 23
    I. Tolerances, Wear Limits, and Settings 23
    II. Tightening Torques 23

TABLES

a. Brake Troubleshooting 6
b. Brake Pressure Specifications 11
c. Front Rotor Reconditioning Specifications 14
d. Brake Drum Reconditioning Specifications 18
e. Rear Rotor Reconditioning specifications 21

Brakes

Introduction

All cars covered by this manual are equipped either with front disc brakes and rear drum brakes, or with disc brakes at all four wheels. The brake system is a diagonal, dual-circuit design, hydraulically actuated by the master cylinder, with a vacuum-powered booster to reduce braking effort. A pressure regulator, or proportioning valve, helps prevent the rear brakes from locking during heavy braking.

A properly functioning brake system is essential to safe driving. If the red brake/parking warning indicator lights up while driving, indicating low pressure in one of the brake circuits, then it is imperative that the system be given a thorough check, even if braking action still seems satisfactory. The brakes should be regularly inspected, and all brake work must be done with extreme cleanliness, careful attention to specifications, and proper working procedures.

All information needed for performing routine inspection and maintenance is given here, although some of the information may only be of value to the professional mechanic. If you lack the skills, the tools, or a clean workplace for servicing the brake system, we suggest you leave these repairs to an authorized Volkswagen dealer or other qualified shop. We especially urge you to consult your authorized Volkswagen dealer before beginning repairs on a car which may be subject to Volkswagen warranty coverage.

12

1. GENERAL DESCRIPTION

Fig. 1-1 is a schematic diagram of the dual-diagonal hydraulic brake system. The master cylinder, operated mechanically by the brake pedal, creates pressure in the hydraulic system. At the wheels, the hydraulic pressure acts on the calipers or wheel cylinders to mechanically apply the brakes. The use of hydraulics makes it possible for the driver to generate high braking forces with a comparatively small amount of effort.

WARNING ━━━

•*Friction materials such as brake linings or brake pads may contain asbestos fibers. Do not create dust by grinding, sanding, or cleaning the pads with compressed air. Avoid breathing any asbestos fibers or dust. Breathing asbestos may result in serious diseases such as asbestosis or cancer, or may result in death.*

•*Brake fluid is poisonous. Wear safety glasses when working with brake fluid, and wear rubber gloves to prevent brake fluid from entering the bloodstream through cuts or scratches. Do not siphon brake fluid by mouth.*

CAUTION ━━━

Brake fluid is very damaging to paint. Immediately wipe up any brake fluid that spills on the vehicle.

Master Cylinder, Vacuum Booster, and Brake Lines

The master cylinder has two separate chambers for two separate hydraulic circuits. The front chamber operates the brakes on the right front and left rear wheels, while the rear chamber operates the brakes on the left front and right rear wheels. In the event of a loss of pressure in one circuit, the other will still supply approximately half of the normal braking force.

The vacuum booster uses engine vacuum to assist braking effort. The rigid brake lines transmit hydraulic pressure to the wheels and resist expansion and pressure loss. Flexible hoses between the rigid lines and the brakes accommodate wheel movement due to steering and suspension action.

Disc Brakes

The disc brakes use a cast-iron caliper with a single hydraulic cylinder to clamp the rotor (disc) between two brake pads. Front rotors are mounted to the wheel hub. Rear rotors are

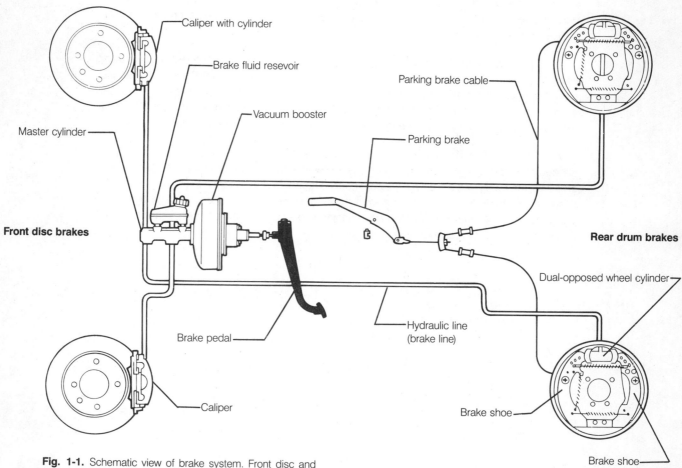

Fig. 1-1. Schematic view of brake system. Front disc and rear drum brakes shown. Four-wheel disc brake system is similar.

integral with the wheel hub; they house the wheel bearings and are held in place by the axle nut. Disc brakes automatically adjust for brake pad and rotor wear.

Rear Drum Brakes

The self-adjusting rear drum brakes use a dual-opposed hydraulic wheel cylinder to apply pressure to the brake shoes, forcing the friction linings against the inside of the brake drum.

Pressure Regulator and Proportioning Valves

To prevent rear-wheel lock-up during hard stops, all cars covered by this manual are equipped with a pressure regulating device that limits the amount of hydraulic pressure applied to the rear brakes. Depending on the model, the car is equipped either with a load-sensing pressure regulator in the brake lines, or with two pre-set proportioning valves which are mounted on the master cylinder. See Fig. 1-2 and Fig. 1-3.

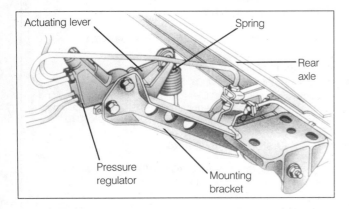

Fig. 1-2. Rear brake pressure regulator.

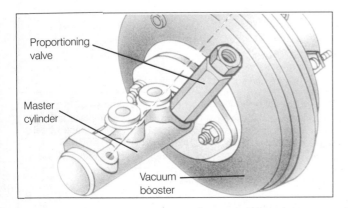

Fig. 1-3. Installed position of one brake proportioning valve. A second valve (not shown) is also mounted on the master cylinder.

Parking Brakes

The cable-operated parking brake mechanically actuates either the rear brake shoes or the rear caliper pistons. The position of the parking brake lever is held by a thumb-release ratchet.

1.1 Brake Applications and Identification

Golf, Golf GL, Golf GT, Jetta, and Jetta GL models, both gasoline and diesel, are equipped with front disc brakes and rear drum brakes. GTI, Jetta GLI, and Jetta Carat models are equipped with four-wheel disc brakes, and internally ventilated front brake rotors for better cooling. All GTI and Jetta models use the load-sensing type of pressure regulator. All Golf models use the master cylinder mounted proportioning valves.

2. MAINTENANCE

The following routine maintenance operations should be performed at the time or mileage intervals listed in **LUBRICATION AND MAINTENANCE**. Instructions can be found in **LUBRICATION AND MAINTENANCE**, or in this section under the listed numbered headings.

1. Checking brake fluid level

2. Inspecting brake hoses and lines for leaks

3. Checking brake pad and/or lining wear

4. Replacing the brake fluid every two years. **4.2**

3. TROUBLESHOOTING

This heading describes symptoms of trouble with the brake system, and suggests possible causes and appropriate corrective actions.

The brake system has the sole function of generating the required friction to stop the car from any speed. Brake problems are usually obvious because they affect the manner in which the car slows and stops. Problems which affect the car's handling or create noise may also be caused by faults in the suspension or steering systems. Information on troubleshooting these systems can be found in **SUSPENSION AND STEERING**. For more help in selecting the appropriate section, see the discussion of troubleshooting in **FUNDAMENTALS** at the front of the manual.

3.1 Basic Troubleshooting Principles

As with any troubleshooting, analysis of the observed symptoms is the key to isolating and identifying braking problems. Reliable brake system performance depends on creating and applying hydraulic pressure in the system. Brake performance is affected by three things: the brake fluid, the system's ability to maintain pressure, and the friction components.

Air in the brake fluid, because it is compressible, will make the brake pedal feel spongy during braking, or will increase the force required at the brake pedal to stop the car. Moisture- or dirt-contaminated fluid will dramatically increase internal corrosion and wear.

12

Seals are used throughout the system to maintain hydraulic pressure. Faulty seals or wear and corrosion on the sealing surfaces will reduce braking efficiency. A symptom of this condition is the need to pump the pedal to get good braking. Simple leaks at the brake line or hose unions may cause the same problems.

Worn or contaminated brake linings are an obvious cause of poor braking performance. The friction material is slowly consumed by use of the brakes and must be periodically replaced. Also, pads and linings which are oil-contaminated or glazed due to overheating cannot produce as much friction, and stopping distances will increase.

When troubleshooting the brake system, consider how quickly the problem occurred. Sudden brake system failure is most likely caused by the failure of one component, such as a burst hose or a disconnected vacuum booster vacuum line. A gradual decline in braking efficiency probably indicates the general state of wear in the system, and more than one component may need to be repaired or replaced.

Table a lists symptoms of problems commonly associated with the brakes, their probable causes, and suggested corrective actions. The numbers in bold type in the corrective action column refer to numbered headings in this section where the suggested repairs are described.

Table a. Brake Troubleshooting

Symptom	Probable cause	Corrective action
1. Brake squeak or squeal	a. Normal condition	a. See **3.3 Brake Noise**
	b. Incorrectly installed brake pads or brake shoes	b. Check installation. **5.1, 6.1, 7.1**
	c. Brake pad carriers or backing plates dirty or corroded	c. Clean calipers and/or backing plates. **3.3, 5.1, 6.1, 7.1**
	d. Brake shoe return springs weak	d. Replace return springs. **6.1**
	e. Pad anti-rattle springs faulty or missing	e. Install/replace anti-rattle springs. **5.1, 7.1**
	f. Brake pads or linings heat-glazed or oil-soaked	f. Replace brake pads/linings. Clean rotors/drums. Replace leaking calipers/wheel cylinders as required. **5.1, 6.1, 7.1** Replace wheel bearing grease seals as required. See **SUSPENSION AND STEERING**
	g. Wheel bearings misadjusted	g. See **SUSPENSION AND STEERING**
2. Pedal goes to floor when braking	a. Insufficient brake fluid	a. Check fluid level. See **LUBRICATION AND MAINTENANCE** Check for leaks. Fill and bleed system. **4.2**
	b. Master cylinder faulty	b. Replace master cylinder. **4.3**
3. Low pedal even after brake adjustment and bleeding	a. Master cylinder faulty	a. Replace master cylinder. **4.3**
4. Pedal feels spongy or brakes work only after pedal is pumped	a. Insufficient brake fluid	a. Check fluid level. See **LUBRICATION AND MAINTENANCE** Check for leaks. Fill and bleed system. **4.2**
	b. Air in brake fluid	b. Bleed system. **4.2**
	c. Master cylinder spring weak	c. Replace master cylinder. **4.3**
	d. Leaking line and hose unions	d. Repair or replace lines and hoses. Bleed system. **4.2**
5. Excessive braking effort with little effect	a. Brake pads or linings wet	a. Use light pedal pressure to dry brakes while driving.
	b. Brake pads or linings heat-glazed or oil soaked	b. Replace brake pads/linings. Clean rotors/drums. Replace leaking calipers/wheel cylinders as required. **5.1, 6.1, 7.1** Replace wheel bearing grease seals. See **SUSPENSION AND STEERING**
	c. Vacuum booster or vacuum line faulty	c. Inspect vacuum lines. Test booster and replace as required. **4.3**
6. Brakes pulsate, chatter, or grab	a. Warped disc brake rotors	a. Recondition or replace rotors. **5.1, 7.1**
	b. Brake drums worn or out-of-round	b. Recondition or replace brake drums. **6.1**.
	c. Brake pads or linings worn	c. Recondition brakes. **5.1, 6.1, 7.1**
	d. Brake pads or linings heat-glazed or oil-soaked	d. Replace brake pads/linings. Clean rotors/drums. Replace leaking calipers/wheel cylinders as required. **5.1, 6.1, 7.1** Replace wheel bearing grease seals as required. See **SUSPENSION AND STEERING**

continued on next page

Table a. Brake Troubleshooting (continued)

Symptom	Probable cause	Corrective action
7. Uneven braking, car pulls to one side, rear brakes lock	**a.** Incorrect tire pressures	**a.** Check and correct tire pressures. See **LUBRICATION AND MAINTENANCE**
	b. Brake pads or linings heat-glazed or oil-soaked	**b.** Replace brake pads/linings. Clean rotors/drums. Replace leaking calipers/wheel cylinders as required. **5.1, 6.1, 7.1** Replace wheel bearing grease seals as required. See **SUSPENSION AND STEERING**
	c. Pressure regulator or proportioning valves faulty	**c.** Adjust or replace pressure regulator. Replace proportioning valves **4.4**
	d. Caliper/wheel cylinders or brake pads/shoes binding	**d.** Clean and recondition brakes. **5.1, 6.1, 7.1**
	e. Drum brake self-adjusters faulty	**e.** Clean, repair, or replace self-adjusting mechanism. **6.2**
	f. Brake fluid contaminated	**f.** Drain, flush, refill, and bleed brake system. **4.2**
	g. Worn tires or suspension components	**g.** See **SUSPENSION AND STEERING**
8. Brakes drag, bind, or overheat	**a.** Brake shoe return springs weak	**a.** Replace springs. **6.1**
	b. Brake caliper/wheel cylinder or brake pad/shoe binding	**b.** Clean and recondition brakes. **5.1, 6.1, 7.1**
	c. Master cylinder faulty	**c.** Replace master cylinder. **4.3**

3.2 Diagnostic Tests

Some general checks of brake system function and component inspection can help isolate problems.

Test the vacuum booster first by pumping the brake pedal a few times with the engine off, and then holding the pedal down. When the engine is started, the pedal should fall slightly. The booster diaphragm rarely fails, but leaks in the vacuum line or a faulty check valve will decrease the vacuum assist. Check the valve by removing it from the booster vacuum line and blowing through it. Air should pass through in the direction of the arrow on the check valve, but not through the opposite way. On cars with diesel engines, vacuum booster problems may be caused by a faulty vacuum pump.

Test the rear brakes by applying the parking brake. It should be able to hold the car, perhaps even stalling the engine, when you try to drive away. If not, the brakes probably need adjustment or reconditioning.

Test the master cylinder by holding the pedal down hard with the car stopped and the engine running. The pedal should feel solid and stay solid. If the pedal slowly falls to the floor, then the master cylinder is faulty and should be replaced.

3.3 Brake Noise

Occasional groaning or squealing sounds coming from the brakes, especially disc brakes, are usually caused by vibrations transmitted through the brake pads. The problem is not unique to Volkswagens. New brake friction materials, using little or no asbestos for health reasons, may contribute to an increase in brake noise problems in all makes. These noises, though discomforting, are normal and rarely indicate a problem in brake system function or effectiveness.

Although there is no permanent solution, proper maintenance and repair can help minimize brake noise. Disc brake caliper assemblies include anti-rattle springs, designed to minimize vibration and noise. As much as possible, brake pads and calipers should be kept free of foreign matter and corrosion which may inhibit smooth operation. Always resurface or replace brake rotors when changing brake pads.

A reduction in brake noise may be possible by installing a shim kit with the pads. The kit, Volkswagen part no. 171 698 993, contains self-adhesive shims which attach to the backs of the brake pads to damp vibration. The backs of the pads must be cleaned down to the metal for good adhesion, and the shims can only be installed on thinner, partially worn pads. The combined thickness of the pad and shim must not exceed the thickness of a new pad. See **5.1 Checking Brake Pad Wear** for specifications.

Rear drum brake squeak may be more easily corrected. A lubricant is available to coat the points on the backing plate where the brake shoes make contact with the plate (raised or embossed points). The lubricant is Wolfracote grease, part number G 000 650, and is available from authorized Volkswagen dealers.

CAUTION ▬

Part numbers are subject to change. Always rely on an authorized Volkswagen dealer parts department for the latest and most accurate information.

To eliminate squeaking drum brakes, remove the brake shoes as described in **6.1 Reconditioning Rear Drum Brakes,** and apply a small amount of Wolfracote grease to the contact points of the brake backing plate, then reinstall the brake shoes.

12

4. BRAKE SYSTEM SERVICE

This section provides the requirements for the brake fluid, the methods for bleeding the brake system, and the servicing of the master cylinder, vacuum booster, and pressure regulator.

4.1 Brake Fluid

Brake fluid is the heart of the hydraulic system. It transmits the mechanical braking force at the pedal to the brake mechanisms at the wheels. Any contamination of the fluid will have a direct influence on braking efficiency. Dirt in the system will clog small passages and wear rubber parts.

Brake fluid absorbs moisture. Moisture in the fluid lowers its boiling point, allowing it to be boiled more easily by the heat generated during braking. Boiling the fluid will create bubbles in the system and, since bubbles are compressible, will reduce braking efficiency. Moisture in the system also causes corrosion.

When adding brake fluid, use only new fluid from unopened containers. Do not reuse brake fluid that has been bled from the system, even if it is brand new. The bleeding operation aerates the fluid. See **LUBRICATION AND MAINTENANCE** for brake fluid specifications. For best performance and system reliability, use only Volkswagen-approved brake fluid.

Because it readily absorbs moisture, brake fluid should be changed every two years, regardless of the number of miles driven annually. The brake system should also be bled of air after any repairs in which brake lines are disconnected. See **Replacing Brake Fluid** for more information.

WARNING ——

Brake fluid is poisonous. Wear safety glasses when working with brake fluid, and wear rubber gloves to prevent brake fluid from entering the bloodstream through cuts or scratches. Do not siphon brake fluid by mouth.

CAUTION ——

Brake fluid is very damaging to paint. Immediately wipe up any brake fluid that spills on painted surfaces.

4.2 Bleeding Brakes

Bleeding brakes is the process of purging aerated or contaminated brake fluid from the system and replacing it with new, clean fluid. Bleeding brakes periodically is good preventive maintenance, but it is also essential if brake lines or components have been disconnected, or any time air is introduced into the system. Vague or spongy brakes may indicate the need to bleed air from the system.

There are three widely used methods of bleeding brakes. Each employs some means of forcing the fluid through the system to the calipers or wheel cylinders, and releasing contaminated fluid through the bleeder valves. The system can be

bled using a pressure bleeder, using a hand-held vacuum bleeder, or manually using the brake pedal and a helper. Each method accomplishes the same result. Pressure bleeding, if available, is fastest. Manual bleeding requires no special tools.

For the best possible results, bleeding should start at the wheel farthest from the master cylinder and end at the wheel closest to the master cylinder. This bleeding sequence is as follows:

1. Right rear caliper or wheel cylinder
2. Left rear caliper or wheel cylinder
3. Right front caliper
4. Left front caliper

For best access to the bleeder valves when bleeding the brakes, the car should be raised and firmly supported on jack stands designed for the purpose. The engine should be off and the vacuum hose and check valve should be disconnected from the vacuum booster. On models equipped with the load-sensing pressure regulator, the actuator lever must be held toward the axle beam when bleeding the rear brakes to allow maximum fluid flow. The bleeder valves on both disc brake calipers and drum brake wheel cylinders are opened and closed using an 8 mm (5/16 in.) box wrench. Use a clear container to catch the expelled fluid and a piece of 4 mm (5/32 in.) inside diameter clear, flexible tubing connected to the bleeder valve, as shown in Fig. 4-1, so that outgoing air bubbles are visible.

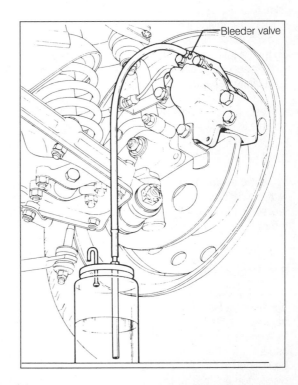

Fig. 4-1. Container (partially filled with brake fluid) connected to caliper bleeder valve with clear tubing for bleeding brakes. Bleeding rear drum brake wheel cylinder is similar (car shown is not one of those covered by this manual).

Pressure Bleeding

Pressure bleeding, using special equipment and compressed air, is the method used by most commercial repair shops. It is the quickest method and the best way to prevent contaminants and air from entering the brake system. The pressure bleeder is connected to the brake fluid reservoir and fills the system with fluid under pressure. Follow the instructions supplied by the equipment manufacturer.

Vacuum Bleeding

Vacuum bleeding uses an inexpensive hand pump connected at the bleeder valve to draw the fluid through the system. It is a practical, do-it-yourself alternative to pressure bleeding, is faster than manual bleeding, and can be accomplished by only one person. Pumps of this general type are available from auto parts and supply outlets.

Follow the pump manufacturer's instructions very carefully. Make sure that the hose connection to the brake bleeder valve is secure and air-tight. Check the brake fluid level in the master cylinder often to guard against emptying the reservoir.

Manual Bleeding

Bleeding the brake system by pumping the brake pedal is the most economical method. The only disadvantage is that it requires a helper.

When manually bleeding the brakes, first fill the brake fluid reservoir on top of the master cylinder until the level is well above the MAX mark, and replace the cap to prevent contamination of the fluid.

Starting with the right rear caliper or cylinder, clean the area around the bleeder valve and remove the dust cap. Fit the box wrench to the bleeder valve, then slip one end of the hose onto the valve and submerge the other end in clean brake fluid in the clear container. Have a helper slowly pump the brake pedal about three times and, on the last time, hold it down. Slowly open the bleeder valve approximately one-half turn. When the brake pedal goes to the floor and fluid stops flowing from the bleeder valve, close the bleeder valve, then release the brake pedal.

CAUTION ——

Until some pressure has built up in the system, only depress the pedal approximately halfway. This will prevent overrunning the master cylinder's normal stroke, which may damage the master cylinder piston seals.

CAUTION ——

Be sure that the bleeder valve is fully closed before releasing the brake pedal to avoid drawing air back into the bleeder valve.

Repeat the procedure until clear fluid with no air bubbles is coming from the bleeder valve, then fully tighten the valve and replace the dust cap. Using the sequence described above, follow the same procedure at the other three wheels. Check the fluid level in the master cylinder frequently, and add more to keep the level at the MAX mark.

Replacing Brake Fluid

Replace the brake fluid by using the procedure described above to expel the old fluid. Remove the filter/strainer from the brake fluid reservoir and clean it in new, unused brake fluid, then fill the reservoir with new, unused brake fluid and bleed the brake system. Remove at least 1 pint (500 cc) of brake fluid at each caliper or wheel cylinder to completely expel the old fluid and replace it. See **LUBRICATION AND MAINTENANCE** for brake fluid specifications. Use only Volkswagen-recommended brake fluid.

Flushing the Brake System

Do not rely on flushing alone to clean a brake system contaminated with dirt or corrosion. The flushing procedure may actually force dirt in the lines into the wheel cylinders. The brake system must be disassembled and the parts individually cleaned. Use only brake fluid to flush the lines. Alcohol must not be used since it will encourage the accumulation of water in the system.

4.3 Master Cylinder and Vacuum Booster

The master cylinder, its vacuum booster, and the brake pedal assembly are shown in Fig. 4-2. The vacuum booster and master cylinder are mounted to the firewall in the engine compartment. The pedal operates the master cylinder via a pushrod which passes through the firewall. The master cylinder piston acts on the brake fluid to create pressure in the system. The brake fluid reservoir is mounted atop the master cylinder.

The vacuum booster, mounted between the pedal mechanism and the master cylinder, uses the difference between engine vacuum and atmospheric pressure to help actuate the master cylinder and reduce pedal effort. Diesel engines, because of their very low engine vacuum, are equipped with an auxiliary vacuum pump.

When the engine is running, vacuum is applied equally to both sides of the booster diaphragm. When the brake pedal is pressed, atmospheric pressure reaches the pedal side of the diaphragm and creates the brake-boosting pressure differential. A check valve in the vacuum hose holds vacuum in the booster when the engine is stopped. The pedal pushrod is directly connected to the master cylinder so that a failure of the vacuum booster, although it will increase braking effort, will not result in total brake failure.

12

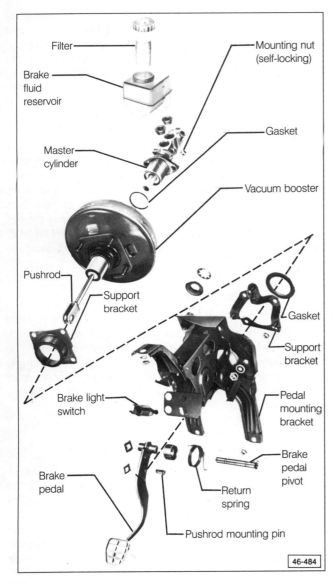

Filter

Brake
fluid
reservoir

Mounting nut
(self-locking)

Gasket

Master
cylinder

Vacuum booster

Pushrod

Support
bracket

Gasket

Support
bracket

Brake light
switch

Pedal
mounting
bracket

Brake
pedal

Brake
pedal
pivot

Return
spring

Pushrod mounting pin

46-484

Fig. 4-2. Exploded view of the brake pedal, vacuum booster,
and master cylinder assembly.

Removing and Installing Master Cylinder

Master cylinder parts or rebuild kits are not available. Volkswagen specifies that a faulty master cylinder must be replaced.
It can be removed and installed with ordinary hand tools. On
installation, use a new gasket between the cylinder and the
vacuum booster, and new self-locking mounting nuts. Make
sure to have an adequate supply of new, unopened brake fluid
on hand, as bleeding the brakes will be necessary after installation. See **4.2 Bleeding Brakes**.

To remove and install:

1. Disconnect the battery negative (−) terminal. Disconnect the electrical connector from the brake fluid reservoir cap.

2. Remove the reservoir cap and, using a clean syringe,
   empty the brake fluid reservoir.

> **WARNING** ━━
> *Brake fluid is poisonous. Do not siphon the brake
> fluid with your mouth.*

3. Disconnect the brake lines from the master cylinder.
   Remove the two nuts holding the master cylinder to the
   vacuum booster, then remove the master cylinder. On
   Golf models, remove the proportioning valves.

4. If necessary, remove the brake fluid reservoir from the
   top of the master cylinder by prying it out of the rubber
   mounting grommets, and install the reservoir on the new
   master cylinder.

5. Using a new gasket and self-locking nuts, install the new
   master cylinder. Torque the nuts to 20 Nm (15 ft. lb.).
   Connect the brake lines and, on Golf models, the proportioning valves. Torque the valves and the brake line
   unions to 15 to 20 Nm (11 to 15 ft. lb.).

> **CAUTION** ━━
> *Do not exceed recommended mounting torque
> of master cylinder mounting nuts. Overtight-
> ening may cause damage to the vacuum
> booster.*

> **NOTE** ━━
> The master cylinder pushrod does not require
> adjustment prior to installation of the master
> cylinder, even if a new vacuum booster has
> been installed.

6. Fill the reservoir with new brake fluid and bleed the
   system as described in **4.2 Bleeding Brakes**. Reconnect the battery negative (−) terminal and the fluid
   reservoir cap connector. Road test the car and repeat the
   brake bleeding operation if necessary.

Removing and Installing Vacuum Booster

A faulty vacuum booster is not repairable, and must be
replaced. It can be removed and installed with ordinary hand
tools. Replacing the vacuum booster requires removing and
installing the master cylinder. See **Removing and Installing
Master Cylinder** above.

To remove the vacuum booster, disconnect the vacuum
hose from the booster, and disconnect the pushrod from the
brake pedal. Working in the engine compartment, remove the
four nuts that mount the vacuum booster to its support bracket,
and remove the booster. Installation is the reverse of removal.
Use new self-locking nuts when installing the booster.

4.4 Brake Pressure Regulator and Proportioning Valves

The load-sensing brake pressure regulator used on all GTI and Jetta models is shown in Fig. 4-3. It is mounted underneath the car with an actuating lever connected to the rear axle beam by a small spring. When the axle changes position, due to a heavy load or during hard braking, the pressure regulator varies the pressure to the rear brakes. The regulator is adjustable.

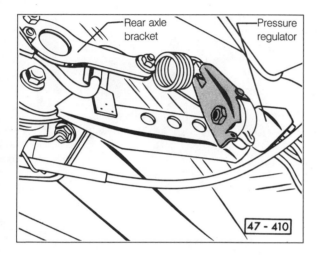

Fig. 4-3. Rear brake pressure regulator used on all GTI and Jetta models, as viewed from beneath car.

Golf models use proportioning valves, mounted in the brake lines at the master cylinder, to control the pressure to the rear wheels. The proportioning valves are not adjustable and have no load-sensing capability.

Quick-checking Brake Pressure Regulator

With the car resting on all four wheels and the fuel tank full, observe the pressure regulator actuating lever while a helper depresses and quickly releases the brake pedal. The lever should move slightly when the brake is quickly released. If not, the regulator is faulty and should be replaced.

NOTE ▬

For this check to be accurate, the helper must not sit in the car.

Pressure Testing Regulator or Proportioning Valves

Testing the pressure-regulating function of either system requires measuring brake system pressure at each wheel, using two pressure gauges with a range of at least 160 bar (2320 psi) connected in place of the brake bleeder valves. Because of the need for this specialized equipment, we recommend having this test performed by an authorized Volkswagen dealer or other qualified repair shop.

The gauges are connected to one front and the diagonally opposite rear brake to test one hydraulic circuit, and then to the other front brake and its diagonally opposite rear brake to test the other hydraulic circuit. The system must be bled at the gauges each time they are connected. Have a helper depress the brake pedal while observing the pressure readings on the gauges. The fuel tank should be full and the suspension must be in its normal resting position, either on the ground or held with spring tensioners.

Table b lists the brake pressure specifications for different conditions and models. Load-sensing pressure regulators can be adjusted by moving the bolt which attaches the spring to the rear axle bracket, to increase or decrease tension on the spring. Replace the regulator if it cannot be adjusted to operate within specifications.

CAUTION ▬

Do not make adjustments with the brake pedal depressed.

5. FRONT DISC BRAKES

An exploded view of a front disc brake is shown in Fig. 5-1. The single-piston caliper is a floating design. When the brakes are applied, the caliper pushes the inside brake pad against the rotor. This moves the caliper body at the same time, pulling the outside pad against the rotor.

Because the front brakes do more of the work of stopping the car, they are likely to wear faster and require service more frequently than the rear brakes. The brake pads and rotors are subjected to the greatest wear, and are the components most often needing attention.

12

Table b. Brake Pressure Specifications

Front caliper pressure (all models)	Rear wheel cylinder pressure (Golf, Golf GL, GT)	Rear wheel cylinder pressure (Jetta, Jetta GL)	Rear caliper pressure (GTI, Jetta GLI, Jetta Carat)	Rear caliper pressure (Jetta GLI 16V)
50 bar(725 psi) 100 bar(1450 psi)	35–39 bar(507–565 psi) 56–60 bar(812–870 psi)	38–42 bar(551–609 psi) 59–63 bar(855–914 psi)	31–33 bar(450–479 psi) 52–54 bar(754–783 psi)	30–36 bar(435–522 psi) 51–57 bar(739–826 psi)

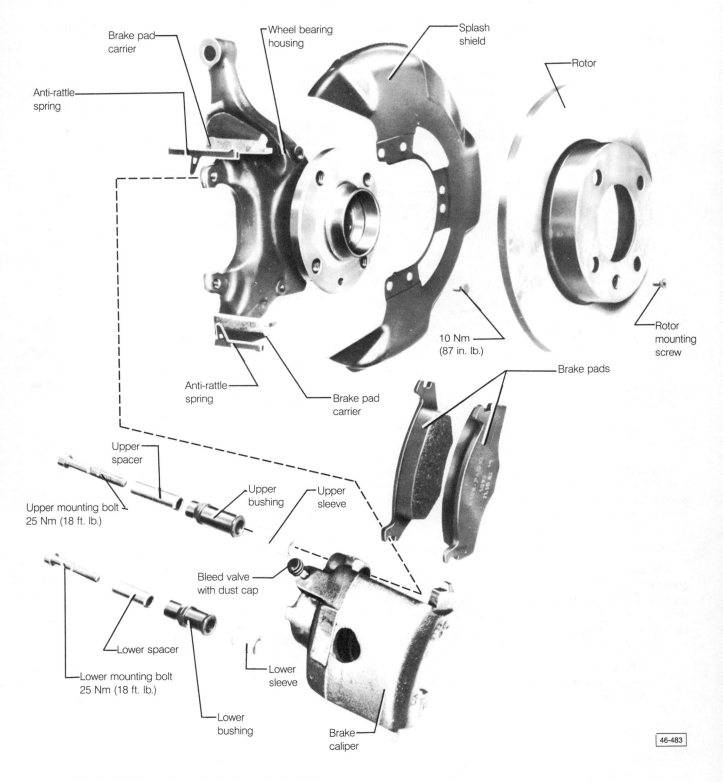

Fig. 5-1. Exploded view of front disc brake assembly.

The brake pads are designed to be routinely replaced as they wear out. While it is possible to restore the brakes by replacing only the brake pads, full braking performance and minimum pad wear can only be achieved if the rotors are resurfaced or replaced at the same time.

WARNING ——

Brake pad friction materials may contain asbestos fibers. Do not create dust by grinding, sanding, or cleaning the pads with compressed air. Avoid breathing any asbestos fibers or dust. Breathing asbestos may result in serious diseases such as asbestosis or cancer, or may result in death.

Checking Brake Pad Wear

The inspection procedure and specifications for checking the brake pads are found in **LUBRICATION AND MAINTE-NANCE**. For more complete inspection of pad condition, the pads must be removed as described in **5.1 Reconditioning Front Disc Brakes**.

5.1 Reconditioning Front Disc Brakes

Reconditioning of the front disc brakes typically includes replacing the brake pads and resurfacing or replacing the brake rotors. Unless the calipers and hoses are damaged, extremely worn, or leaking fluid, more extensive front brake repairs are not normally required.

If the brake pads are soaked with oil, grease, or brake fluid, the cause of the contamination must be found and corrected before new pads are installed. Brake rotors must be replaced when resurfacing exceeds specified limits. See **Removing, Reconditioning, and Installing Brake Rotors** for rotor thickness and runout specifications.

Removing and Installing Brake Pads

Although the calipers must be removed to change the brake pads, this can be done without disconnecting the flexible brake hose. Keeping the hydraulic system sealed eliminates the need to bleed the brakes afterward.

Brake pads and the surfaces of the rotors wear slightly differently. Always replace brake pads in complete sets. If old pads are to be reinstalled, such as after inspecting them, always make sure they are refitted in their original locations.

To remove:

1. Raise the front of the car and support it securely on jack stands. Remove the front wheels.

2. Using a hex wrench, remove the two brake caliper mounting bolts, the spacers, and the sleeves. Push the caliper up slightly and swing it out from the bottom, as shown in Fig. 5-2, to remove it from the pad carrier. Suspend the caliper from the car body with a stiff wire to avoid stretching the brake hose.

   NOTE ━

   If the piston creeps out of the caliper due to residual pressure in the brake lines, place a rubber band around the piston and caliper to hold the piston.

3. Lift out the pads and the anti-rattle springs from the pad carrier.

   CAUTION ━

   If the pads are to be reused, mark the pads so that they can be reinstalled in their original position.

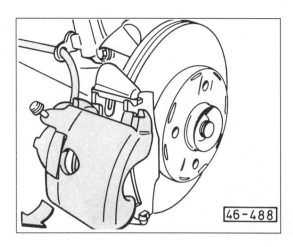

Fig. 5-2. Brake caliper being removed from pad carrier. Slide caliper out from bottom first (arrow).

To install:

1. Install the anti-rattle springs on the pad carrier and hold them in place with the inner brake pad, as shown in Fig. 5-3. Then, install the outer pad.

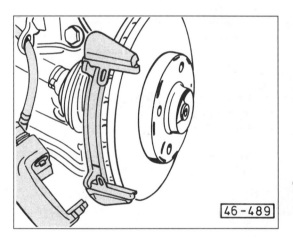

Fig. 5-3. Anti-rattle springs and inner brake pad installed in brake pad carrier.

2. When installing new brake pads, slowly push the piston back into the caliper to provide clearance for the thicker new brake pads.

   NOTE ━

   Pushing in the caliper pistons to gain clearance for the thicker new brake pads will cause brake fluid to overflow the master cylinder fluid reservoir. To prevent this, use a clean syringe to first remove some fluid from the reservoir.

3. Engage the caliper with the upper part of the pad carrier, and pivot the bottom of the caliper into position over the pads, as shown in Fig. 5-4. Be careful not to damage the caliper piston dust seal.

12

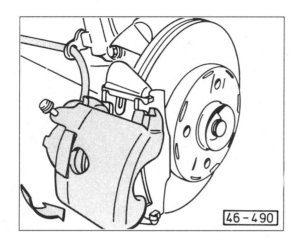

Fig. 5-4. Brake caliper being pivoted into position on pad carrier over brake pads. Engage top part first and follow with bottom (arrow).

4. Install the spacers, the sleeves, and the caliper mounting bolts. The longer parts should be installed in the upper mount. Torque the socket-head mounting bolts to 25 Nm (18 ft. lb.).

> **CAUTION** ▬
>
> *Make sure that the caliper mounting bolts, the sleeves, the bushings, and the spacers are clean and free of corrosion.*

5. Mount the wheel and loosely install the lug bolts. Lower the car and then torque the lug bolts to 110 Nm (81 ft. lb.).

6. Depress the brake pedal several times to adjust the caliper and brake pads to the rotor.

7. Check the level of brake fluid in the reservoir. If necessary, add new brake fluid to fill the reservoir to the MAX mark.

> **WARNING** ▬
>
> *New brake pads require some break-in. Allow for slightly longer stopping distances for the first 100 to 150 miles of city driving, and avoid hard stops.*

Removing, Reconditioning, and Installing Brake Rotors

To remove the brake rotors, first remove the caliper and brake pads as described above. Remove the countersunk flathead screw between two of the wheel bolt holes, and pull the rotor off the wheel hub. Use a soft-faced mallet to free a stuck rotor.

> **CAUTION** ▬
>
> *Do not try to remove the rotor without first removing the caliper. Excessive force may damage the rotor or the wheel bearing housing.*

Installation is the reverse of removal. Make sure that the rotor and wheel hub mounting surfaces mate properly and are free of dirt and corrosion.

> **NOTE** ▬
>
> New replacement brake rotors should be cleaned with a grease-free solvent, such as a commercially available brake cleaner, before installing the caliper and brake pads.

Brake rotors should always be resurfaced in pairs, with an equal amount of material removed from both sides of each rotor. Brake rotors can be resurfaced by most local automotive machine shops. **Table c** lists dimensions for solid and ventilated rotors. Rotors which are worn beyond the wear limit are too thin to be safely used, and should be replaced. Resurfaced rotors should be at least 0.5 mm (.020 in.) thicker than the wear limit, to allow for additional wear. If not, they should be replaced. Rotors which are cracked or warped should always be replaced.

Table c. Front Rotor Reconditioning Specifications

	Solid Rotors	Ventilated Rotors
Thickness new	12.0 mm (.472 in.)	20.0 mm (.787 in.)
Minimum thickness	10.0 mm (.393 in.)	18.0 mm (.708 in.)

5.2 Calipers

Fig. 5-5 is an exploded view of the front disc brake caliper. The piston seal holds the hydraulic pressure in the system as the piston moves, and also provides the caliper's self-adjusting action.

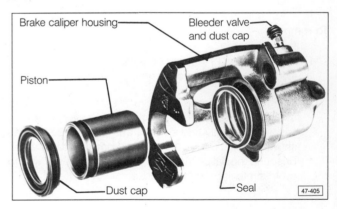

Fig. 5-5. Exploded view of front disc brake caliper.

The caliper is self-adjusting. When the piston moves and presses on the brake pads, the seal is distorted slightly. When the pressure is removed, the seal pulls the piston back slightly, creating a small gap to minimize brake pad wear. As the pads wear, the seal is repositioned on the piston, so that the gap remains approximately the same.

Brake fluid leaks around the brake caliper piston are the result of a failed or damaged piston seal, perhaps caused by corrosion, scoring, or pitting of the piston or caliper bore. The seal can be replaced, but a damaged piston, which is not available as a replacement part, will promptly destroy the new seal. To remedy a leaking caliper piston seal and avoid future problems, complete replacement of the caliper is recommended. A damaged caliper dust seal can be replaced separately.

Remove front brake calipers as described in **Removing and Installing Brake Pads**. Disconnect the brake hose from the caliper and drain the brake fluid into a container. Cap the end of the brake line to prevent dirt and moisture from entering the brake system.

Installation is the reverse of removal. Torque the brake hose union to 15 Nm (11 ft. lb.). Bleed the brake system as described in **4.2 Bleeding Brakes**. Do not let brake fluid contaminate the brake pads or brake rotor surface.

6. REAR DRUM BRAKES

Fig. 6-1 is an exploded view of the rear drum brake assembly. Retaining springs hold the brake shoes in place. The shoes

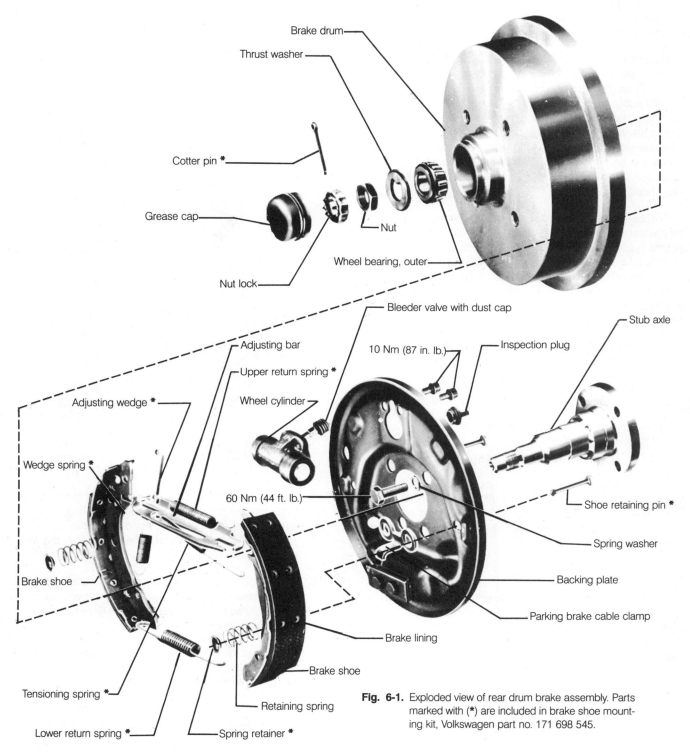

Fig. 6-1. Exploded view of rear drum brake assembly. Parts marked with (*) are included in brake shoe mounting kit, Volkswagen part no. 171 698 545.

12

rest against a fixed bracket at the bottom of the backing plate. When the brakes are applied, the wheel cylinder pushes against the tops of the shoes to force them against the brake drum. Return springs retract the brake shoes when the brakes are released.

The rear brakes are equipped with a self-adjusting mechanism which compensates for wear. At the top of the backing plate, the brake shoes rest against the slotted adjusting bar. As the brake lining wears and brake shoe travel increases, the spring-loaded adjusting wedge fills the gap between the brake shoe and the adjusting bar, essentially lengthening the adjusting bar and keeping the brake shoes from retracting too far from the drum.

Because the rear brakes do less of the work of stopping the car, they are not likely to wear as quickly or require service as frequently as the front brakes. Unless problem symptoms are actually observed at the rear brakes, troubleshooting of brake problems should always include the front brakes. If the rear brakes are worn and require service, then at the very least the front brakes should also be thoroughly inspected. The brake shoes, the drums, and the attaching and adjusting parts are subjected to the greatest wear, and are the components most often needing attention.

The brake shoes are designed to be routinely replaced as they wear out. While it is possible to restore the brakes by replacing only the brake shoes, full braking performance and minimum lining wear can only be achieved if the drums are resurfaced or replaced at the same time. Removal of the brake drums requires cleaning, repacking, and adjusting the wheel bearings during reassembly, as described in **SUSPENSION AND STEERING**.

> **WARNING ——**
>
> *Brake pad friction materials may contain asbestos fibers. Do not create dust by grinding, sanding, or cleaning the pads with compressed air. Avoid breathing any asbestos fibers or dust. Breathing asbestos may result in serious diseases such as asbestosis or cancer, or may result in death.*

Checking Brake Lining Wear

The inspection procedure and specifications for checking the brake lining wear are found in **LUBRICATION AND MAINTENANCE**. For more complete inspection of lining condition, the drums must be removed, as described in **6.1 Reconditioning Rear Drum Brakes**.

6.1 Reconditioning Rear Drum Brakes

Reconditioning of the rear drum brakes typically includes replacing the brake shoes, resurfacing or replacing the brake drums, replacing the attaching and adjusting hardware, and cleaning and repacking the wheel bearings. Unless the wheel cylinders or hoses are damaged or leaking fluid, more extensive rear drum brake repairs are not normally required.

If the brake linings are soaked with grease or brake fluid, the cause of the contamination must be found and corrected before new brake shoes are installed. Brake drums must be replaced when resurfacing exceeds specified limits. See **Reconditioning Brake Drums** for specifications.

Removing and Installing Brake Shoes

The brake shoes only need to be removed when they are being replaced. If the backing plate must be removed for other repairs, the brake shoes can remain attached to it. Bleeding the brake system will not be necessary as long as the brake lines or hoses are not disconnected. The brake drums can be removed with or without the wheel in place.

To remove:

1. Raise the rear of the car and support it securely on jack stands. Remove the wheels, or simply remove one of the wheel lug bolts from each side.

2. With the parking brake released, rotate the brake drum until the adjusting wedge can be seen through a wheel bolt hole. Using a screwdriver as shown in Fig. 6-2, push the adjusting wedge up as far as possible.

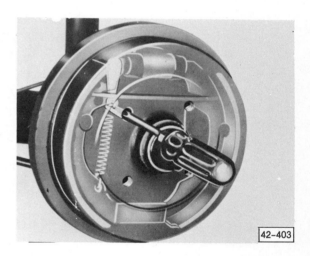

42–403

Fig. 6-2. Phantom view of rear drum brake showing adjusting wedge being pushed up with screwdriver to back off adjustment.

3. Pry off the wheel bearing grease cap and remove the cotter pin, the nut lock, and the axle nut. Tugging on the brake drum slightly if necessary, remove the thrust washer and the outer wheel bearing. Remove the wheel and the brake drum.

4. While supporting the head of one shoe retaining pin from behind the backing plate, push the spring retainer in and rotate it 90° to remove it. See Fig. 6-3. Repeat the step for the other retainer.

5. Disengage the brake shoes from the lower brake shoe support at the bottom of the backing plate, and remove the lower return spring.

6. Unhook the parking brake cable from the lever that is attached to the rear brake shoe. See Fig. 6-4.

Fig. 6-3. Rear brake assembly showing brake shoe retaining pins and spring retainers (light arrows), and lower brake shoe support (dark arrows).

Fig. 6-4. Parking brake cable attachment to lever on rear brake shoe (arrow).

7. Unhook the spring from the bottom of the adjusting wedge, and remove the upper return spring. Remove the brake shoes.

> **CAUTION ——**
>
> *Used brake shoes should not be interchanged. If the shoes are to be reused, mark each shoe's position for reinstallation.*

8. Clamp the adjusting bar in a vise, and use pliers to remove the tensioning spring.

To install:

1. Clamp the front brake shoe in a vise. Lubricate the points where the brake shoe, the adjusting bar, the tensioning spring, and the adjusting wedge contact each other. Use Wolfracote grease, Volkswagen part no. G 000 650.

2. Install the adjusting bar and the tensioning spring as shown in Fig. 6-5, then install the adjusting wedge. The lug on the adjusting wedge should face the backing plate.

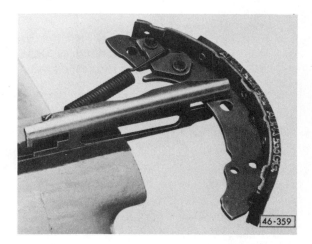

Fig. 6-5. Adjusting bar and tensioning spring being installed on brake shoe. Brake shoe and spring attachment are shown from behind.

3. Attach the rear brake shoe (with parking brake lever) as shown in Fig. 6-6, then install the upper return spring.

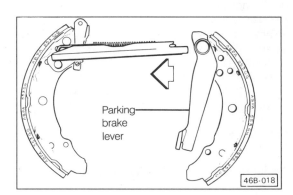

Parking brake lever

Fig. 6-6. Rear brake shoe with parking brake lever being attached to front shoe and adjusting bar. Shoes are held together by upper return spring.

4. Holding the brake shoes near the backing plate, attach the parking brake cable.

5. Using a small amount of Wolfracote grease, lubricate the points on the backing plate where the edges of the brake shoes make contact.

> **WARNING ——**
>
> *Do not allow grease to contaminate the brake linings.*

6. Place the upper ends of the brake shoes around the wheel cylinder piston, install the lower return spring, and engage the bottom ends of the shoes on the lower support.

12

7. Install the shoe retaining pins, the springs, and the spring retainers. Turn the retainers 90° to lock them in place.

8. Reinstall the adjusting wedge spring, then push the wedge up to fully retract the brake shoes for installing the drum.

9. Install the brake drum and repack and adjust the wheel bearings as described in **SUSPENSION AND STEERING**. Use a new cotter pin to secure the axle nut lock.

10. If the wheel was removed from the brake drum, mount the wheel and install the wheel lug bolts. Lower the car and then torque the lug bolts to 110 Nm (81 ft. lb.).

11. After completing the installation on both rear brakes, firmly apply the brake pedal once to set the self-adjusting wedge.

WARNING ━━
New brake linings require some break-in. Allow for slightly longer stopping distances for the first 100 to 150 miles of city driving, and avoid hard stops.

Reconditioning Brake Drums

Both rear brake drums should be resurfaced whenever new brake shoes are installed. **Table d** lists the specifications for resurfacing brake drums, including maximum diameter for the resurfaced drums. Drums which exceed the maximum diameter are too thin to be reliably used and should be replaced.

Brake drums can be resurfaced by most local automotive machine shops. Torquing a wheel to a brake drum changes its shape slightly. If possible, the drums should be resurfaced with the wheel mounted to the drum and the bolts torqued to 110 Nm (81 ft. lb.).

Table d. Brake Drum Reconditioning Specifications

Inside diameter, new . . . . .180.0 mm (7.087 in.)	
Maximum diameter after resurfacing . . . . .180.5 mm (7.106 in.)	
Wear limit . . . . .181.0 mm (7.126 in.)	

Inspecting and Replacing Wheel Cylinder

The wheel cylinder is mounted at the top of the backing plate between the brake shoes. It is reached by removing the brake drum as described in **Removing and Installing Brake Shoes**. Inspect the wheel cylinder by observing the action of the brake shoes while an assistant slowly depresses the brake pedal. Replace the cylinder if the pistons stick, or if the brake shoes do not move out the same distance at a uniform rate. Also replace the cylinder if there are signs of brake fluid leakage under the dust boot. To replace a wheel cylinder the brake line must be disconnected, and it will be necessary to bleed the brakes. See **4.2 Bleeding Brakes**.

NOTE ━━
When the brake drum is removed, insert two screwdrivers behind the backing plate flange and press them against the brake shoes to limit their travel.

To replace the wheel cylinder, first disconnect the brake line from the cylinder behind the backing plate. Seal the brake line to prevent contamination. Unhook the upper return spring and the adjusting bar tensioning spring. Push the adjusting wedge down to spread the brake shoes apart. Remove the two bolts that hold the wheel cylinder to the backing plate, and then remove the wheel cylinder.

Installation is the reverse of removal. Torque the wheel cylinder mounting bolts to 10 Nm (87 in. lb.), and torque the brake line union to 15 Nm (11 ft. lb.). Install the brake drum as described in **Removing and Installing Brake Shoes**, and bleed the brake system as described in **4.2 Bleeding Brakes**.

6.2 Parking Brake (Drum Brakes)

The parking brake lever and its cable connections are shown in Fig. 6-7. The mechanical parking brake operates only on the rear wheels, and is independent of the hydraulic brake system. Each of the two parking brake cables is connected to a lever on one of the rear brakes shoes. See Fig. 6-6 above. When the parking brake lever is pulled, the brake shoes are forced out against the brake drum.

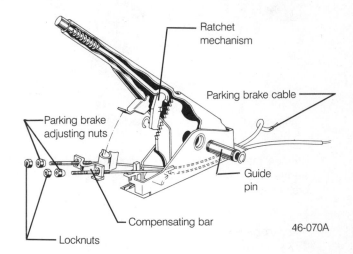

Fig. 6-7. Cut-away view of parking brake lever assembly showing cable connections and internal ratchet.

Adjusting Parking Brake

Adjusting the parking brake should only be necessary if the cable is replaced. Failure of the brake to hold the car most likely indicates worn brake shoes or a faulty self-adjusting mechanism. Check to see that the parking brake functions properly whenever the cables have been detached for rear brake service.

To adjust:

1. Raise the rear of the car and support it securely on jack stands.

2. With the parking brake fully released, firmly apply the brakes one time.

3. Move the parking brake lever to the second detent (second click) from the bottom.

4. Loosen the locknuts and tighten the adjusting nuts by equal amounts just until neither rear wheel can be rotated by hand.

5. Check that when the parking brake is fully released, both rear wheels rotate freely. Readjust if necessary.

6. Tighten the locknuts.

Replacing Parking Brake Cables

The cables can be replaced separately. Remove the locknut and the adjusting nut that hold the cable to the compensating bar. Remove the rear brake drum as described in **Removing and Installing Brake Shoes**, and then unhook the parking brake cable from the lever on the rear brake shoe. It may be necessary to partially disassemble the brakes. Pull the cable and conduit out of the backing plate and remove the cable from the guides and hangers which secure it to the trailing arm.

Pull the old cable out of the body from the rear. Lubricate the new cable with multipurpose grease before inserting it. Feed the cable into the backing plate without kinking it, and hook the end of the cable to the lever on the rear brake shoe. Reinstall the rear brake drum as described in **Removing and Installing Brake Shoes**. At the parking brake lever inside the car, install the compensating bar, the adjusting nut, and the locknut on the cable and adjust the parking brake as described above in **Adjusting Parking Brake**.

7. REAR DISC BRAKES

The components of the rear disc brakes are shown in Fig. 7-1. The rear disc brakes operate in much the same way as the front disc brakes described in **5. Front Disc Brakes**, except that the rear disc rotor doubles as the wheel hub and wheel bearing housing, and the rear calipers can be mechanically activated by the parking brake cables. The wheel lug bolts thread directly into the rotor, and the inner diameter of the rotor hub houses the wheel bearings.

Because the rear brakes do less of the work of stopping the car, they are not likely to wear as quickly or require service as frequently as the front brakes. Unless problem symptoms are actually observed at the rear brakes, troubleshooting of brake problems should always include the front brakes. If the rear brakes are worn and require service, then at the very least the front brakes should also be thoroughly inspected. The brake pads and rotors are subjected to the greatest wear, and are the components most often needing attention.

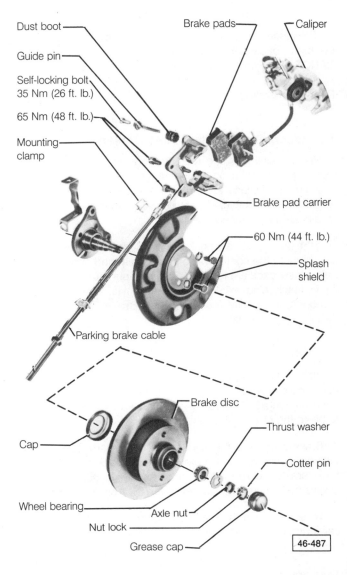

Fig. 7-1. Exploded view of rear disc brake assembly.

The brake pads are designed to be routinely replaced as they wear out. While it is possible to restore the brakes by replacing only the brake pads, full braking performance and minimum pad wear can only be achieved if the rotors are resurfaced or replaced at the same time. Removal of the brake rotors requires cleaning, repacking, and adjusting the wheel bearings during reassembly, as described in **SUSPENSION AND STEERING**.

WARNING ━━

Brake pad friction materials may contain asbestos fibers. Do not create dust by grinding, sanding, or cleaning the pads with compressed air. Avoid breathing any asbestos fibers or dust. Breathing asbestos may result in serious diseases such as asbestosis or cancer, or may result in death.

12

Checking Brake Pad Wear

The inspection procedure and specifications for checking the brake pads are found in **LUBRICATION AND MAINTENANCE**. For more complete inspection of pad condition, the pads must be removed, as described in **7.1 Reconditioning Rear Disc Brakes**.

7.1 Reconditioning Rear Disc Brakes

Reconditioning of the rear disc brakes typically includes replacing the brake pads and resurfacing or replacing the brake rotors. Unless the calipers and hoses are damaged, extremely worn, or leaking fluid, more extensive rear brake repairs are not normally required.

If the brake pads are soaked with oil, grease, or brake fluid, the cause of the contamination must be found and corrected before new pads are installed. Brake rotors must be replaced when resurfacing exceeds specified limits. See **Removing, Reconditioning, and Installing Rear Brake Rotors** for rotor thickness specifications.

Removing and Installing Rear Brake Pads

Although the calipers must be removed to change the brake pads, this can be done without disconnecting the flexible brake hose. Keeping the hydraulic system sealed eliminates the need to bleed the brakes afterward.

Brake pads and the surfaces of the rotors wear slightly differently. Always replace brake pads in complete sets. If old pads are to be reinstalled, such as after inspecting them, always make sure they are refitted in their original locations.

When replacing the brake pads, the two upper self-locking caliper mounting bolts should be replaced.

To remove:

1. Raise the rear of the car and support it securely on jack stands. Remove the rear wheels. Release the parking brake.

2. Remove the wire clip that secures the parking brake cable to the brake caliper, as shown in Fig. 7-2, and unhook the cable from the actuating lever. Slide the cable out of the cable guide.

3. Remove the upper self-locking caliper mounting bolt from the brake caliper. See Fig. 7-2. Hold the guide pin with an open-end wrench to remove the bolt. Pivot the caliper downward off the brake pads, as shown in Fig. 7-3.

4. Lift out the brake pads.

> **CAUTION** ━━
>
> *Do not interchange used pads. If the pads are to be reused, mark them for reinstallation in their same positions.*

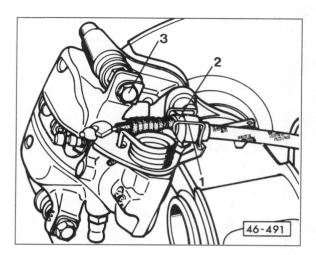

Fig. 7-2. Wire clip (**1**) to be removed when disconnecting parking brake cable from cable guide (**2**). Upper caliper mounting bolt is at **3**.

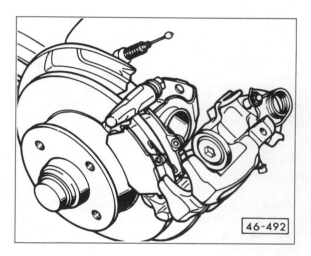

Fig. 7-3. Upper caliper mounting bolt removed and caliper pivoted downward on lower guide pin for removal of brake pads.

To install:

1. Place the brake pads in position on the brake pad carrier.

2. When installing new brake pads, adjust the caliper to provide clearance for the thicker new brake pads. Use a hex wrench in the piston socket to turn the caliper piston clockwise all the way into the caliper housing, as shown in Fig. 7-4.

> **NOTE** ━━
>
> Turning in the caliper pistons to gain clearance for the thicker new brake pads will cause brake fluid to overflow the master cylinder fluid reservoir. To prevent this, use a clean syringe to first remove some fluid from the reservoir.

Fig. 7-4. Rear caliper piston being turned into caliper with hex wrench.

3. Pivot the caliper back into position and install a new upper self-locking mounting bolt. Hold the guide pin with an open-end wrench, and torque the self-locking bolt to 35 Nm (26 ft. lb.).

4. If new brake pads were installed, adjust the parking brake as described in **7.2 Parking Brake**.

5. Mount the wheel and loosely install the lug bolts, then lower the car and torque the bolts to 110 Nm (81 ft. lb.).

6. Before running the engine or moving the car, pump the brake pedal at least 40 times to reset the automatic adjustment of the rear calipers.

> **CAUTION ▬**
>
> *Running the engine and providing vacuum boost to the brakes while resetting the automatic adjustment may jam the caliper.*

7. Check the level of brake fluid in the reservoir. If necessary, add new brake fluid to fill the reservoir to the MAX mark.

> **WARNING ▬**
>
> *New brake pads require some break-in. Allow for slightly longer stopping distances for the first 100 to 150 miles of city driving, and avoid hard stops.*

Removing, Reconditioning, and Installing Rear Brake Rotors

To remove the rear brake rotors, first remove the brake pads as described above. Remove the two bolts holding the brake pad carrier to the stub axle, and suspend the caliper and pad carrier from the suspension or body. Avoid stretching or kinking the hose. If the brake hose remains connected, it will not be necessary to bleed the brakes.

> **NOTE ▬**
>
> Be careful when suspending the caliper assembly. The guide pins are lubricated and will allow the caliper to separate from the pad carrier.

Remove the wheel bearing grease cap from the center of the brake rotor, and then remove the cotter pin, the nut lock, and the axle nut from the stub axle. Tugging on the brake rotor slightly if necessary, remove the thrust washer and the outer wheel bearing. Remove the brake rotor. Use a screwdriver to pry out the dust cap and grease seal from the back of the rotor hub, and remove the inner bearing parts.

Installation is the reverse of removal. See **SUSPENSION AND STEERING** for information on cleaning the wheel bearings, packing them with new grease, and adjusting them after installation. Install a new inner grease seal. Torque the brake pad carrier mounting bolts to 65 Nm (48 ft. lb.). Reinstall the brake pads as described in **Removing and Installing Rear Brake Pads**.

> **NOTE ▬**
>
> New replacement brake rotors should be cleaned with a grease-free solvent, such as a commercially available brake cleaner, before installing the caliper and brake pads.

Brake rotors should always be resurfaced in pairs, with an equal amount of material removed from both sides of each rotor. **Table e** lists the minimum requirements for resurfacing brake rotors—the minimum thickness of a rotor which can still be resurfaced, and the minimum allowable thickness after resurfacing. Rotors which fail to meet either minimum are too thin to be reliably used and should be replaced. Brake rotors can be resurfaced by most any local automotive machine shop.

Table e. Rear Rotor Reconditioning Specifications

Thickness new	10.0 mm (.394 in.)
Minimum thickness	8.0 mm (.315 in.)
Maximum runout	0.06 mm (.002 in.)

7.2 Parking Brake (Disc Brakes)

The parking brake operates only on the rear wheels. It is mechanically actuated, and is independent of the hydraulic brake system. Fig. 6-7 above is a cut-away view of the parking brake lever assembly. The lever operates two separate, replaceable cables connected to the rear brake calipers. When the lever is pulled, the actuating lever on the caliper applies pressure to the brake caliper piston.

Adjusting Parking Brake

The parking brake should only have to be adjusted if the cable, the brake rotor, the brake caliper, or brake pads are replaced. Failure of the brake to hold the car most likely indicates worn brake pads or a faulty caliper. Check to see that the parking brake functions properly whenever the cables have been detached for rear brake service.

CAUTION ━━━

Before adjusting the parking brake cables, adjust the rear disc brakes by retracting the caliper pistons and pumping the brake pedal to reset the automatic adjustment, as described in **Removing and Installing Rear Brake Pads**.

To adjust:

1. Raise the rear of the car and support it securely on jack stands. Remove the rear wheels. Release the parking brake if it is applied.

2. Loosen the parking brake cable locknuts and adjusting nuts under the parking brake lever just until tension on the cables is relieved.

NOTE ━━━

The actuator levers on the calipers should be against their stops as shown in Fig. 7-5. If not, then the caliper's automatic adjustment mechanism may be faulty.

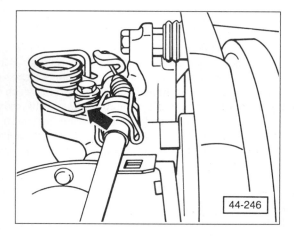

Fig. 7-5. Actuator lever against stop (**arrow**) on brake caliper.

3. Set and release the parking brake three times to stretch and seat the cables.

4. Tighten the adjusting nuts so that when the parking brake is applied, the following conditions are met: at the first detent (one click) the rear rotors should turn by hand with moderate drag; at the second detent the rotors should turn only with considerable effort; at the third detent it should not be possible to turn the rotors by hand.

NOTE ━━━

When the parking brake is released, the rotors should again turn freely.

5. Check the gap between the actuator lever and the stop on the caliper. When the parking brake is correctly adjusted, it should be no greater than 1.0 mm (.039 in.). If it is, loosen the cable adjusting nuts in small increments until the gap is correct.

6. Tighten the parking brake cable locknuts. Mount the wheels and loosely install the lug bolts. Lower the car and torque the lug bolts to 110 Nm (81 ft. lb.).

Replacing Parking Brake Cable

The cables can be replaced separately. Remove the locknut and the adjusting nut that hold the cable to the compensating bar. Remove the wire clip that holds the parking brake cable to the caliper. Unhook the cable from the actuator lever on the caliper and remove the cable from the guides and hangers which secure it to the trailing arm.

Pull the old cable out of the body from the rear. Lubricate the new cable with multipurpose grease before inserting it. Feed the cable into place without kinking it, through the cable guide on the caliper. Hook the cable to the caliper actuating lever and secure it with the wire clip. At the parking brake lever inside the car, install the compensating bar, the adjusting nut, and the locknut on the cable, and adjust the parking brake as described above in **Adjusting Parking Brake**.

7.3 Calipers

Fig. 7-6 is an exploded view of the rear disc brake caliper. The rear calipers differ from those used at the front, mainly in the addition of the automatically adjusting parking brake actuating mechanism.

Brake fluid leaks around the brake caliper piston are the result of a failed or damaged piston seal, perhaps caused by corrosion, scoring, or pitting of the piston or caliper bore. The seal can be replaced, but a damaged piston, which is not available as a replacement part, will promptly destroy the new seal. To remedy a leaking caliper piston seal and avoid future problems, complete replacement of the caliper is recommended. A damaged caliper dust seal can be replaced separately.

To replace a caliper, first remove the parking brake cable from the caliper, as described in **7.2 Parking Brake (Disc Brakes)**. It may be necessary to loosen the cable adjusting nuts under the parking brake lever. Remove the two self-locking caliper mounting bolts and pull the caliper away from the brake pads and carrier. Hold the guide pins with an open-end wrench to remove the bolts. Disconnect the brake hose from the caliper and drain the brake fluid into a container. Cap the end of the brake line to prevent dirt and moisture from entering the brake system.

Installation is the reverse of removal. Pre-bleed the caliper by laying it on its side, as shown in Fig. 7-7. Fill the piston chamber with brake fluid through the bleeder valve until clear fluid runs out of the brake hose connection, then close the bleeder valve. Torque the brake hose union to 15 Nm (11 ft. lb.). Use new self-locking bolts to mount the caliper to the brake pad carrier, and torque them to 35 Nm (26 ft. lb.). Bleed the brake system as described in **4.2 Bleeding Brakes**. Reconnect the parking brake cable and adjust it as described in **Adjusting Parking Brake**. Do not let brake fluid contaminate the brake pads or brake rotor surface.

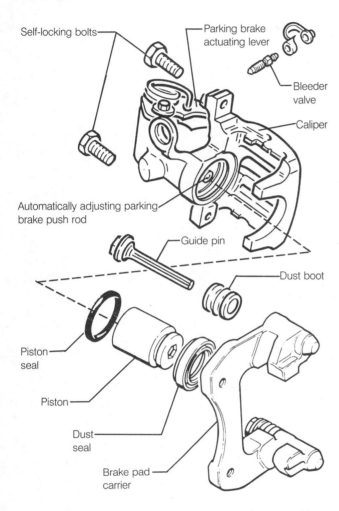

Fig. 7-6. Exploded view of rear brake caliper assembly.

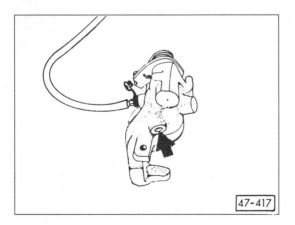

47-417

Fig. 7-7. Rear brake caliper being pre-bled prior to installation. Piston faces down. Bleeder valve and brake hose connection (arrow) face up. Fill until fluid escaping is free of air.

8. TECHNICAL DATA

I. Tolerances, Wear Limits, and Settings

Brake disc, solid front
    thickness, new part . . . . .12.00 mm (.472 in.)
    thickness, minimum . . . . .10.00 mm (.393 in.)

Brake disc, front ventilated
    thickness, new part . . . . .20.00 mm (.787 in.)
    thickness, minimum . . . . .18.00 mm (.709 in.)

Brake drum, rear
    inside diameter, new drum . . . . .180.00 mm (7.087 in.)
    inside diameter,
    maximum after resurfacing . . . . . . .180.50 mm (7.106 in.)
    inside diameter, maximum. . . . . . . .181.00 mm (7.126 in.)

Brake disc, rear
    thickness, new part . . . . .10.00 mm (.394 in.)
    thickness, minimum. . . . . .8.00 mm (.315 in.)
    runout, maximum permissible . . . . .0.06 mm (.002 in.)

II. Tightening Torques

Brake caliper (front) to wheel bearing
    housing (bolt) . . . . .25 Nm (18 ft. lb.)
Brake disc splash shield to wheel bearing
    housing (bolt). . . . . .10 Nm (87 in. lb.)

Rear brake backing plate and stub axle
    to axle beam (bolt) . . . . .60 Nm (44 ft. lb.)
Rear wheel cylinder to backing plate (bolt) . . .10 Nm (87in. lb.)

Brake caliper (rear) to brake pad carrier
    (self-locking bolt) . . . . .35 Nm (26 ft. lb.)
Brake pad carrier to stub axle flange (bolt). . . .65 Nm (48 ft. lb.)

Brake hose to brake caliper . . . . .15 Nm (11 ft. lb.)
Brake hose to wheel cylinder . . . . .15 Nm (11 ft. lb.)
Brake hoses — except to caliper or
    wheel cylinder . . . . .15–20 Nm (11–15 ft. lb.)
Brake line unions (union nuts) . . . . .15–20 Nm (11–15 ft. lb.)
Brake lines to master cylinder. . . . . . .15–20 Nm (11–15 ft. lb.)
Proportioning valves to master cylinder .15–20 Nm (11–15 ft. lb.)

Master cylinder to vacuum booster . . . . . . .20 Nm (15 ft. lb.)
Vacuum booster to support
    bracket (nut). . . . . .20 Nm (15 ft. lb.)

Wheel to brake disc or brake
    drum (lug bolt). . . . . .110 Nm (81 ft. lb.)

12

BODY AND INTERIOR

Contents

Introduction 3

1. General Description 4
  1.1 Instrument Panel and Instrument Cluster 4
  1.2 Seats, Seat Belts, and Interior 4
  1.3 Ventilation, Heating, and Air Conditioning 4
  1.4 Body 5

2. Maintenance 5

3. Troubleshooting 5

4. Interior 5
  4.1 Instrument Cluster and Instrument Panel 5
       Removing and Installing Speedometer Cable
       and Drive Gear 8
  4.2 Radio and Antenna 8
  4.3 Interior Lights 9
       Replacing Interior Light Bulbs 9
  4.4 Heater and Controls (without air conditioning) . 9
       Heater Core 10
       Replacing and Adjusting Heater
       Control Cables 11
       Fresh Air Blower 12
  4.5 Heater and Controls (with air conditioning) . . . 12
       Heater core 12
       Checking Vacuum System 13
       Replacing Control Head 13
       Fresh Air Blower 13
  4.6 Seat Belts 14
       Inspecting Seat Belts 14
       Installing or Replacing Seat Belts 14

       Front Seat Belt Height Adjustment 16
       Child Restraint Tethering (Jetta only) 17
  4.7 Front Seats 18
       Heated Seats 18
  4.8 Rear Seats 19
  4.9 Headliner 19

5. Doors 20
  5.1 Door Assembly 20
       Interior Trim 20
       Window Regulator 21
       Power Window Regulator 21
       Handles and Locks 21
  5.2 Central Locking System 22
       Bi-Pressure System Troubleshooting 22
       Removing and Installing Door Activators 24
       Bi-pressure pump 24
       Rear Lid Activator 24
       Gas Tank Flap Activator 24
  5.3 Side Mirrors 24

6. Exterior 26
  6.1 Headlights 26
       Aiming Headlights 27
  6.2 Taillight Assembly 27
  6.3 Side Marker and Front Turn Signal Lights . . . 28
  6.4 Trim, Bumpers, and Body 28
       Removing Front Body Parts and Grille 28
       Removing and Installing Body Trim 30
       Removing and Installing Bumpers 31
       Removing Plastic Bumper Cover 32
       Hood Lock Cable 32

2 BODY AND INTERIOR

Rear Lid and Hatchback 32

Windshield. 33

7. Sunroof. 33

7.1   Removing and Installing Sunroof. 33

7.2   Adjusting Sunroof Fit. 34

Removing and Installing Rear Guides
with Cables 35

8. Body Assembly Materials 35

9. Air Conditioning. 36

9.1   System Description 36

Safety Features 37

9.2   Inspections and Tests 37

Checking Refrigerant Charge 37

A/C Performance Test 37

9.3   Air Conditioning Specifications 38

TABLES

a. Bulb Application and Part Numbers. 9

b. Heating and Ventilation Vacuum System Test 13

c. Body Assembly Materials 36

d. Air Conditioning Specifications 38

Body and Interior

Introduction

The Volkswagen Golf, Jetta, and GTI have unit construction steel bodies that are exceptionally strong and light. Their lightness contributes greatly to the outstanding performance and fuel economy of the cars. Because very few screws and bolts are used in assembling the body, fewer rattles are likely to develop. The ride is quieted further by the application of sound-dampening material to the floor plates and the body panels.

During manufacture, the various body panels and subassemblies, plus a number of smaller pressed-steel panels and plates, are joined by electric welding. Although all body panels are available as replacement parts, replacement panels must be butt-welded to the undamaged parts of the body after the damaged panels have been cut away. This work should only be undertaken by an experienced body repair technician.

The front fenders, however, are bolted to the main body structure so that they can be easily and economically replaced in the event of damage. The hood, the grille, the doors, and the luggage compartment lid are also removable. These bolt-on components are easily replaced by persons with little or no knowledge of auto body repair. If you lack the skills, special equipment, or a suitable workshop for extensive body repairs, we suggest that you leave this work to an authorized Volkswagen dealer or other qualified repair shop. We especially urge you to consult a Volkswagen dealer before beginning repairs on a vehicle that may be subject to Volkswagen's warranty coverage.

Also covered in this section is the ventilation and heating system. Electrical repairs to the instrument cluster, including the gauges and lights, are covered in **ELECTRICAL SYSTEM**. Care of the body, trim, upholstery, and windows is described in **LUBRICATION AND MAINTENANCE**.

13

1. GENERAL DESCRIPTION

1.1 Instrument Panel and Instrument Cluster

The padded instrument panel houses the instrument cluster and the ventilation and heating system. It is fastened to the body and can be removed using ordinary hand tools. The instrument cluster is removable as a unit without removing the instrument panel. All electrical repairs to the instrument cluster are covered in **ELECTRICAL SYSTEM**.

1.2 Seats, Seat Belts, and Interior

The front seats are individually mounted to the floor. Bench-style rear seats are clipped to the body. Folding rear seats are bolted to the floor. Both styles are easily removed for access to the rear seat belt mountings and for access to the fuel gauge sending unit.

Two types of seat belts are installed on the cars covered by this manual: a typical three-point seat belt that crosses the hips and the shoulder, and a two-point passive restraint system that crosses the chest and has an additional knee bar. Two-point sytems have an ignition interlock that disables the ignition if the seat belts are undone when starting the engine.

All interior trim including the headliner is easily removed using ordinary hand tools.

1.3 Ventilation, Heating, and Air Conditioning

Ventilation is by a flow-through system. Fresh air enters the car at the air intake in the right side of the plenum chamber in the body cowl. Interior air exits through vents located in the side trim panels of the luggage compartment. A three-speed fresh air blower assists air flow.

A blend heating system is used for faster reaction and less fluctuation in passenger compartment temperature levels. In a blend system, coolant always flows through the heater core. Temperature is regulated by a blending door which controls the amount of air that passes through the heater core before it enters the passenger compartment. Two other doors control the flow of air to the windshield and the passenger compartment. See Fig. 1-1.

Cars with air conditioning also use a blend system. Fresh air is first cooled and dehumidified by the evaporator. A portion of the air can then be directed by the blending door through the heater core to maintain the desired temperature. In very hot conditions the interior air can be recirculated for maximum cooling.

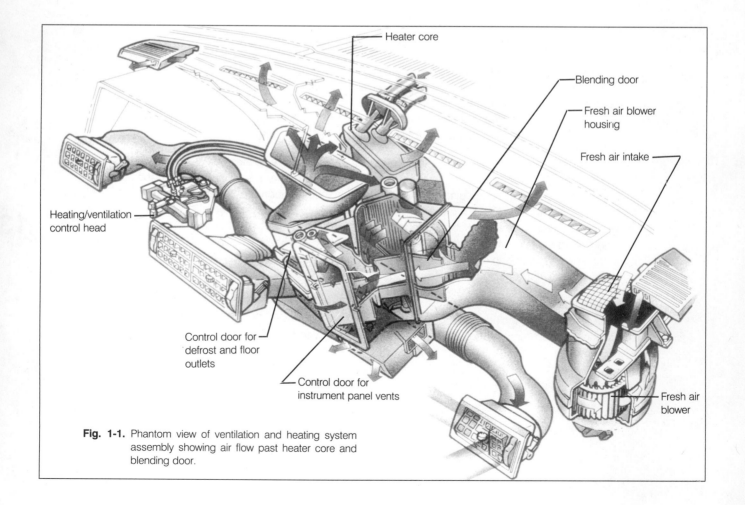

Fig. 1-1. Phantom view of ventilation and heating system assembly showing air flow past heater core and blending door.

1.4 Body

The body is of welded, unitized construction, meaning it does not have a separate frame. See Fig. 1-2. This design forms a very rigid passenger compartment, with large crumple zones in the front and rear for energy absorption in the event of a collision.

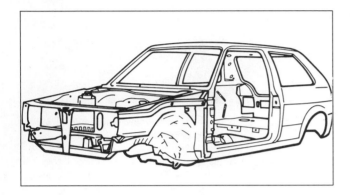

Fig. 1-2. Unitized construction of Golf body. Jetta is similar.

Because the engine, the transaxle, and the driving wheels are all located at the front of the vehicle, the longitudinal hump in the front floor panel does not house the driveshaft. Instead, it serves as a strengthening member and houses the exhaust system, the parking brake cables, and the brake lines.

For corrosion protection, all steel is treated and has a multi-layer finish, and the body seams are sealed using a PVC compound. The front fenders are flanged to allow moisture evaporation, and zinc plates are installed between the fender and the body to act as an anode. The body is undercoated and all interior cavities are flooded with a hot wax.

2. MAINTENANCE

The following routine maintenance operations should be performed at the time and mileage intervals listed in **LUBRI-CATION AND MAINTENANCE**. Maintenance procedures are also described there.

1. Checking heating and ventilation system operation

3. TROUBLESHOOTING

Because the components and assemblies covered in this section vary widely, specific troubleshooting is covered with the repair information. For more help when troubleshooting electrical problems, see **ELECTRICAL SYSTEM**, or see the discussion of troubleshooting in **FUNDAMENTALS** at the beginning of the manual.

4. INTERIOR

This section covers the removal and replacement of interior components. Repairs to interior electrical components are described in **ELECTRICAL SYSTEM**. Information concerning interior door trim, door locks, window controls, and other mechanical parts of the door are covered in **5. Doors**.

4.1 Instrument Cluster and Instrument Panel

The instrument cluster can be removed without removing the instrument panel, however, the instrument cluster must be removed to remove the instrument panel.

To remove the instrument cluster:

1. Disconnect the negative (−) terminal from the battery.

2. Remove the center console. On manual transmission cars first remove the gearshift lever knob and the gearshift boot. On automatic transmission cars remove the selector lever cover plate. Finally, depending on the center console as shown in Fig. 4-1 and Fig. 4-2, remove the retaining screws and partially remove the console. Separate any electrical connectors from behind.

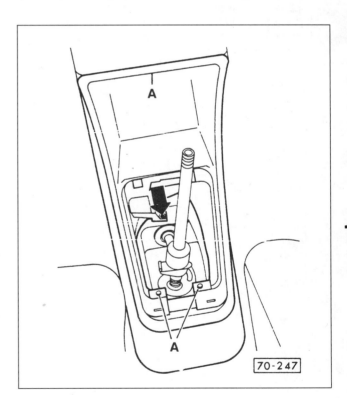

Fig. 4-1. First type of center console showing screw (arrow) to be removed. Additional screws may be located behind ash tray. Pull console back from retaining guides **A** and up.

13

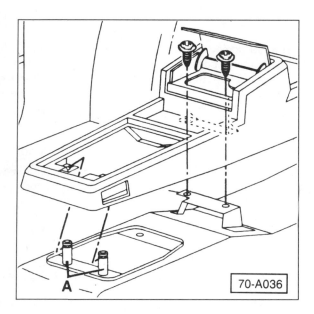

Fig. 4-2. Second type of center console showing screws to be removed. Pull console up off retaining guides **A**.

3. Remove the lower-left instrument panel tray by removing the screws indicated in Fig. 4-3. On some Golf and GTI models the tray may run the full length of the instrument panel, or on models with passive restraint there may be a knee bar. With full-length trays it is necessary to remove two screws securing the fuse panel to the tray. Kneebars are held with two bolts at either end.

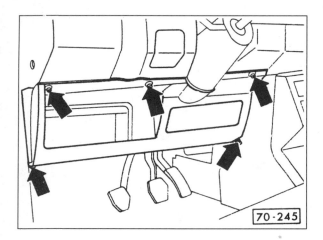

Fig. 4-3. Retaining screws (arrows) to be removed from left-side instrument panel tray.

4. Remove the speedometer cable. Reach behind the instrument cluster and pinch the cable retaining clip, sliding it off the cable end. See Fig. 4-4. Pull the cable from the cluster.

5. Remove the steering wheel and lower steering column cover as described in **SUSPENSION AND STEERING**.

Fig. 4-4. Speedometer cable retaining clip. Arrows indicate clips to be pinched.

6. Remove the heating and ventilation control head from the instrument panel. Pull the control levers straight out, unclip the trim plate, disconnect the wires to it, and remove the plate. Then remove the three control head mounting screws. See Fig. 4-5.

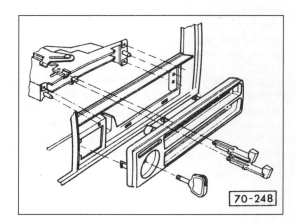

Fig. 4-5. Exploded view of ventilation control head showing removal of control levers.

7. Remove the radio, if applicable.

8. On Jettas, pry the electrical switches from the center of the instrument panel trim plate and remove the switches by disconnecting the electrical connectors.

9. On Golf and GTI models, remove the headlight switch.

10. Remove the instrument panel trim plate. On Golf and GTI models, the plate is held in place by ten spring clips. Work around the rim of trim plate, gently freeing each clip. On Jettas, the plate is held in place by the retaining screws shown in Fig. 4-6.

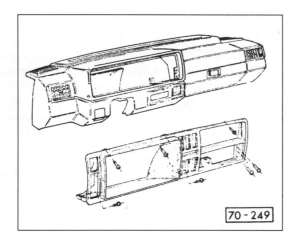

Fig. 4-6. Retaining screws to be removed from instrument panel trim plate on Jettas.

11. Remove the two instrument cluster retaining screws indicated in Fig. 4-7 and partially remove the cluster. On Golf and GTI models, the right screw is behind one of the blank switch covers.

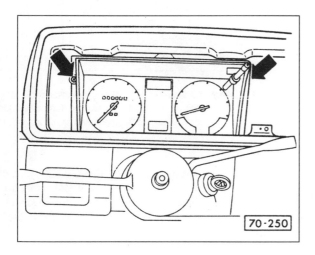

Fig. 4-7. Retaining screws (arrows) to be removed from instrument cluster.

12. Working from the rear, disconnect all electrical and vacuum connections, and label the vacuum lines. Remove the instrument cluster.

Installation is the reverse of removal.

To remove instrument panel:

1. Remove the instrument cluster as described above.

2. Remove the right-side lower instrument panel tray where applicable by removing the screws shown in Fig. 4-8.

3. Pry out the left, center, and right ventilation grilles from their housings as shown in Fig. 4-9, then remove the retaining screws and the housings

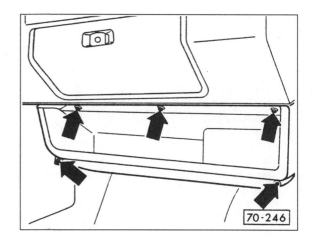

Fig. 4-8. Retaining screws (arrows) to be removed from right-lower instrument panel tray

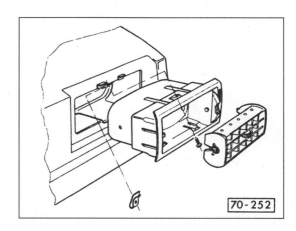

Fig. 4-9. Ventilation grille and related parts.

4. Remove the speaker grilles and, if applicable, the speakers. Remove the grille retaining screw and slide the grille toward the rear of the car. See Fig. 4-10. On Golfs and GTIs, the screw is covered by a full-length trim piece.

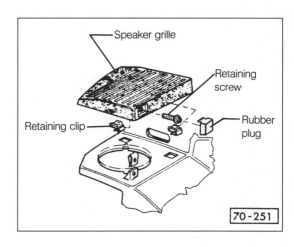

Fig. 4-10. Exploded view of speaker grille mounting hardware. Jetta grille is shown, Golf and GTI are similar.

13

5. On diesel-engined vehicles, remove the cold start handle from the cold start cable. Consult **FUEL SYSTEM (Diesel)** if necessary.

6. On Golf and GTI models, remove the electrical switches from the center of the instrument panel. Remove the nuts holding the switch bracket in place and disconnect all electrical connectors.

7. On Golf and GTI models, remove the relay panel from its bracket underneath the left side of the instrument panel, and disconnect all electrical connections from the left side of the instrument panel.

8. Pry out the glove box light assembly and remove its wiring connector. Remove the glove box by removing the screws around its rim.

9. Remove the drip tray from the base of the windshield in the engine compartment, then remove the screws and nuts shown in Fig. 4-11. Partially pull the instrument panel away from the body. Remove any other electrical connections to the panel, and then pull it from the vehicle.

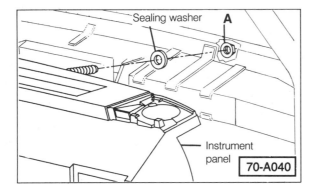

Fig. 4-11. Location of instrument panel padding retaining screws **B**, **C**, and nuts **A** to be removed. Nuts are in air plenum in engine compartment.

Installation is the reverse of removal. Make sure that the sealing washers on the instrument panel studs are in place as shown in Fig. 4-12 before the panel is installed, and double check all electrical connections.

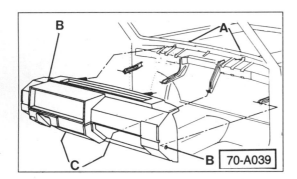

Fig. 4-12. Sealing washer installation for instrument panel studs. Stud nut is at **A**.

Removing and Installing Speedometer Cable and Drive Gear

The speedometer cable runs from a drive gear in the transmission to the back of the speedometer. On automatic transmissions, the cable is mounted directly to the transmission with a union nut. On manual transmissions, the speedometer cable is held by a bolt and hold-down clamp to the transmission and separate drive gear as shown in Fig. 4-13. On U.S. and Canada cars with oxygen sensors, the cable is in two pieces. The first part runs from the transmission to the oxygen sensor (OXS) mileage counter mounted on the firewall. The second part runs from the oxygen sensor (OXS) counter to the speedometer. On diesel cars and Canada cars with automatic transmission, the speedometer cable is in one piece.

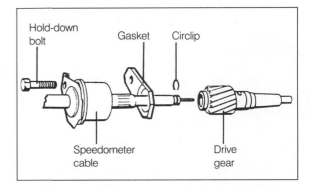

Fig. 4-13. Transmission end of speedometer cable on vehicles with manual transmission. On diesel models, drive gear has 16 teeth and is natural color. On fuel injected models, gear has 15 teeth and is marked red.

To remove a speedometer cable, disconnect the battery ground strap then remove the lower instrument panel tray as described above. Remove the cable from the back of the speedometer as shown in Fig. 4-4 above. Unbolt the cable from the transmission.

To prevent premature failure of the new speedometer cable, do not grease the speedometer end of the cable, and position the cable so that it is free of sharp bends.

New cables for cars with manual transmissions do not come with a drive gear. To install the old drive gear on a new cable, pull the drive gear off of the old cable. Install a new circlip to the new cable and push on the drivegear until the circlip can be seen through the hole in the gear. The circlip's gap should be offset 180° from the hole in the gear.

4.2 Radio and Antenna

The factory-installed radio is removed using two U-shaped clips inserted into the face plate of the radio at the corners. To remove the radio, disconnect the battery ground strap. Push the clips in until they click into position, and then withdraw the radio. Remove the clips before installing the radio, and make sure that the rubber mounting plug is properly engaged. Additional U-shaped clips are available separately from an authorized Volkswagen dealer, tool no. VW 160 (order no. TV0 160 000 90 ZEL).

Factory or after-market radios can be installed on models with or without the factory-installed prep kit. Disconnect the battery ground strap. All wiring for installing a radio is accessible after removing the radio face plate and instrument panel trim plate as described in **4.1 Instrument Cluster and Instrument Panel**. See the wiring diagrams in **ELECTRICAL SYSTEM** marked **Radio**, or **Stereo Radio** to help identify connectors, or to find a power source and ground.

Speakers can be installed in the instrument panel in all cars, in the rear hat shelf on Jettas, and in the hat shelf extension on Golf and GTI models. See Fig. 4-10 above when removing the front speaker grilles.

To replace the roof-mounted antenna on 16-valve models, the radio must be removed, and the headliner must be removed as described in **4.9 Headliner**.

To replace a fender-mounted antenna, remove the instrument cluster as described in **4.1 Instrument Cluster and Instrument Panel**, and remove the wheel house liner as described in **6.4 Trim, Bumpers, and Body**. Working from the engine compartment, remove the plenum drip tray and pull the antenna cable and its grommet out of the firewall. Note the cable routing in the foam tube behind the instrument cluster, and reinstall the same way, to make sure that it does not crimp any vacuum hoses after installation. Remove the antenna retaining nut at the base of the antenna, pull the antenna down into the wheelhouse, and remove it from the mounting bracket. When installing the antenna, use multi-purpose grease on the mounting hole and the nut to reduce rusting.

If the antenna is not to be reinstalled, a plug is available to seal the fender hole (part no. 321 821 169) and to seal the hole in the firewall (part no. N 020 027 1) be sure to also plug the hole in the plenum tray.

4.3 Interior Lights

A light failure may be caused by a blown fuse, especially if more than one bulb appears to have failed. Check and, if necessary, replace fuses as described in **ELECTRICAL SYSTEM**. **Table a** lists interior bulb applications and their part numbers. Dashboard lights and their replacement are covered in **ELECTRICAL SYSTEM**.

Table a. Bulb Application and Part Numbers

Bulb	VW Part No.	U.S. Trade No.
Interior dome	N 17 723 2	211
Glove compartment	N 17 726 2	–
Luggage compartment	N 17 723 2 (Jetta)	211
	N 17 725 2 (Golf/GTI)	–
Center stop	N 17 753 2	168

Replacing Interior Light Bulbs

Always turn off the ignition before replacing a bulb. Avoid leaving fingerprints on the bulb. Fingerprints evaporate when the glass gets hot and can dim the light or reflector.

To replace the dome light bulb, press against the spring clip indicated in Fig. 4-14, and withdraw the assembly. Press the assembly back into position after installing the new bulb.

Fig. 4-14. Spring clip (arrow) that holds interior dome light in headliner.

To replace the luggage compartment light bulb, use a small flat-blade screwdriver to pry the light assembly in the direction shown in Fig. 4-15, then withdraw the assembly. Install the wiring connector end first, and press the assembly back into position. Replace the glove compartment bulb the same way.

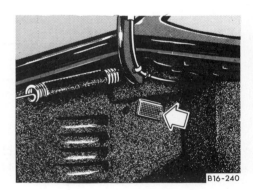

Fig. 4-15. Spring clip that holds luggage compartment light to body for Jetta.

To replace any one of the three center stop light bulbs, remove the bulb housing by pressing the small clips on either side of the assembly inwards to separate the housing from the lens. After installing the new bulb(s), press the bulb housing into position.

4.4 Heater and Controls
(without air conditioning)

The components of the heating and ventilation system and its controls are shown in Fig. 4-16. The heater box contains the heater core, and three doors operated by the control head to regulate air temperature and air flow. The top lever of the control head is connected by cables to the instrument panel vent door, and to the defrost/heater door. The bottom lever is connected by cable to the blending door for temperature regulation.

13

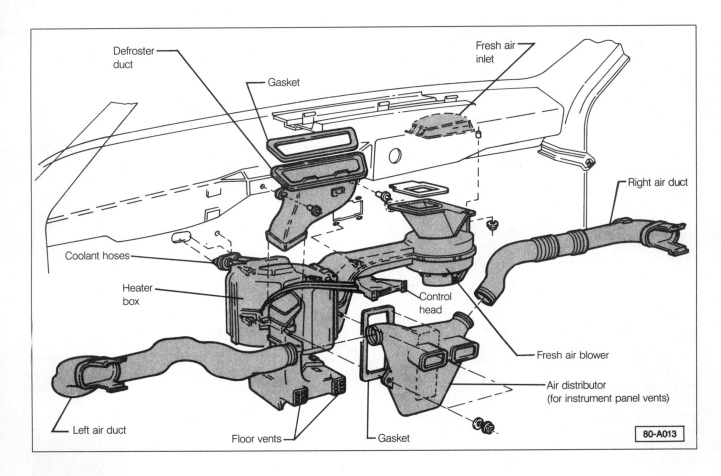

Fig. 4-16. Exploded view of ventilation and heating system used on cars without air conditioning.

Heater Core

Coolant leaking visibly into the passenger compartment is a sign of a faulty core or core seal. A sweet, anti-freeze odor in the car's interior, or a constantly fogged windshield may also indicate a faulty core. Inspect the carpet and the area near the floor vents for any signs of moisture or coolant. A leaking heater core may be caused by overpressurization of the cooling system. See **COOLING SYSTEM** for more information.

To replace heater core:

1. Drain the coolant as described in **COOLING SYSTEM.**

2. Remove the instrument panel as described in **4.1 Instrument Cluster and Instrument Panel.**

3. Remove the two hose clamps and hoses from the heater core. See Fig. 4-17. They are accessible from inside the engine compartment. Plug the core openings to prevent coolant from spilling.

4. Remove the air distributor by removing the two nuts that hold it to the heater box. Separate the distributor from the left and right air ducts.

Fig. 4-17. Heater hose clamps and hoses to be removed from heater core. Remove clips by squeezing tangs.

5. Remove the heater box and control cable assembly by removing the three nuts that hold the box to the car, and by disconnecting the defroster duct and the fresh air blower housing. Discard the old soft seal.

6. Remove the heater core from the heater box by removing the two retaining bolts at the top of the heater box. Make sure that the bottom gasket is in place when the new core is installed into the heater box.

Installation is the reverse of removal. Use a new soft seal where the heater core hose connections pass through the body. Fill the cooling system as described in **COOLING SYSTEM**.

Replacing and Adjusting Heater Control Cables

The three cables that control the heating and ventilation system are identified by their color and length. The long black cable controls the door for the instrument panel vents, the short black cable controls the heater/defroster door, and the blue cable controls the blend door. If a cable or the control head is replaced, the cables should be adjusted.

Replace control cables by first removing the center console and the lower instrument panel trays as described in **4.1 Instrument Cluster and Instrument Panel**. Next, remove the control head from the instrument panel as shown in Fig. 4-5 above. Release the cable housing retaining clips on the heater box and control head, and then pull the cable off of the door control lever. Connect the new cable to the door lever, but do not install the cable housing retaining clip on the heater box. Connect the other end of the new cable to the control head as shown in Fig. 4-18, install the cable housing retaining clip, reinstall the control head in the instrument panel, and adjust the cable as described below. The remainder of installation is the reverse of removal.

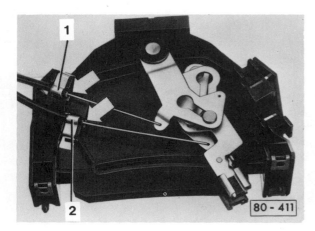

Fig. 4-18. Control cables installed on control head. View is from top. **1** is long black cable, **2** is short black cable. Arrows indicate correct clip installation. Turn head over for installation of blue cable.

To adjust control cables, remove all of the cable housing retaining clips on the heater box. Push the levers in the control head all the way to the left. Push the heater box door levers in turn in the directions indicated in Fig. 4-19, Fig. 4-20, and Fig. 4-21, hold the levers in these positions, and install the cable housing retaining clip.

Fig. 4-19. Long black cable for instrument panel vent door being adjusted. Arrow shows direction to push lever during adjustment.

Fig. 4-20. Short black cable for heater/defroster door being adjusted. Arrow shows direction to push lever during adjustment.

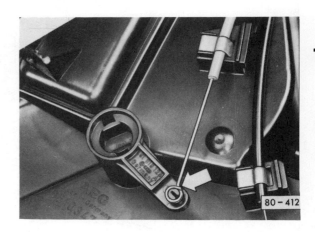

Fig. 4-21. Blue cable for blend door being adjusted. Arrow shows direction to push lever during adjustment.

13

Fresh Air Blower

The fresh air blower is located behind the glove compartment, and is reached by removing the glove compartment and the lower right instrument panel tray as described in **4.1 Instrument Cluster and Instrument Panel.** See **ELECTRICAL SYSTEM.** for electrical tests of the blower motor.

Remove the blower motor by depressing the retaining lug and twisting the assembly off as shown in Fig. 4-22. Disconnect the electrical connector. Installation is the reverse of removal.

Fig. 4-22. Blower motor being removed. Push retaining tab (**A**) and rotate motor in direction of arrow.

4.5 Heater and Controls

(with air conditioning)

The controls of the heating and ventilation system with air conditioning (A/C) are shown in Fig. 4-23. The heater box contains the heater core and three control doors operated by the control head to regulate air temperature and air flow. The fresh air blower housing contains the air conditioning evaporator and a control door for air recirculation. All control doors except the blending door are activated by vacuum servos controlled by the top lever of the control head. The blending door for the heater core is connected to the bottom lever of the control head by a cable.

Insufficient heater or air conditioner output, or air flow that does not correspond to control lever position may be caused by problems with the vacuum system. Check the vacuum system as described below before assuming that another component is faulty.

Heater core

Coolant leaking visibly into the passenger compartment is a sign of a faulty core or core seal. A sweet, anti-freeze odor in the car's interior, or a constantly fogged windshield may also indicate a faulty core. Inspect the carpet and the area near the floor vents for any signs of moisture or coolant. A leaking heater core may be caused by overpressurization of the cooling system. See **COOLING SYSTEM** for more information.

Removal of the heater core on cars with A/C requires that the air conditioning system be discharged. Because of the

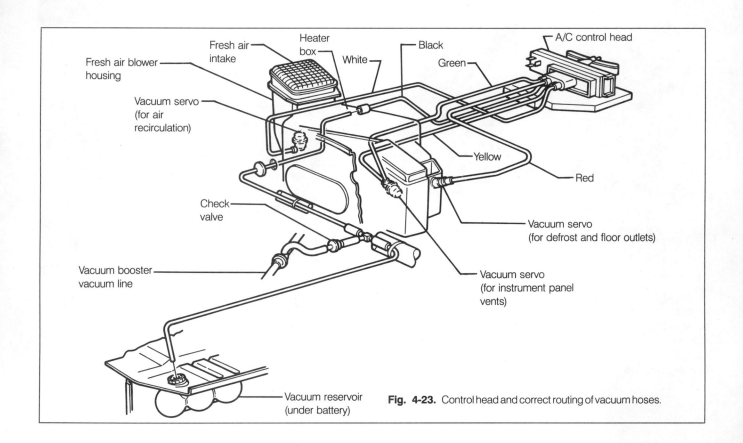

Fig. 4-23. Control head and correct routing of vacuum hoses.

special procedures involved, any work involving the A/C should be performed by an authorized Volkswagen dealer or other qualified shop. For more information see **9. Air Conditioning**.

Checking Vacuum System

The vacuum system supplies engine vacuum, by way of the brake vacuum booster vacuum line, to operate the heating and ventilation control servos. The vacuum system is tested by checking for servo operation and vacuum at the servos when the control lever is moved to its different settings. The servos are reached by removing the center console and lower instrument panel tray(s) as described in **4.1 Instrument Cluster and Instrument Panel**. **Table b** gives vacuum system response to control lever setting. The engine must be running for the tests.

No response from all servos at any control lever setting indicates that there is a problem either with vacuum supply, or with the control head. Check vacuum supply by removing the black hose from the rear of the control head with the engine running. No vacuum at the hose indicates a fault in the hose to the vacuum booster, or a faulty check valve. Vacuum at the hose when it is removed indicates a faulty control head.

If only one or two servos fail to respond to lever position, remove the hose from the malfunctioning servo(s) and check for vacuum. No vacuum indicates a faulty control head or vacuum hose. Vacuum indicates a faulty servo.

Replacing Control Head

To replace a faulty control head, pull the control levers straight out from the control head as shown above in Fig. 4-5. Pry the trim plate from the instrument panel, and remove the screws holding the control head to the panel. Tilt the control head to remove the vacuum lines, electrical connector, and blend door control cable, then remove the control head from the car. Installation is the reverse of removal. Install and adjust the blend door control cable as described above in **4.4 Heater and Controls**. Install the vacuum hoses and electrical connections as shown in Fig. 4-24.

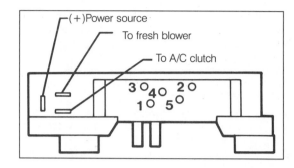

Fig. 4-24. Rear view of heating and ventilation control head showing vacuum connections. Connect black hose (vacuum source) to **1**, white hose (recirculation servo) to **2**, red hose (defrost/floor servo) to **3**, yellow hose (instrument panel top port) to **4**, and green hose (instrument panel side port) to **5**.

Fresh Air Blower

The fresh air blower is located behind the glove compartment, and is reached by removing the glove compartment and the lower right instrument panel tray as described in **4.1 Instrument Cluster and Instrument Panel**. See **ELECTRICAL SYSTEM.** for electrical tests of the blower motor.

Remove the blower motor by removing the three retaining screws and pulling the blower from the evaporator case. Disconnect the electrical connector and remove. Installation is the reverse of removal.

Table b. Heating and Ventilation Vacuum System Test

Control Lever Setting	Air Recirculation Vacuum Servo	Instrument Panel Vacuum Servo	Defrost/Floor Vacuum Servo
Off	Vacuum	Vacuum (upper) Vacuum (lower)	No Vacuum
A/C Max	Vacuum	Vacuum (upper) Vacuum (lower)	No Vacuum
A/C Norm	No Vacuum	Vacuum (upper) Vacuum (lower)	No Vacuum
A/C Bi-level	No Vacuum	Vacuum (upper) No Vacuum (lower)	Vacuum
Vent	No Vacuum	Vacuum (upper) Vacuum (lower)	Vacuum
Heat	No Vacuum	No Vacuum (upper) No Vacuum (lower)	Vacuum
Defrost	No Vacuum	No Vacuum (upper) No Vacuum (lower)	No Vacuum

4.6 Seat Belts

Two types of seat belts are installed on the cars covered by this manual: combination lap-shoulder belts (three-point), and passive restraint belts (two-point). The seat belts should be periodically inspected for webbing defects and proper operation. If the seats belts are removed for any reason, it is of extreme importance to reinstall them correctly. For problems with the seat belt warning light/buzzer system or ignition interlock see **ELECTRICAL SYSTEM**.

WARNING ━

●*For maximum protection from injury, seat belts should be replaced, as a set, if they are subjected to occupant loading in a collision.*
●*Do not bleach or dye seat belt webbing. Webbing that is severely faded or redyed will not meet the strength requirements and must be replaced.*

Inspecting Seat Belts

Inspect front and rear belt webbing, and replace belts with broken or pulled threads, cut loops at the belt edge, bowed webbing, faded areas, or cuts. Pull the belt out fully and let it retract. If it does not move smoothly in either direction, check for dirt, grease, or gum on the webbing. If the belt cannot be cleaned using only a mild soap solution recommended for cleaning upholstery or carpet, replace the belt.

Replace the belt if the buckle cover is cracked, if the push button is loose, or if the buckle does not lock securely. Check all mounting points. The mounting bolts must be tight, yet allow the hardware to swivel freely. Clean any corrosion away from the anchoring points, and replace any corroded hardware.

On three-point front seat belts, check the belt lock-up mechanism by grasping the webbing near the retractor and tugging quickly. Replace any belt that does not lock up.

On two-point seat belts, perform a road test to check the belt lock-up mechanism. Drive in an open area away from other cars. At approximately 5 to 15 mph, with the belt securely fastened, quickly stop the car. Replace any belt that does not lock up.

Inpect the rear seat belt lock-up mechanism by pulling the belt from the extractor and allowing several inches to feed back. Quickly tug on the belt. Replace any belt that does not lock up.

Installing or Replacing Seat Belts

Install all seat belt mounting bolts to the correct torque. Fig. 4-25 through Fig. 4-36 show the anchoring points for the various models covered by this manual, with the correct torques.

WARNING ━

For maximum protection from injury, do not interchange buckle and retractor assemblies with those designated for other seating positions or other models.

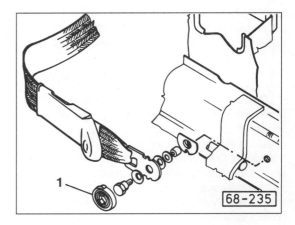

Fig. 4-25. Front seat lower anchor point on two-door models with three-point systems. On Jetta, torque bolt to 40 Nm (29 ft. lb.); on Golf, GTI to 47 Nm (34 ft. lb.). Place spring **1**, end facing up. Preload spring by twisting 270° and installing spring mounting pin.

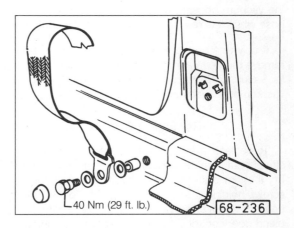

Fig. 4-26. Front seat lower anchor point on four-door models with three-point system.

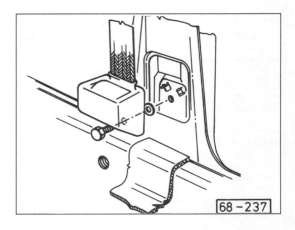

Fig. 4-27. Front seat retractor mounting on three-point systems. On Jetta, torque bolt to 40 Nm (29 ft. lb.); on Golf, GTI to 47 Nm (34 ft. lb.).

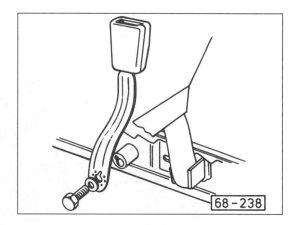

Fig. 4-28. Front seat frame mounting on three-point systems. On Jetta, torque bolt to 50 Nm (36 ft. lb.); on Golf, GTI to 47 Nm (34 ft. lb.).

Fig. 4-29. Front seat upper anchor mounting on three-point systems. On Jetta, torque bolt to 40 Nm (29 ft. lb.); on Golf, GTI to 47 Nm (34 ft. lb.).

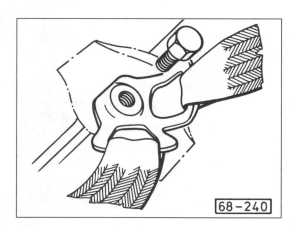

Fig. 4-30. Rear center seat belt mounting points (behind cushion). On Jetta, torque bolt to 40 Nm (29 ft. lb.); on Golf, GTI to 47 Nm (34 ft. lb.).

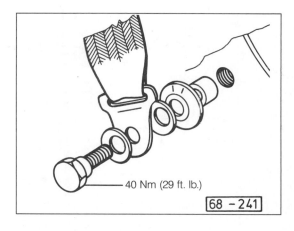

Fig. 4-31. Jetta rear seat belt outer anchor mounting.

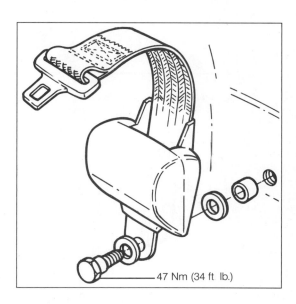

Fig. 4-32. Golf, GTI rear seat belt retractor mounting.

13

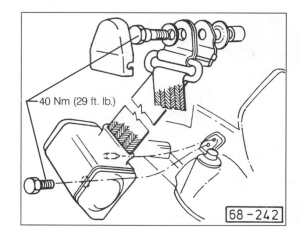

Fig. 4-33. Jetta rear seat belt retractor mounting (behind seat back).

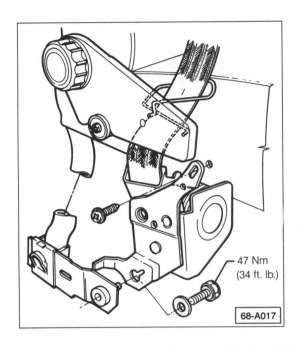

Fig. 4-34. Lower retractor mounting on seat for two-point seat belts (passive restraint).

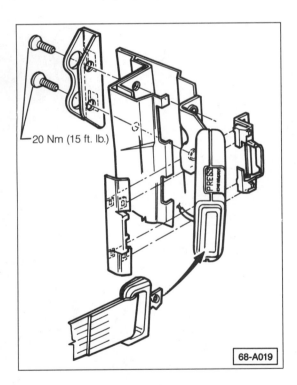

Fig. 4-35. Upper door mounting for two-point seat belts (passive restraint).

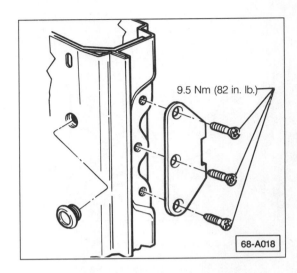

Fig. 4-36. Upper pillar mounting for two-point seat belts (passive restraint).

Front Seat Belt Height Adjustment

The upper anchor points for front three-point seat belts are adjustable on all mid-year 1986 and later Jettas. Although adjustable belts were not factory-installed on earlier Jettas, or on Golf and GTI models, parts are available to allow installation of the adjuster on early 1986 Jettas. Also, a kit is available for remounting the seat belt anchors on 1985 Jettas and 1985 and later Golf and GTI models. All parts are available from an authorized Volkswagen dealer.

The adjuster and its parts for early 1986 Jettas are shown in Fig. 4-37. To install the adjuster, remove the upper seat belt anchor and trim plate. Pry back the door seals slightly, and remove the trim-plate upper mounting bracket. With the new adjusting mechanism set to the second stop from the bottom, install it to the pillar using the allen head bolts. Install the bolts into the old seat belt anchor mounting hole and the hole under the trim-plate upper mounting bracket. Attach the pillar trim plate to the mechanism, and then install the unlocking knob and the upper seat belt anchor.

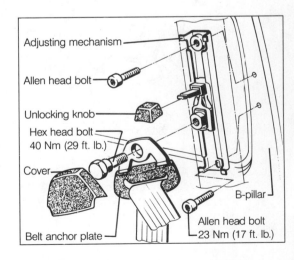

Fig. 4-37. Adjusting mechanism for early 1986 Jettas.

The installed kit for 1985 Jettas and 1985 and later Golf and GTI models is shown in Fig. 4-38.

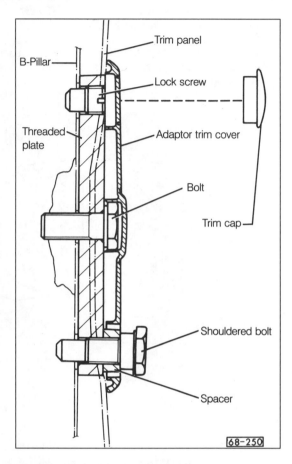

Fig. 4-38. Belt adaptor installed for lowered belt anchor position on 1985 Jettas and 1985 and later Golf and GTI. Lock screw and shoulder bolt can be reversed to raise anchor. Trim cap is used to cover hole if anchor position is changed.

To install the kit, first remove the upper belt anchor and the trim plate, and pry back the door seals. The trim plate should have a rectangle-shaped dotted line on its reverse side. Cut out the rectangle.

Mount the threaded plate vertically to the pillar, by loosely installing the bolt supplied with the kit through the center hole of the threaded plate and into the old belt anchor hole. Coat the lock screw with thread locking compound and, depending on whether the anchor position is being raised or lowered, install it into either the upper or lower hole in the threaded plate until it is flush with the plate. Now torque the center bolt to 40 Nm (29 ft. lb.).

Install the pillar trim piece. Cut an appropriate hole in the adaptor cover and install it into the trim plate so the open bolt hole is accessible. Install the belt anchor using the shouldered bolt and spacer and torque it to 47 Nm (34 ft. lb.).

Child Restraint Tethering
(Jetta only)

Volkswagen recommends the anchoring points shown in Fig. 4-39 for child restraint systems with a tethering strap. Installation requires removal of the rear seat as described in **4.8 Rear Seats**.

WARNING ——

To assure maximum protection, follow manufacturers' instructions when installing a child restraint system.

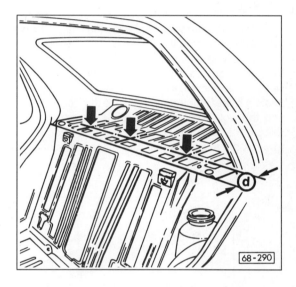

Fig. 4-39. Anchoring points (arrows) for child restraint tethering straps. Line **d** is 195 mm (7.68 in.) from edge of shelf.

Mark the line shown and drill a 8.5 mm ($1\frac{1}{32}$ in.) hole at the intersection of the reinforcing seam and line. Measure and cut a 21 mm ($\frac{7}{16}$ in.) hole in the same location of the hat shelf lining. De-burr all holes and seal them using paint or silicone sealant. Install the carpeting and the seat. Install the anchor fitting supplied with the child seat using the parts shown in Fig. 4-40.

13

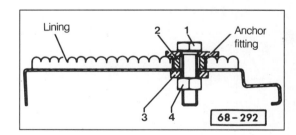

Fig. 4-40. Child restraint anchor installed to rear shelf. Hex bolt **1** is part no. N 014 326 1. Spacer ring **2** is part no. 803 019 825 B. Washer **3** is part no. N 015 401 4. Hex nut **4** is part no. N 011 008 18.

NOTE ▬

If the mounting hardware provided with the child seat does not fit the anchor mounting, contact the child seat manufacturer for suitable parts. Volkswagen specifications are for maximum occupant protection.

4.7 Front Seats

To remove a front seat, first slide the seat all the way forward. Pry up the end of the track cover or remove the screw and slide the cover off of the track as shown in Fig. 4-41. Remove the track stop from the rear of the other rail. On models with heated seats or electric height adjust, disconnect any electrical connectors beneath the seat. Remove the acorn nut, the washer, and the bolt from the front guide shown in Fig. 4-42, and release the retaining rod from the seat while sliding the seat towards the rear of the car and off its tracks. Installation is the reverse of removal.

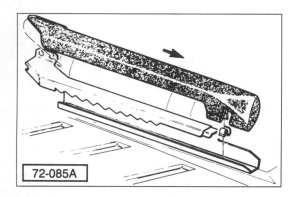

Fig. 4-41. Front seat track cover removed from retaining clip. Slide cover off track in direction of arrow.

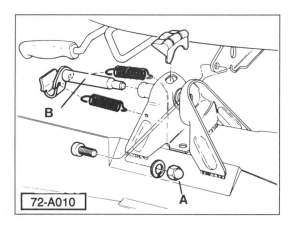

Fig. 4-42. Acorn nut (**A**) and retaining rod (**B**) to be removed when removing seat.

Heated Seats

On models with heated seats, check the electrical circuit to the seats as described in **ELECTRICAL SYSTEM** before assuming that a heating element is faulty.

To replace the heating elements, remove the seat as described above. Separate the backrest wire from the seat wiring connector. See Fig. 4-43.

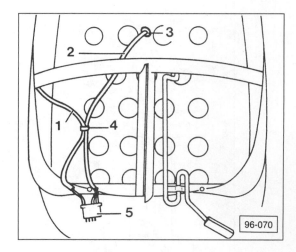

Fig. 4-43. Routing of wires for heated seats beneath driver's seat cushion. Passenger seat is symmetrically opposite. **1** is backrest element wire, **2** is seat element wire, **3** is wiring grommet, **4** is wiring clip, **5** is connector.

Remove the backrest from the seat cushion by removing the left and right trim pieces and the hinge screws. Remove both seat covers and heating elements. Lay the new heating elements against the seat without wrinkling the elements. Install the seat covers and route the wire harness as shown above in Fig. 4-43, and in Fig. 4-44.

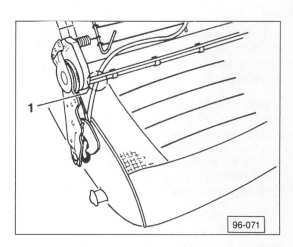

Fig. 4-44. Routing of backrest wire for heated seat. Wire runs between seat cover tensioning wires and seat frame (**1**).

4.8 Rear Seats

Remove the rear bench seat cushion by pushing the cushion toward the rear of the car to release the front catches, then pull the cushion up and out of the car. Remove the rear bench seat backrest by releasing the catches shown in Fig. 4-45. Installation is the reverse of removal.

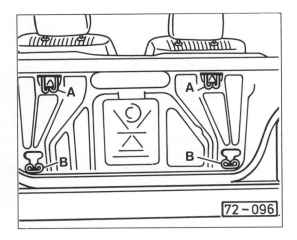

Fig. 4-45. Rear bench seat backrest clips **A** and **B** to be unhooked. Clips are reached from luggage compartment.

Remove a folding rear bench seat by removing the two hinge covers and the two hinge screws shown in Fig. 4-46. Release the rear seat catch and then pull out the seat.

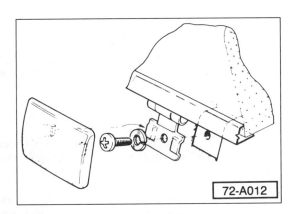

Fig. 4-46. Folding rear seat mounting screws and hinge covers.

On models with folding rear split seats, first remove the two check straps on either side of the seat, shown in Fig. 4-47, and then remove the four hinge covers and screws.

To remove only the seat back(s) on folding rear split seats, fold the seat forward and remove the two shouldered hinge bolts where the backrest joins the seat.

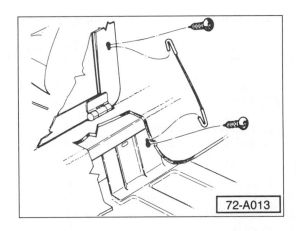

Fig. 4-47. Check straps for folding rear split seat.

4.9 Headliner

The headliner is a one-piece molded panel that is easily removed. Clean the headliner using only mineral spirits, isopropanol, or other mild cleaning solutions.

CAUTION ━━

To avoid damaging the headliner, do not let acetone, paint thinners, or metal primer/polyurethane (a solvent used to install the windshield) contact it.

To remove and install:

1. On Jettas, remove the inside rear view mirror by pulling it away from its mounting.

2. Remove the screws from the sunvisor swivel mounts. On models with lighted visor mirrors, disconnect the wiring. Remove the visors' mounting clips by removing the mounting screws and twisting the clip as shown in Fig. 4-48.

13

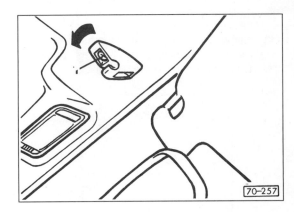

Fig. 4-48. Retaining clip mounting screw (**1**) to be removed, and direction clip is twisted (arrow).

3. On cars with sunroof, remove the sunroof crank handle.

4. Remove the interior dome light, and remove the light trim panel by prying it out from the rear.

5. Remove the upper seat belt anchors from the B-pillars as described in **4.6 Seat Belts**.

6. Remove the grab handles. On Jettas, the grab handle trim covers must be removed for access to the mounting screws.

7. Remove the outer headliner mounts. On Jettas, pry the plastic caps from the headliner and remove the screws shown in Fig. 4-49. On Golf and GTI, pry out the retaining clips.

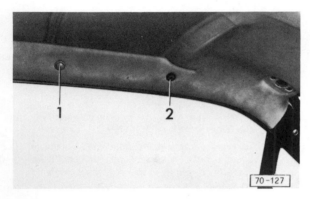

Fig. 4-49. Plastic caps **1** and screws **2**, of retaining clips to be removed.

8. Remove the upper trim panel screw from the A-pillar trim piece and pull from the top to remove it from the lower clip.

9. Remove the two B-pillar trim piece mounting screws. Pull the trim piece from its clips. Pull the weather strips from the pillars and the headliner.

10. Remove the C-pillar trim piece by pulling it off its clips. On Jettas there is one upper clip and two lower clips. On Golf and GTI the clips are along the headliner.

11. Remove the end strip from the headliner and remove the mounting clips from the liner as shown in Fig. 4-50. Lower and remove the headliner.

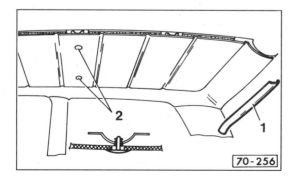

Fig. 4-50. Headliner end strip **1** and trim panel mounting clips **2**.

12. Installation is the reverse of removal. Tighten all seat belt anchors to the correct torque. See **4.6 Seat Belts**.

5. DOORS

The rear half of each door hinge is welded to the door, and the front half is welded to the car body. The only adjustment point of the door hinge is the center mounting bolt. When removing a door, mark the hinge halves so that the door can be reinstalled in its original location.

To remove a door, push the door check bolt from its lock washer. Use an impact driver to loosen the hinge bolts. Support the door, then remove the bolts and the door. On models with electric mirrors, or central locking system, the mirrors must be removed as described in **5.3 Side Mirrors** to remove the wiring from the door, and the vacuum hose and wiring must be removed from the lock actuator as described in **5.2 Central Locking System**.

> **CAUTION** ━━
> *If the door is not supported when the first bolt is removed, the second hinge may bend or break.*

Install the door using the marks made prior to removal. If a replacement door is being installed, it should contact the weather seal evenly and the lock should work smoothly. Set the hinge bolts with an impact driver.

5.1 Door Assembly

The interior door trim, the glass, door handles and locks, side mirrors, and internal door components are all removable with the door installed on the car. The interior trim must be removed for access to the internal door components.

Interior Trim

Although the procedures below apply to front doors, they can be used as a general guide when removing the interior trim from the rear doors on 4-door models.

To remove the interior trim panel, unscrew the lock button and pry out the plastic guide piece. Pry out the trim plate for the inside door operating lever. Pry the trim piece from the front of the pull handle and remove the screws and the handle. Pry the trim piece from the window crank handle, and remove the screw and the handle. The trim panel is held to the door by spring clips at the bottom, and screws at the sides. Carefully remove the interior plastic protective liner without tearing it. Installation is the reverse of removal. Make sure that the liner is installed without gaps. Apply thread locking compound to the window crank handle screw.

Window Regulator

To remove the window regulator, lower the window and remove the interior trim panel and the plastic protective liner from the door as described above. While supporting the glass, remove the bolts shown in Fig. 5-1, and lower the glass into the door. Remove the two bolts from the regulator side rail and the two bolts from the regulator window crank. Remove the window crank and the regulator from the door. If necessary, raise the glass so that the side rail can be removed from the door. Installation is the reverse of removal.

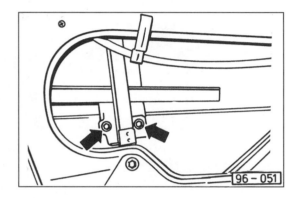

Fig. 5-1. Bolts (arrows) that hold window glass to window regulator guide rail.

Power Window Regulator

Troubleshoot the power window electrical circuit as described in **ELECTRICAL SYSTEM** before assuming that the power regulator is faulty.

To remove the power window regulator, lower the window and remove the interior trim panel and the plastic protective liner as described in **Interior Trim**. While supporting the glass, remove the bolts that hold the window glass to the regulator guide rail as shown above in Fig. 5-1, and lower the glass into the door. Unplug the electrical connector and remove the guide rail mounting bolts and the motor as shown in Fig. 5-2. Remove the entire regulator assembly from the door. Installation is the reverse of removal.

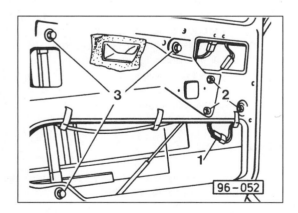

Fig. 5-2. Power window regulator being removed. Wiring connector is at **1**, motor mounting bolts are at **2**, and guide rail bolts are at **3**

Handles and Locks

The outside door handle must first be removed for access to the door lock cylinder. To remove the handle, pry out the trim strip, then remove the two retaining screws and slide the handle off in the direction shown in Fig. 5-3. Installation is the reverse of removal.

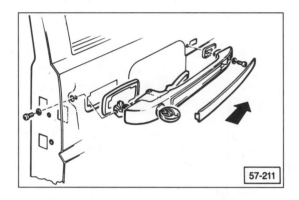

Fig. 5-3. Exploded view of door handle mechanism.

To remove the door lock, remove the interior trim panel and protective liner as described in **Interior Trim**. Remove the two lock-retaining screws and pull the lock part-way out. Remove the two actuating rods from the lock and pull it from the door.

To install the lock, first use a screwdriver to hold the lock lever at a 90° angle as shown in Fig. 5-4.

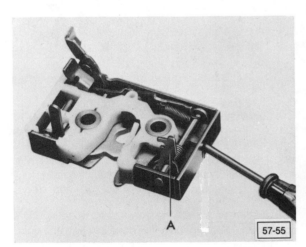

Fig. 5-4. Lock lever **A** being held at 90° angle using screwdriver during installation.

Position the lock to the door, and attach the lock actuating rod to the lock lever, and attach the door lever rod, then remove the screwdriver. See Fig. 5-5. Install and torque the two lock mounting screws to 21 Nm (15 ft. lb.).

To remove the inside door actuating lever, first remove the lock as described above, then remove the strap from the panel and slide the door lever assembly from the door as shown in Fig. 5-6. Installation is the reverse of removal.

13

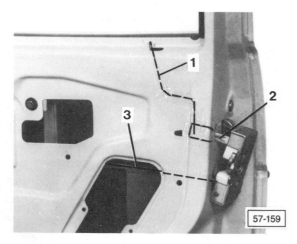

Fig. 5-5. Schematic view of lock actuating rod (**1**) being connected to lock sleeve (**2**), and door lever rod being connected to lock (**3**).

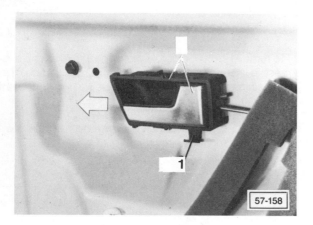

Fig. 5-6. Strap (**1**) to be removed when removing door actuator lever.

A door that is difficult to open from the outside on 1985 and 1986 models may be caused by excess freeplay in the door trigger unit. Later models have a plastic sleeve installed on the lock lever to correct this. The sleeve is available from an authorized Volkswagen dealer for retro-fitting, part no. 176 837 149 (front door), and part no. 176 839 149 (rear door).

To install the plastic sleeve, remove the door lock retaining screws and partially remove the door lock from the door. File off any burrs on the lever. Install the sleeve as shown in Fig. 5-7. Reinstall the lock and torque the screws to 21 Nm (15 ft. lb.). Check lock function before closing the door by pushing the locking pawl into the lock, then releasing it with the handle trigger.

5.2 Central Locking System

The central locking system consists of a special bi-pressure pump in the luggage compartment, connected by vacuum hose to lock activators at each of the doors, at the rear lid, and at the gas tank flap. When the key is turned in the driver's door lock, the master activator turns on the pump to supply pressure to open the locks, or vacuum to close them.

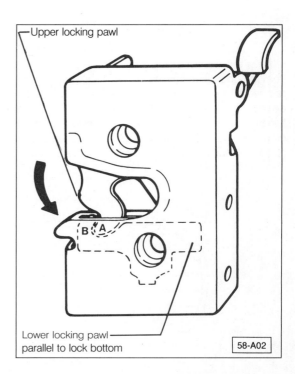

Fig. 5-7. Front door lock with plastic sleeve (arrow) installed. Lock is correctly closed when tab **A** is fully behind **B**. Rear door lock is similar.

This heading covers only the removal and installation of the mechanical parts, and troubleshooting of the bi-pressure system. If the pump does not run when key is turned, the problem may be electrical. Troubleshoot the pump and the master activator as described in **ELECTRICAL SYSTEM.**

NOTE ━

If the central locking system has not been operated for an extended period, the key may have to be turned several times before the system activates.

Bi-Pressure System Troubleshooting

When the key is turned in the master activator, all locks should be activated within 2 seconds. A fault is indicated if the pump runs longer than 5 seconds, or if any of the locks do not activate. A prerequisite for troubleshooting is that the pump runs when the key is turned. The replacement of faulty components follow this heading. Replacement hose is available from an authorized Volkswagen dealer. Troubleshooting should be carried out in the sequence given here, even if only one activator is suspected of being faulty.

To troubleshoot:

1. Remove the bi-pressure pump from its housing as described in **Bi-pressure Pump.**

2. Clamp the hose as shown in Fig. 5-8. Activate the pump using the door key. If the pump runs longer than 5 seconds, either the hose from the pump is leaking, or the pump is faulty. If the pump shuts off within 5 seconds, remove the clamp and continue testing.

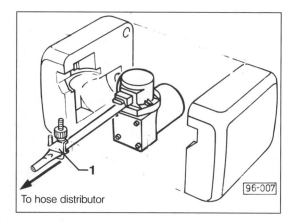

To hose distributor

Fig. 5-8. Bi-pressure pump being tested with hose clamp at **1**.

3. Clamp the hose as shown in Fig. 5-9. If the pump runs longer than 5 seconds when activated, the left rear door activator or the hose to it is faulty. If the pump turns off within 5 seconds, remove the clamp and continue testing.

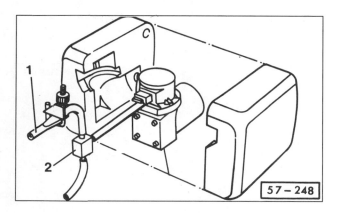

Fig. 5-9. Left rear door activator being tested with hose clamp at **1**, near hose distributor **2**.

4. Clamp the hose as shown in Fig. 5-10. If the pump runs longer than 5 seconds when activated, go to step 6. If the pump turns off within 5 seconds, either the right front or rear door activator, or the hose to them is faulty. Go to step 5. Remove the clamp.

5. To determine which right door activator is faulty, remove the right carpet trim strip and unscrew the lower B-pillar trim. Clamp the hose shown in Fig. 5-11. If the pump runs longer than 5 seconds when activated, the rear door activator or its hose is faulty. If the pump turns off within 5 seconds, the front door activator or its hose is faulty. Remove the clamp.

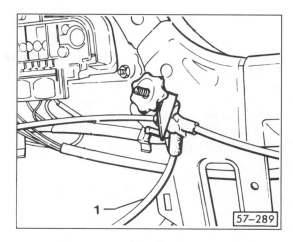

Fig. 5-10. Hose being clamped (**1**) in right rear of car. Clamp blocks air flow to right front and rear doors.

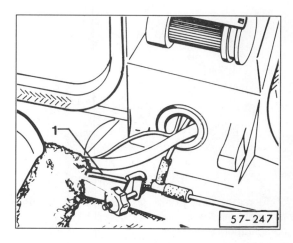

Fig. 5-11. Hose being clamped (**1**) near lower part of B-pillar to block air flow to right front door.

6. Clamp the hose shown in Fig. 5-12. If the pump runs longer than 5 seconds when activated, then the rear lid activator or its hose is faulty. If the pump turns off within 5 seconds, the gas tank flap or its hose is faulty. Remove the clamp.

13

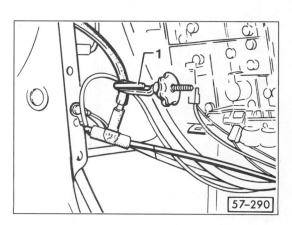

Fig. 5-12. Hose being clamped (**1**) in right rear of car to block air flow to gas tank flap.

Removing and Installing Door Activators

To remove a faulty activator, remove the door trim panel and protective liner as described in **5.1 Door Assembly**. Remove the activator retaining screws and unhook the connecting rod as shown in Fig. 5-13. When removing the master activator from the driver's door, first disconnect the battery ground cable, and disconnect the activator electrical connector. When removing all other activators, pull the hose from the activator. Installation is the reverse of removal.

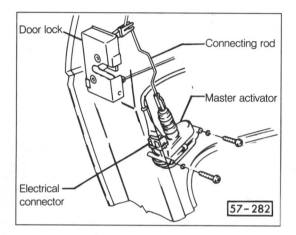

Fig. 5-13. Phantom view of master activator installation. Other door activators are similar.

Bi-pressure pump

To remove the pump, first disconnect the negative (−) terminal from the battery. Remove the trim from the luggage compartment on the driver's side. Remove the retaining strap, and then remove the pump from its housing. Disconnect the electrical connector and the hose, and remove the pump. See Fig. 5-14. Installation is the reverse of removal.

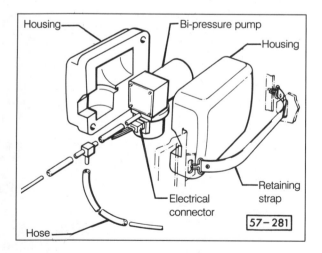

Fig. 5-14. Bi-pressure pump and related components.

Rear Lid Activator

To remove the rear lid activator, open the lid and remove the inside trim panel, where applicable, by unclipping the panel fasteners. Remove the retaining screws, pull the hose from the activator, and unhook the connecting rod as shown in Fig. 5-15. Installation is the reverse of removal.

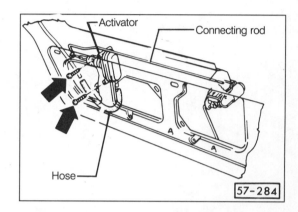

Fig. 5-15. Phantom view of rear lid activator installation.

Gas Tank Flap Activator

To remove the gas tank flap activator, remove the passenger-side trim panel in the luggage compartment. Remove the two screws from the inside of the lugggage compartment, then open the flap and remove the third screw. Remove the activator with its bracket and pull the hose from the activator. See Fig. 5-16. Installation is the reverse of removal.

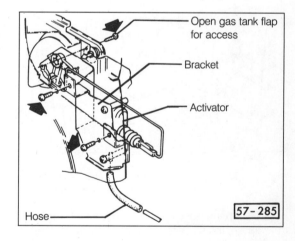

Fig. 5-16. Phantom view of activator for gas tank flap.

5.3 Side Mirrors

To remove manual remote-control side mirrors, first remove the interior door trim panel and proctective liner as described in **5.1 Door Assembly**. Remove the locknut shown in Fig. 5-17. Pry the trim cover loose and remove the mounting screws. Lift the mirror away from the door, guiding the cable through the door. Installation is the reverse of removal.

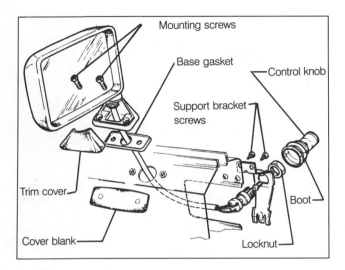

Fig. 5-17. Exploded view of manual remote-control side mirror.

Before assuming that the motor on electric remote-control heated mirrors is faulty, check the electrical circuit as described in **ELECTRICAL SYSTEM**.

To remove and install electric side mirrors:

1. Remove the mirror glass by using a screwdriver to turn the detent through the bottom opening of the mirror. See Fig. 5-18. Hold the mirror still. Disconnect the electrical connectors.

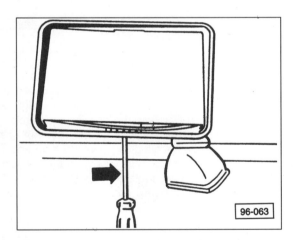

Fig. 5-18. Electric/heated side mirror detent being turned in direction indicated by arrow.

2. Remove the screws from the motor assembly as shown in Fig. 5-19, then disconnect the electrical connectors and remove the motor.

3. Pry the mirror switch from the inside door panel and remove the connector and the switch.

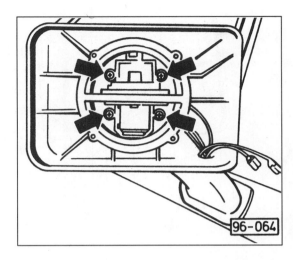

Fig. 5-19. Electric motor mounting screws to be removed.

4. Remove the interior door trim panel and protective liner as described in **5.1 Door assembly**, then disconnect the electrical connectors shown in Fig. 5-20.

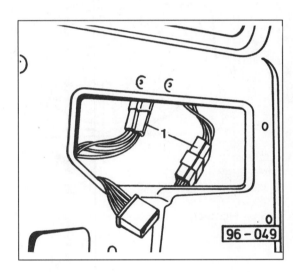

Fig. 5-20. Electrical connectors (**1**) behind door trim panel to be disconnected.

5. Pry the trim cover from the mirror housing, remove the mounting screws, and remove the mirror housing while guiding the wires through the mirror housing.

6. Install the mirror in reverse order. Connect the motor wires as shown in Fig. 5-21. Turn the mirror detent in the direction shown in Fig. 5-22 until it contacts the stop, connect the electrical wires, then place the mirror in the mirror housing and turn the detent in the opposite direction to lock it in position.

13

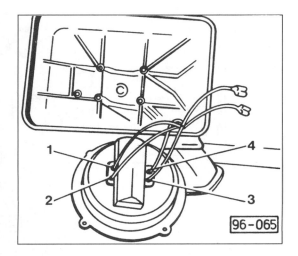

Fig. 5-21. Wire connections to mirror motor. Motor is marked with numbers. Connect blue wire to **1**, brown wire to **2**, white wire to **3**, and black wire to **4**.

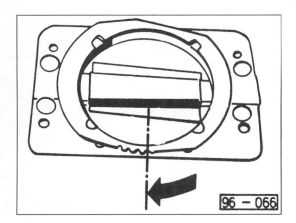

Fig. 5-22. Mirror detent being pushed to its stop prior to mirror installation.

6. EXTERIOR

The exterior body parts and trim discussed under this heading are fastened with conventional fasteners, and are easily removed using ordinary hand tools. A thorough knowledge of automobile body repair is not needed to perform the procedures.

6.1 Headlights

The majority of the cars covered by this manual have aerodynamic headlights with a one-piece lens and reflector assembly and a replaceable halogen bulb. See Fig. 6-1. A lock ring holds the bulb in place, and two screws are used to aim the headlights.

Some 1985 and 1986 Golf models have sealed-beam halogen headlights. Headlight aim is also by two screws, but the bulb and lens must be replaced as one assembly. See Fig. 6-2.

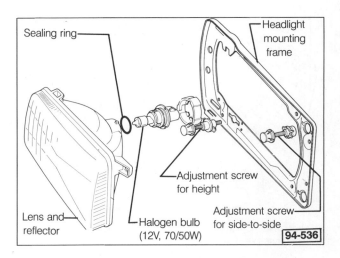

Fig. 6-1. Aerodynamic headlight assembly.

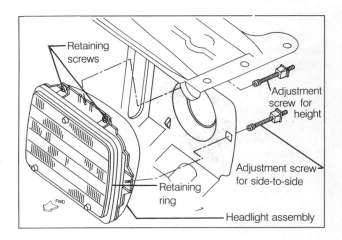

Fig. 6-2. Sealed beam headlight assembly used on some 1985 and 1986 Golf models.

Replace the bulb on aerodynamic headlights with the lights turned off. Open the hood and remove the headlight electrical connector. See Fig. 6-3. Twist the lock ring counterclockwise to release the bulb. The recesses on the new bulb assembly should engage the locating lugs on the lens and reflector housing. Do not touch the bulb glass. Dirt and oil deposits on the glass can cause hot spots and rapid bulb failure. Twist the lock ring clockwise to firmly seat it. Check headlight aim as described in **Aiming Headlights**.

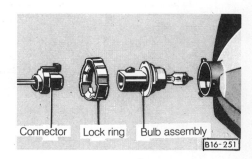

Fig. 6-3. Exploded view of aerodynamic headlight bulb installation. Replacement bulb is Volkswagen part no. N 100 666 01 (U.S. trade no. 9004).

To replace the lens and reflector on aerodynamic headlights, first remove the bulb as described above. Remove the grille as described in **6.4 Trim, Bumpers, and Body.** Working from the front of the headlight, remove the four screws that hold the headlight mounting frame to the body and remove the frame and lens and reflector. Unclip the old lens and reflector from the adjustment screws. Clip on the new lens and reflector, and reinstall the mounting frame, grille, and bulb. Check headlight aim as described in **Aiming Headlights**.

Replace a sealed beam headlight with the lights off. Remove the grille as described in **6.4 Trim, Bumpers, and Body.** Remove the four retaining screws from the retaining ring and remove the ring. Pull the headlight forward and disconnect the wiring. Make sure that the side of the new lens marked UP or TOP, or that the single adjusting lug is uppermost. It should not be necessary to aim the headlight if the adjustment screws have not been touched, however, it is a good idea to check headlight aim as described in **Aiming Headlights**

Aiming Headlights

Special adaptors are supplied with the car's tool kit to aim both aerodynamic and sealed beam headlights. Headlight aiming using the adaptors should be carried out by an authorized Volkswagen dealer or other qualified shop. Headlight aiming can also be done as described below without any special tools, however, the results will not be as exact.

NOTE ———

Check your state laws to see if headlight adjustments must be made by a licensed shop. Some states may also have different aiming specifications from those described here.

To aim the headlights, position the car on a level surface, 7.65 meters (25 ft.) from a vertical wall. The gas tank should be half full and the tire pressures should be correct. Turn the headlights to low beam. With a person in the driver's seat, the low beams must be in the areas shown in Fig. 6-4. If re-aiming is necessary, remove the radiator trim grille and use a phillips head screwdriver on the height and side-to-side adjusting screws to move the headlight.

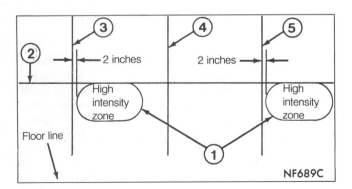

Fig. 6-4. Headlight aiming target on vertical wall. Low beam light intensity areas are at **1**. Line **2** is at height of headlight centers. Line **4** is car centerline. Lines **3** and **5** are distance from centerline to centers of headlights.

6.2 Taillight Assembly

All rear bulbs and the taillight lens are replaced from the luggage compartment. Replacement of the center brake light is covered in **4.3 Interior Lights**.

On Jettas, replace a faulty taillight bulb by first removing the bulb holder. Pinch the two clips on the side of the holder shown in Fig. 6-5 and remove the wire retainer. Push in on the bulb and twist to remove, push in and twist to install. Make sure that both clips are engaged and no wires are pinched when the holder is installed.

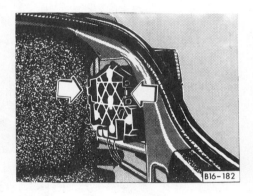

Fig. 6-5. Jetta taillight bulb holder being removed. Pinch clips (arrows) and remove wire retainer. Replacement turn-signal, stop-light and back-up light bulbs are part no. N 017 732 2 (U.S. trade no. 1073). Taillight bulbs are part no. N 017 719 2 (U.S. trade no. 67).

On Golf and GTI models, replace a faulty bulb by first removing the bulb holder. Depress the spring clip at the side of the holder as shown in Fig. 6-6, and turn the holder one-quarter turn counterclockwise. Push in on the bulb and twist to remove, push in and twist to install. Make sure that the gasket is in place when the holder is installed.

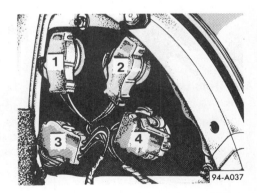

Fig. 6-6. Golf and GTI bulb holders. Replacement bulbs are same as for Jetta. See Fig. 6-5.

The taillight lens is replaced by removing the four nuts in the luggage compartment that hold the lens to the body. Pull the lens off the car with its gasket. On Jettas, it is necessary to first remove the bulb holder as described above. If the gasket is damaged, replace it using a sealing cord, part no. AKD 497 010 R 10, available from an authorized Volkswagen dealer.

13

6.3 Side Marker and Front Turn Signal Lights

To replace a front side marker or turn signal bulb or lens, remove the phillips screw and pull the lens away from the fender or bumper as shown in Fig. 6-7. Turn the bulb holder counterclockwise and pull it out of the rear of the lens assembly. Push in on the bulb and twist to remove, push in and twist to install. Make sure that the tongue on the lens assembly engages the fender or bumper during installation.

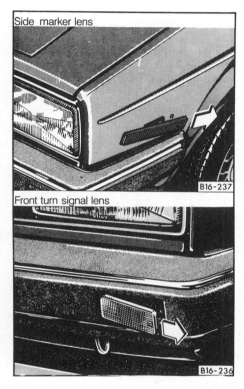

Fig. 6-7. Side marker lens (top) and front turn signal lens (bottom) being removed from bumper. Remove lens in direction of arrow to disengage lens tongue. Replacement side marker bulb is part no. N 900 544 01 (U.S. trade no. 194). Replacement front turn signal bulb is part no. N 017 738 2 (U.S. trade no. 1034).

6.4 Trim, Bumpers, and Body

To prevent corrosion, the fenders, hood, and trunk lid are assembled with zinc plates which act as anodes, and a sealing tape between mating surfaces to prevent moisture from becoming trapped. See Fig. 6-8. The plates are part no. AKL 381 035 50, and the tape is part no. D 001 900.

NOTE ——

The plates and tape are installed as part of the corrosion warranty. If in doubt about warranty protection, consult an authorized Volkswagen dealer.

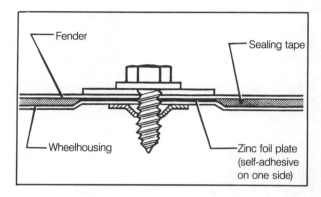

Fig. 6-8. Correct installation of bolt-on body parts.

Removing Front Body Parts and Grille

Fig. 6-9 is an exploded view of the front grille and related body parts.

Remove the plastic grille and lower grille simply by unclipping them. The apron, the spoiler, and the radiator support are held in place by mounting screws. To remove the radiator support, disconnect the hood release cable from the hood latch, and disconnect the horn and headlight electrical connections.

On GTI models, the front spoiler has an integral air duct connected to the brake cooling duct by a rubber bellows. See Fig. 6-10. To remove the front spoiler, first pry the rubber bellows back from the air duct and then remove the spoiler screws and speed nuts. When installing, loosely install the spoiler and screws and speed nuts, fit the bellows on the air duct, and then tighten the screws and nuts.

To replace a fender, first remove the front bumper as described below. Carefully use a heat gun and razor knife to cut through the PVC coating along the A-pillar where the fender meets the body. Remove the mounting bolts shown in Fig. 6-11 and remove the fender. During installation, install the zinc plates and sealing tape as shown above in Fig. 6-8.

CAUTION ——

Use extreme care when applying heat to the body to avoid blistering the paint or discoloring the PVC body coating.

To replace a wheelhouse liner, support that corner of the car securely on a jack stand and remove the wheel. Remove the mounting screws shown in Fig. 6-12. On GTI models, the brake cooling duct must be detached from the liner by removing the two mounting screws and one clip, and prying the rubber bellows off of the air duct. See Fig. 6-10 above. Remove the liner first from the guide, and then pull it from the body. Installation is the reverse of removal. Torque the wheel bolts to 110 Nm (80 ft. lb.) after lowering the car to the ground.

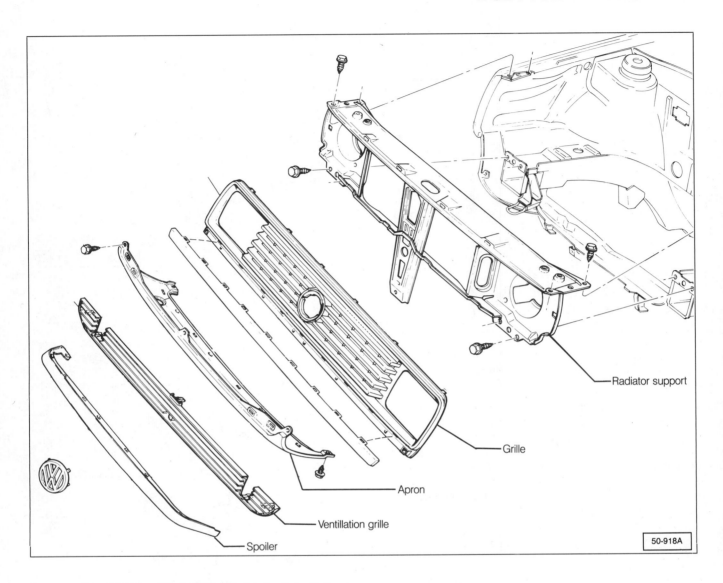

Radiator support

Grille

Apron

Ventillation grille

Spoiler

50-918A

Fig. 6-9. Front grille assembly and related parts for Golf and GTI. Jetta is similar.

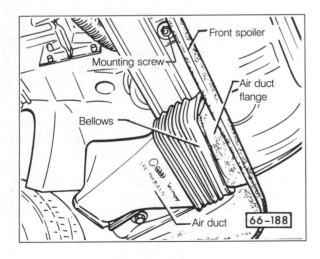

Front spoiler

Mounting screw

Air duct flange

Bellows

Air duct

66-188

Fig. 6-10. GTI front spoiler and air duct.

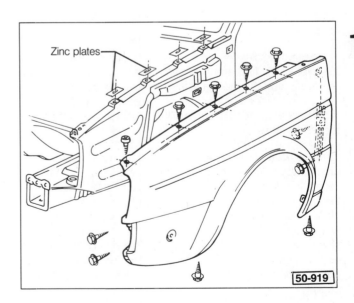

Zinc plates

50-919

13

Fig. 6-11. Exploded view of front fender, mounting bolts, and zinc plates.

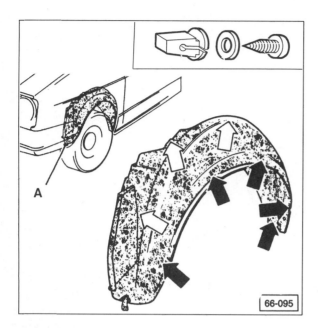

Fig. 6-12. Front wheelhouse liner mounting screw locations (arrows) and liner guide at **A**. Inset shows components of mounting assembly.

To remove the hood, first mark the hinge plate locations on the hood for reinstallation. Loosen the mounting bolts, then with a helper supporting the opposite side, remove the bolts. Install the original hood by aligning the matching marks made earlier. If installing a new hood, loosely install the mounting bolts and adjust the hood so that it contacts the body evenly. During installation, install the zinc plates and sealing tape as shown above in Fig. 6-8.

Removing and Installing Body Trim

Body trim includes the wheelhouse trim pieces, the fender stone guards, the roof moldings, and the body side moldings. When replacing a roof molding, special Volkswagen tools may be necessary. A rivet gun is needed when installing wheelhouse trim. Replacement rivets are available from an authorized Volkswagen dealer.

To remove full-length wheelhouse trim, either drill out or pry the rivet heads from the rivets. See Fig. 6-13. With the heads removed, drive out the rivets, then remove the trim. Use one of the old rivets for comparison when purchasing new rivets. When installing the trim, begin with the center rivet at the top of the wheelhouse.

To remove stone guards, pry the fastening studs on the guard away from the retention clips as shown in Fig. 6-14 On Jettas, the stone guards are additionally held by two rivets at the top and bottom of the guard. Drill out or pry the rivet heads off, then drive out the rivets. Use an old rivet for comparison when purchasing new rivets. On some 1985 Golf models, loose stone guards may be caused by faulty retention clips. Revised retention clips (part no. 191 853 615) and foam washers (part no. 191 853 616) are available from an authorized Volkswagen dealer.

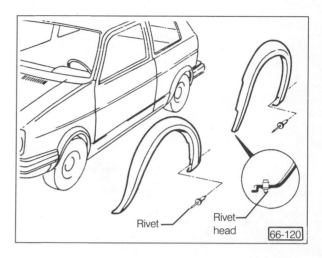

Fig. 6-13. Wheelhouse trim showing installed rivet.

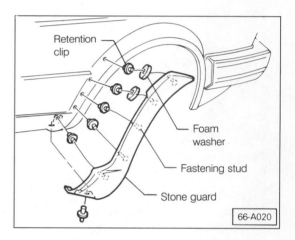

Fig. 6-14. Stone guard attachment to fender.

To remove a roof molding, pull the molding outer lip from the body of the car. Using the special tool or equivalent, spread the molding enough to remove it from the clips. See Fig. 6-15. Work from the rear of the car forward. Replace any clips that are damaged. Before installation, lightly lubricate the inside of the molding. Install the molding from the front of the car back, using the special tool to spread the molding. Position the molding so that there is approximately a 2.0 mm (⁵⁄₆₄ in.) gap between the outer sealing lip and the B-pillar on 2-door models, or the the outer sealing lip and the C-pillar on 4-door models.

To replace a body side molding on 1985 through 1987 cars, use a heat gun and carefully heat the molding to soften the adhesive backing, then pull the molding from the car. Clean the mounting area on the body with a grease and wax removing solvent. Heat the molding and the body area to approximately 95°F (35°C), then remove the backing from the adhesive strip and correctly align the molding. Check that the ends are securely glued.

Body side moldings on 1988 and 1989 cars are mounted with retention clips that snap out from the body for removal.

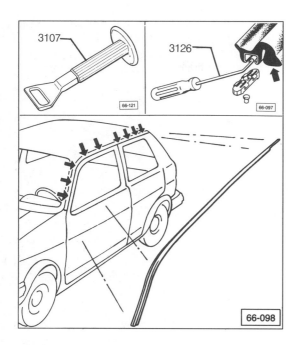

Fig. 6-15. Roof molding and location of mounting clips (arrows). Left inset shows tool used to remove molding. Right inset shows outer sealing lip (arrow) and tool for clip removal/installation.

Removing and Installing Bumpers

The front and rear bumpers are mounted on solid brackets bolted to the frame, with guide brackets attached to the body.

To remove the front bumper, work beneath the car to remove the two bolts from the left and right frame as shown in Fig. 6-16.

Fig. 6-16. Front bumper frame mounting bolts (arrows). Remove bolts from left and right side.

Unclip the lower ventilation grille and remove the bolts from the left and right side of the car shown in Fig. 6-17. Pull the bumper straight out and away from the car.

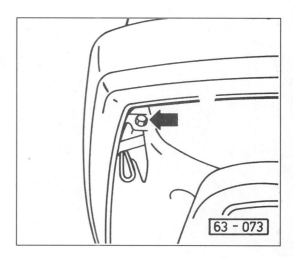

Fig. 6-17. Front bumper mounting bolt on front of car (arrow). Remove bolts from left and right side.

To install the front bumper, slide the bumper onto the body members, making sure that the side guides are correctly positioned. Torque the body frame bolts to 82 Nm (59 ft. lb.). Torque the front bolts to 40 Nm (29 ft. lb.).

To remove the rear bumper, work under the car to remove the bumper mounting bolts from the body frame. See Fig. 6-18.

Fig. 6-18. Rear bumper frame mounting bolts (arrows). Remove bolts from left and right side.

Working in the luggage compartment, remove the bolts shown in Fig. 6-19. Pull the bumper straight out, off of the side guides and away from the car.

To install the rear bumper, slide the bumper into the body members, making sure that the bumper engages the side guides. Torque the frame mounting bolts to 70 Nm (61 ft. lb.). Torque the side body bolts to 40 Nm (29 ft. lb.).

13

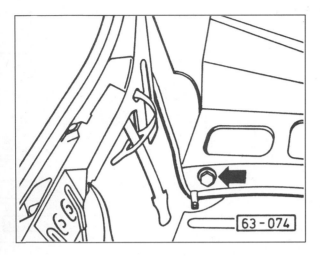

Fig. 6-19. Rear bumper mounting bolt (arrow) in luggage compartment. Remove bolts from left and right side.

Removing Plastic Bumper Cover

The plastic bumper cover can be replaced. A Volkswagen tool and a press will make installation easier. To replace the cover, first remove the bumper as described above. Work the old cover off of its plastic clips. See Fig. 6-20. Align the new cover and press it into the bumper until all the clips are securely engaged.

Fig. 6-20. Bumper being pressed onto bumper cover. Arrows show plastic clips. Inset shows special tool.

Hood Lock Cable

The hood lock cable is non-adjustable. The only repair is replacement. Fig. 6-21 shows the cable routing and attachment points. To remove the cable, it is necessary to remove the front grille as described in **Removing Front Body Parts and Grille**. Separate the cable from the release lever under the radiator support, and pull the cable housing from its retaining clips.

Remove the screws holding the release handle to the body inside the passenger compartment and pull the cable through the firewall. Check that the firewall grommet is correctly seated when installing the new cable for an air-tight seal.

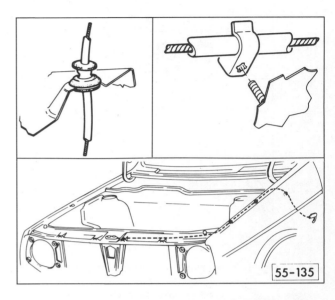

Fig. 6-21. Hood lock cable routing. Right inset shows mounting clips. Left inset shows firewall grommet.

Rear Lid and Hatchback

Fig. 6-22 is a view of the Jetta rear lid and its related components. The grip molding and lock assembly is similar on the Golf and GTI hatchback, but the hatch does not have springs. Instead, gas struts are used to assist raising the hatch. The hatchback hinges are located at the top of the hatch. It is necessary to partially remove the headliner for access to them. If the rear lid or hatchback is to be removed, mark the hinge locations before loosening the mounting bolts.

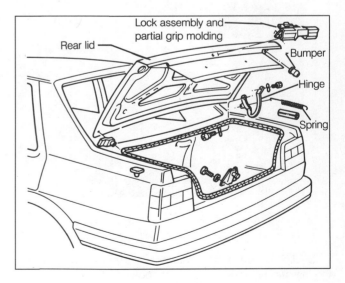

Fig. 6-22. Jetta rear lid.

To remove the Jetta lock assembly and grip molding, remove the six screws holding the grip molding to the rear lid and remove the moldings from either side of the lock. Open the lid and, working from the inside, unclip the actuating lever from the lock assembly. Press in the two lock tabs holding the lock to the lid and remove the lock assembly. To remove the lock assembly from the grip molding, remove the C-clips. Installation is the reverse of removal. Make sure that the lock gasket is intact.

To remove the Golf and GTI hatchback lock assembly, remove the grip molding by removing the four screws. Open the hatchback and remove the inside hatch trim panel by removing its retaining clips. Unclip the actuating lever from the lock assembly, press in the two lock tabs holding the lock assembly to the hatch and remove the lock. Installation is the reverse of removal. Make sure that the lock gasket is intact.

To replace a license plate bulb, remove the screws that hold the lens to the lid. Push and twist the bulb to remove and install it. Tighten the lens screws just until they are snug to avoid cracking the lens. Replacement bulbs are part no. N 017 753 2 (U.S. trade no. 168).

Windshield

The windshield is bonded in place and requires special tools and materials to replace it. A windshield replacement kit, part no. D 004 300, is available from an Authorized Volkswagen dealer, and contains materials and directions for replacing the windshield. In addition, the interior beading and the exterior molding should be replaced with the windshield.

7. SUNROOF

The manual sunroof is controlled by a set of cables which pull the sunroof panel along guide rails when the crank is turned. The sunroof can be adjusted without removing it from the car, however, replacement of the sunroof liner or components such as the cable assembly require sunroof removal. If the sunroof leaks or sticks, adjust it as described in **7.2 Adjusting Sunroof Fit** before deciding that it needs to be removed from the car. Leaks may also be caused by clogged drain hoses. The front hoses lead from the A-pillar into the space between the front fender and the door. The rear hoses are reached after removing the rear bumper. Clean the hoses with a length of flexible cable, such as an old speedometer cable.

7.1 Removing and Installing Sunroof

To remove:

1. Open the sunroof halfway. Use a wooden or plastic wedge to pry the front edge of the trim panel from the sunroof. See Fig. 7-1. Pry as close as possible to each of the clips. Remove the clips and push the panel back into the roof.

2. Close the sunroof and remove the Phillips head screws from the left and right front guides as shown in Fig. 7-2.

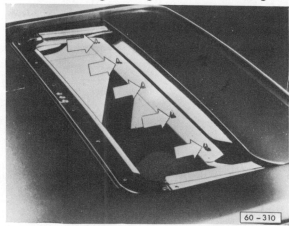

Fig. 7-1. Five clips (arrows) that hold trim panel to sunroof.

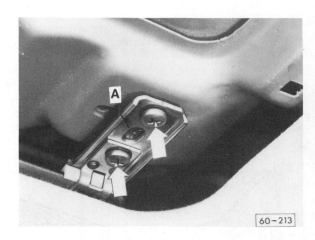

Fig. 7-2. Screws (arrows) to be removed from right and left front guides (**A**).

3. At the rear guides, unhook the left and right leaf springs and swing them inward as indicated in Fig. 7-3.

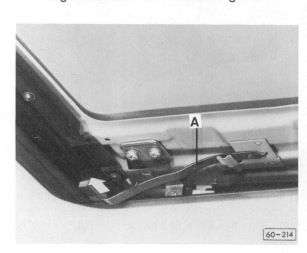

Fig. 7-3. Leaf springs (**A**) being pivoted inward (arrow).

13

4. Remove the screws from the rear guides, then slide the support plate inwards and remove it. See Fig. 7-4. Remove the sunroof through the top of the car.

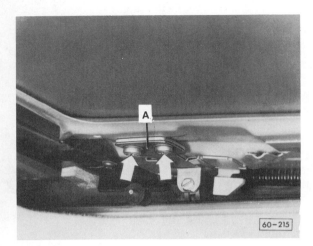

Fig. 7-4. Screws (arrows) to be removed from rear guides and support plate (**A**).

Installation is the reverse of removal. If the interior trim panel was removed from the vehicle, install it into the roof and push it back before installing the sunroof. When the rear guides are installed, align them as shown in Fig 7-5. Adjust the sunroof as described in **7.2 Adjusting Sunroof Fit** before attaching the trim panel.

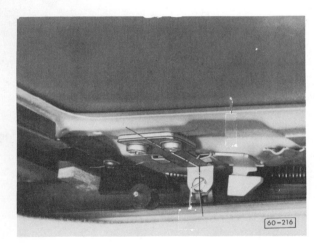

Fig. 7-5. Sunroof correctly aligned to rear guide (broken line). Install support plate between guide and roof panel.

7.2 Adjusting Sunroof Fit

The sunroof should be adjusted whenever the top of the closed sunroof does not lie flush with the roof of the car, if it does not close squarely, if there are wind noises at high speed, if there are water leaks, or if the sunroof has been removed.

To adjust:

1. Open the sunroof halfway. Use a wooden or plastic wedge to pry the front edge of the trim panel from the sunroof. See Fig. 7-1 above. Pry as close as possible to each of the clips. Remove the clips and push the panel back into the roof.

2. Close the sunroof. Loosen the mounting screws that hold the sunroof to the front guides, then turn the adjustment screw shown in Fig. 7-6 until the front of the sunroof is aligned as shown in Fig. 7-7. Tighten the mounting screws.

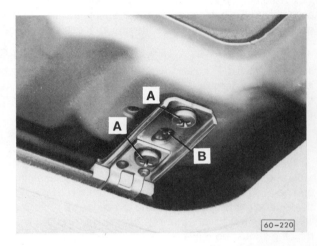

Fig. 7-6. Sunroof front height being adjusted. Screws **A** hold front guide to sunroof. Screw **B** adjusts height.

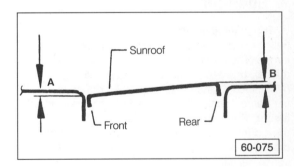

Fig. 7-7. Correctly adjusted sunroof. Dimension **A** and dimension **B** are 0 to 1 mm (0 to .04 in.).

3. Remove the spring from the rear guides. See Fig. 7-3 above. Loosen the screws shown in Fig. 7-8 to adjust rear height by raising or lowering the sunroof by hand. Tighten the screws when the adjustment is correct as shown above in Fig. 7-7, and install the spring.

4. Turn the crank 1/2 turn to open the sunroof, then remove the crank handle. Remove the interior dome light, and pry out the crank handle trim panel at the rear. Remove the mounting screws from the cable drive as shown in Fig. 7-9, and remove the cable drive with the drive gear from above.

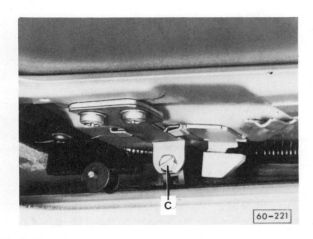

Fig. 7-8. Sunroof rear height being adjusted. Screw **C** is loosened for adjustment.

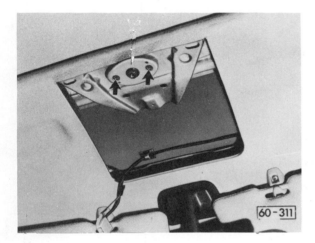

Fig. 7-9. Cable drive retaining screws (arrows) to be removed.

5. Push the sunroof open and shut several times by hand, then adjust the sunroof until it is square with the opening in its partly-open position. Install the cable drive so that the drive gear engages the cables. Install the cable drive screws and crank trim panel, and check that the crank handle rests in the panel when the roof is closed. Open the sunroof half-way and install the trim panel.

Removing and Installing Rear Guides with Cables

The sunroof cables are integral with the rear guides and can only be replaced as a unit.

To remove and install:

1. Remove the sunroof as described in **7.1 Removing and Installing Sunroof.** Remove the screws that hold the wind deflector to the roof and remove it from the car.

2. Remove the window crank and crank trim panel, and then remove the two screws and the cable drive as shown previously in Fig 7-9.

3. Remove the left and right rail cover screws and remove the covers. See Fig. 7-10. Remove the front guides.

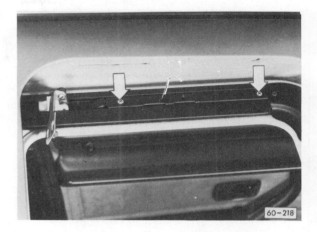

Fig. 7-10. Guide rail cover screws (arrows) to be removed.

4. Pull the cable assembly and the rear guides from the guide rails as shown in Fig. 7-11.

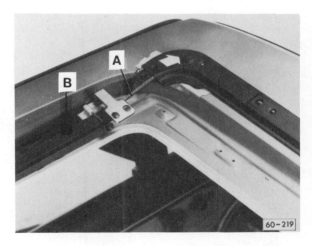

Fig. 7-11. Rear guides with cable assembly (**A**) being removed from guide rails (**B**), in direction of arrow.

5. Installation of the rear guides with cables is the reverse of removal. Reinstall the front guides and rail covers, then adjust the sunroof as described in **7.2 Adjusting Sunroof Fit**.

8. BODY ASSEMBLY MATERIALS

The assembly materials given in **Table c,** are those recommended by Volkswagen, and should be used when performing body and interior repairs for maximum corrosion protection, proper alignment, and trouble-free installation.

Table c. Body Assembly Materials

Application	Type and Volkswagen Part Number
Fastening rear view mirror to windshield	Glass to metal adhesive (part no. D 000 702) Adhesive activator (part no. D 000 701)
Gluing interior leatherette	Synthetic Adhesive (part no. D 001 101)
Gluing carpet, rubber, felt, and fabric to painted metal	Universal Adhesive (part no. D 001 200)
Gluing door seals	Profile rubber adhesive (part no. D 002 100)
Fastening protective liner to door	Two-sided tape (part no. AKL 440 025)
Adhesive cleaning solution	Cleaning solution (part no. D 009 400 1)
Primer for painting	Paint primer (part no. D 009 300)
Sealing gaps in bolts, cables, and wires to panels	Original plastic sealant (part no. D 001 400)

9.   AIR CONDITIONING

Air conditioning (A/C) service and repair requires special equipment and knowledge. Incorrect procedures may not only damage the system, but may also be hazardous. Pressures in excess of 300 psi are created in the system when it is operating. The refrigerant used in the system (R-12) is not poisonous, but in its vapor form it can accumulate in areas with poor ventilation and cause suffocation. Also, in vapor or liquid form R-12 can immediately freeze anything it contacts, including eyes and skin.

Although tests can determine A/C efficiency, it is recommended that all service to the system be left to an authorized Volkswagen dealer or other qualified repair shop. For information concerning the interior A/C operating controls, see **4.5 Heater and Controls**. Dismounting of the A/C compressor and the condenser, without disconnecting the hoses, is covered in **ENGINE**.

9.1 System Description

Fig. 9-1 is a schematic view of a typical automobile air conditioning (A/C) system.

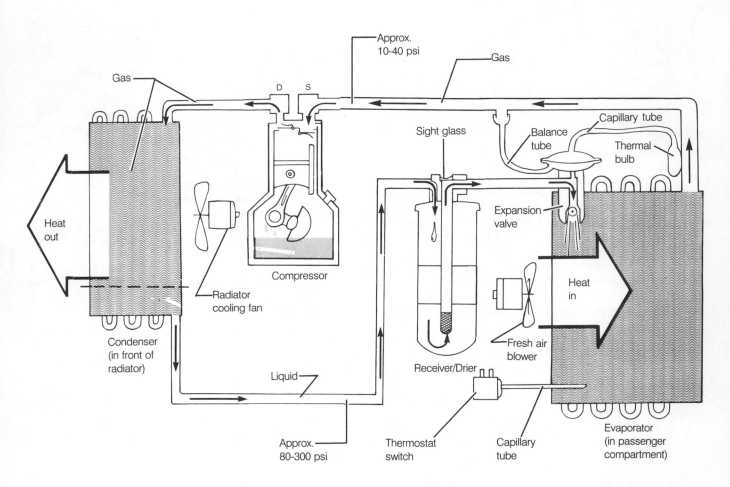

Fig. 9-1. Schematic view of typical air conditioning system. Golf, Jetta, GTI system is similar, except that sight glass is separate from receiver/drier.

The air conditioning system removes heat and moisture from the passenger compartment. It accomplishes this through the application of four principles: materials absorb heat as they change from a liguid to a gas (evaporate); materials give off heat as they change from a gas to a liquid (condense); the boiling point of a liquid varies with its pressure; and, haet always flows from hot to cold. For example, the first principle is demonstrated by wetting your hand and then blowing on it. As the water evaporates, it takes some heat with it and your hand feels cooler.

In the air conditioning system, the heat from the passenger compartment boils (evaporates) the refrigerant (R-12) in the evaporator, causing the heat to be absorbed by the R-12. This heat is then released into the atmosphere when the R-12 is cooled and condensed into a liquid at the condenser. Moisture is removed at the evaporator in the same way that water drops form on a cold glass. The moisture drips onto the water tray beneath the evaporator (located behind the dash) and is routed outside. This is the reason a water puddle may often be seen under the car when the A/C is operating.

The compressor forces the R-12 through the system and at the same time pressurizes the R-12, raising its boiling point to make it more easily condensed. The compressor is engaged by an electro-magnetic clutch which is actuated when the A/C is turned on. The thermostat switch automatically disengages the clutch when the temperature in the passenger compartment reaches the level set on the operating controls. The condenser, which looks like a small radiator, is located in front of the engine radiator. The receiver/drier removes small amounts of moisture and dirt from the system. The expansion valve maintains a steady temperature in the system by metering the flow of R-12 based on the temperature of the refrigerant as it leaves the evaporator.

Safety Features

To prevent system freeze-up, the fresh air blower and the radiator cooling fan come on at low speed whenever the A/C is turned on. A low-pressure switch prevents engagement of the compressor clutch if the R-12 charge is too low. A high-pressure switch runs the radiator cooling fan at high speed to cool the R-12 if the pressure in the system is excessive. A blow-out plug in the receiver/drier releases if system pressure exceeds approximately 500 psi. On diesel-engine cars, a thermoswitch turns the compressor off when the engine coolant temperature rises above 248°F (120°C).

9.2 Inspections and Tests

Periodic inspections will help keep the A/C operating at its peak. There are almost always small leaks in the system which will require that it eventually be recharged with R-12. The V-belt which drives the compressor is subject to wear. The condenser fins can become bent or covered with debris, reducing air flow and raising system pressure to damaging levels.

With the engine off, clean any debris or bugs from the front of the condenser, and straighten any bent fins using a fin comb. Remove the air plenum drip tray and check the fresh air intake

for obstructions. Inspect the compressor, the hoses, and all visible components for any oil leaks, which are often seen at the bottom side of the fittings and components. Inspect the wiring to the pressure switches and compressor clutch. Check the compressor mountings for tightness, and check the condition and tension of the V-belt as described in **LUBRICATION AND MAINTENANCE**.

> **WARNING** ——
> Wear eye protection when inspecting the system. R-12 at normal atmospheric pressures can evaporate and freeze anything it contacts.

The following tests will aid in evaluating system performance.

Checking Refrigerant Charge

Inspect the refrigerant charge of R-12 by starting the engine and turning the air conditioner on to MAX A/C. With the compressor running (clutch cycled on) view the sight glass (located in-line near the condenser in the engine compartment). There should be few or no bubbles visible in the glass. A constant foaming indicates that the system charge is low. Streaks on the interior of the glass may indicate that the system is totally discharged.

If using an aftermarket product to recharge the system, follow the manufacturer's directions closely. To prevent component damage, a totally discharged system must be evacuated (sometimes called pulling a vaccum), using special equipment, to remove any moisture before recharging.

A/C Performance Test

Perform this test if the cooling output seems reduced. A thermometer with a probe is necessary for the test.

> **NOTE** ——
> Reduced cooling output on 1985 to 1987 Jettas may be caused by a malfunctioning expansion valve due to excess engine heat. A special valve insulator, part no. 191 820 692, is available from an authorized Volkswagen dealer to reduce expansion valve temperatures.

To test the A/C, open all instrument panel vents, and place the thermometer into the left center vent as shown in Fig. 9-2. Open one front window, turn on the ignition, and with the upper control lever set to VENT and the lower control lever to FULL COOL, turn the fresh air blower to HIGH. After approximately 30 seconds record the temperature on the thermometer.

With the parking brake firmly set, start the engine and move the upper control lever to MAX A/C. After one minute, record the temperature. It should be at least 15°F (8.3°C) less than the first recorded temperature. If it is not, make sure that the air flow is coming only from the center vents and that the recirculation door is closed. See **4.5 Heater and Controls** for vacuum system troubleshooting. A temperature difference less than the specified value indicates a problem with the system. Inspect the system as described earlier.

13

Fig. 9-2. Thermometer inserted in center vent for A/C test.

9.3 Air Conditioning Specifications

The specifications and graphs listed below in **Table d** and Fig. 9-3 are intended to be used by those experienced in air conditioning service.

Table d. Air Conditioning Specifications

Refrigerant Capacity (R-12). . . .1100 ± 50 grams (40.0 ± 2.0 oz.)
Refrigerant Oil Capacity (Total) . . . . .135 cc
Oil Distribution Through System	
condenser . . . . .20 cc
evaporator . . . . .10 cc
receiver/drier . . . . .25 cc
discharge hose . . . . .5 cc
suction hose. . . . . .5 cc
compressor. . . . . .75 cc
High Pressure Switch	
closes. . . . . .14.5 ± 0.7 bar (210.0 ± 10.2 psi)
opens . . . . .12.0 ± 0.7 bar (174.0 ± 10.2 psi)
Low Pressure Switch	
closes . . . . .3.0 ± 0.3 bar (43.5 ± 4.3 psi)
opens . . . . .2.0 ± 0.3 bar (29.0 ± 4.3 psi)

WARNING ——

Adding refrigerant or servicing the system without the proper tools and equipment may damage the A/C components as well as cause severe personal injury.

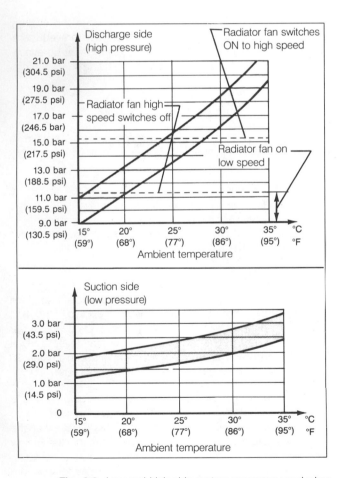

Fig. 9-3. Low and high side system pressures used when checking refrigerant charge and servicing the system. The system pressures should be in the shaded areas according to the ambient air temperatures.

Section 14

ELECTRICAL SYSTEM
Contents

Introduction 3

1. General Description 4
    Voltage and Polarity 4
    Battery 4
    Starter 4
    Charging System 4
    Ignition System 4
    Wiring, Fuses, and Relays 4
    Lights 4
    Heating and Ventilation 4
    Windshield Wipers and Washers 4
    Instruments 4

2. Maintenance 5

3. Troubleshooting 5
  3.1 How To Read Volkswagen Current Flow
      Diagrams 5
      Terminal and Circuit Identification 6
  3.2 Battery, Starter and Charging System
      Troubleshooting 7
  3.3 Basic Electrical Troubleshooting Principles . . . 8

4. Battery 9
  4.1 Testing Battery 9
      Hydrometer Testing 9
      Open-circuit Voltage Test 10
      Load Voltage Testing 10
  4.2 Battery Charging 10

5. Charging system 11
  5.1 Charging System Troubleshooting 11
  5.2 In-Vehicle Testing of Charging System 12
      Testing Alternator and Regulator 12
      Testing Current Drain 12
      Noisy Alternator 13
  5.3 Removing and Installing Alternator and Voltage
      Regulator 13
      Brushes and Voltage Regulator 13

6. Starting System 14
  6.1 Starting System Troubleshooting 14
  6.2 Removing and Installing Starter 14
      Removing and Installing Solenoid Switch . . . 15
      Replacing Starter Bushing (manual transmission
      only) 16

7. Instruments 16
  7.1 Troubleshooting Instrument Cluster
      and Gauges 16
      Testing Instrument Cluster Voltage
      and Ground 16
      Testing and Replacing Voltage Stabilizer 16
      Testing and Replacing Light Emitting Diodes
      (LEDs) and Indicator Bulbs 18
      Testing Upshift Indicator 18
      Testing Dynamic Oil Pressure Warning System
      Control Unit 20

8. Windshield Wipers and Washers 20
  8.1 Windshield Wiper and Washer System
      Troubleshooting 20
      Testing Windshield Wiper Motor 20
      Testing Rear Wiper Motor 20
      Testing Wiper/Washer Switch 21
      Testing Windshield Wiper Intermittent Relay . . 21
  8.2 Windshield Wiper Motor and Linkage 21
      Removing and Installing Windshield Wiper
      Motor 21
      Removing and Installing Rear Wiper Motor . . . 23

9. Horns 24
  9.1 Horn Troubleshooting 24

10. Exterior Lights 24
  10.1 Troubleshooting Exterior Lights 24
      Headlights 25
      Turn Signals and Emergency Flashers 25
      Parking Lights, Taillights, Side Marker Lights,
      and License Plate Lights 25
      Brake Lights 25
      Back-up Lights 25

10.2   Steering Column Switches 25
        Ignition Switch 25

11. Heating, Ventilation and Air Conditioning 26
        Fresh Air Blower 26
        Air Conditioning 26
        Rear Window Defogger 27

12. Power Options and Accessories 27
12.1   Heated Seats 27
12.2   Electric/Heated Outside Mirrors 27
12.3   Central Locking System 27
12.4   Power Windows 28
12.5   Cruise Control 28

13. Fuse/Relay Panel 28
        1985 through 1989 Jetta fuse/relay panel 30
        1985 Golf and GTI relay panel 31
        1985 Golf and GTI fuse panel 32
        1986 through 1989 Golf and GTI relay panel . . 33
        1986 through 1989 Golf and GTI fuse panel . . 34

14. Current Flow Diagrams 35
        Golf and GTI 35
        Jetta 35

Current Flow Diagrams Golf/GTI

        Symbols used in Wiring Diagrams 36
        Ground Circuit 37–43
        Ground Locations 44
        Harness Connectors 45–47
        Power Supply 48–62
        Exterior Lights 63–70
        Brake Lights 71
        Courtesy Lights 72
        Interior Lights 73–75
        Instrument Panel Lights 76–77
        Turn Signals/Flashers 78
        Brake Warning Indicator 79
        Instrument Cluster 80–89
        Horns 90–91
        Windshield Wipers and Washer 92–94
        Rear Wiper and Washer 95–98
        Glow Plugs 99–100
        Electronic Engine Control 101–121
        Fuel Pump System 122
        Cold Start System 123–124
        Idle Speed Boost 125–126
        Coolant Level Warning System 127–128
        Radiator Cooling Fan 129–132
        After-Run Radiator Cooling Fan 133–134

        Seat Belt Warning 135
        Seat Belt Interlock/Park Brake
        Warning 136–139
        Passive Restraint 140–143
        Upshift Indicator 144–147
        Fresh Air Fan 148
        Air Conditioning 149–158
        Cruise Control 159–160
        Radio 161–163
        Power Windows 164–166
        Central Locking 167
        Power Mirrors 168
        Power Mirrors 169–170

Current Flow Diagrams Jetta

        Main Electrical System (1985–1987 Jetta
        Gasoline except GLI) 171–180
        Main Electrical System (1988–1989 Jetta
        Gasoline, 1986–1989 Jetta GLI) 181–195
        Main Electrical System (1985–1989 Jetta
        Diesel) 196–205
        Electronic Engine Controls 206–223
        Automatic Transmission 224–227
        Cruise Control 228–231
        Air Conditioning 232–239
        Multifunction Indicator 240–241
        After-Run Radiator Cooling Fan 242–243
        Heated Seats 244–245
        Electric/Heated Outside Mirrors 246–247
        Central Locking System 248–249
        Power Seat Height Adjustment 250–251
        Power Windows 252–254
        Stereo Radio 255–257
        Stereo Radio with Power Antenna 258–260
        Stereo Radio with Six Speakers and Power
        Antenna 261–264
        Seatbelt interlock for passive restraint . 265–267

Tables

a.   Terminal and Circuit Numbers 7
b.   Battery, Starter and Charging System
      Troubleshooting 7
c.   Specific Gravity of Electrolyte at 80°F (27°C) 10
d.   Open-circuit Voltage and Battery Charge 10
e.   Battery Charging Specifications 10
f.   Warning Light Troubleshooting 11
g.   Starting System Troubleshooting 15
h.   Troubleshooting Upshift Indicator Light System . . . 19
i.   Windshield Wiper Motor Voltage Tests 21
j.   Wiper Switch Continuity Tests 21
k.   Ignition Switch Continuity Tests 25

Electrical System

Introduction

The electrical system is basically an efficient means for transmitting power from the engine to the electrical components of the car. It does this with the help of the alternator which converts some of the engine's mechanical energy into electrical energy. The electrical energy is then carried by wires to the various electrical components such as motors, light bulbs, or electronic control units. The battery in the system supplies electrical power when the engine is not running, and also supplies power to start the engine.

The electrical system is based on negative (−) ground. In other words, the negative terminal of the battery is connected to the car body, and any electrical connection to the body is a connection to ground. This greatly reduces the amount of wire used in the system. Voltage from the battery to the various electrical components is carried by the wiring harness. Most components are then grounded by their physical mounting or electrical connection to the car body. Because of this, the integrity and freedom from corrosion of ground connections in the system, including the negative battery cable and the body ground straps, is one of the most important conditions for trouble-free operation of the electrical system.

The connecting terminals on components and wiring harness connectors can be either pins, or sockets into which pins fit. Most terminals are identified with a number stamped next to the pins on the components. On relays, the terminals are also identified by numbers on the relay. Throughout this section, sockets on the relay panel are identified by referring to the terminal which fits into them. The terminal numbers and the location of all the major electrical connections are given in the current flow diagrams near the end of this section.

All electrical circuits except those required for starting and operating the engine are protected by fuses. To prevent accidental shorts that might blow a fuse or damage wires and electrical components, the ground strap from the negative terminal of the battery should always be disconnected before working on the electrical system. If you lack the skills or the equipment needed for testing and repairing the electrical system, we suggest you leave this work to an authorized Volkswagen dealer or other qualified repair shop. We especially urge you to consult an authorized Volkswagen dealer before beginning repairs on a car that may be subject to Volkswagen's warranty coverage.

14

1. GENERAL DESCRIPTION

A brief description of the principal parts of the electrical system is presented here for familiarization with the system. The components are each discussed in greater detail in later parts of this section.

Voltage and Polarity

The cars covered by this manual have a 12-volt, direct current (DC), negative-ground electrical system. The voltage regulator maintains the voltage in the system at approximately the 12-volt rating of the battery, and all circuits are grounded by direct or indirect connection to the negative (−) terminal of the battery.

Battery

The six-cell, 12-volt lead-acid battery is located on the driver's side of the engine compartment. The battery capacity is determined by the amount of current needed to start the car, and by the amount of current consumed by the electrical system. Volkswagen batteries are rated by ampere/hours (Ah) and cold cranking amps (CCA) rating. The Ah rating is determined by the average amount of current the battery can deliver over time without dropping below a specified voltage. The CCA is determined by the battery's ability to deliver starting current at 0°F (−18°C).

Starter

The starter and its attached solenoid are located at the front of the engine and transaxle assembly on cars with manual transmissions, and at the rear of the engine and transaxle assembly on cars with automatic transmissions. To maximize the amount of current available to the starter, a load-reduction relay interrupts the voltage to many of the electrical accessories when the ignition key is in the START position.

Charging System

The charging system consists of a belt-driven alternator and a voltage regulator. The voltage regulator is an integral part of the alternator brush holder. An alternator manufactured by either Bosch or Motorola is installed on cars covered by this manual. The alternator may be one of three capacities—55 amperes, 65 amperes, or 90 amperes—depending on the type and number of electrical accessories fitted to the car.

Ignition System

The transistorized ignition system is covered in **IGNITION**. To avoid personal injury, as well as damage to the sensitive electronic components of the ignition system, please review the cautions and warnings in that section before troubleshooting or repairing any ignition-related part of the electrical system.

Wiring, Fuses, and Relays

Nearly all parts of the wiring harness connect to components of the electrical system with keyed, push-on connectors which lock into place. Notable exceptions are the heavy battery cables. The wiring is color-coded for circuit identification. Wire colors are indicated in the current flow diagrams near the end of the section.

With the exception of the battery charging system, all electrical power is routed from the ignition switch or the battery through the fuse/relay panel, located behind the instrument panel to the left of the steering column. Fuses prevent excessive current from damaging components and wiring. In addition, Golf and GTI models are equipped with fusible links between the battery and the main wiring harness. Fuses are color coded to indicate their different current capacities.

The relays are electromagnetic switches that operate on low current to switch a high-current circuit on and off. The relays are mounted on the fuse/relay panel. For information concerning relay and fuse locations, see **13. Fuse/Relay Panel** and **14. Current Flow Diagrams**.

Lights

The lighting system includes the parking lights, the side marker lights, the turn signals, the back-up lights, the interior lighting, and the headlights. The headlight dimmer switch is on the steering column. There is no relay in the headlight circuit. High/low beam switching is handled directly from the contacts in the dimmer control. Information on changing bulbs and lenses can be found in **BODY AND INTERIOR**.

Heating and Ventilation

The heating and ventilation system includes a three-speed fresh air blower controlled by a dashboard-mounted switch. The control levers for the air conditioning (A/C) system switch power to the A/C compressor, the fresh air blower, and the radiator cooling fan. Removal and installation of the heating and ventilation components is covered in **BODY AND INTERIOR**.

Windshield Wipers and Washers

The blades of the two-speed windshield wiper system with intermittent operation come to rest in the "park" position automatically when the wiper switch is turned off. The wiper switch includes a windshield washer control. A motor-driven pump supplies the washers with fluid. Golf and GTI models have an additional rear wiper and washer.

Instruments

With the exception of the speedometer, which is gear-driven by a flexible cable from the transaxle, the dashboard instruments are electrical. All differences in instrumentation among models are covered in the current flow diagrams. Removal and installation of the instrument cluster is described in **BODY AND INTERIOR**.

2. MAINTENANCE

No routine lubrication of the alternator, the starter, or other motors is required. The following electrical system maintenance is described in **LUBRICATION AND MAINTENANCE**.

1. Checking the battery

3. TROUBLESHOOTING

This heading describes general procedures for electrical system circuit and component troubleshooting, and provides specific troubleshooting information for the battery, the starter, and the charging system. The later heading **14. Current Flow Diagrams** contains information such as wire colors, terminal identification, and ground and connector locations which is invaluable to electrical troubleshooting.

3.1 How To Read Volkswagen Current Flow Diagrams

The circuit diagrams presented in this manual are organized to indicate current flow, from positive to negative, in the electrical system. This is different from other types of wiring diagrams that actually show the routing of the wiring harness.

As a general rule, current flows from positive (+) at the top of the diagram to negative (−) at the bottom (which represents ground). One exception to this is the fuse/relay panel's internal ground circuit, labeled with the terminal number 31. See **Terminal and Circuit Identification** for further information.

Fig. 3-1 and Fig. 3-2 are examples of Volkswagen current flow diagrams, showing the meanings of the various markings. These are general examples. They do not show all of the schematic symbols used. For a complete listing of the symbols, see **14. Current Flow Diagrams**.

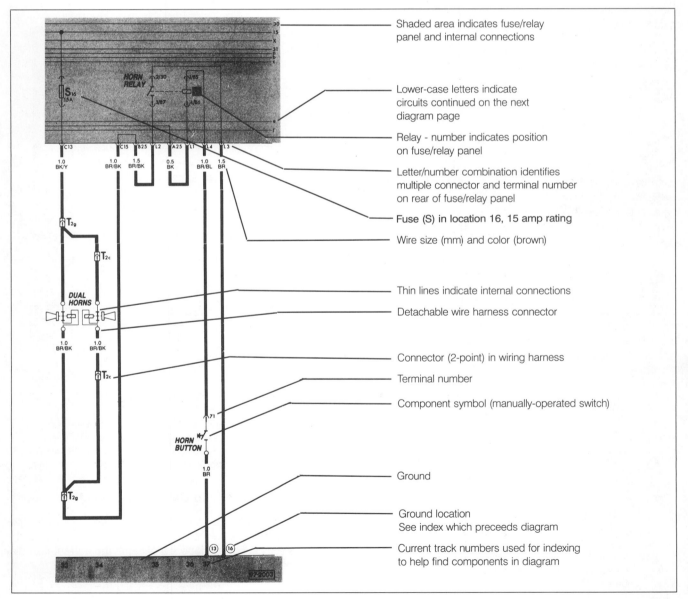

14

Fig. 3-1. Sample current flow diagram for Jetta models.

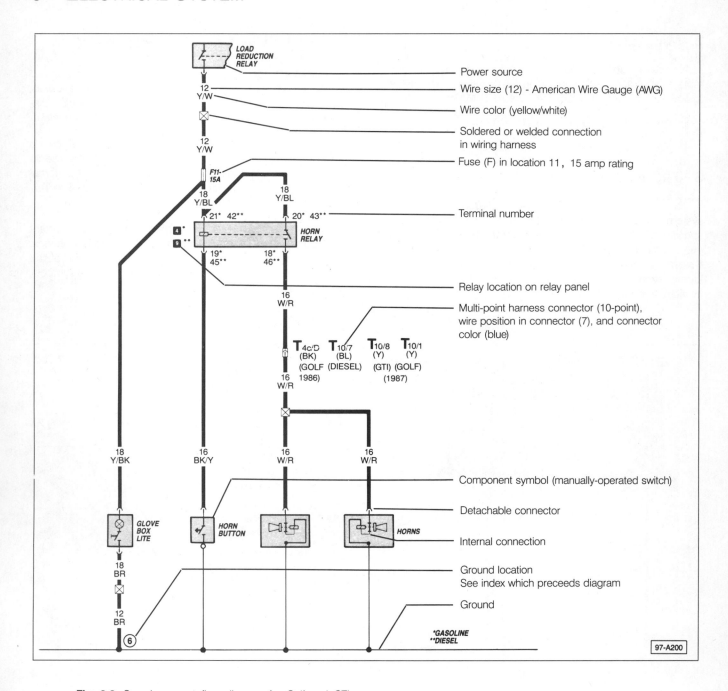

Fig. 3-2. Sample current flow diagram for Golf and GTI models.

Terminal and Circuit Identification

Most terminals are identified by numbers on the components and harness connectors. The terminal numbers for the major electrical connections are given in the current flow diagrams at the end of this section.

Though many terminal numbers are unique, used only once to identify a particular terminal, several numbers appear in numerous places throughout the electrical system and identify certain types of circuits. A letter suffix is sometimes added to the number to distinguish between two different circuits, or between two parts of the same circuit. **Table a** lists several of the most common circuit numbers, and identifies the circuit type and the wire color normally used.

Table a. Terminal and Circuit Numbers

Number	Circuit description	Most common wire color
1	Low voltage ($-$) terminal of coil	Green
4	High voltage center terminal of coil	Black
15	Originates at ignition switch. Supplies power when ignition switch is in ON or START position	Black
X	Load-reduction relay circuit Originates at ignition switch Supplies power only when ignition switch is in ON position. Circuit is interrupted when starter is actuated	Black/yellow
30	Battery positive ($+$) voltage. Supplies power whenever battery is connected. (Not dependent on ignition switch position)	Red

Table a. Terminal and Circuit Numbers (continued)

Number	Circuit description	Most common wire color
31	Ground; battery negative ($-$)	Brown
50	Supplies power from battery to starter solenoid when ignition switch is in START position	Red/black
B+	Originates at alternator and supplies voltage to battery	Red
D+	Alternator warning light and field energizing circuit	—
W	RPM signal from alternator (diesel) on diesel engines	Red/black
85	Ground side ($-$) of switching relay	Brown
86	Power-in side ($+$) of switching relay	—
87	Relay change-over contact	—

3.2 Battery, Starter and Charging System Troubleshooting

The causes of a dead battery or an inoperative starter are often interrelated and hard to pinpoint. **Table b** lists symptoms of trouble with the battery, starter, and charging system, their probable causes, and suggested corrective actions. The bold numbers in the corrective action column refer to the numbered headings in this section where the suggested repairs can be found.

Table b. Battery, Starter and Charging System Troubleshooting

Symptom	Probable cause	Corrective action
1. Engine cranks slowly or not at all, solenoid clicks when starter is operated	a. Battery cables loose, dirty, or corroded b. Battery discharged c. Body ground strap loose, dirty, or corroded d. No voltage reaching starter motor e. Starter motor or solenoid faulty	a. Clean or replace cables. See **LUBRICATION AND MAINTENANCE** b. Charge battery; test and replace if necessary. **4.** c. Inspect ground strap; clean, tighten, and replace as necessary d. Test for voltage at starter. **6.** Test neutral/park/reverse light switch. **10.1** e. Test starter. **6.1**
2. Battery will not stay charged (more than a few days)	a. Shorted circuit draining battery b. Alternator V-belt loose or damaged c. Battery faulty d. Battery cables loose, dirty, or corroded e. Alternator or voltage regulator faulty	a. Test for current drain. **5.2** b. Inspect alternator V-belt. **5.3** c. Test battery and replace if necessary. **4.1** d. Clean or replace cables. See **LUBRICATION AND MAINTENANCE** e. Test alternator and regulator. **5.2**

14

continued on next page

Table b. Battery, Starter and Charging System Troubleshooting (continued)

Symptom	Probable cause	Corrective action
3. Battery losing water	a. Battery being overcharged	a. Test voltage regulator. 5.2
4. Lights dim, light intensity varies with engine speed	a. Alternator V-belt loose or damaged b. Alternator or voltage regulator faulty c. Body ground straps loose, dirty, or corroded	a. Inspect alternator V-belt. 5.3 b. Test alternator and voltage regulator. 5.2 c. Inspect ground straps; clean, tighten, and replace as required.

3.3 Basic Electrical Troubleshooting Principles

Four things are required for current to flow in any electrical circuit: a voltage source, wires or connections to transport the voltage, a consumer or device that uses the electricity, and a connection to ground. Most problems can be found using only a relatively inexpensive multimeter (volt/ohm/amp meter) to check for voltage supply, for breaks in the wiring (infinite resistance or no continuity), or for a path to ground that completes the circuit. In addition, test leads with flat male connectors are needed to prevent damaging terminal connections. For information on using a multimeter or constructing test leads, see **FUNDAMENTALS** at the front of the manual.

Electric current is logical in its flow, always moving from the voltage source toward ground. Keeping this in mind, electrical faults can be located through a process of elimination. Fig. 3-3 is used to illustrate the logic used in locating a sample fault: back-up lights which do not light.

To troubleshoot a circuit:

1. Check to see that all the connections in the circuit are tight and free of corrosion. Especially make sure that all ground connections are clean, dry, tight, and corrosion-free.

2. Check the fuse. In the circuit example shown in Fig. 3-3, the circuit receives power through fuse 15. Fuse and relay locations are given in **13. Fuse/Relay Panel**. A fuse that repeatedly fails indicates an unusually high current flow, probably caused by a damaged wire, a faulty component, or a short directly to ground.

3. Check for voltage reaching the circuit. Connect a voltmeter or test light between a point in the circuit and ground (a clean, unpainted metal part of the car). In the example, the ignition must be switched on since fuse 15 only receives power when the ignition is on. See **3.1 How To Read Volkswagen Current Flow Diagrams**.

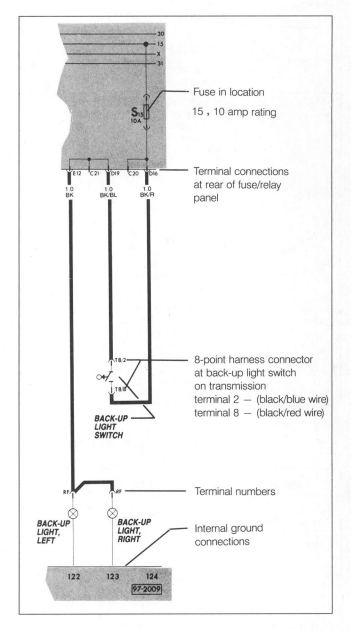

Fuse in location

15 , 10 amp rating

Terminal connections at rear of fuse/relay panel

8-point harness connector at back-up light switch on transmission
terminal 2 — (black/blue wire)
terminal 8 — (black/red wire)

Terminal numbers

Internal ground connections

Fig. 3-3. Sample current flow diagram. See procedure **To troubleshoot a circuit** for example of troubleshooting a circuit.

4. Pick a point where the diagram indicates that there should be voltage. In the example, the terminals "RF" at the connection to the back-up lights should be getting voltage when the ignition is on and the transmission is in reverse. Voltage indicated by the voltmeter (or by the test light lighting up) means that the circuit is doing its job at least as far as that point.

5. If there is no indication of voltage, something has interrupted the circuit between the power source and the test point. Pick a new test point farther "upstream" in the current path. In the example, terminal T8/8 at the back-up light switch would be a good point. If there is voltage at this point, then the fault lies somewhere between the two test points.

6. Check circuit integrity between two points with a continuity test using an ohmmeter to measure resistance between the two points. Continuity (little or no resistance) between two points indicates that that part of the circuit is complete and would allow current flow. No continuity (infinite resistance) indicates that part of the circuit is interrupted and would not allow current flow. In the example, operation of the back-up light switch could be checked by disconnecting the harness connector from the switch and testing for continuity across terminals 2 and 8. There should be continuity only when in reverse gear—otherwise the switch is faulty and should be replaced.

4. BATTERY

The battery does not actually store electricity—it stores energy chemically. The battery contains a number of negative and positive lead plates, along with a liquid solution of sulfuric acid and water called the electrolyte. When an electrical load is placed across the battery, the sulfuric acid combines with the lead in the plates to produce lead sulfate and water. A great number of electrons are released as electrical current flow by this chemical process. Charging the battery reverses the reaction—lead sulfate is released from the plates and sulfuric acid is formed.

Charging the battery does not remove all of the sulfate from the plates. The battery will gradually become sulfated and will no longer hold a sufficient enough charge to start the car. Replacement of the battery is the only remedy. Temperature also affects the efficiency of the battery. The current-producing capacity of a battery at 5°F (−15°C) is only half its capacity at 68°F (20°C), and partly-discharged batteries can freeze due to the higher proportion of water in the electrolyte. A frozen battery produces no current, but can usually be restored when thawed.

Both conventional and maintenance-free batteries are used in cars today. Conventional batteries have filler caps and require that distilled water be added periodically to maintain the electrolyte level. Maintenance-free batteries have no filler caps, and require no maintenance of the electrolyte.

The low-maintenance battery installed by Volkswagen in new cars covered by this manual is a combination of these two types. Although similar in appearance to a conventional battery, the caps on a low-maintenance battery are generally used only for access during hydrometer testing. Under normal operation the battery is maintenance-free, and normal charging can be done without removing the caps.

For more information on checking the battery and on battery maintenance, see **LUBRICATION AND MAINTENANCE**. For information on starting with jumper cables, see **FUNDAMENTALS**.

WARNING ——

Wear goggles, rubber gloves, and a rubber apron when working with battery electrolyte. Battery electrolyte contains sulfuric acid, and can cause severe burns and damage to clothing. If electrolyte is spilled on your skin or clothing, flush the area at once with large quantities of water. If electrolyte gets into your eyes, bathe them with large quantities of clean water for several minutes and call a physician.

WARNING ——

Batteries generate explosive gasses. Keep sparks and open flame away. Do not smoke.

CAUTION ——

Replace batteries with cracked or leaking cases. Leaking electrolyte can damage the car. If acid is spilled on the car, clean the area with a solution of baking soda and water.

4.1 Testing Battery

Battery testing determines the state of battery charge. On conventional or low-maintenance batteries the most common method of testing the battery is that of checking the specific gravity of the electrolyte using a hydrometer. On maintenance-free batteries, because of the sealed case, an open-circuit voltage test is used.

Hydrometer Testing

The hydrometer consists of a glass cylinder with a freely moving float inside. When electrolyte is drawn into the cylinder, the level to which the float sinks indicates the specific gravity of the electrolyte. The more dense the concentration of sulfuric acid in the electrolyte, the less the float will sink, resulting in a higher reading (and state of charge).

Electrolyte temperature affects the reading, so a thermometer should be used to determine electrolyte temperature before making a hydrometer test. Add .004 to the hydrometer reading for every 10°F (6°C) that the electrolyte is above 80°F (27°C); subtract .004 from the reading for every 10°F (6°C) that the electrolyte is below 80°F (27°C).

14▶

Before checking the specific gravity of a battery, load the battery with 15 amps for one minute. This can be done by turning on the headlights without the engine running if the battery is installed in the vehicle. **Table c** lists the percent of charge based on specific gravity values.

Table c. Specific Gravity of Electrolyte at 80°F (27°C)

Specific gravity	State of charge
1.265	Fully charged
1.225	75% charged
1.190	50% charged
1.155	25% charged
1.120	Fully discharged

The battery is in satisfactory condition if the average specific gravity of the six cells is at least 1.225. If the specific gravity is above this level, but the battery lacks power for starting, determine the battery's service condition with a load voltage test, as described below. If the average specific gravity of the six cells is below 1.225, recharge the battery. If, after recharging, the specific gravity varies by more than .050 between any two cells, replace the battery.

Open-circuit Voltage Test

This test is mainly for maintenance-free batteries, but it can also be performed on conventional and low-maintenance batteries if a hydrometer is not available. An open-circuit voltage test checks battery voltage by connecting an accurate digital voltmeter to the battery posts after disconnecting the battery ground cable. Before making an open-circuit voltage test on a battery, first load the battery with 15 amps for one minute. If the battery is installed in a car, this can be done by turning on the headlights without the engine running. Open-circuit voltage levels and their corresponding percentages of charge are given in **Table d**.

Table d. Open-circuit Voltage and Battery Charge

Open-circuit voltage	State of charge
12.6 v or more	Fully charged
12.4 v	75% charged
12.2 v	50% charged
12.0 v	25% charged
11.7 v or less	Fully discharged

The battery is in satisfactory condition if the open-circuit voltage is at least 12.4 volts. If the open-circuit voltage is at this level or above, but the battery lacks power for starting, have a load voltage test performed to determine the battery's service condition. If the open-circuit voltage is below 12.4 volts, recharge the battery. If the battery cannot be recharged to at least 75%, it should be replaced. New maintenance-free batteries should not be installed unless they are at least 75% charged.

Load Voltage Testing

A load voltage battery test should be performed by an authorized Volkswagen dealer or qualified repair facility if, after performing the tests described earlier, the battery appears to be in good condition but still can't provide enough current for starting.

CAUTION ▬

Do not give a maintenance-free battery a load voltage test unless it is at least 75% charged.

4.2 Battery Charging

Discharged batteries can be recharged using a battery charger, but a battery can never be charged to a voltage in excess of that which it is capable of producing electrochemically. During charging, the battery's voltage builds to a peak called the terminal voltage. If charging is continued beyond the terminal voltage, the water in the electrolyte begins to decompose into hydrogen and oxygen. This condition, called gassing, will evaporate the electrolyte to a level that can damage the battery.

Thoroughly read the instructions provided by the battery charger's manufacturer and always follow the instructions carefully. Do not use a charger if the instructions are not available. **Table e** lists charging rates and times that should be followed when charging batteries.

WARNING ▬

The gasses given off by the battery during charging are explosive. Do not smoke. Keep open flames away from the top of the battery, and prevent electrical sparks by turning off the battery charger before connecting or disconnecting it.

CAUTION ▬

Always allow a frozen battery to thaw before attempting to recharge it.

Table e. Battery Charging Specifications

Charging rate (conventional or low-maintenance batteries only)	Specific gravity	Approximate charging time
Fast charge (at 80% to 90% of battery's capacity, example: 43 to 48 amperes for a 54-ampere hour battery)	1.150 or less	1 hour
	1.150 to 1.175	3/4 hour
	1.175 to 1.200	1/2 hour
	1.200 to 1.225	1/4 hour
Slow charge (at 10% of battery's capacity, example: 5.4 amperes for a 54-ampere hour battery)	Above 1.225	Slow charge only, to a specific gravity of 1.250 to 1.265

5. CHARGING SYSTEM

The charging system provides the current necessary to keep the battery charged. The system includes an alternator driven from the engine crankshaft by a V-belt to generate the charging current, and a voltage regulator to control the rate at which the battery is charged.

The charging capacity of the alternator installed on each car depends on the type and number of electrical accessories. The alternator rating can be found on its housing as shown in Fig. 5-1. The voltage regulator is mounted on the end of the alternator housing. Voltage regulators and alternators are available as replacement parts from an authorized Volkswagen dealer. Volkswagen remanufactured alternators are also available as an alternative to new ones.

Fig. 5-1. Location of rating stamp on alternator housing. Example shown is 65-ampere alternator.

To prevent damage to the alternator or regulator when making tests or repairs, make all connections with negative (−) to negative, and positive (+) to positive unless directed otherwise. Even momentary contact with a conductor of the wrong polarity can cause damage to the alternator's diodes. Make certain that the battery ground strap is connected to the battery's negative (−) terminal and that the cable to terminal 30 on the starter is connected to the battery's positive (+) terminal. Never operate the engine with the battery disconnected. Never operate the alternator with its output terminal (B+) disconnected and the other terminals connected. Never short, bridge, or ground any terminals of the charging system except as specifically described in **5.1 Charging System Troubleshooting**.

5.1 Charging System Troubleshooting

Charging system trouble is indicated by an illuminated alternator warning light on the instrument panel, or by an under- or overcharged battery.

The alternator generates electrical current by electrical induction. That is, a magnetic field is placed in motion to induce a current in a stationary coil. When the engine is running and the alternator is spinning, part of the current it produces is used to energize its electromagnetic field. When starting, some other current must be provided to initially energize the field and begin the current generating process. This current is provided by the battery.

The battery current to the alternator rotor is routed through the alternator warning light in the instrument cluster. As soon as the alternator's output equals the battery's voltage, the light goes out. Normally, the warning light should be off when the ignition is off and the engine is stopped. The light should only come on when the ignition is turned on (current to the rotor) and go out again when the engine is started and the battery is being charged. **Table f** describes symptoms of trouble indicated by the warning light, lists tests and probable causes for the problem, and suggests corrective actions. The bold numbers in the corrective action column refer to the numbered headings in this section where the suggested repairs can be found.

14

Table f. Warning Light Troubleshooting

Symptom	Test and probable cause	Corrective action
1. Ignition off, engine not running, warning light glowing or on	(TEST) Disconnect plug from alternator **a.** Light goes out: Faulty diodes **b.** Light does not go out: Short in wiring harness or wiring connector	**a.** Repair or replace alternator. **5.3** **b.** Repair or replace faulty wiring. **14.**
2. Ignition on, engine not running, warning light off	**a.** Battery discharged (TEST) Remove and test warning light bulb **b.** Bulb burned out (TEST) —bulb not burned out Disconnect plug from alternator. Using a voltmeter, test between the plug terminal for the red wires and ground:	**a.** Charge battery. **4.2** **b.** Replace bulb. **7.1**

continued on the next page

Table f. Warning Light Troubleshooting (continued)

Symptom	Test and probable cause	Corrective action
2. Ignition on, engine not running, warning light off (cont'd)	**c.** No voltage: open circuit between plug and battery positive(+) pole	**c.** Repair wire or connections. **14**
	(TEST) — bulb not burned out, voltage reaching connector plug. Disconnect the plug from the alternator. With the ignition on, ground the plug terminal for the blue wire to the engine:	
	d. Light does not come on: Faulty bulb socket, open circuit in blue wire, or open circuit between socket and terminal 15 on the ignition switch	**d.** Replace faulty socket. Repair wires or connections. **14**
	e. Light comes on: Loose connection between regulator and alternator or loose connection between brushes and regulator	**e.** Correct loose connections. **5.3**
	f. Light comes on, regulator properly connected: Internal alternator faults or faulty regulator	**f.** Repair or replace alternator or voltage regulator. **5.3**
3. Engine running at any speed, warning light stays on	**a.** Loose or broken alternator V-belt	**a.** Replace or adjust V-belt. See **LUBRICATION AND MAINTENANCE**
	b. Exciter diodes burned out	**b.** Repair or replace alternator. **5.3**
	c. Faulty regulator or faulty alternator windings	**c.** Test charging system and replace faulty components as needed. **5.2**
	d. High voltage drop between positive (+) battery terminal and alternator due to broken, loose, or corroded wires	**d.** Repair wires or connections. **14**

An undercharged battery is usually associated with starting trouble. Again, make sure that the battery is in good condition and capable of accepting a full charge before blaming the charging system. Causes of an under-charged battery are: the simultaneous use of many electrical accessories for long periods of time, leaving accessories or lights in operation with the engine stopped, frequent long periods of starter usage, and frequent short-trip driving. Broken or frayed charging system wiring or corroded connections at the D+ and B+ terminals of the alternator, as well as worn, corroded, or loose battery cable connections will also prevent adequate charging or increase charging time.

5.2 In-Vehicle Testing of Charging System

The tests described here will help determine the cause of charging system trouble. For the tests, the battery should be fully charged and the alternator V-belt should be tensioned correctly. If in doubt about either, test the battery as described in **4.1 Testing Battery**, and adjust the V-belt as described in **5.3 Removing and Installing Alternator and Voltage Regulator**. The charging system warning light should be operating correctly. All electrical connections should be clean and tight. Replace wires that are hard or cracked.

A general test of charging system output can be made with an accurate digital voltmeter. The most accurate testing is done using an alternator and regulator tester, such as the Sun VAT-40, that applies a high-current load to the alternator. Conclusive tests using this equipment can be performed inexpensively by an authorized Volkswagen dealer or other qualified shop.

CAUTION —

An alternator must never be run with the battery disconnected. This will severely damage the alternator, the voltage regulator, or both. The alternator wiring should be secure, with the plug held by its clip.

Testing Alternator and Regulator

Start the engine and run it at about 3000 rpm with all electrical accessories turned off. Set the voltmeter to the DCV scale and measure the voltage between the positive and negative terminals of the battery. Make sure that the tester is connected to clean areas of the terminals. A reading between 13.5 to 14.5 volts indicates a correctly operating system. A reading higher than 14.5 volts most likely indicates a faulty voltage regulator.

A reading below 13.5 volts means that the battery is not being adequately charged because either the regulator or the alternator is faulty. To determine which, keep the car running at about 3000 rpm and turn on all electrical accessories, then check voltage across the battery. A reading that is the same as the first most likely indicates a faulty regulator. A reading that is lower most likely indicates a faulty alternator.

Testing Current Drain

If tests show that the alternator and regulator are operating correctly, but the battery still continually runs down, there may be a short in the electrical system causing a continuous current drain.

To test for current drain, turn off the ignition switch, the radio, and all lights. Disconnect the clock, if so equipped, by removing its fuse. Turn on the switches for the heated rear window and, if applicable, the air conditioning; this will determine if the load reduction relay is faulty. Disconnect the negative (−) cable from the battery and connect a test light between the cable and the negative post. If the test light comes on, some electrical accessory or a short in the electrical system is draining current from the battery. Isolate the faulty circuit by removing and replacing the fuses one at a time. When the test light goes out, the circuit with the short is located. If no fault is found in this way, a fault may exist in the components without fuses, such as the alternator, the starter motor, the ignition system, and the instrument cluster. Disconnect the items one at a time until the test light goes out.

Low level current drain may not be detectable with a test light. If the light does not come on, but a current drain is still suspected, repeat the test using an ammeter set to the 0 to 200 mA range.

Noisy Alternator

Alternator noises are usually mechanical in origin, but a high, soft whistling sound may be produced by an alternator that is overcharging because of a faulty regulator diode. The same sound may be heard if there is a shorted diode that is placing abnormal electrical strain on the alternator. Some alternators make this sound when operating normally at maximum output.

Alternator mechanical noises are usually the result of misalignment between the V-belt and the pulley, a loose or broken pulley, worn bearings, or a bent rotor shaft. Check for bad bearings by removing the V-belt as described below and rotating the alternator pulley by hand. If the pulley or shaft seem to grind or grate, replace the alternator.

5.3 Removing and Installing Alternator and Voltage Regulator

The alternator is connected to battery current even when the ignition is turned off. To prevent shorts and electrical damage, always disconnect the battery ground strap before removing the alternator.

To remove:

1. Disconnect all wiring at the alternator. On some models there is a main connector plug held in place by a wire. On others, there is an insulator and two nuts that hold the wires to the alternator. If applicable, remove the screw that holds the suppression condenser to the regulator so that it is free from the alternator.

2. On diesel engines with air conditioning, remove the bolt that holds the protective cover to the front of the alternator and remove the cover.

3. Loosen the upper and lower alternator mounting bolts. Loosen the bolt that holds the alternator belt adjusting bracket to the cylinder head or the air-conditioning compressor's mounting bracket.

4. Push the alternator as far as possible toward the engine, then take the V-belt off the alternator pulley.

5. Remove the lower alternator mounting bolt, then remove the upper alternator mounting bolt and remove the alternator from the engine.

Installation is the reverse of removal. Torque the nut on the D+ terminal of the alternator to 3 Nm (27 in. lb.), and torque the nut on the B+ terminal to 16 Nm (12 ft. lb.). On models with a toothed-rack adjusting mechanism, use a torque wrench and a 22 mm crowfoot wrench to tension the V-belt. Turn the larger part of the tensioning gear center bolt counterclockwise until the torque wrench reads 8 Nm (70 in. lb.) on used V-belts or 4 Nm (27 in. lb.) on new V-belts. Hold the wrench steady and tighten the center bolt to 35 Nm (26 ft. lb.). Torque the cylinder head bracket bolt to 20 Nm (15 ft. lb.) and the lower mounting bolt to 26 Nm (19 ft. lb.). See Fig. 5-2.

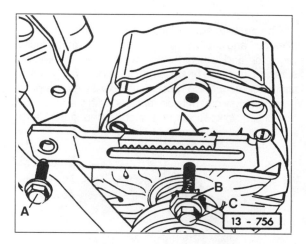

Fig. 5-2. Tensioning alternator V-belt on models with toothed rack adjusting mechanism. Make sure bolt **A** and bolt **C** are loose before adjusting tension. Place crowfoot wrench on outer part of bolt at **B**.

On models without a toothed rack adjusting mechanism, adjust V-belt tension by pushing the alternator away from the engine until the belt can be depressed as shown in Fig. 5-3. When the tension is correct, torque both adjusting bracket bolts to 25 Nm (18 ft. lb.). Torque the lower mounting bolt to 30 Nm (22 ft. lb.).

Brushes and Voltage Regulator

The brushes contact the alternator's slip rings to supply the current that magnetizes the alternator rotor. The voltage regulator maintains a nominal voltage in the electrical system by feeding excess output from the alternator back to ground. In addition, it regulates the amount of current supplied to the alternator rotor, turning it on and off as needed. If either component is faulty, the result will be an over or undercharged battery. The brushes wear under normal use, and will eventually need to be replaced.

14

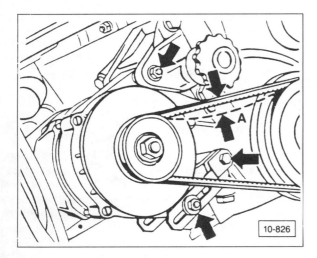

Fig. 5-3. Tensioning alternator V-belt on models without toothed rack adjusting mechanism. Mounting bolts (arrows) should be loose before adjusting tension. Dimension **A** should be between 2 mm and 5 mm (⁵⁄₆₄ in. and ³⁄₁₆ in.)

The brushes and regulator are mounted on the rear of the alternator and can be replaced with the alternator installed. The regulator and brush holder is removed by removing two screws. Check the brush length as shown in Fig. 5-4. On some alternator models the brushes are available as separate parts; on others they can only be replaced with the regulator. See an authorized Volkswagen dealer parts department for more information.

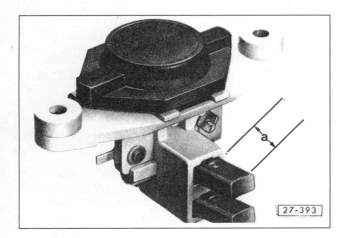

Fig. 5-4. Alternator brush length being checked. Length **a** of new brushes is 13 mm (¹⁷⁄₃₂ in.). Replace brushes worn to 5 mm (⁷⁄₃₂ in.) or less. Regulator and brush holder shown is used on Bosch alternators, Motorola is similar.

6. STARTING SYSTEM

When the ignition key is in the START position, a solenoid switch engages the starter's drive pinion with the ring gear on the engine flywheel or drive plate. To minimize wear and stress on the drive pinion and ring gear, the solenoid does not switch current to the starter until the drive pinion is fully engaged. Also,

the drive pinion has an overrunning clutch to prevent the starter from being driven by the engine.

A number of different starters are used on the cars covered by this manual, based on the engine and transmission combination. Starters are not interchangeable among these different applications. When replacing the starter, make sure that the replacement part is correct for the application.

6.1 Starting System Troubleshooting

The battery and its cables should be in good condition when troubleshooting the starter. If in doubt about the battery, see **4. Battery**. If the outside temperature is at or below 32°F (0°C), check the viscosity of the engine oil, as described in **LUBRICATION AND MAINTENANCE**. The use of an oil of improper viscosity for cold conditions will increase engine friction and can lead to starting difficulties. Troubleshooting information for the starting system appears in **Table g**. The bold numbers in the corrective action column refer to headings in this section where the repair procedures are described.

6.2 Removing and Installing Starter

To remove the starter, first disconnect the ground strap from the negative (−) battery terminal. On cars with automatic transmission, work beneath the car to remove the two bolts that hold the cover plate to the starter, and remove the plate.

Disconnect the wire to terminal 50 and the positive (+) battery cable from the starter solenoid. Remove the bolts that hold the starter to the transaxle bellhousing and remove the starter. On cars with automatic transmission, it is also necessary to remove the bolt holding the starter mounting bracket to the engine.

Inspect the starter. Replace or repair the starter if the drive pinion teeth are worn or broken. On cars with manual transmission, inspect the starter bushing that is pressed into the transaxle's bellhousing. If the bushing is worn or damaged, it should be replaced as described below.

Installation is the reverse of removal. Lubricate the starter bushing with multipurpose grease. On cars with manual transmission, torque the starter mounting bolts to 60 Nm (43 ft. lb.). On cars with automatic transmission, torque the mounting flange bolts to 20 Nm (15 ft. lb.), and torque the starter mounting bracket mounting bolt to 25 Nm (18 ft. lb.). Install the starter wires as shown in Fig. 6-1.

CAUTION ——

Connect wires to the proper terminals. Incorrect installation may damage the electrical system.

Table g. Starting System Troubleshooting

Symptom	Probable cause	Corrective action
1. Starter does not operate when igniton switch is turned to START	a. Ignition switch or wire leading from ignition switch to solenoid faulty (less than 8 volts to solenoid switch)	a. Test for voltage at terminal 50 of solenoid switch with ignition switch at START. If not at least 8 volts, test for voltage at terminal 50 of ignition switch with switch at START. Replace igniton switch (**SUSPENSION AND STEERING**) or eliminate open circuit between igniton switch and solenoid switch. **14.**
	b. Solenoid switch faulty (less than 8 volts to starter motor)	b. Test for voltage at field-winding connecting strap with ignition at START. (See Fig. 6-1 below). If not at least 8 volts, replace solenoid
	c. Starter motor faulty. **6.2**	c. Test for voltage at field-winding connecting strap with ignition at START. If at least 8 volts, repair or replace starter motor. **6.2**
	d. Neutral/park/reverse switch faulty (automatic transmission only)	d. Test switch. **10.1**
2. Starter turns slowly or fails to turn engine	a. Dirty, loose, or corroded starter connections	a. Remove, clean, and tighten connections. **6.2**
	b. Dirty, loose, or corroded ground strap between body and transmission	b. Remove and clean or replace strap. See **MANUAL TRANSMISSION AND CLUTCH** or **AUTOMATIC TRANSMISSION**
	c. Starter faulty	c. Repair or replace starter. **6.2**
3. Starter makes unusual noise, turns erratically, or fails to turn	a. Drive pinion defective	a. Repair or replace starter. **6.2**
	b. Flywheel or driveplate ring gear damaged	b. Replace flywheel or driveplate. See **MANUAL TRANSMISSION AND CLUTCH** or **AUTOMATIC TRANSMISSION**
4. Starter operates, but does not turn engine	a. Starter drive pinion or armature shaft faulty	a. Repair or replace starter. **6.2**
	b. Solenoid switch mechanism faulty	b. Replace starter solenoid switch. **6.2**

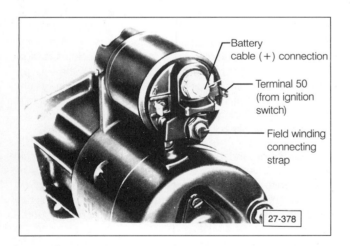

Battery cable (+) connection

Terminal 50 (from ignition switch)

Field winding connecting strap

27-378

Fig. 6-1. Wiring connections to starter solenoid terminals.

Removing and Installing Solenoid Switch

A faulty solenoid switch can be replaced separately. To remove the solenoid switch, first remove the starter as described above. Remove the nut from the field-winding connecting strap shown in Fig. 6-1 above, and remove the strap from the solenoid. Remove the two screws holding the solenoid to the starter, lift the solenoid plunger's pull rod up and off the engaging fork, and remove the solenoid. Installation is the reverse of removal. Apply a sealer to the screw heads after installing the solenoid.

14

Replacing Starter Bushing
(manual transmission only)

Jamming of the starter is usually a sign of a bad starter bushing. A faulty bushing that is not replaced with the starter will cause the starter bearings to quickly fail. The starter bushing is replaceable with the transmission installed and the starter removed. Fig. 6-2 shows the bushing being removed from the bellhousing. To install the bushing, drive the new bushing into the bellhousing until it is firmly seated.

Fig. 6-2. Starter bushing being removed from bellhousing using puller Volkswagen special tool no. VW 228b (order no. TV0 228 B00 027 ZEL).

7. INSTRUMENTS

Fig. 7-1 is an exploded view of the instrument cluster. A flexible printed circuit is used in place of the numerous wires and connectors that would otherwise be required to connect the instruments and switches. Power and electrical signals to the instruments are supplied to the wire terminal housings from two main wire harnesses.

In addition to the visible instruments, the instrument cluster also houses an electronic control unit for the oil pressure warning system and, on certain models, an electronic control unit for the multifunction indicator. These control units are not repairable and should be replaced if faulty.

Troubleshooting or repair of the instrument cluster is easiest with the cluster removed. Removal of the instrument cluster, as well as replacement of the speedometer drive gear and cable, are described in **BODY AND INTERIOR**.

7.1 Troubleshooting Instrument Cluster and Gauges

Begin diagnosing instrument cluster electrical problems by checking the fuses. Make a thorough check in the engine compartment and under the instrument panel for disconnected or damaged wires or connectors. If the fuses, wires, and connectors are intact, then problems are caused by the correct signal not reaching the instrument cluster, or by faulty instrument cluster components.

For an additional aid to troubleshooting the instrument cluster, refer to the current flow diagrams at the end of this section for terminal and connector locations. For information on how to use the diagrams, see **3. Troubleshooting**.

If only one function is affected, the problem is most likely one which affects only that individual circuit. If more than one function of the instrument cluster is affected, it is logical to begin with the instrument cluster's common wiring. Check the main power supply from the ignition switch, the main ground wire, and the voltage stabilizer as described below.

Testing Instrument Cluster Voltage and Ground

If the warning lamps or gauges do not respond with the ignition on, then either battery voltage is not reaching the instrument cluster or the cluster is not properly grounded. With the battery negative (−) terminal disconnected, remove the instrument cluster as described in **BODY AND INTERIOR**. Make sure that the short black and long white 7-point connectors at the rear of the cluster that connect to the wire terminal housings are also disconnected. Reconnect the battery negative cable.

> **CAUTION** ━━━
>
> *Do not allow any unprotected part of the instrument cluster electrical circuitry to touch any metal part of the car while the cluster is removed and the battery is connected.*

Use the current flow diagrams at the end of the section to identify the wire and terminal of the short black connector which supplies power from the ignition switch. With the ignition switched on, use a volt meter or test light to check for voltage between that connector terminal and ground. If there is no voltage, check for voltage at terminal 15 of the ignition switch. If voltage is reaching the switch but the switch will not complete the circuit, then the ignition switch is faulty and should be replaced as described in **SUSPENSION AND STEERING**.

To test for ground, use the ohmmeter or test light to check for continuity between the car body and the ground terminal of the long white connector that goes to ground. (See the appropriate current flow diagram). If there is no continuity, check the wiring harness for faults between the connector and ground.

Testing and Replacing Voltage Stabilizer

Test the voltage stabilizer with the instrument cluster removed, but with the harness connectors connected. Connect a voltmeter to the voltage stabilizer as shown in Fig. 7-2. Connect the ground cable to the battery and turn the ignition on. The meter should read approximately 10 volts. If it is above 10.5 volts or below 9.5 volts, the voltage stabilizer is faulty and should be replaced. Remove the voltage stabilizer by removing its retaining screw and sliding it straight off of its terminals.

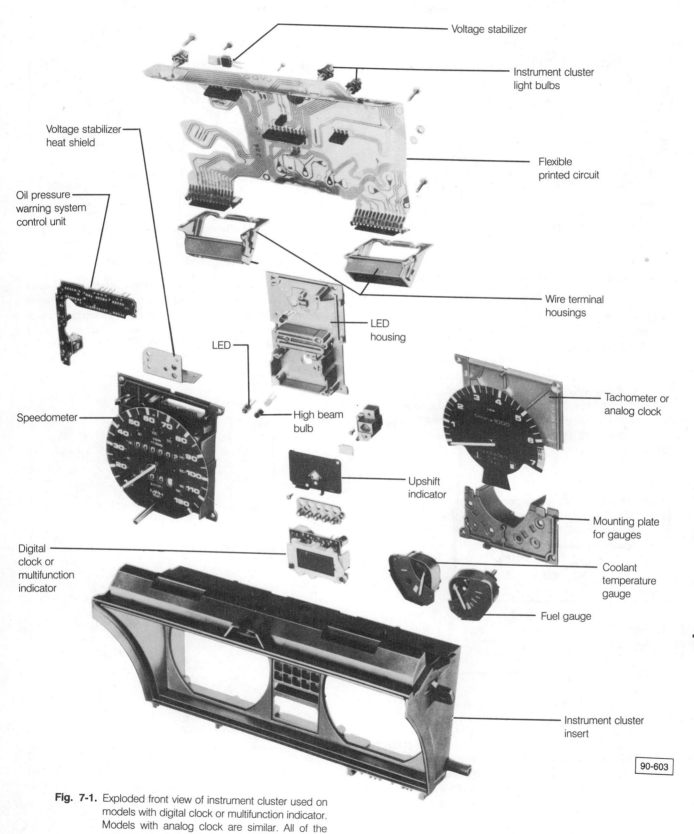

Voltage stabilizer

Instrument cluster
light bulbs

Voltage stabilizer
heat shield

Flexible
printed circuit

Oil pressure
warning system
control unit

Wire terminal
housings

LED
housing

LED

Tachometer or
analog clock

Speedometer

High beam
bulb

Upshift
indicator

Mounting plate
for gauges

Digital
clock or
multifunction
indicator

Coolant
temperature
gauge

Fuel gauge

Instrument cluster
insert

90-603

14

Fig. 7-1. Exploded front view of instrument cluster used on
models with digital clock or multifunction indicator.
Models with analog clock are similar. All of the
components shown are available separately as replacement parts.

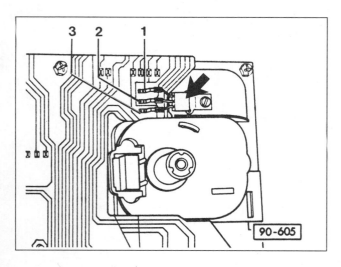

Fig. 7-2. Voltage stabilizer (arrow). Terminal **1** is stabilized voltage output, terminal **2** is ground, terminal **3** is voltage input.

Testing and Replacing Light Emitting Diodes (LEDs) and Indicator Bulbs

Test LEDs and indicator bulbs with the instrument cluster removed and the harness connectors disconnected. Use an external 12-volt power source and jumper wires to apply current to the appropriate terminal in the wire terminal housing. See Fig. 7-3 and **14. Current Flow Diagrams** for terminal identification. If the LEDs or bulbs do not light, check the printed circuit for continuity from the wire terminal housing to the LED or bulb. No continuity indicates that the printed circuit is faulty and should be replaced. If there is continuity, replace the LED or bulb.

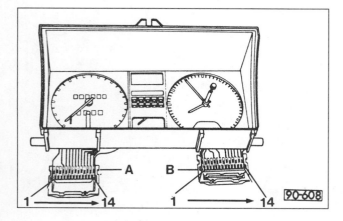

Fig. 7-3. Wire terminal housings **A** and **B** and pins used when testing LEDs or indicator bulbs.

To replace LEDs or indicator bulbs, the instrument cluster must be partially disassembled. Remove the voltage stabilizer as described above, and remove the flexible printed circuit and the LED/bulb holder. Pull the LED or bulb from its holder as shown in Fig. 7-4. When installing new LEDs, take care not to reverse their polarity. The negative (−) terminal of the LED is slightly wider than the positive (+) terminal.

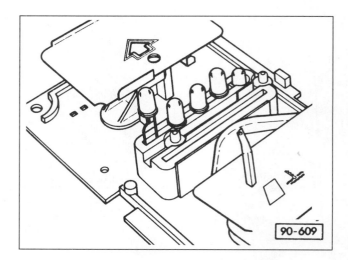

Fig. 7-4. LED being removed from LED holder.

Testing Upshift Indicator

The upshift indicator system on 1985 through 1987 cars with manual transmission indicates the optimum upshift points for maximum fuel efficiency. Fig. 7-5 is a schematic diagram of the system. For more information on the electrical details of the system, see **14. Current Flow Diagrams**.

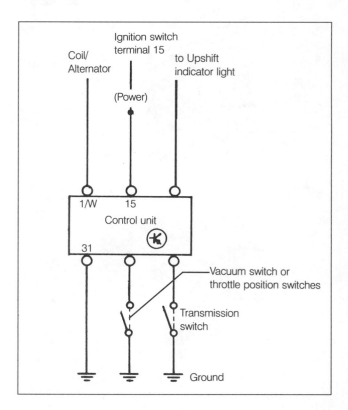

Fig. 7-5. Simplified diagram for upshift indicator light system. Terminal identification depends on whether system is installed in gas or diesel cars.

On gasoline models, the control unit receives an rpm signal from terminal 1 of the ignition coil; on diesel models, from terminal W of the alternator. Engine load is relayed by the vacuum switch on fuel injected models (located in the vacuum line to the ignition distributor), and by two switches mounted on the diesel injection pump on diesel models. The upshift/reverse light switch (located on the transmission) disables the system when either high gear or reverse is selected. The control unit is located in the fuse/relay panel. The indicator light is an LED. **Table h** gives troubleshooting information.

To remove and replace the upshift indicator, remove the printed circuit from the back of the instrument cluster and disassemble the cluster. Remove the screws which mount the upshift indicator front cover and the control unit as shown in Fig. 7-6.

Table h. Troubleshooting Upshift Indicator Light System

Symptom	Probable cause	Corrective action
1. Upshift light on continuously	a. Upshift/reverse light switch faulty	a. Perform continuity test of switch. (Look for continuity only in high gear or reverse). Replace faulty switch
	b. Vacuum switch faulty (Gasoline engines only)	b. Perform continuity test of switch. (There should only be continuity when vacuum is applied to switch)
	c. Throttle position switch(es) faulty	c. Perform continuity test of switches. (There should be continuity only when the switches are depressed
	d. No rpm signal from coil (gas) or alternator (diesel) reaching control unit	d. Check wiring harness and repair as necessary
2. Upshift light does not come on	a. LED or instrument cluster connection faulty	a. Detach coil or alternator wire from control unit and ground it. If LED does not come on (ignition on), LED or LED connection is faulty
	b. Upshift/reverse light switch faulty	b. Detach wiring from switch and test switch's continuity. Should be continuity only in high gear or reverse. Replace if faulty
	c. Vacuum switch or throttle position switches faulty	c. Detach wiring from switch and test switch's continuity. On fuel-injected models there should only be continuity when vacuum is applied to switch; on diesel models only when switches are depressed.
	d. Broken or shorted wire in upshift light harness	d. Test wires for shorts and open circuits.
	e. Control unit faulty	e. Replace control unit if none of the above apply.
3. Upshift light flickers	a. Vacuum switch or throttle position switches faulty	a. Detach wiring from switch and test switch's continuity. On fuel-injected models there should only be continuity when vacuum is applied to switch; on diesel models only when switches are depressed.
	b. Loose connections or broken wires	b. Check wiring for secure connections and continuity while wires are being flexed
	c. Control unit faulty	c. Replace control unit if none of the above applies
4. Upshift light glows before coming on at shift point	a. Control unit faulty	a. Replace control unit (atop fuse/relay panel)

14 ■

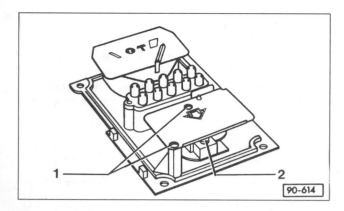

Fig. 7-6. Upshift indicator front cover screws (**1**) and upshift indicator control unit mounting screw (**2**).

Testing Dynamic Oil Pressure Warning System Control Unit

Before troubleshooting the oil pressure warning system, be sure that the system is not indicating actual low oil pressure. Check to make sure that there is normal oil pressure and that the oil pressure switches are functioning correctly, as described in **ENGINE**.

> **NOTE** ——
>
> When first turning on the ignition, it is possible for an impulse from the ignition system to briefly set off the low pressure warning buzzer. This condition is normal and does not indicate a fault.

Remove the instrument cluster as described in **BODY AND INTERIOR** to troubleshoot the control unit. To replace a faulty control unit, remove the instrument illumination bulbs and the voltage stabilizer, and then remove the flexible printed circuit from the instrument cluster. See Fig. 7-1 above. Remove the speedometer and release the locking tabs to lift the control unit printed circuit away as shown in Fig. 7-7. Install the new printed circuit, press in the locking tabs, and reassemble and install the instrument cluster.

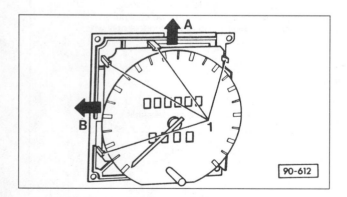

Fig. 7-7. Oil pressure warning system printed circuit being removed. Disengage tabs **1** and pull printed circuit in direction **A** until contacts project, then slide off in direction **B**.

8. WINDSHIELD WIPERS AND WASHERS

The operation of the two-speed windshield wipers and washers is controlled by a lever on the steering column. The wiper blades park automatically when the lever is turned off. The wiper motor is located in the air plenum beneath the drip tray in the engine cowl. A relay on the fuse/relay panel controls the intermittent operation of the wipers, and runs the wipers for several sweeps if the washer is actuated while the wiper switch is in the off position.

On models equipped with a rear wiper, the motor is behind the hatchback trim panel. On 1985 and 1986 models, the rear window washer is operated by a separate motor and reservoir in the right side of the luggage compartment. On 1987 through 1989 models, the rear window washer shares one pump and reservoir with the front washers.

If the wiper or washer motor fails to operate when the steering column lever is moved, see **8.1 Windshield Wiper and Washer Troubleshooting**. If the wiper motor runs but the wiper arms do not move, see **8.2 Windshield Wiper Motor and Linkage**.

8.1 Windshield Wiper and Washer System Troubleshooting

For best results, these troubleshooting tests should be done in the sequence outlined below. Refer to the current flow diagrams for the most complete model-specific information on terminals and connectors.

Testing Windshield Wiper Motor

The windshield wiper motor has three voltage inputs. Terminal 53a is the main power input coming from the fuse panel. The other two inputs are from the wiper/washer switch and provide signals to operate the motor on either low or high speed.

With the ignition on, check the individual terminals of the harness connector for voltage at the various switch positions according to **Table i**. Also check the appropriate connector terminals for continuity to ground. If voltage is reaching the connector as described and the motor still fails to run on one or more speeds, then the motor is faulty and should be replaced. See **Removing and Installing Windshield Wiper Motor**.

If voltage is not reaching the terminals as described above, check the continuity of the wires between the motor's harness connector and the connector for the wiper/washer switch on the steering column. If the wiring harness between the motor and the switch is sound, continue testing the wiper/washer switch as described in **Testing Wiper/Washer Switch**.

Testing Rear Wiper Motor

The rear wiper motor has two voltage inputs. One comes directly from the load reduction relay, and one is from the rear wiper relay. For electrical wiring information pertaining to a specific model, refer to the current flow diagrams at the end of this section.

Table i. Windshield Wiper Motor Voltage Tests

Wiper/Washer switch position	Test terminal	Correct value
Off	53 53b 53a	No voltage No voltage Battery voltage (approximately 12 volts)
Low speed	53 53a 53b	Battery voltage Battery voltage No voltage
High speed	53 53a 53b	Battery voltage Battery voltage Battery voltage

Disconnect the harness connector from the motor and check for voltage. With the ignition on, there should be voltage coming from the load reduction relay. With the rear wiper switch activated, there should be voltage from the relay. Also check for continuity to ground at the third (ground) terminal. If voltage is reaching the connector as described and the motor still fails to run, then the motor is faulty and should be replaced. See **8.2 Windshield Wiper Motor and Linkage**.

If voltage is not reaching the connector as described, check the continuity of the wiring harness. Check for voltage input to the rear wiper relay by removing the relay from the panel and measuring voltage at the appropriate socket terminals with the ignition on. If there is voltage input to the relay but no voltage reaching the motor, then the relay is faulty and should be replaced.

Testing Wiper/Washer Switch

The switch receives power from the ignition switch and the intermittent relay, and routes it depending on the position of the lever. To reach the switch, remove the steering-column cover by removing the Phillips-head screws. The switch terminals are identified in Fig. 8-1.

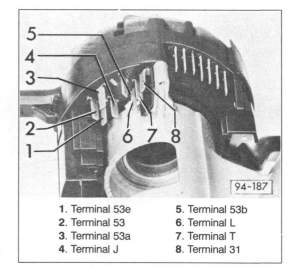

94-187

1. Terminal 53e	5. Terminal 53b
2. Terminal 53	6. Terminal L
3. Terminal 53a	7. Terminal T
4. Terminal J	8. Terminal 31

Fig. 8-1. Wiper/washer switch terminals used to test switch. Make tests of wiring harness using corresponding sockets in harness connector.

Use an ohmmeter to test the switch by making continuity checks as indicated in **Table j**. If the switch fails any of these tests, it is faulty and should be replaced as described in **SUSPENSION AND STEERING**.

Table j. Wiper/Washer Switch Continuity Tests

Wiper/Washer Switch Position	Terminals	Test Result
Off	53 and 53e	Continuity
Low Speed	53 and 53a	Continuity
High Speed Intermittent	53a and 53b 53a and 53 53a and J 53e and 53	Continuity Continuity Continuity Continuity
Washer	53a and T	Continuity
Rear Wiper	53a and L	Continuity

Testing Windshield Wiper Intermittent Relay

Only the low speed function of the wiper motor is wired through the intermittent relay. Before testing the intermittent relay, make sure that the wiper motor and the wiper/washer switch are functioning correctly.

Remove the intermittent relay from the fuse/relay panel. Check for voltage reaching the relay from the ignition switch with the ignition on, and check the ground socket for continuity to ground. By process of elimination, if the relay is getting voltage and has a good ground and no other wiring harness or switch faults can be found, then the relay is faulty and should be replaced.

8.2 Windshield Wiper Motor and Linkage

Both wiper motors and their linkages are readily accessible for replacement. Check with an authorized Volkswagen dealer parts department for information on Volkswagen remanufactured wiper motors. For information on windshield wiper blades, see **LUBRICATION AND MAINTENANCE**.

Removing and Installing Windshield Wiper Motor

Fig. 8-2 is an exploded view of the windshield wiper motor, the wiper motor frame, and the linkage. The wiper motor frame does not need to be removed from the body when removing the motor or linkage. The drive crank should not be removed unless the motor is being replaced.

Disconnect the battery negative (−) terminal and carefully remove the plastic drip tray by unclipping it and pulling it straight up. Disconnect the harness connector from the wiper motor. Disengage the relay rods from the ball pin on the motor's drive crank, then remove the motor mounting bolts and remove the motor from beneath the frame.

14

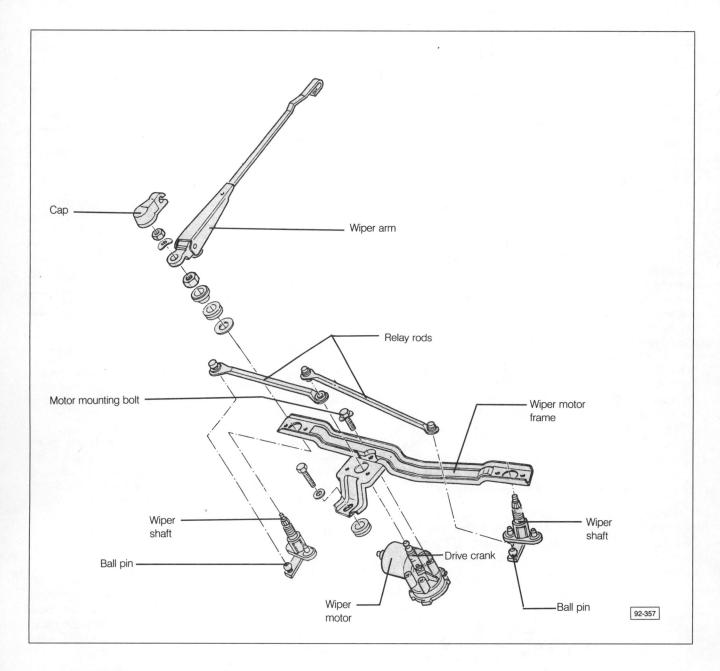

Cap — Wiper arm

Relay rods

Motor mounting bolt — Wiper motor frame

Wiper shaft

Ball pin — Drive crank — Wiper shaft

Wiper motor — Ball pin

92-357

Fig. 8-2. Exploded view of windshield wiper components.

Installation is the reverse of removal. Completely install the motor and connect the battery, but do not connect the relay rods. Turn on the ignition and the wiper switch to run the motor for approximately one minute, then turn off the wiper switch. The motor will stop in its park position. If installing a new motor, transfer the drive crank from the old motor to the new one in the position shown in Fig. 8-3. Lubricate the ball pins with multi-purpose grease and install the relay rods. Check wiper arm position as shown in Fig. 8-4.

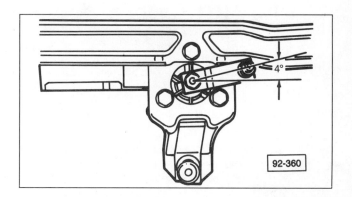

4°

92-360

Fig. 8-3. Windshield wiper drive crank correctly installed in motor (motor in park position).

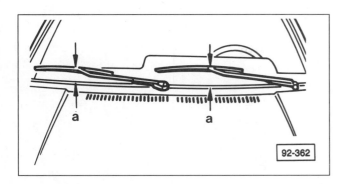

Fig. 8-4. Correct position of windshield wiper arms with relay rods installed and motor in park position. Dimension **a** is 60 mm (2 ⅜ in.).

Removing and Installing Rear Wiper Motor

Fig. 8-5 is a view of the GTI and Golf rear hatch showing the rear wiper motor and linkage assembly. The rear wiper arm attaches to the wiper shaft in the same manner that the front wiper arms are attached.

To remove the motor, disconnect the battery negative (−) terminal and remove the interior hatch trim panel. Pry the relay rod from the drive crank, and then remove the drive crank-mounting nut and the crank. Remove the motor bracket mounting bolts and partially remove the bracket so that the motor's harness connector can be disconnected. Remove the bracket and the motor.

Installation is the reverse of removal. Completely install the motor and connect the battery, but do not connect the relay rods. Turn on the ignition and the wiper switch to run the motor for approximately one minute, then turn off the wiper switch. The motor will stop in its park position. Install the drive crank so that it is parallel to the bottom edge of the hatch, as shown earlier in Fig. 8-5. Lubricate the ball pin with multipurpose grease, and install the relay rod. Mount the wiper arm on the shaft as shown in Fig. 8-6.

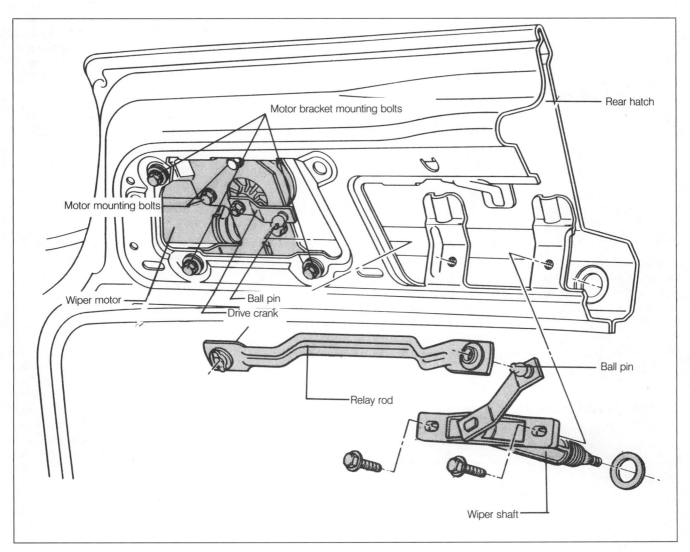

Fig. 8-5. GTI and Golf rear hatch (viewed in open position) showing rear wiper motor and linkage components.

14

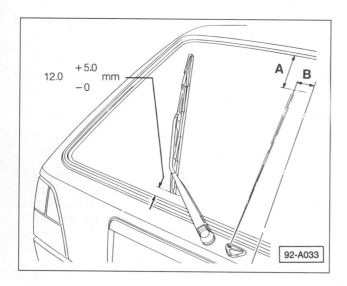

Fig. 8-6. Rear wiper arm installation and washer adjustment. Dimension **A** is 10 mm (⅜ in.). Dimension **B** (from centerline) is 20 mm (¾ in.).

9. HORNS

The components of the horn system are the dual horns, the horn relay, and the horn button on the steering wheel.

On Jettas, the horns and the relay are connected to positive (+) voltage through a fuse whenever the ignition is on. Depressing the horn button activates the horn relay, which in turn completes the circuit to ground to sound the horns.

On GTI and Golf models, the horn relay is also operated by the horn button, however, the horns are permanently grounded and only receive voltage through the relay when the horn button is depressed.

The horn button receives voltage through terminal 71 of the turn signal switch, as shown in Fig. 9-1. On Jettas, the horn button is grounded through the same connector. On GTI and Golf models, the horn button grounds directly through its contact with the steering column. The connector is accessible by removing the steering wheel as described in **SUSPENSION AND STEERING**. See **14. Current Flow Diagrams** for detailed information on terminal and wire identification.

9.1 Horn Troubleshooting

Horns that continually blow indicate either a short in the horn circuit—most likely in the switch or steering column—or a faulty relay. Troubleshoot the circuit using the current flow diagram as a guide.

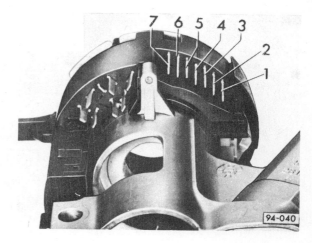

Fig. 9-1. Location of horn and turn signal switch terminals on steering column. Terminal numbers shown do not apply to cars covered by this manual. However, actual terminals are numbered for identification.

If the horns do not sound, check the fuse(s) and all the wiring connections. On GTI and Golf models, the horns are grounded by their mounting to the car body. Make sure that there is a good, corrosion-free ground connection between the horns and the car. Check continuity between the horn and the car using an ohmmeter.

A problem on Golf diesels which causes the glow plug indicator light to glow dimly when the horn button is pushed has been attributed to a faulty horn relay. An improved relay, Volkswagen part no. 431 951 253 H, is available to correct the problem.

10. EXTERIOR LIGHTS

This heading covers exterior light electrical circuits. Replacement of bulbs and lenses for the taillights, side marker lights, turn signals, brake lights, back-up lights, and headlights is covered in **BODY AND INTERIOR**.

10.1 Troubleshooting Exterior Lights

Most of the exterior lighting involves pairs of lights, and this fact is an aid to troubleshooting. If only one of a pair of lights is out—one taillight for example—then the problem is most likely due to a failed bulb or some other problem with that particular light socket or its wiring. A simple test is to exchange the bulb with its counterpart which is known to be good. If the same bulb fails to light in a new location, then the bulb is faulty and should be replaced. If the same light fails to light with the other bulb, then the problem is in the socket or wiring. Many lighting problems are due to dirty or corroded sockets, or loosely-fitting bulb contacts or connectors. Check that voltage is reaching the bulb and that the socket has a good connection to ground.

If a pair of bulbs are both out—both taillights for example—then the problem is most likely in some part of the system which is common to both lights. Begin by checking for a failed fuse. Test switches using simple continuity checks made with an ohmmeter. Check the switch connectors for voltage and continuity to ground.

Headlights

Power to the headlight low beams comes only with the ignition on (terminal 15). Power to the high beams comes directly from the battery, and is routed through the high-beam portion of the turn signal switch.

Turn Signals and Emergency Flashers

Power for the turn signal circuit is routed through the emergency flashers switch only when the ignition is on (terminal 15). The emergency flashers circuit receives power from the battery at all times. When the emergency flashers switch is on, the turn signal switch is bypassed.

The turn signals and the emergency flashers share the same flasher relay, but each circuit has its own fuse. One system working indicates that the flasher relay is good. Look for a failed fuse.

If both the flashers and turn signals are inoperative, then it is probably either the flasher relay or the emergency flasher switch that is faulty. Check to see if power is reaching the relay. Check the flasher switch by checking continuity in the ON and OFF positions, using the current flow diagram as a guide. For failed turn signals, test the turn signal switch as described in **10.2 Steering Column Switches**.

Parking Lights, Taillights, Side Marker Lights, and License Plate Lights

The parking, side marker, tail, and license plate lights all receive power directly from the battery through the light switch in the first or second position, independent of the ignition switch. If these lights fail together, first look for a failed fuse, then for problems in the switch.

Brake Lights

The brake lights receive their power directly from the battery through a fuse and through the brake light switch, independent of the ignition switch. The brake light switch closes when the brake pedal is depressed.

Back-up Lights

On cars with manual transmission, the reverse lights receive power through the back-up/upshift light switch when the transmission is in reverse gear. The switch is mounted on the transmission as shown in Fig. 10-1 and is accessible from the engine compartment.

On cars with automatic transmission, the back-up lights receive their power through the neutral/park/back-up light switch mounted at the base of the shift lever in the passenger compartment. The switch prevents the car from starting if the shift lever is not in the neutral or park position.

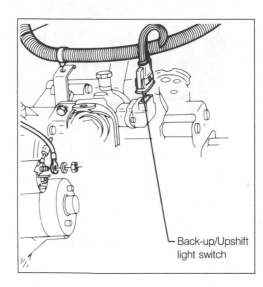

Fig. 10-1. Location of back-up/upshift light switch on manual transaxle housing. Torque mounting bolts to 10 Nm (87 in. lb.).

10.2 Steering Column Switches

The steering column switches can be tested without being removed simply by removing the upper and lower steering column covers and disconnecting the harness connectors. For testing the windshield wiper switch, see **8. Windshield Wipers and Washers**. Replace faulty switches as described in **SUSPENSION AND STEERING**.

Ignition Switch

Fig. 10-2 identifies the terminals of the ignition switch. Terminal 30 brings power in to the ignition switch from the battery. Terminal 15 provides power to the ignition system and other parts of the electrical system when the ignition key is in the ON or START position. Terminal X supplies power through the load reduction relay. It has power when the ignition switch is in the ON position, but has no power when the switch is moved to the START position. Terminal Su is for the seat belt warning/interlock system. **Table k** lists ignition switch continuity checks. A switch which fails any of these tests is faulty and should be replaced.

14

Table k. Ignition Switch Continuity Tests

Switch position	Continuity between terminals
Ignition Off	30 and Su
Ignition On	30 and X 30 and 15
Start	30 and 50 30 and 15

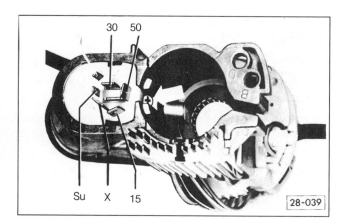

Fig. 10-2. Ignition switch and terminal identification. Switch is held in place by retaining screw (arrow).

11. HEATING, VENTILATION AND AIR CONDITIONING

Fresh Air Blower

The speeds of the fresh air blower motor are controlled by varying resistance. Maximum resistance produces the lowest speed. At high speed, power is supplied directly to the blower motor. On cars with air conditioning, the blower motor receives its power from the air conditioning system.

Before removing a blower motor to test it, check for voltage at the blower motor harness connector with the ignition on. If there is ro voltage reaching the motor, refer to the current flow diagrams for help in troubleshooting the circuit.

If voltage is reaching the connector, remove the blower motor as described in **BODY AND INTERIOR** and check the fuses, the thermofuse, and the series resistors. For access, unclip the blower motor connecting plate as shown in Fig. 11-1.

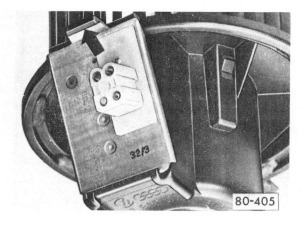

Fig. 11-1. Blower motor connecting plate being removed to reach blower motor fuse and resistors. Push clip in direction of arrow.

Connect an ohmmeter and check the resistance of the thermofuse as shown in Fig. 11-2. The resistance should be approximately zero. If not, the thermofuse is faulty and should be replaced.

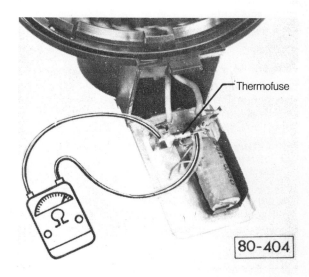

Fig. 11-2. Continuity of blower motor thermofuse being checked with ohmmeter.

Next, test the resisitors as shown in Fig. 11-3. For cars without air conditioning, the resistance ranges from 0.8 ohms (medium blower speed) to 3.3 ohms (low blower speed). There should be a similar range of three resistance values for cars with air conditioning and four blower speeds.

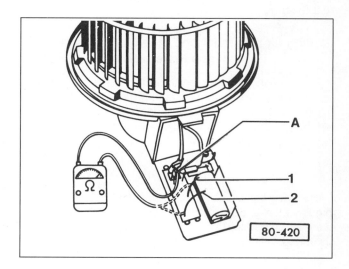

Fig. 11-3. Series resistance of blower motor being measured with ohmmeter. Resistance between terminals **A** and **1** is approximately 3.3 ohms. Resistance between terminals **A** and **2** is approximately 0.8 ohms.

Air Conditioning

The radiator cooling fan and the air conditioning compressor clutch are operated by a relay. Test the blower motor as described above. The control head can be tested after removing it as described in **BODY AND INTERIOR**. Make continuity checks at the electrical connections of the control head with the control lever in its ON and OFF positions. Any other testing of the air conditioning system, including the operation of the pressure switches, requires specialized knowledge and equipment. Servicing by an authorized Volkswagen dealer or other qualified air conditioning shop is highly recommended.

Rear Window Defogger

The rear window defogger is a series of resistance elements that heat up as electrical current passes through them. One or two wires that do not heat up suggests a break in the heating element. Repair material for the element is available from an authorized Volkswagen dealer to repair the breaks as described below. An element that does not operate at all suggests that power is not reaching the heating element. Check for voltage supply to the window element and check for a good connection to ground. Refer to the current flow diagrams at the end of the section for details of the rear window defogger wiring.

To find and repair heating element breaks:

1. Wrap a small piece of aluminum foil around the negative (−) probe of a voltmeter.

2. With the heating element's wiring connected, touch the positive (+) voltmeter probe to the end of the heater element closest to the incoming voltage source.

3. With the ignition and the defogger switch on, place the foil-covered negative probe on the faulty wire near the positive side of the element and slowly slide it toward the negative side. The point at which the voltmeter deflects from zero volts to several volts is where the wire is broken.

4. Apply a strip of masking tape to either side of the break, leaving the break exposed. Apply the repair material over the break and allow it to dry for one hour at room temperature. Remove the tape and retest the wire.

12. POWER OPTIONS AND ACCESSORIES

The power windows, the heated seats, and the heated-/power mirrors are all powered through the load reduction relay. If these systems fail together, one likely cause is a faulty relay.

The central locking system receives its power directly from the battery through a fuse. The cruise control is powered only when the ignition is on.

When troubleshooting these systems, check first for blown fuses. Fuses are simple to check and are a likely cause of trouble. The 1986, 1987, and 1988 Golf and GTI models use a circuit breaker on the fuse/relay panel instead of a fuse for the power windows and mirrors. Current flow diagrams for the major Volkswagen power options and accessories, including the radio, are found in **14. Current Flow Diagrams.**

12.1 Heated Seats

Fig. 12-1 is a schematic view of the heated seats. The control switches are variable resistors (sometimes called rheostats). Current runs through the heating elements, and then to ground. The control units on the fuse/relay panel receive temperature information from a temperature sender in each seat. The heating elements, the switches, and the control units are not repairable. For information on replacing the heating elements, see **BODY AND INTERIOR**. Remove the switch by prying it out using a screwdriver. The control units are removed just like any other relay by pulling them from the fuse/relay panel.

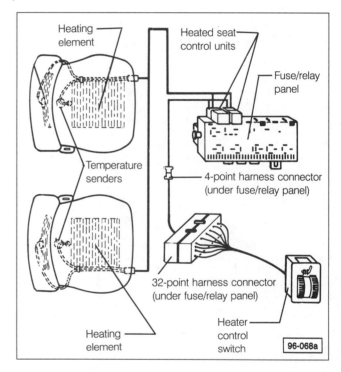

Fig. 12-1. Schematic view of heated seats and controls.

12.2 Electric/Heated Outside Mirrors

The mirror motor is operated by a door-mounted switch. The motor controls the mirror's movement via a magnetic clutch. The mirror heating elements are wired together with the rear window defogger. For removal and replacement of the mirror assemblies or motors, see **BODY AND INTERIOR**. The door-mounted switch is pressed into place and can be carefully pried out for testing.

12.3 Central Locking System

There are two electrical components of the central locking system—the bi-pressure pump in the luggage compartment and the master activator switch in the driver's door. The master activator switch controls the electrical signal to the bi-pressure pump. If the pump does not run when the door key is turned, test the electrical portion of the system as described below. If the pump runs, but the system does not operate, test the bi-pressure system as described in **BODY AND INTERIOR**.

14

NOTE ▬

If the system has not been operated for an extended period of time, several turns of the key may be required to reactivate the system.

To test the system, remove the bi-pressure pump from its housing as described in **BODY AND INTERIOR**, and disconnect the pump's harness connector. Place the driver's door lock button in the up (open) position. There should be voltage at the pump's harness connector as shown in Fig. 12-2. Place the driver's door lock in the down (locked) position. There should be voltage at the pump's wiring connector as shown in Fig. 12-3. If these conditions are not met, test the switch and the circuit wiring. See **14. Current Flow Diagrams**. The inside door trim panel must be removed as described in **BODY AND INTERIOR** to reach the master activator connector.

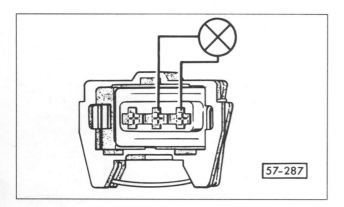

57-287

Fig. 12-2. Test light (shown schematically) connected between terminals of central locking system's bi-pressure pump harness connector for checking for voltage from master activator in driver's door (open position).

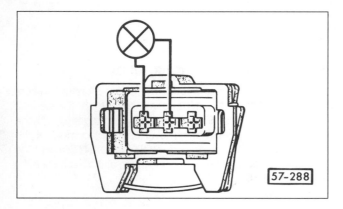

57-288

Fig. 12-3. Test light (shown schematically) connected between terminals of central locking system's bi-pressure pump harness connector for checking for voltage from master activator in driver's door (locked position).

12.4 Power Windows

The power windows are operated by polarity-reversing motors. Depending on the position of the rocker switches, current is routed to change the rotation direction of the motor. On 4-door models, the rear window lockout switch prevents operation of the rear windows by grounding the circuit ahead of the rear window motors.

A single power window that does not operate can be tested without disassembling the door. Remove the rocker switch and disconnect its harness connector. Turn the ignition on and check for voltage at the connector. Also check ground. If voltage is reaching the switch and there is a good ground, perform continuity checks on the switch.

On Jettas, an inoperative rear window may be caused by the window mechanism interfering with the motor wiring harness and detaching it from the window switch. To correct the problem, remove the interior door trim panel as described in **BODY AND INTERIOR**, and secure the harness to the door using a tie-wrap or its equivalent.

12.5 Cruise Control

The components of the cruise control system are an electronic control unit, an induction pick-up in the speedometer head, a vacuum servo at the throttle valve, a vacuum pump, and vacuum valves and electrical switches on the brake and clutch pedals. The cruise control operates at speeds above 22 mph (35 km/h).

The control unit, located under the instrument panel on the driver's side, compares the car's true speed to the speed selected by the driver. True speed is indicated by the speedometer cable pickup. The control unit then either turns on the vacuum pump to contract the vacuum servo to open the throttle or opens a vent at the pump to bleed air into the vacuum lines to release the throttle and slow the car. A vacuum valve and an electric switch vents air into the system and turns off the cruise control whenever either the brake or clutch pedal is depressed.

To leak-test the vacuum servo, remove the vacuum line, squeeze the servo until it is fully depressed, and then plug the vacuum line connection. If the servo does not hold its depressed position, it is faulty and should be replaced.

13. FUSE/RELAY PANEL

On Jettas, the fuses and relays are arranged together in one unit located below the instrument panel on the driver's side of the car, as shown in Fig. 13-1. To reach the fuse/relay panel, pull the upper edge of the recessed storage bin forward and lift out the bin.

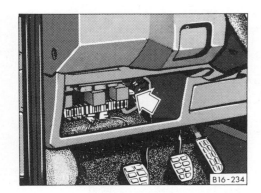

Fig. 13-1. Location of fuse/relay panel on Jetta models. Use special tool (at arrow) to remove fuses.

On Golf and GTI models, the fuses are located behind a small door near the bottom of the instrument panel on the driver's side of the car, as shown in Fig. 13-2. A separate relay panel is reached by removing the canter console and the lower instrument panel tray as described in **BODY AND INTERIOR**.

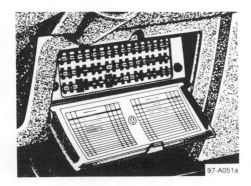

Fig. 13-2. Location of fuse panel on GTI and Golf models.

The fuses come in different colors which correspond to different current ratings. Each fuse is specifically chosen to protect its circuit against any current flow which exceeds the fuse's rating. When replacing fuses, it is never appropriate to substitute a fuse of a higher rating.

CAUTION

Only replace fuses with those of the same rating. If the fuse in one particular location fails repeatedly, that is an indication of a problem in the circuit or in a component which should be repaired.

For 1985 through 1989 Jetta models, fuses and relays are identified in Fig. 13-3.

For 1985 Golf and GTI models, relays are identified in Fig. 13-4. Fuses are identified in Fig. 13-5.

For 1986 through 1989 Golf and GTI models, relays are identified in Fig. 13-6 and fuses are identified in Fig. 13-7.

In the current flow diagrams, most relays are identified by a number in a black box which indicates location on the relay panel. Also, each fuse number is preceded by the letter **S**. For example, S12 in the circuit diagrams indicates fuse number 12 on the fuse panel.

NOTE

Relay locations and fuse designations and locations are subject to change, and may vary from car to car, depending on options. If questions arise, please remember that an authorized Volkswagen dealer is the best source for the most accurate and up-to-date information.

14

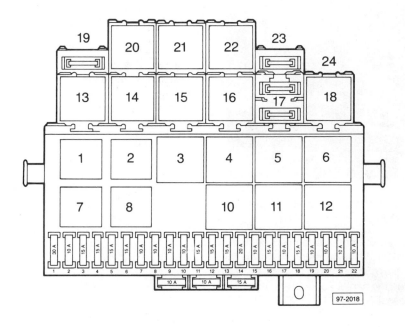

Fig. 13-3. 1985 through 1989 Jetta fuse/relay panel.

Fuses

Fuse No.	Description	Ampere Rating
1	Radiator cooling fan	30
2	Brake lights	10
3	Cigar lighter, radio, clock, interior lights, central locking	15
4	Emergency flashers	15
5	Fuel pump (gasoline engines)	15
6	Open	—
7	Taillights, parking lights, side marker lights (left side)	10
8	Taillights, parking lights, side marker lights (right side)	10
9	Headlights (high beam, right) high beam indicator light	10
10	Headlights (high beam, left)	10
11	Windshield wipers/washers	15
12	Heated seats, electric outside mirrors	15
13	Rear window defogger, heated inside rear view mirror	15
14	Heater blower glove box light	20
15	Back-up lights, automatic transmission console light	10
16	Horn	15
17	Knock sensor control unit	10
18	Dual horn, coolant level and temperature warning light	15
19	Turn signals, brake warning light	10
20	License plate lights	10
21	Headlights (low beam, left)	10
22	Headlights (low beam, right)	10

Relays

Relay No.	Description
1	Open
2	Fuel pump (gasoline) Glow plugs (diesel)
3	Seat belt warning
4	Upshift indicator (1985 - 1987)
5	A/C relay
6	Dual horns
7	Open
8	Load reduction
9	Open
10	Intermittent wipers
11	Open
12	Turn signals, flashers
13	Open
14	Cooling fan after-run (except 16-valve)
15	Passive restraint (1988, 1989)
16	Idle air stabilizer
17	A/C thermofuse
18	Coolant level indicator
19	Power windows
20	Heated seats
21	Heated seats
22	Oxygen sensor system power supply (US cars w/CIS)
23	Power window fuse (30A)
24	Glow plug fuse (Diesel-50A)

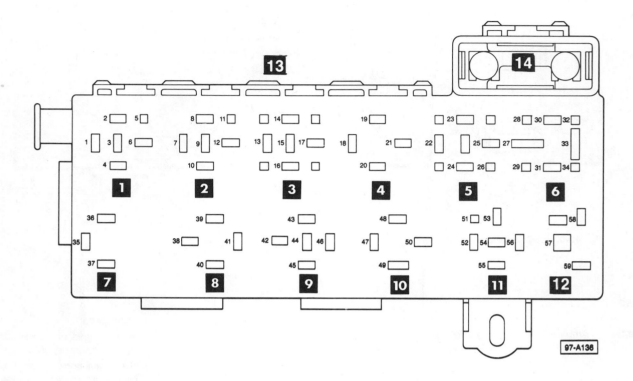

Fig. 13-4. 1985 Golf and GTI relay panel.

Relays

Relay No.	Golf	GTI	Golf diesel
1	Intermittent wiper	Intermittent wiper	Intermittant wiper
2	Upshift indicator	Upshift indicator	Upshift indicator
3	Horns	Low speed radiator colling fan (with A/C)	Open
4	Low speed radiator cooling fan (with A/C)	Open	Low coolant level
5	Open	Open	A/C cutout
6	Fuel pump	Fuel pump	Glow plugs
7	Turn signals, emergency flashers	Turn signals, emergency flasher	Turn signals, emergency flashers
8	Load reduction	Load reduction	Load reduction
9	Idle speed control	Horns	Horns
10	A/C high blower	A/C high blower	Low speed radiator cooling (A/C only)
11	Seat belt interlock	Seat belt warning	Seat belt warning
12	See #11	Open	Open
13	Rear wiper	Rear wiper	Rear wiper
14	–	–	Glow plug fuse

14

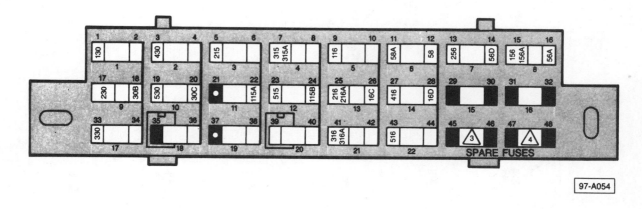

Fig. 13-5. 1985 Golf and GTI fuse panel.

Fuses

Fuse No	Ampere Rating	Description
1	15	Dome light, luggage light, glove box light, clock, Multi-function indicator memory
2	15	Taillights, parking lights, sidemarker lights, license plate lights
3	10	Rear window wiper
4	20	Rear window defogger, horn
5	15	Windshield wiper/washer
6	5	Instrument panel lights
7	10	Headlights, low beam
8	15	Headlights, high beam
9	20	Brake lights, hazard warning lights
10	20	Fuel pump (gasoline engines) Open (diesel engines)
11	—	Open
12	20	Heater

Fuse No	Ampere Rating	Description
13	10	Back-up lights, turn signal lamps, emergency flasher switch
14	10	Relays: (interlock, upshift, OXS, low coolant, glow plug, radiator after-run)
15	—	Open
16	—	Open
17	25	Cigar lighter, A/C clutch, radiator cooling fan (low speed), central locking, diesel vacuum pump
18	—	ACC connector
19	—	Open
20	5	ACC connector, cruise control
21	5	Senders, gauges, warning lamps
22	15	Fuel injection (gasoline engines) Open (diesel engines)

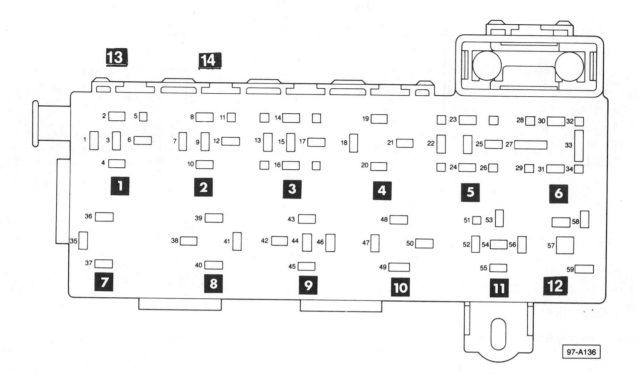

Fig. 13-6. 1986 through 1989 Golf and GTI relay panel.

Relays

Relay No.	Golf, Golf GL	Golf diesel	Golf GT, GTI
1	Intermittent wiper	Intermittent wiper	Intermittent wiper
2	Upshift indicator (1986-1987) **Open (1988, 1989)**	Upshift indicator (1986-1987) **Open (1988, 1989)**	Upshift indicator (1986-1987) **Open (1988, 1989)**
3	Low speed radiator cooling fan (with A/C)	Low speed radiator cooling fan (with A/C)	Low speed radiator cooling fan (with A/C)
4	Horns	Low coolant level	**Horns (1988, 1989 Golf GTI only) Open (except Golf GT)**
5	Rear wiper	Rear wiper	Rear wiper
6	Fuel pump	Glow plugs	Fuel pump
7	Turn signals, flashers	Turn signals, flashers	Turn signals, flashers
8	Load reduction	Load reduction	Load reduction
9	Idle speed control (1986, 1987) **Power supply (1988, 1989)**	Horns	**Horns (except 1988, 1989 Golf GT) Power supply (1988, 1989 Golf GT)**
10	A/C high blower (1986) Fuel injection (1987) **Passive restraint (1988, 1989)**	A/C high blower **A/C cutout (1986, 1987)**	A/C high blower (1986-1987 except 16-valve)
11	Seat belt interlock	Seat belt interlock	Seat belt interlock
12	Bridge	Bridge	Open (1986-1987) **Bridge (1988, 1989)**
13	Radiator cooling fan after-run	Open	Radiator cooling fan after-run
14	Oxygen sensor relay (1987) Low coolant relay (1987) **Open (1988, 1989)**	A/C cutout (1986, 1987) **Passive restraint (1988, 1989)**	**Low coolant indicator (1988, 1989 Golf GT)** Open (except 1988, 1989 Golf GT)

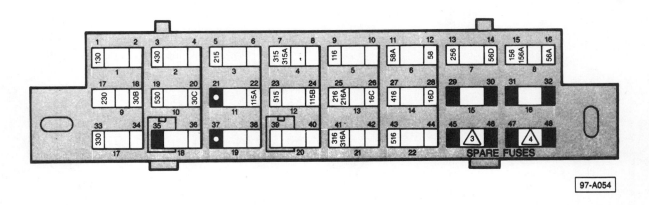

Fig. 13-7. 1986 through 1989 Golf and GTI fuse panel.

Fuses

Fuse No.	Ampere Rating	Description
1	15	Dome light, luggage light, glove box light, clock, Multi-function indicator memory
2	15	Taillights, parking lights, sidemarker lights, license plate lights
3	10	Rear window wiper
4	20	Rear window defogger
5	15	Windshield wiper/washer
6	5	Instrument panel lights
7	10	Headlights, low beam
8	15	Headlights, high beam
9	20	Brake lights, hazard warning lights
10	20	Fuel pump (gasoline engines)
		Open (diesel engines)
11	15	Horn
12	20	Heater (without A/C)
	30	Heater (with A/C)

Fuse No.	Ampere Rating	Description
13	10	Back-up lights, turn signal lamps, emergency flasher switch
14	10	Relays: (interlock, upshift, OXS, low coolant, glow plug, radiator after-run)
15	30	Radiator cooling fan after-run (1988, 1989 except GTI)
		Open (1986-1987)
16		Open
17	25	Cigar lighter, A/C clutch, radiator cooling fan (low speed), central locking, diesel vacuum pump
18	—	ACC connector
	30	Radiator cooling fan after-run (1987 except 16-valve)
19		Open
20	5	ACC connector, cruise control
21	5	Senders, gauges, warning lamps
22	10	Throttle switches and idle stabilizer valve (GTI)
	15	OXS relay (1986-1987 CIS and (1988, 1989 except GTI)

14. CURRENT FLOW DIAGRAMS

Volkswagen wiring diagrams are actually current flow diagrams which are organized to indicate current flow, from positive to negative, in the electrical system. This is different from most other types of wiring diagrams that actually show the routing of the wiring harness. Wire information such as size and color is included, but the diagrams mainly offer information on how a circuit functions rather than what it looks like.

As a general rule, these diagrams indicate current flow from positive (+) at the top of the diagram to negative (−) at the bottom (which represents ground). One exception to this is the fuse/relay panel's internal ground circuit, labeled with the terminal number 31. See **3.1 How To Read Volkswagen Current Flow Diagrams** for information on using the diagrams. See **Terminal and Circuit Identification** for further information on terminal numbers.

At the beginning of the diagrams is a full listing of the wiring and component symbols used in the diagrams, schematic representations of the ground connections for the electrical system, and an index of the connectors which appear on the diagrams with their locations in the car. A complete list of the diagrams is found at the beginning of this section as part of the Table of Contents.

The current flow diagrams in this manual are organized into two broad groups. One group contains the diagrams which apply to all Golf and GTI models. The other group contains the diagrams which apply to all Jetta models.

Golf and GTI

These diagrams cover all Golf and GTI models including Golf, Golf GL, Golf GT, Golf Diesel, GTI, and GTI 16V. There is no main electrical system diagram which covers a whole car. Each diagram covers a particular portion of the electrical system, such as Electronic Engine Control, or a particular accessory such as Power Windows.

Parts of the electrical system may vary from year to year and from model to model. Each diagram's title specifies all model years and models which are covered by that diagram, and exceptions are also included. References to Golf apply to all Golf models unless otherwise noted. References to GTI apply to both GTI and GTI 16V unless otherwise noted.

Jetta

These diagrams cover all Jetta models including Jetta, Jetta GL, Jetta GLI, Jetta GLI 16V, Jetta Carat, Jetta Diesel, and Jetta Turbo Diesel. A Main Electrical System diagram covers all the main features of the basic electrical system. Additional diagrams cover particular subsystems, such as Electronic Engine Control, or particular accessories such as Power Windows.

Parts of the electrical system may vary from year to year and from model to model. Each diagram's title specifies all model years and models which are covered by that diagram, and exceptions are also included. References to Jetta apply to all Jetta models unless otherwise noted. References to Jetta Diesel apply to Diesel and Turbo Diesel unless otherwise noted.

14

Symbols Used in Wiring Diagrams
(page 1 of 1)

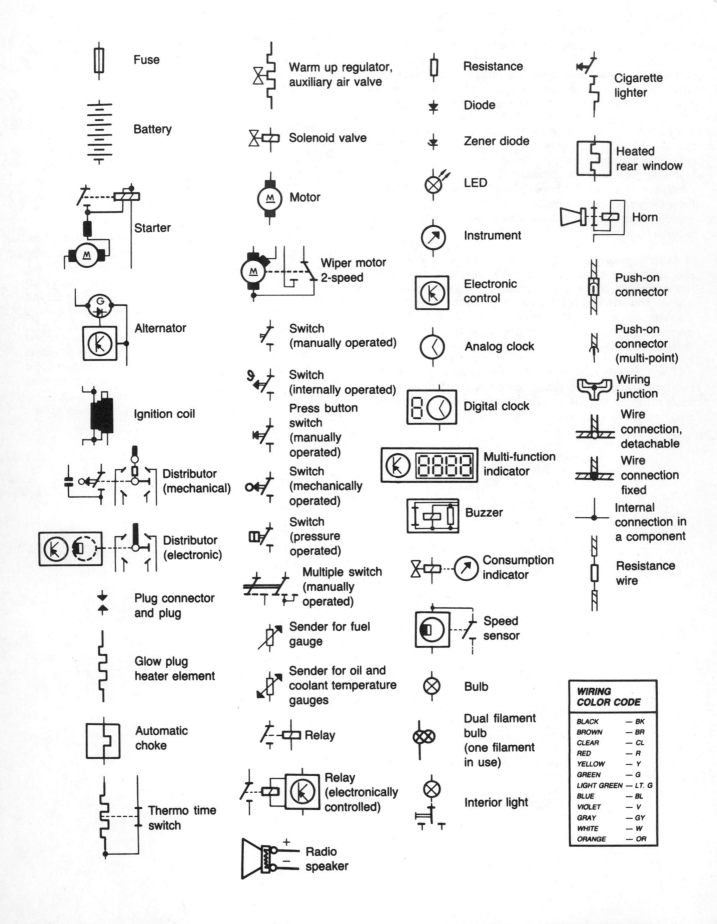

Fuse

Battery

Starter

Alternator

Ignition coil

Distributor (mechanical)

Distributor (electronic)

Plug connector and plug

Glow plug heater element

Automatic choke

Thermo time switch

Warm up regulator, auxiliary air valve

Solenoid valve

Motor

Wiper motor 2-speed

Switch (manually operated)

Switch (internally operated)

Press button switch (manually operated)

Switch (mechanically operated)

Switch (pressure operated)

Multiple switch (manually operated)

Sender for fuel gauge

Sender for oil and coolant temperature gauges

Relay

Relay (electronically controlled)

Radio speaker

Resistance

Diode

Zener diode

LED

Instrument

Electronic control

Analog clock

Digital clock

Multi-function indicator

Buzzer

Consumption indicator

Speed sensor

Bulb

Dual filament bulb (one filament in use)

Interior light

Cigarette lighter

Heated rear window

Horn

Push-on connector

Push-on connector (multi-point)

Wiring junction

Wire connection, detachable

Wire connection fixed

Internal connection in a component

Resistance wire

WIRING COLOR CODE	
BLACK	— BK
BROWN	— BR
CLEAR	— CL
RED	— R
YELLOW	— Y
GREEN	— G
LIGHT GREEN	— LT. G
BLUE	— BL
VIOLET	— V
GRAY	— GY
WHITE	— W
ORANGE	— OR

**Ground Circuit
1985 Golf/GTI
(page 1 of 1)**

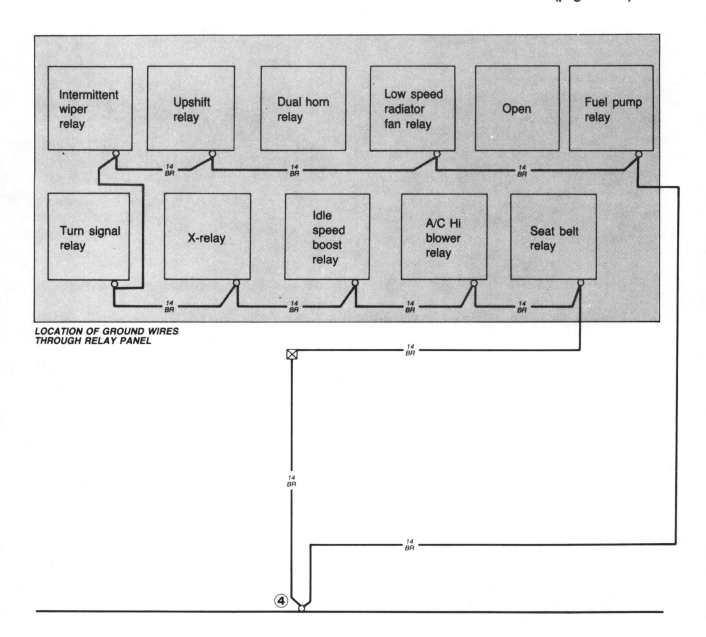

*LOCATION OF GROUND WIRES
THROUGH RELAY PANEL*

Ground location

④ . . . . under LH side of I/P

Ground Circuit
1986 Golf/GTI
(page 1 of 1)

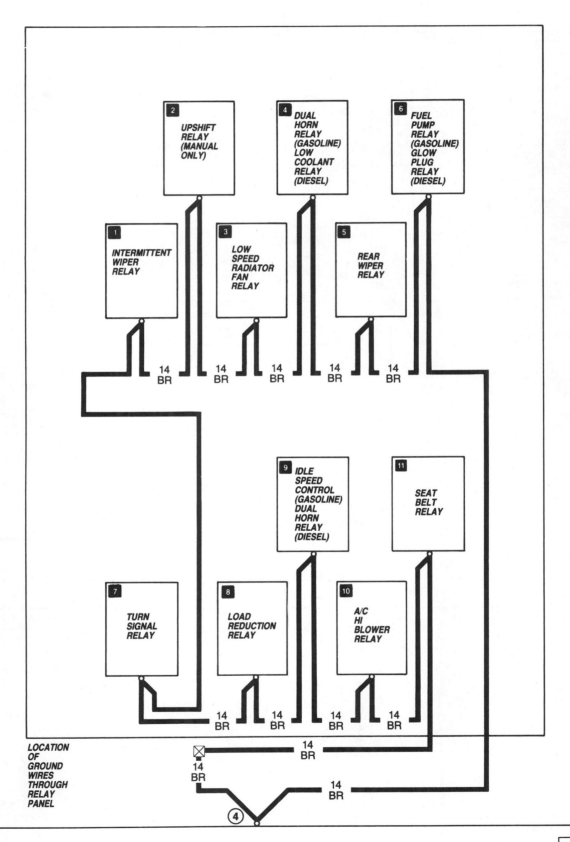

**Ground Circuit
1987 Golf (CIS)
(page 1 of 1)**

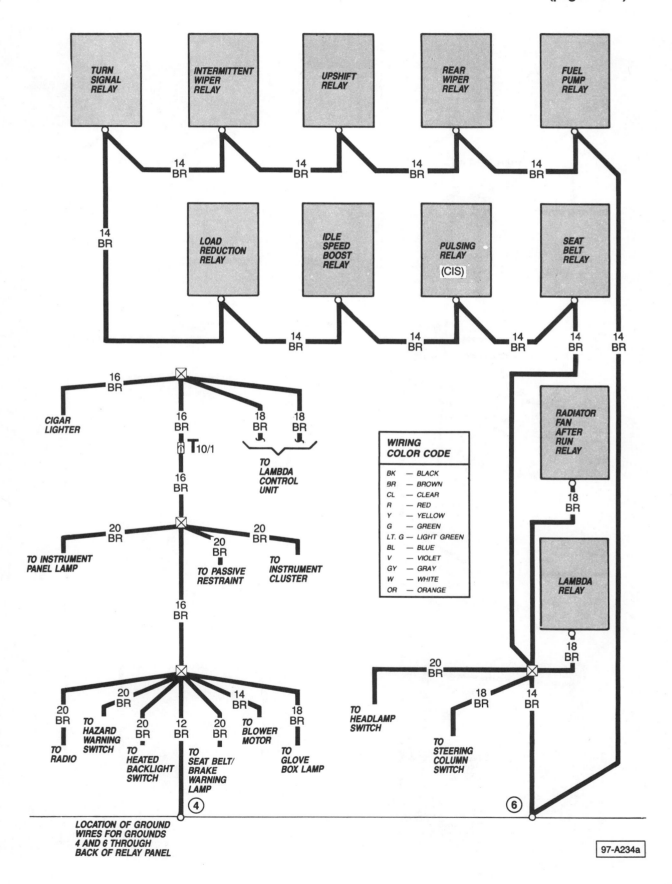

97-A234a

**Ground Circuit
1987 Golf, GTI (CIS-E
except 16-valve)
(page 1 of 1)**

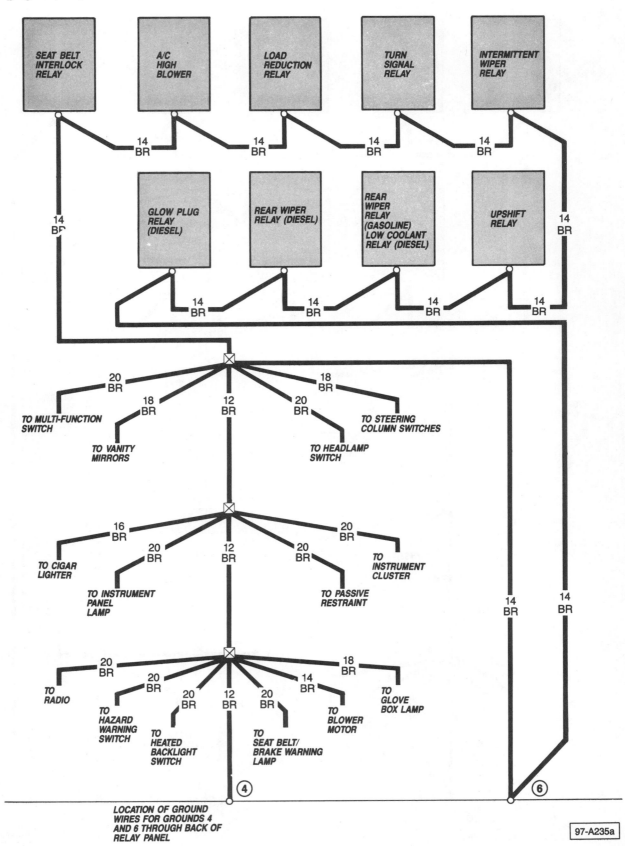

97-A235a

**Ground Circuit
1987-1989 GTI 16-valve
(page 1 of 1)**

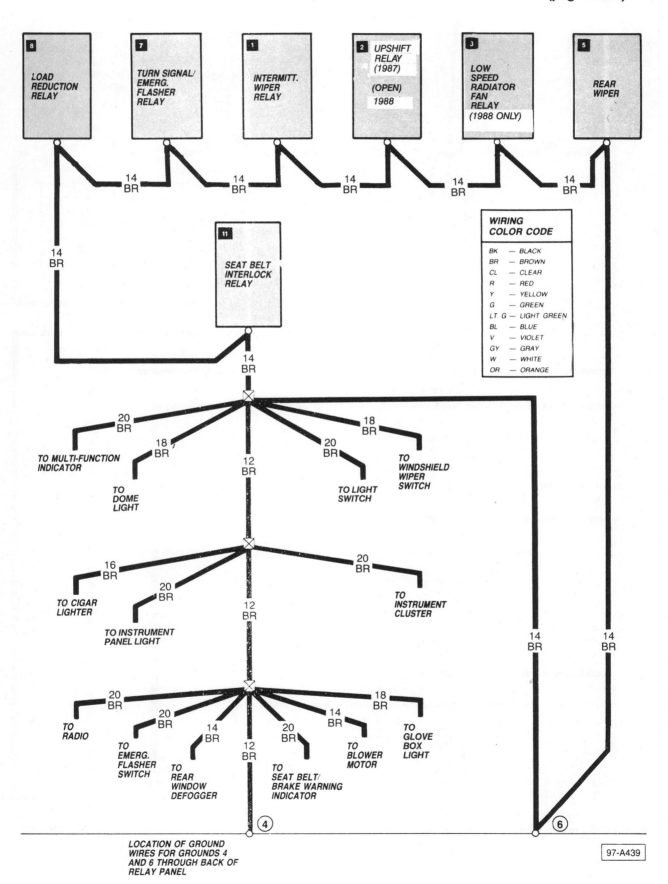

8 LOAD REDUCTION RELAY

7 TURN SIGNAL/ EMERG. FLASHER RELAY

1 INTERMITT. WIPER RELAY

2 UPSHIFT RELAY (1987)

(OPEN) 1988

3 LOW SPEED RADIATOR FAN RELAY (1988 ONLY)

5 REAR WIPER

14 BR
14 BR
14 BR
14 BR
14 BR

14 BR

11 SEAT BELT INTERLOCK RELAY

14 BR

WIRING COLOR CODE	
BK	— BLACK
BR	— BROWN
CL	— CLEAR
R	— RED
Y	— YELLOW
G	— GREEN
LT. G	— LIGHT GREEN
BL	— BLUE
V	— VIOLET
GY	— GRAY
W	— WHITE
OR	— ORANGE

20 BR
TO MULTI-FUNCTION INDICATOR

18 BR
TO DOME LIGHT

12 BR

20 BR
TO LIGHT SWITCH

18 BR
TO WINDSHIELD WIPER SWITCH

16 BR
TO CIGAR LIGHTER

20 BR
TO INSTRUMENT PANEL LIGHT

12 BR

20 BR
TO INSTRUMENT CLUSTER

20 BR
TO RADIO

20 BR
TO EMERG. FLASHER SWITCH

14 BR
TO REAR WINDOW DEFOGGER

12 BR

20 BR
TO SEAT BELT/ BRAKE WARNING INDICATOR

14 BR
TO BLOWER MOTOR

18 BR
TO GLOVE BOX LIGHT

14 BR

14 BR

④

⑥

LOCATION OF GROUND WIRES FOR GROUNDS 4 AND 6 THROUGH BACK OF RELAY PANEL

97-A439

Ground Circuit
1988-1989 Golf (Gasoline only)
(page 1 of 1)

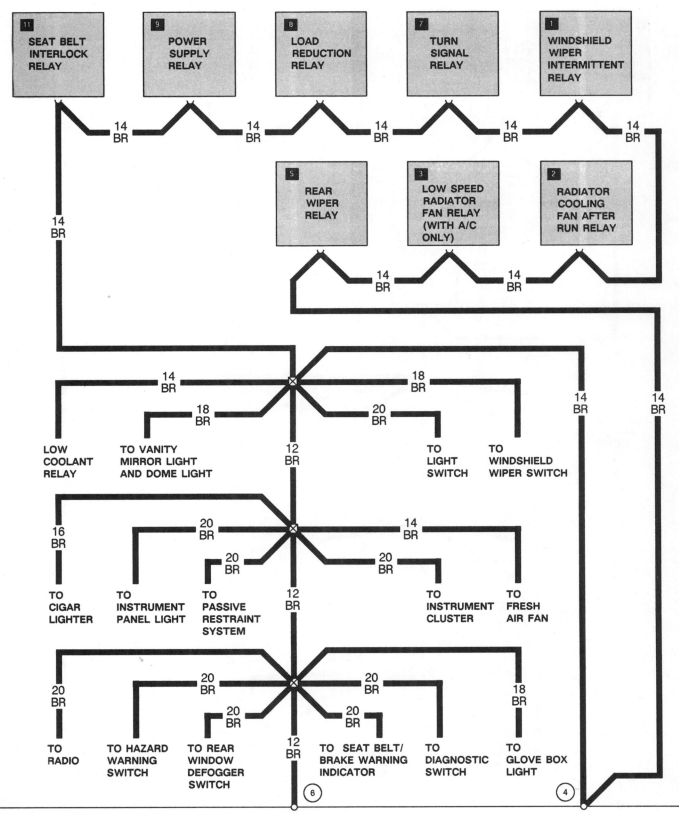

**Ground Circuit
1988-1989 Golf Diesel
(page 1 of 1)**

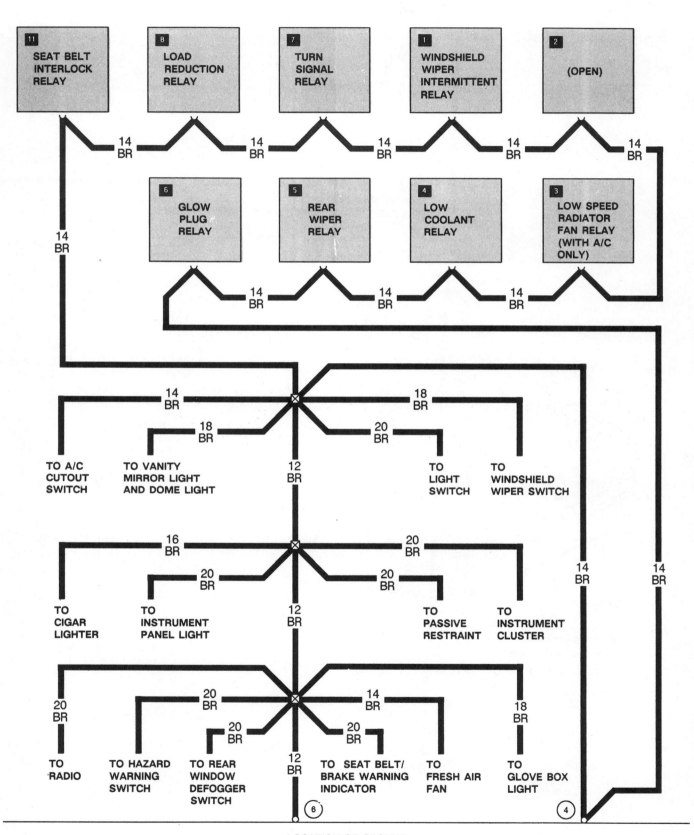

LOCATION OF GROUND
WIRES FOR GROUNDS
4 AND 6 THROUGH
BACK OF RELAY PANEL

**Ground Locations
1985-1989 Golf/GTI
(page 1 of 1)**

Body ground location

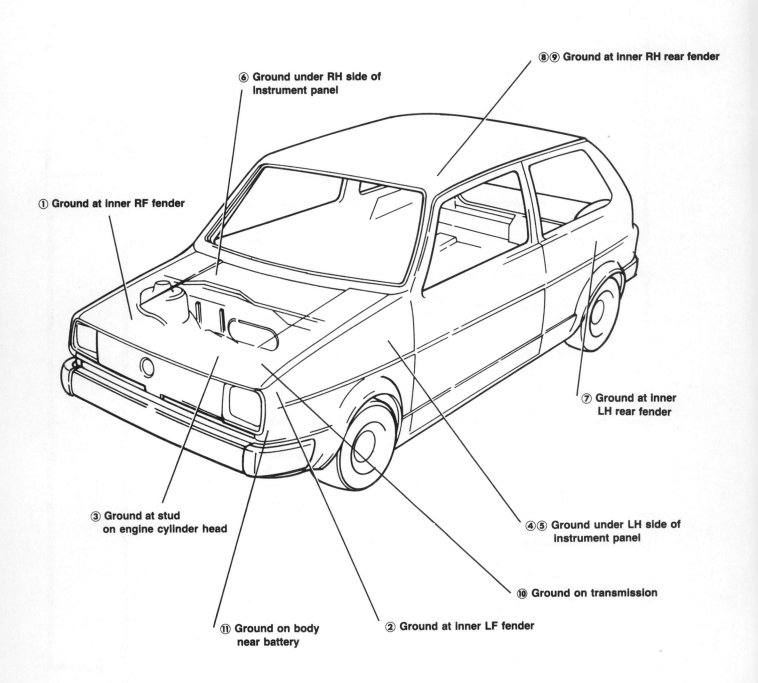

⑥ **Ground under RH side of instrument panel**

⑧⑨ **Ground at inner RH rear fender**

① **Ground at inner RF fender**

⑦ **Ground at inner LH rear fender**

③ **Ground at stud on engine cylinder head**

④⑤ **Ground under LH side of instrument panel**

⑩ **Ground on transmission**

⑪ **Ground on body near battery**

② **Ground at inner LF fender**

Harness Connectors

T1	under instrument panel, LH side
T1a	in engine compartment near alternator
T2 (lights)	luggage compartment, LH side
T2 (air conditioning)	in engine compartment
T2 (cruise control)	behind instrument cluster
T2 (GY)	under instrument panel, LH side
T2a	under instrument panel, LH side
T2b (seat belt interlock)	inside LH door
T2b (cruise control)	under instrument panel, LH side
T2c	under instrument panel, RH side
T2d	inside RH door
T3 (air conditioning)	behind instrument panel
T3 (GY)	under instrument panel, LH side
T3a	under instrument panel, LH side
T4	under instrument panel, LH side
T6	under instrument panel, LH side
T10 (BK)	under instrument panel, LH side
T10 (BL)	under instrument panel, LH side
T10 (G)	under instrument panel, LH side
T10 (GY) (lights)	under instrument panel, LH side
T10 (GY) (air conditioning)	behind air conditioning/heater control
T10 (Y)	under instrument panel, LH side

Harness Connectors
1986-1989 Golf/GTI
(except 16-valve)
(page 1 of 1)

Harness Connectors, 1986–1988 Golf/GTI (except 16-valve)

T1	— on positive battery cable
T1a	— near right front kick panel
T1b	— near left front kick panel
T1c	— near left front kick panel
T1e	— eng. compart. near inj. pump
T1f	— on fire wall, RH side
T1g	— on fire wall, RH side
T1h	— in 'C' pillar, LH side
T1k	— near right front kick panel
T1s	— behind inst. panel, LH side
T2	— near starter
T2a	— in 'C' pillar, LH side
T2b	— behind inst. panel, LH side
T2c	— behind inst. panel, LH side
T2d	— behind hinge of RH sun visor
T2e	— on fire wall, LH side
T2f	— in 'C' pillar, LH side
T2g	— behind inst. panel, LH side
T2h	— behind inst. panel, LH side
T2m	— near intake manifold
T2w	— behind RF door panel
T2x	— behind LF door panel
T2y	— behind RR door panel
T2z	— behind LR door panel
T2AA	— at left front seat belt switch
T3	— near left front kick panel
T3a	— under coolant over flow bottle
T3b	— under carpet at RH 'B' pillar
T3C	— under carpet at LH 'B' pillar
T3d	— near relay panel
T3j	— in left front door panel
T3k	— in left front door panel

T3l	— in right front door panel
T3m	— in right front door panel
'4	— behind inst. panel, LH side
T4a	— near left front kick panel
T4b	— behind inst. panel, LH side
T4c	— behind inst. panel, LH side
T4d	— under coolant over flow bottle
T4e	— behind inst. panel, LH side
T4f	— behind inst. panel, LH side
T4g	— near left front kick panel (1986–1987)
	— near left front door panel (1988)
T6	— under coolant overflow bottle
T6a	— near LF kick panel
T6b	— near LF kick panel
T7/	— on inst. cluster, white, short connectors
T7b/	— on inst. cluster, white, long connectors
T7c/	— on inst. cluster, black, short connectors
T7a/	— on inst. cluster, black, long connectors
T8a/	— behind glove box
T8b/	— upper RH kick panel
T8c/	— upper LH kick panel
T8/e	— right rear of vehicle
T10(BL)	— blue, near relay panel
T10(Y)	— yellow, near relay panel
T10(G)	— green, near relay panel
T10(BK)	— black, near relay panel
T10(GY)	— gray, near relay panel

Harness Connectors, 1987–1988 GTI (16-valve)

T1 — near positive battery cable
T1a — behind instrument panel
T1b — near right front kick panel
T1g — on firewall, middle
T1h — in 'C' pillar, RH side

T2a — in 'C' pillar, LH side
T2b — behind inst. panel, LH side
T2c — behind inst. panel, LH side
T2e — on fire wall, middle
T2f — in 'C' pillar, LH side
T2l — under LF seat
T2m — near A/C refrig. hi-press. sw.
T2w — behind RF door panel
T2x — behind LF door panel
T2y — behind right sunvisor hinge

T3 — behind instrument panel
T3a — near relay panel
T3b — near relay panel
T3j — in left front door panel
T3k — in left front door panel
T3l — in right front door panel
T3m — in right front door panel

T4 — under steering column covers

T4a — under steering column covers
T4g — near left front kick panel

T6 — near LF kick panel
T6a — near LF kick panel

T7/ — on inst. cluster, white, short connectors
T7b/ — on inst. cluster, white, long connectors
T7c/ — on inst. cluster, black, short connectors
T7a/ — on inst. cluster, black, long connectors

T8 — behind relay panel

T8a/ — behind glove box

T8b/ — upper RH kick panel

T8c/ — upper LH kick panel

T10(BL) — blue, near relay panel
T10(Y) — yellow, near relay panel
T10(G) — green, near relay panel
T10(BK) — black, near relay panel
T10(GY) — gray, near relay panel
T10 — under coolant overflow bottle

Power Supply
1985 Golf/GTI (Gasoline only)
(page 1 of 2)

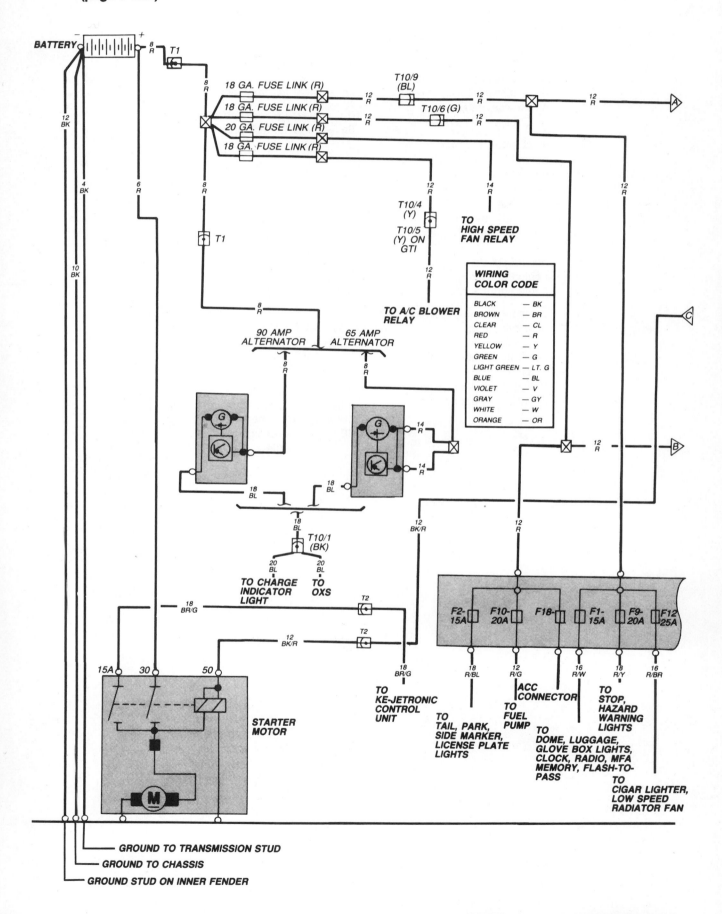

WIRING COLOR CODE

BLACK	— BK
BROWN	— BR
CLEAR	— CL
RED	— R
YELLOW	— Y
GREEN	— G
LIGHT GREEN	— LT. G
BLUE	— BL
VIOLET	— V
GRAY	— GY
WHITE	— W
ORANGE	— OR

GROUND TO TRANSMISSION STUD
GROUND TO CHASSIS
GROUND STUD ON INNER FENDER

Power Supply
1985 Golf/GTI (Gasoline only)
(page 2 of 2)

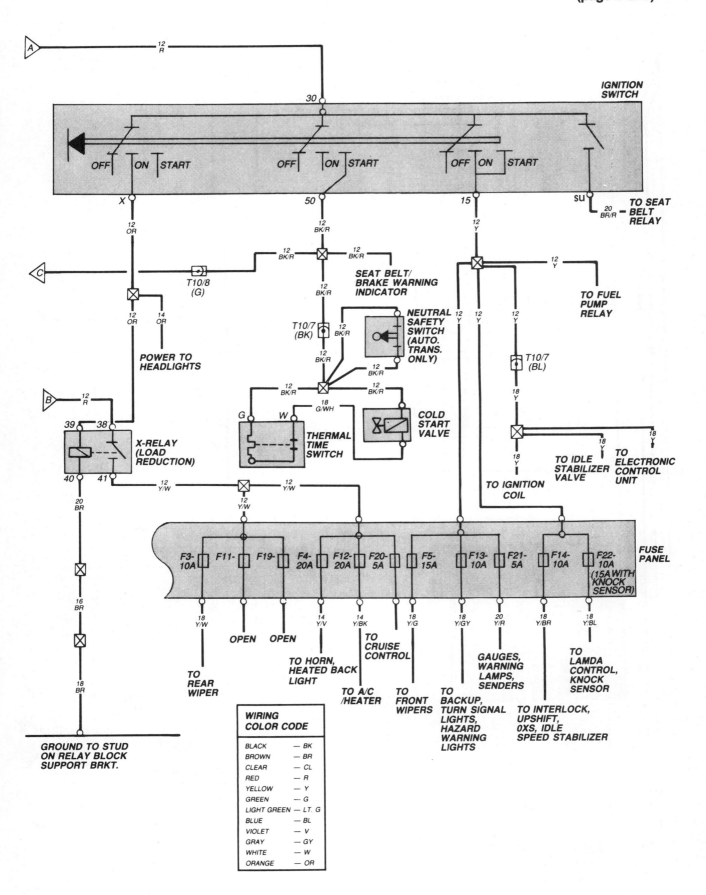

IGNITION SWITCH

OFF | ON | START   OFF | ON | START   OFF | ON | START

30

X   50   15   su   20 BR/R — TO SEAT BELT RELAY

12 OR   12 BK/R   12 Y

C ◁ — T10/8 (G)   12 BK/R ⊠ 12 BK/R   ⊠ 12 Y   12 Y — TO FUEL PUMP RELAY

SEAT BELT/ BRAKE WARNING INDICATOR

12 OR   14 OR   12 BK/R   12 Y 12 Y 12 Y

POWER TO HEADLIGHTS   T10/7 (BK) 12 BK/R   NEUTRAL SAFETY SWITCH (AUTO. TRANS. ONLY)

T10/7 (BL)

B ◁ 12 R   12 BK/R ⊠ 12 BK/R

39 38   18 Y

40 41   G   W   18 G/WH   COLD START VALVE   ⊠

20 BR   THERMAL TIME SWITCH   18 Y   18 Y

X-RELAY (LOAD REDUCTION)   TO IGNITION COIL   TO IDLE STABILIZER VALVE   TO ELECTRONIC CONTROL UNIT

12 Y/W ⊠ 12 Y/W

16 BR   12 Y/W

⊠

18 BR

FUSE PANEL

F3-10A | F11- | F19- | F4-20A | F12-20A | F20-5A | F5-15A | F13-10A | F21-5A | F14-10A | F22-10A (15A WITH KNOCK SENSOR)

18 Y/W   OPEN OPEN   14 Y/V 14 Y/BK 18 Y/G 18 Y/GY 20 Y/R 18 Y/BR 18 Y/BL

TO REAR WIPER

TO HORN, HEATED BACK LIGHT

TO A/C /HEATER

TO CRUISE CONTROL

TO FRONT WIPERS

TO BACKUP, TURN SIGNAL LIGHTS, HAZARD WARNING LIGHTS

GAUGES, WARNING LAMPS, SENDERS

TO INTERLOCK, UPSHIFT, 0XS, IDLE SPEED STABILIZER

TO LAMDA CONTROL, KNOCK SENSOR

GROUND TO STUD ON RELAY BLOCK SUPPORT BRKT.

WIRING COLOR CODE

BLACK	— BK
BROWN	— BR
CLEAR	— CL
RED	— R
YELLOW	— Y
GREEN	— G
LIGHT GREEN	— LT. G
BLUE	— BL
VIOLET	— V
GRAY	— GY
WHITE	— W
ORANGE	— OR

Power Supply
1985 Golf Diesel
(page 1 of 2)

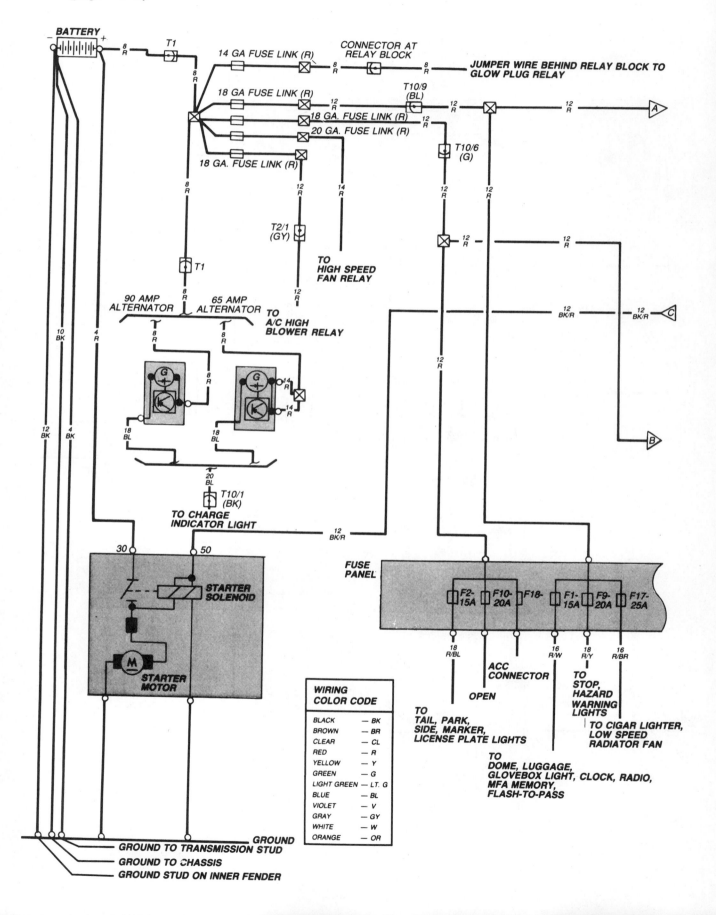

**Power Supply
1985 Golf Diesel
(page 2 of 2)**

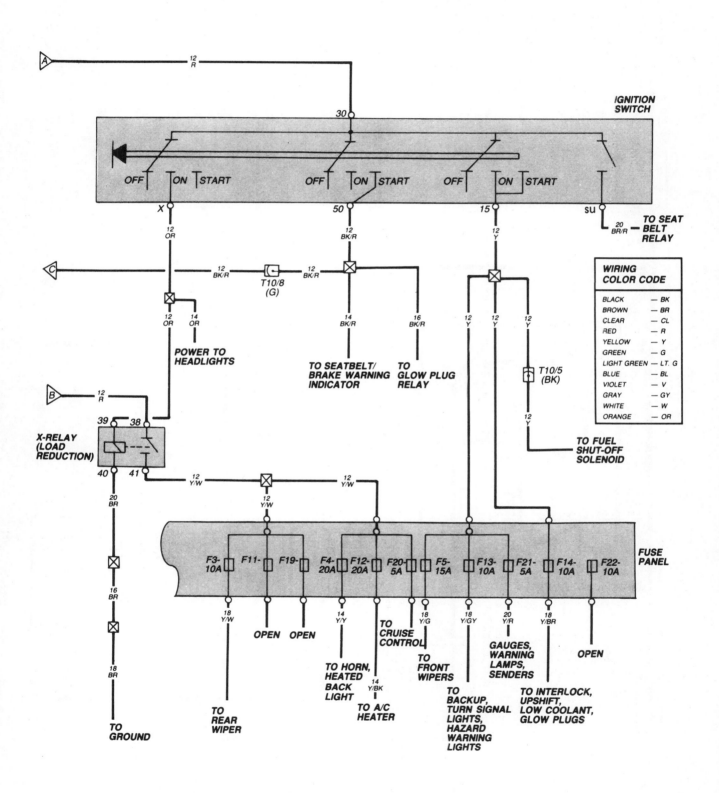

IGNITION
SWITCH

30

OFF ON START   OFF ON START   OFF ON START

X   50   15   su

12
R

12
OR

12
BK/R

12
Y

20
BR/R — TO SEAT
BELT
RELAY

C

12
BK/R

T10/8
(G)

12
BK/R

**POWER TO
HEADLIGHTS**

12
OR

14
OR

14
BK/R

16
BK/R

**TO SEATBELT/
BRAKE WARNING
INDICATOR**

**TO
GLOW PLUG
RELAY**

12
Y

12
Y

12
Y

T10/5
(BK)

12
Y

**TO FUEL
SHUT-OFF
SOLENOID**

WIRING COLOR CODE	
BLACK	— BK
BROWN	— BR
CLEAR	— CL
RED	— R
YELLOW	— Y
GREEN	— G
LIGHT GREEN	— LT. G
BLUE	— BL
VIOLET	— V
GRAY	— GY
WHITE	— W
ORANGE	— OR

B

12
R

**X-RELAY
(LOAD
REDUCTION)**

39   38

40   41

20
BR

16
BR

18
BR

**TO
GROUND**

12
Y/W

12
Y/W

12
Y/W

**FUSE
PANEL**

F3-10A	F11-	F19-	F4-20A	F12-20A	F20-5A	F5-15A	F13-10A	F21-5A	F14-10A	F22-10A

18
Y/W

**TO
REAR
WIPER**

OPEN

OPEN

14
Y/Y

**TO HORN,
HEATED
BACK
LIGHT**

14
Y/BK

**TO A/C
HEATER**

**TO
CRUISE
CONTROL**

18
Y/G

**TO
FRONT
WIPERS**

18
Y/GY

**TO
BACKUP,
TURN SIGNAL
LIGHTS,
HAZARD
WARNING
LIGHTS**

20
Y/R

**GAUGES,
WARNING
LAMPS,
SENDERS**

18
Y/BR

**TO INTERLOCK,
UPSHIFT,
LOW COOLANT,
GLOW PLUGS**

OPEN

Power Supply
1986–1987 Golf/GTI (except
Diesel and 16-valve)
(page 1 of 3)

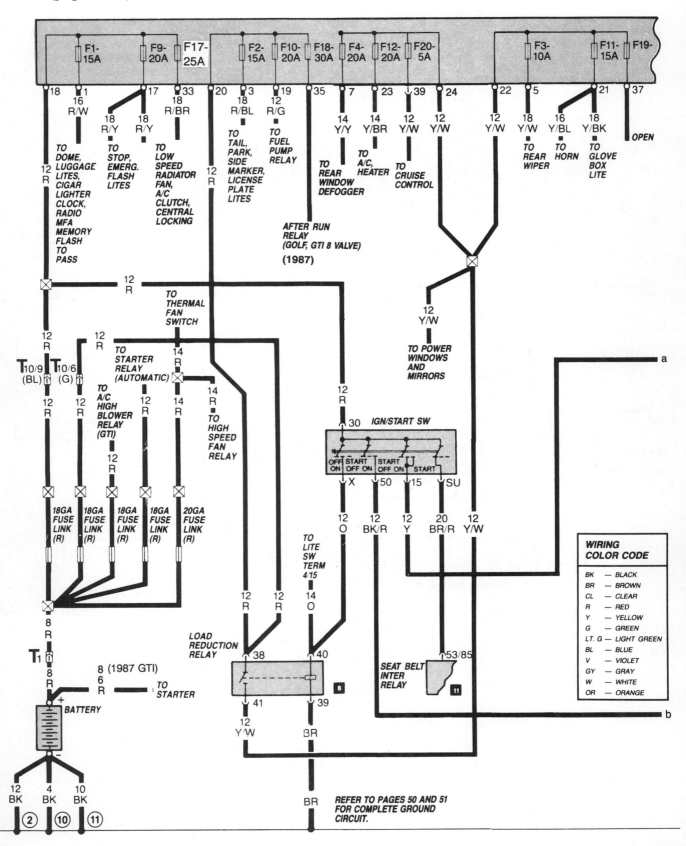

97-A188a

**Power Supply
1986–1987 Golf/GTI (except
Diesel and 16-valve)
(page 2 of 3)**

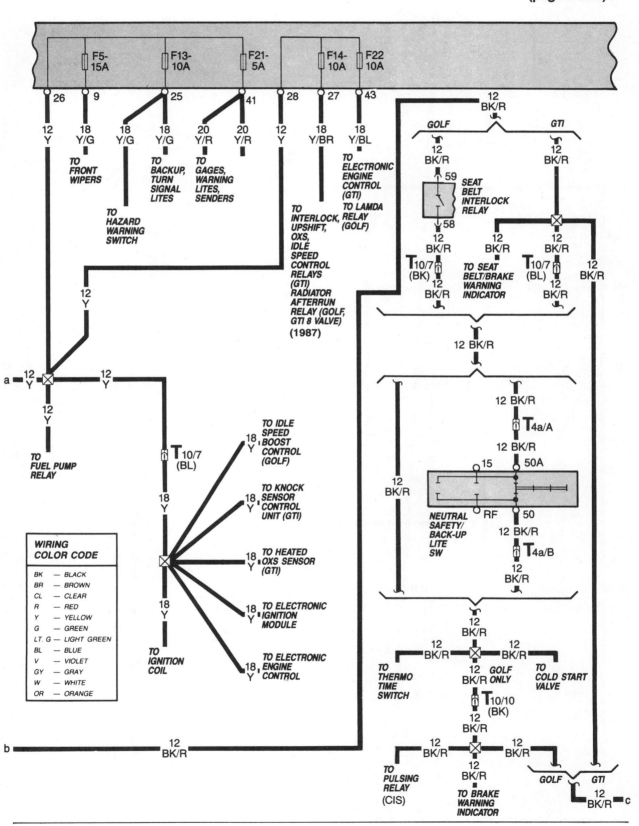

Power Supply
1986–1987 Golf/GTI (except
Diesel and 16-valve)
(page 3 of 3)

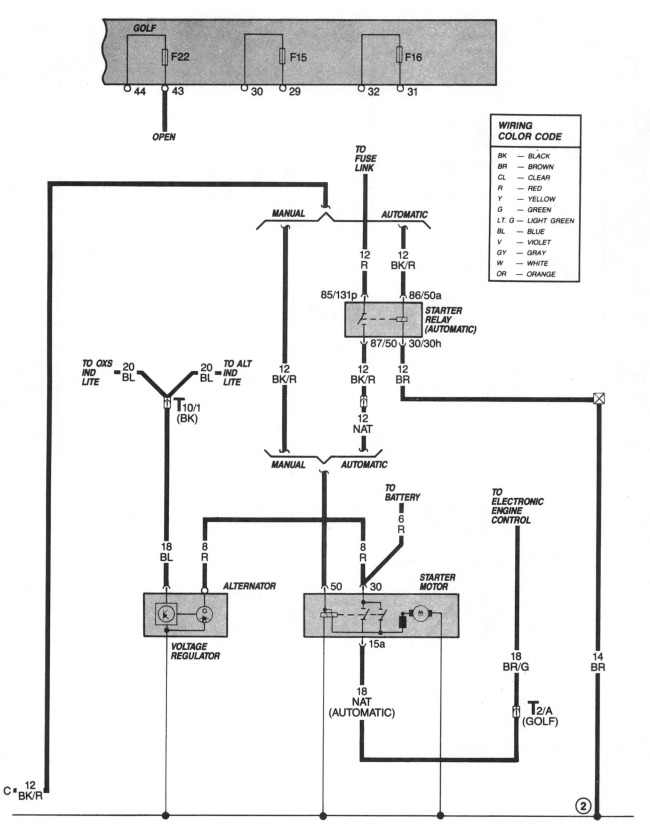

97-A190a

Power Supply
1988-1989 Golf (Gasoline only)
(page 1 of 3)

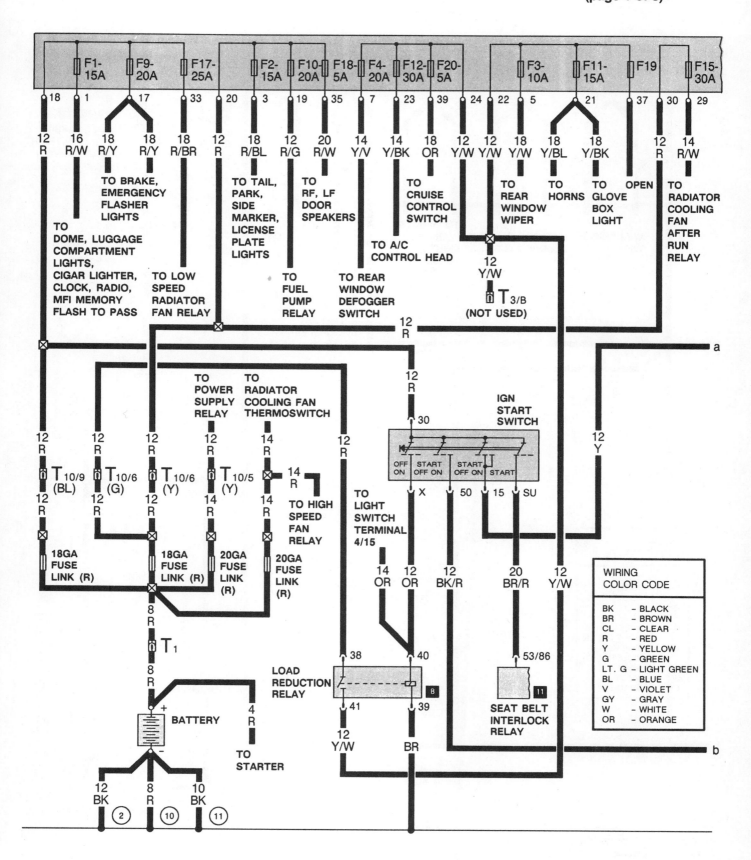

Power Supply
1988-1989 Golf (Gasoline only)
(page 2 of 3)

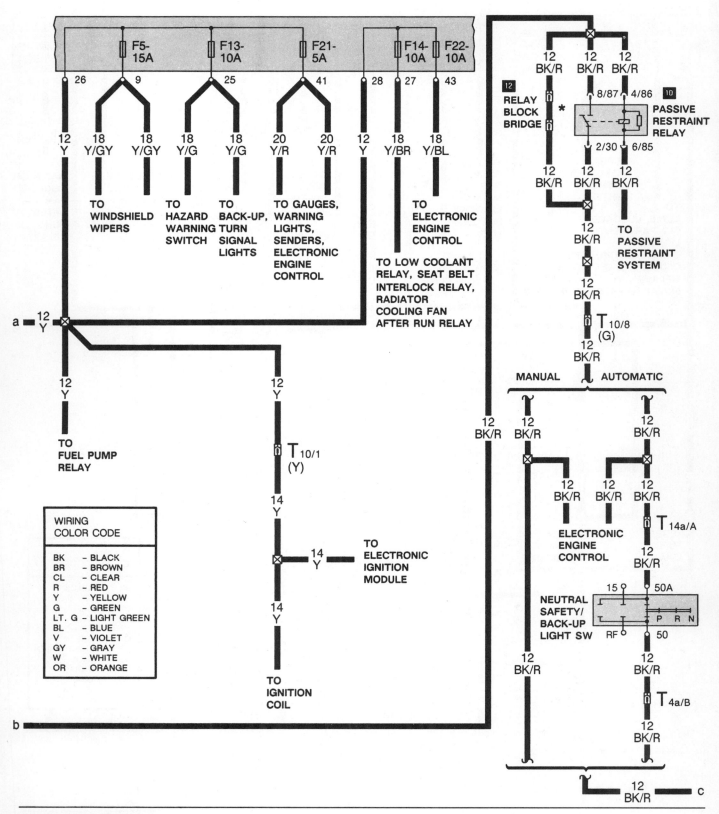

* **BRIDGE FOR USE WITHOUT**
  PASSIVE RESTRAINT
  AT RELAY BLOCK

Power Supply
1988-1989 Golf (Gasoline only)
(page 3 of 3)

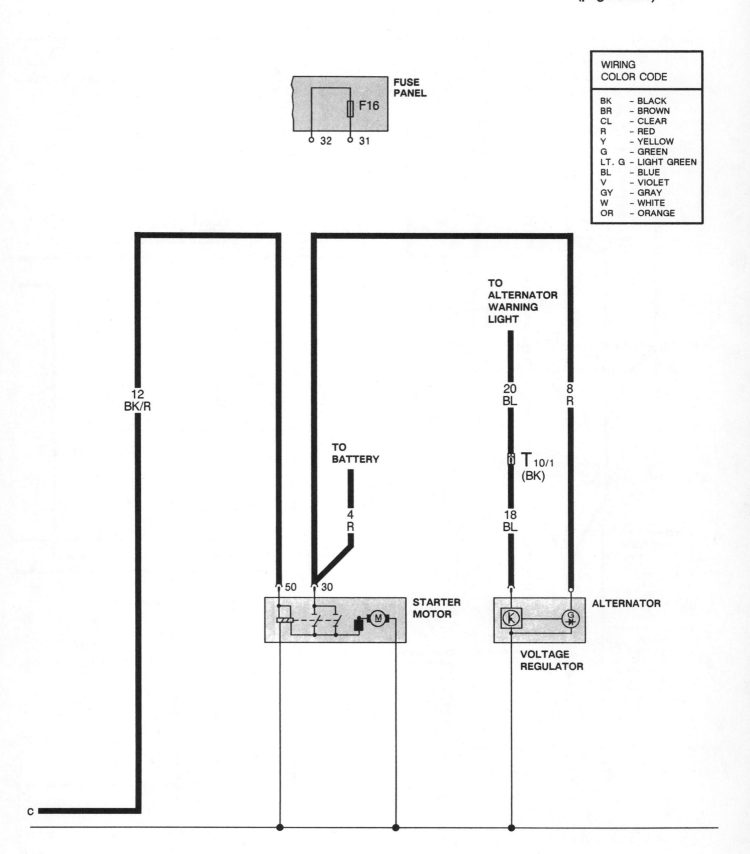

Power Supply
1987-1989 GTI 16-valve
(page 1 of 3)

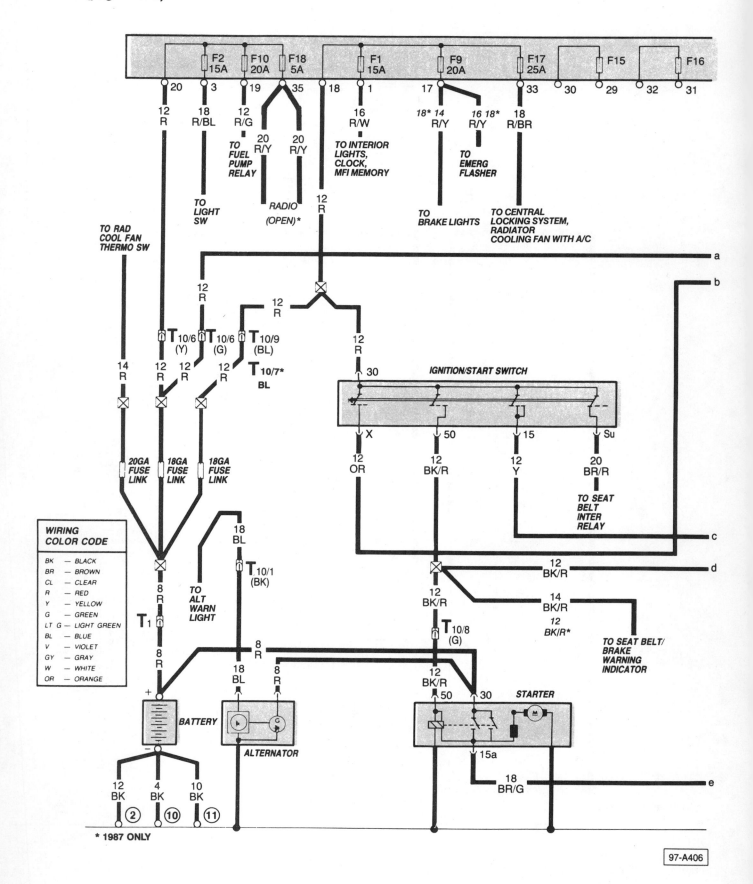

* 1987 ONLY

97-A406

Power Supply
1987-1989 GTI 16-valve
(page 2 of 3)

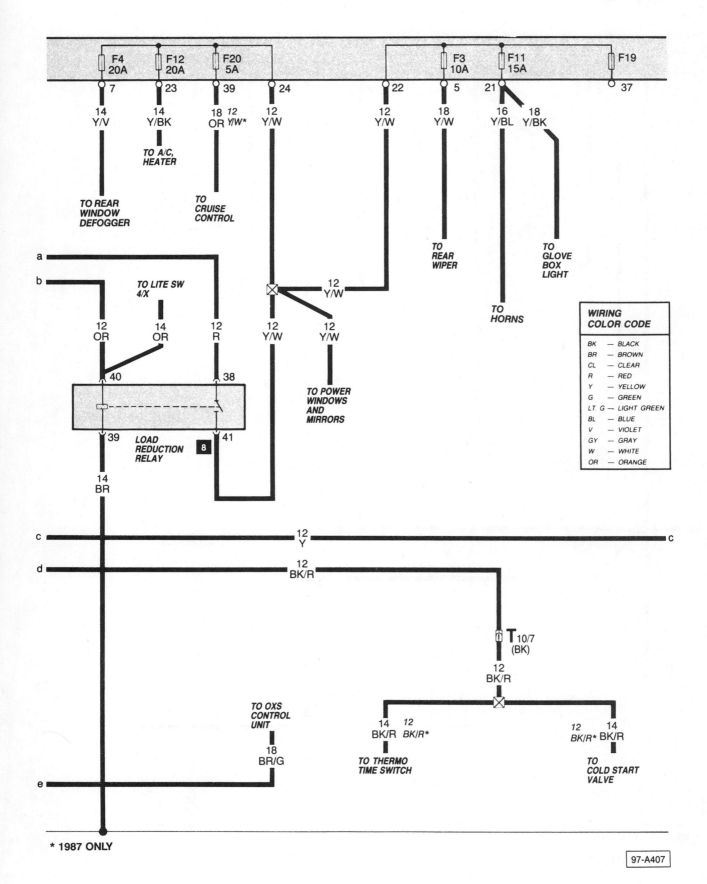

* 1987 ONLY

97-A407

Power Supply
1987-1989 GTI 16-valve
(page 3 of 3)

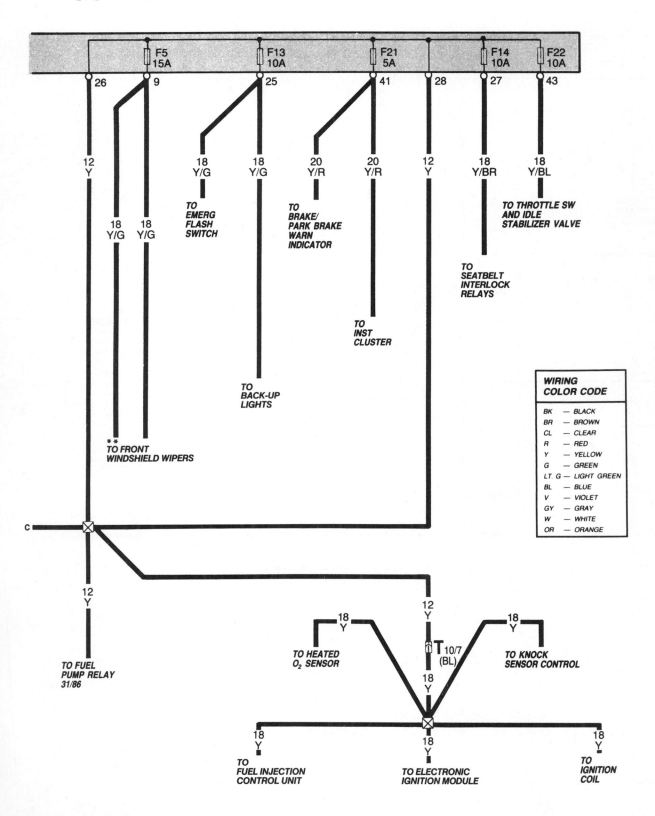

WIRING COLOR CODE		
BK	—	BLACK
BR	—	BROWN
CL	—	CLEAR
R	—	RED
Y	—	YELLOW
G	—	GREEN
LT. G	—	LIGHT GREEN
BL	—	BLUE
V	—	VIOLET
GY	—	GRAY
W	—	WHITE
OR	—	ORANGE

*1988, 1989 MODELS ONLY

97-A408

Power Supply
1986–1989 Golf Diesel
(page 1 of 2)

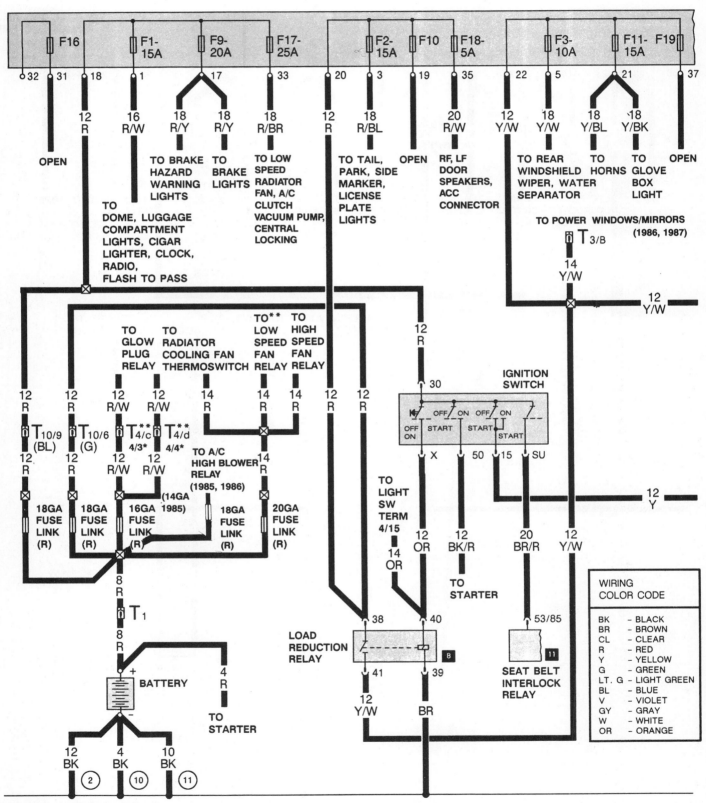

WIRING
COLOR CODE

BK	– BLACK
BR	– BROWN
CL	– CLEAR
R	– RED
Y	– YELLOW
G	– GREEN
LT. G	– LIGHT GREEN
BL	– BLUE
V	– VIOLET
GY	– GRAY
W	– WHITE
OR	– ORANGE

** 1988, 1989 MODELS ONLY

* ALL MODELS EXCEPT 1988, 1989

Power Supply
1986–1989 Golf Diesel
(page 2 of 2)

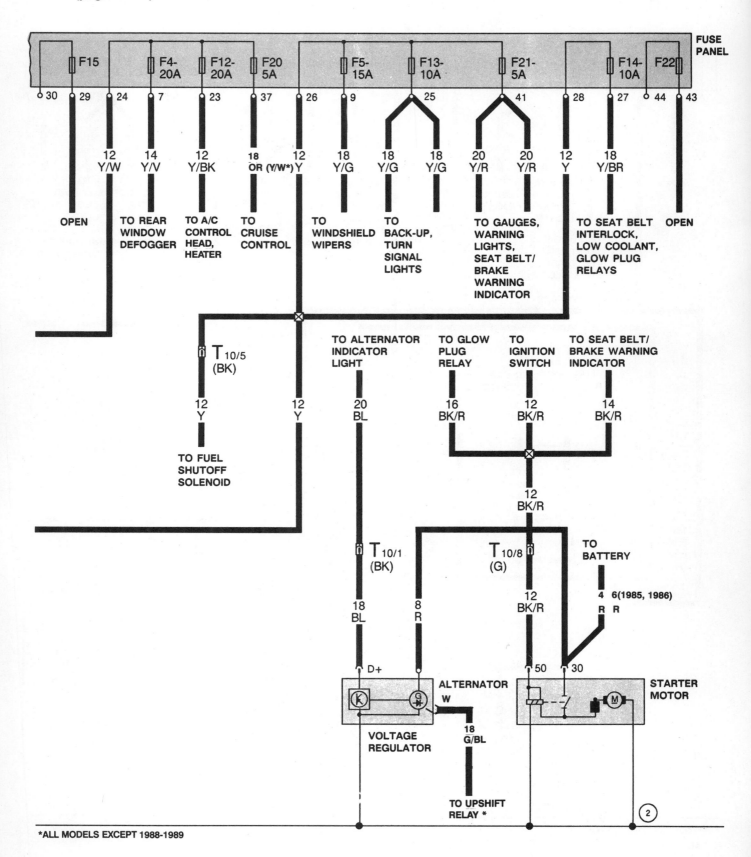

*ALL MODELS EXCEPT 1988-1989

**Exterior Lights
1985 Golf/GTI
(page 1 of 1)**

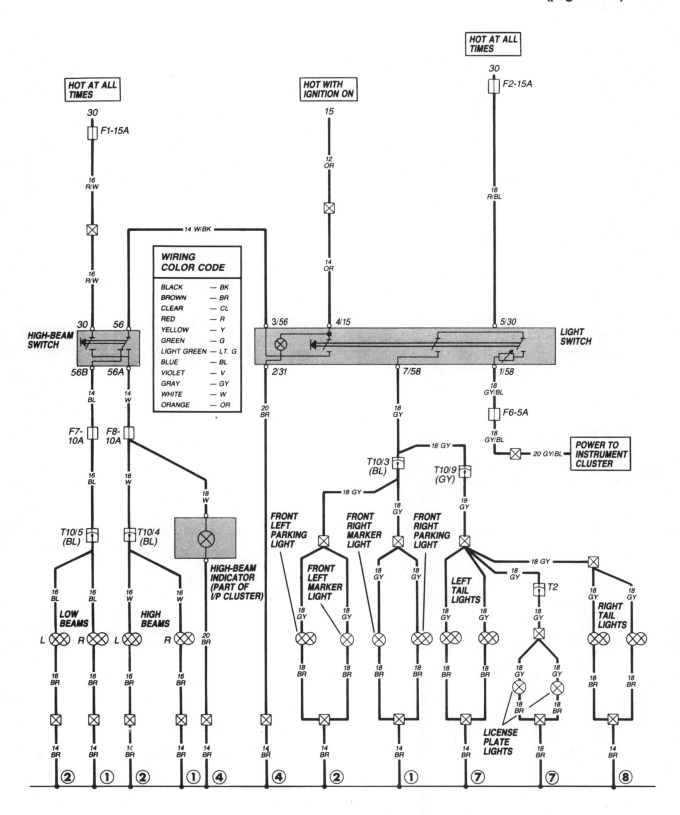

Exterior Lights
1986–1987 Golf,
1986–1989 GTI (page 1 of 2)

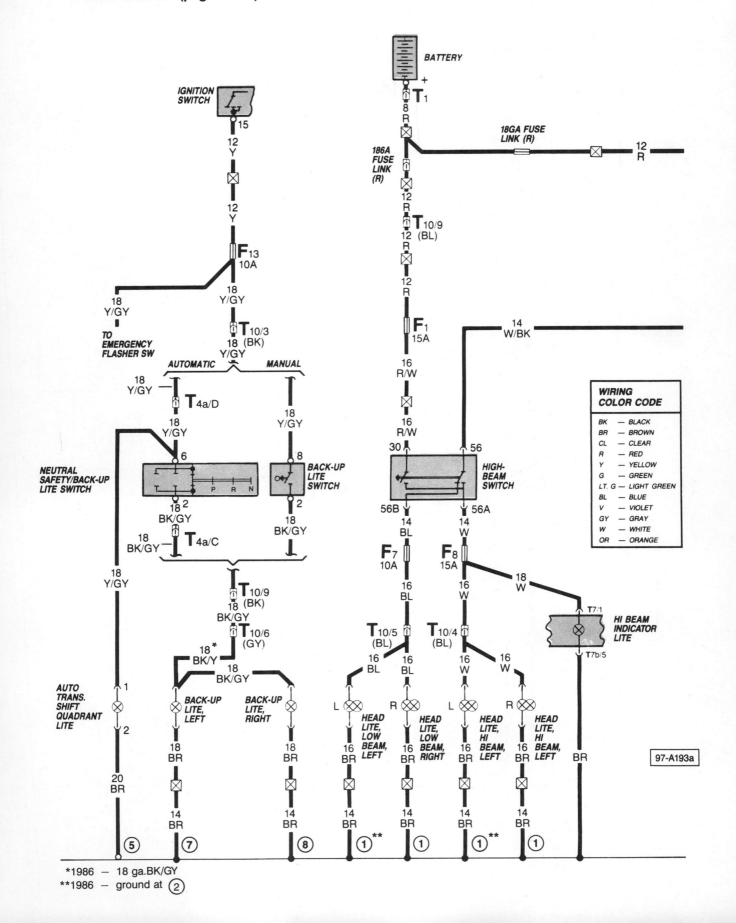

*1986 — 18 ga.BK/GY
**1986 — ground at ②

Exterior Lights
1986–1987 Golf,
1986–1989 GTI (page 2 of 2)

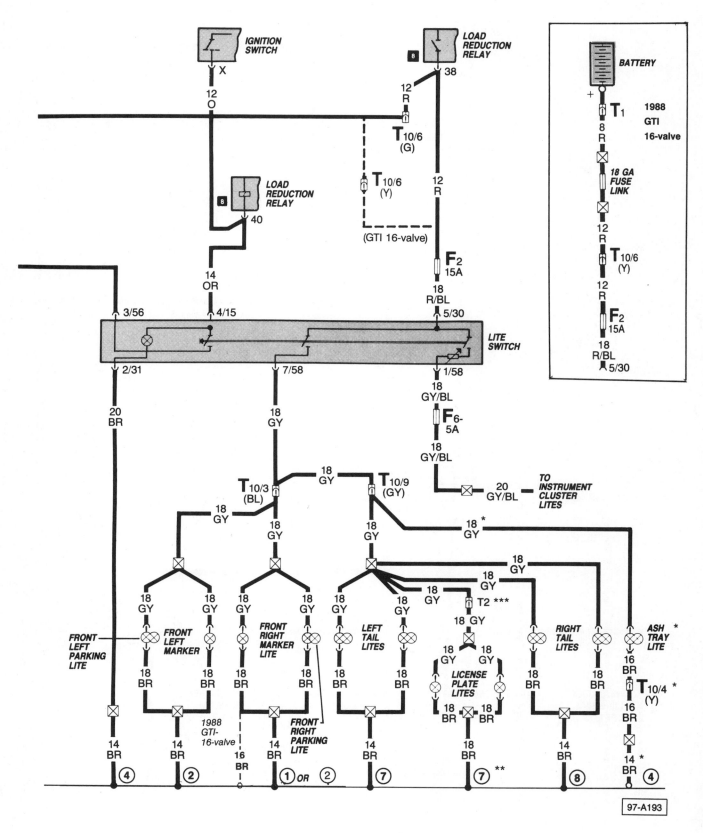

97-A193

*1986 only
**1986 only—1987 ground at ⑨
*** 1987-1989 GTI 16-valve T2f

Exterior Lights
1988-1989 Golf (Gasoline only)
(page 1 of 3)

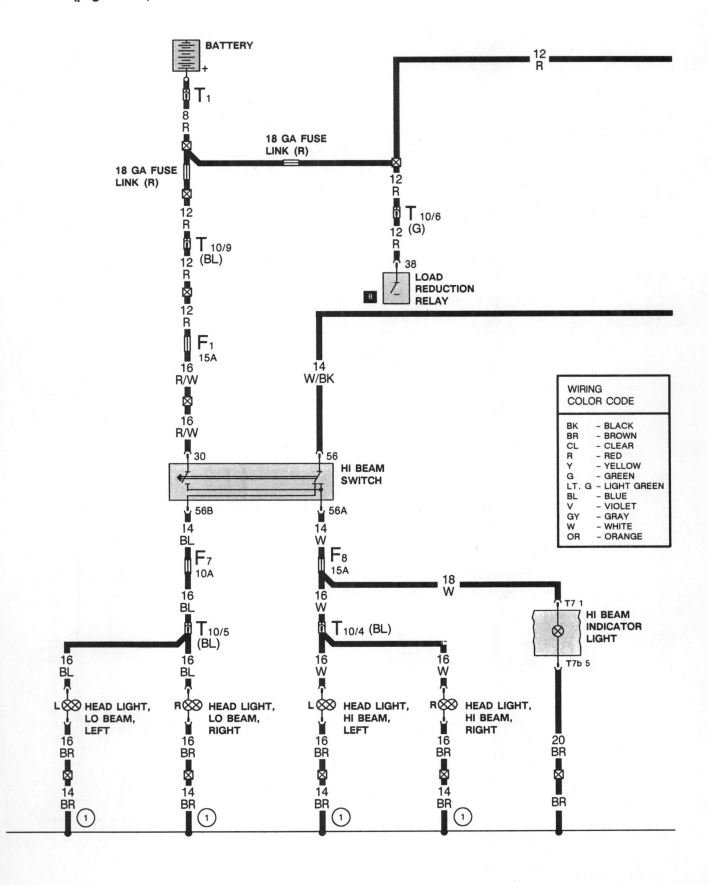

BATTERY

12
R

T₁

8
R

18 GA FUSE
LINK (R)

18 GA FUSE
LINK (R)

12
R

12
R   T 10/6
      (G)

12
R

T 10/9
(BL)

38

12
R

LOAD
REDUCTION
RELAY

12
R

F₁
15A

16
R/W

14
W/BK

16
R/W

30   56

HI BEAM
SWITCH

56B   56A

14   14
BL   W

F₇   F₈
10A   15A

18
W

16   16
BL   W

T 10/5   T 10/4 (BL)
(BL)

T7 1

HI BEAM
INDICATOR
LIGHT

16   16   16   16
BL   BL   W   W

T7b 5

L   HEAD LIGHT,   R   HEAD LIGHT,   L   HEAD LIGHT,   R   HEAD LIGHT,
    LO BEAM,   LO BEAM,   HI BEAM,   HI BEAM,
    LEFT   RIGHT   LEFT   RIGHT

16   16   16   16   20
BR   BR   BR   BR   BR

14   14   14   14
BR   BR   BR   BR   BR

① ① ① ①

WIRING
COLOR CODE

BK   – BLACK
BR   – BROWN
CL   – CLEAR
R   – RED
Y   – YELLOW
G   – GREEN
LT. G – LIGHT GREEN
BL   – BLUE
V   – VIOLET
GY   – GRAY
W   – WHITE
OR   – ORANGE

Exterior Lights
1988-1989 Golf (Gasoline only)
(page 2 of 3)

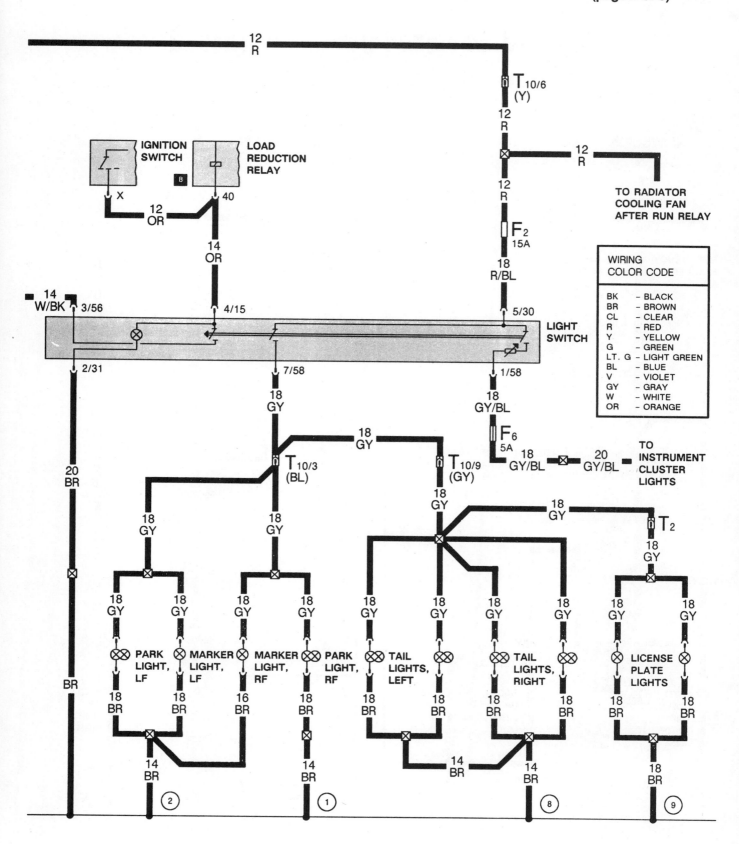

Exterior Lights
1988-1989 Golf (Gasoline only)
(page 3 of 3)

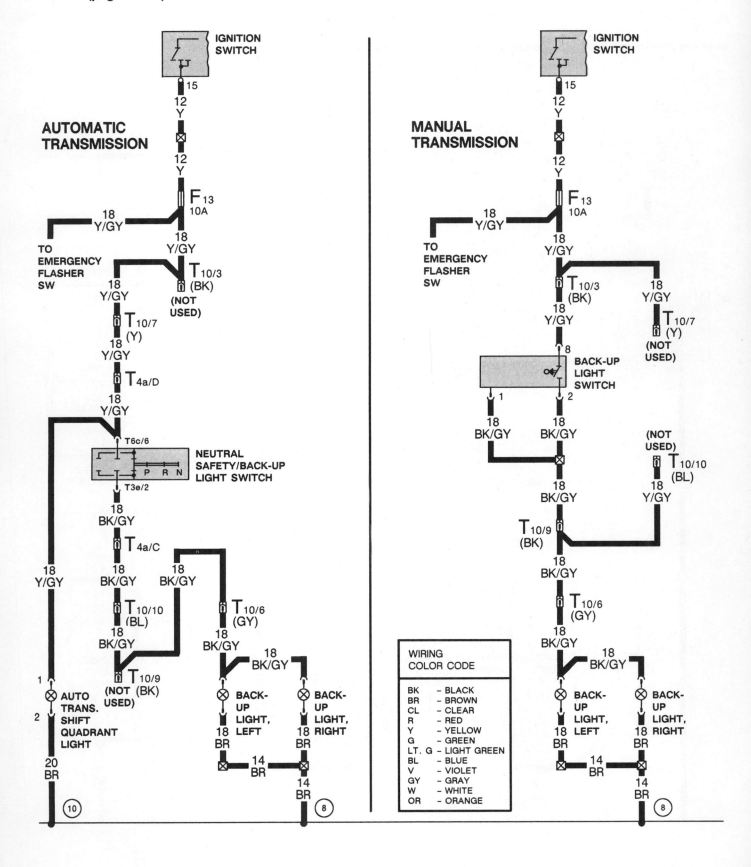

Exterior Lights
1988-1989 Golf Diesel
(page 1 of 2)

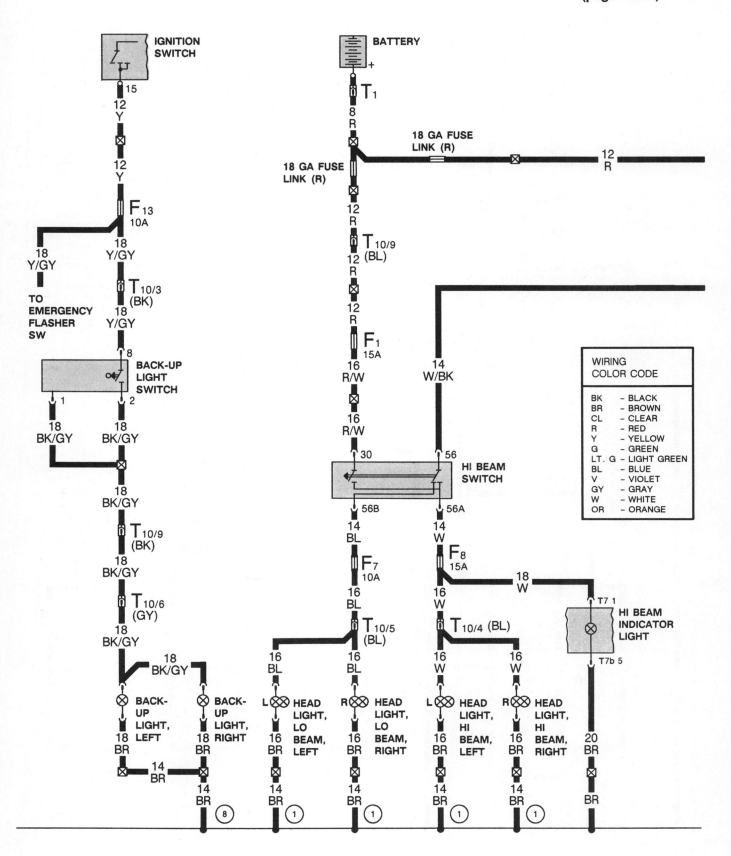

WIRING
COLOR CODE

BK – BLACK
BR – BROWN
CL – CLEAR
R   – RED
Y   – YELLOW
G   – GREEN
LT. G – LIGHT GREEN
BL – BLUE
V   – VIOLET
GY – GRAY
W   – WHITE
OR – ORANGE

Exterior Lights
1988-1989 Golf Diesel
(page 2 of 2)

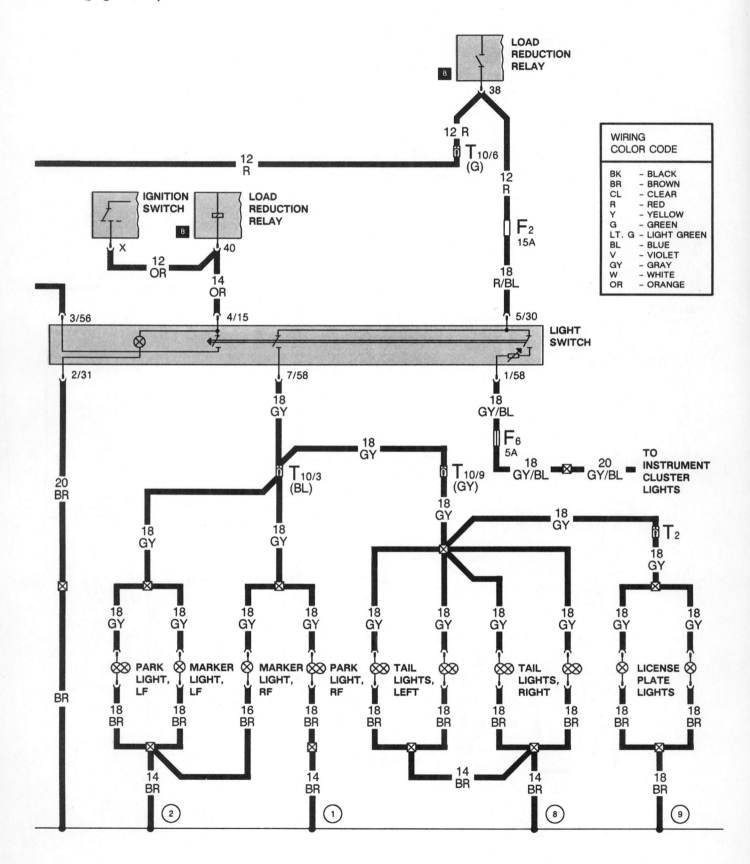

WIRING
COLOR CODE

BK – BLACK
BR – BROWN
CL – CLEAR
R – RED
Y – YELLOW
G – GREEN
LT. G – LIGHT GREEN
BL – BLUE
V – VIOLET
GY – GRAY
W – WHITE
OR – ORANGE

Brake Lights
1985-1989 Golf/GTI
(page 1 of 1)

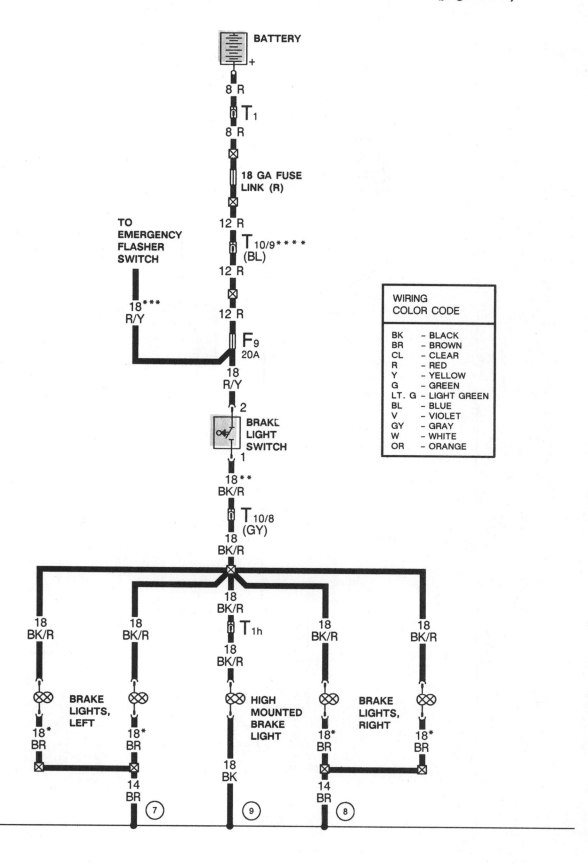

WIRING
COLOR CODE

BK	– BLACK
BR	– BROWN
CL	– CLEAR
R	– RED
Y	– YELLOW
G	– GREEN
LT. G	– LIGHT GREEN
BL	– BLUE
V	– VIOLET
GY	– GRAY
W	– WHITE
OR	– ORANGE

BATTERY

8 R

T_1

8 R

18 GA FUSE
LINK (R)

12 R

$T_{10/9}$ * * * *
(BL)

12 R

12 R

F_9
20A

18
R/Y

TO
EMERGENCY
FLASHER
SWITCH

18 * * *
R/Y

2

BRAKE
LIGHT
SWITCH

1

18 * *
BK/R

$T_{10/8}$
(GY)

18
BK/R

18
BK/R

18
BK/R T_{1h}

18
BK/R

18
BK/R

18
BK/R

18
BK/R

BRAKE
LIGHTS,
LEFT

HIGH
MOUNTED
BRAKE
LIGHT

BRAKE
LIGHTS,
RIGHT

18 *
BR

18 *
BR

18 *
BR

18 *
BR

18
BK

14
BR

14
BR

⑦

⑨

⑧

* 1986 — 16GA

** GTI 16-valve — 14GA

*** GTI 16-valve — 16GA

**** ALL EXCEPT 1985

Courtesy Lights
1985 Golf/GTI
(page 1 of 1)

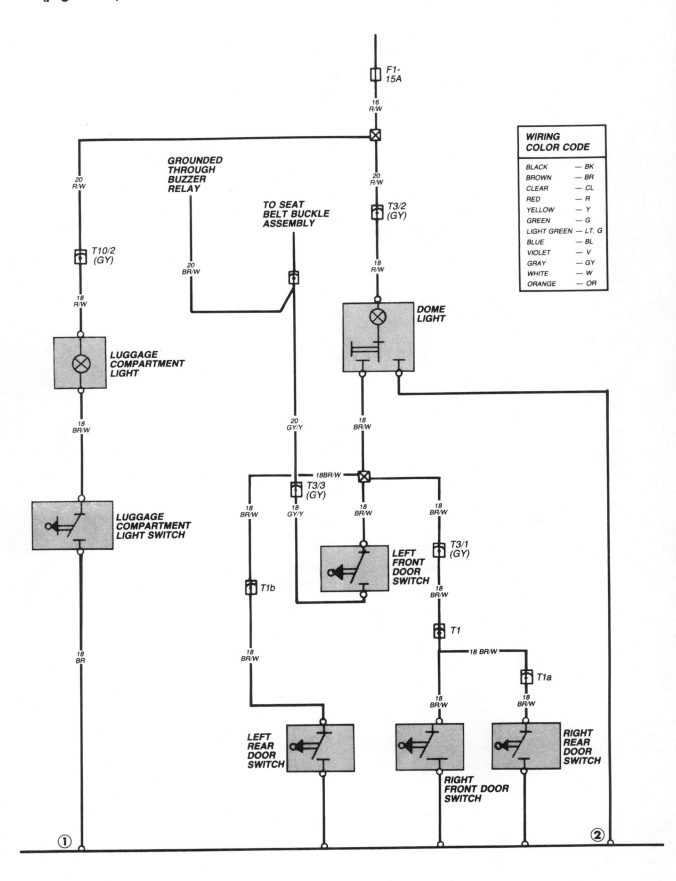

**Interior Lights
1986 Golf/GTI
(page 1 of 1)**

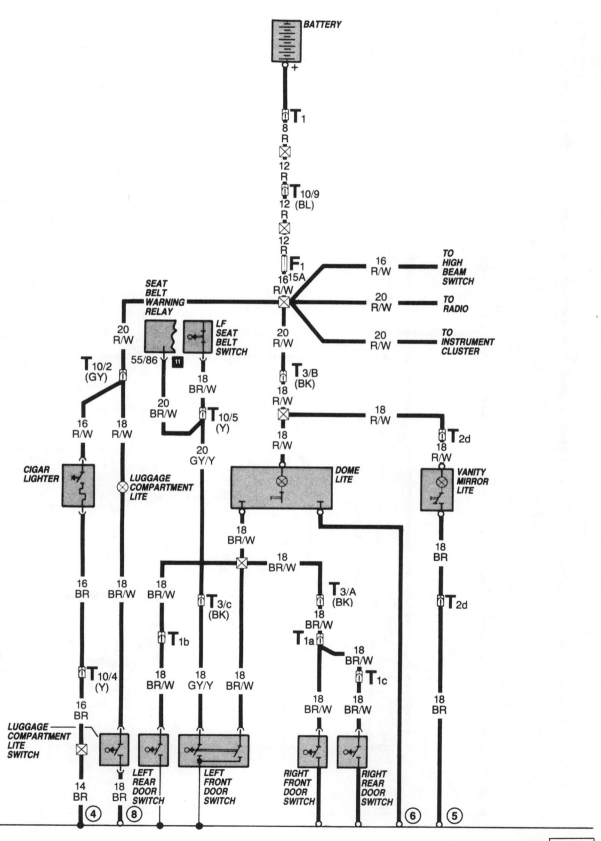

97-A195

Interior Lights
1987-1989 Golf/GTI
(except 16-valve) (page 1 of 1)

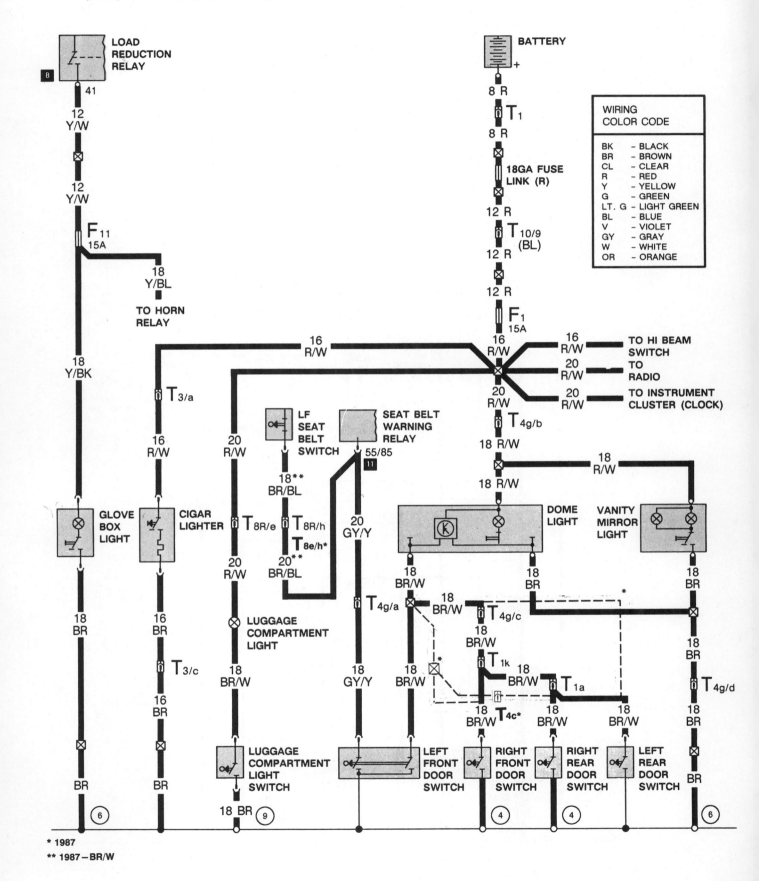

* 1987
** 1987 — BR/W

Interior Lights
1987-1989 GTI 16-valve
(page 1 of 1)

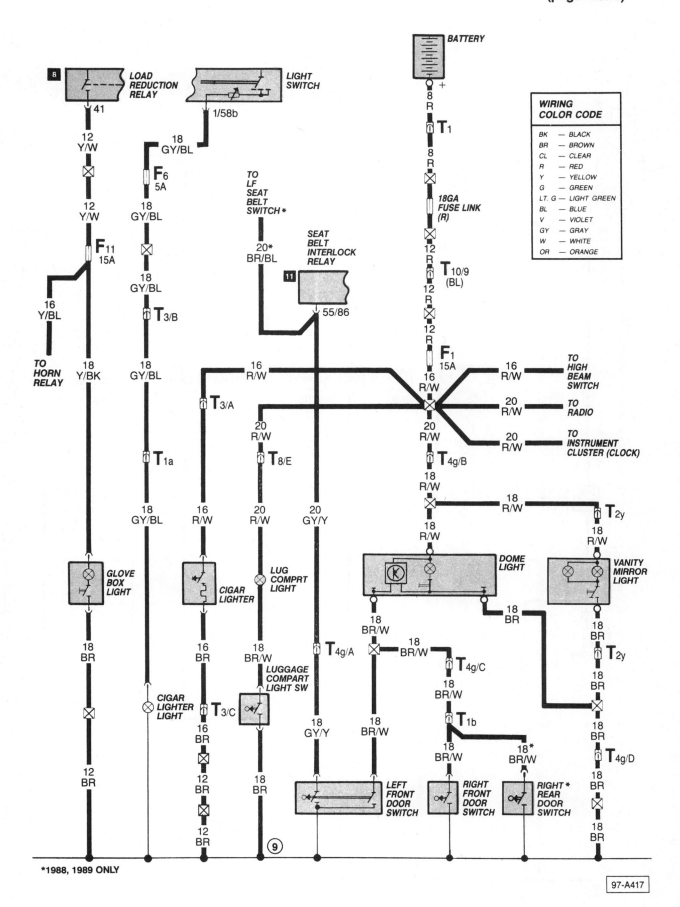

WIRING
COLOR CODE

BK	— BLACK
BR	— BROWN
CL	— CLEAR
R	— RED
Y	— YELLOW
G	— GREEN
LT. G	— LIGHT GREEN
BL	— BLUE
V	— VIOLET
GY	— GRAY
W	— WHITE
OR	— ORANGE

*1988, 1989 ONLY

97-A417

Instrument Panel Lights
1985 Golf/GTI
(page 1 of 1)

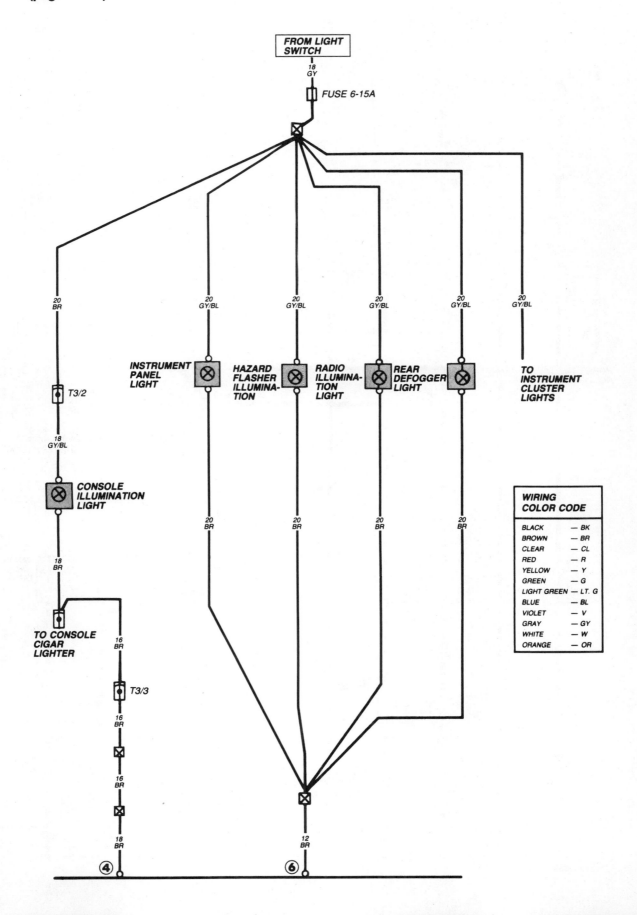

Instrument Panel Lights
1986-1989 Golf/GTI
(page 1 of 1)

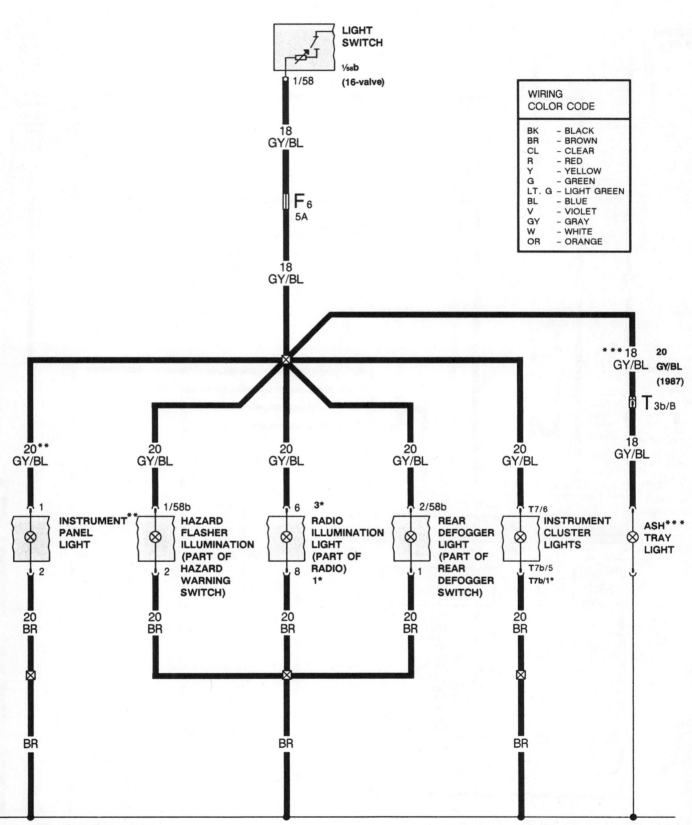

LIGHT
SWITCH

⅛s**b**
1/58   **(16-valve)**

18
GY/BL

F₆
5A

18
GY/BL

WIRING
COLOR CODE

BK – BLACK
BR – BROWN
CL – CLEAR
R   – RED
Y   – YELLOW
G   – GREEN
LT. G – LIGHT GREEN
BL – BLUE
V   – VIOLET
GY – GRAY
W   – WHITE
OR – ORANGE

***18   20
GY/BL GY/BL
       (1987)

T 3b/B

18
GY/BL

20**   20   20   20   20
GY/BL   GY/BL   GY/BL   GY/BL   GY/BL

1   1/58b   6   3*   2/58b   T7/6
INSTRUMENT** HAZARD   RADIO   REAR   INSTRUMENT
PANEL   FLASHER   ILLUMINATION DEFOGGER   CLUSTER
LIGHT   ILLUMINATION LIGHT   LIGHT   LIGHTS
             (PART OF   (PART OF   (PART OF
2   HAZARD   RADIO)   REAR   T7b/5
             WARNING   1*   DEFOGGER   T7b/1*
             SWITCH)   SWITCH)

2   8   1

ASH***
TRAY
LIGHT

20   20   20   20   20
BR   BR   BR   BR   BR

BR   BR   BR

* 1986, 1987 MODELS ONLY

** 1987-1989 MODELS ONLY

*** 1987-1989 MODELS EXCEPT 16-VALVE

Turn Signals/Flashers
1985-1989 Golf/GTI
(page 1 of 1)

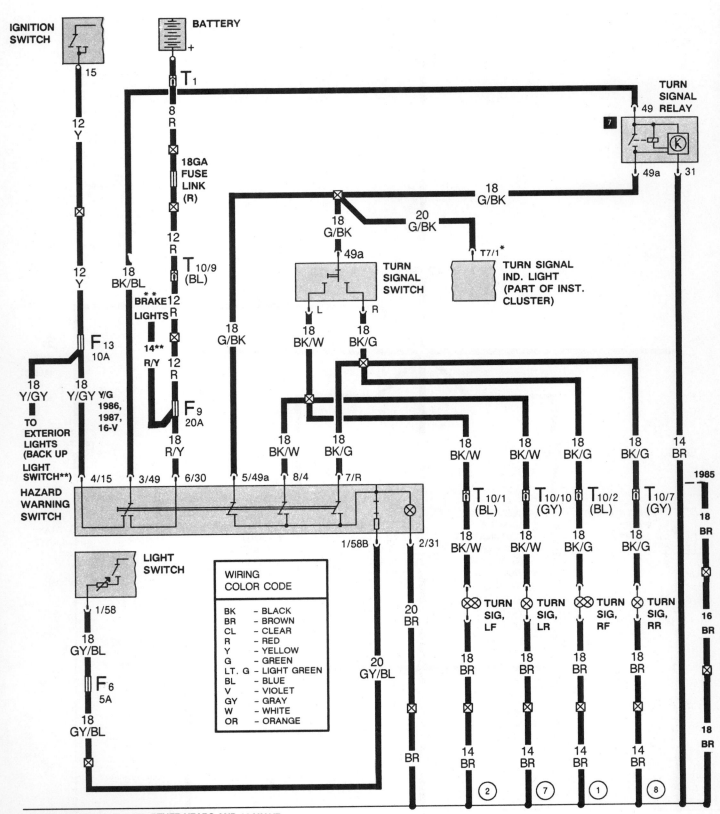

*1988, 1989 ONLY — T⅞ ALL OTHER YEARS AND 16-VALVE

**16-VALVE

Brake Warning Indicator
1985 Golf/GTI
(page 1 of 1)

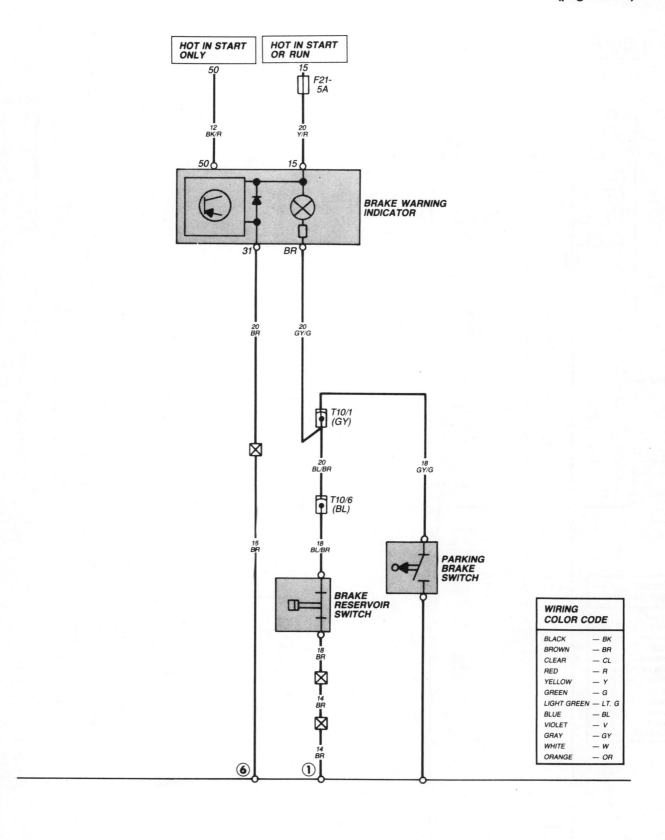

**Instrument Cluster
1985 Golf/GTI
(page 1 of 2)**

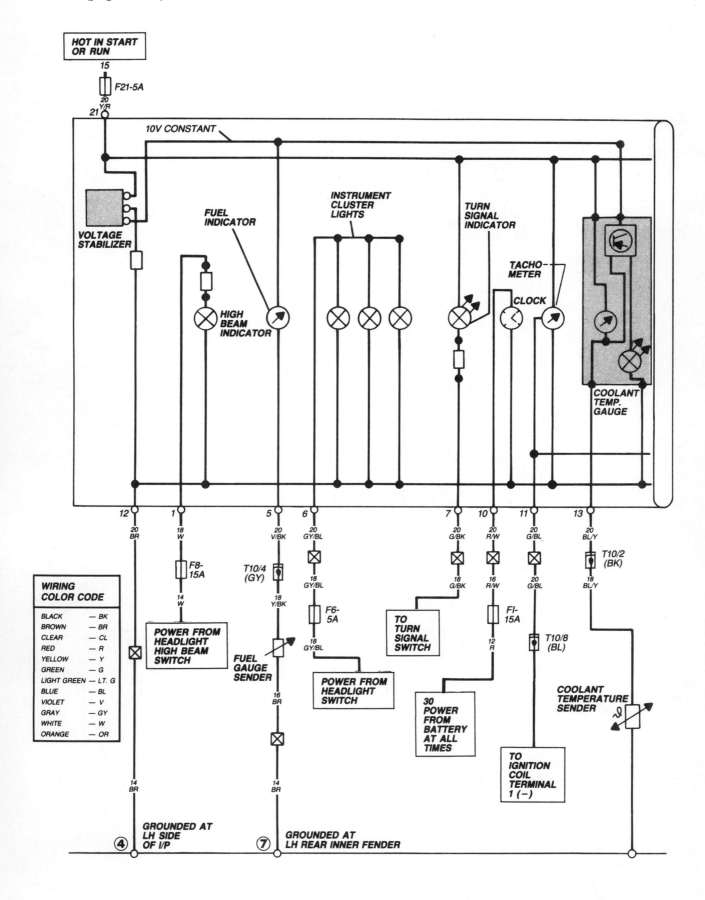

**Instrument Cluster
1985 Golf/GTI
(page 2 of 2)**

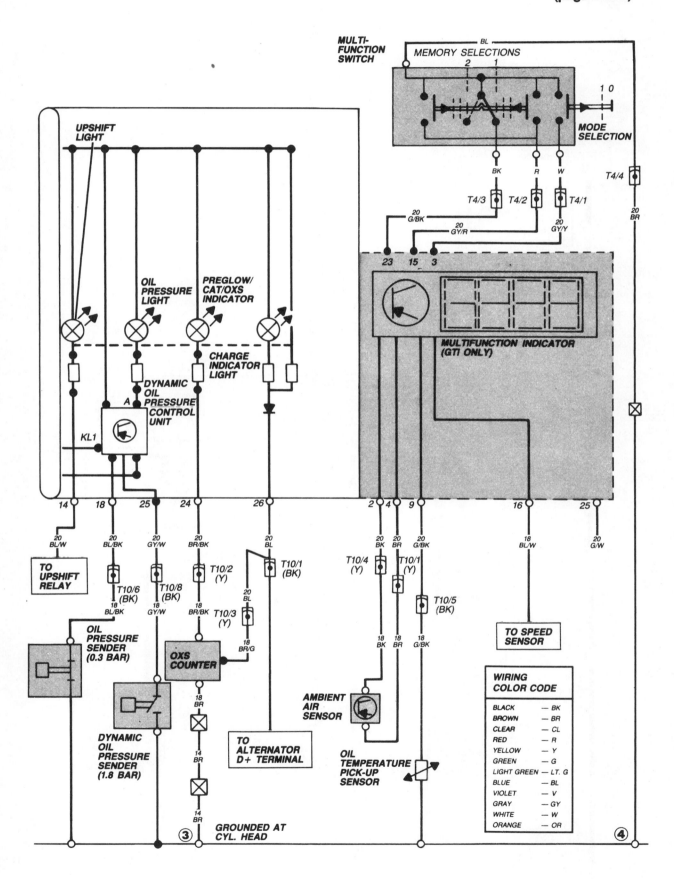

Instrument Cluster
1986 Golf/GTI
(page 1 of 2)

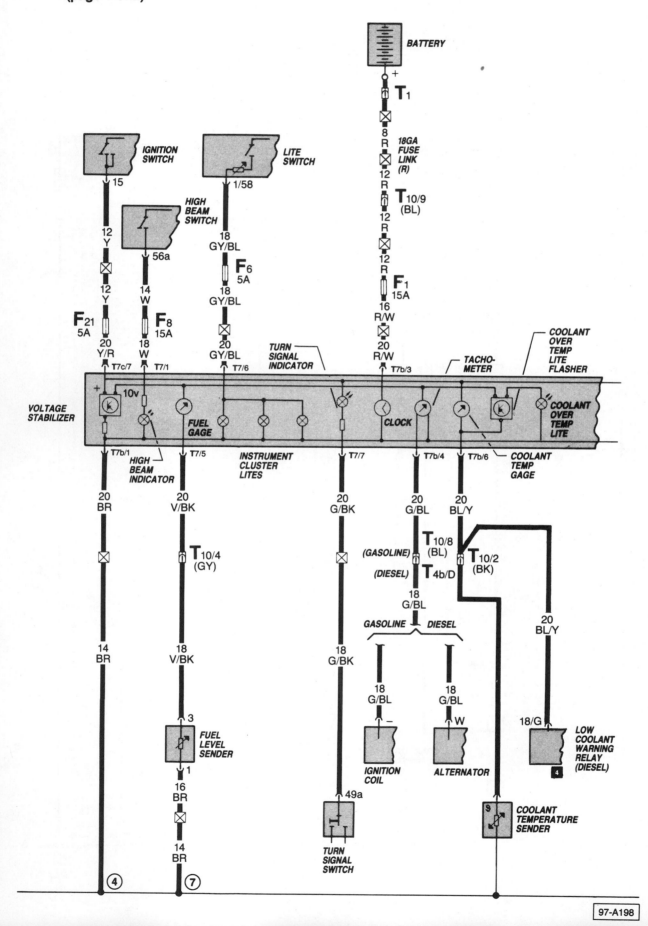

**Instrument Cluster
1986 Golf/GTI
(page 2 of 2)**

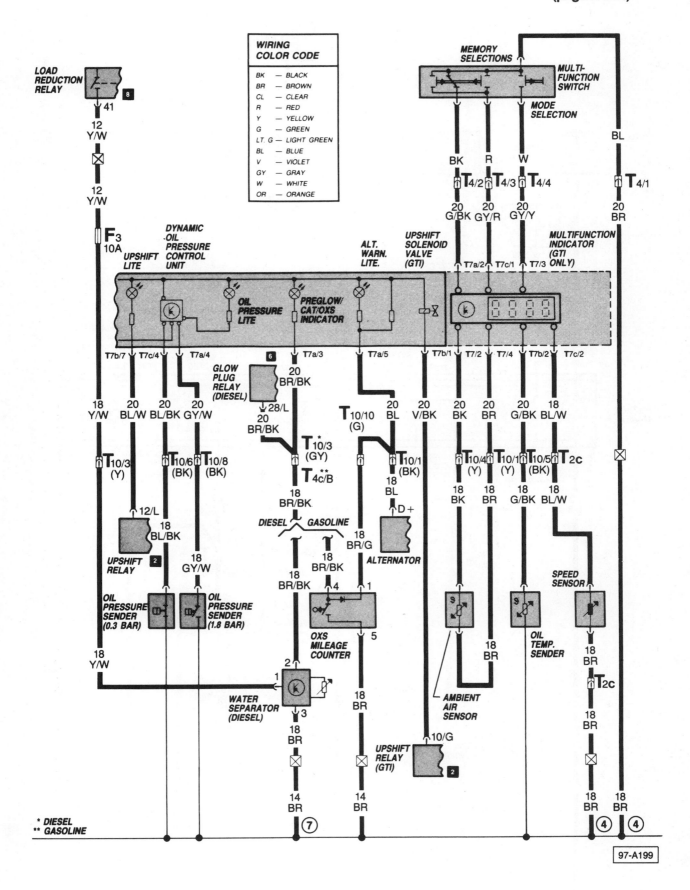

WIRING
COLOR CODE

BK — BLACK
BR — BROWN
CL — CLEAR
R — RED
Y — YELLOW
G — GREEN
LT. G — LIGHT GREEN
BL — BLUE
V — VIOLET
GY — GRAY
W — WHITE
OR — ORANGE

* DIESEL
** GASOLINE

97-A199

Instrument Cluster
1987 Golf/GTI (except 16-valve)
(page 1 of 2)

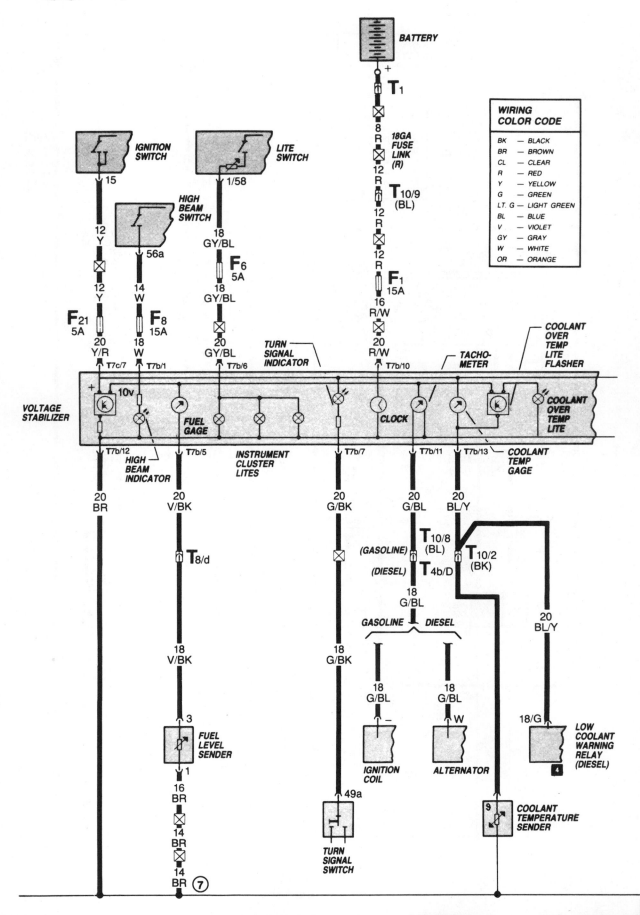

97-A199a

**Instrument Cluster
1987 Golf/GTI (except 16-valve)
(page 2 of 2)**

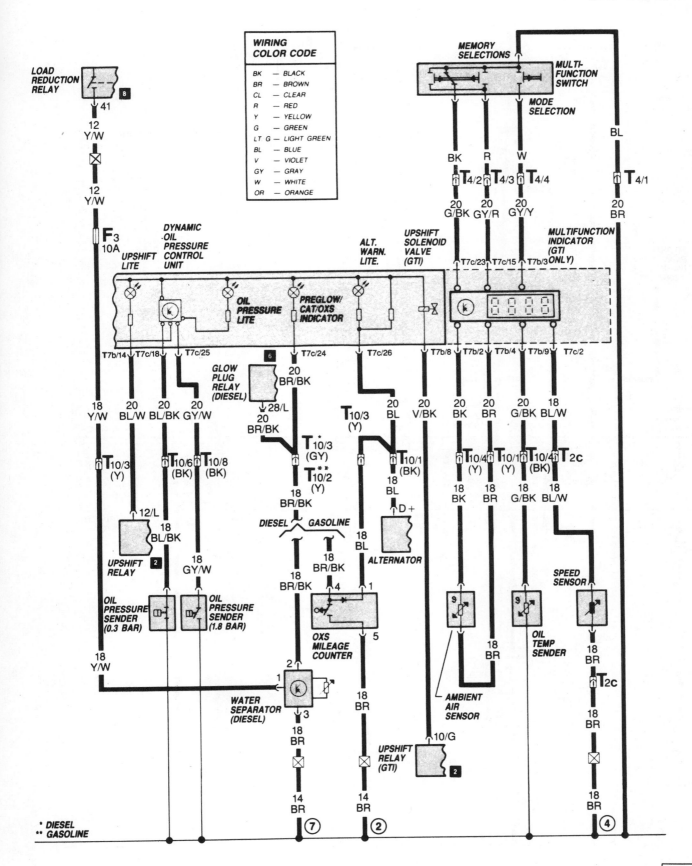

97-A200a

Instrument Cluster
1987-1989 GTI 16-valve
(page 1 of 2)

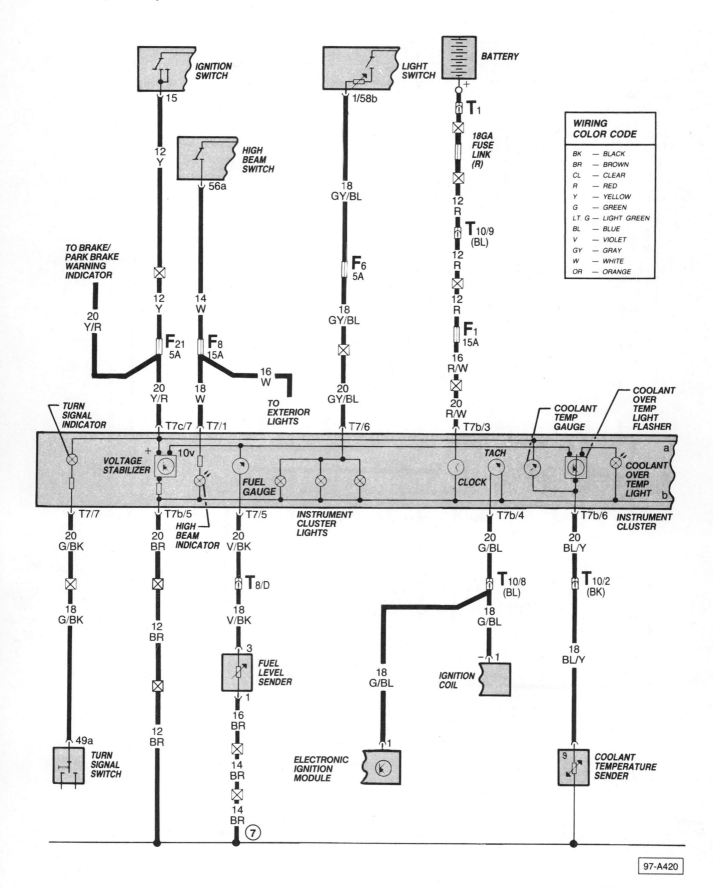

97-A420

**Instrument Cluster
1987-1989 GTI 16-valve
(page 2 of 2)**

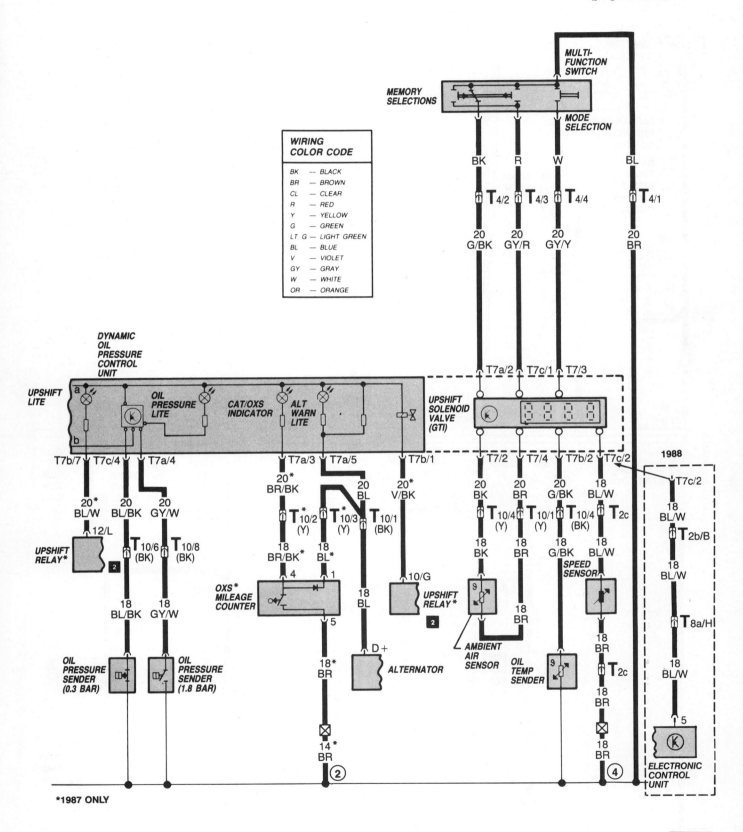

WIRING
COLOR CODE

BK — BLACK
BR — BROWN
CL — CLEAR
R — RED
Y — YELLOW
G — GREEN
LT. G — LIGHT GREEN
BL — BLUE
V — VIOLET
GY — GRAY
W — WHITE
OR — ORANGE

*1987 ONLY

97-A421

Instrument Cluster
1988-1989 Golf
(page 1 of 2)

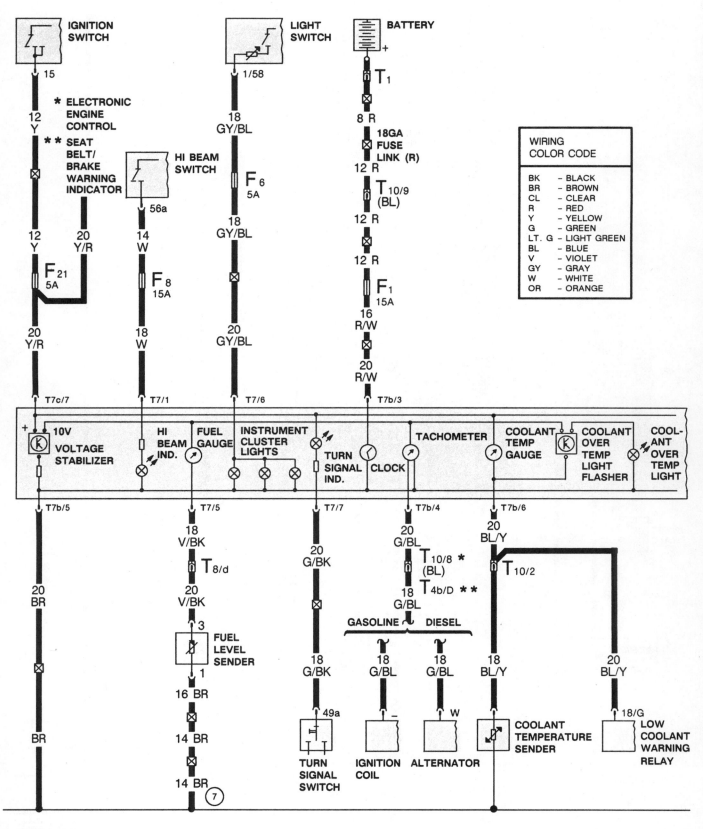

* GAS ONLY
* * DIESEL ONLY

Instrument Cluster
1988-1989 Golf
(page 2 of 2)

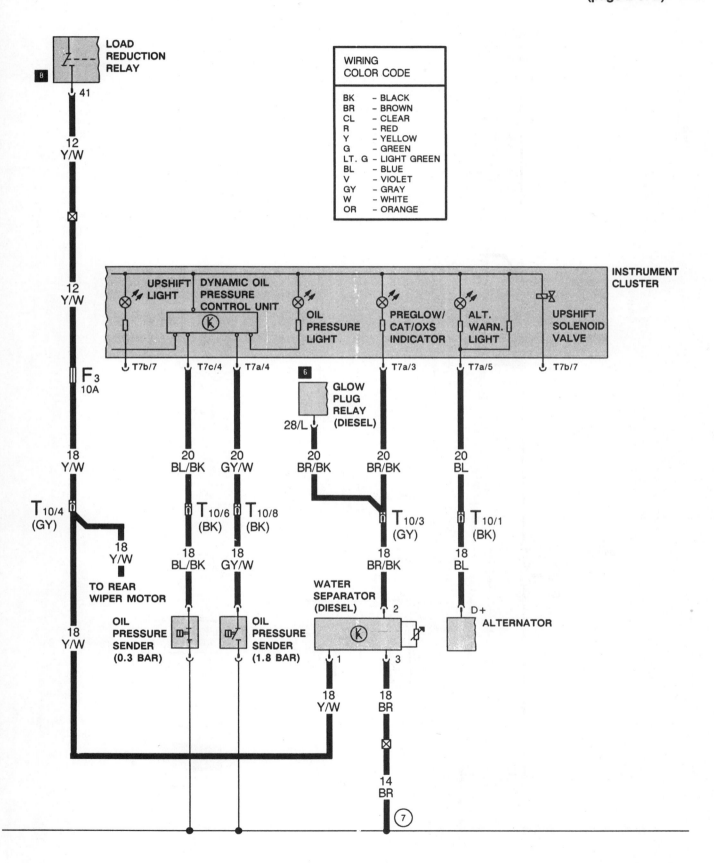

Horns
1985 Golf/GTI
(page 1 of 1)

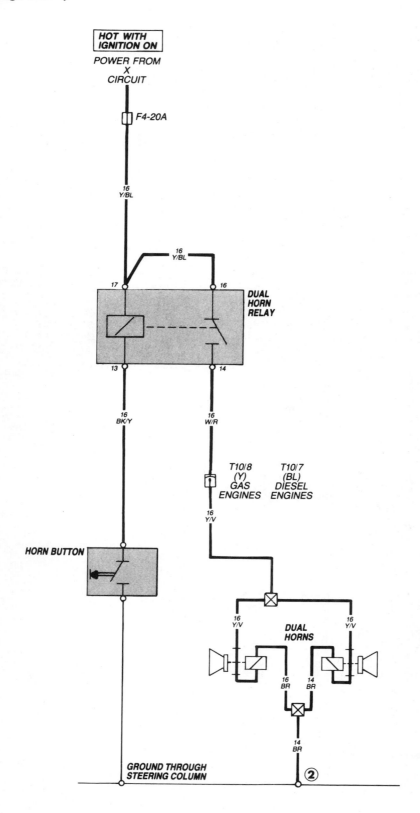

WIRING COLOR CODE	
BLACK	— BK
BROWN	— BR
CLEAR	— CL
RED	— R
YELLOW	— Y
GREEN	— G
LIGHT GREEN	— LT. G
BLUE	— BL
VIOLET	— V
GRAY	— GY
WHITE	— W
ORANGE	— OR

Horns
1986-1989 Golf/GTI
(page 1 of 1)

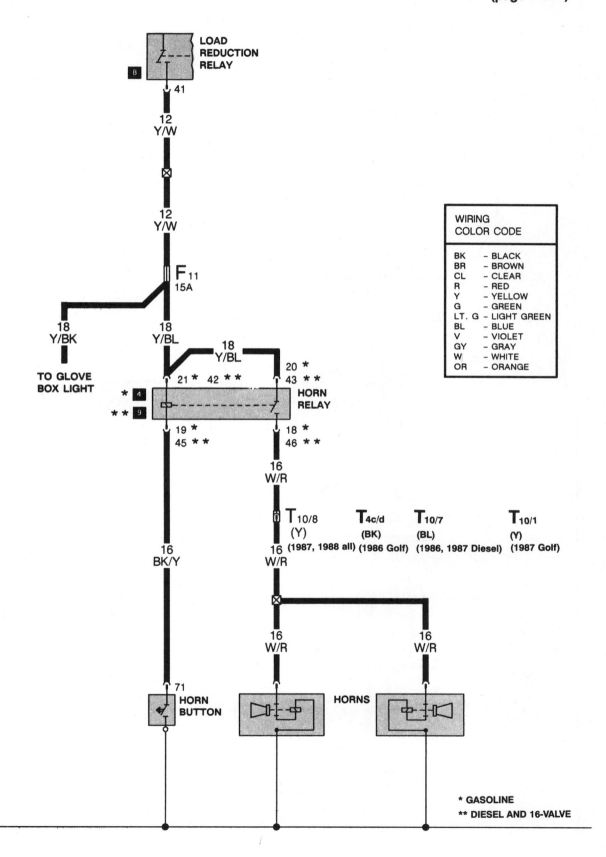

LOAD
REDUCTION
RELAY

B

41

12
Y/W

12
Y/W

F₁₁
15A

18
Y/BK

18
Y/BL

18
Y/BL

TO GLOVE
BOX LIGHT

20 *
43 **

* 4
** 9

21 * 42 **

HORN
RELAY

19 *
45 **

18 *
46 **

16
W/R

T₁₀/₈
(Y)
(1987, 1988 all)

T₄c/d
(BK)
(1986 Golf)

T₁₀/₇
(BL)
(1986, 1987 Diesel)

T₁₀/₁
(Y)
(1987 Golf)

16
BK/Y

16
W/R

16
W/R

16
W/R

71

HORN
BUTTON

HORNS

* GASOLINE
** DIESEL AND 16-VALVE

WIRING
COLOR CODE

BK	– BLACK
BR	– BROWN
CL	– CLEAR
R	– RED
Y	– YELLOW
G	– GREEN
LT. G	– LIGHT GREEN
BL	– BLUE
V	– VIOLET
GY	– GRAY
W	– WHITE
OR	– ORANGE

Windshield Wipers and Washer
1985 Golf/GTI
(page 1 of 1)

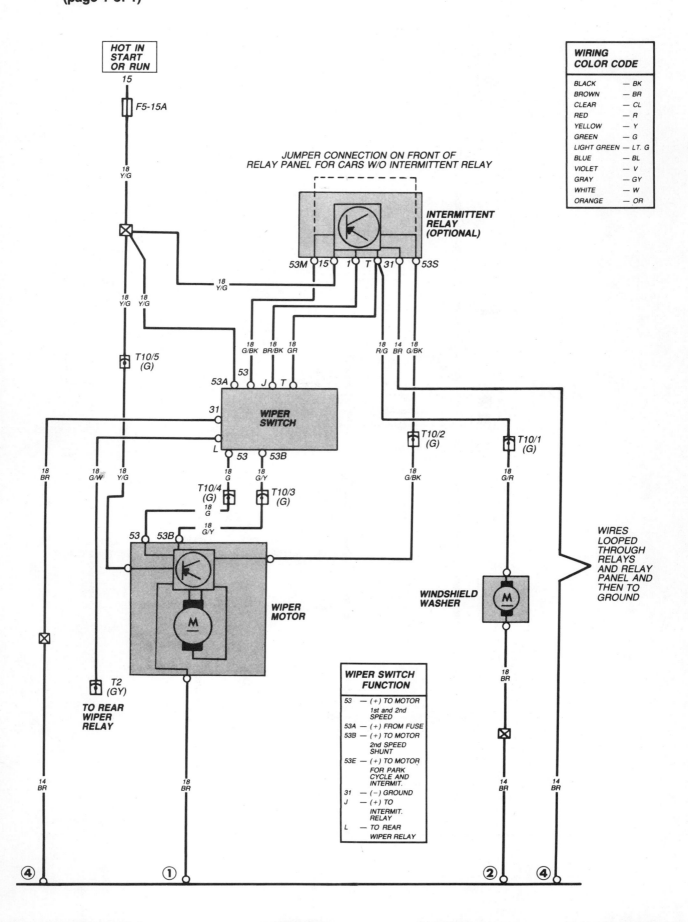

HOT IN
START
OR RUN

15

F5-15A

18
Y/G

JUMPER CONNECTION ON FRONT OF
RELAY PANEL FOR CARS W/O INTERMITTENT RELAY

INTERMITTENT
RELAY
(OPTIONAL)

53M 15   1   T   31   53S

18
Y/G

18   18   18
Y/G   Y/G

18
G/BK

18   18   18
G/BK   BR/BK   GR

18   14   18
R/G   BR   G/BK

T10/5
(G)

53A   53   J   T

31

WIPER
SWITCH

L   53   53B

T10/2
(G)

T10/1
(G)

18
BR

18
G/W

18
Y/G

18
G

18
G/Y

18
G/BK

18
G/R

T10/4
(G)

T10/3
(G)

18
G

18
G/Y

53   53B

WIPER
MOTOR

M

WINDSHIELD
WASHER

M

WIRES
LOOPED
THROUGH
RELAYS
AND RELAY
PANEL AND
THEN TO
GROUND

T2
(GY)

TO REAR
WIPER
RELAY

18
BR

14
BR

18
BR

14
BR

14
BR

WIPER SWITCH FUNCTION

53	— (+) TO MOTOR 1st and 2nd SPEED
53A	— (+) FROM FUSE
53B	— (+) TO MOTOR 2nd SPEED SHUNT
53E	— (+) TO MOTOR FOR PARK CYCLE AND INTERMIT.
31	— (−) GROUND
J	— (+) TO INTERMIT. RELAY
L	— TO REAR WIPER RELAY

4   1   2   4

WIRING COLOR CODE

BLACK	— BK
BROWN	— BR
CLEAR	— CL
RED	— R
YELLOW	— Y
GREEN	— G
LIGHT GREEN	— LT. G
BLUE	— BL
VIOLET	— V
GRAY	— GY
WHITE	— W
ORANGE	— OR

**Windshield Wiper and Washer
1986 Golf/GTI
(page 1 of 1)**

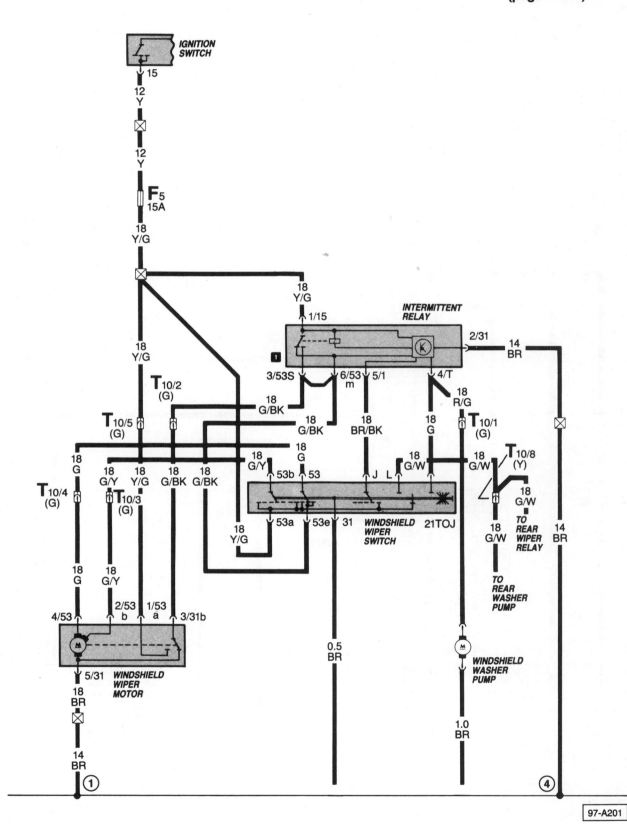

97-A201

Windshield Wipers and Washer
1987-1989 Golf/GTI
(page 1 of 1)

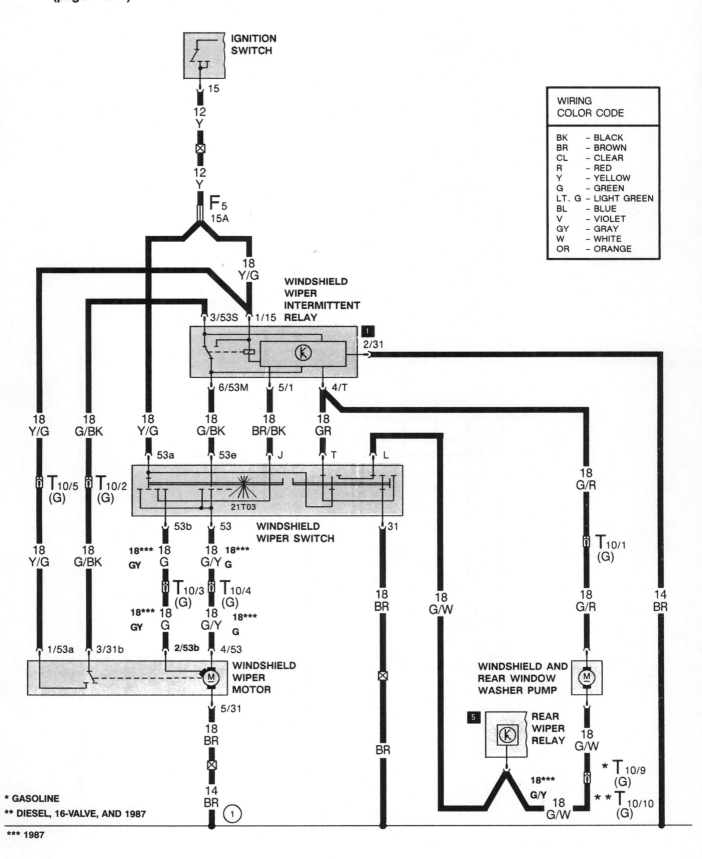

IGNITION SWITCH

WIRING COLOR CODE

BK	– BLACK
BR	– BROWN
CL	– CLEAR
R	– RED
Y	– YELLOW
G	– GREEN
LT. G	– LIGHT GREEN
BL	– BLUE
V	– VIOLET
GY	– GRAY
W	– WHITE
OR	– ORANGE

WINDSHIELD WIPER INTERMITTENT RELAY

WINDSHIELD WIPER SWITCH

21T03

WINDSHIELD WIPER MOTOR

WINDSHIELD AND REAR WINDOW WASHER PUMP

REAR WIPER RELAY

* GASOLINE
** DIESEL, 16-VALVE, AND 1987
*** 1987

**Rear Wiper and Washer
1985 Golf/GTI
(page 1 of 1)**

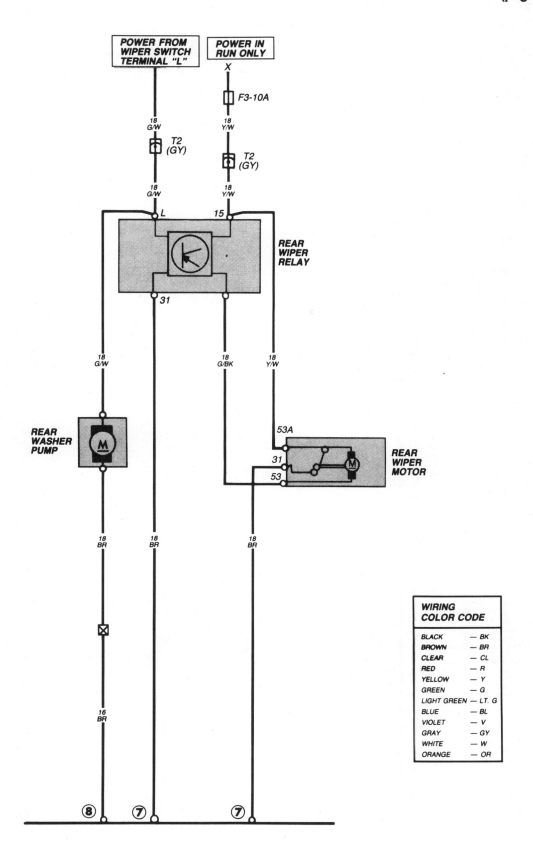

**POWER FROM
WIPER SWITCH
TERMINAL "L"**

**POWER IN
RUN ONLY**

X

F3-10A

18
G/W

18
Y/W

T2
(GY)

T2
(GY)

18
G/W

18
Y/W

L   15

**REAR
WIPER
RELAY**

31

18
G/W

18
G/BK

18
Y/W

**REAR
WASHER
PUMP**

53A

31

53

**REAR
WIPER
MOTOR**

18
BR

18
BR

18
BR

16
BR

⑧   ⑦   ⑦

WIRING COLOR CODE	
BLACK	— BK
BROWN	— BR
CLEAR	— CL
RED	— R
YELLOW	— Y
GREEN	— G
LIGHT GREEN	— LT. G
BLUE	— BL
VIOLET	— V
GRAY	— GY
WHITE	— W
ORANGE	— OR

Rear Wiper and Washer
1986 Golf/GTI
(page 1 of 1)

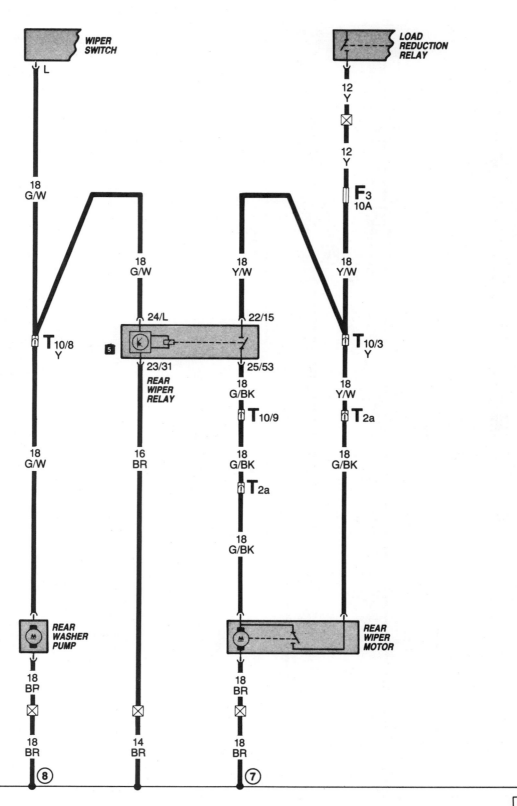

97-A202

**Rear Wiper and Washer
1987-1989 Golf/GTI
(page 1 of 1)**

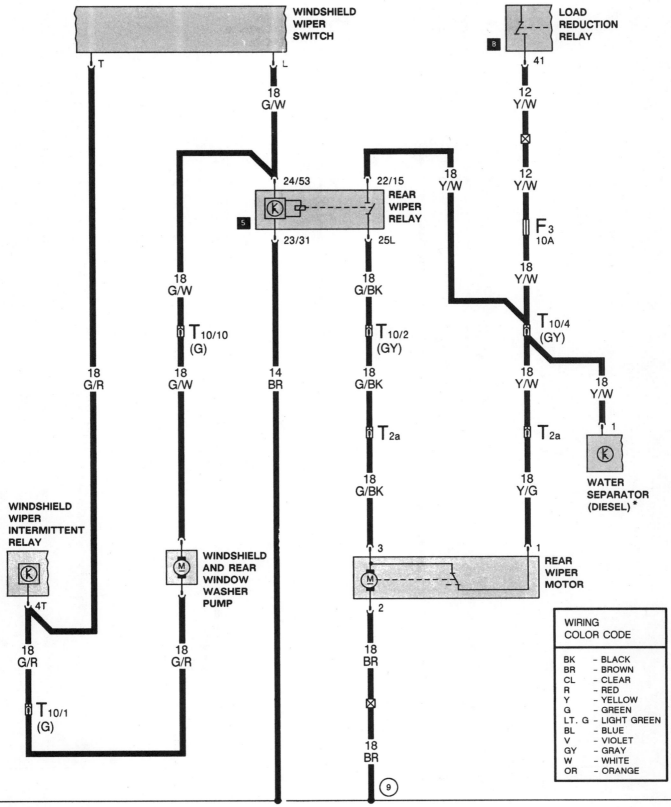

* 1988, 1989

Rear Window Defogger
1985-1989 Golf/GTI
(page 1 of 1)

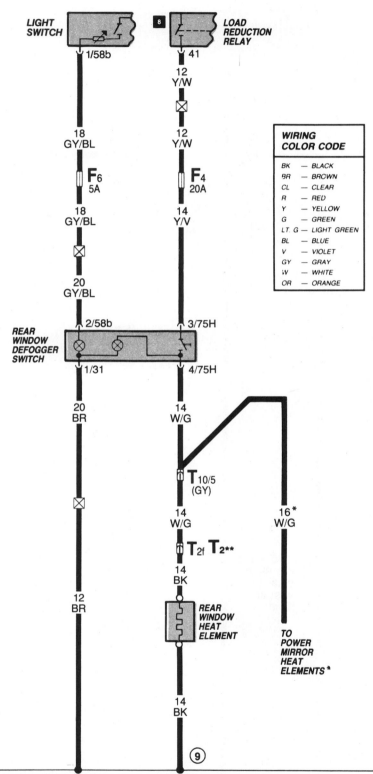

WIRING COLOR CODE	
BK	— BLACK
BR	— BROWN
CL	— CLEAR
R	— RED
Y	— YELLOW
G	— GREEN
LT. G	— LIGHT GREEN
BL	— BLUE
V	— VIOLET
GY	— GRAY
W	— WHITE
OR	— ORANGE

* NOT USED—1985—ALL; 1988, 1989 GOLF, GOLF GL, GOLF GT, GOLF GL DIESEL
** 1985

97-A425

**Glow Plugs
1985 Golf Diesel
(page 1 of 1)**

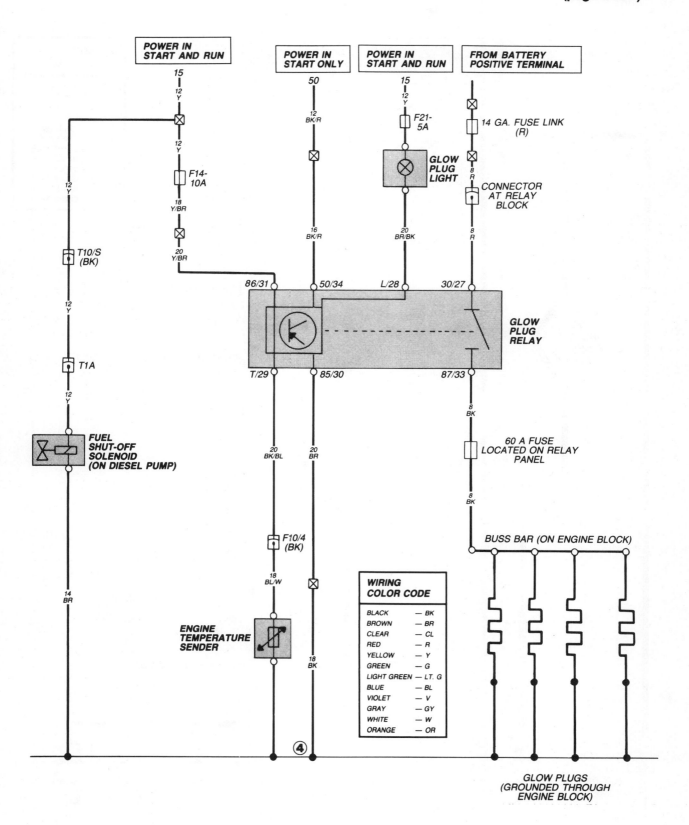

WIRING
COLOR CODE

BLACK	— BK
BROWN	— BR
CLEAR	— CL
RED	— R
YELLOW	— Y
GREEN	— G
LIGHT GREEN	— LT. G
BLUE	— BL
VIOLET	— V
GRAY	— GY
WHITE	— W
ORANGE	— OR

Glow Plugs
1986-1989 Golf Diesel
(page 1 of 1)

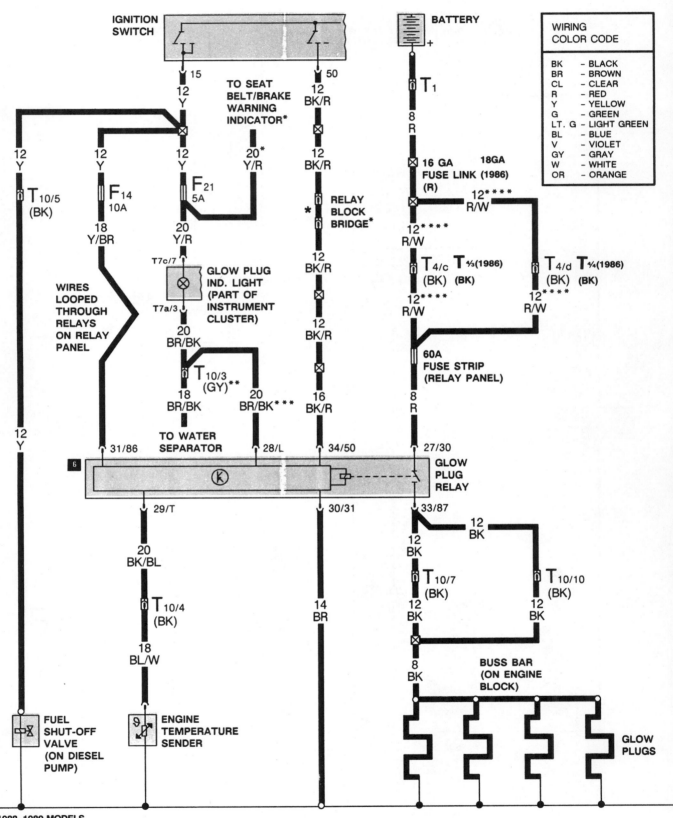

* **1988, 1989 MODELS**

** **1986, 1987 – T10/3 (BK)**

*** **1987 – Y/BR**

**** **1986 – R**

**Electronic Engine Control
1985 Golf (CIS-Canada)
(page 1 of 1)**

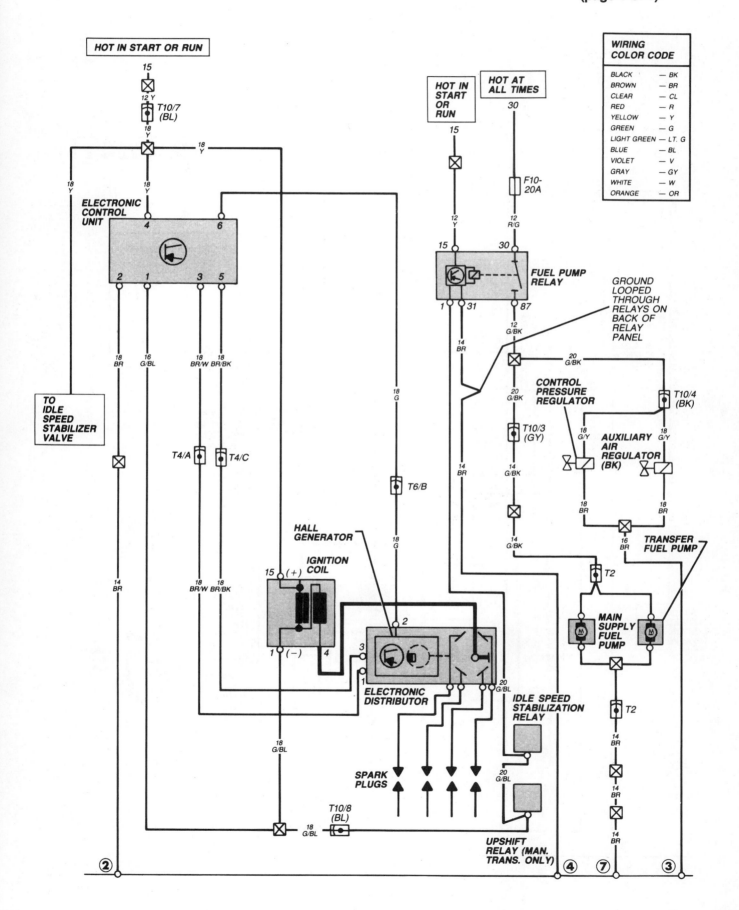

WIRING COLOR CODE	
BLACK	— BK
BROWN	— BR
CLEAR	— CL
RED	— R
YELLOW	— Y
GREEN	— G
LIGHT GREEN	— LT. G
BLUE	— BL
VIOLET	— V
GRAY	— GY
WHITE	— W
ORANGE	— OR

Electronic Engine Control
1985 Golf (CIS-E)
(page 1 of 2)

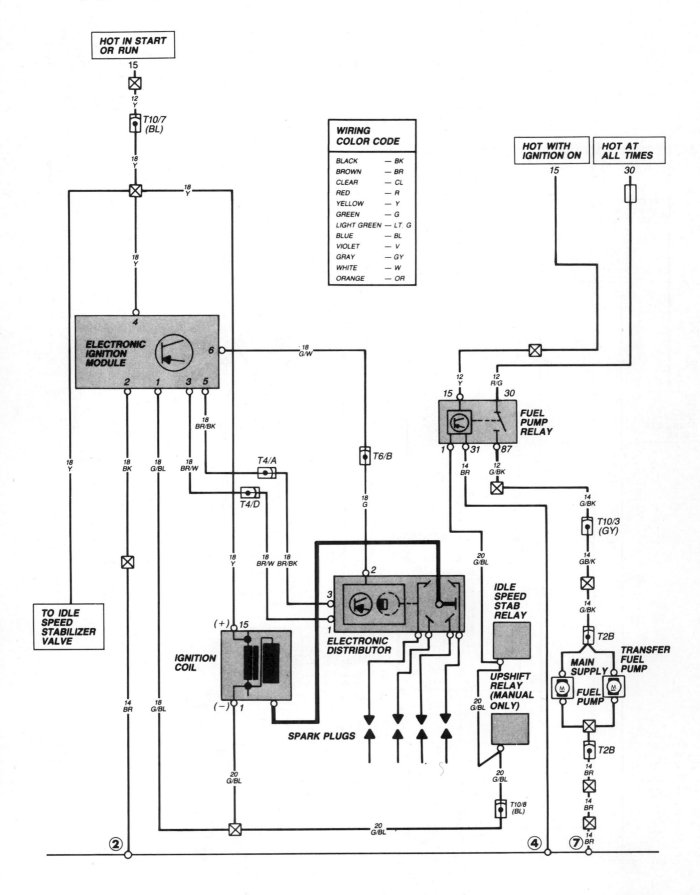

WIRING COLOR CODE	
BLACK	— BK
BROWN	— BR
CLEAR	— CL
RED	— R
YELLOW	— Y
GREEN	— G
LIGHT GREEN	— LT. G
BLUE	— BL
VIOLET	— V
GRAY	— GY
WHITE	— W
ORANGE	— OR

**Electronic Engine Control
1985 Golf (CIS-E)
(page 2 of 2)**

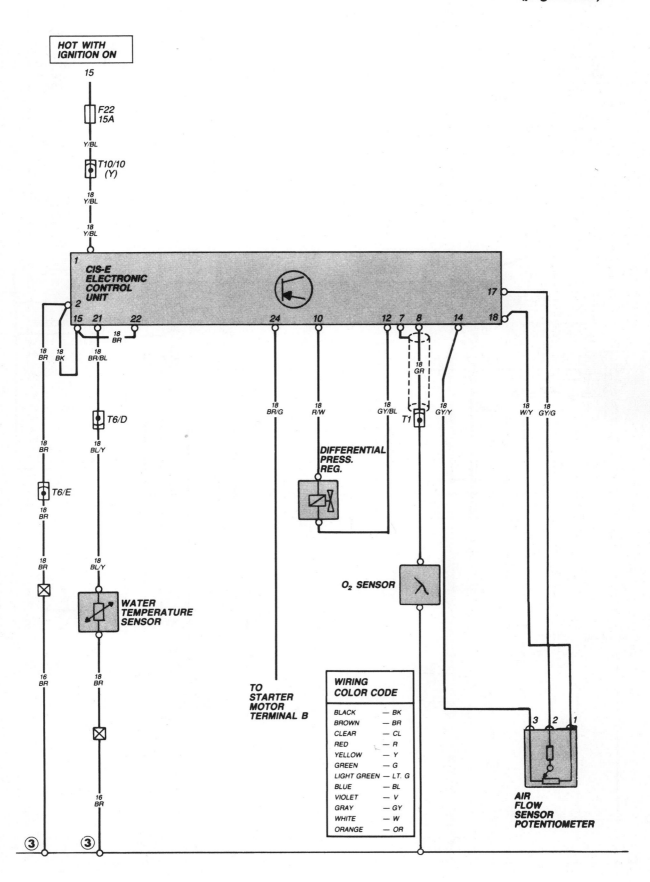

HOT WITH IGNITION ON

15

F22
15A

Y/BL

T10/10
(Y)

18
Y/BL

18
Y/BL

1

**CIS-E
ELECTRONIC
CONTROL
UNIT**

2   17

15   21   22   24   10   12 7 8   14   18

18
BR

18   18   18   18   18   18   18   18   18
BR   BK   BR/BL   BR/G   R/W   GY/BL   GR   GY/Y   W/Y GY/G

T6/D

18   18
BR   BL/Y

T6/E

18
BR

18
BR

T1

18
BR

18
BL/Y

**DIFFERENTIAL
PRESS.
REG.**

**WATER
TEMPERATURE
SENSOR**

O₂ SENSOR

16   18
BR   BR

16
BR

**TO
STARTER
MOTOR
TERMINAL B**

WIRING COLOR CODE	
BLACK	— BK
BROWN	— BR
CLEAR	— CL
RED	— R
YELLOW	— Y
GREEN	— G
LIGHT GREEN	— LT. G
BLUE	— BL
VIOLET	— V
GRAY	— GY
WHITE	— W
ORANGE	— OR

3   2   1

**AIR
FLOW
SENSOR
POTENTIOMETER**

③   ③

**Electronic Engine Control
1985 GTI
(page 1 of 2)**

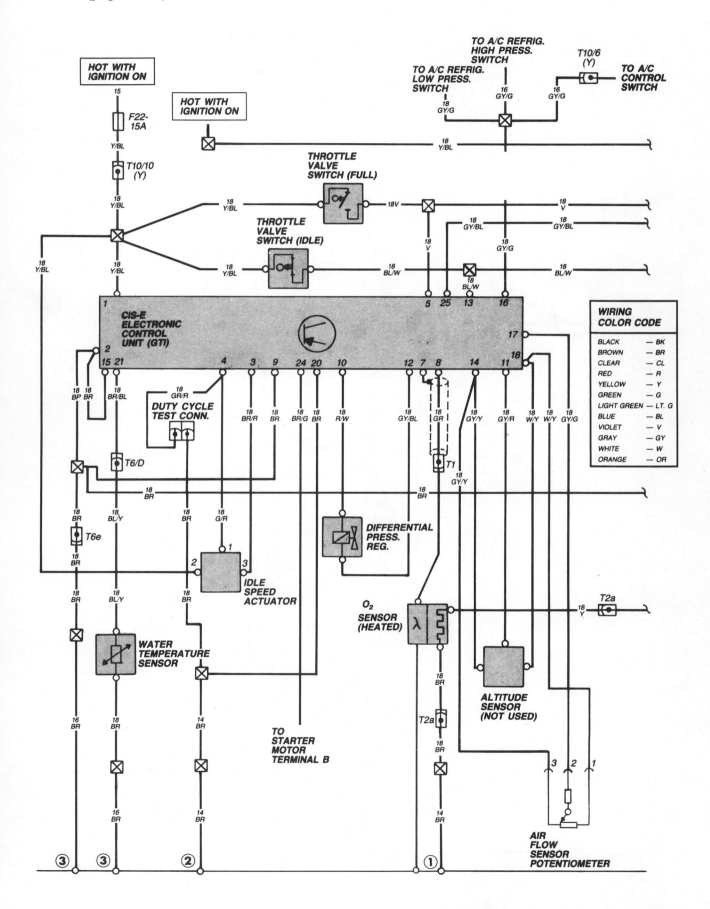

**Electronic Engine Control
1985 GTI
(page 2 of 2)**

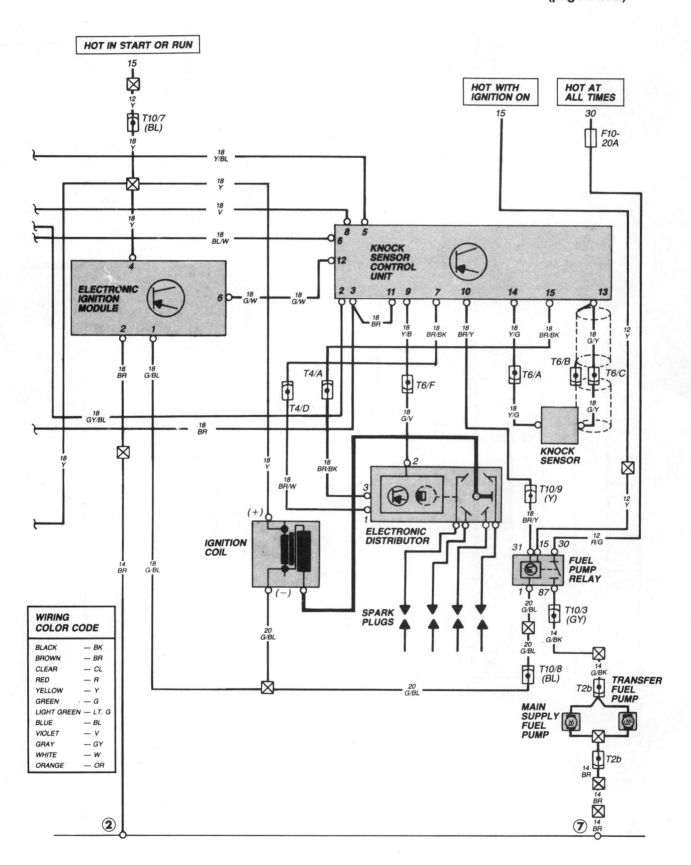

Electronic Engine Control
1986 Golf (CIS)
(page 1 of 2)

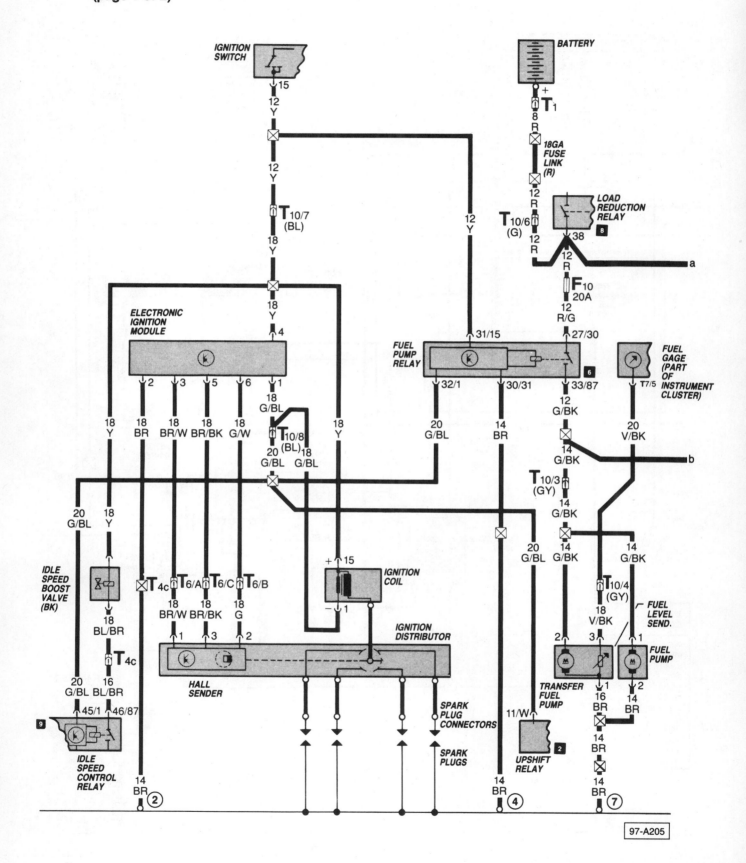

97-A205

Electronic Engine Control
1986 Golf (CIS)
(page 2 of 2)

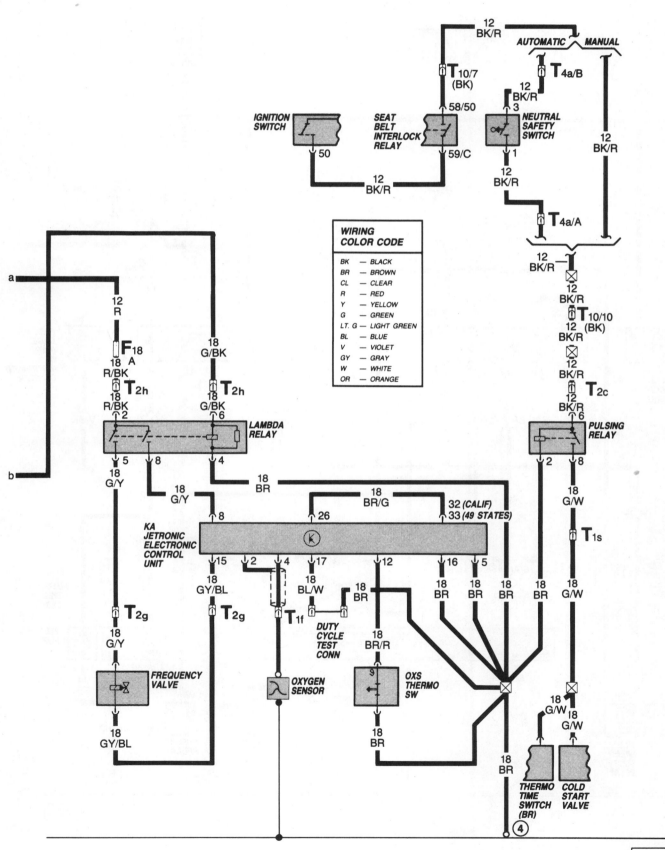

WIRING COLOR CODE

BK	— BLACK
BR	— BROWN
CL	— CLEAR
R	— RED
Y	— YELLOW
G	— GREEN
LT. G	— LIGHT GREEN
BL	— BLUE
V	— VIOLET
GY	— GRAY
W	— WHITE
OR	— ORANGE

97-A210

Electronic Engine Control
1986 Golf (CIS-E)
(page 1 of 2)

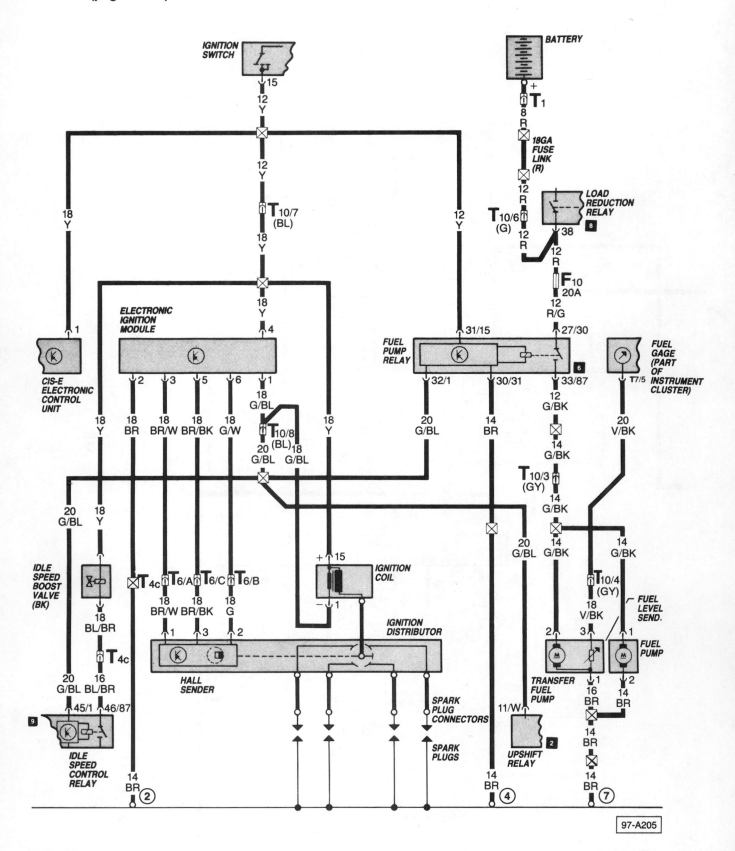

97-A205

**Electronic Engine Control
1986 Golf (CIS-E)
(page 2 of 2)**

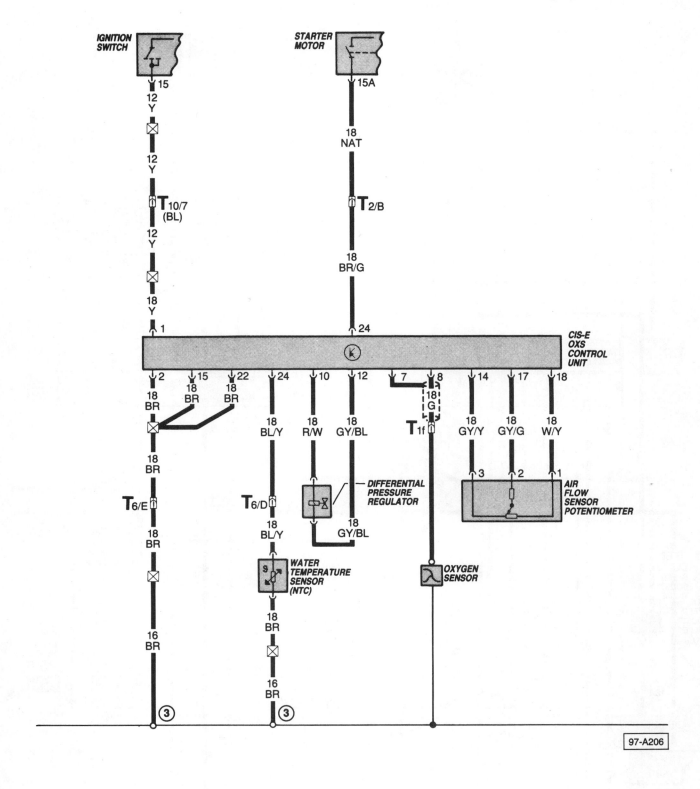

97-A206

Electronic Engine Control
1987 Golf (CIS)
(page 1 of 2)

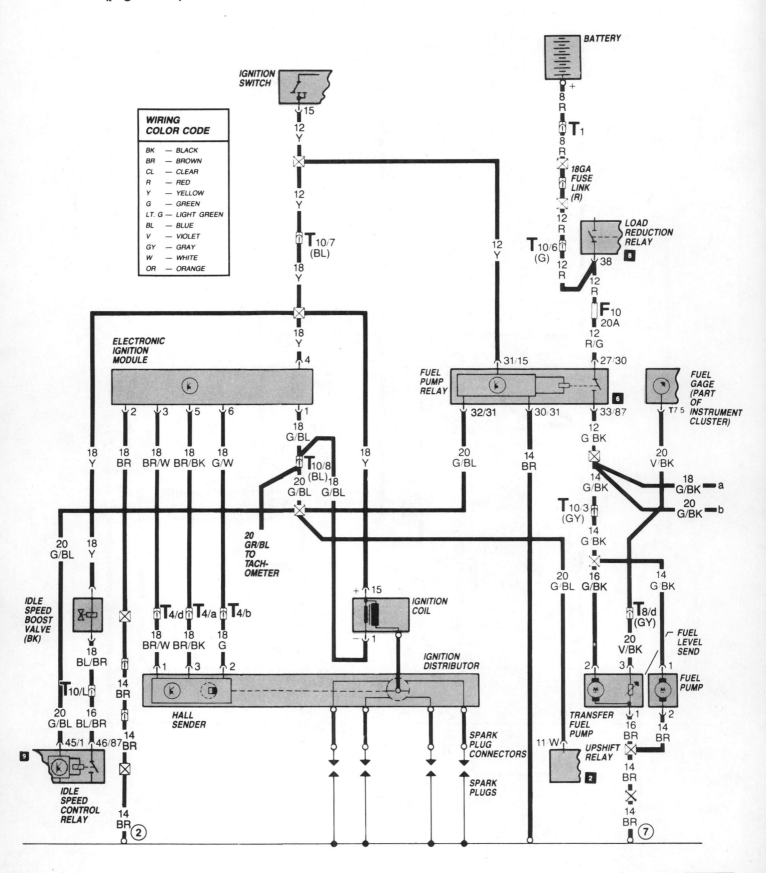

97-A209a

Electronic Engine Control
1987 Golf (CIS)
(page 2 of 2)

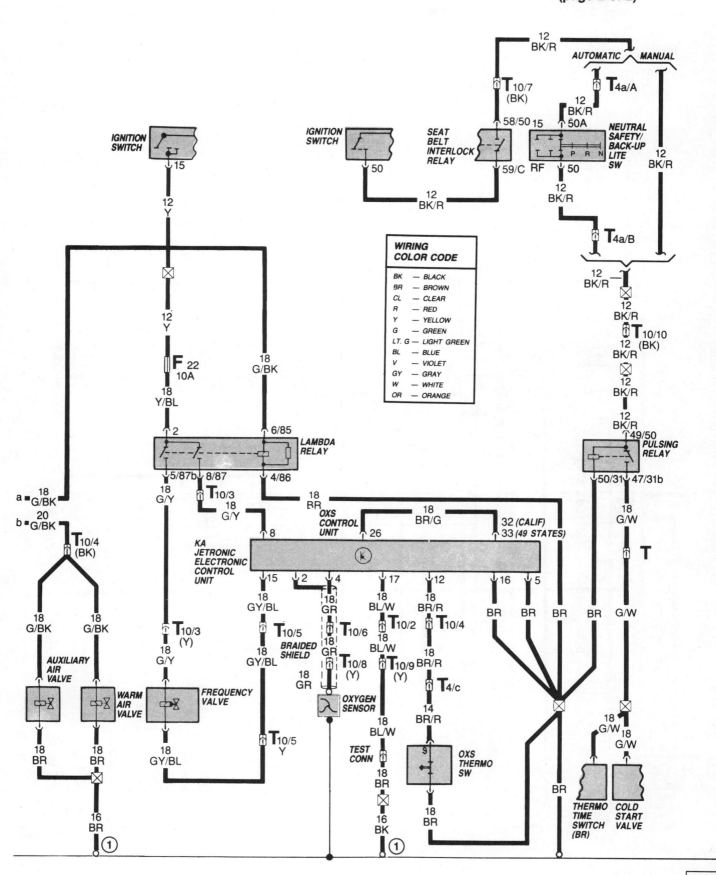

WIRING COLOR CODE

BK — BLACK
BR — BROWN
CL — CLEAR
R — RED
Y — YELLOW
G — GREEN
LT. G — LIGHT GREEN
BL — BLUE
V — VIOLET
GY — GRAY
W — WHITE
OR — ORANGE

97-A210a

Electronic Engine Control
1987 Golf GT, 1986–1987 GTI
(except 16-valve)
(page 1 of 3)

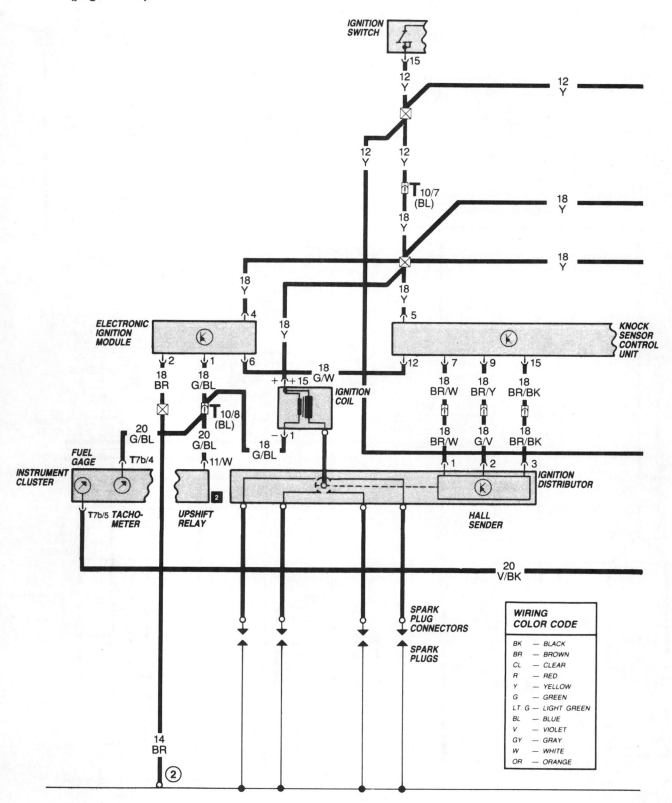

97-A206a

Electronic Engine Control
1987 Golf GT, 1986–1987 GTI
(except 16-valve)
(page 2 of 3)

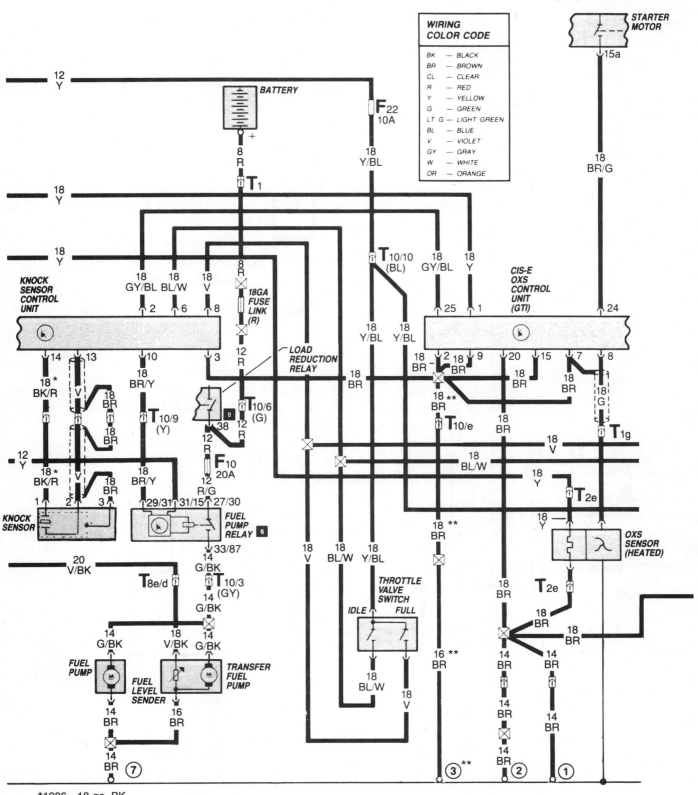

WIRING COLOR CODE

BK	— BLACK
BR	— BROWN
CL	— CLEAR
R	— RED
Y	— YELLOW
G	— GREEN
LT G	— LIGHT GREEN
BL	— BLUE
V	— VIOLET
GY	— GRAY
W	— WHITE
OR	— ORANGE

*1986 – 18 ga. BK
**1987 only

97-A207a

Electronic Engine Control
1987 Golf GT, 1986–1987 GTI
(except 16-valve)
(page 3 of 3)

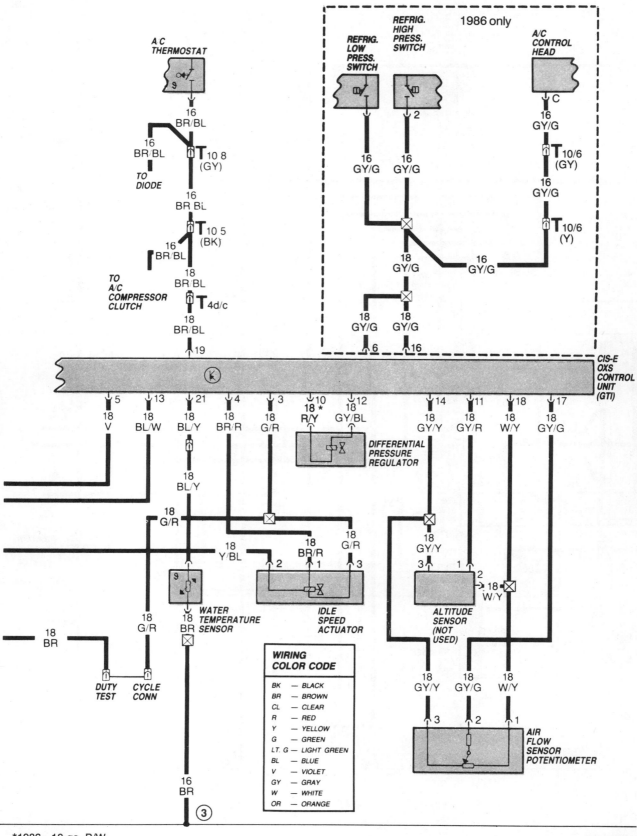

*1986—18 ga. R/W

97-A208a

**Electronic Engine Control
1987-1989 GTI 16-valve
(page 1 of 3)**

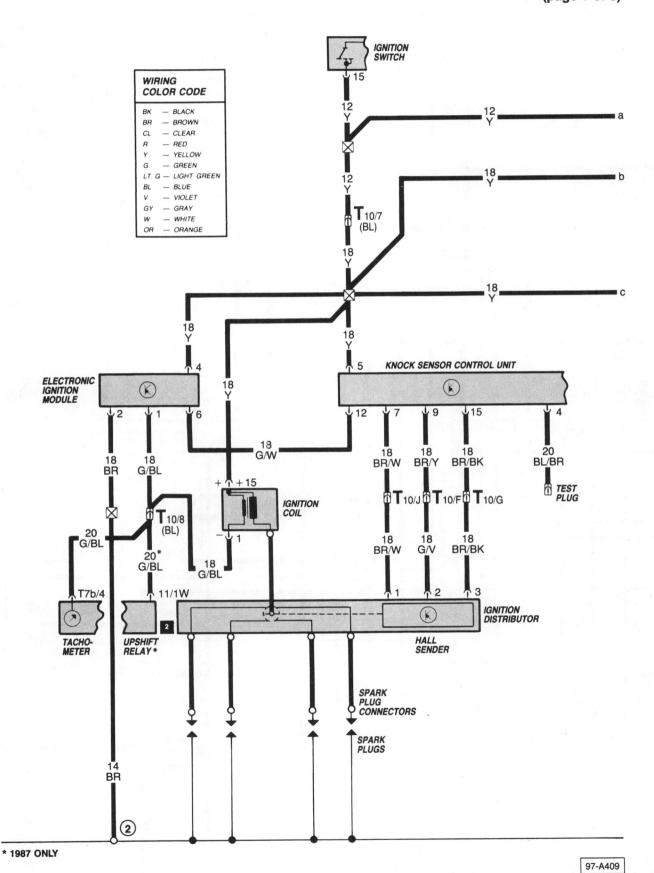

WIRING
COLOR CODE

BK — BLACK
BR — BROWN
CL — CLEAR
R — RED
Y — YELLOW
G — GREEN
LT. G — LIGHT GREEN
BL — BLUE
V — VIOLET
GY — GRAY
W — WHITE
OR — ORANGE

IGNITION
SWITCH

KNOCK SENSOR CONTROL UNIT

ELECTRONIC
IGNITION
MODULE

IGNITION
COIL

TEST
PLUG

TACHO-
METER

UPSHIFT
RELAY *

IGNITION
DISTRIBUTOR

HALL
SENDER

SPARK
PLUG
CONNECTORS

SPARK
PLUGS

* 1987 ONLY

97-A409

Electronic Engine Control
1987-1989 GTI 16-valve
(page 2 of 3)

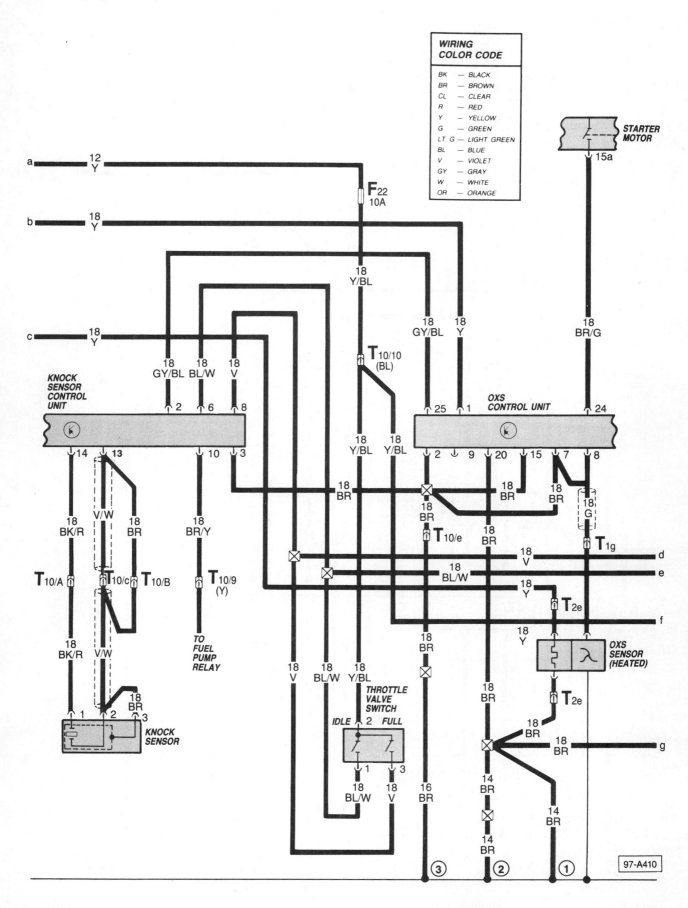

97-A410

**Electronic Engine Control
1987-1989 GTI 16-valve
(page 3 of 3)**

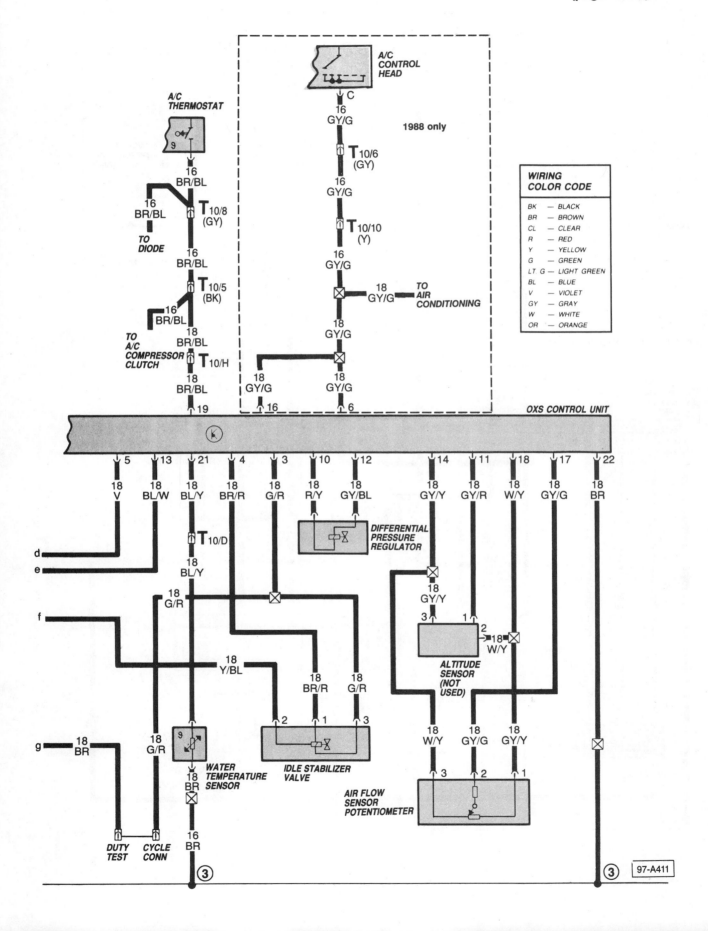

WIRING COLOR CODE	
BK	— BLACK
BR	— BROWN
CL	— CLEAR
R	— RED
Y	— YELLOW
G	— GREEN
LT. G	— LIGHT GREEN
BL	— BLUE
V	— VIOLET
GY	— GRAY
W	— WHITE
OR	— ORANGE

97-A411

Electronic Engine Control
1988-1989 Golf (Digifant II)
(page 1 of 4)

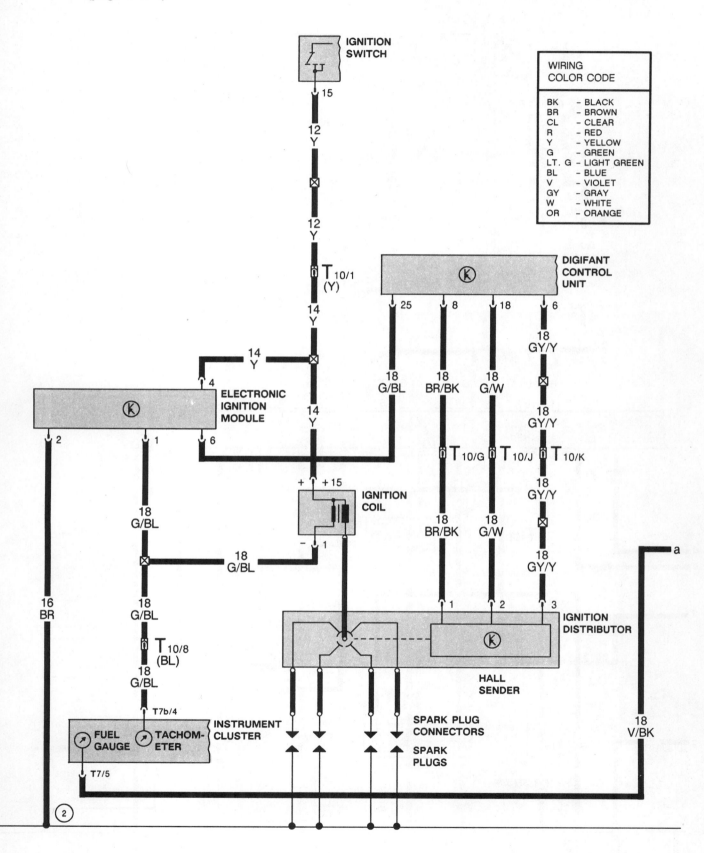

Electronic Engine Control
1988-1989 Golf (Digifant II)
(page 2 of 4)

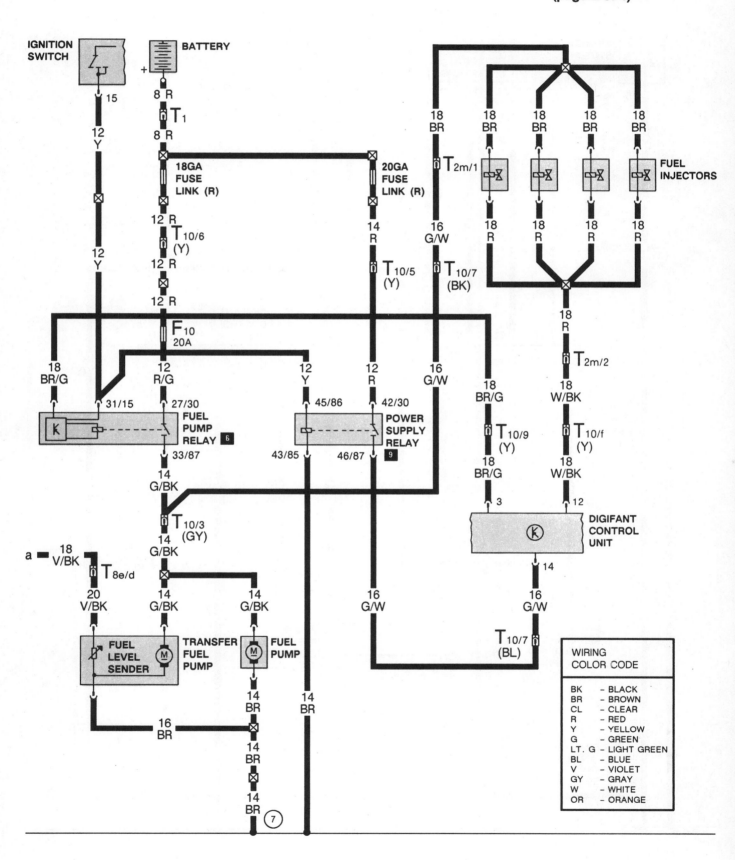

Electronic Engine Control
1988-1989 Golf (Digifant II)
(page 3 of 4)

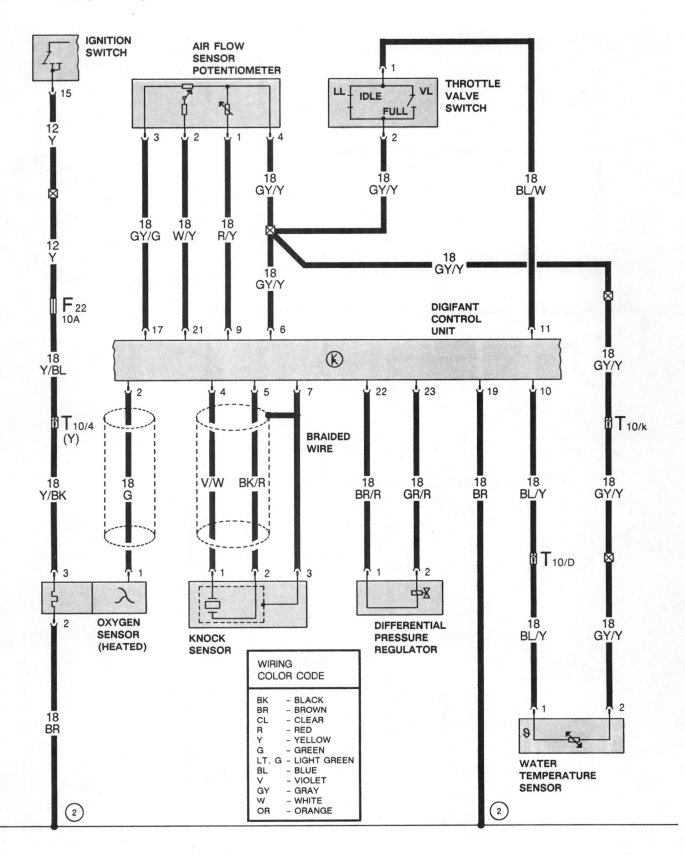

IGNITION SWITCH

AIR FLOW SENSOR POTENTIOMETER

THROTTLE VALVE SWITCH

LL · IDLE · VL
FULL

DIGIFANT CONTROL UNIT

Ⓚ

BRAIDED WIRE

OXYGEN SENSOR (HEATED)

KNOCK SENSOR

DIFFERENTIAL PRESSURE REGULATOR

WATER TEMPERATURE SENSOR

WIRING COLOR CODE

BK	– BLACK
BR	– BROWN
CL	– CLEAR
R	– RED
Y	– YELLOW
G	– GREEN
LT. G	– LIGHT GREEN
BL	– BLUE
V	– VIOLET
GY	– GRAY
W	– WHITE
OR	– ORANGE

Electronic Engine Control
1988-1989 Golf (Digifant II)
(page 4 of 4)

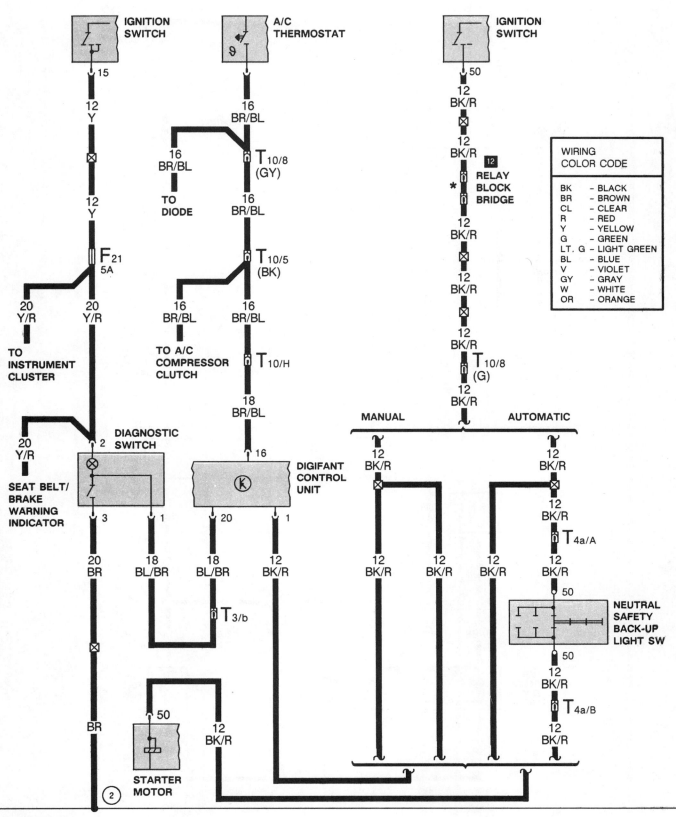

IGNITION
SWITCH

A/C
THERMOSTAT

IGNITION
SWITCH

15

12
Y

16
BR/BL

50

12
BK/R

16
BR/BL

T 10/8
(GY)

12
BK/R

12
Y

12
BK/R

12 RELAY
BLOCK
BRIDGE

TO
DIODE

16
BR/BL

*

F 21
5A

T 10/5
(BK)

12
BK/R

12
BK/R

20
Y/R

20
Y/R

16
BR/BL

16
BR/BL

12
BK/R

TO
INSTRUMENT
CLUSTER

TO A/C
COMPRESSOR
CLUTCH

T 10/H

T 10/8
(G)

12
BK/R

18
BR/BL

MANUAL   AUTOMATIC

20
Y/R

DIAGNOSTIC
SWITCH

2

16

12
BK/R

12
BK/R

SEAT BELT/
BRAKE
WARNING
INDICATOR

DIGIFANT
CONTROL
UNIT

12
BK/R

T 4a/A

3   1

20   1

3

20
BR

18
BL/BR

18
BL/BR

12
BK/R

12
BK/R

12
BK/R

12
BK/R

12
BK/R

50

NEUTRAL
SAFETY
BACK-UP
LIGHT SW

T 3/b

50

12
BK/R

BR

T 4a/B

12
BK/R

50

12
BK/R

BR

STARTER
MOTOR

②

WIRING
COLOR CODE

BK	– BLACK
BR	– BROWN
CL	– CLEAR
R	– RED
Y	– YELLOW
G	– GREEN
LT. G	– LIGHT GREEN
BL	– BLUE
V	– VIOLET
GY	– GRAY
W	– WHITE
OR	– ORANGE

* **FOR WIRING WITH
PASSIVE RESTRAINT,
SEE PAGE 143.**

Fuel Pump System
1987-1989 GTI 16-valve
(page 1 of 1)

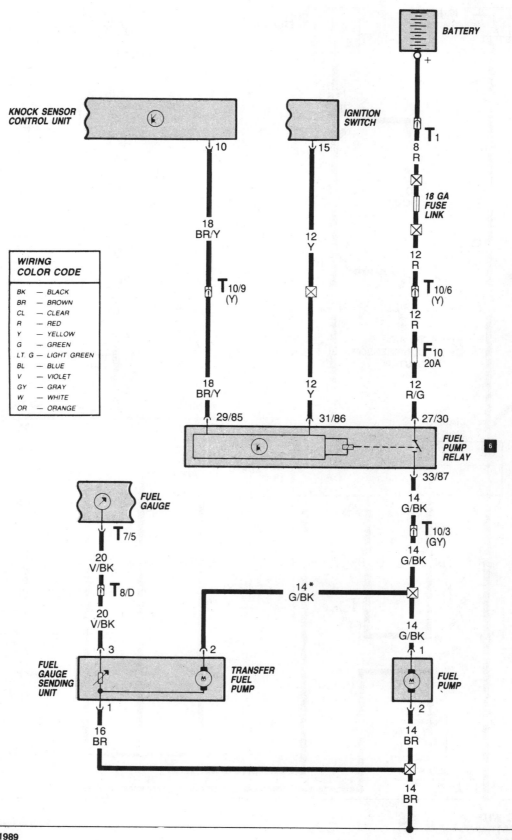

WIRING
COLOR CODE

BK — BLACK
BR — BROWN
CL — CLEAR
R — RED
Y — YELLOW
G — GREEN
LT. G — LIGHT GREEN
BL — BLUE
V — VIOLET
GY — GRAY
W — WHITE
OR — ORANGE

* 16GA 1988,1989

97-A412

**Cold Start System
1985 Golf/GTI (Gasoline only)
(page 1 of 1)**

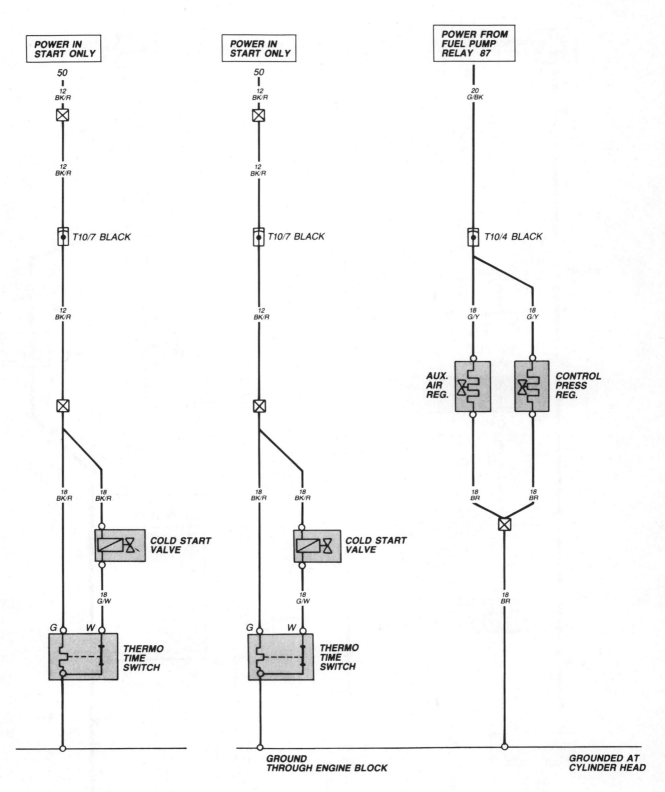

Cold Start System
1986-1989 Golf/GTI (Gasoline only)
(page 1 of 1)

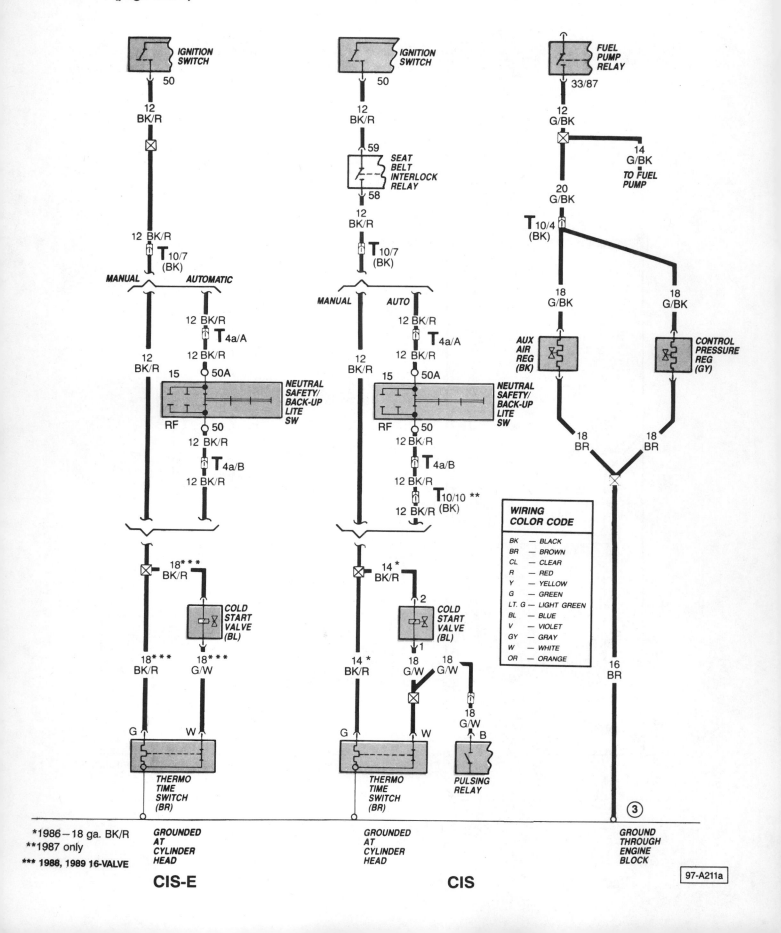

*1986—18 ga. BK/R
**1987 only
***1988, 1989 16-VALVE

GROUNDED
AT
CYLINDER
HEAD

GROUNDED
AT
CYLINDER
HEAD

GROUND
THROUGH
ENGINE
BLOCK

CIS-E   CIS

97-A211a

Idle Speed Boost
1985 Golf (Gasoline only)
(page 1 of 1)

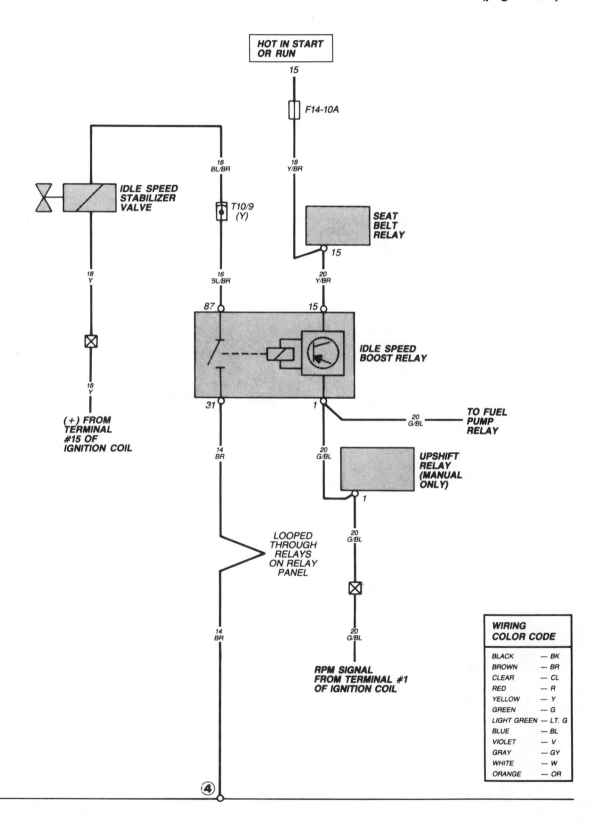

Idle Speed Boost
1986–1987 Golf (Gasoline only)
(page 1 of 1)

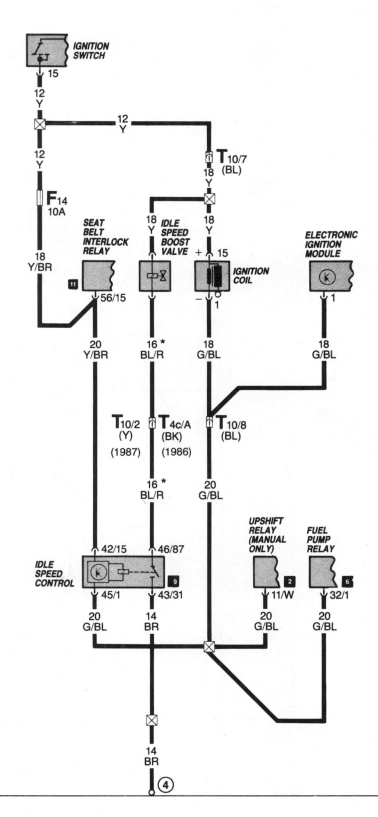

*1987 – 18 ga. BL/BR

97-A212

**Coolant Level Warning System
1985 Golf Diesel
(page 1 of 1)**

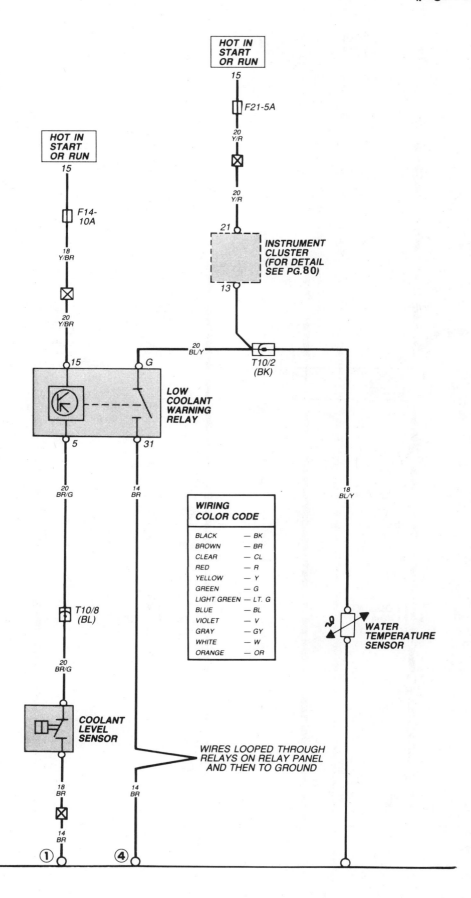

Coolant Level Warning System
1986-1989 Golf Diesel
1988-1989 Golf (page 1 of 1)

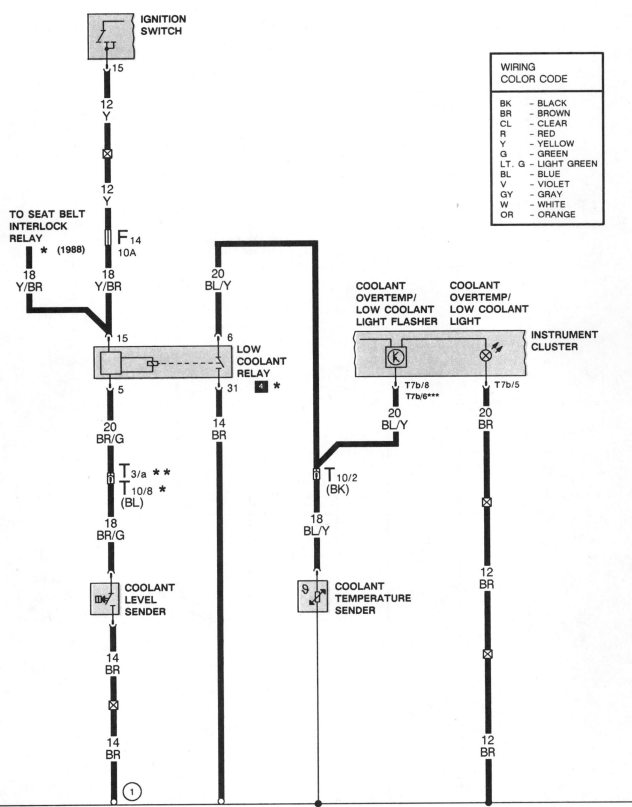

IGNITION
SWITCH

15

12
Y

12
Y

TO SEAT BELT
INTERLOCK
RELAY
    * (1988)

F 14
10A

18
Y/BR

18
Y/BR

20
BL/Y

WIRING
COLOR CODE

BK – BLACK
BR – BROWN
CL – CLEAR
R   – RED
Y   – YELLOW
G   – GREEN
LT. G – LIGHT GREEN
BL – BLUE
V   – VIOLET
GY – GRAY
W   – WHITE
OR – ORANGE

COOLANT
OVERTEMP/
LOW COOLANT
LIGHT FLASHER

COOLANT
OVERTEMP/
LOW COOLANT
LIGHT

INSTRUMENT
CLUSTER

15   6

LOW
COOLANT
RELAY

5   31   4 *

K   ⊗

T7b/8   T7b/5
T7b/6***

20
BR/G

14
BR

20
BL/Y

20
BR

T 3/a **
T 10/8 *
(BL)

T 10/2
(BK)

18
BR/G

18
BL/Y

12
BR

COOLANT
LEVEL
SENDER

COOLANT
TEMPERATURE
SENDER

14
BR

14
BR

12
BR

12
BR

①

* DIESEL ONLY
** GAS ONLY 1988, 1989

*** 1986, 1987

**Radiator Cooling Fan
1985 Golf/GTI
(page 1 of 1)**

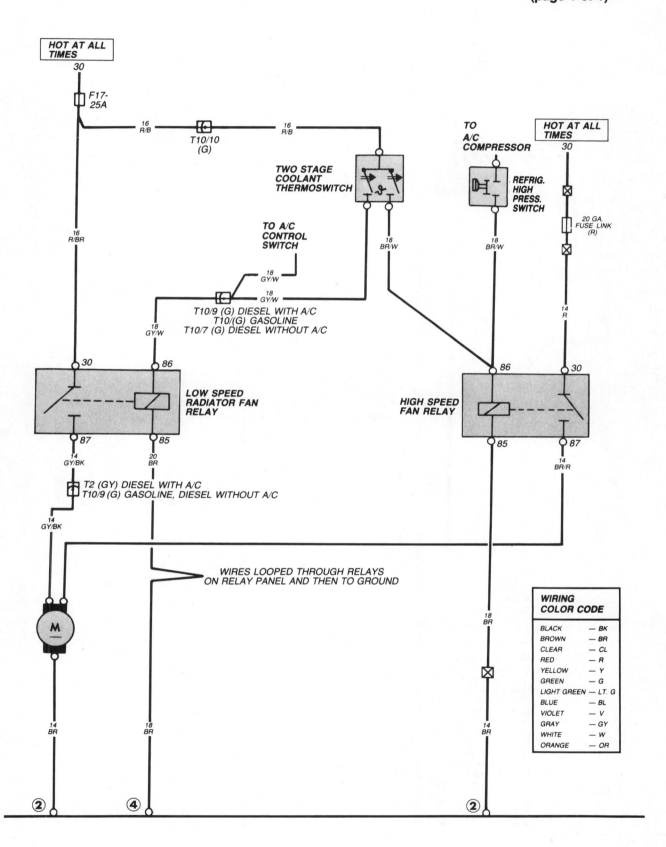

Radiator Cooling Fan
1986-1989 Golf/GTI (without A/C)
(page 1 of 1)

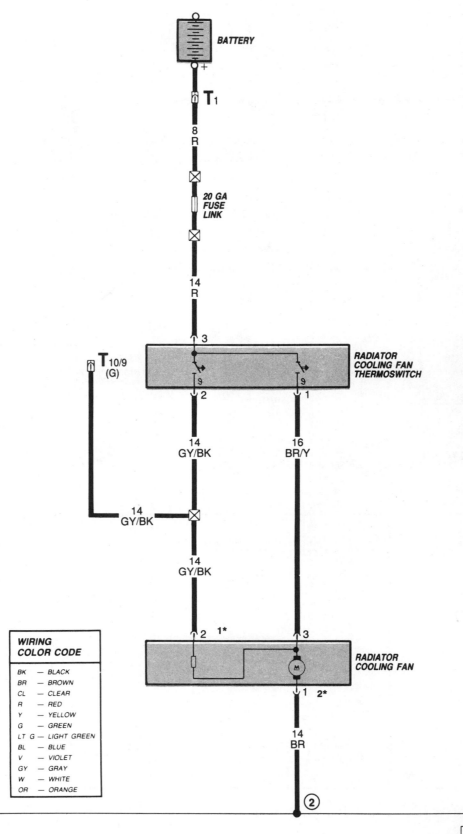

BATTERY

T₁

8
R

20 GA
FUSE
LINK

14
R

3

T 10/9
(G)

RADIATOR
COOLING FAN
THERMOSWITCH

2   1

14
GY/BK   16
                   BR/Y

14
GY/BK

14
GY/BK

WIRING
COLOR CODE

BK	— BLACK
BR	— BROWN
CL	— CLEAR
R	— RED
Y	— YELLOW
G	— GREEN
LT G	— LIGHT GREEN
BL	— BLUE
V	— VIOLET
GY	— GRAY
W	— WHITE
OR	— ORANGE

2   1*   3

M

RADIATOR
COOLING FAN

1   2*

14
BR

②

* 1986, 1987 MODELS

97-A426

Radiator Cooling Fan
1986–1987 Golf (with A/C),
1986-1989 GTI (with A/C)
(page 1 of 1)

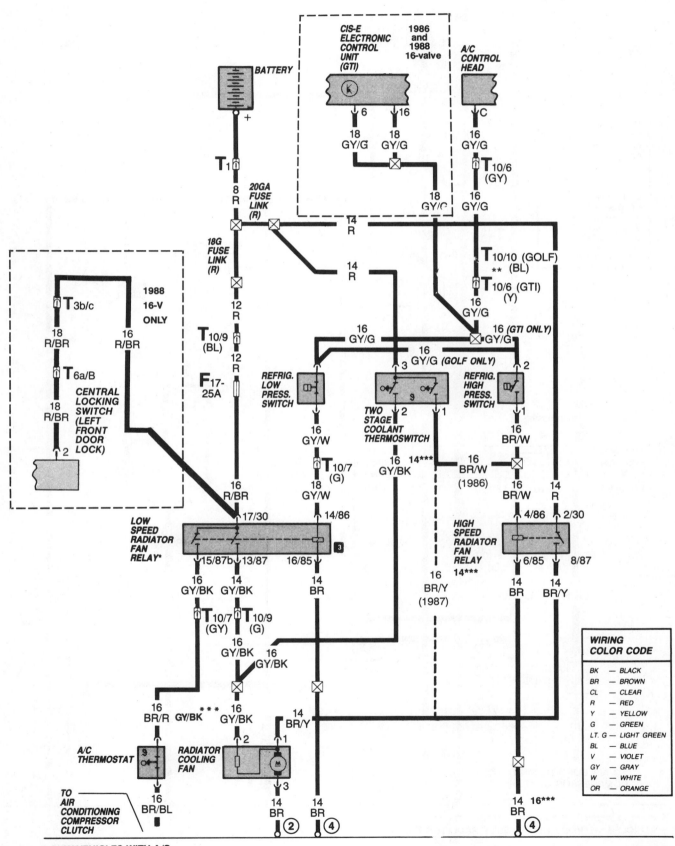

WIRING
COLOR CODE

BK — BLACK
BR — BROWN
CL — CLEAR
R — RED
Y — YELLOW
G — GREEN
LT. G — LIGHT GREEN
BL — BLUE
V — VIOLET
GY — GRAY
W — WHITE
OR — ORANGE

* ONLY VEHICLES WITH A/C

** GTI 16-VALVE — T ¹⁰/₁₀ (Y)

*** 1988, 1989 GTI 16-VALVE

97-A214

Radiator Cooling Fan
1988-1989 Golf Diesel
(page 1 of 1)

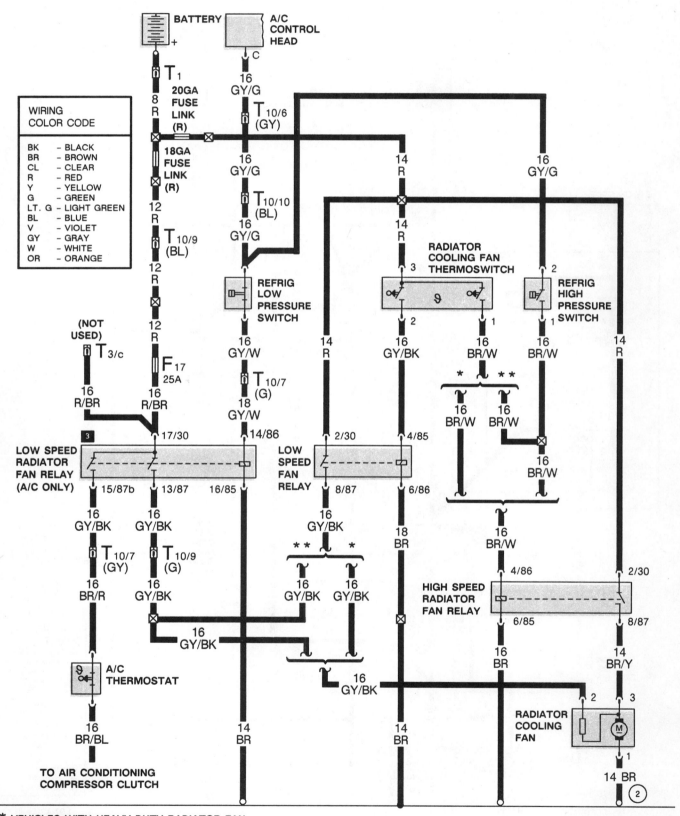

* VEHICLES WITH HEAVY DUTY RADIATOR FAN
** VEHICLES WITHOUT HEAVY DUTY RADIATOR FAN

GROUND CIRCUIT.

After-Run Radiator Cooling Fan
1987 Golf/GTI (except 16-valve)
(page 1 of 1)

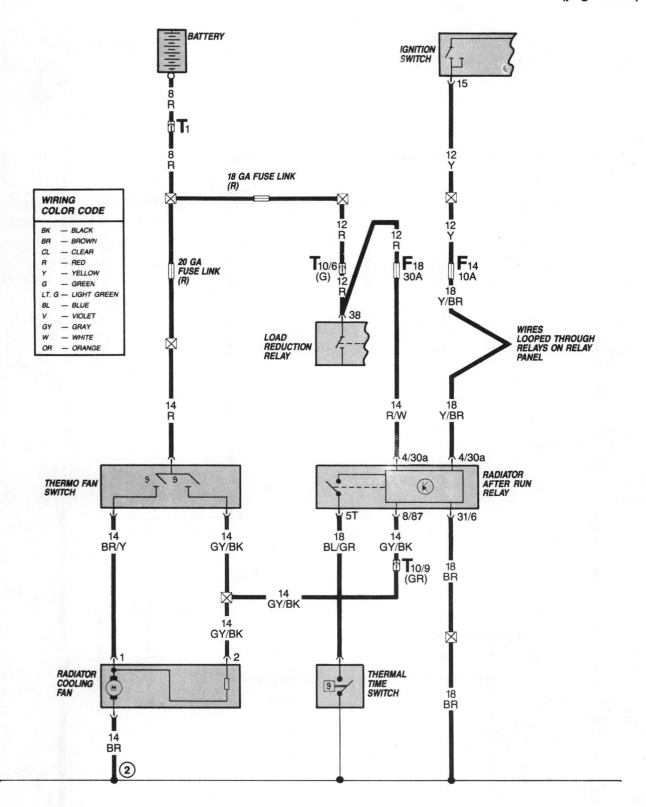

97-A215a

After-Run Radiator Cooling Fan
1988-1989 Golf
(page 1 of 1)

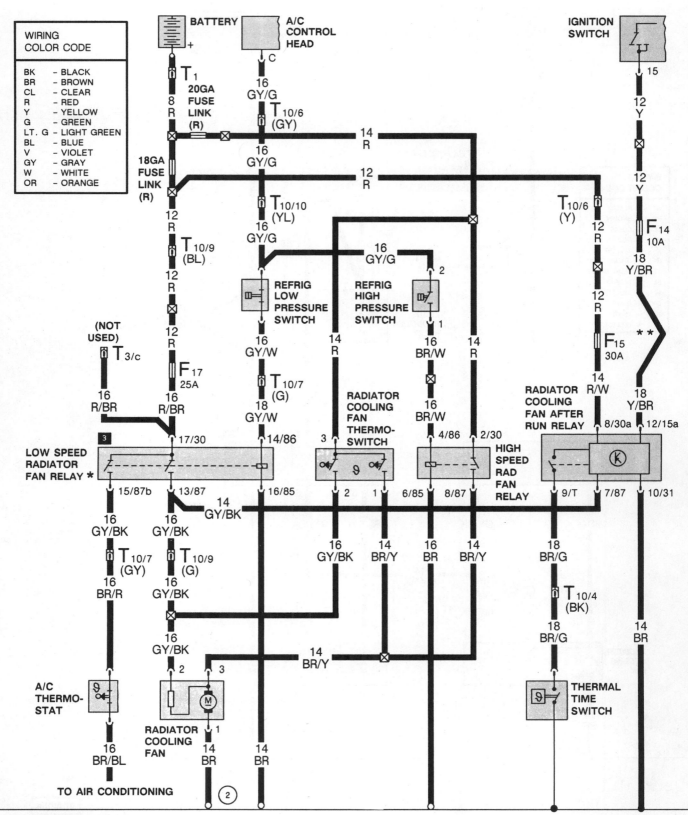

* ONLY VEHICLES WITH A/C
** WIRES LOOPED THROUGH
ON RELAY PANEL

**Seat Belt Warning
1985 Golf
(page 1 of 1)**

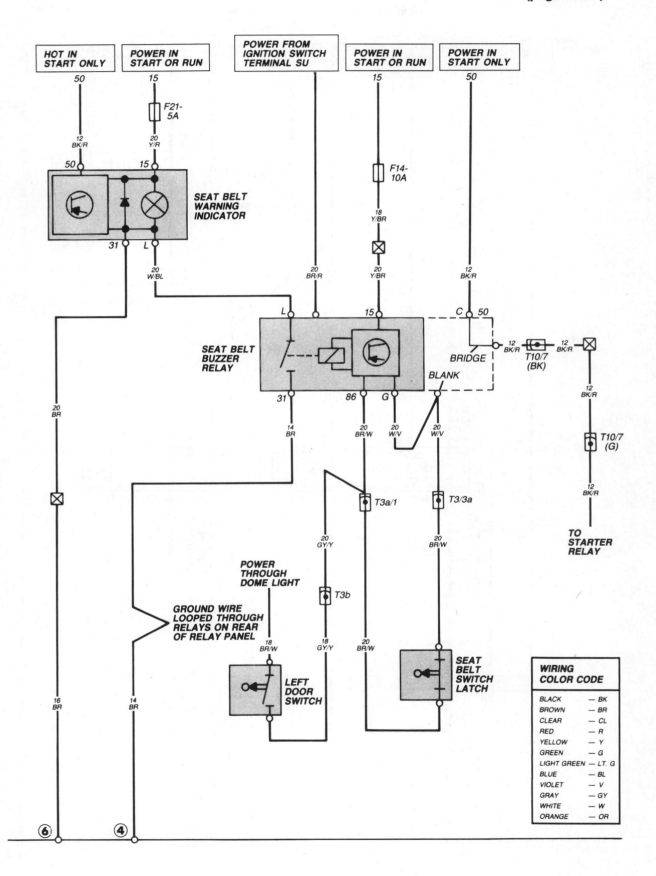

Seat Belt Interlock/Park Brake Warning
1986 Golf/GTI
(page 1 of 1)

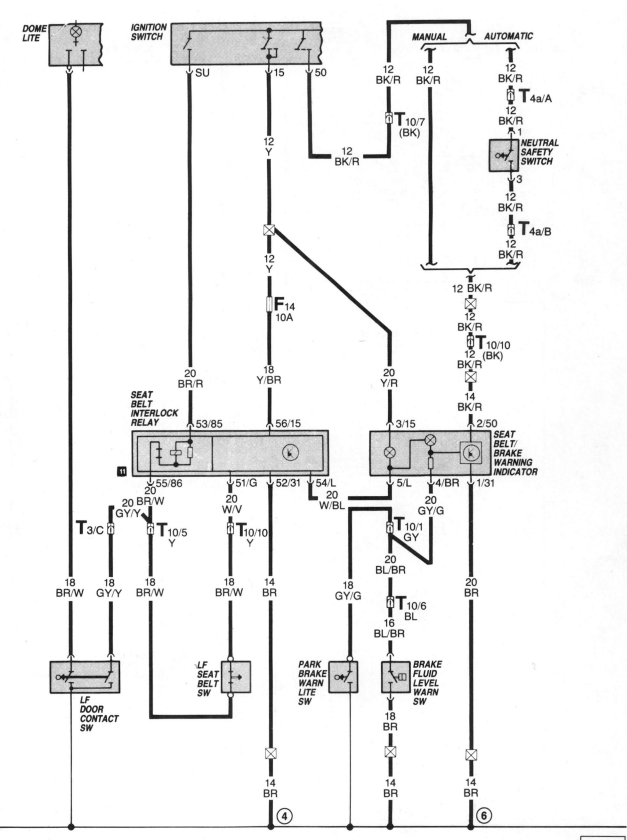

97-A215

Seat Belt Interlock/Park Brake Warning
1987 Golf (except Golf GT)
(page 1 of 1)

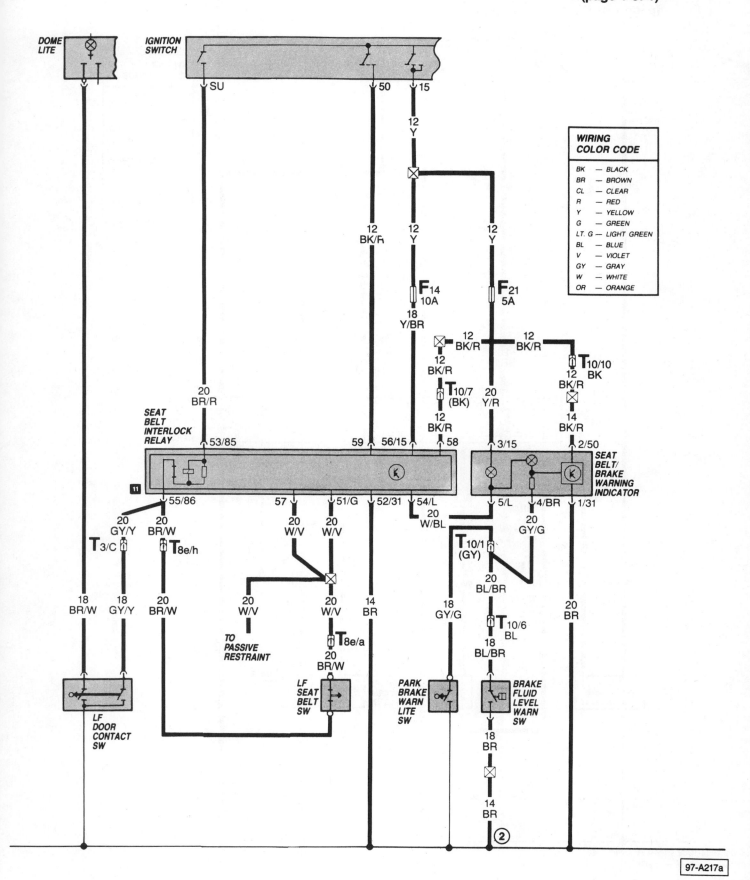

97-A217a

Seat Belt Interlock/Park Brake Warning
1987 Golf GT,
1987-1989 GTI
(page 1 of 1)

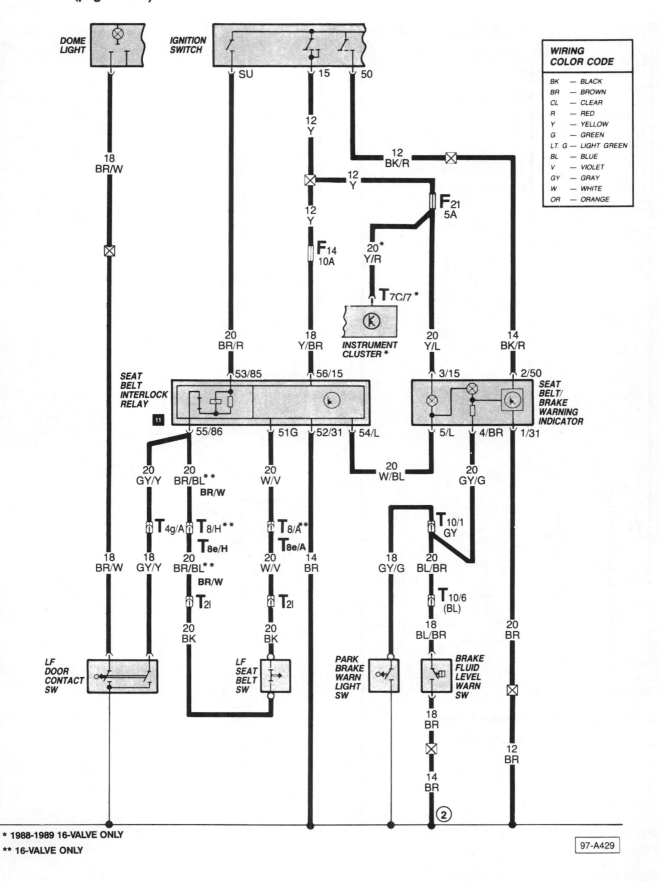

* 1988-1989 16-VALVE ONLY

** 16-VALVE ONLY

97-A429

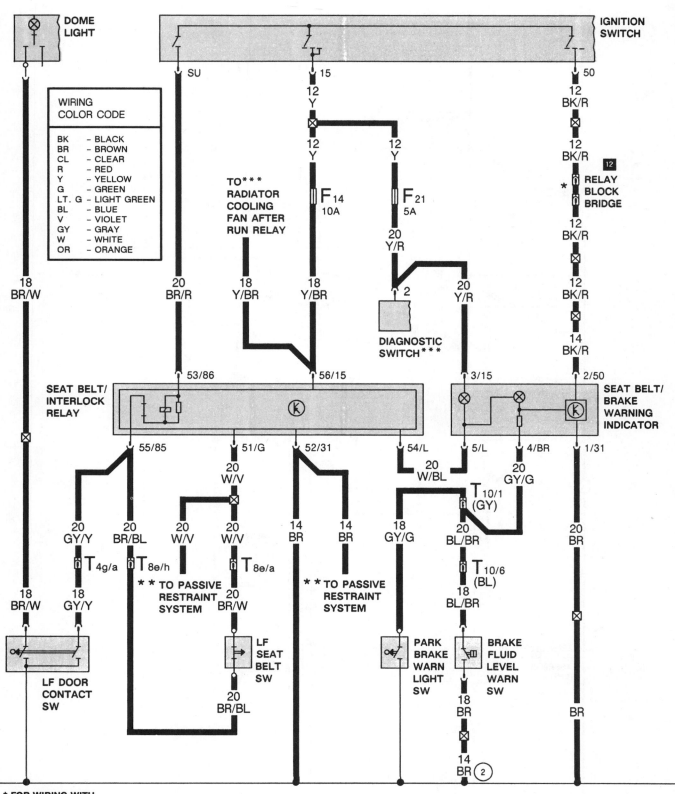

* FOR WIRING WITH
PASSIVE RESTRAINT
** GOLF GL AND DIESEL ONLY
***GAS ONLY

Passive Restraint
1985 Golf/GTI
(page 1 of 1)

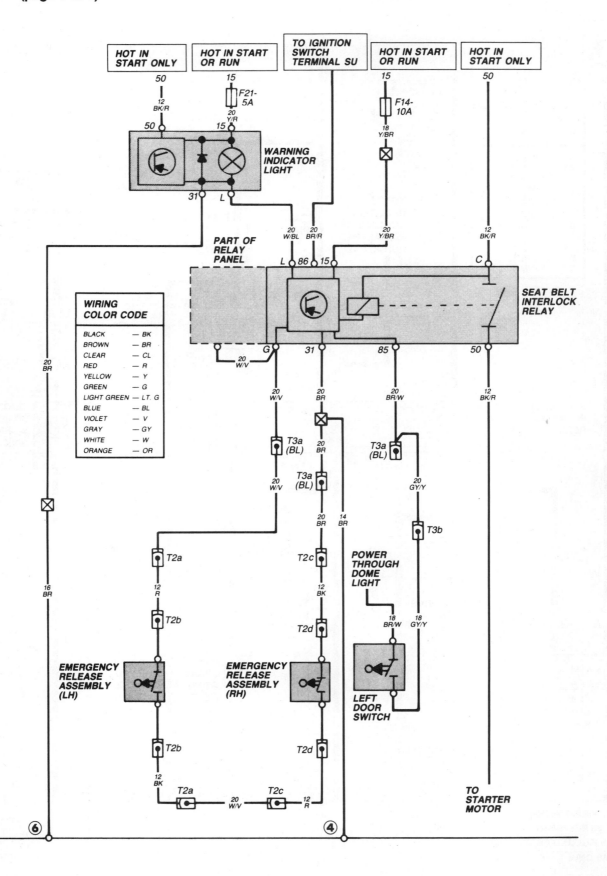

WIRING COLOR CODE

BLACK	— BK
BROWN	— BR
CLEAR	— CL
RED	— R
YELLOW	— Y
GREEN	— G
LIGHT GREEN	— LT. G
BLUE	— BL
VIOLET	— V
GRAY	— GY
WHITE	— W
ORANGE	— OR

Passive Restraint
1987 Golf (early)
(page 1 of 1)

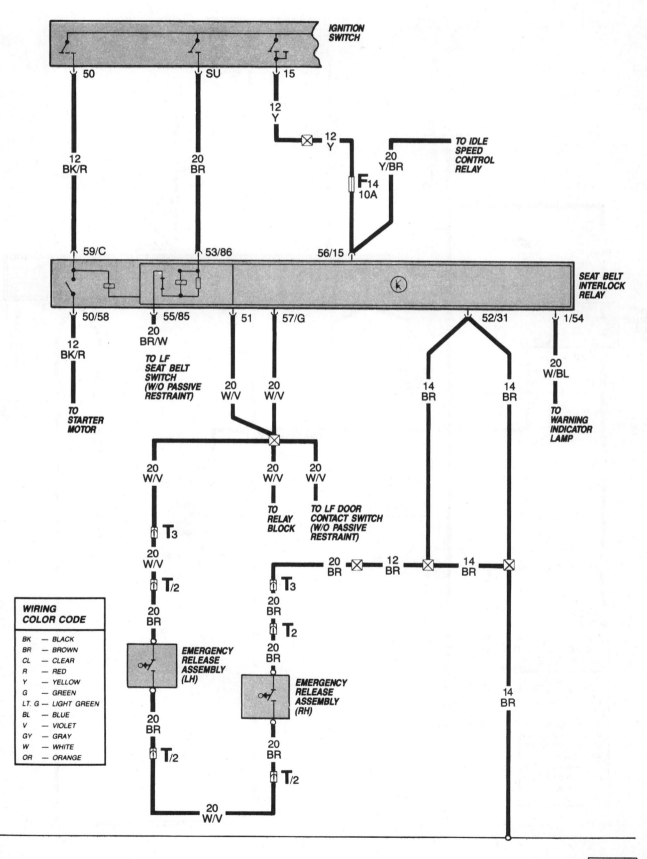

IGNITION
SWITCH

50   SU   15

12
Y

12
Y

TO IDLE
SPEED
CONTROL
RELAY

20
Y/BR

F14
10A

12
BK/R

20
BR

59/C   53/86   56/15

SEAT BELT
INTERLOCK
RELAY

50/58   55/85   51   57/G   52/31   1/54

12
BK/R

20
BR/W

TO LF
SEAT BELT
SWITCH
(W/O PASSIVE
RESTRAINT)

20
W/V

20
W/V

14
BR

14
BR

20
W/BL

TO
STARTER
MOTOR

TO
WARNING
INDICATOR
LAMP

20
W/V

20
W/V

20
W/V

TO
RELAY
BLOCK

TO LF DOOR
CONTACT SWITCH
(W/O PASSIVE
RESTRAINT)

T3

20
W/V

T/2

20
BR

20
BR

12
BR

14
BR

14
BR

T3

20
BR

WIRING
COLOR CODE

BK — BLACK
BR — BROWN
CL — CLEAR
R   — RED
Y   — YELLOW
G   — GREEN
LT. G — LIGHT GREEN
BL — BLUE
V   — VIOLET
GY — GRAY
W   — WHITE
OR — ORANGE

EMERGENCY
RELEASE
ASSEMBLY
(LH)

T2

20
BR

20
BR

EMERGENCY
RELEASE
ASSEMBLY
(RH)

20
BR

14
BR

T/2

20
BR

20
W/V

T/2

**Passive Restraint
1987 Golf (late)
(page 1 of 1)**

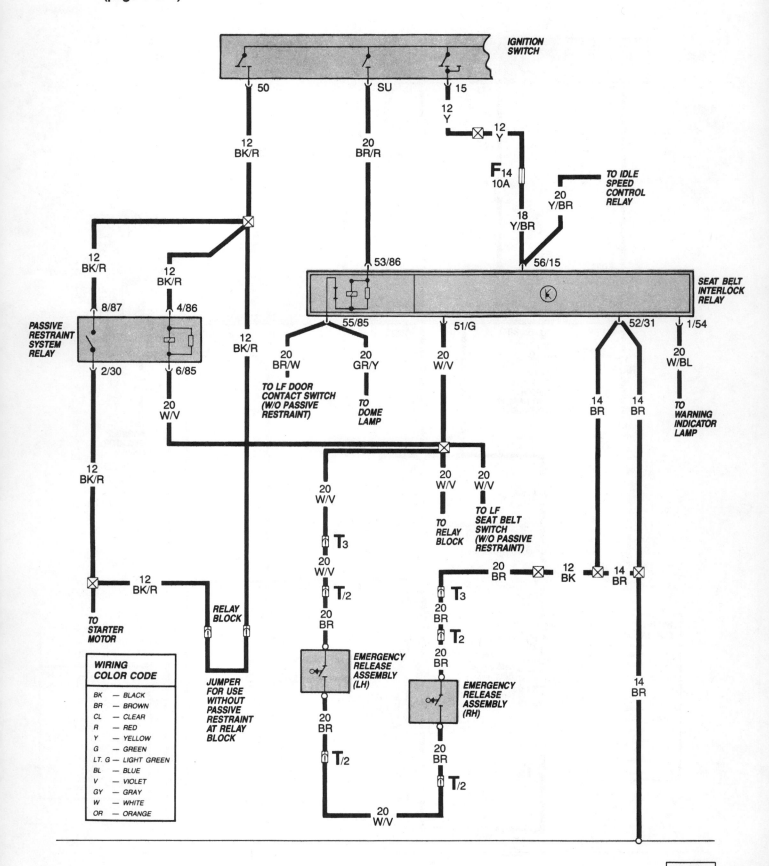

97-A233a

**Passive Restraint
1988-1989 Golf
(page 1 of 1)**

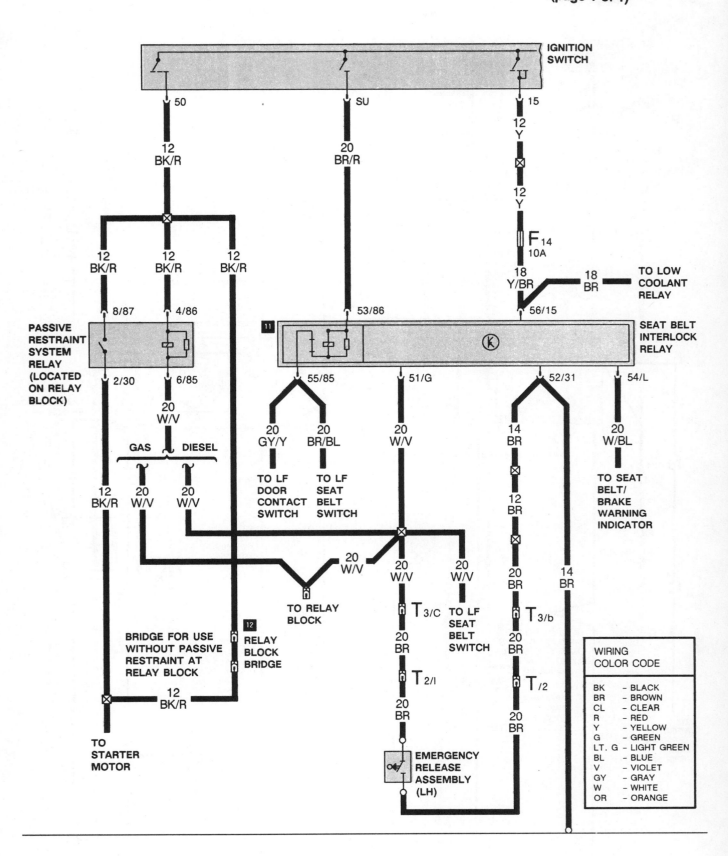

Upshift Indicator
1985 Golf/GTI
(page 1 of 1)

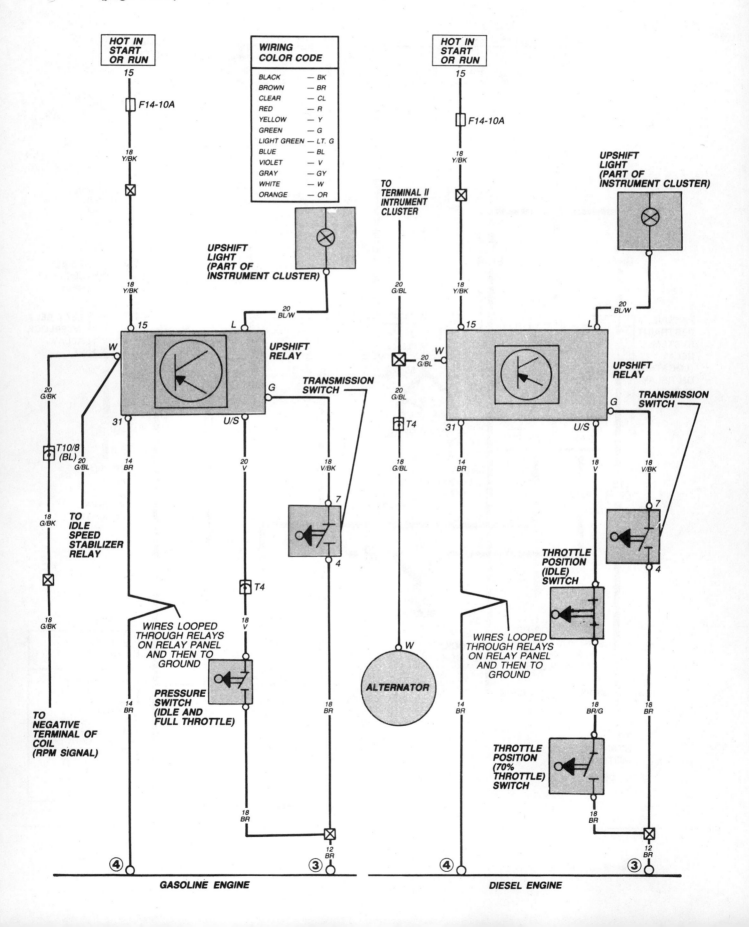

WIRING COLOR CODE	
BLACK	— BK
BROWN	— BR
CLEAR	— CL
RED	— R
YELLOW	— Y
GREEN	— G
LIGHT GREEN	— LT. G
BLUE	— BL
VIOLET	— V
GRAY	— GY
WHITE	— W
ORANGE	— OR

GASOLINE ENGINE

DIESEL ENGINE

Upshift Indicator
1986 Golf/GTI (Gasoline only)
(page 1 of 1)

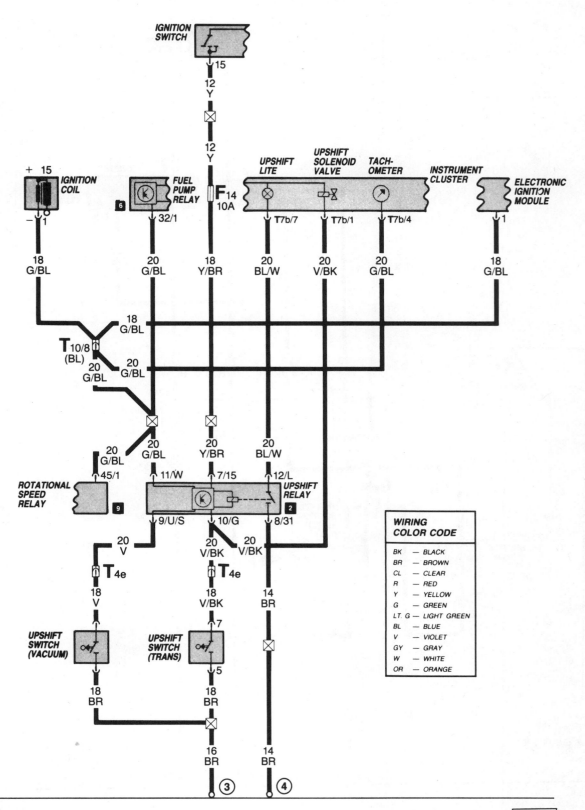

97-A216

Upshift Indicator
1986–1987 Golf Diesel
(page 1 of 1)

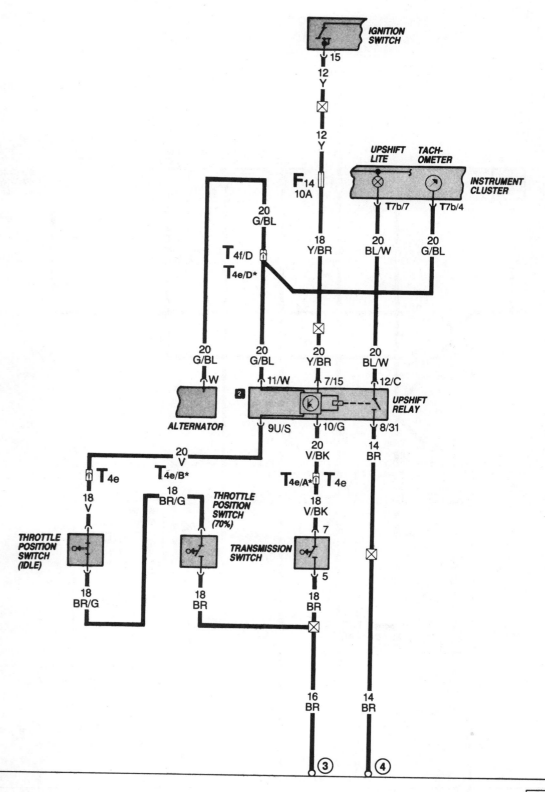

* 1987

97-A217

Upshift Indicator
1987 Golf/GTI (Gasoline only)
(page 1 of 1)

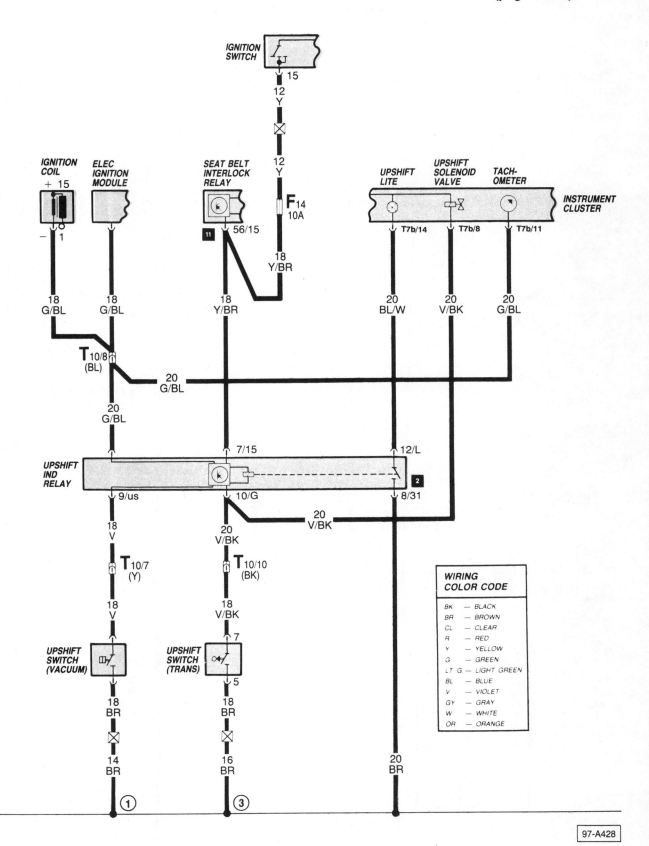

97-A428

Fresh Air Fan
1985-1989 Golf/GTI
(page 1 of 1)

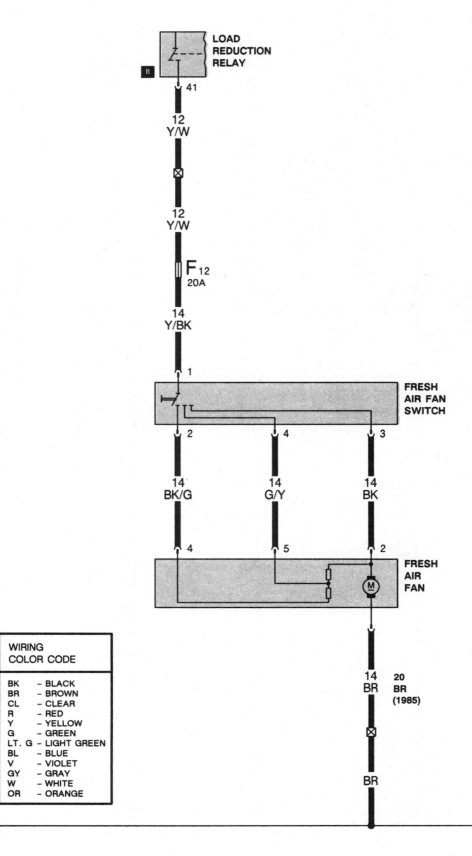

LOAD
REDUCTION
RELAY

8

41

12
Y/W

12
Y/W

F 12
20A

14
Y/BK

1

FRESH
AIR FAN
SWITCH

2   4   3

14   14   14
BK/G   G/Y   BK

4   5   2

FRESH
AIR
FAN

M

14   20
BR   BR
      (1985)

BR

WIRING COLOR CODE	
BK	– BLACK
BR	– BROWN
CL	– CLEAR
R	– RED
Y	– YELLOW
G	– GREEN
LT. G	– LIGHT GREEN
BL	– BLUE
V	– VIOLET
GY	– GRAY
W	– WHITE
OR	– ORANGE

Air Conditioning
1985 Golf/GTI (Gasoline only)
(page 1 of 1)

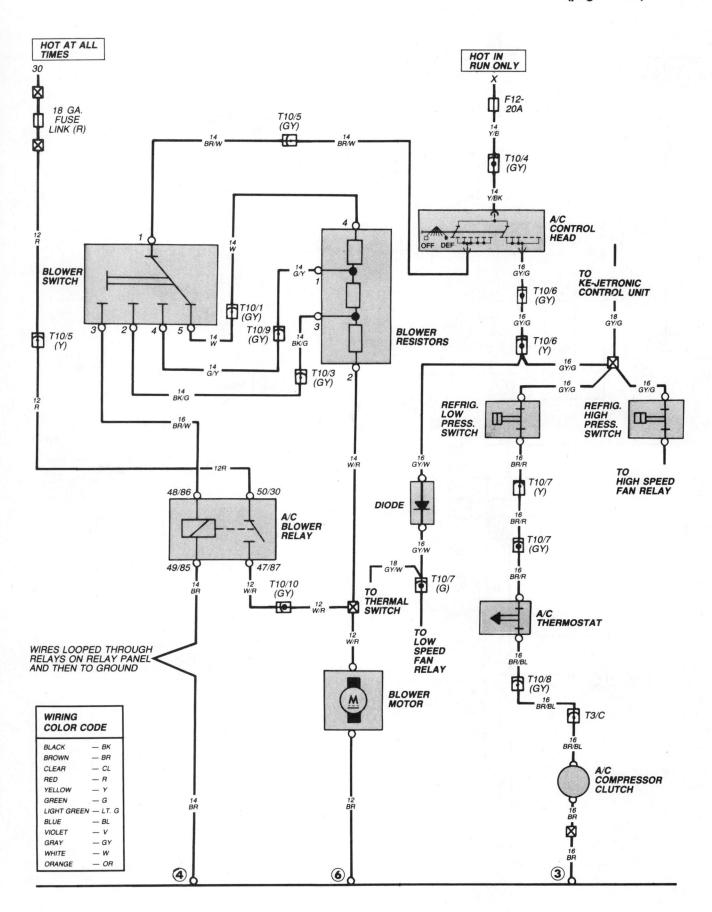

**Air Conditioning
1985 Golf Diesel
(page 1 of 1)**

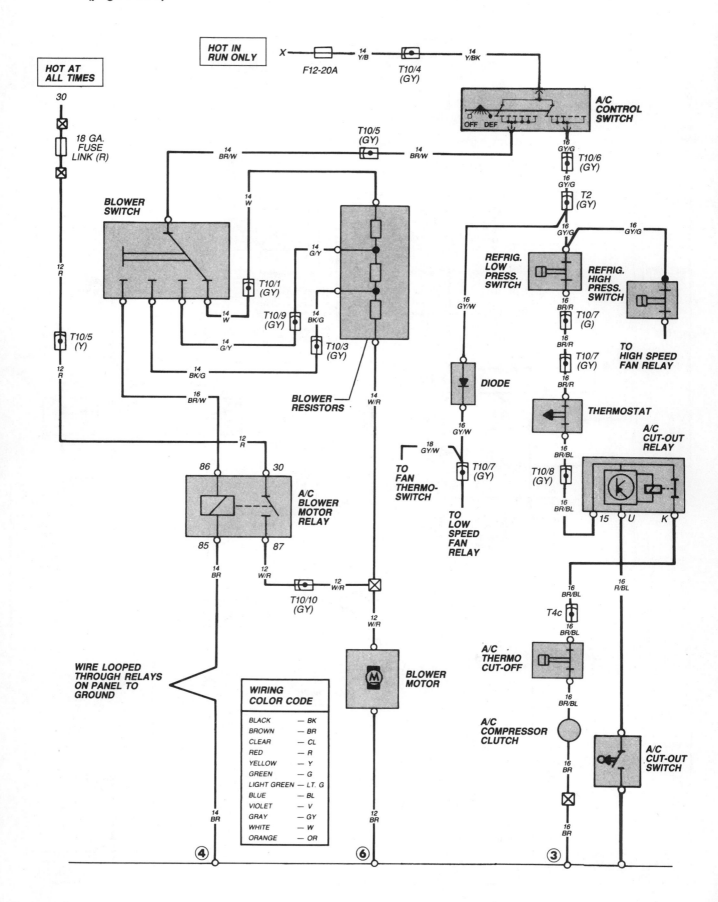

Air Conditioning
1986 Golf/GTI (Gasoline only),
1987 Golf GT/GTI (except 16-valve)
(page 1 of 1)

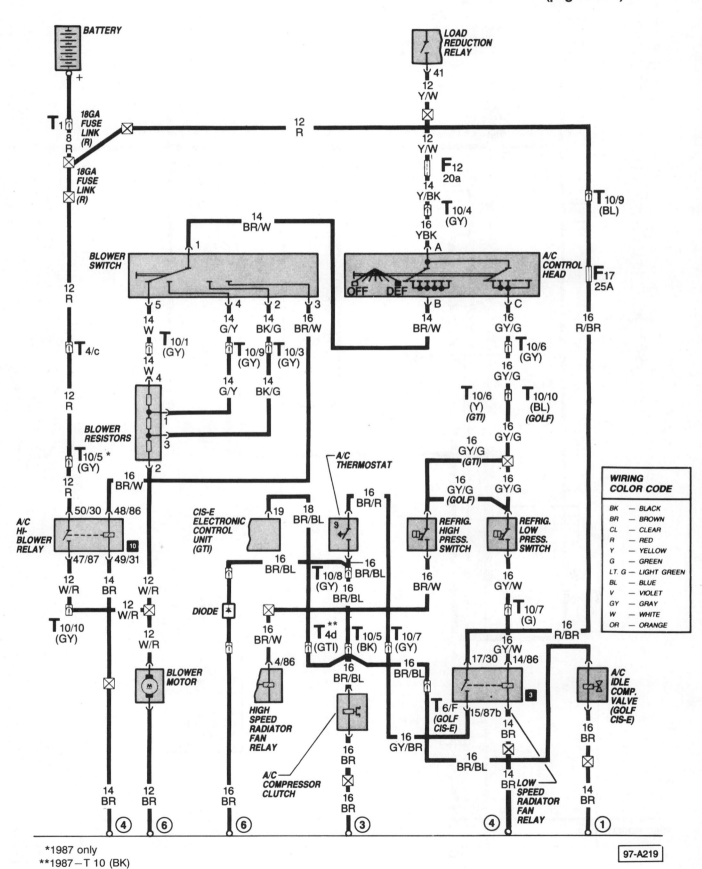

*1987 only
**1987—T 10 (BK)

97-A219

Air Conditioning
1986–1987 Golf Diesel
(page 1 of 2)

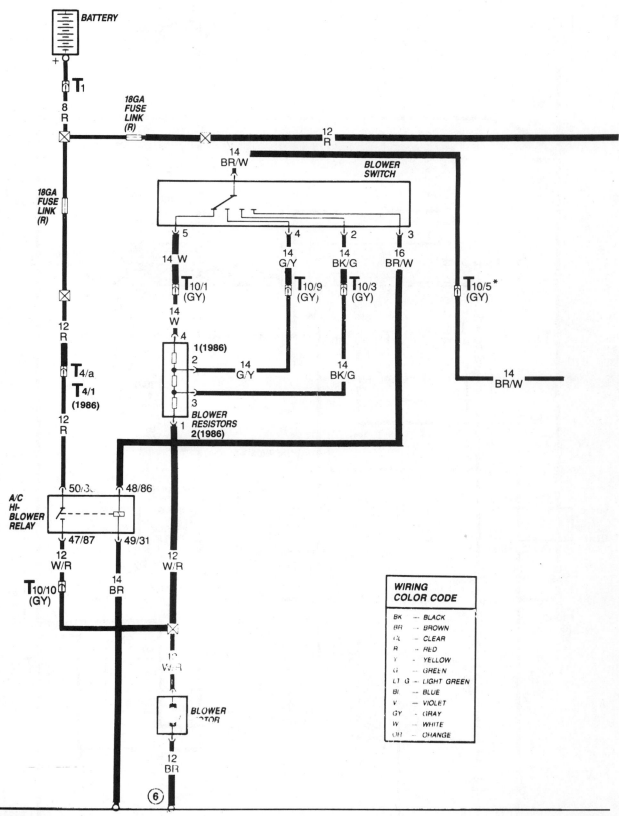

WIRING COLOR CODE

BK	—	BLACK
BR	—	BROWN
CL	—	CLEAR
R	—	RED
Y	—	YELLOW
G	—	GREEN
LT G	—	LIGHT GREEN
BL	—	BLUE
V	—	VIOLET
GY	—	GRAY
W	—	WHITE
OR	—	ORANGE

*1987 MODELS ONLY

97-A223a

**Air Conditioning
1986–1987 Golf Diesel
(page 2 of 2)**

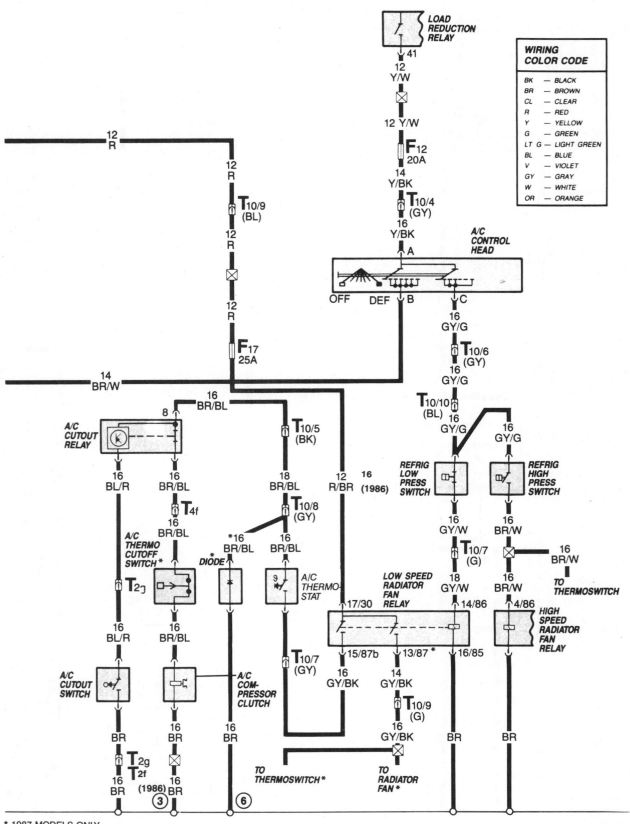

WIRING COLOR CODE	
BK	— BLACK
BR	— BROWN
CL	— CLEAR
R	— RED
Y	— YELLOW
G	— GREEN
LT G	— LIGHT GREEN
BL	— BLUE
V	— VIOLET
GY	— GRAY
W	— WHITE
OR	— ORANGE

LOAD REDUCTION RELAY

A/C CONTROL HEAD

A/C CUTOUT RELAY

A/C THERMO CUTOFF SWITCH *

A/C CUTOUT SWITCH

DIODE *

A/C THERMO- STAT

A/C COM- PRESSOR CLUTCH

LOW SPEED RADIATOR FAN RELAY

HIGH SPEED RADIATOR FAN RELAY

REFRIG LOW PRESS SWITCH

REFRIG HIGH PRESS SWITCH

TO THERMOSWITCH

TO THERMOSWITCH *

TO RADIATOR FAN *

* 1987 MODELS ONLY

97-A224a

Air Conditioning
1988-1989 Golf/GTI (except 16-valve)
(page 1 of 3)

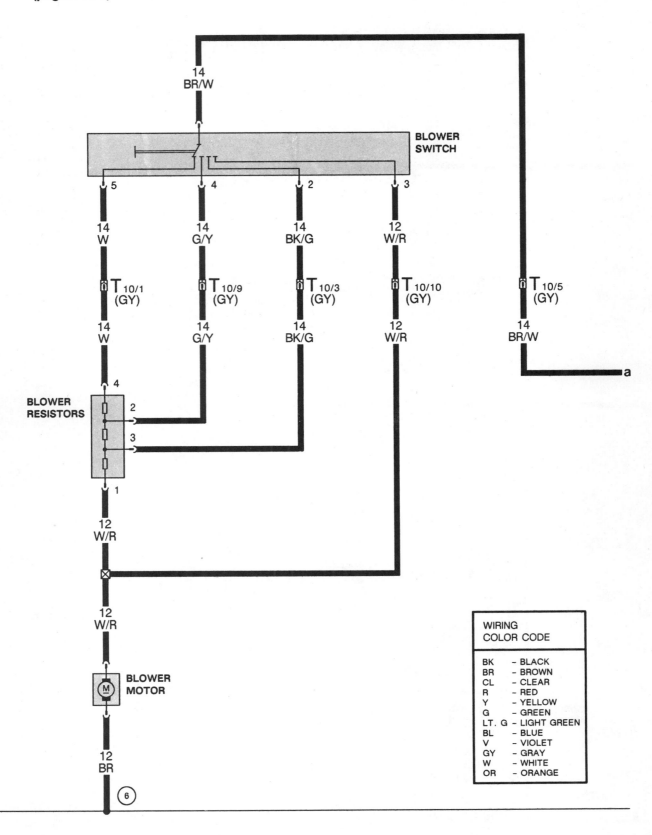

WIRING COLOR CODE	
BK	– BLACK
BR	– BROWN
CL	– CLEAR
R	– RED
Y	– YELLOW
G	– GREEN
LT. G	– LIGHT GREEN
BL	– BLUE
V	– VIOLET
GY	– GRAY
W	– WHITE
OR	– ORANGE

**Air Conditioning
1988-1989 Golf/GTI (except 16-valve)
(page 2 of 3)**

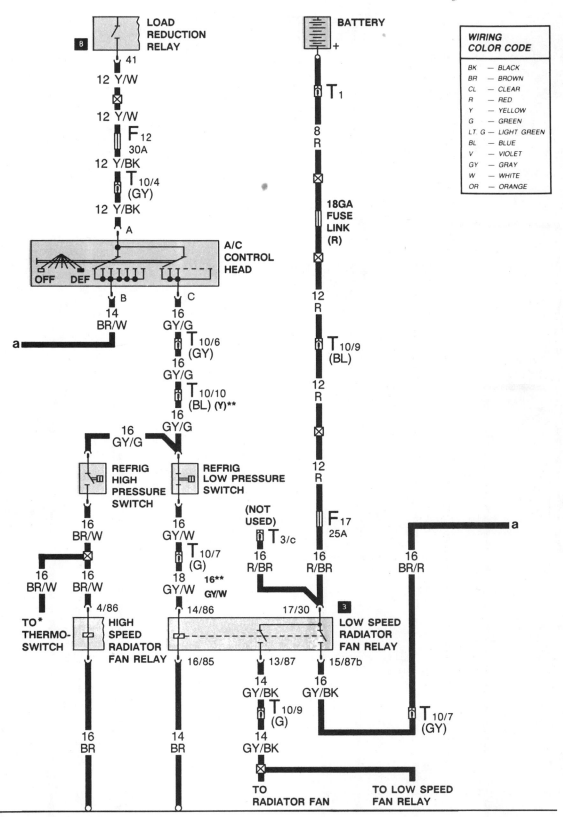

* DIESEL MODELS

** GAS MODELS

Air Conditioning
1988-1989 Golf/GTI (except 16-valve)
(page 3 of 3)

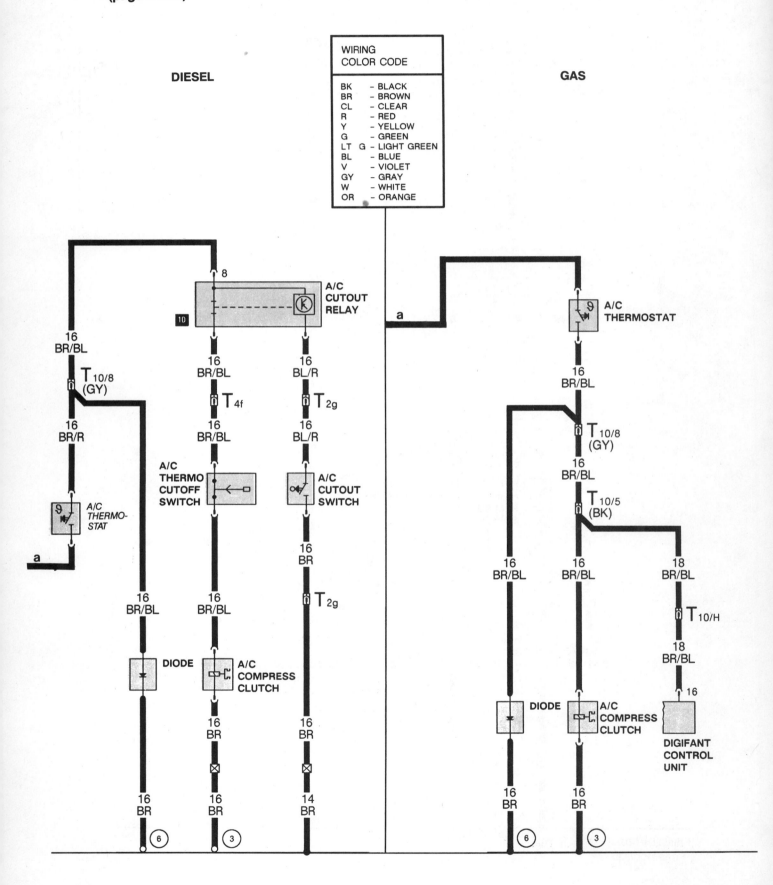

Air Conditioning
1987 Golf (Gasoline only Except Golf GT),
1987-1989 GTI 16-valve
(page 1 of 2)

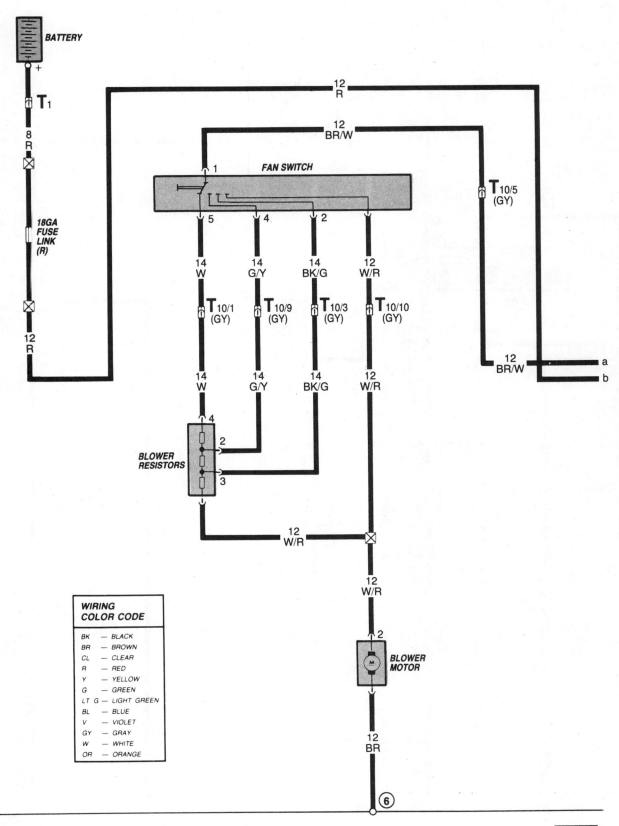

BATTERY

T₁

8
R

18GA
FUSE
LINK
(R)

12
R

12
R

12
BR/W

FAN SWITCH

1

5   4   2

14
W

14
G/Y

14
BK/G

12
W/R

T 10/1
(GY)

T 10/9
(GY)

T 10/3
(GY)

T 10/10
(GY)

T 10/5
(GY)

12
BR/W   a

b

14
W

14
G/Y

14
BK/G

12
W/R

4

2

3

*BLOWER
RESISTORS*

12
W/R

12
W/R

12
W/R

WIRING
COLOR CODE

BK — BLACK
BR — BROWN
CL — CLEAR
R   — RED
Y   — YELLOW
G   — GREEN
LT G — LIGHT GREEN
BL — BLUE
V   — VIOLET
GY — GRAY
W   — WHITE
OR — ORANGE

2

M   *BLOWER
MOTOR*

12
BR

⑥

97-A431

Air Conditioning
1987 Golf (Gasoline only   Except Golf GT),
1987-1989 GTI 16-valve
(page 2 of 2)

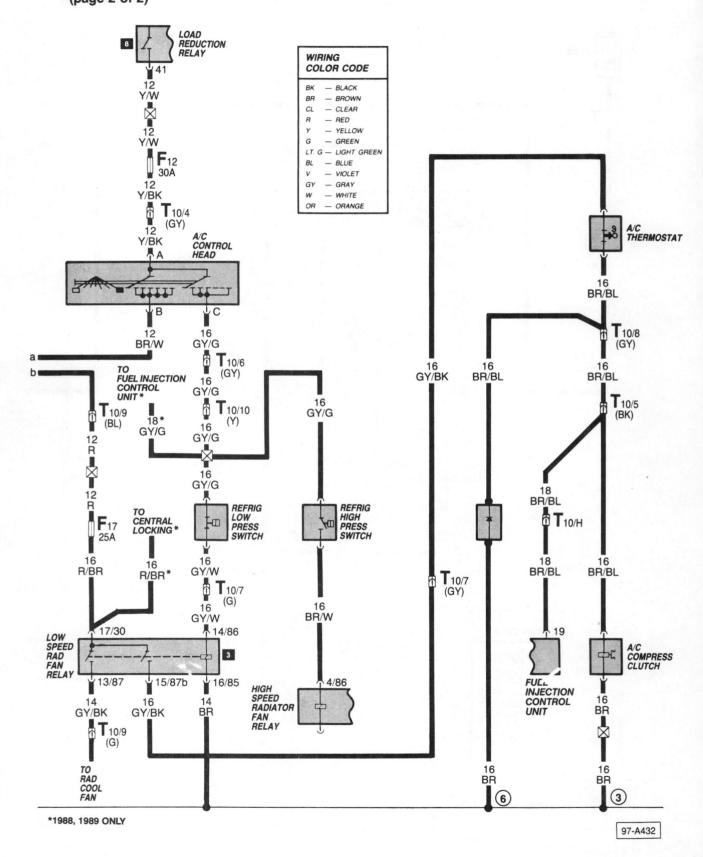

WIRING COLOR CODE	
BK	— BLACK
BR	— BROWN
CL	— CLEAR
R	— RED
Y	— YELLOW
G	— GREEN
LT. G	— LIGHT GREEN
BL	— BLUE
V	— VIOLET
GY	— GRAY
W	— WHITE
OR	— ORANGE

8 LOAD REDUCTION RELAY

41
12 Y/W
12 Y/W
F12 30A
12 Y/BK
T10/4 (GY)
12 Y/BK
A
A/C CONTROL HEAD
B   C
12 BR/W   16 GY/G
a
b   TO FUEL INJECTION CONTROL UNIT *
T10/6 (GY)
16 GY/G
T10/10 (Y)
16 GY/G
T10/9 (BL)
18* GY/G
12 R
16 GY/G
16 GY/G
F17 25A
TO CENTRAL LOCKING *
REFRIG LOW PRESS SWITCH
16 GY/G
REFRIG HIGH PRESS SWITCH
16 R/BR   16 R/BR*
16 GY/W
T10/7 (G)
16 GY/W
17/30   14/86
LOW SPEED RAD FAN RELAY   3
13/87   15/87b   16/85
14 GY/BK 16 GY/BK 14 BR
T10/9 (G)
16 BR/W
HIGH SPEED RADIATOR FAN RELAY
4/86
TO RAD COOL FAN

16 GY/BK
16 BR/BL
16 BR/BL
16 BR/BL
A/C THERMOSTAT
T10/8 (GY)
T10/5 (BK)
18 BR/BL
T10/H
18 BR/BL
19
FUEL INJECTION CONTROL UNIT
A/C COMPRESS CLUTCH
16 BR
T10/7 (GY)

16 BR   6
16 BR   3

*1988, 1989 ONLY

97-A432

Cruise Control
1985–1987 Golf/GTI,
1988-1989 Golf
(page 1 of 1)

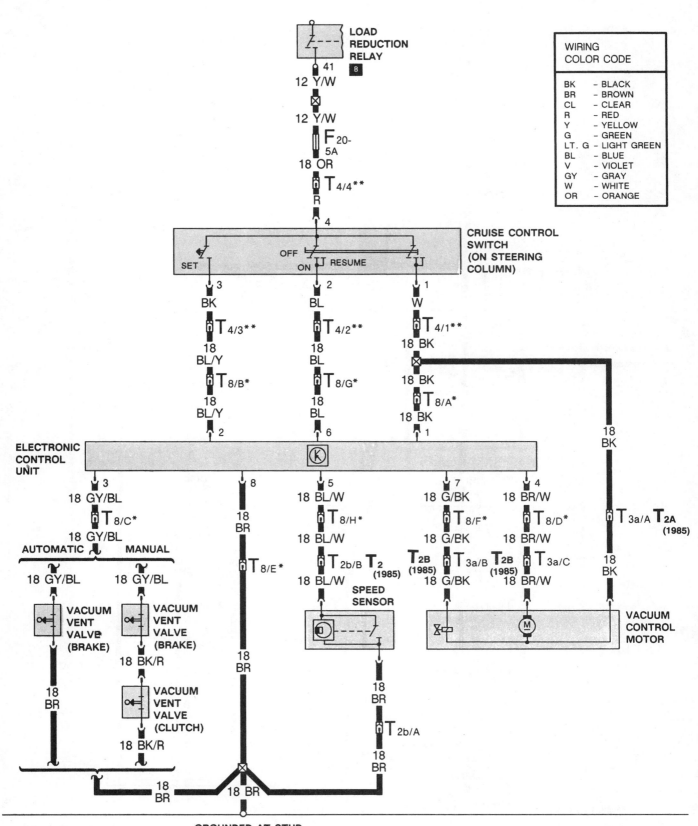

WIRING
COLOR CODE

BK – BLACK
BR – BROWN
CL – CLEAR
R – RED
Y – YELLOW
G – GREEN
LT. G – LIGHT GREEN
BL – BLUE
V – VIOLET
GY – GRAY
W – WHITE
OR – ORANGE

LOAD REDUCTION RELAY

CRUISE CONTROL SWITCH (ON STEERING COLUMN)

ELECTRONIC CONTROL UNIT

VACUUM VENT VALVE (BRAKE)

VACUUM VENT VALVE (BRAKE)

VACUUM VENT VALVE (CLUTCH)

SPEED SENSOR

VACUUM CONTROL MOTOR

AUTOMATIC   MANUAL

GROUNDED AT STUD
AT RELAY PANEL

*1988, 1989 MODELS ONLY

** 1987 16-VALVE MODELS USE CONNECTORS T4a

Cruise Control
1988-1989 GTI 16-valve
(page 1 of 1)

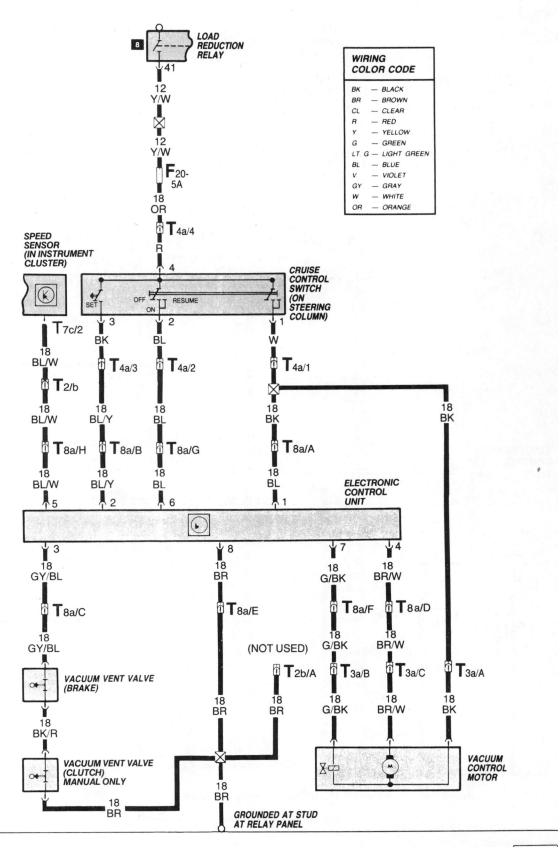

WIRING COLOR CODE	
BK	— BLACK
BR	— BROWN
CL	— CLEAR
R	— RED
Y	— YELLOW
G	— GREEN
LT. G	— LIGHT GREEN
BL	— BLUE
V	— VIOLET
GY	— GRAY
W	— WHITE
OR	— ORANGE

97-A434

Radio
1985–1987 Golf/GTI
(page 1 of 1)

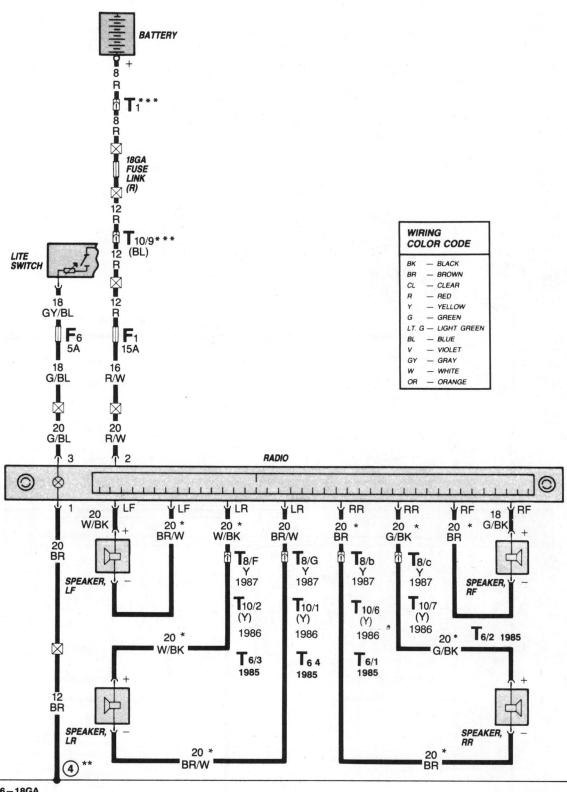

WIRING
COLOR CODE

BK	—	BLACK
BR	—	BROWN
CL	—	CLEAR
R	—	RED
Y	—	YELLOW
G	—	GREEN
LT. G	—	LIGHT GREEN
BL	—	BLUE
V	—	VIOLET
GY	—	GRAY
W	—	WHITE
OR	—	ORANGE

* 1985, 1986 — 18GA
** 1985, 1986 — ⑥
*** 1985 — NOT USED

Radio
1988-1989 Golf/GTI
(page 1 of 2)

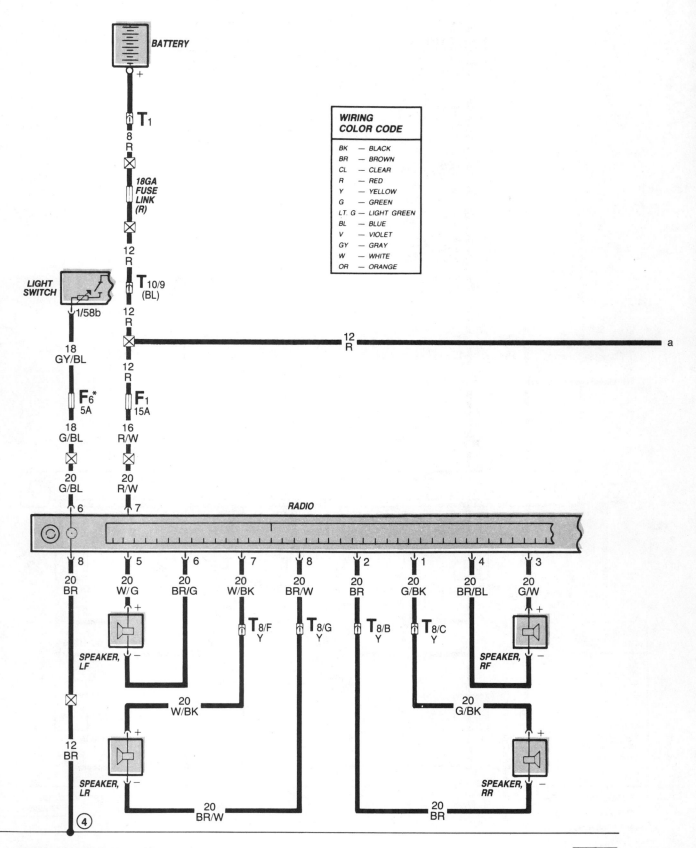

WIRING
COLOR CODE

BK	—	BLACK
BR	—	BROWN
CL	—	CLEAR
R	—	RED
Y	—	YELLOW
G	—	GREEN
LT. G	—	LIGHT GREEN
BL	—	BLUE
V	—	VIOLET
GY	—	GRAY
W	—	WHITE
OR	—	ORANGE

* Fuse 1, 15 AMPS ON ALL MODELS EXCEPT 16-VALVE

97-A433

Radio
1988-1989 Golf/GTI
(page 2 of 2)

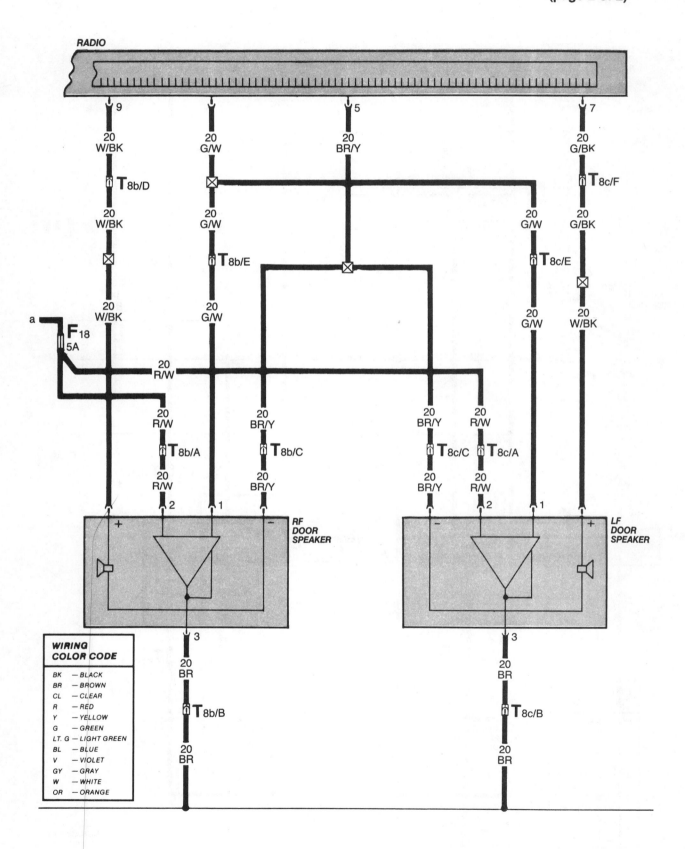

WIRING COLOR CODE

BK	— BLACK
BR	— BROWN
CL	— CLEAR
R	— RED
Y	— YELLOW
G	— GREEN
LT. G	— LIGHT GREEN
BL	— BLUE
V	— VIOLET
GY	— GRAY
W	— WHITE
OR	— ORANGE

Power Windows
1986–1987 Golf/GTI (except 16-valve)
(page 1 of 2)

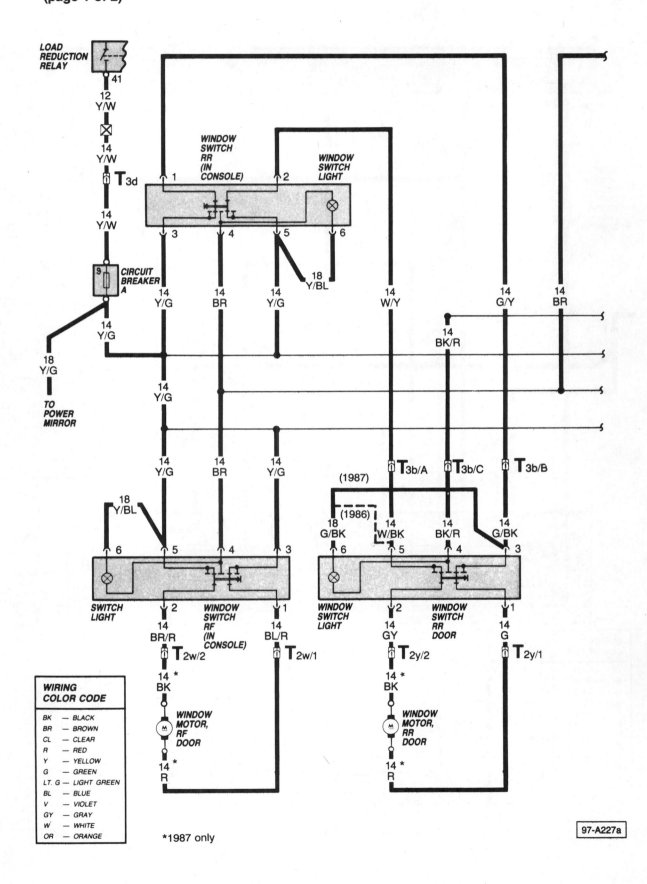

97-A227a

*1987 only

Power Windows
1986–1987 Golf/GTI (except 16-valve)
(page 2 of 2)

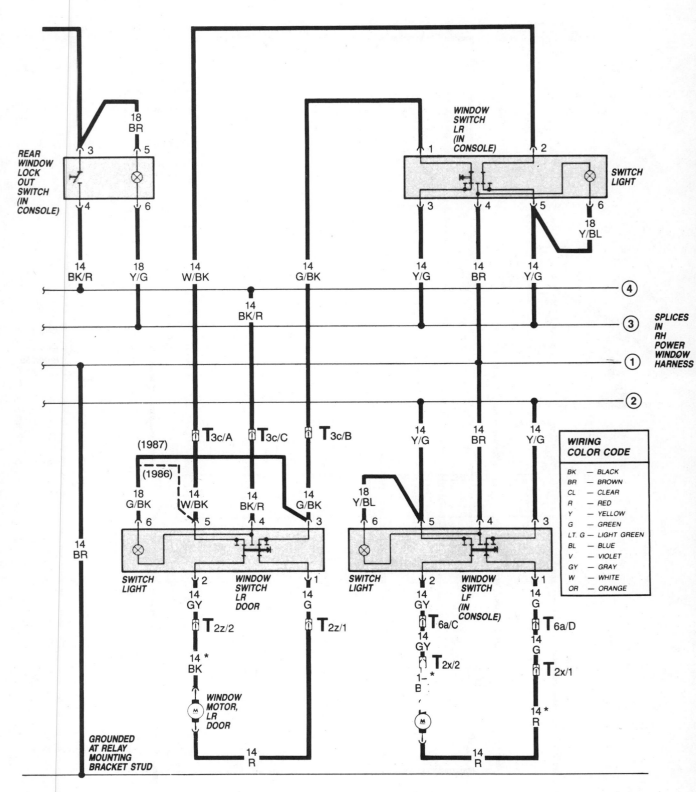

WINDOW
SWITCH
LR
(IN
CONSOLE)

SWITCH
LIGHT

REAR
WINDOW
LOCK
OUT
SWITCH
(IN
CONSOLE)

18
BR

3

5

4

6

1

2

3

4

5

6

18
Y/BL

14
BK/R

18
Y/G

14
W/BK

14
G/BK

14
Y/G

14
BR

14
Y/G

④

14
BK/R

③ SPLICES
IN
RH
POWER
WINDOW
HARNESS

①

②

T3c/A

T3c/C

T3c/B

14
Y/G

14
BR

14
Y/G

(1987)

(1986)

18
G/BK

14
W/BK

14
BK/R

14
G/BK

18
Y/BL

SWITCH
LIGHT

6

5

4

3

WINDOW
SWITCH
LR
DOOR

2

1

SWITCH
LIGHT

6

5

4

3

WINDOW
SWITCH
LF
(IN
CONSOLE)

2

1

14
GY

14
G

14
GY

14
G

T2z/2

T2z/1

T6a/C

T6a/D

14 *
BK

14
GY

14
G

T2x/2

T2x/1

1- *
B

14 *
R

WINDOW
MOTOR,
LR
DOOR

M

M

14
R

14
R

WIRING COLOR CODE

BK	— BLACK
BR	— BROWN
CL	— CLEAR
R	— RED
Y	— YELLOW
G	— GREEN
LT. G	— LIGHT GREEN
BL	— BLUE
V	— VIOLET
GY	— GRAY
W	— WHITE
OR	— ORANGE

14
BR

GROUNDED
AT RELAY
MOUNTING
BRACKET STUD

*1987 only

97-A228a

Power Windows
1987-1989 GTI 16-valve
(page 1 of 1)

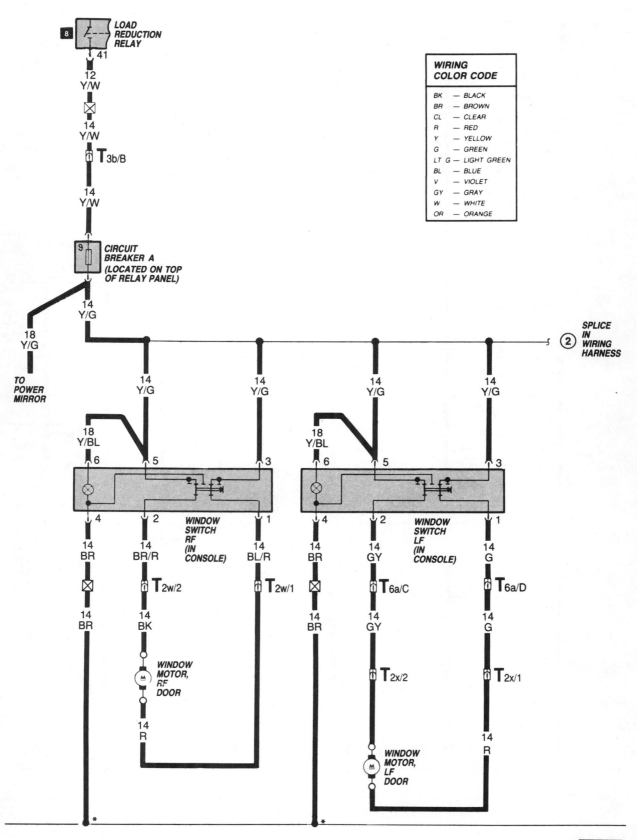

WIRING COLOR CODE	
BK	— BLACK
BR	— BROWN
CL	— CLEAR
R	— RED
Y	— YELLOW
G	— GREEN
LT G	— LIGHT GREEN
BL	— BLUE
V	— VIOLET
GY	— GRAY
W	— WHITE
OR	— ORANGE

* 1986 — SPLICE IN WIRING HARNESS

97-A437

Central Locking
1986-1989 Golf/GTI
(page 1 of 1)

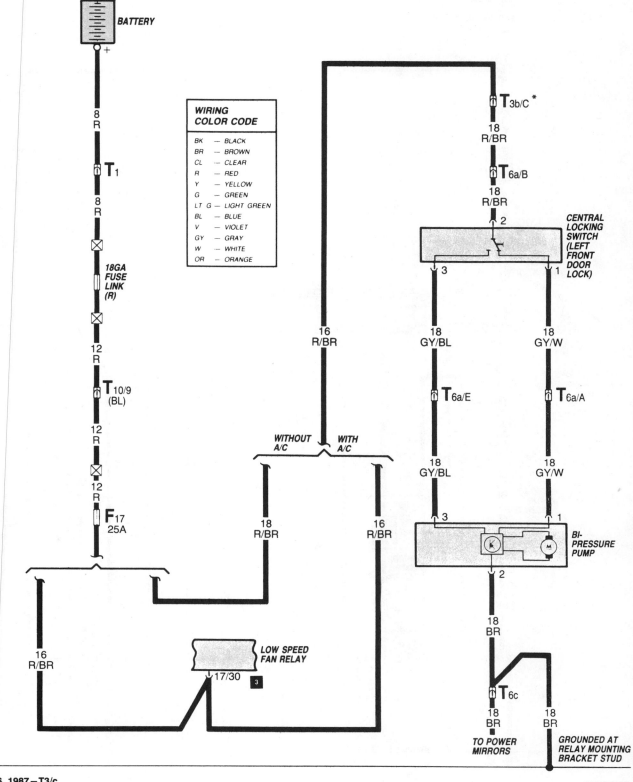

WIRING
COLOR CODE

BK — BLACK
BR — BROWN
CL — CLEAR
R — RED
Y — YELLOW
G — GREEN
LT G — LIGHT GREEN
BL — BLUE
V — VIOLET
GY — GRAY
W — WHITE
OR — ORANGE

BATTERY

8
R

T_1

8
R

18GA
FUSE
LINK
(R)

12
R

$T_{10/9}$
(BL)

12
R

F_{17}
25A

$T_{3b/C}$ *

18
R/BR

$T_{6a/B}$

18
R/BR

2

CENTRAL
LOCKING
SWITCH
(LEFT
FRONT
DOOR
LOCK)

3   1

16
R/BR

18
GY/BL

18
GY/W

$T_{6a/E}$

$T_{6a/A}$

WITHOUT
A/C

WITH
A/C

18
R/BR

16
R/BR

18
GY/BL

18
GY/W

3   1

BI-
PRESSURE
PUMP

K   M

2

16
R/BR

LOW SPEED
FAN RELAY

17/30

3

18
BR

T_{6c}

18
BR

18
BR

TO POWER
MIRRORS

GROUNDED AT
RELAY MOUNTING
BRACKET STUD

* 1986, 1987 — T3/c

97-A438

Power Mirrors
1986 Golf/GTI
(page 1 of 1)

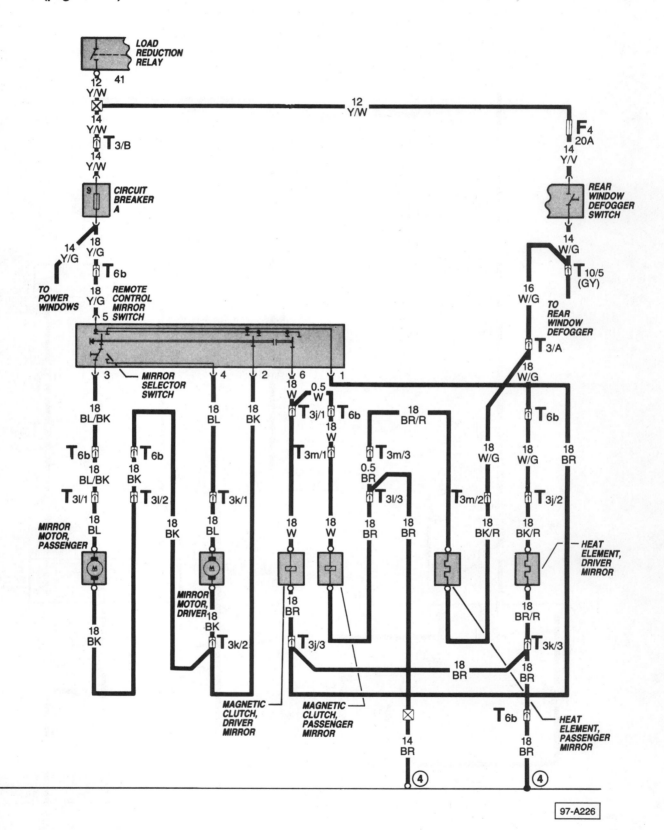

97-A226

Power Mirrors
1987-1989 Golf/GTI
(page 1 of 2)

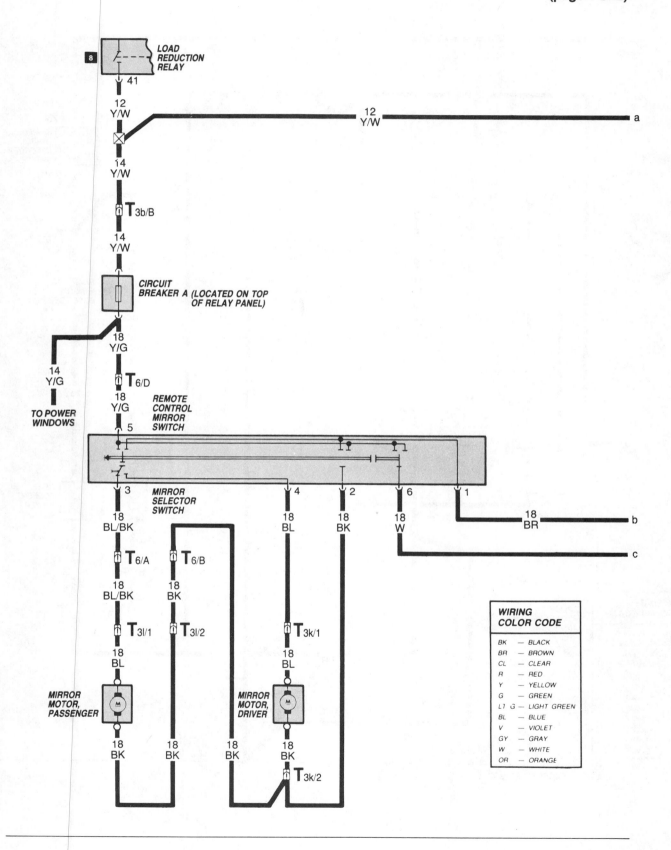

WIRING
COLOR CODE

BK	—	BLACK
BR	—	BROWN
CL	—	CLEAR
R	—	RED
Y	—	YELLOW
G	—	GREEN
LT G	—	LIGHT GREEN
BL	—	BLUE
V	—	VIOLET
GY	—	GRAY
W	—	WHITE
OR	—	ORANGE

97-A435

Power Mirrors
1987-1989 Golf/GTI
(page 2 of 2)

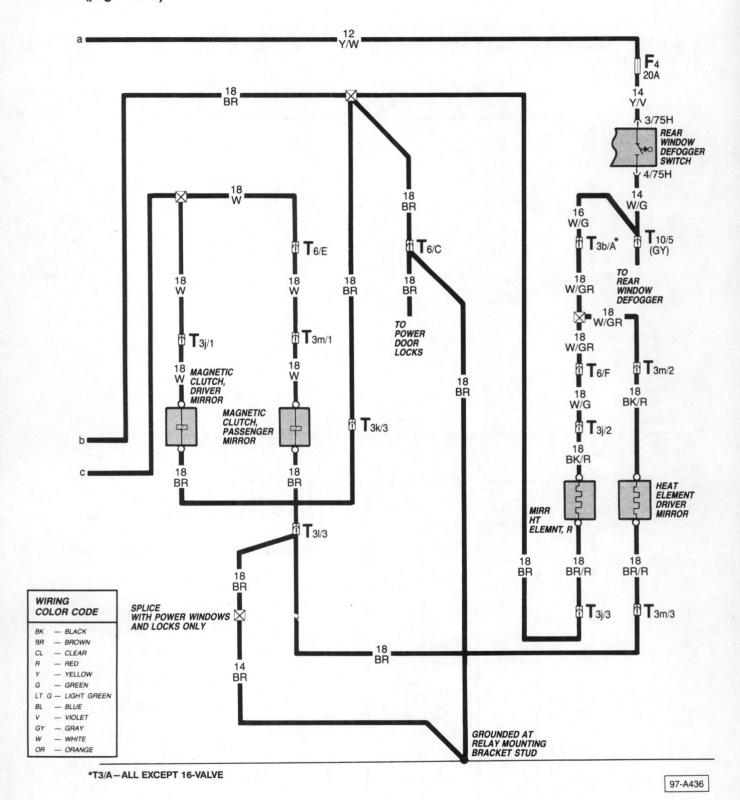

*T3/A—ALL EXCEPT 16-VALVE

97-A436

Main Electrical System
1985–1987 Jetta (Gasoline only except GLI)
(page 1 of 10)

Description	Current Track
Air flow sensor	19, 23
Alternator	1, 2
Alternator warning light	42
Auxiliary air regulator	32
Back-up light, left	122
Back-up light, right	123
Back-up light switch	123
Battery	3
Brake fluid level switch	70
Brake light, left	111
Brake light, right	110
Brake light switch	100
Brake/parking brake indicator light	68, 69
CAT mileage counter	54, 55
Cigarette lighter	80
Cigarette lighter light	81
Clock	73
Clock light	78
Cold start valve	8
Coolant over temp. light	51, 52
Coolant temp. gauge	50
Coolant temp. sending unit	72
Differential pressure regulator	21
Door contact/buzzer switch, left front	64, 65
Door contact switch, left rear	61
Door contact switch, right front	63
Door contact switch, right rear	62
Emergency flasher relay	105, 106
Emergency flasher switch	103-109
Emergency flasher warning light	109
Engine oil press. control unit	42-43
Engine oil press. switch (0.3 bar)	57
Engine oil press. switch (1.8 bar)	56
Engine oil press. warning light	48
Fresh air fan	112, 113
Fresh air fan switch	112, 113
Fuel gauge	49
Fuel gauge sending unit	28
Fuel pump	31
Fuel pump (transfer pump)	29
Fuel pump relay	28-30
Glove compartment light	114
Glove compartment light switch	114
Hall generator	10, 11
Headlight dimmer/flasher switch	85, 86
Headlight hi-beam warn. light	46
Headlight, left	87, 89
Headlight, right	88, 90
Headlight switch light	75
Horns	33, 34
Horn button	37
Horn relay	35, 36

Description	Current Track
Idle speed stabilizer control unit	16-17
Idle speed stabilizer valve	18
Ignition coil	13, 14
Ignition control unit	9-13
Ignition distributor	12-15
Ignition/start switch	38-40
Instrument panel light	77
Instrument panel light switch/ dimmer	79
Interior light with delay switch	60, 61
License plate light	84, 85
Light switch	74-79
Luggage compartment light	58
Luggage compartment light switch	58
Make-up mirror light	59
OXS control unit	17-23
OXS mileage indicator	53
Oxygen sensor	23
Radiator cooling fan	130, 131
Radiator cooling fan relay	128-130
Radiator cooling fan thermoswitch	128, 129
Rear window defogger ind. light	133
Rear window defogger switch	132-134
Rear window defogger switch light	132
Rear window heater element	135
Seat belt switch, left	66
Seat belt warning light	67
Seat belt warning system relay	65-67
Side marker lights, front	91, 94
Spark plugs	12-15
Spark plug connectors	12-15
Starter	4-6
Tachometer	42
Tail light, left	98
Tail light, right	97
Temperature sensor (NTC)	22
Thermoswitch	7, 8
Time delay relay (X-contact)	73, 74
Turn signal indicator light	48
Turn signal light, left front	96
Turn signal light, left rear	99
Turn signal light, right front	93
Turn signal light, right rear	100
Turn signal switch	106, 107
Upshift control light	41
Upshift ind. control unit	24-27
Vacuum switch, upshift indicator	25
Voltage stabilizer	49
Washer/wiper intermittent relay	119, 120
Windshield washer pump	121
Windshield wiper intermittent switch	118-120
Windshield wiper motor	116, 117

Wire Connectors

T1a	— single, eng. compartment right
T1b	— single, under fuse/relay panel
T1c	— single, eng. compart. near coil
T2a	— double, eng. compart. near coil
T1d	— single, under instrument panel
T2b	— double, in luggage compartment
T2c	— double, engine compart., front
T2g	— double, engine compart., front
T8	— 8 point, on transmission
T1f	— single, under fuse/relay panel
T7	— 7 point, on instrument cluster
T7a	— 7 point, on instrument cluster
T7b	— 7 point, on instrument cluster
T7c	— 7 point, on instrument cluster
T1e	— single, under fuse/relay panel
T1g	— single, under fuse/relay panel
T1h	— single, under fuse/relay panel
T2e	— double, on roof bow
T2f	— double, under fuse/relay panel
T32	— 32 point, under instrument panel
T1p	— single, luggage compart., left
T2h	— double, under instrument panel
T3a	— 3 point, under fuse/relay panel
T4	— 4 point, under instrument panel
T7	— 7 point, on instrument cluster
T7b	— 7 point, on instrument cluster
T32	— 32 point, under instrument panel
T2i	— double, near right headlights
T2k	— double, near left headlights
T3b	— 3 point, near right headlights
T3c	— 3 point, near left headlights
T1i	— single, under instrument panel
T2l	— double, under instrument panel
T2n	— double, under instrument panel
T32	— 32-point, under instrument panel
T8	— 8 point, on transmission
T1k	— single, on radiator fan shroud
T1l	— single, on radiator fan shroud
T1m	— single, in luggage comp., left
T2p	— double, in coolant line
T2q	— double, on radiator fan shroud
T2r	— double, on radiator fan shroud
T2s	— double, on radiator fan shroud
T32	— 32 point, under instrument panel

Ground Connectors

(1)	— battery ground cable
(8)	— on intake manifold
(10)	— near fuse/relay panel
(13)	— near steering column
(15)	— in front wiring harness
(16)	— in instrument panel wiring
(17)	— in instrument cluster wiring harness
(18)	— in luggage compartment, left
(19)	— in luggage compartment, right
(20)	— crimped connector in instrument panel wiring harness

Main Electrical System
1985–1987 Jetta (Gasoline only except GLI)
(page 2 of 10)

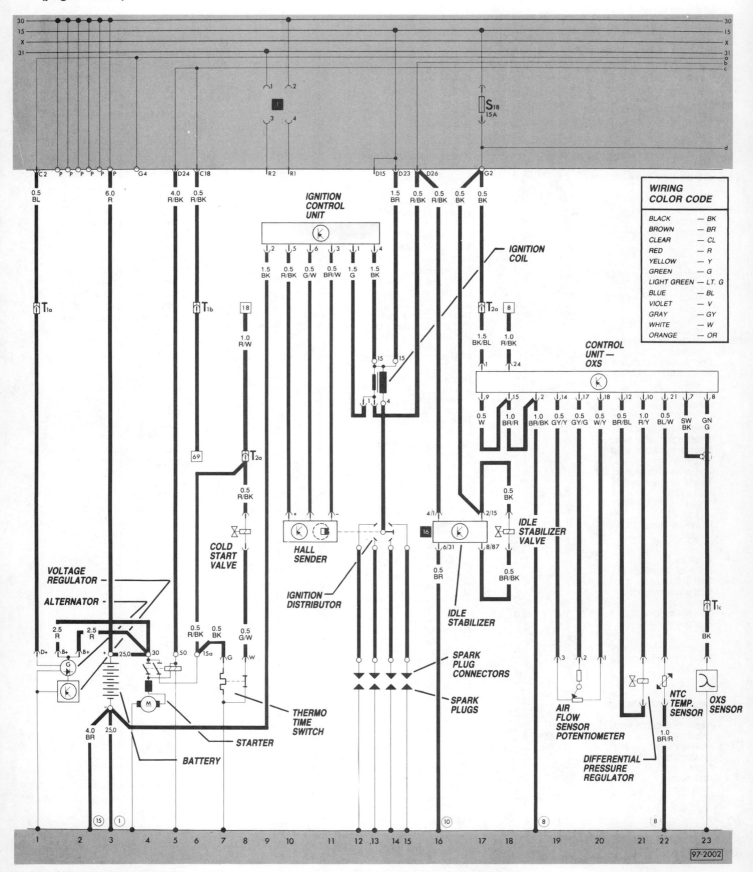

For CIS refer to page 206 , GLI refer to page 182 , CIS Canada refer to page 210

Main Electrical System
1985–1987 Jetta (Gasoline only except GLI)
(page 3 of 10)

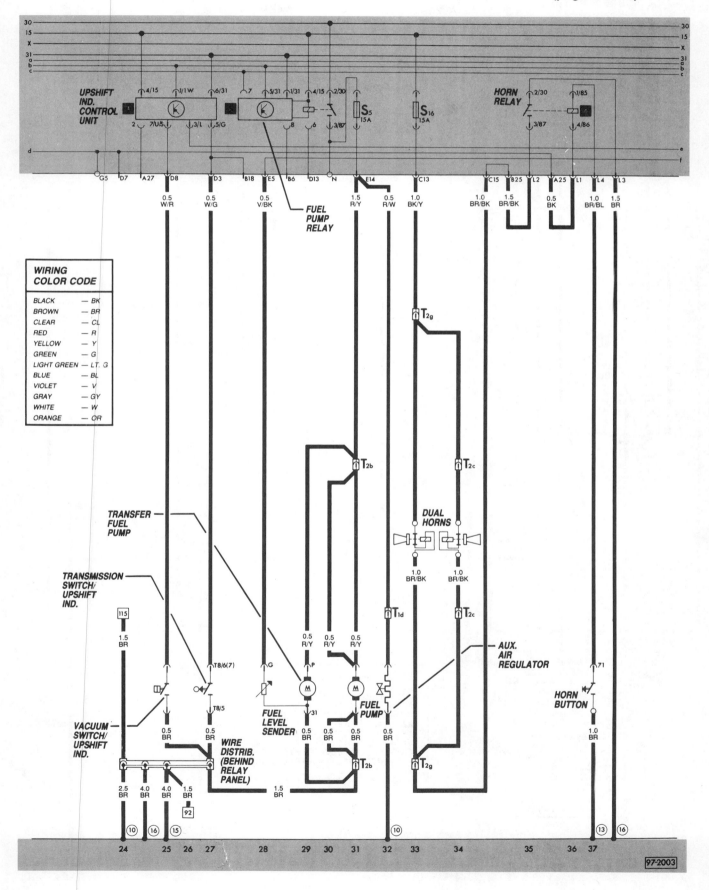

97-2003

Main Electrical System
1985–1987 Jetta (Gasoline only except GLI)
(page 4 of 10)

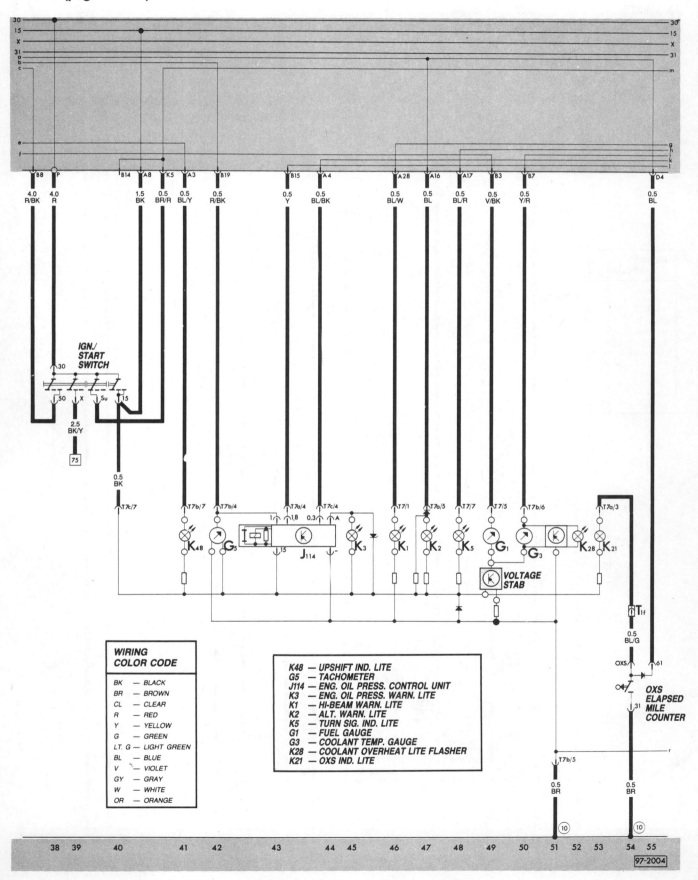

WIRING
COLOR CODE

BK — BLACK
BR — BROWN
CL — CLEAR
R — RED
Y — YELLOW
G — GREEN
LT. G — LIGHT GREEN
BL — BLUE
V — VIOLET
GY — GRAY
W — WHITE
OR — ORANGE

K48 — UPSHIFT IND. LITE
G5 — TACHOMETER
J114 — ENG. OIL PRESS. CONTROL UNIT
K3 — ENG. OIL PRESS. WARN. LITE
K1 — HI-BEAM WARN. LITE
K2 — ALT. WARN. LITE
K5 — TURN SIG. IND. LITE
G1 — FUEL GAUGE
G3 — COOLANT TEMP. GAUGE
K28 — COOLANT OVERHEAT LITE FLASHER
K21 — OXS IND. LITE

IGN./
START
SWITCH

VOLTAGE
STAB

OXS
ELAPSED
MILE
COUNTER

38   39   40   41   42   43   44   45   46   47   48   49   50   51   52   53   54   55

97-2004

Main Electrical System
1985–1987 Jetta (Gasoline only except GLI)
(page 5 of 10)

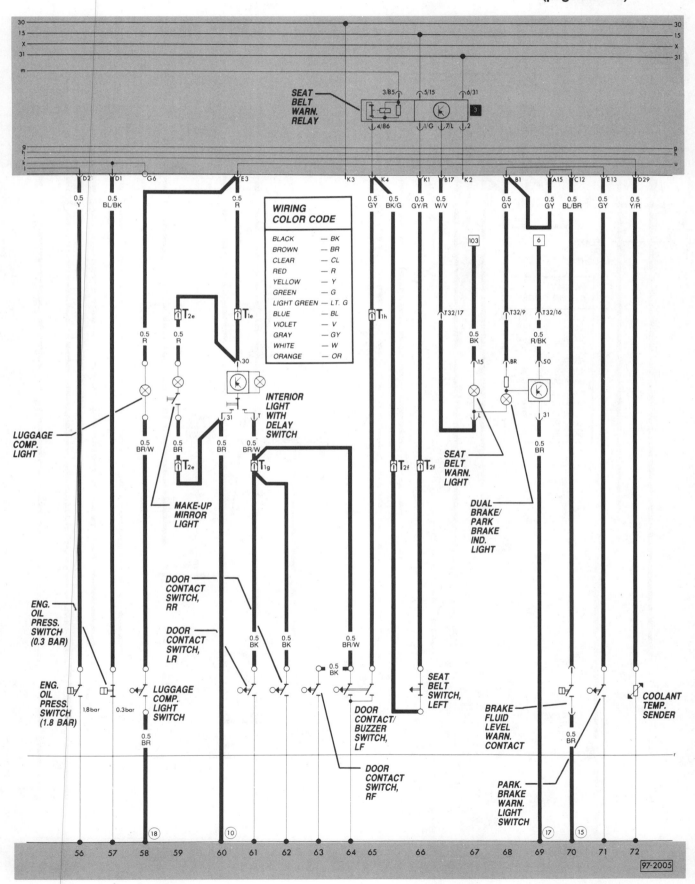

Main Electrical System
1985–1987 Jetta (Gasoline only except GLI)
(page 6 of 10)

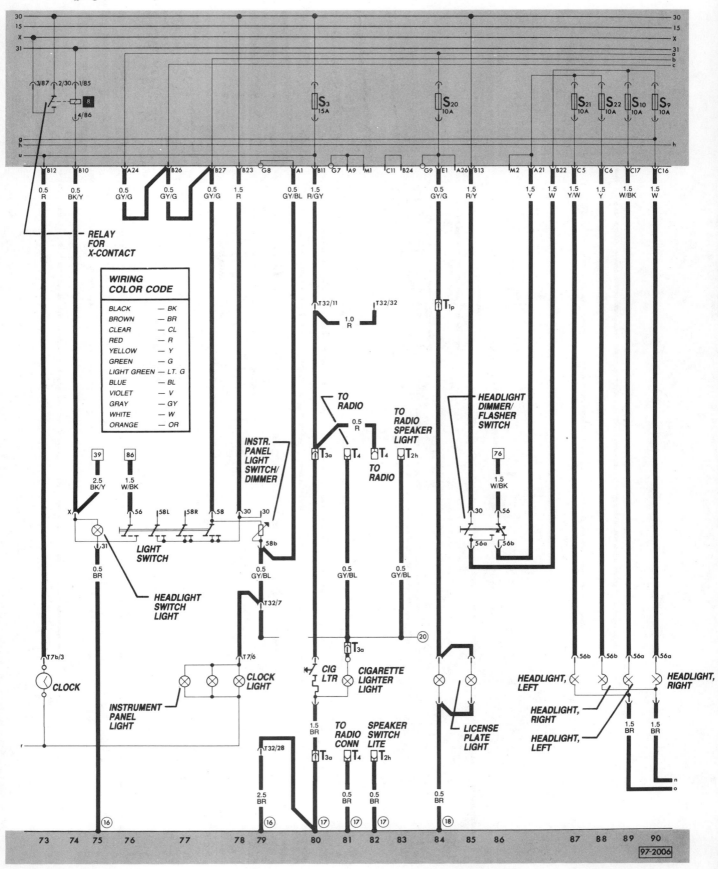

WIRING
COLOR CODE

BLACK	— BK
BROWN	— BR
CLEAR	— CL
RED	— R
YELLOW	— Y
GREEN	— G
LIGHT GREEN	— LT. G
BLUE	— BL
VIOLET	— V
GRAY	— GY
WHITE	— W
ORANGE	— OR

RELAY
FOR
X-CONTACT

INSTR.
PANEL
LIGHT
SWITCH/
DIMMER

HEADLIGHT
SWITCH
LIGHT

LIGHT
SWITCH

TO RADIO

TO
RADIO
SPEAKER
LIGHT

TO
RADIO

HEADLIGHT
DIMMER/
FLASHER
SWITCH

CLOCK

INSTRUMENT
PANEL
LIGHT

CLOCK
LIGHT

CIGARETTE
LIGHTER
LIGHT

CIG
LTR

TO
RADIO
CONN

SPEAKER
SWITCH
LITE

LICENSE
PLATE
LIGHT

HEADLIGHT,
LEFT

HEADLIGHT,
RIGHT

HEADLIGHT,
RIGHT

HEADLIGHT,
LEFT

HEADLIGHT,
RIGHT

Main Electrical System
1985–1987 Jetta (Gasoline only except GLI)
(page 7 of 10)

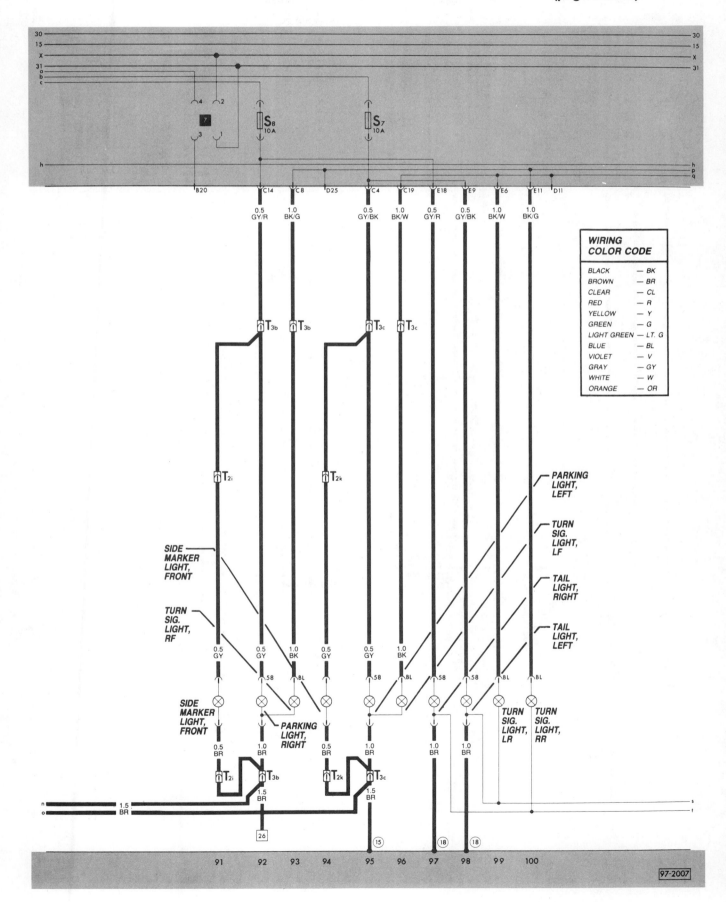

WIRING COLOR CODE	
BLACK	— BK
BROWN	— BR
CLEAR	— CL
RED	— R
YELLOW	— Y
GREEN	— G
LIGHT GREEN	— LT. G
BLUE	— BL
VIOLET	— V
GRAY	— GY
WHITE	— W
ORANGE	— OR

97-2007

Main Electrical System
1985–1987 Jetta (Gasoline only except GLI)
(page 8 of 10)

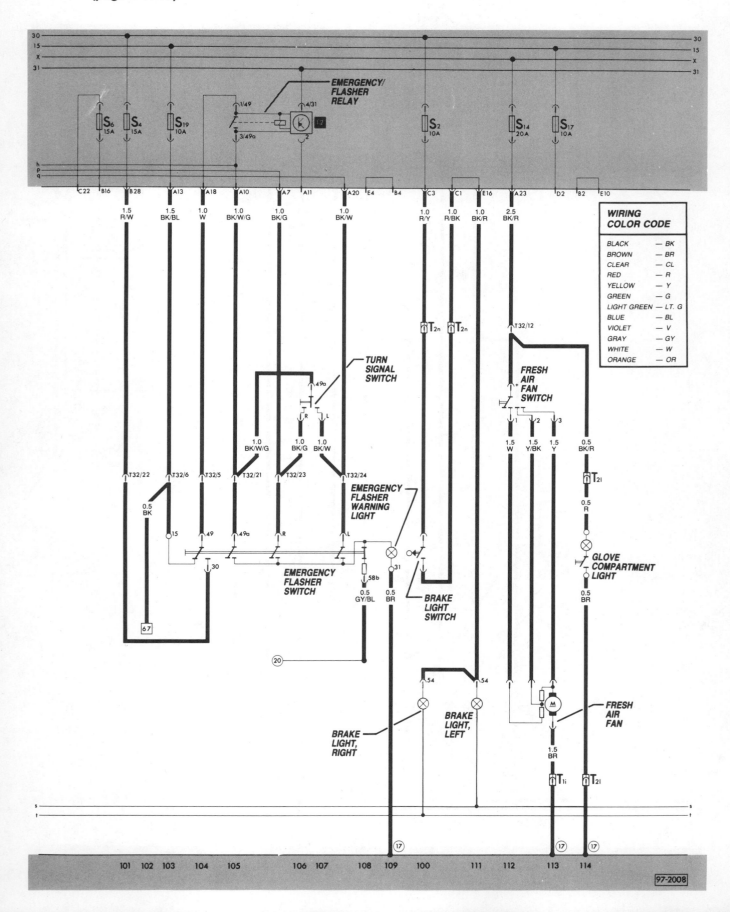

WIRING COLOR CODE	
BLACK	— BK
BROWN	— BR
CLEAR	— CL
RED	— R
YELLOW	— Y
GREEN	— G
LIGHT GREEN	— LT. G
BLUE	— BL
VIOLET	— V
GRAY	— GY
WHITE	— W
ORANGE	— OR

97-2008

Main Electrical System
1985–1987 Jetta (Gasoline only except GLI)
(page 9 of 10)

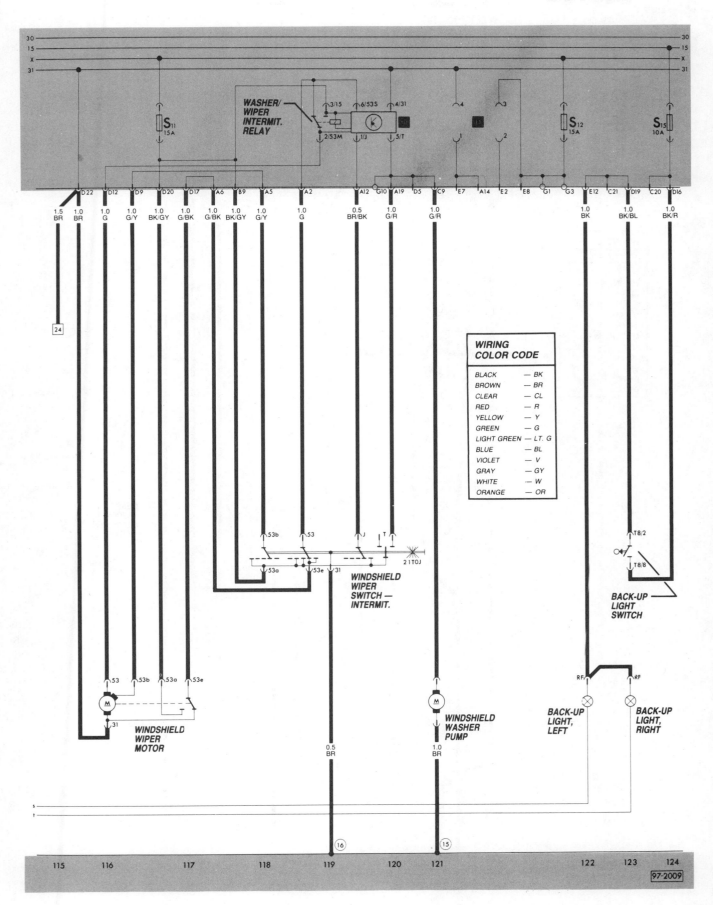

WASHER/
WIPER
INTERMIT.
RELAY

WIRING
COLOR CODE

BLACK	— BK
BROWN	— BR
CLEAR	— CL
RED	— R
YELLOW	— Y
GREEN	— G
LIGHT GREEN	— LT. G
BLUE	— BL
VIOLET	— V
GRAY	— GY
WHITE	— W
ORANGE	— OR

WINDSHIELD
WIPER
SWITCH —
INTERMIT.

BACK-UP
LIGHT
SWITCH

WINDSHIELD
WIPER
MOTOR

WINDSHIELD
WASHER
PUMP

BACK-UP
LIGHT,
LEFT

BACK-UP
LIGHT,
RIGHT

Main Electrical System
1985–1987 Jetta (Gasoline only except GLI)
(page 10 of 10)

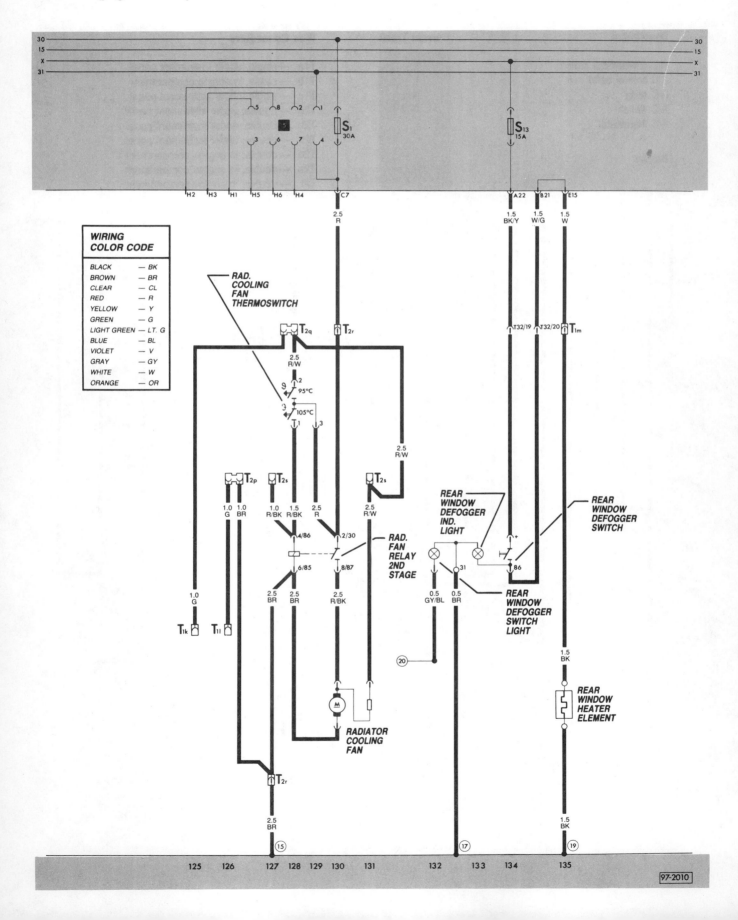

WIRING
COLOR CODE

BLACK	— BK
BROWN	— BR
CLEAR	— CL
RED	— R
YELLOW	— Y
GREEN	— G
LIGHT GREEN	— LT. G
BLUE	— BL
VIOLET	— V
GRAY	— GY
WHITE	— W
ORANGE	— OR

RAD.
COOLING
FAN
THERMOSWITCH

RAD.
FAN
RELAY
2ND
STAGE

RADIATOR
COOLING
FAN

REAR
WINDOW
DEFOGGER
IND.
LIGHT

REAR
WINDOW
DEFOGGER
SWITCH

REAR
WINDOW
DEFOGGER
SWITCH
LIGHT

REAR
WINDOW
HEATER
ELEMENT

97-2010

Main Electrical System
1988-1989 Jetta (except Diesel)
1986–1989 Jetta GLI
(page 1 of 15)

Description	Current track
Air flow sensor potentiometer	26, 27
Alternator	1, 2
Alternator warning lite	55
Back-up lite switch	109
Back-up lite, left	108
Back-up lite, right	110
Battery	3
Brake and parking brake indicator lite	77
Brake fluid level warning contact	79
Brake lite switch	119
Brake lite, left	119
Brake lite, right	120
Cigarette lighter	88
Cigarette lighter lite	89
Clock lite	65
Cold start valve	8
Coolant overheat warning lite	59
Coolant temperature gauge	58
Coolant temperature sending unit	81
Door contact switch, left front	74, 75
Door contact switch, left rear	71
Door contact switch, right front	73
Door contact switch, right rear	72
Emergency flasher relay	113-116
Emergency flasher switch	112-118
Emergency flasher warning lite	118
Engine oil pressure control unit	50-52
Engine oil pressure sw (0.3 bar)	67
Engine oil pressure sw (1.8 bar)	66
Engine oil pressure warning lite	53
Engine oil temperature sensor	61
Fresh air control lever lite	90
Fresh air fan	135, 136
Fresh air fan switch	135, 136
Fuel enrichment switch	19
Fuel gauge	57
Fuel gauge sending unit	32
Fuel pump	35
Fuel pump relay	32-35
Glove compartment lite	137
Hall generator	12, 13
Headlite dimmer/flasher switch	92, 93
Headlite high beam warning lite	54
Headlite switch lite	84
Headlite, left	94, 96
Headlite, right	95, 97
Horn button	41
Horn relay	39, 40
Horns	37, 38
Idle speed stabilizer valve	21, 22
Idle switch	20
Ignition coil	10
Ignition control unit	9-11
Ignition distributor	10,11
Ignition/starter switch	44, 47
Instrument panel lite	65
Instrument panel lite dimmer sw	87
Interior lite with delay switch	70, 71
Junction box	29-32
Knock sensor	16, 17
Knock sensor control unit	12-19
License plate lite	91, 93
Lite switch	83-87
Load reduction relay	82, 83
Luggage compartment lite	68
Luggage compartment lite switch	68

Description	Current track
Make-up mirror lite	69
Memory switch (multi-function ind.)	64, 65
Multi-function indicator	60-65
Multi-function indicator recall button	63
Outside air temperature sensor	62
OXS control unit	15-28
OXS elapsed mileage counter	42, 43
OXS elapsed mileage indicator	44
Oxygen sensor	24
Oxygen sensor heater	25
Parking brake warning lite switch	80
Parking lite, left	102
Parking lite, right	99
Pressure gradient valve	23
Radiator cooling fan	132, 133
Radiator cooling fan after run control unit	128, 129
Radiator cooling fan after run relay	133, 134
Radiator cooling fan after run thermoswitch	128, 130, 131
Rear window defogger indicator lite	139
Rear window defogger switch	138-140
Rear window defogger switch lite	138
Rear window heater element	141
Safety belt switch, left	73
Seat belt warning lite	76
Seat belt warning relay	72-76
Side marker lites, front	98, 101
Spark plug connectors	10, 11
Spark plugs	10, 11
Speed sensor	58
Starter	4, 5
Tachometer	50
Tail lite, left	105
Tail lite, right	104
Temperature sensor (NTC)	28
Thermo time switch	7, 8
Transfer fuel pump	33
Turn signal indicator lite	56
Turn signal lite, left front	103
Turn signal lite, left rear	106
Turn signal lite, right front	100
Turn signal lite, right rear	107
Turn signal switch	114-116
Up-shift Indicator lite	49
Up-shift indicator control unit	29-31
Upshift switch, transmission	31
Upshift switch, vacuum	30
Vacuum sensor	47, 48
Voltage regulator	1, 2
Voltage stabilizer	57
Washer/wiper intermittent relay	125, 126
Windshield washer pump	127
Windshield wiper motor	122, 123
Windshield-wiper intermittent switch	124-126

Wire connectors

T — junction box
T1a — single, in engine compartment, right
T1b — single, behind relay panel plate
T1c — single, in engine compartment
T1d — single
T1e — single, in engine compartment near ignition coil

Wire connectors

T1f — single, in engine compartment near cylinder head cover
T1g — single, behind relay panel plate
T1h — single, in engine compartment, rear
T1i — single, behind dash
T1k — single, behind relay panel plate
T1m — single, in luggage compartment, left
T1o — single, behind relay panel plate
T1p — single, in luggage compartment, left
T1q — single, behind relay panel plate
T2a — double, in engine compartment near intake manifold
T2b — double, in luggage compartment
T2c — double, in engine compartment near brake booster
T2d — double, in engine compartment, front
T2e — double, near interior light
T2f — double, in plenum chamber, right
T2g — double, in engine compartment, front
T2h — double, behind relay panel plate
T2i — double, near headlight, right
T2k — double, near headlight, left
T2l — double, behind dash
T2m — double, behind relay panel plate
T2n — double, behind dash
T2p — double, on fan shroud
T2t — double, behind radiator grille, right
T2u — double, on fan shroud
T2v — double, on fan shroud
T2w — double, on fan shroud
T2x — double, rear seat, left
T3a — 3 point, in engine compartment, center
T3b — 3 point, in engine compartment near throttle valve housing
T3c — 3 point, in plenum chamber, left
T3d — 3 point, behind relay panel plate
T3e — 3 point, near headlight, right
T3f — 3 point, near headlight, left
T3y — 3 point, in engine compartment near ignition coil
T4a — 4 point, behind steering column switch cover
T7 — 7 point, on instrument cluster
T7a — 7 point, on instrument cluster
T7b — 7 point, on instrument cluster
T7c — 7 point, on instrument cluster
T8 — 8 point, on radio
T32 — 32 — point, behind dash

Ground connections

① — ground strap battery to body
③ — ground strap engine to body
⑰ — intake manifold
㉚ — beside relay plate
㊷ — beside steering column
㊿ — luggage compartment, left
(51) — luggage compartment, right
⑧⓪ — 1 — in instrument panel wiring harness
⑧① — in dashboard wiring harness
⑧② — 1 — in wiring harness front/left
⑨⓪ — in wiring harness CIS-E

Plus connections

Ⓐ11 — plus connection (58b) in instrument panel wiring harness

Main Electrical System
1988-1989 Jetta (except Diesel)
1986-1989 Jetta GLI
(page 2 of 15)

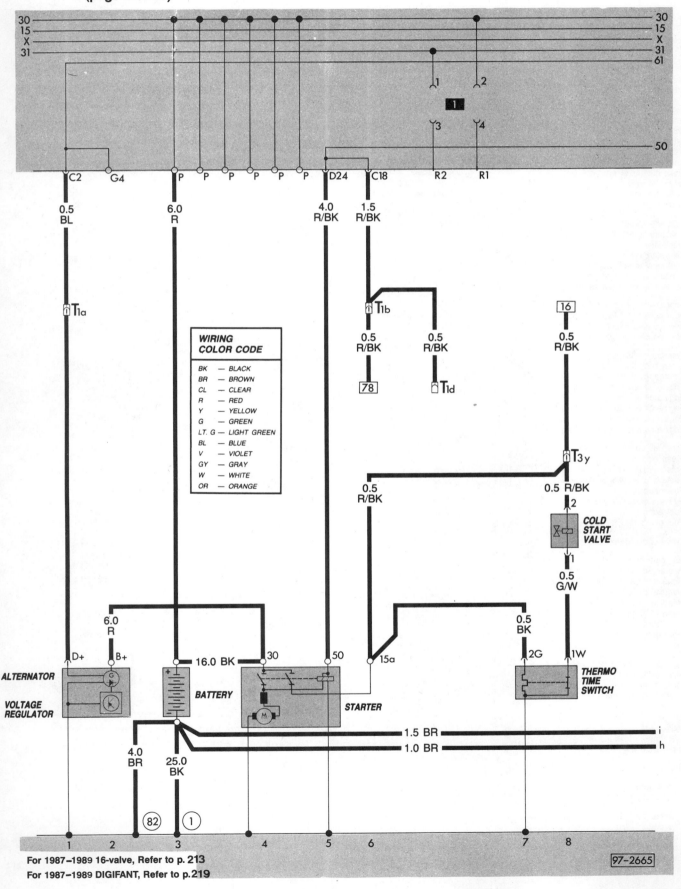

WIRING COLOR CODE

BK	— BLACK
BR	— BROWN
CL	— CLEAR
R	— RED
Y	— YELLOW
G	— GREEN
LT. G	— LIGHT GREEN
BL	— BLUE
V	— VIOLET
GY	— GRAY
W	— WHITE
OR	— ORANGE

For 1987–1989 16-valve, Refer to p. 213
For 1987–1989 DIGIFANT, Refer to p. 219

97–2665

Main Electrical System
1988-1989 Jetta (except Diesel)
1986-1989 Jetta GLI
(page 3 of 15)

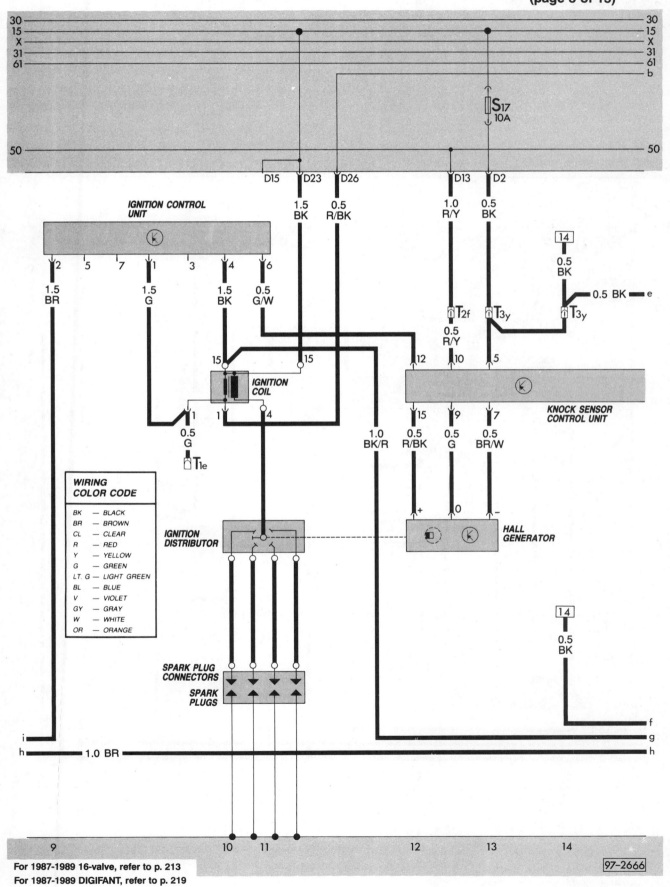

WIRING COLOR CODE

BK — BLACK
BR — BROWN
CL — CLEAR
R — RED
Y — YELLOW
G — GREEN
LT. G — LIGHT GREEN
BL — BLUE
V — VIOLET
GY — GRAY
W — WHITE
OR — ORANGE

For 1987-1989 16-valve, refer to p. 213
For 1987-1989 DIGIFANT, refer to p. 219

97-2666

Main Electrical System
1988-1989 Jetta (except Diesel)
1986-1989 Jetta GLI
(page 4 of 15)

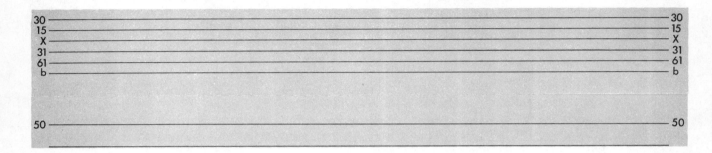

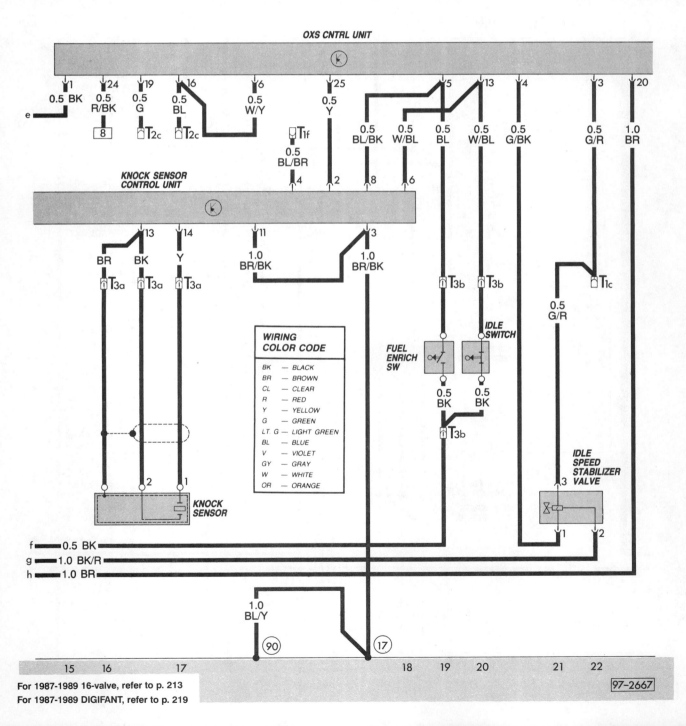

WIRING
COLOR CODE

BK	— BLACK
BR	— BROWN
CL	— CLEAR
R	— RED
Y	— YELLOW
G	— GREEN
LT. G	— LIGHT GREEN
BL	— BLUE
V	— VIOLET
GY	— GRAY
W	— WHITE
OR	— ORANGE

For 1987-1989 16-valve, refer to p. 213
For 1987-1989 DIGIFANT, refer to p. 219

97-2667

Main Electrical System
1988-1989 Jetta (except Diesel)
1986-1989 Jetta GLI
(page 5 of 15)

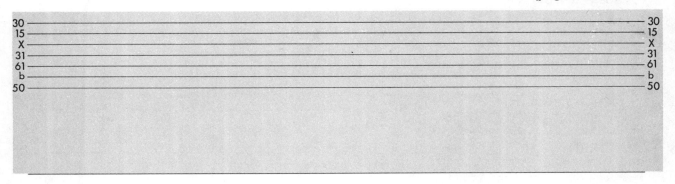

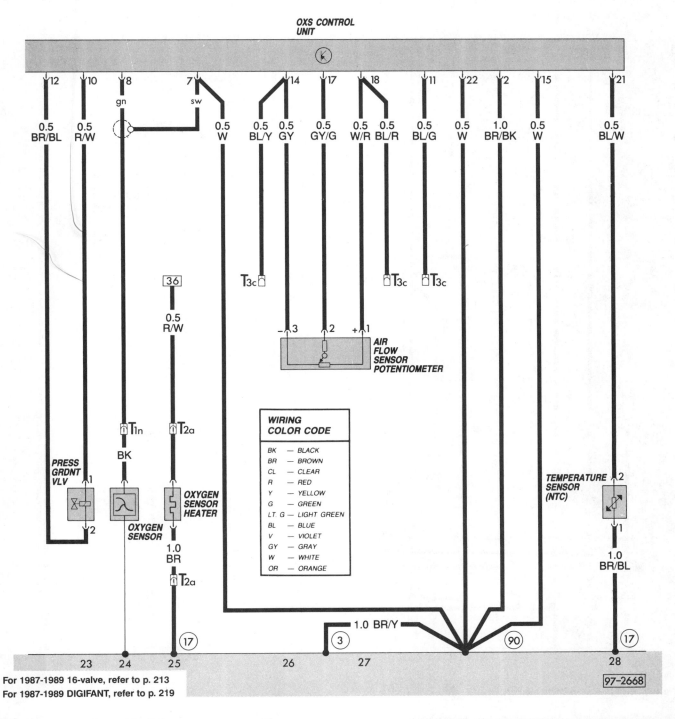

WIRING
COLOR CODE

BK	—	BLACK
BR	—	BROWN
CL	—	CLEAR
R	—	RED
Y	—	YELLOW
G	—	GREEN
LT. G	—	LIGHT GREEN
BL	—	BLUE
V	—	VIOLET
GY	—	GRAY
W	—	WHITE
OR	—	ORANGE

For 1987-1989 16-valve, refer to p. 213
For 1987-1989 DIGIFANT, refer to p. 219

97-2668

Main Electrical System
1988-1989 Jetta (except Diesel)
1986-1989 Jetta GLI
(page 6 of 15)

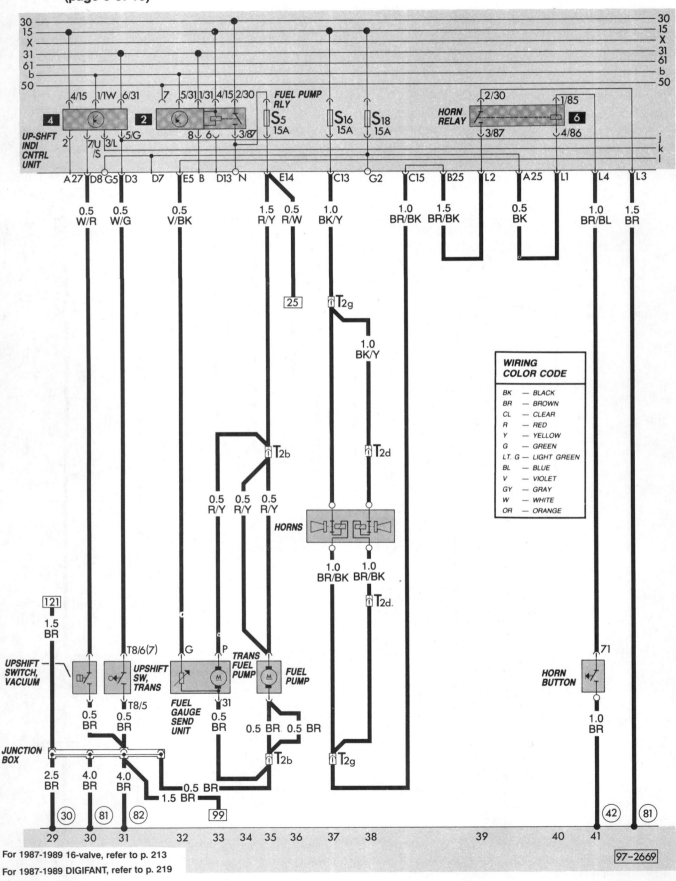

For 1987-1989 16-valve, refer to p. 213

For 1987-1989 DIGIFANT, refer to p. 219

97-2669

**Main Electrical System
1988-1989 Jetta (except Diesel)
1986-1989 Jetta GLI
(page 7 of 15)**

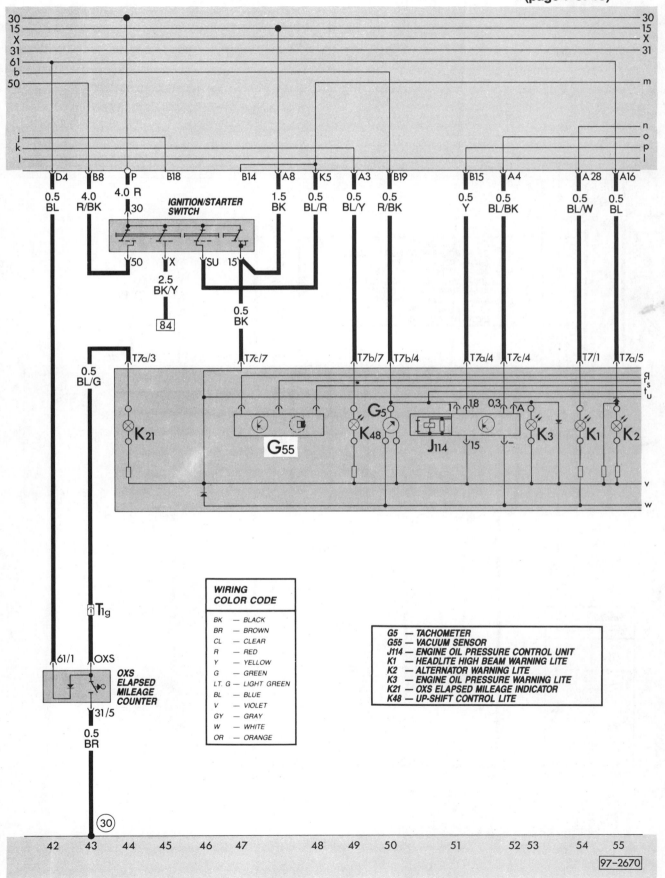

WIRING
COLOR CODE

BK — BLACK
BR — BROWN
CL — CLEAR
R — RED
Y — YELLOW
G — GREEN
LT. G — LIGHT GREEN
BL — BLUE
V — VIOLET
GY — GRAY
W — WHITE
OR — ORANGE

G5 — TACHOMETER
G55 — VACUUM SENSOR
J114 — ENGINE OIL PRESSURE CONTROL UNIT
K1 — HEADLITE HIGH BEAM WARNING LITE
K2 — ALTERNATOR WARNING LITE
K3 — ENGINE OIL PRESSURE WARNING LITE
K21 — OXS ELAPSED MILEAGE INDICATOR
K48 — UP-SHIFT CONTROL LITE

97-2670

Main Electrical System
1988-1989 Jetta (except Diesel)
1986-1989 Jetta GLI
(page 8 of 15)

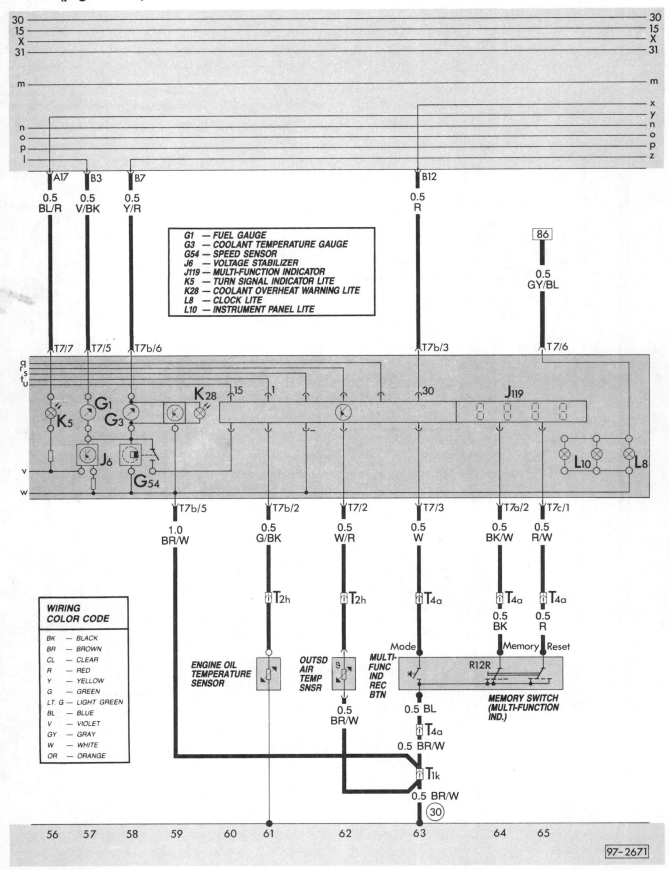

G1	— FUEL GAUGE
G3	— COOLANT TEMPERATURE GAUGE
G54	— SPEED SENSOR
J6	— VOLTAGE STABILIZER
J119	— MULTI-FUNCTION INDICATOR
K5	— TURN SIGNAL INDICATOR LITE
K28	— COOLANT OVERHEAT WARNING LITE
L8	— CLOCK LITE
L10	— INSTRUMENT PANEL LITE

WIRING COLOR CODE

BK	—	BLACK
BR	—	BROWN
CL	—	CLEAR
R	—	RED
Y	—	YELLOW
G	—	GREEN
LT. G	—	LIGHT GREEN
BL	—	BLUE
V	—	VIOLET
GY	—	GRAY
W	—	WHITE
OR	—	ORANGE

ENGINE OIL TEMPERATURE SENSOR

OUTSD AIR TEMP SNSR

MULTI-FUNC IND REC BTN

R12R

MEMORY SWITCH (MULTI-FUNCTION IND.)

97-2671

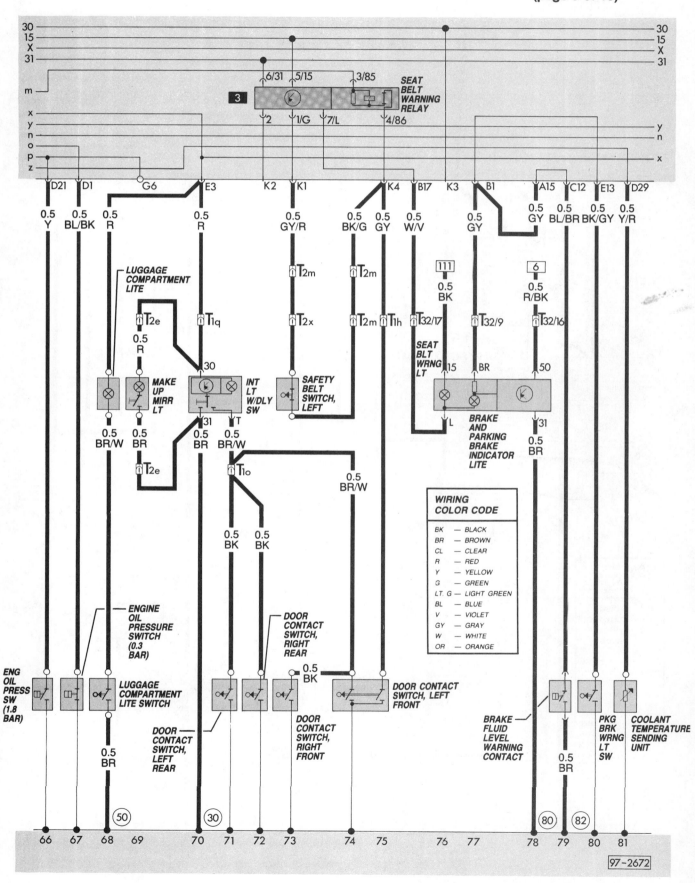

97-2672

Main Electrical System
1988-1989 Jetta (except Diesel)
1986-1989 Jetta GLI
(page 10 of 15)

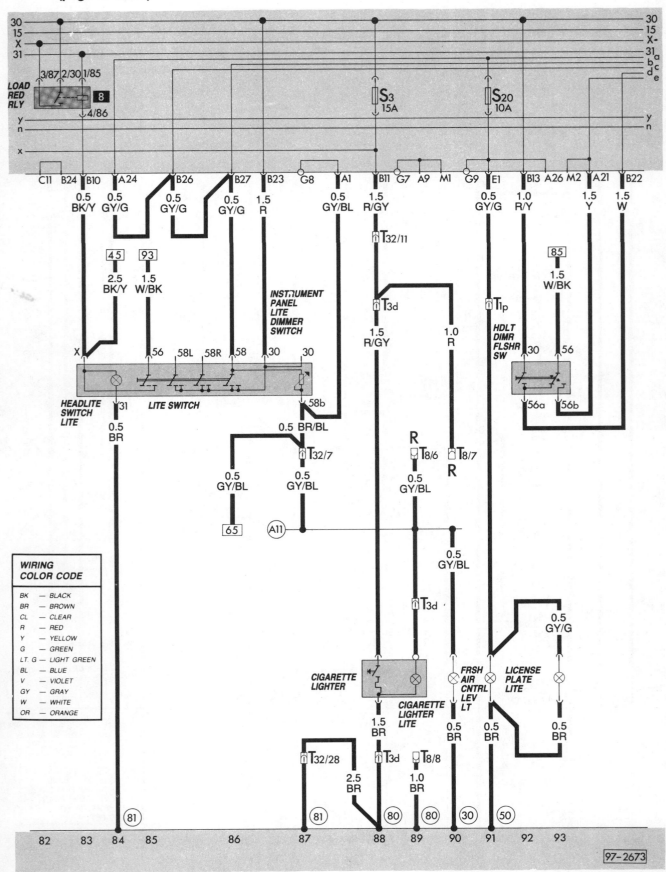

97-2673

**Main Electrical System
1988-1989 Jetta (except Diesel)
1986-1989 Jetta GLI
(page 11 of 15)**

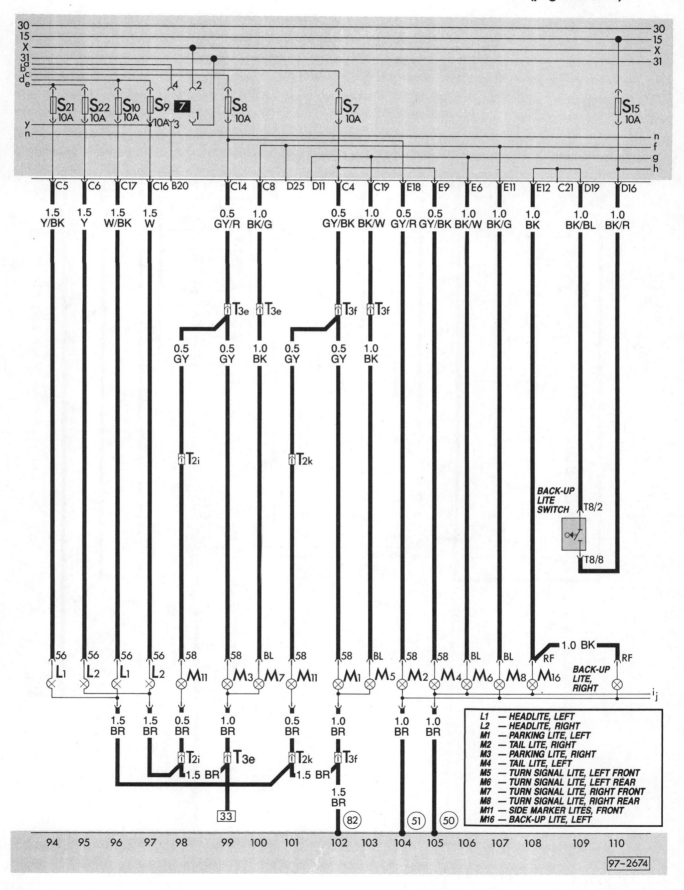

L1	— HEADLITE, LEFT
L2	— HEADLITE, RIGHT
M1	— PARKING LITE, LEFT
M2	— TAIL LITE, RIGHT
M3	— PARKING LITE, RIGHT
M4	— TAIL LITE, LEFT
M5	— TURN SIGNAL LITE, LEFT FRONT
M6	— TURN SIGNAL LITE, LEFT REAR
M7	— TURN SIGNAL LITE, RIGHT FRONT
M8	— TURN SIGNAL LITE, RIGHT REAR
M11	— SIDE MARKER LITES, FRONT
M16	— BACK-UP LITE, LEFT

97-2674

Main Electrical System
1988-1989 Jetta (except Diesel)
1986-1989 Jetta GLI
(page 12 of 15)

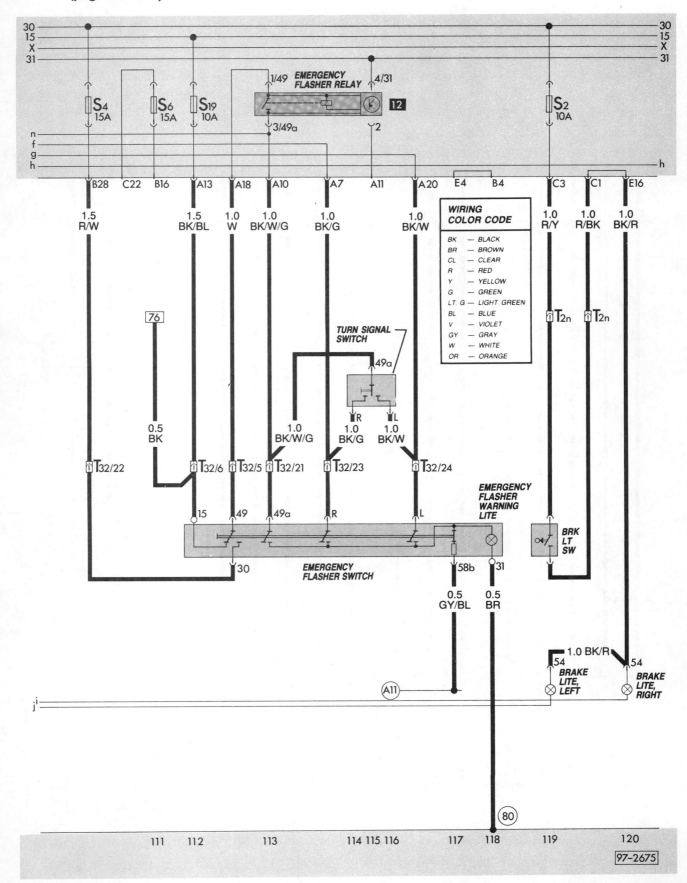

Main Electrical System
1988-1989 Jetta (except Diesel)
1986-1989 Jetta GLI
(page 13 of 15)

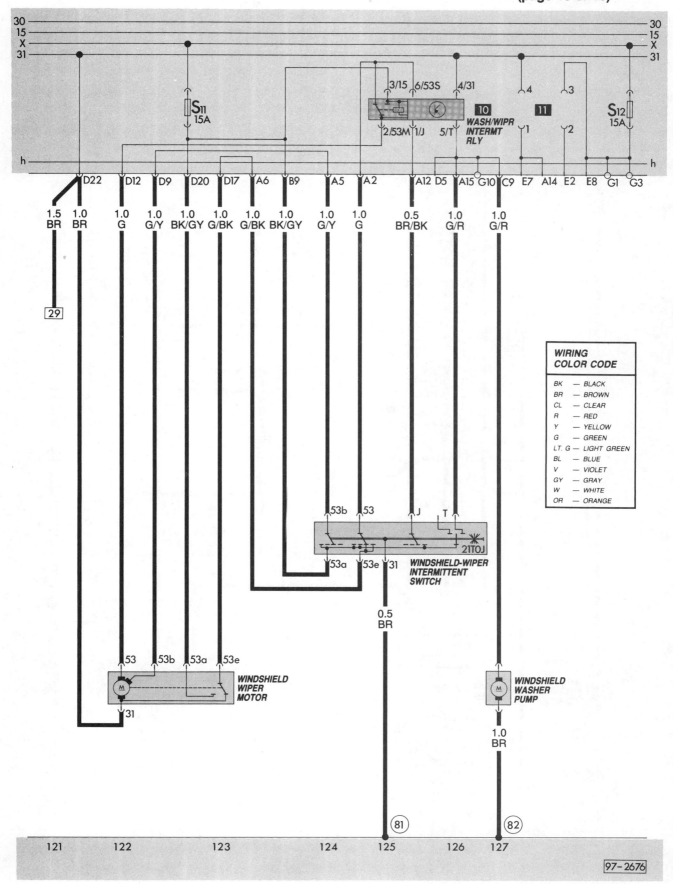

WIRING
COLOR CODE

BK	— BLACK
BR	— BROWN
CL	— CLEAR
R	— RED
Y	— YELLOW
G	— GREEN
LT. G	— LIGHT GREEN
BL	— BLUE
V	— VIOLET
GY	— GRAY
W	— WHITE
OR	— ORANGE

97-2676

Main Electrical System
1988-1989 Jetta (except Diesel)
1986-1989 Jetta GLI
(page 14 of 15)

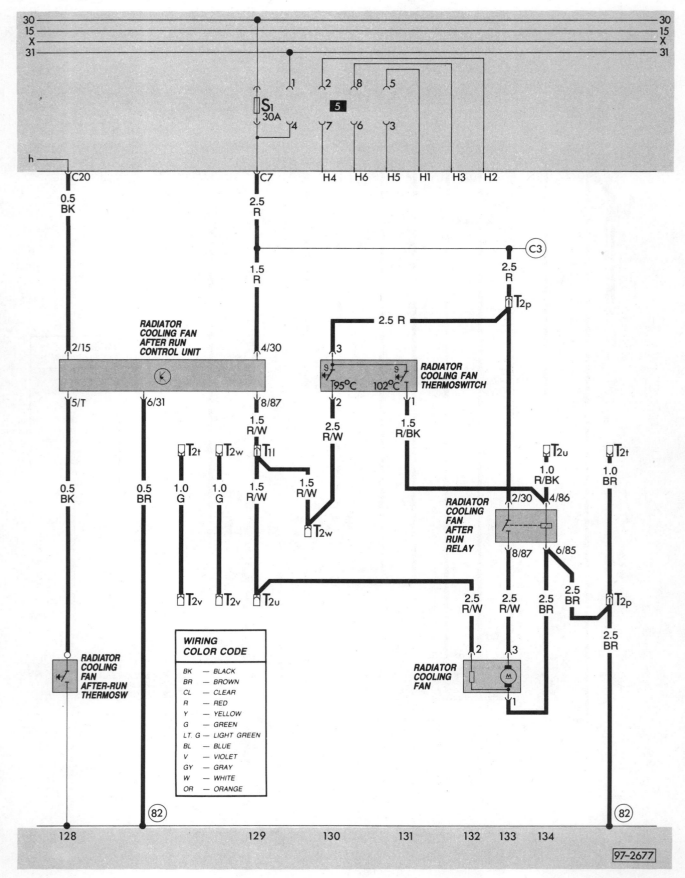

Main Electrical System
1988-1989 Jetta (except Diesel)
1986-1989 Jetta GLI
(page 15 of 15)

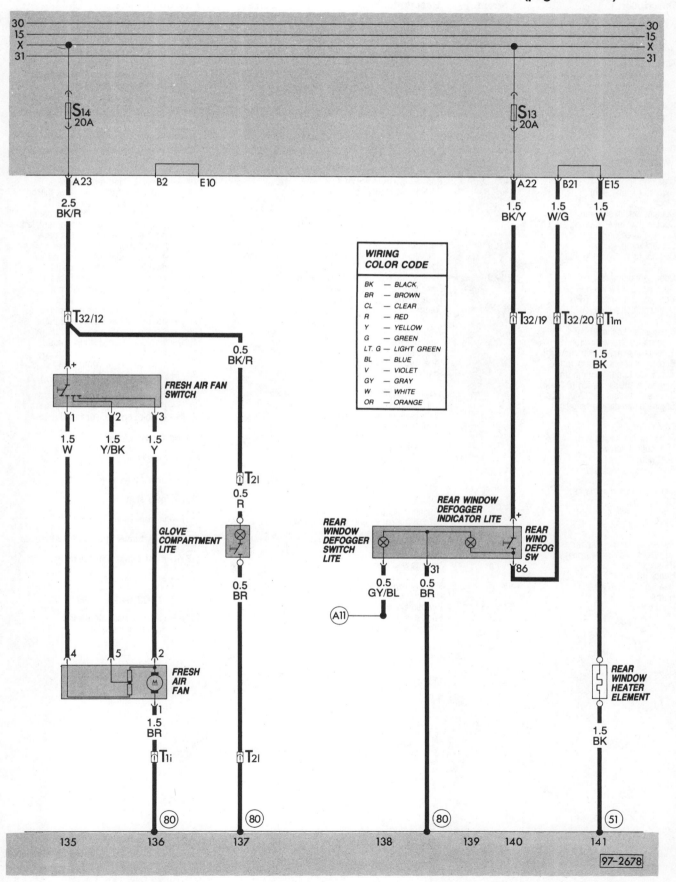

WIRING
COLOR CODE

BK — BLACK
BR — BROWN
CL — CLEAR
R — RED
Y — YELLOW
G — GREEN
LT. G — LIGHT GREEN
BL — BLUE
V — VIOLET
GY — GRAY
W — WHITE
OR — ORANGE

97-2678

**Main Electrical System
1985-1989 Jetta Diesel
(page 1 of 10)**

Description	Current Track	Description	Current Track	Wire Connectors
Alternator	1, 2	Ign/starter switch	12-14	T1a — single, behind relay panel
Alternator warning light	25	Interior light with delay	44, 45	T2 — double engine compartment, right
		Instrument panel light	61, 62	T2a — double, engine compartment, right
Back-up light, left	106	Instrument panel light switch/dimmer	62, 63	T7 — 7 point, on instrument cluster
Back-up light, right	107			T7a — 7 point, on instrument cluster
Back-up light switch	107	License plate light	68-69	T7b — 7 point, on instrument cluster
Battery	3	Light switch	60-62	T7c — 7 point, on instrument cluster
Brake fluid level sender	54	Luggage compartment light	42	T8 — 8 point, on transmission
Brake light, left	95	Luggage compartment light switch	42	T2c — double, in engine compartment, front
Brake light, right	94			T2g — double, in engine compartment, front
Brake light switch	94	Make-up mirror light	43	T1e — single, behind relay panel
				T1g — single, behind relay panel
Cigarette lighter	64	Parking brake indicator light	52-53	T1h — single, behind relay panel
Cigarette lighter light	65	Parking brake warning light switch	55	T2e — double, by inside rearview mirror
Clock	57	Parking light, left	79	T2f — double, behind relay panel
Coolant low level control unit	37, 38	Parking light, right	76	T3z — 32 point, under instrument panel
Coolant low level warning switch	38			T1p — single, in engine compartment, left
Coolant over temp. warning light	30	Radiator cooling fan	114-115	T2h — double, under instrument panel
Coolant temp. gauge	28, 29	Radiator cooling fan relay	112-114	T3a — 3 point, behind relay panel
Coolant temp. sending unit	39	Radiator cooling fan thermoswitch	112, 113	T4 — 4 point, under instrument panel
		Radio connection	65, 66	T2i — double, near right headlight
Door contact/buzzer switch, LF	48, 49	Rear window defogger indicator light	117	T2k — double, near left headlight
Door contact switch, LR	45	Rear window defogger switch	118	T3b — 3 point, near right headlight
Door contact switch, RF		Rear window defogger switch light	116	T3l — 3 point, near left headlight
Door contact switch, RR	46	Rear window heat element	119	T11i — 11 point, under instrument panel
				T2l — double, under instrument panel
Emergency flasher relay	89, 90	Seat belt switch	50	T2n — double, under instrument panel
Emergency flasher switch	87-92	Seat belt warning light	51	T1k — single, on radiator fan shroud
Emergency flasher warning light	93	Seat belt warning relay	49, 51	T1l — single, on radiator fan shroud
Engine oil press. control unit	22	Side marker lights, front	75, 78	T1m — single, in lugg. comp., left
Engine oil temp. sending unit	7	Starter	4, 5	T2p — double, in water hose
Engine oil press. switch (0.3 bar)	41			(near generator)
Engine oil press. switch (1.8 bar)	40	Tail light, left	82	T2q — double, on radiator fan shroud
Engine oil press. warning light	23	Tail light, right	81	T2t — double, on radiator fan shroud
		Time delay relay (x-contact)	57, 58	T2s — double, on radiator fan shroud
Fresh air fan	96, 97	Turn signal indicator light	26	
Fresh air fan switch	96, 97	Turn signal light, LF	80	**Ground Connections**
Fuel cut-off valve	6	Turn signal light, LR	83	
Fuel gauge	27	Turn signal light, RF	77	(1) — battery ground cable
Fuel gauge sending unit	11	Turn signal light, RR	84	(10) — near relay panel
		Turn signal switch	90, 91	(13) — near steering column
Glove compartment light	98			(15) — in front wiring harness
Glow plugs	8, 9	Upshift control light	20	(16) — in instrument panel wiring harness
Glow plug indicator light	31	Upshift indicator control unit	17-21	(17) — in instrument cluster wiring
Glow plug relay	7, 8	Upshift indicator switch (full throttle)	17	(18) — in luggage comp., left
		Upshift indicator switch (idle)	17	(19) — in luggage comp., right
Headlight dimmer/flasher switch	69, 70			(20) — crimp in instrument wiring
Headlight hi-beam warning light	24	Voltage regulator	1, 2	cluster harness
Headlight, left	71-73	Voltage stabilizer	27	
Headlight, right	72-74			
Headlight switch light	58, 59	Washer/wiper intermit. relay	103, 104	
Horns	32, 33	Water separator sender	10, 11	
Horn button	36	Windshield washer motor	105	
Horn relay	34, 35	Windshield wiper intermit. switch	102-104	
		Windshield wiper motor	100, 101	

Main Electrical System
1985-1989 Jetta Diesel
(page 2 of 10)

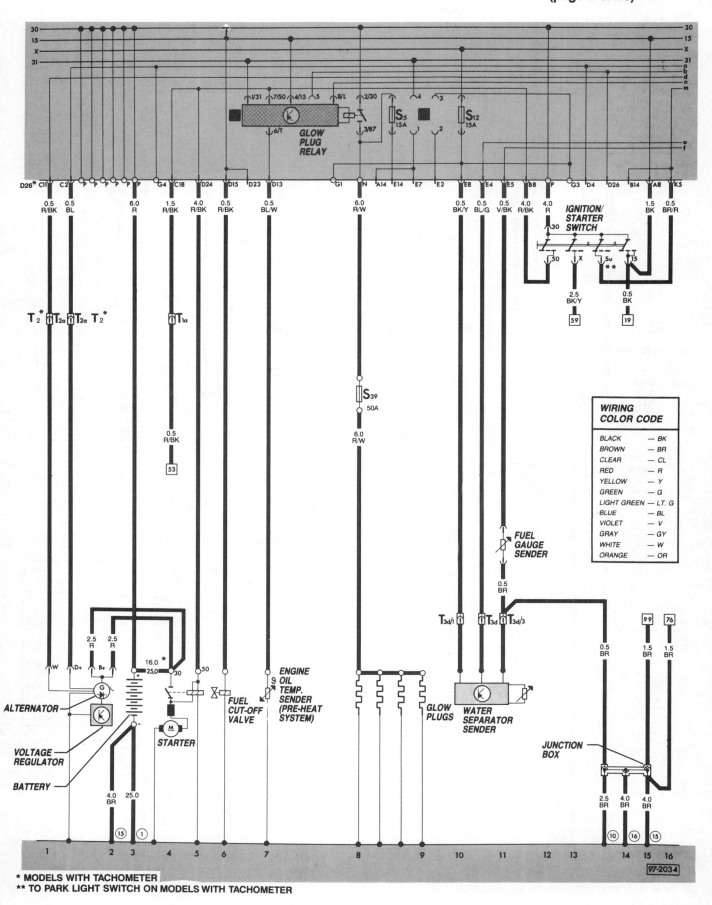

WIRING
COLOR CODE

BLACK	— BK
BROWN	— BR
CLEAR	— CL
RED	— R
YELLOW	— Y
GREEN	— G
LIGHT GREEN	— LT. G
BLUE	— BL
VIOLET	— V
GRAY	— GY
WHITE	— W
ORANGE	— OR

GLOW PLUG RELAY

IGNITION/STARTER SWITCH

ENGINE OIL TEMP. SENDER (PRE-HEAT SYSTEM)

FUEL CUT-OFF VALVE

GLOW PLUGS

FUEL GAUGE SENDER

WATER SEPARATOR SENDER

JUNCTION BOX

ALTERNATOR

VOLTAGE REGULATOR

BATTERY

STARTER

* MODELS WITH TACHOMETER
** TO PARK LIGHT SWITCH ON MODELS WITH TACHOMETER

97-2034

Main Electrical System
1985-1989 Jetta Diesel
(page 3 of 10)

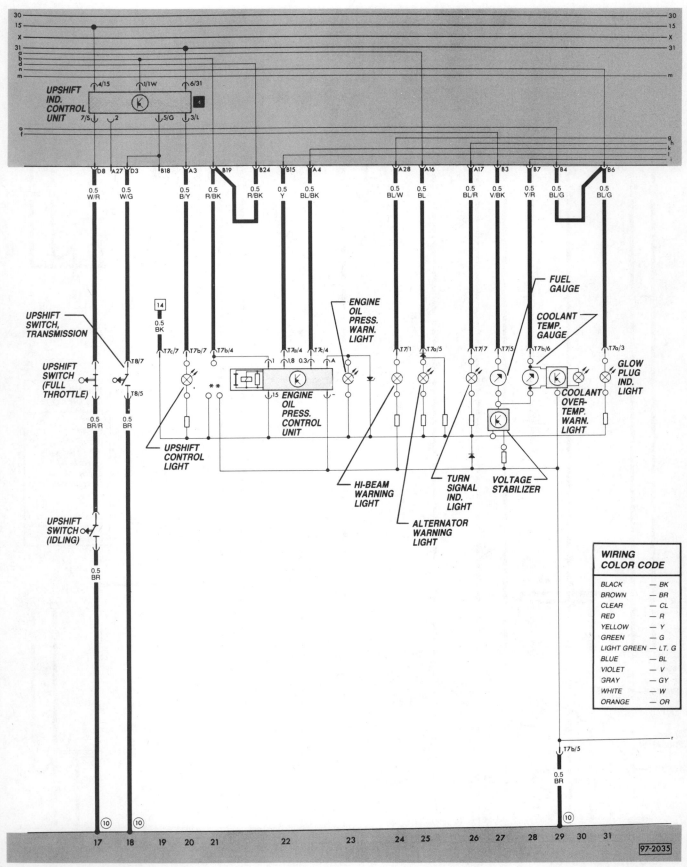

** TACHOMETER ON MODELS WITH TACHOMETER

**Main Electrical System
1985-1989 Jetta Diesel
(page 4 of 10)**

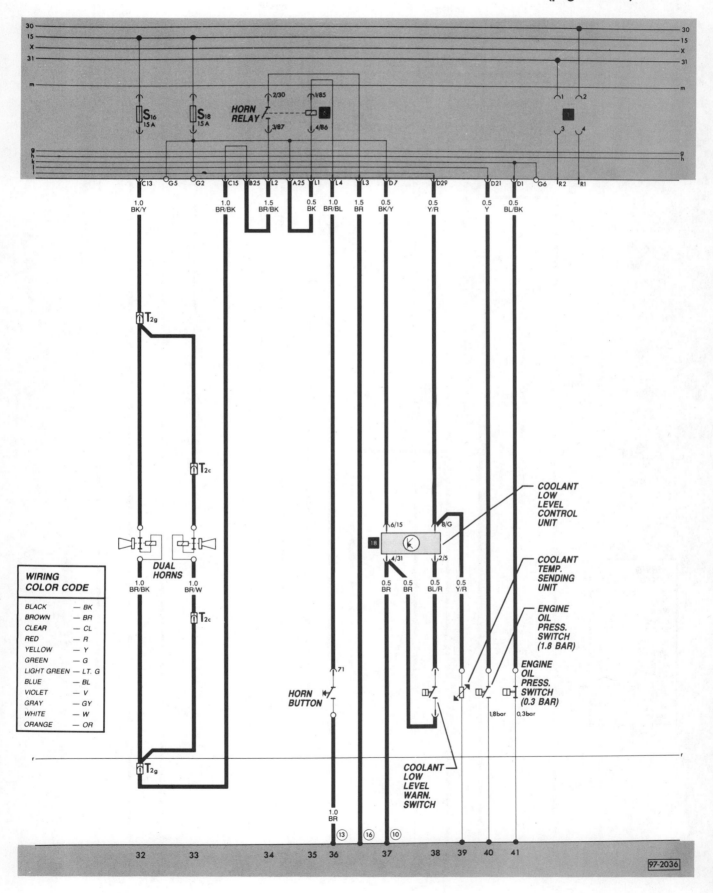

WIRING
COLOR CODE

BLACK	— BK
BROWN	— BR
CLEAR	— CL
RED	— R
YELLOW	— Y
GREEN	— G
LIGHT GREEN	— LT. G
BLUE	— BL
VIOLET	— V
GRAY	— GY
WHITE	— W
ORANGE	— OR

HORN RELAY

DUAL HORNS

COOLANT LOW LEVEL CONTROL UNIT

COOLANT TEMP. SENDING UNIT

ENGINE OIL PRESS. SWITCH (1.8 BAR)

ENGINE OIL PRESS. SWITCH (0.3 BAR)

HORN BUTTON

COOLANT LOW LEVEL WARN. SWITCH

97-2036

Main Electrical System
1985-1989 Jetta Diesel
(page 5 of 10)

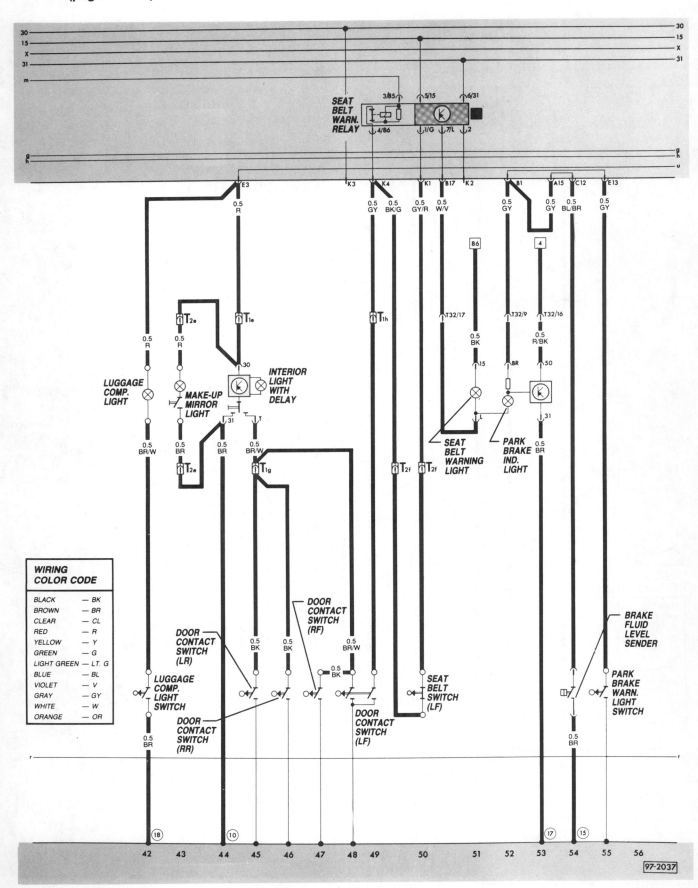

WIRING COLOR CODE

BLACK	— BK
BROWN	— BR
CLEAR	— CL
RED	— R
YELLOW	— Y
GREEN	— G
LIGHT GREEN	— LT. G
BLUE	— BL
VIOLET	— V
GRAY	— GY
WHITE	— W
ORANGE	— OR

97-2037

**Main Electrical System
1985-1989 Jetta Diesel
(page 6 of 10)**

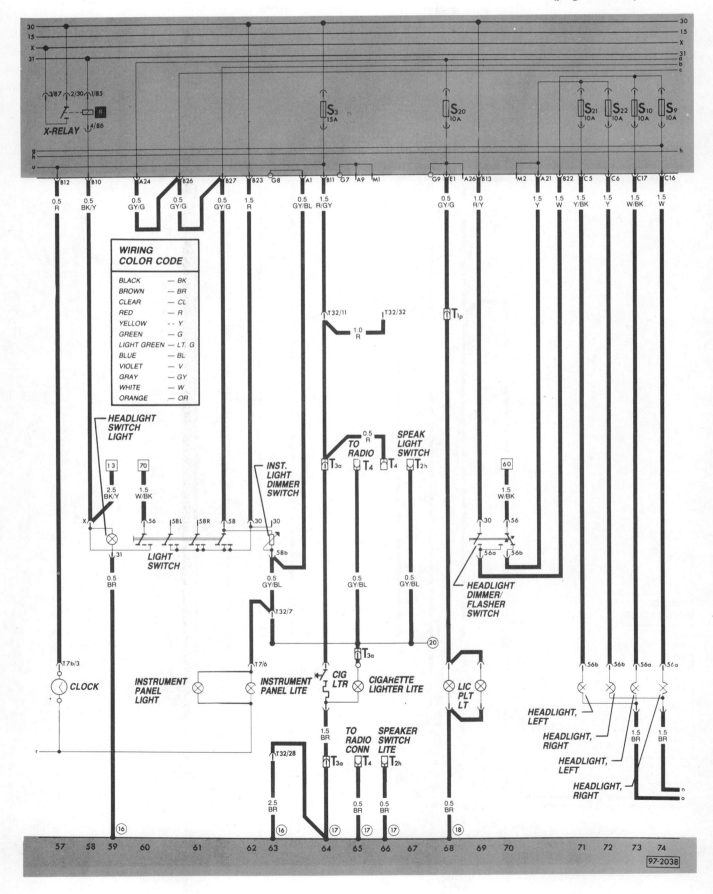

WIRING COLOR CODE

BLACK — BK
BROWN — BR
CLEAR — CL
RED — R
YELLOW -- Y
GREEN — G
LIGHT GREEN — LT. G
BLUE — BL
VIOLET — V
GRAY — GY
WHITE — W
ORANGE — OR

HEADLIGHT SWITCH LIGHT

INST. LIGHT DIMMER SWITCH

TO RADIO

SPEAK LIGHT SWITCH

LIGHT SWITCH

HEADLIGHT DIMMER/ FLASHER SWITCH

CLOCK

INSTRUMENT PANEL LIGHT

INSTRUMENT PANEL LITE

CIG LTR

CIGARETTE LIGHTER LITE

LIC PLT LT

HEADLIGHT, LEFT

HEADLIGHT, RIGHT

TO RADIO CONN

SPEAKER SWITCH LITE

HEADLIGHT, LEFT

HEADLIGHT, RIGHT

97-2038

Main Electrical System
1985-1989 Jetta Diesel
(page 7 of 10)

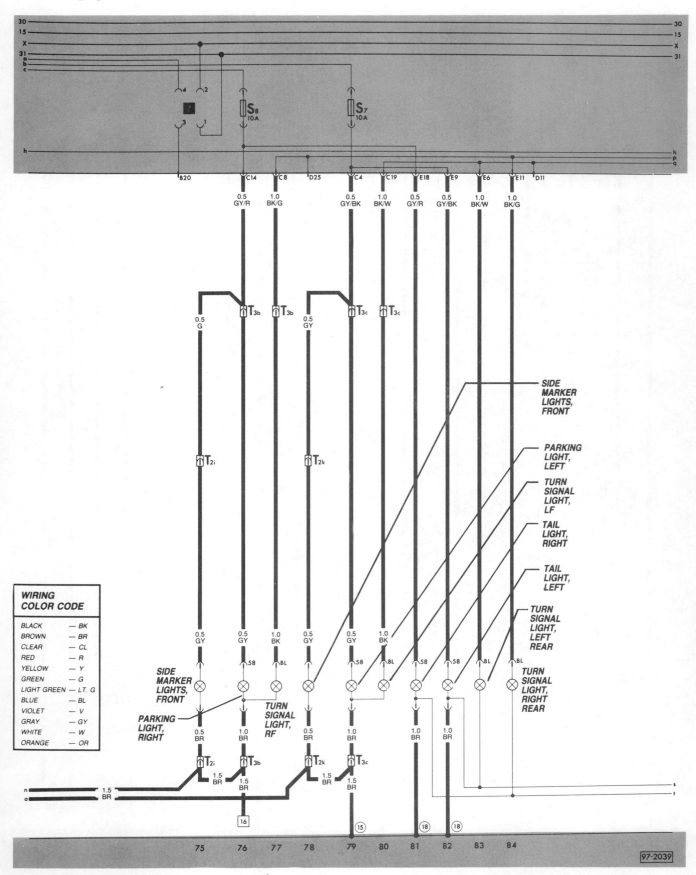

WIRING
COLOR CODE

BLACK	— BK
BROWN	— BR
CLEAR	— CL
RED	— R
YELLOW	— Y
GREEN	— G
LIGHT GREEN	— LT. G
BLUE	— BL
VIOLET	— V
GRAY	— GY
WHITE	— W
ORANGE	— OR

SIDE MARKER LIGHTS, FRONT

PARKING LIGHT, LEFT

TURN SIGNAL LIGHT, LF

TAIL LIGHT, RIGHT

TAIL LIGHT, LEFT

TURN SIGNAL LIGHT, LEFT REAR

TURN SIGNAL LIGHT, RIGHT REAR

SIDE MARKER LIGHTS, FRONT

PARKING LIGHT, RIGHT

TURN SIGNAL LIGHT, RF

97-2039

**Main Electrical System
1985-1989 Jetta Diesel
(page 8 of 10)**

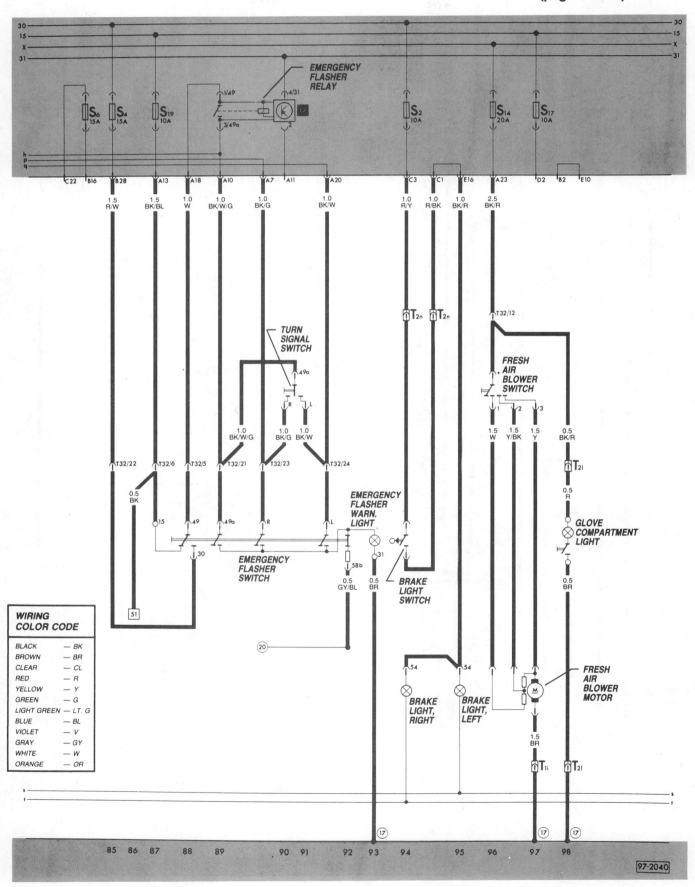

WIRING
COLOR CODE

BLACK	— BK
BROWN	— BR
CLEAR	— CL
RED	— R
YELLOW	— Y
GREEN	— G
LIGHT GREEN	— LT. G
BLUE	— BL
VIOLET	— V
GRAY	— GY
WHITE	— W
ORANGE	— OR

97-2040

Main Electrical System
1985-1989 Jetta Diesel
(page 9 of 10)

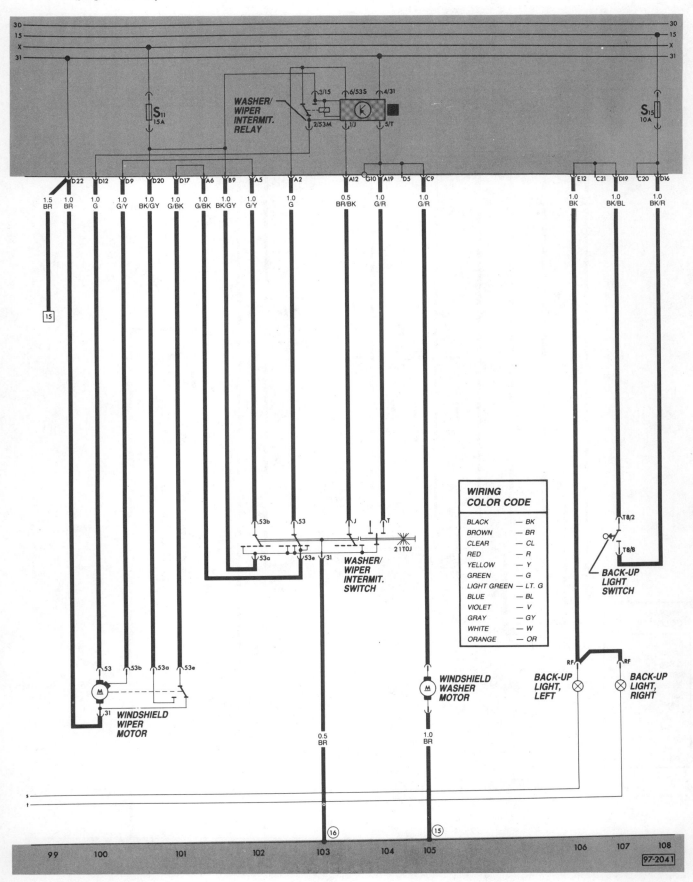

WASHER/
WIPER
INTERMIT.
RELAY

WASHER/
WIPER
INTERMIT.
SWITCH

WINDSHIELD
WIPER
MOTOR

WINDSHIELD
WASHER
MOTOR

BACK-UP
LIGHT
SWITCH

BACK-UP
LIGHT,
LEFT

BACK-UP
LIGHT,
RIGHT

WIRING COLOR CODE	
BLACK	— BK
BROWN	— BR
CLEAR	— CL
RED	— R
YELLOW	— Y
GREEN	— G
LIGHT GREEN	— LT. G
BLUE	— BL
VIOLET	— V
GRAY	— GY
WHITE	— W
ORANGE	— OR

97-2041

**Main Electrical System
1985-1989 Jetta Diesel
(page 10 of 10)**

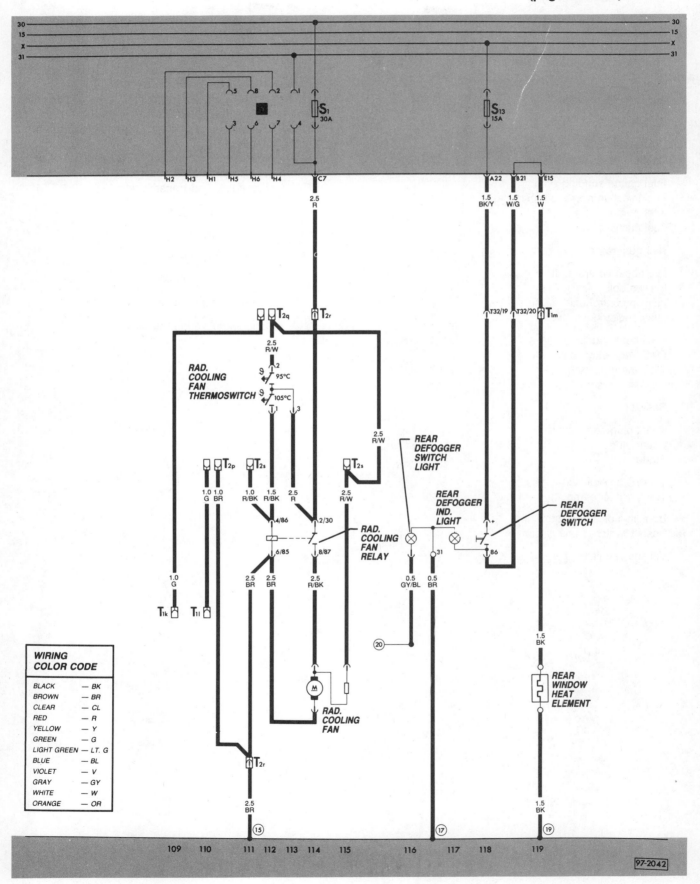

WIRING
COLOR CODE

BLACK	— BK
BROWN	— BR
CLEAR	— CL
RED	— R
YELLOW	— Y
GREEN	— G
LIGHT GREEN	— LT. G
BLUE	— BL
VIOLET	— V
GRAY	— GY
WHITE	— W
ORANGE	— OR

RAD.
COOLING
FAN
THERMOSWITCH

RAD.
COOLING
FAN RELAY

RAD. COOLING
FAN

REAR
DEFOGGER
SWITCH
LIGHT

REAR
DEFOGGER
IND.
LIGHT

REAR
DEFOGGER
SWITCH

REAR
WINDOW
HEAT
ELEMENT

**Electronic Engine Controls
1985–1987 Jetta (CIS)
(page 1 of 4)**

Description	Current track
2-way idle speed boost valve	16
Alternator	1,2
Auxiliary air regulator	32
Battery	3
Cold start valve	5
Control pressure regulator	34
Fuel gauge sending unit	28
Fuel injection power supply relay	17-19
Fuel pump	30
Fuel pump relay	29-31
Hall generator	9,10
Idle boost control unit	14,15
Ignition coil	11,12
Ignition control unit	8-11
Ignition distributor	11-13
OXS control unit	19-22
OXS frequency valve	18
OXS thermoswitch	21
Oxygen sensor	20
Resistor	18
Spark plug connectors	11-13
Spark plugs	11-13
Starter	4,5
Thermo time switch	6,7
Transfer fuel pump	29
Up-shift indicator control unit	24-27
Upshift switch, transmission	26
Voltage regulator	1,2

Wire connectors

T   — wire distributor, under fuse/relay panel
T1a — single, under fuse/relay panel
T1c — single, under instrument panel
T1d — single, in eng compart, right
T2a — double, in eng compart, near ign. coil
T2b — double, in lugg compart, near fuel gauge
        sender
T2c — double, in eng compart, near ign coil
T2h — double, under fuse/relay panel
T8/ — eight-point, and transmission

Ground connectors

① — battery ground strap
⑧ — near cold start valve
⑩ — near fuse/relay panel
⑮ — in front wiring harness
⑯ — in inst panel wiring harness

**Electronic Engine Controls
1985–1987 Jetta (CIS)
(page 2 of 4)**

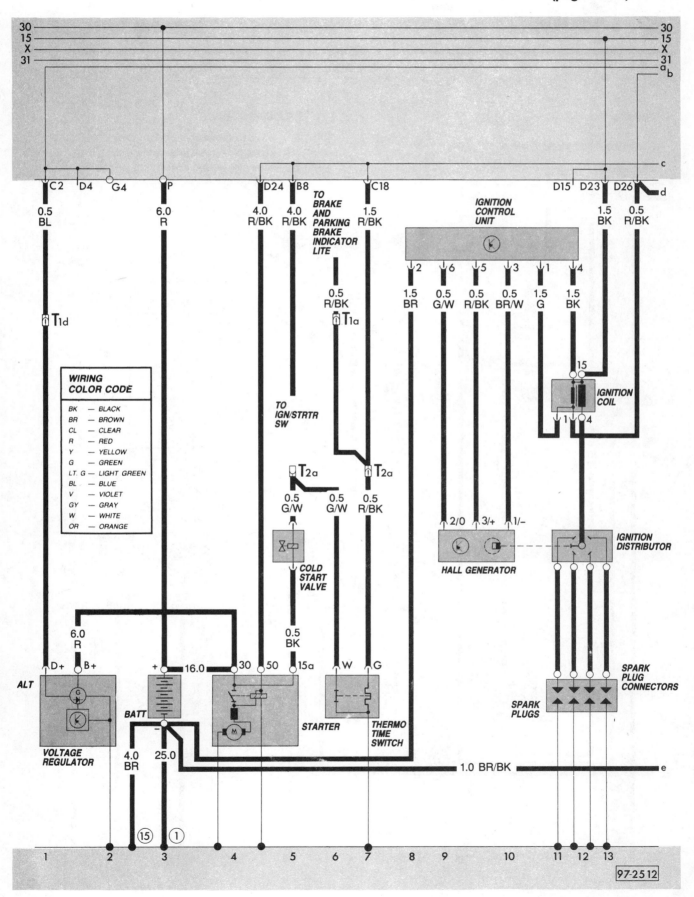

97-2512

Electronic Engine Controls
1985–1987 Jetta (CIS)
(page 3 of 4)

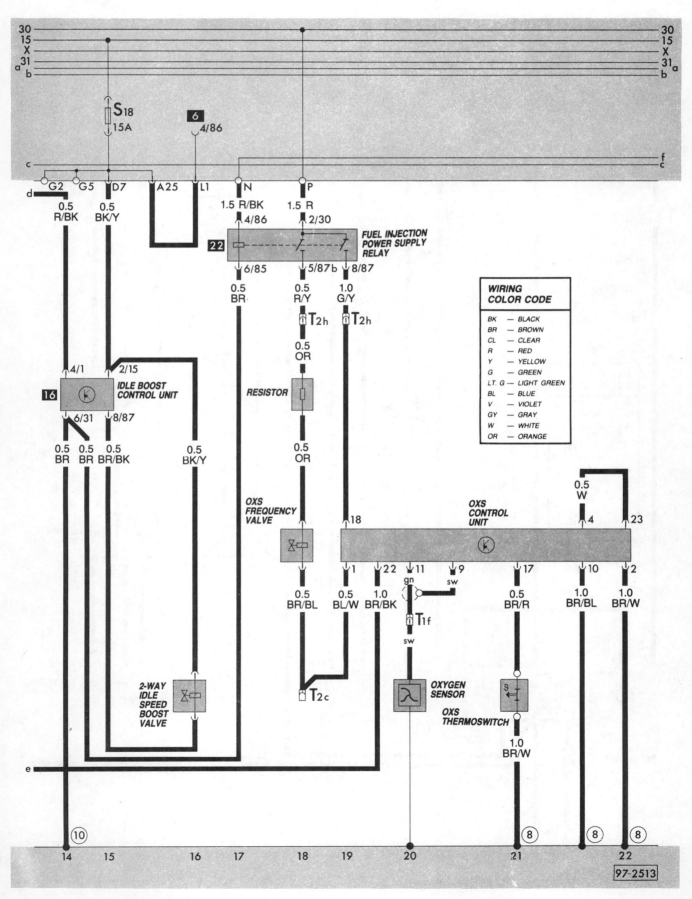

WIRING COLOR CODE	
BK	— BLACK
BR	— BROWN
CL	— CLEAR
R	— RED
Y	— YELLOW
G	— GREEN
LT. G	— LIGHT GREEN
BL	— BLUE
V	— VIOLET
GY	— GRAY
W	— WHITE
OR	— ORANGE

97-2513

**Electronic Engine Controls
1985–1987 Jetta (CIS)
(page 4 of 4)**

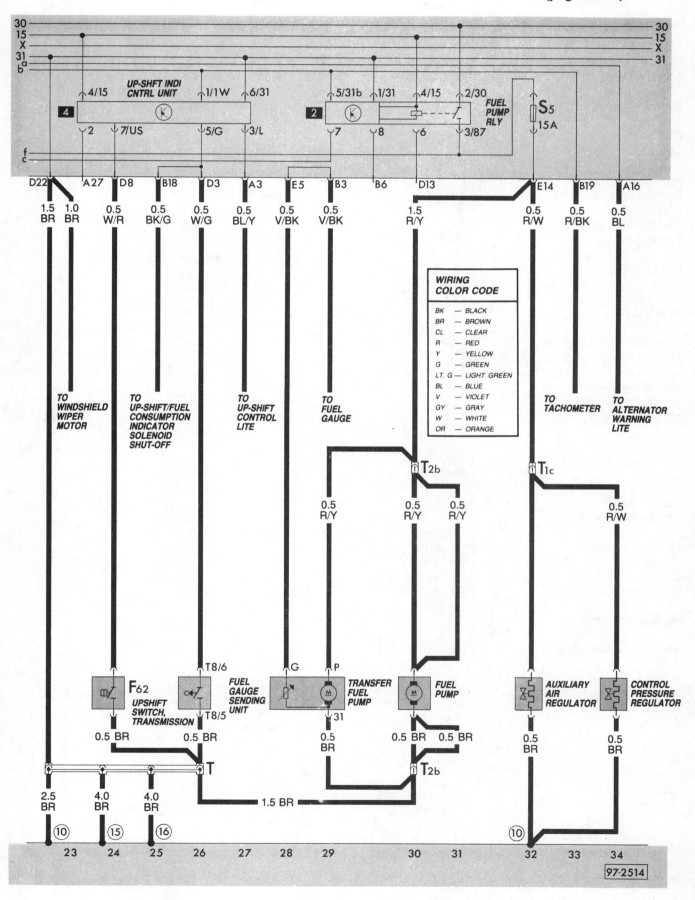

WIRING
COLOR CODE

BK	— BLACK
BR	— BROWN
CL	— CLEAR
R	— RED
Y	— YELLOW
G	— GREEN
LT. G	— LIGHT GREEN
BL	— BLUE
V	— VIOLET
GY	— GRAY
W	— WHITE
OR	— ORANGE

97-2514

Electronic Engine Controls
1985–1987 Jetta (CIS Canada)
(page 1 of 3)

Description	Current Track
Alternator	1-3
Alternator warning light	4
Auxiliary air regulator	27
Battery	4
Cold start valve	7
Control pressure regulator	28
Fuel gauge	30
Fuel gauge sending unit	23
Fuel pump	26
Fuel pump (in tank)	24
Fuel pump relay	23-25
Hall sender	10, 11
Horns	29, 31
Horn button	34
Horn relay	32, 33
Idle speed stab. control unit	16, 17
Idle speed stab. valve	17
Ignition coil	13, 14
Ignition/start switch	7
Ignition control unit	16, 17
Ignition distributor	17
Spark plugs	12-15
Spark plug connectors	12-15
Starter	5, 6
Tachometer	8
Thermo time switch	7, 8
Upshift control light	21
Upshift ind. control unit	19-22
Upshift switch, trans.	22
Upshift switch, vacuum	20
Voltage regulator	1-3
Windshield wiper motor	18

Wire Connectors

T	— junction box, behind fuse/relay panel
T2b	— double, in luggage compartment
T2c	— double, in eng. compart., front
T2g	— double, in eng. compart., front
T1d	— single, eng. compart., right
T2a	— double, eng. compart., near ign. coil

Ground Connections

①	— battery ground strap
⑩	— near fuse/relay panel
⑬	— near steering column
⑮	— in front wiring harness
⑯	— in instrument panel wiring harness

Electronic Engine Controls
1985–1987 Jetta (CIS Canada)
(page 2 of 3)

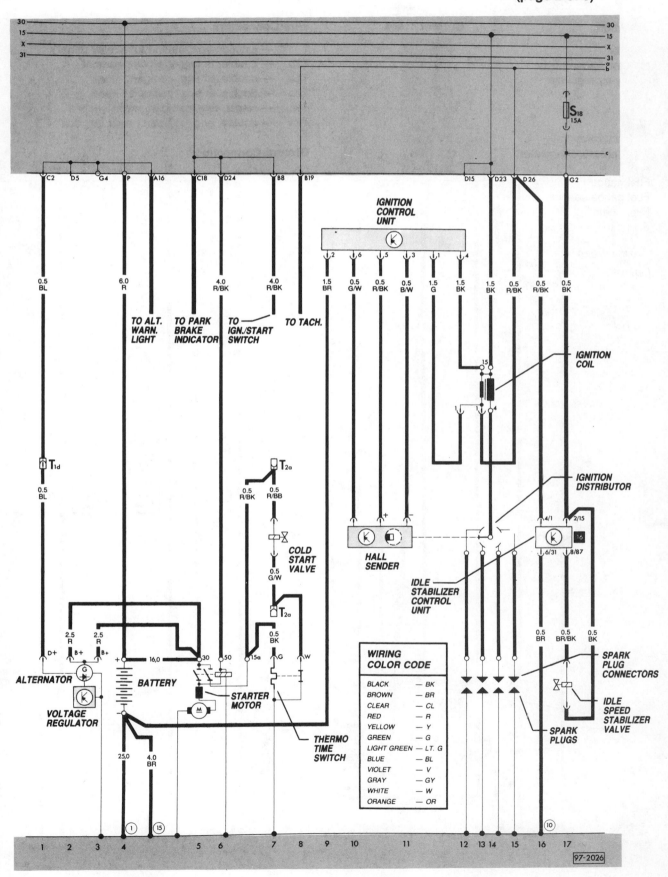

Electronic Engine Controls
1985–1987 Jetta (CIS Canada)
(page 3 of 3)

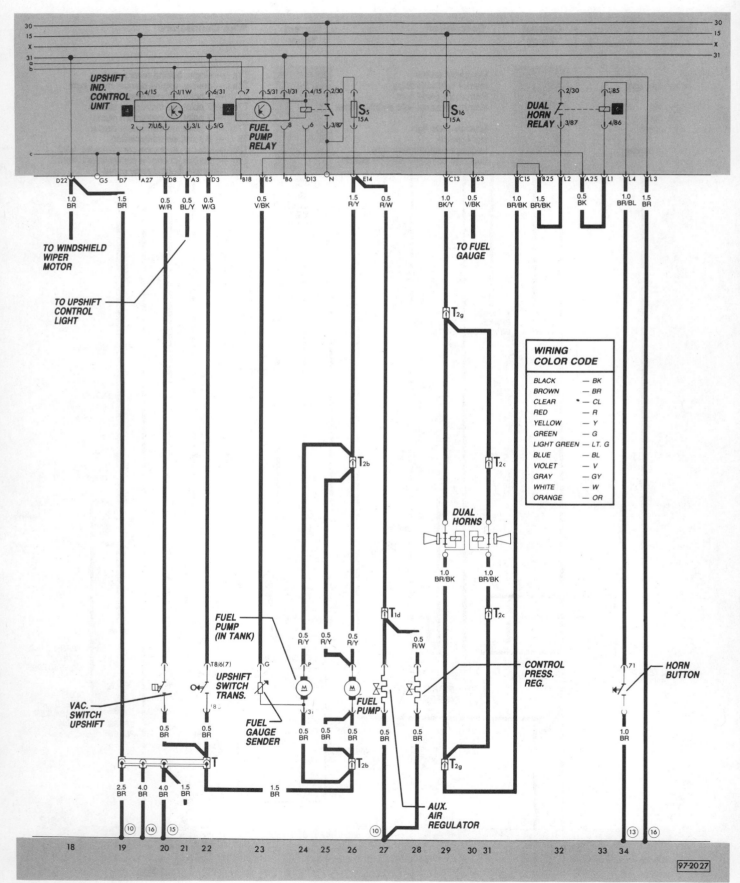

WIRING COLOR CODE

BLACK	— BK
BROWN	— BR
CLEAR	— CL
RED	— R
YELLOW	— Y
GREEN	— G
LIGHT GREEN	— LT. G
BLUE	— BL
VIOLET	— V
GRAY	— GY
WHITE	— W
ORANGE	— OR

97-2027

**Electronic Engine Controls
1988-1989 Jetta GLI 16-valve
(page 1 of 6)**

Description	Current track
Air flow sensor potentiometer	29
Alternator	1, 2
Battery	3, 4
Cold start valve	8
Fuel enrichment switch	22
Fuel gauge sending unit	38
Fuel pump	43
Fuel pump relay	41, 42
Hall generator	17, 18
Ignition coil	12, 13
Idle speed stabilizer valve	24, 25
Idle switch	23
Ignition control unit	10-14
Ignition distributor	13-15
Junction box	33-37
Knock sensor	19, 20
Knock sensor control unit	17-21
OXS control unit	19-31
Oxygen sensor	28
Oxygen sensor heater	44
Pressure gradient valve	27
Spark plug connectors	12-15
Spark plugs	12-15
Starter	5, 6
Temperature sensor (NTC)	31
Thermo time switch	8, 9
Transfer fuel pump	40
Up-shift indicator control unit	34-37
Upshift switch, transmission	37
Upshift switch, vacuum	35
Voltage regulator	1-2

Wire connectors

T1a — single in engine compartment near battery
T1b — single behind relay panel plate
T1c — single in engine compartment near ignition coil
T1d — single behind relay panel plate
T1e — single in engine compartment near ignition coil
T1f — single, near ignition coil
T1g — single behind dash
T2b — double in luggage compartment
T2c — double, near ignition coil
T2e — double in engine compartment near ignition coil
T2f — double in engine compartment
T3a — 3 point, near warm-up regulator
T3b — 3 point, near throttle body
T3c — 3 point in plenum chamber, left
T3d — 3 point in engine compartment
T8/ — eight-point, on transmission

Ground connections

(1) — ground strap battery to body

(18) — Ground-connection, on engine block

(24) — Ground connection on cold starting valve

(30) — near fuse/relay panel

(82) — Ground connection -1- in wiring harness front/left

(90) — Ground connection, in wiring CIS-E harness

Electronic Engine Controls
1988-1989 Jetta GLI 16-valve
(page 2 of 6)

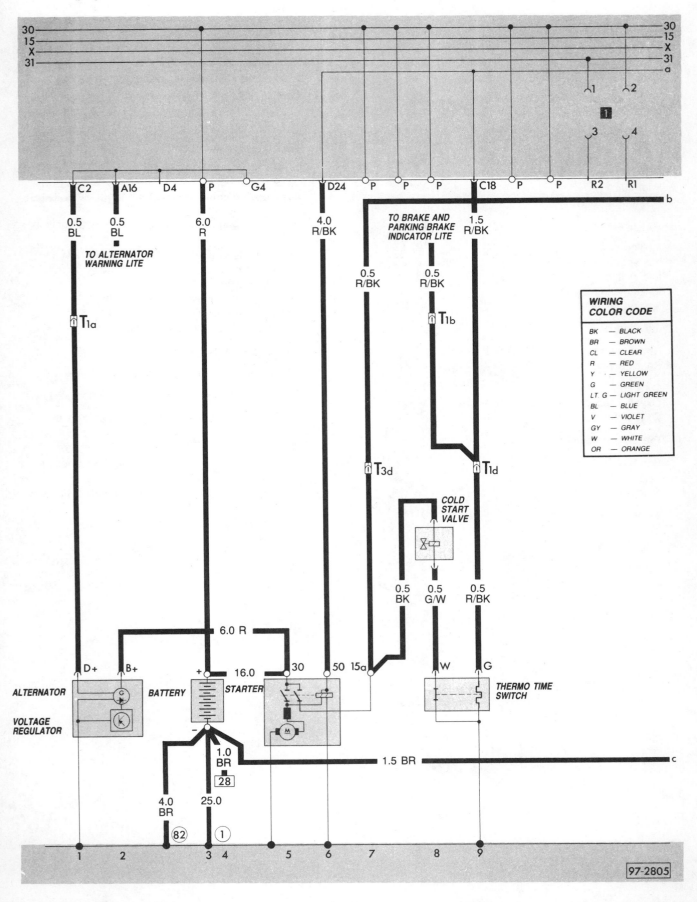

WIRING
COLOR CODE

BK	—	BLACK
BR	—	BROWN
CL	—	CLEAR
R	—	RED
Y	—	YELLOW
G	—	GREEN
LT. G	—	LIGHT GREEN
BL	—	BLUE
V	—	VIOLET
GY	—	GRAY
W	—	WHITE
OR	—	ORANGE

97-2805

Electronic Engine Controls
1988-1989 Jetta GLI 16-valve
(page 3 of 6)

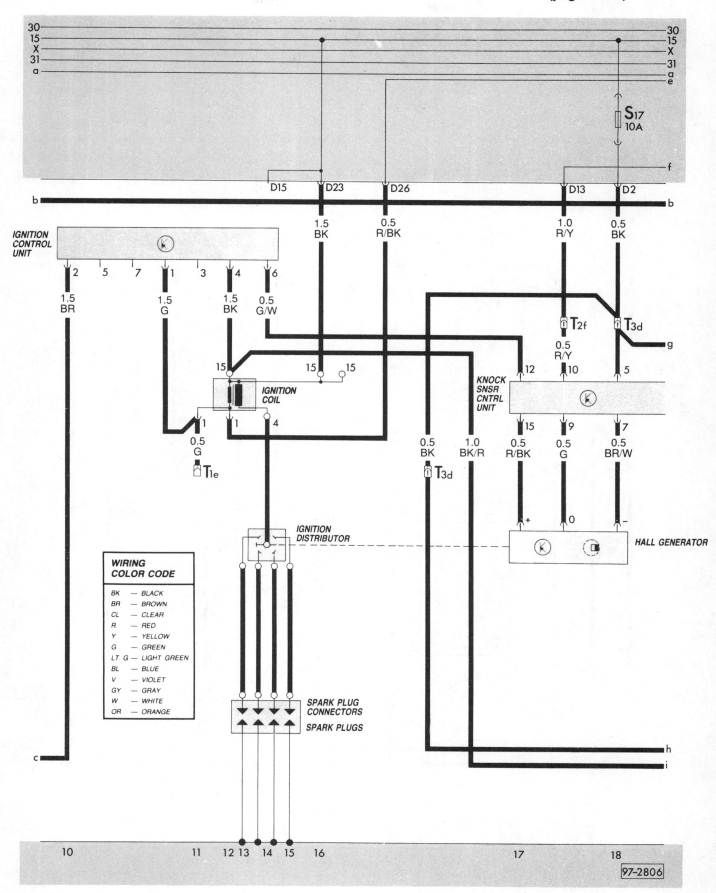

WIRING
COLOR CODE

BK — BLACK
BR — BROWN
CL — CLEAR
R — RED
Y — YELLOW
G — GREEN
LT. G — LIGHT GREEN
BL — BLUE
V — VIOLET
GY — GRAY
W — WHITE
OR — ORANGE

97-2806

Electronic Engine Controls
1988-1989 Jetta GLI 16-valve
(page 4 of 6)

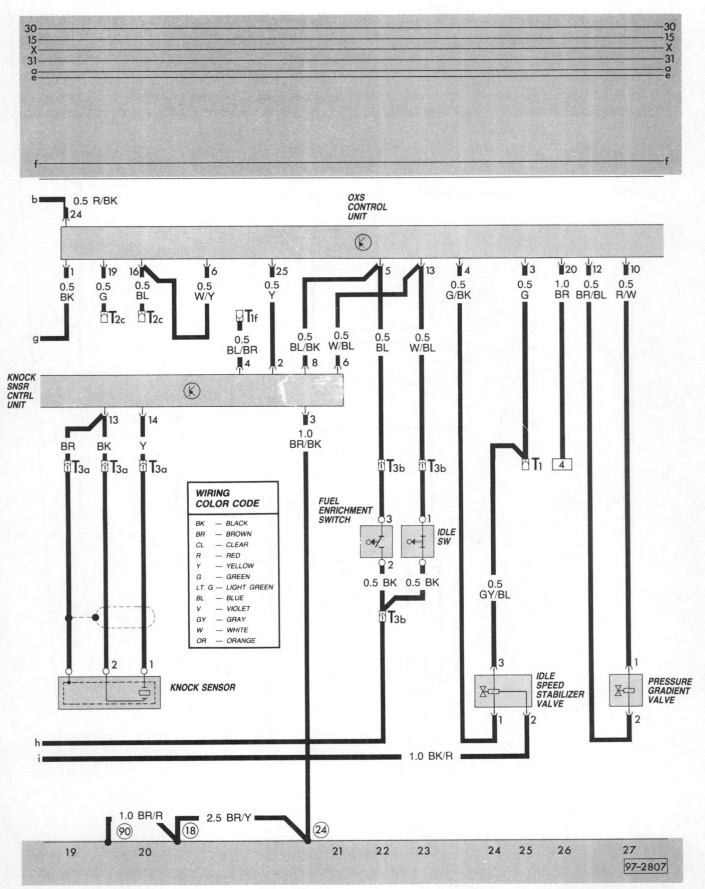

Electronic Engine Controls
1988-1989 Jetta GLI 16-valve
(page 5 of 6)

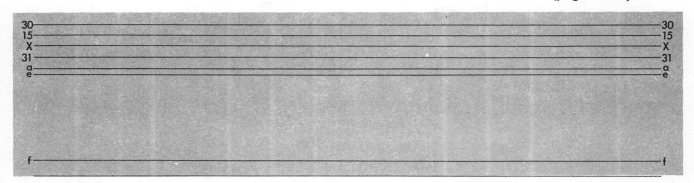

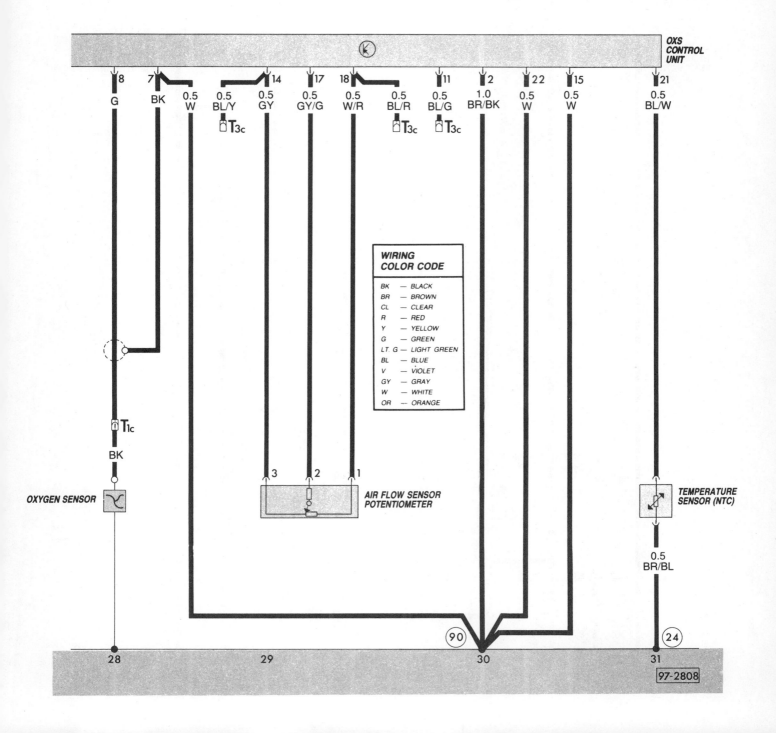

OXS CONTROL UNIT

8	7			14	17	18		11	2	22	15	21
G	BK	0.5 W	0.5 BL/Y	0.5 GY	0.5 GY/G	0.5 W/R	0.5 BL/R	0.5 BL/G	1.0 BR/BK	0.5 W	0.5 W	0.5 BL/W

T3c   T3c   T3c

WIRING COLOR CODE

BK	—	BLACK
BR	—	BROWN
CL	—	CLEAR
R	—	RED
Y	—	YELLOW
G	—	GREEN
LT. G	—	LIGHT GREEN
BL	—	BLUE
V	—	VIOLET
GY	—	GRAY
W	—	WHITE
OR	—	ORANGE

T1c

BK

3   2   1

OXYGEN SENSOR

AIR FLOW SENSOR POTENTIOMETER

TEMPERATURE SENSOR (NTC)

0.5 BR/BL

(90)   (24)

28   29   30   31

97-2808

Electronic Engine Controls
1988-1989 Jetta GLI 16-valve
(page 6 of 6)

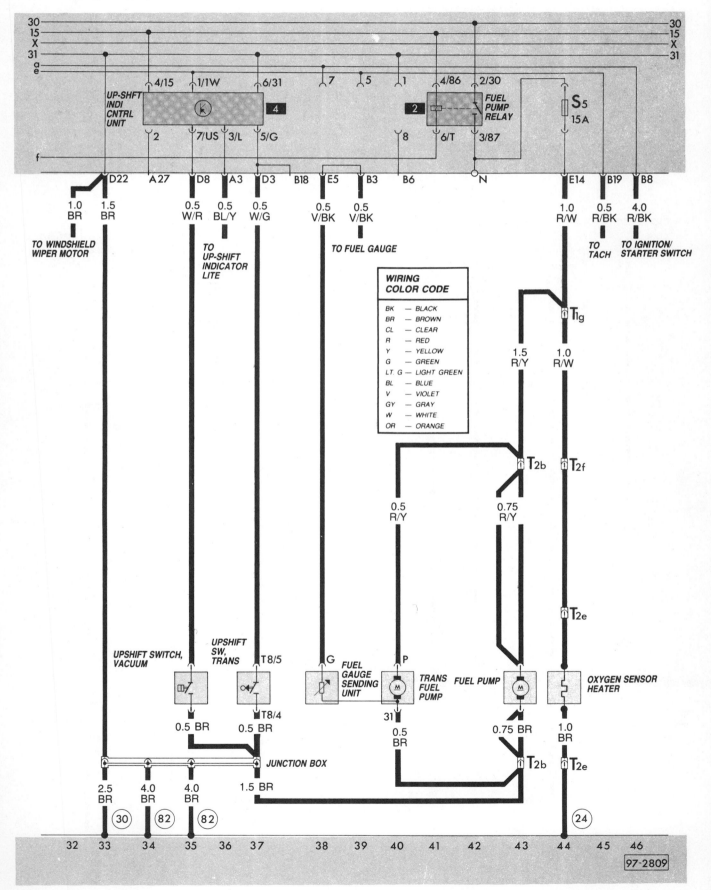

97-2809

Electronic Engine Controls
1987-1989 Jetta (Digifant II)
(page 1 of 5)

Description	Current track
Air flow sensor potentiometer	18,19
Alternator	1,2
Battery	3
Digifant control unit	13-21
Digifant control unit	23-30
Digifant control unit relay	29-31
ECS-Malfunction indicator light and switch	21,22
Eng. coolant temp. sensor	17
Fuel enrichment switch	14
Fuel gauge sending unit	36
Fuel pump	38
Fuel pump relay	37
Hall generator	13-15
Idle speed stabilizer valve	26,27
Idle switch	16
Ignition coil	9-11
Ignition control unit	8-12
Ignition distributor	10-12
Injector, cyl. 1	28
Injector, cyl. 2	30
Injector, cyl. 3	31
Injector, cyl. 4	32
Intake air temp. sensor (in air flow sensor housing)	18-19
Knock sensor	20,21
Oxygen sensor	24,25
Spark plug connectors	10-12
Spark plugs	10-12
Starter	6,7
Transfer fuel pump	37
Voltage regulator	1,2

Wire connectors

T — wire junction, behind fuse/relay panel
T1 — single in engine compartment, right
T1a — single behind relay panel plate
T1b — single behind relay panel plate
T1g — Wire connector, single behind relay panel plate
T2b — Wire connector, double in luggage compartment
T2m— double in plenum chamber, left
T2x — double near intake manifold
T2z — double, in plenum chamber
T2y — double near intake manifold
T3 — 3 point near ignition distributor
T3 — 3 point in plenum chamber, left
T32 — 32-point behind dash

Ground corrections

(1) — ground strap, battery to body
(17) — intake manifold
(18) — on engine block
(30) — near fuse/relay panel
(80) — -1- in instrument panel wiring harness
(81) — in instrument panel wiring harness
(82) — -1- in wiring harness, front left

Welded wiring connections

(G3) — (+) in fuel injector wiring harness
(G4) — in fuel injector wiring harness
(94) — in Digifant wiring harness

Electronic Engine Controls
1987-1989 Jetta (Digifant II)
(page 2 of 5)

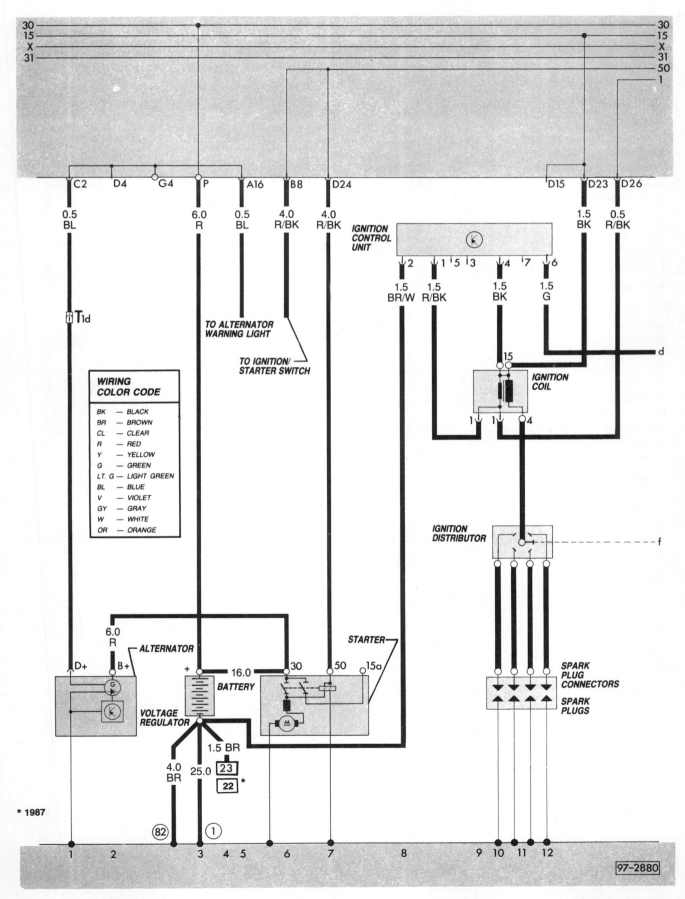

WIRING COLOR CODE

BK	—	BLACK
BR	—	BROWN
CL	—	CLEAR
R	—	RED
Y	—	YELLOW
G	—	GREEN
LT. G	—	LIGHT GREEN
BL	—	BLUE
V	—	VIOLET
GY	—	GRAY
W	—	WHITE
OR	—	ORANGE

97-2880

Electronic Engine Controls
1987-1989 Jetta (Digifant II)
(page 3 of 5)

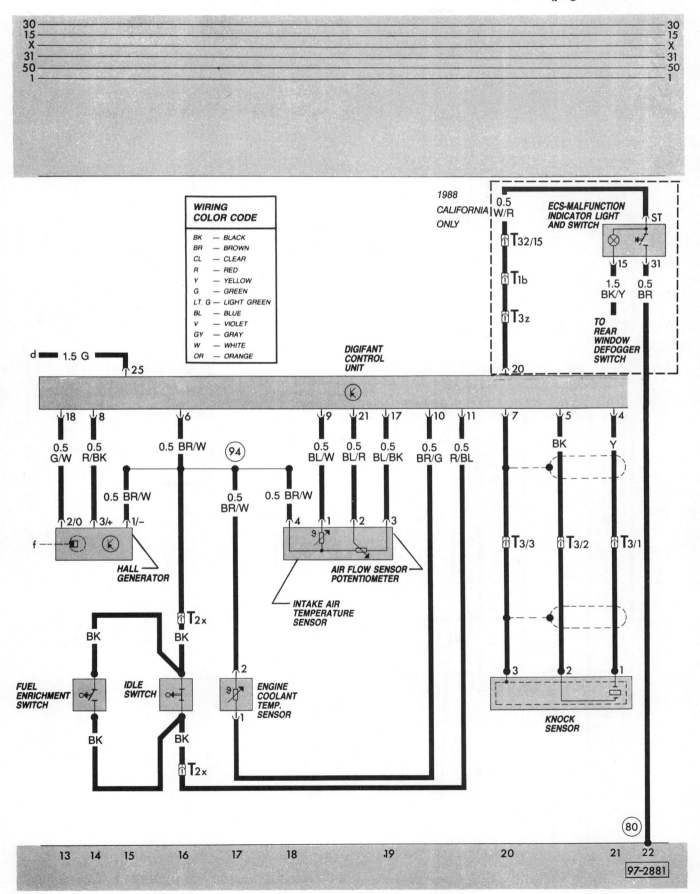

WIRING
COLOR CODE

BK	— BLACK
BR	— BROWN
CL	— CLEAR
R	— RED
Y	— YELLOW
G	— GREEN
LT. G	— LIGHT GREEN
BL	— BLUE
V	— VIOLET
GY	— GRAY
W	— WHITE
OR	— ORANGE

1988
CALIFORNIA
ONLY

ECS-MALFUNCTION
INDICATOR LIGHT
AND SWITCH

TO
REAR
WINDOW
DEFOGGER
SWITCH

DIGIFANT
CONTROL
UNIT

HALL
GENERATOR

AIR FLOW SENSOR
POTENTIOMETER

INTAKE AIR
TEMPERATURE
SENSOR

FUEL
ENRICHMENT
SWITCH

IDLE
SWITCH

ENGINE
COOLANT
TEMP.
SENSOR

KNOCK
SENSOR

97-2881

Electronic Engine Controls
1987-1989 Jetta (Digifant II)
(page 4 of 5)

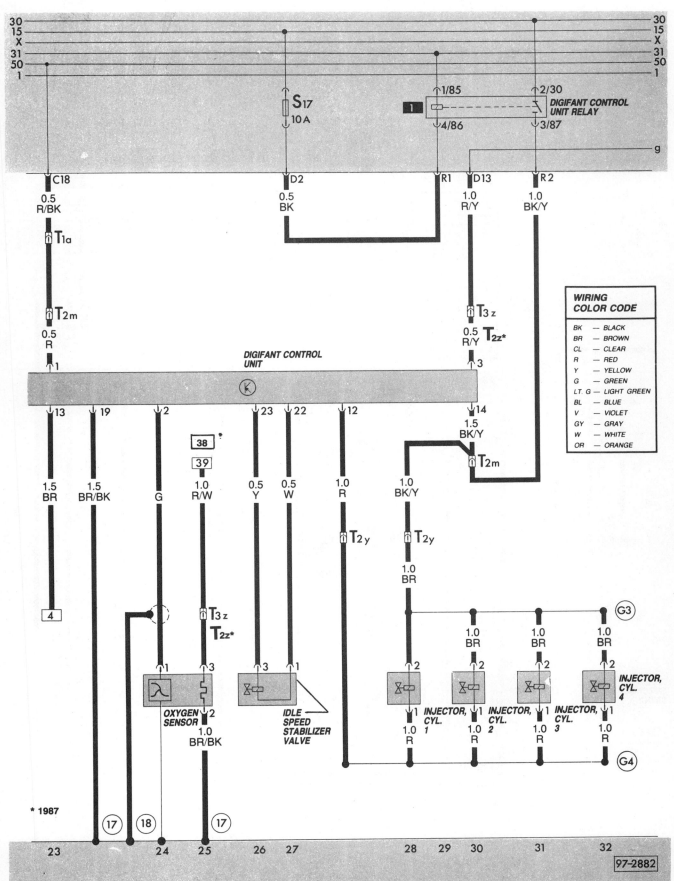

WIRING
COLOR CODE

BK — BLACK
BR — BROWN
CL — CLEAR
R — RED
Y — YELLOW
G — GREEN
LT. G — LIGHT GREEN
BL — BLUE
V — VIOLET
GY — GRAY
W — WHITE
OR — ORANGE

97-2882

**Electronic Engine Controls
1987-1989 Jetta (Digifant II)
(page 5 of 5)**

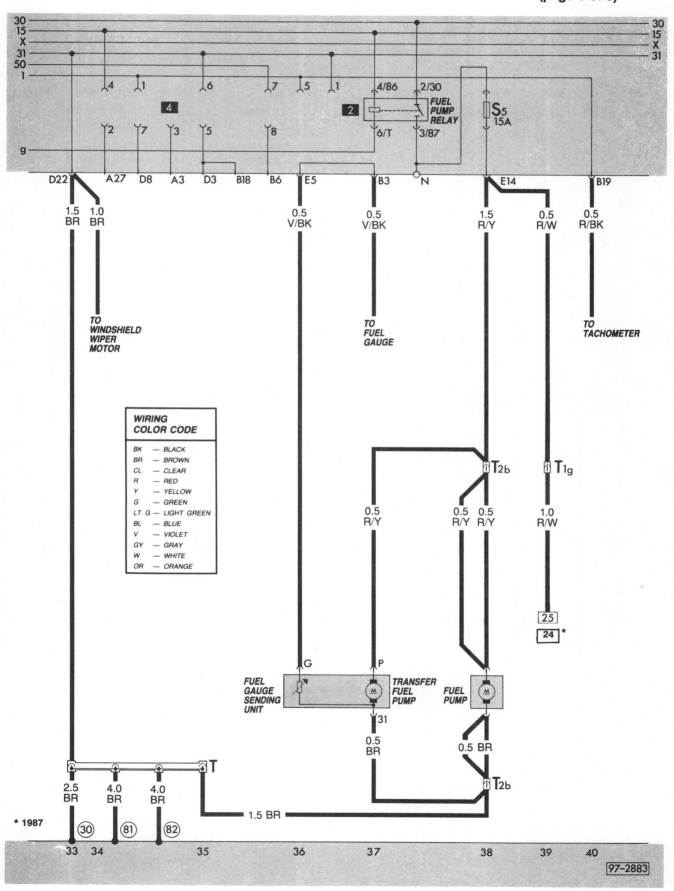

WIRING
COLOR CODE

BK	— BLACK
BR	— BROWN
CL	— CLEAR
R	— RED
Y	— YELLOW
G	— GREEN
LT. G	— LIGHT GREEN
BL	— BLUE
V	— VIOLET
GY	— GRAY
W	— WHITE
OR	— ORANGE

TO
WINDSHIELD
WIPER
MOTOR

TO
FUEL
GAUGE

TO
TACHOMETER

FUEL
PUMP
RELAY

S_5
15A

FUEL
GAUGE
SENDING
UNIT

TRANSFER
FUEL
PUMP

FUEL
PUMP

* 1987

97-2883

**Automatic Transmission
1986–1987 Jetta (Gasoline only)
(page 1 of 2)**

Description	Current Track
Alternator	5
Back-up light, left	4
Back-up light, right	5
Battery	6
Brake light, left	3
Brake light, right	5
Cold start valve	10
Console light	11
Ign/start switch	2
Neutral safety switch	6-8
Starter	6-8
Tail light, left	1
Thermo time switch	9
Turn signal light, LR	2

Wire Connectors

T4 — 4 point, under instrument panel
T2a — double, near ignition coil
T2b — double, engine compartment (water tray)

Ground Connections

(18) — engine compartment, left
(21) — near seat track, left

Automatic Transmission
1986–1987 Jetta (Gasoline only)
(page 2 of 2)

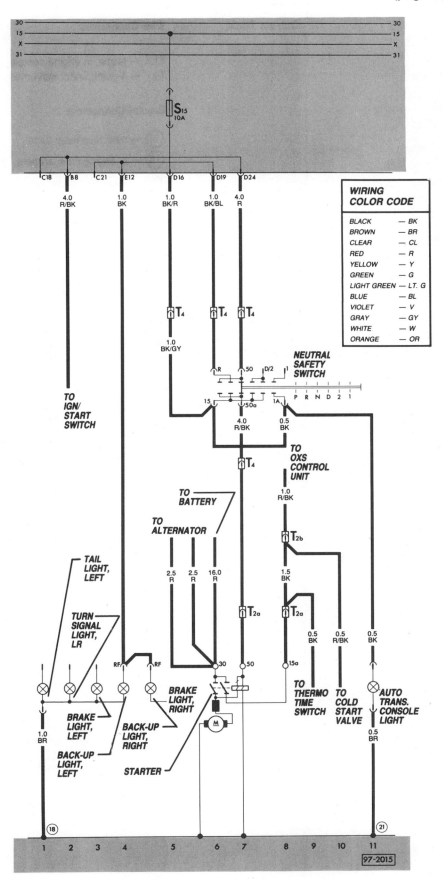

WIRING COLOR CODE	
BLACK	— BK
BROWN	— BR
CLEAR	— CL
RED	— R
YELLOW	— Y
GREEN	— G
LIGHT GREEN	— LT. G
BLUE	— BL
VIOLET	— V
GRAY	— GY
WHITE	— W
ORANGE	— OR

97-2015

Automatic Transmission
1985-1989 Jetta Diesel
(page 1 of 2)

Description	Current Track
Alternator	9
Auto-transmission relay	8-11
Back-up light, left	2
Back-up light, right	1
Battery	10
Brake light, left	3
Brake light, right	1
Console light	7
Ignition/start switch	4
Neutral safety switch	7, 8
Starter	10, 11
Tail light, left	6
Turn signal light, LR	4

Wire Connectors

T1 — single, in engine compartment
T4 — 4-point, under instrument panel

Ground Connectors

⑩ — near fuse/relay panel
⑱ — in engine compartment, left
㉑ — near seat track, left

Automatic Transmission
1985-1989 Jetta Diesel
(page 2 of 2)

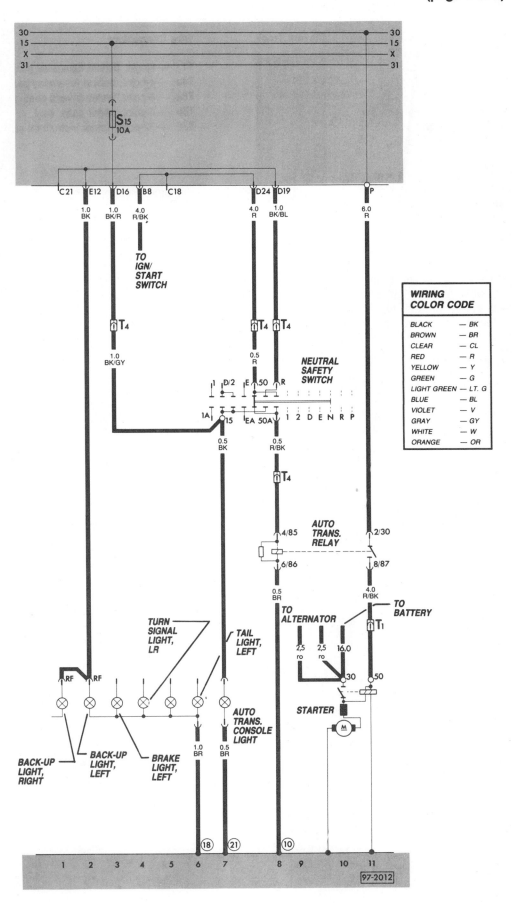

WIRING COLOR CODE	
BLACK	— BK
BROWN	— BR
CLEAR	— CL
RED	— R
YELLOW	— Y
GREEN	— G
LIGHT GREEN	— LT. G
BLUE	— BL
VIOLET	— V
GRAY	— GY
WHITE	— W
ORANGE	— OR

97-2012

Cruise Control
1985-1989 Jetta (manual trans.)
(page 1 of 2)

Description	Current track
Brake lite switch	2,3
Brake lite, left	1
Brake lite, right	2
Cruise control inductive sender	6
Cruise control switch	5-7
Cruise control, main control unit	4-8
Horn relay	8
Vacuum control motor	7-9
Vacuum vent valve, brake	4
Vacuum vent valve, clutch	4

Wire connectors

T1a — single, under relay panel
T2a — double, under relay panel
T2c — double, under relay panel
T3 — three point, under relay panel
T4 — four point, under relay panel
T4b — four point, under steering column cover

Ground connections

(10) — near relay panel

Cruise Control
1985-1989 Jetta (manual trans.)
(page 2 of 2)

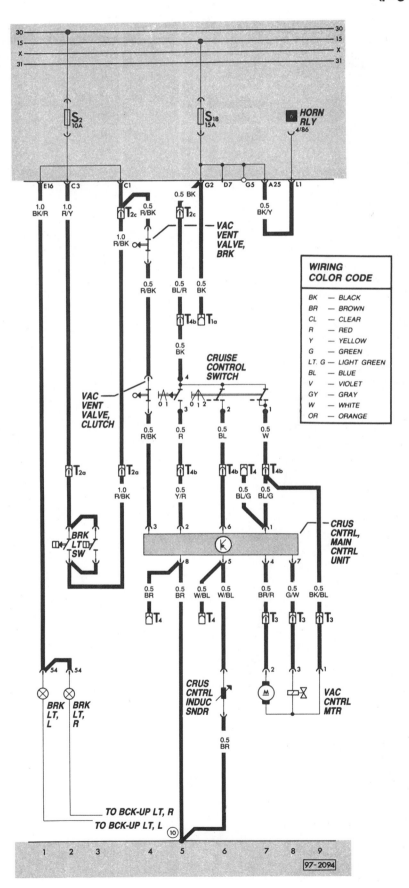

Cruise Control
1985-1989 Jetta (automatic trans.)
(page 1 of 2)

Description	Current track
Automatic transmission console lite	13
Back-up lite, left	15
Back-up lite, right	14
Brake lite switch	2,3
Brake lite, left	1
Brake lite, right	2
Cruise control inductive sender	6
Cruise control switch	5-7
Cruise control, main control unit	4-8
Starter	9-11
Starter cut-out/back-up lite switch	9-11
Vacuum control motor	7-9
Vacuum vent valve, brake	4

Wire Connectors

T1a — single, under relay panel
T1c — single, in eng. compart. near ign. coil
T2a — double, under relay panel
T2c — double, under relay panel
T3   — three point, under relay panel
T4   — four point, under center console
T4a — four point, under relay panel
T4b — four point, under steering column cover

Ground Connections

(10) — near relay panel

(21) — by neutral safety switch

Cruise Control
1985-1989 Jetta (automatic trans.)
(page 2 of 2)

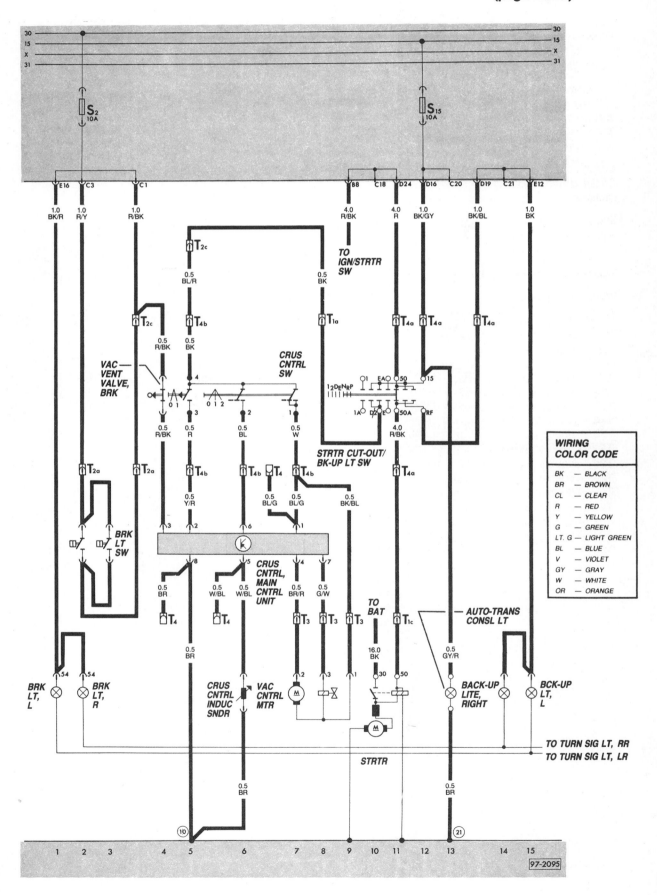

Air Conditioning
1985-1987 Jetta
(page 1 of 2)

Description	Current Track
2-way idle speed boost valve	10
A/C compressor clutch	11
A/C refrigerant high pressure switch	12
A/C refrigerant low pressure switch	11
A/C relay	7-13
A/C switch	3-7
A/C thermostat	11
A/C thermoswitch (Diesel only)	11
Battery	1
Fresh air blower series resistance	3
Fresh air fan	3
Fresh air fan switch	3-6
Glove compartment lite	2
Radiator cooling fan	12
Radiator cooling fan after run relay	13,14
Radiator cooling fan thermoswitch	13

Wire connectors

T1a — single, under instrument panel
T1b — single, in engine compartment
T1c — single, under instrument panel
T2q — double, under instrument panel
T2b — double, under instrument panel
T2c — double, under instrument panel
T2d — double, in engine compartment
T2e — double, in engine compartment
T2f — double, in engine compartment
T2g — double, in engine compartment
T4a — 4-point, under instrument panel
T5a — 5-point, under instrument panel
T32 — 32-point, under instrument panel

**Air Conditioning
1985-1987 Jetta
(page 2 of 2)**

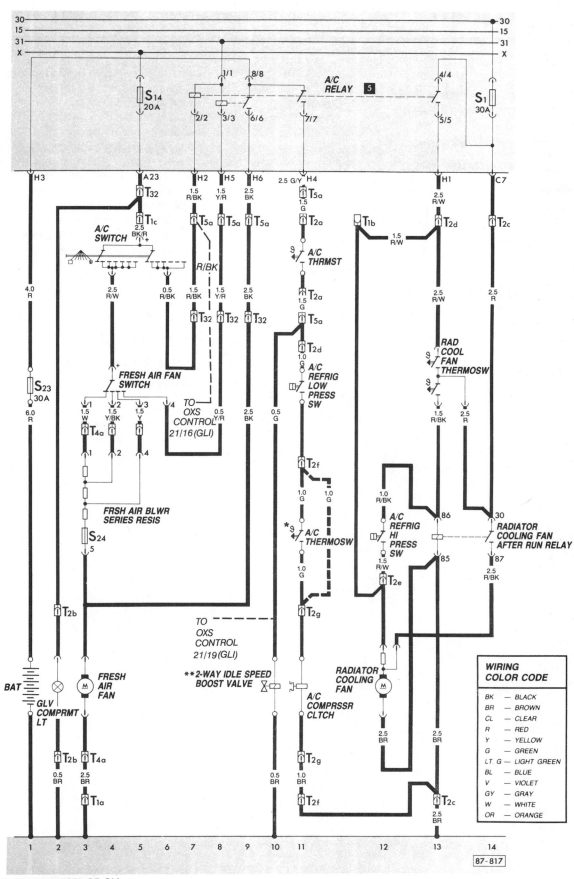

* Diesel

** NOT USED IN TURBO DIESEL OR GLI

**Air Conditioning
1988-1989 Jetta (Gasoline only)
(page 1 of 3)**

Description	Current track
2-way idle speed boost valve	12
A/C compressor clutch	16
A/C refrigerant high pressure switch	18
A/C refrigerant low pressure switch	14
A/C relay	10-14
A/C switch	2-6
A/C thermostat	14
A/C thermoswitch	16
Fresh air blower series resistance	2-5
Fresh air fan	5
Fresh air fan switch	2-5
Glove compartment light	1
Radiator cooling fan	17-19
Radiator cooling fan after run relay	21-24
Radiator cooling fan thermoswitch	20-23
Radiator cooling fan thermoswitch	20

Wire connectors

T1 — single, on Digifant control unit
T1a — single behind instrument panel
T1b — single, on radiator cooling fan after-run relay
T1c — single behind instrument panel
T2a — double behind instrument panel
T2b — double behind instrument panel
T2c — double in engine compartment
T2d — double in engine compartment, front
T2e — double in engine compartment
T2f — double in engine compartment
T2g — double in engine compartment
T3a — 3 point behind instrument panel
T5a — 5 point behind instrument panel
T5b — 5 point behind instrument panel
T32 — 32-point behind instrument panel

Ground connections

(30) — near fuse relay panel

(80) — in instrument panel wiring harness

(82) — in wiring harness front/left

Air Conditioning
1988-1989 Jetta (Gasoline only)
(page 2 of 3)

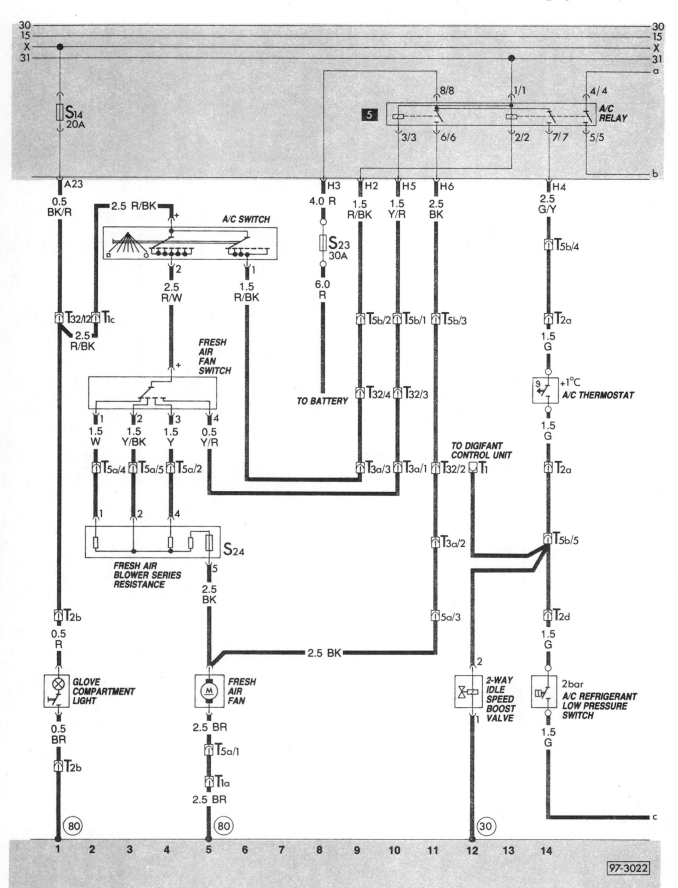

97-3022

Air Conditioning
1988-1989 Jetta (Gasoline only)
(page 3 of 3)

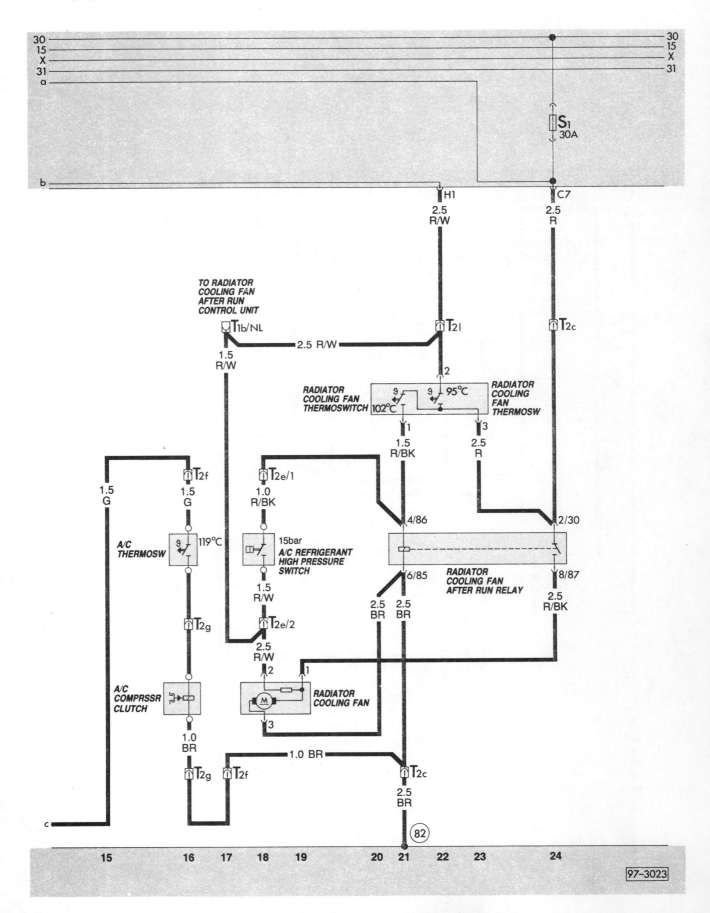

97–3023

Air Conditioning
Diesel 1988-1989
(page 3 of 3)

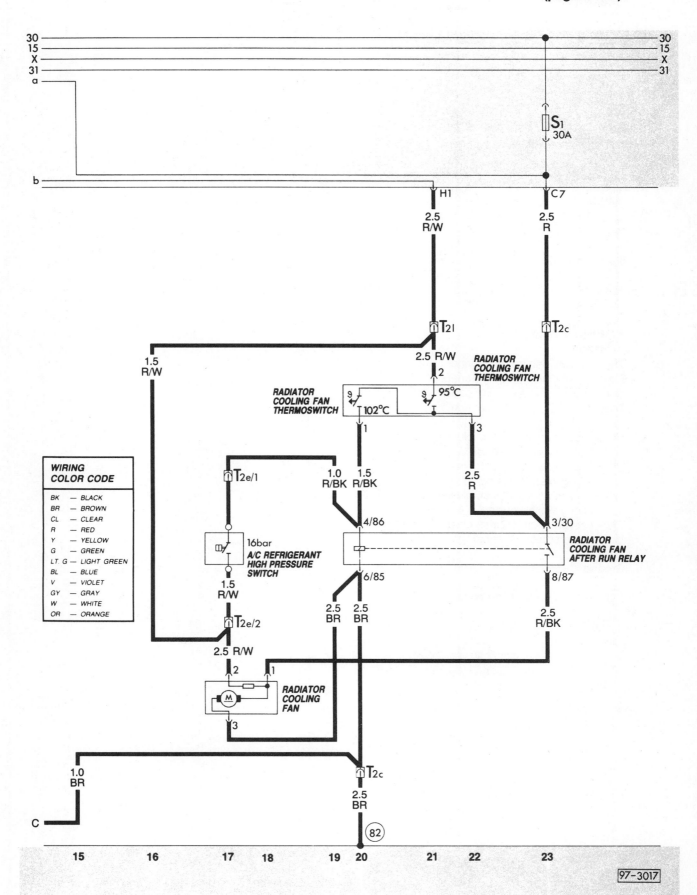

WIRING
COLOR CODE

BK — BLACK
BR — BROWN
CL — CLEAR
R — RED
Y — YELLOW
G — GREEN
LT. G — LIGHT GREEN
BL — BLUE
V — VIOLET
GY — GRAY
W — WHITE
OR — ORANGE

97-3017

Multifunction Indicator
1985-1989 Jetta
(page 1 of 2)

Description	Current Track
Ignition coil	1
Ignition/start switch	3
Memory switch (MFI)	7-9
Multifunction indicator (MFI)	3-9
Oil temp. sender	4
Outside temp. sensor	5
Recall switch (MFI)	6
Speed sensor	2
Vacuum sender	4-6
Voltage stabilizer	1

Wire Connectors

T1e — single, behind relay panel
T1g — single, behind relay panel
T2a — double, behind relay panel
T4a — four point, under steering
    column trim
T7 — seven point, on inst. cluster
    (short white housing)
T7a — seven point, on inst. cluster
    (long black housing)
T7b — seven point, on inst. cluster
    (long white housing)
T7c — seven point, on inst. cluster
    (short black housing)

Ground Connectors

⑫ — on cylinder head cover

**Multifunction Indicator
1988-1989 Jetta
(page 2 of 2)**

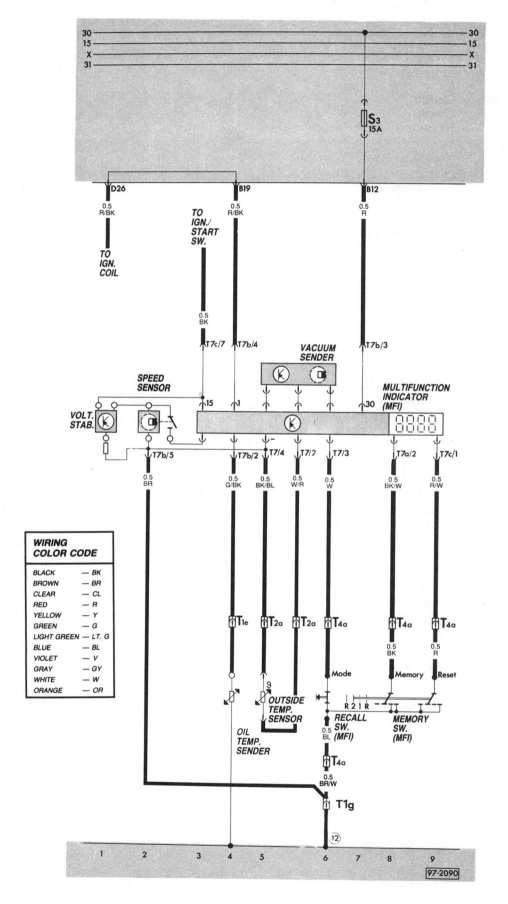

After-Run Radiator Cooling Fan
1986–1989 Jetta
(page 1 of 2)

Description	Current track
Radiator cooling fan	4,5
Radiator cooling fan after run control unit	1-3
Radiator cooling fan thermoswitch	4,5
Radiator cooling fan thermoswitch	1

Wire connectors

T1 — single, in eng compart, on fan shroud
T2 — double, near rad cool fan

Welded connections

(30) — plus connection, in front wiring harness

Ground connections

(15) — in front wiring harness

After-Run Radiator Cooling Fan
1986–1989 Jetta
(page 2 of 2)

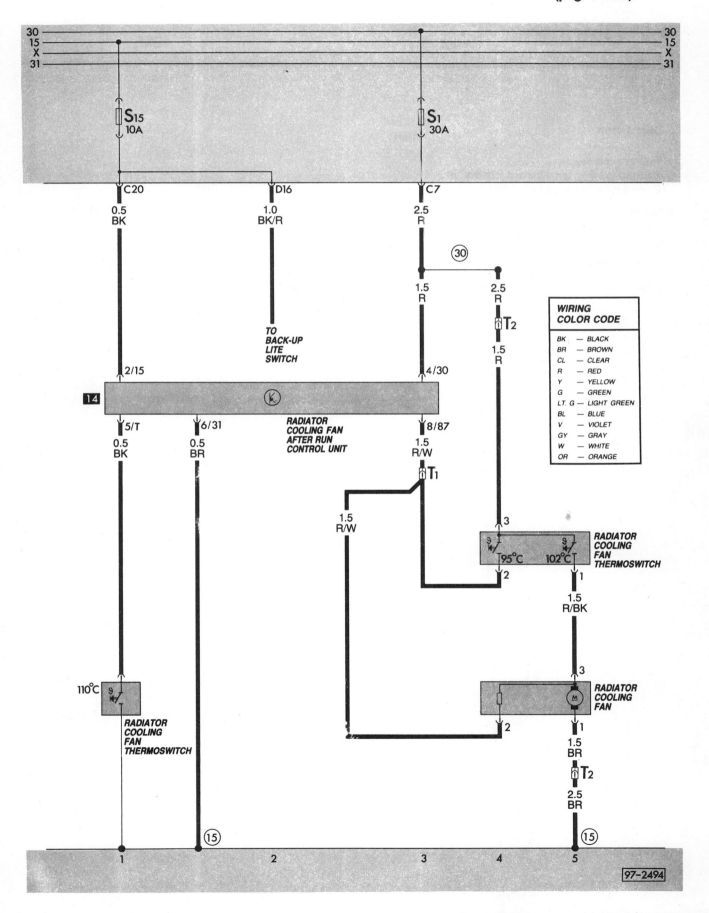

WIRING COLOR CODE	
BK	— BLACK
BR	— BROWN
CL	— CLEAR
R	— RED
Y	— YELLOW
G	— GREEN
LT. G	— LIGHT GREEN
BL	— BLUE
V	— VIOLET
GY	— GRAY
W	— WHITE
OR	— ORANGE

97-2494

Heated Seats
1985-1989 Jetta
(page 1 of 2)

Description	Current Track
Control unit, driver's seat	7-9
Control unit, pass. seat	10
Heat element, driver's backrest	9
Heat element, driver's seat	9
Heat element, pass, backrest	1
Heat element, pass. seat	1
Heat regulating switch, driver's seat	5-6
Heat regulating switch, pass. seat	3-4
Indicator light	10
Thermostat, driver's seat	7
Thermostat, pass. seat	2

Wire Connectors

T1   — single, behind fuse/relay panel
T4a — 4-point, behind fuse/relay panel
T6a — 6-point, under driver's seat
T6b — 6-point, under pass. seat
T32 — 32-point, under instrument panel

Ground connections

(10) — near fuse/relay panel

(17) — in instrument panel wiring harness

**Heated Seats
1985-1989 Jetta
(page 2 of 2)**

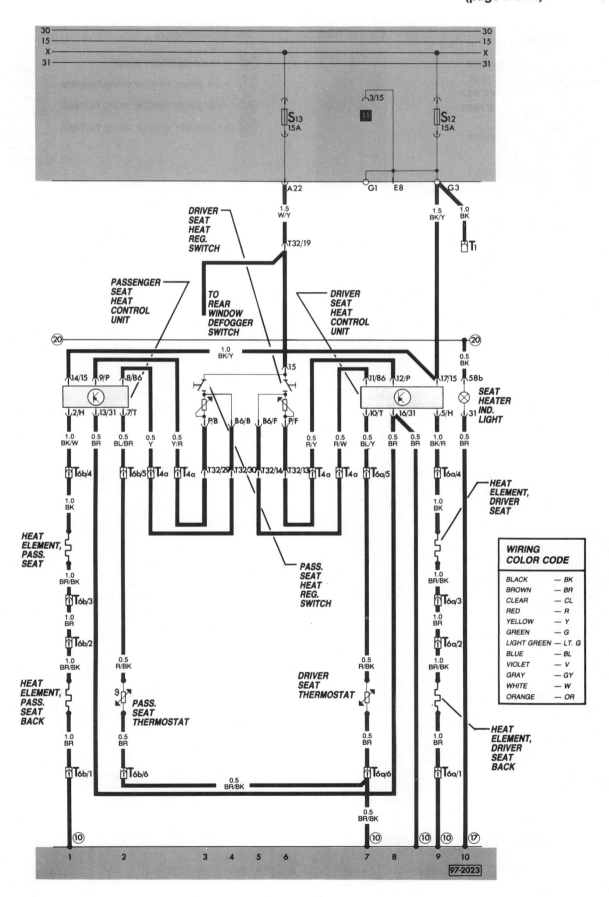

WIRING COLOR CODE	
BLACK	— BK
BROWN	— BR
CLEAR	— CL
RED	— R
YELLOW	— Y
GREEN	— G
LIGHT GREEN	— LT. G
BLUE	— BL
VIOLET	— V
GRAY	— GY
WHITE	— W
ORANGE	— OR

97-2023

Electric/Heated Outside Mirrors
1985-1989 Jetta
(page 1 of 2)

Description	Current Track
Heater element, driver mirror	8
Heater element, passenger mirror	7
Magnetic clutch, driver mirror	4
Magnetic clutch, passenger mirror	5
Mirror motor, driver	3
Mirror motor, passenger	1
Mirror motor, remote control switch	1-5
Mirror selector switch	1-3
Rear window defogger switch	6
Rear window heat element	7

Wire Connectors

T1	— single, behind fuse/relay panel
T1m	— single, behind fuse/relay panel
T3b	— 3 point, behind left front door panel
T3c	— 3 point, behind left front door panel
T3d	— 3 point, behind right front door panel
T3e	— 3 point, behind right front door panel
T6	— 6 point, behind fuse/relay panel
T32	— 32 point, under instrument panel

Ground Connections

(10) — near fuse/relay panel

**Electric/Heated Outside Mirrors
1985–1989 Jetta
(page 2 of 2)**

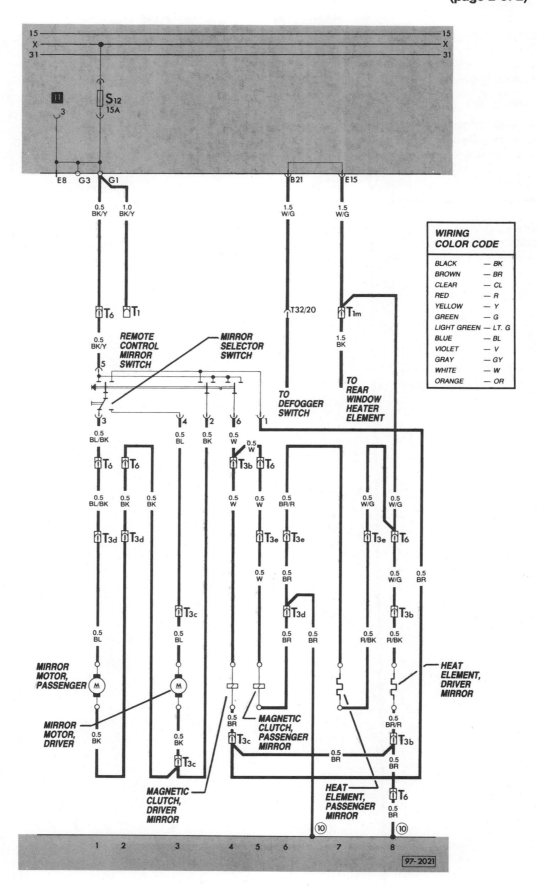

WIRING COLOR CODE	
BLACK	— BK
BROWN	— BR
CLEAR	— CL
RED	— R
YELLOW	— Y
GREEN	— G
LIGHT GREEN	— LT. G
BLUE	— BL
VIOLET	— V
GRAY	— GY
WHITE	— W
ORANGE	— OR

97-2021

Central Locking System
1985–1989 Jetta
(page 1 of 2)

Description	Current Track
Central locking system motor	4,5
Central locking system switch	4,5

Wire connectors

T1h — single, under fuse/relay panel
T3h — three point, under instrument panel
T32 — 32 point, under instrument panel

Ground connectors

(18) — in luggage compartment, left side

Central Locking System
1985–1989 Jetta
(page 2 of 2)

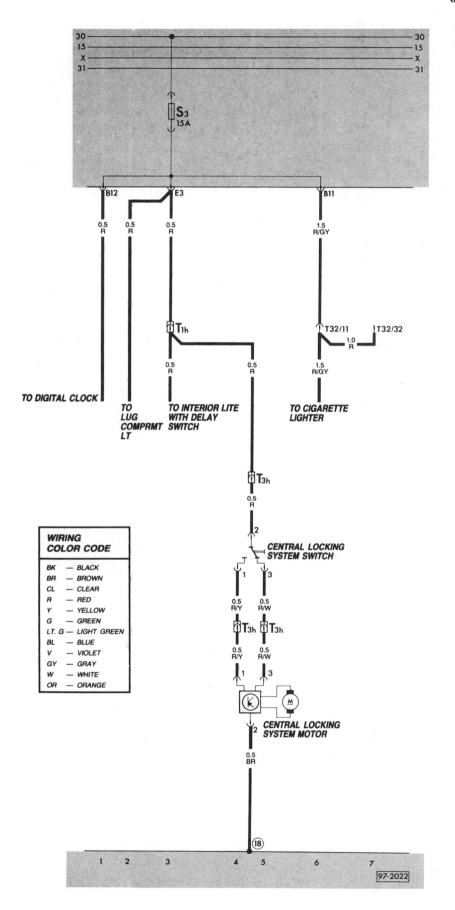

WIRING
COLOR CODE

BK — BLACK
BR — BROWN
CL — CLEAR
R — RED
Y — YELLOW
G — GREEN
LT. G — LIGHT GREEN
BL — BLUE
V — VIOLET
GY — GRAY
W — WHITE
OR — ORANGE

TO DIGITAL CLOCK

TO LUG COMPRMT LT

TO INTERIOR LITE WITH DELAY SWITCH

TO CIGARETTE LIGHTER

CENTRAL LOCKING SYSTEM SWITCH

CENTRAL LOCKING SYSTEM MOTOR

97-2022

Power Seat Height Adjust
1985-1989 Jetta
(page 1 of 2)

Description	Current track
Driver seat rear height adjusting motor	1
Driver seat rear height adjusting switch	1,2
Memory seat adjusting circuit breaker	1
Passenger seat rear height adjusting motor	3
Passenger seat rear height adjusting switch	3,4

Wire connectors

T2a — two-point, under driver's seat
T2b — two-point, under passenger's seat

Ground connections

(10) — near fuse/relay panel

**Power Seat Height Adjust
1985–1989 Jetta
(page 2 of 2)**

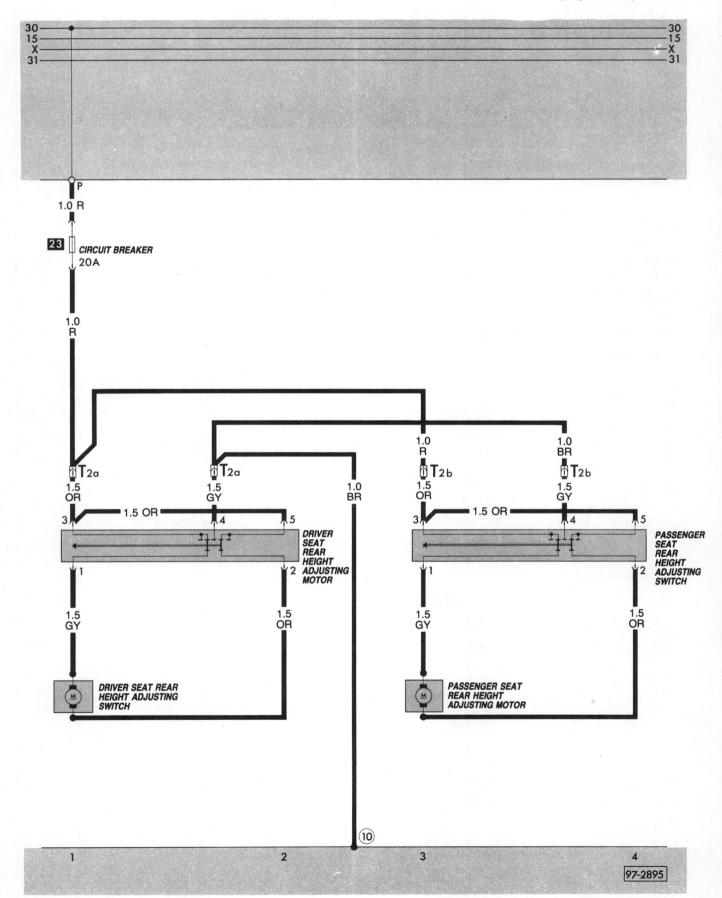

97-2895

Power Windows
1985-1989 Jetta
(page 1 of 3)

Description	Current Track
Rear window lockout switch (in console)	10-11
Rear window lockout switch lite	12
Window motor, LF	7
Window motor, LR	4
Window motor, RF	3
Window motor, RR	6
Window switch lite, LF (in console)	15
Window switch lite, LR (in console)	18
Window switch lite, LR (in door)	13-14
Window switch lite, RF (in console)	2
Window switch lite, RR (in console)	5
Window switch lite, RR (in door)	6-7
Window switch, LF (in console)	16-17
Window switch, LR (in console)	16-17
Window switch, LR (in door)	13-14
Window switch, RF (in console)	3-4
Window switch, RR (in console)	3-4
Window switch, RR (in door)	6-7

Wire connectors

T1 — single, behind fuse/relay panel
T1s — single, behind fuse/relay panel
T2i — double, behind RF door panel
T2r — double, behind RR door panel
T2s — double, behind LR door panel
T2t — double, behind LF door panel
T2v — double, near lower right "A" pillar
T2z — double, near lower left "A" pillar
T3f — three point, near lower right "B" pillar
T3g — three point, near lower left "B" pillar

Ground connections

(10) — near fuse/relay panel

Welded wiring points

(21) — in power window wiring harness (negative)

(22) — in power window wiring harness

(23) — in power window wiring harness (positive)

**Power Windows
1985-1989 Jetta
(page 2 of 3)**

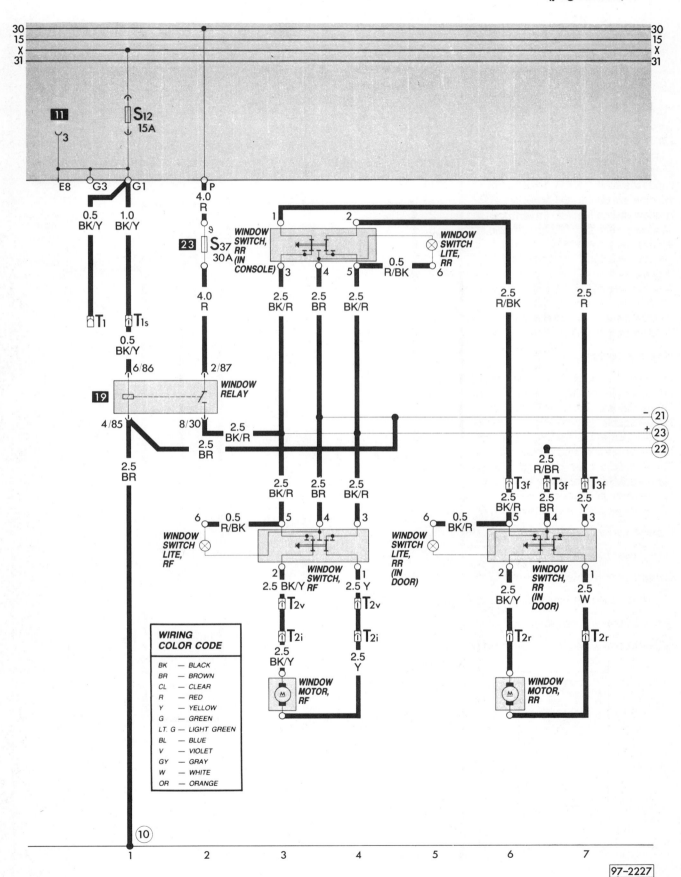

WIRING
COLOR CODE

BK	— BLACK
BR	— BROWN
CL	— CLEAR
R	— RED
Y	— YELLOW
G	— GREEN
LT. G	— LIGHT GREEN
BL	— BLUE
V	— VIOLET
GY	— GRAY
W	— WHITE
OR	— ORANGE

97–2227

Power Windows
1985-1989 Jetta
(page 3 of 3)

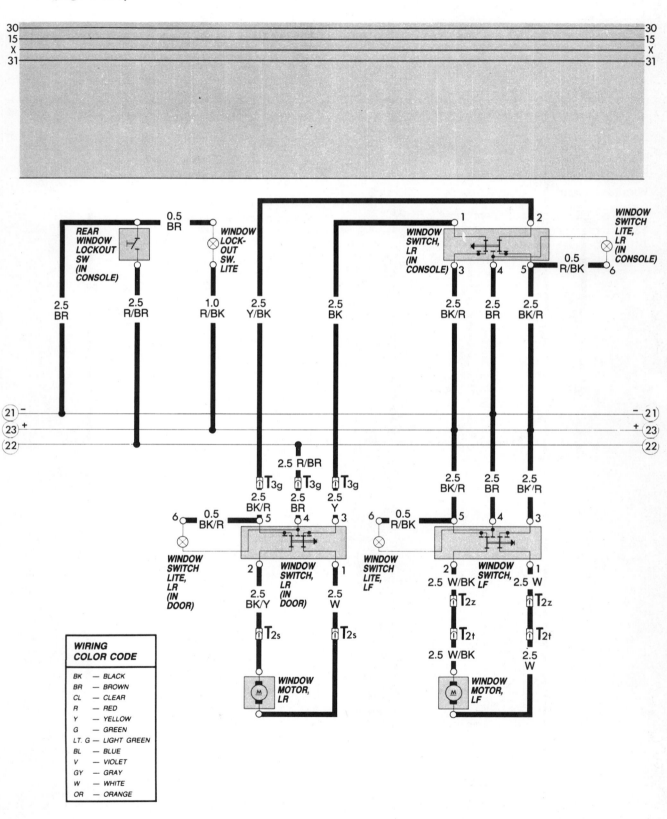

WIRING
COLOR CODE

BK	— BLACK
BR	— BROWN
CL	— CLEAR
R	— RED
Y	— YELLOW
G	— GREEN
LT. G	— LIGHT GREEN
BL	— BLUE
V	— VIOLET
GY	— GRAY
W	— WHITE
OR	— ORANGE

10   11   12   13   14   15   16   17   18

97-2228

Description	Current Track
Cigar lighter	1
Cigar lighter lite	3
Power antenna	9-10
Speaker, LF	4
Speaker, LR	6
Speaker, RF	5
Speaker, RR	7

Wire Connectors

T2a — double, under instrument panel, middle

T3a — three point, under fuse/relay panel

T4 — four point, under instrument panel, middle

T7b/— seven point, on instrument panel wiring harness

Ground Connections

(10) — near fuse/relay panel

(16) — in instrument panel wiring harness

(17) — in instrument cluster wiring harness

Stereo Radio
1985–1986 Jetta
(page 2 of 3)

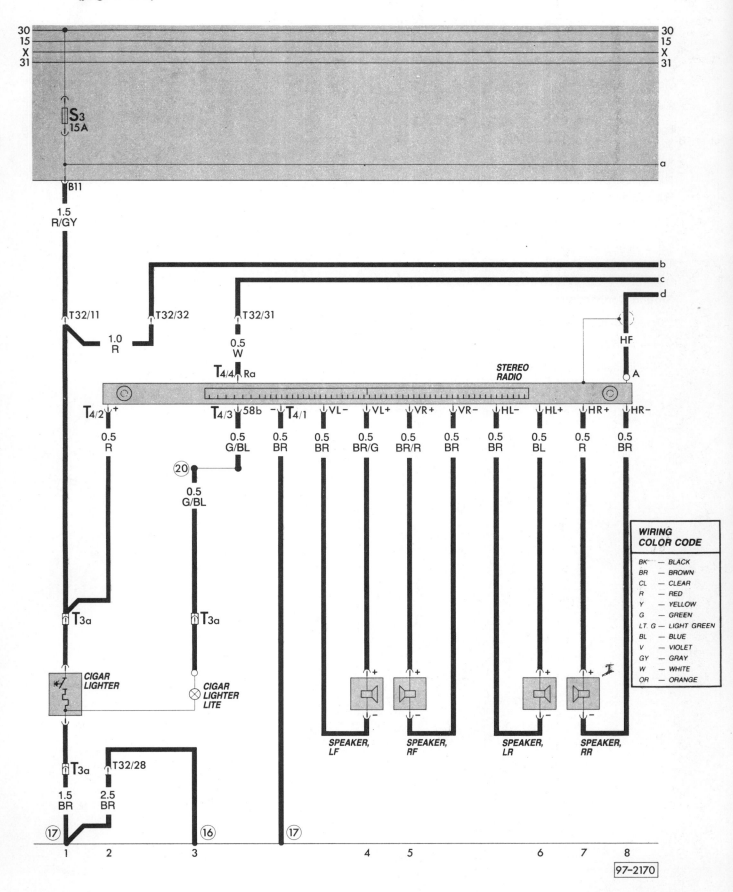

WIRING
COLOR CODE

BK — BLACK
BR — BROWN
CL — CLEAR
R — RED
Y — YELLOW
G — GREEN
LT G — LIGHT GREEN
BL — BLUE
V — VIOLET
GY — GRAY
W — WHITE
OR — ORANGE

97-2170

**Stereo Radio
1985–1986 Jetta
(page 3 of 3)**

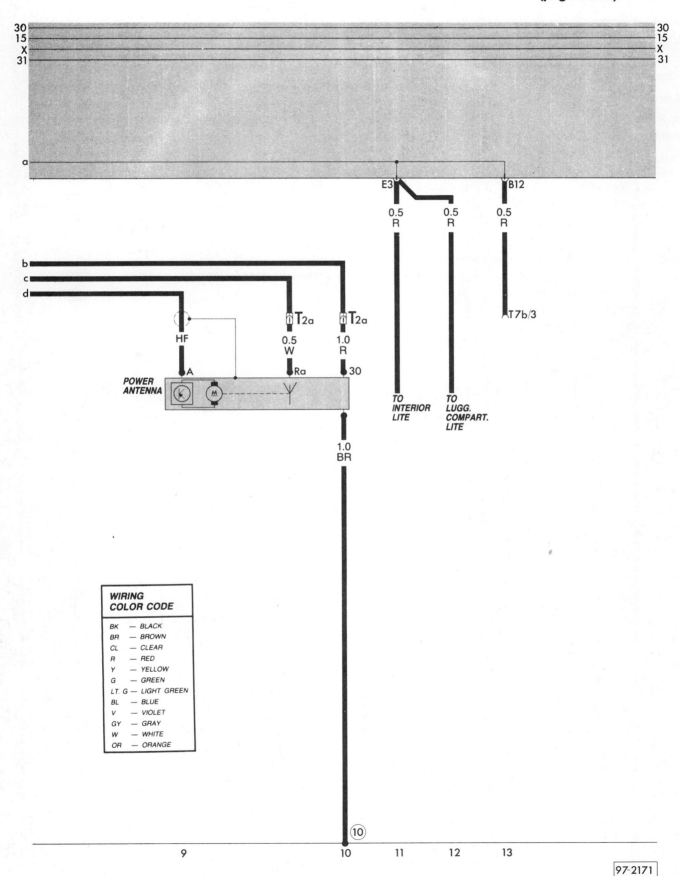

WIRING COLOR CODE	
BK	— BLACK
BR	— BROWN
CL	— CLEAR
R	— RED
Y	— YELLOW
G	— GREEN
LT. G	— LIGHT GREEN
BL	— BLUE
V	— VIOLET
GY	— GRAY
W	— WHITE
OR	— ORANGE

97-2171

**Stereo Radio with Power Antenna
1986–1987 Jetta
(page 1 of 3)**

Description	Current track
Cigarette lighter lite	3
Electrical antenna	9,10
Radio connection	2-8
Refrigerator 12V connector	1
Speaker, left front	4
Speaker, left rear	6
Speaker, right front	5
Speaker, right rear	7

Wire connectors

T2a — double, under instrument panel, middle
T3a — three-point, under fuse/relay panel
T4/ — four-point, right front footwell
T7b — seven-point, on instrument cluster
(long white housing)
T8/ — eight-point, on radio
T8a — eight-point, on radio
T32 — 32-point, under instrument panel

Ground connections

(30) — near fuse/relay panel

(80) — in instrument panel wiring harness

(81) — in instrument panel wiring harness

Plus (+) connections

(A11) — plus connection (58b) in instrument panel
wiring harness

Stereo Radio with Power Antenna
1986–1987 Jetta
(page 2 of 3)

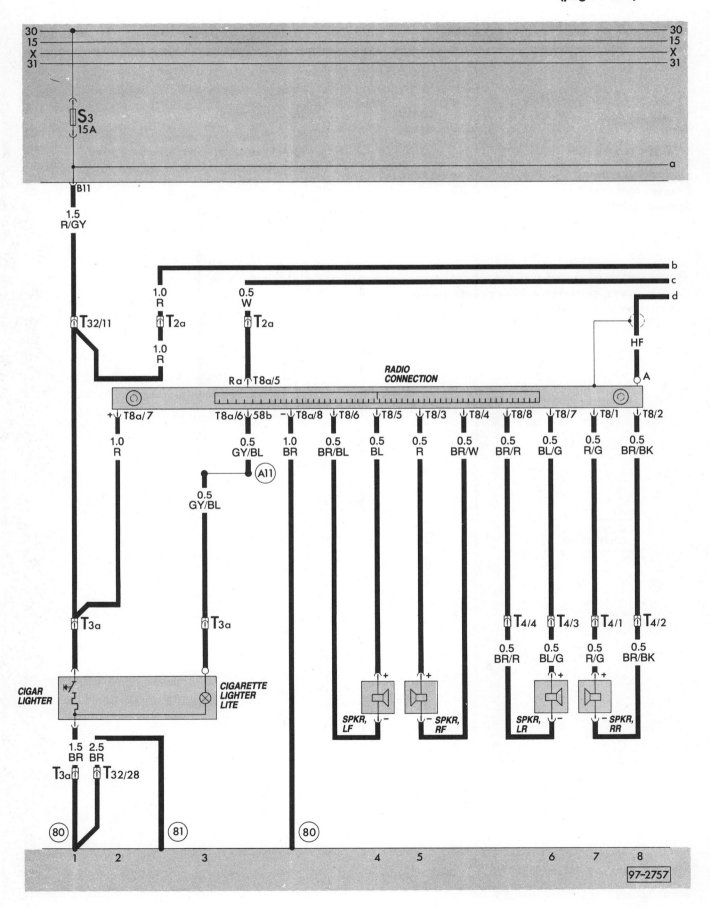

Stereo Radio with Power Antenna
1986–1987 Jetta
(page 3 of 3)

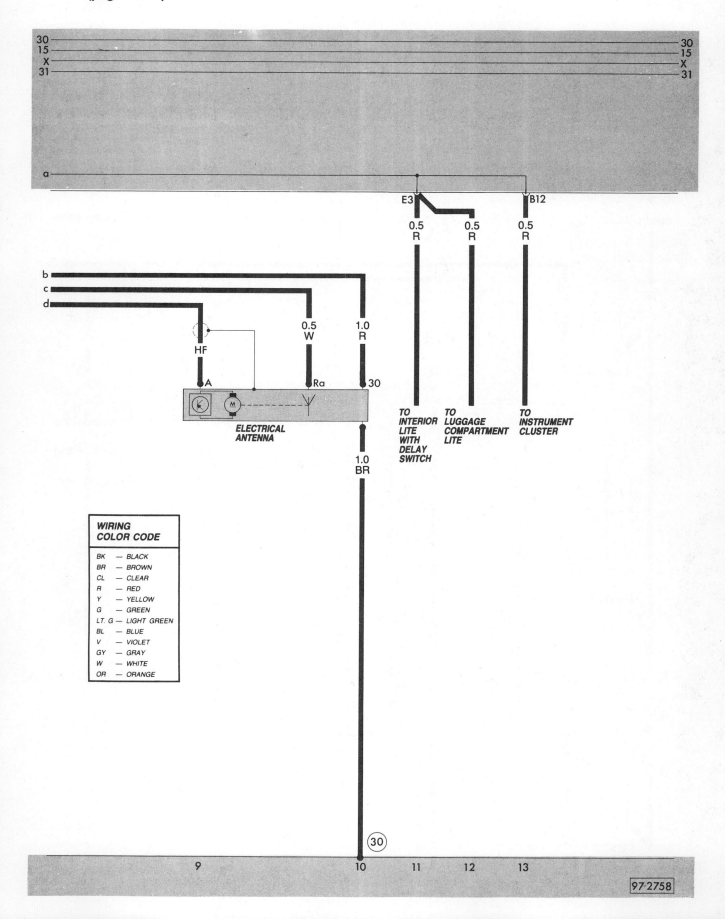

WIRING
COLOR CODE

BK	— BLACK
BR	— BROWN
CL	— CLEAR
R	— RED
Y	— YELLOW
G	— GREEN
LT. G	— LIGHT GREEN
BL	— BLUE
V	— VIOLET
GY	— GRAY
W	— WHITE
OR	— ORANGE

ELECTRICAL
ANTENNA

TO
INTERIOR
LITE
WITH
DELAY
SWITCH

TO
LUGGAGE
COMPARTMENT
LITE

TO
INSTRUMENT
CLUSTER

97-2758

**Stereo Radio with Six Speakers
and Power Antenna
1988-1989 Jetta
(page 1 of 4)**

Description	Current track
Amplified speaker, left front	10,11
Amplified speaker, right front	12,13
Cigarette lighter	1
Cigarette lighter light	3
Electrical antenna	15,16
High tone speaker, left front	5
High tone speaker, right front	6
Power antenna	15,16
Radio connection	4-8
Radio connection	9-14
Speaker, left rear	7
Speaker, right rear	8

Wire connectors

T2a — double, under instrument panel, middle
T2b — double, on LF amplified speaker
T2c — double, on RF amplified speaker
T3a — three-point, under relay panel
T3b — three-point, under instrument panel, middle
T3c — three-point, on LF amplified speaker
T3d — three-point, on RF amplified speaker
T4 — four-point, near RF kick panel
T5a — five-point, on upper left 'A' pillar
T5b — five-point, on upper right 'A' pillar
T7b — seven point, on instrument cluster (long white
　　　connectors)
T8 — eight-point, on radio
T8a — eight-point, on radio
T10 — ten-point, on radio
T32 — thirty-two point, under instrument panel

Ground connections

(30) — near fuse/relay panel
(46) — near fuse/relay panel

Welded wiring connections

(80) — ground connection, in instrument panel wiring
　　　harness
(81) — ground connection, in instrument panel wiring
　　　harness
(A11) — plus (+) connection, terminal 58 in instrument
　　　panel wiring harness

**Stereo Radio with Six Speakers
and Power Antenna
1988-1989 Jetta
(page 2 of 4)**

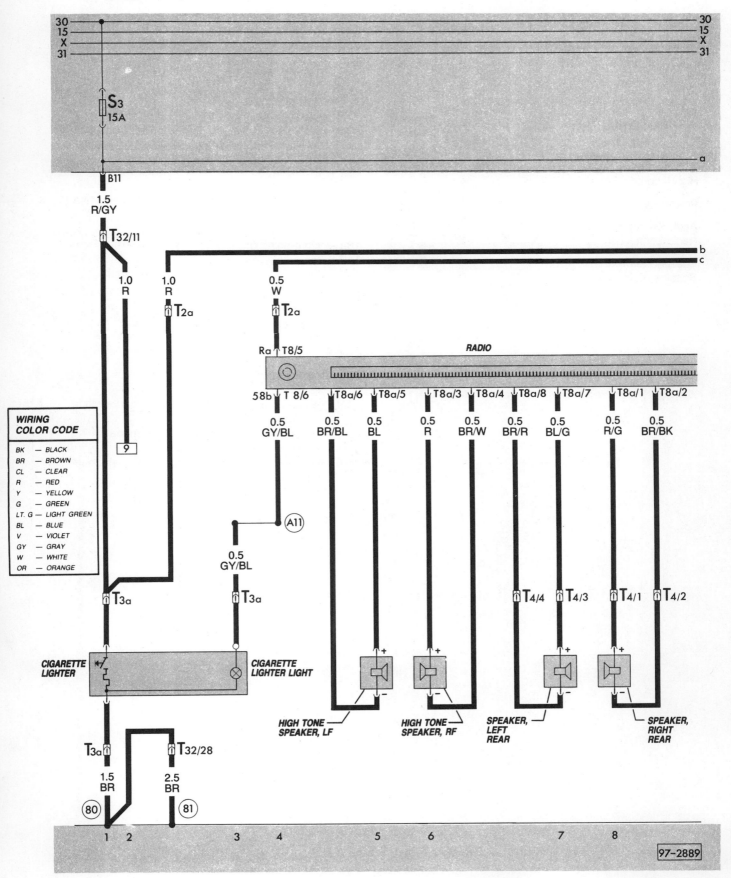

WIRING
COLOR CODE

BK	— BLACK
BR	— BROWN
CL	— CLEAR
R	— RED
Y	— YELLOW
G	— GREEN
LT. G	— LIGHT GREEN
BL	— BLUE
V	— VIOLET
GY	— GRAY
W	— WHITE
OR	— ORANGE

97-2889

**Stereo Radio with Six Speakers
and Power Antenna
1988-1989 Jetta
(page 3 of 4)**

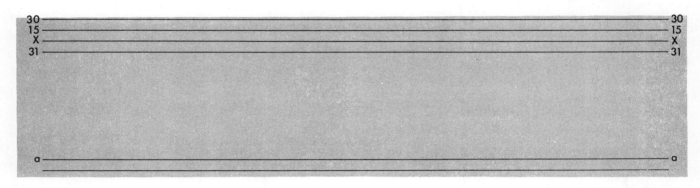

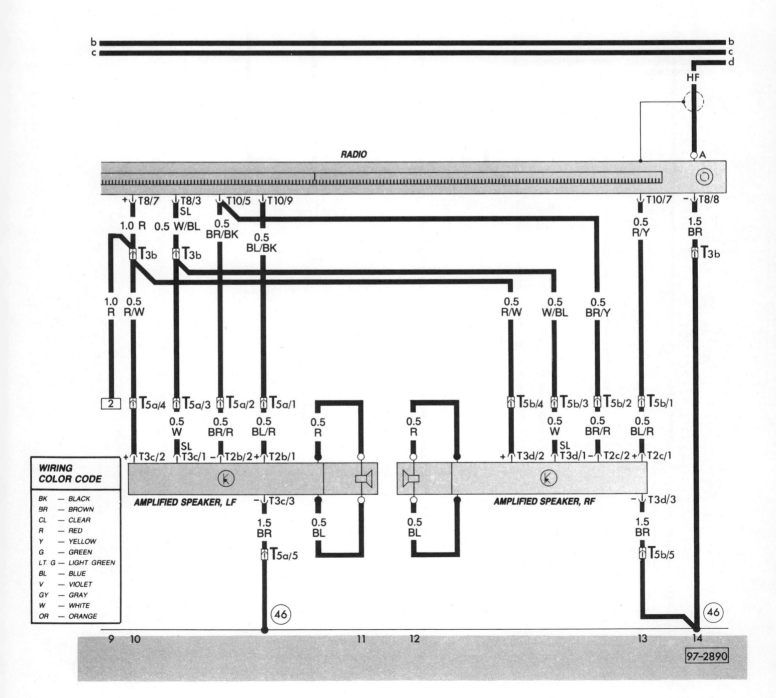

WIRING COLOR CODE	
BK	BLACK
BR	BROWN
CL	CLEAR
R	RED
Y	YELLOW
G	GREEN
LT. G	LIGHT GREEN
BL	BLUE
V	VIOLET
GY	GRAY
W	WHITE
OR	ORANGE

97-2890

**Stereo Radio with Six Speakers
and Power Antenna
1988-1989 Jetta
(page 4 of 4)**

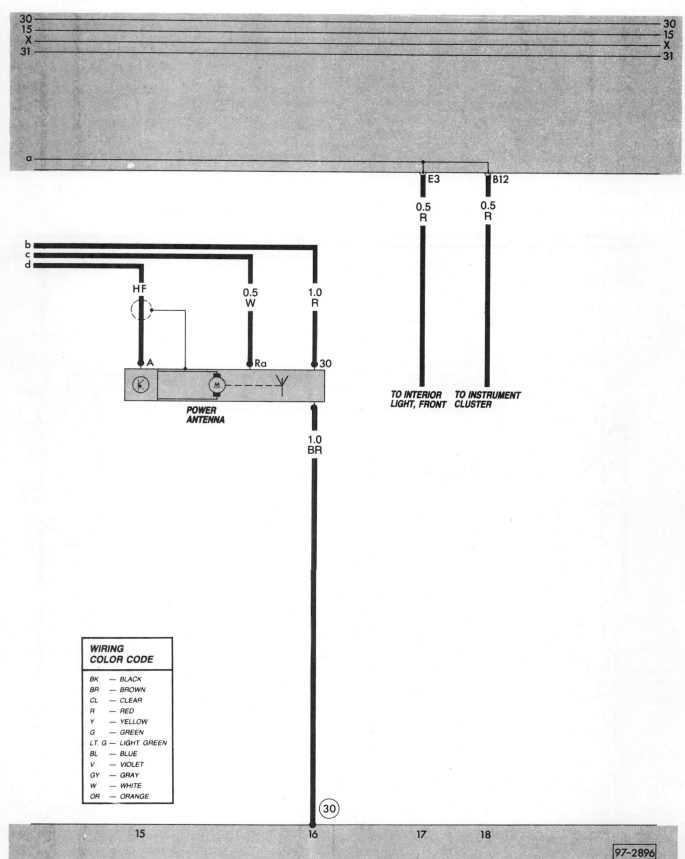

POWER
ANTENNA

TO INTERIOR
LIGHT, FRONT

TO INSTRUMENT
CLUSTER

**WIRING
COLOR CODE**

BK	— BLACK
BR	— BROWN
CL	— CLEAR
R	— RED
Y	— YELLOW
G	— GREEN
LT. G	— LIGHT GREEN
BL	— BLUE
V	— VIOLET
GY	— GRAY
W	— WHITE
OR	— ORANGE

15   16   17   18

97–2896

**Seat Belt Interlock
Passive Restraint
1988-1989 Jetta
(page 1 of 3)**

Description	Current track
Brake and parking brake indicator light	17
Brake fluid level warning contact	18
Door contact switch, left front	8,9
Door contact switch, right front	6
Ignition/starter switch	3-6
Parking brake warning light switch	19
Seat belt switch, left	12
Seat belt warning light	14
Seat belt warning relay	9-12
Starting interlock relay	10,11

Wiring connectors

T1a — single behind relay panel plate
T1b — single behind relay panel plate
T1c — single behind relay panel plate
T2a — double front footwell, left
T7c — 7 point on instrument cluster
T32/ — 32-point behind dash

Ground connectors

(30) — beside relay plate

(80) — in instrument panel wiring harness

(82) — in wiring harness front/left

**Seat Belt Interlock
for passive restraint
1988-1989 Jetta
(page 2 of 3)**

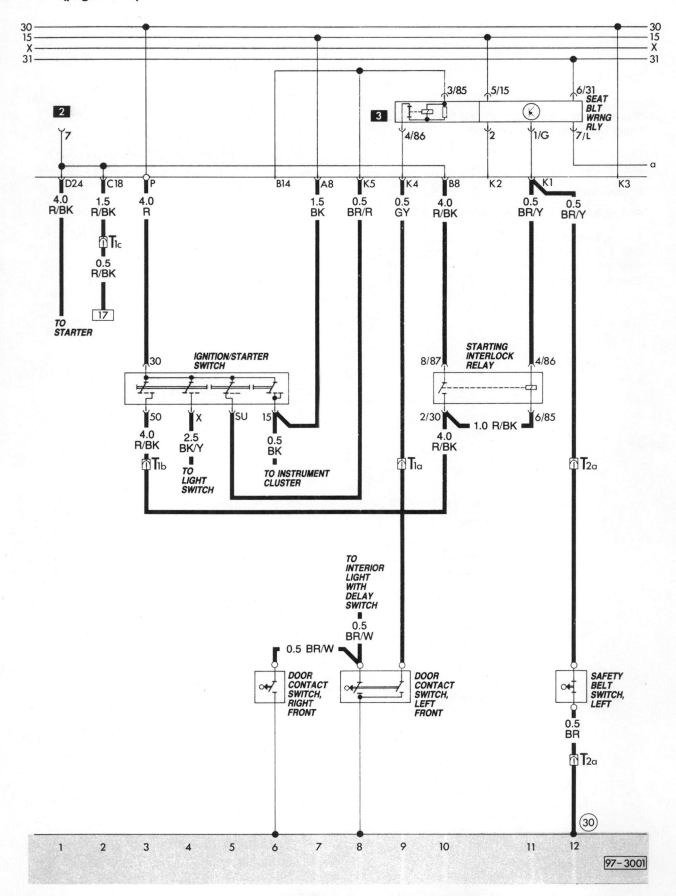

Seatbelt interlock
Passive Restraint
1988-1989 Jetta
(page 3 of 3)

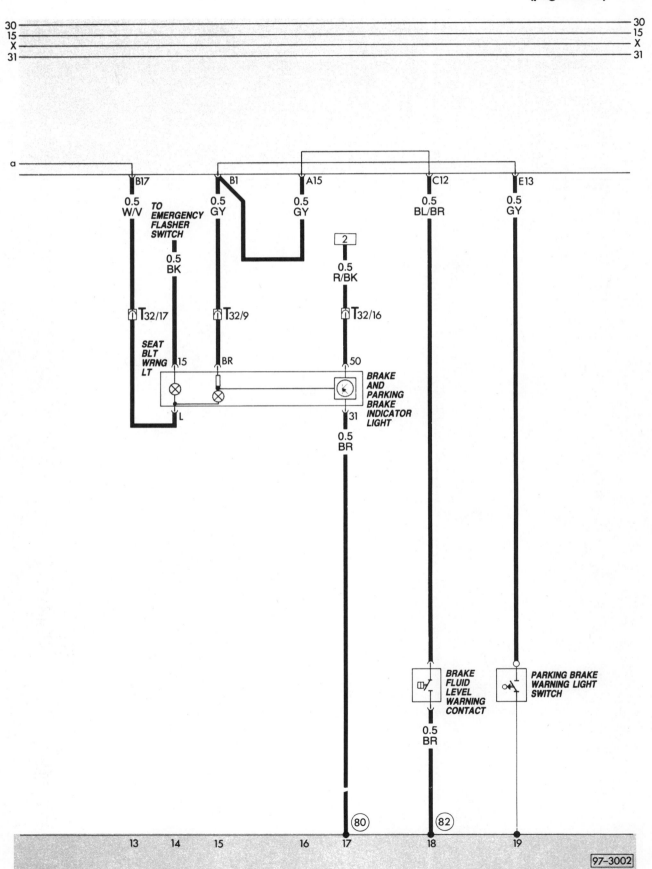

97-3002

INDEX

Subjects are indexed by section number in **bold**, followed by the page number(s) within the section in ordinary type, followed by the numbered heading in **bold** in parentheses. Thus, **10**:12 (**4.1**) refers to page 12 in section **10. Automatic Transmission**, under heading **4.1**.

A

Accelerator cable (auto. trans.)
  10:12 (**4.1**)
  adjusting (gasoline engines) **10**:12
    (**4.2**)
    (diesel engines) **10**:13 (**4.2**)
    (fuel injection) **6**:12 (**5.2**)
  checking and adjusting **6**:13 (**5.2**)
  replacing **6**:12 (**5.2**)
Air conditioning **13**:36 (**9.**)
  electrical components **14**:26 (**11.**)
  general description **13**:4 (**1.3**)
  inspection **13**:37 (**9.2**)
  performance test **13**:37 (**9.2**)
  refrigerant charge
    checking **13**:37 (**9.2**)
  safety features **13**:37 (**9.1**)
  specifications **13**:38 (**9.3**)
  system description **13**:36 (**9.1**)
  tests **13**:37 (**9.2**)
Air filter **2**:14 (**5.1**)
Alignment (*see Wheels*)
Alternator and Regulator
  brushes and voltage regulator **14**:13
    (**5.3**)
  noisy alternator **14**:13 (**5.2**)
  removing and installing **14**:13 (**5.3**)
  testing **14**:12 (**5.2**)
  testing current drain **14**:12 (**5.2**)
Anti-freeze **2**:11 (**3.**)
ATF pump (*see Transmission, automatic*)
Axle (*see Suspension*)

B

Back-up Lights **14**:25 (**10.1**)
Ball joints **11**:19 (**5.3**)
Battery **14**:9 (**4.**)
  charging **14**:10 (**4.2**)
    and **2**:19 (**6.1**)
  checking and cleaning **2**:18 (**6.1**)
  general description **14**:4 (**1.**)
  hydrometer testing **14**:9 (**4.1**)
  load voltage testing **14**:10 (**4.1**)
  open-circuit voltage test
    14:10 (**4.1**)
  replacing **2**:19 (**6.1**)
  testing **14**:9 (**4.1**)
  troubleshooting **14**:7 (**3.2**)
Body and Interior
  body assembly materials **13**:35 (**8.**)
  care of finish **2**:28 (**9.1**)
    polishing **2**:28 (**9.1**)

Body and Interior (cont'd)
  special cleaning **2**:28 (**9.1**)
  washing **2**:28 (**9.1**)
  washing chassis **2**:28 (**9.1**)
  waxing **2**:28 (**9.1**)
  doors (*see Doors*)
  drive gear
    removing and installing **13**:5
    (**4.1**)
  exterior **13**:26 (**6.**)
  front body parts,
    removing **13**:28 (**6.4**)
  grille, removing **13**:28 (**6.4**)
  hatchback **13**:32 (**6.4**)
  headliner **13**:19 (**4.9**)
    removing and installing **13**:19
    (**4.9**)
  heater and controls (*see Heating*)
  hood lock cable **13**:32 (**6.4**)
  instrument cluster **13**:5 (**4.1**)
  instrument panel **13**:5 (**4.1**)
    removing **13**:7 (**4.1**)
  interior **13**:5 (**4.**)
  interior lights (*see Interior lights*)
  maintenance **13**:5 (**2.**)
  rear lid **13**:32 (**6.4**)
    removing **13**:5 (**4.1**)
  seats (*see Seats*)
  seat belts (*see Seat belts*)
  speedometer cable removing and
    installing **13**:5 (**4.1**)
  sunroof (*see Sunroof*)
  troubleshooting **13**:5 (**3.**)
    bi-pressure system **13**:22 (**5.2**)
Brake lights **14**:25 (**10.1**)
Brakes
  bleeding brakes **12**:8 (**4.2**)
    manual bleeding **12**:9 (**4.2**)
    pressure bleeding **12**:9 (**4.2**)
    vacuum bleeding **12**:9 (**4.2**)
  brake fluid **12**:8 (**4.1**)
    replacing **12**:9 (**4.2**)
    specifications **2**:11 (**3.**)
  brake pressure regulator
    quick-checking **12**:11 (**4.4**)
  brake system service **12**:8 (**4.**)
  calipers **12**:14 (**5.2**)
  flushing the brake system **12**:9 (**4.2**)
  front disc brakes **12**:11 (**5.**)
    reconditioning **12**:13 (**5.1**)
    removing and installing **12**:13 (**5.1**)
  general descriptions **12**:4 (**1.**)
  hoses and lines **2**:23 (**7.2**)
  maintenance **12**:5 (**2.**)

Brakes (cont'd)
  master cylinder **12**:9 (**4.3**)
    removing and installing **12**:10 (**4.3**)
  pad wear, checking **12**:13 (**5.**)
  pressure testing regulator **12**:11 (**4.4**)
  proportioning valves **12**:11 (**4.4**)
  rotors removing, reconditioning
    and installing **12**:14 (**5.1**)
  technical data **12**:23 (**8.**)
  troubleshooting **12**:5 (**3.**)
    basic troubleshooting
      principles **12**:5 (**3.1**)
    brake noise **12**:7 (**3.3**)
    diagnostic tests **12**:7 (**3.2**)
  vacuum booster **12**:9 (**4.3**)
    removing and installing **12**:10 (**4.3**)
Brakes, rear disc **12**:19 (**7.**)
  calipers **12**:22 (**7.3**)
  pads wear, checking **12**:20 (**7.**)
    removing and installing **12**:20 (**7.1**)
  parking brake, adjusting **12**:21 (**7.2**)
    cable, replacing **12**:22 (**7.2**)
  reconditioning **12**:20 (**7.1**)
  rotors removing, reconditioning,
    and installing **12**:21
Brakes, rear drum **12**:15 (**6.**)
  brake lining wear,
    checking **12**:16 (**6.**)
  brake shoes
    removing and installing **12**:16 (**6.1**)
  parking brake **12**:18 (**6.2**)
    adjusting **12**:18 (**6.2**)
    cables replacing **12**:19 (**6.2**)
  reconditioning **12**:18 (**6.1**)
  wheel cylinder
    inspecting and replacing **12**:18 (**6.1**)
Bumpers **13**:28 (**6.4**)
  removing and installing **13**:31 (**6.4**)
  plastic cover, removing **13**:32 (**6.4**)

C

Calipers, brake (*see Brakes*)
Camber (*see Wheels*)
Camshaft (*see Engine*)
Catalytic converter **7**:12 (**4.2**)
  checking **7**:13 (**4.2**)
  general description **7**:4 (**1.20**)
  removing and installing **7**:13 (**4.2**)
Central locking system **14**:27 (**12.3**)
Clutch **9**:10 (**5.**)
  cable **9**:10 (**5.1**)
  general description **9**:4 (**1.1**)

2 INDEX

Subjects are indexed by section number in **bold**, followed by the page number(s) within the section in ordinary type, followed by the numbered heading in **bold** in parentheses. Thus, **10**:12 (**4.1**) refers to page 12 in section **10. Automatic Transmission**, under heading **4.1**.

Clutch (cont'd)
  removing and installing **9**:13 (**5.2**)
  shift mechanism (see *Transmission, manual*)
Coil, ignition (see *Ignition system*)
Compression test **2**:17 (**5.7**)
Constant velocity joints (see *Suspension*)
Continuous Injection System (see *Fuel system — gasoline*)
Cooling system
  coolant, checking level **2**:20 (**6.3**)
    draining and filling **4**:7 (**4.1**)
  coolant pump **4**:9 (**4.3**)
    inspecting and replacing **4**:9 (**4.3**)
  cooling fan and radiator thermoswitch
    testing **4**:10 (**4.4**)
  cooling system service **4**:6 (**4.**)
  general descriptions **4**:4 (**1.**)
  hoses **4**:6 (**4.1**)
    inspecting **2**:20 (**6.3**)
    replacing **4**:7 (**4.1**)
  maintenance **4**:4 (**2.**)
  radiator **4**:11 (**4.5**)
    removing and installing **4**:11 (**4.5**)
  radiator cooling fan **4**:10 (**4.4**)
    removing and installing **4**:11 (**4.4**)
  radiator cooling fan after-run system
    4:11 (**4.4**)
  technical data **4**:12 (**5.**)
  thermostat **4**:8 (**4.2**)
    removing and installing **4**:8 (**4.2**)
    testing **4**:8 (**4.2**)
  troubleshooting **4**:4 (**3.**)
    basic troubleshooting
    principles **4**:4 (**3.1**)
    cooling system and expansion tank cap
    diagnostic tests **4**:5 (**3.2**)
    pressure testing **4**:5 (**3.2**)
    temperature gauge and sending unit
    quick-check **4**:6 (**3.2**)
Cruise control **14**:28 (**12.5**)
Current flow diagrams **14**:34 (**14.**)
  how to read **14**:5 (**3.1**)
  Golf and GTI **14**:34 (**14.**)
    after-run radiator cooling fan **14**:133–
    134 (**14.**)
    air conditioning **14**:149–158 (**14.**)
    brake lights **14**:71 (**14.**)
    brake warning indicator
    14:79 (**14.**)
    central locking **14**:167 (**14.**)
    cold start system **14**:123
    –124 (**14.**)
    coolant level warning system
    14:127–128 (**14.**)

Current flow diagrams (cont'd)
  Golf and GTI (cont'd)
    courtesy lights **14**:72 (**14.**)
    cruise control **14**:159–160 (**14.**)
    electronic engine control
    14:101–121 (**14.**)
    exterior lights **14**:63–70 (**14.**)
    fresh air fan **14**:148 (**14.**)
    fuel pump system **14**:122 (**14.**)
    glow plugs **14**:99–100 (**14.**)
    ground circuit **14**:37–43 (**14.**)
    ground locations **14**:44 (**14.**)
    harness connectors **14**:45–47
    (**14.**)
    horns **14**:90–91 (**14.**)
    idle speed boost **14**:125–126 (**14.**)
    instrument cluster **14**:80–89 (**14.**)
    instrument panel lights **14**:76–
    77 (**14.**)
    interior lights **14**:73–75 (**14.**)
    passive restraint **14**:140
    –143 (**14.**)
    power mirrors **14**:168–170 (**14.**)
    power supply **14**:48–62 (**14.**)
    power windows **14**:164–166 (**14.**)
    radiator cooling fan **14**:129–
    132 (**14.**)
    radio **14**:161–163 (**14.**)
    rear wiper and washer **14**:95–
    98 (**14.**)
    seat belt interlock/park brake
    warning **14**:136–139 (**14.**)
    seat belt warning **14**:135 (**14.**)
    symbols used in wiring diagrams
    14:36 (**14.**)
    turn signals/flashers **14**:78 (**14.**)
    upshift indicator **14**:144–
    147 (**14.**)
    windshield wipers and washer
    14:92–94 (**14.**)
  Jetta **14**:34 (**14.**)
    after-run radiator cooling fan
    14:236–237 (**14.**)
    air conditioning **14**:232–233 (**14.**)
    automatic transmission **14**:224–
    227 (**14.**)
    central locking system **14**:242–
    243 (**14.**)
    cruise control **14**:228–231 (**14.**)
    electric/heated outside mirrors
    14:240–241 (**14.**)
    electronic engine controls
    14:206–223 (**14.**)
    heated seats **14**:238–239 (**14.**)

Current flow diagrams (cont'd)
  Jetta (cont'd)
    main electrical system
      1985–1987 Jetta Gasoline except GLI
      14:171–180 (**14.**)
      1988 Jetta Gasoline **14**:181–
      195 (**14.**)
      1986–1988 Jetta GLI **14**:181–
      195 (**14.**)
      1985–1988 Jetta Diesel
      14:196–205 (**14.**)
    mulifunction indicator
    14:234–235 (**14.**)
    power seat height adjustment
    14:244–245 (**14.**)
    power windows **14**:246
    –248 (**14.**)
    stereo radio **14**:249–251 (**14.**)
    stereo radio with power antenna
    14:252–254 (**14.**)
    stereo radio with six speakers and
    power antenna **14**:255–258 (**14.**)
    terminal and circuit identification
    14:6 (**3.1**)
Cylinder head (see *Engine*)

D

Diesel engine and fuel system (see *Engine and Fuel system — diesel*)
Digifant II (see *Fuel system — gasoline*)
Disc brakes (see *Brakes*)
Distributor, ignition **8**:21 (**5.**)
  disassembling and assembling **8**:23
  (**5.3**)
    all engines except 16-valve **8**:24
    (**5.3**)
    16-valve engines **8**:24 (**5.3**)
  distributor cap **2**:16 (**5.3**)
    removing and installing **8**:22
    (**5.1**)
    replacing **8**:22 (**5.1**)
  removing and installing **8**:23 (**5.2**)
  rotor removing and installing
    8:22 (**5.1**)
    replacing **8**:22 (**5.1**)
  spark plug wires
    removing and installing **8**:22 (**5.1**)
    replacing **8**:22 (**5.1**)
Doors **13**:20 (**5.**)
  assembly **13**:20 (**5.1**)
  bi-pressure pump **13**:24 (**5.2**)
  central locking system **13**:22
  (**5.2**)

Subjects are indexed by section number in **bold**, followed by the page number(s) within the section in ordinary type, followed by the numbered heading in **bold** in parentheses. Thus, **10**:12 (**4.1**) refers to page 12 in section **10. Automatic Transmission**, under heading **4.1**.

Doors (cont'd)
  door activators removing and installing **13**:24 (**5.2**)
  gas tank flap activator **13**:24 (**5.2**)
  handles **13**:21 (**5.1**)
  interior trim **13**:20 (**5.1**)
  locks **13**:21 (**5.1**)
  rear lid activator **13**:24 (**5.2**)
  side mirrors **13**:24 (**5.3**)
    electrical removing and installing **13**:25 (**5.3**)
Drum brakes (*see Brakes*)

E

EGR system **2**:17 (**5.5**)
  (*see also Exhaust system and emission controls*)
Electrical system
  general description **14**:4 (**1.**)
  maintenance **14**:5 (**2.**)
  troubleshooting **14**:5 (**3.**)
  (*see also Current flow diagrams*)
Emergency flashers **14**:25 (**10.1**)
Emergencies **1**:25 (**6.**)
  car will not start **1**:26 (**6.2**)
  changing a tire **1**:25 (**6.1**)
  coolant temperature warning light— dim lights **1**:27 (**6.6**)
  oil pressure warning light **1**:27 (**6.5**)
  towing **1**:27 (**6.7**)
Emission controls **7**:4 (**1.1**)
  (*see Exhaust system and emission controls*)
Engine
  camshaft removing and installing **3**:17 (**4.5**)
    camshaft and cam followers **3**:24 (**4.9**)
    camshaft drive belt (except diesel engines) **3**:12 (**4.2**)
    camshaft oil seal **3**:14 (**4.3**)
  components **3**:4 (**1.1**)
    connecting rods and pistons **3**:4 (**1.1**)
    crankshaft and bearings **3**:4 (**1.1**)
    cylinder head **3**:4 (**1.1**)
    intermediate shaft **3**:4 (**1.1**)
    valve train **3**:4 (**1.1**)
  crankshaft and intermediate shaft **3**:37 (**6.2**)
  cylinder block and pistons **3**:33 (**6.**)
    cylinder block oil seals **3**:33 (**6.1**)
  cylinder head **3**:11 (**4.**)
    assembly (16-valve engine) **3**:22 (**4.9**)
    (gasoline engines except 16-valve) **3**:23 (**4.9**)

Engine (cont'd)
  (diesel and turbo diesel engines) **3**:24 (**4.9**)
  cylinder head cover and gasket **3**:12 (**4.1**)
    disassembly, assembly, and reconditioning **3**:22 (**4.9**)
    removing and installing **3**:20 (**4.8**)
  diagnostic testing **3**:10 (**3.2**)
    compression test **3**:10 (**3.2**)
    leak-down test **3**:11 (**3.2**)
    wet compression test (gasoline engines only) **3**:11 (**3.2**)
  diesel and turbo diesel engines **3**:5 (**1.3**)
  diesel and turbo diesel engines (cont'd)
    connecting rods and pistons **3**:5 (**1.3**)
    cylinder head and valve train **3**:5 (**1.3**)
    valve train **3**:6 (**1.3**)
  disassembly, assembly, and reconditioning **3**:34 (**6.2**)
  dynamic oil pressure warning system **3**:40 (**7.1**)
    (high rpm) checking **3**:40 (**7.1**)
  engine and transaxle
    aligning **3**:33 (**5.**)
    removing and installing **3**:28 (**5.**)
    separating **3**:31 (**5.**)
  flywheel or drive plate **3**:38 (**6.2**)
  front crankshaft oil seal
    replacing **3**:33 (**6.1**)
  general descriptions **3**:4 (**1.**)
  hydraulic cam followers **3**:18 (**4.6**)
    checking **3**:19 (**4.6**)
  identification codes and specifications **3**:6 (**1.4**)
    finding engine letter codes **3**:6 (**1.4**)
  intermediate shaft oil seal
    replacing **3**:34 (**6.1**)
  low oil pressure warning system
    checking **3**:40 (**7.1**)
  lubrication system **3**:39 (**7.**)
  maintenance **3**:7 (**2.**)
  troubleshooting **3**:7 (**3.**)
    basic troubleshooting principles **3**:7 (**3.1**)
    engine not running **3**:9 (**3.1**)
    excessive oil consumption **3**:8 (**3.1**)
    fluid leaks **3**:8 (**3.1**)
    noise **3**:7 (**3.1**)
    poor fuel consumption and low power **3**:9 (**3.1**)
    smoking **3**:8 (**3.1**)

Engine (cont'd)
  oil cooler **3**:41 (**7.3**)
  oil pressure switches testing **3**:40 (**7.1**)
  oil pump **3**:40 (**7.2**)
  oil spray nozzles **3**:41 (**7.2**)
  pistons and connecting rods **3**:34 (**6.2**)
  piston height, diesel and turbo diesel **3**:36 (**6.2**)
  piston rings **3**:36 (**6.2**)
  technical data **3**:42 (**8.**)
  valves and valve springs **3**:25 (**4.9**)
  valve adjustment (1985 and early 1986 diesel and turbo diesel only) **3**:15 (**4.4**)
  valve guides **3**:26 (**4.9**)
  valve seats **3**:26 (**4.9**)
  valve stem oil seals **3**:19 (**4.7**)
  16-valve engine **3**:4 (**1.2**)
    cylinder block **3**:4 (**1.2**)
    cylinder head **3**:5 (**1.2**)
    intermediate shaft **3**:5 (**1.2**)
    pistons **3**:5 (**1.2**)
    valve train **3**:5 (**1.2**)
Engine compartment maintenance **2**:18 (**6.**)
Exhaust system and emission controls
  exhaust gas recirculation (EGR) system **7**:19 (**6.**)
  EGR thermo-pneumatic valve testing and replacing **7**:20 (**6.**)
  EGR valve
    testing and replacing **7**:19 (**6.**)
  exhaust system **7**:7 (**4.**)
    installing **7**:12 (**4.1**)
    removing **7**:10 (**4.1**)
  front pipe spring clamps
    removing and installing **7**:10 (**4.1**)
  general descriptions **7**:4 (**1.**)
  maintenance **7**:5 (**2.**)
  technical data **7**:24 (**8.**)
  troubleshooting **7**:5 (**3.**)
    basic troubleshooting principles **7**:5 (**3.1**)

F

Final drive lubricant
  checking and filling **2**:26 (**7.6**)
Fluid and lubricant
  specifications **2**:10 (**3.**)
  brake fluid **2**:11 (**3.**)
  engine coolant (anti-freeze) **2**:11 (**3.**)

4 INDEX

Subjects are indexed by section number in **bold**, followed by the page number(s) within the section in ordinary type, followed by the numbered heading in **bold** in parentheses. Thus, **10**:12 (**4.1**) refers to page 12 in section **10. Automatic Transmission**, under heading **4.1**.

Fluid and lubricant specifications (cont'd)
  engine oil **2**:11 (**3.**)
    changing oil and filter **2**:12 (**4.1**)
  gasoline additive **2**:12 (**3.**)
  gear oil - man. trans. and final drive
    2:11 (**3.**)
  greases **2**:12 (**3.**)
Front suspension
  lubrication and maintenance **2**:27 (**7.7**)
  (see Suspension, front)
Fuel filters **2**:16 (**5.4**)
  diesel fuel filter **2**:17 (**5.4**)
    draining water from **2**:18 (**5.8**)
  main fuel filter
    (gasoline) **2**:16 (**5.4**)
  mini fuel filter **2**:16 (**5.4**)
Fuel injection **6**:10 (**5.**)
  accelerator cable **6**:12 (**5.2**)
  camshaft/injection pump drive belt
    (diesel engines only) **6**:14 (**5.4**)
    installing and adjusting **7**:16 (**5.4**)
    removing **6**:14 (**5.4**)
  cold start cable removing, installing
    and adjusting **6**:13 (**5.3**)
  cold start system **6**:13 (**5.3**)
    general descriptions **6**:4 (**1.**)
  idle speed and maximum rpm
    adjustments **6**:10 (**5.1**)
  idle speed checking and adjusting
    (1985 models without idle speed boost)
    6:10 (**5.1**)
    (1986 and later models with idle speed
    boost) **6**:11 (**5.1**)
  injection pump **6**:17 (**5.5**)
    correcting leaks **6**:21 (**5.5**)
    installing **6**:18 (**5.5**)
    removing **6**:17 (**5.5**)
    timing checking and adjusting **6**:19
    (**5.5**)
    valves **6**:21 (**5.5**)
  injectors **6**:21 (**5.6**)
    inspecting and repairing **6**:22
    (**5.6**)
    pressure testing **6**:22 (**5.6**)
    removing and installing **6**:22 (**5.6**)
  maximum rpm checking and adjusting
    (all 1985 through 1988 diesel and
    turbo diesel models) **6**:12 (**5.1**)
  stop solenoid
    inspecting and replacing **6**:20 (**5.5**)
    quick-check **6**:20 (**5.5**)
  troubleshooting **6**:4 (**3.**)
  turbo diesel boost enrichment **6**:23
    (**5.7**)

Fuel pump **5**:15 (**4.3**)
  check valve
    replacing (CIS and CIS-E only) **5**:18
    (**4.3**)
  electrical tests **5**:16 (**4.3**)
  operating for test **5**:13 (**4.1**)
  replacing **5**:17 (**4.3**)
Fuel system—diesel
  fuel gauge sender **6**:9 (**4.2**)
    removing **7**:9 (**4.2**)
  fuel supply **6**:8 (**4.**)
  maintenance **6**:4 (**2.**)
  technical data **6**:24 (**6.**)
  troubleshooting **6**:4 (**6.**)
    basic principles **6**:5 (**3.1**)
    checking fuel supply
    to injectors **6**:6 (**3.2**)
    diagnostic testing **6**:6 (**3.2**)
    idle speed drop test **6**:7 (**3.2**)
Fuel system—gasoline
  accelerator cable **5**:21 (**4.6**)
  air flow measurement **5**:28 (**5.1**)
  charcoal canister bypass valve
    testing **5**:21 (**4.5**)
  continuous injection system
    (CIS) **5**:27 (**5.**)
  diaphragm pressure regulator—
    CIS-E **5**:19 (**4.4**)
  evaporative emission controls **5**:20
    (**4.5**)
  fuel delivery testing **5**:23 (**4.7**)
    quick-checking **5**:23 (**4.7**)
  fuel injectors—CIS and CIS-E **5**:22
    (**4.7**)
    cleaning **5**:24 (**4.7**)
  fuel injectors—digifant II **5**:24 (**4.8**)
    removing and installing **5**:26 (**4.8**)
    testing **5**:25 (**4.8**)
  fuel metering **5**:28 (**5.1**)
  fuel pressure regulator **5**:19 (**4.4**)
    digifant II **5**:19 (**4.4**)
  fuel pump (see Fuel pump)
  fuel supply **5**:12 (**4.**)
  fuses and relays **5**:12 (**4.1**)
  maintenance **5**:6 (**2.**)
  pressure relief valve—CIS **5**:19 (**4.4**)
  throttle valve basic adjustment **5**:28
    (**5.1**)
  transfer pump **5**:13 (**4.2**)
  troubleshooting **5**:6 (**3.**)
    basic troubleshooting principles **5**:6
    (**3.1**)
    CIS troubleshooting **5**:7 (**3.2**)
    CIS-E troubleshooting **5**:8 (**3.3**)

Fuel system—gasoline (cont'd)
    digifant II troubleshooting **5**:1 (**3.4**)
Fundamentals
  emergencies (see Emergencies)
  alternator **1**:11 (**1.6**)
  battery **1**:11 (**1.6**)
  body **1**:4 (**1.1**)
  brakes **1**:10 (**1.5**)
  buying parts **1**:17 (**3.4**)
  clutch or torque converter **1**:8 (**1.3**)
  cooling system **1**:6 (**1.2**)
  drive axles **1**:9 (**1.3**)
  drivetrain **1**:7 (**1.3**)
  electrical system **1**:11 (**1.6**)
  engine **1**:4 (**1.2**)
  exhaust system **1**:7 (**1.2**)
  final drive **1**:8 (**1.3**)
  fuel system **1**:6 (**1.2**)
  general advice for the beginner
    1:14 (**3.2**)
    planning ahead **1**:14 (**3.2**)
    cleanliness **1**:14 (**3.2**)
    tightening bolts **1**:14 (**3.2**)
    bolt torque **1**:15 (**3.2**)
    gaskets **1**:15 (**3.2**)
    seals **1**:15 (**3.2**)
    wire repairs **1**:15 (**3.2**)
    cleaning **1**:16 (**3.2**)
    electrical testing **1**:16 (**3.2**)
    making an LED test light **1**:17
    (**3.2**)
    disconnecting wiring harness
    connectors **1**:17 (**3.2**)
  getting started **1**:12 (**3.**)
  how to use this manual **1**:11 (**2.**)
  ignition system **1**:5 (**1.2**)
  lifting the car **1**:13 (**3.1**)
  lubrication system **1**:7 (**1.2**)
  safety **1**:12 (**3.1**)
  suspension and steering **1**:9
    (**1.4**)
  tools **1**:19 (**4.**)
  transmission **1**:8 (**1.3**)
  troubleshooting fundamentals **1**:24
    (**5.**)
  wiring harness and circuits **1**:11 (**1.6**)
Fuses general description **14**:44 (**1.**)
Fuse/Relay Panel **14**:28 (**13.**)
  Golf and GTI 1985
    fuse panel **14**:32 (**13.**)
    relay panel **14**:31 (**13.**)
  Golf and GTI 1986 through 1988
    fuse panel **14**:34 (**13.**)
    relay panel **14**:33 (**13.**)

Subjects are indexed by section number in **bold**, followed by the page number(s) within the section in ordinary type, followed by the numbered heading in **bold** in parentheses. Thus, **10**:12 (**4.1**) refers to page 12 in section **10. Automatic Transmission**, under heading **4.1**.

Fuse/Relay panel (cont'd)
  Jetta 1985 through 1988
    14:30 (**13.**)

G

Glow plug system (diesel engine) **8**:24
    (**6.**)
  general description **8**:5 (**1.4**)
  glow plugs
    testing and replacing **8**:24 (**6.1**)
  glow plug relay, checking **8**:26 (**6.2**)
  glow plug system circuits
    testing and repairing **8**:25 (**6.2**)
  glow plug system voltage checks **8**:25
    (**6.2**)
  wiring, checking **8**:25 (**6.2**)

H

Hall sender (*see Ignition system*)
Headlights **13**:26 (**6.1**)
  aiming headlights **13**:26 (**6.1**)
Heated seats **14**:27 (**12.1**)
Heating
  heater and controls—with air
    conditioning **13**:12 (**4.5**)
    control head, replacing **13**:13 (**4.5**)
    fresh air blower **13**:13 (**4.5**)
    heater core **13**:12 (**4.5**)
    vacuum system, checking **13**:13 (**4.5**)
  heater and controls—without air
    conditioning **13**:9 (**4.4**)
    fresh air blower **13**:12 (**4.4**)
    heater control cables, replacing
      and adjusting **13**:11 (**4.4**)
    heater core **13**:10 (**4.4**)
Heating, ventilation and air conditioning
    14:26 (**11.**)
  fresh air blower **14**:26 (**11.**)
  general description **14**:4 (**1.**)
Horns **14**:24 (**9.**)
  troubleshooting **14**:24 (**9.1**)

I

Identification codes **3**:6 (**1.4**)
Idle speed **2**:17 (**5.6**)
Ignition
  distributor (*see Distributor, ignition*)
  general description **8**:4 (**1.**)
    digifant II ignition system **8**:4 (**1.3**)
    electronic ignition system **8**:4 (**1.1**)
    knock sensor system **8**:4 (**1.2**)

Ignition (cont'd)
  system identification **8**:5 (**1.5**)
    applications **8**:5 (**1.5**)
  glow plug system (*see Glow plug system*)
  maintenance **8**:6 (**2.**)
  technical data **8**:26 (**7.**)
  transistorized coil ignition
    (TCI-h) system **8**:12 (**4.**)
    centrifugal and vacuum spark advance
      (basic TCI-h only, engine codes
      GX and MZ) **8**:17 (**4.2**)
    digifant II ignition timing advance
      (engine codes RV and PF)
      checking **8**:17 (**4.3**)
    electronic timing advance
      (TCI-h with knock control
      engine codes HT, RD, PL, RV, PF)
      8:17 (**4.3**)
    ignition timing
      basic **8**:15 (**4.1**)
      adjusting **8**:16 (**4.1**)
      checking **8**:15 (**4.1**)
    knock sensor
      removing and installing **8**:20 (**4.6**)
      knock sensor system components
        checking **8**:20 (**4.5**)
      knock sensor system diagnosis
        (engine codes HT, RD, PL) **8**:18
        (**4.4**)
      knock sensor system voltage checks
        8:19 (**4.5**)
      knock sensor system wiring
        checking **8**:18 (**4.5**)
    rpm-dependent timing advance
      (engine codes HT, RD, PL)
      checking **8**:17 (**4.3**)
    vacuum-dependent ignition timing
      advance
      (engine codes HT, RD, PL)
      checking **8**:17 (**4.3**)
  troubleshooting **8**:6 (**3.**)
    basic troubleshooting principles **8**:6
      (**3.1**)
    coil and spark plug wires
      testing **8**:9 (**3.3**)
    hall sender, testing **8**:10 (**3.4**)
    hall sender switching function **8**:11
      (**3.4**)
    ignition control unit
      testing **8**:10 (**3.4**)
    ignition control unit response
      to hall sender signal **8**:12 (**3.4**)
    ignition control unit voltage
      to coil **8**:11 (**3.4**)

Ignition (cont'd)
    ignition system, quick-check **8**:7
      (**3.1**)
    knock sensor system **8**:18 (**4.5**)
    switch **14**:25 (**10.2**)
    test equipment **8**:7 (**3.1**)
    visual inspection **8**:8 (**3.2**)
    voltage supply and ground
      to hall sender **8**:11 (**3.4**)
    voltage supply and ground
      to ignition control unit **8**:10 (**3.4**)
Injectors (*see Fuel injection*)
Instruments **14**:4 (**1.**)
  (*see also Body and interior*)
  dynamic oil pressure warning system
    control unit testing **14**:20 (**7.1**)
  general description **14**:4 (**1.**)
  instrument cluster and gauges
    troubleshooting **14**:16 (**7.1**)
    testing voltage and ground **14**:16
      (**7.1**)
  LED and indicator bulbs
    testing and replacing **14**:18 (**7.1**)
  upshift indicator
    testing **14**:18 (**7.1**)
  voltage stabilizer
    testing and replacing **14**:16 (**7.1**)
Interior, care of **2**:28 (**9.2**)
  (*see also Body and interior*)
Interior lights **13**:9 (**4.3**)
  bulbs, replacing **13**:9 (**4.3**)

J

Jump-starting **1**:26 (**6.3**)

K

Kickdown operation checking **2**:26 (**7.6**)
Knock sensor (*see Ignition system*)

L

Lifting the car **1**:13 (**3.1**)
Lights (*see also specific type of lights*)
  back-up Lights **14**:25 (**10.1**)
  brake lights **14**:25 (**10.1**)
  exterior **14**:24 (**10.**)
    troubleshooting **14**:24 (**10.1**)
  general description **14**:4 (**1.**)
  headlights **14**:25 (**10.1**)
  license plate lights **14**:25 (**10.1**)
  taillights **14**:25 (**10.1**)
  turn signals **14**:25 (**10.1**)

15

Subjects are indexed by section number in **bold**, followed by the page number(s) within the section in ordinary type, followed by the numbered heading in **bold** in parentheses. Thus, **10**:12 (**4.1**) refers to page 12 in section **10**. **Automatic Transmission**, under heading **4.1**.

Lights (cont'd)
    side marker lights **14**:25 (**10.1**)
Lubrication and maintentance **2**:3
    general descriptions **2**:4 (**1.**)
Lubrication system **3**:39 (**7.**)
    (*see also Engine*)

M

Maintenance
    engine oil change **2**:4 (**1.3**)
    scheduled **2**:4 (**1.1**)
Master cylinder (*see Brakes*)
Mirrors
    electric/heated outside **14**:27 (**12.2**)

O

Oil filter, changing **2**:12 (**4.1**)
Oil seals (*see Transmission, automatic*)
Overheating **1**:27 (**6.4**)
Oxygen sensor system **7**:13 (**5.**)
    general description **7**:5 (**1.2**)
    testing (CIS) **7**:14 (**5.1**)
        frequency valve, checking **7**:15 (**5.1**)
        frequency valve duty cycle measuring **7**:14 (**5.1**)
        oxygen sensor, checking **7**:16 (**5.1**)
        oxygen sensor control unit checking **7**:15 (**5.1**)
        quick checking **7**:14 (**5.1**)
        replacing **7**:16 (**5.1**)
        thermoswitch, checking **7**:14 (**5.1**)
    testing (CIS-Electronic) **7**:17 (**5.2**)
        control unit response checking **7**:17 (**5.2**)
        oxygen sensor control unit replacing **7**:18 (**5.2**)
        oxygen sensor replacing **7**:18 (**5.2**)
        testing **7**:17 (**5.2**)
    testing (Digifant II) **7**:18 (**5.3**)
        digifant control unit, replacing **7**:19 (**5.3**)
        oxygen sensor, replacing **7**:19 (**5.3**)
        oxygen sensor function testing **7**:18 (**5.3**)
        oxygen sensor wiring checking **17**:18 (**5.3**)
    troubleshooting **7**:5 (**3.**)
        oxygen sensor circuits **7**:16 (**5.1**)
Oxygen sensor warning light counter, resetting **2**:21 (**6.5**)

P

Pads, brake (*see Brakes*)
Parking brake (*see Brakes*)
Parking lights **14**:25 (**10.1**)
Parts **1**:17 (**3.2**)
    buying parts **1**:17 (**3.3**)
    genuine Volkswagen parts **1**:17 (**3.3**)
    non-returnable parts **1**:18 (**3.3**)
    spare parts kit **1**:28 (**6.8**)
    Volkswagen remanufactured parts **1**:18 (**3.3**)
Pistons (*see Engine*)
Power steering **2**:21 (**6.4**)
    (*see also Steering*)

R

Radiator (*see Cooling system*)
Radio **13**:8 (**4.2**)
    antenna **13**:8 (**4.2**)
Rear suspension (*see Suspension, rear and Steering*)
Rear window defogger **14**:27 (**11.**)
Relays, general description **14**:4 (**1.**)
Rotor (*see Ignition*)
Rotors, brake (*see Brakes*)

S

Safety **1**:12 (**3.1**)
Seats
    front **13**:18 (**4.7**)
    heated **13**:18 (**4.7**)
    rear **13**:19 (**4.8**)
Seat belts **13**:14 (**4.6**)
    child restraint tethering (Jetta only) **13**:17 (**4.6**)
    cleaning and preserving **2**:28 (**9.**)
    front seat belt height adjustment **13**:16 (**4.6**)
    inspecting **13**:14 (**4.6**)
    installing or replacing **13**:14 (**4.6**)
Shift mechanism (*see Transmission, manual*)
Shock absorbers (*see Suspension*)
Spark plugs **2**:15 (**5.2**)
    wires **2**:16 (**5.3**)
Speedometer cable
    removing and installing **13**:5 (**4.1**)
Steering **11**:29 (**7.**)
    column **11**:30 (**7.1**)
        switches, removing and installing **11**:31 (**7.1**)

Steering (cont'd)
    gearbox, adjusting **11**:34 (**7.2**)
        removing and installing **11**:35 (**7.2**)
    ignition/steering lock cylinder replacing **11**:32 (**7.1**)
    manual steering rack centering **11**:34 (**7.2**)
    power-assisted steering **11**:35 (**7.3**)
    power steering fluid draining and filling **11**:37 (**7.3**)
    power steering pump **11**:37 (**7.3**)
    power steering system pressure testing **11**:37 (**7.3**)
    steering gear and tie rods **11**:32 (**7.2**)
    steering wheel removing and installing **11**:30 (**7.1**)
    tie rods (*see Tie rods*)
    technical data **11**:38 (**8.**)
    troubleshooting **11**:6 (**3.**)
        basic troubleshooting principles **11**:6 (**3.1**)
        diagnostic inspection and testing **11**:8 (**3.2**)
        isolating pulling symptoms **11**:8 (**3.2**)
        vibration **11**:8 (**3.2**)
Stop solenoid (*see Fuel injection*)
Sunroof **13**:33 (**7.**)
    rear guides with cables removing and installing **13**:35 (**7.2**)
    removing and installing **13**:33 (**7.1**)
    sunroof fit, adjusting **13**:34 (**7.2**)
Suspension, front **11**:11 (**5.**)
    ball joints **11**:19 (**5.3**)
    bearings and bushings **11**:20 (**5.4**)
    constant velocity joints **11**:13 (**5.2**)
        removing and installing **11**:14 (**5.2**)
    control arm ball joints inspecting and replacing **11**:19 (**5.3**)
    control arm bushings **11**:22 (**5.4**)
    drive axles **11**:13 (**5.2**)
        removing and installing **11**:14 (**5.2**)
    drive axle vibration damper removing and installing **11**:19 (**5.2**)
    front suspension struts **11**:11 (**5.1**)
        disassembling and assembling **11**:13 (**5.1**)
        removing and installing **11**:12 (**5.1**)
    general description **11**:4 (**1.**)
    maintenance **11**:6 (**2.**)
    shock absorbers, checking **11**:12 (**5.1**)
        disassembling and inspecting **11**:16 (**5.2**)
    subframe mounting repairing **11**:23 (**5.4**)

Subjects are indexed by section number in **bold**, followed by the page number(s) within the section in ordinary type, followed by the numbered heading in **bold** in parentheses. Thus, **10**:12 (**4.1**) refers to page 12 in section **10**. **Automatic Transmission**, under heading **4.1**.

Suspension, front (cont'd)
  technical data **11**:38 (**8.**)
  troubleshooting **11**:6 (**3.**)
    basic troubleshooting principles **11**:6 (**3.1**)
    diagnostic inspection and testing **11**:8 (**3.2**)
    isolating pulling symptoms **11**:8 (**3.2**)
    vibration **11**:8 (**3.2**)
  wheel bearings
    removing and installing **11**:20 (**5.4**)
  wheel bearing housings
    removing and installing **11**:20 (**5.4**)
Suspension, rear
  removing and installing
    as a unit **11**:27 (**6.3**)
  axle beam bushings, replacing **11**:28 (**6.3**)
  axle beam, rear **11**:27 (**6.3**)
  shock absorbers, rear **11**:24 (**6.1**)
    removing and installing **11**:24 (**6.1**)
  springs **11**:24 (**6.1**)
  technical data **11**:38 (**8.**)
  troubleshooting **11**:6 (**3.**)
    basic troubleshooting principles **11**:6 (**3.1**)
    diagnostic inspection and testing **11**:8 (**3.2**)
    isolating pulling symptoms **11**:8 (**3.2**)
    vibration **11**:8 (**3.2**)
  wheel bearings, rear **11**:24 (**6.2**)
    adjusting **11**:27 (**6.2**)
    removing and installing **11**:24 (**6.2**)

T

Taillights, assembly **13**:27 (**6.2**)
Thermostat (*see Cooling system*)
Throttle cable **10**:12 (**4.1**)
  adjusting (gasoline engines) **10**:12 (**4.2**)
  (diesel engines) **10**:13 (**4.2**)
Tie rods
  replacing and adjusting **11**:33 (**7.2**)
  tie rod boots, inner
    replacing **11**:32 (**7.2**)
  tie rod ends
    inspecting **11**:32 (**7.2**)
Tires and wheels **2**:22 (**7.1**)
  (*see also Wheels*)
  changing **1**:25 (**6.1**)
  tire inflation pressure **2**:22 (**7.1**)
  tire rotation **2**:22 (**7.1**)
  wheel alignment **2**:23 (**7.1**)

Tools **1**:19 (**4.**)
  basic tool requirements **1**:19 (**4.**)
  duty cycle meter or dwell meter **1**:23 (**4.**)
  feeler gauges **1**:23 (**4.**)
  jack stands **1**:21 (**4.**)
  jumper wires **1**:24 (**4.**)
  micrometers **1**:23 (**4.**)
  oil change equipment **1**:22 (**4.**)
  tachometer **1**:22 (**4.**)
  timing light **1**:22 (**4.**)
  test light **1**:23 (**4.**)
  torque wrench **1**:22 (**4.**)
  Volkswagen special tools **1**:24 (**4.**)
  volt-ohm meter or multimeter **1**:23 (**4.**)
Torque converter (*see Transmission, automatic*)
Towing **1**:27 (**6.7**)
Transmission, automatic
  accelerator cable (*see Accelerator cable*)
  ATF pump **10**:5 (**1.1**)
  control cables
    removing and installing **10**:11 (**4.1**)
  controls **10**:10 (**4.**)
  external transmission adjustments **10**:12 (**4.2**)
  drive flange oil seals **10**:18 (**5.2**)
    replacing **10**:18 (**5.2**)
  final drive **10**:6 (**1.1**)
  hydraulic controls **10**:6 (**1.1**)
  identification codes **10**:6 (**1.2**)
  maintenance **10**:6 (**2.**)
  oil seals **10**:17 (**5.2**)
  planetary gear system **10**:5 (**1.1**)
  selector lever cable
    adjusting **10**:12 (**4.2**)
    replacing **10**:11 (**4.1**)
  specifications **10**:7 (**1.2**)
  technical data **10**:19 (**6.**)
  throttle cable (*see Throttle cable*)
  torque converter **10**:5 (**1.1**)
  torque converter oil seal **10**:17 (**5.2**)
    checking bushing **10**:17 (**5.2**)
    replacing oil seal **10**:17 (**5.2**)
  transaxle assembly **10**:14 (**5.**)
    removing and installing **10**:14 (**5.1**)
  transmission 010 **10**:4 (**1.1**)
  troubleshooting **10**:7 (**3.**)
    basic troubleshooting principles **10**:7 (**3.1**)
    diagnostic tests **10**:9 (**3.2**)
    pressure test **10**:10 (**3.2**)
    stall speed test **10**:9 (**3.2**)

Transmission, automatic (cont'd)
  2nd gear brake band
    adjusting **10**:14 (**4.2**)
Transmission, manual
  external adjustments **9**:16 (**6.1**)
  general descriptions **9**:4 (**1.**)
  maintenance **9**:6 (**2.**)
  shift lever
    removing and installing **9**:10 (**4.1**)
  shift mechanism **9**:8 (**4.**)
    disassembling, assembling, and adjusting **9**:8 (**4.1**)
  shift rod
    removing and installing **9**:10 (**4.1**)
  technical data **9**:22 (**7.**)
  transaxle, removing and installing **9**:20 (**6.3**)
  transaxle oil seals **9**:16 (**6.2**)
  transmission and final drive **9**:15 (**6.**)
  troubleshooting **9**:6 (**3.**)
    basic troubleshooting principles **9**:6 (**3.1**)
    diagnostic tests **9**:6 (**3.2**)
Transaxle (*see Transmission, automatic*)
Trim **13**:28 (**6.4**)
  removing and installing **13**:30 (**6.4**)
Troubleshooting
  automatic transmission **10**:7 (**3.**)
    (*see also Transmission, automatic*)
  brakes **12**:5 (**3.**) (*see also Brakes*)
  body **13**:5 (**3.**) (*see also Body and Interior*)
  clutch **9**:6 (**3.**) (*see also Transmission, manual*)
  cooling system **4**:4 (**3.**) (*see also Cooling system*)
  emission controls **7**:5 (**3.**) (*see also Exhaust system and emission controls*)
  engine **3**:7 (**3.**) (*see also Engine*)
  exhaust system **7**:5 (**3.**) (*see also Exhaust system and emission controls*)
  fuel system—diesel **6**:4 (**3.**) (*see also Fuel system—diesel*)
  fuel system—gasoline **5**:6 (**3.**) (*see also Fuel system—gasoline*)
  ignition system **8**:6 (**3.**) (*see also Ignition system*)
  interior **13**:5 (**3.**) (*see also Body and interior*)
  manual transmission **9**:6 (**3.**) (*see also Transmission, manual*)
  oxygen sensor circuit **7**:5 (**3.**)

15

8 INDEX

Subjects are indexed by section number in **bold**, followed by the page number(s) within the section in ordinary type, followed by the numbered heading in **bold** in parentheses. Thus, **10**:12 (**4.1**) refers to page 12 in section **10**. **Automatic Transmission**, under heading **4.1**.

Troubleshooting (cont'd)
   (*see also Oxygen sensor system*)
   steering **11**:6 (**3.**) (*see also Steering*)
   suspension **11**:6 (**3.**) (*see also Suspension*)
   tires **11**:6 (**3.**) (*see also Wheels*)
Turbocharger (turbo diesel only) **7**:20 (**7.**)
   removing and installing **7**:21 (**7.1**)
   blow-off valve, replacing **7**:23 (**7.2**)
   general description **7**:4 (**1.1**)
   turbocharger wastegate and blow-off valve testing **7**:22 (**7.2**)
Turn signal lights, front **13**:28 (**6.3**)

V

Valves (*see Engine*)
Ventilation **13**:4 (**1.3**)

W

Wheels **11**:8 (**4.**)
   alignment **11**:9 (**4.2**)
   alignment specifications **11**:11 (**4.3**)
   camber adjustment **11**:10 (**4.2**)
   centerline adjustment (four-wheel alignment only) **11**:10 (**4.2**)
   tires **11**:8 (**4.1**)
   toe adjustment **11**:10 (**4.2**)
   troubleshooting **11**:6 (**3.**)
      tire wear **11**:8 (**3.2**)
   winter tires **11**:9 (**4.1**)
Wheel bearings (*see Suspension and Steering*)
Wheel cylinder (*see Brakes*)
Windshield Wipers and Washers **14**:20 (**8.**)
   blades **2**:27 (**8.1**)
   general description **14**:4 (**1.**)
   intermittent relay testing **14**:21 (**8.1**)
   rear wiper motor removing and installing **14**:23 (**8.2**)
      testing **14**:20 (**8.1**)
   troubleshooting **14**:20 (**8.1**)
   windshield **13**:33 (**6.4**)
   windshield wiper motor removing and installing **14**:21 (**8.2**)
      testing **14**:20 (**8.1**)

Windshield (cont'd)
   windshield wiper motor linkage **14**:21 (**8.2**)
   wiper and washer switch testing **14**:21 (**8.1**)
Windows
   window regulator **13**:21 (**5.1**)
      power **13**:21 (**5.1**) and **14**:28 (**12.4**)
Wiring
   general description **14**:4 (**1.1**)
   (*see also Current flow diagrams*)

Maintenance History

Date	Mileage	Description

Maintenance History

Date	Mileage	Description

Maintenance History

Date	Mileage	Description

Maintenance History

Date	Mileage	Description